THE ROUGH GUIDE TO

Spain WITHDRAWN

This fifteenth edition updated by

Simon Baskett, Geoff Garvey, Matthew Hancock,
Laurie Isola, Helen Ochyra, AnneLise Sorensen,
Joanna Styles, Ros Walford, Greg Ward and
Simon Willmore

ROUGH
GUIDES

roughguides.com

Contents

Introduction to
Spain

First time visitors be warned: Spain is addictive. You might book a city break, villa holiday or hiking trip, but soon you'll be find yourself distracted by something quite different – swept up in the excitement of a fiesta, hooked on the local cuisine, or stunned by Barcelona's otherworldly architecture. Even in the best-known destinations – from Madrid to the *costas*, from the high Pyrenees to the Moorish cities of the south – there are genuinely surprising attractions at every turn, whether it's cool restaurants in the Basque country, the wild landscapes of the central plains, or cutting-edge galleries in the industrial north. Soon, you'll notice that there is not just one Spain but many – and indeed, Spaniards themselves often speak of Las Españas (the Spains).

This diversity is partly down to an almost obsessive regionalism, stemming from the creation in the late 1970s of seventeen *comunidades autonomías* (autonomous regions) with their own governments, budgets and cultural ministries, even police forces. You might think you are on holiday in Spain but your hosts may be adamant that you're actually visiting Catalunya, and will point to a whole range of differences in language, culture and artistic traditions, not to mention social attitudes and politics. Indeed, the old days of a unified nation, governed with a firm hand from Madrid, seem to have gone forever, as the separate kingdoms that made up the original Spanish state reassert themselves in an essentially federal structure.

Does any of this matter for visitors? As a rule – not really, since few tourists have the time or inclination to immerse themselves in contemporary Spanish political discourse. Far more important is to look beyond the clichés of paella, matadors, sangría and siesta if you're to get the best out of a visit to this amazingly diverse country.

Even in the most over-touristed resorts of the Costa del Sol, you'll be able to find an authentic bar or restaurant where the locals eat, and a village not far away where an age-old bullfighting tradition owes nothing to tourism. The large cities of the north,

ABOVE SANTIAGO DE COMPOSTELA, GALICIA **RIGHT** PARQUE NACIONAL DE ORDESA Y MONTE PERDIDO, ARAGÓN

from Barcelona to Bilbao, have reinvented themselves as essential cultural destinations (and they don't all close down for hours for a kip every afternoon). And when the world now looks to Spain for culinary inspiration – the country has some of the most acclaimed chefs and innovative restaurants in the world – it's clear that things have changed. Spain, despite the current economic uncertainty, sees itself very differently from a generation ago. So should you – prepare to be surprised.

Where to go

Spain's cities are among the most vibrant in Europe. Exuberant **Barcelona**, for many, has the edge, thanks to Gaudí's extraordinary *modernista* architecture, the lively promenade of the Ramblas, five kilometres of sandy beach and one of the world's best football teams. The capital, **Madrid**, may not be as pretty, but it claims as many devotees – immortalized in the movies of Pedro Almodóvar, and shot through with a contemporary style that informs everything from its major-league art museums to its carefree bars and summer terrazas. Then there's **Seville**, home of flamenco and all the clichés of southern Spain; **Valencia**, the vibrant capital of the Levante, with a thriving arts scene and nightlife; and **Bilbao**, a not-to-miss stop on Spain's cultural circuit, due to Frank Gehry's astonishing Museo Guggenheim.

Rias Altas

A Coruña

Santiago de
Compostela

GALICIA

Lugo

Gijón

Cangas
de Onis

Oviedo

ASTURIAS

Santander

Bilbao

PAIS VASCO

PICOS DE
EUROPA

Rio Ebro

León

CANTABRIA

Rias Bajas

Pontevedra

Vigo

Tui

A Guarda

Caminha

Valença

Braga

Porto

Ourense

Rio Miño

Verin

Chaves

Braganza

Ponferrada

Astorga

Palencia

Burgos

Rio Duero

Zamora

Valladolid

Vila Real

CASTILLA Y
LEÓN

Salamanca

Segovia

SIERRA DE
GUADARRAMA

Viseu

Ávila

Guadalajara

Coimbra

Ciudad
Rodrigo

SIERRA DE GREDOS

MADRID

COMUNIDAD DE MADRID

PORTUGAL

Castelo
Branco

Plasencia

Aranjuez

Rio Tajo

Rio Tajo

Toledo

Santarem

Cáceres

Trujillo

EXTREMADURA

Rio Guadiana

Ciudad
Real

LISBON

Évora

Mérida

Badajoz

Valdepeñas

Jerez de los
Caballeros

Zafra

CASTILLA-LA MANCHA

Beja

Aracena

Córdoba

Úbeda

Jaén

Baeza

Vila Real
de Santo
Antonio

Seville

Rio Guadalquivir

Ecija

ANDALUCÍA

Ayamonte

Huelva

Granada

Faro

PARQUE
NACIONAL
DE DOÑANA

SIERRA NEVADA

LAS
ALPUJARRA

Antequera

Ronda

Málaga

Costa del Sol

Costa de la Luz

Jerez

Cádiz

Arcos de
la Frontera

Marbella

Gibraltar

Algeciras

Ceuta

Tangier

MOROCCO

Tétouan

Canary Islands

Melilla

–·–·–	AVE High-speed Line
+++++	F.E.V.E. Private Railway
═══	Standard Motorway
═══	Toll Motorway

0   150

kilometres

FACT FILE

• Spain's land **area** is around half a million square kilometres – about twice the size of the UK or Oregon. The **population** is around 47 million – some eighty percent of whom declare themselves nominally Catholic, though religious observance is patchy.

• Politically, Spain is a **parliamentary monarchy**; democracy was restored in 1977, after the death of General Franco, the dictator who seized power in the Civil War of 1936–39.

• Spaniards read fewer **newspapers** than almost any other Europeans – tellingly, the best-selling daily is *Marca*, devoted purely to football.

• **Spanish** (Castilian) is the main official language, but sizeable numbers of Spaniards also speak variants of **Catalan** (in Catalunya, parts of Valencia and Alicante provinces, and on the Balearic Islands), **Galician** and **Basque**, all of which are also officially recognized languages.

• A minority of Spaniards attend **bullfights**; it doesn't rain much on the **plains**; and they only dance **flamenco** in the southern region of Andalucía.

• The highest **mountain** on the Spanish peninsula is Mulhacén (3483m), the longest **river** is the Rio Tajo (716km).

• Spain has 44 sites on **UNESCO's World Heritage** list – more than twice as many as the USA.

• Between them **Real Madrid** and **Barcelona** have won the Spanish league title over fifty times and the European Cup (Champions League) fourteen times and counting.

Not only are Spain's modern cities and towns lively and exciting, they are monumental – literally so. History has washed over the country, adding an architectural backdrop that varies from one region to another, dependent on their occupation by Romans, Visigoths or Moors, or on their role in the medieval Christian Reconquest or in the later Golden Age of imperial Renaissance Spain. Touring **Castilla y León**, for example, you can't avoid the stereotypical Spanish image of vast cathedrals and hundreds of *reconquista* castles, while the gorgeous medieval university city of Salamanca captivates all who visit. In northerly, mountainous **Asturias** and the **Pyrenees**, tiny, almost organically evolved, Romanesque churches dot the hillsides and villages, while in **Galicia** all roads lead to the ancient, and heartbreakingly beautiful cathedral city of Santiago de Compostela. **Andalucía** has the great mosques and Moorish palaces of Granada, Seville and Córdoba; **Castilla-La Mancha** boasts the superbly preserved medieval capital of Toledo; while the harsh landscape of **Extremadura** cradles ornate *conquistador* towns built with riches from the New World.

The Spanish **landscape**, too, holds just as much fascination and variety as the country's urban centres. The evergreen estuaries of Galicia could hardly be more different from the high, arid plains of Castile, or the gulch-like desert landscapes of Almería. In particular, Spain has some of the finest **mountains** in Europe, with superb walking – from short hikes to week-long treks – in a dozen or more protected ranges or *sierras* – especially the Picos de Europa and the Pyrenees. There are still brown bears and lynx in the wild, not to mention boar, storks and eagles, while a near-five-thousand-kilometre coastline means great opportunities for fishing, whale-watching and dolphin-spotting.

Agriculture, meanwhile, makes its mark in the patterned hillsides of the wine- and olive-growing regions, the baking wheat plantations and cattle

FROM TOP LA TOMATINA IN BUÑOL, VALENCIA; CALA D'HORT, THE BALEARIC ISLANDS

ranches of the central plains, the *meseta*, and the rice fields of the eastern provinces of Valencia and Murcia, known as the Levante. These areas, although short on historic monuments and attractions, produce some of Spain's most famous exports, and with the country now at the heart of the contemporary European foodie movement, there's an entire holiday to be constructed out of simply exploring Spain's rich **regional cuisine** – touring the Rioja and other celebrated wine regions, snacking your way around Extremadura and Andalucía in search of the world's best *jamón serrano* (cured mountain ham), or tucking into a paella in its spiritual home of Valencia.

And finally, there are the **beaches** – one of Spain's greatest attractions, and where modern tourism to the country began in the 1960s. Here, too, there's a lot more variety than the stereotypical images might suggest. Long tracts of coastline – along the **Costa del Sol** in Andalucía in particular – have certainly been

SPANISH TIME

Spanish time is notionally one hour ahead of the UK – but conceptually Spain might as well be on a different planet. Nowhere else in Europe keeps such late hours. Spaniards may not take a traditional midday **siesta** as much as they used to, but their diurnal rhythms remain committedly nocturnal. They'll saunter out around 8pm or 9pm in the evening for a **paseo**, to greet friends and maybe have a drink and tapas, and if they're eating out, they'll normally start at 10pm or 11pm, often later in Madrid, where it's not unusual for someone to phone around midnight to see if you're going out for the evening.

Like everything else, practices differ somewhat by region. Madrid – its inhabitants nicknamed **los gatos** or "the cats" for their nocturnal lifestyle – is famed for staying up the latest, with Andalucía a close second. In the north, particularly in Catalunya, they keep more northern European hours. And, of course, **summer nights** never seem to really end.

Author picks

Our hard-travelling authors have visited every corner of Spain – from the *rías* of Galicia to the white towns of Andalucía – to bring you some unique travel experiences. These are some of their own, personal favourites.

Fiestas and *ferias* Get boozy at Sanlúcar de Barrameda's sherry festival (p.228), play with fire at Valencia's Las Fallas (p.802), or join the celebrations at Seville's Feria de Abril (p.228).

Seafood heaven Fill up on aromatic Valencian paella (p.795) or feast on L'Escala anchovies (p.725). Adventurous eaters can try *percebes*, prestigious little crustaceans from Galicia (p.547), or *ortiguillas*, deep-fried sea anemones from the Cádiz area (p.292).

Classic journeys The legendary Camino de Santiago route (p.552) is a life must-do. For train thrills the Catalan Cremallera (p.752) is a blast.

Delightful towns Not famous, no fanfares, but thoroughly lovely – Beget in Catalunya (p.744), El Burgo de Osma in Castilla y León (p.403) and Andalucía's Zahara de la Sierra (p.261).

Amazing views The jagged remains of Las Médulas are eerily captivating (p.442), while the views from the walls of Ávila (p.154) and Barcelona from the cross-harbour cable-car (p.663) are unforgettable.

Hip and hot nightlife Join the gin craze in Barcelona (p.694), let your hair down at *Ibiza Rocks* in Ibiza (p.860), or hit *Coco's* fashionable dancefloors in Madrid (p.116).

Fine sands In a land of long sandy stretches and limpid, turquoise waters the competition for best beach is tough. Top of the table are: Conil in Andalucía (p.291), Águilas in Murcia (p.843) and Ibiza's Cala D'Hort (p.858).

Stunning architecture Gaudí's Parc Güell (p.678), Chillida in San Sebastián (p.453) and the vertical garden in Madrid's CaixaForum (p.88) are all eye-popping city masterpieces.

> Our author recommendations don't end here. We've flagged up our favourite places – a perfectly sited hotel, an atmospheric café, a special restaurant – throughout the guide, highlighted with the ★ symbol.

LEFT JAMÓN, ANDALUCÍA **RIGHT FROM TOP** SARDINES AND ANCHOVIES; CAMINO DE SANTIAGO; EL BURGO DE OSMA, CASTILLA Y LEÓN

massively and depressingly over-developed, but delightful pockets remain, even along the biggest, concrete-clad *costas*. Moreover, there are superb windsurfing waters around Tarifa and some decidedly low-key resorts along the **Costa de la Luz**. On the **Costa Brava**, in the northeast in Catalunya, the string of idyllic coves between Palamos and Begur is often overlooked, while the cooler Atlantic coastline boasts the **surfing beaches** of Cantabria and Asturias, and the unspoilt coves of Galicia's estuaries. Offshore, the **Balearic Islands** – Ibiza, Formentera, Mallorca and Menorca – also have some superb sands, with party-fuelled Ibiza in particular offering one of the most hedonistic backdrops to beachlife in the whole Mediterranean.

Hedonism, actually, brings us full-circle, back to one of the reasons why Spain is pretty much irresistible and infectious. Wherever you are in the country, you can't help but notice the Spaniards' wild – often over-bearing – enthusiasm for **having a good time**. Festivals are a case in point – these aren't staid, annual celebrations, they are raucous reaffirmations of life itself, complete with fireworks, fancy dress, giants, devils, bonfires, parties, processions and sheer Spanish glee. But even outside *fiesta* time there's always something vibrant and noisy happening – from local market to late-night bar, weekend football match to beachside dance club. Meals are convivial affairs – for most Spaniards the rushed sandwich or chain-restaurant takeaway just won't do – and long lunches and late dinners are the norm throughout the country. And with family at the heart of Spanish society, there's a genuine welcome for, and interest in, you and yours, whether at resort hotel or rustic guesthouse. "*A pasarlo bien!*" (Have a good time!), as the Spanish say.

ON THE TAPAS TRAIL

Everyone thinks they know tapas – the little nibbles served up in bars – yet nothing can prepare you for the variety available on their home soil. If all you've ever encountered is deep-fried squid and spicy potatoes, then a treat awaits. That's not even to say that those dishes aren't authentic – but the truth is that your first beachfront plate of Andalucían **calamares** or **patatas bravas** in back-street Barcelona will really make you sit up and take notice. The proper way to eat tapas is to wander from one bar to another to sample a particular speciality, since the best bars tend to be known for just one or two dishes... and the locals wouldn't dream of ordering anything else. So you might duck into one place for **jamón serrano** (cured ham), another for **pulpo gallego** (pot-cooked octopus), a third for **pimientos de Padrón** (small green peppers – about one in ten being fiery-hot), and then maybe on to a smoky old bar that serves just **fino** (dry sherry) from the barrel along with slices of **mojama** (dried, pressed roe). And that's not counting the creative, new-wave bars where sculpted **montaditos** (canapés), yucca chips, samosas, sushi-fusion titbits or artisan-produced cheese and meat are all vying for your attention. Once you've nibbled your way around town, it's time to tackle the serious business of dinner.

When to go

If Spain is a country of many regions, it's also a country of many **climates** (see p.51). The high central plains (which include Madrid) suffer from fierce extremes – stiflingly hot in summer, bitterly cold and swept by freezing winds in winter. The Atlantic coast, in contrast, has a tendency to be damp and misty, with a relatively brief, humid summer. The Mediterranean south is warm virtually all year round, and in parts of Andalucía it's positively subtropical – it's often pleasant enough to take lunch outside, even in the winter months. On a general holiday or city break, in most regions spring, the early part of summer and autumn are the best times to visit. Temperatures will be fairly mild, sites and attractions open, and tourist numbers relatively low – worth considering, especially if your destination is one of the beach resorts or main cultural attractions. Spain is one of the most visited countries on the planet – it plays host to about sixty million tourists a year, rather more than the entire population – and all main tourist destinations are packed in high summer. Even the Pyrenean mountains aren't immune, swapping winter ski crowds for summer hikers and bikers. August is Spain's own holiday month – when the *costas* are at their most crowded, though inland cities (including Madrid) are, by contrast, pretty sleepy, since everyone who can, leaves for their annual break.

LEFT VALENCIA

28

things not to miss

It's not possible to see everything that Spain has to offer in one trip – and we don't suggest you try. What follows, in no particular order, is a selection of the country's highlights, including spectacular architecture, outstanding natural wonders, flamboyant local festivals and a few culinary treats. Each entry has a page reference to take you straight into the Guide, where you can find out more. Coloured numbers refer to chapters in the Guide section.

1

1 FLAMENCO IN SEVILLE

The stamp of heels and heart-rending lament of a *cante jondo* encapsulate the soul of the Spanish south.

2 SHERRY TASTING IN JEREZ

There are few greater pleasures than a chilled glass of fino or manzanilla, and there's no better place to sample them than in the sherry heartland of Jerez.

3 BURGOS CATHEDRAL

Perhaps Spain's finest Gothic cathedral dominates the likeable small city of Burgos, destined to be European City of Culture in 2016.

4 IBIZA AND FORMENTERA'S HIDDEN COVES

The islands' little-developed beaches range from gem-like coves to sweeps of white sand.

9

10

11 PARADORES
Page 37

Converted castles, monasteries and special monuments provide many of Spain's most atmospheric hotels.

12 BODEGAS YSIOS
Page 483

Raise a glass to the Rioja region's amazing designer temple of wine.

13 LAS ALPUJARRAS
Page 350

Drive over lemons and walk old mule paths in this picturesque region of mountain villages nestled in the southern folds of the Sierra Nevada.

14 SEMANA SANTA
Page 228

Easter week sees processions of masked penitents, with the biggest events in Seville and Málaga.

15 FUNDACIÓ JOAN MIRÓ
Page 667

Admire the instantly recognizable colours, shapes and forms of Joan Miró's life's work in this Barcelona museum.

16 SANTIAGO DE COMPOSTELA
Page 546

The pilgrim route to Santiago de Compostela left a swathe of Gothic and Renaissance churches, not least the great Catedral.

17 PARQUE NACIONAL COTO DE DOÑANA
Page 306

Doñana's unique habitats host myriad birds and other wildlife, including the Iberian lynx.

14

15

16

17

18

19

20

18 UNIVERSIDAD DE SALAMANCA

Page 378

Spain's most famous and historic university sits at the heart of this gorgeous honey-coloured city.

19 PICOS DE EUROPA

Page 514

Take a hike along the stunning Cares Gorge, the most popular walk in glorious Picos de Europa National Park.

20 MUSEO DEL PRADO, MADRID

Page 77

Spain's greatest art museum is an obligatory visit on any trip to the capital.

21 SITGES

Page 772

Sitges is Spain's biggest gay resort and throws simply spectacular parties, especially at Carnival time.

22 ROMAN RUINS OF MÉRIDA

Page 211

Wander at will around the ancient Roman ruins of Mérida, the most extensive such remains in the country.

23 MUSEO GUGGENHEIM, BILBAO

Page 469

Frank Gehry's flagship creation of undulating titanium has become one of the iconic buildings of our age.

24

25

26

27

28

Itineraries

Spain is a vast and varied country, and you can't cover all of it in a single trip. Our Grand Tour concentrates on Spain's major cities and outstanding sights, while our other suggested routes focus on two captivating regions, one in the south, one in the north. Each itinerary will take a packed two weeks to cover; if you only have one week to spare you can cover part of one route and get a flavour of the whole country or a feel for one of its fascinating regions.

GRAND TOUR OF SPAIN

Two weeks in Spain and no idea where to start? Our "Grand Tour" puts you on the right track.

❶ Madrid The vibrant capital is at the heart of all that makes modern Spain tick, from world-class art collections to a buzzing café society and a wild nightlife. **See p.60**

❷ Toledo With time for just one side-trip from Madrid, head to Toledo. This old rock-bound city is the home of El Greco and is packed with magnificent buildings. **See p.126**

❸ Seville You could spend weeks exploring Andalucía (see opposite) – but for a taster, Seville combines gorgeous buildings with a vibrant flamenco and tapas scene. **See p.263**

❹ Valencia The rapidly changing city of Valencia – cultural hub of the east, not to mention the spiritual birthplace of paella – breaks up the long journey up the coast. **See p.795**

❺ Barcelona Leave Spain – as the locals would have you believe – for the cool Catalan capital, with its Art Nouveau architecture, designer shops, and stylish bars and clubs. **See p.642**

❻ Figueres The two-hour journey from Barcelona towards the French border is made with only one destination in mind – the extraordinary Teatre-Museu Dalí. **See p.740**

❼ Logroño This handsome city sits at the heart of the Rioja region, and while it's only small there's nothing modest about its superb tapas and wine bars. From here, you could detour along the northern coast (see opposite). **See p.409**

❽ Valladolid Re-live Spain's Golden Age in the capital of Castilla y León, whose majestic Plaza Mayor has no equal. **See p.392**

❾ Salamanca The most beautiful city in Spain has buildings fashioned from a honey-coloured stone that glows as the sun sets. **See p.374**

THE BEST OF ANDALUCÍA

❶ Málaga This transport hub is the obvious place to start, but it's also worth lingering for a day to enjoy this vibrant coastal city. **See p.229**

❷ Ronda Sited astride a towering gorge is the queen of Andalucía's white towns. **See p.256**

❸ Seville The essence of all things *andaluz*, with a stunning cathedral, Moorish Alcázar and atmospheric old quarter. **See p.263**

❹ Córdoba A must-see destination, boasting one of the world's greatest Moorish buildings, the Mezquita, at its heart. **See p.313**

❺ Baeza and Úbeda These twin Renaissance architectural jewels are filled with a wealth of monuments in golden stone. **See p.325**

ABOVE LA CIUDAD DE LAS ARTES Y LAS CIENCIAS, VALENCIA

❻ Cazorla Natural Park A stunning array of wildlife inhabits the rugged mountains, gorges and forested valleys of Cazorla. **See p.328**

❼ Granada Overlooked by the seductive Alhambra, the historic city of Granada is one of Spain's most compelling attractions. **See p.331**

❽ Almuñécar The Costa Tropical's main resort has great beaches and plenty of places to eat, drink and dance the night away. **See p.243**

NORTHERN SPAIN, ALONG THE ATLANTIC COAST

❶ Bilbao Revitalized by the success of its Guggenheim Museum, the energetic city of Bilbao is set amid the spectacular green hills of the Basque Country. **See p.468**

❷ San Sebastián This elegant seaside resort boasts one of Europe's best city beaches; its superb cuisine is at its most affordable in the *pintxos* bars of the old quarter. **See p.452**

❸ Pamplona An intriguing destination, which comes alive during the bull-running of July's San Fermín festival. **See p.484**

❹ Santillana del Mar Often hailed as Spain's prettiest village, Santillana is an exquisite medieval ensemble with some gorgeous hotels. **See p.509**

❺ Picos de Europa Just a few kilometres back from the sea, these snowy peaks are interspersed with lush meadows and ancient settlements, and offer superb hiking. **See p.514**

❻ Llanes Delightful seaside towns dot the Asturian coast, but bustling little Llanes, close to superb beaches and soaring mountains, is perhaps the finest of all. **See p.528**

❼ Oviedo Ravishing little Visigothic churches pepper the hills here – though you'll have to tear yourself away from the city's cider-houses to see them. **See p.536**

❽ The Rías of Galicia The fjord-like estuaries that slice into Galicia cradle dramatic scenery and splendid beaches, with the wild Rías Altas in the north and the busier, gentler Rías Baixas to the south. **See p.561 & p.572**

❾ Santiago de Compostela For over a thousand years, this magnificent cathedral city has welcomed footsore pilgrims; its historic core, bursting with bars and restaurants, remains irresistible. **See p.546**

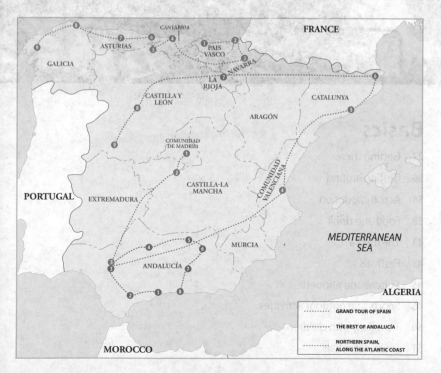

FERIA DE ABRIL, SEVILLE

Basics

Getting there

Madrid and Barcelona are the two main Spanish airports, though the summer holiday trade to the costas and the Balearics, and the rapid growth of European budget airlines, has opened up regional airports right across Spain. Taking the train to Spain is a greener option and has much to recommend it – and now you can do the whole journey from London to Barcelona or Madrid in a day. Driving is more of an adventure, but there are several routes that can save you time, like the direct ferry services from Portsmouth and Plymouth to Santander and Portsmouth to Bilbao.

Flights from the UK and Ireland

Flight time to Spain is two to three hours, depending on the route, and usually the cheapest flights are with the no-frills **budget airlines** such as easyJet (Weasyjet.com), flybe (Wflybe.com), Jet2 (Wjet2.com) and Ryanair (Wryanair.com), who between them fly from over twenty regional UK airports direct to **destinations all over Spain** – not just Madrid and Barcelona, but also to smaller regional Spanish airports like Málaga, Alicante, Santander, Valencia and those in the Balearics. Note that London flights tend to depart from Stansted or Luton, while it's always worth double-checking the exact Spanish airport used – some "Barcelona" flights, for example, are actually to Girona (1hr to the north) or Reus (1hr 15min to the south). **Fares** for flights on all routes start at around £20 each way. However, book last minute in the summer and you can expect to pay considerably more, up to £100 each way depending on the route.

For flights **to the costas and Balearics**, it's also worth checking holiday and charter companies such as Monarch (Wmonarch.co.uk), First Choice (Wfirstchoice.co.uk), Thomas Cook (Wflythomascook.com) and Thomson (Wthomsonfly.com). You might not get the rock-bottom deals of the budget airlines, as schedules and prices are geared towards the summer holiday season, but flights depart from convenient regional airports around the UK.

The widest range of **scheduled flights** is with the now-merged Iberia (Wiberia.com) and British Airways (Wba.com), with direct services from London Gatwick or Heathrow to half a dozen Spanish cities (most frequently to Madrid and Barcelona, but also Valencia, Málaga and Alicante) and connections on to most other airports in Spain. You'll also be able to arrange add-on sections to London from regional English airports such as Manchester or Newcastle or from Scotland. Special offers start at around £100 return, though a typical late-booking summer rate will be more like £200 return.

From Ireland, you can fly with Iberia from Dublin to Madrid, or with Aer Lingus (Waerlingus .com) from Dublin or Cork to several Spanish airports (including Barcelona, Bilbao, Málaga and Alicante). Ryanair also connects Dublin and Shannon with most of the same destinations, plus places like Seville, Valencia and Murcia. Prices start at around €40 each way, though these rise sharply for last-minute bookings or to popular summer destinations.

Flights from the US and Canada

The widest choice of scheduled flights **from the United States** to Spain is with Iberia (Wiberia.com), which flies direct, nonstop from New York to Madrid or Barcelona, and from Miami and Chicago to Madrid. Journey time (typically overnight) is between seven hours ten minutes and eight hours thirty minutes, depending on the route. Fares start at around US$1100 return. The advantage of flying with Iberia is that it offers connecting flights to almost anywhere in Spain, which can be very good value if booked with your transatlantic flight.

Other airlines offering Spain routes (some on a code-share basis with Iberia or other airlines) include American Airlines (Waa.com), Delta (Wdelta.com) and United (Wunited.com). Or you can fly to Spain with airlines such as Air France, KLM,

---

A BETTER KIND OF TRAVEL

At Rough Guides we are passionately committed to travel. We believe it helps us understand the world we live in and the people we share it with – and of course tourism is vital to many developing economies. But the scale of modern tourism has also damaged some places irreparably, and climate change is accelerated by most forms of transport, especially flying. All Rough Guides' flights are carbon-offset, and every year we donate money to a variety of environmental charities.

Lufthansa, TAP or British Airways, for example, which tend to fly via their respective European hubs – in which case, you can add three to four hours to your total travel time, depending on the connection.

From Canada, Air Canada (W aircanada.com) flies nonstop from Toronto to Barcelona. It also sells connecting and/or code-sharing flights from Toronto and Montréal to Madrid, Barcelona, Valencia, Malaga and Bilbao. Alternatively, you can fly with one of the major European airlines via their respective hubs – fares in all cases start from around Can$1250 return.

Flights from Australia, New Zealand and South Africa

There are no direct flights to Spain **from Australia or New Zealand**, but many airlines offer through-tickets with their partners via their European or Asian hubs. Flights via Asia are generally the cheaper option, but fares don't vary as much between airlines as you might think, and in the end you'll be basing your choice on things like flight timings, routes and possible stop-offs on the way. If you're seeing Spain as part of a wider European trip, you might want to aim first for the UK, since there's a wide choice of cheap flights to Spain from there. Or consider a Round-the-world fare, with most basic options able to offer Madrid or Barcelona as standard stopovers.

From **South Africa**, there are no direct flights to Spain, but you can fly from Johannesburg to Madrid via Frankfurt with South Africa Airlines (W flysaa .com), or from Cape Town or Johannesburg with one of the major European airlines via their home hubs; it's around fifteen hours if you fly via London.

Package holidays, tours and city breaks

The basic, mass-market **package holidays** to the traditional resorts on the Costa del Sol, Costa Brava, Costa Blanca and others are not to everyone's taste, but bargains can be found online or at any UK high-street travel agent, from as little as £150 for a seven-night flight-and-hotel package. There are often really good deals for families, either in hotels or in self-catering apartments, though, of course, if you are tied to school holidays you will pay significantly more.

A huge number of **specialist tour operators** offer a wider range of activity holidays or tours,

from hiking in the Pyrenees to touring the artistic highlights of Andalucía. We've given a flavour of what's available in the listed reviews at the end of this section, but the options are almost endless. Prices vary wildly depending on the quality of accommodation offered and whether the tours are fully inclusive or not. Many hiking or bicycle tours, for example, can either be guided or done on a more independent (and cheaper) self-guided basis. Spanish-based tour operators offer some of the more interesting, off-the-beaten-track options, but for these you'll usually have to arrange your own flights to Spain, while many foreign-based operators also tend to quote for their holidays exclusive of airfares.

Some operators and websites specialize in **city breaks**, with destinations including Barcelona, Madrid, Seville and Granada. UK prices start at around £140 for three-day (two-night) breaks, including return flights, airport transfer and B&B in a centrally located one-, two- or three-star hotel. Adding extra nights or upgrading your hotel is possible, too, usually at a fairly reasonable cost. The bigger US operators, such as American Express and Delta Vacations, can also easily organize short city breaks to Spain on a flight-and-hotel basis, while from Australia Iberian specialist Ibertours (W ibertours.com.au) can arrange two- or three-night packages in most Spanish cities.

Other deals worth considering are fly-drive offers, where you'll get a **flight, accommodation and car rental** arranged through your tour operator. Some companies specialize in villas and apartments, or off-the-beaten-track farmhouses and the like, while on other holiday packages you can tour the country's historic paradores, with car rental included.

ADVENTURE OPERATORS

Adventure Center US ☎ 1 800 228 8747, W adventurecenter .com. Active vacations in the Picos de Europa, Catalunya, Andalucía and the Sierra Nevada, including self-guided treks along the Camino de Santiago and cycling trips from the Pyrenees to the Med, starting at $1300 (excluding airfares).

Alto-Aragon UK ☎ 0034 616 452337, W altoaragon.co.uk. An established English-run company offering summer hiking and activity holidays (from around £400, land-only) in the high Pyrenees and the Basque Country.

Exodus Travels UK ☎ 0845 287 3647, W exodus.co.uk. Walking and cycling in Andalucía, Mallorca, the Picos de Europa and the Pyrenees (and most minor mountain ranges), as well as cycling or multi-adventure (climbing, caving, rafting, etc), cultural and sightseeing trips. There's a big range of tours at all prices, but a typical example is a week's walking in the Sierra de Aitana, from £950 including flights.

BACKPACKER TRAVEL

Busabout UK ☎ 0845 0267 514, Ⓦ busabout.com. The European backpacker bus service offers a seven-day Southern Spain/Portugal bus tour staying in Seville, Granada, the Algarve and Lisbon (from £539) plus island-hopping in the Balearics (from £619), all aimed at a young, party crowd.

CYCLING TOURS

Bravobike Spain ☎ 917 582 945, Ⓦ bravobike.com. Offers a variety of cycle tours from one day in Madrid, Segovia or Toledo, for example, to themed week-long tours in *conquistador* country or along the Camino de Santiago. Prices vary from €31 for a half-day trip round Madrid, up to €1900 for a guided wine tour of Rioja.

Easy Rider Tours US ☎ 1 800 488 8332, Ⓦ easyridertours.com. Guided cycling and sightseeing tours in Andalucía, the foothills of the Pyrenees, and along the pilgrims' way to Santiago de Compostela. Tours are all-inclusive and fully supported, from around $3300 for a week, though airfares are extra.

Iberocycle Spain ☎ 020 3286 4124, Ⓦ iberocycle.com. An English-run, Spain-based company specializing in supported or self-guided cycling tours of northern Spain in particular (Cantabria, Asturias, Basque Country, Catalunya). Short five-night trips start at around €550.

FOOD AND DRINK TOURS

Arblaster & Clarke UK ☎ 01730 263111, Ⓦ arblasterandclarke .com. The most notable wine-tour specialist, with quality trips to all Spain's wine-producing regions, including agreeable accommodation and tastings at both famous and little-known wineries. From £1800, excluding flights

A Taste of Spain Spain ☎ 856 079 626, Ⓦ atasteofspain.com. Organizes gourmet culinary tours of Catalunya, the Basque region/La Rioja, Andalucía and central Spain, with tastings, meals and cookery lessons. From around €420 for a day's excursion to taste Iberico ham, up to €3000 for a week following La Mancha's saffron route.

HISTORY, ART AND CULTURE TOURS

Abercrombie and Kent UK ☎ 0845 485 1535, Ⓦ abercrombie kent.co.uk; US ☎ 1 800 554 7016, Ⓦ abercrombiekent.com. Upmarket independent or fully escorted tailor-made tours, with the ten-day "Classic Spain" trip (Barcelona, Madrid, Cordoba, Seville, from £4750) typically providing high-speed train travel, luxury hotels and a private guide for monument visits.

Madrid and Beyond Spain ☎ 917 580 063, Ⓦ madridandbeyond .com. Classy customized holidays and special experiences, from private gallery tours to fashion-expert-led shopping trips in Barcelona and Madrid. Variable prices.

Martin Randall Travel UK ☎ 020 8742 3355, Ⓦ martinrandall .com. The leading cultural-tour specialists, offering small-group, expert-led trips to Catalunya, Madrid, Salamanca, Bilbao and Seville, among others. Trip themes range from a five-day Madrid art tour for around £1700 to the thirteen-day "Wellington in the Peninsula" trip visiting key battle sites for £3300.

HORSERIDING TOURS

Fantasia Adventure Holidays Spain ☎ 610 943 685 Ⓦ fantasiaadventureholidays.com. British-run company offering riding breaks on the Costa de la Luz, from full-board weekends to week-long holidays (from £555, excluding flights).

SURFING HOLIDAYS

Surf Spain UK Ⓦ surfspain.co.uk. Surf camps and tailor-made surfing holidays in the north and south of Spain, with six-night breaks from £409 per person (excluding flights).

WALKING TRIPS

ATG-Oxford UK ☎ 01865 315678, Ⓦ atg-oxford.co.uk. Sustainable-tourism outfit with off-the-beaten-track walking holidays in La Rioja or the volcanic countryside around Girona, plus Mallorca, Catalunya and the Camino de Santiago. Five-day holidays start from £490.

Inntravel UK ☎ 01653 617722, Ⓦ inntravel.co.uk Self-guided walking tours in Andalucia, Picos de Europa, the Pyrenees, the Balearics and Catalunya. Each night's destination is a small family-run hotel where your baggage is waiting. A typical seven-day walking holiday starts at around £600.

Olé Spain US ☎ 1 888 869 7156, Ⓦ olespain.com. Small-group cultural walking tours in Catalunya, Andalucía and Extremadura, with prices starting at $2500 for an eight-day trip (excluding airfares).

Ramblers Worldwide Holidays UK ☎ 01707 331 133, Ⓦ ramblersholidays.co.uk. Long-established walking-tour operator, with hiking holidays in most Spanish mountain regions, as well as vineyard rambles and tours of classical Andalucía. From around £700 for a week's walking in Southern Spain (includes hotel, dinner, guide and airfare).

Trains

Travelling **by train from the UK to Spain** is a viable – and fun – option, with total journey times from London of under twelve hours to Barcelona, and fifteen hours to Madrid. You can now do the journey in one (admittedly very long) day, if you take the 9.15am **Eurostar** (Ⓦ eurostar.com) from London St Pancras International to Paris and change there for the double-decker TGV Duplex, which arrives in Barcelona (via Figueres and Girona) at about 8.40pm. From Barcelona, you can catch a high-speed AVE train, which will get you to Madrid (via Zaragoza) at around midnight. **Fares** start at £69 return for the Eurostar to Paris (through-tickets available from UK towns and cities), plus €118 return for the TGV to Barcelona; return fares from Barcelona to Madrid by high-speed AVE start at €64. You'll have to book well in advance on all services to get the lowest prices. If you don't mind the journey to Spain taking a whole lot longer, there are also minor routes that cross the central Pyrenees (via Canfranc or Puigcerdà), though you may have to spend the night at either of the border towns if you want to see the mountains in daylight.

The best first stop for information about train travel to Spain is the excellent **W seat61.com**, which provides full route, ticket, timetable and contact information. You can book the whole journey online with **Loco2** (**W** loco2.com), or contact a specialist rail agent like Ffestiniog Travel (**W** ffestiniogtravel.co.uk) or the Spanish Rail Service (**W** spanish-rail.co.uk). If you live outside the UK, try **W** voyages-sncf.com, which can book Eurostar and TGV tickets and advise about **rail passes** (principally InterRail and Eurail), which have to be bought before leaving home (see opposite).

Buses

You can reach most major towns and cities in Spain by bus from the UK with **Eurolines** services (**W** eurolines.co.uk). The main routes are from London (though inexpensive add-on fares are available from any British city) to Barcelona (27hr), Madrid (29hr) and Valencia (33hr), with connections on to other Spanish destinations, but it's a long time to spend cooped up in a bus. Standard return fares are £150 to Barcelona, £170 to Madrid, though there are advance deals and special offers – it's always cheapest to book online. Eurolines also has a **Eurolines Pass**, which allows unlimited travel on Eurolines routes between forty-odd cities, but only between Madrid, Barcelona and Alicante within Spain, so it's not much use for a Spanish tour.

Driving to Spain

Driving to Spain from the UK is an interesting way to get there, but with fuel, road toll and overnight costs it doesn't compare in terms of price with flying or taking the train. It's about 1600km from London to Barcelona, for example, which, with stops, takes almost two full days to drive; it's another 600km on to Madrid.

Many people use the conventional **cross-Channel ferry links**, principally Dover–Calais, though services to Brittany or Normandy might be more convenient depending on where you live (and they cut out the trek around Paris). However, the quickest way of crossing the Channel is to use the **Eurotunnel** (**W** eurotunnel.com), which operates drive-on, drive-off shuttle trains between Folkestone and Calais/Coquelles. The 24-hour service runs every twenty minutes throughout the day; though you can just turn up, booking is advised, especially at

weekends and in summer holidays, or if you want the best deals (from £50 one-way).

The best way to cut driving time is to use one of the direct **UK–Spain ferry crossings**, especially if you're heading for the Basque region, Galicia, Castilla y León or even Madrid. Brittany Ferries (**W** brittany-ferries.co.uk) operates car and passenger ferry services from **Portsmouth to Santander** (2 weekly; 24hr) and **Bilbao** (2 weekly; 24–32hr) and **Plymouth to Santander** (1 weekly; 20hr). Fares start at £264 one-way for a car and two passengers, but it costs significantly more in summer, particularly August – it's cheaper for foot-passengers, though everyone has to book some form of seating or cabin accommodation.

Any ferry company or travel agent can supply up-to-date schedules and ticket information, or you can consult the encyclopedic **W** directferries.com, which has details about, and links to, every European ferry service.

Getting around

Most of Spain is well covered by public transport. The rail network reaches all the provincial capitals and the main towns along the inter-city lines, and there's an expanding high-speed network that has slashed journey times on major cross-country routes from Madrid. Inter-city bus services are often more frequent and cheaper than the regular trains, and will usually take you closer to your destination, as some train stations are a few kilometres from the town or village they serve. Driving a car, meanwhile, will give you the freedom to head away from the major tourist routes and take in some of the spectacular scenery at your own pace.

One important point to remember is that all public transport, and the bus service especially, is drastically reduced on **Sundays and public holidays** – don't even consider travelling to out-of-the-way places on these days. The words to look out for on timetables are *diario* (daily), *laborables* (workdays, including Sat), and *domingos y festivos* (Sun and public hols).

By train

Spanish trains, operated by **RENFE** (**W** renfe.com), tend to be efficient and comfortable, and nearly

ALL ABOARD

As well as the main Spanish rail system, there are also several private and regional train lines offering a different view of some spectacular parts of the country, mainly in the north.

The best is probably the **narrow-gauge railway** (see p.500), which runs right across the wild northwest, from Santander in Cantabria, through Asturias to Ferrol in Galicia. Catalunya has its own local commuter line, the **FGC** (see p.703), which operates the mountain rack-railway to **Montserrat**, as well as the **Cremallera**, the "zipper" (see p.752), another rack-and-pinion line that slinks up a Pyrenean valley to the sanctuary and ski station of Núria.

In the Sierra Guadarrama, just north of Madrid, the narrow-gauge line from **Cercedilla** to the ski station at Puerto de Navacerrada and then on to Cotos is a great way to see the mountainous landscape (see p.148).

always run on time. There's a confusing array of services, though the website has a useful English-language version on which you can check timetables and buy tickets with a credit card (printing them out at home before you travel).

Cercanías are local commuter trains in and around the major cities, while **media distancia** (regional) and **larga distancia** (long-distance) trains go under a bewildering number of names, including Avant, Alaris, Intercity (IC), Regional and Talgo services. The difference is speed, service and number of stops, and you'll always pay more on the quickest routes (sometimes quite a lot more).

The premier services are the high-speed trains, such as the **Euromed** from Barcelona to Alicante, or the fast-expanding **AVE** (Alta Velocidad Española) network from Madrid to Seville, Málaga, Valencia, Segovia/Valladolid, Zaragoza, Barcelona, Alicante and Huesca; and from Barcelona to Seville and Málaga; and from Valencia to Seville. The AVE trains have cut travelling times dramatically, with Madrid to Seville, for example, taking two and a half hours compared with six to nine hours on the slower trains. The AVE network also runs across the border from Madrid and Barcelona to Marseille, and from Barcelona to Paris, Lyons and Toulouse, and is set to expand right across the peninsula over the next decade, northwest to Castilla y León, the Basque Country and Asturias, and west to Lisbon in Portugal.

Tickets, fares and rail passes

Although you can just turn up at the station for short hops, **advance booking** is essential (and seat reservations obligatory) for long-distance journeys. Advance tickets can be bought at stations between sixty days and five minutes before departure, but don't leave it to the last minute, as there are usually long queues (and often separate windows for the different types of train). Automatic **ticket machines**

at main stations take some of the hassle out of queuing.

The best deals are always available **online** on the RENFE website, which has a range of different promotional fares offering discounts of up to sixty percent on the full fares. Otherwise, **return fares** (*ida y vuelta*) are discounted by ten to twenty percent, depending on the service – you can buy a single, and so long as you show it when you buy the return, you'll still get the discount. There's also a whole range of other **discounted fares** of between 25 and 40 percent for those over 60 or under 26, the disabled, children aged 4 to 11 years, and those travelling in groups.

Actual fares vary wildly, but as an example, you'll pay around €23 on the regional service from Madrid to Salamanca (2hr 40min trip), while on the Madrid to Barcelona route you could pay €74 on the high-speed AVE service (around 3hr).

The major pan-European **rail passes** (InterRail and Eurail) are only worth considering if you're visiting the country as part of a wider European tour. Both schemes also have single-country Spain rail passes available, which might be better value depending on your Spanish itinerary. The **InterRail Spain Pass** (🌐 interrailnet.com) is only available to European residents and allows three, four, six or eight days' train travel within one month, with under-26 years, second- and first-class versions available. For anyone else, **Eurail** (🌐 raileurope.com) has various Spain passes available, typically offering three days' travel in two months, again in various classes. You can check current prices on the websites, but bear in mind that it often works out cheaper to buy individual tickets in Spain as you need them, and it's certainly more convenient to be free to choose long-distance buses on some routes. All passes have to be bought before you leave home, and you'll still be liable for supplements and seat reservations on long-distance and high-speed trains.

By bus

Buses will probably meet most of your transport needs, especially if you're venturing away from the larger towns and cities. Many smaller villages and rural areas are only accessible by bus, almost always originating in the capital of their province. Services are pretty reliable, whether it's the two-buses-a-day school or market run or the regular services between major cities (the latter often far more conveniently scheduled than the equivalent train services). **Fares** are very reasonable, too: Madrid to León (3hr 30min), for example, costs around €25, Madrid to Santander (6hr) around €31. On inter-city runs, you'll usually be assigned a seat when you buy your ticket. Some destinations are served by more than one **bus company**, but main bus stations have posted timetables for all services (and, sometimes, someone who can speak English). Or you can check timetables on the company websites, which, while not always up to date, do at least give an idea of available services. Major companies like Alsa (Ⓦalsa.es/en) and Avanzabus (Ⓦavanzabus.com) have nationwide services, and both have English-language versions of their websites.

There are only a few cities in Spain (Madrid, Barcelona and Valencia, for example) where you'll need to use the **local bus** network, and all the relevant details are given in the Guide. You'll also sometimes need to take a local bus out to a campsite or distant museum or monastery; fares are very cheap, rarely more than a euro or two.

By car

Spain has an extensive system of highways, both free and with tolls. The **autopistas** are the most comfortable and best-kept roads. The second-grade roads, **autovías (prefixed E)**, often follow similar routes, but their speed limits are lower. Many *autopistas* and some *autovías* are toll roads, relatively expensive by local standards but worth paying for the lighter traffic encountered. You can usually pay with a credit card, although it's wise to have enough cash just in case. Toll roads are usually designated by an "AP" or "R" or the words "*peaje/Telpeaje/Via T*".

The Spanish **drive on the right**, and **speed limits** are enforced throughout the country. On most *autopistas* it is 120km/h, on the *autovía* 90km/h, and in towns and villages 50km/h. Police have the power to fine drivers on the spot for speeding or any other transgressions, and if you don't have any cash, they will escort you to the nearest cash machine and issue you with a receipt there and then. You can pay by credit card at most petrol stations for **fuel** (*gasolina*), the main companies being Cepsa and Repsol.

An EU **driver's licence** is sufficient to drive in Spain. US, Canadian, Australian and New Zealand licences should also be enough, though you may want to get an International Driver's Licence as well, just to be on the safe side. If you are bringing your own car, you will need your vehicle registration and insurance papers – and check with your insurers that you are covered to drive the car abroad. It's also

---

THE SPANISH DRIVING EXPERIENCE

If it's your first time out on a Spanish road, especially in one of the bigger cities, you could be forgiven for thinking you've stumbled upon the local chapter of *Mad Max* devotees, out for a burn-up. In fact, those wild-eyed, dangerously speeding, non-signalling, bumper-hogging, mobile-talking, horn-sounding road warriors are normal law-abiding Spanish citizens on their way to work. **Traffic lights** and **pedestrian crossings** in particular present a difficult conceptual challenge – if you are going to stop at either, make sure you give plenty of warning to avoid another vehicle running into the back of you, and keep an eye out for cars crossing your path who have jumped the lights. **Signposting** is universally poor (yes, *that* was the turn you wanted), even on main roads and highways, while joining and exiting **autopistas/autovías** can be particularly dangerous, as it's almost a point of honour not to let anyone in or out. Many of the worst **accidents** are on the N roads, which have only a single carriageway in each direction, so take particular care on these. Major roads are generally in good **condition**, though some minor and mountain roads can be rather hairy and are little more than dirt tracks in the more remote regions. Sheep, goats and cattle are also regular hazards. Having said all this, things are (slowly) improving and drivers are a bit more careful because of increased use of radar and speed controls. The police are also setting up more **drink-driving** controls than before, though you have to remember that this is a country where it's considered a good idea to have bars in motorway service stations.

SPAIN'S BEST DRIVES

There are some fantastic driving routes in this land of big scenery, big horizons and big surprises – here's our choice of Spain's best drives.

Alt Empordà Track the coastline in northern Costa Brava as you take in Greek and Roman ruins at Empúries and Salvador Dalí's former home outside the picturesque town of Cadaqués. See p.725.

Cañón de Río Sil Gaze upon Galicia's most arresting landscape along this dramatic canyon that is also home to one of the country's foremost wine-producing regions. See p.590.

The Cincó Villas Lose yourself in small-town Aragón on the 80km drive linking the historic "five towns," from Tauste to Sos del Rey Católico. See p.608.

El Escorial to Ávila The most scenic route out of Madrid province, an hour's drive from Felipe II's colossal monastery and over the hills to the historic walled city of Ávila. See p.151.

Gipuzkoa Head inland from San Sebastián and immerse yourself in Basque culture at Tolosa's lively carnival and historic Oñati, with its distinctive *casas torres*. See p.461.

Inland from Benidorm It's the juxtaposition between hedonistic sun-and-sand and quiet, rural inland Valencia that marks this leisurely 55km excursion, from Calpe to Alcoy. See p.826.

Puerto de las Palomas to Zahara de la Sierra One of the most dramatic descents in Andalucía starts from the "Pass of the Doves" and corkscrews dizzily downwards to the ancient Moorish village of Zahara, with spectacular views across the sierras. See p.260.

Sierra de la Demanda Mountain monasteries, verdant valleys and bare upland vistas on the two-hour drive (LR113) from La Rioja to the Castilla y León heartland. See p.416.

Through the Valle de Jerte Track the Río Jerte for 70km (N110 out of Plasencia towards Barco de Ávila) on one of the most picturesque drives in Spain – carpeted in cherry blossom every spring. See p.195.

Valldemossa to Lluc The Ma10 tracks the dramatic coastline of northern Mallorca, a roller coaster of a ride through hilltop villages via the island's highest peaks. See p.876.

Vielha to Esterri d'Aneau Snowy peaks, thickly forested slopes and, above all, utter mountain stillness – this 42km drive over the Bonaigua Pass (2072m) is pure Pyrenees. See p.766.

compulsory to carry two hazard triangles and reflective jackets in case of accident or breakdown. Rear seat belts are also compulsory, as are child seats for infants. An official first-aid kit and a set of spare bulbs is also recommended.

Parking can be a big pain in the neck, especially in big cities and old-town areas. Metered parking zones usually have stays limited to a couple of hours, though parking between 8pm and 8am, on Saturday afternoons and all Sundays tends to be free. Green or blue bays signify pay-parking areas in most cities, but it's always worth double-checking that you're allowed to park where you've just left your car, as any illegally parked vehicle will be promptly towed. Some cities (like Granada) have also introduced old-town **congestion charges**, which you might unwittingly trigger as a casual visitor. It's nearly always best to pay extra for a hotel with parking or use a pay car park, for which you'll need to budget anything from €12 to €20 a day.

Car rental

Car rental is cheapest arranged in advance through one of the large multinational agencies (Avis, Budget, EasyCar, Europcar, Hertz, Holiday Autos, National or Thrifty, for example). There are hundreds of pick-up offices in Spain, including regional airports and major train stations. Rates start from around £120/$200 a week for a two-door Renault Clio or similar, more for larger vehicles and in peak holiday periods. Local Spanish companies (such as Pepecar; ⓦpepecar.com) can sometimes offer better value for money and you can also get some very good low-season rates.

You'll need to be 21 or over (and have been driving for at least a year) to rent a car in Spain. You will also need a credit card to cover the initial deposit and have both your licence photo card and the paper licence document. It's essential to check that you have adequate **insurance cover** for your rental car, and that all visible damage on a car you're picking up is duly marked on the rental sheet. It's definitely worth considering paying the extra charge to reduce the "excess" payment levied for any damage, but these waiver charges (by the day) soon add up. However, you can avoid all **excess charges** in the event of damage by taking out an annual insurance policy (from £40) with ⓦinsurance4carhire.com, which also covers windscreen and tyre damage.

By bike

Bike rental is not common, save in resort areas or in tourist-oriented cities such as Barcelona and Madrid, where you can expect to pay €15–20 a day, or around €25 for a half-day bike tour. Barcelona, Seville and some other cities also have bike-transit schemes, where you join (by paying a deposit) and then pick up bikes (free or low-cost) to ride around

DISTANCE CHART (KM)

	Alicante	Barcelona	Bilbao	Burgos	Córdoba	Granada	Jaén	León	Madrid
Alicante	–	552	814	645	513	372	417	762	420
Barcelona	552	–	609	629	893	889	840	818	630
Bilbao	814	609	–	160	795	820	730	350	400
Burgos	645	629	160	–	640	664	581	178	245
Córdoba	513	893	795	640	–	238	110	736	404
Granada	372	889	820	664	238	–	98	761	424
Jaén	417	840	730	581	110	98	–	677	342
León	762	818	350	178	736	761	677	–	349
Madrid	420	630	400	245	404	424	342	349	–
Málaga	480	1022	930	776	168	125	211	871	543
Murcia	82	602	785	634	482	297	342	749	408
Pamplona	723	490	152	210	841	869	791	404	456
Salamanca	630	835	398	248	604	634	543	208	219
San Sebastián	769	525	249	300	924	949	854	489	534
Santander	837	715	103	186	820	856	762	280	428
Santiago de Compostela	1033	1165	596	526	1009	1032	949	364	607
Seville	606	1055	861	711	149	261	300	674	537
Toledo	439	710	472	317	391	413	326	412	78
Valencia	183	365	651	590	536	510	454	702	361

the city from one depot to another. However, dedicated cycle paths are rare (again, Barcelona is an exception), and cycling around most major Spanish cities can be a hair-raising, if not downright dangerous, business.

Outside towns and cities, cycling is a great way to see parts of the country that might otherwise pass you by, though bear in mind that Spain is one of the most mountainous countries in Europe and there are often searing high-summer temperatures with which to contend. You also need to be extremely careful on the road (single file only, at all times), since Spanish drivers don't generally expect to see cyclists and don't take much care when they do. Off-road biking is a far better idea, and increasing numbers of mountain bikers are taking to the trails in national parks or following long-distance routes like the Camino de Santiago.

Ferries and planes

Anyone heading from the Spanish mainland to the Balearic Islands will probably do so by **ferry** or **catamaran** express ferry (from Alicante, Barcelona, Dénia or Valencia) – all the details are in the relevant city and island chapters. However, there's also an extensive network of internal Spanish **flights**, including to and between the Balearics, with Iberia (Ⓦ iberia.com) and other smaller operators. These can be worth it if you're in a hurry and need to cross

the entire peninsula, or if you can snap up a bargain web fare, but otherwise tourists rarely use flights to get around Spain. The main exception has always been Europe's busiest air route, that between Madrid and Barcelona, though this is now facing stiff competition from the high-speed AVE train, which is comparable in overall centre-to-centre journey time, and often cheaper.

Accommodation

There's a great variety of accommodation in Spain, ranging from humble family-run pensions to five-star luxury hotels, often in dramatic historic buildings. The mainstay of the coastal resort is the typical beachfront holiday hotel, though renting an apartment or a villa gives you more freedom, while farm stays, village B&Bs, rural guesthouses and mountain inns are all increasingly popular options.

Compared with other European countries, accommodation in Spain is still pretty good value. In almost any town, you'll be able to get a no-frills double room in a *pensión* or small hotel for around €50, sometimes even less, especially outside the main resorts. As a rule, you can expect to pay from €100 for something with a bit of boutique styling,

Málaga	Murcia	Pamplona	Salamanca	San Sebastián	Santander	Santiago de Compostela	Seville	Toledo	Valencia
480	82	723	630	769	837	1033	606	439	183
1022	602	490	835	525	715	1165	1055	710	365
930	785	152	398	249	103	596	861	472	651
776	634	210	248	300	186	526	711	317	590
168	482	841	604	924	820	1009	149	391	536
125	297	869	634	949	856	1032	261	413	510
211	342	791	543	854	762	949	300	326	454
871	749	404	208	489	280	364	674	412	702
543	408	456	219	534	428	607	537	78	361
–	414	993	674	1065	967	1124	231	527	649
414	–	772	604	812	817	1015	531	420	233
993	772	–	453	97	264	742	924	529	524
674	604	453	–	554	370	437	467	273	573
1065	812	97	554	–	350	836	2022	631	612
967	817	264	370	350	–	499	896	508	769
1124	1015	742	437	836	499	–	901	672	970
231	531	924	467	2022	896	901	–	507	684
527	420	529	273	631	508	672	507	–	378
649	233	524	573	612	769	970	684	378	–

and from €150–250 for five-star hotels, historic paradores and luxury beachfront resorts. However, the trend is bucked by Madrid and Barcelona, in particular, and some fashionable coastal and resort areas, where rooms are often appreciably more expensive in all categories.

Advance reservations are essential in major cities and resort areas at peak holiday, festival or convention times. Local festivals and annual events also tend to fill all available accommodation weeks in advance. That said, as a general rule, if you haven't booked, all you have to do is head for the cathedral or main square of any town, which is invariably surrounded by an old quarter full of *pensiones* and hotels. You don't always pay more for a central location; indeed, the newer three- and four-star properties tend to be located more on the outskirts. **Families** will find that most places have rooms with three or even four beds at not a great deal more than the double-room price; however, **single travellers** often get a comparatively bad deal, and can end up paying sixty to eighty percent of the price of a double room.

Accommodation prices are **seasonal**, but minimum and maximum rates should be displayed at reception. In high season on the costas, many hotels only take bookings for a minimum of a week, while some also require at least a half-board stay. However, it's worth noting that high season isn't always summer, in ski resorts for example, while inland cities such as Madrid tend to have cheaper prices in August, when everyone heads for the coast.

Where possible, **website** bookings nearly always offer the best deals, especially with the larger **hotel groups** that have made big inroads into Spain – it's always worth checking NH Hoteles (Ⓦnh-hotels .com), Accor (Ⓦaccorhotels.com) and Sol Meliá (Ⓦsolmelia.com) for current deals.

Private rooms and B&Bs

The cheapest beds are usually in **private rooms**, in someone's house or above a bar or restaurant. The signs to look for are *habitaciones* (rooms) or *camas* (beds), or they might be touted at resort bus and train stations in summer as you arrive. The rooms should be clean, but might well be very simple and timeworn; you'll probably share a communal bathroom.

The number of private **"bed-and-breakfast"** establishments (advertised as such) is on the increase, and while some are simply the traditional room in someone's house, others – especially in the major cities – are very stylish and pricey home from homes.

Pensiones, hostales and hotels

Guesthouses and hotels in Spain go under various anachronistic names – *pensión, fonda, residencia,*

ACCOMMODATION PRICES

We give a room price for all establishments reviewed in this guide. Unless otherwise stated, this represents the price for the **cheapest available double or twin room in high season** (ie usually Christmas/New Year, Easter, and June–September, though local variations apply – summer prices might be high-season on the Costa del Sol but will be low-season in scorching inland Andalucía, for example). Consequently, at many times of the year, or during special promotions, you'll often find a room for a lower price than that suggested. For **youth hostels** and anywhere else with **dorm beds**, we also give the per-person overnight rate. Note that **eight percent tax** (IVA) is added to all accommodation bills, which might not be specifically stated until it is time to pay, so always ask if you're uncertain.

Hotel prices don't usually include breakfast, which is almost always an optional extra; often it's much cheaper to find a nearby bar to eat in.

hostal, etc – though only **hotels and pensiones** are recognized as official categories. These are all star-rated (hotels, one- to five-star; *pensiones*, one- or two-star), but the rating is not necessarily a guide to cost or ambience. Some smaller, boutique-style *pensiones* and hotels have services and facilities that belie their star rating; some four- and five-star hotels have disappointingly small rooms and an impersonal feel.

At the budget end of the scale are **pensiones** (marked P), **fondas** (F) – which traditionally had a restaurant or dining room attached – and **casas de huéspedes** (CH), literally an old-fashioned "guest-house". In all such places you can expect straightforward rooms, often with shared bathroom facilities (there's usually a washbasin in the room), while occasionally things like heating, furniture (other than bed, chair and desk) and even external windows might be too much to hope for. On the other hand, some old-fashioned *pensiones* are lovingly cared for and very good value, while others have gone for a contemporary, boutique style.

Next step up, and far more common, are **hostales** (Hs) and **hostal-residencias** (HsR), which are not hostels, in any sense, but budget hotels, generally offering good, if functional, rooms, usually with private bathrooms and – in the better places – probably heating and air conditioning. Many also have cheaper rooms available without private bathrooms. Some *hostales* really are excellent, with good service and up-to-date furnishings and facilities.

Fully-fledged **hotels** (H), meanwhile, have a star-rating dependent on things like room size and staffing levels rather than any intrinsic attraction. There's often not much difference in price between a one-star hotel and a decent *hostal*, for example, and the *hostal* might be nicer. At three and four stars, hotel prices start to increase and you can expect soundproofing, an elevator, an English-language channel on the TV and a buffet breakfast

spread. At five stars, you're in the luxury class, with pools, gyms, Jacuzzis, and prices to match, and some hotels differentiate themselves again as five-star "deluxe" or "gran classe" (GL).

You can pick up lists of local accommodation from any Spanish tourist office, and there are countless websites to look at, too, including the excellent **Rusticae** (Ⓦ rusticae.es), which highlights scores of stylish rural and urban hotels across the country.

Paradores

Spain has over ninety superior hotels in a class of their own, called **paradores** (Ⓦ parador.es), which are often spectacular lodgings converted from castles, monasteries and other Spanish monuments (although some are purpose-built). They can be really special places to stay, sited in the most beautiful parts of the country, or in some of the most historic cities, and prices are very good when compared with the five-star hotels with which they compete. Overnight rates depend on location and popularity, and start at around €100 a night, though €150–180 is more typical. That said, a whole host of special offers and web deals (through the official website) offer discounted rates for the over-55s, the under-30s, or for multi-night stays.

A popular approach is to take a fly-drive holiday based around the paradores. There is no end of routes you could choose, but good options include the area around Madrid and through the Sierra de Gredos; along the Cantabrian coast, past the Picos de Europa; or along the French–Spanish border and through the foothills of the Pyrenees. Another popular route takes you through Galicia, and on to *Hostal dos Reis Católicos*, one of the most sumptuous paradores of all in Santiago de Compostela. Three-night **packages**, where you stay in a different parador every night, start at €159 per person (based on two sharing, car rental not included). All the details are on the website, or contact the official parador **agents**, Keytel in the UK (Ⓦkeytel.co.uk) or Petrabax in the US (Ⓦpetrabax.com).

Villas, apartments and rural tourism

Most UK and European tour operators can find you a self-catering **villa** or **apartment**, usually on one of the costas or in the Balearics. They are rented by the week, and range from simple town-centre apartments to luxury coastal villas with private pools. Prices, of course, vary wildly, but the best deals are often packages, including flights and car rental, with endless **villa agencies** including First Choice (Ⓦfirstchoice.co.uk/villas) or Iglu Villas (Ⓦigluvillas.com).

Casas rurales (rural houses), or *casas de pagès* in Catalunya, are where many Spanish holiday-makers stay. It's a wide-ranging concept, from boutique cave dwellings to restored manor houses, many with pools and gardens. You can rent by the room, or by the property, either on a B&B basis or self-catering, depending on the accommodation. Many places also offer outdoor activities such as horse-riding, walking, fishing and cycling. They are generally excellent value for money, starting at around €30 per person, even cheaper if you're in a group or staying for longer than a night or two.

ASETUR (Ⓦecoturismorural.com), the association for rural tourism in Spain, has an excellent website where you can search thousands of properties by region, while many Spanish tourist-office websites also carry information on *casas rurales*. Holiday companies in your own country may also have

Spanish rural properties available, or contact Spain-based **agencies** like Ruralia (Cantabria and Asturias; Ⓦruralia.com), Rustic Blue (Andalucía; Ⓦrusticblue .com), Agroturisme (Catalunya; Ⓦagroturisme.org), Casas de Gredos (Ⓦcasasgredos.com; Ávila and Gredos area), and Top Rural (Ⓦtoprural.com; Spain-wide).

Youth hostels

There are around 250 youth hostels (*albergues juveniles*) in Spain under the umbrella of the **Red Española de Albergues Juveniles** (REAJ; Ⓦreaj .com), the Spanish youth hostel association that is affiliated to the international organization, Hostelling International (HI; Ⓦhihostels.com) There are full details of each hostel on the REAJ website (English-language version available), and we've included some of the best in the Guide.

However, many HI hostels are only open in the spring and summer, or tend to be inconveniently located in some cities; they may also be block-booked by school/youth groups. You'll need an HI membership card, though you can buy one at most hostels on your first night. And at €16–25 a night in high season (less for under-26s, and out of season) for a bunk bed with shared facilities, they're no cheaper than a basic double room in a *hostal* or *pensión*. That said, hostels are good places to meet other travellers, and there are some really gorgeously located ones, especially in Andalucía and in the hiking regions of northern Spain.

Some cities and resort areas also have a wide range of **independent backpacker hostels**. Prices are similar, they tend to be far less institutional, and open all year round, and you won't need a membership

---

PICK OF THE PARADORES

Nearly all Spain's **paradores** have a quirky history, a story to tell or a magnificent location – here's our choice of the best, from former palaces to pilgrims' hospitals.

Hostal dos Reis Católicos, Santiago de Compostela
Apparently the oldest hotel in the world, the *Hostal dos Reis Católicos* is impressively set in a fifteenth-century hospital at the end of the Camino de Santiago. See p.559.
Parador Carlos V, Jarandilla Majestic former imperial palace, set in the verdant Vera valley. See p.194.
Parador Castillo de Santa Catalina, Jaén Occupying a stunning, crag-bound thirteenth-century Moorish fortress, this is one of the most spectacular locations in Spain. See p.325.
Parador Condes de Alba y Aliste, Zamora Occupying a grand palace in the middle of a quiet town, Zamora's parador is gentility defined. See p.390.

Parador Hostal de San Marcos, León One of León's major historic buildings, once a pilgrims' hostel, later a very grand sixteenth-century monastery. See p.437.
Parador de Lerma, Lerma A remarkable ducal palace facing a broad plaza of elegant beauty. See p.426.
Parador Marqués de Villena, Alarcón There are just fourteen rooms in this atmospheric Arabic castle perched on the rocky promontory above the Río Júcar. See p.184.
Parador Nacional Castell de la Suda, Tortosa Tortosa's highest point, the splendid Castillo de la Suda, looms majestically over the lush Ebre valley. See p.784.

card. Also, many are brand-new, often with private rooms as well as dorms, and with excellent facilities (en-suite rooms, cafés, wi-fi, bike rental, tours, etc).

Mountain refuges, monasteries and pilgrim accommodation

In mountain areas and some of the national parks, climbers and trekkers can stay in **refugios**, simple dormitory huts, generally equipped only with bunks and a very basic kitchen. They are run by local mountaineering organizations, mostly on a first-come-first-served basis, which means they fill up quickly in high summer, though you can book in advance at some (or bring a tent and camp outside). Overnight prices start around €15 per person (or €30–40 with a meal included).

It is sometimes possible to stay at Spanish **monasterios** or **conventos**, which may let empty cells for a small charge. You can just turn up and ask – many will take visitors regardless of gender – but if you want to be sure of a reception, it's best to approach the local *turismo* first, or phone ahead. There are some particularly wonderful monastic locations in Galicia, Castilla y León, Catalunya and Mallorca. If you're following the Camino de Santiago, you can take full advantage of monastic accommodation specifically reserved for **pilgrims** along the route (see p.556).

Camping

There are literally hundreds of authorized campsites in Spain, mostly on the coast and in holiday areas. They work out at about €5 or €6 per person plus the same again for a tent, and a similar amount for each car or caravan. The best-located sites, or the ones with top-range facilities (restaurant, swimming pool, bar, supermarket), are significantly more expensive. If you plan to camp extensively, buy the annual *Guía de Campings*, which you can find in large bookshops, or visit Ⓦ vayacamping.net. The price quoted in our campsite reviews in this Guide refers to the cost for two people, a pitch and a car.

In most cases, **camping outside campsites** is legal – but there are certain restrictions. You're not allowed to camp "in urban areas, areas prohibited for military or touristic reasons, or within 1km of an official campsite". What this means in practice is that you can't camp on the beach, while in national parks camping is only allowed in officially designated areas. Aside from these restrictions, however, and with a little sensitivity, you can set up a tent for a short period almost anywhere in the countryside. Whenever possible, ask locally first.

Food and drink

Spanish cuisine has come a long way in recent years, and Spanish chefs are currently at the forefront of contemporary European cooking. You know a power shift has taken place when *Restaurant* magazine's annual "World 50 Best Restaurants" list regularly cites three or four Spanish eateries in the top ten, and when there are more gourmet places in the Basque Country worth making a

special trip for than in Paris. There's some fantastic food to be had in every region, and not just the fancy new-wave stuff either – the tapas, gazpacho, *tortilla* and paella that you may know from home are simply in a different league when made with the correct ingredients in their natural surroundings.

Of course, not every restaurant is a gourmet experience and not every dish is a classic of its kind. Tourist resorts – after all, where many people go – can be disappointing, especially those aimed at a foreign clientele, and a week on one of the costas can just as easily convince you that the Spanish national diet is egg and chips, *sangría*, pizza and Guinness. However, you'll always find a good restaurant where the locals eat, and few places in Europe are still as good value, especially if you have the *menú del día*, the bargain fixed-price lunch that's a fixture across the country.

Breakfast, snacks and sandwiches

The traditional Spanish **breakfast** (*desayuno*) is *chocolate con churros* – long, extruded tubular doughnuts served with thick drinking chocolate or coffee. Some places specialize in these but most bars and cafés also serve cakes and pastries (*bollos* or *pasteles*), croissants and toast (*tostadas*), or crusty sandwiches (*bocadillos*) with a choice of fillings (try one with omelette, *tortilla*). A "sandwich", incidentally, is usually a less appetizing ham or cheese sandwich in white processed bread. Other good places for snacks are **cake shops** (*pastelerías* or *confiterías*) or the local bakery (*panadería*), where they might also have savoury pasties and turnovers.

Bars, tapas and raciones

One of Spain's glories is the phenomenon of **tapas** – the little portions of food that traditionally used to be served up free with a drink in a bar. (The origins are disputed but the word is from *tapar*, "to cover", suggesting a cover for drinks' glasses, perhaps to keep the flies off in the baking sun.) A *menú de tapeo* (tapas menu) is found in many restaurants or bars and can include just about anything – a handful of olives, a slice or two of cured ham, a little dish of meatballs or chorizo, spicy fried potatoes or battered squid. They will often be laid out on the counter, so you can see what's available, or there might be a blackboard menu. Most bars have a speciality; indeed, Spaniards will commonly move from bar to bar, having just the one dish that they consider each bar does well. Conversely, if you're in a bar with just some pre-fried potatoes and day-old Russian salad on display, and a prominent microwave, go somewhere else to eat.

Aside from a few olives or crisps sometimes handed out with a drink, you often pay for tapas these days (the provinces of Granada and Jaén, León and parts of Galicia are honourable exceptions), usually around €2–4 a portion. **Raciones** or a **media racion** (around €6–12) are simply bigger

---

IT'S FOOD, JIM, BUT NOT AS WE KNOW IT

King of molecular gastronomy, and godfather of Spanish contemporary cuisine, **Ferran Adrià**, started it all, with his liquid-nitrogen-frozen herbs, seafood-reduction Rice Krispies and exploding olive-oil droplets. Although his multi-Michelin-starred *El Bulli* restaurant on the Costa Brava has now closed and turned into a cookery foundation and "centre for creativity" (see p.730), the influences of Spain's best-known chef have shaken the restaurant scene, as his former employees, acolytes and disciples have gone on to make the country one of the most exciting places to eat in the world.

The style city of Barcelona, not surprisingly, is at the forefront of this innovative form of cooking, with **Carles Abellán**'s *Comerç 24* (see p.691) typical of the breed, while the **Roca brothers**' celebrated *Celler de Can Roca* in Girona (see p.739) keeps Catalunya firmly in the vanguard of new-wave cuisine. However, it's in the Basque Country that many of the hottest chefs are currently in action: **Andoni Aduriz** at *Mugaritz*, Errenteria, San Sebastián (see p.460), father-and-daughter team **Juan Mari and Elena Arzak** at *Arzak*, San Sebastián (see p.459), and **Martín Berasategui** at *Restaurante Martín Berasategui*, Lasarte-Oria, San Sebastián (see p.460), are all cooking sensational food in restaurants that regularly feature in lists of the world's best. Maybe it's a northern thing, but there's less fuss in the south of the country about the so-called *cocina de autor*; in Madrid, perhaps only **Sergi Arola** cuts the new-wave mustard with his *Gastro* (see p.110), or his newer, more affordable venture *Vi-Cool* (see p.108).

plates of tapas: a *ración*, or two or three half *raciones* are enough for a meal – you're sometimes asked if you want a *tapa* or a *ración* of whatever it is you've chosen.

There are big regional variations in tapas. They are often called **pinchos** (or *pintxos*) in northern Spain, especially in the Basque provinces, where typically tapas come served on a slice of baguette, held together with a cocktail stick. When you've finished eating, the sticks are counted up to work out your bill. This kind of tapas can be as simple as a cheese cube on bread or a far more elaborately sculpted concoction; they are also known as **montaditos** (basically, *canapés*). Famously good places across

Spain for tapas-tasting include Madrid, León, Logroño, San Sebastián, Granada, Seville and Cádiz.

Most cafés and bars have some kind of tapas available, while you'll also find a decent display in **tascas**, **bodegas** and **tabernas** (kinds of taverns) and **cervecerías** (beer-houses). It's always cheapest to stand at the bar to eat; you'll pay more to sit at tables and more again to sit outside on a terrace.

Restaurants

The simplest kind of restaurant is the **comedor** (dining room), often a room at the back of a bar or the dining room of a *hostal* or *pensión*. Traditionally,

---

SPANISH CUISINE

There really is no such thing as traditional "Spanish" cuisine, since every region claims a quite separate culinary heritage. That said, you'll find similar dishes cropping up right across the country, whatever their origin, while typical Mediterranean staples are ubiquitous – olive oil, tomatoes, peppers, garlic, onions, lemons and oranges.

It's usual to start your meal with a **salad** or a plate of cold cuts, while **soups** might be fish or seafood or, in the north especially, hearty broths such as the Galician cabbage-and-potato *caldo gallego*. Boiled potatoes with greens, or a thick minestrone of vegetables, are also fairly standard starters, while depending on the season you might be offered grilled asparagus or artichokes, or stewed beans with chunks of sausage.

Anywhere near the coast, you really should make the most of what's on offer, whether it's the fried fish of Málaga, Basque shellfish or the seafood specialities in Galicia, notably octopus (*pulpo*). Fish stews (*zarzuelas*) can be memorable, while seafood rice dishes range from *arroz negro* ("black rice", cooked with squid ink) to the better-known **paella**. This comes originally from Valencia (still the best place for an authentic one), though a proper paella from there doesn't include fish or seafood at all but things like chicken, rabbit, beans and snails.

Meat is most often grilled and served with a few fried potatoes. Regional specialities include *cordero* (lamb) from Segovia, Navarra and the Basque Country, as well as *cochinillo* (suckling pig) or *lechal* (suckling lamb) in central Spain. **Cured ham**, or *jamón serrano*, is superb, produced at its best from acorn-fed Iberian pigs in Extremadura and Andalucía, though it can be extremely expensive. Every region has a local **sausage** in its locker – the best known is the spicy chorizo, made from pork, though others include *morcilla* (blood sausage; best in Burgos, León and Asturias), and *butifarra*, a white Catalan sausage made from pork and tripe. **Stews** are typified by the mighty *fabada*, a fill-your-boots Asturian bean-and-meat concoction.

Cheeses to look out for include Cabrales, a tangy blue cheese made in the Picos de Europa; Manchego, a sharp, nutty cheese made from sheep's milk in La Mancha; Mahon, a cow's-milk cheese from Menorca, often with paprika rubbed into its rind; Idiazábal, a smoked cheese from the Basque Country; and Zamorano, made from sheep's milk in Castilla y León.

In most restaurants, **dessert** is nearly always fresh fruit or *flan*, the Spanish crème caramel, with the regions often having their own versions such as *crema catalana* in Catalunya and the Andalucian *tocino de cielo*. There are also many varieties of *postre* – rice pudding or assorted blancmange mixtures – and a range of commercial ice-cream dishes.

If you want to know more about the food in the region where you're travelling, turn to the special **features**:

Andalucía See p.229	**Basque Country** See p.459	**Extremadura** See p.194
Aragón See p.606	**Castilla-La Mancha** See p.178	**Galicia** See p.547
Around Madrid See p.139	**Castilla y León and La Rioja**	**Madrid** See p.108
Asturias See p.529	See p.375	**Valencia and Murcia** See p.795
Balearics See p.851	**Catalunya** See p.715	

they are family-run places aimed at lunching workers, usually offering a straightforward set meal at budget prices. The highway equivalent are known as **ventas** or **mesones** (inns), dotted along the main roads between towns and cities. These have been serving Spanish wayfarers for centuries – some of them quite literally – and the best places are immediately picked out by the line of cars and trucks outside. Proper restaurants, **restaurantes**, come in a myriad of guises, from rustic village restaurants to stylish Michelin-starred eateries; **asadores** specialize in grilled meats, **marisquerías** in fish and seafood.

Almost every restaurant serves a weekday, fixed-price lunchtime meal, the **menú del día**, generally three courses including wine for €10–15, occasionally even cheaper, depending on where you are in Spain. This is obviously a terrific deal; the *menú del día* is only sporadically available at night, and sometimes prices are slightly higher (and the menu slightly fancier) at weekends. The very cheapest places are unlikely to have a written menu, and the waiter will tell you what the day's dishes are. In smarter restaurants in bigger cities and resorts, there will still be a *menú del día*, though it might be a shadow of the usual à la carte menu, and drinks may be excluded. Even so, it's a way of eating at a restaurant that might normally cost you three or four times as much. Top city restaurants often also feature an upmarket *menú* called a **menú de degustación** (tasting menu), which again can be excellent value, allowing you to try out some of the country's finest cooking for anything from €50 to €100 a head.

Otherwise, in bars and so-called *cafeterías*, meals often come in the form of a **plato combinado** – literally a combined dish – which will be a one-plate meal of something like steak, egg and chips, or *calamares* and salad, often with bread and a drink included. This will generally cost in the region of €5–10.

If you want a menu in a restaurant, ask for **la carta**; *menú* refers only to the fixed-price meal. In all but the most rock-bottom establishments it is customary to leave a small **tip**, though five percent of the bill is considered sufficient and service is normally included in a *menú del día*. IVA, the eight percent **tax**, is also charged, but it should say on the menu if this is included in the price or not.

Spaniards generally eat very late, with **lunch** served from around 1pm (you'll be the first person there at this time) until 4pm, and **dinner** from 8.30pm or 9pm to midnight. Obviously, rural areas are slightly earlier to dine, but making a dinner reservation for 10.30pm or even later is considered perfectly normal in many cities in Spain. Most restaurants **close one day a week**, usually Sunday or Monday. The opening hours given in this Guide provide a rough idea, but bear in mind that many restaurants in Spain will close early or not open at all during quiet periods.

Vegetarians

Vegetarians generally have a fairly hard time of it in Spain, though there's an increasing number of veggie restaurants in the bigger cities, including some really good ones in Madrid (see box, p.106) and Barcelona (see box, p.693). In more rural areas, there's usually something to eat, but you may get weary of fried eggs and omelettes. However, many tapas favourites, especially in the south, are veggie (like fried aubergine, or spinach and chickpeas in Seville), while superb fresh fruit and veg, and excellent cheese, is always available in the markets and shops.

In restaurants, you're faced with the extra problem that pieces of meat – especially ham, which the Spanish don't regard as real meat – and tuna are often added to vegetable dishes and salads. You'll also find chunks of chorizo and sausage turning up in otherwise veg-friendly soups or bean stews. The phrases to get to know are *Soy vegetariano/a. Como sólo verduras. Hay algo sin carne?* ("I'm a vegetarian. I only eat vegetables. Is there anything without meat?"); you may have to add *y sin marisco* ("and without seafood") and *y sin jamón* ("and without ham") to be really safe.

Some salads and vegetable dishes are strictly **vegan**, but they're few and far between. Fruit and nuts are widely available, nuts being sold by street vendors everywhere.

Coffee, tea and soft drinks

Café (coffee) is invariably an espresso (*café solo*); for a large cup of weaker, black coffee, ask for an *americano*. A *café cortado* is a *café solo* with a drop of milk; a *café con leche* is made with lots of hot milk. Coffee is also frequently mixed with brandy, cognac or whisky, all such concoctions being called *carajillo*. Iced coffee is *café con hielo*. **Chocolate** (hot chocolate) is a popular breakfast drink, or for after a long night on the town, but it's usually incredibly thick and sweet. For a thinner, cocoa-style drink, ask for a brand name, like Cola Cao.

Spaniards usually drink **té** (tea) black, so if you want milk it's safest to ask for it afterwards, since ordering *té con leche* might well get you a glass of warm milk with a tea bag floating on top. Herbal teas (*infusions*) are widely available, like *manzanilla* (camomile), *poleo* (mint tea) and *hierba luisa* (lemon verbena).

Local soft drinks include **granizado** (crushed ice) or **horchata** (a milky drink made from tiger nuts or almonds), available from summer street stalls, and from milk bars (*horchaterías*, also known as *granjas* in Catalunya) and ice-cream parlours (*heladerías*). Although you can drink the **water** almost everywhere, it tastes revolting in some cities and coastal areas – inexpensive *agua mineral* comes either sparkling (*con gas*) or still (*sin gas*).

Wine

One of the great pleasures of eating out in Spain is the chance to sample some of the country's excellent **wines**. Over fifty percent of the European Union's vineyards lie in Spain and *vino* is the invariable accompaniment to every meal. At lunchtime, a glass or small pitcher of the house wine – often served straight from the barrel – is usually included in the *menú del día*; otherwise, restaurant wine starts at around €5–10 a bottle, although the sky's the limit for the really good stuff. And there's plenty of that, since in recent years Spanish wine has enjoyed an amazing renaissance, led largely by the international success of famous wine-producing regions like La Rioja and Ribera del Duero. Other regions – not perhaps so well-known abroad – are also well worth investigating, like Galicia or the Priorat in Catalunya, and every wine-producing area is set up for *bodega* (winery) visits, tastings and tours. In Andalucía, meanwhile, the classic wine is **sherry** –

> ### SPAIN'S TOP 6 BODEGA VISITS
>
> **Bodegas Codorníu, Penedès** Spain's first producers of cava, located in outstanding Catalan Art Nouveau premises. See p.771.
> **Bodegas Marqués de Riscal, La Rioja Alavesa** Terrific wine, and an extraordinary Frank Gehry-designed building to boot. See p.483.
> **Bodegas Ysios, La Rioja Alavesa** Located in a stunning building by Santiago Calatrava. See p.483.
> **Condes de Albarei, Galicia** Cooperative *bodega* turning out excellent Albariño wines. See p.574.
> **González Byass, Jerez** One of the biggest sherry producers, makers of the Tio Pepe brand. See p.302.
> **Costers del Siurana, Priorat** Investigate the Priorat region wines in deepest Catalunya. See p.783.

vino de jerez – while champagne in Spain means the Catalan sparkling wine, **cava**.

The festival and tourist drink is, famously, **sangría**, a wine and fruit punch that's often deceptively strong; a variation in Catalunya is *sangría de cava*. *Tinto de verano* is a similar red-wine-and-soda or -lemonade combination; variations on this include *tinto de verano con naranja* (red wine with orangeade) or *con limón* (lemonade).

Beer

Beer (*cerveza*) is nearly always lager, though some Spanish breweries also now make stout-style brews, wheat beers and other types. It comes in 300ml bottles (*botellines*) or, for about the same price, on tap – a *caña* of draught beer is a small glass, a *caña doble* larger, and asking for *un tubo* (a tubular glass) gets you about half a pint. Mahou, Cruz Campo, San Miguel, Damm, Estrella de Galicia and Alhambra are all decent beers. A **shandy** is a *clara*, either with fizzy lemon (*con limón*) or lemonade (*con casera* or *con blanca*).

Spirits and shots

In mid-afternoon – or, let's face it, sometimes even at breakfast – Spaniards take a *copa* of liqueur with their coffee, such as *anís* (similar to Pernod) or *coñac*, the local **brandy**, which has a distinct vanilla flavour. Most brandies are produced by the great sherry houses in Jerez (like Lepanto, Carlos I and Cardinal Mendoza), but two good ones that aren't are the Armagnac-like Mascaró and Torres, both from Catalunya. Instead of brandy, at the end of a meal many places serve **chupitos** – little shot glasses of flavoured schnapps or local firewater, such as Patxarán in Navarra and the Basque Country, Ratafía in Catalunya or Orujo in Galicia. One much-loved Galego custom is the *queimada*, when a large bowl of *aguardiente* (a herb-flavoured fiery liqueur) with fruit, sugar and coffee grains is set alight and then drunk hot.

You should order **spirits** by brand name, since there are generally less expensive Spanish equivalents for standard imports, or simply specify *nacional*. Larios gin from Málaga, for instance, is about half the price of Gordon's. Measures are staggeringly generous – bar staff generally pour from the bottle until you suggest they stop. Long drinks include the universal Gin-Tónic and the Cuba Libre (rum and Coke), and there are often Spanish Caribbean rums (*ron*) such as Cacique from Venezuela or Havana Club from Cuba.

The media

The ubiquitous Spanish newspaper kiosk is your first stop for regional and national newspapers and magazines, though hotels and bars nearly always have a few kicking around for customers. The bigger cities, tourist towns and resorts will also have foreign newspapers available (some of which are actually published in Spain), generally on the day of issue or perhaps a day late. Television is all-pervasive in bars, cafés and restaurants, and you're going to find yourself watching more bullfighting, basketball and Venezuelan soap operas than perhaps you'd bargained for. Most hotel rooms have a TV, too, though only in the fancier places will you get any English-language programming, and then probably only the BBC News, CNN or Eurosport satellite channels.

Newspapers

Of the Spanish **national newspapers** the best are the Madrid-based centre-left El País (Ⓦelpais.es) and the centre-right El Mundo (Ⓦelmundo.es), both of which have good arts and foreign news coverage, including comprehensive regional "what's on" listings and supplements every weekend. The **regional press** is generally run by local magnates and is predominantly right of centre, though often supporting local autonomy movements. Nationalist press includes Avui in Catalunya, printed in Catalan, and the Basque papers El Correo, Deia and Gara, the last of which has close links with ETA. All that said, the paper with the highest circulation is Marca (Ⓦmarca.com), the country's top **sports daily**, mainly football-dominated; there's also As (Ⓦas.com), El Mundo Deportivo (Ⓦelmundodeportivo.es) and Sport (Ⓦsport.es). The main cities are also awash with **free newspapers**, which are dished out at bus and metro stops.

Magazines

There's a bewildering variety of **magazines** specializing in celebrity gossip (known collectively as la prensa rosa), ranging from the more traditional Hola to the sensationalist QMD! (Qué Me Dices). El Jueves ("The Thursday" – strapline: "The magazine that comes out on Wednesdays") is a weekly comic-strip-style satirical magazine, while the online daily El Confidencial (Ⓦelconfidencial.com) gives the inside track on serious economic and political stories. There are also various **English-language magazines** and papers produced by and for the expatriate communities in the main cities and on the costas, such as InMadrid (Ⓦin-madrid.com), Barcelona Metropolitan (Ⓦbarcelona-metropolitan .com), and – for southern Spain – Sur in English (Ⓦwww.surinenglish.com) and The Olive Press (Ⓦtheolivepress.es).

Radio

There are hundreds of local radio channels, broadcasting in Spanish and regional languages, alongside a handful of national ones. The state-run Radio Nacional de España, or RNE (Ⓦrtve.es/radio), covers five stations: Radio Nacional, a general news and information channel; Radio Clásica, broadcasting mainly classical music and related programmes; the popular music channel Radio 3; Radio 4, in Catalan; and the rolling news and sports channel Radio 5. Radio Exterior is RNE's international shortwave service. Other **popular channels** include Cadena Ser and Onda Cero (news, talk, sports and culture), the Catholic Church-run COPE, Los 40 Principales (for the latest hits, Spanish and otherwise) and Cadena 100 (music and cultural programming). Radio Marca (dedicated sports radio) is also very popular.

Television

RTV (Ⓦrtve.es/television) provides the main, state-run channels, namely La 1 (ie, "Uno"), a general entertainment and news channel, and its sister La 2 ("Dos"). Private national stations are Antena 3, Cuatro (Four), Telecinco (Five) and La Sexta (Sixth). There are also plenty of **regional channels**, the most important being Catalunya's TV3 and Canal 33, both broadcast in Catalan, and the Basque Country's ETB channels (in Basque), though there are also stations in Galicia (TVG) and Andalucía (Canal Sur) with local programming. The main satellite channel is Canal+.

Festivals

It's hard to beat the experience of arriving in some small Spanish village, expecting no more than a bed for the night, to discover the streets decked with flags and streamers, a band playing in the plaza and the entire population out celebrating the local fiesta. **Everywhere in Spain, from the tiniest hamlet to the great cities, devotes at least a couple of days a year to partying, and participating in such an event propels you right into the heart of Spanish culture.**

Local saints' days aside, Spain has some really major events worth planning your whole trip around, from the great Easter processions of Semana Santa (Holy Week) to the famous bull-running during July's Fiesta de San Fermín in Pamplona. There are also fiestas celebrating deliverance from the Moors, safe return from the sea, or the bringing in of the grapes – any excuse will do. One thing they all tend to have in common is a curious blend of religious ceremony and pagan ritual – sombre processions of statuary followed by exuberant merrymaking – in which fire plays a prominent part.

The **annual festival calendar in this section** concentrates on the country's most notable fiestas. For more regional and local fiestas turn to the **feature boxes** found in the Guide.

Outsiders are always welcome at fiestas, the only problem being that it can be hard to find a hotel, unless you book well in advance. The other thing to note is that while not every fiesta is a national **public holiday** (see p.56), or vice versa, you may well get stuck if you arrive in town in the middle of an annual event, since pretty much everything will be closed.

JANUARY

5: Cabalgata de Reyes When the "Three Kings" (*reyes*) arrive to bring the children their presents for Epiphany. Most cities stage a spectacular cavalcade as the Three Kings are driven through the streets throwing sweets to the crowds.

16–17: Sant Antoni Bonfires and saint's day processions, especially on the Balearic Islands.

FEBRUARY

Week preceding Ash Wednesday and Lent: Carnaval An excuse for wild partying and masques, most riotous in Cádiz (Andalucía), Sitges, Catalunya and Águilas (Valencia).

TOP 5 FIESTAS

Semana Santa Andalucía. See p.228
Feria de Abril Seville. See p.228
Fiesta de San Fermín Pamplona.
See p.486
Las Fallas Valencia. See p.802
La Tomatina Buñol. See p.813

MARCH

12–19: Las Fallas Valencia has the biggest of the bonfire festivals held for San José, climaxing on the Nit de Foc (Night of Fire) when enormous caricatures are burnt, and firecrackers let off in the streets. See p.802.

EASTER

March/April: Semana Santa Holy Week is celebrated across Spain, most theatrically in Seville, Málaga, Murcia and Valladolid, where *pasos* – huge floats of religious scenes – are carried down the streets, accompanied by hooded penitents atoning for the year's misdeeds. Maundy Thursday and Good Friday see the biggest, most solemn processions.

APRIL

22–24: Fiestas de Moros y Cristianos Mock battle between Moors and Christians in Alcoy, Valencia. See p.826.

23: Sant Jordi A day of celebration across the region, especially Barcelona (see p.646) for Catalunya's patron saint – Sant Jordi, St George. Being the birth date of Cervantes, it's also celebrated as National Book Day throughout Spain.

Last week: Feria de Abril Spectacular week-long fair in Seville, with a major bullfighting festival.

MAY

Early May: Horse Fair Jerez (Andalucía). Horsey high jinks – show-jumping, parades and the famous "dancing Andalusian horses" – turn Jerez into equine heaven.

15: San Isidro Madrid's patron saint's day sees a two-week fiesta either side of the actual date.

Seventh Sunday after Easter: Pentecostés Pentecost is celebrated by the Romería del Rocío – the great pilgrimage-fair – at El Rocío, near Huelva (Andalucía). See p.307.

Thursday after Trinity Sunday: Corpus Christi Religious processions accompanied by floats and penitents, notably in Toledo, Granada and Valencia, plus the spectacular costumed events of Berga's Festa de la Patum, Catalunya (see p.750).

Last week: Feria de la Manzanilla The big annual sherry festival celebrates the famous tipple of Sanlúcar de Barrameda (Andalucía).

JUNE

Second or third week: Sónar Europe's biggest electronic music and multimedia bleep-fest, held over three days in Barcelona. See p.646.

23–24: San Juan Midsummer's eve is celebrated with bonfires and fireworks all over Spain, marking a hedonistic welcome to the summer – particularly in San Juan de Alicante and in Barcelona.

JULY

7–14: San Fermín The famed "Running of the Bulls" at Pamplona. See p.486.

25: Santiago Spain's patron saint, St James, is honoured at Santiago de Compostela, with fireworks and bonfires.

Last three weeks: Pirineos Sur World music festival on a floating stage at Lanuza, near Sallent de Gállego, in the Pyrenees.

AUGUST

10–11: Misteri d'Elx Elche, Valencia (see p.833) hosts mock battles between Christians and Moors, ending with a centuries-old mystery play.

Last week: Los Santos Niños *Gigantones* (giant puppets) are paraded in Alcalá de Henares, near Madrid.

Last Wednesday: La Tomatina Buñol, near Valencia, hosts the country's craziest fiesta, a one-hour tomato fight. See p.813.

SEPTEMBER

First week: Vendimia The grape harvest is celebrated wildly in Valdepeñas (Castilla-La Mancha), Jerez (Andalucía) and many other wine towns.

21: San Mateo The annual Rioja wine harvest bash coincides with the local saint's day in Logroño (La Rioja).

Third Week: Festa de Santa Tecla Human castles (*castells*) and processions of *gegants* (giant puppets) in Tarragona.

24: La Mercè Barcelona's biggest annual party (either side of the saint's day, 24th) sees a week's worth of giants' parades, fireworks and human-castle-building.

OCTOBER

1: San Miguel Villages across the country celebrate their patron saint's day.

12: La Virgen del Pilar Honouring the patron saint of Aragón is an excuse for bullfights, dancing and celebrations in Zaragoza and elsewhere.

DECEMBER

24: Nochebuena Christmas Eve is particularly exuberant, with parties and carousing early in the evening before it all suddenly stops in time for family dinner or Mass.

31: Nochevieja New Year is celebrated by eating a grape for every stroke of the clock in Plaza del Sol in Madrid, Pza. de Catalunya in Barcelona, and main squares and bars throughout the country.

Culture and etiquette

Spain is a fantastically welcoming, vibrant country, characterized by its love of life. With a population of over 44 million it's a diverse place, too, with regional identities as characteristic as their local landscapes, and the Basques, Galicians and Catalans all add their own languages and cultures to the mix. No matter where you decide to visit though, many of the clichés of Spanish life, such as the siesta, busy bars and restaurants open late into the night, and towns celebrating lively festivals, still pretty much ring true.

Social life and etiquette

One of the most important aspects of Spanish life is the **family**; no celebration would be complete without an extended gathering, although this is more common away from the busy cities where modern life takes its toll. Even so, the elderly are respected, and it's not uncommon to have older relatives being cared for in the family home. Likewise, children are absolutely adored, and included in everything.

Food plays an important part in Spanish family life, with lunch (*la comida*) the biggest meal of the day, often lasting from 2 to 4pm. It's common for shops and whole villages to come to a standstill for the afternoon meal and **siesta**, especially in more out-of-the-way places. Evening meals, which often start as late as 10pm, are usually preceded by a leisurely stroll, or **paseo**, when you may take in an aperitif in a bar or two.

Friends are more likely to meet in restaurants for meals, but if you are **invited to someone's house** for dinner, you should take a small gift for any children, along with chocolates, a bottle of wine, or some flowers (though avoid dahlias, chrysanthemums and flowers in odd numbers as these would only be given at funerals). Also bear in mind that **drinking** too much isn't common; although there seems to be a bar on every corner, this is more for coffee and socializing than heavy boozing.

The Spanish are among the biggest **smokers** in Europe, with an estimated thirty percent of the population smoking regularly. Attitudes are changing, however, and the law now bans smoking in all public places, including shops, public transport, bars and restaurants.

Tipping is common in Spain, although not always expected, but locals are small tippers and twenty cents on a bar table or five percent in a restaurant is usually enough. It is also common practice to tip taxi drivers, hotel porters and the like in small change.

If you are planning to indulge in any topless **sunbathing**, consider local feelings first, and try to stick to beaches where people are already doing it. You also need to make sure you are properly covered if you enter a **church**; shorts and sleeveless tops should be avoided.

Greetings

If you're **meeting someone** for the first time, you should shake their hand. If you become friends, you may well move on to hugging (men) or kisses on each cheek (women), starting with the left. Men are also more likely to kiss women hello and goodbye, than to shake their hand. To say **hello**, use *Buenos días* before lunch and *Buenos tardes* after that. Bear in mind that in Spain the sense of time is somewhat elastic, so unless you're meeting for business (when being late is very bad form) don't be offended if you are left waiting for a good ten or twenty minutes.

Sports and outdoor activities

Spain is nothing if not enthusiastic about sport, with football and basketball all but national obsessions, and bullfighting – whether or not you agree it's a "sport" – one of its cultural highlights. There are also plenty of opportunities to get out and enjoy the country's stunning outdoors, whether it's ambling around a golf course, skiing in the southern slopes, chasing surf off the Basque Country coast or canyoning in the Pyrenees.

Basketball

In Spain, **basketball** (*baloncesto*) comes second only to football in national interest, and the 2014 World Championships (Ⓦspain2014.org) were held here, the second time the country has hosted the world's biggest basketball tournament. Domestically, there are eighteen professional teams competing in the national league, **ACB** (Ⓦacb.com), whose season runs from September to June; while other big competitions include the Copa del Rey and the Europe-wide Euroleague. The two biggest teams are, not entirely coincidentally, owned by the two most successful football teams, Barcelona and Real Madrid, and have won the ACB (until 1983 known as the Liga Nacional) dozens of times between them. There's more basketball information on the Federacion Española de Baloncesto website (Ⓦfeb.es). Games are broadcast on TV, and match tickets cost from around €20.

Bullfighting

The **bullfight** is a classic image of Spain, and an integral part of many fiestas. In the south, especially, any village that can afford it will put on a *corrida* for an afternoon, while in big cities such as Madrid or Seville, the main festival times are accompanied by a season of prestige fights. However, with the exception of Pamplona, bullfighting is far more popular in Madrid and all points south than it is in the north or on the islands. Indeed, many northern cities don't have bullrings, while the regional governments of both Catalunya and the Canary Islands have gone so far as to **ban bullfighting**. Spain's main opposition to bullfighting is organized by **ADDA** (Asociación Defensa Derechos Animal; Ⓦaddaong.org), whose website has information (in English) about international campaigns and current actions.

Los Toros, as Spaniards refer to bullfighting, is certainly big business, with the top performers, the matadors, on a par with the country's biggest pop and sports stars. To aficionados (a word that implies more knowledge and appreciation than mere "fan"), the bulls are a ritual part of Spanish culture – with the emphasis on the way man and bull "perform" together – in which the *arte* is at issue rather than the cruelty. If pressed on the issue of the slaughter of an animal, they generally fail to understand. Fighting bulls are, they will tell you, bred for the industry; they live a reasonable life before they are killed, and, if the bullfight went, so, too, would the bulls.

If you decide to attend a *corrida*, try to see a big, prestigious event, where star performers are likely to despatch the bulls with "art" and a successful, "clean" kill. There are few sights worse than a matador making a prolonged and messy kill, while the audience whistles and chucks cushions. The most skilful events are those featuring mounted matadors, or *rejoneadores*; this is the oldest form of *corrida*, developed in Andalucía in the seventeenth century.

The **bullfight season** runs from March to October, and **tickets** for *corridas* start from around €6 – though you can pay much more (up to €150) for the prime seats and more prominent fights. The cheapest seats are *gradas*, the highest rows at the back, from where you can see everything that happens without too much of the detail; the front rows are known as the *barreras*. Seats are also divided into *sol* (sun), *sombra* (shade) and *sol y sombra* (shaded after a while), though these distinctions have become less crucial as more and more bullfights start later in the day, at 6pm or 7pm, rather than the traditional 5pm. The *sombra* seats are more expensive, not so much for the spectators' personal comfort as the fact that most of the action takes place in the shade.

The corrida

The **corrida** begins with a procession, to the accompaniment of a *pasodoble* by the band. Leading the procession are two *alguaciles*, or "constables", on horseback and in traditional costume, followed by the three matadors, who will

BASQUE GAMES AND SPORTS

It's a whole different ball game in the Basque Country, where sporting obsessions are of a very distinct kind. **Pelota** (a version of which is known as **jai alai**, Basque for "happy party") is played all over Spain, but in Euskal Herria even the smallest village has a *pelota* court or *fronton*, and betting on the sport is rife. **Rowing** is also hugely popular, and regattas are held every weekend in summer. During local fiestas, you'll also see other unique Basque sports including **aizkolaritza** (log-chopping), **harri-jasotzea** (stone-lifting), **soka-tira** (tug-of-war) and **segalaritza** (grass-cutting). The finest exponents of the first two in particular are popular local heroes (the world champion stone-lifter Iñaki Perurena's visit to Japan resulted in the sport being introduced there – he remains the only lifter to surpass the legendary 315kg barrier).

each fight two bulls, and their *cuadrillas*, their personal "team", each comprising two mounted *picadores* and three *banderilleros*.

Once the ring is empty, the first bull appears, to be "tested" by the matador or his *banderilleros* using pink and gold capes. These preliminaries conducted (and they can be short, if the bull is ferocious), the **suerte de picar** ensues, in which the *picadores* ride out and take up position at opposite sides of the ring, while the bull is distracted by other *toreros*. Once they are in place, the bull is made to charge one of the horses; the *picador* drives his short-pointed lance into the bull's neck, while it tries to toss his padded, blindfolded horse, thus tiring the bull's powerful neck and back muscles. This is repeated up to three times, until the horn sounds for the *picadores* to leave. For many, this is the least acceptable stage of the *corrida*, and it is clearly not a pleasant experience for the horses, who have their ears stuffed with oil-soaked rags to shut out the noise, and their vocal cords cut out to render them mute.

The next stage, the **suerte de banderillas**, involves the placing of three sets of *banderillas* (coloured sticks with barbed ends) into the bull's shoulders. Each of the three *banderilleros* delivers these in turn, attracting the bull's attention with the movement of his own body rather than a cape, and placing the *banderillas* while both he and the bull are running towards each other.

Once the *banderillas* have been placed, the **suerte de matar** begins, and the matador enters the ring alone, having exchanged his pink-and-gold cape for the red one. He (or she) salutes the president and then dedicates the bull either to an individual, to whom he gives his hat, or to the audience by placing his hat in the centre of the ring. It is in this part of the *corrida* that judgements are made and the performance is focused, as the matador displays his skills on the (by now exhausted) bull. He uses the movements of the cape to attract the bull, while his body remains still. If he does well, the band will start to play, while the crowd *olé* each pass. This stage

lasts around ten minutes and ends with the kill. The matador attempts to get the bull into a position where he can drive a sword between its shoulders and through to the heart for a *coup de grâce*. In practice, they rarely succeed in this, instead taking a second sword, crossed at the end, to cut the bull's spinal cord; this causes instant death.

If the audience is impressed by the matador's performance, they will wave their handkerchiefs and shout for an award to be made by the president. He can award one or both ears, and a tail – the better the display, the more pieces he gets – while if the matador has excelled himself, he will be carried out of the ring by the crowd, through the *puerta grande*, the main door, which is normally kept locked.

Popular **matadors** include the veteran Enrique Ponce, Julián "El Juli" López, Granada's David "El Fandi" Fandila, César Jiménez and Manuel Jesús Cid Sala "El Cid". But the *torero* who sets most male aficionados' hearts aflutter (and many female ones, too) is the moody, quixotic and media-shy José Tomás Román Martín; fighting under the name José Tomás, his fans claim that his courageous, high-risk style – he has been seriously gored on numerous occasions – has taken the art back to its roots.

Football

Until its poor performance in the 2014 World Cup, Spain had one of the greatest national teams of all time. Spain became World Cup winners in 2010 and won back-to-back European championships in 2008 and 2012. Meanwhile, Barcelona – mercurial *tiki-taka* (pass-and-move) masters – and big spenders Real Madrid are regular finalists of the European Champions League. Certainly, if you want the excitement of a genuinely Spanish sporting event, watching a Sunday-evening game in **La Liga** (w lfp.es) usually produces as much passion as anything you'll find in the bullring.

For many years, the country's two dominant teams have been **Real Madrid** and **FC Barcelona**, each boasting one of the world's two best footballers in Cristiano Ronaldo and Lionel Messi. Their monopoly was broken by **Atlético Madrid**, who surprised everyone by winning the league title in 2014, but other challengers struggle to keep up. These usually include Valencia, the Andalucian powerhouse of **Sevilla** and the emerging force of **Villarreal**, who have experienced a rags-to-riches success story under president and ceramics tycoon Fernando Roig. Also powerful are **Athletic Bilbao**, who only draw on players from Euskal Herria (the Basque Country in both Spain and France and Navarra) and those who come through the club's youth ranks.

The league **season** runs from late August until May, and most games kick off at 5pm or 7pm on Sundays, though live TV usually demands that one key game kicks off at 10pm on Saturday and 9pm on Sunday. With the exception of local derbies, major European games, and the so-called *clásicos* between Real Madrid and Barcelona, **tickets** are not too hard to get. They start at around €30 for La Liga games, with the cheapest in the *fondo* (behind the goals); *tribuna* (pitchside stand) seats are much pricier, while to see an average Real Madrid (see p.95) or Barcelona (see p.678) game could easily cost you up to €100.

Golf

When Cantabria boy Severiano "Seve" Ballesteros died in 2011, aged just 54, the whole nation mourned. He and his fellow golfers, like José María Olazábal, Sergio García and Miguel Ángel Jiménez, have raised the country's golf profile immeasurably in recent years, while with around three hundred **golf courses** Spain is one of the best European destinations for the amateur golfer too. Temperatures, especially favourable in the south, mean that you can play more or less year-round on the Costa del Sol, while a number of courses have been built away from the traditional centres, for example along the Costa de la Luz and the Atlantic coast, which, while not as nice in winter, tend to be a little cheaper. There are increasing concerns, however, about the amount of water used by courses in a country that is experiencing a severe water crisis.

Plenty of tour operators can arrange golf-holiday packages, while for more information visit the very useful **Golf Spain** website (🌐 golfspain.com), which details all the country's golf courses and golf schools, plus green fees and golf-and-resort packages.

Hiking and mountain sports

Spain is one of the most mountainous countries in Europe, and as such is hugely popular with walkers. Aside from the classic long-distance routes, there are fantastic day-hikes, climbs and circuits possible almost everywhere, though you'll need to be properly equipped with a map, compass or GPS, hiking boots and mountain gear.

SPAIN'S CLASSIC HIKES

The country's **major footpaths** are known as GR (Grande Recorrido) or PR (Pequeño Recorrido), some of which make up part of the trans-European walking routes that extend across the entire continent. GR paths are the longest, and are marked by red-and-white stripes, while the smaller PR routes (yellow-and-white) can usually be done in a day. The best-known routes are the GR11, which crosses the Pyrenees from coast to coast, via Andorra; the GR65 and its variants, the Camino de Santiago; and the GR7, which starts from Tarifa in Andalucía, heads through the Sierra Nevada and up the Catalan coast before reaching the Pyrenees.

Baixa Garrotxa A 28-kilometre loop through the spectacular Garrotxa volcanic region of northeastern Catalunya. See p.746.

Camino de Santiago The legendary, month-long pilgrimage route runs from the Pyrenees to Santiago de Compostela, by way of Romanesque architecture in Navarra (see p.491), mighty Gothic cathedrals in Castilla y León (see p.426), fine wines in La Rioja and beautiful green Galicia scenery (see p.558).

Cañón de Añisclo Much less visited and wilder than its neighbour Ordesa, this spectacular river gorge is overlooked by wedding-cake palisades. See p.635.

Carros de Foc The trans-park circuit takes in the most scenic corners of the Parc Nacional d'Aigüestortes i Estany de Sant Maurici, a challenging route linking nine overnight refuges. See p.762.

Circo de las Cinco Lagunas A scintillating one-day walk in the Sierra de Gredos, with sparkling mountain lakes and the half-tame Gredos ibex to see. See p.157.

Circo de Soaso The best sampling of Aragón's Parque Nacional de Ordesa – upstream along the valley to a superb waterfall, and back via a spectacular corniche route called the Faja de Pelay. See p.635.

Desfiladero de Cares The classic Picos de Europa hike – through the Cares Gorge – is a dramatic 12km route along a path hewn out of the cliff face. See p.524.

Pedraforca One of the most revered peaks in Catalunya is a relatively easy one to bag, with a variety of routes up. See p.754.

In Andalucía, the **Sierra Nevada** mountain range and national park offers spectacular walking among the highest peaks in Europe after the Alps. It can be pretty hard going, but there are less challenging hikes in the foothills, particularly the lush valleys of Las Alpujarras. For the best trekking in central Spain, head for the **Sierra de Gredos**, two hours' drive from Madrid, where there are lots of excellent one- and two-day hikes in the shadow of the highest peak, Almanzor (2592m). To the north, in the Pyrenees, the largest concentration of peaks lies in the eastern half of the range, particularly in Catalunya's **Parc Nacional d'Aigüestortes i Estany de Sant Maurici**, where there are walks of all levels, from afternoon rambles to multi-day expeditions. Further challenges abound to the west, where the **Aragonese Pyrenees** are home to the two highest peaks in the range, Aneto (3404m) and Posets (3375m), while in Aragón's **Parque Nacional de Ordesa** there are both rewarding day-hikes and more intensive climbs. If asked to choose just one corner of Spain, though, many would plump for the rugged **Picos de Europa** in Cantabria and Asturias, which, although only 40km or so across, offers a surprising diversity, from easy day-treks to full-blown expeditions.

Rafting and canyoning

There's **rafting** (see p.759) in various rivers across Spain, though the fast-flowing Noguera Pallaresa in the eastern Pyrenees is the most popular choice for expeditions. The season runs roughly from March to October, during which time you can fling yourself down the rapids in an inflatable raft from around €50 for a two-hour trip, and more like €180 for an all-day trip with lunch.

The Parque Natural Sierra de Guara (🅦 guara.org) and the Parque Nacional de Ordesa (🅦 ordesa.net) provide some of the best locations in Europe for **canyoning** (*barranquismo*) – hiking, climbing, scrambling and abseiling in caves, gorges and rivers. Operators in most of the local villages (including Alquézar and Torla) offer equipment and guides, with prices starting from around €70 for a full day's expedition. The park websites have more information on routes and local organizations.

Skiing and snowboarding

Spain offers a decent range of slopes, and often at lower prices than its more mountainous European neighbours. It is also home to the southernmost skiing in Europe, in the form of the Sol y Nieve resort in the **Sierra Nevada** (Andalucía), which has the longest season in Spain, running from November to April and sometimes even May, allowing you to ski in the morning and head to the beach in the afternoon – really, the only thing the resort's got going for it. Much more challenging skiing is to be had in the north of the country in the Pyrenees. The **Aragonese Pyrenees** are home to a range of resorts catering for beginners to advanced skiers, while the resorts in the **Catalan Pyrenees**, to the east, encompass Andorra; the biggest resort here is Soldeu/El Tarter. Other options include the more intimate **Alto Campoo**, near Santander, and, for a day's excursion, easy-to-intermediate skiing just outside Madrid at **Valdesqui** and **Navacerrada**.

There are ski deals to Spain from tour operators in your home country, though it often works out cheaper if you go through a local Spanish travel agent or even arrange your trip directly with local providers. Many local hotels offer ski deals, and we've covered some options in the Guide. Equipment rental will set you back around €20–30 a day as a general rule, and weekly lift-passes from around €120, although the longer you rent or ski for, the cheaper it will be.

Watersports

Spain offers a vast range of watersports, especially along the Mediterranean coast where most resorts offer **pedalo, kayak, paddle board and canoe rental** (from €10/hour), sailing/kitesurfing tuition, and **boat rental** (€40/hour) and **waterskiing** (from €30/15min).

Surfing is best on the Atlantic coast, backed up by the fact that the area plays regular host to a number of prestigious competitions such as the Billabong Pro, Ferrolterra Pantín Classic and the Goanna Pro. Breaks such as the legendary Mundaka (Costa Vasca), considered by many as the best left-hander in Europe, along with a superb run of beaches with waves for all abilities, make the region's reputation. The surfing season runs roughly from September to April, meaning that a full wet suit is a basic requirement in the cold Atlantic waters. If you prefer to surf in warmer waters, the Andalucian coastline has a few decent spots. For more information, see 🅦 beach wizard.com, an excellent website giving full details of all the best spots in Spain, along with reviews, maps and travel information.

Tarifa on the Costa de la Luz is *the* spot in Spain – indeed, in the whole of Europe – for **windsurfing and kitesurfing**, with strong winds almost guaranteed, and huge stretches of sandy beach to enjoy.

You'll also find schools dotted around the rest of the coast, with another good spot being the rather colder option of the Atlantic coast in Galicia. Prices are around €27 for an hour's board and sail rental, while lessons start at €50 for two hours including board rental.

Travelling with children

Spain is a good country to travel with children of any age; they will be well received everywhere, and babies and toddlers, in particular, will be the centre of attention. You will probably have to change your usual routine, since young children stay up late in Spain, especially in the summer. It's very common for them to be running around pavement cafés and public squares after 10 or 11pm, and yours will no doubt enjoy joining in. It's expected that families dine out with their children, too, so it's not unusual to see up to four generations of the same family eating tapas in a bar, for example.

Holidays

Many holiday hotels and self-contained club-style resorts offer things like kids' clubs, babysitting, sports and entertainment. The only caveat is that, of course, you're unlikely to see much of Spain on these family-oriented holidays. The two best cities to take children, hands down, are Madrid and Barcelona, which have loads of child-friendly attractions. Otherwise, Spain has various theme parks and leisure activities specifically aimed at kids, while the long Spanish coastline has a bunch of popular **water parks**.

Museums, galleries and sights throughout Spain either offer **discounts** or **free entry** for children (it's often free for under-4s or even under-7s), and it's the same on trains, sightseeing tours, boat trips and most other usual tourist attractions.

Accommodation

If you're travelling independently, finding **accommodation** shouldn't be a problem, as *hostales* and *pensiones* generally offer rooms with three or four beds. Bear in mind that much budget accommodation in towns and cities is located on the upper storeys of buildings, often without lifts. It's also

worth noting that some older-style *pensiones* don't have heating systems – and it can get very cold in winter. If you want a cot provided, or baby-listening or **baby-sitting** services, you'll usually have to stay in a more expensive hotel – and even then, never assume that these facilities are provided, so always check in advance. **Self-catering accommodation** offers the most flexibility; even in major cities, it's easy to rent an apartment by the night or week and enjoy living like a local with your family.

Products, clothes and services

Baby food, disposable nappies, formula milk and other standard items are widely available in pharmacies and supermarkets, though not necessarily with the same range or brands that you will be used to at home. Organic baby food, for example, is hard to come by away from the big-city supermarkets, and most Spanish non-organic baby foods contain small amounts of sugar or salt. Fresh milk, too, is not always available; UHT is more commonly drunk by small children. If you require anything specific for your baby or child, it's best to bring it with you or check with the manufacturer about equivalent brands. Remember the airline restrictions on carrying liquids in hand luggage if you're planning to bring industrial quantities of Calpol to see you through the holiday.

For **babies' and children's clothing**, Prénatal (ⓦ prenatal.es) and Chicco (ⓦ www.chicco.es) are Spain's market leaders, with shops in most towns and cities. Or you can always try the local El Corte Inglés department store.

Families might eat out a lot, but things like **highchairs and special children's menus** are rare, except in the resorts on the costas and islands. Most bars and cafés, though, will be happy to heat milk bottles for you. **Baby-changing areas** are also relatively rare, except in department stores and shopping centres, and even where they do exist they are not always up to scratch.

Attitudes

Most establishments are **baby-friendly** in the sense that you'll be made very welcome if you turn up with a child in tow. Many museum cloakrooms, for example, will be happy to look after your pushchair as you carry your child around the building, while restaurants will make a fuss of your little one. However, **breast-feeding** in public is not widespread, though it's more acceptable in big resorts and the main cities; the local village café is probably not the place to test rural sensibilities. **Noise** is the other factor that often stuns visiting parents. Spain is a loud country, with fiesta fireworks, jackhammers, buzzing mopeds and clamouring evening crowds all adding to the mix. Babies sleep through most things, but you might want to pick and choose accommodation with the location of bars, clubs, markets, and the like, firmly in mind.

Travel essentials

Addresses

Addresses are written as: C/Picasso 2, 4° izda. – which means Picasso Street (*calle*) no. 2, fourth floor, left- (*izquierda*) hand flat or office; dcha. (*derecha*) is right; cto. (*centro*) centre. Where no house number is know s/n (*sin número*) is commonly used in Spain. Avenida is often abbreviated to Avda. (Avgda. in Barcelona, Catalunya and the Balearics) in addresses.

Other confusions in Spanish addresses result from the different spellings, and sometimes words, used in Catalan, Basque and Galician – all of which are replacing their Castilian counterparts; for example, *carrer* (not *calle*) and *plaça* (not plaza) in Catalan.

Climate

Overall, spring, early summer and autumn are ideal times for a Spanish trip – though the weather varies enormously from region to region. Note that the chart below shows **average temperatures** – and while Seville, the hottest city in Spain, can soar high into the 90s at midday in summer, it is a fairly comfortable 23–27°C (75–80°F) through much of the morning and late afternoon. Equally, bear in mind that temperatures in the north or west, in Extremadura or León for example, can approach freezing at night in winter, while mountainous regions can get extremely cold much of the year.

Complaints

By law, all establishments (including hotels) must keep a *libro de reclamaciones* (**complaints book**). If you have any problems, you can usually produce an immediate resolution by asking for the book, since most establishments prefer to keep them empty, thus attracting no unwelcome attention from officialdom. If you do make an entry, English is acceptable but write clearly and simply; add your home address, too, as you are entitled to be informed of any action, including – but don't count on it – compensation. Or take your complaint to any local *turismo*, which should attempt to resolve the matter while you wait.

Costs

There are few places in Europe where you'll get a better deal on the cost of simple meals and drinks.

AVERAGE TEMPERATURES						
	Jan	Mar	May	Jul	Sept	Nov
ALICANTE, COSTA BLANCA						
°C/°F	16/61	20/68	26/78	32/90	30/86	21/70
BARCELONA, CATALUNYA						
°C/°F	13/56	16/61	21/70	28/83	25/77	16/61
MADRID, CASTILE						
°C/°F	9/49	15/59	21/70	31/88	25/77	13/56
MÁLAGA, COSTA DEL SOL						
°C/°F	17/63	19/67	23/74	29/84	29/84	20/68
MALLORCA, BALEARICS						
°C/°F	14/58	17/63	22/72	29/84	27/80	18/65
PONTEVEDRA, GALICIA						
°C/°F	14/58	16/61	20/68	25/77	24/75	16/61
SANTANDER, CANTABRIA						
°C/°F	12/54	15/59	17/63	22/72	21/70	15/59
SEVILLE, ANDALUCÍA						
°C/°F	15/59	21/70	26/78	35/95	32/90	20/68

Public transport remains very good value, as does car rental, certainly out of season..

It's difficult to come up with **a daily budget** for the country, as your euro glass of wine and €40 *pensión* room in rural Andalucía might be €3 and €60, respectively, in Madrid or Barcelona. However, as a very rough guide, if you always stay in youth hostels or the cheapest hotels, use public transport and stick to local restaurants, you could get by on between €50 and €80 a day. Stay somewhere a bit more stylish or comfortable, eat in fancier restaurants, and go out on the town, and you'll need more like €100–150 a day, though, of course, if you're holidaying in Spain's paradores or five-star hotels, this figure won't even cover your room.

Visiting museums, galleries, churches and monasteries soon adds up – if you visited every site we cover in Salamanca alone, for example, you'd be out of pocket by €30 or so – check to see if there are tourist cards available that give discounts on entry. Accordingly, it pays to take along any **student/ youth or senior citizen cards** you may be entitled to, as most attractions offer discounts (and make sure you carry your passport or ID card). Some museums and attractions are **free** on a certain day of the week or month (though note that this is sometimes limited to EU citizens only; you'll need to show your passport). Any **entrance fees** noted in the Guide are for the full adult price; children (as well as seniors) usually get a discount, and the under-4s are often free.

Crime and personal safety

The police in Spain come in various guises. The **Guardia Civil**, in green uniforms, is a national police force, formerly a military organization, and has responsibility for national crime, as well as roads, borders and guarding public buildings. There's also the blue-uniformed **Policía Nacional**, mainly seen in cities, who deal with crime, drugs, crowd control, identity and immigrant matters, and the like. Locally, most policing is carried out by the **Policía Municipal**, who wear blue-and-white uniforms, and these tend to be the most approachable if you're reporting a crime for example. In

certain of the autonomous regions, there are also regional police forces, which are gradually taking over duties from the Guardia Civil and Policía Nacional. The **Mossos d'Esquadra** in Catalunya (blue uniforms with red-and-white trim) and the Basque **Ertzaintza** (blue and red, with red berets) have the highest profile, though you're most likely to encounter them on traffic and highways duty.

If you do get robbed, go straight to the police, where you'll need to make an official statement known as a **denuncia**, not least because your insurance company will require a police report. Expect it to be a time-consuming and laborious business – you can do it online (details on Ⓦ policia .es), but you'll still have to go into the station to sign it. If you have your passport stolen, you need to contact your embassy or consulate.

Avoiding trouble

Pickpocketing and **bag-snatching** is, unfortunately, a fact of life in major Spanish cities and tourist resorts, though no more so than anywhere else in Europe. You need to be on guard in crowded places and on public transport, but there's no need to be paranoid. Drivers shouldn't leave anything in view in a **parked car**; take the SatNav or iPod with you. **On the road**, be cautious about accepting help from anyone other than a uniformed police officer – some roadside thieves pose as "good Samaritans" to persons experiencing car and tyre problems, some of which, such as slashed tyres, may have been inflicted at rest stops or service stations in advance. The thieves typically attempt to divert your attention by pointing out a problem and then steal items from the vehicle while you are looking elsewhere.

Incidentally, if you are stopped by a proper police officer for a **driving offence**, being foreign just won't wash as an excuse. They'll fine you on the spot, cash or card.

Sexual harassment

Spain's macho image has faded dramatically, and these days there are relatively few parts of the country where **women travelling alone** are likely to feel intimidated or attract unwanted attention. There is little of the pestering that you have to contend with in, say, the larger Italian cities, and the outdoor culture of terrazas (terrace bars) and the tendency of Spaniards to move around in large, mixed crowds, help to make you feel less exposed. *Déjame en paz* ("leave me in peace") is a fairly standard rebuff, and if you are in any doubt, take a taxi, always the safest way to travel late at night.

> ## EMERGENCY NUMBERS
>
> ☏ **112** All emergency services
> ☏ **061** Ambulance
> ☏ **080** Fire service
> ☏ **062** Guardia Civil
> ☏ **091** Policía Nacional

STAYING SAFE IN SPANISH CITIES

Certain Spanish cities – Madrid, Barcelona and Seville particularly – have a bad rep as far as petty crime is concerned. While it's easy to get spooked by lurid tales of local thievery (hoteliers often go to great pains to warn guests of the dangers), taking the usual sensible **precautions** should help make your stay safe.

Know where your belongings are at all times (eg, don't leave **bags** unattended, even if you're looking at rooms upstairs in a *hostal*). Carry handbags slung across your neck, not over your shoulder; don't put wallets in your back pocket; leave passport and tickets in the hotel safe; and keep a photocopy of your passport, plus notes of your credit card helplines and so on.

On the street, beware of people standing unusually close at street kiosks or attractions, or of those trying to distract you for any reason (pointing out "bird shit" – in reality, planted shaving cream – on your jacket, shoving a card or paper to read right under your nose). Next thing you know, your purse has gone.

The major **resorts** of the costas have their own artificial holiday culture, where problems are more likely to be caused by other alcohol-fuelled holiday-makers. You are actually more vulnerable in isolated, **rural regions**, where you can walk for hours without coming across an inhabited farm or house, though it's rare that this poses a threat – help and hospitality are much more the norm. Many single women happily tramp the long-distance pilgrim footpath, for example, though you are always best advised to stay in rooms and *pensiones* rather than camping wild.

Electricity

The current in most of Spain is 220v – bring an adaptor (and transformer) to use UK and US laptops, mobile phone chargers, and other electronic devices.

Entry requirements

EU citizens (and those of Norway, Iceland, Liechtenstein and Switzerland) need only a valid national identity card or passport to enter Spain. Other Europeans, and citizens of the **United States**, **Canada**, **Australia** and **New Zealand**, require a passport but no visa, and can stay as a tourist for up to ninety days. Other nationalities (including South Africans) will need to get a visa from a Spanish embassy or consulate before departure. Visa requirements do change, and it's always advisable to check the current situation before leaving home.

Most EU citizens who want to stay in Spain for longer than three months, rather than just visit as a tourist, need to register at a provincial **Oficina de Extranjeros** (Foreigners' Office), where they'll be issued with a residence certificate; you'll find a list of offices (eventually) on the Ministry of Interior website (Ⓦ mir.es). You don't need the certificate if

you're an EU citizen living and working legally in Spain, or if you're legally self-employed or a student (on an exchange programme or otherwise). US citizens can apply for one ninety-day extension, showing proof of funds, but this must be done from outside Spain. Other nationalities wishing to extend their stay will need to get a special visa from a Spanish embassy or consulate before departure.

Health

The **European Health Insurance Card (EHIC)** gives EU citizens access to Spanish state public-health services under reciprocal agreements. While this will provide free or reduced-cost medical care in the event of minor injuries and emergencies, it won't cover every eventuality – and it only applies to EU citizens in possession of the card – so travel insurance is essential.

No **inoculations** are required for Spain, and the worst that's likely to happen to you is that you might fall victim to an upset stomach. To be safe, wash fruit and avoid tapas dishes that look as if they were prepared last week. Water at public fountains is fine, unless there's a sign saying "*agua no potable*", in which case don't drink it.

For minor complaints, go to a **farmacia** – pharmacists are highly trained, willing to give advice (often in English) and able to dispense many drugs that would be available only on prescription in other countries. They keep usual shop hours (Mon–Fri 9am–1.30pm & 5–8pm), but some open late and at weekends, while a rota system (displayed in the window of every pharmacy) keeps at least one open 24 hours in every town.

If you have special medical or dietary requirements, it is advisable to carry a letter from your doctor, translated into Spanish, indicating the nature of your condition and necessary treatments.

With luck, you'll get the address of an English-speaking **doctor** from the nearest *farmacia*, police station or tourist office – it's obviously more likely in resorts and big cities. Treatment at **hospitals** for EU citizens in possession of the EHIC card is free; otherwise, you'll be charged at private-hospital rates, which can be very expensive.

In **emergencies**, dial ☎ 112 for an ambulance.

Insurance

You should take out a comprehensive **insurance policy** before travelling to Spain, to cover against loss, theft, illness or injury. A typical policy will provide cover for loss of baggage, tickets and – up to a certain limit – cash or travellers' cheques, as well as cancellation or curtailment of your journey. When securing baggage cover, make sure that the per-article limit will cover your most valuable possession. Most policies exclude so-called **dangerous sports** unless an extra premium is paid: in Spain, this can mean that most watersports are excluded (plus rafting, canyoning, etc), though not things like bike tours or hiking.

If you need to make a claim, you should keep receipts for medicines and medical treatment, and in the event you have anything stolen, you must obtain an official statement from the police.

Internet

Wireless internet access (wi-fi, pronounced "wee-fee" in Spain) is widespread in cafés, bars, hotels and other public "hotspots" – Barcelona city council, for example, operates Spain's largest free public wi-fi network. Otherwise, you can get online at computer shops and phone offices (*locutorios*), where you'll pay as little as €1 an hour, though it can cost two or three times as much. Since most accommodation in Spain has free wi-fi, reviews in the Guide only highlight places where there is no wi-fi or you have to pay for it.

Laundry

You'll find a few coin-operated self-service laundries (*lavanderías automáticas*) in the major cities, but you normally have to leave your clothes for a service wash and dry at a *lavandería*. A dry cleaner is a *tintorería*. Note that by law you're not allowed to leave laundry hanging out of windows over a street, and many *pensiones* and *hostales* expressly forbid washing clothes in the sink. To avoid an international incident, ask first if there's somewhere you can wash your clothes.

Mail

Post offices (*Correos*; Ⓦ correos.es) are normally open weekdays from 8am to 2pm and again from 5pm to 7.30pm, though branches in bigger places may have longer hours, may not close at midday and may open on Saturday mornings. There's an office-finder on the website, which also gives exact opening hours and contact details for each post office in Spain. As you can also pay bills and buy phonecards in post offices, queues can be long – it's often easier to buy **stamps** at tobacconists (look for the brown-and-yellow *estanco* sign).

Outbound mail is reasonably reliable, with letters or cards taking around three days to a week to the UK and the rest of Europe, a week to ten days to North America, New Zealand and Australia, although it can be more erratic in the summer. There's also a whole host of express-mail services (ask for *urgente* or *exprés*).

Maps

You'll find a good selection of **road maps** in most Spanish bookshops, street kiosks and service stations. Most widely available are the regional Michelin maps (1:400,000), covering the country (including the Balearics) in a series of nine maps, though there are also whole-country maps and atlas-format versions available. Other good country and regional maps are those published by Distrimapas Telstar (ⓦdistrimapas-telstar.es), which also produces reliable indexed **street plans** of the main cities. Any good book or travel shop in your own country should be able to provide a decent range of Spain maps, or buy online from specialist stores such as ⓦstanfords.co.uk or ⓦrandmcnally.com.

You can buy **hiking/trekking maps** from specialist map/travel shops in Spain, including La Tienda Verde in Madrid (ⓦtiendaverde.es), and Librería Quera (ⓦllibreriaquera.com) or Altaïr (ⓦaltair.es) in Barcelona. These and other bookshops stock the full range of **topographical maps** issued by two government agencies – the Instituto Geográfico Nacional and the Servicio Geográfico del Ejército – available at scales of 1:200,000, 1:100,000, 1:50,000 and occasionally 1:25,000. The various SGE series are considered to be more up to date, although neither agency is hugely reliable. A Catalunya-based company, Editorial Alpina (ⓦeditorialalpina.com), produces useful 1:40,000 or 1:25,000 map/booklet sets for most of the Spanish **mountain and foothill areas** of interest, and these are also on sale in many bookshops.

Money

Spain's currency is the **euro** (€), with notes issued in denominations of 5, 10, 20, 50, 100, 200 and 500 euros, and coins in denominations of 1, 2, 5, 10, 20 and 50 cents, and 1 and 2 euros. Up-to-the-minute currency **exchange rates** are posted on ⓦoanda.com.

By far the easiest way to get money is to use your bank **debit card** to withdraw cash from an **ATM**, found in villages, towns and cities all over Spain, as well as on arrival at the airports and major train stations. You can usually withdraw up to €300 a day, and instructions are offered in English once you insert your card. Make sure you have a personal identification number (PIN) that's designed to work overseas, and take a note of your bank's emergency contact number in case the machine swallows your card. Some European debit cards can also be used directly in shops to pay for purchases; you'll need to check first with your bank.

All major **credit cards** are accepted in hotels, restaurants and shops, and for tours, tickets and transport, though don't count on being able to use them in every small *pensión* or village café. You can also use your credit card in an ATM to withdraw cash, though remember that these advances will be treated as loans, with interest accruing daily from the date of withdrawal. If you use a foreign credit card in some shops, you may also be asked for photo ID, so be prepared to show a driving licence or passport. Make sure you make a note of the number for reporting lost or stolen cards to your credit card company.

Spanish **bancos** (banks) and **cajas de ahorros** (savings banks) have branches in all but the smallest villages. **Banking hours** are usually Monday to Friday 8.30am to 2pm, with some city branches open Saturday 8.30am to 1pm (except June–Sept when all banks close on Sat), although times can vary from bank to bank. Outside these times, it's usually possible to change cash at larger hotels (generally with bad rates and high commission) or with travel agents – useful for small amounts in a hurry.

In tourist areas, you'll also find specialist **casas de cambio**, with more convenient hours (though rates vary), while some major tourist offices, larger train stations and most branches of El Corte Inglés department store have exchange facilities open throughout business hours.

Opening hours

Almost everything in Spain – shops, museums, churches, tourist offices – closes for a **siesta** of at least two hours in the middle part of the day. There's a lot of variation (and the siesta tends to be longer in the south), but you'll get far less aggravated if you accept that the early afternoon is best spent asleep, or in a bar, or both.

Basic **working hours** are Monday to Friday 9.30am to 2pm and 5pm to 8pm. Many **shops** open slightly later on a Saturday (at 10am) and close for the day at 2pm, though you'll still find plenty of places open in cities, and there are regional variations. Moreover, department and chain stores and shopping malls tend to open a straight Monday to Saturday 10am to 9pm or 10pm.

Museums and galleries, with very few exceptions, also have a break between 1pm or 2pm and 4pm. On Sundays, most open mornings only, and on Mondays many close all day (museums are also usually closed Jan 1 & 6, May 1, Dec 24, 25 & 31). Opening hours vary from year to year, though often not by more than half an hour or so. Some are also seasonal, and usually in Spain, "summer" means from Easter until September, and "winter" from October until Easter.

The most important **cathedrals, churches and monasteries** operate in the same way as museums, with regular visiting hours and admission charges. Other churches, though, are kept locked, generally opening only for worship in the early morning and/or the evening (between around 6pm and 9pm).

Public holidays

Alongside the Spanish **national public holidays** (see box below) there are scores of regional holidays and local fiestas (often marking the local saint's day), any of which will mean that everything except hotels, bars and restaurants locks its doors.

In addition, **August** is traditionally Spain's own holiday month, when the big cities are semi-deserted, with many shops and restaurants closed for the duration. In contrast, it can prove nearly impossible to find a room in the more popular coastal and mountain resorts at these times; similarly, seats on planes, trains and buses in August should if possible be booked in advance.

Shopping

The great city **markets** of Spain are attractions in their own right – bustling, colourful and hugely photogenic – but even so they are emphatically not "just for tourists". Local people still do their daily shop in places like La Boqueria in Barcelona, Valencia's Mercado Central or Madrid's refurbished Mercado de San Miguel, while a visit to any town's local market is a sure way to get a handle on regional produce and specialities. Independent **food shops** thrive too, from traditional bakeries to classy delis serving the finest cured meats, while the bigger cities support whole enclaves of foodie shops – in Barcelona's La Ribera neighbourhood, for example, you can flit from alley to alley to buy hand-crafted chocolates, artisan-made cheeses, home-roast coffee, organic olive oil and the like.

Leatherwork, such as belts, bags, purses and even saddles, are best sourced in Andalucía. The town of Ubrique (Cádiz) has been a centre of leather production since medieval times, and you can browse and buy from the workshops that line the main street (which also make branded items for the big international fashion names).

Ceramics are widely available, but are especially good in Andalucía (Córdoba region, and around Seville) and in Catalunya (at La Bisbal, northwest of Palafrugell).

In Andalucía you'll also be able to pick up the most authentic **flamenco** accessories such as dresses, fans, shawls and lace.

Smoking laws

Since 2006, smoking in public places in Spain has been regulated by law, and tougher restrictions introduced in 2011 mean that it's now forbidden to smoke in all public buildings and transport facilities, plus bars, restaurants, clubs and cafés. Compared to other countries with smoking restrictions in force, you'll find there's still an awful lot of puffing going on, though the ban is generally observed.

Taxes

Local sales tax, **IVA** (pronounced "eeba"), is ten percent in hotels and restaurants, and twenty-one percent in shops. It's usually included in the price though not always, so some hotel or restaurant bills can come as a bit of a surprise – though quoted prices should always make it clear whether or not tax is included. **Non-EU residents** are able to claim back the sales tax on purchases that come to over €90. To do this, make sure the shop you're buying from fills out the correct paperwork, and present this to customs before you check in at the airport for your return flight.

Telephones

Spanish **telephone numbers** have nine digits; mobile numbers begin with a 6 or 7, freephone numbers begin 900, while other 90-plus- and 80-plus-digit numbers are nationwide standard-rate or special-rate services. To **call Spain from abroad**, dial your country's international access code + 34 (Spain's country code) + the nine-digit Spanish number.

Public telephones have instructions in English, and accept coins, credit cards and phonecards. **Phonecards** (*tarjetas*) with discounted rates for calls are available in tobacconists, newsagents and post offices, issued in various denominations either by Telefónica (the dominant operator) or one of its rivals. Credit cards are not recommended for local

---

SPANISH NATIONAL PUBLIC HOLIDAYS

Jan 1 *Año Nuevo,* New Year's Day
Jan 6 *Epifanía,* Epiphany
March/April *Viernes Santo,* Good Friday
May 1 *Fiesta del Trabajo,* May Day
Aug 15 *La Asunción,* Assumption of the Virgin
Oct 12 *Día de la Hispanidad,* National Day
Nov 1 *Todos los Santos,* All Saints
Dec 6 *Día de la Constitución,* Constitution Day
Dec 8 *Inmaculada Concepción*
Dec 25 *Navidad,* Christmas Day

and national calls, since most have a minimum charge that is far more than a normal call is likely to cost. It's also best to avoid making calls from the phone in your hotel room, as even local calls will be slapped with a heavy surcharge.

You can make international calls from any public payphone, but it's cheaper to go to one of the ubiquitous phone centres, or **locutorios**, which specialize in discounted overseas connections. **Calling home from Spain**, you dial ☎00 (Spain's international access code) + your country code (44 for the UK) + city/area code minus initial zero + number. For **reverse-charge calls**, dial the international operator (☎1008 Europe, ☎1005 rest of the world).

Most European **mobile phones** will work in Spain, though it's worth checking with your provider whether you need to get international access switched on and whether there are any extra charges involved. Even though prices are coming down, it's still expensive to use your own mobile extensively while abroad, and you will pay for receiving incoming calls, for example.

Time

Spain is one hour ahead of the UK, six hours ahead of Eastern Standard Time, nine hours ahead of Pacific Standard Time, eight hours behind Australia, ten hours behind New Zealand, and the same time as South Africa. In Spain, the clocks go forward in the last week in March and back again in the last week in October. It's worth noting, if you're planning to cross the border, that Portugal is an hour behind Spain throughout the year.

Toilets

Public toilets are generally reasonably clean but don't always have any paper. They can very occasionally still be squat-style. They are most commonly referred to and labelled *Los Servicios*, though signs may point you to *baños*, *aseos* or *lavabos*. *Damas* (Ladies) and *Caballeros* (Gentlemen) are the usual distinguishing signs for sex, though you may also see the potentially confusing *Señoras* (Women) and *Señores* (Men).

Tourist information

The Spanish national tourist office, **Turespaña** (🖥spain.info), is an excellent source of information when planning your trip. The website is full of ideas, information and searchable databases, and there

are links to similar websites of Turespaña offices in your own country.

There are **oficinas de turismo** (tourist offices) in virtually every Spanish town, usually open Monday to Friday 9am to 2pm and 4pm to 7pm, Saturday and Sunday 9am to 2pm, but hours vary considerably from place to place. In major cities and coastal resorts the offices tend to remain open all day Saturday and on Sunday morning between April and September.

The information and help available in *oficinas de turismo* also varies: some are very good, and some do little more than hand out a map and ask where you're from. Not all staff speak English, especially in the more rural and out-of-the-way destinations. There's also often more than one information office, especially in bigger towns and cities, where responsibility for local tourism is split between municipal and provincial offices. As a rough rule, the municipal offices are better for specific city information, the provincial offices best for advice about where to go in the region.

Travellers with disabilities

The classic tourist images of Spain – the medieval old towns, winding lanes, the castles and monasteries – don't exactly fill you with confidence if you're in a wheelchair. However, Spain is changing and facilities are improving rapidly, especially in the more go-ahead, contemporary cities. There are accessible rooms and hotels in all major Spanish cities and resorts and, by law, all new public buildings (including revamped museums and galleries) are required to be fully accessible. Public transport is the main problem, since most local buses and trains are virtually impossible for wheelchairs, though again there are pockets of excellence in Spain. The AVE high-speed train service, for example, is fully accessible, as is every city and sightseeing bus in Barcelona (and large parts of its metro and tram network, too). In many towns and cities, acoustic traffic-light signals and dropped kerbs are common.

Some organizations at home may be able to advise you further about travel to Spain, like the very useful UK-based **Tourism For All** (🖥www.tourismforall.org.uk). **Access Travel** (🖥access-travel.co.uk) offers Barcelona city breaks and holidays to five other Spanish resorts, and at the very least, local tourist offices in Spain should also be able to recommend a suitable hotel or taxi company. In Barcelona – the single most clued-up city – there's lots more information on the local tourism website, 🖥barcelonaturisme.com (click on "Accessible Barcelona").

Madrid

GRAN VÍA AT DUSK

1

Madrid

Madrid became Spain's capital simply by virtue of its geographical position at the heart of Iberia. When Felipe II moved the seat of government here in 1561, his aim was to create a symbol of the unification and centralization of the country, and a capital from which he could receive the fastest post and communication from every corner of the nation. The site itself had few natural advantages – it is 300km from the sea on a 650-metre-high plateau, freezing in winter, boiling in summer – and it was only the determination of successive rulers to promote a strong central capital that ensured Madrid's survival and development.

Today, Madrid is a vast, predominantly modern city, with a population of some four million and growing. The journey in – through a stream of soulless suburbs and high-rise apartment blocks – isn't pretty, but the streets at the heart of the city are a pleasant surprise, with pockets of medieval buildings and narrow, atmospheric alleys, dotted with the oddest of shops and bars, and interspersed with eighteenth-century Bourbon squares. Compared with the historic cities of Spain – Toledo, Salamanca, Seville, Granada – there may be few sights of great architectural interest, but the monarchs did acquire outstanding picture collections, which formed the basis of the **Prado** museum. This, together with the **Reina Sofía** and the **Thyssen-Bornemisza** museums, state-of-the-art homes to fabulous arrays of modern Spanish painting (including Picasso's *Guernica*) and European and American masters, has made Madrid a top port of call on the European art tour.

Aside from these heavyweight cultural attractions, there is a host of smaller museums and palaces which can be almost as rewarding. Sports fans will inevitably be drawn to the Santiago Bernabéu, home to Real Madrid, one of the most glamorous and successful clubs in world football, while a scattering of parks and gardens provide a welcome respite from the hustle and bustle of the city centre.

However, monuments and sights are not really what Madrid is about and as you get to grips with the place, you soon realize that it's the lifestyle of the inhabitants – the **madrileños** – that is the capital's key attraction: hanging out in traditional cafés or summer terrazas, packing the lanes of the Sunday Rastro flea market or playing hard and very late in a thousand **bars**, clubs, discos and *tascas*. Whatever Barcelona, Valencia or San Sebastián might claim, the Madrid scene, immortalized in the movies of Pedro Almodóvar, remains the most vibrant and fun in the country.

The arrival of the new millennium saw Madrid undergo a series of urban rehabilitation programmes focused on the city's older *barrios* (districts). Improvements

LA CHATA TAPAS BAR, LA LATINA

Highlights

❶ Palacio Real Marvel at the over-the-top opulence in this grandiose former residence of the Spanish monarchs. **See p.71**

❷ El Rastro Take a Sunday stroll from Plaza Mayor through Madrid's shambolic flea market. **See p.72**

❸ The Prado The Goya, Velázquez and Bosch collections alone make the trip to one of the world's greatest art museums a must. **See p.77**

❹ Guernica See this icon of twentieth-century art set in context at the Reina Sofía. **See p.83**

❺ Museo Arqueológico Nacional Given a new lease of life following a lengthy refurbishment,

the archeological museum contains a stunning display of ancient treasures. **See p.93**

❻ Real Madrid Watch the ten-times European champions' dazzling roster of big-name players parade their footballing skills at the Santiago Bernabéu stadium. **See p.95**

❼ Tapas Sample the vast array of tasty specialities as you hop from bar to bar in the Huertas, La Latina, Chueca or Malasaña districts. **See p.105**

❽ A night on the tiles Start late at a bar, then go on to a club and try to make it into the early hours before collapsing over *chocolate con churros*. **See p.113**

HIGHLIGHTS ARE MARKED ON THE MAP ON PP.62–63

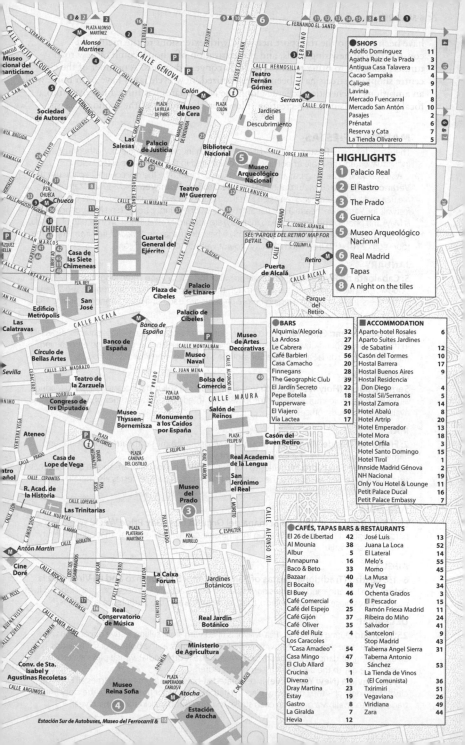

SHOPS

Adolfo Domínguez	11
Agatha Ruiz de la Prada	3
Antigua Casa Talavera	12
Cacao Sampaka	4
Caligae	9
Lavinia	1
Mercado Fuencarral	8
Mercado San Antón	10
Pasajes	2
Prénatal	6
Reserva y Cata	7
La Tienda Olivarero	5

HIGHLIGHTS

1. Palacio Real
2. El Rastro
3. The Prado
4. Guernica
5. Museo Arqueológico Nacional
6. Real Madrid
7. Tapas
8. A night on the tiles

BARS

Alquimia/Alegoría	32
La Ardosa	27
Le Cabrera	29
Café Barbieri	56
Casa Camacho	20
Finnegans	28
The Geographic Club	39
El Jardín Secreto	22
Pepe Botella	18
Tupperware	21
El Viajero	50
Vía Lactea	17

ACCOMMODATION

Aparto-hotel Rosales	6
Aparto Suites Jardines de Sabatini	12
Casón del Tormes	10
Hostal Barrera	17
Hostal Buenos Aires	9
Hostal Residencia Don Diego	4
Hostal Sil/Serranos	5
Hostal Zamora	14
Hotel Abalú	8
Hotel Artrip	20
Hotel Emperador	13
Hotel Mora	18
Hotel Orfila	3
Hotel Santo Domingo	15
Hotel Tirol	1
Innside Madrid Génova	2
NH Nacional	19
Only You Hotel & Lounge	11
Petit Palace Ducal	16
Petit Palace Embassy	7

CAFÉS, TAPAS BARS & RESTAURANTS

El 26 de Libertad	42	José Luís	13
Al Mounia	38	Juana La Loca	52
Albur	5	El Lateral	14
Annapurna	16	Melo's	55
Baco & Beto	33	Momo	45
Bazaar	40	La Musa	2
El Bocaito	48	My Veg	34
El Buey	46	Ochenta Grados	3
Café Comercial	6	El Pescador	15
Café del Espejo	25	Ramón Frieza Madrid	11
Café Gijón	37	Ribeira do Miño	24
Café Oliver	35	Salvador	41
Café del Ruiz	4	Santceloni	9
Los Caracoles "Casa Amadeo"	54	Stop Madrid	43
Casa Mingo	47	Taberna Angel Sierra	31
El Club Allard	30	Taberna Antonio Sánchez	53
Crucina	1	La Tienda de Vinos (El Comunista)	36
Diverxo	10	Txirimiri	51
Dray Martina	23	Vegaviana	26
Estay	19	Viridiana	49
Gastro	8	Zara	44
La Giralda	7		
Hevia	12		

1

have been made to the transport network, with extensions to the metro, the construction of new ring roads, and the excavation of a honeycomb of new road tunnels designed to bring relief to Madrid's congested streets. A number of the city centre shopping streets have been pedestrianized, new cycle lanes have been built, while an ambitious regeneration scheme along the Manzanares has turned the river into a focal point for leisure and recreation. However, the impact of the economic crisis,

MADRID'S FIESTAS

There are dozens of **fiestas** in Madrid, some of which involve the whole city, others just an individual *barrio*. The more important dates celebrated in the capital are listed below.

Also well worth checking out are cultural festivals organized by the city council, in particular the **Veranos de la Villa** (July–Aug) and **Festival de Otoño a Primavera** (Nov–June). Many events are free and, in the summer, often open air, taking place in the city's parks and squares. Annual festivals for alternative theatre (Feb), flamenco (Feb–March & June), books (end May), dance (April & May) and photography (mid-June to mid-July) are also firmly established on the cultural agenda. Full programmes are published in the monthly what's-on magazine *esMadrid*, free from any of the tourist offices (see p.99) and from the city's tourist website (Ⓦ esmadrid.com).

JANUARY

5: Cabalgata de Reyes To celebrate the arrival of the gift-bearing Three Kings there is a hugely popular, gigantic evening procession through the city centre in which children are showered with sweets. It's held on the evening before presents are traditionally exchanged in Spain.

FEBRUARY

Week before Lent: Carnaval An excuse for a lot of partying and fancy-dress parades, especially in the gay zone around Chueca. The end of *Carnaval* is marked by the bizarre and entertaining parade, El Entierro de la Sardina (The Burial of the Sardine), on the Paseo de la Florida.

MARCH/APRIL

Semana Santa (Holy Week) Celebrated with a series of solemn processions around Madrid, although for a more impressive backdrop head for Toledo (routes and times of processions are available from tourist offices).

MAY

2: Fiesta del Dos de Mayo Held throughout Madrid, with music, theatre productions and flamenco shows though a bit low-key in recent years.

15: Fiestas de San Isidro Festivities to honour Madrid's patron saint are spread a week either side of this date, and are among the country's biggest festivals. The fiestas also herald the start of the bullfighting season.

JUNE/JULY

End June/beginning July: La Semana del Orgullo Gay (Gay Pride Week) Week-long party throughout Chueca, culminating in a massive carnival-style parade that brings the city centre to a standstill.

AUGUST

6–15: Castizo (Traditional fiestas of San Cayetano, San Lorenzo and La Virgen de la Paloma) in La Latina and Lavapiés *barrios*. Much of the activity – processions, dancing and live music – takes place around C/Toledo, the Pza. de la Paja and the Jardines de las Vistillas.

DECEMBER

25: Navidad During Christmas, Pza. Mayor is filled with stalls selling festive decorations and displaying a large model of a Nativity scene. El Corte Inglés, at the bottom of C/Preciados, has an all-singing, all-dancing clockwork Christmas scene (Cortylandia), which plays at certain times of the day to the delight of assembled children.

31: Nochevieja (New Year's Eve) is celebrated at bars, restaurants and parties all over the city. Puerta del Sol is the customary place to gather, waiting for the strokes of the clock – it is traditional to swallow a grape on each stroke to bring good luck in the coming year.

1

combined with chronic overspending and the failure of three consecutive bids for the Olympics, has stalled the momentum. High levels of unemployment, a battery of austerity measures, endemic political corruption and local government ineptitude have certainly taken the gloss off the Spanish capital, but the *madrileños* themselves are incredibly resilient folk and the city remains one of the most vibrant and welcoming destinations for any visitor.

A brief history

Madrid's history dates back to the ninth century when **Muslims** established a defensive outpost on the escarpment above the River Manzanares which later became known as "Mayrit" – the place of many springs.

It remained a relatively insignificant backwater until 1561 when Felipe II designated the city his **imperial capital** by virtue of its position at the heart of the recently unified Spain. The cramped street plan in the city centre provides a clue as to what the city would have been like at this time and the narrow alleys around the Pza. Mayor are still among Madrid's liveliest and most atmospheric. With the **Bourbons** replacing the Habsburgs at the start of the eighteenth century, a touch of French style, including the sumptuous Palacio Real, was introduced into the capital by Felipe V.

It was the "King-Mayor" **Carlos III**, however, who tried to convert the city into a home worthy of the monarchy after he ascended to the throne in 1759, ordering the streets to be cleaned, sewers and lighting to be installed and work to begin on the Prado museum complex.

Upheaval and political polarization

The early **nineteenth century** brought invasion and turmoil to Spain as Napoleon established his brother Joseph (or José to Spaniards) on the throne. Madrid, however, continued to flourish, gaining some very attractive buildings and squares, including the Pza. de Oriente and Pza. de Santa Ana. With the onset of the **twentieth century**, the capital became the hotbed of the political and intellectual discussions that divided the country; *tertulias* (political/philosophical discussion circles) sprang up in cafés across the city (some of them are still going) as the country entered the turbulent years of the end of the monarchy and the foundation of the Second Republic.

The Civil War

Madrid was a Republican stronghold during the **Civil War**, with fierce battles raging around the capital as Franco's troops laid siege to the city, eventually taking control in

---

ORIENTATION

Madrid's layout is fairly straightforward. At the city's heart is the large oval-shaped plaza **Puerta del Sol** (often referred to as just "Sol"). Around it lie the oldest parts of Madrid, neatly bordered to the west by the **River Manzanares**, to the east by the park of **El Retiro** and to the north by the city's great thoroughfare, the **Gran Vía**.

Madrid's main sights occupy a compact area between the **Palacio Real** and the gardens of **El Retiro**. The great trio of museums – the **Prado**, **Thyssen-Bornemisza** and **Reina Sofía** – lie in a "golden triangle" just west of El Retiro and close to Paseo del Prado. Over towards the river are the oldest parts of the city, centred on the splendid, arcaded **Pza. Mayor**, an area known as **Madrid de los Austrias** after the Habsburg monarchs who built it.

To get a feel for the city you should experience the contrasting character and life of the various neighbourhoods (*barrios*). The most central and rewarding of these are the areas around **Pza. de Santa Ana and C/Huertas**, east of Sol; **La Latina and Lavapiés**, south of Pza. Mayor, where the Sunday market, El Rastro, takes place; and **Malasaña and Chueca**, north of Gran Vía. By happy circumstance, these *barrios* have some of Madrid's finest concentrations of tapas bars and restaurants.

1

1939. The Civil War, of course, caused untold damage, and led to forty years of isolation. The city's great spread to **suburbia** began during the Franco era and it has continued unabated ever since, with unbridled property speculation taking its toll on the green spaces that surround the capital. Franco also extended the city northwards along the spinal route of the Paseo de la Castellana, to accommodate his ministers and minions during development extravaganzas of the 1950s and 1960s.

The post-Franco era

The Spanish capital has changed immeasurably, however, in the four decades since Franco's death, initially guided by a poet-mayor, the late **Tierno Galván**. His efforts – the creation of parks and renovation of public spaces and public life – left an enduring legacy, and were a vital ingredient of the *movida madrileña* "the happening Madrid" with which the city broke through in the 1980s. Since the early 1990s, the centre-right Partido Popular has been in control, bringing with it a more restrictive attitude towards bar and club licensing. Mayor Alberto Ruiz Gallardón was the catalyst for a succession of gigantic pharaoh-style urban renewal schemes. These undoubtedly improved the city environment, but at the same time he and regional president Esperanza Aguirre presided over rampant property speculation and subsequent collapse that have bequeathed the city a number of white elephant civic projects and a seemingly insurmountable debt crisis.

In recent years there has been a tendency towards homogenization with the rest of Europe, as franchised fast-food joints and coffee bars have sprung up all over the city centre. Nevertheless, in making the transition from provincial backwater to major European capital, Madrid has still managed to preserve its own stylish and quirky identity.

Madrid de los Austrias

Madrid de los Austrias (Habsburg Madrid) was a mix of formal planning – at its most impressive in the expansive and theatrical Pza. Mayor – and areas of shanty town development, thrown up as the new capital gained an urban population. The central area of old Madrid still reflects both characteristics, with its twisting grid of streets, alleyways and steps, and its Flemish-inspired architecture of red brick and grey stone, slate-tiled towers and Renaissance doorways.

Puerta del Sol

Ⓜ Sol

The obvious starting point for exploring Madrid de los Austrias (and most other areas of the centre) is the **Puerta del Sol**. This square marks the epicentre of the city – and, indeed, of Spain. It is from this point that all distances are measured, and here that six of Spain's *Rutas Nacionales* officially begin. On the pavement outside the clock-tower building on the south side of the square, an inconspicuous stone slab shows **Kilometre Zero**.

The square, which conceals a new subterranean transport hub, is a popular meeting place, especially by the statue of a bear pawing a *madroño* (strawberry tree) – the city's emblem – at the start of C/Alcalá and the equestrian bronze of King Carlos III. Statues apart, there's little of note in the square apart from the **Casa de Correos**, built in 1766, originally the city's post office and now home to the main offices of the Madrid regional government. At New Year, the square is packed with people waiting for the clock that crowns the Neoclassical facade to chime midnight. Sol's main business, however, is shopping, with giant branches of the **department stores** El Corte Inglés and the French chain FNAC in C/Preciados, at the top end of the square.

MADRID'S FREEBIES

Free entrance can be gained to many of Madrid's premier attractions. Sites classed as Patrimonio Nacional, such as the Palacio Real, the Convento de la Encarnación, El Pardo and the Monasterio de las Descalzas, are free to EU citizens at various times during the week (bring your passport). Museums run by Madrid City Council, including the Museo de San Isidro, La Ermita de San Antonio, the Templo de Debod and the Museo de Historia de Madrid, do not charge admission. Most museums are free for children, and give substantial discounts to retirees and students (bring ID in all cases). In addition, many museums and sights that normally charge entry set aside certain times when entrance is free, and nearly all are free on World Heritage Day (April 18), International Museum Day (May 18), La Noche en Blanco (early Sept), the Día de Hispanidad (Oct 12) and Día de la Constitución (Dec 6). The following are free at these times:

Museo de América Sun 10am–3pm.
Museo Reina Sofía Mon, Wed–Sat 7–9pm, Sun 3pm–7pm.
Museo Arqueológico Nacional Sat 2–8pm, Sun 9.30am–noon.
Museo de Artes Decorativas Thurs 5–8pm, Sun 10am–3pm.
Museo Cerralbo Thurs 5–8pm, Sat 2–3pm & Sun 10am–3pm.
Museo Lázaro Galdiano Mon, Wed, Thurs, Fri &–Sat 3.30–4.30pm, Sun 10am–3pm.
Museo del Prado Mon–Sat 6–8pm, Sun 5–7pm, Nov 19 & May 18.
Museo del Romanticismo Sat 2–6.30pm, Sun 10am–3pm.
Museo Sorolla Sat 2–8pm, Sun 10am–3pm.
Museo Thyssen-Bornemisza Mon noon–4pm.
Museo del Traje Sat 2.30–7pm, Sun 10am–3pm.
Palacio Real Oct–March: Mon–Thurs 4–6pm, April–Sept: 6–8pm.
Real Academia de Bellas Artes Wed 10am–3pm.

Plaza Mayor

Ⓜ Sol

Follow C/Mayor (the "Main Street" of the medieval city) west from the Puerta del Sol and you could easily walk right past Madrid's most important landmark: **Plaza Mayor**. Set back from the street and entered by stepped passageways, it appears all the more grand in its continuous sweep of arcaded buildings. It was planned by Felipe II – the monarch who made Madrid the capital – as the public meeting place of the city, and was finished thirty years later in 1619 during the reign of Felipe III, who sits astride the stallion in the central statue. The architect was Juan Gómez de Mora, responsible for many of the civic and royal buildings in this quarter.

The square, with its hundreds of balconies, was designed as a theatre for public events, and it has served this function throughout its history. It was the scene of the Inquisition's *autos-de-fé* (trials of faith) and the executions that followed; kings were crowned here; festivals and demonstrations passed through; plays by Lope de Vega and others received their first performances; bulls were fought; and gossip was spread. The more important of the events would be watched by royalty from their apartments in the central **Casa Panadería**, a palace named after the bakery that it replaced. It was rebuilt after a fire in 1692 and subsequently decorated with frescoes. However, the present delightful, and highly kitsch, array of allegorical figures that adorn the facade was only added in 1992. Today, the palace houses municipal offices and a tourist office (daily 9.30am–8.30pm).

Nowadays, Plaza Mayor is primarily a tourist haunt, full of expensive outdoor cafés and restaurants (best stick to a drink), buskers and caricaturists. However, an air of grandeur clings to the plaza, which still performs public functions. In the summer months and during the major *madrileño* fiestas, it becomes an outdoor **theatre** and **music stage**; and in the winter, just before Christmas, it becomes a **bazaar** for festive decorations and religious regalia. Every Sunday, too, stamp and coin sellers set up their stalls.

1

Mercado de San Miguel

Set back from the road, near the entrance to the Pza. Mayor, is the splendid decorative ironwork of the **Mercado de San Miguel**. Built in 1916, it was formerly one of the old-style food markets scattered throughout the city, but it has now been refurbished and converted into a stylish, though pricey, tourist-oriented emporium complete with oyster and champagne bar.

The alley taverns

In the alleys just below the square, such as C/Cuchilleros and C/Cava de San Miguel, are some of the city's oldest *mesones*, or **taverns**. Have a drink in these in the early evening and you are likely to be serenaded by passing *tunas* – musicians and singers dressed in traditional costume of knickerbockers and waistcoats who wander around town playing and passing the hat. These men-only troupes are attached to various faculties of the university and are usually students earning a bit of extra cash to make ends meet.

Plaza de la Villa and around

West along C/Mayor, towards the Palacio Real, is **Plaza de la Villa**, an example of three centuries of Spanish architectural development. Its oldest surviving building is the eye-catching fifteenth-century **Torre de los Lujanes**, a fine Mudéjar (Moors working under Christian rule) tower, where Francis I of France is said to have been imprisoned in 1525 after his capture at the Battle of Pavia in Italy. Opposite is the former town hall, the **ayuntamiento (Casa de la Villa)**, begun in the seventeenth century, but remodelled in Baroque style. Finally, fronting the square is the **Casa de Cisneros**, which was built by a nephew of Cardinal Cisneros in the sixteenth-century Plateresque ("Silversmith") style.

A WALKING TOUR OF MADRID DE LOS AUSTRIAS

To get a feel for what the old city might have been like when it was first designated the Spanish capital in the sixteenth century take a stroll around the area known as **Madrid de los Austrias**.

Start off at **Pza. de la Villa**, probably the oldest square in the city and home to some of its most ancient buildings, including the fifteenth-century Torre de los Lujanes. Then take the narrow, elbow-shaped C/Codo out of the northeastern corner of the plaza, passing the Convento de los Carboneras where the nuns still sell traditional cakes and biscuits, continuing downhill to the tranquil backstreet C/San Justo. If you bear left past the splendid **Baroque Basílica de San Miguel** you will emerge on to bustling C/Segovia, one of the ancient entrances into the old city. From here wander down Cava Baja with its succession of traditional *tascas*, former coaching inns and stylish tapas bars. You will end up in **Pza. Humilladeros**, which buzzes with people sitting at the terrace bar in the middle of the square and is flanked by the graceful lines of the Iglesia de San Andrés and the mansion that is now home to the Museo de San Isidro. Walk past the splendid domed church and turn right into **Pza. de la Paja**, one of the old market squares that once littered the medieval city. Wealthy families would have lived in the mansions that line the square, each with a small garden similar to the peaceful Jardín de Anglona situated at the bottom of the plaza.

Take a right along C/Príncipe de Anglona and shady C/Nuncio to rejoin C/Segovia and bear left up **C/Cuchilleros**, named after the knife-makers who once plied their trade on the street. Here you will pass the renowned restaurant **Botín**, a *madrileño* institution that lays claim to be the oldest eating establishment in the world, followed by a string of cellar bars offering flamenco and traditional tapas. Don't miss the beautiful wrought-iron work of the **Mercado de San Miguel** before finishing up with a circuit of the arcaded splendour of the **Pza. Mayor**.

Basílica de San Miguel

C/San Justo 4 • July–Sept 14 Mon–Sat 10am–1.15pm & 6–9.15pm, Sun 9.45am–1.30pm & 6.30–9.15pm; Sept 15–June 30 Mon–Sat 9.45am–1.30pm & 5.30–9pm, Sun 9.45am–2.15pm & 6–9.15pm • Free • Ⓜ La Latina

Just around the corner from Pza. de la Villa is the flamboyant **Basílica de San Miguel**. Designed by Italian architects at the end of the seventeenth century, the Basílica is one of the few examples of a full-blown Baroque church in Madrid.

Ópera and the Palacio Real

Dominated by the imposing **Palacio Real** and the elegant Pza. de Oriente, **Ópera** is one of the most pleasant and relaxed *barrios* in the city. The area contains the lavishly decorated **Teatro Real**, the tranquil gardens of the **Campo del Moro** and the **city cathedral**, while the two unobtrusive monastery complexes of **La Encarnación** and **Las Descalzas Reales** conceal an astounding array of treasures.

San Ginés

C/Arenal 13 • Daily 8.45am–1pm & 6–9pm • Free • Ⓜ Sol/Ópera

Situated midway between Sol and Ópera along C/Arenal is the ancient church of **San Ginés**. Of Mozarabic origin (built by Christians under Moorish rule), it was completely reconstructed in the seventeenth century. There is an El Greco canvas of the moneychangers being chased from the temple on show in the **Capilla del Cristo** (on show Mon 12.30pm). Alongside, in somewhat uneasy juxtaposition, stands a cult temple of the twentieth century, the *Joy Madrid* nightclub, and, behind it, the **Chocolatería San Ginés**, a Madrid institution, which at one time catered for the early-rising worker but now churns out *chocolate con churros* for the late nightclub crowd (see box, p.116).

Descalzas Reales

Pza. de las Descalzas Reales 3 • Guided tours (some in English) Tues– Sat 10am–2pm & 4–6.30pm, Sun & some public hols 10am–3pm • €6, joint ticket with Convento de la Encarnación €8, valid for 48hrs, free for EU citizens on Wed & Thurs 4–6.30pm • Ⓦ patrimonionacional. es • Ⓜ Sol/Callao

A couple of blocks north of San Ginés is one of the hidden treasures of Madrid, the **Monasterio de las Descalzas Reales**. It was founded in 1557 by Juana de Austria, daughter of the Emperor Carlos V, sister of Felipe II, and, at the age of 19, already the widow of Prince Don Juan of Portugal. In her wake came a succession of titled ladies (*Descalzas Reales* means "Barefoot Royals"), who brought fame and, above all, fortune to the convent, which is unbelievably rich, though beautiful and tranquil, too. It is still in use, with shoeless nuns tending patches of vegetable garden.

Whistle-stop **guided tours** conduct visitors through the cloisters and up an incredibly elaborate stairway to a series of chambers packed with art and treasures of every kind. The **former dormitories** are perhaps the most outstanding feature, decorated with a series of Flemish tapestries based on designs by Rubens and a striking portrait of St Francis by Zurbarán. These were the sleeping quarters for all the nuns, including St Teresa of Ávila for a time, although the empress María of Germany preferred a little more privacy and endowed the convent with her own luxurious private chambers. The other highlight of the tour is the **Joyería** (Treasury), piled high with jewels and relics of uncertain provenance. The nuns kept no records of their gifts, so no one is quite sure what many of the things are – there is a bizarre cross-sectional model of Christ – nor which bones came from which saint. Whatever the case, it's an exceptional hoard.

Convento de la Encarnación

Pza. de la Encarnación • Guided tours (usually in Spanish only) Tues–Sat 10am–2pm & 4–6.30pm, Sun & some public hols 10am–3pm • €6, joint ticket with the Monasterio de las Descalzas €8, valid for 48hrs, free for EU citizens on Wed & Thurs 4–6.30pm; guided tours only • ⓦ patrimonionacional.es • ⓜ Ópera

Just to the north of Pza. de Oriente is the **Convento de la Encarnación**. This was founded a few years after Juana's convent, by Margarita, wife of Felipe III, though it was substantially rebuilt towards the end of the eighteenth century. It houses an extensive but somewhat disappointing collection of seventeenth-century Spanish art, and a wonderfully bizarre library-like reliquary, reputed to be one of the most important in the Catholic world. The most famous relic housed here is a small glass bulb said to contain the blood of the fourth-century doctor martyr, St Pantaleon, whose blood supposedly liquefies at midnight every July 26 (the eve of his feast day). The tour ends with a visit to the Baroque-style church, which features a beautifully frescoed ceiling.

Teatro Real

Pza. de Isabel II • General tours daily 10.30am–1pm; closed mid-July to mid-Sept; • €8 (under-26s €6, under-7s free); tickets on sale from the box office from 9.15am • Info and reservations ☎ 915 160 660, ⓦ teatro-real.com • ⓜ Ópera

West of Sol, C/Arenal leads to the **Teatro Real**, or **Ópera**, which gives this area its name. Built in the mid-nineteenth century, it almost sank a few decades later as a result of subsidence caused by underground canals and was forced to close in 1925; it finally reopened in 1997 after an epic ten-year refurbishment that ended up costing a mind-boggling €150 million. The interior is suitably lavish and merits a visit in its own right, and it makes a truly magnificent setting for opera, ballet and classical concerts (see p.119). You can take a general tour or a tour focusing on the artistic or technical elements of productions.

Plaza de Oriente

ⓜ Ópera

The opera house is separated from the Palacio Real by the **Plaza de Oriente**, one of the most graceful and agreeable open spaces in Madrid and used in the bad old days by Franco as the venue for his public addresses; small groups of neo-Fascists still gather here on the anniversary of his death on November 21. One of the square's main attractions – and the focus of its life – is the Parisian-style *Café de Oriente*, whose summer terraza is one of the stations of Madrid nightlife. The café (which is also a prestigious restaurant) looks as traditional as any in the city but was in fact opened in the 1980s by a priest, Padre Lezama, who ploughs his profits into various charitable schemes.

The café apart, the dominant features of Plaza de Oriente are **statues**: 44 of them, depicting Spanish kings and queens, which were originally designed to go on the palace facade but found to be too heavy (some say too ugly) for the roof to support. The **statue of Felipe IV** on horseback, in the centre of the square, clearly belongs on a different plane; it was based on designs by Velázquez, and Galileo is said to have helped with the calculations to make it balance.

Catedral Nuestra Señora de la Almudena

C/Bailén 8–10 • Daily: 9am–8.30pm (July & Aug 10am–9pm); not open for visits during Mass: Mon–Sat noon, 6pm & 7pm, Sun & hols 10.30am, noon, 1.30pm, 6 & 7pm (July & Aug daily noon & 8pm) • Free (€1 donation requested) • ☎ 915 422 400, ⓦ catedraldelaalmudena .es • **Museum** Mon–Sat 10am–2.30pm • €6, €4 for Madrid residents and students • **Crypt** daily 10am–8pm • ⓜ Ópera

Facing the Palacio Real to the south, across the shadeless Pza. de la Armería, is Madrid's cathedral, **Nuestra Señora de la Almudena**. Planned centuries ago, bombed out in the Civil War, worked upon at intervals since, and plagued by lack of funds, it was eventually opened for business in 1993 by Pope John Paul II. The building's bulky

Neoclassical facade was designed to match the Palacio Real opposite, while its cold neo-Gothic interior is largely uninspiring.

To one side of the main facade is a small **museum** containing some of the Catedral's treasures, though the main reason to visit is to gain access to the dome from where you can enjoy some fantastic views over the city and out towards the Sierra. The entrance to the **crypt**, with its forest of columns and dimly lit chapels, is to be found on C/Mayor.

The Moorish wall and Jardines de las Vistillas

C/Bailén crosses C/Segovia on a high **viaduct** (now lined with panes of reinforced glass to prevent once-common suicide attempts); this was constructed as a royal route from the palace to the church of San Francisco el Grande, avoiding the rabble and river that flowed below. Close by is a patch of **Moorish wall** (*muralla árabe*) from the medieval fortress here, which the original royal palace replaced. Across the aqueduct, the **Jardines de las Vistillas** ("Gardens of the Views") beckon, with their summer terrazas looking out across the river and towards the distant Sierra.

Palacio Real

C/Bailén • Daily: April–Sept 10am–8pm; Oct–March 10am–6pm; closed occasionally for state visits • €10; free for EU citizens Oct–March: Wed & Thurs 4–6pm, April–Sept: 6–8pm • ⓦ patrimonionacional.es • Ⓜ Ópera

The **Palacio Real**, or Royal Palace, scores high on statistics. It claims more rooms than any other European palace; a library with one of the biggest collections of books, manuscripts, maps and musical scores in the world; and an armoury with an unrivalled assortment of weapons dating back to the fifteenth century. If you're around on the first Wednesday of the month (except July–Sept) between noon and 2pm, look out for the **changing of the guard** outside the palace, a tradition that has recently been revived.

Guided tours in various languages are available (€7), but a more relaxing option is to hire an audio-guide (€4) and make your own way through the luxurious royal apartments, the Royal Armoury Museum and the Royal Pharmacy. This will give you more time to appreciate the extraordinary opulence: acres of Flemish and Spanish tapestries, endless Rococo decoration, bejewelled clocks, and pompous portraits of the monarchs.

The palace also houses an impressive exhibition space, the **Galería de Pinturas**, which displays work by Velázquez, Caravaggio and Goya, among others, and also hosts temporary **exhibitions**.

The palace

The Habsburgs' original palace burnt down on Christmas Day, 1734. Its replacement, the current building, was based on drawings made by Bernini for the Louvre. It was constructed in the mid-eighteenth century and was the principal royal residence from then until Alfonso XIII went into exile in 1931; both Joseph Bonaparte and the Duke of Wellington also lived here briefly. The present royal family inhabits a considerably more modest residence on the western outskirts of the city, using the Palacio Real on state occasions only.

The **Salón del Trono** (Throne Room) is the highlight for most visitors, containing the thrones installed for Juan Carlos and Sofía, the current monarchs, as well as the splendid ceiling by Tiepolo, a giant fresco representing the glory of Spain – an extraordinary achievement for an artist by then in his seventies. Look out, too, for the marvellous **Sala de Porcelana** (Porcelain Room) and the incredible oriental-style **Salón de Gasparini**.

The outbuildings and annexes

The palace outbuildings and annexes include the **Armería Real**, a huge room full of guns, swords and armour, with such curiosities as the suit of armour worn by Carlos

1

V in his equestrian portrait by Titian in the Prado. Especially fascinating are the complete sets of armour, with all the original spare parts and gadgets for making adjustments. There is also an eighteenth-century **Farmacia**, a curious mixture of alchemist's den and laboratory, whose walls are lined with jars labelled for various remedies. The **Biblioteca Real** (Royal Library) can now only be visited by prior arrangement for research purposes.

The gardens

Jardines de Sabatini April–Sept 9am–10pm; Oct–March 9am–9pm **Campo del Moro** April–Sept daily 10am–8pm; Oct–March daily 10am–6pm; occasionally closed for state visits

Immediately north of the palace are the **Jardines de Sabatini**, which provide a shady retreat and venue for summer concerts, while to the rear is the larger, and far more beautiful, **Campo del Moro** (access only from the far west side, off the Paseo de la Virgen del Puerto), a leafy English-style garden with shady paths, monumental fountains and a splendid view of the western facade of the palace.

South of Plaza Mayor

The areas south of Plaza Mayor have traditionally been tough, working-class districts, with tenement buildings thrown up to accommodate the expansion of the population in the eighteenth and nineteenth centuries. In many places, these old houses survive, huddled together in narrow streets, but the character of **La Latina** and **Lavapiés** has changed as their inhabitants, and the districts themselves, have become younger, more fashionable and more cosmopolitan. The streets of Cava Baja and Cava Alta in La Latina, for example, include some of the city's most popular bars and restaurants. These are attractive *barrios* to explore, particularly for bar-hopping or during the Sunday-morning flea market, **El Rastro** (see below), which takes place along and around the Ribera de Curtidores (Ⓜ La Latina/Tirso de Molina).

Around La Latina

La Latina is a short walk south from Pza. de la Villa and, if you're exploring Madrid de los Austrias, it's a natural continuation, as some of the squares, streets and churches here date back to the early Habsburg period. One of the most attractive pockets is around **Pza. de la Paja**, a delightful square behind the large church of **San Andrés**, and

---

EL RASTRO

Madrid's flea market, **El Rastro**, is as much a part of the city's weekend ritual as a Mass or a *paseo*. This gargantuan, thriving shambles of a street market sprawls south from Metro La Latina to the Ronda de Toledo, especially along Ribera de Curtidores. Through it, crowds flood between 10am and 3pm every Sunday – and increasingly on Fridays, Saturdays and public holidays, too. On offer is just about anything you might – or more likely might not – need, from secondhand clothes and military-surplus items to flamenco fans and antiques.

Some of the goods are so far gone that you can't imagine any of them ever selling. Others may be quite valuable, but on the whole it's the stuff of markets around the world you'll find here: pseudo-designer clothes, bags and T-shirts. Don't expect to find fabulous bargains, or the hidden Old Masters of popular myth: the serious antique trade has mostly moved off the streets and into the surrounding shops, while the real junk is now found only on the fringes. Nonetheless, the atmosphere of El Rastro is always enjoyable, and the bars around these streets are as good as any in the city. One warning: keep a close eye on your bags, pockets, cameras (best left at the hotel) and jewellery. The Rastro rings up a fair percentage of Madrid's tourist thefts.

once home to one of the city's medieval markets. In summer, there are a couple of terrazas here, tucked well away from the traffic.

Iglesia de San Andrés, Capilla del Obispo and Capilla de San Isidro

Pza. de San Andrés & Pza. de la Paja • **Iglesia de San Andrés** Mon–Thurs & Sat 9am–1pm & 6–8pm, Fri 6–8pm, Sun 10am–1pm • Free • **Capilla del Obispo** Tues 10am–12.30pm, Thurs 4–5.30pm; closed July & Aug • €2 • ☎ 915 592 874 (reservation only), ⓦ museocatedral .archimadrid.es/capilla-del-obispo • Ⓜ La Latina

The **Iglesia de San Andrés** and the **Capilla de San Isidro** can be reached from Pza. de San Andrés. Inside is a beautifully sculpted dome depicting angels laden with fruit and a red-marble backdrop fronted by black columns and sculptures of saints. The chapel of San Isidro was built in the mid-seventeenth century to hold the remains of Madrid's patron saint (since moved to the Iglesia de San Isidro). The adjoining Gothic **Capilla del Obispo** (entrance on Pza. de la Paja), with its impressive polychromed altarpiece and alabaster tombs, reopened in 2010 following a forty-year restoration saga.

Museo de San Isidro

Pza. San Andrés 2 • Aug: Tues–Sun 9.30am–8pm • Free • ☎ 913 667 415, ⓦ www.madrid.es/museosanisidro • Ⓜ La Latina

Alongside the church of San Andrés is one of the city's newer museums, the **Museo de San Isidro**, housed in a sixteenth-century mansion owned by the counts of Paredes and supposedly once the home of Madrid's patron saint. The city's **archeological collection**, which consists of relics from the earliest settlements along the River Manzanares and nearby Roman villas, is in the basement. The rest of the museum is given over to exhibits on the later history of the city and also **San Isidro** and his miraculous activities, including the well from which he is said to have rescued his own son.

San Francisco el Grande

Pza. de San Francisco 11 • Aug Tues–Sun 10.30am–12.30pm & 5–7pm; rest of year Tues–Fri 10.30am–12.30pm & 4–6pm, Sat 10.30am–1.30pm; €3 with guided tour • ☎ 913 653 800 • Ⓜ La Latina

A couple of minutes' walk southwest of the Museo de San Isidro down the hill is one of Madrid's grandest, richest and most elaborate churches, **San Francisco el Grande**. Built towards the end of the eighteenth century as part of Carlos III's renovations of the city, it has a dome even larger than that of St Paul's in London. The interior, which you can only visit with a guided tour, contains paintings by, among others, Goya and Zurbarán, and some magnificent frescoes by Bayeu.

Iglesia de San Isidro

C/Toledo 37 • Daily 7.30am–1pm & 6–9pm • Ⓜ La Latina

The vast **Iglesia de San Isidro** was originally the centre of the Jesuit Order in Spain. After Carlos III fell out with the Order in 1767, he redesigned the interior and dedicated it to the city's patron, whose remains are entombed within. The church acted as the city's cathedral prior to the completion of the Almudena by the Palacio Real, but relics and altarpiece aside, its chief attribute is its size.

Next door is the **Instituto Real**, a school that has been in existence considerably longer than the church and counts among its former pupils such literary notables as Calderón de la Barca, Lope de Vega, Quevedo and Pío Baroja.

Puerta de Toledo

Ⓜ Puerta de Toledo

If you proceed south to the end of Ribera de Curtidores, whose antique shops (some, these days, extremely upmarket) stay open all week, you'll see a large arch, the **Puerta de Toledo**, at one end of the Ronda de Toledo. The only surviving relation to the Puerta de Alcalá in the Pza. de la Independencia, this was built originally as a triumphal arch to honour the conquering Napoleon. After his defeat in the Peninsular Wars, it became

1

a symbol of the city's freedom. Just in front of the arch, the Mercado Puerta de Toledo, once the site of the city's fish market, is in the process of being turned into a teaching centre for one of the local universities.

Estadio Vicente Calderón

Paseo Virgen del Puerto 67 • ☎ 913 664 707 or ☎ 902 260 430, ⓦ clubatleticodemadrid.com • **Match tickets** From around €35 • ☎ 902 530 500 and via the website • **Club shop** Mon–Sat 10am–2.30pm & 3.30–8pm, match days 11am–kickoff • **Museum** Tues–Sun 11am–7pm • €10 with guided tour (noon, 1pm, 4.30pm & 5.30pm), children 4–12 €5 • ⓜ Pirámides

Alongside the newly regenerated River Manzanares is the **Estadio Vicente Calderón**, home to 2014 League champions Atlético Madrid, arch-rivals of the more glamorous Real (see p.95). The 54,000-capacity stadium houses a decent **club shop** and a **museum** detailing the history and achievements of the club, who are planning to move to an out-of-town site in the not too distant future.

Lavapiés

A good point at which to start exploring the multicultural *barrio* of **Lavapiés** is the Pza. Tirso de Molina (ⓜ Tirso de Molina). From here, you can follow C/Mesón de Paredes, stopping for a drink at one of the city's most traditional bars, the *Taberna Antonio Sánchez* at no. 13, past rows of wholesale clothes shops to **La Corrala**, on the corner of C/Sombrerete. This is one of many traditional *corrales* – tenement blocks – in the quarter, built with balconied apartments opening onto a central patio. Plays, especially farces and *zarzuelas* (a kind of operetta), used to be performed regularly in Spanish *corrales*, and the open space here usually hosts a few performances in the summer. It has been sympathetically renovated and declared a national monument.

From Metro Lavapiés, you can take C/**Argumosa** towards the Museo Reina Sofía. Don't miss out on the opportunity to sample some of the excellent local bars on this pleasant tree-lined street while you're here.

Cine Doré

C/Santa Isabel 3 • Closed Mon • Films €2.50 • ☎ 913 691 125 • ⓜ Antón Martín

To the north of the quarter is the **Cine Doré**, the oldest cinema in Madrid, dating from 1922, with a late modernist/Art Nouveau facade. It has been converted to house the Filmoteca Nacional, an art-film centre (see p.119) with bargain prices, and has a pleasant and inexpensive **café/restaurant** (5pm–12.45am).

East of Sol: Plaza de Santa Ana to Plaza de Cibeles

The **Plaza de Santa Ana/Huertas** area lies at the heart of a triangle, bordered to the east by the Paseo del Prado, to the north by C/Alcalá and along the south by C/Atocha, with the Puerta del Sol at the western tip. The city reached this district after expanding beyond the Palacio Real and the Pza. Mayor, so the buildings date predominantly from the nineteenth century. Many of them have literary associations: there are streets named after Cervantes and Lope de Vega (where one lived and the other died), and the *barrio* is host to the Atheneum club, Círculo de Bellas Artes (Fine Arts Institute), Teatro Español and the Congreso de los Diputados (parliament). Just to the north, there is also an important museum, the **Real Academia de Bellas Artes de San Fernando**.

For most visitors, though, the major attraction is that this district holds some of the best and most beautiful **bars** and **tascas** in the city. They are concentrated particularly around Plaza de Santa Ana and the streets that run into Huertas.

Plaza de Santa Ana and around

Ⓜ Sol/Sevilla

1

The bars around **Plaza de Santa Ana** really are sights in themselves. On the square itself, the dark wood-panelled *Cervecería Alemana* was a firm favourite of Hemingway's and has hardly changed since the turn of the twentieth century. Opposite, *La Suiza* café is a great place for a coffee and a cake while watching the world go by. Flanking one side of the plaza is the elegant facade of the emblematic *ME Madrid Reina Victoria* hotel, once a favourite of bullfighters and now the designer showpiece for the Sol-Meliá chain, while at the other end are the polished lines of the nineteenth-century Neoclassical pile, the Teatro Español.

Viva Madrid, on the northeast corner at C/Manuel Fernández y González 7, should be another port of call, if only to admire the fabulous tilework, original zinc bar and a ceiling supported by wooden caryatids. One block east from here is **C/Echegaray**, home to a string of great bars and restaurants, including the wonderfully dilapidated sherry bar, *La Venencia*, at no. 7.

Huertas

The area around pedestrianized **C/Huertas** itself is workaday enough – sleepy by day but buzzing by night – and, again, packed with bars. North of here, and parallel, are two streets named in honour of the greatest figures of Spain's seventeenth-century literary golden age, Cervantes and Lope de Vega. Bitter rivals in life, both are probably spinning in their graves now, since Cervantes is interred in the **Convento de las Trinitarias** on the street named after Lope de Vega, while the latter's house, the **Casa de Lope de Vega**, finds itself on C/Cervantes. Forensic scientists began a search for the precise location of Cervantes' body in the convent in 2014 using ground-penetrating radar.

Casa de Lope de Vega

C/Cervantes 11 • Tues–Sun 10am–3pm; closed mid-July to mid-Aug • Free • Guided tours: wait for a group to be formed; ring ☎ 914 299 216 to reserve a tour in English • Ⓜ Antón Martín

The charming little **Casa de Lope de Vega** provides a fascinating reconstruction of life in seventeenth-century Madrid; ring the bell and you will be taken on a tour of the Spanish Golden Age dramatist's former home, which includes a delightful little patio garden.

El Congreso

C/San Jerónimo s/n • Tours Sat every 30min, 10.30am–12.30pm; closed Aug; passport essential • Ⓦ congreso.es • Ⓜ Sevilla

El Congreso de Los Diputados is an unprepossessing nineteenth-century building where the Congress (the lower house) meets. Sessions can be visited by appointment only, though anyone can turn up for the tour on Saturday mornings. You're shown, among other things, the bullet holes left by Colonel Tejero and his Guardia Civil associates in the abortive coup attempt of 1981.

Círculo de Bellas Artes

C/Alcalá 42 • Exhibitions usually Tues–Sun 11am–2pm & 5–9pm • Ⓦ circulobellasartes.com • Ⓜ Sevilla

Cut across to C/Alcalá from Pza. de las Cortes and you'll emerge close to the **Círculo de Bellas Artes**, a strange-looking 1920s building crowned by a statue of Pallas Athene. This is Madrid's foremost centre, and includes a theatre, music hall, cinema, exhibition galleries and a very pleasant bar (daily 9am–1am; Fri & Sat til 3am) – all marble and leather decor, with a nude statue reclining in the middle of the floor. It attracts the capital's arts and media crowd but is not in the slightest exclusive, nor expensive, and there's an adjoining terraza and a great rooftop bar, too. The Círculo is theoretically a members-only club, but it issues €1 day-membership on the door, for which you get access to all areas.

1

Plaza de la Cibeles and Real Academia de Bellas Artes

Close to the Círculo and past an imposing array of grandiose buildings on C/Alcalá lies one of Spain's leading art galleries, the **Real Academia de Bellas Artes**, one for art buffs who have some appetite left after the Prado, Thyssen-Bornemisza and Reina Sofía. Half a kilometre to the east is **Plaza de la Cibeles**. Awash in a sea of traffic in the centre of the square are a **fountain** and statue of the goddess Cibeles, which survived the bombardments of the Civil War by being swaddled from helmet to hoof in sandbags. It was designed, as were the two other fountains gushing magnificently along the Paseo del Prado, by Ventura Rodríguez. The fountain is the scene of celebrations for victorious Real Madrid fans (Atlético supporters bathe in the fountain of Neptune just down the road).

Palacio de Cibeles and Casa de América

Casa de América Tours Sat & Sun 11am, noon & 1pm (open more often in Aug, but check the website for details) • ⓦ casamerica.es /visitas • Ⓜ Banco de España

The monumental wedding-cake building on the eastern side of Plaza de Cibeles was until quite recently Madrid's main post office. Constructed from 1904 to 1917, **Palacio de Cibeles** is vastly more imposing than the parliament and runs the Palacio Real pretty close. The city council took a shine to it and it now provides a home for the burgeoning **municipal offices**. It is also home to a smart new exhibition space **CentroCentro** (Tues–Sun 10am–8pm), with a viewing gallery (Tues–Sun 10.30am–1.30pm & 4–7pm; €2, under-12s €0.50), a café (daily 10am–midnight), expensive restaurant and an overpriced terrace bar (daily 10am–2am). Adjacent, a palatial eighteenth-century mansion built by the Marqués de Linares is now home to the **Casa de América**, a cultural organization promoting Latin American art and hosting temporary exhibitions.

Real Academia de Bellas Artes de San Fernando

C/Alcalá 13 • Tues–Sun 10am–3pm • €6, free Wed • ☎ 915 240 864 ⓦ realacademiabellasartessanfernando.com • Ⓜ Sevilla

The **Real Academia** has traditionally been viewed as one of the most important art galleries in Spain. Admittedly, you have to plough through a fair number of dull academic canvases, but there are some hidden gems. These include a group of small panels by **Goya**, in particular *The Burial of the Sardine* and two revealing self-portraits, and a curious *Family of El Greco*, which may be by the great man or his son. Two other rooms are devoted to foreign artists, in particular Rubens. Upstairs, there is a series of sketches by Picasso, and a brutally graphic set of sculptures depicting the *Massacre of the Innocents* by José Ginés. It is also home to the national chalcography (copper or brass engraving) collection (Mon–Thurs 8.30am–5pm; Fri 9am–3pm, July & Sept Mon–Fri 9am–3pm; closed Aug), which includes a number of Goya etchings used for his *Capricho* series on show at the Prado.

The Paseo del Arte

Madrid's three world-class art museums, the Prado, Thyssen-Bornemisza and Reina Sofía, are all along or close to the Paseo del Prado within a kilometre of each other in what is commonly known as the **Paseo del Arte**. The most famous of the three galleries is the **Prado**, which houses an unequalled display of Spanish art, an outstanding Flemish collection and an impressive assemblage of Italian work. The **Thyssen-Bornemisza** provides an unprecedented excursion through Western art from the fourteenth to the late twentieth centuries. The final member of the trio, the **Reina Sofía**, is home to the Spanish collection of contemporary art, including the Miró and Picasso legacies and the jewel in the crown – *Guernica*.

PASEO DEL ARTE COMBINED ENTRY TICKET

If you plan to visit all three art museums on the Paseo del Prado during your stay, it's worth buying the under-advertised **Paseo del Arte ticket** (€25.60), which is valid for a year and allows one visit to each museum at a substantial saving, although it does not include the temporary exhibitions. It's available at any of the three museums and will save you just under €7 on full-price tickets.

Museo del Prado

C/Ruiz de Alarcón 23 • Mon–Sat 10am–8pm, Sun 10am–7pm; Jan 6, Dec 24 & Dec 31 10am–2pm; closed Jan 1, May 1 & Dec 25 • €14, free for under-18s, students under 25 and disabled people; free Mon–Sat 6–8pm, Sun & hols 5–7pm; combined admission with Paseo del Arte ticket (see box above) • ☎ 902 107 077, ⓦ museodelprado.es • Ⓜ Banco de España/Atocha

The **Museo del Prado** is Madrid's premier attraction – well over two million visitors enter its doors each year – and one of the oldest and greatest collections of art in the world. Built as a natural science museum in 1775, the Prado opened to the public in 1819, and houses the finest works collected by Spanish royalty – for the most part, avid, discerning and wealthy buyers – as well as Spanish paintings gathered from other sources over the past two centuries. Finding enough space for displaying the works has always been a problem, but after fourteen years of arguments, delays and controversy, the €152 million Rafael Moneo-designed **extension**, which includes a stylish glass-fronted building incorporating the eighteenth-century cloisters of the San Jerónimo church, was finally opened in 2007. The new wing houses the restaurant and café areas, an expanded shop, an auditorium, temporary exhibition spaces, restoration and conservation workshops and a new sculpture gallery.

The museum's highlights are its early Flemish collection – including almost all of **Bosch**'s best work – and, of course, its incomparable display of Spanish art, in particular that of **Velázquez** (including *Las Meninas*), **Goya** (including the *Majas* and the *Black Paintings*) and **El Greco**. There's also a huge section of Italian painters (**Titian**, notably) collected by Carlos V and Felipe II, both great patrons of the Renaissance, and an excellent collection of seventeenth-century Flemish and Dutch pictures gathered by Felipe IV, including **Rubens**' *Three Graces*. The museum has also hosted an increasing number of critically acclaimed temporary displays in recent years. Even in a full day you couldn't hope to do justice to everything here, and it's perhaps best to make a couple of more focused visits.

INFORMATION AND TOURS   MUSEO DEL PRADO

Tickets are purchased at the Puerta de Goya opposite the *Hotel Ritz* on C/Felipe IV, and the **entrances** are round the back at the Puerta de los Jerónimos, which leads into the new extension, or at the side at the Puerta de Goya Alta. If you want to avoid the lengthy queues for tickets, a better option is to buy them in advance via the museum website (ⓦ museodelprado.es). The Puerta de Murillo entrance, opposite the botanical gardens, is now for school and university groups only.

Tours What follows is, by necessity, only a brief guide to the museum contents. If you want more background on the key paintings pick up an audio-guide (€3.50) or the extensive guide (€19.50) in the bookshop. There are also some useful colour booklets (€1) on Velázquez, Goya, El Greco, Titian and Bosch available at the information desk and in their respective galleries. A lunchtime or early evening visit is often a good plan if you want to avoid the worst of the crowds and tour groups.

Exploring the museum

To follow the **route** proposed by the museum, bear right after the Puerta de los Jerónimos entrance and head into the central hallway – the Sala de las Musas. From here you are guided through the early Flemish, Italian and Spanish collections on the ground floor before being directed upstairs. A tour of the sixteenth- and seventeenth-century Italian and French collections in the northern wing gives way to the Flemish and Dutch galleries on the second floor where work from Rubens and Rembrandt is to the fore. Back on the first floor, visitors are ushered through the Spanish Golden Age

1

collections with their heavyweight contributions from El Greco, Velázquez and Murillo before enjoying the delights of Goya which stretch up to the second floor once again. From there you return to the ground floor for Goya's *Black Paintings* before concluding the visit with a tour of the grandiose historical epics that make up the remainder of the nineteenth-century Spanish collection.

Spanish painting
The Prado's collections of Spanish painting begin on the ground floor (rooms 12–18) with the striking cycles of twelfth-century **Romanesque frescoes** reconstructed from a pair of churches from the Mozarabic (Muslim rule) era in Soria and Segovia. **Early panel paintings** – exclusively religious fourteenth- and fifteenth-century works – include a huge *retablo* (altarpiece) by Nicolás Francés; the anonymous *Virgin of the Catholic Monarchs*; Bermejo's *Santo Domingo de Silos*; and Pedro Berruguete's *Auto-da-Fé*.

The Golden Age: Velázquez and El Greco
Upstairs, the collections from Spain's Golden Age – the late sixteenth and seventeenth centuries under Habsburg rule – are prefigured by a fabulous array of paintings by **El Greco** (1540–1614), the Cretan-born artist who worked in Toledo from the 1570s. You really need to have taken in the works in Toledo to appreciate fully his extraordinary genius, but the portraits and religious works here (rooms 38–40), ranging from the Italianate *Trinity* to the visionary late *Adoration of the Shepherds*, are a good introduction.

PRADO HIGHLIGHTS

The Prado is much too big for a single visit to do the collection justice; however, if you are pressed for time here is a list of some of the **works you should not miss**.

The Garden of Earthly Delights by Bosch. A surrealistic masterpiece years ahead of its time.

The Triumph of Death by Pieter Brueghel. A disturbing and macabre depiction of hell by the Flemish master.

The Annunciation by Fra Angelico. A ground-breaking early Renaissance work.

Self-portrait by Dürer. Insightful self-portrait by the German genius.

The Descent from the Cross by Van der Weyden. An emotive and colourful depiction of the Deposition.

The Romanesque frescoes. Stunning frescoes from the Romanesque churches in Segovia and Soria.

David and Goliath by Caravaggio. The Italian's theatrical use of chiaroscuro at its best.

The Adoration of the Shepherds by El Greco. One of a series of revolutionary Mannerist works by the Greek-born painter.

Las Meninas by Velázquez. One of the most technically adroit and fascinating paintings in Western art.

Artemisa by Rembrandt. The Dutchman used his wife Saskia as a model for this portrayal of the heroic queen.

Sir Endymion Porter by Van Dyck. A superlative work by the Dutch court painter famous for his portraits of Charles I.

The Three Graces by Rubens. One of the great classically inspired works by the Flemish genius.

Charles V at Múhlberg by Titian. A magnificent equestrian portrait of the Holy Roman Emperor.

The Lavatorio by Tintoretto. Epic masterpiece depicting Christ washing the feet of the disciples, that once belonged to Charles I.

La Maja Desnuda and **La Maja Vestida** by Goya. A pair of supremely seductive portraits of a woman reclining on a bed of pillows, one clothed, one naked.

Dos and **Tres de Mayo** by Goya. Timeless and iconic images on the horror of war.

Goya's Black Paintings. A series of penetrating and haunting images from the latter part of Goya's career.

In rooms 41 and 49–52, you confront the greatest painter of Habsburg Spain, **Diego Velázquez** (1599–1660). Born in Portugal, Velázquez became court painter to Felipe IV, whose family is represented in many of the works: "I have found my Titian," Felipe is said to have remarked on his appointment. Velázquez's masterpiece, *Las Meninas*, is displayed in the octagonal central gallery (room 50) alongside studies for the painting. Manet remarked of it, "After this, I don't know why the rest of us paint," and the French poet Théophile Gautier asked "But where is the picture?" when he saw it, because it seemed to him a continuation of the room. *Las Hilanderas* and *Vulcan's Forge* showing the royal tapestry factory at work, *Christ Crucified* and *Los Borrachos* (*The Drunkards*) are further magnificent paintings. In fact, almost all of the fifty or so works on display (around half of the artist's surviving output) warrant close attention. Don't overlook the two small panels of the *Villa Medici*, painted in Rome in 1650, in virtually Impressionist style. There are several Velázquez canvases, including *The Surrender at Breda*, in the stunning collection of royal portraits and works depicting Spanish military victories.

In the adjacent rooms are examples of just about every significant Spanish painter of the seventeenth century, including many of the best works of **Francisco Zurbarán** (1598–1664), **Bartolomé Esteban Murillo** (1618–82), **Alonso Cano** (1601–67), **Juan de Valdés Leal** (1622–60) and **Juan Carreño** (1614–85). Note, in particular, Carreño's portrait of the last Habsburg monarch, the drastically inbred and mentally retarded Carlos II, rendered with terrible realism. There's also a fine selection of paintings by **José Ribera** (1591–1625), who worked mainly in Naples, and was influenced there by Caravaggio. His masterpieces are considered to be *The Martyrdom of St Philip* and the dark, realist portrait of *St Andrew*; look out, too, for the bizarre *Bearded Lady*.

Goya

The final suite of Spanish rooms (69–73), which continue up on to the second floor (74–79) and down on to the ground floor (87–89), provides an awesome and fabulously complete overview of the output of **Francisco de Goya** (1746–1828), the largest and most valuable collection of his works in the world, with some 140 paintings and 500 drawings and engravings. Goya was the greatest painter of Bourbon Spain, a chronicler of Spain in his time and an artist whom many see as the inspiration and forerunner of Impressionism and modern art. He was an enormously versatile artist: contrast the voluptuous *Maja Vestida* and *Maja Desnuda* (*The Clothed Belle* and *The Naked Belle*) with the horrors depicted in the *Dos de Mayo* and *Tres de Mayo* (moving, on-the-spot portrayals of the rebellion against Napoleon in the streets of Madrid and the subsequent reprisals). Then there is the series of pastoral cartoons – designs for tapestries – and the extraordinary *Black Paintings* (rooms 87 & 88), a series of disconcerting murals painted on the walls of his home by the deaf and embittered painter in his old age. The many portraits of his patron, Carlos IV, are remarkable for their lack of any attempt at flattery, while those of Queen María Luisa, whom he despised, are downright ugly.

The nineteenth century

The Prado's collection of melodramatic nineteenth-century Spanish art was originally housed in the nearby Casón del Buen Retiro (now the museum's centre for investigation), but has been relocated to magnificent effect on the ground floor in rooms 90–100. Dramatic works by Eduardo Rosales and Antonio Gisbert are combined with some fine luminous canvases by Spanish Impressionist Joaquin Sorolla.

Italian painting

The Prado's early Italian galleries on the ground floor are distinguished principally by **Fra Angelico**'s *Annunciation* (c.1445) and by a trio of panels by **Botticelli** (1445–1510). The latter illustrate a deeply unpleasant story from the *Decameron* about a woman hunted by hounds; the fourth panel (in a private collection in the US) gives a happier conclusion.

With the sixteenth-century Renaissance, and especially its Venetian exponents on the first floor, the collection really comes into its own. The Prado is said to have the most complete collection of Titians and painters from the Venetian School of any single museum. There are major works by **Raphael** (1483–1520), including a fabulous *Portrait of a Cardinal*, and epic masterpieces from the Venetians **Tintoretto** (1518–94), such as the beautifully composed *Lavatorio*, bought by Felipe IV when Charles I of England was beheaded and his art collection was auctioned off, and **Veronese** (1528–88), as well as **Caravaggio** (1573–1610), with his brutal *David with the Head of Goliath* another highlight. The most important works, however, are by **Titian** (1487–1576) in rooms 19–24. These include portraits of the Spanish emperors *Carlos V* and *Felipe II* (Carlos' suit of armour is preserved in the Palacio Real), and a famous, much-reproduced piece of erotica, *Venus, Cupid and the Organist* (two versions are displayed here), a painting originally owned by a bishop.

Flemish, Dutch and German painting

The biggest name in the **early Flemish collection** (room 3) is **Hieronymus Bosch** (1450–1516), known in Spain as "El Bosco". The Prado has several of his greatest triptychs: the early-period *Hay Wain*, the middle-period *Garden of Earthly Delights*, and the late *Adoration of the Magi* – all familiar from countless reproductions but infinitely more chilling in the original. Bosch's hallucinatory genius for the macabre is at its most extreme in these triptychs, but is reflected here in many more of his works, including three versions of *The Temptations of St Anthony* (though only the smallest of these is definitely an original). Don't miss, either, the amazing table-top of *The Seven Deadly Sins*.

Bosch's visions find an echo in the works of **Pieter Brueghel the Elder** (1525–69), whose *Triumph of Death* must be one of the most frightening canvases ever painted. Another elusive painter, **Joachim Patinir**, is represented by four of his finest works. From an earlier generation, **Rogier van der Weyden**'s *Descent from the Cross* is outstanding; its monumental forms make a fascinating contrast with his miniature-like *Pietà*. There are also important works by Memling, Bouts, Gerard David and Massys.

The collection of **later Flemish and Dutch art** is on the second floor (rooms 30–34), with enough works here to make an excellent comparison between the flamboyant Counter-Reformation propaganda of Flanders and the more austere bourgeois tastes of Holland. **Rubens** (1577–1640) is extensively represented, with the beautifully restored *Three Graces, The Judgement of Paris* and a series of eighteen mythological subjects designed for Felipe IV's hunting lodge in El Pardo (though Rubens supervised rather than executed these). There is, too, a fine collection of canvases by his contemporaries, including **Van Dyck**'s dramatic and deeply moving *Piedad*, and his magnificent portrait of himself and Sir Endymion Porter. **Jan Brueghel**'s representations of the five senses and **David Teniers**' scenes of peasant lowlife also merit a closer look. For political reasons, Spanish monarchs collected few works painted from seventeenth-century Protestant Holland; an early **Rembrandt**, *Artemisa*, in which the artist's pregnant wife served as the model, is, however, an important exception (room 34).

The **German room** (9) on the ground floor is dominated by **Dürer** (1471–1528) and **Lucas Cranach the Elder** (1472–1553). Dürer's magnificent *Adam and Eve* was saved from destruction at the hands of the prudish Carlos III only by the intervention of his court painter, Mengs, whose own paintings are on the first floor in room 64. The most interesting of Cranach's works is a pair of paintings depicting Carlos V hunting with Ferdinand I of Austria.

French and British painting

Most of the **French** work held by the Prado is from the seventeenth and eighteenth centuries (rooms 25, 26 and 63 on the first floor). Among the outstanding painters represented is **Nicolas Poussin** (1594–1665), with his Baroque work shown to best effect in *Triumph of David*, *Landscape with St Jerome* and *Mount Parnassus*. The romantic landscapes and sunsets of **Claude Lorraine** (1600–82) are well represented, and look out for **Hyacinthe Rigaud**'s (1659–1743) portrayal of the imperious *Louis XIV*.

British painting is thin on the ground – a product of the hostile relations between the Spanish and English from the sixteenth to nineteenth centuries. There is, however, a small sample of eighteenth-century portraiture from **Joshua Reynolds** (1723–92) and **Thomas Gainsborough** (1727–88) in room 65 on the first floor.

The Tesoro del Dauphin

The museum's basement houses the **Tesoro del Dauphin** (Treasure of the Dauphin), a display of part of the collection of jewels that belonged to the Grand Dauphin Louis, son of Louis XIV and father of Felipe V, Spain's first Bourbon king. The collection includes goblets, cups, trays, glasses and other pieces richly decorated with rubies, emeralds, diamonds, lapis lazuli and other precious stones.

Museo Thyssen-Bornemisza

Paseo del Prado 8 · Mon noon–4pm; Tues–Sun 10am–7pm (extended opening in summer months, check website for details); closed Jan 1, May 1 & Dec 25 · €10 for permanent collection, €9–11 for temporary exhibitions, combined ticket €13.50–17 or Paseo del Arte ticket (see box, p.77); free for under-12s and on Mon for all · ☎ 902 760 511, ⓦ museothyssen.org · Ⓜ Banco de España

The **Museo Thyssen-Bornemisza** occupies the old Palacio de Villahermosa, diagonally opposite the Prado, at the end of Pza. de las Cortes. This prestigious site played a large part in Spain's acquisition – for a knock-down $350 million in June 1993 – of what many argue was the world's greatest private art trove after that of the British royals: some seven hundred paintings accumulated by father-and-son German–Hungarian industrial magnates. The son, Baron Hans Heinrich Thyssen, died in April 2002 aged 81. Another trump card was the late baron's fifth wife, Carmen Cervera (aka "Tita" Cervera), a former Miss Spain, who steered the works to Spain against the efforts of Britain's Prince Charles, the Swiss and German governments, the Getty foundation and other suitors.

The museum had no expense spared on its design – again in the hands of the ubiquitous Rafael Moneo, responsible for the remodelling of Estación de Atocha and the extension at the Prado – with stucco walls (Carmen insisted on salmon pink) and marble floors. A terribly kitsch portrait of Carmen with a lapdog hangs in the great hall of the museum, alongside those of her husband and King Juan Carlos and Queen Sofía. Pass beyond, however, and you are into seriously premier-league art: **medieval to eighteenth-century** on the second floor, **seventeenth-century Dutch** and **Rococo and Neoclassicism to Fauves and Expressionists** on the first floor, and **Surrealists**, **Pop Art** and the **avant-garde** on ground level. Highlights are legion in a collection that displays an almost stamp-collecting mentality in its examples of nearly every major artist and movement: how the Thyssens got hold of classic works by everyone from Duccio and Holbein, through El Greco and Caravaggio, to Schiele and Rothko, takes your breath away.

Carmen has a substantial collection of her own (over 600 works), which has been housed in the **extension**, built on the site of an adjoining mansion and cleverly integrated into the original format of the museum. It is particularly strong on nineteenth-century landscape, North American, Impressionist and Post-Impressionist work. The ground floor is home to a large temporary exhibition space, which has staged a number of interesting and highly successful shows.

There's a handy cafeteria and restaurant in the new extension; there's also a shop, where you can buy a wide variety of art books, guides to the museum, postcards and other souvenirs. In July and August the museum opens a restaurant on the top-floor terrace: *El Mirador*. Advance tickets for the museum, a good idea in high season, are available via the website.

1

The second floor: European old masters and Carmen's collection

Take a lift to the second floor and you will find yourself at the chronological start of the museum's collections: European painting (and some sculpture) from the fourteenth to the eighteenth century. The core of these collections was accumulated in the 1920s and 30s by the late baron's father, Heinrich, who was a friend of the art critics Bernard Berenson and Max Friedländer. He was clearly well advised. The early paintings include incredibly good (and rare) devotional panels by the Sienese painter **Duccio di Buoninsegna**, and the Flemish artists **Jan van Eyck** and **Rogier van der Weyden**. You then move into a fabulous array of Renaissance portraits (room 5), which include three of the very greatest of the period: **Ghirlandaio**'s *Portrait of Giovanna Tornabuoni*, **Hans Holbein**'s *Portrait of Henry VIII* (the only one of many variants in existence that is definitely genuine) and **Raphael**'s *Portrait of a Young Man*. *A Spanish Infanta* by **Juan de Flandes** may represent the first of Henry VIII's wives, Catherine of Aragón, while the *Young Knight* by **Carpaccio** is one of the earliest-known full-length portraits of the king. Beyond these is a collection of **Dürer**s and **Cranach**s to rival that in the Prado, and as you progress through this extraordinary panoply, display cases along the corridor contain scarcely less spectacular works of sculpture, ceramics and gold- and silverwork.

Next in line, in room 11, are **Titian** and **Tintoretto**, and three paintings by **El Greco**, one early, two late, which make an interesting comparison with each other and with those in the Prado. **Caravaggio**'s monumental *St Catherine of Alexandria* (room 12) is the centrepiece of an important display of works by followers of this innovator of chiaroscuro. As you reach the eighteenth century, there is a room containing three flawless **Canaletto** views of Venice (room 17). Tagged onto this floor are the first galleries (lettered A–H) that make up the initial section of Carmen's collection. **Luca Giordano**'s monumental *Judgement of Solomon* and a **Van Dyck** *Crucifixion* (room A) are two of the early highlights. Gallery C traces the development of landscapes from early Flemish works through to the nineteenth century. Beyond are some interesting works by North American and European artists that complement the baron's collection and some soothing Impressionist offerings by **Degas**, **Renoir**, **Pissarro**, **Monet** and **Sisley**. Constable's *Lock*, however, is no longer in the collection, Carmen having controversially sold it for £22.4 million in 2012 because she had "no liquidity", a decision that prompted the resignation of museum trustee Sir Norman Rosenthal.

The first floor: Americans, Impressionists and Expressionists

The route now takes you downstairs through the remainder of Carmen's collection (rooms I–P), beginning with further Impressionist work, taking in some delightful canvases by **Gauguin** and the Post-Impressionists and ending with some striking Expressionist pieces by **Kandinsky** and **Robert Delaunay**.

From room P, walk along the corridor to rejoin the baron's collection. After a comprehensive round of seventeenth-century Dutch painting of various genres, Rococo and Neoclassicism, you reach some **English portraiture** by Gainsborough, Reynolds and Zoffany (room 28) and **American painting** in rooms 29 and 30. The collection, one of the best outside the US, concentrates on landscapes and includes James Goodwyn Clonney's wonderful *Fishing Party on Long Island Sound*, and works by James Whistler, Winslow Homer and John Singer Sargent.

As with Carmen's collection, **Impressionism** and **Post-Impressionism** are another strong point, with a choice selection of paintings by Vincent van Gogh, including one of his last and most gorgeous works, *Les Vessenots* (room 32). **Expressionism**, meanwhile, is represented by some stunning works by Ernst Ludwig Kirchner, Franz Marc, Wassily Kandinsky and Max Beckmann.

The ground floor: avant-garde

Works on the ground floor run from the beginning of the twentieth century through to around 1970. The good baron didn't, apparently, like contemporary art:

"If they can throw colours, I can be free to duck," he explained, following the gallery's opening.

The most interesting work in his "experimental avant-garde" sections is from the **Cubists**. There is an inspired, side-by-side hanging of parallel studies by Picasso (*Man with a Clarinet*) and Braque (*Woman with a Mandolin*). Later choices include a scattering of Joan Miró, Jackson Pollock, Dalí, Rauschenberg and Lichtenstein. In the **Synthesis of Modernity** section, there are some superbly vivid canvases by Max Ernst and Marc Chagall, a brilliant portrait of George Dyer by Francis Bacon, and a fascinating **Lucian Freud**, *Portrait of Baron Thyssen*, posed in front of the Watteau *Pierrot* hanging upstairs.

Museo Reina Sofía

C/Santa Isabel 52 • Mon & Wed–Sat 10am–9pm, Sun 10am–2.30pm; closed Jan 1 & 6, May 1 & 15, Sept 9, Nov 10, Dec 24, 25 & 31 • €8, free Mon–Sat 7–9pm, Sun 3–7pm; free for under-18s and over–65s; or Paseo del Arte ticket *(see box, p.77)* • ☎ 917 741 000, Ⓦ museoreinasofia.es • Ⓜ Atocha

It is fortunate that the **Museo Reina Sofía**, facing Estación de Atocha at the end of Paseo del Prado, keeps slightly different opening hours and days to its neighbours. For this leading exhibition space and permanent gallery of modern Spanish art – its centrepiece is Picasso's greatest picture, *Guernica* – is another essential stop on the Madrid art circuit, and one that really shouldn't be seen after a Prado–Thyssen overdose.

The museum, a vast former hospital, is a kind of Madrid response to the Pompidou Centre in Paris, with transparent lifts shuttling visitors up the outside of the Sabatini building to the permanent collection. Like the other two great art museums, it has also undergone a major **extension** programme – the French architect Jean Nouvel added a massive state-of-the-art metal-and-glass wing behind the main block in 2005. If the queues at the main entrance are too long, try the alternative one in the new extension on the Ronda de Atocha. You can also buy tickets in advance via the website.

The Santini building

It is for **Picasso's Guernica** that most visitors come to the Reina Sofía, and rightly so. Superbly displayed, this icon of twentieth-century Spanish art and politics carries a shock that defies all familiarity. Picasso painted it in response to the bombing of the Basque town of Gernika by the German Luftwaffe, acting in concert with Franco, in the Spanish Civil War. In the fascinating preliminary studies, displayed around the room, you can see how he developed its symbols – the dying horse, the woman mourning her dead, the bull, the sun, the flower, the light bulb – and then return to the painting to marvel at how he made it all work.

The painting was first exhibited in Paris in 1937, as part of a Spanish Republican Pavilion in the Expo there, and was then loaned to the Museum of Modern Art in New York, until, as Picasso put it, Spain had rid itself of Fascist rule. The artist never lived to see that time, but in 1981, following the restoration of democracy, the painting was, amid much controversy, moved to Madrid to hang (as Picasso had stipulated) in the Prado. Its transfer to the Reina Sofía in 1992 again prompted much soul-searching and protest, though for anyone who saw it in the old Prado annexe, it looks truly liberated in its present setting. Many Basques believe the painting's rightful home is with them, but studies have revealed cracks and fissures that make the painting too fragile to move once again.

Guernica hangs midway around Collection 1 on the second floor. It is displayed adjacent to rooms dedicated to the Spanish Pavilion in the 1937 Expo. There are strong sections on **Cubism** and the **Paris School**, in the first of which Picasso is again well represented, alongside work by French artist Georges Braque and Spaniard Juan Gris.

Dalí and **Miró** make heavyweight contributions to the nearby halls. Miró, who once claimed that he wanted "to assassinate painting", is represented with a series of

1

characteristically striking but impenetrable canvases. The development of Dalí's work and his variety of techniques are clearly displayed here, with works ranging from the classic *Muchacha en la Ventana* to famous surrealist works such as *El Gran Masturbador* and *El Enigma de Hitler*. There is an impressive collection of Spanish sculpture to be found in the final rooms.

The fourth floor, which houses Collection 2, covers themes from the postwar years up to the late 1960s and includes Spanish and international examples of **abstract** and **avant-garde** movements. Outstanding pieces from **Francis Bacon** (*Reclining Figure*), **Henry Moore** and **Graham Sutherland** give a British context, while challenging work from **Antoni Tapiès**, **Antonio Saura** and **Eduardo Chillida** provide the Spanish perspective. If the avant-garde work all gets too much, there are also some more accessible offerings from the Spanish realists.

The Area Nouvel

The extension, or the **Nouvel wing** as it is now known, consists of three brand-new buildings built around an open courtyard topped by a striking delta-shaped, metallic, crimson-coloured roof. It is home to Collection 3 which deals with themes from the final years of the Francoist dictatorship through to the present day. The new wing also houses an auditorium, a library, a café-restaurant and a bookshop (Mon & Wed–Sat 10am–7pm, Sun 10am–2.15pm) that sells a wide range of glossy coffee-table volumes, as well as more academic tomes and the informative museum guidebook (€22), which examines eighty key works in detail.

Parque del Retiro and around

When you get tired of sightseeing, Madrid's many parks are great places to escape for a few hours. The most central and most popular of them is **El Retiro**, a delightful mix of formal gardens and wider open spaces. Nearby, in addition to the Prado, Thyssen-Bornemisza and Reina Sofía galleries, are a number of the city's **smaller museums**, plus the startlingly peaceful **Jardines Botánicos**.

Parque del Retiro

Winter daily 6am–10pm; summer 6am–midnight • ⓜ Retiro

Originally the grounds of a royal retreat (*retiro*) and designed in the French style, the **Parque del Retiro** has been public property for more than a hundred years. In its 330 acres you can jog, row in the lake (you can rent boats by the Monumento a Alfonso XII), picnic (though officially not on the grass), have your fortune told and – above all – promenade. The busiest day is Sunday, when half of Madrid, replete with spouses, in-laws and kids, turns out for the *paseo*. Dressed for show, the families stroll around, nodding at neighbours and building up an appetite for a long Sunday lunch.

Strolling aside, there's almost always something going on in the park, including a good programme of **concerts** and **fairs** organized by the city council. Concerts tend to be held in the Quiosco de Música in the north of the park. The most popular of the fairs is the Feria del Libro (Book Fair), held in early June, when every publisher and half the country's bookshops set up stalls and offer a 25 percent discount on their wares. At weekends, there are **puppet shows** by the Puerta de Alcalá entrance, and on Sundays you can often watch groups of South American musicians performing by the lake.

A number of **stalls and cafés** along the Paseo Salón del Estanque sell drinks, *bocadillos* and *pipas* (sunflower seeds), and there are terrazas, too, for *horchata* and *granizados*. The park has a safe reputation, at least by day; in the late evening, it's best not to wander alone.

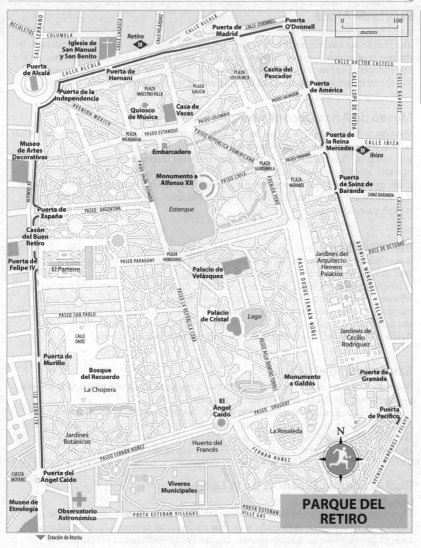

Palacio de Velázquez, Palacio de Cristal, Casa de Vacas and the Bosque del Recuerdo

Palacio de Velázquez & Palacio de Cristal April–Sept daily 10am–10pm; Oct–March 10am–6pm • Free • ☎ 915 746 614 for information • **Casa de Vacas** • Opening hours vary depending on exhibitions but usually daily 10am–9pm; closed Aug • Free

Temporary art exhibitions are frequently housed in the beautifully tiled **Palacio de Velázquez**, the splendid glass and wrought-iron **Palacio de Cristal** and the more modest **Casa de Vacas**, all of which are inside the park. Look out, too, for **El Ángel Caído** (Fallen Angel), the world's only public statue to Lucifer, in the south of the park. There is also the **Bosque del Recuerdo**, 192 olive trees and cypresses planted in the Paseo de la Chopera in memory of those who died in the train bombings at the nearby Atocha station on March 11, 2004.

1

Puerta de Alcalá

Ⓜ Retiro/Banco de España

The Parque del Retiro's northwest corner gives access to the Pza. de la Independencia, in the centre of which is one of the two remaining gates from the old city walls. Built in the late eighteenth century, the **Puerta de Alcalá** was the biggest in Europe at that time and, like the bear and *madroño* tree, has become one of the city's monumental emblems.

Museo de Artes Decorativas

C/Montalbán 12 • Tues–Sat 9.30am–3pm, also open Thurs & Fri 5–8pm in winter and spring, Sun 10am–3pm • €3, free Thurs pm and Sun • ☎ 915 326 499, Ⓦ mnartesdecorativas.mcu.es • Ⓜ Banco de España/Retiro

Just south of Puerta de Alcalá is the **Museo de Artes Decorativas**, housed in a graceful-looking mansion close to the Retiro. The eclectic collection of furniture, glass, carpets, toys, clocks, jewellery and fans is interesting enough but the highlight is undoubtedly the beautifully tiled Valencian kitchen on the fourth floor with its superb painted *azulejos*.

Museo Naval

Paseo del Prado 5 • Tues–Sun 10am–7pm • Aug 10am–3pm • Free (bring ID), though a voluntary €3 donation is requested • ☎ 915 238 516, Ⓦ www.armada.mde.es/museonaval • Ⓜ Banco de España

A couple of blocks west of the Museo de Artes Décorativas in a corner of the Naval Ministry is the **Museo Naval**, strong, as you might expect, on models, charts and navigational aids from or relating to the Spanish voyages of discovery. Exhibits include the first map to show the New World, drawn in 1500, cannon from the Spanish Armada and part of Cortés' standard used in the conquest of Mexico.

San Jerónimo el Real

C/Ruiz de Alarcón 19 • Mon–Sat 10am–1pm & 5–8.30pm, Sun 9.30am–2.30pm & 5.30–8.30pm, July & Aug Mon–Sat 10am–1pm & 6–8.30pm, Sun 9.30am–1.30pm & 6–8.30pm • Ⓜ Banco de España/Atocha

Just behind the Prado is **San Jerónimo el Real**, Madrid's society church, where in 1975 Juan Carlos (like his predecessors) was crowned. Despite significant remodelling and the addition of two Gothic towers, the old form of the church is still clearly visible; but the seventeenth-century cloisters have fallen victim to the Prado extension.

Real Academía Española de la Lengua

C/Felipe IV 4 • Ⓜ Banco de España/Atocha

Opposite the church is the **Real Academia Española de la Lengua** (Royal Language Academy), whose job it is to make sure that the Spanish language is not corrupted by foreign or otherwise unsuitable words. The results are entrusted to their official dictionary – a work that bears virtually no relation to the Spanish you'll hear spoken on the streets.

Real Jardín Botánico

Pza. de Murillo 2 • Daily 10am–dusk • €3, under-10s free • Ⓦ www.rjb.csic.es • Ⓜ Atocha

Immediately south of the Prado is the delightful, shaded **Real Jardín Botánico**. Opened in 1781 by Carlos III (known as *El Alcalde* – "The Mayor" – for his urban-improvement programmes), the garden once contained over 30,000 plants. The numbers are down these days, though the gardens were renovated in the 1980s, after years of neglect, and the worldwide collection of flora is fascinating for any amateur

FROM TOP PLAZA MAYOR (P.67); BOATING LAKE, PARQUE DEL RETIRO (P.84) >

1

botanist; don't miss the hothouse with its tropical plants and amazing cacti or the bonsai collection of former prime minister Felipe González. Temporary exhibitions take place in the Palacio Villanueva within the grounds.

La CaixaForum

Paseo del Prado 36 • Daily 10am–8pm • €4 • ⓦ obrasocial.lacaixa.es • Ⓜ Atocha

Opposite the botanical gardens is **La CaixaForum**, an innovative and stylish exhibition space opened in 2008 by the powerful Catalan bank, which complements the existing attractions on the Paseo del Arte. The centre, which hosts a variety of high-quality temporary art shows, concerts and workshops, is flanked by an eye-catching vertical garden designed by French botanist Patrick Blanc in which some 15,000 plants form an organic carpet extending across the wall. Inside, there's a decent art bookshop and a neat top-floor café that serves a fine €12 lunchtime set menu.

Estación de Atocha

Ⓜ Atocha

On the far side of the botanical gardens from La CaixaForum is the sloping Cuesta de Moyano, lined with **bookstalls**; although it's at its busiest on Sundays, many of the stalls are open every day. Across the way, the **Estación de Atocha** is worth a look even if you're not travelling out of Madrid. It's actually two stations, old and new, the latter now sadly infamous as the scene of the horrific train bombings that killed 191 people and injured close to 2000 in March 2004. The original station, a glorious 1880s glasshouse, was revamped in the early 1990s with a spectacular tropical-garden centrepiece. It's a wonderful sight from the walkways above, and train buffs and architects will want to take a look at the high-speed AVE trains and the station beyond.

Museo Nacional de Antropología/Etnología

C/Alfonso XII 68 • Tues–Sat 9.30am–8pm, Sun 10am–3pm • €3, under-18s & over-65s free, free Sat after 2pm & Sun • ☎ 915 306 418, ⓦ mnantropologia.mcu.es • Ⓜ Atocha

Also in this area is the **Museo Nacional de Antropología/Etnología** designed to give an overview of different cultures of the world, in particular those intertwined with Spanish history. The most unusual exhibits are to be found in a side room on the ground floor – a macabre collection of deformed skulls, a Guanche (the original inhabitants of the Canary Islands) mummy and the skeleton of a circus giant (2.35m tall).

Real Fábrica de Tapices

C/Fuentarrabia 2 • Mon–Fri 10am–2pm; closed Aug • €4 • Tours every half-hour (guides usually speak English) • ☎ 914 340 550, ⓦ realfabricadetapices.com • Ⓜ Atoche Renfe/Menéndez Pelayo

The **Real Fábrica de Tapices** still turns out handmade tapestries, many of them based on the Goya cartoons in the Prado. They are fabulously expensive, but the entrance fee is a bargain, with the tour tracing the fascinating manufacturing process, barely changed in the three hundred years of the factory's existence.

The Gran Vía, Chueca and Malasaña

The **Gran Vía**, Madrid's great thoroughfare, runs from Pza. de Cibeles to Pza. de España, effectively dividing the old city to the south from the newer parts northwards. Permanently jammed with traffic and crowded with shoppers and sightseers, it's the commercial heart of the city, and – if you spare the time to look up – quite a

1

monument in its own right, with its early twentieth-century, palace-like banks, offices and cinemas. Look out for the **Edificio Metrópolis** (1905–11) on the corner of C/Alcalá, complete with cylindrical facade, white stone sculptures, zinc-tiled roof and gold garlands, and the towering **Telefónica** building which was the chief observation post for the Republican artillery during the Civil War, when the Nationalist front line stretched across the Casa de Campo to the west.

North of the Telefónica building, C/Fuencarral heads north to the Glorieta de Bilbao. To either side of this street are two of Madrid's most characterful *barrios*: **Chueca**, to the east, and **Malasaña**, to the west. Their chief appeal lies in an amazing concentration of bars, restaurants and, especially, nightlife. However, there are a few reasons – cafés included – to wander around here by day.

Chueca

Once rather down at heel, Chueca is now one of the city's most vibrant *barrios* and the focal point of Madrid's **gay scene**. At the centre is the lively **Pza. de Chueca** (ⓂChueca), which is fronted by one of the best old-style *vermut* bars in the city, *Bodega Ángel Sierra*. The whole area has become gentrified in recent years with the rise of a host of stylish bars, cafés and restaurants and the opening of the newly refurbished Mercado de San Antón.

Paseo de Recoletos

From Pza. de Chueca east to **Paseo de Recoletos** (the beginning of the long Paseo de la Castellana) are some of the city's most enticing streets. Offbeat restaurants, small private art galleries, and odd corner shops are in abundance, and the C/**Almirante** has some of the city's most fashionable clothes shops, too. To the north, on Paseo de Recoletos, are a couple of the city's most lavish **traditional cafés**, the *Café Gijón* at no. 21 and *Café del Espejo* at no. 31 (see p.112).

Sociedad General de Autores

C/Fernando VI 4 • Ⓜ Alonso Martínez

On the edge of the Santa Bárbara *barrio*, is the **Sociedad de Autores** (Society of Authors), housed in the only significant *modernista* building in Madrid designed by José Grasés Riera, who was part of the Gaudí school, and featuring an eye-catching facade that resembles a melted candle.

Museo Nacional del Romanticismo

C/San Mateo 13 • May–Oct Tues–Sat 9.30am–8.30pm (closes 6.30pm Nov–April), Sun 10am–3pm • €3, free on Sat after 2pm, Sun • ☎ 914 481 045, ⓦ museoromanticismo.mcu.es • Ⓜ Tribunal

Reopened in 2009 after a nine-year, seven-million-euro restoration, the **Museo Nacional del Romanticismo** has been given a new lease of life with an imaginative and inspiring refurbishment. The museum aims to show the lifestyle and outlook of the late Romantic era through the re-creation of a typical bourgeois residence in the turbulent reign of Isabel II (1833–68), and this it does brilliantly. Overflowing with a marvellously eclectic and often kitsch hoard of memorabilia, the mansion is decorated with some beautiful period furniture and ceiling frescoes. There's also a relaxing garden café serving a selection of teas, coffees and cakes.

Museo de Historia de Madrid

C/Fuencarral 78 • Tues–Fri 9.30am–8pm, Sat & Sun 10am–2pm, Aug Tues–Fri 9.30am–2pm, Sat & Sun 10am–2pm • Free • ☎ 917 011 863, ⓦ munimadrid.es/museomunicipal • Ⓜ Tribunal

Just around the corner from the Museo del Romanticismo, the **Museo de Historia de Madrid** is in the final throes of yet another lengthy restoration programme. The building itself features a flamboyant churrigueresque facade by Pedro de Ribera. At present there is a small taster of the museum's holdings including a fascinating 1830s

1

scale model of the city, but once fully open it will house a large chronological collection of paintings, photos, maps, sculptures and porcelain, all relating to the history of the city since it was designated capital in 1561.

Malasaña

The heart, in all senses, of **Malasaña** is the **Pza. Dos de Mayo**, named after the insurrection against Napoleonic forces on May 2, 1808; the rebellion and its aftermath are depicted in Goya's famous paintings at the Prado. The surrounding district bears the name of one of the martyrs of the uprising, 15-year-old Manuela Malasaña, who is also commemorated with a street (as are several other heroes of the time). On the night of May 1, Madrid honours its heroes, though the plaza is no longer the site of the traditional festivities.

More recently, the quarter was the focus of the *movida madrileña*, the "happening scene" of the late 1970s and early 1980s. As the country relaxed after the death of Franco and the city developed into a thoroughly modern capital under the leadership of the late mayor, Tierno Galván, Malasaña became a focal point for the young. Bars appeared behind every doorway, drugs were sold openly in the streets, and there was an extraordinary atmosphere of new-found freedom. Times have changed and a good deal of renovation has been going on in recent years, but the *barrio* retains a somewhat alternative – nowadays rather grungy – feel, with its bar custom spilling onto the streets, and an ever-lively scene in the Pza. Dos de Mayo terrazas.

The streets have an interest of their own and are home to some fine traditional bars, while on C/Manuela Malasaña you can take your pick from some of the trendiest cafés in town. There are also some wonderful old shop signs and architectural details, best of all the **Antigua Farmacia Juanse** on the corner of C/San Andrés and C/San Vicente Ferrer, with its irresistible 1920s *azulejo* scenes depicting cures for diarrhoea, headaches and suchlike.

San Antonio de los Alemanes
Corredera de San Pablo 16 • Mon–Sat 10.30am–2pm; closed Aug • €2 • ⓜ Callao

One of the few specific sights in this quarter is **San Antonio de los Alemanes**, a delightful, elliptical church with dizzying floor-to-ceiling frescoes by Neapolitan artist Luca Giordano depicting the life of St Anthony.

Plaza de España, Moncloa and beyond

Plaza de España provides a breathing space from the densely packed streets to the east. Beyond the square lies a mixture of leafy suburbia, university campus and parkland, including the green swathes of Parque del Oeste and Casa de Campo. Sights include some fascinating minor museums and, further out, the royal palace of *El Pardo*. The airy terrazas along Paseo del Pintor Rosales provide ample opportunity for refreshment.

Plaza de España
ⓜ Plaza de España

The **Plaza de España** at the west end of Gran Vía was home, until the flurry of corporate building in the north of Madrid, to two of the city's tallest buildings: the **Torre de Madrid** and the **Edificio de España**. These rather stylish 1950s buildings preside over an elaborate monument to Cervantes in the middle of the square, which in turn overlooks the bewildered-looking bronze figures of Don Quixote and Sancho Panza.

The plaza itself is a little on the seedy side, especially at night. However, to its north, **C/Martín de los Heros** is a lively place, day and night, with a couple of the city's best cinemas, and behind them the **Centro Princesa**, with shops, clubs, bars and a 24-hour branch of the ubiquitous VIPS – just the place to buy a box of chocolates or a bite to eat before heading on to a small-hours club.

Conde Duque

Ⓜ Plaza de España

Up the steps opposite the Centro Princesa is **C/Conde Duque**, an atmospheric street that contains an intriguing selection of cafés, restaurants and shops, and one that is dominated by the massive former barracks of the royal guard, constructed in the early eighteenth century by Pedro de Ribera. The barracks have been turned into a dynamic cultural centre, **El Centro Cultural de Conde Duque** (Ⓦcondeduquemadrid.es; free). Just to the east of this is the **Pza. de las Comendadoras** – named after the convent that occupies one side of the square – which is a tranquil space bordered by a variety of interesting craft shops, bars and cafés.

Museo Cerralbo

C/Ventura Rodríguez 17 • Tues, Wed, Fri & Sat 9.30am–3pm, Thurs 9.30am–3pm & 5–8pm, Sun & hols 10am–3pm; July & Aug Tues–Sat 9.30am–2pm, Sun & hols 11am–2pm • €3, free Thurs 5–8pm, Sat after 2pm, Sun • Ⓣ 915 473 646, Ⓦ museocerralbo.mcu.es • Ⓜ Plaza de España

A block to the west of Pza. de España a beautiful mansion houses the refurbished **Museo Cerralbo**, endowed with the collections of the reactionary politician, poet, traveller and archeologist, the seventeenth Marqués de Cerralbo. The rooms, stuffed with paintings, furniture, armour and artefacts, provide a fascinating insight into the lifestyle of the nineteenth-century aristocracy, though there is little of individual note.

Parque del Oeste

Pza. de España • Ⓜ Argüelles/Ventura Rodríguez

The **Parque del Oeste** stretches northwest from the Pza. de España, following the rail tracks of Príncipe Pío up to the suburbs of Moncloa and Ciudad Universitaria. In summer, there are numerous terrazas in the park, while, year-round, a **teleférico** shuttles its passengers high over the river from Paseo del Pintor Rosales to the middle of the Casa de Campo, where there's a bar/restaurant with pleasant views back towards the city. Just below the starting point of the *teleférico* (April–Sept daily noon–8 or 9pm; Oct–March Sat, Sun & public hols noon–dusk; €4 single, €5.80 return; Ⓣ902 345 002, Ⓦteleferico.com) is the beautiful **Rosaleda** (10am–7.30pm), a vast rose garden at its best in May and June.

Templo de Debod

C/Ferraz 1 • April–Sept Tues–Fri 10am–2pm & 6–8pm, Sat & Sun 9.30am–8.30pm; Oct–March Tues–Fri 9.45am–1.45pm & 4.15–6.15pm, Sat & Sun 9.30am–8pm • Free • Ⓦ www.madrid.es/templodebod • Ⓜ Plaza de España

On the south side of the park, five minutes' walk from Pza. de España, is the **Templo de Debod**, a fourth-century BC Egyptian temple given to Spain in recognition of the work done by Spanish engineers on the Aswan High Dam (which inundated its original site). Reconstructed here stone by stone, it seems comically incongruous, and even more so with the multimedia exhibition on the culture of Ancient Egypt housed inside.

La Ermita de San Antonio de la Florida

Glorieta de la Florida 5 • Tues–Fri 10am–8pm, Sat & Sun 10am–2pm; July 13–23 closed afternoons • Free • Ⓦ madrid.es/ermita • Ⓜ Príncipe Pío

Almost alongside the famous roast chicken and cider restaurant *Casa Mingo* is **La Ermita de San Antonio de la Florida**. This little church on a Greek-cross plan was built by an Italian, Felipe Fontana, between 1792 and 1798, and decorated by **Goya**, whose frescoes are the reason to visit. In the dome is a depiction of a miracle performed by St Anthony of Padua. Around it, heavenly bodies of angels and cherubs hold back curtains to reveal the main scene: the saint resurrecting a dead man to give evidence in

1

favour of a prisoner (the saint's father) falsely accused of murder. Beyond this central group, Goya created a gallery of highly realist characters – their models were court and society figures – while for a lesser fresco of the angels adoring the Trinity in the apse, he took prostitutes as his models. The *ermita* also houses the artist's mausoleum, although his head was stolen by phrenologists for examination in the nineteenth century.

Moncloa

The wealthy suburb of **Moncloa** contains the Spanish prime ministerial residence and merits a visit even if you are not using the bus terminal for El Pardo and El Escorial. The metro will bring you out next to the mammoth building housing the Air Ministry and the giant Arco de la Victoria, built by Franco in 1956 to commemorate the Nationalist victory in the Civil War. Beyond this lie the leafy expanses of the Parque del Oeste and the campuses of the **Ciudad Universitaria**. During termtime, the area becomes one giant student party on weekend evenings, with huddles of picnickers and singing groups under the trees.

Museo de América

Avda. de los Reyes Católicos 6 • Tues, Wed, Fri & Sat 9.30am–3pm, Thurs 9.30am–7pm, Sun 10am–3pm • €3, free on Sun • ☎ 915 492 641, ⓦ mecd.gob.es/museodeamerica • ⓜ Moncloa

Near the Arco de la Victoria is the **Museo de América**, which contains a fine collection of artefacts, ceramics and silverware from Spain's former colonies in Latin America in a thematic layout. The highlight is the fabulous Quimbayas treasure – a breathtaking collection of gold objects and figures from the Quimbaya culture of Colombia.

Museo del Traje

Avda. de Juan de Herrera 2 • Tues–Sat 9.30am–7pm, Sun & hols 10am–3pm (July & Aug open late from 9.30am–10.30pm on Thurs) • €3; free for under-18s, Sat after 2.30pm and all day Sun • ☎ 915 504 708, ⓦ museodeltraje.mcu.es • ⓜ Moncloa

Across the busy road from the Museo de América down towards the university is the **Museo del Traje**, a fascinating excursion through the history of clothes and costume. Exhibits include clothes from a royal tomb dating back to the thirteenth century, some stunning eighteenth-century ball gowns and a selection of Spanish regional costumes, as well as shoes, jewellery and underwear. Modern Spanish and international designers are also featured, with a Paco Rabanne miniskirt and stylish dresses from Pedro del Hierro. The upmarket restaurant in the grounds has a cool garden terrace for summer use.

Casa de Campo

ⓜ Batán/Lago, bus (#33) from Príncipe Pío or *teleférico* (see p.91)

If you want to jog, play tennis, swim (pool open daily June–Sept 11am–8pm; €5), picnic, go to the fairground or see pandas, then the **Casa de Campo** is the place. This enormous expanse of heath and scrub is in parts surprisingly wild for a spot so easily accessible from the city; other sections have been tamed for more conventional pastimes.

Picnic tables and café-bars are dotted throughout the park and there's a **jogging track** with exercise posts, a municipal open-air **swimming pool** close to ⓜ Lago, tennis courts, and rowing boats for rent on the **lake** (again near ⓜ Lago). Sightseeing attractions include a large and well-organized **zoo** and a popular amusement park, the **Parque de Atracciones** (see p.120), complete with the obligatory selection of heart-stopping, stomach-churning gravity rides. Be aware that some of the **access roads** through the park are frequented by prostitutes, though there are few problems during daylight hours.

El Pardo

Nine kilometres northwest of Madrid in the former royal hunting ground of **El Pardo** is where Franco had his principal residence. A garrison still remains in the town – where most of the Generalísimo's staff were based – but the stigma of the place has lessened over the years, and it is now a popular weekend excursion for *madrileños*, who come here for long lunches in the terraza restaurants, or to play tennis or swim at one of the nearby sports clubs.

Palacio del Pardo

C/Manuel Alonso • April–Sept daily 10am–8pm; Oct–March daily 10am–6pm; closed occasionally for official visits • Guided tours €9, 5–16-year-olds, over-65s €4, free Wed & Thurs 5–8pm (April–Sept), 3–6pm (Oct–March) for EU citizens • ⓦ patrimonionacional.es • Buses (#601) from Moncloa (daily 6.30am–midnight, every 10–15 min; 25min)

Rebuilt by the Bourbons on the site of a hunting lodge of Carlos V, the **Palacio del Pardo** is the tourist focus of the area. The interior is pleasant enough, with its chapel and theatre, a portrait of Isabel la Católica by her court painter Juan de Flandes, and an excellent collection of tapestries, many after the Goya cartoons in the Prado. Guides detail the uses Franco made of the *palacio*, but pass over some of his stranger habits – he kept by his bed, for instance, the mummified hand of St Teresa of Ávila. The country-house retreat in the grounds known as the **Casita del Príncipe** was, like the *casitas* (pavilions) at El Escorial, designed by Prado architect Juan de Villanueva, and is highly ornate.

Salamanca and the Paseo de la Castellana

Salamanca, the area north of the Parque del Retiro, is a smart address for apartments and, even more so, for shops. The *barrio* is the haunt of *pijos* – universally denigrated rich kids – and the grid of streets between C/Goya and C/José Ortega y Gasset contains most of the city's designer emporiums. Most of the buildings are modern and undistinguished, though there are some elegant nineteenth-century mansions and apartment blocks. A scattering of museums, galleries and exhibition spaces might tempt you up here, too – in particular the **Sorolla** and the **Lázaro Galdiano** museums, two little gems that are often ignored by visitors.

Plaza de Colón and around

If you tackle the area from south to north, the first point of interest is **Plaza de Colón** (ⓜColón), endowed at street level with a statue of Columbus (Cristóbal Colón), and some huge stone blocks arranged as a megalithic monument to the discovery of the Americas. Below the plaza and underneath the cascading waterfall facing the city's longest, widest and busiest avenue, the Paseo de la Castellana, is the **Teatro Fernán Gómez** arts centre.

Museo Arqueológico Nacional

C/Serrano 13 • Tues–Sat 9.30am–8pm, Sun 9.30am–3pm, free Sat after 3pm and Sun am • €3 • ⓣ 915 777 912, ⓦ man.es • ⓜ Colón/Serrano

Adjacent to Pza. de Colón is the revitalized **Museo Arqueológico Nacional**, open after a lengthy refurbishment. The collections have been given a new lease of life with their arrangement around a naturally lit central atrium, while the labelling and video explanations (in English and Spanish) put the exhibits into context. As befitting a national collection, the museum holds some very impressive pieces, among them the celebrated Celtiberian busts known as *La Dama de Elche* and *La Dama de Baza*, and a wonderfully rich hoard of Visigothic treasures found at Toledo. The museum also contains outstanding Roman, Egyptian, Greek and Islamic finds.

Museo de Arte Público

Paseo de la Castellana 41 • Free • ⓜ Rubén Darío

North from the Museo de la Biblioteca Nacional, up the Paseo de la Castellana, the **Museo de Arte Público** is an innovative attempt at using the space underneath the Juan

1

Bravo flyover. However, its haphazard and rather stark collection of sculptures, including the six-tonne suspended block titled *The Meeting* by the late Eduardo Chillada, appears to be more appreciated by the city's skateboard community.

Museo Sorolla

C/Martínez Campos 37 • Tues, Thurs–Sat 9.30am–8pm, July & Aug closes 2.30pm, Sun 10am–3pm • €3, free under-18s, Sat 2–8pm, Sun • ☎ 913 101 584, ⓦ museosorolla.mcu.es • Ⓜ Gregorio Marañon/Iglesia

Not far north of here, across the Paseo de la Castellana, is a little jewel of a gallery, the **Museo Sorolla**, with a large collection of work by the painter **Joaquín Sorolla** (1863–1923), tastefully displayed in his beautifully preserved old home. The most striking of his paintings, which include beach scenes, portraits and landscapes, are impressionistic plays on light and texture. His old studio is much as he left it, and the house itself, with its cool and shady Andalucian-style courtyard and gardens, is worth the visit alone and makes a wonderful escape from the traffic-choked streets.

Museo Lázaro Galdiano

C/Serrano 122 • Mon & Wed–Sat 10am–4.30pm, Sun 10am–3pm • €6; free under-12s, 3.30–4.30pm & Sun 2–3pm • ☎ 915 616 084, ⓦ flg.es • Ⓜ Gregorio Marañon/Rubén Darío

The **Museo Lázaro Galdiano** is just northeast of the Museo Sorolla at the intersection of C/Serrano and C/María Molina. This formerly private collection was given to the state by José Galdiano in 1948 and spreads over the four floors and thirty-seven rooms of his former home. It is a vast jumble of artworks, with some very dodgy attributions, but includes some really exquisite and valuable pieces. Among painters represented are El Greco, Bosch, Gerard David, Dürer and Rembrandt, as well as a host of Spanish artists, including Berruguete, Murillo, Zurbarán, Velázquez and Goya. Other exhibits include a collection of clocks and watches, many of them once owned by Carlos V.

Museo de Ciencias Naturales

C/José Gutiérrez Abascal 2 • Tues–Fri & Sun 10am–5pm, Sat 10am–8am (July & Aug 10am–3pm), Sun 10am–2.30pm • €6; 4–16 year-olds €3 • ☎ 914 111 328, ⓦ mncn.csic.es • Ⓜ Gregorio Marañon

Set back from the busy road, halfway along the Paseo de la Castellana, is the **Museo de Ciencias Naturales** (Natural History Museum), whose displays are split between two buildings. One is now home to a renovated exhibition space focusing on biodiversity and Mediterranean fauna with a collection of stuffed animals, skeletons and audiovisual displays on the evolution of life on earth, the other is home to some rather dull fossil and geological exhibits.

To the Bernabéu

North along the Paseo de la Castellana, you reach the **Zona Azca** (Ⓜ Nuevos Ministerios/Santiago Bernabéu), a business quarter, once home to the city's tallest skyscraper, the 157-metre Torre Picasso designed by Minori Yamasaki (also the architect of New York's infamous Twin Towers), although now dwarfed by the four new towers erected beyond Pza. Castilla. It is only a short hop across the Castellana to Real Madrid's magnificent **Santiago Bernabéu** stadium, easily the most famous sight in this part of town.

Santiago Bernabéu

C/Concha Espina 1 • Tour Mon–Sat 10am–7pm, Sun 10.30am–6.30pm (closes 5hr before kickoff on match days) • €19, under-14s €13 • ☎ 913 984 300, ⓦ realmadrid.com • Ⓜ Santiago Bernabéu

The **Santiago Bernabéu** stadium provides a suitably imposing home for one of the most famous clubs in world football, Real Madrid. Even if you can't get to see a match, you can take the **stadium tour** which, though exorbitantly priced, is understandably popular. It starts with a panoramic view of the massive 80,000-capacity stadium and takes in a visit to the dressing rooms and a walk through the tunnel onto the pitch.

FÚTBOL IN MADRID

The "Galactico" era of the likes of David Beckham, Zinedine Zidane, Ronaldo and Luís Figo may be over, but **Real Madrid** remains one of the most glamorous teams in club football with an ample quota of superstars including the world's two most expensive players in Gareth Bale and Cristiano Ronaldo. The ten-time winners of the European Cup and 32-time Spanish champions play at the **Bernabéu**, venue of the 1982 World Cup final and a ground that ranks as one of the world's most fabled sporting arenas.

Tickets to games – which have become more difficult to get hold of in recent years – cost from €30 up to €500 for big matches and usually go on sale a couple of weeks before a game; Real runs a telephone and online booking service (☎ 902 324 324, ⊕ realmadrid.com). They can be purchased by credit card on the ticket line or online for all but the biggest matches. If you don't get lucky, you can still catch a glimpse of the hallowed turf by taking the stadium tour.

The capital is also home to another of the country's biggest teams, 2014 league champions **Atlético Madrid** (☎ 902 530 500, ⊕ clubatleticodemadrid.com; tickets from around €35, on sale via the website), who play at the **Estadio Vicente Calderón** in the south of the city (Ⓜ Pirámides), though a stadium move is in the pipeline. The more modest Getafe (☎ 916 959 643, ⊕ getafecf.com; tickets from around €30) and Rayo Vallecano (☎ 914 782 253, ⊕ rayovallecano.es; tickets from around €25) are both based in working-class suburbs of the city.

Also included is the **trophy exhibition**, complete with endless cabinets of gleaming silverware, with pride of place given to the team's nine European Cups and video footage of their greatest triumphs. The tour ends with the obligatory visit to the overpriced club shop – where you soon come to realize why Real is one of the richest football clubs in the world. The stadium also has a surprisingly affordable café (*Realcafé*) and a more expensive **restaurant** (*Puerta 57*), both open to the public and affording views over the pitch (though they are not open during games).

Plaza Castilla

Ⓜ Plaza Castilla

The Paseo de la Castellana ends with a flourish at **Plaza Castilla** with four giant skyscrapers constructed on Real Madrid's former training ground, the result of a controversial deal that allowed the club to solve many of its financial problems. The two tallest towers, one of which is designed by Norman Foster, soar some 250m into the sky.

ARRIVAL AND DEPARTURE   MADRID

Whatever your point of **arrival** in Madrid, it's an easy business getting into the centre of the Spanish capital. The airport is connected by a speedy metro link, shuttle buses and taxis, while the city's main train and bus stations are all linked to the metro system only a short ride from the centre.

BY PLANE

Aeropuerto Adolfo Suárez Madrid-Barajas (general information ☎ 902 404 704/913 211 000, ⊕ aena.es), recently renamed in honour of the late Spanish prime minister who oversaw the transition to democracy after the death of Franco, is 16km east of the city, on the A2 road. It has four terminals, including the vast new T4 building designed by Richard Rogers and Carlos Lamela, which has helped double the capacity to some seventy million passengers a year. All Iberia's domestic and international flights, as well as airlines that belong to the Oneworld group, such as British Airways and American Airways, use T4 (a 10min shuttle-bus ride from the other terminals);

other international flights and budget airlines, including Aer Lingus, EasyJet and Ryanair, go from T1, while Air France, KLM and SAS use T2.

Metro link From the airport, the metro link (Line 8) takes you from T4 and T2 to the city's Nuevos Ministerios station in just 12min (daily 6am–2am; €3 supplement plus €1.50 fare). From there it's a 15min metro ride to most city-centre locations.

Airport buses The route by road to central Madrid is more variable, depending on rush-hour traffic, anything from 20min to 1hr. The bright y... express buses run round the clock (every 15– 11pm; every 35min at night) from each termi...

1

and Atocha (stops only at Cibeles 11.30pm–6am; €5) with a journey time of around 40min.

Taxis are always available outside, too, and cost around €25–30 (including a €5.50 airport supplement) to the centre, depending on traffic.

Train A *cercanías* train line takes you from T4 to Chamartín in the north of the city in around 11min or to Atocha in the south in 25min (6am–11.30pm; €2.40).

Car rental Half a dozen or so car rental companies have stands at the airport terminals and can generally supply clients with maps and directions.

Airport facilities Other airport facilities include 24hr currency exchange, ATMs, a post office, left-luggage lockers, a RENFE office for booking train tickets, chemists, tourist offices and hotel reservations desks.

BY TRAIN

Two main stations, Estación de Chamartín and Estación de Atocha, serve destinations throughout Spain and further afield.

Estación de Chamartín Serves trains from France or northern and western Spain (including the high-speed links to Segovia and Valladolid); a modern terminal isolated in the north of the city, connnected by metro with the centre, and by regular commuter trains (*cercanías*) with Estación de Atocha.

Destinations A Coruña (5–7 daily; 6hr–9hr 20min); Ávila (20–25 daily; 1hr 20min–2hr 10min); Bilbao (2 daily; 5hr); Burgos (7 daily; 2hr 15min–4hr 35min); Ferrol (1–3; 7hr 35min–11hr); Gijón (4–6 daily; 5hr 25min); León (10–12 daily; 2hr 45min–5hr 10min); Lisbon (daily; 10hr 40min); Oviedo (4–7 daily; 4hr 55min–5hr 5min); Pamplona (5–8 daily; 3hr 10min–3hr 50min); Pontevedra (3–5 daily; 6hr 45min–9hr 30min); Salamanca (7–10 daily; 2hr 20min–3hr); San Sebastián (7 daily; 5hr 20min–7hr 30min); Santander (3–5 daily; 4hr 20min–6hr 10min); Santiago (4–5 daily; 5hr 30min–8hr 30min); Segovia (AVE 12–14 daily; 25min; 7 daily 1hr 50min–2hr); Sigüenza (4–6 daily; 1hr 30min–1hr 50min); Soria (2–3 daily; 2hr 40min–3hr); Valladolid (AVE 20 daily; 56min–1hr 10min; 7 daily–2hr 50min); Vigo (7–9 daily; 6hr 10min–10hr 35min); Vitoria (AVE 2 daily 3hr 40min; 3 daily; 5hr 30min); Zamora (3–6 daily; 1hr 55min–3hr 15min). Plus most other destinations in the northeast and northwest.

Estación de Atocha Centrally located at the end of the southern end of Paseo del Prado, it has two interconnected terminals: one for local services, the other for all points in southern and eastern Spain, including the high-speed AVE trains to Barcelona, Seville, Toledo, Málaga, Valencia and Zaragoza.

Destinations Albacete (15–20 daily; 1hr 20min–2hr 55min); Alcalá de Henares (every 5–20min; 35min); Algeciras (3 daily; 5hr 15min–6hr 5min); Alicante (10–14 ¹ly; 2hr 20min–3hr 35min); Almería (3 daily; 6hr

20min–8hr 40min); Aranjuez (every 15–30min; 45min); Badajoz (3–5 daily; 5hr 35min–6hr 30min); Barcelona (19–32 daily; 2hr 50min–3hr 10min); Cáceres (3–6 daily; 3hr 45min–4hr 10min); Cádiz (7–13 daily; 3hr 58min–5hr 15min); Cartagena (2–4 daily; 4hr 50min–5hr 15min); Ciudad Real (20–25 daily; 50min–1hr); Córdoba (30 daily; 1hr 40min–2hr); Cuenca (AVE 9–11 daily; 50min; Regional 4 daily; 3hr); El Escorial (every 20–30min; 1hr 5min); Granada (4 daily; 4hr 25min); Guadalajara (AVE 9 daily; 25min; regional every 15–30min; 55min); Huelva (5–8 daily; 3hr 40min–5hr 20min); Huesca (2–4 daily; 2hr 15min–3hr 35min); Jaén (2–4 daily; 4hr 15min); Jerez (10–13 daily; 3hr 20min–4hr 35min); Lleida (10 daily; 2hr); Málaga (13–15 daily; 2hr 20min–2hr 50min); Marseilles (daily; 7hr); Mérida (5 daily; 4hr 50min–5hr 50min); Seville (20–24 daily; 2hr 20min–2hr 45min); Toledo (15–18 daily; 33min); Valencia (19 daily; 1hr 40min–3hr 30min); Zaragoza (20 daily; 1hr 15min). Plus most destinations in the south and west.

Príncipe Pío If you're coming from local towns around Madrid, you may arrive at Príncipe Pío (aka Estación del Norte), fairly close to the centre below the Palacio Real, which is also connected to the metro network.

Information and reservations Call ☎ 902 320 320 or go to ⊚ renfe.com. Tickets can be bought at the individual stations, at Aeropuerto de Barajas arrivals in T1 and T4 and at registered travel agents. Bear in mind that you'll need to book in advance for most long-distance trains, especially at weekends or holiday time.

BY BUS

Bus terminals are scattered throughout the city. The largest – used by all of the international bus services – is the Estación Sur de Autobuses at C/Méndez Álvaro 83 on the corner of C/Retama, 1.5km south of the Atocha station (☎ 914 684 200, ⊚ www.etacionautobusesmadrid.com; Ⓜ Méndez Álvaro). There are other bus stations at the *intercambiadoras* in Avda. de América (Ⓜ Avda. de América), Conde de Casal (Ⓜ Conde de Casal), Moncloa (an underground terminal just above Ⓜ Moncloa), Príncipe Pío (Ⓜ Príncipe Pío) and Pza. Elíptica (Ⓜ Plaza Elíptica). Leading bus companies that operate from Madrid include Alsa (⊚ alsa.es), Arriva (⊚ arriva.es) Avanzabus (⊚ avanzabus.com), Samar (⊚ samar.es), La Sepulvedana (⊚ lasepulvedana.es), and Socibus (⊚ www.socibus.es).

Estación Sur de Autobuses destinations Albacete (10–20 daily; 2hr 45min–3hr 35min); Alicante (6 daily; 4hr 50min–5hr); Almería (5 daily; 6hr 30min); Aranjuez (Mon–Fri every 30 min, Sat & Sun hourly; 40min); Arenas de San Pedro (4–5 daily; 2hr); Ávila (5–10 daily; 1hr 20min–1hr 45min); Badajoz (7–8 daily; 5hr 5hr 45min); Cáceres (7 daily; 3hr 55min–4hr 55min); Ciudad Real (2–3 daily; 2hr 30min); Córdoba (6 daily; 4hr 45min); Cuenca (7–9 daily; 2hr 10min–2hr 30min); Gijón (11 daily; 5hr 30min–6hr 30min);

Granada (13 daily; 4hr 30min–5hr 30min); Jaén (15 daily; 4hr 30min–5hr); León (11 daily; 3hr 30min–4hr 30min); Lisbon (3 daily; 7hr); Málaga (5–7 daily; 6hr); Marbella (6 daily; 7hr); Mérida (8 daily; 4–5hr); Oviedo (12 daily; 5hr–5hr 45min); Palencia (5 daily; 3hr 15min); Pontevedra (6 daily; 8hr); Salamanca (20 daily; 2hr 30min); Santiago (4 daily; 8–9hr); Seville (8 daily; 6hr 30min); Trujillo (10–15 daily; 2hr 40min–4hr); Valencia (10 daily; 4hr 15min); Valladolid (14 daily; 2hr 15min–2hr 30min); Zamora (6 daily; 3hr–3hr 15min); and international services to France.
Intercambiador de Avda. de América destinations Alcalá (every 15min; 45min); Barcelona (12 daily; 7hr 50min–8hr 20min); Bilbao (10–15 daily; 4hr 10min–4hr 45min); Guadalajara (every 30min; 40–55min); Logroño (7 daily; 4hr); Pamplona (7 daily; 5hr 15min–6hr 45min); San Sebastián (10 daily; 5hr 10min–6hr 20min); Santander (8 daily; 4hr 30min–5hr 30min); Soria (9 10 daily; 2hr 30min); Vitoria (10 daily; 4hr 10min–4hr 30min); Zaragoza (20 daily; 4hr).
Intercambiador de Moncloa destinations El Escorial (approx every 15–30min; 55min–1hr). Onward connections to El Valle de los Caídos.
Intercambiador de Plaza Elíptica destination Toledo (every 30min; 1hr–1hr 30min).
Intercambiador de Príncipe Pío destination Segovia (every 30min; 1hr 45min).

Intercambiador Conde de Casal destination Chinchón (daily every 30min–1hr; 45–55min).

BY CAR

All the main roads into Madrid bring you right into the city centre, although eccentric signposting and even more eccentric driving can be very unnerving. The two main ring roads – the M40 and the M30 – and the Paseo de la Castellana are all notorious bottlenecks, although virtually the whole city centre can be close to gridlock during the peak rush-hour periods (Mon–Fri 7.30–9.30am & 6–8.30pm). Be prepared for a long trawl around the streets to find parking, and even then in most central areas you'll have to buy a ticket at one of the roadside meters (up to €2.95 for a maximum stay of 2hr in the blue-coloured bays; up to €2.40 for a maximum stay of 1hr in the green-coloured bays). Charges apply Mon–Fri 9am–9pm, Sat and Aug 9am–3pm. Another option is to put your car in one of the many signposted parkings (up to €2/hr and around €31.50/day). Your own transport is really only of use for out-of-town excursions, so it's advisable to find a hotel with or near a car park and keep your car there during your stay in the city. If you are staying more than a couple of weeks, you can get long-term parking rates at some neighbourhood garages.

Free maps of the whole central area of Madrid are available from any of the *turismos* (see p.99).

GETTING AROUND

Madrid is a pretty easy city to **get around**. The central areas are walkable; the metro is modern, extensive and efficient; buses are also good and serve some of the more out-of-the-way districts; and taxis are always available.

THE METRO

The clean and highly efficient metro (Ⓦ www .metromadrid.es) is by far the quickest way of getting around Madrid, serving most places you're likely to want to get to. It runs from 6am until 2am, and the flat fare is €1.50 for the central zone (€2 if you want to venture further afield), or €12.20 for a ten-trip ticket (*bono de diez viajes*), which can be used on buses, too. The network has undergone massive expansion in recent years and some of the outlying commuter districts are now connected by light railways, which link with the existing stations (separate

tickets are needed for some of these). Lines are numbered and colour-coded, and the direction of travel is indicated by the name of the terminus station. You can pick up a free colour map of the system (*plano del metro*) at any station.

BUSES

The comprehensive urban bus network (Ⓦ emtmadrid .es) is another good way to get around and see the sights: in the text, where there's no metro stop, we've indicated which bus to take. There are information booths in the Pza. de Cibeles and Puerta del Sol, which dispense a huge route

---

THE TOURIST TRAVEL PASS

If you're using public transport extensively, it could be worth getting a **tourist pass (abono túristico)**, covering the metro, train and bus. These are non-transferable, and you'll need to show your passport or identity card at the time of purchase. **Zone A** cards cover central Madrid, **Zone T** cards cover the whole region including buses to Toledo and Guadalajara but not those to the airport. They are available for a duration of one to seven days and range in cost from €8.40 for a Zone A daily card to €70.80 for a weekly one for Zone T (under-11s are half-price; under-4s travel free) and can be purchased at all metro stations, the airport and tourist offices. If you're staying longer, passes (*abonos*) covering the metro, train and bus, and available for each calendar month, are worthwhile.

Schematic map of the subway network

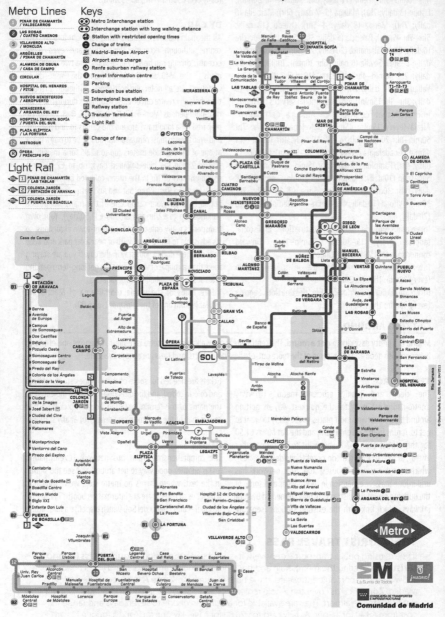

map (*plano de los transportes de Madrid*), and – along with other outlets – sell bus passes. Fares are the same as for the metro, at €1.50 a journey, or €12.20 for a ten-trip ticket (*bono de diez viajes*), which can be used on both forms of transport, but note that you can only buy the single tickets on the buses themselves (try to have the right money). Buses run from 6am to midnight. In addition, there are *búho* (owl) night buses that operate on twenty routes around the central area and out to the suburbs: departures are half-hourly from midnight to 5.30am, from Pza. de Cibeles.

TAXIS

One of the best things about getting round Madrid is that there are thousands of taxis – white cars with a diagonal red stripe on the side – which are reasonably cheap; €8–10 will get you to most places within the centre and, although it's common to round up the fare, you're not expected to tip. The minimum fare is €2.40–2.90 and supplements are charged for the airport, train and bus stations, the IFEMA congress centre, going outside the city limits, and for night trips (10pm–6am). In any area in the centre, day and night, you should be able to wave down a taxi (available ones have a green light on top of the cab) in a short time, although it is more difficult at weekends when half the population is out on the town. To phone for a taxi, call ☎915 478 600 (also for wheelchair-friendly cabs) ☎914 051 213, ☎913 712 131 or ☎914 473 232. If you want to make a complaint take the driver's number and ask for the *hoja de reclamaciones* (a claim form). If you leave something in a taxi, ring ☎915 279 590.

LOCAL TRAINS

The local train network, or *cercanías*, is the most efficient way of connecting between the main train stations and provides the best route out to many of the suburbs and to nearby towns such as Alcalá de Henares. Most trains are air-conditioned, fares are cheap, and there are good connections with the metro. Trains generally run every 15 to 30min from 6am to midnight. For more information, go to the RENFE website at ⓦrenfe.com and click on the *cercanías* section for Madrid.

BICYCLES

Madrid is not a particularly bike-friendly city, but things are improving. A new network of cycle paths is being constructed in some of the central areas and a municipal bike hire scheme known as BiciMad (☎915 298 210, ⓦbicimad.com) has also been introduced though it is still in its infancy and has experienced a number of teething problems. You can pick up and return a bike at one of the stations dotted all over the city centre, though you will have to pay a credit card deposit of €150. Prices for occasional users are €2 for the first hour and €4 thereafter (charged once you return the bike).

CITY TOURS

The *turismo* in Pza. Mayor (see below) can supply details of a variety of guided English-language walking tours around the city (tickets from €5.90; ☎902 221 424 info at ⓦesmadrid.com). For a bus tour of all the major city sights, wait at the pick-up points outside the Prado, Pza. de España, Pza. de Colón and Pza. de Cibeles. Tickets cost €21 (under-16s €10, under-6s free; ⓦmadridcitytour .es) and allow you to jump on and off throughout the day at various places throughout the city.

INFORMATION

There are **Turismo** at the following locations, which are open all year round:

Barajas International Airport in T1 (Mon–Fri 8am–8pm, Sat & Sun 9am–2pm; ☎913 058 656), T2 and T4 (daily 9am–8pm; ☎913 338 248).
Estación de Atocha (Mon–Fri 9am–8pm, Sat & Sun 9am–1pm; ☎913 159 976).
Estación de Chamartín (Mon–Fri 8am–8pm, Sat 9am–2pm; ☎913 159 976).

Pza. Mayor 27 (daily 9.30am–8.30pm; ⓜSol/Ópera).
Pza. de Colón In the underground passageway, accessed at the corner of C/Goya (daily 9.30am–8.30pm; ⓜColón).
CentroCentro, Palacio de Cibeles (Tues–Sun 8am–8pm; ⓜBanco de España).
Turismo booths Next to the Reina Sofía, in Pza. de Cibeles and in Pza. de Cibeles off Gran Vía

---

THE MADRID CARD

The **Madrid Card** (☎902 877 996, ⓦmadridcard.com) gives the holder the right of admission to over 50 museums and sights, a tour of the Bernabéu, the *teleférico*, an open-top bus tour and a guided walking tour of the old city, as well as discounts at a number of shops and restaurants. It costs €45 for one day (€55 for two, €65 for three; discounts for under-12s) and is on sale via the internet, at T2 at Barajas and at the Plaza Mayor tourist office. Do your sums before you splash out, though, as you would need to cram a lot into a day's sightseeing to get your money's worth. If you just want to concentrate on the big-three art galleries, the Paseo del Arte ticket (see p.77) may be better value, and will allow you to take things at a more leisurely pace.

1

(daily 9.30am–8.30pm).

Website and phone numbers The Madrid tourist board is at ⓦ esmadrid.com, while the regional authority has one covering the whole of the province (ⓦ turismomadrid.es). There's tourist information available in English on ☎ 902 100 007, a premium number that links all the regional tourist offices mentioned above, and on ☎ 914 544 410.

ACCOMMODATION

Business hotels apart, most of Madrid's **accommodation** is pretty central. With increasing competition, many *hostales* and hotels have been busy upgrading their facilities and a new breed of stylish, design-conscious, medium-priced hotel has emerged. Many of the expensive hotels do special weekend offers, and prices drop substantially in August when temperatures soar towards 40ºC (air-conditioning is usual and a welcome extra). You'll notice that buildings in the more popular hotel/*hostal* areas often house two or three separate establishments, each on **separate floors**; these are generally independent of each other. One thing to bear in mind is **noise**; bars, clubs, traffic and roadworks all contribute to making Madrid a high-decibel city, so avoid rooms on the lower floors, or choose a place away from the nightlife if you want a bit of peace and quiet. Madrid has just one **campsite**, located well out of the centre, but there are a couple of very handy backpackers' **hostels** right in the heart of the city.

If you want to be at the heart of the old town, the areas around **Puerta del Sol, Pza. de Santa Ana** and **Pza. Mayor** are the ones to go for; if you're into nightlife, **Malasaña** or **Chueca** may also appeal; for a quieter location and a bit of class, you should opt for the **Paseo del Prado, Recoletos** or **Salamanca** areas; if you have children the areas around the parks are good options.

SOL, ÓPERA AND MADRID DE LOS AUSTRIAS

This really is the heart of Madrid, and prices, not surprisingly, are a bit higher than some of the other central areas, though you can still find bargains in the streets around the Pza. Mayor.

Los Amigos Hostal C/Arenal 26, 4º ☎ 915 592 472, ⓦ losamigoshostel.com; ⓜ Ópera/Sol; map pp.102–103. Great backpacking option just a few minutes from Sol. Dormitories cater for 4–6 people, and there are a couple of communal rooms. Lockers are available, but bring your own padlock. The friendly staff speak English, and bed linen and use of the kitchen are included in the price. Dorms €17, en-suite double €50

Chic & Basic Mayerling C/Conde de Romanones 6 ☎ 914 201 580, ⓦ chicandbasic.com; ⓜ Tirso de Molina; map pp.102–103. A stylish mid-range hotel with 22 rooms, housed in a former textile warehouse close to C/Atocha. Clean lines and black-and-white decor predominate in the simple, neat rooms. Continental breakfast is included in the price and there's free internet as well as a sun terrace. €75

Hostal La Macarena Cava de San Miguel 8, 2º ☎ 913 659 221, ⓦ silserranos.com; ⓜ Sol; map pp.102–103. A comfortable *hostal* in a characterful street just off the Pza. Mayor. Some of the well-kept rooms are a little on the small side though they all have satellite TV and a/c. Great location but can be a little noisy. €59

★**Hotel Meninas** C/Campomanes 7 ☎ 915 412 805, ⓦ hotelmeninas.com; ⓜ Ópera; map pp.102–103. A stylish, 37-room hotel owned by the same group as the nearby *Ópera*, and similarly good value. Very helpful staff, excellent attic rooms, flat-screen TVs and free broadband internet access. Breakfast included for internet reservations. €100

Hotel Palacio de San Martín C/Pza. de San Martín 5 ☎ 917 015 000, ⓦ hotel-inturpalaciosanmartin.com; ⓜ Ópera/Sol; map pp.102–103. Situated in a historic building in an attractive square alongside the Monasterio de las Descalzas Reales. Stylish and spacious rooms with period decor, a small gym and sauna, plus a restaurant with a terrace in the plaza. €97

★**Petit Palace Arenal** C/Arenal 16 ☎ 915 644 355, ⓦ petitpalace.com; ⓜ Sol/Ópera; map pp.102–103. A member of the Petit Palace chain, with 64 sleek, modern rooms. All have a/c and free broadband, and there are some family-friendly rooms too. Two other members of this chain, the *Posada del Peine* (ⓦ hpetitpalaceposadadelpeine .com) and the *Puerta del Sol* (ⓦ hpetitpalacepuertadelsol .com), are close at C/Postas 17 and C/Arenal 4. €70

Posada del Leon de Oro C/Cava Baja 12 ☎ 911 191 494, ⓦ posadadelleondeoro.com; ⓜ La Latina; map pp.102–103. This former inn has been converted into a chic, designer hotel with seventeen large, individually decorated rooms complete with walk-in showers. €100

Room Mate Mario C/Campomanes 4º ☎ 915 488 548, ⓦ room-matehotels.com; ⓜ Ópera; map pp.102–103. Hip, designer hotel with a perfect spot on a pleasant street close to the Teatro Real. Compact, ultra-cool rooms, neat bathrooms, friendly staff and free internet. Buffet breakfast is included. There is another member of the chain, the *Laura*, at nearby Travesía de Trujillos 3 (☎ 917 011 670). Family rooms from €139. €90

AROUND PLAZA DE SANTA ANA AND HUERTAS

Pza. de Santa Ana and the Huertas area are at the heart of Madrid nightlife, with bars and cafés open until very late at night. The following are all within a few blocks of the square, with the metro stations Antón Martín, Sevilla and Sol close by. Go for rooms on the higher floors if you want to avoid the worst of the noise.

Hostal Alaska C/Espoz y Mina 7, 4º ☎915 249 208, ☻hostalalaska.es; ⓜSol; map pp.102–103. A selection of brightly decorated but simple rooms all with bathroom, a/c and TV, in this well-run *hostal*. Quadruple room from around €70 and a six-bed family apartment available from €150. **€55**

Hostal Barrera C/Atocha 96, 2º ☎915 275 381, ☻hostalbarrera.com; ⓜAntón Martín; map pp.62–63. A friendly, good-value fourteen-room *hostal* only a short distance from Atocha station and run by an English-speaking owner. Smart a/c rooms are a cut above the rest in this category. Internet access available. **€68**

★ **Hotel Urban** Carrera San Jeronimo 34 ☎917 877 770, ☻hotelurban.com; ⓜSevilla/Sol; map pp.102–103. Ultra-cool, fashion-conscious, five-star hotel offering a glut of designer rooms, a rooftop pool, summer terrace and *pijo* cocktail bar. It even has its own small museum, consisting of items from owner Jordi Clos' collection of Egyptian and Chinese art. Look out for special deals online. **€200**

International Hostel Posada de Huertas C/Huertas 21 ☎914 295 526, ☻posadadehuertas.com; ⓜAntón Martín/Sevilla; map pp.102–103. A modern hostel right at the heart of things, close to Pza. Santa Ana. Dormitories range in size from four to ten people, though doubles are also available. There's a common room with TV and internet access, plus laundry facilities and individual lockers. Breakfast is included. Dorms **€17**

ME Madrid Reina Victoria Pza. Santa Ana 14 ☎917 016 000, ☻memadrid.com; ⓜSol; map pp.102–103. Once a favourite haunt of bullfighters, this giant white wedding-cake of a hotel is now part of Melià's exclusive ME chain. Minimalist decor, designer furnishings, high-tech fittings, a super-cool penthouse bar and a chic restaurant serving fusion-style food. Special offers can bring the price down to around €175. **€200**

★ **NH Palacio Tepa** C/San Sebastian 2 ☎913 896 490, ☻nh-hoteles.com; ⓜAntón Martín; map pp.102–103. This luxurious new five-star, 85-room hotel is right in the heart of Huertas, close to Pza. Santa Ana and a stone's throw from the big museums. It has a range of large, plush rooms including some two-storey suites and wooden-beamed attics. Celebrity chef Paco Roncero runs the hotel's designer tapas bar *Estado Puro*. **€175**

★ **Room Mate Alicia** C/Prado 2 ☎913 896 095, ☻room-matehotels.com; ⓜSol/Sevilla; map pp.102–103. Perched on the corner of the plaza, the 34-room *Alicia* is in a great location – if a little noisy. Seriously cool decor, stylish rooms and great value. **€90**

AROUND PASEO DEL PRADO AND ATOCHA

This is a quieter area, though still very central, and it is close to the main art museums, the Parque del Retiro and Estación de Atocha. Some of the city's most expensive hotels are here – as well as a few more modest options.

★ **Hostal Gonzalo** C/Cervantes 34, 3º ☎914 292 714, ☻hostalgonzalo.com; ⓜAntón Martín; map pp.102–103. This has to be one of the most welcoming *hostales* in the city. It has fifteen bright, en-suite rooms – all of which have a/c and modern bathrooms – and a charming owner. **€50**

Hotel Artrip C/Valencia 11 ☎915 393 282, ☻artriphotel.com; ⓜLavapiés; map pp.62–63. A new arrival on the scene, this self-styled *Art Hotel* is conveniently located close to the Reina Sofia and other art galleries in the area. Its seventeen sleek, design-conscious rooms combine the modern with the traditional. Buffet breakfast for an extra €5. **€130**

Hotel Mora Paseo del Prado 32 ☎914 201 569, ☻hotelmora.com; ⓜAtocha; map pp.62–63. A good-value, slightly old-fashioned 62-room hotel perfectly positioned for all the galleries on the Paseo del Arte. It's not as smart as the nearby *Nacional*, but it's cheaper, and some of the a/c rooms have pleasant views along the Paseo del Prado. **€86**

Hotel Palace Pza. de los Cortes 7 ☎913 608 000, ☻westinpalacemadrid.com; ⓜAtocha/Banco de España; map pp.102–103. A colossal, sumptuous hotel with every imaginable facility, a spectacular, glass-covered central patio, and luxurious rooms – plus none of the snootiness of the *Ritz* across the road. Look out for website offers. **€239**

NH Nacional Paseo del Prado 48 ☎914 296 629, ☻nh-hoteles.com; ⓜAtocha; map pp.62–63. A large, plush hotel, part of the NH chain, attractively situated opposite the Jardines Botánicos. Special offers can reduce the price substantially. **€115**

La Pepa Chic B&B Pza. de los Cortes 4, 7º dcha. ☎648 474 742, ☻lapepa-bnb.com; ⓜBanco de España; map pp.102–103. Boutique accommodation in this neat B&B in the heart of the art museum quarter. The fourteen rooms have a brilliant white and red colour scheme, clean lines and functional furnishings. **€70**

★ **Radisson Blu Madrid Prado** C/Moratín 52 ☎915 242 626, ☻radissonblu.com/pradohotel-madrid; ⓜAtocha; map pp.102–103. Designer hotel located along the Paseo del Prado featuring sleek rooms in black, brown and white, photos of the Madrid skyline adorning the walls, black-slate bathrooms and coffee machines. There is a small gym, a spa and indoor pool, a whisky bar and a restaurant too. **€134**

Villa Real Pza. de las Cortes 10 ☎914 203 767, ☻derbyhotels.es; ⓜSevilla; map pp.102–103. Aristocratic hotel with its own art collection owned by Catalan entrepreneur Jordi Clos. Each of the 96 luxurious double rooms has a spacious sitting area and many have balconies over the plaza. The rooftop restaurant, whose walls are decorated with Andy Warhol originals, affords splendid views over the Congresos de Diputados and down towards the Paseo del Prado. **€140**

1

PLAZA DE ESPAÑA, GRAN VÍA AND BEYOND

The huge old buildings along the Gran Vía – which stretches all the way from Pza. España to C/Alcalá – hide a vast array of hotels and *hostales* at every price, often with a delightfully decayed elegance, though they also suffer from traffic noise. After dark, the area can feel somewhat seedy.

Aparto-hotel Rosales C/Marqués de Urquijo 23 ☎ 915 420 351, ⓦ apartohotel-rosales.com; ⓜ Argüelles; map pp.62–63. Large, comfortable apartments with separate bedroom, living area and kitchenette. Close to the Parque del Oeste and in one of the quieter areas of town, so a good option if you're travelling with children. Two persons **€110**, four persons **€150**

■ ACCOMMODATION

Los Amigos Hostal	8
Chic & Basic Mayerling	21
Hostal Alaska	13
Hostal Andorra	2
Hostal Gala	3
Hostal Gonzalo	18
Hostal La Macarena	15
Hotel de las Letras	4
Hotel Meninas	5
Hotel Palace	14
Hotel Palacio de San Martín	7
Hotel San Lorenzo	1
Hotel Urban	10
International Hostel	
Posada de Huertas	20
ME Madrid Reina Victoria	16
NH Palacio Tepa	19
La Pepa Chic B&B	11
Petit Palace Arenal	9
Posada del Leon de Oro	22
Radisson Blu Madrid Prado	23
Room Mate Alicia	17
Room Mate Mario	6
Villa Real	12

● TAPAS BARS & RESTAURANTS

Al Natural	12	La Ccava	42
El Abuelo	26	Cervecería Cervantes	36
Almendro 13	52	La Chata	50
Artemisa	21	Círculo de Belles Artes	8
Asador Arizmendi	57	Cornucopia	7
La Barraca	1	La Finca de Susana	11
La Bola	2	La Gloria de Montera	6
El Botín	37	El Lacón	31
Las Bravas	19	Lhardy	15
Café de Oriente	9	La Mallorquina	13
Casa del Abuelo	25	Mercado de San Miguel	28
Casa González	38	Mezklum Tech	27
Casa Labra	10	La Musa Latina	48
Casa Lastra	59	Museo del Jamón	14
Casa Lucio	56	La Oreja del Oro	22
Casa Paco	40		

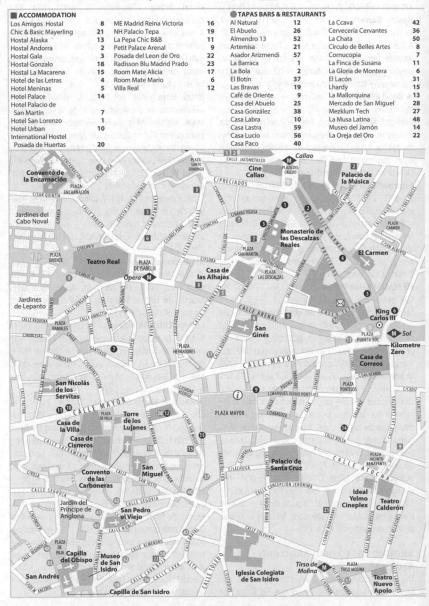

Aparto Suites Jardines de Sabatini Cuesta San Vicente 16 ☎915 425 900, ⓦjardinesdesabatini.com; Ⓜ Plaza España/Príncipe Pío; map pp.62–63. Convenient location in between Pza. España and Príncipe Pío station, this upmarket apartment complex with a rooftop terrace overlooking the royal palace offers studios and suites with small kitchen areas that sleep up to three people. Studio **€85**, suite **€150**

Casón del Tormes C/Río 7 ☎915 419 746, ⓦhotelcasondeltormes.com; Ⓜ Plaza de España; map pp.62–63. A neat and functional 63-room hotel in a surprisingly quiet street off Pza. España, the *Casón del Tormes* is a very good option in this price range. Rooms are comfortable, en suite and a/c, and the English-speaking staff are helpful. Triples available from €115. **€84**

		● BARS		■ CLUBS		● SHOPS	
Palacio de Anglona	43	Alhambra	20	Coco	4	El Arco Artesania	15
Paradis Madrid	16	Cervecería Alemana	35	Joy Madrid	6	Area Real Madrid	5
La Platería	49	Cervecería Santa Ana	33	Torero	9	Casa de Diego	6
Posada de la Villa	47	Del Diego	3			Casa Mira	8
Prada a Tope	23	Delic	55	■ MUSIC VENUES		Casa Yustas	9
La Sanabresa	51	Dos Gardenias	46	Cardamomo	8	La Central	1
Taberna La Dolores	41	La Fidula	44	Café Berlín	2	Desnivel	16
Tapassentao	45	The Glass Bar	18	Café Central	11	El Flamenco Vive	7
La Tapería del Prado	54	Gin Club/Mercado		Café Jazz Populart	12	FNAC	10
El Tempranillo	58	de la Reina	5	Las Carboneras	10	Geppetto	2
La Trucha	29	Museo Chicote	4	Casa Patas	13	Imaginarium	4
La Vaca Veronica	53	Naturbier	34	La Coquette	5	José Ramírez	14
Vadebaco	32	La Venencia	24	Oba Oba	1	La Librería	11
Vi-cool	39	Viva Madrid	30	El Sol	3	Mariano Madrueño	3
Yerbabuena	17			El Son	7	Mercado de San Miguel	12
						Seseña	13

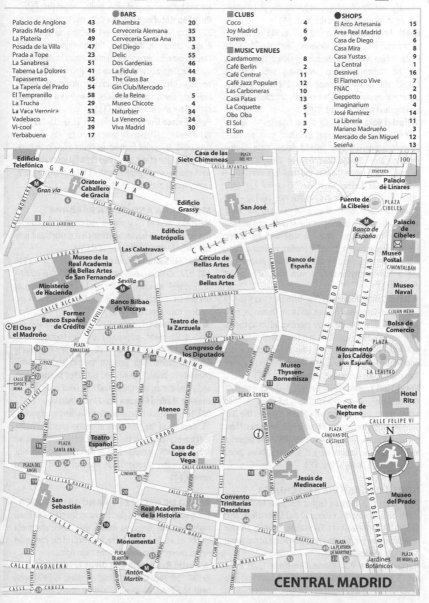

CENTRAL MADRID

1

Hostal Andorra Gran Vía 33, 7º ☎915 323 116, ⓦhostalandorra.com; ⓂCallao; map pp.102–103. Simple, clean and homely *hostal*, with bathrooms and a/c in all the compact rooms. **€45**

Hostal Buenos Aires Gran Vía 61, 2º ☎915 420 102, ⓦhostalbuenosaires-madrid.com; ⓂPlaza de España; map pp.62–63. Twenty-five pleasantly decorated rooms with a/c, satellite TV and modern bathrooms, plus double-glazing to keep out much of the noise. **€61**

Hotel Emperador Gran Vía 53 ☎915 472 800, ⓦemperadorhotel.com; ⓂSanto Domingo/Plaza de España; map pp.62–63. The main reason to come here is for the stunning rooftop swimming pool with its magnificent views. Otherwise, this 232-room hotel is rather impersonal, though the recently refurbished rooms are large and well decorated. **€100**

★**Hostal Gala** C/Costanilla de los Ángeles 15. ☎915 419 692, ⓦhostalgala.com; ⓂCallao; map pp.102–103. An upmarket, very tasteful *hostal* close to the shopping areas around Gran Vía. The slickly decorated rooms have a/c, power showers and small balconies. **€70**

Hotel de las Letras Gran Vía 11 ☎915 237 980, ⓦhoteldelasletras.com; ⓂGran Vía; map pp.102–103. Design-conscious hotel housed in a beautiful early nineteenth-century building at the smarter end of Gran Vía. The stylish rooms come complete with flat-screen TVs and pillow menus. There's a rooftop cocktail terrace, while downstairs, there's a smooth bar and lounge area and a high-quality restaurant with reasonably priced dishes. **€132**

★**Hotel Santo Domingo** C/San Bernardo 1 ☎915 479 800; ⓦhotelsantodomingo.es. ⓂSanto Domingo; map pp.62–63. What with the jungle paintings adorning the car park, the private art collection and the rooftop swimming pool with views over the city, this Mercure hotel is full of nice surprises. Rooms have tasteful individual decor, carpeted floors, large beds and walk-in shower rooms. **€111**

Hotel Tirol C/Marqués de Urquijo 4 ☎915 481 900, ⓦt3tirol.com; ⓂArgüelles; map pp.62–63. A good option if you are travelling with young children, the *Tirol* provides family rooms with a double bed and bunks. There is a play area too and the Parque del Oeste and *teleférico* into the Casa de Campo are just a stone's throw away; €120–180 for a family of four. **€80**

NORTH OF GRAN VÍA AND CHUECA

North of Gran Vía, there are further wedges of *hostales* and hotels on and around C/Fuencarral and C/Hortaleza, near ⓂGran Vía. To the east of C/Fuencarral, Chueca is another nightlife centre and the city's *zona gay*, home to numerous bars, clubs and restaurants.

Hostal Zamora Pza. Vázquez de Mella 1, 4º izqda ☎915 217 031, ⓦhostalzamora.com; ⓂGran Vía; map pp.62–63. There are seventeen well-kept, simple rooms in this pleasant *hostal* overlooking the plaza. All have modern bathrooms, TV and a/c. There are good-value family rooms, too. **€51**

Hotel San Lorenzo C/Clavel 8 ☎915 213 057, ⓦhotel-sanlorenzo.com; ⓂGran Vía; map pp.102–103. A former *hostal* that has been upgraded to a neat and tidy three-star hotel offering clean and comfortable rooms with a/c and bathrooms; quadruples available from €80. **€50**

Only You Hotel and Lounge C/Barquillo 21 ☎910 052 222, ⓦonlyyouhotels.com; ⓂChueca; map pp.62–63. A new arrival on the scene, this boutique-style hotel, housed in a refurbished nineteenth-century building is in a great location between Chueca and Recoletos. There are seventy very swish, individually decorated rooms, including seven upmarket suites, as well as a gastro and cocktail bar and a small gym. **€135**

Petit Palace Ducal C/Hortaleza 3, 3º ☎915 211 043, ⓦhotelpetitpalaceducalchueca.com; ⓂGran Vía; map pp.62–63. Upgraded from an old *hostal* a few years back, this is now one of the self-styled Petit Palace chain. Its 58 sleek rooms come complete with all manner of mod cons. Family rooms available. **€100**

MALASAÑA AND SANTA BÁRBARA

Malasaña, west of C/Fuencarral and centred around Pza. Dos de Mayo, is a former working-class district, and now one of the main nightlife areas of Madrid.

Hostal Sil/Serranos C/Fuencarral 95, 2º & 3º ☎914 488 972, ⓦsilserranos.com; ⓂTribunal; map pp.62–63. Two well-managed *hostales*, run by a friendly owner, at the quieter end of C/Fuencarral, functional rooms with a/c, modern bathrooms and TV. **€55**

★**Hotel Abalú** C/Pez 19 ☎915 314 744, ⓦhotelabalu.com; ⓂNoviciado; map pp.62–63. This boutique hotel, which is a little north of Gran Vía, has some individually designed rooms with personal touches such as mini-chandeliers, butterfly prints and patterned mirrors. Suites and a two-person apartment available. Good value. **€75**

Innside Madrid Genova Pza. Alonso Martínez 3 ☎912 062 160, ⓦhotelabalu.com; Ⓜmelia.com; map pp.62–63. Another of the new wave of design-conscious hotels that have sprung up in the city in recent years, the *Genova* is blessed with an excellent location on the plaza, 65 airy, modern rooms, a cocktail bar, small gym and breakfast room. **€140**

PASEO DE RECOLETOS AND SALAMANCA

This is Madrid at its most chic: the Bond Street/Rue de Rivoli region of smart shops and equally well-heeled apartment blocks. It's a safe, pleasant area, just north of the Parque del Retiro, though a fair walk from the main sights.

★**Hostal Residencia Don Diego** C/Velázquez 45, 5º ☎914 350 760, ⓦhostaldondiego.com; ⓂVelázquez; map pp.62–63. Although officially a *hostal*, this is much more like a hotel. All the neat, quiet and comfortable rooms have a/c and satellite TV. Reasonably priced for this upmarket area. English-speaking staff. **€65**

Hotel Orfila C/Orfila 6 ☎917 027 770, ⊛hotelorfila .com; Ⓜ Colón/Alonso Martínez; map pp.62–63. Exclusive boutique hotel housed in a beautiful nineteenth-century mansion on a quiet street north of Alonso Martínez. Twelve of the exquisite rooms are suites, and there's an elegant terrace for tea and drinks, as well as an

upmarket restaurant, too. Of course, none of this comes cheap. **€255**

Petit Palace Embassy C/Serrano 46 ☎914 313 060, ⊛www.petitpalace.com; Colón/Goya; map pp.62–63. A four-star member of the sleek Petit Palace Hotels chain, close to Pza. Colón and in the middle of the upmarket Salamanca shopping district. The *Embassy* has 75 rooms, including ten family rooms for up to four people. Free broadband internet access and flat-screen TVs. **€100**

EATING

Madrid's range of **eating** establishments is legion, and includes tapas bars, cafés, *marisquerías* (seafood bars) and *restaurantes*. At almost any of our recommendations you could happily eat your fill – money permitting – though at bars, *madrileños* usually eat just a tapa or share a *ración* of the house speciality, then move on to repeat the procedure down the road. While cafés do serve food, they are much more places to drink coffee, have a *copa* or *caña*, or read the papers. Some also act as a meeting place for the semi-formal *tertulia* – a kind of discussion/drinking group, popular among Madrid intellectuals of the past and revived in the 1980s.

SOL, PLAZA MAYOR AND ÓPERA

The central area is the most varied in Madrid in terms of price and food. Indeed, there can be few places in the world that rival the streets around Puerta del Sol for sheer number of places to eat and drink. Around the smarter Ópera district, you need to be more selective, while on Pza. Mayor itself, stick to drinks. Unless indicated otherwise, all these places are easily reached from Metro Sol.

CAFÉS

Café de Oriente Pza. de Oriente 2; Ⓜ Ópera; ⊛grupolezama.es; map pp.102–103. Sophisticated Parisian-style affair with a popular *terraza* looking out towards the Palacio Royal. Daily 8.30am–1.30am.

La Mallorquina Puerta del Sol 2; Ⓜ Sol; ⊛pastelerialamallorquina.es; map pp.102–103. Old-fashioned pastry shop right on Sol and good for breakfast or snacks – try one of their *napolitanas* (cream slices) in the sunny upstairs salon. Daily 9am–9.15pm.

TAPAS BARS

El Abuelo C/Núñez de Arce 5; map pp.102–103. There's a *comedor* at the back of this down-to-earth bar, where you can order a selection of delicious *raciones* – the *croquetas* are especially good – and a jug of house wine. Mon–Thurs 1–4pm & 7pm–midnight, Fri & Sun noon–4pm & 7pm–1am.

Las Bravas C/Alvarez Gato 3; ⊛lasbravas.com; map pp.102–103. As the name suggests, *patatas bravas* (spicy potatoes) are the tapa to try at this bar, which has patented its own version of the sauce; the *tortilla* is pretty good, too. On the outside of the bar are novelty mirrors, a hangover from the days when this was a barber's and the subject of a story by Valle Inclán. Standing room only and bright lights mean it is not to everyone's liking, though. Other branches nearby at C/Espoz y Mina 13 and Pasaje Mathéu 5. Daily

12.30–4.30pm & 8.30pm–midnight.

★**Casa del Abuelo** C/Victoria 12; ⊛lacasadelabuelo .es; map pp.102–103. Sister bar to the nearby *El Abuelo*, this tiny, highly atmospheric *madrileño* institution just serves its cloyingly sweet red house wine, beer and great cooked prawns – try them *al ajillo* (in garlic) or *a la plancha* (fried). Mon–Thurs & Sun noon–midnight, Fri & Sat noon–2am.

Casa Labra C/Tetuán 12 ☎915 310 081, ⊛casalabra .es; map pp.102–103. A great, traditional place, where the Spanish Socialist Party was founded in 1879. Order a drink at the bar and a *ración* of *bacalao* (cod fried in batter) or some of the best *croquetas* in town at the counter to the right of the door. There's a fairly expensive restaurant at the back with classic *madrileño* food on offer. Bar: daily 9.30am–3.30pm & 5–11pm. Restaurant: daily 1.15–3.30pm & 8.15–10pm.

Lhardy C/San Jerónimo 8 ☎915 213 385, ⊛lhardy .com; map pp.102–103. Dating back over 175 years, *Lhardy* is one of Madrid's most famous and expensive restaurants. Once the haunt of royalty, it's a beautiful place but greatly overpriced (minimum €60). Downstairs, however, there's a wonderful bar/shop, where you can snack on *canapés*, *fino* (dry sherry) and *consommé*, without breaking the bank. Mon–Sat breakfast 9–11.45am, lunch 1–3.15pm, dinner 8.30–10.45pm; Sun breakfast 9–11.15am, lunch 1–3.15pm; July daily 9am–3.30pm; closed Aug.

★**Mercado de San Miguel** Pza. de San Miguel ⊛mercadodesanmiguel.es; map pp.102–103. Transformed from a traditional neighbourhood market into a hip location for an *aperitivo* and a spot of tapas, this beautiful wrought-iron *mercado* is worth exploring at almost any time of day. There's something for everyone, from vermouth and champagne to salt cod, oysters and sushi. Mon, Wed & Sun 10am–midnight, Thurs–Sat 10am–2am.

Museo del Jamón C/San Jerónimo 6; map pp.102–103. The largest branch of this ubiquitous Madrid chain,

1

from whose ceilings are suspended hundreds of *jamones* (hams). The best – and they are not cheap – are the *jabugos* from the Sierra Morena, though a ham croissant certainly won't break the bank. Daily 9am–midnight.

La Oreja de Oro C/Victoria 9; map pp.102–103. Standing room only in this spit-and-sawdust bar just opposite *La Casa del Abuelo*. Try the excellent *pulpo a la Gallega* (sliced octopus layered over a bed of potatoes and seasoned with cayenne pepper) washed down with Ribeiro wine served in terracotta bowls. The speciality *oreja* (pig's ear) is also on offer of course. Mon–Thurs & Sun noon–midnight, Fri & Sat noon–2am; closed Aug.

RESTAURANTS

El Botín C/Cuchilleros 17 ☎913 664 217, ⊛botin.es; ⓜSol/Tirso de Molina; map pp.102–103. Established in 1725, the picturesque *El Botín* is cited in the *Guinness Book of Records* as Europe's oldest restaurant. Favoured by Hemingway, inevitably it's become a tourist haunt but not such a bad one, with quality Castilian roasts – especially suckling pig (*cochinillo*) from Segovia and roast lamb (*cordero asado*). Around €45 per head. Daily 1–4pm & 8pm–midnight.

★ El Buey Pza. de la Marina Española 1 ☎915 413 041, ⊛restauranteelbuey.com; ⓜSanto Domingo; map pp.62–63. A meat-eaters' paradise specializing in steak – which you fry up yourself on a sizzling hotplate. Very good side dishes, too, including a superb leek and seafood pie,

and excellent home-made desserts. All for around €35 a head. Mon–Sat 1–4pm & 9pm–midnight, Sun 1–4pm.

Casa Paco Pza. Puerta Cerrada 11 ☎913 663 166, ⊛casapaco1933.com; ⓜLa Latina/Sol; map pp.102–103. This classic, traditional *comedor*, with no-nonsense service, dishes out some of the best-prepared meat dishes in town. Specializes in sirloin steak (*solomillo*), and another delicious cut known as *cebón de buey*. Count on spending about €35. Mon–Sat 7am–11.30pm; closed Aug.

La Finca de Susana C/Arlabán 4 ⊛lafinca-restaurant.com; ⓜSevilla; map pp.102–103. One of two great-value restaurants set up by a group of Catalan friends (the other is *La Gloria de Montera* just off Gran Vía (map pp.102–103). Best at lunchtime, with the tasty €10 set menu consisting of simple dishes served with a little imagination. Tables are close together and you'll need to arrive early to avoid queuing, as you can't book. Daily 1–3.30pm & 8.30–11.30pm.

PLAZA DE SANTA ANA AND HUERTAS

You should spend at least an evening eating and drinking at the historic, tiled bars in this central area. Restaurants are good, too, and frequented as much by locals as tourists.

TAPAS BARS

★ Casa González C/Leon 12 ⊛casagonzalez.es; map pp.102–103. As you'd expect, this great little bar on the busy C/Leon has an extensive range of wines and cheese on

---

MADRID'S VEGETARIAN RESTAURANTS

Madrid has a growing number of good-value **vegetarian restaurants**, scattered about the centre. These include:

Al Natural C/Zorrilla 11 ☎913 694 709, ⊛alnatural.biz; ⓜSevilla; map pp.102–103. On the scene some 20 years, this vegetarian continues to serve up good-quality dishes often made from its own produce. The ever-changing set lunch costs €12.20 while the more elaborate taster menu, with options such as mushroom and chestnut risotto and pumpkin gnocchi, is €23. Mon–Sat 1–4pm & 8.30–11.30pm, Sun 1–4pm.

Artemisa C/Ventura de la Vega 4 ☎914 295 092, ⊛restaurantesvegetarianosartemisa.com; ⓜSevilla; C/Tres Cruces 4 ☎915 218 721; ⓜGran Vía; map pp.102–103. Two branches of this long-standing popular vegetarian (you may have to wait for a table), good for veggie pizzas and paellas, superb vegetable dishes and an imaginative range of salads and soups. Reasonable prices at around €25 per head, lunchtime set menu at €11.90. Daily 1.30–4pm, 9pm–midnight.

Crucina C/Divino Pastor 30 ☎914 453 364; ⊛web mastercrucina.wix.com/crucina ⓜSan Bernardo/Bilbao; map pp.62–63. Innovative "raw vegan" food

such as seaweed salad and apricot crêpes. A three-course meal costs under €30. Mon–Thurs 1–4pm & 8–11.45, Fri & Sat 1–4pm & 8–midnight, Sun 1–4.30pm.

Vegaviana C/Pelayo 35 ☎913 080 381; ⓜChueca; map pp.62–63. There's a wide range of vegetarian options with an international twist at this small eatery in the heart of Chueca. There's a free-range chicken option for non-veggies, too. Very good value, with big portions meaning you'll struggle to break the €20 mark. Tues–Sat 1.30–4pm & 9–11.30pm.

★ Yerbabueba C/Bordadores 3 ☎915 480 811, ⊛yerbabuena.ws; ⓜÓpera; map pp.102–103. A cut above most of its competitors, this friendly vegetarian has an extensive and well-presented range of dishes. Crêpes with courgettes, leek and potato stuffing, tempura aubergines with sugar-cane syrup and a hearty pumpkin pie are among the mains. There is a children's menu and some excellent desserts too. Mon–Sat 1–4.30pm & 8pm–midnight, Sun 1–4.30pm.

CLOCKWISE FROM TOP LEFT *CAFÉ COMERCIAL* (P.111); MUSEO ARQUEOLÓGICO (P.93); EL RASTRO (P.72); REINA SOFÍA (P.83) >

1

MADRID CUISINE

Thanks to its status as Spanish capital, Madrid has long provided a home to **almost every regional style of Spanish cooking** from Castilian roasts, Galician seafood and Andalucian fried fish, to Asturian stews, Valencian paellas and Basque *nueva cocina*.

The city also has its own range of home-spun dishes with the famous *cocido madrileño*, a three-course stew of various cuts of meat, chorizo, chickpea and vegetables, topping the list. Other traditional favourites include *callos* (tripe in a spicy tomato sauce), *oreja* (pig's ears), *caracoles* (snails) and a range of offal-based dishes.

But Madrid is becoming increasingly cosmopolitan and dozens of **foreign cuisines** have appeared on the scene in recent years. There are some good Peruvian, Argentinian, Middle Eastern and Italian places and a growing number of oriental-influenced restaurants with some inventive fusion-style cuisine.

offer, but it also serves up other great tapas including a fantastic *salmorejo*, a range of speciality sausages from around Spain, and some imaginative *tostas* covered in a variety of tasty patés. Mon–Thurs 9.30am–midnight, Fri & Sat 9.30am–1pm, Sun 11am–6pm.

Cervecería Cervantes Pza. de Jesús 7 Ⓜ Antón Martín; map pp.102–103. Prawns are the speciality here – the *tosta de gambas* is delicious – but there's a wide range of other tapas, and the beer is good, too. An excellent place for an *aperitivo*. Mon–Sat noon–midnight, Sun noon–4pm.

El Lacón C/Manuel Fernández y González 8 Ⓦ meson ellacon.com; Ⓜ Sol; map pp.102–103. A large Galician bar-restaurant with plenty of seats upstairs. Great *pulpo*, *caldo gallego* (meat and vegetable broth) and *empanadas*. They also do a *menú exprés* at lunchtime consisting of a single course and a drink for just €4. Daily 1–4pm & 8pm– midnight; closed Aug.

★**Taberna La Dolores** Pza. de Jesús 4; Ⓜ Antón Martín; map pp.102–103. Splendid *canapés* at this popular and friendly tiled bar at the bottom of Huertas. The beer is good, and the food specialities include Roquefort and anchovy, and smoked-salmon *canapés*. Get here early if you want a space at the bar. Mon–Thurs & Sun 11am–1am, Fri & Sat 11am–2am.

La Trucha C/Manuel Fernández y González 3 Ⓣ 914 295 833; Ⓜ Antón Martín; map pp.102–103. An ever-popular tapas bar and moderately priced restaurant sandwiched between Santa Ana and C/Echegaray. Andalucian-style *pescaito frito*, delicious smoked fish and *pimientos de Padrón* are specialities. Mon–Sat noon–4pm & 7.30pm–midnight; closed Sun.

RESTAURANTS

Mezklum Tech C/Príncipe 16 Ⓣ 915 218 911, Ⓦ mezklum.com; Ⓜ Sevilla; map pp.102–103. A hyper-cool restaurant decked out in shades of mauve and white and serving a fine array of Mediterranean dishes, with good salads and pastas. It has a good-value lunch time set menu for €11, while there are taster menus in the evening

for €20 or €25. Mon–Thurs 1.30–4pm & 9pm–12.30am, Fri & Sat 1.30–4.30pm & 9pm–1am, Sun 1.30–4.30pm.

Prada a Tope C/Príncipe 11 Ⓣ 914 295 221; Ⓜ Sevilla; map pp.102–103. Quality produce from El Bierzo in León at this branch of the restaurant chain; the *pimientos asados*, *morcilla* and *tortilla* are extremely tasty. Expect to pay €25 for a full meal. Tues–Sat noon–4pm & 8pm–midnight, Sun noon–4pm.

La Sanabresa C/Amor de Diós 12 Ⓣ 914 290 338; Ⓜ Antón Martín; map pp.102–103. A real local, with a TV in one corner, and an endless supply of customers who come for its good-quality and reasonably priced dishes. Don't miss the grilled aubergines. *Menú del día* for around €10, otherwise €20. Mon–Sat 1–4.30pm & 8.30pm–midnight.

★**La Vaca Verónica** C/Moratín 38 Ⓣ 914 297 827, Ⓦ lavacaveronica.es; Ⓜ Antón Martín; map pp.102– 103. Excellent Argentinian-style meat, really good fresh pasta in imaginative sauces, quality fish dishes and tasty vegetables. Try the *filet Verónica* and the *carabinero con pasta*. The lunchtime menu is a good deal at €15 and there is an evening and weekend one for €20. The service is friendly too. Mon–Sat 1.30–4.30pm & 8.30pm– midnight, Sun 1.30–4.30pm.

Vadebaco C/Prado 4 Ⓣ 915 417 017, Ⓦ vadebaco.com; Ⓜ Sevilla/Antón Martín; map pp.102–103. Creative tapas and a vast range of wines are on offer at this relatively new arrival just off Pza. Santa Ana. The grilled octopus with spicy potatoes and mushroom risotto are both recommended. Cocktail bar and a €12 lunchtime menu. Mon–Sat 1–5pm & 8pm–2am, Sun 1–5pm.

★**Vi-cool** C/Huertas 12 Ⓣ 914 294 913, Ⓦ vi-cool.com; Ⓜ Antón Martín; map pp.102–103. Catalan celebrity chef Sergi Arola's latest – and most affordable – venture in Madrid. The low-key, minimalist interior provides the setting for some simple, but classy and creative offerings including marinated sardines in tomato oil, fried langoustines in a curry and mint sauce, as well as gourmet hamburgers and pizzas. The set lunch is just under €13 while the tapas selection is €20. Daily 1–4pm & 8pm–midnight.

1

LA LATINA AND LAVAPIÉS

South from Sol and Huertas are the quarters of La Latina and Lavapiés, whose patchwork of tiny streets retains an appealing neighbourhood feel, and are home to a great selection of bars and restaurants.

TAPAS BARS

★**Almendro 13** C/Almendro 13; ⓜLa Latina; map pp.102–103. Always packed at weekends, this fashionable wood-panelled bar serves great *fino* from chilled black bottles. Tuck into the house specials of *huevos rotos* (fried eggs on a bed of crisps) and *roscas rellenas* (rings of bread stuffed with various meats). Daily 1–4pm & 7pm–midnight.

Los Caracoles "Casa Amadeo" Pza. Cascorro 18; ⓜLa Latina; map pp.62–63. A favourite since the 1940s, and as the name suggests the *caracoles* (snails) are the thing to eat. The place to come after a trek around the Rastro – although it will be heaving and keep an eye on the bill. Tues–Fri 11am–4pm, Sat 11am–4pm & 7–10pm, Sun 10.30am–4pm.

★**La Chata** C/Cava Baja 24; ⓜLa Latina; map pp.102–103. One of the most traditional, and popular, tiled tapas bars in Madrid, with hams hanging from the ceiling, taurine and football mementoes on the walls, and a good selection of *raciones*, including excellent *rabo de toro* (oxtail) and *pimientos del piquillo rellenos* (stuffed peppers). Mon 1.30–4.30pm & 8.30pm–1am, Wed 8.30pm–1am, Thurs–Sun 1–4.30pm & 8.30pm–1am.

★**Juana La Loca** Pza. Puerta de Moros 4 ⓦjuanalalocamadrid.com; ⓜLa Latina; map pp.62–63. Fashionable hangout serving inventive tapas – a great *tortilla* with caramelized onion, tuna carpaccio and smoked salmon with curry sauce – and a great selection of very tasty, but fairly pricey, *canapés*. Mon 8pm–midnight, Tues–Thurs 1–5pm & 8pm–midnight, Fri 1–5pm & 8pm–1am, Sat 1pm–1am, Sun 1pm–midnight.

Melo's C/Avemaría 44; ⓜLavapíes; map pp.62–63. It's standing room only at this very popular Galician bar serving huge *zapatillas* (slippers of Galician country bread filled with *lacón* and *queso*) and great *pimientos de Padrón*. Tues–Sat 8pm–1am; closed Aug.

La Musa Latina C/Costanilla San Andrés 12 ⓦgrupo lamusa.com; ⓜLa Latina; map pp.102–103. Another style-conscious restaurant on the La Latina scene. Serves a great €11 menu and a decent selection of modern tapas. It has a cool brick-walled bar downstairs with DJ sessions in the evenings. Mon–Wed 1pm–1am, Thurs 1pm–1.30pm, Fri 1pm–2am, Sat 10am–2pm, Sun 10am–1pm.

Taberna de Antonio Sánchez C/Mesón de Paredes 13 ☎915 397 826, ⓦtabernaantoniosanchez.com; ⓜTirso de Molina; pp.62–63. Said to be the oldest *taberna* in Madrid, this Lavapiés bar has an appropriately dark, wooden interior complete with stuffed bulls' heads (one of which killed Antonio Sánchez, the son of the founder). *Rabo de toro* (oxtail), *tortilla*, *callos* (tripe) and *caracoles* (snails) are among the classic *madrileño* tapas on offer. Mon–Sat noon–4pm & 8pm–midnight, Sun noon–4.30pm.

★**Tapassentao** C/Príncipe Anglona 1; ⓜLa Latina; map pp.102–103. Just opposite the church of San Pedro, this popular bar serves up a wide range of interesting tapas. Favourites include fried aubergines, vegetable tempura and battered mushrooms. Tues–Thurs 12.30pm–midnight, Fri–Sun 12.30pm–2am.

★**El Tempranillo** Cava Baja 38; ⓜLa Latina; map pp.102–103. A stylish little bar serving tasty tapas and a vast range of Spanish wines by the glass – a great place to discover a new favourite. Daily 1–4pm & 8pm–midnight; closed 2 weeks in Aug.

★**Txirimiri** C/Humilladero 6 ⓦtxirimiri.es; ⓜLa Latina; map pp.62–63. Fantastic range of tapas and *pintxos* in this friendly and very popular bar just beside the Mercado de la Cebada. Mouthwatering combinations include *tortilla* with caramelized onion, langoustine *croquetas*, mushroom risotto and the house speciality, the Unai hamburger *pintxo*. Daily noon–midnight.

RESTAURANTS

Asador Arizmendi Pza. Tirso de Molina 7, 1° (entrance on C/Jesús y María) ☎914 295 030, ⓦasadorarizmendi .com; ⓜTirso de Molina; map pp.102–103. The new ownership has retained this restaurant's traditional appeal with Basque-Navarran specialities. There's a €25 executive menu (Mon–Thurs and Friday lunch) with choices that include

---

SUMMER IN MADRID

Although things have changed as Madrid comes into line with the rest of Europe, the Spanish capital experiences a **partial shut-down in the summer**; from the end of July, you'll suddenly find that many of the bars, restaurants and offices are closed, and their inhabitants gone to the coast and countryside. Only in September does the city open fully for business again.

Luckily for visitors, and those *madrileños* who choose to remain, the main sights and museums stay open, and the summer nightlife takes on a momentum of its own in outdoor terrace bars, or *terrazas*. In addition, the city council organizes a major programme of entertainment, Los Veranos de la Villa, and overall it's not a bad time to be in town, so long as you can cope with the soaring temperatures and you're not trying to get anything done.

1

TOP CHEFS IN MADRID

Aside from the burgeoning international cuisine scene in Madrid, further good news for gastronomes is that several of the **country's top chefs** have established flagship restaurants in the capital.

El Club Allard (C/Ferraz 2 ☎915 590 939, ⓦ elcluballard.com; ⓜ Argüelles; map pp.62–63. María Marte took over at the Michelin-starred *El Club Allard* after head chef Diego Guerrero departed. The Dominican, who worked her way up from office cleaner to leading the kitchen, has maintained the high standard at this former club and offers three supremely creative set menus at €86, €98 and €116. Tues–Sat 1.30–4pm & 9pm–midnight.

Diverxo C/Pensamiento 28 ☎915 700 766, ⓦ diverxo.com; ⓜ Tetuán; map pp.62–63; scheduled to move to the NH Hotel Eurobuilding at C/Padre Damián 23. Madrid's only restaurant in possession of three Michelin stars, *Diverxo* is run by chef David Muñoz and has a deserved reputation for stunning presentation, mouthwatering food and unpretentious service. As you would expect, prices are sky-high, with taster menus starting at €75 a head but the final bill often ending up close to the €200 mark. Tues–Sat 2–4.30pm & 9–11.30pm.

Gastro C/Zurbano 31 ☎913 102 169, ⓦ sergiarola .es; ⓜ Alonso Martínez; map pp.62–63. Sergi Arola has set up this Michelin-starred restaurant, which offers a constantly changing range of fixed courses on a set menu (€49–135 without wine). Tues–Sat 2–3.30pm & 9–11.30pm. Arola has also opened the more accessible *Vi-Cool* at C/Huertas 12 (see p.108).

Ramón Freixa Madrid C/Claudio Coello 67 ☎917 818 262, ⓦ ramonfreixamadrid.com; ⓜ Serrano; map pp.62–63. Catalan chef Ramon Freixa's flagship restaurant is situated in the luxury surroundings of the *Selenza* hotel and is now the proud owner of two Michelin stars. Creative and impeccably presented dishes from an ever-changing menu featuring superb meat and fish options and new twists on Spanish classics. À la carte dishes range from €35 to €60, while there is a selection of taster menus available from €80 to €125 (excluding wine). Only space for 35 diners, so book well in advance. Tues–Sat 1.30–3.30pm & 9–11pm; closed Easter, Aug & Christmas.

Santceloni Hotel Hesperia Paseo de la Castellana 57 ☎912 108 840, ⓦ restaurantesantceloni.com; ⓜ Gregorio Marañon; map pp.62–63. Óscar Velasco runs this Michelin-starred restaurant, with stunning, but hugely expensive menus at €150 and €180. Closed Sat lunch, Sun & Aug.

---

leek and prawn pie, steak and mandarin sorbet. Tues–Sat 1.30–4pm & 8.30–midnight, Sun 1.30–4pm; closed Aug.

Casa Lastra C/Olivar 3 ☎913 690 837; ⓜ Lavapiés/ Antón Martín; map pp.102–103. Very popular local restaurant serving classic Asturian fare, including *entrecot al cabrales* (steak in a strong blue-cheese sauce), *fabada* and, of course, *sidra* (cider). Big portions, and the set lunch is very good value at around €13. Mon, Tues, Thurs–Sat 1–4pm & 8pm–midnight, Sun 1–4pm.

Casa Lucio C/Cava Baja 35 ☎913 653 252, ⓦ casalucio .es; ⓜ La Latina; map pp.102–103. A Madrid institution famous for its Castilian specialities such as *cocido*, *callos* (tripe) and roasts, cooked to perfection. Booking is essential. Count on around €50 a head. If you can't stretch to a full meal, try some of the specialities in the front bar. Daily 1–4pm & 8.30pm–midnight; closed Aug.

LaCcava C/Segovia 8 ☎915 423 716, ⓦ laccava.com; ⓜ La Latina; map pp.102–103. On the ground floor of an eighteenth-century building this is a cocktail bar and café; downstairs it's a restaurant serving a stylish range of modern tapas and fusion dishes perfect for sharing, and at very competitive prices (€13–15 for larger dishes). Good salads and vegetarian options too. The decor is based on a Mini Cooper theme so a fun place to go with kids. Tues &

Wed 8pm–12.30am, Thurs 8pm–2am, Fri 8pm–2.30am, Sat 1.30pm–2.30am, Sun 1.30–8pm.

Palacio de Anglona C/Segovia 13 ☎913 653 753, ⓦ palaciodeanglona.com; ⓜ La Latina/Ópera; map pp.102–103. Housed in the cellars of an old mansion and decked out in black and white decor, this good-value restaurant has a range of imaginative dishes such as salmon and mussels and spinach salad with goats' cheese, raisins and walnuts (around €8–9 for mains). Tues–Sun 1.30–4pm & 8.30pm–2am.

★**Posada de la Villa** C/Cava Baja 9 ☎913 661 860, ⓦ posadadelavilla.es; ⓜ La Latina; map pp.102–103. The most attractive-looking restaurant in La Latina, spread over three floors of a seventeenth-century mansion. Cooking is typically *madrileña*, including superb roast lamb. Reckon on a good €50 per person for the works – though you could get away with less. Mon–Sat 1–4pm & 8pm–midnight, Sun 1–4pm; closed Aug.

GRAN VÍA, PLAZA DE ESPAÑA AND BEYOND

On the Gran Vía, burger bars and fast-food joints tend to fill most of the gaps between shops and cinemas. However, there are a few good restaurants in and around the great avenue.

1

RESTAURANTS

★**La Barraca** C/Reina 29 ☎915 327 154, ⓦlabarraca .es; ⓂGran Vía/Banco de España; map pp.102–103. Step off the dingy street into this little slice of Valencia for some of the best paellas in town. Service is attentive but not overfussy, the starters are excellent, and there's a refreshing lemon sorbet for dessert. A three-course meal with wine will set you back around €30 a head. Daily 1–4.15pm & 8–11.45pm.

La Bola C/Bola 5 ☎915 476 930, ⓦlabola.es; ⓂSanto Domingo; map pp.102–103. Established in 1870, this is one of the places to go for *cocido madrileño* (soup followed by chickpeas and other vegetables and then a selection of meats), only served at lunchtime (€19). Don't plan on doing anything energetic afterwards, as it is incredibly filling. Service can be a little surly. No cards. Mon–Sat 1.30–5pm & 8.30–11pm, Sun 1.30–5pm; July–Sept 7; closed Sat eve and Sun.

★**Casa Mingo** Paseo de la Florida 34 ☎915 477 918, ⓦcasamingo.es; ⓂPríncipe Pío; map pp.62–63. Noisy, crowded and fun, *Casa Mingo* is a reasonably priced (around €15 a head) Asturian chicken and cider house just up the road from the Príncipe Pío. Tables are like gold dust, so loiter with your bottle of *sidra* in hand. Daily 10am–midnight.

Cornucopia C/Navas de Tolosa 9 ☎915 213 896, ⓦrestaurantecornucopia.com; ⓂCallao; map pp.102–103. Fusion-style food is on offer in this good-value restaurant on a quiet street between Callao and Ópera. The lunchtime menu, which is also available on Saturdays, is €11.50, while they also offer a special menu for €21.90 that includes dishes such as grilled tuna in soya sauce and couscous and pork steak stuffed with brie and apricots. Vegetarian options available. Daily 1.30–4.30pm & 7.30pm–midnight.

CHUECA AND SANTA BÁRBARA

Chueca – and Santa Bárbara to its north – have a combination of some superb traditional old bars and stylish new restaurants, as well as a vast amount of nightlife.

CAFÉS

Café Comercial Glorieta de Bilbao; ⓂBilbao; map pp.62–63. One of the city's most popular meeting points – a lovely traditional café, well positioned for the Chueca/ Santa Bárbara area. Daily 7.30am–1am.

TAPAS BARS

Baco & Beto C/Pelayo 24 ☎915 228 441, ⓦbaco-beto .com; ⓂChueca; map pp.62–63. Exceedingly tasty, creative tapas with great *tostas* and *canapés*. Try the courgette with melted brie and the *croquetas*. An excellent selection of wines, too. Mon–Fri 8pm–1am, Sat 2–4.30pm & 8pm–1am.

★**El Bocaito** C/Libertad 4–6 ☎915 321 219 ⓦbocaito .com; ⓂChueca; map pp.62–63. Munch away on a variety of delicious *canapés* and tapas, washed down with a cold beer, at this busy bar; their *Luisito* is the hottest *canapé* your tastebuds are ever likely to encounter. Mon–Sat 1–4pm & 8.30pm–midnight; closed two weeks in Aug.

Stop Madrid C/Hortaleza 11 ☎915 218 887, ⓦstopmadrid.es; ⓂGran Vía; map pp.62–63. An old-time bar specializing in *jamón*, chorizo and manchego cheese, as well as *vermut* on tap. The *Canapé Stop* of ham and tomato doused in olive oil is well worth a try. Daily 12.30pm–2am.

★**Taberna Angel Sierra** C/Gravina 11, Pza. Chueca ☎915 310 126; ⓂChueca; map pp.62–63. One of the classic bars of Madrid, with a traditional zinc counter, constantly washed down. Everyone drinks *vermut*, which is on tap and delicious, and free tapas of the most exquisite *boquerones en vinagre* are despatched; *raciones*, however, are a bit pricey. Daily noon–2am.

RESTAURANTS

El 26 de Libertad C/Libertad 26 ☎915 218 223; ⓂChueca; map pp.62–63. Enjoy creative cuisine at this newly refurbished restaurant popular with the Chueca locals. A good lunchtime set menu is available in the week, with more imaginative – and expensive – offerings in the evenings, but service can be slow. Around €25 a head. Mon & Sun 1.30pm–4pm, Tues–Sat 1.30pm–1.30am.

Annapurna C/Zurbano 5 ☎913 198 716, ⓦannapurna restaurante.com; ⓂColón; map pp.62–63. One of the best Indian restaurants in Madrid, especially if you go for the tandoori dishes or *thali*. Stylish decor and attentive service. There's a taster menu for €33 (Mon–Fri lunch). Mon–Sat 1.45–4pm & 9pm–midnight.

Bazaar C/Libertad 21 ☎915 233 905, ⓦrestaurant bazaar.com; ⓂChueca; map pp.62–63. Fusion-style cuisine with Mediterranean and Asian influences in this good-value Chueca restaurant decked out in white wood. The lunchtime set menu is around €11, though service is impersonal. No reservations, so arrive early to avoid a wait. Sun–Wed 1.15–4pm & 8.30–11.30pm, Thurs–Sat 1.15–4pm & 8.15pm–midnight.

Café Oliver C/Almirante 12 ☎915 217 379, ⓦcafeoliver.com; ⓂChueca; map pp.62–63. There are strong French and Moroccan influences at this trendy Chueca restaurant, with an imaginative set lunch at €15. A filling brunch of pastries, eggs and pancakes is on offer for the popular but overpriced Sunday brunch (€25). Mon–Thurs 1.30–4pm & 9pm–midnight, Fri & Sat 1.30–4pm & 9pm–1am, Sun 11.30am–4pm & 9pm–midnight; closed Sun eve & Mon in July & Aug.

Dray Martina C/Argensola 7 ☎910 810 056, ⓦdraymartina.com; ⓂAlonso Martínez; map pp.62–63. This new gastrobar is a café, restaurant and *bar de copas* all rolled into one. Trendy vintage-style decor provides the backdrop for this popular corner restaurant which serves up a

1

fresh and imaginative set lunch for around €12. Mon–Fri 8.30am–2am, Sat & Sun 10am–2am.

Momo C/Libertad 8 ☎915 327 348; ⓜChueca; map pp.62–63. Relocated a few hundred metres from its original home, this well-established eatery is the place to go for a lunchtime set menu with that little bit extra: interesting flavours, sauces and other creative touches. A selection of set menus available at midday, evening and weekends for €11.50–20. Mon–Thurs 1–4pm & 9pm–midnight, Fri & Sat 1–4pm & 9pm–1am.

My Veg C/Valverde 28 ☎915 311 702; ⓦmyveg.es; ⓜChueca/Gran Vía; map pp.62–63. Not, as the name would suggest, a vegetarian restaurant but vegetables are, nevertheless, given pride of place in this new arrival in Chueca. The menu changes according to the season but delights such as cream of asparagus with peppers, lemon and parmesan or fried squid with avocado and tomato sauce are on offer. Mains around €10–14. Mon 10am–6pm, Tues–Sat 10am–2am.

Salvador C/Barbieri 12 ☎915 214 524, ⓦcasasalvador madrid.com; ⓜChueca; map pp.62–63. A blast from the past, with bullfighting decor and specialities such as *rabo de toro* (bull's tail), *gallina en pepitoria*, fried *merluza* (hake) and *arroz con leche* (rice pudding), all of which are excellent. Set menu at €22 and à la carte around €30–35. Mon 1.30–4pm, Tues–Sat 1.30–4pm & 9–11.30pm.

La Tienda de Vinos (El Comunista) C/Augusto Figueroa 35 ☎915 217 021; ⓜChueca; map pp.62–63. A long-established, down-to-earth, no frills *comedor*; its unofficial (but always used) name dates back to its time as a student haunt under Franco. The garlic soup is recommended as are the lentejas (lentils) and the *croquetas*. Mains €7.50–12. Daily noon–4pm & 8pm–midnight.

Zara C/Barbieri 8 ☎915 322 074; ⓦrestaurantezara .com; ⓜChueca/Gran Vía; map pp.62–63. Excellent food at very good prices at this Cuban restaurant that has just relocated round the corner from its original home. *Ropa vieja* (strips of beef), fried yucca, minced beef with fried bananas and other specialities; the *daiquiris* are very good, too. Prices are moderate (under €30). Tues–Sat 1–4.30pm & 8–11.30pm; closed public hols.

MALASAÑA AND CHAMBERÍ

Malasaña is another characterful area, with a big nightlife scene and dozens of bars. Farther north, in Chamberí, the area around Pza. de Olavide – a real neighbourhood square – offers some good-value places, well off the tourist trail.

CAFÉS

Café del Ruiz C/Ruiz 11 ☎914 461 232; ⓜTribunal/Bilbao; map pp.62–63. A traditional café, serving coffee, cakes and cocktails. A top spot for a late drink or a pep-up coffee before going on to one of the nearby clubs. Mon–Sat 3.30pm–2am, Sun 3.30pm–midnight.

TAPAS BARS

Albur C/Manuela Malasaña 15 ☎915 942 733, ⓦrestaurantealbur.com; ⓜBilbao; map pp.62–63. Wooden tables, rustic decor and excellent food, although the service can be a little slow. The spicy mussels and the baked octopus are both worth sampling; the well-kept wines are the ideal accompaniment. There is a decent €11.50 *menú del día* too. Mon–Thurs 12.30–5pm & 7.30pm–midnight, Fri 12.30–5pm & 7.30pm–1.30am, Sat 1pm–1.30am, Sun 1pm–midnight.

★**La Musa** C/Manuel Malasaña 18 ☎914 487 558, ⓦgrupolamusa.com; ⓜBilbao; map pp.62–63. It's easy to see why *La Musa* – a café, bar and restaurant all rolled into one – has become such a firm favourite on the Malasaña scene. A variety of imaginative – and very tasty – tapas, generous helpings, a strong wine list and chic decor are all part of the recipe for success. Mon–Thurs 9am–1pm, Fri 9am–2am, Sat 1pm–2am, Sun 1pm–1am.

RESTAURANTS

La Giralda C/Hartzenbusch 12 ☎914 457 779, ⓦrestauranteslagiralda.com; ⓜBilbao; map pp.62–63. An *andaluz* fish and seafood restaurant of very high quality: perfectly cooked *chipirones*, *calamares* and all the standards, plus wonderful *mero* (grouper). A second branch, across the road at no. 15, does a similarly accomplished job on *pescados fritos*. Around €30–35 per person. Mon–Sat 1–4pm & 8pm–midnight, Sun 1–4pm; closed public hols.

★**Ochenta Grados** C/Manuela Malasaña 10 ☎914 458 351, ⓦochentagrados.com; ⓜBilbao; map pp.62–63. The idea behind *Ochenta Grados* is to serve traditional main-course dishes in miniature and it works wonderfully. Forget the idea of a starter and a main; just order a selection of dishes to share from the inventive menu, maybe steak tartare with mustard, parmesan ice cream or prawn risotto. Each dish is around about €5. Mon–Thurs & Sun 1.30–4pm & 8.30pm–midnight, Fri –Sat 1.30–4.30pm & 8.30pm–2am.

★**Ribeira do Miño** C/Santa Brígida 1 ☎915 219 854, ⓦmarisqueriaribeiradomino.com; ⓜTribunal; map pp.62–63. A fabulous-value *marisquería*, serving a seafood platter for two for around €35. Go for the slightly more expensive Galician white wine Albariño to accompany it. Fast, efficient and friendly service. Tues–Sun 1–4pm & 8pm–midnight; closed Aug.

PASEO DEL PRADO, PASEO DE RECOLETOS AND EL RETIRO

This is a fancier area with few bars of note but some extremely good, if expensive, restaurants, well worth considering, even if you're not staying at the *Ritz*.

CAFÉS

★**Café del Espejo** Paseo de Recoletos 31 ☎913 191 122, ⓦrestauranteelespejo.com; ⓜColón; map pp.62–63. Opened in 1991 but you wouldn't guess it – mirrors, gilt and a wonderful glass pavilion, plus a leafy outside terraza. Daily 9am–1am.

Café Gijón Paseo de Recoletos 21 ☎915 215 425, ⓦcafegijon.com; ⓜBanco de España; map pp.62–63. A famous literary café – and a centre of the intellectual/arty *movida* in the 1980s – decked out in Cuban mahogany and mirrors. Has a summer terraza. Daily 7.30am–1am.

Círculo de Bellas Artes C/Alcalá 42 ☎913 605 400, ⓦcirculobellasartes.com; ⓜBanco de España; map pp.102–103. A stylish bar, where you can loll on sofas and have drinks at "normal" prices. Outside, in summer, there's a comfortable terraza. Daily 9.30am–1am.

TAPAS BARS

La Platería C/Moratín 49 ☎914 291 722; ⓜAtocha/ Banco de España; map pp.102–103. Just across the square from *La Tapería* (see below), this touristy but conveniently placed bar has an enormously popular summer terraza and a good selection of reasonably priced tapas. Daily 7.30am–1pm.

La Tapería del Prado Pza. Platerías de Martínez 1 ☎914 294 094, ⓦlataperia.es; ⓜAtocha/Banco de España; map pp.102–103. A modern and slightly pricey bar opposite the Prado serving up an inventive range of tapas and *raciones*, plus a decent set lunch at €12. Mon–Fri 8am–2am, Sat & Sun 10am–2am.

RESTAURANTS

Al Mounia C/Recoletos 5 ☎914 350 828, ⓦalmounia .es; ⓜColón/Banco de España; map pp.62–63. High-quality Moroccan cooking in the most established Arabic restaurant in town, offering a romantic setting with attentive service. Lunchtime menu available Mon–Fri at €32 and a taster menu in the evening at €49. Mon–Sat 1.30–4pm & 9–11.30pm, Sun 1.30–4pm; closed Aug.

Paradis Madrid C/Marqués de Cubas 14 ☎914 297 303, ⓦrestaurantearadismadrid.es; ⓜBanco España; map pp.102–103. Upmarket Catalan restaurant often frequented by the politicians from the nearby parliament, serving light, high-quality and inventive Mediterranean food on the menu with superb starters, fish and rice dishes. Menus available from €35. Mon–Fri 1.30–4pm & 9pm–midnight, Sat 9pm–midnight.

Viridiana C/Juan de Mena 14 ☎915 315 222, ⓦrestauranteviridiana.com; ⓜRetiro/Banco de España; map pp.62–63. A bizarre temple of Madrid *nueva cocina*, offering mouthwatering creations from chef Abraham Garcia whose menu changes with the seasons, plus a superb

selection of wines. The bill for a three-course meal will come to over €100 a head, but it's an unforgettable experience. Daily 1.30–4pm & 8.30–midnight; closed Aug.

SALAMANCA

Salamanca is Madrid's equivalent of Bond Street or Fifth Avenue, full of designer shops and expensive-looking natives. The recommendations below are correspondingly pricey but high quality.

TAPAS BARS

Hevia C/Serrano 118 ☎915 623 075, ⓦheviamadrid .com; ⓜNúñez de Balboa; map pp.62–63. Plush venue and wealthy clientele who come for expensive but excellent tapas and *canapés*. The smoked fish, *salmorejo* and squid are superb. Mon–Sat 9am–1pm; closed part of Aug.

José Luís C/Serrano 89 ☎915 630 958, ⓦjoseluis.es; ⓜSerrano; map pp.62–63. An upmarket tapas bar with dainty and delicious sandwiches laid out along the bar. You take what you fancy and cough up at the end, in the safe knowledge that the owner will have notched up another few hundred euros to expand his chain of bars in the Americas. Daily 1am–1pm.

El Lateral Paseo de la Castellana 89 ⓦlateral.com; ⓜSantiago Bernabéu/Nuevos Ministerios; map pp.62–63. A swish place serving a good variety of classic dishes such as *croquetas* and *pimientos rellenos* (stuffed peppers) with a modern twist. Other branches at Castellana 42, C/ Velazquez 57 and C/Fuencarral 43. Sun–Wed noon–midnight, Thurs–Sat noon–1am.

RESTAURANTS

Estay C/Hermosilla 46 ☎915 780 470, ⓦestay restaurante.com; ⓜVelázquez; map pp.62–63. There's Basque-style cuisine in miniature (*canapés* and mini-casseroles) in this pleasant and roomy restaurant. A great range of *pintxos*, including *jamón* with roquefort cheese, langoustine vol-au-vents and a fine wine list too. A meal will cost €25–30. Mon–Sat 1–4pm & 8pm–midnight.

El Pescador C/José Ortega y Gasset 75 ☎914 021 290, ⓦwww.marisqueriaelpescador.net; ⓜLista; map pp.62–63. One of the city's best seafood restaurants, run by Gallegos and with specials flown in from the Atlantic each morning. The clientele can be a bit intimidating, but you'll rarely experience better seafood cooking. Around €60–70. If the restaurant is too much you can always sample some of the dishes in the bar. Mon–Sat 12.30–4.30pm & 8pm–12.30am; closed Easter & Aug.

DRINKING AND NIGHTLIFE

Madrid **nightlife** is a pretty serious phenomenon. This is one of the few cities in Europe where you can get caught in traffic jams in the early hours of the morning when the clubbers are either going home or moving on to the dance-past-dawn discos. As with everything *madrileño*, there is a bewildering variety of nightlife venues. Most common are the **discobares** – attuned

1

to all musical and sexual persuasions, whose unifying feature is background (occasionally live) pop, rock, dance or salsa music. These get going from around 11pm and stay open routinely until 2am, as will the few quieter **cocktail bars** and **pubs**.

For *discotecas*, entry charges are quite common (€5–18), but tend to cover you for a first drink. Free passes can often be picked up from public relations personnel who hang around in the streets outside, in tourist offices or bars. Be aware that many *discotecas* are fairly ephemeral institutions and frequently only last a season before opening up somewhere else under a different name, so it's a good idea to consult listing magazines *La Guía del Ocio*, *Metrópoli*, *esMadrid* or the website ⓦ clubbingspain.com for the very latest information.

BARS

Madrid's bar scene caters to every conceivable taste in terms of drinks, music and atmosphere, though in recent years, the notoriously late opening hours have been somewhat curtailed by the local authorities, who are attempting to get bars to close by 2am.

SOL, PLAZA DE SANTA ANA AND HUERTAS

Alhambra C/Victoria 5 ☏915 210 718; ⓜSol; map pp.102–103. A friendly tapas bar by day, *Alhambra* transforms itself into a fun *discobar* by night with the crowds spilling over into the *El Buscón* bar next door. Mon–Wed 11am–1.30am, Thurs 11am–2am, Fri & Sat 11am–3.30am.

Cervecería Alemana Pza. Santa Ana 6 ☏914 297 033, ⓦcerveceriaalemana.com; ⓜSol; map pp.102–103. Refurbished once again but it remains a stylish old beer house, once frequented by Hemingway. Order a *caña* and go easy on the tapas, as the bill can mount up fast. Daily except Tues 10am–12.30am, Fri & Sat until 2am.

Cervecería Santa Ana Pza. Santa Ana 10 ☏914 294 356, ⓦcerveceriasantaana.com; ⓜSol; map pp.102–103. Old-styled wood-panelled bar which has actually only been around since the mid 1980s. Cheaper than the *Alemana*, with tables outside, friendly service and a good selection of tapas. Daily 11am–1.30am (Fri & Sat until 2.30am).

Dos Gardenias C/Santa María 13; ☏627 003 571; ⓜAntón Martín; map pp.102–103. Intimate and relaxed little bar in the Huertas area where you can chill out in their comfy chairs, sip on a mojito, and escape from the hubbub of the city outside. Tues–Sat 9.30am–2.30am.

La Fídula C/Huertas 57 ☏914 292 947, ⓦmyspace .com/lafidula; ⓜAntón Martín; map pp.102–103. Re-opened after a brief period out of action, you can sip *fino* to the accompaniment of live music – usually flamenco – performed on the tiny stage (€10, including drink when there's a live act). Daily 8pm–3am.

The Glass Bar C/San Jeronimo 34 ☏914 877 710, ⓦhotelurban.com; ⓜSevilla; map pp.102–103. Housed in the ultra-chic five-star *Hotel Urban*, this glamorous, glass-fronted cocktail bar has become a compulsory stop for the well-heeled crowd. In summer, there's a terrace bar on the sixth floor. Mon–Sat 11am–3am.

Naturbier Pza. Santa Ana 9 ☏913 600 597 ⓦnaturbier .com; ⓜSol; map pp.102–103. Next door to the

Cervecerías Alemana and *Santa Ana*, the *Naturbier* brews its own tasty, cloudy beer and serves a variety of German sausages to accompany it. You can book tours of the brewery with a tasting session at the end for €20. Daily 8pm–3am.

★**La Venencia** C/Echegaray 7 ☏914 297 313; ⓜSol; map pp.102–103. For a real taste of old Madrid, this is a must: a dilapidated wood-panelled bar, serving just sherry – try the extra-dry *fino* or the crisp *manzanilla* – cured tuna (*mojama*) and delicious olives. The decoration has remained unchanged for decades, with ancient barrels and yellowing posters, while the bill is chalked up old-style on the wooden bar. Daily 1–3.30pm & 7.30pm–1.30am; closed Aug.

Viva Madrid C/Manuel Fernández y González 7 ☏914 203 596; ⓜAntón Martín; map pp.102–103. A fabulous tiled bar – both outside and in – with quite pricey wines and sherry, plus basic tapas. Nearly always packed. Daily 1pm–2.30am.

GRAN VÍA

★**Del Diego** C/Reina 12 ☏915 233 106, ⓦdeldiego .com; ⓜGran Vía; map pp.102–103. An elegant New York-style cocktail bar set up by a former *Museo Chicote* waiter and now better than the original place. There's a friendly, unhurried atmosphere, and it's open until the early hours. The house special is the vodka-based Del Diego, but the mojitos and margaritas are great, too. Mon–Sat 7pm–3am; closed Aug.

Gin Club/Mercado de la Reina Gran Vía 12 ☏915 213 198, ⓦmercadodelareina.es; ⓜGran Vía; map pp.102–103. Multipurpose tapas bar, restaurant and *bar de copas*. At the back, with its mirror ceilings, black leather chairs, is the chill-out cocktail bar, the *Gin Club*, offering over 20 different brands at between €9 and €12, although you can also get a decent mojito here if you prefer something different. Daily 9am–2am.

El Jardín Secreto C/Conde Duque 2 ☏915 418 023, ⓦeljardinsecretomadrid.com; ⓜPlaza de España; map pp.62–63. Cosy, fairy-tale style bar and eatery on the corner of a tiny square close to Pza. de España, serving reasonably priced drinks and cocktails. Service is friendly and the atmosphere unhurried. Mon–Thurs & Sun 5.30pm–12.30am, Fri & Sat 6.30pm–2.30am.

Museo Chicote Gran Vía 12 ☏915 326 727, ⓦmuseo -chicote.com; ⓜGran Vía; map pp.102–103. Opened back in 1931, *Chicote* was once a haunt of Buñuel and Hemingway.

TERRAZAS

With the introduction of a new law banning smoking inside bars and restaurants, **terrazas** have become more popular than ever in Madrid and many places now have at least a few tables set up on the city pavements year-round.

In summer many more bars migrate on to the streets. Beyond **Pza. de Colón** and up to the **Bernabéu** more fashionable terrazas with music, a posey clientele and higher prices often appear in the summer. Be aware, however, that many of the terrazas run by clubs vary their sites year by year as they fall foul of the increasingly strict licensing and noise regulations.

Atenas Parque de Atenas (just off C/Segovia) ⓦ terrazaatenas.com; ⓜ Ópera. Lively summer terraza set in the park down by the river in the shadow of the Catedral and not far from the bars and clubs of La Latina.

Paseo del Pintor Rosales ⓜ Argüelles. There is a clutch of terrazas catering for all tastes and popular with families along this avenue on the edge of the Parque del Oeste.

Paseo de Recoletos and, Paseo de la Castellana On the nearer reaches of Paseo de Recoletos is the refined garden terraza at the *Casa de América* (no. 2) and those of the old-style cafés *Gijón* (no. 21) and *Espejo* (no. 31), popular meeting points for *madrileños* of all kinds.

Pza. de Comendadoras ⓜ Ventura Rodríguez. One of the city's few traffic-free squares, this has a couple of very popular terrazas – attached to the *Café Moderno* and to the Mexican restaurant next door.

Pza. de Oriente ⓜ Ópera. The *Café de Oriente* terraza is a station of Madrid nightlife and enjoys a marvellous location next to the opera house, gazing across the plaza to the Palacio Real.

Pza. de la Paja ⓜ La Latina. One of the most pleasant terrazas in the heart of old Madrid can be found in this former market square in La Latina.

Pza. San Andrés ⓜ La Latina. Just the other side of the church of San Andrés a host of bars spills out onto this atmospheric plaza. The place is buzzing in the summer, and makes a great meeting place before a bar crawl around the area.

Pza. de Santa Ana ⓜ Sol. Several of the *cervecerías* here have outside seating, and there's a *chiringuito* (a makeshift bar) in the middle of the square throughout the summer.

Terraza de Las Vistillas C/Bailén (on the south side of the viaduct); ⓜ Ópera. This popular terraza is good for a relaxing drink while enjoying the *vistillas* ("little vistas") over towards the Almudena Catedral and the Guadarrama mountains to the northwest.

It's lost some of its charm but is still a very fashionable place, with evening music sessions. Mon–Sat 5pm–1.30am.

LA LATINA AND LAVAPIÉS

Café Barbieri C/Ave María 45 ☎ 915 273 658; ⓜ Lavapiés; map pp.62–63. A relaxed bar/café in the heart of Lavapiés, with unobtrusive music, old-style decor, newspapers and a wide selection of coffees. Tues & Wed 4pm–midnight, Thurs 4pm–1.30am, Fri & Sat 4pm–2.30am, Sun 4–11.30pm.

Delic Pza. de la Paja 8 ☎ 913 645 450, ⓦ delic.es; ⓜ Antón Martín; map pp.102–103. Serving home-made cakes, fruit juices and coffee, this is a pleasant café by day, transforming into a crowded but friendly cocktail bar by night. Wed–Sun 11am–2am; closed first half of Aug.

El Viajero Pza. de la Cebada ☎ 913 669 064, ⓦ elviajeromadrid.com; ⓜ La Latina; map pp.62–63. Bar, disco, restaurant and summer terraza on different floors of this fashionable La Latina nightspot. Great views of San Francisco el Grande from the terraza at the top. Reasonably priced *raciones* to share, while there are grilled meats and steaks for mains (€13–22). Restaurant: Mon–Fri 12.30pm–1am; Sat 11.30am–2am; Sun 11.30am–midnight; closed first half Jan, second half Aug.

CHUECA, MALASAÑA AND SANTA BÁRBARA

★**La Ardosa** C/Colón 13 ☎ 915 214 979, ⓦ www .laardosa.com; ⓜ Tribunal; map pp.62–63. One of the city's classic *tabernas*, offering limited but very tasty tapas including great *croquetas*, *salmorejo* and an excellent home-made *tortilla*. Prides itself on its draught beer and Guinness and serves a great pre-lunch *vermút* too. Daily 8.30am–2am.

★**Le Cabrera** C/Bárbara de Braganza 2 ☎ 915 775 955, ⓦ lecabrera.com; ⓜ Colón; map pp.62–63. A chic addition to the Madrid scene serving drinks and creative tapas in the dazzling gastro bar on the ground floor and expertly mixed cocktails in the cosier basement area. There's another branch in the Casa de América at Paseo de Recoletas 2. Gastrobar: Mon–Thurs 1.30–4pm & 8.30pm–midnight; Fri & Sat til 2am; Sun 1.30–5pm. Cocktail bar: Mon–Fri 4pm–2am; Sat 1pm–2.30am; Sun 1.30pm–2am.

Casa Camacho C/San Andrés 2 (just off Pza. Dos de Mayo) ☎ 915 313 598; ⓜ Tribunal; map pp.62–63. An irresistible old neighbourhood *bodega*, with a traditional bar counter, *vermút* on tap and basic tapas. An ideal place to start the evening. Packed out at weekends. Daily noon–1.30am.

Finnegans Pza. de las Salesas 9 ☎ 913 100 521, ⓦ finnegans.es; ⓜ Colón/Alonso Martínez; map

1

CHOCOLATE BEFORE BED

If you stay up through a Madrid night, then you must try one of the city's great institutions – the **Chocolatería San Ginés** (ⓦchocolateriasangines.com; daily 9.30am–7am; map pp.102–103) on Pasadizo de San Ginés, off C/Arenal between the Puerta del Sol and Teatro Real. Established in 1894, this serves *chocolate con churros* to perfection – just the thing after a night's excess. There's an almost mythical *madrileño* custom of winding up at San Ginés after the clubs close (not that they do any longer), before heading home for a shower and then off to work.

pp.62–63. A large Irish bar with several rooms, complete with bar fittings and wooden floors brought over from the Emerald Isle. English-speaking staff, and TV sports. Daily 8am–2am.

Pepe Botella C/San Andrés 12 (on Pza. Dos de Mayo) ☎915 224 309, ⓦfacebook.com/cafepepebotella; ⓜTribunal; map pp.62–63. An old-style elegance still clings to this little bar, with its friendly staff, marble-topped tables, low-volume music and no fruit machines. Daily 11am–3am; Aug from 3pm.

Tupperware C/Corredera Alta de San Pablo 26 ☎914 485 016; ⓜTribunal; map pp.62–63. You'll find a refreshingly cosmopolitan musical diet at this classic Malasaña nightspot. Daily 9pm–3.30am.

Vía Lactea C/Velarde 18 ☎914 467 581; ⓜTribunal; map pp.62–63. Call in here to see where the *movida* began. *Vía Lactea* was a key meeting place for Spain's designers, directors, pop stars and painters in the 1980s, and it retains its original decor from the time, billiard tables included. There's a stage downstairs. It attracts a young, studenty clientele and is packed at weekends. Daily 8pm–3am.

SALAMANCA

Alquimia/Alegoría C/Villanueva 2 (entrance on C/Cid) ⓦalegoria-madrid.es; ⓜRetiro; map pp.62–63. A restaurant-bar-club modelled on an English gentlemen's club, with over-the-top Baroque decor. It's a popular backdrop for media presentations and pop videos. Thurs–Sat 9pm–5am; Sun 7pm–midnight; entrance €10.

The Geographic Club C/Alcalá 141 ⓦthe geographicclub.com; ⓜGoya; map pp.62–63. Nineteenth-century travel-themed bar/restaurant just north of the Retiro furnished with lots of dark wood and glass cabinets full of objets d'art. Go for the large range of decent-value cocktails and drinks rather than the food. Sun–Wed 1pm–1.30am, Thurs 1pm–2am, Fri & Sat 1pm–3am.

DISCOTECAS

Discotecas – or clubs – aren't always that different from *discobares*, though they tend to be bigger and flashier, with a lot of attention to the lighting, sound system and decor. They start late and stay open until around 4am, some till 6am and a couple till noon. In summer, some of the trendier clubs suspend operations and set up outdoor terrazas (see box, p.115).

SOL, ÓPERA AND PZA. DE SANTA ANA

Coco C/Alcalá 20 ⓦcocomadrid.com; ⓜSevilla; map pp.102–103. Über-modern decor in this slick club that is one of the most fashionable stations of the night on the Madrid scene. House, funk and hip-hop in the *Really* and *Mondo Disko* sessions on Thursday to Saturday nights from midnight. €15 with first drink.

Joy Madrid C/Arenal 11 ⓦwww.joy-eslava.com; ⓜSol/Ópera; map pp.102–103. *Joy* may not be at the cutting edge of the club scene, but judging by the queues, it remains one of the city's most popular and successful clubs. If you can't get in, console yourself with the *Chocolatería San Ginés* on the street behind (see box above). Daily midnight–6am; €12–15, including first drink.

Torero C/Cruz 26 ⓜSol/Sevilla; map pp.102–103. A very popular and enjoyable two-storey disco right in the heart of the Santa Ana area, but the door policy is pretty strict and it can become rather overcrowded at weekends. Closed Sun & Mon; €10.

PASEO DEL PRADO/ATOCHA

Azucar Salsa C/Atocha 107 ⓦazucarsalsadisco.com; ⓜAtocha/Antón Martín; map pp.62–63. Fun salsa disco, which also runs dance classes, with frequent Cuban and Bachata nights and amateur dance competitions where the virtuosos get a chance to strut their stuff. Wed–Sat 11.30pm–6am; €8–10 including first drink, women usually given free entry.

Kapital C/Atocha 125 ⓦgrupo-kapital.com/kapital; ⓜAtocha; map pp.62–63. A seven-storey macro-disco, complete with three dancefloors, lasers, go-go dancers, a cocktail bar and a top-floor terrace. House, funk and R&B. Thurs–Sat midnight–6am, plus Sun-night session from 8pm; usually free entry before 1am after that €16 (including two drinks).

GRAN VÍA AND PLAZA. DE ESPAÑA

Bash Pza. de Callao 4 ⓦtripfamily.com; ⓜCallao; map pp.62–63. *Bash* is one of the major venues on the Madrid club scene. There's the *OHM Dance Club* techno-house session on Fri & Sat and for those with real stamina, there's also a Sun-night session popular with the gay crowd. Sessions usually begin around midnight; €12–15 including first drink.

Morocco C/Marqués de Leganés 7 ⓦmoroccoclub.es; ⓜSanto Domingo; map pp.62–63. Fun, unpretentious disco with a slightly older clientele and a varied diet of Spanish pop. Fri & Sat midnight–6am; €10 entry with drink.

CHUECA/SANTA BÁRBARA

T-Club C/Barceló 11 ⓦ tclub.es; ⓜ Tribunal; map pp.62–63. Formerly known as *Pachá*, this club, housed in a fantastic Art Deco building, remains a popular station of the Madrid night scene with its varied offering of resident DJ sessions, concerts and themed nights; €15 including first drink. Wed–Sat midnight–6am and occasional session on Sun.

SALAMANCA AND THE NORTH

Moma 56 C/José Abascal 56 ⓦ momafiftysix.com;

ⓦ Gregorio Marañon; map pp.62–63. An exclusive, New York-style club, popular with *pijos* and the upmarket glamour crowd. Also inside are the *Kashira* Japanese and Italian restaurant and a bar serving cocktails and light Mediterranean and fusion food; €10 entry. Club open Thurs–Sat midnight–6am.

69 Pétalos C/Alberto Alcocer 32 ⓦ grupo69petalos .com; ⓜ Colombia/Cuzco; map pp.62–63. Despite the upmarket location, this is a light-hearted club determined to keep the clientele happy with its party atmosphere, actors and go-gos. There is a popular summer terraza too. Disco Thurs–Sat midnight–6am, terraza Mon–Sat midnight–2am.

MUSIC, FILM AND THEATRE

Most nights in Madrid, you can take in performances of **flamenco**, **salsa**, **rock**, **jazz**, **classical music** and **opera**. Often, it's the smaller, offbeat clubs that are the more enjoyable, though there are plenty of large auditoria for big-name concerts. In summer, events are supplemented by the council's **Veranos de la Villa** cultural programme, and in autumn by the **Festival de Otoño**. These also encompass **theatre** and **film**, both of which have healthy year-round scenes.

FLAMENCO

Flamenco underwent something of a revival in Madrid in

the 1990s, in large part owing to the "new flamenco" artists, like Ketama and Joaquín Cortés, who were unafraid to mix it

---

GAY AND LESBIAN MADRID

Much of Madrid's nightlife has a big gay input and **gay men** especially will feel at home in most of the listings in our "Discotecas" section. However, Pza. Chueca and the surrounding streets, especially C/Pelayo, harbour at least a dozen exclusively gay bars and clubs, as well as a café that's traditionally gay – the *Café Figueroa* at C/Augusto Figueroa 17. The **lesbian scene** is more disparate.

The main gay organization in Madrid is **Coordinadora Gay de Madrid**, C/Puebla 9 (Mon–Fri 10am–2pm & 5–8pm; Aug from 7pm; ☎ 915 230 070, ⓦ cogam.org; ⓜ Gran Vía), which can give information on health, leisure and gay rights. Feminist and lesbian groups are based at the Centro de la Mujer, C/Barquillo 44, 1º izda. ☎ 913 081 233. For a good one-stop shop with lots of info on the gay scene, try Berkana Bookshop, C/Hortaleza 62 (Mon–Sat 10.30am–9pm, Sun noon–2pm & 5–9pm; ⓦ libreriaberkana.com; ⓜ Chueca).

BARS AND DISCOTECAS

Café Acuarela C/Gravina 10 ⓦ caféacuarela.es; ⓜ Chueca. Comfortable café, with kitsch Baroque-style decor. The perfect place for a quiet drink, and popular with a mixed crowd. Daily, about 11am–2am.

Cool Ballroom C/Isabel la Católica 6; ⓜ Santo Domingo. Futuristic, style-conscious mixed club with a large gay following, especially for the Saturday night LOL session. Expect to pay €10–15 entry fee, and don't arrive until late. Thurs–Sat midnight–6am, Sun 9pm–2am.

Escape C/Gravina 13 ⓦ escapechueca.com; ⓜ Chueca. Originally a lesbian club, but now popular with the gay crowd too. A fun and friendly atmosphere. Thurs–Sat midnight–5am.

Liquid C/Barbieri 7; ⓦ www.liquid.es; ⓜ Chueca. Popular gay bar, lined with plasma screens playing music videos. Gets packed so worth arriving early to avoid the queues. Mon–Sat 9pm–3am.

La Lupe C/Torrecilla del Leal 12; ⓦ lalupedehuertas .com; ⓜ Antón Martín. A mixed gay, lesbian and alternative bar. Good music, cheap drinks and occasional cabaret. Tues–Sat 9am–3pm.

Medea C/Cabeza 33; ⓜ Tirso de Molina/Antón Martín. A women-only disco with a huge dancefloor and wide-ranging selection of music. Gets going from about 1am.

Ricks C/Clavel 8; ⓜ Gran Vía. A varied-clientele *discobar* that gets packed at weekends when every available space is used for dancing. Open and light, with a friendly atmosphere – but drinks are pricey. Daily 11.30pm–5.30am.

Truco C/Gravina 10; ⓜ Chueca. A long-established women's bar with a popular summer terraza that spills out onto Chueca's main plaza. Mon–Thurs 5pm–3am, Fri & Sat noon–3am.

1

with a bit of blues, jazz, even rock. A new generation of younger but more traditional artists such as Niña Pastori and Estrella Morente is now more popular. Madrid has its own flamenco festival (Suma Flamenca) in May–June, when you stand a chance of catching some of the bigger names such as Tomatito or José Mercé. For up-to-date and authoritative information on the flamenco scene, try ⓦ flamenco-world .com. The club listings below span the range from purist flamenco to crossover experiments, and most artists – even major stars – appear in them. Although the following may open earlier, be aware that in many cases performances won't really get going until around midnight.

Almonte C/Juan Bravo 35 ☏ 915 632 504, ⓦ almontesalarociera.com; Ⓜ Diego de León. There's a little slice of Andalucía in this *sala rociera* where it's easy to imagine you've been transported to Seville as you watch the locals strut their stuff. A few more *finos* and you'll pluck up the courage to have a go yourself. Sun–Thurs 10pm–5am, Fri & Sat 10pm–6pm.

Café de Chinitas C/Torija 7 ☏ 915 595 135, ⓦ chinitas .com; Ⓜ Santo Domingo; map pp.62–63. One of the oldest flamenco clubs in Madrid, with a dinner-dance spectacular. It's expensive, but the music is authentic. Reservations are essential (sessions at 8pm & 10.30pm) and you can either opt for the show and drink at €35 or have a meal too for €48. Mon–Sat 8pm–midnight.

Candela C/Olmo 2 ☏ 914 673 382; Ⓜ Antón Martín; map pp.62–63. A legendary bar frequented by musicians – the late, great Camarón de la Isla is reputed to have sung here until 11am on one occasion. Tues–Sun 10.30pm–2am.

Las Carboneras C/ Conde de Miranda ☏ 915 428 677, ⓦ tablaolascarboneras.com; Ⓜ Sol; map pp.102–103. A relative newcomer to the restaurant/*tablao* scene, geared to the tourist market but a good alternative if you want to get a taste of flamenco; around €34 for the show and a drink, between €65 and €70 if you want dinner as well. Shows: Mon–Thurs 8.30pm & 10.30pm, Fri & Sat 8.30pm & 11pm.

Cardamomo C/Echegaray 15 ⓦ cardamomo.net; Ⓜ Sevilla/Sol; map pp.102–103. This flamenco bar has evolved into a well-respected fully blown *tablao* in recent years. The show with a drink will cost you €39, while dinner will set you back an extra €33. Check the website for the schedule.

★**Casa Patas** C/Cañizares 10 ☏ 913 690 496, ⓦ casapatas.com; Ⓜ Antón Martín; map pp.102–103. A small but very popular flamenco *tablao* that gets its share of big names. The best nights are Thurs and Fri. Costs €35, including drink. Mon–Sat 9pm–2am.

Corral de la Morería C/Morería 17 ☏ 913 658 446, ⓦ corraldelamoreria.com; Ⓜ La Latina; map pp.62–63. A renowned and atmospheric venue for some serious flamenco acts but, again, expensive at about €42 for show plus a drink and double that if you want to dine in the restaurant. Daily 7pm–2am, shows at 8.30pm & 10.30pm.

POP, ROCK AND BLUES

Madrid is very much on the international rock-tour circuit and you can catch big (and small) American and British acts in front of enthusiastic audiences. Sports arenas such as Atlético Madrid's Vicente Calderón football stadium and Las Ventas bullring are used for some of the biggest acts, while in the smaller clubs, you have a chance of seeing a very wide range of local bands.

CLUBS AND BARS

La Coquette C/Hileras 14; Ⓜ Ópera; map pp.102–103. A small, crowded basement bar, where people sit around in the near-dark watching blues bands perform on a tiny stage. Daily 8pm–2.30am; live music most nights with blues on Wed & Thurs.

Honky Tonk C/Covarrubias 24 ☏ 914 456 886, ⓦ clubhonky.com; Ⓜ Alonso Martínez; map pp.62–63. This late-opening bar just north of Alonso Martínez has nightly blues and rock sets. Daily 9.30pm–5am, live acts 12.30am.

Libertad 8 C/Libertad 8 ☏ 915 321 150, ⓦ libertad8cafe .es; Ⓜ Chueca; map pp.62–63. *Libertad 8* made its name during the *movida*, but this friendly little bar in Chueca still acts as a venue for up-and-coming singer-songwriters and even has its own record label. Tues–Sun 1pm–2am.

Siroco C/San Dimás 3 ☏ 915 933 070, ⓦ siroco.es; Ⓜ San Bernardo; map pp.62–63. Live bands play fairly regularly at this popular little club, not far north of the Gran Vía; €5–10. Closed Sun.

El Sol C/Jardines 3 ☏ 915 326 494, ⓦ elsolmad.com; Ⓜ Sol/Gran Vía; map pp.102–103. Over thirty years on the scene, this down-to-earth club hosts around twenty live concerts a month, but continues afterwards (usually

MADRID LISTINGS

Listings information is in plentiful supply in Madrid. The newspapers *El País* (ⓦ elpais.es) and *El Mundo* (ⓦ elmundo.es) have excellent daily listings, and on Fridays both publish magazine sections devoted to events, bars and restaurants in the capital.

If your time in Madrid doesn't coincide with the Friday supplements, or you want maximum info, pick up the weekly listings magazine *La Guía del Ocio* (ⓦ guiadelocio.com; €1) at any kiosk. The *ayuntamiento* publishes a monthly pamphlet *esMadrid* (in English and Spanish), which is free from any of the tourist offices and lists forthcoming events in the city (also see ⓦ esmadrid.com).

from about 1.30am) as a disco, playing house, soul and acid jazz. Tues–Sat midnight–5.30am.

MAJOR EVENT VENUES

Circo Price Ronda de Atocha 35 ☎915 279 8656, ⓦteatrocircoprice.es; ⓜAtocha/Lavapiés; map pp.62–63. Big enough to hold some major shows and concerts, but small enough to retain a sense of intimacy, the Circo Price hosts a popular Christmas circus, an annual magic season and many of the concerts in the Veranos de la Villa season.

Palacio de Deportes Avda. Felipe II s/n ☎912 586 016, ⓦpalaciodedeportes.com; ⓜGoya; map pp.62–63. The city's sports arena that replaced the old one that burned down in 2001. It's used for big shows of the Miley Cyrus, Kylie Minogue, Rihanna variety.

Palacio de Vistalegre C/Uterbo 1 ☎915 639 493, ⓦpalaciovistalegre.com; ⓜOporto/Vista Alegre. This covered bullring in the south of the city has become one of the favoured venues of touring artists.

La Riviera Paseo Bajo Virgen del Puerto s/n, Puente de Segovia ☎913 652 415, ⓦsalariviera.com; ⓜPuerta del Ángel; map pp.62–63. A fun disco (weekends only) and concert venue right next to the river, which has hosted its fair share of big groups including Coldplay and the Black Eyed Peas.

LATIN MUSIC

Madrid attracts big-name Latin artists, who tend to play at the venues below. The local scene is a good deal more low-key, but there's enjoyable salsa, nonetheless, in a handful of clubs.

Galileo Galilei C/Galileo 100 ☎915 347 557, ⓦsalagalileogalilei.com; ⓜIslas Filipinas. A bar, concert venue and disco all rolled into one. Latin music is regularly on offer, but you'll need to check the website to find out which night, as it also hosts cabaret, flamenco and singer-songwriters. Mon–Sat 9pm–3am.

Oba-Oba C/Jacometrezo 4 ☎617 933 770; ⓜCallao; map pp.102–103. Samba and lambada, with lethal *caipirinhas* from the bar. Daily 11pm–5.30am.

El Son C/Victoria 6; ☎915 232 609 ⓦdiscotecaelson .com; ⓜSol; map pp.102–103. Threre's live salsa music (Mon–Thurs) at this small Latin club, which has picked up where its predecessor *Massai* left off. There's no space to stand and watch, so make sure you bring your dancing shoes. Daily from 7pm.

JAZZ

Madrid doesn't rank up there with London, Paris or New York on the jazz front, but the clubs are friendly, unpretentious places. Look out for the annual jazz festival staged at a variety of venues in November.

Bogui Jazz C/Barquillo 29 ☎915 211 568, ⓦboguijazz .com; ⓜChueca; map pp.62–63. Back In action after a licensing wrangle with the local council, *Bogui* has jazz sets

every evening from Thurs–Sat followed by a disco; €10 entry for concerts. Wed–Sun 10.30pm–5am.

★**Café Berlín** C/Jacometrezo 4 ☎915 215 752, ⓦberlincafe.es; ⓜCallao/Santo Domingo; map pp.102–103. Jazz and blues sessions often take place in this good-looking Art Nouveau café just off the Gran Vía. It also stages soul, flamenco and tango concerts too. Mon–Sat 11pm–5am, Fri & Sat til 6am.

Café Central Pza. del Ángel 10 ☎913 694 143, ⓦcafecentralmadrid.com; ⓜSol; map pp.102–103. A small and relaxed jazz club that gets the odd big name, plus strong local talent. The Art Deco café is worth a visit in its own right. €12–14 for gigs, otherwise free. Daily 1.30pm–2.30am.

Café Jazz Populart C/Huertas 22 ☎914 298 407, ⓦpopulart.es; ⓜAntón Martín; map pp.102–103. Nightly sets from jazz and blues bands. Daily from 6pm, sets start 11pm & 12.30am.

Clamores C/Alburquerque 14 ☎914 457 938, ⓦsalaclamores.com; ⓜBilbao; map pp.62–63. A large, low-key and enjoyable jazz bar with accomplished (if not very famous) artists, not too exorbitant drinks and a nice range of snacks. €5–12 for gigs, otherwise free. Sets start around 10.30pm; bar is open until 4am.

CLASSICAL MUSIC AND OPERA

The Teatro Real is the city's prestigious opera house and the Auditorio Nacional de Musica is home to the Orquesta Nacional de España. Equally enjoyable are the salons and small auditoria for chamber orchestras and groups.

Auditorio Nacional de Música C/Príncipe de Vergara 146 ☎913 370 140, ⓦwww.auditorionacional.mcu.es; ⓜCruz del Rayo. Home of the Spanish National Orchestra and host to most international visiting orchestras.

Teatro Real Pza. Isabel II; info ☎915 160 660, box office ☎915 160 606, ticket line ☎902 244 848, ⓦteatro-real.com; ⓜÓpera. Madrid's opulent opera house, and a fantastic setting for some prestigious productions. Tickets range from €8 to €380, but you'll need to book well in advance for the best seats.

Teatro Zarzuela C/Jovellanos 4 ☎915 245 400, ⓦteatrodelazarzuela.mcu.es; ⓜSevilla. The main venue for Spanish operetta.

FILM

Cines – cinemas – can be found all over the central area, and there's a handful of grand old picture houses strung out along the length of the Gran Vía. These offer major releases dubbed into Spanish, though a number of cinemas have regular original language screenings, with subtitles; these are listed in a separate *versión original/subtitulada* (*v.o.*) section in the newspapers. Tickets for films cost around €9, but most cinemas have a *día del espectador* (usually Mon or Wed) when they cost from €4. Be warned that on Sunday night half of

1

TICKETS

Tickets for most big rock concerts are sold by Fnac, C/Preciados 28 ☎915 956 190 (Ⓜ Callao), and El Corte Inglés, C/Preciados 1–4 ⓦ elcorteingles.es (Ⓜ Sol). For theatre and concert tickets try Entradas.com ☎902 221 622, ⓦ entradas.com; Caixa Catalunya/Tele Entrada ☎902 101 212, ⓦ telentrada.com; Ticketmaster ☎902 150 025, ⓦ ticketmaster.es; and Servi-Caixa ☎902 332 211, ⓦ servicaixa.com. The website ⓦ atrapalo.com also sells discount tickets for the theatre and musicals.

Madrid goes to the movies, and queues can be long.

Filmoteca/Cine Doré C/Santa Isabel 3 Ⓜ Antón Martín. A beautiful old cinema, now home to an art-film centre, with imaginative programmes of classic and contemporary films, all shown in *v.o.* at an admission price of just €2.50 (closed Mon). In summer, there are open-air screenings on a little terraza – they're very popular, so buy tickets in advance.

Golem and **Renoir** C/Martín de los Heros 12 and C/ Princesa 3 ⓦ golem.es, ⓦ cinesrenoir.com; Ⓜ Plaza de España. These two multiscreen cinemas, within 200m of each other, show regular *v.o.* films.

Ideal Yelmo Cineplex C/Doctor Cortezo 6 ⓦ yelmocineplex.es; Ⓜ Sol/Tirso de Molina. A centrally located, nine-screen complex that shows a good selection of *v.o.* films.

THEATRE AND CABARET

Madrid is enjoying a renaissance in theatre; you can catch anything from Lope de Vega to contemporary and experimental productions, and there's also a new wave of cabaret and comedy acts. Look out, too, for the annual Festival de Otoño a Primavera which runs from September to May.

Teatro de Bellas Artes C/Marqués de Riera 2 ☎915 324 437, ⓦ teatrobellasartes.es; Ⓜ Banco de España. The *teatro* stages a wide range of productions from Shakespeare to Red Riding Hood.

Teatro Español C/Príncipe 25 ☎913 601 480, ⓦ teatroespanol.es; Ⓜ Sol/Sevilla. A classic Spanish theatre on the site of one of the city's old *corrales*.

Teatro Fernán Gómez Pza. de Colón ☎914 362 540, ⓦ teatrofernangomez.esmadrid.com; Ⓜ Colón. A range of dramas, dance and musical productions are on at this arts centre named after the late Spanish actor.

Teatro María Guerrero C/Tamayo y Baus 4 ☎913 102 949 or ☎913 101 500, ⓦ cdn.mcu.es; Ⓜ Colón. This is the headquarters of the Centro Dramático Nacional, which stages high-quality Spanish and international productions in a beautiful neo-Mudéjar interior.

Teatro Nuevo Apolo Pza. Tirso de Molina 1 ☎913 690 637, ⓦ summummusic.com; Ⓜ Tirso de Molina. Madrid's principal venue for major musicals and dance spectacles.

Teatro Valle-Inclán C/Pza. de Lavapiés ☎915 058 801, ⓦ cdn.mcu.es; Ⓜ Lavapiés. Opened in 2006, the state-of-the-art Valle-Inclán provides a second home for the Centro Dramático Nacional.

Teatros del Canal C/Cea Bermúdez 1 ☎915 802 070, ⓦ teatroscanal.com; Ⓜ Ríos Rosas. Two large theatres in this complex host music, dance and drama. One of the spaces is used for the regional theatre festival in the spring and for acclaimed touring productions.

CHILDREN

Many of the big sights may lack child-specific services or activities, but there's plenty to keep kids occupied for a short stay. There are various **parks** (El Retiro being a particular favourite), a host of well-attended public **swimming pools** and an increasing number of **child-oriented attractions**. Children are welcome in nearly all cafés and restaurants.

IN THE CITY

Imax Madrid Parque Tierno Galván ☎914 674 800, ⓦ imaxmadrid.com; Ⓜ Méndez Alvaro. Futuristic cinema with three different types of screen showing natural history-style features in Spanish. €8.55–9.55.

Museo de Cera (Wax Museum) Paseo de Recoletos 41 ☎913 199 330, ⓦ museoceramadrid.com; Ⓜ Colón. Expensive, tacky, and the figures bear little resemblance to the originals, but nevertheless popular with children. There's also a train of horrors and a film history of Spain. €17, under-10s & over-65s €12, under-4s free. Mon–Fri 10am–2.30pm & 4.30–8.30pm, Sat, Sun & public hols 10am–8.30pm.

Museo del Ferrocarril Paseo de las Delicias 61 ☎902 228 822, ⓦ museodelferrocarril.org; Ⓜ Delicias. An impressive collection of engines, carriages and wagons that once graced the railway lines of Spain. Of more interest to the younger ones is the fascinating collection of model railways and the mini-railway (Sat 11.30am–2pm; €1). There's an atmospheric little cafeteria housed in one of the more elegant carriages. The station was used as a backdrop in the film classic *Doctor Zhivago*. €6, 4–12-year-olds €4, under-4s free; Sun €2.50. Tues–Fri 9.30am–3pm, Sat 10am–8pm, Sun 10am–3pm.

1

Parque de Atracciones Casa de Campo ☎ 902 345 009, ⓦ parquedeatracciones.es; ⓜ Batán/bus #33 & #65. A theme park packed full of rides, whose attractions include the 100km/hr Abismo roller coaster, the swirling Tarantula ride, the 63m vertical drop La Lanzadera and the whitewater-rafting ride Los Rápidos. €29.90 for a day-ticket which includes most rides for anyone over 1.20m tall, €23.90 for children between 90cm and 1.20m tall (reductions for advance purchases via the website), children under 90cm tall go free. Oct–March Sat, Sun & public hols noon–8pm; April–Sept most days noon–midnight (see website).

Planetario Parque Tierno Galván ☎ 914 673 461, ⓦ planetmad.es; ⓜ Méndez Álvaro. Exhibition halls, audiovisual displays and projections on a variety of astronomical themes (all in Spanish). €3.60; under-14s €1.65.

Zoo–Aquarium Casa de Campo ☎ 917 119 950, ⓦ zoomadrid.com; ⓜ Casa de Campo/Batán, bus #33 from Príncipe Pío. Over 2000 different species, including big cats, gorillas, pandas, koalas and venomous snakes, plus an impressive aquarium with sharks, a children's zoo, a parrot show and a dolphinarium. €22.90, under-7s €18.55, under-3s free (reductions for advance purchases via the website). Daily 10.30am–dusk.

SWIMMING POOLS AND AQUAPARKS

Outdoor swimming pools are open between June and September. The Piscina Canal Isabel II, Avda. de Filipinas 54 (daily 10am–8.30pm; ⓜ Ríos Rosas), is a large and well-maintained pool, and the best central option. Alternatively, try the open-air *piscina* in the Casa de Campo (daily 10am–8.30pm; ⓜ Lago). There are also two aquaparks around the city, the closest being Aquópolis de San Fernando (ⓦ san-fernando.aquopolis.es), 16km out on the N-II Barcelona road (buses #221, #224A and #226 from the *intercambiador* at Avda. de América).

OUT OF THE CITY

Faunia Avda. de las Comunidades 28 ☎ 913 016 210, ⓦ faunia.es; ⓦ Valdebernardo, bus #71 from Pza. Manuel Becerra (ⓜ Manuel Becerra). An innovative nature park re-creating a series of ecosystems that provide a home to 720 different animal species. Highlights are the Arctic dome with its penguins, the komodo dragons and the storms in the indoor tropical rainforest. An entertaining and educational experience for children of all ages. €25.95, under-12s €19.95, under-3s free (reductions for advance purchases via the website). Daily 10.30am–dusk.

Palacio de Hielo C/Silvano 77 ☎ 917 160 159, ⓦ sporthielo.com; ⓜ Canillas. There's an 1800-square-metre ice rink, a 24-lane bowling alley and an indoor play park in this massive leisure/shopping complex on the eastern side of the city. Ice rink: Sept–May: Wed & Thurs 8.45–10.15pm, Fri 5.30pm–midnight, Sat 12.30–3pm & 5.30pm–midnight, Sun 12.30–3pm & 5.30–10.20pm; €7–12.50.

SHOPPING

Shopping districts in Madrid are distinctly defined. The biggest range of stores is along the Gran Vía and the streets running north out of Puerta del Sol, which is where the **department stores** – such as El Corte Inglés – have their main branches. For **fashion** (*moda*), the smartest addresses are calles Serrano, Goya, Ortega y Gasset and Velázquez in the Salamanca *barrio*, while more alternative designers are in Malasaña and Chueca (C/Almirante, especially). For street fashion, there's plenty on offer around C/Fuencarral and the nearby area known as triBall. The **antiques** trade is centred towards the Rastro, on and around C/Ribera de Curtidores, while for **general weirdness**, it's hard to beat the shops just off Pza. Mayor, where luminous saints rub shoulders with surgical supports and Fascist memorabilia. If you want international shops or chain stores, head for Madrid 2, a large shopping centre next to ⓜ Barrio de Pilar. There is a smaller, more upmarket mall at ABC Serrano, with entrances at C/Serrano 61 and Paseo de la Castellana 34 (ⓜ Rubén Darío).

Most areas of the city have their own **mercados del barrio** – indoor markets, devoted mainly to food. Among the best are the refurbished **Mercado de San Miguel** (just west of Pza. Mayor) and **Mercado de San Antón** in Chueca (ⓜ Chueca), while there are more traditional markets in the Pza. de la Cebada (ⓜ La Latina) and C/Santa Isabel (ⓜ Antón Martín). The city's biggest market is, of course, **El Rastro** – the flea market – which takes place on Sundays in La Latina, south of Pza. Cascorro (see box, p.72). Other specialized markets include the secondhand bookstalls on Cuesta del Moyano, near Estación de Atocha, and the stamp and coin markets in Pza. Mayor on Sundays.

CRAFTS AND MISCELLANEOUS

★**Antigua Casa Talavera** C/Isabel la Católica 2 ☎ 915 473 417, ⓦ antiguacasatalavera.com; ⓜ Santo Domingo; map pp.62–63. Packed to the rafters with a massive selection of traditional Spanish ceramics, this old-fashioned family business is a great place to pick up a souvenir. Mon–Fri 10am–1.30pm & 5–8pm, Sat 10am–1.30pm.

El Arco Artesania Pza. Mayor 9 ☎ 913 652 680; ⓜ Sol; map pp.102–103. This shop may be at the heart of tourist Madrid, but the goods are a far cry from the swords, lace and castanets that fill most stores in the area. Crafts include ceramics, leather, wood, jewellery and textiles. There's a gallery space for exhibitions, too. Mon–Sun 11am–9pm.

Area Real Madrid C/Carmen 3 ☎ 915 217 950; ⓜ Sol; map pp.102–103. Club store just off Sol where you can pick up replica shirts and all manner of – expensive – souvenirs related

1

to the club's history. Mon–Sat 10am–9pm, Sun 11am–8pm. There is another branch in the shopping centre at Real's Bernabéu stadium at C/Padre Damián gate 55. (MSantiago Bernabéu). Mon–Sat 10am–9pm, Sun 11am–7.30pm.

★**Casa de Diego** Puerta del Sol 12 ☎915 226 643, ℹ casadediego.com; Ⓜ Sol; map pp.102–103. An old-fashioned shop with helpful staff selling a fantastic array of Spanish fans (*abanicos*) ranging from cheap offerings at €12 to beautifully hand-crafted works of art costing up to €1500. Mon–Sat 9.30am–8pm.

Casa Yustas Pza. Mayor 30 ☎913 665 084, ℹ casayustas .com; Ⓜ Sol; map pp.102–103. Madrid's oldest hat shop, established in 1894. Pick from traditional designs for men's and women's hats (*sombreros*), caps (*gorras*) and berets (*boinas*). There's also a large range of souvenir-style goods including Lladró porcelain figurines. Mon–Sat 9.30am–9.30pm, Sun & public hols 11am–9.30pm.

El Flamenco Vive C/Condé de Lemos 7 ☎915 473 917, ℹ elflamencovive.com; Ⓜ Ópera; map pp.102–103. A fascinating little piece of Andalucía in Madrid, specializing in all things flamenco, from guitars and CDs to polka-dot dresses and books. Mon–Sat 10.30am–2pm & 5–9pm.

José Ramírez C/Paz 8 ☎915 314 229, ℹ guitarrasramirez.com; Ⓜ Sol; map pp.102–103. The Ramírez family have been making hand-crafted guitars since 1882 and, even if you are not a budding flamenco artist, this beautiful shop still merits a visit to appreciate these works of art. Mon–Fri 10am–2pm & 5–8pm, Sat 10am–2pm.

Seseña C/Cruz 23; ☎915 316 840, ℹ sesena.com; Ⓜ Sol; map pp.102–103. A tailor specializing in traditional *madrileño* capes for royalty and celebrities. Clients have included Luis Buñuel, Gary Cooper and Hillary Clinton. Mon–Sat 10am–1.30pm & 4.30–8pm.

BOOKS AND MAPS

La Central C/Postigo de San Martín 8 ☎917 909 930, ℹ lacentral.es; Ⓜ Callao; map pp.102–103. Stunning new bookshop over four floors of a beautifully decorated building just off Pza. Callao. A comprehensive collection of Spanish, Latin American and English classics. Mon–Fri 9.30am–10pm, Sat 10am–10pm, Sun 10am–9.30pm.

Desnivel Pza. Matute 6 ☎902 248 848, ℹ libreriadesnivel .com; Ⓜ Antón Martín; map pp.102–103. This centrally located bookshop stocks a good range of guides and maps covering mountaineering and hiking in all parts of Spain. Mon–Fri 10am–8.30pm, Sat 11am–8.30pm.

FNAC C/Preciados 28 ☎902 100 632, ℹ fnac.es; Ⓜ Callao; map pp.102–103. The book department of this huge store is a good place to sit and peruse books and magazines in all languages. Also sells CDs, computer equipment and electronic goods. Mon–Sat 10am–9.30pm, Sun & hols 11.30am–9.30pm.

La Librería C/Mayor 80 ☎914 540 018, ℹ edicioneslalibreria.com; Ⓜ Sol; map pp.102–103.

A tiny place full of books just about Madrid. Most are in Spanish, but many would serve as coffee-table souvenirs. It's also a good place to pick up old prints and photos of the city. Mon–Fri 10am–2pm & 4.30–7.30pm, Sat 11am–2pm.

Pasajes C/Genova 3 ☎913 101 245, ℹ pasajeslibros .com; Ⓜ Alonso Martínez/Colón; map pp.62–63. Specializes in English and foreign-language books. Also has a useful noticeboard service for flat-sharing and Spanish classes. Mon–Sat 9.30am–9.30pm.

CLOTHES AND SHOES

Adolfo Domínguez C/Serrano 5 ☎902 231 226, ℹ adolfodominguez.com; Ⓜ Retiro; map pp.62–63. Domínguez has a massive five-storey flagship store for his classic modern Spanish designs – a wide range of colours and lines for both men and women. Mon–Sat 10am–8.30pm.

Agatha Ruiz de la Prada C/Serrano 27 ☎913 190 501, ℹ agatharuizdelaprada.com; Ⓜ Colón/Goya; map pp.62–63. Outlet for the brightly coloured clothes and accessories of this *movida* designer. There's a children's line, stationery and household goods, too. Mon–Sat 10am–8.30pm.

Caligae C/Augusto Figueroa 27 ☎915 320 240; Ⓜ Chueca; map pp.62–63. One of a string of shoe shops located on this busy Chueca street, selling discounted designer footwear. Mon–Fri 10am–2pm & 5–8pm, Sat 10.30am–2pm & 5–8pm.

Mercado Fuencarral C/Fuencarral 45 ☎915 214 152, ℹ mdf.es; Ⓜ Tribunal/Gran Vía; map pp.62–63. Funky shopping mall catering for the young fashion-conscious crowd, filled with clubwear shops, record stores, jewellers, a café and a tattoo parlour. Mon–Sat 11am–9pm.

FOOD AND DRINK

★**Cacao Sampaka** C/Orellana 4 ☎913 195 840, ℹ cacaosampaka.com; Ⓜ Alonso Martínez/Colón; map pp.62–63. Every conceivable colour, shape and flavour of chocolate is available in this chocoholics' paradise. The only surprise is that the restaurant has some non-chocolate snacks on the menu. Daily 10am–9pm; closed Aug.

Casa Mira C/San Jerónimo 30; ☎914 296 796, ℹ casamira .es; Ⓜ Sol; map pp.102–103. An old, established *pastelería*, setting up 150 years ago and selling delicious *turrón*, *mazapán*, *frutas glaseadas* and the like. Daily 10am–2pm & 5–9pm; closed Sun June–Sept and mid-July to Sept.

Lavinia C/José y Gasset 16 ☎914 260 604, ℹ lavinia.es; Ⓜ Núñez de Balboa; map pp.62–63. Massive wine shop in the upmarket *barrio* of Salamanca, with a great selection from Spain and the rest of the world. Mon–Sat 10am–9pm.

Mariano Madrueño C/Postigo San Martín 3 ☎915 211 955, ℹ marianomadrueno.es; Ⓜ Callao; map pp.102–1063. The place to get wines and liqueurs such as *Pacharán* sloe gin. Mon–Fri 9.30am–2pm & 5–8pm, Sat 9.30am–2pm.

★**Mercado San Antón** C/Augusto Figueroa 24 ☎913

300 730, ⓦmercadosananton.com; ⓜChueca; map pp.62–63. Like the Mercado San Miguel near Pza. Mayor, this local market has been transformed into a trendy meeting place on the Chueca scene, with gourmet food stands, a wine bar, a café, a sushi stall and a stylish terrace restaurant. Market open Mon–Sat 10am–10pm, Sun 10am–3pm; terrace and restaurant Mon–Thurs & Sun 10am–midnight, Fri & Sat 10am–1.30am.

★**Reserva y Cata** C/Conde de Xiquena 13 ☎913 190 401, ⓦreservaycata.com; ⓜColón/Chueca; map pp.62–63. Well-informed staff at this friendly specialist shop will help you select from some of the best new wines in the Iberian Peninsula. Mon 5–9pm, Tues–Fri 11am–3pm & 5–9pm, Sat 11am–3pm.

★**Tienda Olivarero** C/Mejia Lequerica 1 ☎915 321 876, ⓦpco.es; ⓜAlonso Martínez; map pp.62–63. Outlet for olive growers' cooperative boasting around ninety different varieties of olive oil. Mon–Fri 10am–2pm & 5–8pm, Sat 10am–2pm.

CHILDREN

Geppetto C/Mayor 78 ☎915 360 748, ⓦgeppettoitalia .com; ⓜSol; map pp.102–103. Handmade wooden toys and trinkets from Italy which make perfect gifts for small children. Daily 10.30am–8.30pm.

Imaginarium C/Carmen 15 ☎915 238 729, ⓦimaginarium.es; ⓜSol; map pp.102–103. Toys, games and activities with an educational twist for children of all ages. Mon–Sat 10am–9pm.

Prénatal C/Goya 99 ☎915 315 930; ⓜGoya; map pp.62–63; Madrid 2, La Vaguada, Avda. Monforte de Lemos; ⓜBarrio del Pilar. Spanish equivalent of Mothercare, with more branches around the city – and often a little cheaper. Mon–Sat 10am–10pm, Sun 11am–9pm.

DIRECTORY

Bicycles To rent a bike or for tours outside the city, get in touch with Bravo Bike at Juan Mendizábal 19 bajo izda (☎917 582 945 or ☎607 448 440, ⓦbravobike.com; ⓜVentura Rodríguez) or Bike Spain at Pza. de la Villa 1 (☎915 590 653 or ☎677 356 586, ⓦbikespain.info; ⓜÓpera).

Bullfights Madrid's main Pza. de Toros, the monumental Las Ventas (C/Alcalá 237 ⓦlas-ventas.com; ⓜVentas), hosts some of the year's most prestigious events, especially during the May *San Isidro* festivities, though the main season runs from March to October. Tickets (€5–120) are available at the box office at Ventas (March–Oct Thurs–Sun 10am–2pm & 5–8pm, from 10am on day of fight; ☎902 150 025, via the official website and from ⓦwww.taquillatoros.com; as well as the authorized booths along C/Victoria near Sol).

Disabled access Madrid is slowly getting geared up for disabled visitors (*minusválidos*). The local authority has produced a practical guide known as Accessible Madrid at ⓦwww.esmadrid.com/en/access-madrid. The Organización Nacional de Ciegos de España (ONCE; National Organization for the Blind, C/Prim 3 ☎915 325 000, ⓦwww.once.es) provides more specialist advice, as does the Federación de Asociaciones de Minusválidos Físicos de la Comunidad de Madrid (FAMMA; C/Galileo 69 ☎915 933 550, ⓦfamma .org); ⓦdiscapnet.es is also a useful source of information (Spanish only). Wheelchair-friendly taxis can be ordered from Eurotaxi (☎630 026 478 or ☎687 924 027) and Radio Taxi (☎915 478 200 or ☎915 478 600).

Embassies Australia, Torre Espacio, Paseo de la Castellana 259D (☎913 536 600, ⓦspain.embassy.gov.au; ⓜBegoña); Britain, Torre Espacio, Paseo de la Castellana 259D (☎917 146 300 or ☎902 109 356, ⓦukinspain.fco. gov.uk; ⓜBegoña); Canada, Torre Espacio, Paseo de la Castellana 259D (☎913 828 400, ⓦcanadainternational .gc.ca; ⓜBegoña); Ireland, Paseo de la Castellana 46 (☎914 364 093, ⓦembassyofireland.es; ⓜRubén Darío);

New Zealand, C/Pinar 7, 3º (☎915 230 226, ⓦnzembassy .com/spain; ⓜGregorio Marañon); USA, C/Serrano 75 (☎915 872 200, ⓦembusa.es; ⓜRubén Darío); South Africa, C/Claudio Coello 91 (☎914 363 780, ⓦwww.dirco .gov.za/madrid; ⓜRubén Darío).

Health First-aid stations are scattered throughout the city and open 24hr, including Carrera San Jerónimo 32, close to Puerta del Sol (☎913 690 491; ⓜSol). Central hospitals include El Clínico San Carlos, C/Profesor Martín Lagos s/n (☎913 303 000; ⓜIslas Filipinas); Hospital Gregorio Marañon, C/Dr Esquerdo 46 (☎915 868 000; ⓜO'Donnell); Ciudad Sanitaria La Paz, Paseo de la Castellana 261 (☎917 277 000; ⓜBegoña). English-speaking doctors are available at the Anglo-American Medical Unit, C/Conde de Aranda 1 (☎914 351 823; Mon–Fri 9am–8pm, Sat 10am–3pm; ⓜRetiro). The Clinica Dental Pza. Prosperidad at Pza. Prosperidad 3, 2ºB (☎914 158 197, ⓦclinicadental plazaprosperidad.com; ⓜProsperidad), has some English-speaking dentists as does the Clinica Dental Cisne at C/Magallanes 18 (☎914 463 221, ⓦcisnedental.com; ⓜQuevedo).

Left luggage Facilities (*consignas*) at Barajas Airport in terminals 1 & 4 (2–24hr; €10 per item); the Estación Sur bus station (€3.50–5/day); and lockers at Atocha (Mon–Fri 5.30am–10.15pm, Sat open 6.15am, Sun open 6.30am; €3.10–5.20/day) and Chamartín (7am–11pm; €3.10–5.20/day).

Pharmacies Open 24hr: C/Mayor 59 (☎915 480 014; ⓜSol); C/Toledo 46 (☎913 653 458; ⓜLa Latina); C/Atocha 46 (☎913 692 000; ⓜAntón Martín); C/Goya 12 (☎915 754 924; ⓜSerrano).

Police Stations (*comisarías*) at C/Leganitos 19 (☎915 487 945; ⓜPlaza de España/Santo Domingo), C/Huertas 76 (☎913 221 027; ⓜAntón Martín) and C/Luna 29 (☎915 211 236; ⓜCallao).

Around Madrid

A VIEW OF TOLEDO

Around Madrid

The lack of historic monuments in Madrid is more than compensated for by the region around the capital. Within a radius of 100km – and within an hour's travel by bus and train – are some of Spain's greatest cities. Not least of these is Toledo, which preceded Madrid as the country's capital. Immortalized by El Greco, who lived and worked there for most of his later career, the city is a living museum to the many cultures – Visigothic, Moorish, Jewish and Christian – which have shaped the destiny of Spain. If you have time for just one trip from Madrid, make it this.

That said, **Segovia**, with its extraordinary Roman aqueduct and irresistible Disney-prototype castle, puts up strong competition, while Felipe II's vast palace-cum-mausoleum of **El Escorial** is a monument to out-monument all others. And there are smaller places, too, less known to foreign tourists: **Aranjuez**, an oasis in the parched Castilian plain, famed for its asparagus, strawberries and lavish Baroque palace and gardens; the beautiful walled city of **Ávila**, birthplace of St Teresa; and Cervantes' home town, **Alcalá de Henares**, with its sixteenth-century university. For walkers, too, trails amid the sierras of **Gredos and Guadarrama** provide enticing escapes from the midsummer heat.

All of the towns in this chapter can be visited as easy day-trips from Madrid, but they also offer interesting jumping-off points into Castile and beyond.

Toledo

TOLEDO remains one of Spain's great cities. Redolent of past glories, it is packed with memorable sights – hence the whole city's status as a National Monument and UNESCO Patrimony of Mankind – and enjoys an incomparable setting. Be aware, however, that the extraordinary number of day-trippers can take the edge off what was once the most extravagant of Spanish experiences.

Set in a landscape of abrasive desolation, Toledo sits on a rocky mound where every available inch has been built upon: churches, synagogues, mosques and houses are heaped upon one another in a haphazard, cobblestoned spiral.

To see the city at its best, it is advisable to avoid peak holiday periods and weekends and stay at least a night: a day-trip will leave you hard-pressed to see everything. More importantly, in the evening with the crowds gone and the city lit up by floodlights – resembling one of **El Greco**'s moonlit paintings – Toledo is a different place entirely.

There are two main entrances to the old city of Toledo: via the mechanical staircase that scales the hill from the Puerta de Bisagra opposite the tourist office and leaves you close to the Convento de Santo Domingo Antiguo, or up C/Real del Arrabal to the Pza. Zocodover. Once there, the street **layout** can appear confusing, but the old core is so small that it should never take too long to get back on track; part of the city's charm is that it's a place to wander in and absorb. Don't leave without seeing at least the

THE AQUEDUCT AT SEGOVIA

Highlights

❶ A tour of El Greco's Toledo Explore the churches and museums of this historic city in search of evocative masterpieces by the Greek painter. **See p.132 & p.134**

❷ Toledo's Catedral An astonishing construction featuring a heady mixture of opulent decorations and styles befitting a former capital. **See p.132**

❸ Savour strawberries and cream at Aranjuez Indulge in the town's famous sweet treat at the street cafés by the royal palace. See **p.140**

❹ El Escorial Marvel at Felipe II's massive monastery complex perched spectacularly in the foothills of the Sierra de Guadarrama. **See p.143**

❺ Hiking in the sierra Head for the hills of Guadarrama or Gredos for a break from the city heat. **See p.148 & p.156**

❻ A walk along the walls at Ávila Superb views of the town and the harsh Castilian landscape. **See p.154**

❼ The aqueduct at Segovia A marvel of Roman engineering situated at the entrance to the historic mountain city. **See p.158**

❽ The fountains at La Granja A beautiful display at the royal retreat near Segovia. **See p.166**

HIGHLIGHTS ARE MARKED ON THE MAP ON P.128

El Grecos (many of which have been redisplayed since the four hundredth anniversary of the painter's death in 2014), the Catedral, the synagogues and Alcázar, but give it all time and you may stumble upon things not listed in this or any other guidebook. Enter any inviting doorway and you'll find stunning patios, rooms and ceilings, often of Mudéjar workmanship.

Brief history

Toledo was known to the Romans, who captured it in 192 BC, as Toletum, a small but well-defended town. Taken by the Visigoths, who made it their capital, it was already an important cultural and trading centre by the time the **Moors** arrived in 712. The period that followed, with Moors, Jews and Mozárabes (Christians subject to Moorish rule) living together in relative equality, was one of rapid growth and prosperity and

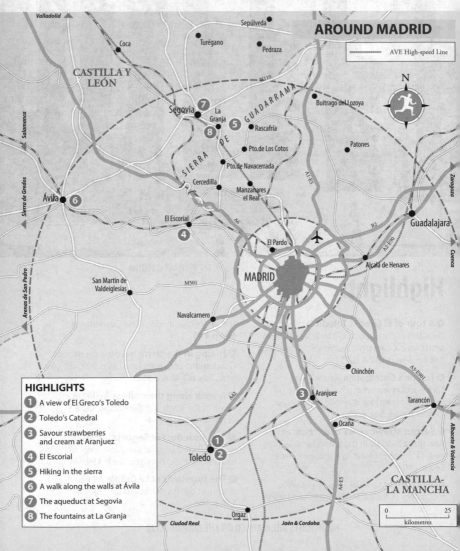

AROUND MADRID

AVE High-speed Line

N

CASTILLA Y LEÓN

CASTILLA-LA MANCHA

HIGHLIGHTS

1 A view of El Greco's Toledo

2 Toledo's Catedral

3 Savour strawberries and cream at Aranjuez

4 El Escorial

5 Hiking in the sierra

6 A walk along the walls at Ávila

7 The aqueduct at Segovia

8 The fountains at La Granja

0 ———— 25 kilometres

FIESTAS

FEBRUARY–APRIL

First Sunday in February: Santa Agueda Women's Festival Married women take over city administration and parade and celebrate in traditional costume.

Semana Santa (Holy Week): Formal processions in Toledo and a Passion play on Saturday in the Pza. Mayor at Chinchón.

Mid-April: Fiesta del Anís y del Vino, Chinchón Ample tastings of these two local products.

MAY–AUGUST

Thursday after Trinity, possibly in June: Corpus Christi Solemn, costumed religious procession in Toledo when the Catedral's magnificent sixteenth-century *custodia* is paraded around.

June 24–29: San Juan y San Pedro Lively procession with floats and music in Segovia.

August 15: Virgen de la Asunción Chinchón's celebrations include an *encierro*, with bulls running through the street.

August 15: Virgen del Sagrario Amazing fireworks display in Toledo.

August 17–25: Entertaining fiestas in La Granja (near Segovia) Parades, bullfighting, fireworks and the fountains in full flow, and in Orgaz (near Toledo) which honours its patron saint with further celebrations.

Last week in August: Spectacular parades of giant puppets, and theatre, music and dance in Alcalá de Henares.

SEPTEMBER & OCTOBER

First weekend in September: Motín de Aranjuez Re-enactment of the Mutiny of Aranjuez in Aranjuez.

September 27: La Virgen de la Fuencisla The image of Segovia's patron saint is carried from the sanctuary in the Eresma valley to the Catedral.

October 25: San Frutos Fiestas, Segovia Concerts, celebrations and parades in honour of the city's patron saint.

Toledo became the most important northern outpost of the Muslim emirates. Though there are few physical remains of this period, apart from the enchanting miniature mosque of **Cristo de la Luz**, the long domination has left a clear mark on the atmosphere and shape of the city.

When the Christian king Alfonso VI "reconquered" the town in 1085, with the assistance of El Cid, Moorish influence scarcely weakened. Although Toledo became the capital of Castile and the base for campaigns against the Moors in the south, the city itself was a haven of cultural tolerance. Not only was there a school of translators revealing the scientific and philosophical achievements of the East, but Arab craftsmen and techniques remained responsible for many of the finest buildings of the period: look, for example, at the churches of **San Román** or **Santiago del Arrabal** or at any of the old **city gates**.

At the same time Jewish culture remained powerful. There were, at one time, at least seven **synagogues** – of which two, **Santa María la Blanca** and **El Tránsito**, survive – and Jews occupied many positions of power. The most famous was Samuel Levi, treasurer and right-hand man of Pedro the Cruel until the king lived up to his name by murdering Levi and stealing his fortune. From this period, too, dates the most important purely Christian monument, Toledo's awesome **Catedral**.

This golden age ended abruptly in the sixteenth century with the transfer of the capital to Madrid, following hard on the heels of the Inquisition's mass expulsion of Muslims and Jews; some of the latter responded by taking refuge in Catholicism, becoming known as *conversos*. The city played little part in subsequent Spanish history until the Civil War with the siege of the Alcázar (see box, p.133) and it remains, despite the droves of tourists, essentially the medieval city so often painted by El Greco.

2

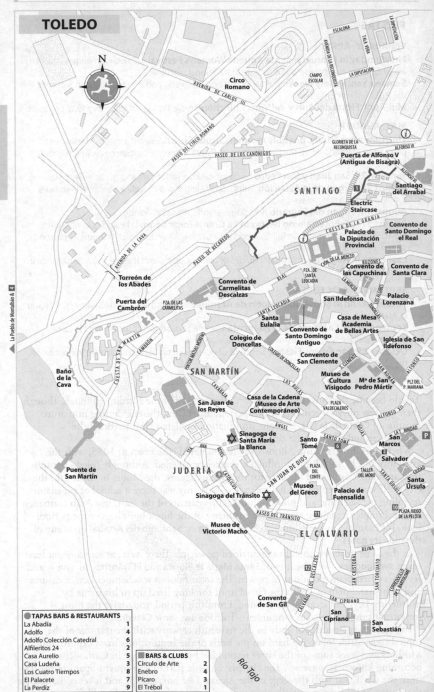

TOLEDO

N

La Puebla de Montalbán & 4

Circo
Romano

CAMPO
ESCOLAR

ESCALONA

T.H.A. VERA

LA DIPUTACIÓN

AVENIDA DE LA RECONQUISTA

LA DIPUTACIÓN

AVENIDA DE CARLOS III

PASEO DEL CIRCO ROMANO

PASEO DE LOS CANÓNIGOS

GLORIETA DE LA
RECONQUISTA

ALFONSO VI

**Puerta de Alfonso V
(Antigua de Bisagra)**

ALFONSO VI

**Santiago
del Arrabal**

SANTIAGO

**Electric
Staircase**

CUESTA DE LA GRANJA

**Convento de
Santo Domingo
el Real**

**Palacio de
la Diputación
Provincial**

CON. DE LA MERCED

PZA. DE
SANTA
LEOCADIA

LA MERCED

BUZONES

**Convento de
las Capuchinas**

**Convento de
Santa Clara**

ALBERES

**Palacio
Lorenzana**

PASEO DE RECAREDO

AVENIDA DE LA CAVA

**Torreón de
los Abades**

**Puerta del
Cambrón**

PZA. DE LAS
CARMELITAS

**Convento de
Carmelitas
Descalzas**

REAL

SANTA LEOCADIA

San Ildefonso

TENDILLAS

**Casa de Mesa
Academia
de Bellas Artes**

**Iglesia de San
Ildefonso**

**Santa
Eulalia**

**Colegio de
Doncellas**

**Convento de
Santo Domingo
Antiguo**

COLEGIO DE DONCELLAS

S. CLEMENTE

**Convento de
San Clemente**

SAN ROMÁN

ALFONSO

PLZ. DEL
P. MARIANA

**Museo de
Cultura
Visigodo**

**Mº de San
Pedro Mártir**

ALFONSO XII

**Baño
de la
Cava**

CUESTA DE SAN MARTÍN

CAMBRÓN

PINTOR MATÍAS MORENO

LAVABÁJA

SAN MARTÍN

LAS BULAS

**Casa de la Cadena
(Museo de Arte
Contemporáneo)**

**San Juan de
los Reyes**

ÁNGEL

PLAZA
VALDECALEROS

ROJAS

**San
Marcos**

LA.T. TRINIDAD

**El
Salvador**

SANTA ÚRSULA

**Santa
Úrsula**

P

CIUDAD

**Puente de
San Martín**

STA.
ANA

REYES

CATÓLICOS

**Sinagoga de
Santa María
la Blanca**

JUDERÍA

SAN JUAN DE DIOS

SANTO TOMÉ

**Santo
Tomé**

PLAZA
DEL
CONTE

**Museo
del Greco**

TALLER
DEL MORO

**Palacio de
Fuensalida**

PLAZA JUEGO
DE LA PELOTA

Sinagoga del Tránsito

PASEO DEL TRÁNSITO

**Museo de
Victorio Macho**

EL CALVARIO

REINA

SAN CRISTÓBAL

SAN TORCUATO

LOS DESCALZOS

CALVARIO

SAN CIPRIANO

CONSOCUELO DE S. BARTOLOMÉ

**Convento
de San Gil**

**San
Cipriano**

**San
Sebastián**

Río Tajo

● TAPAS BARS & RESTAURANTS

La Abadía	1
Adolfo	4
Adolfo Colección Catedral	6
Alfileritos 24	2
Casa Aurelio	5
Casa Ludeña	3
Los Cuatro Tiempos	8
El Palacete	7
La Perdiz	9

■ BARS & CLUBS

Círculo de Arte	2
Enebro	4
Pícaro	3
El Trébol	1

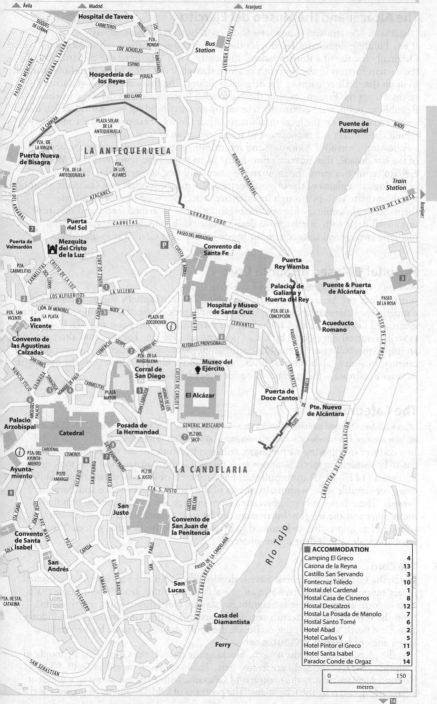

■ ACCOMMODATION	
Camping El Greco	4
Casona de la Reyna	13
Castillo San Servando	3
Fontecruz Toledo	10
Hostal del Cardenal	1
Hostal Casa de Cisneros	8
Hostal Descalzos	12
Hostal La Posada de Manolo	7
Hostal Santo Tomé	6
Hotel Abad	2
Hotel Carlos V	5
Hotel Pintor el Greco	11
Hotel Santa Isabel	9
Parador Conde de Orgaz	14

0   150
metres

▼ 14

2

The Alcázar and the Museo del Ejército

C/Unión s/n • Thurs–Tues 10am–5pm • €5, under-18 free, free Sun • ☎ 925 238 800, ⓦ www.museo.ejercito.es

If one building dominates Toledo, it's the bluff, imposing fortress of the **Alcázar**. Originally the site of a Roman palace, Emperor Carlos V ordered the construction of the current fortress in the sixteenth century, though it has been burned and bombarded so often that little remains of the original building. The monument enjoyed iconic status during the Franco era after the Nationalist forces inside, under siege by the Republican town, were eventually relieved by an army heading for Madrid which took severe retribution on the local inhabitants. After the war, Franco's regime completely rebuilt the fortress as a monument to the glorification of its defenders.

Following a tortuous relocation and refurbishment programme lasting the best part of the last decade, the Alcázar is now home to an impressive state-of-the-art **Museo del Ejército** (army museum). Encompassing a new building constructed over the archeological remains of the original fortress, the museum offers two fascinating routes which navigate visitors through its extensive collections – one historic and one thematic. Spain's military history, the organization of its armed forces and the art of war are all dealt with in exhaustive detail, while exhibits include everything from medieval swords and suits of armour to toy soldiers and Civil War memorabilia.

Hospital y Museo de Santa Cruz

C/Cervantes 3 • Mon–Sat 10am–6.30pm, Sun 2–6.30pm • Free • ☎ 925 221 036

Just north of the Alcázar, off Pza. de Zocodover, is the **Hospital y Museo de Santa Cruz**, a superlative Renaissance building with a fine Plateresque facade, housing some of the greatest El Grecos in Toledo, including *The Immaculate Conception* and *The Holy Family* as well as outstanding works by Luca Giordano and Ribera. The **museum** also contains an impressive collection of exhibits dating from prehistory through to the twentieth century, including archeological finds, ceramic and sculpture. Don't miss the patio with its ornate staircase – the entrance is beside the ticket office.

The Catedral

C/Cardenal Cisneros • Areas that need tickets: Mon–Sat 10am–6.30pm & Sun 2– 6.30pm; New Museums closed Mon • €8, €11 including bell tower and upper cloister; free Sun after 2pm for Spanish citizens • ☎ 925 222 241, ⓦ catedralprimada.es

In a country overflowing with massive religious institutions, the metropolitan **Catedral** has to be something special – and it is. A robust Gothic construction that took over 250 years (1227–1493) to complete, it has a richness of internal decoration in almost every conceivable style, with masterpieces of the Gothic, Renaissance and Baroque periods. The exterior is best appreciated from outside the city, where the hundred-metre spire and the weighty buttressing can be seen to greatest advantage. From the street it's less impressive, so hemmed in by surrounding houses that you can't really sense the scale or grandeur of the whole.

The Coro

Inside the Catedral, the central nave is divided from four aisles by a series of clustered pillars supporting the vaults, 88 in all, the aisles continuing around behind the main altar to form an apse. There is magnificent **stained glass** throughout, mostly dating from the fifteenth and sixteenth centuries, particularly beautiful in two rose windows above the north and south doors. Beside the south door (Puerto de los Leones) is a huge, ancient **fresco of St Christopher**.

At the physical heart of the church, blocking the nave, is the **Coro**, itself a panoply of sculpture. The wooden stalls are in two tiers. The lower level, carved in 1489–95 by Rodrigo Alemán, depicts the conquest of Granada, with each seat showing a different village being taken by the Christians. The portraits of Old Testament characters on the stalls above were executed in the following century, on the north side by Philippe Vigarni and on the south by Alonso Berruguete, whose superior technique is evident. He also carved the large **Transfiguration** here from a single block of alabaster. The *reja* (grille) that encloses the Coro is said to be plated with gold, but it was covered in iron to disguise its value from Napoleon's troops and has since proved impossible to renovate.

The Capilla Mayor and Transparente

The **Capilla Mayor** stands directly opposite the Coro. Its gargantuan altarpiece, stretching clear to the roof, is one of the triumphs of Gothic art, overflowing with intricate detail and fanciful embellishments. It contains a synopsis of the entire New Testament, culminating in a Calvary at the summit.

Directly behind the main altar is an extraordinary piece of fantasy – the Baroque **Transparente**. Wonderfully extravagant, with marble cherubs sitting on fluffy marble clouds, it's especially magnificent when the sun reaches through the hole punched in the roof for just that purpose. A red cardinal's hat hangs from the vaulting just in front. Spanish primates are buried where they choose, with the epitaph they choose and with their hat hanging above them, where it stays until it rots. One of them chose to be buried here, and there are other pieces of headgear dotted around the Catedral.

The Capillas

There are well over twenty **chapels** embedded into the walls of the catedral, all of which are of some interest. Many of them house fine tombs, particularly the **Capilla de Santiago**, the octagonal **Capilla de San Ildefonso** and the gilded **Capilla de Reyes Nuevos**.

In the **Capilla Mozárabe**, Mass is still celebrated daily according to the ancient Visigothic rites. When the Church tried to ban the old ritual in 1086 the people of Toledo were outraged. The dispute was put to a combat, which the Mozárabe champion won, but the Church demanded further proof: trial by fire. The Roman prayer book was blown to safety, while the Mozárabe version remained, unburnt, in the flames. Both sides claimed victory, and in the end the two rituals were allowed to coexist. If you want to attend Mass, be there at 9am and look out for the priest – you may well be the only congregation.

The Tesoro, Sacristía and Sala Capitular

The **Tesoro** (Treasury) houses the riches of the Catedral, most notably a solid silver *custodia* (repository for Eucharist wafers) commissioned by Cardinal Cisneros in 1515; it's three metres high and weighs over two hundred kilos.

THE SIEGE OF THE ALCÁZAR

At the outset of the **Spanish Civil War**, on July 20, 1936, Colonel José Moscardó – a leading Nationalist rebel – and the cadets of the military academy under his command were **driven into the Alcázar**. They barricaded themselves in with a large group that included six hundred women and children, and up to a hundred left-wing hostages (who were never seen again).

After many phone calls from Madrid to persuade them to surrender, a Toledo attorney phoned Moscardó with an ultimatum: within ten minutes the Republicans would shoot his son, captured that morning. Moscardó declared that he would never surrender and told his son, "If it be true, commend your soul to God, shout Viva España, and die like a hero." (His son was actually shot with others a month later in reprisal for an air raid.) Inside, though not short of ammunition, the defenders had so little food they had to eat their horses.

The number of Republican attackers varied from 1000 to 5000. Two of the three mines they planted under the towers exploded but nothing could disturb the solid rock foundations, while spraying petrol all over the walls and setting fire to it had no effect. Finally, General Franco decided to relieve Moscardó and diverted an army that was heading for Madrid. On September 27, General José Varela commanded the successful attack on the town, which was followed by the usual bloodbath. The day after Franco entered Toledo to consolidate his victory, he was declared head of state.

An even more impressive accumulation of wealth is displayed in the **Sacristía** (Sacristy) with its magnificent ceiling fresco of the *Clothing of Saint Ildephonsus* by Luca Giordano, while the paintings include a *Disrobing of Christ* and portraits of the Apostles by El Greco, Velázquez's portrait of *Cardinal Borja* and Goya's *Christ Taken by the Soldiers*. The adjoining rooms house works of art that were previously locked away or poorly displayed. Among them are paintings by Caravaggio, Gerard David and Morales, and El Greco's most important piece of sculpture, a polychromed wooden group of *San Ildefonso and the Virgin*.

The **Sala Capitular** (Chapter House) has a magnificent sixteenth-century *artesonado* (wooden sculptured) ceiling and portraits of all Spain's archbishops to the present day.

Santo Tomé and the Burial of the Count of Orgaz

Pza. del Conde 4 • Mid-March to mid-Oct 10am–6.45pm; mid-Oct to mid-March 10am–5.45pm • €2.50, free Wed after 4pm for EU citizens • ☎ 925 256 098, ⊛ santotome.org

A little way to the west of the Catedral is one of Toledo's outstanding attractions: El Greco's masterpiece, **The Burial of the Count of Orgaz**. It's housed, alone, in a small annexe to the church of **Santo Tomé** and depicts the count's funeral, at which SS Stephen and Augustine appeared in order to lower him into the tomb. It combines El Greco's genius for the mystic, exemplified in the upper half of the picture where the count's soul is being received into heaven, with his great powers as a portrait painter and master of colour. The identity of the sombre-faced figures watching the burial has been a source of endless speculation. On two identities, however, there is universal agreement; El Greco painted himself seventh from the left, looking out at the viewer, and his son in the foreground. Less certain are the identities of the rest of the mourners, but the odds are on for Felipe II's presence among the heavenly onlookers, even though he was still alive when it was painted. A search for the count's bones came to an end in early 2001 when they were unearthed from a tomb located, appropriately enough, directly below the painting.

Museo del Greco

Paseo del Tránsito • April–Sept Tues–Sat 9.30am–8pm, Sun 10am–3pm; Oct–March Tues–Sat 9.30am–6.30pm, Sun 10am–3pm • €3, €5 combined entry with Museo Sefardí; free Sat after 2pm & Sun • ☎ 925 223 665, ⊛ museodelgreco.mcu.es

From Santo Tomé, the C/Alamillo leads down to the old **Judería** (Jewish quarter) and the **Museo del Greco** devoted to the life and work of the Greek-born artist so closely associated with the city. This refurbished exhibition space houses his famous *View and Map of Toledo*, a full series of the *Twelve Apostles*, completed later than the set in the Catedral and subtly different in style, and a fascinating selection of other work by the painter and his disciples. Several of the rooms also re-create the atmosphere of the artist's original living quarters in the city, though this is not the actual house in which he lived. The exhibits are well explained in both Spanish and English, and short videos explain the artist's life and the techniques he used.

Sinagoga del Tránsito and the Museo Sefardí

C/Samuel Levi • April–Sept Tues–Sat 9.30am–8pm, Sun 10am–3pm; Oct–March Tues–Sat 9.30am–6.30pm, Sun 10am–3pm • €3, €5 combined entry with Museo del Greco, free Sat pm & Sun • ☎ 925 223 665

Almost next door to the Museo del Greco is the **Sinagoga del Tránsito**. Built along Moorish lines by Samuel Levi in 1366, it became a church run by the military order of Calatrava after the expulsion of the Jews. The interior is a simple galleried hall, brilliantly decorated with polychromed stuccowork and superb filigree windows. Hebrew inscriptions praising God, King Pedro and Samuel Levi adorn the walls. It houses a small **Museo Sefardí** (Sephardic Museum) tracing the distinct traditions and development of Jewish culture in Spain.

Museo de Victorio Macho

Pza. de Victorio 2 Macho • Mon–Sat 10am–7pm, Sun 10am–3pm • €3 • ☎ 925 284 225, ⊛ realfundaciontoledo.es

Opposite the Sinagoga del Tránsito, splendidly situated on a spur overlooking the Río Tajo and in a delightfully tranquil garden, is the **Museo de Victorio Macho**, which contains the sculptures, paintings and sketches of the Spanish artist Victorio Macho (1887–1966). The auditorium on the ground floor shows a documentary (available in English) about the city and its history.

Sinagoga de Santa María la Blanca

C/Reyes Católicos 4 • Daily 10am–5.45pm, summer closes 6.45pm • €2.50, free Wed pm for EU citizens • ☎ 925 227 257

The only other surviving synagogue apart from the Sinagoga del Tránsito, **Santa María la Blanca** is a short way further down C/Reyes Católicos. Like El Tránsito, which it predates by over a century, it has been both church and synagogue, though, as it was built by Mudéjar craftsmen, it actually looks more like a mosque. Four rows of octagonal pillars each support seven horseshoe arches, all of them with elaborate and individual designs moulded in plaster, while a fine sixteenth-century *retablo* has been preserved from the building's time as a church. The whole effect is quite stunning, accentuated by a deep-red floor tiled with decorative *azulejos*.

Monasterio de San Juan de los Reyes

C/San Juan de los Reyes 2 • Daily 10am–6.45pm, winter closes 5.45pm • €2.50, free Wed after 4pm for EU citizens • ☎ 925 223 802,
⊛ sanjuandelosreyes.org

Down C/Reyes Católicos from Santa María la Blanca you come to the superb church of **San Juan de los Reyes**, its exterior bizarrely festooned with the chains worn by Christian prisoners from Granada released on the reconquest of their city. It was originally a Franciscan convent founded by the "Catholic Kings", Fernando and Isabel, to celebrate their victory at the Battle of Toro. Designed in the decorative Gothic Hispano-Flemish style sometimes referred to as Isabelline (after the queen), its double-storeyed cloister is quite outstanding: the upper storey has an elaborate Mudéjar ceiling, and the crests of Castile and Aragón – seven arrows and a yoke – are carved everywhere in assertion of the new unity brought by the royal marriage.

EL GRECO AND TOLEDO

Even if you've never seen **Toledo** – and even if you've no idea what to expect – there's an uncanny familiarity about your first view of it, with the Alcázar and the Catedral spire towering above the tawny mass of the town. This is due to **El Greco**, whose constant depiction of the city (as background, even, for the Crucifixion) seems to have stuck, albeit unwittingly, somewhere in everyone's consciousness.

Domenikos Theotokopoulos, "the Greek", was born in Crete in 1541 and worked in Venice and Rome before going to Spain. He had originally hoped to get work on the decoration of El Escorial, but after being rejected by Felipe II, he arrived in Toledo in about 1577. His first major commission was to produce the altarpiece for the church of Santo Domingo el Antiguo and many others followed, including his most famous work: *The Burial of the Count of Orgaz*. El Greco remained in the city until his death in 1614 which came while he was working on a commission for the Hospital de Tavera. He was buried in Santo Domingo el Antiguo.

Many of El Greco's extraordinary paintings – some of the most individual, most intensely spiritual visions of all Spanish art – remain scattered throughout the city. Years ahead of his time, his work went on to influence artists for centuries to come, including Manet, Cezanne and Picasso.

Hortension Félix Paravicino, a Spanish preacher and poet who was a subject of one of El Greco's paintings, commented "Crete gave him life and the painter's craft, Toledo a better homeland, where through death he began to achieve eternal life."

Convento de Santo Domingo el Antiguo

Pza. Santo Domingo el Antiguo • Mon–Sat 11am–1.30pm & 4–7pm, Sun 4–7pm • €2.50 • ☎ 925 222 930

A little way to the north of San Juan de los Reyes and close to the mechanical staircase leading out of the old city is the **Convento de Santo Domingo el Antiguo**. The church's chief claim to fame is that it contains El Greco's remains, which can be glimpsed through a peephole in the floor. The nuns display their art treasures in the old choir, but more interesting is the high altarpiece of the church, El Greco's first major commission in Toledo. Unfortunately, most of the canvases have gone to museums and are here replaced by copies, leaving only two *St John*s and a *Resurrection*.

Iglesia de San Ildefonso (Iglesia de los Jesuitas)

Pza. Juan de Mariana 1 • April–Sept daily 10am–5.45pm; Oct–March daily 10am–6.45pm • €2.50 • ☎ 925 251 507

A short distance to the south of the Convento de Santo Domingo el Antiguo stretching along C/San Román and facing on to the Pza. Juan de Mariana is the imposing Baroque facade of the **Iglesia de San Ildefonso**, more commonly known as the **Iglesia de los Jesuitas**. The church, modelled on the Jesuit headquarters, the Gesú in Rome, was completed in 1765, over 150 years after work began and only two years before the brotherhood was expelled from Spain by Carlos III. Although the interior is pleasing enough, the main reason to visit is to make your way up the tower for some magnificent views of the city.

The Puerta del Sol and Mezquita del Cristo de la Luz

Cuesta de los Carmelitos Descalzos 10 • March–Sept Mon–Fri 10am–2pm & 3.30–6.40pm; Oct–Feb Mon–Fri 10am–2pm & 3.30–5.45pm, Sat & Sun 10am–5.45pm • €2.50, free on Wed after 4pm for EU citizens • ☎ 925 254 191

If you leave the old city by the Cuesta de Armas, which runs out of the Pza. de Zocodover and down the hill, you will come across the battlements of the **Puerta del Sol**, a great fourteenth-century Mudéjar gateway. Tucked behind the gateway on the Cuesta de los Carmelitas Descalzos is the tiny mosque of **Mezquita del Cristo de la Luz**. Although this is one of the oldest Moorish monuments in Spain (it was built by Musa Ibn Ali in the tenth century on the foundations of a Visigothic church), only the nave, with its nine different cupolas, is the original Arab construction. The apse was added when the building was converted into a church, and is claimed to be the first product of the Mudéjar style. According to legend, as King Alfonso rode into the town in triumph, his horse stopped and knelt before the mosque. Excavations revealed a figure of Christ, still illuminated by a lamp, which had burned throughout three and a half centuries of Muslim rule – hence the name Cristo de la Luz. The outstandingly elegant mosque, set in a small park and open on all sides to the elements, is so small that it seems more like a miniature summer pavilion, but it has an elegant simplicity of design that few of the town's great monuments can match.

Santiago del Arrabal and the Puerta Bisagra

Pza. Santiago del Arrabal 4

Below the Puerta del Sol on the way out of the old city is the intriguing brickwork exterior of the Mudéjar church of **Santiago del Arrabal**, while at the foot of the hill and marooned in a constant swirl of traffic is Toledo's main gate, the sixteenth-century **Puerta Nueva de Bisagra**. Its patterned-tile roofs bear the coat of arms of Carlos V. Alongside is the gateway that it replaced, the ninth-century Moorish portal through which Alfonso VI and El Cid led their triumphant armies in 1085.

Hospital de Tavera

C/Duque de Lerma 2 • Mon–Sat 10am–1.30pm & 3–5.30pm, Sun 10am–1.30pm • €4.50, €2.50 to visit just the building • ☎ 925 220 451

Beyond the city walls along the Paseo de Merchán is the **Hospital de Tavera**. This

Renaissance palace with beautiful twin patios houses the private collection of the Duke of Lerma. The gloomy interior is a reconstruction of a sixteenth-century mansion dotted with fine paintings, including a *Day of Judgement* by Bassano; the portrait of Carlos V by Titian is a copy of the original in the Prado. The hospital's archives are kept here, too: thousands of densely handwritten pages chronicling the illnesses treated. The museum contains several works by El Greco, and Ribera's celebrated portrait of a freak "bearded woman" breast-feeding a baby. Also here is the death mask of Cardinal Tavera, the hospital's founder, and in the church of the hospital is his ornate marble tomb – the last work of Alonso de Berruguete.

2

ARRIVAL AND DEPARTURE
TOLEDO

By train A high-speed train service departs from Atocha station in Madrid (15–18 daily; 35min; €20 return; it's essential to book in advance at the station or via the website ⓦrenfe.com). Toledo's magnificent neo-Mudéjar train station is some way out on the Paseo de la Rosa, a 20min walk – take the left-hand fork off the dual carriageway and cross the Puente de Alcántara – or a bus ride (#5 or #6 or the tourist shuttle) to the heart of town. Destinations Albacete (2–5 daily; 2hr 25min–2hr 55min); Cuenca (2–3 daily; 1hr 50min–2hr 50min).

By bus Every 30min from the Pza. Elíptica terminal in Madrid (1hr; €11.26 return). The bus station is on Avda. de Castilla la Mancha in the modern, lower part of the city; bus

#5 runs to Pza. Zocodover, though if you take shortcuts through the *barrio* at the bottom of the hill just inside the walls, it's a mere 10min walk to the Puerta Nueva de Bisagra. Destinations Ciudad Real, for the south 4 daily; 1hr 30min–2hr); Cuenca (Mon–Fri 2 daily; 2hr); Guadamur (3–5 daily; 20min); Orgaz (3–13 daily; 35min); Talavera de la Reina, for Extremadura (6–14 daily; 1hr).

By car The best places to park are in the streets beyond the Circo Romano in the new town (Mon–Fri 10am–2pm & 5–8pm, Sat 10am–2pm; €0.85/hr) or in the underground car park close to the mechanical staircase (Mon–Fri 7am–10pm, Sat, Sun & hols 8am–10pm) that leads up into the old city.

GETTING AROUND

On foot Walking is the only way to see the city itself, but be aware that resident cars have a tendency to roar along even the tiniest alleyways in the centre. Information on an array of

walking tours is available at the *turismo* (see below). You can also check out ⓦtoledopaisajes.com and ⓦtoledo3culturas .com (from €10 for a 90min tour of the main sights).

INFORMATION

Regional tourist office Opposite Puerta Nueva de Bisagra outside the city walls (summer Mon–Sat 9am–7pm, winter Mon–Fri 9am–6pm, Sun & hols 9am–3pm; ☎925 220 843, ⓦturismocastillamancha.com).

Local tourist offices In the train station (daily 9.30am–5pm; ☎925 239 121); at the top of the mechanical staircase leading into the city from the Puerta de Bisagra (Cuesta de la Granja s/n; Mon–Fri 10am–5pm, Sat & Sun 10am–3.50pm; ☎925 248 232); the kiosk in Pza. Zocodover (daily 10am–7pm) and in the plaza next to the

Catedral (daily 10am–6pm; ☎925 254 030, ⓦtoledo -turismo.com).

Tickets You can save on the entry fees to a number of the sights such as the synagogue of Santa María la Blanca, San Juan de los Reyes, Santo Tomé and the Iglesia de los Jesuitas if you invest in the €8 tourist wristband. Alternatively, depending on how much you want to visit, there is a range of discount tourist cards available for between €18 and €65 from ⓦtoledocard.com, on sale at the high-speed train station and many of the larger hotels.

ACCOMMODATION

Booking a room in advance is important in Toledo, especially at weekends, or during the summer. The tourist offices have lists of all the **accommodation** available in town. Be aware that prices in many places almost double at Easter, bank holidays and at Corpus Christi, but that outside these times and midweek, hotels often offer substantially reduced rates.

Casona de la Reyna C/San Sebastián 26 ☎925 282 052, ⓦcasonadelareyna.com. Situated in the quiet San Cipriano area of the old town close to the Judería, this functional mid-range hotel has 25 spacious, classically decorated rooms with a/c and private parking. __€60__

Castillo San Servando Across the Puente de Alcántara and just off Paseo de la Rosa on Cuesta de San Servando

☎925 224 554, ⓦjuventud.jccm.es/sanservando/es. Toledo's youth hostel is across the river from the Alcázar and in a wing of the fourteenth-century Mudéjar-style Castillo San Servando, a 15min walk (signposted) from the train station. It has a fine view of the city, and a pool and communal areas. Booking is advised and a YH card required; accommodation is in two- or four-room

2

dormitories. Closed mid-Aug to mid-Sept. Under-30s **€14.05**, over-30s **€16.90**

Fontecruz Toledo Pza. del Juego de la Pelota 7 ☎ 925 274 690, ⊛ fontecruzhoteles.com. Luxury boutique-style hotel in the heart of the old town close to the Catedral with its own spa and a top-notch restaurant. **€109**

★ **Hostal del Cardenal** Paseo de Recaredo 24 ☎ 925 224 900, ⊛ hostaldelcardenal.com. A splendid old mansion with 27 very comfortable, classically decorated rooms, a well-regarded, but pricey restaurant and delightful patio gardens, located outside the city wall, near Puerta Nueva de Bisagra. Discounts available on the website. **€92**

Hostal Casa de Cisneros C/Cardenal Cisneros ☎ 925 228 828, ⊛ hostal-casa-de-cisneros.com. Upmarket boutique-style *hostal* in a refurbished sixteenth-century townhouse with ten en-suite, wood-beamed a/c rooms situated opposite the Puerta de Leones entrance of the Catedral. **€66**

Hostal Descalzos C/Descalzos 30 ☎ 925 222 888, ⊛ hostaldescalzos.com. Very good-value, centrally located *hostal*, handy for the main sights. Some of the modern, but straightforward en-suite rooms have lovely views, plus there's a small open-air pool. **€48**

★ **Hostal La Posada de Manolo** C/Sixto Ramón Parro 8 ☎ 925 282 250, ⊛ laposadademanolo.com. An atmospheric *hostal* in a carefully refurbished period house close to the Catedral, with small brick-lined and beamed rooms, all with a/c. **€80**

Hostal Santo Tomé C/Santo Tomé 13 ☎ 925 221 712, ⊛ hostalsantotome.com. Relatively new *hostal* next door to the church of the same name with a range of simple, comfortable a/c rooms including a four-bed attic family room. They also have their own garage (a rarity in Toledo) for those travelling by car. **€52**

Hotel Abad C/Real del Arrabal 1 ☎ 925 283 500, ⊛ hotelabad.com. A smart hotel situated in a former ironworks close to the Mezquita de la Luz. The 22 tastefully decorated rooms have brick-lined walls and warm colours, and those in the loft are particularly nice. There are family apartments available from €100. **€65**

Hotel Carlos V Pza. Horno de la Magdalena 4 ☎ 925 222 105, ⊛ carlosv.com. Tucked away in a little side street close to the Alcázar, the rooms in this well-established hotel have been given a makeover with a choice between the more traditional standard option and the slightly slicker, clean-lined premium ones. The big attraction of this hotel is the terrace bar with some great views over the city. **€120**

★ **Hotel Pintor el Greco** C/Alamillos de Tránsito 13 ☎ 925 285 191, ⊛ hotelpintorelgreco.com. A well-equipped and nicely furnished hotel in a refurbished seventeenth-century bakery situated in the old Jewish quarter. It has sixty comfortable rooms, many with fine views across the Tajo, and private parking. Special offers available. **€80**

Hotel Santa Isabel C/Santa Isabel 24 ☎ 925 253 120, ⊛ hotelsantaisabel.net. A mid-range hotel occupying a converted nobleman's house right in the centre of town. It has neat, unfussy rooms (some with views), wood-panelled floors and safe parking (€10 per night). **€45**

Parador Conde de Orgaz Cerro del Emperador s/n ☎ 925 221 850, ⊛ www.paradores.com. Superb views of the city from the terrace of Toledo's top hotel, but the drawback is that it's a fair walk from the centre. Light and airy rooms and a splendid outdoor pool that's tempting if the heat gets too much in summer. **€135**

CAMPING

Camping El Greco Carretera de Toledo–Puebla de Montalbán ☎ 925 220 090, ⊛ campingelgreco.es. There are great views of the city from this riverside campsite – and a bar to enjoy them from – plus a swimming pool to cool off in after a hard day's sightseeing. A 30min walk from the Puerta de Bisagra: cross the Puente de la Cava towards Puebla de Montalbán, then follow the signs. **€20**

EATING AND DRINKING

Toledo is a major tourist centre and inevitably many of its **cafés**, **bars** and **restaurants** are geared to passing trade. However, the city is also popular with Spanish visitors, so decent, authentic places do exist – and there's a bit of nightlife, too.

★ **La Abadía** Pza. San Nicolás 3 ☎ 925 251 140, ⊛ abadiatoledo.com. There's a constantly changing €12 lunchtime menu in this popular restaurant which also serves some good specialities such as partridge and venison. They do breakfast options from €2.50. Daily around 8am–midnight.

Adolfo C/Hombre de Palo 7 ☎ 925 227 321, ⊛ grupoadolfo.com. One of the most prestigious restaurants in town, tucked behind a marzipan café, in an old Jewish townhouse (ask to see the painted ceiling in the eleventh-century cellar downstairs), and serving imaginative, high-quality but over-priced food, using local ingredients such as partridge, with a meal costing in the region of €70–90. Mon–Sat 1–4pm & 8pm–midnight, Sun 1–4pm.

Adolfo Colección Catedral C/Nuncio Viejo 1 ☎ 925 224 244, ⊛ grupoadolfo.com. If you can't afford to eat at the *Adolfo* restaurant (above), have a glass of wine and some designer tapas or the €12.90 lunchtime menu at this elegant little bar run by the same people. Mon–Thurs noon–midnight, Fri & Sat noon–12.30am, Sun noon–11.30pm.

★**Alfileritos 24** C/Alfileritos 24 ☎ 925 239 625, ⓦ alfileritos24.com. A cool, relaxed, brick-lined bar-restaurant serving an imaginative and tasty €10.50 lunchtime bar menu and a more elaborate but excellent €18.50 restaurant version. In the evening à la carte options include some creative salad dishes, quail and vegetable rice dishes, and goat stew with mushrooms and sesame. The taster menu with its array of starters, meat and fish dishes will set you back €39 but certainly won't leave you hungry. Daily around 1.30–4pm and 8.30–11.30pm.

Casa Aurelio C/Sinagoga 1 & 6 ☎ 925 224 105, ⓦ casa-aurelio.com. Two branches of a popular Toledano group of restaurants (there's another one next to the Catedral in the Pza. del Ayuntamiento which closes on Tuesdays) serving up good, classic Castilian food. Mains range from €20–25, while the lunchtime menu is €23.50. Mon & Sun 1–4.30pm, Tues & Thurs–Sat 1–4.30pm & 8–11.30pm.

Casa Ludeña Pza. Magdalena 13. One of many places around this square, but this down-to-earth bar-restaurant is the most authentic. It offers some of the best *carcamusa* in town and a full meal for around €15 a head. Daily 1–4pm.

★**Los Cuatro Tiempos** C/Sixto Ramón Parro 5 (close to the Catedral) ☎ 925 223 782, ⓦ restaurante loscuatrotiempos.com. An excellent restaurant with local specialities such as *cochinillo*, *perdiz* and *cordero* given a modern twist. The set menu is around €20, à la carte around €35 a head. Mon–Sat 1–4pm & 8.30–11.30pm, Sun 1–4pm.

El Palacete C/Soledad 2 ☎ 925 225 375, ⓦ www .restauranteelpalacete.com. Located in a beautifully restored building dating back to the eleventh century, this high-quality restaurant serves well-presented meat and fish dishes and offers a €36 taster menu. Mon & Sun 1.30–4pm, Tues–Sat 1.30–4.30pm & 8.30–11.30pm.

La Perdiz C/Reyes Católicos 7 ☎ 925 252 919, ⓦ grupoadolfo.com. A popular place which does a good set lunch at €12.90 and has a fine selection of local wines. Owned by the same people as *Adolfo* (see opposite). Tues–Sat 1–4pm & 8–11.30pm, Sun 1–4pm; closed third week in Jan and first 2 weeks in Aug.

NIGHTLIFE

By Spanish standards, Toledo's **nightlife** is rather tame. You'll find most late-night bars running along C/Sillería and its extension C/Alfileritos, west of Pza. de Zocodover. In the old core, there are several discobars close to Pza. de Zocodover, while in the new town the area around Pza. de Cuba is packed with bars and clubs. Out of the tourist season, between September and March, classical concerts are held in the Catedral and other churches; details can be obtained from the *oficina de turismo*.

Círculo de Arte Pza. de San Vicente ☎ 925 265 653, ⓦ circuloartetoledo.org. A converted chapel now used as a venue for live music, exhibitions, poetry reading and the like. Also makes a classy location for a coffee or drink. Daily from 10am to late (depends on live acts).

Enebro Pza. Santiago Caballeros 1 ☎ 925 254 269. A good-value bar with pleasant terrace that makes a good early-evening stop, serving free tapas with each drink. There's another branch at Pza. San Justo 9. Daily from 10am to midnight.

Pícaro C/Cadenas 6 ☎ 925 221 301 ⓦ picarotoledo.com. Popular discobar/café with regular concerts and DJ sessions. spread over three levels in this nightspot not far from Pza. de Zocodover. Daily 3pm–4am (until 6am at weekends).

CUISINE AROUND MADRID

The **food** to be found in most of the areas **around Madrid** owes much to **Castilian tradition**, with roast meats such as *cochinillo* (suckling pig) and *cordero* (roast lamb) providing the signature dishes in many restaurants. Cooked to perfection so the meat is deliciously tender and falling off the bone (in some restaurants they even cut the *cochinillo* with plates), meals are served with almost no side dishes, bar the odd chip or potato.

But one of the chief pleasures of eating in the areas around the Spanish capital is that **local specialities** still remain. In Toledo, for example, many of the more traditional restaurants offer *carcamusa* – a meat in a spicy tomato sauce, and game such as partridge (*perdiz*), pheasant (*faisán*) and quail (*cordoniz*). In Segovia Castilian roasts are to the fore, while in nearby La Granja the rather healthier *judiones* (large white beans) are on offer. Like La Granja, Ávila is also renowned for its beans, this time haricot beans with sausage (*judias del barco*), as well as its delicious, and massive, T-bone steaks (*chuletón de Ávila*), and for the most sickly sweet of desserts, the *yemas de Santa Teresa* (candied egg yolks). If all that proves too much, head for the oasis of Aranjuez where vegetables (in particular asparagus) and fresh strawberries are the local speciality.

El Trébol C/Santa Fé 15 ☎ 925 281 297. Very popular bar between Pza. Zocodover and the Museo de Santa Cruz serving some great tapas and the house speciality *bombas* (potatoes stuffed with meat and fried). A tasty range of *bocadillos* and some good tortilla too. Daily 10am–3.30pm & 7pm–midnight.

Aranjuez

A short train journey from Madrid is **ARANJUEZ**, a little oasis at the confluence of the Tajo and Jarama rivers on the southern edge of the province of Madrid, where the eighteenth-century Bourbon rulers set up a spring and autumn retreat. The beauty of Aranjuez is its greenery – it's easy to forget just how dry and dusty most of central Spain is until you come upon this town, with its lavish palaces and luxuriant gardens, which inspired the composer Joaquín Rodrigo to write the famous *Concierto de Aranjuez*. Famed for its summer strawberries (served with cream – *fresas con nata* – at roadside stalls) and asparagus, Aranjuez functions principally as a weekend escape from Madrid and most people come out for the day, or stop en route to or from Toledo.

Palacio Real

Palace Tues–Sun: April–Sept 10am–8pm; Oct–March 10am–6pm • €9 (ticket includes entry to the Casa del Labrador and Museo de Faluas Reales), free Wed & Thurs 5–8pm (3–6pm Oct–March) for EU citizens **Gardens** Daily 8am–dusk • Free • ☎ 918 911 344, ⓦ patrimonionacional.es

The showpiece eighteenth-century **Palacio Real** and its **gardens** were an attempt by the Spanish Bourbon monarchs to create a Versailles in Spain; Aranjuez clearly isn't in the same league, but it's a very pleasant place to while away a few hours. The palace, placed by the river, is more remarkable for the ornamental fantasies inside than for any virtues of architecture. There seem to be hundreds of rooms, all exotically furnished, most amazingly so the **Porcelain Room**, which is entirely covered in decorative ware from the factory that used to stand in Madrid's Retiro park. Most of the palace dates from the reign of the "nymphomaniac" Queen Isabel II, and many of the sexual scandals and intrigues that led to her removal from the throne in 1868 were played out here.

Outside, on a small island, are the fountains and neatly tended gardens of the **Jardín de la Isla**. The **Jardín del Príncipe**, on the other side of the main road, is more attractive, with shaded walks along the river and plenty of spots for a siesta.

Real Casa del Labrador

Tues–Sun: April–Sept 10am–8pm; Oct–March 10am–6pm • Included with entrance to the Palacio Real • ☎ 918 911 344, ⓦ patrimonionacional.es

At the far end of the **Jardín del Príncipe** is the **Casa del Labrador**, an opulent house containing more silk, marble, crystal and gold than would seem possible in so small a place, as well as a huge collection of fancy clocks. The guided tour goes into great detail about the weight and value of every item.

Museo de Faluas Reales

Tues–Sun: April–Sept 10am–8pm; Oct–March 10am–6pm • Included with entrance to the Palacio Real • ☎ 918 911 344, ⓦ patrimonionacional.es

In the gardens, by the river, is the small **Casa de los Marinos** or **Museo de Faluas Reales**, which houses the brightly coloured launches in which royalty would take to the river. You can do the modern equivalent and take a boat trip through the royal parks from the jetty by the bridge next to the palace (Tues–Sun 11am–sunset; €7).

ARRIVAL AND DEPARTURE ARANJUEZ

By train An old wooden steam train (May–July & Sept to mid-Oct Sat & Sun; €29.90, under-10s €14.90; ☎ 902 228 822), the *Tren de la Fresa*, also runs between Madrid and Aranjuez; it leaves the Museo del Ferrocarril at Paseo de las

Delicias 61 in Madrid at 10.00am and returns from Aranjuez at 6pm, arriving back at Atocha at 7pm. The price includes a guided bus tour in Aranjuez, entry to the main monuments and *fresas* on the train. The less romantic, but highly efficient, standard trains leave every fifteen to thirty minutes from Atocha, with the last train returning from Aranjuez at about 11.30pm (€4 each way).

By bus Buses run every half-hour during the week and every hour at weekends from Estación Sur (€4.20 each way; 40min).

INFORMATION AND GETTING AROUND

Turismo Casa de Infantes, facing the Pza. de San Antonio (daily 10am–6pm; ☏ 918 910 427, ⓦ aranjuez.es).

Getting around A bus service occasionally connects the various sights and if you have children the *chiquitren*, a motorized mini-train (March–Sept: Tues–Sun 10am–8pm; €5, children €3) that departs from the Palacio Real, is a good option, but everything is within easy walking distance, and the town's a very pleasant place to stroll around.

ACCOMMODATION

It's essential to reserve a room in advance, as **accommodation** is not plentiful.

★ **Hotel El Cocherón 1919** C/Montesinos 22 ☏ 918 754 350, ⓦ elcocheron1919.com. Boutique-style hotel close to the Palacio and gardens with 18 individually decorated rooms, a large and tranquil central patio area and a small bar/cafeteria. There is a family room for €110. **€64**

Hotel Don Manuel C/Príncipe 71 ☏ 918 754 086, ⓦ donmanuelhotel.com. A comfortable hotel, with a good range of rooms, close to the royal palace and across the road from the Jardín del Príncipe. **€65**

NH Príncipe de la Paz C/San Antonio 22 ☏ 918 099 222, ⓦ nh-hoteles.com. A smart NH hotel complete with all the usual business facilities, bar and restaurant, and conveniently located next to the palace. **€100**

CAMPING

Camping Internacional Aranjuez On a far bend of the Río Tajo ☏ 918 911 395, ⓦ campingaranjuez.com. This large campsite with 162 pitches is equipped with a swimming pool, a supermarket and a children's club, and rents out bicycles and canoes. **€22**

EATING AND DRINKING

The splendid nineteenth-century **Mercado de Abastos** on C/Stuart is a good place to buy your own food for a picnic (including, in season, the famous locally grown strawberries and asparagus).

La Alegria de la Huerta Carretera de Madrid 4 ☏ 918 912 938, ⓦ laalegriadelahuerta.com. This place, near to the bridge across the Tajo on the main road in from Madrid, offers a speciality *arroz con bogavante*, pheasant and *cochinillo*. Lunchtime menu has dishes such as stuffed aubergines and the obligatory strawberries and cream for €15. Mon–Thurs & Sun noon–4pm, Fri & Sat noon–4pm & 9pm–midnight; closed first 2 weeks in Aug.

Casa José C/Abastos 32 ☏ 918 911 488, ⓦ casajose.es. Renowned restaurant serving high-quality *nouvelle cuisine* featuring local produce. Offers an excellent seasonal taster menu at €75 and a standard menu at around €60 which includes offerings such as glacéed artichokes and suckling pig in orange and parsley. Tues–Sat 1–4pm & 9pm–midnight, Sun 1–4pm.

Casa Pablete C/Stuart 108 ☏ 918 910 381. A traditional bar good for tapas and *raciones* with excellent *montados de calamares* and *solomillo*. Tues–Sat 1–4pm & 9pm–midnight, Sun 1–4pm; closed Aug.

Casa Pablo C/Almíbar 42 ☏ 918 911 451, ⓦ casapablo. net. Castilian food at a reasonable price served in traditional surroundings in this long-standing Aranjuez favourite, whose walls are covered with pictures of local dignitaries and bullfighters. Daily 1.30–4pm & 8.30pm–midnight; closed Aug.

El Rana Verde Pza. Santiago Rusiñol s/n ☏ 918 019 171, ⓦ elranaverde.com. Probably the best-known restaurant in the area, but mainly because of its pleasant riverside location. It dates back to the late nineteenth century and serves up a range of decent, if unspectacular menus for €16.50 and €27.50. Daily around 1.30–4pm & 8.30pm–midnight.

Chinchón

CHINCHÓN, 45km southeast of Madrid, is an enchanting little place, with a fifteenth-century castle and a picture-postcard **Pza. Mayor**, encircled by whitewashed buildings festooned with wooden balconies. Providing the backdrop to the Pza. Mayor is the Neoclassical **Iglesia de la Asunción**, which houses Goya's depiction of the Assumption.

The town is best known for being the home of *anís* – a mainstay of breakfast drinkers across Spain. Your best bet for a sample of the spirit is one of the local bars or the Alcoholera de Chinchón, a shop on the Pza. Mayor. The **Museo Etnológico** (Tues–Fri 11am–2pm & 4–8pm, Sat & Sun 11am–3pm & 4–8pm; free; ⓦmuseolaposada.es), at C/Morata 5, off the Pza. Mayor has some of the traditional *anís*-making machines on display.

ARRIVAL AND INFORMATION

By bus From Aranjuez #430 from Avda. de las Infantas (Mon–Fri hourly, Sat & Sun 8 daily; 55min); from Madrid #337 every 30min from the bus station at Avda. Mediterraneo 49 (ⓜ Conde Casal); 45–55min.

CHINCHÓN

Turismo Pza. Mayor (summer: Mon–Fri 10am–3pm & 5–8pm, Sat & Sun 10am–3pm, winter daily 10am–7pm; ☏918 935 323, ⓦ ciudad-chinchon.com).

ACCOMMODATION

Hostal Chinchón C/Grande 16 ☏918 935 398, ⓦhostalchinchon.com. Near the Pza. Mayor, modest but pleasant with ten decent-sized a/c doubles and triples. There is a terrace pool and restaurant/bar. **€50**
★ **Parador de Chinchón** C/Los Huertos 1 ☏ 918 940 836, ⓦwww.paradores.com. Situated in a sixteenth-century former Augustinian monastery close to the Pza. Mayor, this historic parador has an outdoor pool, tranquil patio gardens, large rooms and a very good restaurant. Look out for offers on the website. **€145**

EATING AND DRINKING

★ **Casa de Pregonero** Pza. Mayor 4 ☏918 940 696, ⓦlacasadelpregonero.com. Adds modern touches to traditional dishes and has some mouthwatering starters and desserts such as strawberry and asparagus gazpacho and mandarin sorbet with rum. There are set menus at €23 and €30, but reckon on at least €40 a head if you go à la cartre. Wed–Mon 1.30–4.30pm & 8.30–11.30pm.
★ **Mesón La Balconada** Pza. Mayor ☏918 941 303, ⓦrestaurantelabalconada.com. Excellent restaurant in one of the balconied buildings overlooking the plaza, serving top-quality Castilian specialities such as *cochinillo* and *cordero* as well as some quality fish dishes. An extensive wine list too. Expect to pay around €45 per person. Mon, Tues & Thurs–Sun around 1.30–4pm & 8.30pm–midnight.
Mesón del Comendador Pza. Mayor ☏918 940 420, ⓦchinchonrestaurante.com. One of a cluster of good restaurants on the plaza serving classic Castilian fare, but the prices here are rather more modest. Mon, Tues & Thurs–Sun around 1.30–4pm & 8.30pm–midnight.
Mesón Cuevas del Vino C/Benito Hortelano 13 ☏918 940 206, ⓦcuevasdelvino.com. Situated in an old olive oil mill, with its own *bodega*, this restaurant first opened its doors back in 1964, with luminaries such as Orson Welles and Yul Brynner passing through its doors in the early years. There is a taster menu, which includes *cordero* or *cochinillo*, available at €38.50. Mon–Fri noon–4.30pm & 8–11pm, Sat noon–midnight, Sun noon–8pm.
Mesón del Duende C/Grande 36 ☏918 940 807, ⓦmesonelduende.com. One of the more reasonably priced restaurants in town in a little courtyard not far from the Pza. Mayor, serving traditional Castilian food with a set lunch at under €20. Tues–Sun 1.30–4pm & 8.30–11pm.

San Lorenzo del Escorial and Valle de los Caídos

Northwest of Madrid, in the foothills of the Sierra de Guadarrama, is one of Spain's best known and most visited sights – Felipe II's vast monastery-palace complex of **El Escorial**. The vast granite building, which contains a royal palace, a monastery, a mausoleum, four thousand rooms, fifteen cloisters and one of the finest libraries of the Renaissance, embodies all that was important to one of the most powerful rulers in European history. The town around the monastery, **San Lorenzo del Escorial**, is an easy day-trip from Madrid; for onward travel, rail and road routes continue to Ávila and Segovia. The heart of the **Sierra de Guadarrama** lies just to the north, and is Madrid's easiest mountain escape.

Tours from Madrid to El Escorial often take in the grim Francoist monument **El Valle de los Caídos** where the dictator and many Civil War dead are buried.

El Escorial

Tues–Sun: April–Sept 10am–8pm; Oct–March 10am–6pm • €10 (entry covers monastery, Palacio de los Borbones, outlying lodges and gardens); extra €7 for a guided tour, €4 for audio-guide; free Wed & Thurs 5–8pm (3–6pm Oct–March) for EU citizens • ☎918 905 902, Ⓦ patrimonionacional.es

The monastery of **El Escorial** was the largest Spanish building of the Renaissance: rectangular, overbearing and austere, from the outside it resembles a prison more than a palace. Built between 1563 and 1584 to commemorate the victory over the French at the battle of San Quentin on August 10, 1557 (San Lorenzo's Day), it was originally the creation of Juan Bautista de Toledo, though his one-time assistant, **Juan de Herrera**, took over and is normally given credit for the design. **Felipe II** planned the complex as both monastery and mausoleum, where he would live the life of a monk and "rule the world with two inches of paper". Later monarchs had less ascetic lifestyles, enlarging and richly decorating the palace quarters, but Felipe's simple rooms remain the most fascinating.

Visits to the **Real Monasterio del Escorial** have become more relaxed in recent years, and you can use your ticket (purchased in the **visitors' entrance**) to enter, in whatever sequence you like, the basilica, sacristy, chapterhouses, library and royal apartments. To escape the worst of the crowds avoid Wednesday and Thursday afternoons in the high season and try visiting just before lunch or late in the day.

The Biblioteca and Patio de los Reyes

A good starting point is the west gateway, the traditional **main entrance**, facing the mountains. Above it is a gargantuan statue of San Lorenzo holding the gridiron on which he was martyred. Within is the splendid **Biblioteca** (Library), adorned with shelves designed by Herrera to harmonize with the architecture, and frescoes by Tibaldi and his assistants that show the seven Liberal Arts. Its collections include the tenth-century *Codex Albeldensis*, St Teresa's personal diary, some gorgeously executed Arabic manuscripts and a Florentine planetarium of 1572 demonstrating the movement of the planets according to the Ptolemaic and Copernican systems. Beyond is the **Patio de los Reyes**, named after the six statues of the kings of Israel on the facade of the basilica straight ahead. Off to the left is a school, and to the right the monastery, both of them still in use.

Basílica

In the **Basílica**, notice the flat vault of the *coro* above your head as you enter, which is apparently entirely without support, and the white marble Christ carved by Benvenuto Cellini and carried here from Barcelona on workmen's shoulders. The east end is decorated by Italian artists: the sculptures are by the father-and-son team of Leone and Pompeo Leoni, who also carved the two facing groups of Carlos V with his family and Felipe II with three of his wives; Mary Tudor is excluded. The reliquaries near the altar are said to hold the entire bodies of ten saints, plus 144 heads and 306 arms and legs.

Sacristía, Salas Capitulares and the Panteón Real

The **Sacristía** and **Salas Capitulares** (Chapter Houses) contain many of the monastery's religious treasures, including paintings by Titian, Velázquez and José Ribera. Beside the sacristy a staircase leads down to the **Panteón Real**, the final resting place of all Spanish monarchs since Carlos V, with the exception of Felipe V and Fernando VI. The deceased monarchs lie in exquisite gilded marble tombs: kings (and Isabel II) on one side, their spouses on the other.

Just above the entry is the Pudridero Real, a separate room in which the bodies (which are covered in lime) rot for twenty years or so before the cleaned-up skeletons are moved to the final resting place. The royal children are laid in the **Panteón de los Infantes**; the tomb of Don Juan, Felipe II's bastard half-brother, is grander than any of the kings', while the wedding-cake babies' tomb with room for sixty infants is more than half full.

Museos Nuevos, Salones Reales and Claustro Grande

What remains of the Escorial's art collection – works by Bosch, Gerard David, Dürer, Titian, Zurbarán and many others, which escaped transfer to the Prado – is kept in the elegant suite of rooms known as the **Museos Nuevos** (New Museums). Don't miss the **Sala de las Batallas**, a magnificent gallery lined with an epic series of paintings depicting the most notable imperial battles. The surprisingly modest **Salones Reales** (Royal Apartments) contain the austere **quarters of Felipe II**, with the chair that supported his gouty leg and the deathbed from which he was able to contemplate the high altar of the basilica. However, Felipe's successors occupied the more lavish **Palacio de los Borbones**, which takes up the northeastern corner of the complex.

Claustro Grande and Patio de los Evangelistas

You can wander at will in some of the Escorial's courtyards; most notable is the **Claustro Grande**, with frescoes of the *Life of the Virgin* by Tibaldi, and the secluded gardens of the **Patio de los Evangelistas** which lie within, while on the southern flank lies a series of parterre gardens known as the Jardín de los Frailes.

Outlying lodges

April–Sept Tues–Sun 10am–8pm, Oct–March 10am–6pm • €5 Casita del Príncipe, €3 Casita del Infante

The **Casita del Príncipe** (aka Casita de Abajo) and the **Casita del Infante** (aka Casita de Arriba) are two eighteenth-century royal lodges located within the grounds of El Escorial, both full of decorative riches, and built by Juan de Villanueva, Spain's most accomplished Neoclassical architect – so worth seeing in themselves as well as for their formal gardens.

The Casita del Infante, which served as the present King Juan Carlos' student digs, is a short way up into the hills and affords a good view of the Escorial complex; follow the road to the left from the main entrance and then stick to the contours of the mountain around to the right – it's well signposted.

The Casita del Príncipe, in the Jardines del Príncipe below the monastery, is larger and more worthwhile, with an important collection of Giordano paintings and four pictures made from rice paste.

Silla de Felipe

Around 3km out of town is the **Silla de Felipe** – "Felipe's Seat" – a chair carved into a rocky outcrop with a great view out towards the palace. His majesty is supposed to have sat here to watch the construction going on. You can reach it on foot by following the path through the arches beyond the main entrance to the monastery by the Biblioteca; keep to the left as you go down the hill and then cross the main road and follow the signs. If you have a car, take the M 505 Ávila road and turn off at the sign after about 3km.

El Valle de los Caídos

April–Sept Tues–Sun 10am–7pm, Oct–March 10am–6pm • €9, free Wed & Thurs 4–7pm (3–6pm Oct–March) for EU citizens • ☎ 918 905 411, ⓦ patrimonionacional.es and ⓦ www.valledeloscaidos.es

Nine kilometres north of El Escorial nestled among the mountains is **El Valle de los Caídos** (The Valley of the Fallen). This is an equally megalomaniac yet far more chilling monument: an underground basilica hewn under Franco's orders, allegedly as a memorial to the Civil War dead of both sides, though in reality as a shrine to the *generalísimo* and his regime.

It remains a controversial place to this day. The socialist government of José Luis Rodríguez Zapatero tried to depoliticize the site and passed a law that prevents its use

FROM TOP EL ESCORIAL (P.143); THE CITY WALLS AT ÁVILA (P.151) >

2

COMING TO TERMS WITH THE PAST

El Valle de los Caídos is probably the most controversial and emotive physical expression of the Francoist dictatorship that still remains in present-day Spain. Partly built by Popular Front prisoners in the 1940s and 1950s, this pharaonic memorial to the fascist triumph in the Civil War towers over a valley that conceals tens of thousands of corpses moved there under Franco's orders. After the burial of the founder of the Falange Party, José Antonio Primo de Rivera, and Franco himself, the mausoleum became a place of homage for neo-fascists who continued to commemorate the dictator's death every November 20 by parading their fascist paraphernalia at the site. But the future of the monument has finally been exposed to official scrutiny following the decision of the former socialist government to set up a committee to decide how to turn the site into a monument to reconciliation.

The removal of Franco's remains is one option, but the destruction of the giant cross appears to have been dismissed as has the possibility of evicting the Benedictine monks who inhabit the site. The most likely outcome is the establishment of a museum or interpretation centre which will put the monument in its context and use it as a reminder of the horrors that resulted from the Civil War. But the debate has shown how raw feelings remain in Spain and how problematic the country has found the experience of coming to terms with its traumatic past.

It was not until 2007, over thirty years after the death of the dictator, that the then socialist government introduced what became known as the "historical memory" law, which recognized victims of the Franco regime, prohibited political events at the Valle de los Caídos and provided some state help for the identification and eventual exhumation of the victims of Francoist repression whose corpses still lie in over two thousand mass graves scattered across Spain. Even that step was resisted by opponents who preferred to turn a blind eye to the deep wounds left by the Civil War and its aftermath. But grassroots campaigns, often led by relatives of the victims, to dig up the mass graves forced the government to break its silence and confront the issue.

The conservative Partido Popular government, which came to power in 2011, has been reluctant to follow up the initiative of their predecessors and have cut funding for the exhumations but the pressure is on to try to force Spain to come to terms with matters that have been swept under the carpet for so many years. As Catalan photographer Francesc Torres, a leading light in the movement to shed light on Spain's unexamined past, has said: "History is resilient. You can cover it, but it's not going away."

by Falangist supporters keen to glorify the Franco era, while it also set up a commission to decide how to turn it into a monument symbolizing reconciliation rather than Nationalist victory and oppression (see box above).

To get to the monument itself you have to travel some 6km along a road which winds its way up from the main entrance gate. Above is a vast 150-metre-high cross, reputedly the largest in the world, and visible for miles along the A6 motorway towards Segovia.

The **basilica complex** denies its claims of memorial "to the Civil War dead of both sides" almost at a glance. The debased and grandiose fascist-style architectural forms employed, the grim martial statuary, the constant inscriptions "Fallen for God and for Spain" and the proximity to El Escorial intimate the complex's true function: the glorification of General Franco and his regime. The dictator himself lies buried behind the high altar, while the only other named tomb, marked simply "José Antonio", is that of his guru, the Falangist leader José Antonio Primo de Rivera, who was shot dead by Republicans at the beginning of the war. The "other side" is present only in the fact that the complex was built by the Republican army's survivors – political prisoners on quarrying duty.

ARRIVAL AND INFORMATION   SAN LORENZO DEL ESCORIAL

By train There are trains every 15–30min from Madrid (5.45am–11.30pm; 1hr) from Atocha, calling at Chamartín. If you arrive by train, get straight on the local bus that shuttles you up to the centre of town – they leave promptly and it's a long uphill walk.

Destinations Ávila (7 daily; 1hr); Madrid (30 daily; 1hr). If you want to go on to Segovia you will have to backtrack down the train line to Villalba and then take one of the trains from Madrid.

By bus Buses (#661 & #664 from the *intercambiador* at

Moncloa) run every 15min on weekdays and hourly at weekends and take around an hour to arrive. Stay on the bus and it will take you right up to the monastery. To get to El Valle de los Caídos from El Escorial, you can get a local bus #C660A that runs from the bus station at C/Juan de Toledo 3, just north of the visitors' entrance to the monastery (departs 3.15pm, returns 5.30pm).

Destinations Guadarrama (every 30min–1hr; 15min); Madrid (every 15–30min; 1hr); Valle de los Caídos (daily; 15min).
Turismo C/Grimaldi 4 (Tues–Sat 10am–2pm & 3–6pm, Sun 10am–2pm; ☎918 905 313, ⓦsanlorenzoturismo .org), on the small street to the north of the visitors' entrance to the monastery, running into C/Floridablanca.

ACCOMMODATION

Most **hotels** are close to the monastery. In summer the town is a favourite retreat from the heat of Madrid, so it's wise to book in advance.

HOTELS AND HOSTALES
Hotel Botánico C/Timoteo Padrós 16 ☎918 907 879, ⓦbotanicohotel.com. Twenty individually decorated rooms (including suites and superior rooms) available in this plush hotel set in the verdant grounds of a former palace. **€96**
Hotel Florida C/Floridablanca 12–14 ☎918 901 520, ⓦhflorida.com. A well-appointed mid-range place, with a restaurant and café serving a buffet breakfast for an extra €8. There are fifty rooms with a/c and for an extra €16 you get a superior room with views of the monastery. **€65**
NH Hotel Victoria Palace C/Juan de Toledo 4 ☎918 969 890, ⓦnh-hoteles.es. Now part of the NH chain, El Escorial's top hotel has its own pool, views of the monastery, sleek rooms and all the facilities you would expect in this category. **€107**
Posada Don Jaime C/San Antón 24 ☎918 903 000, ⓦposadadonjaime.es. Three cosy doubles and five suites (ranging in price from €66 to €106) in this homely hotel in an old mansion house in the centre of the town. There is

parking, a small garden and a tiny indoor pool open in summer. **€66**

HOSTEL
El Escorial C/Residencia 14 ☎918 905 924, ⓦreaj.com. A large 58-berth youth hostel situated up on the hill above the monastery. There is another, smaller, hostel down in the park beside the monastery, the *Santa María del Buen Aire* (☎918 903 640), which has a pool and camping space, but it is usually packed with school groups (YH cards needed for both hostels); prices include breakfast. Under-30s **€16.94**, over-30s **€21.78**

CAMPING
Caravaning El Escorial Carretera de Guadarrama a El Escorial km 3.5 ☎902 014 900, ☎918 902 412, ⓦcampingelescorial.com. A very well-equipped campsite with several swimming pools and three tennis courts situated 6km out on the road back towards Guadarrama. A little noisy during summer weekends. **€22.20**

EATING AND ENTERTAINMENT

Scattered about town are plenty of small **bars**, which offer snacks and tapas. For evening **entertainment** the eighteenth-century Teatro Coliseo at C/Floridablanca 20 offers flamenco, jazz and classical concerts and theatrical productions year-round. Details of shows can be picked up from the *oficina de turismo*, or check out website ⓦsanlorenzoturismo.org.

El Charolés C/Floridablanca 24 ☎918 905 975. Renowned for its fish and stews, this old-school restaurant with attentive service is at the top end of the scale. It does a €35 menu on weekdays with an excellent *cocido* on Wed & Fri, otherwise expect to pay around €50 a head. Daily 1–4.15pm & 9pm–midnight.
La Cueva C/San Antón 4 ☎918 901 516, ⓦmesonlacueva.com. An atmospheric wooden-beamed *mesón* that is a good bet for both tapas and a larger meal. Menus available at €19.80 or €28.50 with mains such as salmon in cava and suckling pig. There is *cocido* on Thursdays for €22. Tues–Sat 1–4pm & 9–11pm, Sun 1–4pm.
★ **La Fonda Genara** Pza. de San Lorenzo 2 ☎918 901 636, ⓦrestaurantegenara.com. Popular, but slightly overpriced, place on this lively plaza and inside the *centro*

coliseo, which is filled with theatrical mementos and has a wide-ranging menu of good-quality Castilian fare. The extensive lunchtime menu is €15.50 (€25 weekends) without drinks, while there is an evening menu for €28 per person featuring mains such as duck confit and sirloin steak with caramelized onion. Mon–Sat 1–4pm & 9–11pm, Sun 1–4pm.
El Sartén por el Mango C/Juan de Toledo 19 ☎918 961 313, ⓦrestaurantelasartenporelmango.es. A host of creative as well as more classic *raciones* served up in this well-regarded restaurant, just a short walk from the monastery. There are superior set lunches available for €17 on weekdays and €24 at the weekend. Sun–Thurs 8.30am–8pm, Fri & Sat noon–midnight (June–Sept daily 10am–midnight).

The Sierra de Guadarrama

The routes from Madrid and El Escorial to Segovia strike through the heart of the **Sierra de Guadarrama** (w sierraguadarrama.info), and it is a beautiful journey. The road is occasionally marred by suburban development, especially around **Navacerrada**, Madrid's main ski station, but from the train it's almost entirely unspoilt. There are plenty of opportunities for walking, but make sure you buy the appropriate maps in Madrid.

If you want to base yourself in the mountains for a while you'd do best to head for **Cercedilla**. Alternatively, over to the east, there is **Manzanares el Real**, with its odd medieval castle and reservoir-side setting.

In the shadow of the mountains to the north lies the Valle de Lozoya. At the western end are the village of **Rascafría** and the nearby Benedictine monastery of El Paular, and to the east the old fortified town of **Buitrago**, with its medieval core and small Picasso museum.

Cercedilla

CERCEDILLA is an alpine-looking village perched at the foot of the valley leading up to the Puerto de la Fuenfría and makes an excellent base for summer walking. It is much frequented by *madrileños* at weekends, as it has the advantage of being accessible.

The village is the starting point for a very pleasant five-hour round-trip **walk** along the pine-fringed Calzada Romana (old Roman road) up to the Puerto de la Fuenfría (1796m), with its striking views down into Segovia province. Follow the signs up to Las Dehesas where there is an **information centre tourismo** (see below) which provides maps and advice on walks in the area, then head past the meadows and follow the clearly indicated path up to the Puerto.

ARRIVAL AND INFORMATION

CERCEDILLA

By bus Every half-hour (50min–1hr 10min) from the *intercambiador* in Moncloa.

By train Madrid–Segovia line, over 20 daily 6am–11pm from Atocha calling at Chamartín, 3–4 daily going on to Segovia; 40–50min; Cotos (4 daily; 40min); Puerto de Navacerrada (4 daily; 25min).

Turismo (Fri & Sat 11am–3pm & 4–8pm, Sat & Sun 11am–3pm; ☏ 918 523 704); Las Dehesas (Mon–Fri 10am–3pm; Sat, Sun & hols 10am–6pm; ☏ 918 522 213, w cercedilla.es).

ACCOMMODATION AND EATING

Los Frutales Carretera de las Dehesas 41 ☏ 918 520 244, w los-frutales.com. A delightful bucolic setting for this hotel-restaurant with six charming rooms (breakfast included in price). The restaurant serves good *croquetas*, *trucha* (trout) and meat dishes, and has a cool terrace in summer. **€105**

Hostal Longinos – El Aribel C/Emilio Serrano 71 ☏ 918 521 511, w hostalaribel.com. Convenient location close to the railway station, but otherwise nothing special, this alpine-style *hostal* has 23 en-suite rooms and a café-bar. **€45**

Luces del Poniente C/Lina de Ávila 4 ☏ 918 525 587, w lucesdelponiente.com. A tranquil rural hotel with thirteen spacious, individually decorated rooms, a covered pool and spa area (April–Oct) and a relaxing garden terrace area. Rooms start at €75 from November to March but the spa is closed then. **€110**

Villa Castora Carretera de Las Dehesas 29 ☏ 918 520 334, w reaj.com. Youth hostel with double, quadruple and five-bed dormitories, conveniently located close to the town. YH card essential; prices include breakfast. Under-30s **€16.94**, over-30s **€21.78**

Puerto de Navacerrada and Cotos

From Cercedilla, you can embark on a wonderful little train ride to the **Puerto de Navacerrada**, the most important pass in the mountains and the heart of the ski area, or a little farther on to **Cotos** where a number of well-maintained walks around the **Parque Natural de Peñalara** (w parquenaturalpenalara.org) begin. The train runs hourly over weekends and holidays but is expensive (€17.10 return) and passes through the *parque natural*, an extension of the upper Manzanares basin: watch out for roe deer and wild boar. In winter it is possible to ski in both Navacerrada and Cotos, but be prepared for long queues and traffic jams at weekends.

Hiking in the high peaks

Navacerrada is also the starting point for a number of impressive walks along the **high peaks**, while Cotos is the gateway to the highest peak in the Sierra, Peñalara (2430m). It can be reached in about four hours, but is a reasonably tough ascent. Less challenging but very enjoyable is the easy, well-indicated hike to the glacial lake, the Laguna Grande.

2

INFORMATION   COTOS

Information There is a small information booth just above the small café close to the Cotos train station that will give advice on all routes (summer Mon–Fri 10am–6pm, Sat, Sun & hols 10am–8pm; winter daily 10am–6pm; ☎918 520 857).

Monasterio del Paular and Rascafría

Guided tours Mon–Wed & Fri noon, 1pm & 5pm, Sat noon, 1pm, 5pm & 6pm, Sun 1pm, 5pm & 6pm (Nov to mid-April the afternoon visits on Sat & Sun are at 4pm & 5pm) · In Spanish only · Free · ⓦ monasteriopaular.com · Buses #194 link with Madrid (intercambiador Pza. Castilla) 2–3 times a day; 2hr 5min

Some 10km below Cotos in the beautiful Valle de Lozoya just outside the pleasant mountain village of **Rascafría** stands the **Monasterio de Santa María de El Paular**, originally a Carthusian monastery founded at the end of the fourteenth century, and now home to a handful of Benedictine monks who provide guided tours of the silent cloisters and the main church.

ACCOMMODATION   RASCAFRÍA

Los Calizos On the road to Miraflores ☎918 691 112, ⓦloscalizos.com. A tranquil, twelve-room hotel, a little way out of Rascafría, with a fine restaurant and extensive grounds. Price includes breakfast and an evening meal for two. **€130**

Hostal Rural El Valle Avda. del Valle 39 ☎918 691 213, ⓦ hotelruralelvalle.com. A cheap but cosy option close to the village. Thirty rooms, some of which have cooking facilities. **€50**

Manzanares el Real

Castle Tues–Sun 10am–6pm · €5, under-14 €3 · Dramatized visits Oct–June: Sat & Sun noon and 1.45pm, July–Sept Fri 9pm & 10pm, Sat noon & 1.45pm; €8 · ☎918 530 008

Some 50km north of Madrid, on the shores of the Santillana *embalse* (reservoir), lies **MANZANARES EL REAL**, a town which in former times was disputed between the capital and Segovia. Nowadays it's geared to Madrid weekenders, whose villas dot the landscape for miles around. The town's one attraction is the **castle**, which despite its eccentric appearance is a perfectly genuine fifteenth-century construction, built around an earlier chapel. It was soon modified into a palace by the architect Juan Guas, who built an elegant gallery on the south side and false machicolations on the other, and studded the tower with stones resembling cannonballs. The interior has been heavily restored, but it makes for an interesting visit.

ARRIVAL AND INFORMATION   MANZANARES EL REAL

By bus From the *intercambiador* in Pza. de Castilla (ⓜPlaza de Castilla) hourly; 45min.
Turismo (Mon–Fri noon–3pm, Sat, Sun & hols 10am–3pm; ⓦmanzanareselreal.org). For information about the region as a whole consult the website ⓦsierranorte.com.

ACCOMMODATION

La Fresneda Carretera M608, km19.5 ☎918 477 213, ⓦcampingfresneda.com. This recently upgraded campsite on the road towards Soto del Real has a pool bar area, small playground and shady pitches. **€18**

El Ortigal C/Montañero 19 ☎918 530 120. Campsite at the foot of La Pedriza, with great views and its own pool, situated on the northern side of the town. **€18**

EATING AND DRINKING

Restaurante Parra C/Panaderos 15 ☎ 918 539 577, ⓦ restauranteparra.net. Better value than many of the Sierra restaurants, this one serves up similar fare with Castilian meat dishes and paellas topping the bill. A decent wine list too. There is a lunchtime menu for €10 (€19 at weekends), but if you go à la carte expect to pay around €35 a head. Tues–Thurs 8am–5.30pm, Fri–Sun 8am–11.30pm.

2

La Pedriza

Access limited to 350 cars a day at weekends • Free • Information centre daily 10am–6pm • ☎ 918 539 978 • Buses from the *intercambiador* in Pza. de Castilla in Madrid (daily every 30min 7.30am–9.30pm; 45min–1hr)

Rising behind Manzanares el Real is the ruggedly beautiful **La Pedriza**, a spur of the Sierra de Guadarrama that has been declared a regional park. There are some enjoyable walks by the river and around the granite dome El Yelmo, as well as some much-revered technical climbs, notably the ascent to the jagged Peña del Diezmo. The park is also home to a very large colony of **griffon vultures**.

Buitrago de Lozoya

East of La Pedriza, beyond the road to Burgos, lies the attractive little town of **BUITRAGO DE LOZOYA**, a fortified settlement with defensive walls that date from the twelfth century, a castle (Sat 10.15am–5.45pm, Sun 10.15am–1.45pm) a fine Mudéjar church (daily 9am–2pm & 4–8pm) and, more surprisingly, a small **Picasso museum** (Tues, Thurs & Fri 11am–1.45pm & 4–6pm, Wed 11am–1.45pm, Sat 10am–2pm & 4–7pm, Sun 10am–2pm; free). The collection, based on work donated by the artist to his friend and local barber Eugenio Arias, features an interesting selection of sixty minor pieces dating from between 1948 and 1972.

ARRIVAL AND INFORMATION   BUITRAGO DE LOZOYA

By bus Hourly buses (#191) from the *intercambiador* in Pza. de Castilla; 1hr 20min.

Turismo C/Tahona 19 (Wed–Sat 10am–2pm & 4–6pm, Sun 10am–2pm; ⓦ buitrago.org).

Patones de Arriba

On the southern edge of the so-called Sierra Pobre is the picturesque mountain village of **PATONES DE ARRIBA**, abandoned in the 1930s but since restored and now a fashionable weekend destination for many *madrileños*. The black slate architecture of the village is undeniably beautiful, the views are good, and you can be assured of a fine meal, but there is little else to detain the casual visitor. The village is closed to cars, so you will need to leave vehicles in the car park in nearby **Patones de Abajo** and walk the 2.5km up the signposted path.

ARRIVAL AND INFORMATION   PATONES DE ARRIBA

By bus Two or three buses (#197) daily from the *intercambiador* in the Pza. de Castilla in Patones Abajo.

Turismo ⓦ patones.net.

ACCOMMODATION

★ El Tiempo Perdido Travesía del Ayuntamiento 5 y 7 ☎ 918 432 152, ⓦ eltiempoperdido.com. Luxury boutique hotel with seven individually decorated rooms (some with small balconies) housed in one of the beautiful slate cottages in this tranquil village. The owner Paco Bello is also the chef at the excellent *El Poleo* restaurant which is contained within the hotel. Open only at weekends and the eve of holidays. €100

EATING AND DRINKING

El Abuelo Manolo C/Buenavista 29 ☎ 918 432 947. Traditional restaurant with excellent views and a great summer terrace serving red-meat staples and some delicious home-made *croquetas*. Eating à la carte will cost around

€30–35 a head, but there is a set menu for under €20. Also houses a café serving a range of teas and some very tasty cakes. Mon & Thurs–Sun 1.30–4pm & 8.30pm–midnight. **El Poleo** Travesía del Arroyo 3 ☎918 432 101, ⓦeltiempoperdido.com. Attached to the hotel *El Tiempo*

Perdido and owned by Cordobés chef Paco Bello, this restaurant takes a creative angle on the local cuisine with dishes such as roast lamb with honey and couscous. You can eat outside on the picturesque patio in summer. Set menus at €22 and €25. Fri–Sun 1.30–4pm & 8.30pm–midnight.

Ávila

2

Two things distinguish **ÁVILA**: its eleventh-century **walls**, two perfectly preserved kilometres of which surround the old town, and the mystic writer **Santa Teresa**, who was born here and whose shrines are a major focus of religious pilgrimage. Set on a high plain, with the peaks of the Sierra de Gredos as a backdrop, the town is quite a sight, especially if you approach with the evening sun highlighting the golden tone of the walls and the details of the 88 towers. The walls make orientation straightforward, with the **Catedral** and most other sights contained within. Just outside the southeast corner is the city's main square, **Pza. Santa Teresa**, and the most imposing of the old gates, the **Puerta del Alcázar**.

Convento de Santa Teresa

Pza. de la Santa 2 • **Chapel** Daily 9.30am–1pm & 3.30–7.30pm • Free • **Reliquary** Daily 9.30am–1.30pm & 3.30–7pm • Free • **Museum** Daily April–Sept 10am–2pm & 4–7pm; Oct–March 10am–1.30pm & 3.30–5.30pm • €2 • ☎920 211 030

The obvious place to start a tour of Teresa's Ávila is the **Convento de Santa Teresa**, built over the saint's birthplace just inside the south gate of the old town and entered off the Paseo del Rastro. Most of the convent remains *de clausura*, but you can see the very spot where she was born, now a fabulously ornate chapel in the Baroque church, which is decorated with scenes of the saint demonstrating her powers of levitation to various august bodies. A small **reliquary**, beside the gift shop, contains memorials of Teresa's life, including not only her rosary beads, but also one of the fingers she used to count them with. In the crypt of the monastery is a **museum** dedicated to the saint's life and work. Packed full of memorabilia, accounts of her miraculous deeds and numerous translations of her work, it provides a truly hagiographic vision of Teresa's life.

Monasterio de la Encarnación

Paseo de la Encarnación s/n • May–Sept Mon–Fri 9.30am–1pm & 4–7pm, Sat & Sun 10am–1pm & 4–7pm; Oct–April Mon–Fri 9.30am–1pm & 3.30–6pm, Sat & Sun 10am–1pm & 4–6pm • €2 • ☎920 211 212

Heading through the old town, and leaving by the Puerta del Carmen, you can follow a lane, C/Encarnación, to the **Monasterio de la Encarnación**. The entrance to the museum is in the patio – ring the bell and wait if it appears to be unattended and you will eventually be ushered in. Teresa lived here for much of the time between 1535 and 1574, the last three years as the prioress. Each room is labelled with a miraculous act she performed or vision that she witnessed, while everything she might have touched or looked at is also on display. A small museum section also provides a reasonable introduction to the saint's life, with maps showing the convents, papal bulls, and a selection of her sayings – the pithiest, perhaps, "Life is a night in a bad hotel".

Convento de San José

Pza. de las Madres 4 • Daily: April–Oct 10am–1.30pm & 4–7pm; Nov–March 10am–1.30pm & 3–6pm • €1.40 • ☎920 222 127

A third Teresan sight lies five minutes east of the cathedral outside the city walls. This is the **Convento de San José**, the first monastery that the saint founded, in 1562. Its museum contains relics and memorabilia, including the coffin in which Teresa once

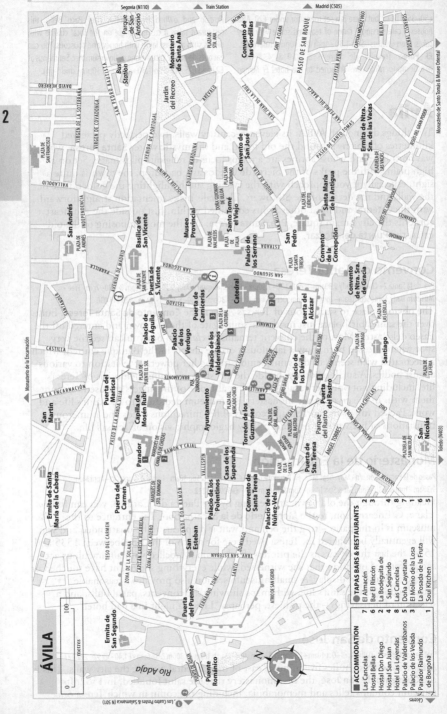

ÁVILA

0   metres   100

ACCOMMODATION

Las Cancelas	7
Hostal Bellas	6
Hostal Don Diego	2
Hostal San Juan	4
Hotel Las Leyendas	8
Palacio de Valderrábanos	5
Palacio de los Velada	3
Parador Raimundo	6
de Borgoña	1

TAPAS BARS & RESTAURANTS

El Almacén	2
Bar El Rincón	3
La Bodeguita de	
San Segundo	4
Las Cancelas	7
Doña Cayetana	8
El Molino de la Losa	1
La Posada de la Fruta	6
Soul Kitchen	5

slept and a signed handkerchief stained with her blood. The tomb of her brother Lorenzo is in the larger of the two churches, which was the work of one of the El Escorial architects, Francisco de Mora.

Los Cuatro Postes

You might want to make your way up to **Los Cuatro Postes**, a little four-posted shrine, 1.5km along the Salamanca road west of town and a fine vantage point from which to admire the walls of the town. It was here, aged 7, that the infant Teresa was recaptured by her uncle, running away with her brother to seek Christian martyrdom fighting the Moors.

The Catedral

Pza. de la Catedral • Jan–Feb & Nov–Dec Mon–Fri 10am–4.30pm, Sat 10am–6pm, Sun noon–3pm; March–June & late Sept–Nov Mon–Fri 10am–6pm, Sat 10am–7.30pm, Sun noon–3pm; July to late Sept Mon–Fri 10am–7pm, Sat 10am–8pm, Sun noon–3pm; last tickets given out 45min before closing • €4 • ☎ 920 211 641, ⓦ catedralavila.com

Ávila's **Catedral** was started in the twelfth century but has never been finished, as evidenced by the missing tower above the main entrance. The earliest Romanesque parts were as much fortress as church, and the apse actually forms an integral part of the city walls.

Inside, the succeeding changes of style are immediately apparent; the **Romanesque** parts are made of a strange red-and-white mottled stone, then there's an abrupt break and the rest of the main structure is pure white stone with **Gothic** forms. Although the proportions are exactly the same, this newer half of the Catedral seems infinitely more spacious. The *coro*, whose elaborate carved back you see as you come in, and two chapels in the left aisle, are **Renaissance** additions. Here you can admire the elaborate marble tomb of a fifteenth-century bishop known as El Tostado (the "toasted" or "swarthy"), while the thirteenth-century *sacristía* with its star-shaped cupola and gold inlay decor, and the treasury-museum with its monstrous silver *custodia* and ancient religious images are also worth a visit.

Basílica de San Vicente

Pza. de San Vicente 1 • May–Oct Mon–Sat: 10am–7pm, Sun 4–6pm; Nov–April Mon–Sat 10am–1.30pm & 4–7pm, Sun 4–6pm (no visits during Mass) • €2 • ☎ 920 255 230

The **Basílica de San Vicente** marks the site where San Vicente was martyred, and his tomb narrates the gruesome story of torture and execution by the Romans. Legend has it that following the martyrdom a rich Jew, who had been poking fun at the martyrs, was enveloped and suffocated by a great serpent that miraculously emerged from the rocks. On the verge of asphyxiation he repented and converted to Christianity, later building the church on the very same site, and he, too, is said to be buried here. In the crypt you can see part of the rocky crag where San Vicente and his sisters were executed and from which the serpent later supposedly appeared. Like the Catedral, the building is a mixture of architectural styles. The warm pink glow of the sandstone of the church is a characteristic feature of Ávila, also notable in the **church of San Pedro** (daily 10.30am–noon & 7–8pm) in Pza. de Santa Teresa.

Capilla de Mosén Rubí

Pza. de Mosén Rubí 9 • Tues–Sat summer 5–7pm; winter 4–6pm, Sun 11am–1.30pm • Free

One of the most eye-catching of the city's monuments, the polygonal **Capilla de Mosén Rubí** was started in the fifteenth century, but owing to a lengthy legal dispute and a lack of funds it was not completed until the following century. The delay explains the chapel's two distinct architectural styles – Gothic and Renaissance – which are evident in the interior design. The magnificent marble tombs of the benefactors take pride of place in the centre of the chapel.

2

SANTA TERESA DE ÁVILA

Santa Teresa (1515–82) was born to a noble family in Ávila and from childhood began to experience visions and religious raptures. Her religious career began at the Carmelite convent of La Encarnación, where she was a nun for 27 years. From this base, she went on to reform the movement and found convents throughout Spain. She was an ascetic, but her appeal lay in the mystic sensuality of her experience of Christ, as revealed in her autobiography, for centuries a bestseller in Spain. As joint patron saint of Spain (together with Santiago), she remains a central pillar in Spanish Catholicism and schoolgirls are brought into Ávila by the busload to experience first-hand the life of the woman they are supposed to emulate. She died in Alba de Torres just outside Salamanca, and the Carmelite convent, which contains the remains of her body and a dubious reconstruction of the cell in which she passed away, is another major target of pilgrimage. On a more bizarre note, one of Santa Teresa's mummified hands has been returned to Ávila after spending the Franco years by the bedside of the dictator.

City walls

April–Oct Tues–Sun 10am–8pm; Nov–March Tues–Sun 10am–6pm • €5; children €3.50 (free Tues 2–4pm) • ☎ 920 350 000, ⓦ muralladeavila.es

The **city walls**, a mixture of red limestone, granite and brick, were built under Alfonso VI, following his capture of the city from the Moors in 1090; they took his Muslim prisoners nine years to construct. At closer quarters, they prove a bit of a facade, as the old city within is sparsely populated, most of modern life having moved into the new developments outside the fortifications. It's possible to walk along two sections of the walls from Puerta de Carnicerías to Puerta del Carmen and from Puerta del Alcázar to Puerta del Rastro, the former being the best with some memorable views of the town. There have been some experiments with night-time opening in the summer (usually 10pm–12.30am Sun–Wed), but check with the tourist office. Tickets are available from the green kiosk by the Puerta del Alcázar and the tourist office at Puerta de Carnicerías.

Museo de Ávila

Pza. del Navaillos 3 • Tues–Sat July–Sept10am–2pm & 4–8pm; Oct–June 10am–2pm & 5–8pm; Sun 10am–2pm • €1.20, free Sat & Sun • ☎ 920 211 003, ⓦ museoscastillayleon.jcyl.es

Just outside the city walls, through the Puerta de Carnicerías, is the small **Museo de Ávila (Museo Provincial)**, housed in the sixteenth-century Palacio de los Deanes where the Catedral's deans once lived. Today, its eclectic exhibits include collections of archeological remains, ceramics, agricultural implements and traditional costumes, as well as some fine Romanesque statues and a wonderful fifteenth-century triptych depicting the *Life of Christ*. The ticket also allows you entry to the museum storeroom in the church of Santo Tomé El Viejo just opposite.

Monasterio de Santo Tomás

Pza. de Granada 1 • Sept–June 10.30am–2pm & 3.30–7.30pm; July & Aug 10.30am–9pm • €4 (including audio-guide); closed Feb 1–6, Oct 15 & Dec 25; Museo Oriental and Museo de Ciencias Naturales share the same hours as monastery • €3 • ☎ 920 352 237, ⓦ monasteriosantotomas.com

The **Monasterio de Santo Tomás** is a fifteen-minute walk south of the old city. Established by the Reyes Católicos Fernando and Isabel in the later fifteenth century, the monastery is set around three cloisters and contains a fine, carved Gothic choir in the main church. Within are the tombs of Don Juan, the only son of the Reyes Católicos, and the notorious Torquemada, Isabel's confessor and later head of the Inquisition. Alongside is the **Museo Oriental**, which contains memorabilia brought back from the Far East by Dominican missionaries and a small natural history collection.

ARRIVAL AND DEPARTURE

ÁVILA

By train From Madrid (Chamartín station) there are around twenty trains a day to Ávila (1hr 25min–2hr 10min). The train station is a 15min walk to the east of the old town, and a local bus connects it with Pza. Victoria, a little west of the cathedral. On foot, follow the broad Paseo de la Estación to its end, by the large church of Santa Ana, and head straight on to reach Pza. Santa Teresa.

Destinations El Escorial (6 daily; 1hr); Madrid (20–25 daily; 1hr 25min–2hr 10min); Medina del Campo (12 daily; 40–50min); Salamanca (10 daily; 1hr 10min–1hr 30min).

By bus Buses are less frequent (Estación del Sur; 8–11 daily; 1hr 25min–1hr 45min) and use a terminal on the Avda. de Madrid, a little closer in: walking from here, cross the small park opposite, then up C/Duque de Alba, or take a local bus to Pza. Victoria.

Destinations Arenas de San Pedro (daily Mon–Fri; 1hr 30min); Madrid (8–11 daily; 1hr 25min–1hr 45min); Salamanca (4 daily; 1hr 30min); Segovia (4 daily; 55min).

By car Follow signs for the walls (*murallas*) or the parador and you should be able to park just outside the old town.

INFORMATION

Visitors' centre Avda. de Madrid 39, just beyond the Basílica de San Vicente (daily summer 9am–8pm, winter 9am–5.30pm; ☎ 920 354 045, ⓦ www.avilaturismo.com, ⓦ www.avila.es). Here you can buy the Ávila tourist pass for €15 (under-12s free) which will provide entry to most of the leading sights for a period of 48 hours.

Turismo Casa de las Carnicerías, C/San Segundo 17 (July to mid-Sept Mon–Sat 9.30am–2pm & 5–8pm, Sun 9.30am–5pm; mid-Sept to June Mon–Sat 9.30am–2pm & 4–7pm, Sun 9.30am–5pm; ☎ 920 211 387, ⓦ turismocastillayleon.com).

ACCOMMODATION

There are numerous cheap **hostales** around the train station and along Avda. José Antonio, but you should be able to find something nearer the walled centre of town.

★**Las Cancelas** C/Cruz Vieja 6 ☎ 920 212 249, ⓦ lascancelas.com. Fourteen functional a/c rooms in this converted fifteenth-century building, some of which have good views of the Catedral and walls. There's a decent bar and a pleasant patio restaurant serving regional specialities, too. €60

Hostal Bellas C/Caballeros 19 ☎ 920 212 910, ⓦ hostalbellas.com. Eager-to-please owners run this centrally located *hostal*. Most rooms have showers and there are discounts out of season. €37

Hostal Don Diego C/Marqués de Canales y Chozas 5 ☎ 920 255 475, ⓦ hostaldondiego.es. A friendly, family-run and good-value *hostal* just opposite the parador with its own parking and restaurant. All twelve simple but neatly decorated rooms have bath or shower. €32

Hostal San Juan C/Comuneros de Castilla 3 ☎ 920 251 475, ⓦ hostalsanjuan.es. There are seventeen functional en-suite rooms in this relatively new *hostal* in the centre of the old town. Family rooms available with a free cot for children under two. €38.50

★**Hotel Las Leyendas** C/Francisco Gallego 3 ☎ 920 352 042, ⓦ lasleyendas.es. A recent arrival on the Ávila hotel scene, this sixteenth-century mansion has nineteen

tastefully refurbished rooms, with exposed brick and stone work on some of the walls, wooden beams and minimalist decor. Some rooms have views of the Sierra. Its restaurant, *La Bruja*, serves up a refreshing mix of creative tapas and Castilian classics. €69

Palacio de Valderrábanos Pza. de la Catedral 9 ☎ 920 211 023, ⓦ palaciovalderrabanoshotel.com. This slightly fading but perfectly situated hotel, housed in a former bishop's palace next to the Catedral, has large, old-style but comfortable rooms and frequently offers great cut-price deals. €65

★**Palacio de los Velada** Pza. de la Catedral 10 ☎ 920 255 100, ⓦ veladahoteles.com. A beautifully converted sixteenth-century palace with a stunning cloistered bar. The large, airy rooms – many with views over the patio – are all very competitively priced if you book via the website. €95

Parador Raimundo de Borgoña C/Marqués de Canales y Chozas 2 ☎ 920 211 340, ⓦ www.paradores .com. A converted fifteenth-century mansion close to the city walls. While not the most exciting parador in Spain, it is pleasant enough and has all the usual comforts. Offers can bring the price down to around €80. €145

EATING AND DRINKING

Ávila has a decent if unexceptional array of **bars** and **restaurants**, some of them sited just outside the walls. Local specialities include the Castilian *cordero asado* (roast lamb), *judías del barco con chorizo* (haricot beans with sausage), *mollejas* (cow's stomach) and *yemas de Santa Teresa* (candied egg yolk) – the last of these sold in confectioners all over town. For nightlife head outside the city walls to C/Capitán Peña where the strip of four *bares de copas* next to each other keeps the walking to a minimum.

2

★ **El Almacén** Carretera Salamanca 6 ☎ 920 254 455. One of the best restaurants in the province, situated in a former storehouse across the river, close to Los Cuatro Postes, with great views of the city walls. It serves quality meat and fish dishes with a creative touch and excellent desserts, and boasts a lengthy wine list. Somewhat overpriced, however, at around €50 a head. Tues–Sat 1–4pm & 9–11pm, Sun 1–4pm; closed Sept.

Bar El Rincón Pza. Zurraquín 6. To the north of Pza. de la Victoria, this down-to-earth bar attached to a *hostal* serves up a generous three-course menu for around €10. Excellent *calamares* and seafood dishes on offer too. Daily around 1.30–4pm and 8.30pm to midnight.

★ **La Bodeguita de San Segundo** C/San Segundo 19. Buried into the wall by the Puerta de Carnicerías, this critically acclaimed wine bar has a fantastic selection from Rioja, Ribera de Duero, Rueda, Penedes, Somantano and Galicia, and serves up a tasty range of accompanying tapas too. Daily around 1.30–4pm & 8.30pm–midnight.

Las Cancelas C/Cruz Vieja 6 ☎ 920 212 249. Next to the Catedral and in the hotel of the same name, this friendly restaurant with a great interior patio is popular with locals and serves up some excellent *cordero asado* (roast lamb) and *chuletón de Ávila* (succulent locally bred steak). À la carte will cost around €35. Daily around 1.30–4pm & 8.30pm–midnight.

Doña Cayetana Pza. de Pedro Dávila 6 ☎ 920 256 139.

Popular, and very good-value, two-storey restaurant with a nice interior patio in this plaza by the Puerta del Rastro, specializing in Castilian meat dishes and fish, with a lunch menu at €10.50. Mon–Sat 1.30–4pm & 8.30pm–midnight, Sun 1.30–4pm.

El Molino de la Losa C/Bajada de la Losa 12 ☎ 920 211 101, ⊕ elmolinodelalosa.com. A converted fifteenth-century mill out by Los Cuatro Postes, with a deserved reputation for quality cuisine. However, it is on the expensive side with mains costing around €20. Daily 1.30–4pm & 9–11pm.

La Posada de la Fruta Pza. de Pedro Dávila 8 ☎ 920 254 702, ⊕ posadadelafruta.com. With an attractive, sunny, covered courtyard, this is a nice place for a drink, and it also serves some tasty regional cuisine, with a good-value €12 menu and à la carte at around €25. Daily noon–4pm & 8–11.30pm; usually closed part of July.

Soul Kitchen C/Caballeros 13 ☎ 920 213 483, ⊕ soulkitchen.es. A new arrival on the Ávila scene – and a breath of fresh air, too – with its sleek minimalist lines, stripped wood tables and creative menu. Gourmet hamburgers, cuttlefish *croquetas* and grilled salmon with wasabi mayonnaise give a taste of what's on offer. There is an excellent €10.50 set lunch and a decent wine list too. Mon 10am–5pm, Wed & Thurs 10am–11.30pm, Fri 10am–2am, Sat 11am–2am, Sun 11am–11.30pm.

The Sierra de Gredos

The **Sierra de Gredos** continues the line of the Sierra de Guadarrama, enclosing Madrid to the north and west. A major mountain range, with peaks in excess of 2500m, Gredos offers the best trekking in central Spain, including high-level routes across the passes, as well as more casual walks around the villages.

By bus, the easiest access to this spectacular region is from Madrid to Arenas de San Pedro, from where you can explore the range, and then move on west into the valley of La Vera in Extremadura. If you have your own transport, you could head into the range south from Ávila along the N502. Stop at any one of the villages on the north side of the range, along the Tormes valley, such as Hoyos del Espino or Navarredonda and explore the spectacular circular walks from there.

Arenas de San Pedro and around

ARENAS DE SAN PEDRO is a sizeable town with a somewhat prettified fifteenth-century castle, the Castillo de la Triste Condesa, a Gothic church and the half-built eighteenth-century palace, the Palacio del Infante Don Luis de Borbón.

Grutas del Águila

Daily 10.30am–1pm & 3–6pm, closes an hour later in the afternoon in summer • €7.50; under-5s free • ☎ 920 377 107, ⊕ grutasdelaguila.es

Some 9km away, close to the village of Ramacastañas, are the caves known as the **Grutas del Águila**, lined with an impressive array of bizarre limestone formations stained with orange, yellow and brown from the trace elements in the rocks.

Walks to the Gredos watershed

The main reason to stop at Arenas is to make your way up to the villages of **EL HORNILLO** and **El ARENAL**, respectively 6km and 9km to the north, the trailheads for **walks up to the Gredos watershed**. There are no buses but it's a pleasant walk up from Arenas to El Arenal on a track running between the road and the river – start out past the sports centre and swimming pool in Arenas.

Valle del Tormes

On the north side of Gredos is the beautiful **Valle del Tormes**, which enjoys spectacular views across to the highest peaks in the range. The village of **HOYOS DEL ESPINO**, 20km west along the AV941, makes a good base, as there are several places to stay, a few decent bars, and shops where you can stock up on supplies. A few kilometres to the east is **Navarredonda**, another good base from which to explore the area, while the nearby picturesque village of San Martín del Pimpollar is the base of the excellent **Gredos Guides** (☎920 348 817, ☎626 066 223, ⊕gredosguides.es), a small business run by local expert and fluent English-speaker Juanfran Redondo who organizes a fantastic range of personally tailored ecological and adventure activities throughout the local area, from bird watching and hiking to mushroom hunting and snow-shoe walking.

ARRIVAL AND DEPARTURE   SIERRA DE GREDOS

By bus Buses run from the Estación Sur in Madrid to Arenas de San Pedro (2–6 daily; 2hr) and to Hoyos del Espino (1 bus daily; 4hr). There are daily buses from Ávila that call at Hoyos on their way to Barco de Ávila and a twice-daily service to Arenas.

WALKS IN GREDOS

The **two classic walks** in the Gredos mountains are best approached from the so-called Plataforma, at the end of a twelve-kilometre stretch of paved road running from the village of Hoyos del Espino (see above), where you can purchase detailed maps of the area. You could also reach this point by walking up from El Hornillo or El Arenal on the southern side of the range, although it makes for a tougher challenge. A functional pamphlet of the area can be obtained from the tourist office at C/Triste Condesa 1, in Arenas de San Pedro (Tues–Sun 10am–3pm, July & Aug daily 10am–3pm; ☎920 370 245, ⊕arenasdesanpedro.es).

CIRCO DE LAGUNA GRANDE

The **Circo de Laguna Grande** is the centrepiece of the Gredos range, with its highest peak, Almanzor (2593m), surrounded by pinnacles sculpted into utterly improbable shapes. The path begins at the car park at the end of the road coming from Hoyos and climbs towards the high Pozas meadow. From there you can reach the large glacial lake at the end of the valley, a spectacular two-hour walk that winds its way down the slopes on a well-defined path. The route is best done in late spring, summer or early autumn, as snow makes it a treacherous walk in winter.

CIRCO DE LAS CINCO LAGUNAS

For a tougher and much longer route – the **Circo de las Cinco Lagunas** – you can continue on from the Laguna Grande, where there is a *refugio* and camping area, to the Cinco Lagunas (allow 8hr from the Plataforma). Take the signposted path to the right just before the lake, which follows an old hunting route used by Alfonso XIII, up to the Portilla del Rey pass. From there you will be able to look down on the lakes – which are reached along a sharp, scree-laden descent. The drop is amply rewarded by virtual solitude, even in midsummer, and sightings of *Capra pyrenaica victoriae*, the graceful (and almost tame) Gredos mountain goat. There are also species of salamander and toad found only in the area. It is another four to five hours on to the village of Navalperal de Tormes, which is 14km west of Hoyos del Espino.

ACCOMMODATION

The *casas rurales* that are scattered throughout the villages often make a good base, especially if you are travelling in a group (information line ☎ 920 206 204, ⓦ casasgredos.com).

ARENAS AND GUISANDO

Hostal El Fogón de Gredos C/Linarejo 6 ☎ 920 374 018, ⓦ fogondegredos.com. If you want a mountain location, then this is your best bet. Situated a couple of kilometres outside Guisando on the flanks of the mountains, this two-star *hostal* has simple, comfortable rooms and a decent restaurant. Breakfast included. **€52**

Posada de la Triste Condesa C/Dr Juan Torres 9 ☎ 920 372 567, ⓦ posadatristecondesa.com. Rustic accommodation with five cosy, tastefully designed double rooms around a delightful plant-strewn interior patio. Breakfast included. **€60**

VALLE DEL TORMES

Camping Gredos On the road from Hoyos del Espino towards the Plataforma ☎ 920 207 585, ⓦ elcamping degredos.com. A riverside campsite by the Puente del Duque with plenty of shady pitches and wooden bungalows for rent. Closed mid-Oct to Easter. **€14.50**

Camping Navagredos Navarredonda ☎ 920 207 476, ⓦ navagredos.com. Large, pine-forested campsite with 300 pitches on the fringes of the Sierra and close to the Río Tormes. Wooden bungalows on offer. Closed Oct–April. **€16.40**

★ **Casa de Arriba** C/Cruz 19, Navarredonda ☎ 920 348 024, ⓦ casadearriba.com. Cosy and comfortable *casa rural* at the top of the hill in Navarredonda, serving breakfasts and meals too. A pleasant garden area for relaxing when the sun is out. **€79**

★ **Hotel Milano Real** Hoyos del Espino ☎ 920 349 108, ⓦ elmilanoreal.com. Wonderful hotel on the outskirts of the village with a high-quality restaurant serving some excellent regional and Spanish specialities and a seasonal menu at €30. Eight suites (€200), each decorated according to an international theme from Arabic to Japanese, Colonial to Manhattan, five comfortable doubles and a delightful garden area. **€152**

★ **Hotel Rural las 4 Calles** C/Mayor 57, San Martín del Pimpollar ☎ 920 348 817, ☎ 626 066 223, ⓦ gredosguides.es. Very friendly local hotel in this picturesque village with five en-suite rooms and a cosy little seating area. The owner, Juanfran, can organize a range of outdoor activities for visitors, from birdwatching to hikes and mountain biking. Price includes breakfast. **€50**

Parador de Gredos Navarredonda, km 10 on the AV941 ☎ 920 348 048, ⓦ www.paradores.com. Spain's first-ever parador, which has undergone a major refurbishment programme in recent years and enjoys some great views across the mountains from the terraces. The rustic rooms are large and comfortable while the restaurant serves up some high-quality local produce. **€95**

Youth hostel Navarredonda ☎ 920 348 005 ⓦ reaj .com. Well-situated youth hostel not far from the parador on the outskirts of the village, with a large summer pool, good communal areas and some great views of the mountains. Two- and four-bed rooms. YH card needed. **€12.71**, under-30s **€9.32**

Segovia

After Toledo, **SEGOVIA** is the standout trip from Madrid. A relatively small city, strategically sited on a rocky ridge, it is deeply and haughtily Castilian, with a panoply of squares and mansions from its days of Golden Age grandeur, when it was a royal resort and a base for the Cortes (parliament). It was in Segovia that Isabel la Católica was proclaimed queen of Castile in 1474.

For a city of its size, there is an extraordinary array of architectural monuments. Most celebrated are the breathtaking **Roman aqueduct**, the Gothic **Catedral** and the fairy-tale **Alcázar**, but the less obvious attractions – the cluster of ancient churches and the many mansions found in the lanes of the old town, all in a warm, honey-coloured stone – are what really make it worth a visit. If you have time, take a walk out of the city alongside the river and out to the fascinating church of **Vera Cruz**.

The aqueduct

The most photographed sight in Segovia is the magnificent **aqueduct**. Over 800m of granite, supported by 166 arches and 120 pillars and at its highest point towering some 30m above the Pza. de Azoguejo, it stands up without a drop of mortar or cement. No one knows exactly when it was built, but it was probably around the end of the first century AD under either Emperor Domitian or Trajan. It no longer carries water from the Río Acebeda to the city, and in recent years traffic vibration and pollution have been threatening to undermine the entire structure, but the completion of a meticulous restoration programme should ensure it remains standing for some time to come. If you climb the stairs beside the aqueduct you can get a view looking down over it from a surviving fragment of the city walls.

Museo Zuloaga

Pza. de Colmenares s/n • Wed 9am–4pm • €1.20, Sat & Sun free • ☎ 921 463 348

Some 200m up the hill to the right of the aqueduct and nestled against the walls is the **Museo Zuloaga**, a museum dedicated to the ceramicist Daniel Zuloaga and housed in the Romanesque Iglesia San Juan de los Caballeros, where the noble families of the city used to meet. Its limited opening hours mean that Wednesdays are the only time you can see the striking display of the artist's work, including some marvellous painted tiles and a scene of the Apostles with Christ that was designed to surround the family fireplace and which were modelled on those at the Monasterio de Santo Domingo de Silos in Burgos.

Casa de los Picos and the Alhóndiga

Passing under the aqueduct and up the hill along C/Cervantes and C/Juan Bravo, you will be directed towards the old city past the curious fifteenth-century **Casa de los Picos** (House of Spikes), with its waffle-like facade made up of pyramid-shaped stones to your right, and the former corn exchange, the **Alhóndiga**, down a few steps on your left.

Plaza de San Martín

A short distance northwest of Casa de los Picos is the **Plaza de San Martín**, one of the city's grandest squares, whose ensemble of buildings includes the fourteenth-century **Torreón de Lozoya** (normally open for art exhibitions Mon–Fri 6–9pm, Sat & Sun noon–2pm & 6–9pm) and the twelfth-century **church of San Martín**, which demonstrates all the local stylistic peculiarities. It has the characteristic covered portico, a fine arched tower and a typically Romanesque aspect; like most of Segovia's churches, it can be visited only when it's open for business, during early morning or evening services. In the middle of the plaza is a **statue of Juan Bravo**, a local folk hero who led the *comuneros* rebellion against Carlos V in protest against tax increases, the undermining of local power and the influence of foreign advisers.

La Trinidad and Plaza San Esteban

Tues–Sat 10am–2pm & 4–7pm (July–Sept opens and closes an hour later in the afternoon), Sun 10am–2pm • €1.20; free Sat & Sun

North of Pza. de San Martín, the church of **La Trinidad** preserves the purest Romanesque style in Segovia: each span of its double-arched apse has intricately carved capitals, every one of them unique. Nearby – and making a good loop to or from the Alcázar – is the **Plaza San Esteban**, worth seeing for its superb, five-storeyed, twelfth-century church tower.

The Catedral

Pza. Mayor • Daily April–Sept: 9.30am–6.30pm, Oct–March: 9.30am–5.30pm, except during Mass • €3, free Sun 9.30am–1.15pm (museum and cloisters closed) • Guided tours at 11am & 4.30pm • ☎ 921 462 205

C/Juan Bravo eventually leads on to the bar-filled **Pza. Mayor**. Dominating one corner of the plaza are the exuberant lines of the **Catedral**. Construction began in 1525, on

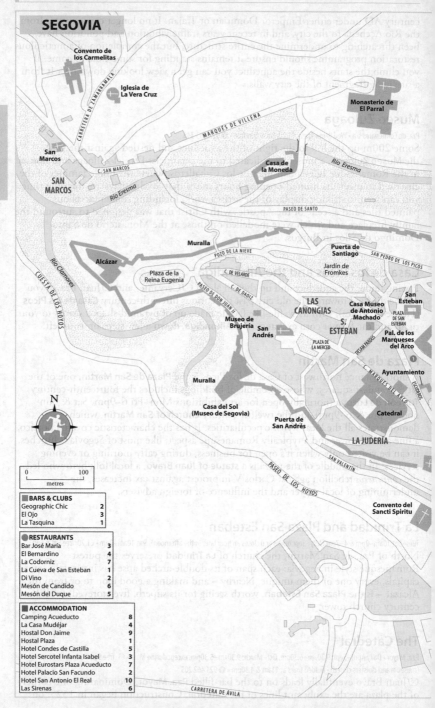

SEGOVIA

Convento de los Carmelitas

Iglesia de La Vera Cruz

Monasterio de El Parral

CARRETERA DE ZAMARRAMALA

MARQUES DE VILLENA

San Marcos

C. SAN MARCOS

SAN MARCOS

Río Eresma

Casa de la Moneda

Río Eresma

Río Eresma

PASEO DE SANTO

Muralla

Río Clamores

Alcázar

Plaza de la Reina Eugenia

POZO DE LA NIEVE

C. DE VELARDE

PASEO DE DON JUAN II

C. DE DAOIZ

Puerta de Santiago

SAN PEDRO DE LOS PICOS

Jardín de Fromkes

LAS CANONGIAS

Museo de Brujería

San Andrés

PLAZA DE LA MERCED

S. ESTEBAN

DCSM PAXIOLS

Casa Museo de Antonio Machado

San Esteban

PLAZA DE SAN ESTEBAN

Pal. de los Marqueses del Arco

C. MARQUES DEL ARCO

Ayuntamiento

ESCUDEROS

Catedral

CUESTA DE LOS HOYOS

Muralla

Casa del Sol (Museo de Segovia)

Puerta de San Andrés

LA JUDERÍA

SAN VALENTÍN

PASEO DE LOS HOYOS

Convento del Sancti Spiritu

N

0   100
metres

CARRETERA DE ÁVILA

BARS & CLUBS

Geographic Chic	2
El Ojo	3
La Tasquina	1

RESTAURANTS

Bar José María	3
El Bernardino	4
La Codorniz	7
La Cueva de San Esteban	1
Di Vino	2
Mesón de Candido	6
Mesón del Duque	5

ACCOMMODATION

Camping Acueducto	8
La Casa Mudéjar	4
Hostal Don Jaime	9
Hostal Plaza	1
Hotel Condes de Castilla	5
Hotel Sercotel Infanta Isabel	3
Hotel Eurostars Plaza Acueducto	7
Hotel Palacio San Facundo	2
Hotel San Antonio El Real	10
Las Sirenas	6

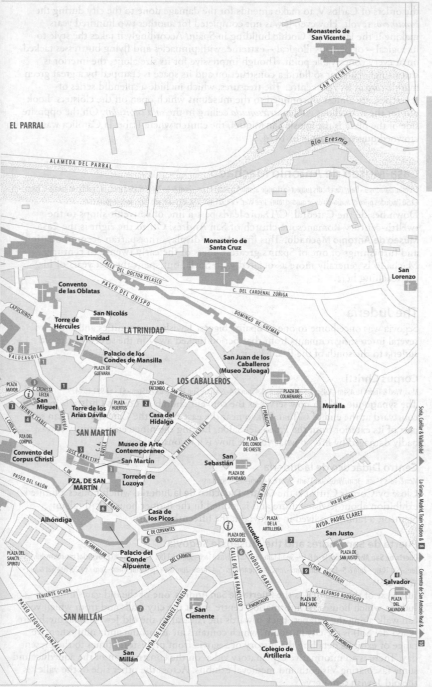

EL PARRAL

Río Eresma

ALAMEDA DEL PARRAL

Monasterio de
San Vicente

SAN VICENTE

Monasterio de
Santa Cruz

San
Lorenzo

CALLE DEL DOCTOR VELASCO

C. DEL CARDENAL ZÚÑIGA

Convento
de las Oblatas

PASEO DEL OBISPO

San Nicolás

DOMINGO DE GUZMÁN

CAPUCHINOS

Torre de
Hércules

La Trinidad

LA TRINIDAD

Palacio de los
Condes de Mansilla

San Juan de los
Caballeros
(Museo Zuloaga)

VALDEAGUILA

PLAZA DE
GUEVARA

PZA SAN
FACUNDO

LOS CABALLEROS

C. SAN AGUSTÍN

PLAZA DE
COLMENARES

PLAZA
MAYOR

CRONISTA
LECEA

San
Miguel

Torre de los
Arias Dávila

Casa del
Hidalgo

Muralla

INFANTA ISABEL

HERRERÍA

PLAZA
HUERTOS

C./PERUCHA

C. DE LA ROCA

SAN MARTÍN

C. A.
DÁVILA

Museo de Arte
Contemporáneo

E. MARTÍN HIGUERA

PLAZA
DEL CONDE
DE CHESTE

PZA DEL
CORPUS

JOSÉ CANALEJAS

San Martín

San
Sebastián

C. SAN JUAN

Convento del
Corpus Christi

C. DE

Torreón de
Lozoya

PLAZA
DEL CONDE
DE CHESTE

PASEO DEL SALÓN

PZA. DE SAN
MARTÍN

PLAZA DE
AVENDAÑO

JUAN BRAVO

VIA DE ROMA

Alhóndiga

Casa de
los Picos

PLAZA
DE LA
ARTILLERÍA

AVDA. PADRE CLARET

San Justo

Acueducto

DE SAN MILLÁN

C. DE CERVANTES

PLAZA DEL
AZOGUEJO

PLAZA DE
SAN JUSTO

PLAZA DEL
SANCTI
SPIRITU

Palacio del
Conde Alpuente

DEL CARMEN

CALLE DE SAN FRANCISCO

TEODOSIO GARCÍA

C. OCHOA ONDÁTEGUI

El
Salvador

TENIENTE OCHOA

C. S. ALFONSO RODRÍGUEZ

PLAZA DEL
SALVADOR

SAN MILLÁN

AVDA. DE FERNÁNDEZ LADREDA

San
Clemente

C. MONTALVO

PLAZA DE
DÍAZ SANZ

CALLE LAS MORENAS

PASEO EZEQUIEL GONZÁLEZ

San
Millán

Colegio de
Artillería

Soria, Cuéllar & Valladolid ▶

La Granja, Madrid, Train Station & 8 ▶

Convento de San Antonio Real & 10 ▶

2

the orders of Carlos V, to make amends for the damage done to the city during the *comuneros* revolt. However, it was not completed for another two hundred years, making it the last major Gothic building in Spain. Accordingly it takes the style to its logical – or perhaps illogical – extreme, with pinnacles and flying buttresses tacked on at every conceivable point. Though impressive for its size alone, the interior is surprisingly bare for so florid a construction and its space is cramped by a great green marble *coro* at its very centre. The treasures, which include a splendid series of tapestries, are almost all confined to the **museums** which open off the cloisters. Look out for the marvellous golden *artesonado* ceiling in the *sala capitular*. On the opposite side of the plaza is the **Iglesia San Miguel**, the church where Isabel la Católica was crowned queen of Castile in 1474.

Casa-Museo de Antonio Machado

C/Desamparados 5 • Daily (but hours subject to change at short notice) 11am–2pm & 4–7pm (guided tours in Spanish at 1pm & 6.30pm) • €2.50 (includes price of audio-guide or guided tour), free Wed • ☎ 921 460 377, ⓦ machado.turismodesegovia.com

Down beside the Catedral, C/Daoiz leads past a line of souvenir shops to the twelfth-century Romanesque church of San Andrés. Off to the right is the **Casa-Museo de Antonio Machado**. This little house displays the spartan accommodation and furnishings of one of Spain's greatest poets of the early twentieth century; Machado is generally more associated with Soria, but spent the last years of his life teaching here.

The Judería

Segovia was once home to one of Spain's biggest Jewish communities and there are several interesting remnants from that period tucked away in the streets of the old **Judería** to the south of the Pza. Mayor.

Corpus Christi

Mon, Wed & Thurs 10.45am–1.45pm, Sat 10.45am–1.45pm & 4–6.45pm, Sun 10.45am–2.45pm • €1 • ☎ 921 463 429

The **synagogue**, which now serves as the convent church of **Corpus Christi**, is in a little courtyard at the end of C/Juan Bravo near the east end of the Catedral. You can see part of its exterior from the Paseo del Salón. During the nineteenth century it was badly damaged by fire, so what you see now is a reconstruction.

Centro Didáctico de la Judería

Mon & Tues 11am–3pm, Wed–Sun 11am–2pm & 4–7pm • €2; free Thurs

Close by Corpus Christi is the **Centro Didáctico de la Judería**, which houses a limited exhibition about Jewish culture and is located in the former house of Abraham Senneor, a rabbi who lived in Segovia in the fifteenth century.

Puerta de San Andrés and the Museo de Segovia

Puerta de San Andrés Mon–Wed & Fri–Sun 11am–6.30pm, Thurs 11am–3pm • €1 (for parapet walk) **Provincial museum** July–Sept Tues–Sat 10am–2pm & 5–8pm, Sun 10am–2pm; Oct–June Tues–Sat 10am–2pm & 4–7pm, Sun 10am–2pm • €1.20, free Sat & Sun • ☎ 921 460 613

Just west of the Catedral is the **Puerta de San Andrés**, one of the old gates into the Judería which houses an information centre about the city walls and from which you can walk along the parapet. Back towards the Alcázar in the old Jewish slaughterhouse (Casa del Sol) is the **city museum**, which contains an absorbing and comprehensive range of exhibits detailing the history of Segovia from prehistoric times to the present day. There is an informative explanatory video on the construction of the aqueduct and some fascinating Visigoth and medieval exhibits. Across the other side of the valley is the old **Jewish cemetery**.

The Alcázar

Daily: April–Sept 10am–7pm; Oct–March 10am–6pm • €5, access to the tower an additional €2 (audio-guide €3), free third Tues in the month for EU citizens • ☎ 921 460 759, ⍟ alcazardesegovia.com

Beyond the Pza. Mayor and the Judería, perched on the northwestern tip of the city walls, is the **Alcázar**. An extraordinary fantasy of a castle, with its narrow towers and flurry of turrets, it will seem eerily familiar to just about every visitor, having apparently served as the model for the Disneyland castle in Orlando. It is itself a bit of a sham; although it dates from the fourteenth and fifteenth centuries, it was almost completely destroyed by a fire in 1862 and rebuilt as a deliberately hyperbolic version of the original. Nevertheless the rooms contain some fascinating furnishings and artefacts and it is worth the entry fee alone for the beautiful *artesonado* ceilings and the magnificent panoramas from the tower.

Vera Cruz and the Convento de las Carmelitas

Tues 4–7pm, Wed–Sun 10.30am–1.30pm & 4–7pm, Oct–March closes 6pm; closed Nov • €2 (free Tues) • ☎ 921 432 475

The most striking of Segovia's ancient churches is undoubtedly **Vera Cruz**, a remarkable twelve-sided building outside town in the valley facing the Alcázar, which can be reached by taking the path down to Paseo San Juan de La Cruz. It is traditionally thought to have been built by the Knights Templar in the early thirteenth century on the pattern of the church of the Holy Sepulchre in Jerusalem, and once housed part of the True Cross (hence its name; the sliver of wood itself was moved to the nearby village church of La Magdalena at Zamarramala). Inside, the nave is circular with ghostly vestiges of beautiful murals still visible on the walls, and its heart is occupied by a strange two-storeyed chamber – again twelve-sided – in which the knights, as part of their initiation, stood vigil over the cross. Climb the tower for a highly photogenic vista of the city.

While you're over here you could take in the prodigiously walled **Convento de las Carmelitas** (April–Sept Tues–Sun 10am–1.30pm & 4–8pm; Oct–March same times, but closes an hour earlier in the eve; free/voluntary donation), which is also referred to as the monastery of San Juan de la Cruz, and contains the gaudy mausoleum of its founder saint.

Casa de la Moneda

C/Moneda Tues 10am–3pm, Wed–Sun 10am–7pm • €3; free Wed • ☎ 921 475 109, ⍟ casamoneda.es

Located in a picturesque setting down by the River Eresma, a little further east of Vera Cruz, is the **Casa de la Moneda**, the former royal mint established by Felipe II in the late sixteenth century and designed by El Escorial architect Juan de Herrera. Inside is a museum tracing the history and the methods used in the production of royal coinage

---

WALKS AROUND SEGOVIA

Segovia is an excellent city for **walks**. Drop down onto the path that winds its way down into the valley from the Alcázar on the north side of the city wall and you'll reach the Río Eresma. Head west and you'll pass close to Vera Cruz and the Convento de los Carmelitas, with some great views of the Alcázar, before turning back towards the city; head east and you can follow the beautiful tree-lined path alongside the river and wend your way back up the hill to the old town in a round trip of a little over an hour. On your way you can visit the **Monasterio de El Parral** (Wed–Sun visits at 11am & 5pm; donation); or better still, follow the track that circles behind Vera Cruz to the monastery. El Parral is a sizeable and partly ruined complex occupied by Hieronymites, an order found only in Spain. Ring the bell for admission and you will be shown the cloister and church; the latter is a late Gothic building with rich sculpture at the east end. Gregorian Masses can be heard on Sundays at noon.

For the best view of all of Segovia, take the main road north for 2km or so towards **Cuéllar**. A panorama of the whole city, including the aqueduct, gradually unfolds.

and an interpretation centre (Oct–March Mon & Tues 10am–3pm, Wed–Sun 10am–6pm; April–Sept Wed–Sun 10am–7pm) about the aqueduct. There is a refreshing riverside café too.

Convento de San Antonio Real

Tues 4–7pm, Wed–Sat 10am–2pm & 4–7pm, Sun 10.30am–2pm • €2

If you follow the line of the aqueduct away from the old city you will come to the **Convento de San Antonio Real**, a little gem of a palace, and now also serving as a luxury hotel (see opposite). Originally founded by Enrique IV in 1455, it contains, an intriguing collection of Mudéjar and Hispano-Flemish art, some outstanding *artesonado* ceilings and a wonderful fifteenth-century wooden calvary.

San Millán and San Justo

San Millán Mass 10.30am & 8pm, Sun 10am, 11.30am, 12.30pm & 8pm San Justo Mon–Sat 10.45am–1.45pm & 4–7pm (though subject to changes)

Back towards the city, but still outside the old walls, stand two fine Romanesque churches. Between the bus station and the aqueduct is the church of **San Millán**, with a fine Mozárabe tower and open porticoes. Its interior has been restored to its original form though it is only open during services. Facing the aqueduct is **San Justo**, which has a wonderful Romanesque wall painting in the apse and a twelfth-century sculpture of Christ complete with hinged arms.

ARRIVAL AND DEPARTURE   SEGOVIA

By train The high-speed train from Chamartín station in Madrid (12–14 daily; return tickets from around €20) takes just 25min, though the train station is quite a way out of town (take the #11 bus, which goes to the aqueduct every 15min). If you take a regional train it will take you a lot longer (3 daily; 2hr 5min), but it goes to the old station nearer to the centre (then take bus #8) and costs around €13.
Destinations Cercedilla (4–5 daily; 35–40min); Madrid

(20 daily; 30min–1hr 50min).
By bus There are regular buses from Madrid (operated by La Sepulvedana, Intercambiador de Moncloa; ⓜ Moncloa; every 30min, 1hr 15min; €8.09 single) that drop you at the bus station to the west of the aqueduct.
Destinations Ávila (2–4 daily; 1hr); La Granja (20 daily; 25min); Madrid (every 30min; 1hr 15min); Salamanca (2 daily; 2hr 45min); Valladolid (hourly; 1hr 50min–2hr 30min).

INFORMATION

Turismo Offices at: Pza. Mayor 10 (Mon–Sat 9.30am–2pm & 4–7pm, Sun 9.30am–5pm, ☎ 921 460 334, ⓦ turismo castillayleon.com); the high-speed train station Camino de la Ermita de Juarrillos (Mon–Fri 8.15am–3.15pm, Sat & Sun 10.30am–1.30pm & 4–6.30pm); and the bus station on Paseo Ezequiel González (Wed–Sun 10am–4pm).
Local council visitors' reception office Pza. de

Azoguejo, just beneath the aqueduct (☎ 921 466 720, ⓦ turismodesegovia.com; daily 10am–6.30pm). You can sign up for a guided tour (Mon–Fri 11.15am & 4.30pm, Sat & Sun 11.45am & 4.30pm; €13.50, €10.50 children over 5). For a modest €3 you can purchase a Segovia Tourist Card which will give you a range of discounts on entry fees and at restaurants and hotels.

ACCOMMODATION

Most of the **accommodation** is to be found in the streets around the Pza. Mayor and Pza. de Azoguejo, but rooms can be hard to come by even out of season, so it's worth booking ahead. Be warned that in winter, at over 1000m, the nights can be very cold and sometimes snowy.

★ **La Casa Mudéjar** C/Isabel Católica 8 ☎ 921 466 250, ⓦ lacasamudejar.com. Characterful hotel located in a restored mansion sandwiched between the Pza. Mayor and the Judería. Well-appointed rooms with historic touches such as beautiful carved *artesonado* ceilings, a patio

restaurant that serves some traditional *sefardí* dishes with fruit sauces, and a small spa area (from €20 for an 80min circuit). **€85**
Hostal Don Jaime C/Ochoa Ondátegui 8 ☎ 921 444 787, ⓦ hostaldonjaime.com. An excellent budget option,

this old-style, but comfortable sixteen-room *hostal* is close to the aqueduct. All doubles have their own bathroom. **€55**
Hostal Plaza C/Cronista Lecea 11 ☎921 460 303, ⓦhostal-plaza.com. A smart *hostal*, centrally located just off the Pza. Mayor, with twenty small a/c doubles and four triples, all with simple but stylish decor. It also has its own garage. **€51**
★**Hotel Condes de Castilla** C/José Canalejas 5 ☎921 463 529, ⓦhotelcondesdecastilla.com. Refurbished, reformed and rebranded, this hotel, housed in a beautiful old building overlooking the church of San Martín, now has thirteen imaginatively decorated rooms, each named after a Castilian noble. **€110**
Hotel Sercotel Infanta Isabel Pza. Mayor 12 ☎921 461 300, ⓦhotelinfantaisabel.com. A very comfortable hotel, now part of the Sercotel chain, with 37 rooms (including four triples and eight superior class doubles) done out with nineteenth-century-style furnishings and ideally positioned right on the Pza. Mayor. **€85**
Hotel Eurostars Plaza Acueducto Avda. Padre Claret 2–4 ☎921 413 403, ⓦeurostarsplazaacueducto.com. Probably the best view of the aqueduct in the whole city is from the terrace bar in this well-appointed, modern four-star hotel. Many of the rooms also have great views over this masterpiece of Roman engineering. Child rooms and

triples also available. **€110**
Hotel Palacio San Facundo Pza. San Facundo 4 ☎921 463 061, ⓦhotelpalaciosanfacundo.com. An old Segovian mansion not far from the Pza. Mayor converted into a swish business-style hotel with slickly decorated rooms and a stylish, covered patio bar. Look out for offers on the website. **€150**
★**Hotel San Antonio El Real** San Antonio El Real s/n ☎921 413 455, ⓦsanantonioelreal.es. Luxury hotel located inside a splendid old convent just up from the aqueduct. The 51 rooms are large, sumptuously decorated and with all the facilities you could want, while the garden cloister is the perfect place for a relaxing drink. **€140**
Las Sirenas C/Juan Bravo 30 ☎921 462 663, ⓦhotelsirenas.com. Chintz decor, classic Castilian furnishings, big rooms, a neat garden and terrace all at a very reasonable price in this two-star hotel. **€50**

CAMPING
Camping Acueducto Avda. Don Juan de Borbón 49 ☎921 425 000, ⓦcampingacueducto.com. The nearest campsite, 3km out on the road to La Granja; take a #6 "Nueva Segovia" bus from the Pza. Mayor. A quiet site with a swimming pool that has great views of the sierra and plenty of shade. Closed mid-Oct to Easter. **€24**

EATING AND DRINKING

Segovia takes its cooking seriously, with restaurants of Madrid quality – and prices to match. Culinary specialities include *cochinillo asado* (roast suckling pig) and *judiones*, large white beans from La Granja.

Bar José María C/Cronista Lecea 11, just off Pza. Mayor ⓦrtejosemaria.com. Bar-annexe to one of Segovia's best restaurants serving delicious and modestly priced tapas. Daily 1–4pm & 8–11.30pm.
★**El Bernardino** C/Cervantes 2 ☎921 462 477, ⓦelbernardino.com. A friendly place serving the Castilian classics of *cochinillo* and *cordero*, but better value than some of the city's more famous restaurants. The *menú segoviano* with *cochinillo* is under €30, while they also do a decent-value kids' menu. Daily around 1.30–4pm & 8.30pm–midnight.
La Codorniz C/Hermanos Barral 3 ☎921 463 897, ⓦrestaurantelacodorniz.com. There's a decent-value tourist menu with suckling pig for €25, some great *tortilla* and lots of *combinados* involving *codorniz* (quail) at this unpretentious place opposite San Millán church. Daily around 1.30–4pm & 8.30pm–midnight.
La Cueva de San Esteban C/Valdelaguila 15, off the top end of Pza. San Esteban ☎921 460 982, ⓦlacuevadesanesteban.com. A cavern-restaurant and bar serving draught beer, an extensive range of tapas and Castilian classics, popular with locals and good value. There is a *menú del día* at €10 though eating à la carte will cost more in the region of €25 a head. Daily noon–midnight.

★**Di Vino** C/Valdeáguila 7 ☎921 460 789, ⓦrestaurantedivino.com. A smart restaurant housed in an old convent owned by the same people as *La Cueva de San Esteban* (see above). Expect excellent food, good service and imaginative touches to Castilian classics. Menu prices start at €25 (€16 for children). Mon & Wed–Sun 1–4pm & 8–midnight.
Mesón de Cándido Pza. Azoguejo 5 ☎921 428 103, ⓦmesondecandido.es. In the shadow of the aqueduct you will find the city's most celebrated restaurant: the place for *cochinillo* and other roasts cooked to perfection. Allow around €40 per person. Daily around 1.30–4pm & 8.30pm–midnight.
Mesón del Duque C/Cervantes 12 ☎921 462 487, ⓦrestauranteduque.es. Rival to the nearby *Cándido*, and also specializing in Castilian roasts, though it claims to be the oldest restaurant in the city. Offers a range of different menus including the obligatory *cochinillo* and *cordero* in the €30 to €40 bracket. Daily around 1.30–4pm & 8.30pm–midnight.

OUT OF TOWN
La Posada de Javier In the village of Torrecaballeros, 8km northeast on the N110 ☎921 401 136,

2

ⓦ laposadadejavier.es. Serious *madrileño* – and *segoviano* – gourmands eat out in the neighbouring villages, and this lovely old farmhouse is one of the most popular choices. It isn't cheap, however, with a menu costing at least €30. Booking is essential at weekends. Tues–Thurs & Sun 1–4pm, Fri & Sat 1–4pm & 8.30–11.30pm; closed July.

NIGHTLIFE

Pza. Mayor, with its cathedral backdrop, makes a great place for a drink and a snack, but the biggest clusters of **bars** can be found in the narrow streets that lead off the plaza and back down by the aqueduct along Avda. Fernández Ladreda.

Geographic Chic C/Infanta Isabel 20 ☎ 921 434 185. Bar-club modelled on an English-style pub with dark wood furnishings, comfy sofas and a varied diet of music. Daily 8pm–3am.

El Ojo Pza San Martín 6 ☎ 921 462 680. Small *bar de copas* perched on the edge of this charming little plaza and serving well poured draught beer accompanied by a soundtrack of jazz, rock and pop. Tues–Thurs 4–11pm, Fri 4pm–2am, Sat noon–2.30am, Sun noon–11pm.

La Tasquina C/Valdeláguila 3 ☎ 921 461 954. Popular wine bar close to the Pza. Mayor serving some tasty tapas to accompany a wide selection of wines and cavas. Daily 1.30–4pm & 8.30–11pm.

Around Segovia

Segovia has a major outlying attraction in the elegant Bourbon summer palace and gardens of **La Granja**, 10km southeast of the town on the CL601 Madrid road, and connected by regular bus services. True Bourbon aficionados, with time and transport, might also want to visit a second palace and hunting museum 12km west of La Granja at **Riofrío**.

La Granja

Pza. de España 17 • April–Sept Tues–Sun 10am–7pm; Oct–March Tues–Sun 10am–8pm (last entry an hour before closing); gardens daily 10am–dusk • €9, joint ticket with the Palacio Real at Riofrío €10, free Wed & Thurs 3–6pm (April–Sept 5–8pm) for EU citizens • ☎ 921 470 019, ⓦ patrimonionacional.es

The **Palacio Real de la Granja de San Ildefonso** was built by the reluctant first Bourbon king of Spain, Felipe V, no doubt homesick for the luxuries of Versailles. Its glories are the mountain setting and the extravagant wooded grounds and gardens, but it's also worth casting an eye over the **palace**. Though destroyed in parts and damaged throughout by a fire in 1918, much has been well restored and is home to a superlative collection of sixteenth-century tapestries, one of the most valuable in the world. Everything is furnished in plush French imperial style, but it's almost all of Spanish origin; the majority of the huge chandeliers, for example, were made in the **glass factory** in the village of San Ildefonso (April–Sept: Tues–Sat 10am–6pm, Sun 10am–3pm; Oct–March: Tues–Fri & Sun 10am–3pm, Sat 10am–6pm; €5, under-10s free; ⓦ fcnv.es). Here you can visit an exhibition on the history of the craft and still see the glass being blown and decorated in the traditional manner.

The highlight of the **gardens** is its series of **fountains**, which culminates in the fifteen-metre-high jet of La Fama. They're fantastic and really not to be missed, which means timing your visit for 5.30pm on Saturdays or 1pm on Sundays (€4) when some are switched on (they may not be switched on during periods of water shortage, so it's best to check on ☎ 921 470 019 or the website beforehand). Only on three saints' days in the year – normally May 30 (San Fernando), July 25 (Santiago) and August 25 (San Luís) – are all of the fountains set to work, with accompanying crowds to watch. The enormous monumental fountain known as the Baños de Diana usually operates on Saturday nights in summer (10.30–11.30pm mid-July to early Sept 4; €2) and is illuminated together with the palace facade.

Riofrío

April–Sept Tues–Sun 10am–8pm; Oct–March Tues–Sun 10am–6pm (last entry an hour before closing) • €7; joint ticket with the Palacio Real at La Granja €10, free Wed & Thurs 3–6pm (April–Sept 5–8pm) for EU citizens • ⓦ patrimonionacional.es, ☎ 921 470 019

The palace at **Riofrío** was built by Isabel, the widow of Felipe V, in the fear that she would be banished from La Granja by her stepson Fernando VI. He died, however, leaving the throne for Isabel's own son, Carlos III, and Riofrío was not occupied until the nineteenth century, when Alfonso XII moved in to mourn the death of his young queen Mercedes. He, too, died pretty soon after, which is perhaps why the palace has a spartan and slightly tatty feel.

The complex, painted in dusty pink with green shutters, is surrounded not by manicured gardens but by a **deer park**, into which you can drive but not wander. Inside the palace, you have to join a guided tour, which winds through an endless sequence of rooms, none stunningly furnished. About half the tour is devoted to a **museum of hunting**; the most interesting items here are reconstructions of cave paintings, including the famous Altamira drawings.

ARRIVAL AND INFORMATION   AROUND SEGOVIA

By bus Buses depart to La Granja from the bus station in Segovia (20 daily, 10 daily at weekends; 25min).

By train There are four to five local trains a day from Segovia to Navas de Riofrío (10min; €1.85). From there it is a 1km walk to Riofrío. Regional line trains from Chamartín station in Madrid to Segovia also stop at Navas de Riofrío (3–5 daily; 1hr 45min–2hr; €7.70).

Turismo La Granja Pza. de los Dolores 1 (Tues–Sun 10am–1.30pm & 3.30–7.30pm; ☎ 921 473 953, ⓦ turismorealsitiodesanildefonso.com).

NORTH FROM SEGOVIA: A CASTLE TOUR

Of some five hundred **castles** that remain in reasonable state of repair in Spain, Segovia province has an especially rich selection. Drivers en route to Valladolid and the Río Duero (see p.401) can construct an enjoyable route to see the best of them; there are buses (from Segovia or Valladolid), but you may end up spending the night in places that really only warrant a quick stop.

Fifty kilometres northwest of Segovia, the fortress (Mon–Fri 10.30am–1pm & 4.30–6/7pm, Sat & Sun 11am–1pm & 4/4.30–6/7pm, closed first Tues of each month; €2.70; ⓦ castillodecoca .com) at the small town of **Coca** is the prettiest imaginable, less a piece of military architecture than a country house masquerading as one. Built in about 1453, as the base of the powerful Fonseca family, it's constructed from pinkish bricks, encircled by a deep moat and fantastically decorated with octagonal turrets and elaborate castellation – an extraordinary design strongly influenced by Moorish architecture. There are five **buses** a day here from Segovia, though Coca itself is fairly unremarkable; drivers should push on to **Medina del Campo** in Castilla y León for lunch (see p.399), itself the site of another fabulous castle.

The castle at **Turégano** (Wed–Sun 11am–2pm & 4–6pm; summer 5–8pm; €6), 28km north of Segovia, is essentially a fifteenth-century structure enclosing an early thirteenth-century church. However, it's east of here, off the main Segovia–Soria road (N110), that the most rewarding diversions are to be made. Eight kilometres east of Turégano, **Pedraza** in particular is almost perfectly preserved from the sixteenth century. The village is protected on three sides by a steep valley; the only entrance is the single original gateway (which used to be the town prison), from where the narrow lanes spiral up towards a large Pza. Mayor, still used for a bullfighting festival in the first week in September. The **Castillo de Pedraza** (Wed–Sun 11am–2pm & 4–7pm) is where the 8-year-old dauphin of France and his younger brother were believed to be imprisoned in 1526, given up by their father François I who swapped his freedom for theirs after he was captured at the battle of Pavia. **Sepúlveda**, a little further north (and off the highway between Madrid and Burgos), is less of a harmonious whole, but has an even more dramatic setting, strung out high on a narrow spit of land between the Castilla and Duratón river valleys. Its physical and architectural high point is the distinctive Romanesque church of **El Salvador**, perched high above its ruined castle. Ask at the tourist office (Pza. del Trigo 6 Sepúlveda; Wed 10.30am–2pm, Thurs–Sun 10.30am–2.30pm & 4–6pm; ☎ 921 540 237, ⓦ sepulveda.es) for details of routes down into the spectacular gorge that is home to one of the country's biggest colonies of griffon vultures.

ACCOMMODATION

Hotel Roma C/Guardas 2 ☎ 921 470 752, ⓦ hotelroma .org. Friendly two-star hotel right outside the palace gates with sixteen slightly dated but comfortable rooms and a restaurant serving local specialities. €70

★**Isabel de Farnesio** Travesia de La Reina 4 ☎ 921 471 078, ⓦ hotelisabeldefarnesio.com. This chic hotel has 23 immaculately decorated doubles and a handful of luxurious suites. Its spa area provides a selection of beauty treatments and a gastrobar. €90

Parador de la Granja Casa de los Infantes, C/Fuentes 3, San Ildefonso de la Granja ☎ 921 010 750, ⓦ www. paradores.com. A plush parador with a rooftop pool and spa area housed in the eighteenth-century Casa de los Infantes built by Carlos III for two of his sons. Large, modern rooms and an excellent restaurant specializing in local dishes such as *judiones*, lamb and suckling pig. €135

EATING AND DRINKING

Casa Zaca C/Embajadores 6 ☎ 921 470 087, ⓦ casazaca.com. Great place in La Granja to stop off for lunch, this former post-house has been serving up quality home-style local cuisine, including the local speciality broad beans, since 1940 and remains a family business. Good value too with a meal and wine costing in the region of €35. Tues–Sun 1.30–4pm.

Martinho C/Valenciana 5 ☎ 921 470 198, ⓦ restaurantemartinho.es. Close to the Palacio Real, this little ochre-fronted restaurant is a delight, especially if you want something that goes beyond the standard Castilian dishes: delicately cooked fish, creative meat dishes and some great desserts. Worth taking the chef's advice on the specials which can range from chickpeas and langoustines to steak burgers stuffed with paté. Mains around the €15–18 mark which is good value considering the quality ingredients.

Alcalá de Henares

ALCALÁ DE HENARES, a little over 30km east from Madrid, is one of Europe's most ancient university towns, and renowned as the birthplace of **Miguel de Cervantes**. In the sixteenth century the university was a rival to Salamanca's, but in 1836 the faculties moved to Madrid and the town went into decline. Almost all the artistic heritage was lost in the Civil War and nowadays it's virtually a suburb of Madrid. It is not somewhere you'd want to stay longer than it takes to see the sights.

Universidad Antigua

Pza. San Diego • Regular 45min guided tours usually in Spanish daily 10am–2pm & 4–7/8pm • €4.50 • ☎ 918 856 487, ⓦ visitasalcala.es

The **Universidad Antigua** stands at the heart of the old town. It was endowed by Cardinal Cisneros (also known as Cardinal Jiménez) at the beginning of the sixteenth century, and features a fabulous Plateresque facade and a Great Hall, the **Paraninfo**, with a gloriously decorated Mudéjar *artesonado* ceiling. Next door, the **Capilla de San Ildefonso** has another superb ceiling, intricately stuccoed walls and the Italian marble tomb of Cardinal Cisneros, although his actual remains are buried in the Catedral in Pza. de los Santos Niños.

Museo Casa Natal de Cervantes

C/Mayor 48 • Tues–Sun 10am–6pm • Free • ☎ 918 899 654, ⓦ museo-casa-natal-cervantes.org

The **Museo Casa Natal de Cervantes** on the porticoed C/Mayor claims to have been the birthplace of Cervantes in 1547 though the house itself was actually constructed in 1956. It's authentic in style, furnished with genuine sixteenth-century objects, and contains a small museum with a few early editions of *Don Quixote* and other curiosities related to the author.

Corral de Comedias

Pza. de Cervantes 15 • Guided tours Tues–Sun 11.30am, 12.30pm, 1.30pm, 4.30pm, 5.30pm • €3 • ☎ 918 771 950, ⓦ corraldealcala.com

Just off the central Pza. Cervantes is the oldest surviving public theatre in Europe, the **Corral de Comedias**, which has been brought to life once more after a twenty-year restoration programme. Originally dating from 1601, the theatre was discovered beneath a crumbling old cinema by three drama students in 1980. Like Shakespeare's Globe, it was a hub of rowdy heckling and lively dramatics throughout the first half of the seventeenth century.

La Catedral

Pza. de los Santos Niños • Mon–Sat 9am–1pm & 5–8.30pm, Sun 10am–1.30pm & 6–8.30pm • €0.50, €3.50 with audio-guide, tower €2.50 • Ⓦ visitascatedraldealcala.org • ☎ 918 880 930

Elevated to the status of **Catedral** in 1991 when Alcalá separated from the diocese of Madrid, the Gothic church of San Justo and San Pastor was restored in the late twentieth century after being badly damaged in the Civil War. The remains of Cardinal Cisneros, regent of Spain on two separate occasions during the era of the Catholic Kings, lie within. The best views of the historic core of the city are from the tower.

Complutum

Camino del Juncal • Tues–Sun 10am–2pm & 5–8pm (Oct–May 4–6pm) • €1 • ☎ 918 771 750, Ⓦ complutum.com

The ruins of the forum of the Roman town of **Complutum**, on the outskirts of Alcalá, have been rescued and recently re-excavated after being partially destroyed by construction work in the 1960s. The original complex dates from the first century AD, although it was replaced by another two centuries later. You can make out the remains of buildings, roads and other Roman urban infrastructure, including the market and the baths on the site.

Museo Arqueológico and the Casa de Hippolytus

Museo Arqueológico Tues–Sat 11am–7pm, Sun 11am–3pm • Free • **Casa de Hippolytus** May–Oct Tues–Fri 10am–2pm, Sat & Sun 10am–2pm & 5–8pm; Nov–April Tues–Fri 10am–2pm, Sat & Sun 10am–2pm & 4–7pm • €1 ☎ 918 771 750

Next to the Monasterio de San Bernardo, the regional **Museo Arqueológico** houses an array of Roman finds. On the outskirts of town on Avenida de Madrid are the foundations of a Roman villa, the **Casa de Hippolytus**, which was originally a school for the children of wealthy Romans, complete with a temple, baths, and a garden containing exotic animals. The centrepiece is a magnificent mosaic signed by Hippolytus, depicting fishermen at sea and a vast array of aquatic life.

ARRIVAL AND INFORMATION   ALCALÁ DE HENARES

By train From Madrid's Chamartín or Atocha stations; daily every 15–30min from 5.30am–11.45pm from Madrid. For a more atmospheric trip you could catch the *Tren de Cervantes*, which leaves Atocha at 11.05am on Saturdays (April to mid June; €20, €15 for children aged 4–11; ☎ 918 892 694), complete with staff in period costume, and including a guided tour of the main sights, before returning to Madrid at 6.50pm.

By bus Daily every 15min, from the *intercambiador* at Avda. de América in Madrid.

Turismo Just off the central Pza. de Cervantes (daily: 10am–2pm & 4–7pm (June to mid Oct 5–8pm); ☎ 918 892 694, Ⓦ turismoalcala.es); also at Pza. de los Santos Niños (same hours; ☎ 918 810 634). Arranges guided tours (usually leaving at noon & 5pm; €8–10) and has maps and other handy information.

EATING AND DRINKING

Goya C/Goya 2 ☎ 918 826 034 Ⓦ restaurantegoya.com. Not far from the railway station, this bar/restaurant serves a comprehensive range of tapas and tostas, a good quality set lunch for €13.50 (*cocido* on Thursdays) and some stylish meat and fish dishes. Mon–Fri 8am–midnight, Sat 9am–midnight; closed Easter.

★ **Hostería del Estudiante** C/Los Colegios 3 ☎ 918

880 330 Ⓦ www.paradores.com. Run by the Parador chain and situated in part of the old university this is probably the best restaurant in town, serving up local cuisine such as *migas* (breadcrumbs, garlic, chorizo and pepper) and roast meats. Expect to pay €35–40 per person. Daily 1–4pm & 8.30–midnight; closed mid-July to first week in Sept.

Castilla-La Mancha and Extremadura

HANGING HOUSE, CUENCA

Castilla-La Mancha and Extremadura

The vast area covered by this chapter is some of the most travelled, yet least visited, country in Spain. Once south of Toledo, most tourists thunder nonstop across the plains of Castilla-La Mancha to Valencia and Andalucía, or follow the great rivers through Extremadura into Portugal. At first sight this is understandable. Castilla-La Mancha, in particular, is Spain at its least welcoming: a huge, bare plain – the name La Mancha comes from the Arab *manxa*, meaning steppe – burning hot in summer, chillingly exposed in winter. But this impression is not an entirely fair one – away from the main highways the villages are as friendly as any in the country, and in the northeast, where the mountains start, are the extraordinary cliff-hanging city of Cuenca and the historic cathedral town of Sigüenza. Castilla-La Mancha is also the agricultural and wine-growing heartland of Spain and the country through which Don Quixote cut his despairing swathe.

It is in **Extremadura**, though, that there is most to be missed by just passing through. This harsh environment was the cradle of the *conquistadores*, men who opened up a new world for the Spanish Empire. Remote before and forgotten since, Extremadura enjoyed a brief golden age when its heroes returned with their gold to live in splendour. **Trujillo**, the birthplace of Pizarro, and **Cáceres** were built with *conquistador* wealth, the streets crowded with an array of perfectly preserved and very ornate mansions of returning empire builders. Then there is **Mérida**, the most completely preserved Roman city in Spain, and the monasteries of **Guadalupe** and **Yuste**, the one fabulously wealthy, the other rich in imperial memories. Finally, for some wild scenery and superb fauna, northern Extremadura has the **Parque Natural de Monfragüe**, where even the most casual birdwatcher can look up to see eagles and vultures circling the cliffs.

Castilla-La Mancha

The region that was for so long called **New Castile** – and that until the 1980s held Madrid in its domain – is now officially known as **Castilla-La Mancha**. The main points of interest are widely spaced on an arc drawn from Madrid, with little between. If you are travelling east on **trains and buses** towards Aragón, the only worthwhile stops are Sigüenza (en route to Zaragoza) or Cuenca (en route to Teruel). To the south, Toledo has bus links within its own province, but if heading for Andalucía or Extremadura you'd do better returning to Madrid and starting out again; the Toledo rail line stops at the town.

If you have a **car**, and are **heading south**, the Toledo–Ciudad Real road, the Montes de Toledo and the wetland Parque Nacional de las Tablas de Daimiel all provide good

TEATRO ROMANO, MÉRIDA

Highlights

❶ Museo de Arte Abstracto, Cuenca
One of the famous hanging houses is the wonderful setting for this gem of a museum. **See p.181**

❷ La Ciudad Encantada Explore the weird and wonderful limestone formations near Cuenca. **See p.183**

❸ Jamón Treat yourself to a *ración* of the cured dried ham washed down with *pitarra* wine. **See p.194**

❹ Cherry blossoms, Valle de Jerte Take in the spectacular display in this picturesque valley when the trees burst into bloom for ten days in spring. **See p.195**

❺ Vulture spotting, Parque Natural de Monfragüe You don't have to be a dedicated ornithologist to be impressed by these prehistoric-looking creatures. **See p.200**

❻ Trujillo A visit to the birthplace of Pizarro is worthwhile for the view of the town from the Cáceres road alone. **See p.201**

❼ Evening in Cáceres Wander around the atmospheric historic core at night. **See p.206**

❽ The Roman ruins in Mérida Marvel at the stunning array of Roman buildings and artefacts. **See p.213**

HIGHLIGHTS ARE MARKED ON THE MAP ON PP.174–175

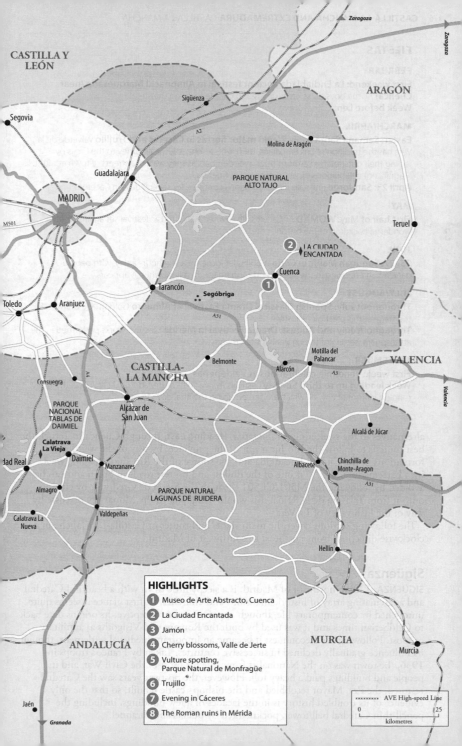

HIGHLIGHTS

1 Museo de Arte Abstracto, Cuenca

2 La Ciudad Encantada

3 Jamón

4 Cherry blossoms, Valle de Jerte

5 Vulture spotting, Parque Natural de Monfragüe

6 Trujillo

7 Evening in Cáceres

8 The Roman ruins in Mérida

AVE High-speed Line

0 — 25 kilometres

FIESTAS

FEBRUARY
First weekend: La Endiablada ancient festival in Almonacid Marquesado (near Cuenca) All the boys dress up as devils and parade through the streets.
Week before Lent *Carnaval* everywhere.

MARCH/APRIL
Easter: Semana Santa (Holy Week) major fiestas in Cáceres and Trujillo Valverde de la Vera has the tradition of Los Empalaos, men who re-enact Jesus's journey to the Cross by roping their outstretched arms to huge wooden bars as they walk the streets of town at night. Magnificent celebrations (floats, penitents) in Cuenca.
April 23: San Jorge Enthusiastic celebrations continue for several days in Cáceres.

MAY
First half of May: WOMAD At Cáceres. Renowned world music festival set against the wonderful backdrop of the historic core.

JUNE
23–27: San Juan Manic in Coria A bull is let loose for a few hours a day, with people dancing and drinking in the streets and running for their lives when it appears.

JULY/AUGUST
Throughout July: Spanish Classical Drama Festival at Almagro Golden-age drama takes the stage at this prestigious festival.
Throughout July and August: Drama Festival in Mérida Classical works performed in the atmospheric setting of the original Roman theatre.

SEPTEMBER
First week: Vendimia celebrations at Valdepeñas
Week leading up to third Sunday Festivals in Jarandilla and Madrigal de la Vera with bulls running in front of cows – which are served up on the final day's feast.

alternatives to the sweltering A4 *autopista*. **Heading east**, through Cuenca to Teruel, the best route is to follow the Río Júcar out of the province, by way of the weird rock formations in the Ciudad Encantada and the source of the Río Tajo. **Heading west**, into Extremadura, the A5 is one of the dullest and hottest roads in Spain and can be avoided by following the M501/CL501 through the Sierra de Gredos or by cutting onto it from Talavera de la Reina; this would bring you to the Monastery of Yuste by way of the lush valley of La Vera.

The following sections cover the main sights and routes of Castilla-La Mancha in a clockwise direction, from northeast to southwest of Madrid.

Sigüenza

SIGÜENZA, 120km northeast of Madrid, is a sleepy little town with a beautiful Catedral and a fascinating array of historic mansions and churches. At first glance it seems quite untouched by contemporary life, though appearances are deceptive. Its origins date back to Celtiberian times and it was used by both the Romans and Visigoths as a military outpost. Following the Reconquest it became an important medieval settlement, though its influence gradually declined in successive centuries. Taken by Franco's troops in 1936, the town was on the Nationalist front line for most of the Civil War, and its people and buildings paid a heavy toll. However, the postwar years saw the Catedral restored, the Pza. Mayor recobbled and the bishop's castle rebuilt, so that the only evidence of its troubled history is in the facades of a few buildings, including the pencil-thin Catedral bell tower, pockmarked by bullets and shrapnel.

Catedral

C/Serrano Sanz • Open daily for worship 9.30am–2pm & 4.30–8pm; frequent guided tours of chapels usually Tues–Sun: noon, 1pm, 4.30pm & 5.30pm • €4

Sigüenza's main streets lead you towards the **Catedral**, which is built in the pinkish yellow stone that characterizes the town. Begun in 1150 by the town's first bishop, Bernardo of Agen, it is essentially Gothic, with three rose windows, though it has been much altered over the years. Facing the main entrance is a huge marble *coro* with an altar to a thirteenth-century figure of the Virgin. To the right of the *coro* is the cathedral's principal treasure, the alabaster tomb of Martín Vázquez de Arce, known as El Doncel (the page boy); a favourite of Isabel la Católica, he was killed fighting the Moors in Granada. On the other side of the building is an extraordinary doorway: Plateresque at the bottom, Mudéjar in the middle and Gothic at the top – an amazing amalgam, built by a confused sixteenth-century architect. Take a look, too, at the sacristy, whose superb Renaissance ceiling has 304 heads carved by Covarrubias. In a chapel opening off this (with an unusual cupola, best seen in the mirror provided) is an El Greco *Annunciation*. More treasures are displayed in the rooms off the **cloister**.

3

SIGÜENZA

■ ACCOMMODATION
Hostal Posta Real	2
Hotel El Doncel	3
Hotel HC Sigüenza	4
Parador de Sigüenza	1

● TAPAS BARS AND RESTAURANTS
Cafetería Atrio	3
Gurugu de la Plazuela	2
Mesón Los Soportales	4
Nöla	1

Museo Diocesano del Arte Sacro

Pza. Obispo Don Bernardo • Wed, Thurs & Sun 11am–2pm & 4–7pm; Fri & Sat 11am–2pm & 4–8pm; closed Jan to mid-March • €3

Housed in a refurbished sixteenth-century mansion close to the Catedral, the **Museo Diocesano del Arte Sacro** displays artworks from the Stone Age to the twentieth century, including Greek and Roman sculptures, textiles, manuscripts and a vast array of sacred paintings including work by Morales, Madrazo and a particularly saccharine *Mary as a Child* by Zurbarán.

Castillo

Pza. del Castillo

From **Pza. Mayor**, C/Mayor leads up to the castle passing close by the **church of San Vicente**. The **Castillo** started life as a Roman fortress, was adapted by the Visigoths and further improved by the Moors as their Alcazaba. Reconquered in 1124, it became the official residence of the warlike Bishop Bernardo and his successors. The Civil War virtually reduced the castle to rubble, but it was almost completely rebuilt in the 1970s and converted into a parador. You can visit the central patio even if you are not staying at the hotel.

Casa del Doncel

Sat & Sun 11am–2pm • Free

Opposite the church of San Vicente is the striking Gothic construction known as the **Casa del Doncel**, dating back to the thirteenth century and one of the most emblematic buildings in Sigüenza. The Mudéjar-style interior, which has undergone recent refurbishment, is worth a peek if you are here at the weekend.

ARRIVAL AND DEPARTURE
SIGÜENZA

By train Around six trains a day run from Madrid to Sigüenza (1hr 30min–1hr 40min). RENFE operates a special "tren medieval" excursion which leaves Chamartín station in Madrid (most Sat late April to late June & mid-Sept to mid-Nov; departs Chamartín 10am, arrives Sigüenza 11.25am, returns 7.40pm arriving at Chamartín 8pm or 9.15pm; €30, children 4–13 €16; price includes a guided tour of the town and entry to the main sights). The train station is 5min from the centre of this compact town. Destinations Madrid (5–6 daily; 1hr 40min); Medinaceli (daily; 20min); Zaragoza (2 daily; 2hr–2hr 30min).

INFORMATION

Turismo To the west of the Catedral at C/Serrano Sanz 9 (Mon–Thurs 10am–2pm & 4–6pm, Fri 10am–2pm & 4–8pm, Sat 10am–2.30pm & 4–7pm, Sun 10am–2pm; summer opens and closes an hour later Mon–Sat pm; ☎ 949 347 007, ⓦ siguenza.es). The office runs guided tours of the town for groups of ten or more people (Mon–Sat noon & 4.30pm (5.15pm May–Sept), Sun noon; €7).

CASTILLA-LA MANCHA CUISINE

La Mancha is renowned for its simple, down-to-earth **cuisine** based on local ingredients and traditional recipes made famous in Cervantes' classic *Don Quixote*. Dishes such as *gazpacho manchego* (a stew usually made from rabbit mixed with pieces of unleavened bread), *atascaburras* (puréed potato with salted cod and garlic) and *pisto manchego* (a selection of fried vegetables in a tomato sauce and often topped with a fried egg) are among the staples. The region is famed for its garlic and saffron, but perhaps the most celebrated of all foods from the region is **Manchego cheese** of which there is a bewildering array, though it can be divided into two main types: *semi-curado* (semi-cured) and *curado* (cured) – both must come from the local Manchegan breed of sheep, though the latter is stronger and more expensive. To accompany the cheese, there is nothing better than a glass of wine: the Valdepeñas vineyards which have traditionally been known more for the quantity than the quality of their product have improved significantly in recent years.

ACCOMMODATION

The town makes for a relaxing stopover en route to Soria and the north or as a base for exploring the rest of the region.

Hostal Posta Real C/San Vicente 1 ☎ 949 390 490, ⓦ postareal.com. In the centre of the old town, this *hostal* has 23 simple, but comfortable and quite stylish en-suite rooms as well as a cafeteria. **€60**

Hotel El Doncel Paseo de la Alameda 1 ☎ 949 390 001, ⓦ eldoncel.com. A stylishly refurbished eighteen-room hotel, with smart rooms mixing the traditional and the modern. The *Doncel* is also home to a very good restaurant serving some high-quality regional cuisine, including a €45 taster menu. **€70**

Hotel HC Sigüenza C/Alfonso VI 7 ☎ 949 391 974, ⓦ hotelhcsiguenza.com. Next to the shady Alameda park with its summer terraza bars, this modern three-star hotel, with its individually decorated rooms, is a good mid-range option. **€70**

★**Parador de Sigüenza** Pza. del Castillo s/n ☎ 949 390 100, ⓦ www.paradores.com. Located in the town's twelfth-century castle, this atmospheric parador enjoys a stunning hilltop location, with fine views from the rooms on the upper floors. High-quality local specialities and seasonal produce are served up in the imposing dining room. **€156**

EATING AND DRINKING

For **meals**, as well as the options below, try the hotel restaurants at *El Doncel* and the *Parador de Sigüenza*.

Cafetería Atrio Pza. Obispo Don Bernardo 6. In the shadow of the Catedral, this relaxed bar serves excellent tapas and has a great summer terraza. Daily around 1.30–4pm & 8.30pm–midnight.

★**Gurugu de la Plazuela** Travesaña Alt, 17, next to the Plazuela de la Cárcel ☎ 949 390 134, ⓦ gurugu delaplazuela.com. Dating back to the seventeenth century, this laidback tavern specializes in wild mushrooms with some sixteen different varieties on the menu. Very reasonable prices too at around €20 a head. Thurs–Sat 12.30–4pm & 8pm–midnight, Sun 12.30–4pm & open Wed & on Sun eve June–Sept.

Mesón Los Soportales Pza. Mayor 3 ☎ 949 347 349. A great location opposite the Catedral, this bar makes a good base for a drink and a spot of tapas. Daily around 1.30–4pm & 8.30pm–midnight.

Nöla C/Mayor 41 ☎ 949 393 246, ⓦ nolarestaurante .es. A new arrival on the Sigüenza scene, this classy restaurant serves up a creative seasonal menu with mains such as duck confit with pears and desserts that include fruit mousse with rosemary and yoghurt ice cream. Taster menus are available at €27, €35 and €45. Wed 8.30–10.30pm, Thurs–Mon 1.30–3.30pm & 8.30–10.30pm.

Cuenca and around

The mountainous, craggy countryside around **CUENCA** is as dramatic as any in Spain. Located 166km east of Madrid, the city, the capital of a sparsely populated province, is an extraordinary-looking place, enclosed on three sides by the deep gorges of the Huécar and Júcar rivers, with balconied houses hanging over the clifftop – the finest of them tastefully converted into a wonderful museum of abstract art. No surprise, then, that this is a popular weekend outing from Madrid; to get the most from a visit, try to come on a weekday, and stay overnight; with this much time, you can make the short trip to see the bizarre limestone formations of the **Ciudad Encantada** and visit the picturesque source of the Río Cuervo.

The Ciudad Antigua

At the centre of the rambling **Ciudad Antigua** is the Pza. Mayor, a fine space, entered through the arches of the Baroque *ayuntamiento* and ringed by cafés and ceramic shops. Follow the road out of the Pza. and up the hill and you get some fantastic views of the surrounding countryside.

The Catedral and Tesoro Catedralicio

Pza. Mayor • Oct–May: Mon–Fri 10am–2pm & 4–5pm, Sat 10am–6pm, Sun 10am–5pm; June, July & Sept: Mon–Fri 10am–2pm & 5–7pm, Sat & Sun 10am–7pm; Aug daily 10am–7pm • €3.80 (€5 with joint entry to Museo Diocesano), free first Mon of the month • ☎ 969 224 626

Occupying most of the east side of the Pza. Mayor is the **Catedral**, whose incongruous, unfinished facade betrays a misguided attempt to beautify a simple Gothic building

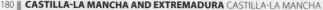

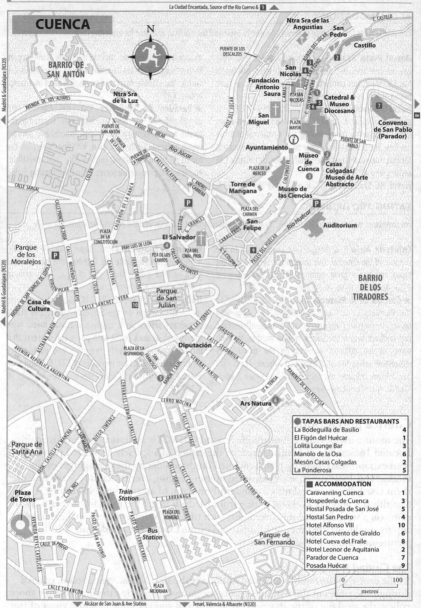

CUENCA

N

TAPAS BARS AND RESTAURANTS
La Bodeguilla de Basilio	4
El Figón del Huécar	1
Lolita Lounge Bar	3
Manolo de la Osa	6
Mesón Casas Colgadas	2
La Ponderosa	5

ACCOMMODATION
Caravanning Cuenca	1
Hospedería de Cuenca	3
Hostal Posada de San José	5
Hostal San Pedro	4
Hotel Alfonso VIII	10
Hotel Convento de Giraldo	6
Hotel Cueva del Fraile	8
Hotel Leonor de Aquitania	2
Parador de Cuenca	7
Posada Huécar	9

after the tower collapsed. The interior is much more attractive, especially the carved Plateresque arch at the end of the north aisle and the chapel next to it, with distinctly un-Christian carvings round its entrance.

Alongside is a small **Tesoro Catedralicio**, which contains some beautiful gold and silver work, as well as wooden doors by Alonso Berruguete.

Museo Diocesano

C/Obispo Valero 3 • Tues–Sat 10am–2pm & 4–6pm, Sun 11am–2pm, July & Aug: Tues–Sat 10am–2pm & 5–7pm, Sun 11am–2pm •
€2.50 (€5 joint entry with the Catedral) • ☎ 969 224 210, ⓦ museodiocesanocuenca.jimdo.com

Next to the Catedral, further religious treasures are to be found in the adjacent **Museo Diocesano**, including two canvases by El Greco, a magnificent *Crucifixion* by Gerard David and a Byzantine diptych unique in Spain. The museum also houses a marvellous collection of tapestries and carpets.

Museo de Cuenca

C/Obispo Valero 12 • Summer Tues–Sat 10am–2pm & 5–7pm, Sun 10am–2pm; winter Tues–Sat 10am–2pm & 4–7pm, Sun 11am–2pm •
€3, free Sat & Sun

Right opposite the Museo Diocesano is the excellent **Museo de Cuenca**, which traces the city's history from prehistoric times and showcases a good Roman collection from local finds.

Museo de Arte Abstracto

Casas Colgadas • Tues–Fri 11am–2pm & 4–6pm, Sat 11am–2pm & 4–8pm, Sun 11am 2.30pm; closed Sept 18–21 • €3, under-10s free •
ⓥ 969 212 983, ⓦ march.es/arte/cuenca

The artistic highlight of Cuenca has to be the nearby **Museo de Arte Abstracto**, a gallery established in the 1960s by Fernando Zóbel, one of the leading artists in Spain's "abstract generation". It is now run by the prestigious Fundación Juan March, which displays works from a core collection of abstract painting and sculpture by, among many others, Eduardo Chillida, José Guerrero, Lucio Muñoz, Antonio Saura, Antonio Tàpies and Fernando Zóbel, and hosts some of the best exhibitions to be found in provincial Spain. The museum itself is a stunning conversion of one of the extraordinary Casas Colgadas ("Hanging Houses"), a pair of fifteenth-century houses, with cantilevered balconies, literally hanging from the cliff face.

For the best views of the houses cross the Puente de San Pablo **footbridge** that heads across the gorge to the parador.

Fundación Antonio Saura

Pza. San Nicolás 4 • Summer Mon & Wed–Sat 11am–2pm & 5–8pm, Sun 11am–2pm; winter Mon & Wed–Sat 11am–2pm & 4–7pm,
Sun 11am–2pm • €2.50 • ⓦ fundacionantoniosaura.es

Housed in the eighteenth-century mansion known as the Casa Zavala is the **Fundación Antonio Saura**, which contains some important and striking work by the renowned Spanish surrealist who died in Cuenca in 1998. The foundation also hosts regular exhibitions of paintings, photographs and sculpture.

Museo de las Ciencias

Pza. de la Merced 1 • Tues–Sat 10am–2pm & 4–7pm (mid-June to mid-Sept opens an hour later in the afternoon), Sun 10am–2pm • €3;
free Wed, Sat pm & Sun • ☎ 969 240 320, ⓦ pagina.jccm.es/museociencias

Housed in an old convent and an adjoining modern extension, the **Museo de las Ciencias** is an ambitious and largely successful attempt to explain the origins of the universe and the history of the earth in the context of the local region. It has recently been remodelled and now contains a host of fascinating interactive exhibits and makes a great visit if you are with children.

Ars Natura

C/Río Gritos 5, Cerro Molina • Tues–Sat 10am–2pm & 4–7pm (closes an hour later in summer), Sun 10am–2pm • €3, under-18s free •
☎ 969 271 717, ⓦ centroarsnatura.es

The **Ars Natura** is a state-of-the-art interpretation centre focusing on the flora, fauna, geology and climate of the Castilla-La Mancha region and man's interaction with it. It features plenty of child-friendly interactive exhibits, a garden area that displays local plant species and an upmarket restaurant (see p.183).

3

ARRIVAL AND DEPARTURE

By train Cuenca has recently been connected to the AVE high-speed train network and is now just a 50min trip from Madrid on the line to Valencia. The Fernando Zóbel AVE station is some 3km out of town and has regular bus connections to the city centre (line #12). The slower but considerably cheaper regional trains stop at the more central station at C/Mariano Catalina 10, which has a regular bus link to the old town.

Destinations Madrid (AVE 11 daily, 50min; around €50 return; regional 4 daily, 3hr; €30 return); Valencia (AVE 7 daily, 1hr; regional 4 daily, 3hr–3hr 30min).

INFORMATION

Turismo Pza. Mayor 1 (daily 9am–2pm & 4–6.30pm, summer same hours except Sat & Sun 9am–9pm; ☎ 969 241 051, ⓦ cuenca.es and ⓦ turismocuenca.com). There is also a visitor reception centre at C/Cruz Roja 1 on the

CUENCA AND AROUND

By bus The bus station is on the southern edge of the modern part of town close to the old train station at C/Fermin Caballero 20.

Destinations Albacete (2–5 daily; 1hr 45min); Madrid (7–10 daily; 2hr–2hr 30min); Valencia (2 daily; 3hr–3hr 15min).

By car The old town of Cuenca – the Ciudad Antigua – stands on a high ridge, looped to the south by the Río Huécar and the modern town and its suburbs. If you're driving in, follow signs for the Catedral and try one of the car parks beyond that up at the top of the old town.

way into town on the Madrid road (Mon–Sat 10am–2pm & 5–7pm, Sun 10am–2pm; ☎ 969 241 050, ⓦ turismocuenca.com)

ACCOMMODATION

You'll find many **places to stay** in the new town, with a concentration of *hostales* along C/Ramón y Cajal, but there are several reasonably priced options in the old town.

Hospedería de Cuenca C/San Pedro 27 ☎ 969 239 117, ⓦ hospederiadecuenca.com. Stylish boutique hotel in the old town just up the hill from the Pza. Mayor. Fourteen individually decorated rooms with sleek wooden furnishings, flat-screen TVs and swish bathrooms scattered over the six floors of this old mansion. **€85**

★**Hostal Posada de San José** C/Julián Romero 4 ☎ 969 211 300, ⓦ posadasanjose.com. A lovely old building with a tranquil garden in the old town near the Catedral. It has only 22 pleasantly decorated rooms, so be sure to book ahead. There's a good-quality restaurant, too, and an extra €15 will get you a room with a view over the gorge. **€88**

Hostal San Pedro C/San Pedro 34 ☎ 969 234 543, ⓦ hostalsanpedro.es. This comfortable little *hostal* in a great position up in the old town close to the Catedral, has eight neat rooms, some with views and seating areas, and all with smart bathrooms. **€80**

Hotel Alfonso VIII C/Parque de San Julián 3 ☎ 969 212 512, ⓦ hotel-alfonsoviii.com. A nicely located functional three-star hotel in the new town, facing the park. They also offer two-room apartments (from €99, depending on the time of year), which make a good family option. **€51**

Hotel Convento de Giraldo Ctra. C/San Pedro 12 ☎ 969 232 700, ⓦ hotelconventodelgiraldo.com. An upmarket 34-room, four-star hotel housed in a refurbished seventeenth-century mansion in the heart of the old town. Simple but smart, comfortable rooms, which combine the old and the new. **€99**

Hotel Cueva del Fraile Ctra. Cuenca-Buenache km 7 ☎ 969 211 571, ⓦ hotelcuevadelfraile.com. A sixteenth-century former monastery 5km out from Cuenca. The rooms are pleasantly furnished in antique style and the extensive grounds include a pool. It also has its own restaurant serving local specialities. **€44**

★**Hotel Leonor de Aquitania** C/San Pedro 58–60 ☎ 969 231 000, ⓦ hotelleonordeaquitania.com. One of Cuenca's prime hotels, beautifully situated in an eighteenth-century nobleman's house in the old town. Tastefully decorated rooms, some with sitting areas and superb views (available for between €71 and €88). There is a new spa and fitness area and the restaurant is a great spot for a meal, too. **€60**

Parador de Cuenca Convento de San Pablo ☎ 969 232 320, ⓦ www.paradores.com. Expensive, but not that special, although it does have a pool and great views across the gorge to the Casas Colgadas. **€176**

Posada Huécar C/Paseo del Huécar 3 ☎ 969 214 201, ⓦ posadahuecar.com. A characterful inn on the banks of the Río Huécar with pleasant rustic furnishings in the rooms, all of which have en-suite bathrooms. Provides free cots for babies and also hires bikes if you fancy exploring the area. **€50**

CAMPING

Carvanning Cuenca 6km north of the city on the CM2105 (no bus) ☎ 969 231 656, ⓦ campingcuenca .com. There's a riverside location for this extremely well-appointed campsite with a great pool, surrounded by shady pines. Closed mid-Oct to mid-March. **€21.80**

EATING, DRINKING AND NIGHTLIFE

The Pza. Mayor is the place to head for evening *copas*, with its vibrant and diverse range of **bars**. The liveliest joints are on C/Severo Catalina and in the little alleyways overlooking the Río Júcar. Another popular area is on and around C/Parque del Huécar by the Júcar, while there are a host of *barses de copas* around the stations and C/Fermín Caballero.

La Bodeguilla de Basilio C/Fray Luis de León 3 ☎ 969 235 274. Head for the crowded bar rather than the *comedor* at the back and order a drink and you will get the chance to sample a decent range of *raciones*, frequently accompanied by a free tapa while you wait. Good value and enjoyable, as long as you don't mind standing. Mon–Sat 1–4pm & 8pm–midnight, Sun 1–4pm.

★ **El Figón del Huécar** C/Julián Romero 6 ☎ 969 240 062, ⓦ figondelhuecar.es. Inventive cuisine in this place up in the old town. Dishes range from lamb stuffed with raisins, pine nuts and paté to gilthead bream baked with prawn and sesame seeds. Mains cost €18–22 or you could go ffor the taster menu with venison or lamb for €36. Tues–Sat 1.30–4pm & 9–11pm, Sun 1.30–4pm.

Lolita Lounge Bar Travesia Clavel 7 ☎ 679 693 634, ⓦ lolitaloungebar.es. Sleek space-age decor in this cocktail bar specializing in gin and tonic and conveniently located close to the Pza. Mayor. There is a good outdoor summer terrace area too. Thurs & Fri 7.30pm–late, Sat & Sun noon–late.

★ **Manolo de la Osa** Ars Natura, C/Río Gritos 5, Cerro Molina ☎ 969 219 512, ⓦ manueldelaosa.com. Opened up by renowned chef Manolo de la Osa at the Ars

Natura interpretation centre on the edge of town, this exceptional restaurant serves up a range of original and creative takes on traditional dishes. Set menus for €50 and €70 include some fantastic salads and delicious options such as prawns in basil and apple, cumin soup with cheese, and sweetbreads with potato and truffle. Tues–Sat 1.30–4pm & 8.30pm–midnight, Sun 1–30–4pm.

★ **Mesón Casas Colgadas** C/Canónigos 3 ☎ 969 223 509, ⓦ mesoncasascolgadas.com. The location of this restaurant – in one of the Hanging Houses in the old town – could not be better and the food is excellent too. There are two set-menu options, one at €38 which features suckling pig, roast lamb and Manchego specialities and the other at €27 which includes a fish dish and lamb stew. Mon 1.30–4pm, Wed–Sun 1.30–4pm & 9–11pm.

La Ponderosa C/San Francisco 20. Standing room only in this popular and long-established bar in the new town near to the Parque San Julián. Serves up quality *raciones* including *mollejas* (sweet meats), local tomatoes and a range of local specialities. Daily around 11–4pm & 8.30pm–midnight.

La Ciudad Encantada

Daily: May–Sept 10am–8pm; Oct–April 10am–6pm • €4, 7- to 12-years-olds €3, guided tours €5 • ⓦ ciudadencantada.es

The classic excursion from Cuenca is to the **Ciudad Encantada**, a twenty-square-kilometre "park" of karst limestone outcrops, sculpted by natural erosion into a bizarre series of abstract, natural and animal-like forms. A few of the names – "fight between an elephant and a crocodile", for example – stretch the imagination a little, but the rocks are certainly amazing, and many of the creations really do look knocked into shape by human hands. The fantasy landscape was used as a backdrop for Arnold Schwarzenegger's first major film, *Conan the Barbarian*.

The most interesting area of sculptures is enclosed and the extensive car park and restaurants outside testify to its popularity with weekending *madrileños*. However, off season, or during the week, you can have the place almost to yourself. Just outside the entrance there are signs to the **Mirador de Uña**, providing excellent views over the valley. You will need your own transport to get to the park, which is around 20km northeast of Cuenca, on signed back roads towards Albarracín. If you get stuck, you might like to seek out the quiet and functional **hostal**, the *Ciudad Encantada* (☎ 969 288 194, ⓦ hostalciudadencantada.es; €55), opposite the entrance gate.

Another 30km farther north on the CM2106 past Tragacete is the **source of the Río Cuervo**, a moss-covered crag peppered with waterfalls.

Uña and around

The route east from the Ciudad Encantada towards Albarracín is a delight, edging through the verdant **Júcar Gorge** and across the wild, scarcely populated Serranía de Cuenca; you'll need your own transport. En route, still in Cuenca province, you might stop at **UÑA**, a village sited between a lagoon and a barrage. Just over the provincial border, in Teruel province, the road between Uña and Frías de Albarracín runs past a point known as García, close to the **source of the Río Tajo** where the great river begins its journey across Iberia to the Atlantic.

ACCOMMODATION   UÑA AND AROUND

Hotel Castillo de Uña C/Egido 23, Uña ☎ 969 282 917, ⊕ castillodeuna.es. This lakeside hotel has decent rooms, as well as a panoramic restaurant and a pleasant garden bar. **€52**

Segóbriga

April–Sept Tues–Sun 10am–3pm & 4–6pm; Oct–March 10am–3pm & 4–7.30pm • €5, 6- to 11-year-olds €1 • ☎ 629 752 257, ⊕ patrimoniohistoricoclm.es

Just south of the A3 motorway that runs between Madrid and Valencia, near the village of Saelices, **SEGÓBRIGA** makes a worthy detour for anyone interested in Roman ruins. References to the town date back to the second century BC and it developed into a prosperous settlement largely thanks to the presence of nearby gypsum mines. The town reached its peak about four centuries later, but declined under the Visigoths and was effectively abandoned during the Arab occupation. The best-preserved structures are the theatre and amphitheatre – which had a capacity for 5500 people – but there are also some interesting additions made by the Visigoths. An informative interpretation centre on the site recounts the history of what was a fairly important settlement.

Alarcón

Just off the old NIII road between Honrubbia and Motilla del Palancar is the lively little town of **ALARCÓN**, occupying an imposing defensive site sculpted by the burrowing of the Río Júcar. Almost completely encircled and walled, the village is accessible by a spit of land just wide enough to take a road that passes through a succession of **fortified gateways**.

At the top of the village is an exquisite **castle**, eighth century in origin and captured from the Moors in 1184 after a nine-month siege.

ACCOMMODATION   ALARCÓN

Hostal Don Juan C/Marqués de Villena 4 ☎ 618 875 893, ⊕ hostaldonjuan.es. An affordable option, this newish *hostal* has five neat doubles, some with seating areas. Book ahead in summer and at weekends. **€63**

★**Parador Marqués de Villena** ☎ 969 330 315, ⊕ www.paradores.com. The Arabic fortress has now been converted into one of the country's smallest and most atmospheric paradores, with just fourteen, brick-lined doubles. Book ahead in summer and at weekends. **€211**

EATING AND DRINKING

The parador, with its atmospheric dining hall, is probably the best **place to eat**, and there is cheaper fare served at the bars on the main Pza. de Don Juan Manuel.

La Cabaña de Alarcón C/Alvaro de Lara 21 ☎ 969 330 373, ⊕ restaurantelacabanadealarcon.es. A good-value restaurant with a cool library-like interior and a terrace overlooking the valley, serving up a range of well-presented locally inspired dishes. Mains cost €10–16. Daily noon–4pm & 8pm–midnight.

Albacete province

Travelling between Madrid or Cuenca and Alicante or Murcia, you'll pass through **Albacete province**, one of Spain's more forgettable corners. Hot, arid plains for the most part, the province shelters the lovely **Alcalá del Júcar** and the humdrum provincial capital, **Albacete**. Scenically, the only relief is in the hyperactive **Río Júcar**, which, in the north of the province, sinks almost without warning into the plain.

Alcalá del Júcar

If you are driving, it's certainly worth making a detour off the main roads east to take the scenic route along the banks of the Río Júcar, between Valdeganga and the stunning village of **ALCALÁ DEL JÚCAR**. Almost encircled by the river, the village is an amazing sight, with its houses built one on top of the other and burrowed into the white cliff face. Several of these **cuevas** (caves) have been converted into bars and restaurants and make a great place for a drink, with rooms carved up to 170m through the cliff and windows overlooking the river on each side of the loop. They're open daily in summer but otherwise only at weekends.

Alcalá also boasts a **castle** (May–Sept 11am–2pm & 5–8pm; Oct–April 11am–2pm & 3–6pm; €2) – adapted at intervals over the past 1500 years, though today just a shell – with great views.

ACCOMMODATION	ALCALÁ DEL JÚCAR
Hostal Pelayo Avda. Constitución 4 ☎ 967 473 099, ⓦ hotelpelayo.net. Decent rooms (some with balconies) and its own restaurant and terrace next to the river. Breakfast included. **€45**	**Hostal Rambla** Paseo de los Robles 2 ☎ 967 474 064, ⓦ hostalrambla.es. Another good option in a shady spot by the river. Simple, pleasantly decorated, comfortable rooms, some with small balconies, and a restaurant. **€55**

EATING AND DRINKING

La Asomada C/La Asomada 107 ☎ 652 182 440. Restaurant/*bodega* by the castle that serves quality tapas based on ecological ingredients which the owner produces herself. Fri 8pm–midnight, Sat, Sun & hols 11am–4pm & 8pm–midnight.

Las Cuevas del Diablo C/Tal y Cual 12 ☎ 637 418 297, ⓦ cuevasdeldiablo.com. A series of bars, a disco and even a small museum have been carved out of this seventy-metre tunnel that ends in a fantastic *mirador* across the valley. The "diablo" is eccentric owner Juan José Martínez, a self-confessed Don Juan character with a comedy Dalí-esque moustache. Entry fee €3, drink included. Mon–Fri 9am–9pm, Sat & Sun 10am–9pm (disco hours vary); knock at the door in C/San Lorenzo to enter.

Albacete

ALBACETE was named **Al-Basit** – "the plain" – by the Moors, but save for a few old backstreets, it is basically a modern city. The **Catedral** is noteworthy for the presence of Ionic columns instead of normal pillars astride its nave. The **Pasaje Lodares** is also worth seeking out. A stunning iron-and-glass gallery constructed in 1925, it is adorned with neo-Baroque and modernist decoration and lined with shops.

Museo de Albacete

Parque de Abelardo Sánchez • Tues–Sat 10am–2pm & 4.30–7pm, Sun 10am–2pm, open mornings only in summer • €3, free Wed & Sat 4.30–7pm & Sun • ☎ 967 228 307, ⓦ patrimoniohistoricodm.es

The **Museo de Albacete**, whose prize exhibits are five small Roman dolls, perfectly sculpted and jointed, and an array of local Roman mosaics, has a more than respectable archeological and ethnographical collection. Local-born painter Benjamin Palencia donated 120 works that form the basis of the art collection.

Museo de la Cuchillería

Pza. de la Catedral • Tues–Sat 10am–2pm & 5–8pm, Sun 10am–2pm • €3, under-18s free • ☎ 967 616 600, ⓦ museo-mca.com

For Spaniards, Albacete is synonymous with high-quality knives and the **Museo de la Cuchillería**, housed in the intriguing green-tiled mock-Gothic Casa Hortelano by the Catedral, will tell you all you want to know about this speciality that, as with Toledo, can be traced back to the Moors.

Museo del Niño

C/Méjico • Mon–Fri 9.30am–1.30pm • Free • ⓦ museodelnino.es

The family-oriented **Museo del Niño** has exhibits on the history of childhood with sections covering school life, recreation and home. Exhibits include dolls, toys, puppets and comics. The museum will move into a new base in another former school in the course of the next few years.

ARRIVAL AND DEPARTURE
ALBACETE

By train Albacete is connected to the high-speed train network on the route between Madrid and Valencia. The new train station is on C/Federico García Lorca on the northeastern edge of the city.
Destinations Alicante (9 daily; 50min–1hr 15min); Madrid (18 daily; 1hr 30min–2hr 30min); Valencia (6 daily; 1hr 40min).

By bus The bus from Madrid takes around 3hr and drops you at the terminus by the high-speed train station on C/ Federico García Lorca.
Destinations Alicante (9 daily; 2hr–2hr 20min); Cuenca (3–5 daily; 2hr 25min–3hr); Madrid (20 daily; 2hr 45min–3hr).

INFORMATION

Turismo Pza. Altozano (summer: Mon–Sat 10am–2pm & 5–9pm, Sun 10am–2pm; winter: Mon–Sat 10am–2pm & 4–8pm, Sat & Sun 10am–2pm; ☎967 630 004, ⓦalbaceteturistico.es).

ACCOMMODATION

Hotel San José C/San José de Calasanz 12 ☎967 507 402, ⓦhotelsanjose-albacete.es. This three-star hotel offers modern business-style comfort with large rooms close to the pleasant city-centre park. **€65**

EATING AND DRINKING

The city is full of **tapas bars** and **restaurants** serving high-quality local produce with several good options to be found in the streets around the Catedral.

Casa Paco C/La Roda 26 ☎967 220 041. Well-known and popular restaurant serving up a mixture of regional specialities such as partridge and *gazpacho manchego* together with more creative offerings from around €9. Tues–Sat 1–5pm & 8.30–midnight, Sun 1–5pm.

Nuestro Bar C/Alcalde Conangla 102 ☎967 243 373, ⓦnuestrobar.es. Renowned local bar serving great tapas and a vast range of regional cuisine, all at reasonable prices, with many *raciones* under €10. Mon–Sat 1.30–5pm & 9pm–midnight, Sun 1.30–5pm.

Ciudad Real and the heartland of La Mancha

There is a huge gap in the middle of the tourist map of Spain between Toledo and the borders of Andalucía, and from Extremadura almost to the east coast. This, the province of **Ciudad Real**, comprises the heartland of **La Mancha**. The tourist authorities try hard to push their Ruta de Don Quixote across the plains, highlighting the windmills and other Quixotic sights: the signposted central part of the route, which starts at Belmonte and finishes at Consuegra, can be done in a day, but much of it is fanciful and, unless you're enamoured with the book, it's only of passing interest.

Nonetheless, a few places merit a visit if you've got time to spare, most notably **Consuegra**, for its magnificent windmills, **Almagro**, for its arcaded square and medieval theatre, and **Calatrava**, for the castle ruins of its order of knights. It is also the heart of wine-producing country, and many of the *bodegas* in **Valdepeñas** offer free tastings. The **websites** ⓦquijote.es and ⓦturismocastillalamancha.es both give more information about the area.

Consuegra

CONSUEGRA lies just to the west of the A4 *autovía*, roughly midway from Madrid to Andalucía, and has the most picturesque and typical of Manchegan settings, below a ridge of eleven restored (and highly photogenic) windmills. The first of these is occupied by the town's **turismo** while others house shops and workshops. They share their plateau with a ruined **castle** (June–Sept Mon–Fri 10.10am–1.40pm & 4.40–6.40pm, Sat & Sun open 10.40am; Oct–May Mon–Fri 10.10am–1.40pm & 3.40–5.40pm, Sat & Sun open 10.40am; €4; ☎925 095 339, ⓦcastillodeconsuegra.es).

DON QUIXOTE

Not a novel in the modern sense, **Miguel de Cervantes'** *Don Quixote de La Mancha* (published in 1604) is a sequence of episodes following the adventures of a country gentleman in his fifties, whose mind has been addled by romantic tales of chivalry. In a noble gesture, he changes his name to Don Quixote de La Mancha, and sets out on horseback, in rusty armour, to right the wrongs of the world. At his side throughout is Sancho Panza, a shrewd, pot-bellied rustic given to quoting proverbs at every opportunity. During the course of the book, Quixote, an instantly sympathetic hero, charges at windmills and sheep (mistaking them for giants and armies), makes ill-judged attempts to help others and is mocked by all for his efforts. Broken-hearted but wiser, he returns home and, on his deathbed, pronounces: "Let everyone learn from my example … look at the world with common sense and learn to see what is really there."

Cervantes' life was almost as colourful as his hero's. The son of a poor doctor, he fought as a soldier in the sea battle of Lepanto, where he permanently maimed his left hand and was captured by pirates and put to work as a slave in Algiers. Ransomed and sent back to Spain, he spent the rest of his days writing novels and plays in relative poverty, dying ten years after the publication of *Don Quixote*, "old, a soldier, a gentleman and poor".

Spanish academics have spent as much time dissecting the work of Cervantes as their English counterparts have Shakespeare's. Most see *Don Quixote* as a satire on the popular romances of the day, with the central characters representing two forces in Spain: Quixote the dreaming, impractical nobility, and Sancho the wise and down-to-earth peasantry. There are also those who read in it an ironic tale of a visionary or martyr frustrated in a materialistic world, while others see it as an attack on the Church and establishment. Debates aside, this highly entertaining adventure story is certainly one of the most influential works to have emerged from Spain.

which was once the headquarters of the Order of St John in the twelfth century and offers splendid views of the plain from its windswept ridge. The town below is also attractive, with a lively Pza. Mayor and many Mudéjar churches.

INFORMATION

Turismo Occupies the first windmill (usually open June–Sept Mon–Fri 9am–2pm & 4.30–7pm, Sat & Sun 10.30am–2pm & 4.30–7pm; Oct–May Mon–Fri 9am–2pm

CONSUEGRA

& 3.30–6pm, Sat & Sun 10.30am–2pm & 4.30–7pm; 🔮 turismoconsuegra.com). Good for information on the Ruta de Don Quixote.

ACCOMMODATION AND EATING

Vida de Antes C/Colón 2 ☎ 925 480 609, 🔮 lavidadeantes .com. A cosy little hotel with nine individually designed rooms laid out around an interior patio of a traditional Manchego house. Breakfast is an extra €4–6. **€70**

Hostal-Restaurante San Poul Avda. Alcázar de San Juan ☎ 925 481 315, 🔮 sanpoul.es. Small, old-fashioned, but very welcoming, *hostal* with a decent restaurant, situated on the eastern side of town below the windmills. **€50**

Ciudad Real

The city of **CIUDAD REAL**, capital of the province at the heart of this flat country, makes a good base for excursions and has connections by bus with most villages in the area. It has a few sights of its own, too, including a Mudéjar gateway, the **Puerta de Toledo**, which fronts the only surviving fragment of its medieval walls, at the northern edge of the city on the Toledo road. Further in, take a look at the fourteenth-century **church of San Pedro**, an airy, Gothic edifice, housing some exquisite chapels and an elaborate fifteenth-century alabaster *retablo*. The Pza. Mayor with its impressive neo-Gothic town hall and clock with its mechanical figures of Cervantes, Don Quixote and Sancho Panza, is also worth a visit.

Museo Provincial

C/Prado 4 • Sept to mid-July Tues–Sat 10am–2pm & 5–8pm, Sun 10am–2pm, mid-July & Aug Tues–Sat 9am–2pm, Sun 10am–2pm • Free • ☎ 926 226 896

The **Museo Provincial** is made up of two buildings, the first a modern one opposite the Catedral, which exhibits local archeological finds, and the former Convento de la

Merced, which houses a decent art collection including work by Dalí, Chillida, Tàpies and Saura.

Museo de Don Quijote

Ronda de Alarcos 1 • Tues–Sat 10am–2pm & 5–8pm, July & Aug Tues–Sat 10am–2pm (closed for refurbishment as we went to press) • Free • ☎ 926 200 457

In the entertaining **Museo de Don Quijote** personalities from the story guide you round the exhibits that include some smart audiovisuals bringing the tale to life.

ARRIVAL AND DEPARTURE   CIUDAD REAL

By train Ciudad Real's train station, with high-speed AVE connections to Madrid and south to Seville and Córdoba, lies out of town at the end of Avda. de Europa; bus #5 connects with the central Pza. de Pilar.
Destinations Almagro (6 daily; 15min); Cordoba (21 daily; 50min–1hr 5min); Madrid (25 daily; 55min–1hr); Sevilla

3

NATIONAL PARKS AND RESERVES IN LA MANCHA

A respite from the arid monotony of the Castilian landscape, and a treat for birdwatchers, is provided by the oasis of **La Mancha Húmeda** ("Wet La Mancha"). This is an area of lagoons and marshes, both brackish and fresh, along the high-level basin of the Río Cigüela and Río Guadiana. Drainage for agriculture has severely reduced the amount of water in recent years, so that the lakes effectively dry up in the summer, but there is still a good variety of interesting plant and bird life. You're best off visiting from April to July when the water birds are breeding, or from September to midwinter when migrating birds pass through.

PARQUE NACIONAL DE LAS TABLAS DE DAIMIEL

Major parks between Ciudad Real and Albacete include the **Parque Nacional de las Tablas de Daimiel**, 11km north of Daimiel itself, which is renowned for its bird life (over 200 species visit the park over the course of the year). There's an information centre (daily: summer 9am–9pm; winter 9am–7pm; ☎ 926 693 118, ⓦ lastablasdedaimiel.com) alongside the marshes. The park is accessible only by car or taxi, and Daimiel has little accommodation on offer.

Hostal Las Brujas Paseo del Carmen, Daimiel ☎ 926 852 289, ⓦ restaurantelasbrujas.es. Excellent-value place on the outskirts of town with simply furnished rooms, a popular restaurant and a summer terrace. **€38**

Hotel Las Tablas C/Virgen de la Cruces 5, Daimiel ☎ 926 852 108, ⓦ hotellastablasdaimiel.com. Comfortable 30-room hotel in the centre of town from which you can organize guided trips of the park. Price includes breakfast. **€77**

PARQUE NATURAL DE LAS LAGUNAS DE RUIDERA

More traveller-friendly, but crowded in the summer months, is the **Parque Natural de las Lagunas de Ruidera**, northeast of Valdepeñas (frequent buses from Albacete). You'll find an information centre (July & Aug daily 9am–9pm; Sept–June Wed–Sun 9am–7pm; ☎ 926 528 116) on the roadside, as you enter Ruidera from Manzanares, and several nature trails inside the park, as well as swimming and boating opportunities. Accommodation includes:

Hotel Albamanjon Laguna de San Pedro, Ossa de Montiel ☎ 926 699 048, ⓦ albamanjon.net. Picturesque rural hotel/restaurant overlooking one of the lakes. The large rooms have terraces and seating areas. **€112**

Los Batanes Ctra. Las Lagunas km 8, Ruidera ☎ 926 699 076, ⓦ losbatanes.com. Campsite with a large pool and grassy sunbathing area close to the Laguna Redondilla. **€24**

Doña Ruidera Pedazo de lo Alto, Ruidera ☎ 926 525 064, ⓦ hotelruidera.es. Good-value aparthotel

with large rooms and a couple of two-bedroom apartments with views of the lake at €150 each. **€55**

Hostal La Noria Avda. Castilla-La Mancha 69, Ruidera ☎ 926 528 032, ⓦ hostallanoria.com. Down-to-earth and friendly nineteen-room (some with balconies) *hostal* in the village of Ruidera. **€38**

Hotel Entrelagos Ctra. Las Lagunas ☎ 926 528 022, ⓦ entrelagos.com. Two-star hotel with simple en-suite rooms and its own little beach on the edge of one of the lakes. **€60**

(13 daily; 1hr 45min–2hr).
By bus The bus station is on the Ronda de Ciruela.
Destinations Almagro (1–8 daily; 20min); Madrid (3 daily;

2hr 50min); Toledo (3 daily; 1hr 30min–2hr 5min); Valdepeñas (5 daily; 1hr 15min).

INFORMATION

Turismo The main tourist office is on the Pza. Mayor (Tues–Sat 10am–2pm & 5–9pm, Sat & Sun 10am–2pm; summer Tues–Sun 10am–2pm; ☎926 216 486, ⓦciudadreal.es/turismo, ⓦtierradecaballeros.com). There is also an information booth at the train station.

ACCOMMODATION

Keep in mind that finding a **place to stay** is not always easy, so it's worth booking ahead.

Hotel NH Ciudad Real Avda. Alarcos 25 ☎926 217 010, ⓦnh-hotels.com. Centrally located, ninety-room business-style hotel, which is part of the slickly run if slightly faceless NH chain. **€57**

Hotel Santa Cecilia C/Tinte 3 ☎926 228 545, ⓦsantacecilia.com. A competitively priced four-star hotel in the centre of town. Rooms have been recently refurbished and it has its own pool. **€55**

EATING AND DRINKING

Ciudad Real has an impressive range of **tapas bars**. The town's **nightlife** at the weekend generally starts off with tapas on C/Palma, carrying on to the bars along Avenida Torreón del Alcázar and around.

La Casuca C/Palma 10 ☎926 255 480. Home-made cooking at reasonable prices and a decent range of local wines in this popular bar-restaurant close to the centre of town. Daily 1.30–5pm & 9pm–midnight.
Mesón El Ventero Pza. Mayor 9 ☎926 216 588. Look out for local specialities like *migas* (breadcrumbs, garlic,

chorizo and pepper) and *atascaburras* (puréed potato, garlic and cod). Daily 1.30–4pm & 8.30–11.30pm.
Miami Park Ronda Ciruela 34 ☎926 222 043, ⓦmiamigastro.es. A wide range of stylish tapas and *raciones* on offer at this up-market restaurant. Seasonal taster menus also on offer from around €39. Mon–Sat 10am–1am.

Almagro

Twenty kilometres southeast of Ciudad Real is **ALMAGRO**, an elegant little town, which for a period in the fifteenth and sixteenth centuries was quite a metropolis in southern Castile, partly thanks to the influence of the Fuggers, bankers to the Habsburg king and Holy Roman Emperor Carlos I (Charles V).

Corral de las Comedias

Pza. Mayor 18 • March & Oct–Dec Mon–Thurs 10am–2pm & 4–7pm, Fri 10am–2pm & 4–5.45pm, Sat 10am–12.45pm & 4–5.45pm (dramatized visit at 1 & 6pm), Sun 10am–12.45pm & 4–7pm (dramatized visit at 1pm); Dec–Feb daily 10am–2pm & 4–7pm; April–June & Aug–Sept Mon–Thurs 10am–2pm & 5–8pm, Fri 10am–2pm & 5–6.45pm (dramatized visit at 7pm), Sat 10am–12.45pm & 5–6.45pm (dramatized visits at 1 & 7pm), Sun 10am–12.45pm & 5–8pm (dramatized visit at 1pm); July daily 10am–2pm & 6–9pm • €3–4 • ☎926 882 458, ⓦcorraldecomedias.com

Almagro's main claim to fame today is the **Corral de las Comedias**, a perfectly preserved sixteenth-century open-air theatre, unique in Spain. Plays from its sixteenth- and seventeenth-century heyday – the golden age of Spanish theatre – are performed regularly in the tiny auditorium, and throughout July it hosts a fully fledged theatre festival (ⓦfestivaldealmagro.com).

Museo Nacional del Teatro

C/Gran Maestre 2 • Sept–June Tues–Fri 10am–2pm & 4–7pm, Sat 11am–2pm & 4–6pm, Sun 11am–2pm, July & Aug Tues–Fri 11am–2pm & 6–9pm, Sat 11am–2pm & 6–9pm, Sun 11am–2pm • €3 • ☎926 261 014, ⓦmuseoteatro.mcu.es

Across the square from the Corral de las Comedias, the **Museo del Teatro** houses costumes, photos, posters, model theatres and other paraphernalia documenting the history of drama from Greek and Roman times to the present, but is probably only of passing interest to anyone other than theatre buffs.

Museo de Encaje

Callejón del Villar • Jan–March & Oct–Dec Tues–Fri 10am–2pm & 4–7pm, Sat 10am–2pm & 4–6pm, Sun 11am–2pm; April–June, Aug & Sept Tues–Fri 10am–2pm & 5–8pm, Sat 10am–2pm & 5–7pm, Sun 11am–2pm; July Mon–Fri 10am–2pm & 6–9pm, Sat 10am–2pm & 6–8pm, Sun 11am–2pm • €1.50

As well as its theatre festival, Almagro is renowned for its lace and embroidery work showcased in the **Museo de Encaje**, which also looks at the techniques, origins and history of the craft.

Plaza Mayor

The **Plaza Mayor** is magnificent: more of a wide street than a square, it is arcaded along its length, and lined with rows of green-framed windows – a north-European influence brought by the Fugger family, Carlos V's bankers, who settled here. Also resident in Almagro for a while were the Knights of Calatrava (see opposite), though their power was on the wane by the time the **Convento de la Asunción de Calatrava** was built in the early sixteenth century. Further traces of Almagro's former importance are dotted throughout the town in the grandeur of numerous **Renaissance mansions**.

Back in the Plaza Mayor, you can have an open-air snack or browse among the shops in the arcades, where **lacemakers** at work with bobbins and needles are the main attraction. On Wednesday mornings there's a lively **market** in C/Ejido de San Juan.

ARRIVAL AND INFORMATION   ALMAGRO

By train Almagro is connected to Madrid with one train a day (2hr 35min) and to Ciudad Real with five trains (15min); the train station is a short distance from the centre of town along the Paseo de la Estación.
By bus Buses, connecting the city to Ciudad Real, stop near the *Hotel Don Diego* on the Ronda de Calatrava.

Turismo Pza. Mayor 1 (Jan–March & Oct–Dec Tues–Fri 10am–2pm & 4–7pm, Sat 10am–2pm & 4–6pm, Sun 10am–2pm; April–June, Aug & Sept Tues–Fri 10am–2pm & 5–8pm, Sat 10am–2pm & 5–7pm, Sun 10am–2pm; July Tues–Fri 10am–2pm & 6–9pm, Sat 10am–2pm & 6–8pm, Sun 10am–2pm; ☎ 926 860 717, ⓦ ciudad-almagro.com).

ACCOMMODATION

Almagro is a great **place to stay**, although accommodation can be fairly limited during the theatre festival and at holiday weekends, so make sure you book ahead.

★**Casa del Rector** C/Pedro Oviedo 8 ☎ 926 261 259, ⓦ lacasadelrector.com. Some delightful and well-appointed rooms, each with their own individual decor, set in three distinct areas of this stylish hotel; for atmosphere go for the ones around a beautiful interior patio. The hotel also has a spa. **€99**
Hospedería Almagro Ejido de Calatrava s/n ☎ 926 882 087, ☎ 926 882 122. Over forty simple and functional rooms in this neat hotel located next to the convent. Also has a pleasant patio bar and restaurant. **€50**

Hostal Los Escudos C/Bolaños 55 ☎ 926 861 574, ⓦ hostallosescudos.es. Thirteen individually decorated, a/c rooms in this upmarket little *hostal* on one of the main roads into town. **€45**
Parador de Almagro C/Gran Maestre ☎ 926 860 100, ⓦ www.paradores.com. Housed in a sixteenth-century Franciscan convent, this historic parador features some peaceful interior courtyards and a great swimming pool. Look out for offers on the parador website. **€150**

EATING AND DRINKING

Tapas **bars** cluster around the Pza. Mayor; and the *bodega* at the parador is worth a stop for a drink, too.

La Cuerda Pza. del General Jorreto 6 ☎ 926 882 805. Just in front of the train station, this is a friendly place specializing in rice and fish dishes. Eating à la carte will cost around €30 a head, while the lunchtime *menú del día* at closer to €10 is very good value. Closed Mon eve and first 2 weeks in Sept.
★**Mesón El Corregidor** C/Jerónimo Ceballos 2 ☎ 926 860 648, ⓦ elcorregidor.com. The best restaurant in town, with a €25 set menu featuring local specialities,

while à la carte options include lamb, steak and *cochinillo*. There is a very pleasant patio bar in the same building. Tues–Sun 1–4pm & 8–11pm; closed first week in Aug.
La Posada de Almagro C/Gran Maestre 5 ☎ 926 261 201, ⓦ laposadadealmagro.com. There are two beautiful interior patios in this restaurant that specializes in local delicacies and roast lamb. A meal costs in the region of €35 a head. Thurs–Tues 1–4pm & 8.30pm–midnight.

El Campo de Calatrava

The area known as **El Campo de Calatrava**, in between Almagro and Ciudad Real, was the domain of the **Knights of Calatrava**, a Cistercian order of soldier-monks created in the twelfth century which was at the forefront of the reconquest of Spain from the Moors.

So influential were they in these parts that Alfonso X created Ciudad Real as a royal check on their power. Even today, dozens of villages for many kilometres around are suffixed with their name.

Calatrava La Vieja

Carrión de Calatrava • Oct–March Fri, Sat & Sun 10.30am–2pm & 3.30–5.30pm, April, May & Sept Fri, Sat & Sun 10am–2pm & 4–8pm, June, July & Aug Mon–Thurs 10am–2.30pm • €5 • ⓦ patrimoniohistoricoclm.es

Founded by the Moors back in the eighth century, the fortified settlement now known as **Calatrava La Vieja** (Qal'at Rabah in Arabic) acted as the powerbase of the Caliphate of Córdoba in this strategically important region. It was recaptured by the Christians in the mid-twelfth century and subsequently became the first headquarters of the Knights of Calatrava. The medieval walled fortress with its towers and remains of buildings such as the *mezquita* can be clearly seen during the visit.

Calatrava La Nueva

Aldea del Rey • April–Sept Tues–Fri 11am–2pm & 5.30–8.30pm, Sat 10am–2pm & 5.30–8.30pm, Sun 10am–2pm & 5–9pm; Oct–March Tues–Fri 11am–2pm & 4–6pm, Sat 10am–2pm & 4–6pm, Sun 10am–6pm • €3

In the opening decades of the thirteenth century, the knights pushed their headquarters south to a commanding hilltop 25km south of Almagro, protecting an important pass – the Puerto de Calatrava – into Andalucía. Here, in 1216, they founded **Calatrava La Nueva**, a settlement that was part monastery and part castle, and whose main glory was a great Cistercian church. Here you get a good idea of what must have been an enormously rich and well-protected fortress. The church itself is now completely bare but preserves the outline of a striking rose window and has an amazing stone-vaulted entrance hall. On the hill opposite is a further castle ruin, known as **Salvatierra**, which the knights took over from the Moors.

Valdepeñas and beyond

The road from Ciudad Real through Almagro continues to **VALDEPEÑAS**, centre of the most prolific wine region in Spain just off the main Madrid–Andalucía motorway. You pass many of the largest **bodegas** on the slip road into town coming from the north and Madrid; most of them offer free tastings. Another option is the high-tech **Museo del Vino** at C/Princesa 39, close to Pza. de España (Tues–Sat 10am–2pm & 5–8pm, Sun 11am–2pm; summer Tues–Sat 10am–2pm & 6–9pm, Sun 11am–2pm; €3; ☎926 321 111, ⓦmuseodelvinovaldepenas.es). The town holds a popular wine **festival** at the beginning of September. There is also a **windmill**, on C/Francisco Mejía, which the tourist office says "could be the biggest in Europe", and opposite a museum dedicated to the abstract drawings of local artist Gregorio Prieto (Tues–Sat winter: 10am–2pm & 5–8pm, summer 10am–2pm & 6–9pm, Sun 11am–2pm; free; ☎926 324 965, ⓦgregorioprieto .org), though there are also works by Picasso, Matisse, Chagall and Francis Bacon.

Gorge of Despeñaperros

Heading south beyond Valdepeñas, you enter Andalucía through the **Gorge of Despeñaperros**, a narrow mountain gorge once notorious for bandits and still a dramatic natural gateway that signals a change in both climate and vegetation, or as Richard Ford put it (travelling south to north), "exchanges an Eden for a desert".

INFORMATION	VALDEPEÑAS
Turismo Pza. España (June–Sept Mon–Sun 9am–2pm & 5–8pm; Oct–May Tues–Sat 10am–2pm & 4–6pm,	Sun 11.30am–1.30pm; ☎926 312 552, ⓦwww .valdepenas.es).

ACCOMMODATION

Hotel & Spa Veracruz Pza. Veracruz ☎ 926 313 000, ⓦ hotelveracruzplaza.com. A modern well-equipped hotel with large rooms and its own spa. Offers trips of the local *bodegas* and wine-therapy beauty treatments. **€75**

Hotel Central C/Capitán Fillol 4 ☎ 926 313 388, ⓦ hotelcentralval.com. There are 25 straightforward en-suite rooms in this decent-value hotel that has its own parking in the centre of town. **€60**

The Montes de Toledo

The **Montes de Toledo** cut a swathe through the upper reaches of La Mancha, between Toledo, Ciudad Real and Guadalupe. If you're heading into Extremadura, and have time and transport, the deserted little roads across these hills (they rise to just over 1400m) provide an interesting and atmospheric alternative to the main routes. This is an amazingly remote region to find so close to the centre of Spain: its people are so unused to visitors that in the smaller villages you'll certainly get a few odd looks.

Toledo to Navalmoral de la Mata

The CM4000, west of Toledo, provides a direct approach into **Extremadura**, linking with the A5 from Madrid to Trujillo, and with roads north into the valley of **La Vera** (see opposite). It follows the course of the Río Tajo virtually all the way to uninspiring **TALAVERA DE LA REINA**, known for its manufacture of ceramics.

Oropesa and around

OROPESA is best known for its **castle**, a warm, stone building on a Roman site, rebuilt from Moorish foundations in the fifteenth century by Don García Álvarez de Toledo. Below it, stretches of the old town walls survive, along with a few noble mansions and a pair of Renaissance churches. There are great views from the neatly manicured gardens across to the hulking silhouettes of the Gredos mountains on the horizon, beyond which an attractive minor road, from **Oropesa**, with its castle parador, runs to **El Puente del Arzobispo** and south of the river to the Roman site of **Los Vascos**.

ACCOMMODATION OROPESA

Parador Virrey de Toledo Oropesa ☎ 925 430 000, ⓦ www.paradores.com. Installed in part of the splendid village castle, this is the best place to stay in the area, with a great terrace pool, large communal areas and a good restaurant serving a range of local specialities. **€145**

Navalmoral de la Mata

West from Oropesa, **NAVALMORAL DE LA MATA** has nothing to offer other than its road, rail and bus connections to more engrossing places such as the **Monasterio de Yuste** across the rich tobacco-growing area to the north, **Plasencia** to the west, and **Trujillo** and **Guadalupe** to the south.

Into the hills

The most accessible route into the Montes de Toledo from Talavera is via the CM4000 and then the CM4009 and CM403 south of La Puebla de Montalbán, which runs through the backwater village of **Las Ventas Con Peña Aguilera**, overlooked by rock-studded hills, including a curious outcrop shaped like three fat fingers – the name Peña Aguilera means "Crag of Eagles". Southwest of Las Ventas, a tiny road leads to **San Pablo de los Montes**, a delightful village of fine stone houses nestling against the mountains.

If you keep to the CM403 south of Las Ventas, you will come to the main pass over the Montes de Toledo, the **Puerto del Milagro**, with great views of the hills dipping down on either side to meet the plain. Past the Puerto del Milagro, you can drive through lovely scenery towards Ciudad Real, or turn right along the CM4017 at the El Molinillo junction to follow a road through the hills via Retuerta del Bullaque to

Navas de Estena. Here the road curves round to the north, passing a large crag with caves 5km beyond Navas, allowing you to loop round to Navahermosa and on to the CM401 to Guadalupe.

Extremadura

Once neglected and overlooked by many visitors, **Extremadura** has established itself on the tourist trail – and deservedly so. The grand old *conquistador* towns of **Trujillo** and **Cáceres** are excellent staging posts en route south from Madrid or Salamanca; **Mérida** has numerous Roman remains and an exemplary museum of local finds; and there is superb bird life in the **Parque Natural de Monfragüe**. Almost inaccessible by public transport, but well worth visiting, is the great **monastery of Guadalupe**, whose revered icon of the Virgin has attracted pilgrims for the past five hundred years. The lush hills and valley of **La Vera** are the first real patch of green you'll come to if you've driven along the A5 west from Madrid.

La Vera

Characterized by its lovely *gargantas* – streams – **La Vera** lies just south of the Sierra de Gredos, a range of hills tucked above the **Río Tiétar** valley. In spring and summer, the area attracts bands of weekenders from Madrid to the picturesque villages of **Candeleda** and **Jarandilla**. At the heart of the region is the **Monasterio de Yuste**, the retreat chosen by Carlos V to cast off the cares of empire.

Jarandilla and around

The main village in these parts is **JARANDILLA DE LA VERA**, which has good **walking** around it. A track into the hills leads to the village of **El Guijo de Santa Bárbara** (4.5km) and then ends, leaving the ascent of the rocky valley beyond to walkers. An hour's trek away up the Garganta de Jaranda is a pool known as El Trabuquete and a high meadow with shepherds' huts known as Pimesaíllo. On the other side of the valley – a serious trek needing a night's camping and good area maps – is the **Garganta de Infierno** (Stream of Hell) and natural swimming pools known as **Los Pilones**.

The village of **Villanueva de la Vera** to the east of Jarandilla along the EX203 has gained a certain amount of notoriety for its **Peropalo** fiesta, in which a donkey is horribly mistreated while carrying the figure of *Peropalo* through the streets. It seems strange to imagine such cruelty, given the rural idyll hereabouts and the incredibly house-proud appearance of the villages, especially **Losar**, which has an almost surreal display of topiary.

The Monasterio de Yuste

Tues–Sun April–Sept 10am–8pm, Oct–March 10am–6pm • €9, free Oct–March Wed & Thurs 3–6pm, April–Sept Wed & Thurs 5–8pm • ☎ 927 172 197, ⓦ patrimonionacional.es

There is nothing especially dramatic about the **Monasterio de Yuste**, the retreat created by Carlos V after renouncing his empire: just a simple beauty and the rather stark accoutrements of the emperor's last years. The monastery, which is signposted from Cuacos de Yuste on the Jarandilla–Plasencia road, had existed here for over a century before Carlos' retirement and he had earmarked the site for some years, planning his modest additions – which included a pleasure garden – while still ruling his empire from Flanders. He retired here with a retinue that included an Italian clockmaker, Juanuelo Turriano, whose inventions were the emperor's last passion.

The imperial apartments are draped throughout in black, and exhibits include the little sedan chair in which Carlos was brought here, and another designed to support the old man's gouty legs. If you believe the guide, the bed and even the sheets are the very ones in which the emperor died, though since the place was sacked during the Peninsular Wars and deserted for years after the suppression of the monasteries, this seems unlikely. A door by the emperor's bed opens out over the church and altar so that even in his final illness he never missed a service. Outside, there's a snack bar and picnic spots, and you'll find a track signposted through the woods to Garganta La Olla (see below).

Cuacos de Yuste

The Monasterio de Yuste is 2km into the wooded hills from **CUACOS DE YUSTE**, an attractive village with a couple of squares, including the tiny Pza. de Don Juan de Austria, named after the house (its upper storey reconstructed) where Carlos' illegitimate son Don Juan lived when visiting his father. The surrounding houses, their overhanging upper storeys supported on gnarled wooden pillars, are sixteenth-century originals, and from the beams underneath the overhang tobacco is hung out to dry after the harvest.

Garganta La Olla

Just beyond Jaraíz de la Vera, a left turning leads for around 5km to **GARGANTA LA OLLA**, a beautiful, ramshackle mountain village set among cherry orchards. There is a signposted short-cut track to the Monasterio de Yuste, and several other things to look out for: the **Casa de Putas** (a brothel for the soldiers of Carlos V's army, now a butcher's but still painted the traditional blue) and the **Casa de la Piedra** (House of Stone), a house whose balcony is secured by a three-pronged wooden support resting on a rock. The latter is hard to find; begin by taking the left-hand street up from the square and then ask.

ARRIVAL   LA VERA

By bus Buses run from Príncipe Pío to the Monasterio de Yuste (2 daily; 4hr) and to Jarandilla (2 daily; 3hr 50min).

ACCOMMODATION

JARANDILLA AND AROUND
Don Juan de Austria Hotel Rural and Spa Avda. Soledad Vega Ortiz 101 ☎ 927 560 206, ⓦ hoteljaranda .com. Comfortable, well-equipped and furnished rooms, some with views of the Sierra and the castle, and a small spa in this good mid-range option in the village. **€70**
★ **Parador Carlos V** Avda. García Prieto 1 ☎ 927 560 117, ⓦ www.paradores.com. A magnificent parador in the fifteenth-century castle where the emperor stayed

during the construction of Yuste. A splendid palm-fringed courtyard, period furnishings and a very good restaurant serving Extremeño cuisine. **€125**
Posada de Pizarro Cuesta de Carros 1 ☎ 927 560 727, ⓦ laposadadepizarro.com. A comfortable option containing ten en-suite rooms, each decorated with frescoes on the bedroom walls. Buffet breakfast included. **€40**
★ **Ruta Imperial** C/Machoteral ☎ 927 561 330, ⓦ hotelruralrutaimperial.com. Grass lawns (a rarity in

EXTREMEÑO CUISINE

Given that **Extremadura** remains a largely agricultural region, it is hardly surprising its **cuisine** is renowned for high-quality local ingredients, whether it be the trout from the streams in the Gredos mountains, the *pimentón* (paprika) from the Vera, the goats' cheese from Cáceres or the succulent cherries from the Valle de Jerte. Signature dishes include the humble *migas* (breadcrumbs, paprika, ham, garlic and olive oil) and *patatas revolconas* (delicious paprika-flavoured potatoes), but to most Spaniards ham is the gastronomic product they most associate with Extremadura.

Together with the Sierra Morena in Andalucía, the Extremaduran sierra is the only place in the country that supports the pure-bred Iberian pig, source of the best **jamón**. For its ham to be as flavoursome as possible, the pig, a subspecies of the European wild boar exclusive to the Iberian Peninsula, is allowed to roam wild and eat acorns for several months of the year. The undisputed kings of hams in this area, praised at length by Richard Ford in his *Handbook for Travellers*, are those that come from Montánchez, in the south of the region. The village is midway between Cáceres and Mérida, so if you're in the area try some in a bar, washed down with local red wine – but be warned that the authentic product is extremely expensive, a few thinly cut slices often costing as much as an entire meal. The local wine, *pitarra*, is an ideal accompaniment.

central Spain), a terrace restaurant overlooking the Garganta coming down from the mountains, an outdoor pool and comfortable rooms at an affordable price (two family rooms available). **€70–97**

CAMPING

Camping La Mata Just outside Madrigal de la Vera east of Jarandilla along the EX203 ☎ 927 565 238, ⓦ campinglamata.com. Pleasant, grassy campsite with a decent bar/restaurant close to a natural swimming pool on one of the gargantas. **€18.40**

Jaranda Ctra. EX203, km 47 ☎ 927 560 454, ⓦ campingjaranda.es. Attractive campsite by the river with plenty of shady pitches, cabins for rent, a pool and a

supermarket. Closed Oct to mid-March. **€18.80**

CUACOS DE YUSTE

★**Hotel Abadía de Yuste** Avda. Constitución ☎ 927 172 241, ⓦ www.abadiadeyuste.com. Relaxing, fifteen-room hotel close to the Monasterio de Yuste, with atmospheric decor, a swimming pool and two restaurants. **€66**

GARGANTA LA OLLA

Hotel Rural Carlos I Avda. Libertad ☎ 927 179 678, ⓦ hotelcarlosprimero.com. A good-value option in this village. Individually decorated rooms, a couple of larger suites with sitting areas and a bar-restaurant serving up local dishes. **€66**

El Valle de Jerte

Immediately north of La Vera, the main Plasencia–Ávila road follows the valley of the **Río Jerte** (from the Greek *Xerte*, meaning "joyful") to the pass of Puerto de Tornavacas, the boundary with Ávila province. The villages here are more developed than those of La Vera but the valley itself is stunning and renowned for its orchards of cherry trees, which for a ten-day period in spring cover the slopes with white blossom. If you're anywhere in the area at this time, it's a beautiful spectacle.

If you have transport, you can follow a minor route across the sierra to the north of the valley from **Cabezuela del Valle** to **Hervás**, following the highest road in Extremadura, which rises to 1430m.

On the **southern side** of the valley, the main point of interest is the **Puerto del Piornal** pass, just behind the village of the same name. The best approach is via the villages of **Casas del Castañar** and **Cabrero**. Once at the pass you can continue over to Garganta La Olla in La Vera.

Plasencia

Set in the shadow of the Sierra de Gredos, and surrounded on three sides by the Río Jerte, **PLASENCIA** looks more impressive from afar than it actually is. Once you get up into the old city the walls are hard to find – for the most part they're propping up the backs of houses – and the Catedral is barely half-built, but it still merits a visit. Opposite the Catedral is the **Casa del Deán** (Dean's House), with an intriguing balcony like the prow of a ship. Continuing away from the cathedral along C/Blanca you come out at the **Pza. de San Nicolás**, where, according to local tradition, the church was built to prevent two local families from shooting arrows at each other from adjacent houses.

Plasencia has some lively bars, delightful cafés and a fine, arcaded **Pza. Mayor**, the scene of a farmers' **market** every Tuesday morning, held here since the twelfth century.

Parque de la Isla

At the entrance to the city on the main road in from Ávila is the very pleasant **Parque de la Isla** on the banks of the Río Jerte; head here for a relaxing walk or picnic. A little north of here are the remaining 55 arches of the sixteenth-century **aqueduct**, designed by Juan de Flandes, that used to bring in the city's water supply.

La Catedral

Pza. de la Catedral **La Catedral Nueva** Daily 10.30–11am · Free **La Catedral Vieja** Summer Mon–Sat 11am–2pm & 5–8pm, Sun 9–11.30am & 5–8pm; winter Mon–Sat 11am–2pm & 4–7pm, Sun 9–11.30am & 4–7pm · €4

Plasencia's **Catedral** is in fact two churches – old and new – built back to back. Work began on the second church, **La Nueva,** at the end of the fifteenth century, but after numerous technical hitches it was eventually abandoned in 1760 when the open end was simply bricked up. It does have some redeeming features, however, most notably the Renaissance choir stall intricately carved by Rodrigo Alemán and described with some justice by the National Tourist Board as "the most Rabelaisian in Christendom".

The older, Romanesque part of the cathedral, known as **La Vieja**, was built between the thirteenth and fourteenth centuries and now houses a refurbished **museum** and **cloisters**.

Museo Etnográfico Textil Provincial

Plazuela Marqués de la Puebla • July to mid-Sept Mon–Sat 9.30am–2.30pm; mid-Sept to June Wed–Sat 11am–2pm & 5–8pm, Sun 11am–2pm • Free • ⓦ brocense.com

The **Museo Etnográfico Textil Provincial** contains some colourful costumes and local crafts reflecting local traditions. Many of the exhibits are still much in evidence in the more remote villages in the north of Plasencia province.

ARRIVAL AND DEPARTURE

PLASENCIA

By train The train station is some distance away from the centre – take a taxi (around €5) unless you fancy the hike. Destinations Badajoz (1–3 daily; 2hr 50min); Cáceres (2–5 daily; 1hr 10min); Madrid (3–4 daily; 2hr 50min); Mérida (2–3 daily; 1hr 55min–2hr 15min).

By bus The bus station is about 15min walk from the centre, along the gently inclining Avda. del Valle to the west.

Destinations Cáceres (4–5 daily; 1hr 20min); Jarandilla (2–5 daily; 2hr); Madrid (2 daily; 4hr); Salamanca (3 daily; 2hr).

By car Be warned that the town is difficult to navigate, with a warren of narrow one-way streets and poor signing.

INFORMATION

Turismo C/Santa Clara 2, just off the Pza. de la Catedral (Mon–Fri 7.45am–3.15pm & 4–7pm, Sat & Sun 9.30am–2pm & 4–7pm; ☎ 927 423 843, ⓦ plasencia.es). There is also a provincial office in the Pza. Torre Lucia next to the city walls (mid-Sept to mid-June Mon–Fri 8.30am–2.30pm & 4–6pm, Sat & Sun 10am–noon, mid-June to mid-Sept Mon–Fri 8am–3pm, Sat & Sun 10am–2pm; ☎ 927 017 840, ⓦ turismoextremadura.com).

ACCOMMODATION

La Chopera 2.5km out on the Ávila road ☎ 927 416 660, ⓦ campinglachopera.com. A large riverside campsite with decent facilities, bungalows for hire and a swimming pool. €17.50

Hostal La Muralla C/Berrozana 6 ☎ 927 413 874, ⓦ hostallamuralla.es. A professionally run thirteen-room *hostal* with a/c en-suite rooms and a central location close to the Pza. Mayor. €40

Hotel Exe Alfonso VIII C/Alfonso VIII 32 ☎ 927 410 250, ⓦ hotelexealfonsoviii.com. A smart four-star hotel with bright, classically decorated rooms, located on the main road near the post office. All the facilities you'd expect of a hotel of this category. €80

Parador Pza. de San Vicente Ferrer s/n ☎ 927 425 870, ⓦ www.paradores.com. Housed in a beautiful restored fifteenth-century Gothic convent with large rooms, a cloister, stone staircases and a huge dining room, this parador also has a convenient central location. €125

EATING AND DRINKING

This is the land of the **pincho**, a little sample of food provided free with your beer or wine – among which is the local *pitarra* wine. Finding good restaurants is not as easy as finding bars in Plasencia (try the area between the Catedral and the Pza. Mayor): there are over fifty bars in the old town alone, mostly found on C/Patalón (go down C/Talavera from the main square and it's the second turning on the left).

RESTAURANTS

Casa Juan C/Arenillas 2 ☎ 927 424 042, ⓦ restaurante casajuan.com. Good-quality regional dishes with some refined touches in this critically acclaimed restaurant in the old part of town. A good-value €20 menu available weekday lunchtimes. Mon–Wed & Thurs–Sun 1–4pm & 8.30–11.30pm.

Los Monges C/Sor Valentina Mirón 24, just up from Puerta Berronzana ☎ 927 420 808, ⓦ losmonges.com. A good-quality family restaurant serving up some fine local produce with a creative twist. Expect to pay around €40 a head. Daily 1–4pm & 8.30–11.30pm.

Restaurante Succo C/Vidrieras 7 ☎ 927 412 932, ⓦ restaurantesucco.es. Minimalist decor and excellent creative food at decent prices (around €25 a head) in this restaurant close to the Pza. Mayor. The beautifully presented dishes include warm salad with baby squid and langoustines, and goat casserole with mushrooms. Mon–Sat 1–4pm & 8.30–11.30pm, Sun 1–4pm; closed all day Sun in July & Aug.

BARS

La Herradura C/Patalón 28 ☎ 927 421 399. A busy bar that is a good bet for *pinchos*, hot and cold tapas and a glass of *pitarra* wine. Their speciality dish is *torreznos a la plancha* (deliciously unhealthy bits of fried fatty pork). Usually daily noon–4pm & 8–midnight.

Valle del Ambroz

A little further to the west of the Valle de Jerte and almost as pleasing to the eye is the **Valle del Ambroz**. Dotted with picturesque villages set against a backdrop of some magnificent mountain scenery, the valley, which follows the Roman Vía de la Plata, heads up towards the picturesque town of **Hervás** and on towards Bejar in the region of Castilla y León.

Hervás

Pleasant little **HERVÁS**, perched on the flanks of the valley, makes a good base from which to explore the area. It also has attractions of its own including a fascinating, former Jewish quarter and a couple of small museums.

Museo de la Moto Clásica

Carretera de la Garganta • July–Sept Mon–Fri 10.30am–1.30pm & 5–9pm, Sat & Sun 10.30am–9pm; Oct–June Tues–Fri 10.30am–1.30pm & 4–7pm, Sat & Sun 10.30am–1.30pm & 4–8pm • €10, under-12s free • ⓦ museomotoclasica.com

The overpriced **Museo de la Moto Clásica**, housed in a series of conical pavilions on the edge of town, contains an impressive though eccentrically displayed private collection of classic motorbikes, cars, bicycles and carriages, including giant Cadillacs, World War II sidecars and horse-drawn carts.

Museo Pérez Comendador-Leroux

C/Asensio Neila 5 • Tues 4–8pm, Wed–Fri 11am–2pm & 4–8pm, Sat & Sun 10.30am–2pm • €1.20, free Sun • ☎ 927 481 655, ⓦ mpcl.net

The **Museo Pérez Comendador-Leroux**, which is situated in a splendid eighteenth-century mansion, is home to works of local sculptor Enrique Pérez Comendador, his French artist wife Magdalena Leroux and some of their friends and associates.

ARRIVAL AND INFORMATION | HERVÁS

By bus Twice daily from Cáceres via Plasencia (2hr 5min), three times a day from Salamanca (1hr 40min) and from Madrid (3hr 20min).

By car From Plasencia take the N630 north towards Salamanca and then the EX205 to Hervás.

Turismo C/Braulio Navas 6 (Tues–Fri 10am–2pm & 5–7pm, Sat & Sun 10am–2pm; ☎ 927 473 618, ⓦ hervas.es).

ACCOMMODATION AND EATING

★**Jardín del Convento** Pza. del Convento ☎ 927 481 161, ⓦ eljardindelconvento.com. A beautiful and tranquil little hotel in a refurbished former nineteenth-century convent, with six rooms and a small cottage apartment with space for four people that's set in the delightful gardens (€115). €65

★**Restaurante Mesón Nardi** C/Braulio Navas 19 ☎ 927 481 323, ⓦ restaurantenardi.com. Imaginative and well-presented dishes based on local ingredients and specialities are served in this friendly place on a pedestrian street in the centre of town. Expect to pay around €20–30 a head. Mon & Wed–Sun 1–4pm & 8–11.30pm.

Las Hurdes

Las Hurdes, the abrupt rocky lands north of Plasencia, have always been a rich source of mysterious tales. According to legend, the region was unknown to the outside world until the time of Columbus, when two lovers fleeing from the court of the Duke of Alba chanced upon it. The people who welcomed them were supposedly unaware of the existence of other people or other lands. Shields and other remnants belonging to the Goth Rodrigo and his court of seven centuries earlier were discovered by the couple, giving rise to the saying that the *hurdanos* are descendants of kings.

Sixty years ago, the inhabitants of the remoter areas were still so unused to outsiders that they hid in their houses if anyone appeared. In 1932, **Luis Buñuel** filmed an unflatteringly grotesque documentary here, *Las Hurdes: Tierra Sin Pan* ("Land Without Bread"), in which it was hard to discern any royal descent in his subjects. Modernity has crept up on the villages these days, though they can still feel wild and very remote, and the soil is so barren that tiny terraces have been constructed on the riverbeds as the only way of getting the stubborn land to produce anything.

Las Hurdes villages

You could approach Las Hurdes from Plasencia, Salamanca or Ciudad Rodrigo – the region borders the Sierra de Francia (see p.386). If you're coming from Plasencia the village of **PINOFRANQUEADO** marks the start of the region. It has a campsite, *hostales* and a natural swimming pool. Fifteen kilometres farther along on the road at Vegas de Coria you can turn off to reach **NUÑOMORAL**, the village best connected to the outside world. A good base for excursions, it also has a bank alongside its **hostal** – not a common sight in these parts.

A few kilometres to the north of Nuñomoral, the tiny village of **LA HUETRE** is worth a visit; take a left fork just before the village of Casares de las Hurdes. The typical slate-roofed houses are in decent condition and have an impressive setting, surrounded by steep rocky hills. Walkers might also head for the remote and disarmingly primitive settlement of **EL GASCO**, at the top of Valle de Malvellido, the next valley to the south, where there is a huge waterfall beneath the Meancera Gorge.

ARRIVAL AND INFORMATION | LAS HURDES

By bus Early-morning buses connect Nuñomoral to both Ciudad Rodrigo and Plasencia.
By car From Plasencia take the EX370 and then the EX204.
Turismo Avda. de Las Hurdes, Caminomorisco (Wed–Sun 10am–2pm & 4.30–7.30pm; ☎ 927 435 329, ⊛ todohurdes.com). The website ⊛ mancomunidadhurdes .org also has plenty of useful information on the region.

ACCOMMODATION AND EATING

Hotel Hospedería Hurdes Reales C/Factoría, Las Mestas ☎ 927 434 139, ⊛ hospederiasdeextremadura .es. Large rooms, a decent restaurant and a small outdoor pool in this modern hotel in beautiful surroundings in the village of Las Mestas in the northern part of Las Hurdes. €70

Pensión El Hurdano Avda. Padre Rizabala, Nuñomoral ☎ 927 433 012. An excellent and inexpensive *hostal* which also serves very ample dinners. €35

The Sierra de Gata

The **Sierra de Gata** creates a westerly border to Las Hurdes, in a series of wooded hills and odd outcrops of higher ground, in parts stunningly beautiful. To explore the whole region, you need your own transport and certainly a detailed local **map** – regular Spanish road maps tend to be pretty sketchy.

The Sierra de Gata is almost as isolated as Las Hurdes – in some of the villages the old people still speak *maniego*, a mix of Castilian Spanish and Portuguese. For a trip into the heart of the region, take the EX204 south from Las Hurdes to **Villanueva de la Sierra** and follow the EX205 west. A couple of kilometres past the Río Arrago, a very minor road veers north towards **Robledillo de Gata**, a village of old houses packed tightly together. A shorter, easier detour, south of the EX205, around 5km on, goes to the hilltop village of **Santibáñez el Alto**, whose oldest houses are built entirely of stone, without windows. At the top of town, look out for a tiny bullring, castle remains and the old cemetery – there's a wonderful view over the Borbollón reservoir from here. Another 3km along the EX205, a turn-off to the north takes you on a winding road up to the pretty village of **Gata**. Farther west on the EX205 is the largest village of the region, **Hoyos**, which has some impressive mansions. Lastly, farther along the EX205, another turning leads north to **San Martín de Trevejo**, one of the prettiest of the many lonely villages around.

ARRIVAL AND DEPARTURE   SIERRA DE GATA

By car Take the EX370 from Plasencia and then the EX204 northwards before bearing west onto the EX205.

ACCOMMODATION

Campsite Sierra de Gata ☎ 927 672 168, ⓦ camping sierradegata.es. Located 4km from the village of Gata on the banks of a stream, this campsite has a large outdoor pool, a small bar and plenty of shade. **€18**

Finca El Cabezo Villamiel ☎ 927 672 903, ⓦ elcabezo .com. Characterful and cosy *casa rural* with six large, rustic rooms. Breakfast included in the price. **€85**

Hospedería Conventual Sierra de Gata Camino del Convento 39, San Martín de Trevejo ☎ 927 144 021,

ⓦ hospederiasdeextremadura.es. Spa hotel housed in a former convent dating from the fifteenth century and in the foothills of the Sierra de Gata. Rooms are comfortable and spacious, the hotel has its own restaurant and an outdoor pool for use in the summer months. **€70**

Hotel Rural El Redoble Pza. de la Paz 23, Hoyos ☎ 927 514 665, ⓦ el-redoble.com. Simply furnished hotel with nine air-conditioned en-suite rooms and a restaurant/bar. **€40**

Coria

South of the Sierra de Gata, **CORIA** makes an interesting stop. It looks nothing much from the main road, but it's actually a cool, quiet old town with lots of stately whitewashed houses. The fifteenth-century **convent** (Mon–Fri & Sun 9.30am–12.45pm & 4.15–6.45pm, Sat 4.15–6.45pm; €1.50) with its Gothic-Renaissance cloister is enclosed within third- and fourth-century **Roman walls**. For the most part these are built into and around the houses, but a good stretch is visible between the deserted tower of the fifteenth-century castle, built by the dukes of Alba, and the cathedral.

Catedral

Pza. de la Catedral **Catedral** Daily 10am–1.30pm & 4–7pm; summer opens and closes an hour later in the afternoons **Museum** Closed Mon • €2

The **Catedral** has beautifully carved west and north portals in the Plateresque style of Salamanca and, inside, the choir stalls and *retablo* are worth seeing. The building overlooks a striking medieval bridge across fields, the river having changed course three hundred years ago.

Museo Carcel Real

C/Monjas 2 • Wed–Sun 10.30am–2pm & 4.30–7.30pm (opens and closes an hour later in the afternoons in summer) • Free

The former town prison now houses the local archeological museum, **Museo Carcel Real**, with exhibits dating from the time the Celtiberians first settled in the area.

Convento del Palancar

Tues–Sun 10am–1pm & 4.30–6.45pm; ring the doorbell • Voluntary donation

A detour off the EX109, south of Coria, will take you to the **Convento del Palancar**, a monastery founded by San Pedro de Alcántara in the sixteenth century and said to be the smallest in the world at only seventy square metres. It's hard to imagine how a community of ten monks could have lived in these cubbyholes, though San Pedro himself set the example, sleeping upright in his cubicle. A small monastic community today occupies a more modern monastery alongside; ring the bell and a monk will come and show you around.

To reach Palancar, turn left off the EX109 just after Torrejoncillo and follow the road towards **Pedroso de Acim**; a left turn just before the village leads to the monastery.

MONFRAGÜE'S WILDLIFE

There are **over two hundred species of animals in Monfragüe**, including reptiles, deer, wild boar and the ultra-rare Spanish lynx. Most important is the bird population, especially the black stork – this is the only breeding population in western Europe – and birds of prey such as the black vulture (not averse to eating tortoises), the griffon vulture (partial to carrion intestine), the Egyptian vulture (not above eating human excrement), the rare Spanish imperial eagle (identifiable by its very obvious white shoulder patches), the golden eagle and the eagle owl (the largest owl in Europe). Ornithologists should visit Monfragüe in May and June, botanists in March and April, and everybody should avoid July to September, when the heat is stifling.

ARRIVAL AND INFORMATION   CORIA

By car South from the Sierra de Gata along the EX109 towards Cáceres or take the EX08 or EXA1 from Plasencia.
Turismo Inside the *ayuntamiento* on Avda. de Extremadura

(usually Mon–Fri 9.30am–2pm & 4–6pm, Sat & Sun 10am–2pm, summer opens and closes an hour later in the afternoons; ☎ 927 508 000, ⊛ www.coria.org).

ACCOMMODATION

Hotel Los Kekes Avda. Sierra de Gata 49 ☎ 927 504 080, ⊛ hotelkekes.com. A modest hotel which has twenty recently refurbished air-conditioned doubles and an adjoining restaurant. **€50**
Sumaiya El Palacio Pza. de la Catedral ☎ 927 508

117, ⊛ hotelsumaiyaelpalacio.com. Housed in the seventeenth-century former bishop's palace, this elegant four-star hotel has thirty smart rooms with modern facilities and a decent restaurant. **€90**

Parque Natural de Monfragüe

South of Plasencia a pair of dams, built in the 1960s, has turned the **ríos Tajo and Tiétar** into a sequence of vast reservoirs. It's an impressive sight and a tremendous area for wildlife: almost at random here you can look up to see storks, vultures and even eagles circling the skies. The best area for concerted wildlife viewing – and some very enjoyable walks – is the **PARQUE NATURAL DE MONFRAGÜE**, Extremadura's only protected area, which extends over 44,000 acres to either side of the Plasencia–Trujillo road. Transport of your own is an advantage.

Walking in the park

If you're **walking** in Monfragüe, it's best to stick to the colour-coded paths leading from the park's headquarters at **Villarreal de San Carlos**. Each of them is amply paint-blobbed and leads to rewarding birdwatching locations. Elsewhere, it is not easy to tell where you are permitted to wander – it's very easy to find yourself out of the park area in a private hunting reserve.

The Green Route

The **Green Route**, to the Cerro Gimio, is especially good – a two-and-a-half-hour stroll looping through woods and across streams, in a landscape unimaginable from Villarreal, to a dramatic cliff top viewing station.

The Red Route

The longer **Red Route** heads south of Villarreal, over a bridge across the Río Tajo, and past a fountain known as the Fuente del Francés after a young Frenchman who died there trying to save an eagle. Two kilometres farther is a great crag known as the Peñafalcón, which houses a large colony of griffon vultures, and the Castillo de Monfragüe, a castle ruin high up on a rock, with a chapel next to it; there is an observation post nearby. All these places are accessible from the EX208 and if you're coming in on the bus, you could ask to get off here. There are also two routes of

8km and 12km respectively that have been designed for **cars** and include a number of viewing points.

The dehesas

On the south side of the park, towards Trujillo, you pass through the **dehesas**, strange Africa-like plains which are among the oldest woodlands in Europe. The economy of the *dehesas* is based on grazing, and the casualties among the domestic animals provide the vultures of Monfragüe with their daily bread.

ARRIVAL AND DEPARTURE — PARQUE NATURAL DE MONFRAGÜE

By train The nearest train station is Monfragüe, 18km from Villarreal de San Carlos and a stop for slow trains on the Madrid–Cáceres line.

By bus There is just one bus along the road, which runs between Plasencia and Torrejón El Rubio (Mon–Fri; departs from Plasencia bus station 8.30am).

By car The easiest approach to the park is along the EX208 from Plasencia to Trujillo, which runs past the park headquarters at Villarreal de San Carlos.

INFORMATION

Information centre At the park's headquarters at Villarreal de San Carlos (daily: summer 9am–7.30pm; winter 9am–6pm; ☎ 927 199 134, ⊛ parquedemonfrague .com). Pick up a leaflet with a map detailing the three colour-coded walks from the village and details about activities such as horseriding and walking in the park. There is also a seasonal shop, selling wildlife T-shirts and the like, and a useful guide to the park (in Spanish).

ACCOMMODATION AND EATING

VILLARREAL DE SAN CARLOS

Casa Rural El Cabrerin ☎ 927 199 002, ⊛ elcabrerin .com. There are four straightforward a/c en-suite rooms in this little *casa rural* which can also be rented out as a whole for larger groups for €220. **€55**

Casa Rural Al Mofrag ☎ 927 199 205, ☎ 686 454 393, ⊛ casaruralalmofrag.com. Right in the centre of the park, close to the information centre, this *casa rural* has six simple, a/c, comfortable rooms and an outdoor pool open in summer. **€60**

Casa Rural Monfragüe ☎ 927 199 003, ⊛ monfraguerural.com. Owned by the same people as the *Cabrerin*, this *casa rural* has six large, airy a/c rooms with an option in some of them to add an extra bed. **€55**

TORREJÓN EL RUBIO

Hospedería Parque de Monfragüe ☎ 927 455 278, ⊛ hospederiasdeextremadura.es. An upmarket hotel with a pool and a good restaurant offering a range of local specialities and barbecues on the terrace in summer. Clean lines and simple decor in the sixty rooms. **€70**

Hotel Carvajal Pza. de Pizarro 54 ☎ 927 455 260, ⊛ hotelcarvajal.es. Just to the south of the park, this simple thirteen-room hotel-restaurant is friendly and good value for money. **€50**

CAMPING

Camping Monfragüe 12km north of Villarreal on the Plasencia road ☎ 927 459 233, ⊛ camping monfrague.com. A well-equipped, year-round site near the turning to the Monfragüe train station that has a swimming pool and restaurant. It also has bikes for rent to get to Monfragüe. **€16.40**

Trujillo

TRUJILLO is the most attractive town in Extremadura: a classic **conquistador** stage set of escutcheoned mansions, stork-topped towers and castle walls. A very small place, still only a little larger than its extent in *conquistador* times, much of it looks virtually untouched since the sixteenth century, and it is redolent above all of the exploits of the conquerors of the Americas; Francisco Pizarro, the conqueror of Peru, was born here, as were many of the tiny band who with such extraordinary cruelty aided him in defeating the Incas.

Plaza Mayor

At the centre of a dense web of streets is the **Plaza Mayor**, a grand square overlooked by a trio of palaces and churches, and ringed by a half-dozen cafés and restaurants, around which life for most visitors revolves. In the centre is a huge bronze statue of Pizarro –

oddly enough by American sculptor, Carlos Rumsey – which was bought by the Spanish government in the late 1920s.

Palacio de la Conquista

In the square's southwest corner is the **Palacio de la Conquista**, the grandest of Trujillo's mansions with its roof adorned by statues representing the twelve months. Just one of many built by the Pizarro clan, it was originally inhabited by Pizarro's half-brother and son-in-law Hernando, who returned from the conquests to live here with his half-Inca bride Yupanqui (Pizarro's daughter).

Iglesia de San Martín

Mon–Sat 10am–2pm & 4–6.30pm (opens and closes an hour later in the afternoon in summer), Sun 10am–noon & 4–6.30pm (opens and closes an hour later in the afternoon in summer) • €1.40

Diagonally opposite the Palacio de la Conquista, and with a skyline of storks, is the bulky church of **San Martín**. Its tombs include, among others, that of the family of Francisco de Orellana, the first explorer of the Amazon.

Palacio de los Duques de San Carlos

The **Palacio de los Duques de San Carlos** is home to a group of nuns who moved out of their dilapidated convent up the hill and restored this palace in return for the lodgings. The chimneys on the roof boast aggressively of cultures conquered by Catholicism in the New World – they are shaped like the pyramids of Aztecs, Incas and others subjected to Spanish rule.

Palacio de Juan Pizarro de Orellana

Mon–Fri 10am–1pm & 4–6pm, Sat & Sun 11am–2pm & 4.30–6.30pm • Free

Of the many other town mansions, or **solares**, the most interesting is the **Palacio de Orellana-Pizarro**, just west of the main square. Go in through the superb

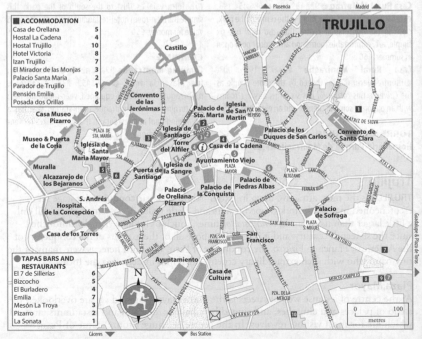

Renaissance arched doorway to admire the courtyard, an elegant patio decorated with the alternating coats of arms of the Pizarros – two bears with a pine tree – and the Orellanas.

North of Plaza Mayor

From the plaza, C/Ballesteros leads up to the walled upper town, past the domed **Torre del Alfiler** (daily: summer 10am–2pm & 4–7pm; winter 10am–2pm & 5–8pm) with its coats of arms and storks' nests, and through the fifteenth-century gateway known as the **Arco de Santiago**.

Iglesia de Santiago

Daily: summer 10am–2pm & 4–7pm; winter 10am–2pm & 5–8pm • €1.40

Built up against the walls of the Arco de Santiago is the **Iglesia de Santiago**, which dates from the thirteenth century and was sometimes used as a venue for council meetings in the Middle Ages, while opposite it is the **Palacio de los Chaves**, which was where the Reyes Católicos, Fernando and Isabel, stayed when they were in town.

Iglesia de Santa María Mayor

Daily 10am–2pm & 4.30–7.30pm, summer opens & closes 30min later in the afternoons • €1.40

The most interesting and important of the town's many churches, **Santa María Mayor** is located a short way up the hill beyond the gateway. The building is basically Gothic but contains a beautiful raised Renaissance *coro* noted for the technical mastery of its almost flat vaults. There is a fine Hispano-Flemish reredos by Fernando Gallego, while tombs include those of the Pizarros – Francisco was baptized here – and Diego García de Paredes, a man known as the "Sansón Extremeño" (Extremaduran Samson). Among other exploits, this giant of a man, armed only with his gargantuan sword, is said to have defended a bridge against an entire French army and to have picked up the font, now underneath the *coro*, to carry holy water to his mother. You are allowed to clamber up the **tower**, which provides magnificent views of the town, the parched plains over towards Cáceres, and the Sierra de Gredos.

Casa Museo Pizarro and Museo de la Coria

Casa Museo Pizarro Daily: summer 10am–2pm & 4–7pm; winter 10am–2pm & 5–8pm • €1.40 **Museo de la Coria** Sat, Sun & public hols 11.30am–2pm • Free

Located in the Pizarros' former residence, the **Casa Museo Pizarro** is a small, relatively dull affair, with little beyond period furniture and a few panels on the conquest of Peru.

For those who want to delve deeper, the **Museo de la Coria**, housed in an old Franciscan convent nearby, has more detailed exhibits on the Conquest.

Castillo

Daily: summer 10am–2pm & 4–7pm; winter 10am–2pm & 5–8pm • €1.40

The **Castillo** is now virtually in open countryside; for the last hundred metres of the climb you see nothing but the occasional broken-down remnant of a wall clambered over by sheep and dogs. The fortress itself, Moorish in origin but much reinforced by later defenders, has been restored, and its main attraction is the panoramic view of the town and its environs from the battlements. As you look out over the town and on towards the distant horizon, the castle's superb defensive position is abundantly evident.

ARRIVAL AND DEPARTURE | TRUJILLO

By bus The town is well served by buses, with up to ten a day to and from Madrid (4–5hr) and eight from Cáceres (45min). Buses arrive in the lower town, a 5min walk from the Pza. Mayor.

By car If you're driving, follow the signs to the Pza. Mayor, and with luck you should be able to park beyond the square and farther along C/García de Paredes.

INFORMATION

Turismo Pza. Mayor (daily 10am–2pm & 5–8pm; ☎ 927 322 677, ⊛ trujillo.es). Sells discount tickets for combined visits to some of the main sites (€4.70–5.30) and provides guided tours (in Spanish) of the town at 11am and 5.30pm (€7).

ACCOMMODATION

Trujillo could be visited easily enough as a day-trip from Cáceres, but it's definitely worth staying the night. **Places to stay** are in high demand – so book ahead if you can. The *turismo* can provide accommodation lists. The best rooms are in the old town close to the Pza. Mayor.

★**Casa de Orellana** C/Palomas 5–7 ☎ 927 659 265, ⊛ casadeorellana.com. Just four doubles and a single in this delightful and exclusive little hotel located in a refurbished fifteenth-century mansion close to the Pza. Mayor. There is a patio garden with a swimming pool and the price includes breakfast. **€100**

Hostal La Cadena Pza. Mayor 8 ☎ 927 321 463, ⊛ mesonhostalacadena.es. A homely *hostal*, with simple, but nicely decorated a/c rooms overlooking all the action, and a decent restaurant. **€36**

Hostal Trujillo C/Francisco Pizarro 4–6 ☎ 638 019 071, ⊛ hostaltrujillo.es. A pleasant *pensión* situated in a fifteenth-century building between the Pza. Mayor and the bus station. Twenty a/c rooms (including some triples and family rooms at €53 and €70) and a good restaurant. **€35**

Hotel Victoria Pza. de Campillo 22 ☎ 927 321 819, ⊛ hotelvictoriatrujillo.es. A friendly three-star hotel in an elegant old nineteenth-century mansion, with a pool, restaurant and comfortable en-suite rooms. **€75**

Izan Trujillo Pza. del Campillo 1 ☎ 927 458 900, ⊛ izanhoteles.es. Situated in the converted Convento de San Antonio, this swish four-star hotel has 72 classically decorated double rooms, a swimming pool and a covered patio-bar area. **€85**

★**El Mirador de las Monjas** Pza. de Santiago 2 ☎ 927 659 223, ⊛ elmiradordelasmonjas.com. Up in the old part of town by the castle, this homely *hostería* has five comfy rooms with modern bathrooms and a good restaurant serving some excellent local produce and a varied €20 set menu. **€50**

Palacio Santa María C/Ballesteros 6 ☎ 927 659 190, ⊛ nh-hotels.com. A chain hotel, but more atmospheric than its brethren, set in a beautiful refurbished sixteenth-century mansion and tucked down a small street behind the Pza. Mayor. Slick, modern facilities, including a rooftop pool. **€105**

Parador de Trujillo Pza. Santa Beatriz de Silva ☎ 927 321 350, ⊛ www.paradores.es. Top-end accommodation in a sixteenth-century former *convento* north of the Pza. Mayor. Two beautiful cloistered patio areas and large rooms. **€130**

Pensión Emilia C/Pza. Campillo 28 ☎ 927 320 083, ⊛ laemilia.com. A clean and comfortable *pensión* located down by the main road into town, with warm decor and a restaurant and bar downstairs. **€55**

★**Posada dos Orillas** C/Cambrones 6 ☎ 927 659 079, ⊛ dosorillas.com. Thirteen individually designed rooms in this converted inn in the heart of the old quarter. It has a delightful patio area where you can have breakfast and a restaurant serving up some imaginative, well-presented salads and local specialities. **€70**

EATING AND DRINKING

There are plenty of **bar-restaurants** on the Pza. Mayor, and for budget eating, all the *pensiones* around Pza. Campillo have reasonably priced set menus on offer. At the weekend, **nightlife** revolves around the streets splaying out of Pza. Mayor and down in the newer parts of town.

El 7 de Sillerías Sillerías 7 ☎ 927 321 856, ⊛ el7desillerias.com. Friendly service, a café/bar area, a pleasant interior patio and a €14 *menú del día* that is a notch above many of the other restaurants in its class. Located close to the Pza. Mayor. Daily 12.30–4pm & 8.30pm–midnight.

Bizcocho Pza. Mayor 11 ☎ 927 322 017, ⊛ restaurante bizcochotrujillo.com. A reliable restaurant serving regional specialities and good meat dishes. It has two separate dining areas and a summer terrace looking out on to the plaza. Around €40 a head. Daily 12.30–5pm & 8pm–midnight.

El Burladero Pza. Mayor 7 ☎ 927 321 501. A good bar to start the night, serving imaginative tapas and a decent selection of wine. Normally daily 1.30–5pm & 8pm–midnight.

Emilia C/Pza. Campillo 28 ☎ 927 321 216, ⊛ laemilia .com. A *pensión* located down towards the main road, which offers one of the most competitive set menus in town. Daily 1–4pm & 9–11.30pm.

Mesón La Troya Pza. Mayor 10 ☎ 927 321 364. Trujillo's best-known restaurant. Offers a huge set menu for €15, although it is a case of quantity over quality and they'll probably serve you a giant *tortilla* as a starter before you have even ordered. Daily 1–4.30pm & 8.30–11.30pm.

★**Pizarro** Pza. Mayor 13 ☎ 927 310 925. Rather better quality food than *La Troya* and more manageable quantities, costing around €30 à la carte, and about half that for the set menu. Mon & Wed –Sun 1–4pm.

La Sonata C/Ballesteros 10 ☎ 927 322 884, ⓦ lasonata .es. Tucked away in a street just north of the Pza. Mayor,

this serves some well-presented Extremeño specialities. It does a decent menu for €10 and a more sophisticated version featuring mains such as duck and lamb for €25. Daily 1–4.30pm & 7.30pm–midnight.

Guadalupe

The small town of **GUADALUPE**, perched up in the sierra to the west of Trujillo, is dominated in every way by the great **Monasterio de Nuestra Señora de Guadalupe**, which for five centuries has brought fame and pilgrims to the area. It was established in 1340, on the spot where an ancient image of the Virgin, said to have been carved by St Luke, was discovered by a shepherd fifty or so years earlier. The delay was simply a question of waiting for the Reconquest to arrive in this remote sierra, with its lush countryside of forests and streams. In the fifteenth and sixteenth centuries, Guadalupe was among the most important pilgrimage centres in Spain: Columbus named the Caribbean island in honour of the Virgin here, and a local version was adopted as the patron saint of Mexico. Much of the monastic wealth, in fact, came from returning **conquistadores**, whose successive endowments led to a fascinating mix of styles. The monastery was abandoned in the nineteenth-century Dissolution, but was later reoccupied by Franciscans, who continue to maintain it.

The town itself is a fitting complement to the monastery and countryside: a network of narrow cobbled streets and overhanging houses constructed around the Pza. Mayor, the whole overshadowed by the monastery's bluff ramparts. There's a timeless feel, only slightly diminished by modern development on the outskirts, and a brisk trade in plastic copies of religious treasures.

The church and monastery

Church Daily 8.30am–9pm • Free **Monastery** Daily 9.30am–1.30pm & 3.30–6.30pm • Guided tour €5, 6–14-year-olds €2.50 • ☎ 927 367 000, ⓦ monasterioguadalupe.com

The **monastery church** opens onto the Pza. Mayor (aka Pza. de Santa María). Its gloomy Gothic interior is, like the rest of the monastery, packed with treasures from generations of wealthy patrons.

The entrance to the **monastery** proper is to the left of the church. The (compulsory) guided tour begins with a Mudéjar **cloister** – two brick storeys of horseshoe arches with a strange pavilion or tabernacle in the middle – and moves on to the **museums**, with an apparently endless collection of rich vestments, early illuminated manuscripts and religious paraphernalia, along with some fine artworks including a triptych by Isenbrandt and a small Goya. The **Sacristía**, beyond, is the finest room in the monastery. Unaltered since it was built in the seventeenth century, it contains eight paintings by Zurbarán, which, uniquely, can be seen in their original context – the frames match the window frames and the pictures themselves are a planned part of the decoration of the room.

Climbing higher into the heart of the monastery, you pass through various rooms filled with jewels and relics before the final ascent to the Holy of Holies – the Camarín. From this tiny room high above the main altar you can look down over the church while a panel is spun away to reveal the highlight of the tour – the bejewelled and richly dressed **image of the Virgin**. The Virgin is one of the few black icons ever made – originally carved out of dark cedarwood, its colour has further deepened over the centuries under innumerable coats of varnish. The story goes that the image was originally carved by St Luke, made its way to Spain and was then hidden during the Arab occupation for over five hundred years. It was eventually rediscovered by a local cowherd on the banks of the Río Guadalupe at the beginning of the thirteenth century.

On the way out, drop in at the **Hospedería del Real Monasterio**, around to the right. The bar, in its Gothic cloister, with lovely gardens outside, is one of the world's more unusual places to enjoy a *Cuba libre*.

ARRIVAL AND DEPARTURE

GUADALUPE

By bus Buses leave from either side of Avda. de Barcelona, uphill from the *ayuntamiento*, 200m from the Pza. Mayor: Mirat operates services to Trujillo and Cáceres, Samar runs buses to Madrid (some change at Talavera de a Reina). Destinations Cáceres (2 daily; 2hr 30min); Madrid (1–2 daily; 3hr 45min); Trujillo (2 daily; 2hr–2hr 30min).

INFORMATION

Turismo Pza. Mayor (daily 10am–2pm & 4–7pm; ☎ 927 154 128, ⊛ oficinadeturismoguadalupe.blogspot.com.es).

ACCOMMODATION

There are plenty of **places to stay** in Guadalupe and the only times you're likely to have difficulty finding a room are during Easter Week or around September 8, the Virgin's festival day.

★ **Hospedaría del Real Monasterio** Pza. Juan Carlos s/n ☎ 927 367 000, ⊛ hotelhospederiamonasterio guadalupe.com. Housed in a wing of the monastery and popular with Spanish pilgrims, this place is much better value than the parador, very atmospheric and serves excellent food in the giant dining room, too. **€72**

Hostal Alba Taruta C/Alfonso Onceno 16 ☎ 927 254 144, ⊛ hostalalbataruta.com. Friendly, family-run *hostal* close to the main plaza with simple old-style rooms. The *comedor* downstairs serves an inexpensive range of *platos*. **€60**

Hostal Casa Isabel C/Nueva de los Capellanes 12 ☎ 927 367 126, ⊛ hostalisabelguadalupe.es. A modern ten-room *hostal* close to the Pza. Mayor offering neat, comfortable en-suite rooms with a bar downstairs. **€50**

Parador de Guadalupe C/Marqués de la Romana 12 ☎ 927 367 075, ⊛ www.paradores.com. A beautiful parador, housed in a fifteenth-century hospital and a former school, with a swimming pool and immaculate patio gardens. **€115**

CAMPING

Las Villuercas ☎ 927 367 139, ⊛ camping lasvilluercasguadalupe.es. Some 2km out of town towards Trujillo, close to the main road. A quiet campsite with a pool and bar-restaurant. Open all year. **€18**

EATING AND DRINKING

You can **eat** at most *hostales* and *pensiones*, with just about everywhere – including the restaurants on Pza. Mayor – serving set menus for around €11.

Hospedaría del Real Monasterio Pza. Juan Carlos s/n ☎ 927 367 000, ⊛ hotelhospederiamonasterio guadalupe.com. A great setting for a meal, with a choice of the grand dining room or the outdoor courtyard. Meals cost €25–35, but they also do a set menu for under €20. Daily 1.30–3.30pm & 9–10.30pm.

Mesón del Cordero C/Alfonso Onceno 27 ☎ 927 367 131. Serves good home cooking with grand views from the dining room thrown in. Roast lamb and local vegetable produce are the specialities. Good value at around €25–30 a head. Tues–Sun 1.30–4pm & 8.30–11.30pm.

The Sierra de Guadalupe

A truly superb view of Guadalupe set in its sierra can also be enjoyed from the road (EX118) north to Navalmoral. Five kilometres out of town, the **Ermita del Humilladero** marks the spot where pilgrims traditionally caught their first glimpse of the monastery.

The surrounding **Sierra de Guadalupe** is a wild and beautiful region, with steep, rocky crags abutting the valley sides. If you have your own transport, you could strike northwest of the EX102 at Cañamero, up to the village of **Cabañas del Castillo**, nestling against a massive crag and ruined castle; the handful of houses are mostly empty, as only twelve inhabitants remain. Beyond here, you can reach the main **Navalmoral–Trujillo road** close to the **Puerto de Miravete**, a fabulous viewpoint, with vistas of Trujillo in the far distance. Another great driving route, again leaving the EX102 at Cañamero, is to follow the narrow road **through Berzocana** to Trujillo.

Cáceres

CÁCERES is in many ways remarkably like Trujillo. It features an almost perfectly preserved walled town, the Ciudad Monumental, packed with *solares* built on the

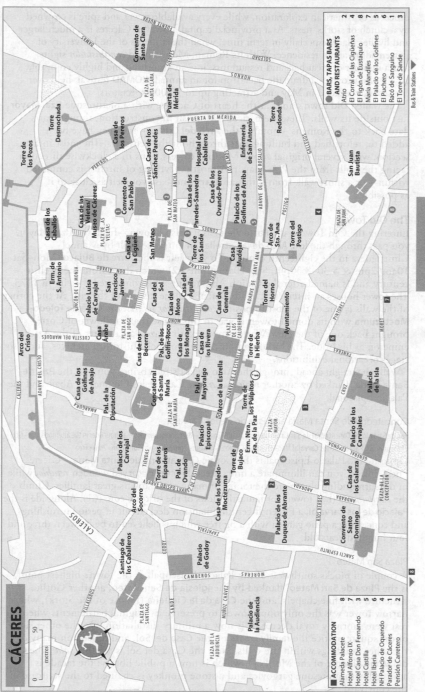

CÁCERES

0   50
metres

BARS, TAPAS BARS AND RESTAURANTS
Atrio	2
El Corral de las Cigüeñas	4
El Figón de Eustaquio	8
María Mandiles	7
El Palacio de los Golfines	5
El Puchero	6
Racó de Sanguino	1
El Torre de Sande	3

Bus & Train Stations ▶

ACCOMMODATION
Alameda Palacete	8
Hotel Alfonso IX	3
Hotel Casa Don Fernando	7
Hotel Castilla	5
Hotel Iberia	6
NH Palacio de Oquendo	4
Parador de Cáceres	1
Pensión Carretero	2

AS & N521 ▶

proceeds of American exploration, while every available tower and spire is crowned by a clutch of storks' nests. As a provincial capital, however, Cáceres is a much larger and livelier place, especially in term time, when the students of the University of Extremadura are in residence. With its Roman, Moorish and *conquistador* sights, and a number of great bars and restaurants, it is an absorbing and highly enjoyable city. It also provides a dramatic backdrop for an annual **WOMAD** festival, held over the second weekend in May and attracting up to 70,000 spectators.

The walled **Old Town** stands at the heart of Cáceres, with a picturesque **Pza. Mayor** just outside its walls. These are basically Moorish in construction, though parts date back to the Romans – notably the **Arco del Cristo** – and they have been added to, refortified and built against throughout the centuries. The most intact section, with several original adobe Moorish towers, runs in a clockwise direction, facing the walls from the Pza. Mayor. Almost everything of interest is contained within – or a short walk from – this area; try and base yourself as close to it as possible.

3

The Old Town

Entering the Old Town – the **Parte Vieja**, as it's also known – from the Pza. Mayor, you pass through the low **Arco de la Estrella**, an entrance built by Manuel Churriguera in the eighteenth century. To your left is the **Torre de Bujaco** (Mon–Sat 10am–2pm & 5.30–8.30pm, Sun 10am–2pm; €2) which dates from the twelfth century and is named after the Caliph Abú-Ya'qub who conquered the city in 1173. The tower houses an interactive exhibition about the history of the city. At the corner of the walls is one of the most imposing *conquistador solares*, the **Casa de Toledo-Moctezuma** with its domed tower. It was to this house that a follower of Cortés brought back one of the New World's more exotic prizes, a daughter of the Aztec emperor, as his bride. The building houses the provincial historical archives, and also stages occasional exhibitions.

Walking straight ahead through the Arco de la Estrella brings you into the **Pza. de Santa María**, flanked by another major *solar*, the Casa de los Golfines de Abajo and the Palacio Episcopal.

Concatedral de Santa María and Palacio de los Carvajal

Pza. de Santa María **Concatedral de Santa María** Daily 10am–2pm & 5–8pm (open and closes an hour later in the afternoon May–Oct) • €1 for museum **Palacio de los Carvajal** Mon–Fri 8am–9.15pm, Sat 10am–2pm & 5–8pm, Sun 10am–2pm • Free

Opposite the Palacio Episcopal is the Gothic **Concatedral de Santa María** – Cáceres' finest. Inside, you can illuminate a fine sixteenth-century carved wooden *retablo*, while in the surrounding gloom are the tombs of many of the town's great families. Climb the *campanario* (bell tower) for fantastic views of the historic core (€1). Alongside is the **Palacio de los Carvajal**, a fifteenth-century mansion decked out in period furnishings and concealing a patio garden with a fig tree which is believed to be between three and four hundred years old.

Plaza San Mateo

A couple of blocks southwest of the Palacio Episcopal, at the town's highest point, is the **Plaza de San Mateo**, flanked by the **Iglesia de San Mateo**, another Gothic structure with fine chapels, and the **Casa de la Cigüeña** (House of the Stork), whose narrow tower was the only one allowed to preserve its original battlements when the rest were shorn by royal decree. It is now a military installation. On the other side of the square, notice the **family crests** on the **Casa del Sol**, and indeed on many of the other buildings within the walls. Near the Casa del Sol is another *solar*, the **Casa del Mono** (House of the Monkey), which is now a public library; the facade is adorned with grotesque gargoyles and a stone monkey is chained to the staircase in the courtyard.

Museo de Cáceres

Pza. de las Veletas • Mid-April to Sept Tues–Sat 9am–3pm & 5–8.30pm, Sun 10am–3pm; Oct to mid-April Tues–Sat 9am–3pm & 4–7.30pm, Sun 10am–3pm • ☎ 927 01 08 77, ⓦ museodecaceres.blogspot.com.es • €1.20, EU citizens free

Just behind Pza. San Mateo, in the Pza. de las Veletas, is the **Casa de las Veletas**, which houses the archeology and ethnology sections of the **Museo de Cáceres**. The collections here take second place to the building itself: its beautifully proportioned rooms are arrayed around a small patio and preserve the *aljibe* (cistern) of the original Moorish Alcázar with its horseshoe arches. It also has an extraordinary balustrade, created from Talavera ceramic jugs.

From here, a footbridge leads to the museum's art collection in the **Casa de los Caballos** (House of Horses), open mornings only. The modern art and sculpture includes works by Miró, Picasso and Eduardo Arroyo, while the highlight of the medieval section is El Greco's *Jesús Salvador*.

Casa Árabe/Museo Yusuf Al Burch

Cuesta del Marqués 4 • Variable hours but generally daily 10am–2pm & 6–8pm • €1.50

A short stroll away along C/Rincón de la Monja is the **Casa Árabe**. The owner of this Moorish house has had the bright idea of decorating it more or less as it would have been when occupied by its original owner. The Alhambra it's not, but it at least provides a context for all the horseshoe arches and curving brick ceilings and it still possesses the original cistern supplied by water from the roof.

Casa de los Golfines de Arriba

Something could be said about almost every other building in the Old Town, but look out, too, for the **Casa de los Golfines de Arriba** on C/Adarve Padre Rosalío, the alleyway that runs alongside the walls parallel to the Pza. Mayor. It was in this latter *conquistador* mansion that Franco had himself proclaimed Generalísimo and head of state in October 1936.

Outside the walls

Outside the walls, it's worth wandering up to the sixteenth-century **church of Santiago de los Caballeros**, which fronts the plaza of the same name, opposite a more or less contemporary mansion, **Palacio de Godoy**, with its corner balcony. The church, open only for Masses, has a fine *retablo* by Alonso Berruguete. For a good **view** of the Old Town, exit the walls through the Arco del Cristo down to the main road and turn right onto C/Fuente Concejo, following the signs for about five minutes or so.

ARRIVAL AND DEPARTURE   CÁCERES

By train or bus Both the train and bus stations are around 3km out from the old town, at the far end of Avda. de Alemania. It's not a particularly enjoyable walk, so it's best to take bus #1, which runs down the *avenida* to Pza. de San Juan, a square adjoining the Pza. Mayor; an irregular shuttle bus from the train station (free if you show a rail ticket) also runs into town, to the Pza. de América, a major traffic junction west of the Old Town.
Train destinations Badajoz (4–6 daily; 1hr 45min); Madrid (4–5 daily; 3hr 45min–4hr); Mérida (4–6 daily; 50min–1hr).

Bus destinations Alcántara (2–4 daily; 1hr 30min); Badajoz (7 daily; 1hr 15min); Coria (2 daily; 1hr 15min); Madrid (7 daily; 3hr 40min–4hr 45min); Mérida (3 daily; 1hr); Plasencia (4–5 daily; 1hr 20min); Salamanca (8 daily; 3hr–3hr 45min); Seville (3–6 daily; 3hr 10min–3hr 45min); Trujillo (8 daily; 45min).
By car If you're driving, be warned that increasing pedestrianization is making access to some streets impossible by car; your best bet is to park on Avda. de España, on the main road in from Madrid, or outside the Old Town.

INFORMATION

Turismo Pza. Mayor (Wed–Fri 9am–2pm & 4–6pm, summer 8am–3pm, Sat & Sun 10am–2pm; ☎ 927 010 834, ⓦ turismoextremadura.com and ⓦ turismo.caceres .es). In addition to this regional *turismo* there is a municipal office (summer Tues–Sun 10am–2pm & 5.30–8.30pm; winter Tues–Sun 10am–2pm & 4.30–7.30pm, ☎ 927 247 172) opposite the parador in the Old Town at C/Olmo 11.

ACCOMMODATION

★**Alameda Palacete** C/Margallo 45 ☎927 211 674, ⓦalamedapalacete.com. Eight fascinatingly decorated rooms, each with its own individual ambience in this delightful little hotel not far from the Pza. Mayor. Suites are available for between €60 and €80. Breakfast included. **€60**

Hotel Alfonso IX C/Moret 20 ☎927 246 400, ⓦhotelalfonsoix.com. Well located on a pedestrianized street off C/Pintores, this 37-room hotel offers smart en-suite rooms with a/c and satellite TV. Apartments are also available through the website. **€50**

★**Hotel Casa Don Fernando** Pza. Mayor 30 ☎927 214 279, ⓦcasadonfernando.com. Perfectly situated on the main plaza, this slick, designer-style hotel has 38 stylishly furnished doubles, including some large attic rooms, and a decent café-bar. Website offers can bring the price down to around €70. **€132**

Hotel Castilla C/Ríos Verdes 3 ☎927 244 404, ⓦhotelcastillacaceres.com. Upgraded from a *hostal* to a hotel, the Castilla has neat, functional en-suite rooms and a

good central location. **€75**

Hotel Iberia C/Pintores 2 ☎927 247 634, ⓦwww .hotelplazamayor.iberiahotel.com. A tastefully restored 38-room hotel, complete with period furnishings, located in a mansion in a corner of the Pza. Mayor. Breakfast included. **€75**

NH Palacio de Oquendo Pza. de San Juan 11 ☎927 215 800, ⓦnh-hotels.com. Now part of the NH chain, this smart, well-appointed hotel is in a sixteenth-century palace, just outside the walls of the Old Town, and is in many ways a nicer and certainly better value place than the parador. **€105**

Parador de Cáceres C/Ancha 6 ☎927 211 759, ⓦwww.paradores.com. The parador occupies an elegant and atmospheric *conquistador* mansion in the Ciudad Monumental – the only hotel within the walls. **€140**

Pensión Carretero Pza. Mayor 22–23 ☎927 247 482, ⓦcaceresjoven.com. Basic, but great-value *pensión* with large doubles and spotless bathrooms – though some rooms can be noisy at the weekend. **€30**

EATING, DRINKING AND NIGHTLIFE

There is a good range of **bars**, **restaurants** and **bodegas** in and around the Pza. Mayor, while the Old Town offers a bit more style at modest prices. Cáceres has the best nightlife in the region – especially during termtime – with the night starting off in the bars along C/Pizarro, south of Pza. de San Juan, moving on to C/Dr Fleming and the discos in the nearby Pza. de Albatros. There are several late-night bars around Pza. Mayor and a string of interesting watering holes in and around C/Donoso Cortés, while live music can be heard in many places along the nearby C/General Ezponda.

RESTAURANTS

★**Atrio** Pza. de San Mateo 1 ☎927 242 928, ⓦrestauranteatrio.com. An exclusive Michelin-starred restaurant, now relocated in the Old Town in a designer hotel of the same name, with an extensive menu and sophisticated food. As you would expect the food is superlative, but so are the prices with the taster menus starting at around €100. Daily 1–4pm & 8.30–11.30pm.

★**El Figón de Eustaquio** Pza. de San Juan 12 ☎927 244 362, ⓦelfigondeeustaquio.com. This long-established and popular restaurant features an extensive list of regional dishes, cooked with care. Allow €25–30 a head, although there are a range of lunchtime menus from €17 to €22. Daily around 1.30–4pm & 8–11.30pm.

El Palacio de los Golfines C/Adarve Padre Rosalío 2 ☎927 242 414, ⓦpalaciogolfines.es. Stylishly presented food in a magnificent setting in an old palace just inside the city walls. There's an extensive wine list, too. Expect to pay around €35. Mon–Sat 1.30–4pm & 8.30–11.30pm, Sun 1.30–4pm.

El Puchero Pza. Mayor 10 ☎927 232 241, ⓦrestauranteelpuchero.com. The cheapest restaurant on the plaza, with an ever-popular *terraza*; home-style cooking and main courses around the €8–12 mark. Tues–Sun 8am–11.30pm.

Racó de Sanguino Pza. de las Veletas 4 ☎927 227 682, ⓦracodesanguino.es. Located in an old square inside the walled down and next to the Museo de Cáceres, this restaurant has an extensive selection of quality regional dishes and wines as well as some creative tapas. There is a good-value €12 set lunch on offer too. Mon noon–4pm, Tues–Sat noon–4pm & 8–11pm.

★**El Torre de Sande** C/Los Condes 3 ☎927 211 147, ⓦtorredesande.com. Another top-class restaurant in the middle of the Old Town, it has refined food and attentive service for around €50 a head. There is a delightful summer terrace serving tapas and *raciones* too. Daily 1–4pm & 7pm–midnight; closed Sun eve & Mon.

BARS

★**El Corral de las Cigüeñas** Cuesta de Aldana 6 ☎927 217 425. A beautiful spot in the Old Town with tables in a large, palm-shaded courtyard. A great place to enjoy a breakfast snack, a lunchtime *aperitivo* or a night-time cocktail. Live music and other acts. Daily winter 7pm–late, summer 1pm–late.

María Mandiles C/Sergio Sanchéz 7. This popular bar a few minutes' walk to the northwest of the Old Town is hard to miss with its pink exterior and dark wooden decor. A good music selection at night with 1980s and 1990s classics at weekends. Daily 8pm–late.

Northwest of Cáceres

Northwest of Cáceres is the vast **Embalse de Alcántara**, one of a series of reservoirs harnessing the power of the Río Tajo in the last few kilometres before it enters Portugal. The scheme swallowed up large tracts of land and you can see the old road and railway to Plasencia disappearing into the depths of the reservoir (their replacements cross the many inlets on double-decker bridges), along with the tower of a castle.

The EX207 loops away to the south of the reservoir, through **Arroyo de la Luz** and **Brozas**, each with fine churches, before reaching **Alcántara**, with its superb Roman bridge across the Tajo. The Portuguese border – and the road to Costelo Branco and Coimbra – is just a dozen kilometres beyond.

Alcántara

The name **ALCÁNTARA** comes from the Arabic for "bridge" – in this case a beautiful six-arched **Puente Romano** spanning a gorge of the Río Tajo. Completed in 105 AD, and held together without mortar, it was reputed to be the loftiest bridge ever built in the Roman Empire, although it's far from certain which bits, if any, remain genuinely Roman.

The bridge is quite a distance from the town itself, which is built high above the river; if you're on foot, don't follow the signs via the road – instead, head to the far side of the town and down the steep cobbled path.

Further Roman remains include a **triumphal arch** dedicated to Trajan and a tiny **classical temple**. The dominating landmark, however, is the restored **Convento San Benito**, erstwhile headquarters of the Knights of Alcántara, one of the great orders of the Reconquest. For all its enormous bulk, the convent and its church are only a fragment; the nave of the church was never built. Outside, the main feature is the double-arcaded Renaissance gallery at the back; it serves as the backdrop for a season of classical plays in August. Entry to the convent (frequent guided tours all day Tues–Sat & Sun morning; free) is through the adjacent Fundación de San Benito, which has been making attempts to restore the cloister and the Plateresque east end with its elaborate wall tombs.

Alcántara also contains the scanty remains of a **castle**, numerous **mansions** and street after street of humble whitewashed houses. The place is marvellous for scenic walks, whether in the town, along the banks of the Tajo or – best of all – in the hills on the opposite bank.

ARRIVAL AND INFORMATION   ALCÁNTARA

By bus Buses, which run twice a day to and from Cáceres, stop at a little square ringed by cafés at the entrance to the historic part of the town.
Turismo Avda. de Mérida 21 (May–Sept Tues–Fri

10am–2pm & 5–7pm, Sat & Sun 10.30am–2.30pm; Oct–April Tues–Fri 10am–2pm & 4.30–6.30pm, Sat & Sun 10.30am–2.30pm; ☎ 927 390 863, ⓦ alcantara.es). Very helpful and can provide a town map.

ACCOMMODATION

Hospedería Conventual Carretera Poblado de Iberdrola s/n ☎ 927 390 368, ⓦ hospederiasdeextremadura.es. A little way to the north of the town, this

good-value thirty-room hotel is housed in a beautifully restored fifteenth-century convent. Large rooms, modern bathrooms, a pool and a good restaurant. **€70**

Mérida

Some 70km to the south of Cáceres on the N630, the former capital of the Roman province of Lusitania, **MÉRIDA** (the name is a corruption of *Emerita Augusta*), contains more **Roman remains** than any other city in Spain. Even for the most casually interested, the extent and variety of the remains here are compelling, with everything from engineering works to domestic villas, by way of cemeteries and places of worship, entertainment and culture. With a little imagination, and a trip to the wonderful modern museum, the Roman city is not difficult to evoke – which is just as well, for the modern city, in which the sites are scattered, is no great shakes.

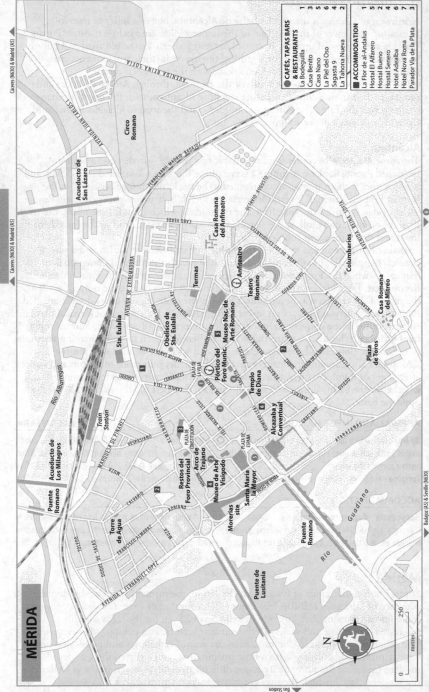

MÉRIDA

CAFÉS, TAPAS BARS & RESTAURANTS
La Bodeguilla 1
Casa Benito 3
Casa Nano 5
La Piel del Oso 6
Sagasta 9 4
La Tahona Nueva 2

ACCOMMODATION
La Flor de al-Andalus 1
Hostal El Alfarero 5
Hostal Bueno 2
Hostal Senero 4
Hotel Adealba 6
Hotel Nova Roma 7
Parador Vía de la Plata 3

Each July and August, the Roman theatre in Mérida hosts a **theatre festival** (wfestivaldemerida.es), including performances of classical Greek plays and Shakespeare's Roman tragedies.

The Roman sites

Built on the site of a Celtiberian settlement and founded by Emperor Augustus in 25 BC as a home for retired legionaries, Mérida became the tenth city of the Roman Empire and the final stop on the Vía de la Plata, the Roman road that began in Astorga in northern Castile. The old city stretched as far as the modern bullring and Roman circus, covering only marginally less than the triangular area occupied by the modern town.

The Puente Romano and Alcazaba

Daily April–Sept 9am–9pm, Oct–March 9.30am–7pm • Combined ticket or €4

The obvious point to begin your tour is the magnificent **Puente Romano**, the bridge across the islet-strewn Río Guadiana. It is sixty arches long (the seven in the middle are fifteenth-century replacements) and was still in use until the early 1990s, when the nearby **Puente de Lusitania** – itself a structure to admire – was constructed by Spanish architect Santiago Calatrava.

Defence of the old bridge was provided by a vast **Alcazaba**, built by the Moors to replace a Roman construction. The interior is a rather barren archeological site, although in the middle there's an *aljibe* to which you can descend by either of a pair of staircases.

Templo de Diana to the Arco Trajano

Museo de Arte Visigodo Tues–Sat: April–Sept 9.30am–8pm; Oct–March 9.30am–6.30pm, Sun 10am–3pm • Free

Northeast of the Alcazaba, past the airy sixteenth-century Pza. de España, the heart of the modern town, is the so-called **Templo de Diana**, adapted into a Renaissance mansion, and farther along are remains of the **Foro**, the heart of the Roman city. To the west of the plaza in C/Santa Julia, the Convento de Santa Clara houses the **Museo de Arte Visigodo**, with a collection of about a hundred lapidary items. It will eventually be housed alongside the Museo Nacional de Arte Romano. Just behind here is the great **Arco Trajano**, once wrongly believed to be a triumphal arch; it was, in fact, a marble-clad granite monumental gate to the forum.

Morerías archeological site

Daily April–Sept 9am–2pm & 5.30–7.30pm, Oct–March 9.30am–2pm & 4–7pm • Combined ticket or €4

Heading to the river from the Arco Trajano you'll also discover the **Morerías archeological site** along C/Morerías, where you can watch the digging and preservation of houses and factories from Roman through Visigoth to Moorish times – particularly of interest are the well-preserved Roman mosaics.

Teatro Romano, Anfiteatro and Casa Romana del Anfiteatro

Daily April–Sept 9am–9pm, Oct–March 9.30am–7pm • **Teatro Romano and Anfiteatro** Combined ticket or €8 • **Casa Romana del Anfiteatro** Combined ticket or €4

A ten-minute walk east of the Pza. de España will take you to Mérida's main archeological site containing the theatre and amphitheatre. The elaborate and beautiful

---

COMBINED TICKET IN MÉRIDA

The best way to see the Roman sights is to buy the excellent-value **combined ticket**, costing €12 (9–16-year-olds, pensioners and holders of student cards €6 if EU citizens) and valid over a number of days. It covers the Teatro Romano and Anfiteatro, the Roman villas Casa del Anfiteatro and Casa del Mitreo, the Columbarios burial ground, the Circo Romano, the archeological site at Morerías, the Alcazaba and the Basílica de Santa Eulalia though not the Museo de Arte Romano, and is available at any of the sites.

Teatro Romano is one of the best preserved anywhere in the Roman Empire. Constructed around 15 BC, it was a present to the city from Agrippa, as indicated by the large inscription above the passageway to the left of the stage. The stage itself, a two-tier colonnaded affair, is in particularly good shape, and many of the seats have been entirely rebuilt to offer more comfort to the audiences of the annual July and August season of classical plays (@ festivaldemerida.es).

Adjoining the theatre is the **Anfiteatro**, a slightly later and very much plainer construction. As many as 15,000 people – almost half the current population of Mérida – could be seated to watch gladiatorial combats and fights with wild animals. The **Casa Romana del Anfiteatro** lies immediately below the museum, and offers an approach to it from the site. It has wonderful mosaics, including a vigorous depiction of grape-treading.

The Museo Nacional de Arte Romano

April–Sept Tues–Sat 9.30am–8pm, Sun 10am–3pm; Oct–March Tues–Sat 9.30am–6.30pm, Sun 10am–2pm • €3, free Sat after 2pm & Sun am

The **Museo Nacional de Arte Romano**, constructed in 1986 above the Roman walls, is a wonderfully light, accessible building, using a free interpretation of classical forms to present the mosaics and sculpture as if emerging from the ruins. The exhibits, displayed on three levels of the basilica-like hall, include statues from the theatre, the Roman villa of **Mitreo** (see below) and the vanished forum, and a number of mosaics – the largest being hung on the walls so that they can be examined at each level. Individually, the finest exhibits are probably the three statues, displayed together, depicting Augustus, the first Roman emperor; his son Tiberius, the second emperor; and Drusus, Augustus' heir apparent until (it is alleged) he was murdered by Livia, Tiberius' mother.

The ruins outside the centre

Santa Eulalia April–Sept 9.30am–2pm & 5–7.30pm, Oct–March 9.30am–2pm & 4–7pm • **Casa del Mitreo and Columbarios burial ground** April–Sept Daily 9am–9pm, Oct–March 9.30am–2pm & 4–7pm • Combined ticket or €4 each

The remaining monuments are on the other side of the train tracks. From the museum, it's a fifteen-minute walk if you cut down the streets towards Avenida de Extremadura and then head east out of the city to the **Circo Romano**, essentially an outline, where up to 30,000 spectators could watch horse and chariot races. Across the road from here, a stretch of the **Acueducto de San Lázaro** leads off towards the Río Albarregas.

The more impressive aqueduct, however, is the **Acueducto de los Milagros**, of which a satisfying portion survives in the midst of vegetable gardens, west of the train station. Its tall arches of granite, with brick courses, brought water to the city in its earliest days from the reservoir at Proserpina, 5km away. The best view of the aqueduct is from a low and inconspicuous **Puente Romano** across the Río Albarregas; it was over this span that the Vía de la Plata entered the city.

Two further sights are the church of **Santa Eulalia**, by the train station, which has a porch made from fragments of a former temple of Mars, and a second Roman villa, the **Mitreo**, in the shadow of the Pza. de Toros, south of the museum and theatres. The villa has a magnificent but damaged mosaic depicting the cosmos. A short walk away is the **Columbarios burial ground**, which has two family sepulchres and an interesting series of exhibits on Roman death rites.

Proserpina and Cornalvo reservoirs

You can swim in the **Embalse de Proserpina**, a Roman-constructed reservoir 5km north of town (special buses from Paseo de Roma, May–Aug; €1.10), and a popular escape to cool off in summer; it's lined with holiday homes, has a campsite and a small beach

area but is best avoided at weekends. Alternatively, if you have transport, head to the **Embalse de Cornalvo**, 18km east of Mérida (turn left after the village of Trujillanos). There's a Roman dyke here, and a small national park has been created in the area with walking trails in the surrounding forest.

ARRIVAL AND DEPARTURE

By train The train station is pretty central, with the theatre site and Pza. de España no more than a 10min walk away.
Destinations Badajoz (7 daily; 45min); Cáceres (5 daily; 55min); Madrid (6 daily; 4hr 40min–5hr 40min); Plasencia (3 daily; 2hr); Seville (daily; 3hr 40min).
By bus The bus station is on the other side of the river and is a grittier 20min walk from the town centre, along Avda.

de Libertad, which extends from the new single-arch bridge.
Destinations Badajoz (9 daily; 50min); Cáceres (2 daily; 1hr); Jerez de los Caballeros (1 daily; 1hr 55min); Madrid (8 daily; 4hr 15min); Salamanca (5 daily; 4hr 10min–5hr 5min); Seville (6 daily; 2hr 50min); Trujillo (4 daily; 2hr); Zafra (8 daily; 1hr 10min).

INFORMATION

Turismo Just outside the gates to the theatre and amphitheatre site (daily 9.30am–2pm & 4.30–7pm; ☎924 330 722, ⓦturismomerida.org). There is another

office (Mon–Sat 9.30am–2pm & 5–8pm; ☎924 380 191) at C/Santa Eulalia 62.

ACCOMMODATION

★ **La Flor de al-Andalus** Avda. Extremadura 6 ☎924 313 356, ⓦlaflordeal-andalus.es. A relatively new self-styled boutique *hostal* close to the train station and with eighteen rooms decorated in Andalucian style, each named after a flower and with a/c. €52
Hostal El Alfarero C/Sagasta 40 ☎924 303 183, ⓦhostalalfarero.com. A very cosy *hostal* with eleven a/c doubles, two triples and one family room. Pastel colours, stylish bathrooms and a neat little patio area. €55
Hostal Bueno C/Calvario 9 ☎924 302 977, ⓦhostal buenomerida.com. A basic but clean *hostal* – all the rooms have tiny bathrooms. Its sister *hostal*, *La Salud*, about 200m away at C/Vespasiano 41, is handy if this one is full. €33
Hostal Senero C/Holguín 12 ☎924 317 207, ⓦhostalsenero.com. A long-established, friendly *hostal*

with neat rooms situated around a quiet courtyard and close to the main plaza. €44
Hotel Adealba C/Ramiro Leal 18 ☎924 388 308, ⓦhoteladealba.com. A recent arrival on the scene, this design-conscious four-star hotel close to the Alcazaba has large rooms with wooden floors and clean lines and a spa (€15 extra). Look out for offers on the website. €120
Hotel Nova Roma C/Suárez Somonte 42 ☎924 311 262, ⓦnovaroma.com. A good location for this functional and well-established 55-room hotel. Rooms are neat, if a little old-fashioned; service is friendly and there is parking, though it will cost €10 a night. €50
Parador Vía de la Plata Pza. Constitución 3 ☎924 313 800, ⓦwww.paradores.com. Well-run and friendly parador in an eighteenth-century Baroque convent, near the Arco de Trajano. €120

EATING AND DRINKING

There is a good selection of **bars** in the area around the Roman sites and close to the train station.

La Bodeguilla C/Moreno de Vargas 2 ☎924 318 854, ⓦbraserialabodeguilla.com. Friendly service, an excellent value €10 set lunch and some very tasty à la carte dishes make this bar/restaurant popular with the locals. Reservation recommended. Daily 1–4pm & 8–11.30pm.
Casa Benito C/San Francisco 3 ☎924 330 769. An array of bullfighters' ephemera lines the walls of this bar, which serves the local speciality tapas, *pitarra* wine and good breakfasts. Mon–Sat 1–4pm & 8–11.30pm.
Casa Nano C/Castelar 3 ☎924 318 257. Pleasant restaurant, offering good fish dishes and a varied *menú del día* at €12 as well as more sophisticated options such as lamb casserole or local speciality lamb

with plums. Mon–Thurs 10am–midnight, Fri & Sat 10am–12.45am.
La Piel del Oso C/Bartolomé Torres Naharro 7. Very pleasant bar/café out past the Casa del Mitreo serving great breakfasts and cakes. Friendly service and smart minimalist decor. Daily around 8.30am–11.30pm.
Sagasta 9 C/Sagasta 9 ☎924 318 257. Smart tapas bar close to the Templo de Diana serving regional specialities with a creative touch. Mon–Thurs 10pm–midnight, Fri & Sat 10am–12.45am.
La Tahona Nueva C/Alvarado 5 ☎924 304 130. Refurbished local which stages regular gigs, exhibitions and other cultural events. Friendly and fun. Mon–Fri 9pm–2am, Sat & Sun 1pm–2am.

Badajoz

The valley of the Río Guadiana, followed by road and rail, waters rich farmland between Mérida and **BADAJOZ**. The main reason for visiting this provincial capital, traditional gateway to Portugal and the scene of innumerable sieges, is still to get across the border. It's not somewhere you'd want to stay very long – crude modern development has largely overrun what must once have been an attractive old centre, and few of the monuments have survived – but food and lodging are cheap, and it does serve as a useful stopover. The city's troubled history, springing from its strategically important position on the Río Guadiana, is its main claim to fame. Founded by the Moors in 1009, the city was taken by the Christian armies of Alfonso IX in 1230, used as a base by Felipe II against the Portuguese in 1580, stormed by British forces under the Duke of Wellington in 1812 and taken by Franco's Nationalist troops in 1936.

Catedral and the museo

Pza. de España • Museo Tues–Sat: summer 11am–1pm & 6–8pm; winter 11am–1pm & 5–7pm • €3

At the heart of old Badajoz is the **Pza. de España** and the squat thirteenth-century **Catedral**, a fortress like building, prettified a little during the Renaissance by the addition of a portal and embellishment of the tower. The **museo** contains work by local-born artist Luís de Morales (1520–86).

3

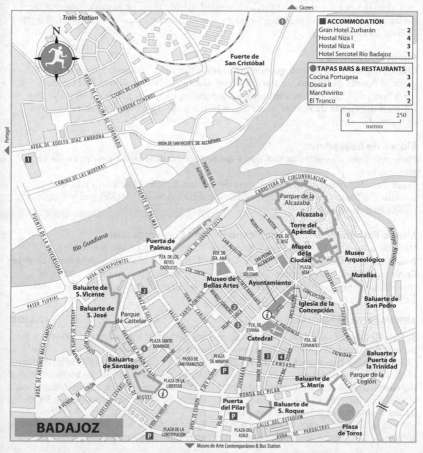

3

TO THE PORTUGUESE BORDER AND BEYOND

The **Portuguese frontier** is 4km west of Badajoz. You can get to Elvas, the first sizeable town on the Portuguese side of the border, by local bus (Mon–Fri 4 daily 7.45am–9.10pm). From here there are up to eight long-distance buses (2hr 45min–3hr 10min) to **Lisbon** each day.

Alcazaba

Museo Arqueológico Tues–Sun 10am–3pm • Free

Northeast of Pza. de España, C/San Juan leads to **Pza. Alta**, once an elegant arcaded concourse, whose facades are decorated with a dazzling Mudéjar-style design, and what remains of the town's fortress, the **Alcazaba**. This is largely in ruins but preserves Moorish entrance gates and fragments of a Renaissance palace inside. Part of it houses a **Museo Arqueológico**, with local Roman and Visigothic finds. Defending the townward side is the octagonal Moorish **Torre del Aprendiz**, or Torre Espantaperros ("dog-scarer" – the dogs in question being Christians).

Museo de la Ciudad

Pza. de Santa María • April–Sept Tues–Sat 10am–2pm & 5–8pm, Sun 10am–2pm • Free

Nearby the Alcazaba is the **Museo de la Ciudad**, which presents an interesting and well-thought-out survey of the city's chequered history from prehistoric times to the present day, as well as containing works by one of the city's most famous sons, the artist Luís de Morales.

Puente de Palmas

One of the city's main distinguishing features is the Río Guadiana, spanned by the graceful **Puente de Palmas**, or Puente Viejo. The bridge was designed by Herrera (architect of El Escorial) as a fitting first impression of Spain, and leads into the city through the **Puerta de Palmas**, once a gate in the walls, now standing alone as a sort of triumphal arch.

Museo de Bellas Artes

C/Duque de San Germán • Summer Tues–Sat 10am–2pm & 6–8pm, Sun 10am–2pm; winter Tues–Sat 10am–2pm & 4–6pm, Sun 10am–2pm • Free

From Pza. de España behind the Puerta de Palmas, C/Santa Lucía will take you towards the **Museo de Bellas Artes**, which includes works by Morales and a couple of good panels by Zurbarán.

Museo Extremeño e Iberoamericano de Arte Contemporáneo

C/Virgen de Guadalupe • Tues–Sat 10am–1.30pm & 5–8pm, Sun 10am–1.30pm • Free • ☎ 924 013 060, ⍟ meiac.es

Near Pza. de la Constitución and off Avenida Calzadillas Maestre is the **Museo de Arte Contemporáneo**. This striking circular, rust-coloured building houses a wealth of modern paintings, installations and sculpture, by artists from Spain, Portugal and Latin America.

ARRIVAL AND DEPARTURE   BADAJOZ

By train The train station is on the far side of the river, up the road that crosses the Puente de Palmas and on C/Carolina Coronado. Buses #1 and #2 go to the Pza. de la Libertad, or it's around €5 in a taxi.
Destinations Cáceres (5 daily; 1hr 40min); Madrid (7 daily; 5hr 25min–8hr 45min); Mérida (6 daily; 35–50min).
By bus If you're arriving by bus, you'll have a 15min-plus walk to the centre, as the station is located on C/José Rebollo López towards the southern edge of the

city. Your best bet is to hop on city bus #3 or #4 to Avda. de Europa.
Destinations Cáceres (3 daily; 1hr 15min–1hr 30min); Córdoba (1–3 daily; 4hr 15min–4hr 30min); Madrid (8 daily; 4hr 40min–5hr 10min); Mérida (8 daily; 45min); Olivenza (9 daily; 30min); Seville (5–7 daily; 3hr 10min); Zafra (5–7 daily; 1hr 10min).
By car For parking follow the signs to Pza. de Minayo where you'll find an attended underground car park.

INFORMATION

Turismo Pasaje San Juan, just off Pza. de España (June–Sept Mon–Fri 10am–2pm & 6–8.30pm, Sat & Sun 10am–2pm; Oct–May Mon–Fri 10am–2pm & 5–7.30pm, Sat & Sun 10am–2pm; ☎ 924 224 981, ☻ turismobadajoz.com).

ACCOMMODATION

There's plenty of **accommodation** available in Badajoz, much of it inexpensive, making it a good stopover on the way into Portugal.

Gran Hotel Zurbarán Gómez de Solís 1 ☎ 924 001 400, ☻ granhotelzurbaranbadajoz.com. A sleek, business-style hotel, with swimming pool and bar-café. Look out for weekend deals that can bring the price down to as low as €50. **€65**

Hostal Niza I and II C/Arco Agüero 34 & 45 ☎ 924 223 881, ☻ hostalnizabadajoz.com. Very simple but clean rooms with en-suite bathroom in these two well-located *hostales*. **€43**

Hotel Sercotel Río Badajoz Avda. Adolfo Díaz Ambrona s/n ☎ 924 272 600, ☻ www.hotelriobadajoz.com. At the far end of Puente de la Universidad, this upmarket 101-room hotel has a swimming pool, parking and a good restaurant. Plenty of offers available via the website. **€65**

EATING, DRINKING AND NIGHTLIFE

The area around C/Muñoz Torrero, a couple of blocks below the Pza. de España, is the most promising for reasonably priced **food** and **tapas**.

Cocina Portugesa C/Muñoz Torrero 7 ☎ 924 224 150, ☻ cocinaportuguesa.com. The best budget bet in Badajoz, with tasty, reasonably priced Portuguese cooking (mains cost between €7 and €12) and a selection of good-value menus starting at €9. Daily around 1.30–4pm & 8.30–11.30pm.

Dosca II Avda. de Colón 3, just off Pza. Santo Domingo ☎ 924 224 240, ☻ cafeteriarestaurantedoscaii.com. This place is very popular with locals, serving a wide range of satisfying, well-cooked specialities in the nautically themed restaurant. Does a generous €13.50 menu. Daily around 1.30–4pm & 8–11pm.

Marchivirito Nuestra Señora de Bótoa 37 ☎ 924 274 215. High-quality restaurant out of town on the Cáceres road with a great summer terrace, excellent starters and meat dishes and a very good wine list. The steak tartare is one of the star dishes. Prices are high, though; expect to pay around €40 a head. Mon–Sat 2–4.30pm & 9.30pm–midnight, Sun 2–4.30pm.

El Tronco C/Muñoz Torrero 16 ☎ 924 236 253. *El Tronco* has a vast range of superb-value bar snacks and excellent regional food and wine in the restaurant for well under €10 a *ración*. Mon–Sat 1.30–4pm & 8.30–11.30pm, Sun 1.30–4pm.

Southern Extremadura

The routes **south from Mérida** or **Badajoz** cross territory that is mostly harsh and unrewarding, fit only for sheep and the odd cork or olive tree, until you come upon the foothills of the Sierra Morena, on the borders of Andalucía. En route, **Olivenza**, a town that has spent more time in Portugal than Spain, is perhaps the most attractive stop, and offers a road approach to Évora, the most interesting city of southern Portugal.

Olivenza

Twenty-five kilometres southwest of Badajoz, whitewashed **OLIVENZA** seems to have landed in the wrong country; long disputed between Spain and Portugal, it has been Spanish since 1801. Yet not only are the buildings and the town's character clearly Portuguese, the oldest inhabitants still cling to this language. There's a local saying here: "The women from Olivenza are not like the rest, for they are the daughters of Spain and the granddaughters of Portugal."

The walls, castle and the Museo Etnográfico

Museo Oct–April Tues–Fri 10.30am–2pm & 4–7pm, Sat 10am–2.15pm & 4–7pm, Sun 10am–2.15pm; May–Sept Tues–Fri 10.30am–2pm & 5–8pm, Sat 10am–2.15pm & 5–8pm, Sun 10am–2.15pm • €2 • ☎ 924 49 0 222, ☻ elmuseodeolivenza.com

The town has long been strongly fortified, and traces of the **walls and gates** can still be seen, even though houses have been built up against them. They extend up to the **castle**, which has three surviving towers and holds the **Museo Etnográfico**, which displays

LAND OF THE CONQUISTADORES

Extremadura is a tough country that bred tough people, if we are to believe the names of places like Valle de Matamoros (Valley of the Moorslayers), and one can easily understand the attraction that the New World and the promise of the lush Indies must have held for its inhabitants.

Francisco Pizarro, the conqueror of Peru, and **Francisco de Orellano**, the explorer of the Amazon, both came from Trujillo, while the ruthless **Hernán Cortés**, who led the destruction of the Aztec empire, hailed from Medellín in Badajoz. Jerez de los Caballeros also produced its crop of *conquistadores*. The two most celebrated are **Vasco Núñez de Balboa**, discoverer of the Pacific, and **Hernando de Soto** (also known as the Conqueror of Florida), who in exploring the Mississippi became one of the first Europeans to set foot in North America.

an interesting and comprehensive range of exhibits detailing all aspects of life in the region and a room containing part of a 150kg meteorite that fell in the area in 1924.

Iglesias Santa María del Castillo and Santa María Magdalena

Tues–Sat 10am–2pm & 5–7pm, Sun 10am–2pm

Right beside the castle is the seventeenth-century church of **Santa María del Castillo** and around the corner, **Santa María Magdalena**, built a century later. The latter is in the distinctive Portuguese Manueline style, with arcades of twisted columns; the former is a more sober Renaissance affair with three aisles of equal height and a notable work of art in the huge "Tree of Jesse" *retablo*. Just across the street from Santa María Magdalena is a former **palace**, now the public library, with a spectacular Manueline doorway.

INFORMATION   OLIVENZA

Turismo Pza. de España (summer Tues–Fri 9am–2pm & 4–7pm, Sat 10am–2pm & 4–7pm, Sun 10am–2pm; winter Tues–Fri 9am–2pm & 4–6pm, Sat 10am–2pm & 4–7pm, Sun 10am–2pm; ☎ 924 490 151).

ACCOMMODATION AND EATING

★**Hotel Palacio Arteaga** C/Moreno Nieto 5 ☎ 924 491 129, ⓦ palacioarteaga.com. Situated in the centre of town in an elegant mansion, this boutique-style hotel has 24 individually decorated rooms with a/c and a beautiful interior patio area. It also boasts a good restaurant serving a range of Portuguese and Extremeño dishes. **€85**

Jerez de los Caballeros

The road from Badajoz to **JEREZ DE LOS CABALLEROS** is typical of southern Extremadura, striking across a parched landscape whose hamlets – low huts and a whitewashed church strung out along the road – look as if they have been dumped from some low-budget Western set of a Mexican frontier town.

Churches

San Miguel Tues–Sat noon–2pm & 5–7pm **San Bartolomé** Tues–Sat 10am–noon

Jerez de los Caballeros is a quiet, friendly place, through which many tourists pass but few stay. The church towers dominate the walled old town: a passion for building spires gripped the place in the eighteenth century, when three churches had new ones erected: the first is **San Miguel**, in the central Pza. de España, made of carved brick; the second is the unmistakeable red-, blue- and ochre-glazed tower of **San Bartolomé**, on the hill above it, with a striking tiled facade; and the third, rather dilapidated, belongs to **Santa Catalina**, outside the walls.

The Castle and the Iglesia de Santa María de Encarnación

Above the Pza. de España the streets climb up to the restored remains of a **castle** of the Knights Templar (this was once an embattled frontier town), mostly late thirteenth-century but with obvious Moorish influences. Adjoining the castle, and predating it by over a century (as do the town walls), is the **Iglesia de Santa María de Encarnación**. Built on a Visigothic site, it's more interesting seen from the battlements above than from the inside.

INFORMATION	JEREZ DE LOS CABALLEROS

Turismo Ayuntamiento, Pza. de la Constitutión (Mon–Sat 9.30am–2.30pm & 4.30–7pm, Sun 10am–2pm; ☎ 924 730 372, ⓦ turismo.jerezcaballeros.es).

ACCOMMODATION

Posada de las Cigüeñas C/Santiago 7–9 ☎ 924 731 446, ⓦ laposadadelasciguenas.com. A seven-room *posada* with a pool, bar area, a sun terrace and restaurant. Some of the individually decorated rooms have balconies with great views over the town. **€50**

Zafra

If you plan to stick to the main routes or are heading south from Mérida, **ZAFRA** is rather less of a detour than Olivenza, though it's also much more frequented by tourists. Two beautiful arcaded plazas, the Pza. Grande and the Pza. Chica, adjoin each other in the town centre. But the town is famed mainly for its **castle** – now converted into a parador – which is remarkable for the white marble Renaissance patio. The region is also renowned for its wines, and you can visit the **Bodega Medina**, C/Cestria 4 (Mon–Fri 10.30am–2pm, Sat 10am–2pm; ☎ 924 575 060, ⓦ bodegasmedina.net; by appointment through the *turismo*).

Nuestra Señora de la Candelaria

C/Tetuán • Summer Tues–Fri 11am–2pm & 6–7pm, Sat 11am–2pm & 5–7pm, Sun 11am–1pm

The most attractive of several interesting churches is **Nuestra Señora de la Candelaria**, with nine panels by Zurbarán in the *retablo* and a chapel by Churriguera; the entrance is on C/José through a small gateway, around the side of the church.

Convento de Santa Clara

C/Sevilla • Mid-June to mid-Oct Tues–Sun 10am–2pm, mid-Oct to mid-June Tues–Sun 11am–2pm & 5–6.30pm

The tombs of the Figueroa family (the original inhabitants of the castle) are worth a look. They're within the **Convento de Santa Clara**, just off the main shopping street, which also houses a museum examining the life of the nuns and their links with the town.

INFORMATION	ZAFRA

Turismo Pza. de España 8 (Mon–Fri 10am–2pm & 5–9pm, Sat & Sun 11am–2pm, winter opens and closes an hour earlier in the afternoons; ☎ 924 551 036, ⓦ visit azafra.com, ⓦ rutadelaplata.com).

ACCOMMODATION

★**Casa Palacio Conde de la Corte** C/Pilar Redondo 2 ☎ 924 563 3811, ⓦ condedelacorte.com. A beautiful, luxurious boutique-style hotel with bullfighting-themed rooms, a great Andalucian patio area and pool. Price includes breakfast. **€105**

Hostal Carmen Avda. Estación 9 ☎ 924 551 439, ⓦ hostalcarmen.com. A very tidy *hostal* with facilities closer to that of a hotel. Also boasts an excellent medium-priced restaurant with a varied set lunch. **€46**

Hotel Las Palmeras Pza. Grande 14 ☎ 924 552 208, ⓦ hotellaspalmeras.net. Well-appointed, good-value *hostal* with standard rooms, an elegant patio and bar-restaurant with a summer terraza. **€42**

Parador Pza. Corazón de María 7 ☎ 924 554 540, ⓦ www.paradores.com. Housed in a fifteenth-century castle, and the rooms in this parador are suitably palatial. A splendid courtyard, a tranquil pool and an excellent restaurant too. **€80**

EATING AND DRINKING

★**La Rebotica** C/Boticas 12 ☎ 924 554 289. A small and very popular restaurant in the centre of town (make a reservation first) with a wide selection of high-quality local dishes such as oxtail or steak with figs in brandy sauce. Expect to pay around €35 a head. Tues–Sat 1–4pm & 8.30–11.30pm, Sun 1–4pm.

Andalucía

MEZQUITA, CÓRDOBA

Andalucía

The popular image of Spain as a land of bullfights, flamenco, sherry and ruined castles derives from Andalucía, the southernmost territory and the most quintessentially Spanish part of the Iberian Peninsula. Above all, it's the great Moorish monuments that compete for your attention here. The Moors, a mixed race of Berbers and Arabs who crossed into Spain from Morocco and North Africa, occupied al-Andalus for over seven centuries. Their first forces landed at Tarifa in 710 AD, and within four years they had conquered virtually the entire country; their last kingdom, Granada, fell to the Christian Reconquest in 1492. Between these dates, they developed the most sophisticated civilization of the Middle Ages, centred in turn on the three major cities of Córdoba, Seville and Granada.

Each one of Andalucia's major cities preserves extraordinarily brilliant and beautiful monuments, of which the most perfect is **Granada**'s Alhambra palace, arguably the most sensual building in all of Europe. **Seville**, not to be outdone, has a fabulously ornamented Alcázar and the grandest of all Gothic Catedrals. Today, Andalucía's capital and seat of the region's autonomous parliament is a vibrant contemporary metropolis that's impossible to resist. **Córdoba**'s exquisite Mezquita, the grandest and most beautiful mosque constructed by the Moors, is a landmark building in world architecture and is not to be missed.

These three cities have, of course, become major tourist destinations, but it's also worth leaving the tourist trail and visiting some of the smaller **inland towns** of Andalucía. Renaissance towns such as **Úbeda**, **Baeza** and **Osuna**, Moorish **Carmona** and the stark white hill towns around **Ronda** are all easily accessible by local buses. Travelling for some time here, you'll get a feel for the landscape of Andalucía: occasionally spectacularly beautiful but more often impressive on a huge, unyielding scale.

The region also takes in mountains – including the **Sierra Nevada**, Spain's highest range. You can often ski here in March, and then drive down to the coast to swim the same day. Perhaps more compelling, though, are the opportunities for walking in the

SEMANA SANTA IN MÁLAGA

Highlights

❶ **Semana Santa** Andalucía's major Holy Week festival is memorably celebrated in Seville, Málaga, Córdoba and Granada. **See p.228**

❷ **Seville** The region's pulsating capital city is a treasure house of churches, palaces and museums. **See p.263**

❸ **Flamenco** The passionate dance, song and music of the Spanish south. **See p.283**

❹ **Sipping sherry in Jerez** Andalucía's classic wine is made in Jerez and makes the perfect partner for tapas. **See p.302**

❺ **Coto de Doñana** Explore Europe's largest and most important wildlife sanctuary. **See p.306**

❻ **Mezquita, Córdoba** This 1200-year-old Moorish mosque is one of the most beautiful ever built. **See p.316**

❼ **Alhambra** Granada's Moorish palace is the pinnacle of Moorish architectural splendour in Spain. **See p.332**

❽ **Las Alpujarras** A wildly picturesque region dotted with traditional mountain villages. **See p.350**

HIGHLIGHTS ARE MARKED ON THE MAP ON PP.226–227

lower slopes, **Las Alpujarras**. Alternatively, there's good trekking among the gentler (and much less known) hills of the **Sierra Morena**, north of Seville.

On the **coast**, it's easy to despair. Extending to either side of **Málaga** is the **Costa del Sol**, Europe's most heavily developed resort area, with its poor beaches hidden behind a remorseless density of concrete hotels and apartment complexes. However, the region offers two alternatives, much less developed and with some of the best beaches in all Spain. These are the villages **between Tarifa and Cádiz** on the Atlantic, and those **around**

ANDALUCÍA

HIGHLIGHTS

1. Semana Santa
2. Seville
3. Flamenco
4. Sipping sherry in Jerez
5. Coto de Doñana
6. Mezquita, Córdoba
7. Alhambra
8. Las Alpujarras

Almería on the southeast corner of the Mediterranean. The latter allow warm swimming in all but the winter months; those near Cádiz, more easily accessible, are fine from about June to September. Near Cádiz, too, is the **Parque Nacional Coto de Doñana**, Spain's largest and most important nature reserve, which is home to a spectacular range of flora and fauna.

The realities of life in contemporary Andalucía can be stark. **Unemployment** in the region is the highest in Spain – over forty percent in some areas – and a large

FIESTAS

FEBRUARY

1: San Cecilio Fiesta in Granada's traditionally gypsy quarter of Sacromonte.
Week before Lent: Carnaval An extravagant week-long event in all the Andalucian cities. Cádiz, above all, celebrates, with uproarious street parades, fancy dress and satirical music competitions.

MARCH/APRIL

Easter: Semana Santa (Holy Week) You'll find memorable processions of *pasos* (floats) and penitents at Seville, Málaga, Granada and Córdoba, and to a lesser extent in smaller towns such as Jerez, Arcos, Baeza and Úbeda. All culminate with dramatic candlelight processions at dawn on Good Friday, with Easter Day itself more of a family occasion.
Last week of April: Feria de Abril Week-long fair at Seville: the largest *feria* in Spain.

MAY

First week: Cruces de Mayo Celebrated in Córdoba and includes a "prettiest patio" competition in a town full of prize examples.
Early May (week after Feria de Abril): Feria del Caballo A somewhat aristocratic horse fair is held at Jerez de la Frontera.
Pentecost: Romería del Rocío Horse-drawn carriages and processions converge from all over the south on El Rocío (Huelva).
Last week: Feria de la Manzanilla Prolonged binge in Sanlúcar de Barrameda to celebrate the town's excellent manzanilla wine, with flamenco and sporting events on the river beach.

JUNE

13: San Antonio Fiesta at Trevélez (Las Alpujarras) with mock battles between Moors and Christians.
Third week The Algeciras Feria Real is another major event of the south.
End June/early July: International Festival of Music and Dance Major dance/flamenco groups and chamber orchestras perform in Granada's Alhambra palace, Generalife and Carlos V palace.

JULY

Early July: International Guitar Festival Brings together top international acts from classical, flamenco and Latin American music in Córdoba.
End of month: Virgen del Mar Almería's major annual shindig, with parades, horseriding events, concerts and lots of drinking.

AUGUST

First week The first cycle of horse races along Sanlúcar de Barrameda's beach, with heavy official and unofficial betting; the second tournament takes place two weeks later.
5: Trevélez observes a midnight *romería* to Mulhacén.
13–21: Feria de Málaga One of Andalucía's most enjoyable fiestas for visitors, who are heartily welcomed by the ebullient *malagueños*.
15: Ascension of the Virgin Fair With *casetas* (dance tents) at Vejer and elsewhere.
Noche del Vino Riotous wine festival at Competa (Málaga).
23–25: Guadalquivir festival Bullfights and an important flamenco competition, at Sanlúcar de Barrameda.

SEPTEMBER & OCTOBER

First two weeks of September: Feria de Ronda Ronda's annual *feria*, with flamenco contests and Corrida Goyesca – bullfights in eighteenth-century dress.
First/second week of September: Vendimia Celebrating the vintage at Jerez.
Sept 27–Oct 1: Feria de San Miguel In Órgiva (Las Alpujarras), featuring traditional dancing and a huge paella cook-up.

ANDALUCÍA'S CUISINE

The most striking feature of Andalucía's cuisine is its **debt to the Moors**. In their long period of hegemony over the region the North Africans introduced oranges and lemons as well as spices such as cumin and saffron and refined techniques for growing olives and almonds. Their chilled soups such as *ajo blanco* (made with ground almonds) and gazpacho are still a welcome refresher in high summer temperatures. Of course, gazpacho is today made with tomatoes and green peppers, both brought back from the Americas by Columbus, who sailed from Andalucía.

The region is also the birthplace of **tapas**, the classic titbits that Spaniards love to tuck into as they drink. Between 6pm and 9pm most evenings city bars are humming with conversations of *tapeadores* (as aficionados are termed). One of Andalucía's favourite tapas is **jamón serrano**, mountain-cured ham from prime producing zones in the Sierra de Aracena and the Alpujarras. The most prized ham of all is *jamón ibérico* from black Iberian pigs, and in the curing village of Jabugo this is graded into five levels of quality with the very best accorded five *jotas* or "j's" (for Jabugo). The taste is delicious (for those who can afford it) and far superior to the standard white-pig *jamón* sold in supermarkets.

Andalucía is also known in Spain as the *zona de los fritos* (fried food zone) and **fried fish** is a regional speciality. *Chanquetes* (whitebait), sardines, *calamares* and *boquerones* (anchovies) are all *andaluz* favourites and the seafood *chiringuitos* (beach restaurants) of Málaga are famous for their **fritura malagueña** (assorted fried fish).

Inland, Andalucía is a mountainous region and the specialities here are **carnes de caza** (game). *Jabalí* (wild boar), *venado* (venison), *cabrito* (kid) and *perdiz* (partridge) all make memorable meals in the hands of a competent chef.

The wine par excellence of Andalucía – particularly to accompany tapas – is **fino** (dry sherry) from Jerez de la Frontera, although nearby Sanlúcar de Barrameda's *manzanilla* and *montilla* (produced in Córdoba) are similar and display their own prized characteristics.

4

proportion of the population still scrapes a living from seasonal agricultural work. The *andaluz* villages, bastions of anarchist and socialist groups before and during the Civil War, saw little economic aid or change during the Franco years, and although much government spending has been channelled into improving infrastructure such as hospitals and road and rail links, the lack of employment opportunities away from the coastal tourist zones persists. For all its poverty, however, Andalucía is also Spain at its most exuberant – those wild and extravagant clichés of the Spanish south really do exist and can be absorbed at one of the hundreds of annual **fiestas**, **ferias** and **romerías**.

Málaga

MÁLAGA seems at first an uninviting place. It's the second city of the south (after Seville), with a population of over half a million, and is also one of the poorest: an estimated one in four of the workforce are jobless. Though the clusters of high-rises look pretty grim as you approach, the city does have some compelling attractions. The elegant central zone is now largely pedestrianized with the focal and marble-paved **Calle Marqués de Larios** – lined with fashionable stores – its most elegant thoroughfare. This leads into the **Pza. de la Constitución**, the city's main square, with a monumental fountain flanked by slender palms, and the terraces of numerous cafés and restaurants. The centre has a number of interesting churches and museums, not to mention the **birthplace of Picasso** and the **Museo Picasso Málaga**, housing an important collection of works by Málaga's most famous son. Perched on the hill above the town are the formidable citadels of the **Alcazaba** and **Gibralfaro**, magnificent vestiges of the seven centuries that the Moors held sway here. The city authorities hope that a revamped **seafront** and cleaned-up coastline will make the city attractive as a beach resort and has encouraged new hotels, restaurants and bars along the promenades east and west of the centre. The latest instalment of this project has seen a dramatic overhaul of the port area, now dubbed **Muelle Uno**, featuring a spectacular pergola stretched along a marina lined with shops, bars and restaurants.

Málaga is also renowned for its **fish** and **seafood**, which can be sampled at tapas bars and restaurants throughout the city, as well as at the old fishing villages of **El Palo** and **Pedregalejo**, now absorbed into the suburbs, where there's a seafront *paseo* lined with some of the best **marisquerías** and **chiringuitos** (beachside fish restaurants) in the province.

The Alcazaba

Main entrance at Pza. de la Aduana; alternatively, a lift on C/Guillen Sotelo (slightly east) will transport you to the heart of the palace, saving you the climb • All year Mon 9am–6pm; April–Oct Tues–Sun 9am–8.15pm; Nov–March Tues–Sun 8.30am–7.30pm • €2.25, €3.55 combined ticket with Gibralfaro; free entry Sun from 2pm • ☎ 630 932 987

Visible on its lofty hill from the city below, the **Alcazaba** is a magnificent example of the fortified palaces that were the focus of most Moorish cities. To the left of its

● TAPAS BARS & RESTAURANTS

Antigua Casa de Guardia	14
Antonio	10
Bar Lo Güeno	11
Bar Los Pueblos	13
Bar-Restaurante Palacios	15
Bodegas Quitapeñas	12
Cañadu	6
Il Laboratorio	4
Parador Gilbralfaro	5
Tapadaki	3
El Tapeo de Cervantes	2
El Tintero	8
Uvedoble	9
El Vegetariano	7
Vino Mío	1

■ CLUBS & BARS

Anden	3
Asúcar	2
La Botellita	4
El Pimpi	5
Pub Celtic Druids	1
Puerta Oscura	6

● SHOPPING

El Corte Inglés	4
Librería Luces	3
La Mallorquina	2
Mapas y Compañía	1

MÁLAGA

entrance on C/Acazabilla stands the **Teatro Romano** (Roman Theatre), which was accidentally discovered in 1951, and – following excavation and restoration – is now a venue for various outdoor entertainments. The citadel, too, is Roman in origin, with blocks and columns of marble interspersed among the Moorish brick of the double- and triple-arched gateways.

The main structures, expensively restored at the start of the new millennium, were begun by the Moors in the eighth century, probably soon after their conquest, but the palace higher up the hill dates from the early decades of the eleventh. This was the residence of the Arab emirs of Málaga, who carved out an independent kingdom for themselves upon the break-up of the Western Caliphate. Their independence lasted a mere thirty years, but for a while their kingdom included Granada, Carmona and Jaén. The complex's **palace** was heavily restored in the 1930s, but some fine stuccowork, the ceilings and elegant patios give a flavour of the sumptuous edifice it must once have been. The interior displays Moorish ceramics found during the archeological excavations.

ACCOMMODATION

Albergue Juvenil Málaga	11
Apartamentos San Pablo	2
Hostal La Hispanidad	13
Hostal La Palma	10
Hostal Victoria	8
Hotel California	3
Hotel Ibis	4
Hotel Larios	5
Hotel Lola	12
Hotel Málaga Palacio	7
Hotel Trebol	6
Parador Gibralfaro	1
Pensión Juanita	9

The Gibralfaro

Daily: April–Oct 9am–9pm; Nov–March 9am–6pm • Combined ticket with Alcazaba €3.55; free entry Sun from 2pm • ☎ 952 227 345

Above the Alcazaba, and connected to it by a long double wall (the *coracha*), is the **Gibralfaro castle**. It's reached by climbing a steep, twisting path that skirts the southern walls, passing bougainvillea-draped ramparts and sentry-box-shaped Moorish wells. You can also approach from the town side, as the urban buses and tourist coaches do, but this is a rather unattractive walk and not one to be done alone after sundown. If you want to avoid the climb altogether, you can take bus #35 heading east from the Paseo del Parque, which stops just outside the entrance. This would then enable you to view the Gibralfaro first, descending the hill to the Alcazaba.

Last used in 1936 during the Civil War, the castle, like the Alcazaba, has been wonderfully restored and now houses an interesting **museum** devoted to its history – a scale model lets you see how the city would have looked in Moorish times. A walk around the battlements affords terrific **views** over the city, while the nearby parador (reached by following the road leading out of the castle's car park for 100m and turning right into the parador's grounds) has a pleasant terrace café and restaurant with more fine views.

The Catedral

Mon–Fri 10am–6pm, Sat 10am–5pm; closed Sun am for services; free entry 2–6pm • €5

The city's most conspicuous edifice seen from the heights of the Gibralfaro is the peculiar, unfinished **Catedral**. Constructed between the sixteenth and eighteenth centuries, it still lacks a tower on the west front because a radical *malagueño* bishop donated the earmarked money to the American War of Independence against the British. Unfortunately – and despite its huge scale – it also lacks any real inspiration and is distinguished only by an intricately carved seventeenth-century *sillería* (choir stall) by noted sculptor Pedro de Mena. However, **Iglesia del Sagrario** (same ticket and hours), on the Catedral's northern flank, is worth a look, if only for its fine Gothic portal, dating from an earlier, uncompleted Isabelline church. Inside, a restored and magnificent gilded Plateresque **retablo**, which is brilliantly illuminated during services, is the work of Juan de Balmaseda.

Museo Picasso Málaga

C/San Agustín • July–Aug Mon–Thurs 10am–8pm, Fri–Sat 10am–9pm, Sun 10am–8pm; rest of year same hours but closed Mon; also open on certain Sat evenings throughout the summer • Permanent collection €8, temporary collection €5.50, combined ticket €10; audio-guide included with admission fee; free entry on Sunday after 6pm • ☎ 952 602 731, ⓦ museopicassomalaga.org

Just around the corner from the Catedral is the **Museo Picasso Málaga**, housed in the elegant sixteenth-century mansion of the counts of Buenavista. It was opened by the king and queen in 2003, 112 years after Picasso left Málaga at the age of 10 and to where he returned only once for an unhappy, fleeting visit in his late teens. In later life, he toyed with the idea of "sending two lorries full of paintings" to set up a museum in Málaga but vowed never to set foot in Spain while the ruling General Franco – who described the artist's work as "degenerate" – was still alive. Picasso died in 1973 and was outlived by the dictator by two years.

The **permanent collection** consists of 233 works donated by Christine and Bernard Ruiz-Picasso, the artist's daughter-in-law and grandson, while the **temporary collection** comprises loaned works and special exhibitions (not necessarily connected with Picasso). Though not on a par with the Picasso museums in Paris and Barcelona, the museum does allow you to see some of the lesser-known works that Picasso kept for himself or gave away to his lovers, family and friends – rather harshly described as the "less saleable stuff" by one critic.

The collection

Among the highlights of the collection are, in Room 9, *Olga Koklova con Mantilla* (a portrait of his first wife, draped in a hotel tablecloth) and, in the same room, a moving

MÁLAGA'S FORTHCOMING MUSEUMS

The **Museo de las Bellas Artes** that was formerly housed in the Museo Picasso is due to be relocated to the Aduana (the old customs building on the Paseo del Parque). The refurbishment of this elegant eighteenth-century palace was nearing completion at the time of writing and the new museum (also housing the city's important archeological collection) is scheduled to open in 2015. The collection includes notable works by Murillo and Zurbarán, among others. Two other significant developments are scheduled to raise even further Málaga's profile as a European art venue: negotiations have concluded to open a branch of **Paris's Pompidou Centre** in the **Muelle Uno** harbour development and artists such as Bacon, Magritte, Giacometti and Brancusi are some of the names announced who will have works on show. A second project is slated to transform the old tobacco factory (**La Tabacalera**), along the coast to the west of the centre, into a museum to house a collection from the **Russian State Museum** in St Petersburg. This will consist of about 100 works on permanent loan – including paintings by Kandinsky and Chagall – as well as Byzantine icons and works of socialist realism from the Soviet era. Both museums are scheduled to open in 2015 and either of the tourist offices should have the latest news on this.

portrait of his son Paul, painted in 1923. Other rooms have canvases from the breadth of Picasso's career including his Blue, Pink and Cubist periods, as well as sculptures in wood, metal and stone and a few ceramics. Two other influential women who figured prominently in the artist's long and turbulent love life are also the subject of powerful images: in Room 5, *Cabeza de Mujer 1939* is a portrait of the beguiling yet tragic Dora Maar, and in Room 8, *Jacqueline Sentada* is a seated representation of his second wife, Jacqueline Roque. An interesting, recently acquired work in the same room is *Desnudo acostado* (Reclining nude), where Picasso explores a whole range of body positions in a single image.

The collection is rotated and thus not all the works mentioned above may be on show at any one time.

The archeological remains and the Palacio de Buenavista

An unexpected surprise lies in the museum's basement – **archeological remains** revealed during the building's refurbishment. These include substantial chunks of a Phoenician city wall and tower dating from the seventh century BC which would have protected these early colonists from attacks by the Iberian tribes. From later periods there are parts of a Roman *salazones* factory used to produce the famous *garum*, a fish-based sauce and Roman delicacy, and also vestiges of the cellar of the sixteenth-century **Palacio de Buenavista**. A case nearby displays some of the finds unearthed in the excavations, including Phoenician, Greek and Roman pottery fragments and a sixth-century-BC Egyptian scarab.

Casa Natal de Picasso

Pza. de la Merced 15 • Daily 9.30am–8pm • €2 • ☎ 951 926 060, ⓦ www.fundacionpicasso.es

Picasso was born a couple of hundred metres away from the museum that houses his works in the Pza. de la Merced, where the **Casa Natal de Picasso** is home to the Fundación Picasso, a centre for scholars researching the painter's life and work. A revamped exhibition space now displays lithographs, etchings and washes by Picasso – mainly with women as the subject matter – while on the stairs are photos of the artist at various stages in his long life. The stairs lead to a reconstructed reception room, furnished as it might have looked when Picasso was growing up here at the end of the late nineteenth century. Among the items on display are some embroidered bed linen by the artist's mother, a canvas by his art-teacher father, and the infant Picasso's christening robe used in the ceremony at the nearby Iglesia de Santiago.

Centro de Arte Contemporaneo

C/Alemania s/n • July–Sept Tues–Sun 10am–2pm & 5–9pm; Oct–June Tues–Sun 10am–8pm • Free • ☎ 952 120 055, ⓦ cacmalaga.org

Building on the success of the Picasso museum, the city is now turning itself into an art-lover's hotspot with this superb modern art museum and the Museo Carmen Thyssen. Sited on the east bank of the Río Guadalmedina, the **Centro de Arte Contemporaneo** is an impressive modern art museum housed in a former market building. The tone is set by an amusing sculpture at the entrance, *Man Moving*, by German artist Stephan Balkenhol while inside the permanent collection displays works by international artists Louise Bourgeois, Cindy Sherman, Damien Hirst and Tony Cragg. Spanish artists include Juan Muñoz, Miquel Barceló and Juan Uslé. Check out the centre's website for information on frequent temporary exhibitions.

Museo Carmen Thyssen

C/Compañia 10 • Tues–Sun 10am–8pm • €6 (permanent collection), combined ticket including temporary exhibition €8 • ☎ 902 303 131, ⓦ carmenthyssenmalaga.org

Just off the west side of Pza. de la Constitución and housed in the refurbished sixteenth-century Palacio de Villalón is the **Museo Carmen Thyssen**, named after the spouse of the late baron whose collection forms the core of the Thyssen-Bornemisza museum in Madrid. Opened in 2011, the museum comprises 230 loaned works from Thyssen's personal collection of Spanish nineteenth-century art. Displayed on three floors (the fourth floor houses temporary exhibitions which have featured Monet, Picasso, Matisse, Miró and Van Gogh) and divided into sections titled "Romantic", "Naturalist Landscape", and "Fin-de-siècle", most of the works are perhaps more interesting for the glimpses they give of Spanish and *andaluz* life and times than intrinsic artistic merit or originality.

The exceptions to this are mainly in the third-floor's "Fin-de-siècle" collection where five paintings by nineteenth-century Valencian Impressionist Joaquín Sorolla y Bastida are fine examples of his hallmark high-keyed colouring and vigorous brushwork. The evocative *Lavanderas de Galicia* is perhaps the best of the bunch and demonstrates a deft understanding of light and colour. Other interesting works here include *Julia* by Ramón Casas i Carbó, a rather arrogantly-posed image of the lottery seller who was to become his wife, Gustavo Bacarisas' *Feria*, and paintings by *córdobes* artist Julio Romero de Torres.

The first floor has a somewhat incongruously titled "Old Masters" room displaying a handful of older works including an image of *San Marina* by Zurbarán and a moving polychromed wood sculpture, *The Dead Christ*, an anonymous Italian work from the thirteenth century. The museum also has a *cafetería* as well as a shop selling books on, and reproductions of, the artworks.

Jardín Botánico La Concepción

5km north of Málaga and signposted off the A45 *autovía* • Guided tours Tues–Sat: April–Sept 9.30am–8.30pm; Oct–March 9.30am–5.30pm; last visit 90min before closing • €5.20; Tues free after 4.30pm in summer and 1.30pm in winter • ☎ 951 926 180, ⓦ botanicomalaga.com

A pleasant trip out of Málaga is to the **Jardín Botánico La Concepción**. A spectacular tropical garden, much of which was planted in the nineteenth century, this formerly private estate was founded in the 1850s by Amelia Loring, granddaughter of the British consul, and purchased in 1990 by the Málaga city council, since when it has been open to the public. Specimens on view include exotic blooms, thirty species of palm, and other trees of all shapes and continents, such as the Australian banyan with its serpentine aerial roots.

A **taxi** costs about €15 one-way from the centre. The most convenient way to visit without your own transport, however, is to use the **Málagatour dedicated bus service**

(€1.30) which leaves from the bus station. The summer service (April–Sept) runs seven buses (roughly every 75min) between 11am and 7pm, with the last return bus at 8pm. See the Jardín's website for full timetable and winter schedule.

ARRIVAL AND DEPARTURE   MÁLAGA

BY AIR

From the airport (☎ 902 404 704), the electric train (*ferrocarril*) provides the easiest approach to Málaga (every 30min; 20min; June–Sept 7am–11.45pm; €1.75). From the Arrivals hall or baggage carousels go to the exit and cross the forecourt to the train station "Aereopuerto". Buy a ticket from the machine for the C1 Cercanías line to the Centro-Alameda stop (12min). The train also makes a stop en route at the Málaga train station (María Zambrano) which is also convenient for the bus station next door. Alternatively, city bus Linea A leaves from outside the Terminal 3 Arrivals hall (roughly hourly from 7am–9pm; €3), stopping at the train and bus stations en route to the centre and the Paseo del Parque near the port, from where you can also pick it up in the opposite direction when you're returning to the airport. A taxi (roughly 15min) into town from the rank outside the Arrivals hall will cost around €25 depending on traffic and time of day.

BY TRAIN

The city's impressive recently modernized RENFE train station (María Zambrano) is southwest of the heart of town; bus #3 runs from here to the centre every 10min or so. For current timetables and ticket information, consult RENFE ☎ 902 240 202, ⓦ renfe.es.
Destiinations Algeciras (3 daily, change at Bobadilla; 3hr 30min); Cádiz (3 daily, change at Bobadilla; 4hr 40min); Córdoba (4 daily; 2hr 20min; AVE 11 daily; 1hr); Fuengirola (every 30min from airport; 35min); Granada (6 daily, change at Antequera; 3hr); Madrid (AVE 11 daily; 2hr 40min); Ronda (1 daily, change at Bobadilla; 1hr 47min); Seville (6 daily; 2hr 30min); Torremolinos (every 30min; 25min).

BY BUS

The bus station is just behind the RENFE station, from where all buses (run by a number of different companies) operate. In summer, it's best to arrive an hour or so early for the bus to Granada, since tickets can sell out. Bus timetables can be checked on ⓦ estabus.emtsam.es.
Destinations Algeciras (10 daily; 2hr); Almería (7 daily; 4hr); Almuñécar (9 daily; 2hr); Cádiz (4 daily; 4hr); Córdoba (4 daily; 3hr); Fuengirola (5 daily; 45min); Gibraltar (stops at La Linea de la Concepcion border; 4 daily; 3hr); Granada (20 daily; 2hr); Huelva (1 daily; 4hr 30min); Jaén (4 daily; 3hr); Jerez de la Frontera (3 daily; 4hr 30min); Madrid (11 daily; 6hr); Marbella (20 daily; 45min); Motril (7 daily; 2hr); Nerja (24 daily; 1hr); Ronda (18 daily; 2hr); Salobreña (6 daily; 1hr 45min); Seville (5 daily; 2hr 30min); Úbeda/Baeza (3 daily; 4hr).

BY CAR

Arriving in Málaga by car you face the serious problem of parking and will have little choice but to use one of the many signed car parks around the centre or use a garage connected to your accommodation (you will still need to pay but many hotels offer discounts). Note that **theft** from cars is rampant in Málaga and you should never leave anything valuable on view in a street-parked vehicle, especially overnight.

BY FERRY

Málaga has the remnants of a passenger ferry port, the Estación Marítima, though these days there's a service only to the Spanish enclave of Melilla in Morocco, with Trasmediterranea (7hr; ☎ 902 454 645, ⓦ trasmediterranea .es). If you're heading for Fes and eastern Morocco, this is a useful connection – particularly for taking a car over – though most people go for the quicker services at Algeciras and Tarifa to the west. A useful site for checking the latest ferry schedules is ⓦ directferries.co.uk.
Destinations Melilla (1–2 daily in summer; see website for winter timetables; 4–10hr).

INFORMATION AND TOURS

Turismo Pasaje de Chinitas 4 (Mon–Fri 9am–7.30pm, Sat & Sun 9.30am–3pm; ☎ 952 308 911); can provide information on cultural events and accommodation, and sells a detailed city map.
Turismo municipal On Pza. de la Marina (daily 9am–6pm, April–Sept closes 8pm; ☎ 951 926 020), with other branches at the bus station and in the airport Arrivals hall.

Bus tours One way to get to grips quickly with the city is on an open-topped bus tour. This hop-on, hop-off service is operated by Málagatour (€18, kids €10, tickets valid 24hr; ☎ 902 101 081, ⓦ city-sightseeing.com); buses leave the bus station every 30min (9.15am–7pm) with about a dozen stops around the centre (see website for route map), including the Catedral, Pza. de la Merced, the Alameda and the Gibralfaro.

ACCOMMODATION

Málaga boasts dozens of hotels and *hostales* in all budget categories. The best places to start looking for cheaper **accommodation** are the area just south of the Alameda Principal and the streets east and west of C/Marques de Larios, which cuts between the Alameda and Pza. de la Constitución. Prices quoted are high season rates but many hotels and *hostales* do website and seasonal special offers which often slash prices significantly.

Albergue Juvenil Málaga Pza. de Pio XII ☎952 308 500. Modern youth hostel on the western outskirts of town, with double and single rooms, disabled facilities, its own sun terrace and restaurant. Tends to fill up in season, so book ahead. Bus #18 heading west across the river from the Alameda will drop you nearby. Under-26 €22, over-26 €26

Apartamentos San Pablo C/Trinidad 39 ☎952 300 955, ⓦapartamentossanpablomalaga.com. Excellent new apartments and studios (sleeping two to six people) in a building alongside the church of San Pablo on the west bank of the Rio Guadalmedina. All come with well-equipped kitchen, plasma TV and lounge area. Just the place for a longer stay with welcoming owners and (relatively) easy street parking nearby. Reductions for stays of over three days €60

Camping Torremolinos Loma del Paraiso 2 ☎952 382 602, ⓦcampingtorremolinos.com. Torremolinos' campsite, 10km west of Málaga along the coast, has plenty of shade and good facilities although it's pricey in high season. It's 3km east of the centre of the resort on the main N340 Málaga–Cádiz highway, 500m from the sea. €37.10

Hostal La Hispanidad Explanada de la Estación 5 ☎952 311 135, ⓦwww.hostalhispanidad.com. Facing the train station, this is a useful sleepover if you've got an early train (or bus) to catch. The labyrinthine interior has refurbished en-suite rooms named after different countries of the Americas, with a/c and TV, and there are plenty of eating places nearby. €50

Hostal La Palma C/Martínez 7 ☎952 226 772, ⓦwww.hostallapalma.es. One of the best budget places in town, with a/c en-suite doubles in addition to simpler rooms sharing bath; frequently offers discounts. €35

Hostal Victoria C/Sancha de Lara 3 ☎952 224 224, ⓦwww.hostalvictoriamalaga.com. Pleasant *hostal* with good-value double and single rooms, just north of the Alameda. €55

Hotel California Paseo de Sancha 17, 500m east of the bullring ☎952 215 164, ⓦhotelcalifornianet.com. Charming small hotel near the beach with flower-bedecked entrance. The well-appointed rooms come with a/c and safes, and the hotel has its own garage. Five-night minimum stay in August. Buses #11, #34 and #35 from the Alameda will drop you outside. €76

Hotel Ibis Paseo Guimbarda 5 ☎952 070 741, ⓦibishotel.com. On the west bank of the Guadalmedina, this is part of the international chain, offering functional rooms at attractive prices with frequent website special offers. Can arrange parking. €55

Hotel Larios C/Marqués de Larios 2 ☎952 222 200, ⓦhotel-larios.com. Modern, upmarket and central hotel inside the shell of an original Art Deco edifice; satellite TV, room safes, and a rooftop bar with panoramic views are among the features. Does frequent special offers. €149

Hotel Lola C/Casas de Campos 17 ☎952 579 300, ⓦroom-matehotels.com. Designer-chic boutique hotel where rooms come with plasma TV, DVD player, minibar and room safe. Also has its own bar-restaurant and garage. €119

Hotel Málaga Palacio Cortina del Muelle 1 ☎952 215 185, ⓦwww.marriott.com. This central four-star hotel with harbour-view rooms pampers its guests with free minibar and bathrobes. Facilities include rooftop pool and restaurant with spectacular views and a gym. Online special offers. €159

Hotel Trebol C/Moreno Carbonero 3 ☎952 608 702, ⓦhoteltrebol.com. Pleasant new small hotel in the atmospheric market area with modern a/c rooms. Features include flat-screen TV, and internet connections. Ask for a room facing the street as these get more light and air. €55

★ **Parador Gibralfaro** Monte de Gibralfaro ☎952 221 902, ⓦwww.paradores.es. You won't get a better panoramic view of the coast than from this eagle's nest on top of the Gibralfaro hill. It's quite small as paradores go, which adds to its charm, plus there's a pretty good restaurant (see opposite) and it also squeezes in a pool and has its own garage. See website for offers. €145

Pensión Juanita C/Alarcón Luján 8 ☎952 213 586, ⓦpensionjuanita.es. Central and friendly *pensión* offering rooms with or without bath on the fourth floor (with a lift). Large family rooms also available. €45

EATING AND DRINKING

Málaga has no shortage of **places to eat and drink**, and, though it's hardly a gourmet paradise, the city has a justified reputation for seafood. Its greatest claim to fame is undoubtedly its **fried fish**, acknowledged as the best in Spain. You'll find many fish restaurants grouped around the Alameda, although for some of the very best you need to head out to the suburbs of Pedregalejo and El Palo, served by bus #11 (from Paseo del Parque). On the seafront *paseo* at **Pedregalejo**, almost all of the cafés and restaurants serve up terrific seafood. Farther on, after the *paseo* disappears, you find yourself amid fishing shacks and smaller, sometimes quite ramshackle, cafés in **El Palo**, an earthier sort of area for the most part, with a beach and huts, and – in summer or at weekends – an even better place to eat.

TAPAS BARS

Antigua Casa de Guardia C/Pastora at the junction with the Alameda ☎952 214 680, ⓦantiguacasa deguardia.net. This is one of Málaga's oldest bars, dating from the nineteenth century, and one of the few still serving the traditional sweet Málaga wine (Falstaff's "sack"), made from muscatel grapes and dispensed from huge barrels. Try washing it down with shellfish sold from a stall at the rear of the bar. The new-season wine, *Pedriot*, is incredibly sweet; much more palatable is *Seco Añejo*, which has matured for a year. Mon–Thurs 10am–10pm, Fri–Sat 10am–10.45pm, Sun 10am–3pm.

Bar Lo Güeno C/Marín García 9 ☎952 223 048, ⓦloguena.es. Excellent and atmospheric tapas place; *pincho* (spicy shrimp) and *habas* (broad beans with black sausage) are specials. They have recently added a very good small *asador* (grill house) sited immediately opposite and a *mesón* (restaurant) next door. Daily noon–midnight.

Bodegas Quitapeñas (aka La Manchega) C/Marín García 4 ☎952 602 357, ⓦquitapenas.es. Another fine old drinking den with its own off-site bodega (which can be visited). Good tapas selection and *jibias guisadas* (stewed cuttlefish) is a speciality. You can wash them down with Málaga's traditional Moscatel and Sierras de Málaga wines. Daily noon–4pm & 7.15pm–midnight.

Tapadaki C/Carretería 69 ☎952 217 966, ⓦtapadaki .com. A stylish tapas and *raciones* bar serving a fusion of Asian and Spanish tapas; try their *solomillo de cerdo y shitake* (pork loin with mushrooms) or *cordero estofado con couscous* (stewed lamb with couscous). Does special offers on bottled wines. Tues–Sun 1.30–4.30pm & 8pm–12.30am.

★El Tapeo de Cervantes C/Carcer 8 ☎952 609 458, ⓦeltapeodecervantes.com. This Lilliputian but outstanding bar near the Teatro Cervantes merits at least one visit. Here you'll find a cosy ambience and some creative tapas priced between €3–5; be sure to sample their *atun rojo en salsa coliflor* (tuna in a cauliflower sauce). They have recently added an equally excellent restaurant, *El Mesón de Cervantes*, located just around the corner at C/Alamos 11. Tues–Sat 1–4pm & 7.30–11.30pm, Sun 7.30–11.30pm.

Uvedoble C/Cister 15 ☎952 248 478, ⓦwww .uvedobletaberna.com. Modernistic bar offering "designer" tapas in a minimalist setting with a small but interesting tapas and *raciones* menu. Try their *croquetas caseras ibéricos* (croquettes with *jamón*) or *ensalada de membrillo* (quince salad). Also does tasty desserts. Mon–Sat 12.30–4.30pm & 8pm–midnight.

RESTAURANTS

Antonio C/Fernando Lesseps 7 ☎952 223 397, ⓦmesonantonio.com. Popular small and central restaurant serving well-prepared *malagueño* dishes, with an outdoor terrace in an atmospheric cul-de-sac off the north end of C/Nueva; menu for around €12. Mon–Sat 12–4.30pm & 8pm–midnight.

Bar Los Pueblos C/Ataranzas. ☎951 253 693. This popular and busy diner has undergone a major refurbishment but the welcome is as warm as ever. It serves up satisfying, inexpensive food all day – bean soups and *estofados* are its specialities; gazpacho is served in half-pint glasses. Good-value daily menu for €8. Mon–Sat 7.30am–5.30pm.

Bar-Restaurante Palacios C/Eslava 4 ☎952 358 251 Plain, honest food in a vibrant *comedor popular* with friendly waiters; has a menu for around €9, and specialities include *jamón iberico*, fish *surtido* and a mean paella. Mon–Fri 7.30am–midnight, Sat 7.30am–5pm.

Cañadu Pza. de la Merced 21 ☎952 602 719. Relaxed vegetarian restaurant serving a good selection of salads and pastas as well as couscous and *ajo blanco* (cold garlic soup) accompanied by organic wines and beers. Main dishes €4–9. Daily 1.30–4.30pm & 8–11.30pm.

Il Laboratorio Pza. San Pedro de Alcántara ☎952 224 998. Vibrant Italian-style pizzeria-trattoria serving (besides pizzas) salads and daily specials. They also do breakfasts – try their *revueltos* (scrambled eggs) – and there's a small outdoor terrace under the trees on a charming *plazuela*. Main dishes €4.50–12. Daily 1pm–12.30am.

★Parador Gilbralfaro Monte Gilbralfaro ☎952 221 902. Superior dining on the terrace with spectacular views over the coast and town. The house specialities are *malagueño* fish and meat dishes, and the menu is excellent value at around €30 with reasonable wine prices. There's also a vegetarian menu. Ring to book one of the best tables. Main dishes €10–25. If you can't face the climb, take a taxi or bus #35 east along Paseo del Parque. Daily 1.30–4pm & 8.30–11pm.

El Tintero Pza. del Dedo, El Palo ☎952 206 826. Right at the far eastern end of the seafront, just before the *Club Náutico* (bus #11; ask for "*Tintero*"), this is a huge beach restaurant where the waiters charge round with plates of fish (around €8 each) and you shout for, or grab, anything you like. The bill is totalled according to the number of plates on your table at the end of the meal. The fish to go for are, above all, *mero* (cod) and *rosada* (dogfish and catfish), along with Andalucian regulars such as *boquerones*, *gambas* and *sepia* (cuttlefish). Haute cuisine it certainly isn't, but for sheer entertainment it's a must. Daily 1.30–4.30pm & 8.30–11.30pm.

El Vegetariano Pozo del Rey 5 ☎952 214 858. Atmospheric little veggie place offering a variety of imaginative pasta-, cheese- and salad-based dishes. Main dishes €7.50–11.50. Mon–Sat 1–4pm & 8–11pm.

Vino Mío Pza. Jeronimo Cuervo 2 ☎952 609 093, ⓦrestaurantevinomio.com. Friendly lunchtime-onwards

4

bar-restaurant serving creative tapas and fusion food (Morrocan/Asian/Spanish) with veggie options and a weekday menu for €12.50. They entertain diners with a flamenco show (Mon–Sat 8–9.30pm; €4 supplement) after which it reverts to a normal restaurant. The bar also offers cocktails with a "two for the price of one" happy hour 7–8pm. Kitchen open nonstop from 1–11pm. Daily 1pm–2am.

NIGHTLIFE

Most of Málaga's **nightlife** is northeast of the Catedral along and around **calles Granada and Beatas** and the streets circling the nearby **Pza. de Uncibay**. In the summer months, there's also a scene nearer the sea at **Malagueta**, south of the bullring. At weekends and holidays, dozens of youth-oriented disco bars fill the crowded streets in these areas, and over the summer – though it's dead out of season – the scene spreads out along the seafront to the suburb of **Pedregalejo**. Here the streets just behind the beach host most of the action, and dozens of *discotecas* and smaller music bars lie along and off the main street, Juan Sebastián Elcano. Málaga's daily paper, *Sur*, is good for local entertainment **listings**; there's also an English edition (*Sur in English*) on Fridays, available from *turismos* and hotels.

Anden Pza. de Uncibay 8 ☎650 101 388, ⓦdiscotecaanden.com. Disco-bar with a wild crowd and a playlist featuring Spanish pop, house and reggae. Two big dance rooms are serviced by four bars, and there are often queues to get in. Thurs–Sat 11pm–7am.

Asúcar Junction of C/Juan de Padilla & C/Lazcano ☎628 189 351. The place to come for salsa in Málaga. Thurs–Sun 11.30pm–late.

La Botellita Pasaje Mitjana ☎952 771 404. Wild place packed to the rafters with young local revellers dancing to the tunes of the Spanish Top 40. At the end of this alley, the tiny Pza. Marqués Vado del Maestre is filled with drinking bars and plenty of night-time action. Thurs–Sat 11.30pm–4.30am.

★ **El Pimpi** C/Granada 62 ☎952 228 990, ⓦelpimpi .com. Cavernous and hugely popular *bodega*-style bar serving up, among other concoctions, tasty *vino dulce* by the glass or bottle. There are tapas to go with the drinks and you can do a bit of celebrity-spotting on their wall of photos (which includes a young Antonio Banderas). Don't miss a superb terrace (with Alcazaba view) out the back. A great place to kick-start the evening. Daily 10am–2am.

Pub Celtic Druids Pza. de la Merced 17 ☎952 218 171. A laidback, Irish-themed bar serving breakfasts (until 1pm), bar food during the day and *copas* after dark. Screens sports events in the bar and there's a lively terrace that stays open into the small hours. Daily 9am–3am.

Puerta Oscura C/Molina Lario 5 near the Catedral ☎952 221 900, ⓦpuertaoscuramalaga.com. Slightly incongruous classical-music-cum-cafetería-cum-cocktail bar – sometimes with live performers – which also mounts art exhibitions; serves cocktails, ices and baguettes. T-shirts are definitely a no-no here. Mon–Fri 10am–2am, Sat 4pm–3am, Sun 4pm–midnight.

SHOPPING

El Corte Inglés Avda. de Andalucía 4 ☎952 357 001. A great department store with a basement supermarket that sells a terrific selection of the nation's wines and spirits. Mon–Sat 10am–10pm.

Librería Luces Alameda Principal 16 ☎952 122 100. The town's most central general bookshop stocks a selection of titles in English. Mon–Sat 10am–9pm.

La Mallorquina Pza. Felix Saenz (near the market) ☎952 213 352. This is a good place to pick up *malagueño* cheeses, wines, almonds and dried fruit. Mon–Fri 9.15am–2.15pm & 5–8.30pm, Sat 9.15am–2pm.

Mapas y Compañía C/Compañía 33 ☎952 608 815. Málaga's best travel bookshop sells IGN walking maps, as well as 1:50,000 Mapas Cartografía Militar (military maps). Mon–Sat 10am–1.30pm & 5–8.30pm, Sat 10.30am–2pm.

DIRECTORY

Currency exchange El Corte Inglés will change currency free of charge.

Consulates UK, Edificio Eurocom, C/Mauricio Moro Pareto 2 ☎952 352 300; US, Avda. Juan Gómez 8, Fuengirola ☎952 474 891; Republic of Ireland, Avda. de los Boliches 15, Fuengirola ☎952 475 108.

Football Since gaining promotion to La Liga's top flight in 2008 C.F. Málaga has consolidated its status, first under current Manchester City coach Manuel Pellegrini followed by Bernd Schuster. In the 2011–12 season the club qualified for the Champions League for the first time in its history and reached the quarter finals. Games are at La Rosaleda stadium, Paseo de Martiricos s/n, at the northern end of the Río Guadalmedina. Tickets can be purchased from the stadium (☎952 104 488, ⓦwww.malagacf.es).

Hospital Hospital Carlos Haya, Avda. Carlos Haya, 2km west of the city centre ☎951 290 000.

Left luggage There are lockers and a *consigna* at the train station (daily 6.15am–12.45am), and lockers at the bus station (daily 6.30am–11pm).

Pharmacy Farmacia Caffarena (24hr) on the Alameda at no. 2, near the junction with C/Marqués de Larios ☎ 952 212 858, ⓦ farmaciacaffarena.net.

Police The Policía Local are at Avda. La Rosaleda 19 (☎ 952 126 500); in emergencies, dial ☎ 092 (local police) or ☎ 091 (national).

Post office C/Santa Lucía 7 (Mon–Fri 8.30am–8.30pm, Sat 9.30am–1pm).

Garganta del Chorro

Fifty kilometres northwest of Málaga lies the deep, rugged canyon of the Río Guadalhorce, known as the **Garganta del Chorro**. It's an amazing place – an immense five-kilometre-long cleft in a vast limestone massif, which has become Andalucía's major centre for rock climbers. The gorge's most stunning feature, however, is a concrete catwalk, El Camino del Rey, which threads the length of the gorge, hanging precipitously halfway up its side. Built in the 1920s as part of a hydroelectric scheme, it was one of the wonders of Spain, but has since fallen into a dangerous state of disrepair. Despite being officially "closed" intrepid travellers continued to use it. In the 1990s, following a number accidents and fatalities, access to the catwalk was finally cut at each end of the gorge, making it impossible to reach without a guide and climbing gear. After many false starts the authorities have finally put works in hand to **restore the Camino** and at the time of writing a new catwalk was being constructed one metre above the line of the old one (thus making the old structure impossible to use). The work is scheduled to be completed before the summer of 2015 and information can be obtained on its progress from Finca la Campana (see p.240). The Camino will then be operated by a private company that will charge an entry fee for access. If you have no head for heights it's still possible to explore the rest of the gorge, however, and get a view of the Camino by walking from El Chorro (see below). A glimpse of both gorge and Camino can also be had from any of the trains going north from Málaga – the line, slipping in and out of tunnels, follows the river for a considerable distance along the gorge, before plunging into a last long tunnel just before its head.

ARRIVAL AND DEPARTURE

GARGANTA DEL CHORRO

By train and bus El Chorro is served by two daily direct trains (55min; currently running at 10.43am & 17.30pm), but no buses, from Málaga. There are two daily buses to El Chorro from nearby Álora (currently running 7.25am & 12.30pm Mon–Fri) which is served by ten daily trains from Málaga.

By car To get there with your own transport, take the A357 heading west from Málaga towards Pizarra, turning here along the A343 to Álora. Continue beyond Álora for 15km and turn west at Valle de Abdalajís along the minor MA4401, a journey of around 65km in total.

A WALK FROM EL CHORRO TO THE GORGE

One of the best ways of viewing Garganta del Chorro is to follow a 12km **walk** (vehicles should follow the same route) from the village of **El Chorro**. Take the road from the train station, signposted "Pantano de Guadalhorce", reached by crossing over the dam and turning right, then following the road north along the lake towards the hydroelectric plant. After 8km turn right at a junction to reach – after 2km – the bar-restaurant *El Mirador*, poised above a road tunnel and overlooking the various lakes and reservoirs of the Guadalhorce scheme. From the bar (where you should leave any transport) a dirt track on the right heads towards the gorge. Follow this and take the first track on the right after about 700m. This climbs for some 2km to where it splits into two small trails. The trail to the left leads after 300m to a magnificent **viewpoint** over the gorge from where you can see the Camino del Rey clinging to the rock face. The right-hand track climbs swiftly to an obvious peak, the **Pico de Almochon**, with more spectacular views, this time over the lakes of the Embalse de Guadalhorce.

ACCOMMODATION

Bar-Restaurante Garganta del Chorro ☎ 952 497 219, ⓦ www.lagarganta.com. Near the station, this restaurant and accommodation complex has pleasant rooms inside a converted mill and overlooking a pool. **€92**

Camping El Chorro ☎ 952 495 244. Located in the village, this is an excellent campsite with a pool and restaurant, reached by heading downhill to your right for 400m after getting off the train. They also rent out wood cabins sleeping up to six. Open all year. **€19**, cabins **€55**

★ **Finca La Campana** ☎ 626 963 942, ⓦ www. fincalacampana.com. Signs from the station will direct you 2km to this farmhouse, set in rural surroundings with a bunkhouse and a cluster of attractive cottages (with fully-equipped kitchen) and sharing a pool. Run by qualified Swiss climber Jean Hofer, the place also offers courses in rock climbing and caving, rents out mountain bikes, can arrange kayaks on the nearby lake/reservoir, and does hiking excursions, as well as guided trips along the Camino del Rey. Contact Jean to find out the latest situation regarding the Camino's repair works (see p.239). For longer stays (two nights plus) transfers can be arranged from Álora or Málaga airport and camping is also possible. Camping (per person) **€16**, bunks **€12** cottages **€45**

Antequera and around

ANTEQUERA, some 55km north of Málaga on the main rail line to Granada, is an attractive market town with some important monuments, a clutch of interesting churches and a fine old Pza. de Toros. The most famous of its sights, however, is a group of prehistoric dolmen caves on the northern edge of town that rank among the most important in Spain.

Nuestra Señora del Carmen

Pza. del Carmen • Tues–Fri 11am–1.30pm & 4.30–5.45pm, Sat & Sun 11am–2pm • €2

The finest of Antequera's collection of Baroque churches (the *turismo* can provide a full list) is **Nuestra Señora del Carmen** on Pza. del Carmen. The church's rather plain facade little prepares you for the eighteenth-century interior, now painstakingly restored to its former glory. The main altar's sensational 13m-high *retablo* – one of the finest in Andalucía – is a masterly late Baroque extravaganza of carved wood by Antonio Primo and Diego Márquez, its centrepiece a Virgin in a *camarín* (shrine) flanked by a bevy of polychromed saints and soaring angels.

The dolmen caves

Avda. de Málaga 1 • Tues–Sun 10am–5pm • Free • ☎ 952 702 505

Antequera's most visited monuments are the group of prehistoric dolmen caves on the town's northern edge, now enclosed in a futuristic new "dolmen park" with visitor centre, car park and a Centro de Interpretación. The grandest and most famous of these megalithic monuments is the **Cueva de Menga**, its roof formed by an immense 180-tonne monolith. Dating from around 2500 BC, a columned gallery leads to an oval burial chamber, probably the final resting place of an important chieftain. The nearby **Cueva de Viera**, dating from a century or two later, has cut stones but a smaller burial chamber. To reach the dolmens, take the Granada road out of town – an easy ten-minute walk – to the turning, rather insignificantly signposted, after about 1km on the left.

Two kilometres away, a third cave, **El Romeral**, is different (and later) in structure, with a domed ceiling of flat stones; get instructions (and a map) of how to reach it from the visitor centre.

The Plaza de Toros

Paseo María Cristina s/n • Museum May–Sept Tues–Fri 9.30am–2pm & 6–8pm; Oct–April Tues–Fri 9.30am–2pm & 4–6pm; Sat & Sun (all year) 9.30am–2.30pm • €1

The **Plaza de Toros** in the newer part of town on the Alameda de Andalucía is also worth a look; it staged its first *corrida* in August 1848. Whatever your view on bullfighting, it's difficult not to pick up the atmosphere the old place generates, especially when you survey the amphitheatre from the matador's position in the centre of the burning sand. The ring also has a small museum filled with the usual bullfighting photos, *trajes de luces* (bullfighters' suits) and other *taurino* paraphernalia.

INFORMATION   ANTEQUERA

Turismo Town maps and information on El Torcal are available from a helpful tourist office on the central Pza. San Sebastián (Mon–Sat 9.30am–7pm, Sun 10am–2pm ☎ 952 702 505, ☎ turismoantequera.com), alongside the church of the same name.

ACCOMMODATION

A good base for visits to nearby El Torcal, Antequera has plenty of **accommodation** options and prices are reasonable. The Antequera *turismo* can provide information regarding some attractive *casas rurales* to rent near El Torcal.

Camping El Torcal ☎ 952 111 608, ☎ campingeltorcal. com. Camping is no longer allowed inside the *parque natural*, but this campsite lies on the park's edge just off the A7075, 6km south of Antequera. Also has en-suite *cabañas* (cabins; €30). Closed Oct–March. €16

★ **Hotel Arte de Cozina** C/Calzada 25 ☎ 952 840 014, ☎ artedecozina.com. Comfortable and good-value a/c en-suite rooms with TV plus a friendly welcome make this a winner. Also has a very good restaurant. €40

Hotel Los Dolmenes Cruce del Romeral ☎ 952 845 956, ☎ hotellosdolmenes.com. Pleasant three-star hotel close to the dolmen caves with spacious, comfortable rooms with terrace balcony and views. Ideal if you have a vehicle as their ample car park is free. €50

Hotel Plaza San Sebastián Pza. San Sebastián 4 ☎ 952 844 239, ☎ hotelplazasansebastian.com. Attractive two-star hotel facing the church of San Sebastián offering well-equipped a/c rooms with satellite TV. Ask for one of their lighter exterior rooms. €38

Número Uno C/Lucena 40 ☎ 952 843 134, ☎ hotelnumerouno.com. A relatively new hotel with pleasant a/c en-suite rooms with TV, plus a roof terrace above a popular bar-restaurant. €35

Parque Natural de El Torcal

Centro de Visitantes April–Sept daily 10am–7pm; Oct–March daily 10am–5pm • ☎ 952 243 324, ☎ torcaldeantequera.com

Approaching Antequera along the old road from Málaga (MA3402) via Almogía and Villanueva de la Concepción, you pass the entrance to the popular natural park famed for its haunting rock sculptures. **Parque Natural de El Torcal**, 13km south of Antequera, is one of the most geologically arresting of Spain's natural parks. A massive high plateau of glaciated limestone tempered by a lush growth of hawthorn, ivy and wild rose, it can be painlessly explored using the three walking routes that radiate from the centre of the park, outlined in a leaflet available from the **Centro de Visitantes**.

Trails

The best-designed and most exciting **trails** are the yellow and red routes, the former climaxing with suitable drama on a cliff edge with magnificent views over a valley. The latter gives fantastic vantage points of the looming limestone outcrops, eroded into vast, surreal sculptures. Because of the need to protect flora and fauna, the red route is in a restricted zone and can only be visited with a **guide** (ask at the *centro*). The **green** and **yellow routes** (waymarked) can be walked without a guide, the former taking about forty minutes if you don't dawdle, the latter about two hours. In early summer on the popular green route you may find yourself competing with gangs of schoolkids, who arrive en masse on vaguely educational trips, excitedly trying to spot La Copa (the wine glass), El Lagarto (the lizard) and La Loba (the she-wolf), as well as other celebrated **rock sculptures**. Keep an eye on the skies while you're here, for griffon vultures are frequent visitors and, with their huge wingspans, make a spectacular sight as they glide overhead. The Centro de Visitantes also has it's own **cafetería** with a *menú del día*.

ARRIVAL AND DEPARTURE

By bus Buses run from Málaga (Mon–Fri 5 daily, Sat & Sun daily); ask the driver to drop you at the road for El Torcal from where it's a 4km uphill slog to the visitor centre.

By taxi turístico The most convenient way to visit the park without your own transport is the *taxi turístico*, which

PARQUE NATURAL DE EL TORCAL

can be arranged through the *turismo* in Antequera; for €34 (€42 weekends), a taxi will drop off up to four passengers at the Centro de Visitantes and wait (roughly 1hr) until you have completed the green route before returning you to Antequera.

Nerja

The eastern section of the Costa del Sol ribbons east of the city of Málaga as far as Almería, and is generally uninspiring. Inland there are plenty of attractive sierras to explore but, though far less developed than its twin coastal strip to the west of Málaga, there's little to tempt you to stop before you reach the twin resorts of Nerja and Almuñécar – which are its saving feature. First, some 40km out of Málaga, comes **NERJA**, nestling in the foothills of the Almijara range. This was a village before it was a resort, so it has some intrinsic character, and villa development has been shaped around it.

The focus of the whitewashed old quarter is the **Bálcon de Europa**, a striking palm-fringed belvedere overlooking the sea. The beaches flanking this are also reasonably attractive, with a series of quieter coves within walking distance. There are plenty of other great **walks** around Nerja, too, well documented in the *turismo*'s own leaflets; or, at Smiffs Bookshop, C/Almirante Ferrandiz 10, you can buy individual leaflets detailing walks in the area by local resident and hiker Elma Thompson.

The Cuevas de Nerja

Daily July & Aug 10am–7.30pm; rest of year 10am–2pm & 4–6.30pm • €8.50 • ⓦ cuevadenerja.es

Nerja's chief tourist attraction, the **Cuevas de Nerja**, 3km east from the town, are a heavily commercialized series of caverns, impressive in size – and home to the world's longest-known **stalactite** at 63m – though otherwise not tremendously interesting. They also contain a number of prehistoric paintings, but these are not currently on public view.

ARRIVAL AND INFORMATION

By bus The main bus station (actually a stand) is on C/San Miguel at the north end of town close to Pza. Cantarero; from here hourly buses leave for the *cuevas*. It's a 5min walk south from the bus station to the beach and centre.

NERJA

Turismo C/Carmen 1 (July–Sept daily 10am–2pm & 6–10pm; Oct–June Mon–Fri 10am–2pm & 5–8pm, Sat 10am–1pm; ⓣ952 521 531, ⓦwww.nerja.org), next to the *ayuntamiento* and just west of the Balcón de Europa.

ACCOMMODATION

Camping Nerja ⓣ952 529 714, ⓦnerjacamping.com. Located 4km east of town along the N340, this is a decent campsite with shade, pool, bar and restaurant. €21.75

Hostal Marissal Paseo Balcón de Europa 3 ⓣ952 520 199, ⓦwww.hostalmarissal.com. This excellent *hostal* is in the town's prime location – actually on the belvedere. En-suite balcony rooms come with a/c, TV and strongbox and many (try for rooms 102–5 or 204–5) have sea view; it also rents apartments in the same

location. Doubles €70, apartments €115

Hostal Mena C/El Barrio 15 ⓣ952 520 541, ⓔinfo @hostalmena.es. Central rooms come with bath, sea views and a/c or fans plus a delightful garden at the rear in this very friendly *hostal*. €43

Hotel Paraiso del Mar C/Carabeo 22 ⓣ952 521 621, ⓦhotelparaisodelmar.es. With similar views to the parador, this is a very pleasant hotel where all rooms come with Jacuzzi and many have sea-view balconies (€154).

There's also a pool, gardens and sauna dug out of the cliff face. €135

Parador Nacional C/Almuñécar 8 ☎952 520 050, ⓦ www.parador.es. Overlooking one of Nerja's most popular beaches, Playa de Burriana, to which you descend with a private lift, this is a modern parador with comfortable rooms and a pool situated in attractive gardens. €180

Almuñécar

The lively resort of **ALMUÑÉCAR** is marred by a number of towering holiday apartments, and the rocky grey-sand beaches are rather cramped, but the esplanade behind them, with palm-roofed bars (many serving free tapas with each drink) and restaurants, is fun, and the old quarter – clustered around a sixteenth-century castle – attractive. The two main beaches, the **Playa San Cristóbal** and the **Playa Puerta del Mar** are separated by the towering headland of the Peñon del Santo.

ARRIVAL AND INFORMATION   ALMUÑÉCAR

By bus The bus station, which has frequent connections to Málaga and Granada, is at the junction of avenidas Juan Carlos I and Fenicia, northeast of the centre.

Turismo In an imposing neo-Moorish mansion on Avda.

de Europa (daily 10am–1.30pm & 5–8pm, July & Aug 6–9pm; ☎958 631 125, ⓦ www.almunecar.info), behind the Playa San Cristóbal beach at the west end of the town.

ACCOMMODATION

The pressure on **accommodation** in Almuñécar is not quite as acute as at Nerja. There are more than enough hotels to cope with the summer crush, while good-value *hostales* encircle the central Pza. de la Rosa in the old town.

Hostal Plaza Damasco C/Cerrajos 16 ☎958 630 165. Cosy *hostal* just off the plaza it's named after, offering a/c en-suite rooms with TVs. €65

Hotel California Carretera de Málaga km 313, northwest of the town on the main road ☎958 630 436, ⓦ hotelcaliforniaspain.com. Moorish-style, inviting hotel with balcony rooms and bar offering evening meals with plenty of veggie options. Owners are keen paragliders and can also organize diving and skiing. €60

★ **Hotel Casablanca** Pza. San Cristóbal 4 (aka Pza. Abderramán) ☎958 635 575, ⓦ hotelcasablanca

almunecar.com. The wonderful *Casablanca* is one of the most charming hotels on the coast. Fifty metres from the beach with a splendid neo-Moorish facade, the hotel boasts comfortable a/c terrace balcony rooms with great sea views (on the front). The friendly family proprietors make this an all-round winner. Also has garage parking. €70

Hotel Toboso C/Larache 2 ☎958 639 208, ⓦ hoteltobosoalmunecar.com. Comfortable hotel a block south of the N340 offering a/c rooms with mountain or sea views plus garden and own parking. €99

EATING AND DRINKING

There are numerous **places to eat** along the seafront, many of them offering cheap, if unspectacular fare. Many of the town's more interesting possibilities are set further back in the *casco antiguo* or old quarter.

Bar-Taberna El Cortijillo Pza. Kelibia 4 ☎958 631 465. Lively *freiduría* and *raciones* bar popular with young locals and one of several in an attractive square with a lively scene on summer nights. Main dishes €8–18. Mon, Wed–Sun noon–midnight.

Bodega Francisco c/Real 15, north of Pza. Rosa ☎958 630 168. Wonderful old bar with barrels stacked up to the ceiling and walls covered with ageing *corrida* posters and mounted boars' heads. The *fino* and *montilla* are both excellent, and the bar offers a wide range of tapas and *platos combinados*. There's an adjoining dining area and impromptu flamenco sometimes adds to the fun. Main

dishes €7–14. Daily 10am–4pm & 7–11pm; closed Nov–Easter.

Mesón Antonio C/Manila 9 ☎667 391 947. One of several lively bars in the street and usually packed with locals, this *mesón* specializes in *carne a la brasa* (chargrilled meat) and octopus. Main dishes €7–16. Daily 11am–5.30pm & 8pm–midnight.

Salitre Lute y Jesús Paseo Puerto del Mar ☎958 882 395. One of a chain of three, this busy seafront fish restaurant reputedly serves the best *pulpo a la brasa* in town (chargrilled octopus) as well as plates of tasty fried fish. Main dishes €6–15. Daily noon–5pm & 7pm–midnight; closed Nov.

4

The Costa del Sol resorts

West of Málaga – or more correctly, west of Málaga airport – the real **Costa del Sol** gets going, and if you've never seen this level of tourist development, it's quite a shock. These are certainly not the kind of resorts you could envisage anywhere else in Europe. The 1960s and 1970s hotel and apartment tower blocks were followed by a second wave of property development in the 1980s and 1990s, this time villa homes and leisure complexes, funded by massive international investment. It's estimated that 300,000 foreigners now live on and around the Costa del Sol, the majority of them British and other Northern Europeans, though marina developments such as Puerto Banús have also attracted Arab and Russian money.

Approached in the right kind of spirit, it is possible to have fun in resorts like **Torremolinos**, **Fuengirola** and, at a price, in **Marbella**. But if you've come to Spain to be in Spain keep going at least until you reach Estepona.

Fuengirola

Twenty kilometres southwest of Málaga, beyond the vast, bizarre resort of Torremolinos, lies **FUENGIROLA**, very slightly less developed and infinitely more staid than its neighbour. It's not so conspicuously ugly, but it is distinctly middle-aged and family-oriented. The huge, long beach has been divided up into restaurant-beach strips, each renting out lounge chairs and pedal boats.

4

INFORMATION   FUENGIROLA

Turismo Located at Avda. Jesús S. Rein 6 (Mon–Fri 9am–7.30pm, Sat 9am–2pm; ☎952 467 457, ⓦwww .visitafuengirola.com), close to the train (☎952 128 080) and bus (☎952 475 066) stations.

ACCOMMODATION

Camping Fuengirola Carretera Nacional 340, km 207 ☎952 474 108, ⓦcampingfuengirola.net. The nearest campsite lies 2km to the east of the centre and is reached via a turn-off near the junction of the N340 and the road to Mijas; bus "Línea Roja" from Avda. Ramón y Cajal on the main Marbella road will take you there. €31

Hostal Cuevas C/Capitán 7 ☎952 460 606. Near to Pza. de la Constitución, this is a good option for pleasant a/c en-suite rooms with TV. €50

Hostal Italia C/de La Cruz 1, off the east side of Pza. de la Constitución ☎952 474 193, ⓦhostal-italia.com. This friendly *hostal* is the nicest option around the town's main plaza for a/c en-suite rooms with TV and balcony. €75

Hotel Las Piramides Paseo Marítimo s/n ☎952 583 297, ⓦhotellaspiramides.com. Fuengirola's upmarket option, this four-star giant at the western end of the seafront has sea-view rooms, its own pool and lots of luxury frills. €135

EATING AND DRINKING

The warren of streets to the south of the pedestrianized main square (Pza. Constitución) are lined with **restaurants** of a rather depressing similarity while many of Fuengirola's very best restaurants and tapas bars are slightly outside the normal tourist beat.

GETTING AROUND THE COSTA DEL SOL

One of the major selling points of the **Costa del Sol** is its ease of access. Hundreds of flights arrive here every week, and **Málaga airport** is positioned midway between **Málaga**, the main city on the coast, and **Torremolinos**, its most grotesque resort. You can easily reach either town by taking the electric train (*cercanía*) that runs every thirty minutes (daily 7am–11.45pm) along the coast between Málaga and **Fuengirola**, 20km to the southwest. Frequent bus connections also link all the major coastal resorts, while a toll *autopista* (motorway) between Málaga and Sotogrande has taken the strain off the often overloaded coastal highways. Inland, Granada, Córdoba and Seville are all within easy reach of Málaga; so, too, are **Ronda** and the beautiful "White Towns" to the west, and a handful of relatively restrained coastal resorts, such as **Nerja**, to the east.

★**Bar La Paz Garrido** Avda. de Mijas ☎ 952 478 341. Just north of the Pza. de la Constitución, this hugely popular bar-restaurant serves up some of the best-value seafood in town – the gazpacho, *boquerones a la plancha* (fried anchovies) and *patatas bravas* (spicy sautéed potatoes) are highly recommended. Main dishes €6–12. June–Sept Tues–Sun 1.15–4pm & 8.15pm–midnight; Oct–May Tues–Sun 8.15pm–midnight.

Mesón Don Pé C/la Cruz s/n ☎ 952 478 351. One of the few restaurants worth recommending in the zone south of the Pza. de la Constitución, this specializes in mid-price meat dishes and *cochinillo asado* (suckling pig). Main dishes €8–21. June–Sept daily 6.30pm–midnight; Oct–May Mon–Sat 6.30pm–midnight.

Mesón Salamanca C/Capitán 1, just off the east side of Pza. de la Constitución ☎ 952 592 287. Reliable and popular bar-restaurant with an attractive dining room offering traditional dishes, both fish and meat. It has a range of good-value *menús del día* ranging between €9.50 and €22 (including wine) and has an extensive tapas menu. Daily 1–4pm & 7–11pm.

La Plaza Pza. de la Constitución ☎ 952 463 359, ⊚ barlaplazafuengirola.es. This vibrant bar with a popular terrace on the square opens for breakfast and serves economical tapas, *platos combinados*, snacks and salads throughout the day, with many daily specials. In the evening it serves *copas* (late-night drinks). Main dishes (cafetería) €5–10. Daily 9am–1am.

Marbella and around

Sheltered by the hills of the Sierra Blanca, **MARBELLA** stands in considerable contrast to most of what's come before. Since it attracted the attentions of the smart set in the 1960s the town has zealously polished its reputation as the Costa del Sol's most stylish resort. Glitz comes at a price, of course: many of the chic restaurants, bars and cafés cash in on the hype, and in the old town – where most visitors spend their time – everything costs considerably more. Until the recent financial crash Marbella had the highest per capita income in Europe and more Rolls-Royces than any European city apart from London. In recent years, the Spanish government and authorities have been exercised by the arrival in Marbella of alleged Russian and Italian mafia bosses who have been buying up property and using the town as a base to control their criminal empires, activities that led to the discovery by police in 2005 of Europe's biggest-ever money-laundering operation, channelling billions of dollars from worldwide crime syndicates into Marbella-registered companies. In an ironic twist of history, there's been a massive return of Arabs to the area, especially since the late King Fahd of Saudi Arabia built a White House lookalike, complete with adjacent mosque, on the town's outskirts, where the Saudi royal family and a veritable army of courtiers and servants spend the summer months.

Four South of Marbella's centre, there are three excellent **beaches** stretching east from Playa de la Badajilla and Playa de Venus to Playa de la Fontanilla to the west, which gets progressively less crowded the farther west you go.

The old town

To be fair, Marbella has been spared the worst excesses of concrete architecture and also retains the greater part of its **old town** – set back a little from the sea and the new development. Centred on the attractive Pza. de los Naranjos and still partially walled, the old town is hidden from the main road and easy to miss. Slowly, this original quarter is being bought up and turned into clothes and jewellery boutiques and restaurants, but the process isn't that far advanced. You can still sit in an ordinary bar in a small old square and look up beyond the whitewashed alleyways to the mountains of Ronda.

Puerto Banús

The seriously rich don't stay in Marbella itself. They secrete themselves away in villas in the surrounding hills or laze around on phenomenally large and luxurious yachts at the marina and casino complex of **Puerto Banús**, 6km west of town. As you'd expect, Puerto Banús has more than its complement of big-name designer boutiques, cocktail bars and restaurants, most of them very pricey.

ARRIVAL AND INFORMATION

MARBELLA

By bus From the bus station (☎ 952 764 401) in the north of the town, buses #2 or #7 will drop you close by the old town; otherwise, it's a 20min walk south along C/Trapiche.

Turismo Pza. de los Naranjos (Mon–Fri 9am–8pm, Sat 10am–2pm; ☎ 952 768 707). It can help with accommodation, and provides a street-indexed town map.

ACCOMMODATION

All Marbella's budget **accommodation** is in the old town, or on or around C/Luna just east of there. Pressure on rooms is tight in July and extremely so in August, when you'll need to book ahead.

Albergue Juvenil C/Trapiche 2 ☎ 952 771 491, ⓦ inturjoven.com. To the north of the old town, the *Albergue Juvenil* has economical beds in smart double and four-person en-suite rooms, and there's also a pool. Under-26 **€22**, over-26 **€26**

Hostal Berlin C/San Ramón 21 ☎ 952 821 310, ⓦ hostalberlin.com. Sparkling and very friendly *hostal*; all rooms come with a bath, a/c and satellite TV, and free internet access is available to guests (also wi-fi throughout). Bargain rates outside July and August. **€60**

Hostal El Gallo C/Lobatos 44 ☎ 952 827 998, ⓦ hostalelgallo.es. Good-value en-suite a/c rooms with

TV above a great little *barrio* restaurant. **€63**

Hostal Juan C/Luna 18 ☎ 952 779 475, ⓔ pensionjuan @hotmail.com. This *hostal* has a friendly proprietor and good-value en-suite rooms with TVs and fridges. Situated on a tranquil street. **€45**

★**Hotel La Morada Mas Hermosa** C/Montenebros 16, ☎ 952 924 467, ⓦ lamoradamashermosa.com. Sited to the north of Pza. de los Naranjos, this is an enchanting small hotel in a refurbished eighteenth-century townhouse with elegant, individually styled a/c rooms (most with terraces). **€105**

EATING AND DRINKING

4

Although it now has a Michelin double-starred chef (Dani García at the restaurant of the *Hotel Puente Romano*), Marbella's best-value eating and drinking places aren't always the most obvious. Avoid the touristy and overpriced **restaurants** on the Pza. de los Naranjos, which turn the whole square into their dining terrace after dark – you're better off seeking out some of Marbella's excellent **tapas bars** and less brassy restaurants. And despite it's high-roller reputation, it's possible to dine well in Marbella at normal *andaluz* prices.

TAPAS BARS

Bar Altamirano Pza. de Altamirano 4 ☎ 952 824 932, ⓦ baraltamirano.es. Great place for some of the freshest seafood tapas and *raciones* in town; has a terrace with tables spread across a small square. Thurs–Tues 1–4pm & 7–11.30pm.

Cervecería Simon C/Pablo Casals 1 ☎ 952 779 746. Fine tapas at low prices and a pleasant terrace on which to enjoy them. Specials include *chopitos fritas* (cuttlefish) and *rabo de toro* (stewed bull's tail). Daily 9am–11pm.

El Estrecho C/San Lázaro 12 ☎ 952 770 004, ⓦ barelestrecho.es. Founded in 1954, this is an excellent and atmospheric little tapas bar with a wide range of choice. There's a small dining room off to the side if you want to make a meal of it, and cool jazz sounds often float in the background. Try their *carne mechada* (larded meat) or *mejillones tigres* (tiger mussels). Mon–Sat noon–midnight.

★**Taberna de Santiago** Avda. del Mar 5 ☎ 952 770 078. This is the tapas and *raciones* bar of the famous nearby *Santiago* restaurant (see below). Everything is top quality and the prices are very reasonable: an *ensalada mixta*, *ración* of *bacalao con tomate* (cod in tomato sauce) and half-litre *jarra* of house wine is easily enough for two people and weighs in at under €30; or try a paella at €20 for

two people. It has a pleasant sea-view terrace. Daily noon–5pm & 7–midnight.

RESTAURANTS

El Gallo C/Lobatas 44, ☎ 952 827 998. Good, popular and economical little neighbourhood restaurant serving up traditional *andaluz* dishes such as *langostino pil pil* (prawns with chilli) and *conejo al ajillo* (rabbit in garlic). There's also a great-value menu for €10. Mon–Wed & Fri–Sun 1–4pm & 7–11pm.

★**Gaspar** C/Notario Luís Oliver 19, west of Pza. de los Naranjos ☎ 992 779 098, ⓦ tabernagaspar.es. A gem of a restaurant run by a friendly family from Rioja – which explains the comprehensive wine list. Besides their standard dishes – including *tortilla*, *cordero asado* (charcoal grilled lamb), and *pastel de berenjenas* (aubergine terrine) you can also order a few plates of *raciones* to share. If you have to wait for a table you can peruse the books in the restaurant's library, and impromptu flamenco sometimes happens when *cantantes* (singers) drop in for a meal. Expect to pay around €25. Daily 2–5pm & 8.30pm–midnight.

★**Santiago** Avda. Duque de Ahumada s/n ☎ 952 770 078, ⓦ restaurantesantiago.com. For a splurge, head for *Santiago*, near the Puerto Deportivo, one of Marbella's swankiest and oldest restaurants, founded in the 1950s by

Santiago Domínguez – who started out with a *chiringuito* on the beach opposite. Over fifty years later Santiago is still overseeing his restaurant and bars and is famous throughout Spain as one of the great restaurateurs. The restaurant serves traditional *malagueño* cuisine (both fish and meat) with a creative touch. The "value for money" philosophy is typified by a recommended *menú de degustación* (€50 including wine). There's also an attractive seafront terrace. Daily noon–midnight.

Sociedad de Pesca Deportiva Puerto Deportivo, Local 5, to the left as you enter the port ☎ 952 775 438. The Marbella fishermen's club should know a thing or two about seafood and they serve up reasonably priced delicious fish and *mariscos* at their restaurant with a terrace in the port. Try their *almejas a la marinera* (clams in wine) or *boquerones fritos* (fried anchovies). Menu for €10. Tues–Sun noon–4pm & 7.30pm–midnight.

NIGHTLIFE

Marbella has one of the liveliest **nightlife** scenes on the *costa*, with action centred around Pza. Puente de Ronda, Pza. de Africa in the old town and Pza. de Olivos to the west of here. The once riotious Puerto Deportivo, the seafront yacht harbour, also has a scene, although this has cooled down in recent years due to complaints about noise. It now boasts many laidback *copas* bars with terraces filled with sofas and easy chairs.

Buddha Avda. del Mar 3 ☎ 952 772 891, ⓦ buddhamarbella.net. Central retro *discoteca* and club with themed nights (such as *música Cubana*, salsa, and Sixties sounds). Daily 10pm–6am.

Club Premiere Pza. de Olivos 2 ☎ 652 632 499. Lively music venue often staging live gigs ranging from pop to electronica and acid jazz and regularly features jam sessions with local musicians. One of a clutch of clubs around this square. Daily midnight–7am.

Punto Faro Puerto Deportivo, in front of the lighthouse ☎ 952 820 128. Popular lounge and cocktail bar – try their *daiquiri de fresa* (strawberry) – attracting an over-35s crowd with a classic rock-soul playlist.

El Palique C/Ancha 3 ☎ 669 032 071. Small *andaluz*-style bar which aficionados claim serves up the best mojitos in town. There's live flamenco on Saturday nights and the playlist ranges from flamenco-rock to flamenco-chill. Tues–Sun 5pm–3am.

Estepona and around

The coast continues to be upmarket (or "money-raddled", as Lauric Lee put it) until you reach **ESTEPONA**, about 30km west, which is about as Spanish as the resorts round here get. It lacks the enclosed hills that give Marbella character, but the hotel and apartment blocks that sprawl along the front are restrained in size, and there's space to breathe. The fine sand beach has been enlivened a little by a promenade studded with flowers and palms, and, away from the seafront, the old town is very pretty, with cobbled alleyways and two delightful plazas. At the beginning of July, the Fiesta y Feria week transforms the place, bringing out whole families in flamenco-style garb.

Plaza de Toros museum complex

Mon–Fri 9am–3pm, Sat 10am–2pm • Free

From May onward, Estepona's **bullfighting** season gets under way in a modern **bullring** reminiscent of a Henry Moore sculpture. This building has now taken on an additional role as the location for no fewer than three museums: the **Museo Etnográfico** (folk museum), the **Museo Paleontológico** (paleontology) and, perhaps the most interesting, the **Museo Taurino** (bullfighting), with fascinating exhibits and photos underlining the importance of *taurinismo* in Andalucian culture.

Selwo Adventure Park

July & Aug daily 10am–8pm (see website for rest of year opening times) • €24.50, children (up to age 9) €17; discount tickets offering reductions up to €6 are frequently available from the Estepona *turismo* • ⓦ selwo.es

The **Selwo Adventure Park** is a landscaped zoo 6km to the east of town where the two-thousand-plus resident animals are allowed to roam in "semi-liberty" and there are re-creations of African Zulu and Masai villages. To reach the park, there are signed exits indicated from the N340 and the A7-E15 Autopista del Sol, plus regular buses from all the major Costa del Sol resorts.

Casares

Beyond Estepona, 8km along the coast, a minor road (the MA546) climbs a farther 13km into the hills to **CASARES**, one of the classic *andaluz* White Towns. In keeping with the genre, it clings tenaciously to a steep hillside below a castle, and has attracted its fair share of arty types and expats. But it remains comparatively little known; bus connections are just about feasible for a day-trip (currently leaving 1pm, returning 4pm; 45min) or you may want to consider an overnight stay. Further details from the *turismo*.

ARRIVAL AND INFORMATION

By bus The station is on Avda. de España, to the west of the centre behind the seafront.

Turismo The town's efficient and centrally located *turismo*

ESTEPONA AND AROUND

is located inside the Ayuntamiento at Pza. de las Flores s/n (Mon–Fri 9am–3.30pm, Sat 10am–2pm; ☎ 952 802 002); they will supply town maps and can help you find a room.

ACCOMMODATION AND EATING

Camping Parque Tropical 6km east of town on the A7, km162 ☎ 952 793 618. Estepona's nearest campsite is set back a few hundred metres from the beach in a former tropical garden with plenty of shade plus a spectacular conservatory-pool and restaurant. **€30**

★ **La Escollera** Puerto Pesquero ☎ 952 806 354. Now into its eighth decade and sited at the foot of the lighthouse in the fishing harbour, adjoining the Puerto Deportivo, this is a vibrant, reasonably priced restaurant for excellent fish and *mariscos*. In addition to a great tapas bar there's a wonderful sea-view terrace restaurant. At weekends you'll need to arrive early to get a table or book ahead. Main dishes €8–20. Tues–Sun 1–4.30pm & 8–11.30pm.

Hostal El Pilar Pza. de las Flores ☎ 952 800 018. Friendly *hostal* on a charming plaza offering en-suite balcony rooms with a/c and TV. **€55**

Hotel Mediterráneo Avda. de España 68, on the

seafront to the east of C/Terraza ☎ 952 793 393, ⓦ mediterraneo-estepona.com. Functional but good-value seafront hotel, where rooms have bath, TV and (most) sea views. Ask for a higher room on the front (these are quieter). **€65**

Pensión San Miguel C/Terraza 16 ☎ 952 802 616. Friendly establishment with its own bar, a little west of Pza. de las Flores. All rooms are en suite and come with a/c and TV. **€50**

Restaurante El Gavilán del Mar C/Correo 1 actually on Pza. Arce ☎ 952 802 856. A decent place for seafood (meat dishes are also on offer), specializing in paella, and with a terrace on this charming square. Try their *sardinas asadas* (grilled sardines) or a *zarzuela* (fish casserole) which is enough for two. Main dishes €8–15. Mon & Wed–Sun 11.30am–midnight.

Gibraltar

GIBRALTAR's interest is essentially its novelty: the genuine appeal of the strange, looming physical presence of its rock, and the dubious one of its preservation as one of Britain's last remaining colonies. For most of its history it has existed in a limbo between two worlds without being fully part of either. It's a curious place to visit, not least to witness the bizarre process of its opening to mass tourism from the Costa del Sol. Ironically, this threatens both to destroy Gibraltar's highly individual hybrid society and at the same time to make it much more British, after the fashion of the expat communities and huge resorts of the Costa. In recent years, the economic boom Gibraltar enjoyed throughout the 1980s, following the reopening of the border with Spain, has started to wane, and the future of the colony – whether its population agrees to it or not – is almost certain to involve closer ties with Spain.

The Town

The town has a necessarily simple layout, as it's shoehorned into the narrow stretch of land on the peninsula's western edge in the shadow of the towering Rock. **Main Street** (La Calle Real) runs for most of the town's length, a couple of blocks back from the port. On and around Main Street are most of the shops, together with many of the British-style pubs and hotels.

BRITISH SOVEREIGNTY IN GIBRALTAR

Sovereignty of the Rock (a land area smaller than the city of Algeciras across the water) will doubtless eventually return to Spain, but at present a **stalemate** exists regarding the colony's future. For Britain, it's a question of divesting itself of the colony without incurring the wrath of Gibraltar's citizens who are implacably opposed to any further involvement with Spain. For Spain, there are unsettling parallels with the *presidios* (Spanish enclaves) on the Moroccan coast at Ceuta and Melilla – both at present part of Andalucía. Nonetheless, the British presence is in practice waning and the British Foreign Office clearly wants to steer Gibraltar towards a new, harmonious relationship with Spain. To this end, they are running down the significance of the military base, and now only a token force of under a hundred British troops remains – most of these working in a top-secret high-tech bunker buried deep inside the Rock from where the Royal Navy monitors sea traffic through the Strait (accounting for a quarter of the world's movement of all shipping).

In 1967, just before Franco closed the border in the hope of forcing a quick agreement, the colony voted on the return to Spanish control of the Rock – rejecting it by 12,138 votes to 44. Most people would probably sympathize with that vote – against a Spain that was then still a dictatorship – but almost fifty years have gone by, Spanish democracy is now secure, and the arguments are becoming increasingly tenuous. May 1996 saw a change in the trend of internal politics, with the defeat of the colony's pugnaciously anti-Spanish Labour government (following two previous landslide victories) and the election of a new **Social Democratic administration** led by Peter Caruana. Caruana won further victories in 2000, 2004 and 2007 but was defeated in the 2011 election by a Labour-Liberal coalition, following which Labour leader Fabian Picardo became chief minister.

The ruling PP (Partido Popular) conservative **Spanish administration** also elected in 2011 has repeated the claims over Gibraltar voiced by all its predecessors, and the political stalemate seems set to continue for as long as Britain uses the wishes of the Gibraltarians as a pretext for blocking any change in the colony's status – a policy that infuriates the Spanish government, whose former foreign minister, Abel Matutes, stated that the wishes of the residents "did not apply in the case of Hong Kong".

Yet Gibraltarians stubbornly cling to British status, and all their institutions are modelled on British lines. Contrary to popular belief, however, they are of neither mainly Spanish nor British blood, but an ethnic mix descended from Genoese, Portuguese, Spanish, Menorcan, Jewish, Maltese and British forebears. **English** is the official language, but more commonly spoken is what sounds to an outsider like perfect Andalucian Spanish. It is, in fact, *llanito*, an Andalucian dialect with the odd borrowed English and foreign word reflecting its diverse origins – only a Spaniard from the south can tell a Gibraltarian from an Andalucian.

Trafalgar Cemetery

Prince Edward's Road • Daily 8.30am–sunset

To the south of the town centre, beyond the city walls, lies the evocative **Trafalgar Cemetery**, where some of those who perished at the Battle of Trafalgar are buried. A memorial to the battle stands in the cemetery grounds and a number of graves display a good line in imperial epitaphs.

The Gibraltar Museum

Bomb House Lane • Mon–Fri 10am–6pm, Sat 10am–2pm • £2

The **Gibraltar Museum** is mainly concerned with gilding the imperial story, although the building also holds two well-preserved and beautiful fourteenth-century **Moorish baths** as well as a rather incongruous Egyptian mummy washed up in the bay.

Nelson's Anchorage

Rosia Road • Mon–Sat 9.30am–6.45pm • £1, free with inclusive Rock ticket

At **Nelson's Anchorage** a monstrous **100-tonne Victorian gun** marks the site where Nelson's body was brought ashore – preserved in a barrel of rum – from HMS *Victory* after the Battle of Trafalgar in 1805.

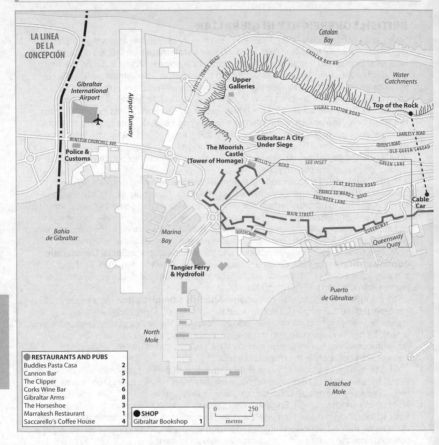

4

RESTAURANTS AND PUBS

Buddies Pasta Casa	2
Cannon Bar	5
The Clipper	7
Corks Wine Bar	6
Gibraltar Arms	8
The Horseshoe	3
Marrakesh Restaurant	1
Saccarello's Coffee House	4

SHOP

Gibraltar Bookshop	1

The Top of the Rock

Cable car: Daily: 9.30am–6pm, last trip down 5.45pm • £10.50 (sterling) return, £8 one-way

From near the southern end of Main Street you can hop on a **cable car**, which will carry you up to the summit – **The Top of the Rock** as it's logically known. Although the cable car's fare structure militates against it, after riding to the top it's possible to walk back down, a pleasant twenty- to thirty-minute stroll. From The Top of the Rock you can look over the Strait of Gibraltar to the Atlas Mountains of Morocco and down to the town, the elaborate water-catchment system cut into the side of the rock, and ponder whether it's worth heading for one of the beaches such as Catalan Bay (see p.252).

Upper Rock Nature Reserve

All sites Daily: summer 9.30am–7.15pm; winter 9.30am–6.15pm • **Nature Reserve** £0.50, inclusive ticket for cave, tower and exhibition €10, under-12s half price

The area at The Top of the Rock, designated the **Upper Rock Nature Reserve**, is home to six-hundred-plus plant and tree species, and also contains the Apes' Den (a fairly reliable viewing point to see the tailless monkeys), St Michael's Cave and other sights; the attractions in this zone cost extra and may only be accessed with an **inclusive ticket,**

available from tourist offices or at each attraction. A grand tour of the Rock takes a half- to a full day.

From the cable-car stop at The Top of the Rock, it's an easy walk south along St Michael's Road through the Nature Reserve, to **St Michael's Cave**, an immense natural cavern that led ancient people to believe the Rock was hollow and gave rise to its old name of Mons Calpe (Hollow Mountain). The cave was used during the last war as a bomb-proof military hospital and nowadays hosts occasional concerts. If you're adventurous, you can arrange at the tourist office for a guided visit to Lower St Michael's Cave, a series of chambers going deeper down and ending in an underground lake.

If you prefer to walk rather than take the cable car to the top, you could visit the **Tower of Homage**, reached via Willis' Road. Dating from the fourteenth century, this is the most visible surviving remnant of the old **Moorish Castle**. Near to the Tower of Homage on Willis' Road itself, and housed in a former ammunition store – with some eighteenth-century graffiti etched into its walls – is the **Gibraltar: A City Under Siege** exhibition, which uses tableaux to explain the various sieges the Rock has endured during its three hundred years as a British colony. Farther up the same road you'll find the **Upper Galleries** (aka the Great Siege Tunnels), which were blasted out of the rock during the Great Siege of 1779–82 in order to point guns down at the Spanish lines.

To **walk down** from The Top of the Rock, follow Signal Station Road and St Michael's Road to O'Hara's Road (passing O'Hara's Battery, a privately restored WWII gun emplacement; entry £3.50) and the **Mediterranean Steps** – a very steep descent most of the way down the east side (not for those who suffer from vertigo), turning the southern corner of the Rock. You'll eventually pass through the **Jews' Gate** and into Engineer Road, from where the return to town is through the Alameda Gardens.

Catalan Bay

There's just one tiny fishing village at **Catalan Bay**, which is where you'll find the Rock's best **beach** backed by a characterless stretch of seafront reminiscent of a hum-drum British holiday resort. The inhabitants of the village like to think of themselves as very distinct from the townies on the other side of the Rock. It's easily reached by following Devil's Tower Road from near the airport (20min walk) or on buses #4 or #8 from Market Square.

ARRIVAL AND DEPARTURE   GIBRALTAR

By air Blands Travel (Cloister Building, Irish Town; ☎ 20079478, ⊛ blandstravel.com; closed Sat & Sun), the leading travel agent in Gibraltar can assist with booking easyJet (4 daily) and Monarch Airlines (daily) flights to London and the latter's (4 weekly) flights to Manchester.

By bus Owing to the relatively scarce and pricey accommodation, you're far better off visiting the Rock on a day-trip from La Línea or Algeciras. The border with Gibraltar is a 5min walk from the centre of La Línea. Just over the border buses (#5; every 15min) make the short journey to Main Street and the town centre. This is also an easy 10min walk across part of the airport runway.

Destinations Buses from Algeciras go to La Línea on the hour and half-hour (30min).

By car If you have a car, don't attempt to bring it to Gibraltar – the queues at the border are always atrocious

and parking is a nightmare owing to lack of space. Use the underground car parks in La Línea – there's one beneath the central Pza. de la Constitución – and either take the bus or walk into Gibraltar.

By ferry (to Morocco) One decidedly functional attraction of Gibraltar is its role as a port for Morocco. A catamaran service, the *Tanger Med*, sails to Tangier (Fri 6pm; 1hr) and back (Sun 7.30pm local time); check with the agent for the current timetable. Tickets – available from the agent Turner, 65/67 Irish Town (☎ 20078305, ✉ turner@gibtelecom.net) – cost £37.50 one-way and £68 return for a foot passenger (email the agent for vehicle charges). Blands Travel (see above) runs twice-weekly day-trips to Tangier on Wednesday and Saturday (£80), which includes a guided tour, camel ride and lunch. A useful site for checking the latest ferry schedules is ⊛ directferries .co.uk.

INFORMATION AND TOURS

Turismo In Casemates Square (Mon–Fri 9am–5.30pm, Sat 10am–3pm, Sun 10am–1pm; ☎ 20045000, ⊛ visitgibraltar.gi), and there's a sub-office in the customs and immigration building at the border (Mon–Fri 9am–4.30pm; ☎ 20074982). Much of Gibraltar – with the exception of the cut-price booze shops – closes down at the weekend, but the tourist sights remain open, and this can be a quiet time to visit.

Currency The Gibraltar pound is used (the same value as the British pound, but different notes and coins); if you pay in euros, you generally fork out about five percent more. It's best to change your money once you arrive in Gibraltar, since the exchange rate is slightly higher than in Spain and

there's no commission charged. Gibraltar pounds can be hard to change in Spain.

Bookshop The Gibraltar Bookshop, 300 Main Street ☎ 20071864, is a good source for stocking up on holiday reading and has a wide selection of books on the Rock's history.

Dolphin-spotting trips Daily dolphin-spotting boat trips, run by companies operating from Marina Bay, including Dolphin Safari (£25, children £12.50; ☎ 20071914, ⊛ dolphinsafari.gi) and Dolphin Adventure (£25, children £12.50; ☎ 20050650, ⊛ www.dolphin.gi). You should ring first to book places or ask the tourist office to do it for you.

ACCOMMODATION

Shortage of space on the Rock means that **places to stay** are at a premium and there's little in the budget category. No **camping** is allowed on the peninsula, and if you're caught sleeping rough or inhabiting abandoned bunkers, you're likely to be arrested and fined.

Bristol Hotel Cathedral Square ☎ 20076800, ⓦ bristolhotel.gi. Long-established three-star with refurbished rooms and a pool (there is a supplement for a sea view). **£86**.

Cannon Hotel 9 Cannon Lane ☎ 20051711, ⓦ cannon hotel.gi. Small, pleasant hotel close to Main St with a/c rooms, some sharing bath. English breakfast included. **£42**

Emile Youth Hostel Montagu Bastion, Line Wall Rd ☎ 20051106, ⓦ emilehostel.net. Gibraltar's privately run youth hostel has the cheapest beds (with shared bathrooms) in town, but it's not the most attractive location. Dorms **£18**, doubles **£40**

Rock Hotel 3 Europa Rd ☎ 20073000, ⓦ rockhotel gibraltar.com. Flagship hotel immediately below the Apes' Den, trading on its imperial connections – rooms are decorated in "colonial style" and come with ceiling fans and a trouser press; some have sea views. **£185**

EATING AND DRINKING

Restaurants are far more plentiful than places to stay, though by Spanish standards are still relatively expensive: pub snacks or fish and chips are reliable stand-bys. Main Street is crowded with touristy places, while Gibraltarian **pubs** mimic traditional English styles (and prices), but are often rowdy, full of soldiers and visiting sailors.

RESTAURANTS

Buddies Pasta Casa 15 Cannon Lane ☎ 20040627. Decent pasta in all its varieties is served up here – as well as the ubiquitous fish and chips. Main dishes £5–11. Daily noon–10pm.

The Clipper 78 Irish Town ☎ 20079791. Spacious diner serving British-style pub grub – a house special is steak-and-ale pie – along with a variety of beers. Main dishes £6–10. Mon–Fri & Sun 9am–10pm, Sat 9am–4pm.

Corks Wine Bar 79 Irish Town ☎ 20075566. This is a tranquil venue and offers a variety of salads and pasta dishes as well as pub-style favourites such as steak-and-Guinness pie. Main dishes £7–16. Daily 10am–10pm; Sat closes 4pm; closed Sun.

Marrakesh Restaurant 9 Governor's Parade ☎ 20075196. An interesting Moroccan option in the centre of town, with a pleasant terrace. A wide-ranging menu offers couscous (chicken, lamb and vegetarian), tagines and other Magrebí dishes. Main dishes £7–13. Mon–Sat noon–3pm & 7–11pm.

Saccarello's Coffee House 57 Irish Town ☎ 20070625. *Saccarello's* is a local institution and a great place for tea and home-made confectionery. It also does lunch dishes such as pies, quiche and lasagne and there's free wi-fi throughout. Main dishes £7–12. Mon 8.30am–4pm, Tues–Sat 8.30am–7.30pm.

PUBS

Cannon Bar Cannon Lane. One of Gibraltar's few (relatively) quiet pubs with friendly staff, decent food and a small terrace. Main dishes £4–10. Daily 9am–midnight.

Gibraltar Arms 186 Main St ☎ 20072133. British-style boozer in the heart of the action with the usual all-day pub food (including their all-day British breakfast). Tends to stay open longer than its neighbours. Main dishes £5–10. Daily 7am–late.

The Horseshoe 193 Main St ☎ 20077444. Decent and hearty pub grub with an outdoor terrace. Serves a range of British and international beers. Main dishes £6–11. Daily 9am–midnight.

Algeciras

ALGECIRAS occupies the far side of the bay from Gibraltar, spewing out smoke and pollution in the direction of the Rock. The last town of the Spanish Mediterranean, it must once have been an elegant resort; today, it's unabashedly a port and industrial centre, its suburbs extending on all sides. When Franco closed the border with Gibraltar at La Línea it was Algeciras that he decided to develop to absorb the Spanish workers formerly employed in the British naval dockyards, thus breaking the area's dependence on the Rock.

Most travellers are scathing about the city's ugliness, and unless you're waiting for a bus or train, or heading **for Morocco**, there's admittedly little reason to stop. However, once you start to explore, you'll discover that the **old town** has some very attractive corners that seem barely to have changed in fifty years, especially around Pza. Alta.

ARRIVAL AND INFORMATION

ALGECIRAS

By train The train station (☎ 956 653 456) is at C/San Bernardo s/n, 1.2km behind the port. At Algeciras, the train line begins again, heading north to Ronda, Córdoba and Madrid. The route to Ronda – through spectacular mountain scenery – is one of the best rail journeys in Andalucía; there are four departures a day.

Destinations Córdoba: (3 daily; 3hr 15min); Granada (3 daily; 4hr 20min); Madrid (2 daily; AVE 5hr 20min); all Algeciras northbound trains go via Ronda (1hr 40min) and the Bobadilla junction.

By bus The main bus station (☎ 956 653 456) is in C/San Bernardo, behind the port, next to the *Hotel Octavio* and just short of the train station.

Destinations Cádiz (hourly 7am–10pm; 2hr 15min); La Línea (for Gibraltar: every 30min; 30min); Madrid (4 daily; 8hr); Seville (8 daily; 1hr 45min); Tarifa (every 30min).

By ferry Morocco is easily visited from Algeciras: in summer, there are crossings to Tangier and to the Spanish *presidio* of Ceuta, little more than a Spanish Gibraltar with a brisk business in duty-free goods, but a relatively painless way to enter Morocco. Tickets cost €25–35 one-way to Tangier or Ceuta (depending on the company), and are sold at scores of travel agents along the waterfront and on most approach roads. For up-to-date information on hydrofoils and fast-ferries, check with the *turismo* or with the ferry companies: Trasmediterránea, on the harbourfront (☎ 956 583 400, ⟨w⟩ trasmediterranea.es), or Viajes Transafric at Avda. Marina 4 (☎ 956 654 311, ⟨w⟩ transafric.com), fronting the port. Viajes Transafric also do a daily all-inclusive day-trip to Tangier by fast-ferry, which includes a guided tour, lunch and time for shopping (€55). Wait till Tangier – or if you're going via Ceuta, Tetouan – before buying any Moroccan currency; rates in the embarkation building kiosks are very poor. A useful site for checking the latest ferry schedules is ⟨w⟩ directferries.co.uk.

Destinations Ceuta (up to 25 daily; 35min); Tangier (up to 30 daily; 1hr–2hr 30min).

Turismo On C/Juan de la Cierva (Mon–Fri 9am–7.30pm, Sat & Sun 9.30am–3pm; ☎ 670 948 731, ⟨w⟩ ayto-algeciras .es), the pedestrianized avenue running east–west between the harbour and the train and bus stations. They can provide a town map, help with finding a room and have up-to-date ferry schedules.

White Towns southwest of Ronda

Andalucía is dotted with small, brilliantly whitewashed settlements – the **Pueblos Blancos** or "White Towns" – most often straggling up hillsides towards a castle or towered church. Places such as **Mijas**, up behind Fuengirola, are solidly on the tourist trail, but even here the natural beauty is undeniable. All of them look great from a distance, though many are rather less interesting on arrival. Arguably the best lie in a roughly triangular area between Málaga, Algeciras and Seville; at its centre, in a region of wild, mountainous beauty, is the spectacular town of **Ronda**.

Castellar de la Frontera

The first White Town on the route proper is **CASTELLAR DE LA FRONTERA**, 27km north of Algeciras, a bizarre village enclosed within the walls of a striking thirteenth-century Moorish castle, whose population, in accord with some grandiose scheme, was moved downriver in 1971 to the "new" town of Nuevo Castellar, turning the castle settlement into a ghost village. Although remote and isolated, much of the village inside the castle has been restored and now has a couple of bars and places to stay.

TOWARDS RONDA FROM THE COAST

Of several possible approaches to Ronda from the coast, the stunningly scenic route up **from Algeciras**, via Gaucín, is the most rewarding – and worth going out of your way to experience. It's possible by either bus or train (a spectacularly scenic option), or, if you've time and energy, can be walked in four or five days. En route, you're always within reach of a river and there's a series of hill towns, each one visible from the next, to provide targets for the day. Casares is almost on the route, but more easily reached from Estepona.

From Málaga, most buses to Ronda follow the coastal highway to San Pedro before turning into the mountains via the modern A376 *autovía*, dramatic enough, but rather a bleak route, with no villages and only limited views of the sombre rock face of the Serranía; an alternative route, via Álora and Ardales, is far more attractive and is taken by a couple of daily buses. The two-hour train ride up from Málaga is another scenic option, with three connecting services daily, including a convenient early-evening departure.

ACCOMMODATION	CASTELLAR DE LA FRONTERA

Casas Rurales de Castellar The same company that runs *Hotel Castellar* also runs *Casas Rurales de Castellar* which consists of a number of restored village houses with a decent restaurant attached. **€68**

Hotel Castellar ☎ 956 693 150, ⊚ tugasa.com. Of the two places to stay inside the castle walls, *Hotel Castellar* occupies part of the castle and has well-equipped rooms with fine views. B&B. **€66**

Jimena de la Frontera and around

JIMENA DE LA FRONTERA, 20km north of Castellar de la Frontera along the A405, is a far larger and more open hill town, rising to a grand Moorish castle with a triple-gateway entrance and round keep. In recent years it has become home to a considerable number of British expats who probably feel the need to be within working and shopping distance of Gibraltar.

Parque Natural de los Alcornocales

Jimena is also a gateway to the **Parque Natural de los Alcornocales**, a vast expanse of verdant hill country stretching south to the sea and north to El Bosque and covered with *alcornocales* (cork oaks). A haven for large numbers of birds and insects, the park is also a paradise for walkers. *Walking in Andalucía* by Guy Hunter-Watts describes half a dozen walks in the park, two starting in Jimena.

ACCOMMODATION AND EATING	JIMENA DE LA FRONTERA

Bar Ventorrillero Pza. de la Constitución 2 ☎ 956 640 997. At the foot of C/Sevilla, the town's main artery, this is a friendly bar-restaurant with a weekday lunchtime menu for €9. Tues–Sun 1–4.30pm & 7.30–11pm.

Camping Los Alcornocales ☎ 956 640 060, ⊚ www.campinglosalcornocales.com. Jimena's campsite occupies a suberb location with great views on the north side of town (reached by following C/Sevilla to the end), and has its own restaurant. **€21**

Hostal El Anon C/Consuelo 34 ☎ 956 640 113, ⊚ hostalanon.com. The charming and friendly *Hostal El Anon* is perhaps the best place to stay, comprising a series of tastefully renovated houses and stables with bar, restaurant and rooftop pool. Offers rooms and apartments. Doubles **€60**, apartments **€72**

Restaurante Bar Cuenca Avda. de los Deportes, on the way into town ☎ 956 640 152. This is perhaps the town's best place to eat, serving tapas and meals in its main room and with a pretty terrace patio at the rear. Main dishes €7–15. Daily 9am–midnight.

Gaucín

Beyond Jimena, it's 23km farther along the A405 passing through woods of cork oak and olive groves to reach **GAUCÍN**. Almost a mountain village, Gaucín commands tremendous views (to Gibraltar and the Moroccan coast on a very clear day), and makes a great place to stop over.

ARRIVAL AND DEPARTURE	GAUCÍN

By bus and train You can reach Gaucín by bus or by train, but the train station (at El Colmenar on the fringes of the Cortés nature reserve) is 13km away. From here it's a bracing and mostly uphill hike to the village; a taxi (around €20 one-way) can be arranged at *Bar-Restaurante Flores* fronting the station (☎ 952 153 026) or from the *taxista* (☎ 630 226 657) when they are closed. The *Flores* also does decent meals (€8 *menú*), and there are several other bars here. The train line between Gaucín and Ronda passes through a handful of tiny villages. En route, you can stop off at the station of Benaoján-Montejaque, from where it's an hour's trek to the prehistoric Cueva de la Pileta (see p.260). From Benaoján, Ronda is just three stops (30min) down the line.

ACCOMMODATION

★ **Ahora Casa Rural** Bda. El Colmenar, 500m downhill from the train station ☎ 952 153 046, ⊚ casaruralahora.com. This is a wonderful little oasis close to the train station with en-suite cabin-style rooms surrounded by greenery. There's a communal room with *chimenea* (stove), library and games in addition to a wellbeing centre offering all kinds of alternative therapies plus a sauna and Jacuzzi. Also has its own restaurant (with a menu for €14). **€55**

Hostal Moncada C/Luís Armiñian, Gaucín ☎ 952 151 324. En-suite a/c rooms above a restaurant and next to the *gasolinera* (where you should enquire; get a room at the back for a view and less noise) as you come into the village from Jimena. €40

Hotel Rural Fructuosa C/Covento 67, Gaucín ☎ 952 151 072, ⚏ lafructuosa.com. A more upmarket option in the village proper is the charming *Hotel Rural Fructuosa*, with its own – very good – mid-priced restaurant nearby. €70

Ronda

The full natural drama of **RONDA**, rising amid a ring of dark, angular mountains, is best appreciated as you enter the town. Built on an isolated ridge of the *sierra*, it's split in half by a gaping river gorge, **El Tajo**, which drops sheer for 130m on three sides. Still more spectacular, the gorge is spanned by a stupendous eighteenth-century arched bridge, the **Puente Nuevo**, while tall, whitewashed houses lean from its precipitous edges.

Much of the attraction of Ronda lies in this extraordinary view, or in walking down by the Río Guadalvín, following one of the donkey tracks through the rich green valley. Birdwatchers should look out for the lesser kestrels nesting in the cliffs beneath the Alameda; lower down you can spot crag martins. The town has a number of **museums** and, surprisingly, has sacrificed little of its character to the flow of day-trippers from the Costa del Sol.

Ronda divides into three parts: on the south side of the bridge is the old Moorish town, **La Ciudad**, and farther south still, its **San Francisco** suburb. On the near north side of the gorge, and where you'll arrive by public transport, is the largely modern **Mercadillo** quarter.

La Ciudad

La Ciudad retains intact its Moorish plan and a great many of its houses, interspersed with a number of fine Renaissance mansions. It is so intricate a maze that you can do little else but wander at random. However, at some stage, make your way across the eighteenth-century **Puente Nuevo** bridge, peering down the walls of limestone rock into the yawning Tajo and the Río Guadalvín, far below.

Puente Nuevo

April–Sept Mon–Fri 10am–7pm; Oct–March Mon–Fri 10am–6pm; Sat & Sun (all year)10am–3pm • €2 • ☎ 649 965 338

The spectacular eighteenth-century **Puente Nuevo** bridge spanning the gorge between the Mercadillo and La Ciudad quarter was originally the town prison, and last saw use during the Civil War, when Ronda was the site of some of the south's most vicious massacres. Hemingway, in *For Whom the Bell Tolls*, recorded how prisoners were thrown alive into the gorge. The bridge itself is a remarkable construction and has its own **Centro de Información**, housed in the former prison above the central arch with exhibits documenting its construction and history; entry is to the side of the parador in Pza. de España.

Casa del Rey Moro gardens

C/Santo Domingo 17 • Daily: April–Oct 10am–7pm; Nov–March 10am–6pm • €4 • ☎ 952 161 002

The somewhat arbitrarily named **Casa del Rey Moro** (House of the Moorish King) is an early eighteenth-century mansion built on Moorish foundations. The gardens (but not the house itself) have recently been opened to the public, and from here a remarkable underground stairway, the Mina, descends to the river; these 365 steps (which can be slippery after rain), guaranteeing a water supply in times of siege, were cut by Christian slaves in the fourteenth century. There's a viewing balcony at the bottom where you can admire El Tajo's towering walls of rock and its bird life, although the long climb back up will make you wonder whether it was worth it.

Palacio del Marqués de Salvatierra
C/Marqués de Salvatierra 26

The **Palacio del Marqués de Salvatierra** is a splendid Renaissance mansion with a fine portal depicting an oddly primitive, half-grotesque frieze of Adam and Eve together with the colonial images of four Peruvian Indians (or possibly Incas) supporting a pediment. Twin sets of Corinthian pillars flank the entrance, topped by an elegantly crafted wrought-iron balcony in the *rondeño* style. The house is still used by the family, and hence prohibits visits.

Baños Árabes
C/San Miguel • Mon–Fri April–Oct 10am–7pm; Nov–March 10am–6pm; all year Sat & Sun 10am–3pm • €3, free on Mon

At the foot of C/Santo Domingo are two old town bridges – the **Puente Viejo** of 1616 and the single-span Moorish **Puente de San Miguel**; nearby, on the southeast bank of the river, are the distinctive hump-shaped cupolas and glass roof-windows of the old **Baños Árabes**. Dating from the thirteenth century and recently restored, the complex is based on the Roman system of cold, tepid and hot baths and is wonderfully preserved; note the sophisticated barrel-vaulted ceiling and brickwork octagonal pillars supporting horseshoe arches.

Santa María La Mayor
Pza. Duquesa de Parcent • Daily: April–Sept 10am–8pm; Oct–March 10am–6pm • €4

At the centre of La Ciudad, on Ronda's most picturesque square, the Pza. Duquesa de Parcent, stands the cathedral church of **Santa María La Mayor**, originally the Moorish town's Friday mosque. Externally, it's a graceful combination of Moorish, Gothic and Renaissance styles with the belfry built on top of the old minaret. The interior is decidedly less interesting, but you can see an arch covered with Arabic calligraphy, and just in front of the street door, a part of the old Arab *mihrab*, or prayer niche, has been exposed.

Casa de Mondragón
Pza. de Mondragón s/n • April–Sept Mon–Fri 10am–7pm, Oct–March 10am–6pm; Sat & Sun (all year) 10am–3pm • €3

Slightly west of Pza. Duquesa lies the fourteenth-century **Casa de Mondragón**, probably the real palace of the Moorish kings. Inside, three of the patios preserve original stuccowork and there's a magnificent carved ceiling, as well as a small museum covering local archeology and aspects of Moorish Ronda.

Museo Lara
C/Armiñán 29 • Daily 11am–7pm • €4

To the northeast of the Pza. Duquesa de Parcent, on C/Armiñán, which bisects La Ciudad, you'll find the **Museo Lara**, containing the collection of *rondeño* Juan Antonio Lara, a member of the family that owns and runs the local bus company of the same name. An avid collector since childhood, Señor Lara has filled the spacious museum with a fascinating collection of antique clocks, pistols and armaments, musical instruments and archeological finds, as well as early cameras and cinematographic equipment.

Museo del Bandolero
C/Armiñán 65 • Daily April–Sept 10.45am–8pm; Oct–March 10.45am–7pm • €3.75

The **Museo del Bandolero** is largely devoted to celebrating the Serranía's illustrious, mainly nineteenth-century bandits and includes displays of their weapons, as well as tableaux and audiovisual presentations.

The southern end of La Ciudad
Near the southern end of La Ciudad, to the right, are the ruins of the **Alcázar**, once impregnable until razed by the French ("from sheer love of destruction", according to

the nineteenth-century hispanist Richard Ford) in 1809. Beyond here the principal gates of the town, the magnificent Moorish **Puerto de Almocábar**, through which passed the Christian conquerors (led personally by Fernando), and the triumphal **Puerta de Carlos V**, erected later during the reign of the Habsburg emperor, stand side by side at the entrance to the suburb of San Francisco.

Mercadillo and Plaza de Toros

Bullring and museum open daily: April–Sept 10am–8pm; Oct–March 10am–6pm • €6.50

The Mercadillo quarter, which grew up in the wake of the Reconquest, is of comparatively little interest, although it is now the town's commercial centre. There is only one genuine monument here, the eighteenth-century **Plaza de Toros** sited on Pza. Teniente Arce, close to the beautiful clifftop *paseo*, Paseo de Orson Welles, offering spectacular views towards the Sierra de Ronda. Ronda played a leading part in the development of bullfighting and was the birthplace of the modern *corrida* (bullfight). The ring, built in 1781, is one of the earliest in Spain and the fight season here is one of the country's most important. At its September *feria*, the *corrida goyesca*, honouring Spain's great artist Goya, who made a number of paintings of the fights at Ronda, takes place in eighteenth-century costume. You can wander around the arena, and there's a **museum** inside stuffed with memorabilia such as famous bullfighters' *trajes de luces* (suits) and photos of the ubiquitous Ernest Hemingway and Orson Welles – both avid aficionados – visiting the ring.

ARRIVAL AND INFORMATION   RONDA

By bus Ronda's bus station – used by all bus companies – is on Pza. Redondo in the Mercadillo quarter, to the northeast of the bullring.
Destinations Arcos de la Frontera (2 daily; 1hr 45min); Cádiz (2 daily; 3hr 15min); Grazalema (2 daily; 35min); Jerez de la Frontera (2 daily; 2hr 15min); Málaga (12 daily; 2hr); Marbella (4 daily; 1hr 15min); San Pedro de Alcantara (5 daily; 1hr); Seville (5 daily; 2hr 30min); Ubrique (2 daily; 1hr 30min); Zahara de la Sierra (2 daily; 55min).
By train Ronda's train station lies a 5min walk east of the bus station on Avda. Andalucía, in the Mercadillo quarter to the northeast of the bullring. The station is 10min walk or an easy bus or taxi ride from the centre.

By car Arriving by car, your best bet for street parking is to park as far out as possible (near the train station is usually feasible where there's also a pay car park), or head straight for one of the central signposted pay car parks.
Turismo-Municipal tourist office The combined Junta de Andalucía and municipal tourist office lies opposite the south side of the bullring (April–Sept Mon–Fri 10am–7pm, Oct–March Mon–Fri 10am–6pm; Sat 10am–2pm & 3–5pm, Sun 10am–2.30pm (both all year); ☎952 187 119) and can help with accommodation and provide a map.
Online The website ⊛ turismoderonda.es is a good source of information.

ACCOMMODATION

Most of the **places to stay** are in the **Mercadillo** quarter, although some more upmarket hotels have recently opened up in the old Moorish quarter, **La Ciudad**, on the south side of El Tajo. Both zones are within easy walking distance of Pza. de España.

Alavera de los Baños C/San Miguel s/n ☎952 879 143, ⊛ alaveradelosbanos.com. Enchanting small hotel with stylish rooms (some with terraces), garden, pool and views from rear rooms of grazing sheep on the hill across the river. Also has a couple of elegant suites. **€95** suites **€107**
Camping El Sur Carretera Ronda–Algeciras km 2.8 ☎952 875 939. Ronda's campsite with pool, bar and restaurant, lies some 2km out of town along the Algeciras road (A369). **€19**
Hotel Andalucía C/Martínez Astein 19 ☎952 875 450, ⊛ hotel-andalucia.net. Pleasant en-suite rooms in leafy

surroundings opposite the train station. **€35**
Hotel Colón C/Pozo 1, on the Pza. de la Merced ☎952 870 218, ⊛ hotelcolon.es. Charming small hotel with a/c en-suite facilities and – in rooms 301 & 302 – your own spacious roof terrace. **€48**
★ **Hotel San Gabriel** C/José Holgado 19, La Ciudad ☎952 190 392, ⊛ hotelsangabriel.com. One of a number of recently opened hotels in La Ciudad, this is a stunning restoration of an eighteenth-century mansion, with beautifully furnished a/c rooms, an amusing five-seater cinema for guests (with a library of classic DVDs)

and welcoming proprietors. €95

Parador de Ronda Pza. de España ☎952 877 500, ⓦwww.parador.es. Ronda's imposing parador offers elegantly furnished rooms with spectacular views overlooking El Tajo, plus a pool, terrace bar and very good restaurant. €180

EATING AND DRINKING

Most of Ronda's bargain **restaurants** are grouped round Pza. del Socorro and nearby Pza. Carmen Abela, though there are also some to be found near Pza. de España.

Bar Bodega San Francisco Ruedo de Alameda 32, La Ciudad ☎952 878 162. Highly popular tapas bar in this atmospheric *barrio* with a terrace on an attractive leafy square. Try their *tortilla de camarones* (shrimp fritters) or *filetito con mojo picón* (steaklet with spicy sauce). Mon–Wed & Fri–Sun 11am–4pm & 7pm–12.30am.

Bar Faustino C/Santa Cecilia 4 ☎952 190 307. Lively place for economical tapas, *raciones* and *platos combinados*, with friendly service and an upstairs dining area. Stays open until well beyond midnight and has an open-air patio. Tues–Sun 11am–midnight.

★**Bar Maestro** C/Espinel 7, near the Pza. de Toros ☎952 871 017. Great hole-in-the-wall (and one of Ronda's oldest tapas venues which opened in 1946) with a tempting menu recited verbally by the proprietor. It's also a bar *taurino*, so the photos of past *torero* greats plus Hemingway and Welles (all one-time customers) gaze down from the walls. Try their *costillas* (pork ribs). Has a small street terrace. Mon–Sat 7am–midnight.

Café Alba C/Espinel 44 ☎952 871 009. Piping-hot *churros* and delicious breakfast coffee with a street terrace on this pedestrian thoroughfare. Daily 8am–4pm.

Parador de Ronda Pza. de España ☎952 877 500. The parador's upmarket restaurant has an excellent choice of local and regional dishes such as *rabo de toro* (bull's tail)

and *solomillo de ciervo* (venison loin), many of them appearing on a menu for €30. Main dishes €12–26. Daily 1–4pm & 8–11pm.

Patatín Patatán C/Borrego 7 ☎610 411 866. Popular tapas bar with a buzzing *ambiente* and a wide range of specials, including *patatas allioli* (potatoes in garlic sauce) and *habas a la rondeña* (broad beans). Mon, Tues & Thurs–Sun 12am–4pm & 8pm–1am.

★**Restaurante Almocábar** Ruedo de Alameda 5, La Ciudad ☎952 875 977. Excellent restaurant serving creative variations on regional dishes along with a range of salads such as the *ensalada almocábar*, which includes figs, cheese, pears and honey. House specials include *paté de perdiz* (partridge) and *cochinillo* (suckling pig). Has a pleasant terrace on this square. Main dishes €8–15. Reservations advised. Mon & Wed–Sun 1–5pm & 7.30pm–midnight.

Tragabuches C/José Aparicio 1 ☎952 190 291. Ronda's most acclaimed restaurant is named after a celebrated eighteenth-century *rondeño* bullfighter-turned-bandit, and, with an adventurous menu and minimalist decor, is perhaps worth a splurge if you're into *El Bulli*-style chemistry, textures, flavours and foam. They offer a range of tasting *menús* for €60–86. Booking advised. Tues–Sat 1.30–3.30pm & 8.30pm–10.30pm; Sun 1.30–3.30pm.

Around Ronda

Ronda makes an excellent base for exploring the superb countryside of the Serranía de Ronda to the south or for visiting the remarkable **Cueva de la Pileta**, with its prehistoric cave paintings, and the Roman ruins of **Ronda la Vieja**.

Ronda la Vieja

Wed–Sun 10am–2pm; hours could be changed; ring ☎951 041 452 or confirm with *turismo* • Free

Some 12km northwest of Ronda are the ruins of a town and **Roman theatre** at a site known as **Ronda la Vieja**, reached by turning right 6km down the main A374 road to Arcos/Seville. At the site a friendly farmer, who is also the guardian, will present you with a plan (in Spanish). Based on Neolithic foundations – note the recently discovered prehistoric stone huts beside the entrance – it was as a Roman town in the first century AD that Acinipo (the town's Roman name) reached its zenith. Immediately west of the theatre, the site's most imposing ruin, the ground falls away in a startlingly steep escarpment offering fine views all around, taking in the picturesque hill village of Olvera to the north.

Cueva de la Pileta

Daily guided visits on the hour 10am–1pm & 4–6pm • €8; limit of 25 persons per tour, booking essential at peak times • ☎ 952 167 343

West from Ronda is the prehistoric **Cueva de la Pileta**, a fabulous series of caverns with some marvellous paintings of animals (mainly bison), fish and what are apparently magic symbols. These etchings and the occupation of the cave date from about 25,000 BC – hence predating the more famous caves at Altamira in northern Spain – to the end of the Bronze Age. The tour lasts an hour on average, but can be longer, and is in Spanish – though the guide does speak a little English. There are hundreds of bats in the cave, and no artificial lighting, so visitors carry lanterns; you may also want to take a jumper, as the caves can be extremely chilly. Be aware if you leave a car in the car park that thieves are active here.

ARRIVAL AND DEPARTURE   CUEVA DE LA PILETA

By train and bus To reach the caves from Ronda, take either an Algeciras-bound local train to Estación Benaoján-Montejaque (4 daily; 25min), or a bus, which drops you a little closer in Benaoján. There's a bar and restaurant at the train station if you want a bite to eat before the 6km walk (1hr) to the caves. Follow the farm track from the right bank of the river until you reach the farmhouse (30min). From here, a track goes straight uphill to the main road just before the signposted turning for the caves.

By car If you're driving, follow the road to Benaoján and take the signed turn-off, from where it's about 4km.

White Towns northwest of Ronda

Ronda has good transport connections in most directions. Almost any route to the north or west is rewarding, taking you past a whole series of White Towns, many of them fortified since the days of the Reconquest from the Moors – hence the mass of "de la Frontera" suffixes.

Perhaps the best of all the routes, though a roundabout one, and tricky without your own transport, is to **Cádiz** via Grazalema, Ubrique and Medina Sidonia. This passes through the spectacular **Parque Natural Sierra de Grazalema** before skirting the nature reserve of **Cortes de la Frontera** (which you can drive through by following the road beyond Benaoján) and, towards Alcalá de los Gazules, running through the northern fringe of **Parque Natural de los Alcornocales**, which derives its name from the forests of cork oaks, one of its main attractions and the largest of its kind in Europe.

Grazalema

Twenty-three kilometres from Ronda, **GRAZALEMA** is a striking white village at the centre of the magnificent Parque Natural Sierra de Grazalema, a paradise for hikers and naturalists. The **Puerto de las Palomas** (Pass of the Doves – at 1350m the second-highest pass in Andalucía) rears up behind the village. Cross this (a superb walk or drive), and you descend to Zahara de la Sierra and the main road west (see opposite).

INFORMATION   GRAZALEMA

Turismo Located on Pza. Asomaderos, off the main square, Pza. de España (daily 10am–2pm & 3.30–7pm; ☎ 956 132 052), can provide information about the park, accommodation in the village and activities such as horseriding, and also sells good walking maps.

ACCOMMODATION AND EATING

The **bars and restaurants** on and around Pza. de España are generally reasonably priced, if not outstanding.

Cádiz El Chico Pza. de España 8 ☎ 956 132 027. Located on the main square, this is one of the town's better restaurants and specializes in dishes of the sierra – *cordero* *al horno de leña* (lamb in a wood-fired oven) is a signature dish. There's a lunchtime weekday menu for €12. Also does good tapas in its bar. Tues–Sat noon–5pm & 8pm–

midnight; Sun noon–5pm; closed Mon.

Camping Tajo Rodillo ☎956 132 418. Grazalema's campsite is located above the village at the end of C/Las Piedras. **€16.50**

Casa de las Piedras C/Las Piedras 6 ☎956 132 014, ⓦcasadelaspiedras.es. The only budget option, this friendly family-run *hostal* is located above the main square. It offers comfortable en-suite rooms and also rents out some apartments nearby. The *hostal*'s revamped mid-priced restaurant serves local dishes with a creative edge. House specials include *gazpacho verde* (green gazpacho made with avocado) and *asado de cerdo* (charcoal grilled pork). There's also a menu for €18 plus a vine-covered patio for alfresco dining. Main dishes €9–17. Daily 1–4pm & 7.30–11pm. Doubles **€48**, apartments **€65**

Lacidulia C/Agua 44 ☎956 132 101. Reliable, traditional bar-restaurant for dishes of the *sierra* including *carillada en*

salsa (pig's cheek), charcoal-grilled meat, soups and *arrozes* (rice dishes). There's also a menu for €8.50 plus a good selection of local wines. Has a street terrace and also does tapas. Main dishes €8–16. Daily 11am–11pm.

★**La Mejorana** C/Santa Clara 6 ☎956 132 327, ⓦlamejorana.net. One of the most attractive places to stay in the village, this welcoming *hostal* offers comfortably furnished rooms (many with views) in an elegant *casa señorial* complete with pool. B&B. **€58**

Hotel Villa de Grazalema Finca El Olivar s/n ☎956 132 032, ⓦwww.villasdeandalucia.com. This recently refurbished three-star hotel lies on the village's northern edge (a 3min walk) and has comfortable rooms with terrace balconies and fine views. It also rents out cottages (sleeping up to four). Facilities include a restaurant and bar, pool and free parking. Doubles **€72**, cottages **€138**

Ubrique

From Grazalema, following the scenic A2302 towards Ubrique takes you through the southern sector of the natural park, a landscape of dramatic vistas and lofty peaks. The road snakes through the charming ancient villages of Villaluenga del Rosario and Benaocaz with plenty of opportunities for hikes – perhaps down Benaocaz's six-kilometre-long paved Roman road – along the way. **UBRIQUE**, 20km southwest of Grazalema, is a natural mountain fortress and was a Republican stronghold in the Civil War. Today, it's a prosperous and bustling town, owing its wealth to the medieval guild craft of **leather working**. The highly skilled leather workers work for many of the big names (including Loewe, Louis Vuitton, Gucci) at unmarked workshops around the town. These high-value products are then whisked away to be sold in Madrid, Paris, Rome and London. Shops selling the output of numerous other workshops (footwear and bags, often at bargain prices) line the main street, Avda. Dr Solis Pascual.

ACCOMMODATION AND EATING   UBRIQUE

Hotel Occuris Avda. Dr Solis Pascual 49 ☎956 463 939, ⓦwww.hoteloccuris.com. Two-star hotel on the main street for pleasant enough en-suite rooms with a/c and TV plus its own tapas bar and restaurant. **€56**

El Laurel de Miguel C/San Juan Bautista 7, just behind

the main street ☎956 115 109. Very good tapas and *raciones* bar with a decent range of tapas and wines plus a street terrace. Try the *pluma ibérica* (pork loin) or *magret de pato* (duck breast). Tues–Sun noon–midnight.

Zahara de la Sierra

Heading directly to Jerez or Seville from Ronda, a scenic rural drive along the Grazalema park's eastern fringes, you pass below **ZAHARA DE LA SIERRA** (or *de los Membrillos* – "of the Quinces"), perhaps the most perfect example of these fortified hill towns. Set above a lake (in reality, the man-made *embalse*, or reservoir, which has dramatically changed the landscape to the north and east of town), Zahara is a landmark for many kilometres around, its red-tiled houses huddling round a church and castle perched on a stark outcrop of rock. Once an important Moorish citadel, the town was captured by the Christians in 1483, opening the way for the conquest of Ronda – and ultimately Granada.

ACCOMMODATION   ZAHARA DE LA SIERRA

Hostal Marqués de Zahara C/San Juan 3 ☎956 123 061. A pleasant and central *hostal* with en-suite balcony

rooms, a shady patio and its own restaurant nearby. **€50**

Hotel Los Tadeos Paseo de la Fuente s/n ☎956 123

086. Smart, refurbished small hotel near the swimming pool on the eastern edge of the village. Terrace balcony a/c rooms have great views and come with wet room or Jacuzzi, plus there's an infinity pool. €63

Hotel Arco de la Villa Camino Nazarí s/n ☎ 956 123 230, ⊚ tugasa.com. On the road leading up to the castle, this is a good-value and recently constructed hotel with spectacular views over the nearby *embalse*. €60

Arcos de la Frontera

Of more substantial interest than Zahara de la Sierra, and another place to break the journey, is **ARCOS DE LA FRONTERA**, taken from the Moors in 1264, over two centuries before Zahara fell – an impressive feat, for it stands high above the Río Guadalete on a double crag and must have been a wretchedly impregnable fortress. This dramatic location, enhanced by low, white houses and fine sandstone churches, gives the town a similar feel and appearance to Ronda – only Arcos is poorer and, quite unjustifiably, far less visited. The streets of the town are if anything more interesting, with their mix of Moorish and Renaissance buildings. At its heart is the Pza. del Cabildo, easily reached by following the signs for the parador, which occupies one side of it. Flanking another two sides are the castle walls and the large Gothic-Mudéjar church of **Santa María de la Asunción**; the last side is left open, offering plunging views to the river valley. Below the town to the north lies **Lago de Arcos** (actually a reservoir) where locals go to cool off in summer.

INFORMATION

Turismo Located on the hill leading up from the new to the old town at Cuesta de Belén 5 (Mon–Sat 9.30am–2pm; ⊚ www.ayuntamientoarcos.org), it can provide a town map and also does guided tours of the old town (April–Oct Mon–Fri 11am & 6pm, Nov–March 11am & 5pm; €4).

ACCOMMODATION

A number of **hostales** providing budget accommodation have recently opened up in the old town, formerly the exclusive preserve of a clutch of upmarket hotels. Staying a little out of town, at the **Lago de Arcos**, where there are two hotels, is another possibility. There's a bus service to the lake.

IN TOWN

★**La Casa Grande** C/Maldonado 10 ☎ 956 703 930, ⊚ lacasagrande.net. Perched along the same clifftop as the parador, this elegant hotel has beautiful rooms inside a restored *casa señorial* with a columned inner patio and a sensational view from the terrace of their bar across the river valley. They also offer more expensive suites. Doubles €90, suites €110

Hostal-Bar San Marcos C/Marqués de Torresoto 6 ☎ 956 700 721. Excellent *hostal* in the old town, offering pleasant rooms with bath. The friendly proprietors run a cosy bar-restaurant downstairs with a menu for €8. B&B. €42

★**Parador de Arcos de la Frontera** Pza. del Cabildo ☎ 956 700 500, ⊚ www.parador.es. Perched on a rock pedestal – with reassuringly reinforced foundations to prevent it from sliding over the cliff – this is one of the smaller paradores, with spacious balcony rooms to enjoy the view. There's a delightful patio (open to the public for drinks and afternoon tea) and the "crow's nest" terrace has the best views in town. Also has a restaurant with a recommended menu for €22. €163

ON LAGO DE ARCOS

Hacienda El Santiscal 3km out of town on the lakeside ☎ 956 708 313, ⊚ santiscal.com. Small country hotel in a beautiful converted *hacienda* with sumptuously decorated and furnished a/c rooms, restaurant and a pool in the grounds. Horseriding available. €75

Hotel Mesón de la Molinera Lago de Arcos ☎ 956 708 002, ⊚ mesondelamolinera.com. Tranquil location on the waterfront with stunning views towards Arcos on its hilltop. The hotel offers well-equipped balcony rooms with safe, while cheaper accommodation is on offer in chalet-style bungalows. Also has its own bar and restaurant. Easy parking. Doubles €80, bungalows €60

EATING AND DRINKING

There are plenty of places to **eat and drink** in Arcos in both the upper old town and the modern lower town.

Alcaraván C/Nueva 1 ☎ 956 703 397. This atmospheric cave restaurant is close to the castle walls and serves tapas and *platos asados* (roasted meats) as well as a variety of salads. Main dishes cost €5–15. Mon–Wed 12.30–4pm, Thurs–Sun 12.30pm–midnight.

Bar-Restaurante Terraza C/Múñoz Vásquez ☎ 956

700 668. Below the old town, with a terrace in the gardens of the Paseo de Andalucía, this is a pleasant place to sit out, and serves a wide variety of inexpensive *platos combinados* and offers a menu for €8. Mon, Tues & Thurs–Sun 9am–midnight.

Mesón Los Murales Pza. de Boticas 1 ☎ 685 809 661. One of the best low-priced options in the old town, close to the church of San Pedro, and serving an economical menu for €9. Has a pleasant street terrace. Main dishes €6–13. Mon–Wed & Fri–Sun 9am–11.30pm.

Seville (Sevilla)

"Seville," wrote Byron, "is a pleasant city, famous for oranges and women." And for its heat, he might perhaps have added, since **SEVILLE**'s summers are intense and start early, in May. Seville has three important monuments and an illustrious history, but what it's essentially famous for is its own living self – the greatest city of the Spanish south, of Carmen, Don Juan and Figaro, and the archetype of Andalucian promise. This reputation for gaiety and brilliance, for theatricality and intensity of life does seem deserved. It's expressed on a phenomenally grand scale at the city's two great festivals – **Semana Santa** (Holy Week at Easter) and the **Feria de Abril** (which starts two weeks after Easter Sunday and lasts a week). Either is worth considerable effort to get to. Seville is also Spain's second most important centre for **bullfighting**, after Madrid.

Despite its elegance and charm, and its wealth, based on food processing, shipbuilding, aircraft construction and a thriving tourist industry, Seville lies at the centre of a depressed agricultural area and has an unemployment rate of over thirty percent – one of the highest in Spain. The total refurbishment of the infrastructure boosted by the 1992 Expo – including impressive new roads, seven bridges, a high-speed rail link and a revamped airport – was intended to regenerate the city's (and the region's) economic fortunes, but has hardly turned out to be the catalyst for growth and prosperity promised at the time. Indeed, some of the colossal debts are still unpaid over two decades later.

Seville's **old city** – where you'll want to spend most of your time – is sited along the east bank of the Guadalquivir. At its heart, side by side, stand the three great monuments: the **Giralda tower**, the **Catedral** and the **Alcázar**, with the cramped alleyways of the **Barrio Santa Cruz**, the medieval Jewish quarter and now the heart of tourist life, extending east of them.

North of here is the main shopping and commercial district, its most obvious landmarks **Pza. Nueva**, **Pza. Duque de la Victoria** and the smart, pedestrianized **C/Sierpes**, which runs roughly between them. From **La Campana**, the small square at the northern end of C/Sierpes, C/Alfonso XII runs down towards the river by way of the **Museo de Bellas Artes**, second in importance in Spain only to the Prado in Madrid. Across the river is the earthier, traditionally working-class district of **Triana**, flanked to the south by the **Los Remedios** *barrio*, the city's wealthier residential zone where the great April *feria* takes place.

The Catedral

July & Aug Mon–Sat 9.30am–4pm; Sun 2.30–6pm; Sept–June Mon 11am–3.30pm, Tues–Sat 11am–5pm, Sun 2.30–6pm; ticket valid for Catedral and the Giralda • €8, under-16s free • ⓦ www.catedraldesevilla.es

Seville's **Catedral** (properly titled Santa María de la Séde) was conceived in 1402 as an unrivalled monument to Christian glory – "a building on so magnificent a scale that posterity will believe we were mad". To make way for this new monument, the Almohad mosque that stood on the proposed site was almost entirely demolished. Meanwhile, the canons, inspired by their vision of future repute, renounced all but a subsistence level of their incomes to further the building.

The Catedral was completed in just over a century (1402–1506), an extraordinary achievement, as it's the largest Gothic church in the world. As Norman Lewis says, "It expresses conquest and domination in architectural terms of sheer mass." Though it is built

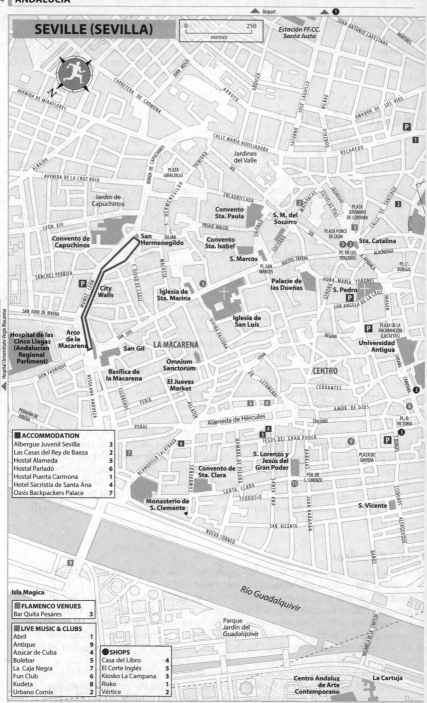

SEVILLE (SEVILLA)

0   250
metres

Airport

Estación FF.CC.
Santa Justa

ACCOMMODATION

Albergue Juvenil Sevilla	3
Las Casas del Rey de Baeza	2
Hostal Alameda	5
Hostal Parladó	6
Hostal Puerta Carmona	1
Hotel Sacristía de Santa Ana	4
Oasis Backpackers Palace	7

FLAMENCO VENUES

Bar Quita Pesares	3

LIVE MUSIC & CLUBS

Abril	1
Antique	9
Azucar de Cuba	4
Bulebar	5
La Caja Negra	7
Fun Club	6
Kudeta	8
Urbano Comix	2

SHOPS

Casa del Libro	4
El Corte Inglés	5
Kiosko La Campana	3
Risko	1
Vértice	2

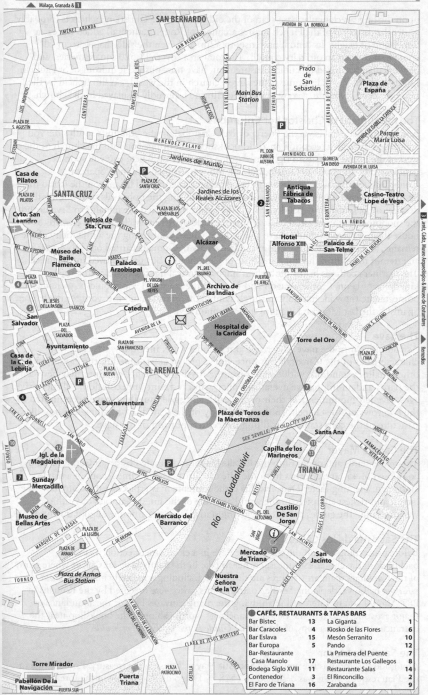

SEE 'SEVILLE: THE OLD CITY' MAP

● **CAFÉS, RESTAURANTS & TAPAS BARS**

Bar Bistec	13	La Giganta	1
Bar Caracoles	4	Kiosko de las Flores	6
Bar Eslava	15	Mesón Serranito	10
Bar Europa	5	Pando	12
Bar-Restaurante		La Primera del Puente	7
Casa Manolo	17	Restaurante Los Gallegos	8
Bodega Siglo XVIII	11	Restaurante Salas	14
Contenedor	3	El Rinconcillo	2
El Faro de Triana	16	Zarabanda	9

upon the huge, rectangular base-plan of the old mosque, the Christian architects (probably under the direction of the French master architect of Rouen cathedral) added the extra dimension of height. Its central nave rises to 42m, and even the side chapels seem tall enough to contain an ordinary church. The total area covers 11,520 square metres, and new calculations, based on cubic measurement, have now pushed it in front of St Paul's in London and St Peter's in Rome as the largest church in the world, a claim upheld by the *Guinness Book of Records*, a copy of whose certificate is proudly displayed in the church.

The monument to Christopher Columbus

Entry to the Catedral is via the Puerta de San Cristóbal on the building's south side; you are guided through a reception area and bookshop that brings you into the church to the west of the portal itself. Turn right once inside to head east, where you will soon be confronted by the **Tomb of Christopher Columbus** (Cristóbal Colón in Spanish). Columbus' remains were originally interred in the cathedral of Havana, on the island that he had discovered on his first voyage in 1492. But during the upheavals surrounding the declaration of Cuban independence in 1902, Spain transferred the remains to Seville, and the monumental tomb – in the late Romantic style by Arturo Mélida – was created to house them. However, doubts have always been voiced concerning the authenticity of the remains, and in 2002 scientists from the University of Granada carried out DNA tests in an attempt to confirm that they are those of Columbus – but these proved inconclusive. The mariner's coffin is held aloft by four huge allegorical figures, representing the kingdoms of León, Castile, Aragón and Navarra; the lance of León should be piercing a pomegranate (now inexplicably missing), symbol of Granada (and the word for the fruit in Spanish), the last Moorish kingdom to be reconquered.

The nave

As you move into the **nave**, sheer size and grandeur are, inevitably, the chief characteristics of the Catedral. But once you've grown accustomed to the gloom, two other qualities stand out with equal force: the rhythmic balance and interplay between the parts, and an impressive overall simplicity and restraint in decoration. All successive ages have left monuments of their own wealth and style, but these have been limited to the two rows of side chapels. In the main body of the Catedral only the great box-like structure of the **coro** stands out, filling the central portion of the nave.

The Capilla Mayor

The *coro* extends and opens onto the **Capilla Mayor**, dominated by a vast **Gothic retablo** composed of 45 carved scenes from the Life of Christ. The lifetime's work of a single craftsman, Fleming Pieter Dancart, this is the supreme masterpiece of the Catedral – the largest and richest altarpiece in the world and one of the finest examples of Gothic woodcarving. The guides provide staggering statistics on the amount of gold involved.

The Sacristía de los Cálices

Before proceeding around the edge of the nave in a clockwise direction it's best to backtrack to the church's southeast corner to take in the **Sacristía de los Cálices** where many of the Catedral's main art treasures are displayed, including a masterly image of *Santas Justa y Rufina* by Goya, depicting Seville's patron saints, who were executed by the Romans in 287. Should you be interested in studying the many canvases here or the abundance of major artworks placed in the various chapels, it's worth calling at the bookshop near the entrance to purchase a copy of the official *Guide to the Cathedral of Seville*.

The Sacristía Mayor

Alongside this room is the grandiose **Sacristía Mayor**, housing the treasury. Embellished in the Plateresque style, it was designed in 1528 by Diego de Riaño, one of the foremost

exponents of this predominantly decorative architecture of the late Spanish Renaissance.
Amid a confused collection of silver reliquaries and monstrances – dull and prodigious
wealth – are displayed the **keys** presented to Fernando by the Jewish and Moorish
communities on the surrender of the city; sculpted into the metal in stylized Arabic script
are the words "May Allah render eternal the dominion of Islam in this city". Through a
small antechamber here you enter the oval-shaped **Sala Capitular** (chapterhouse), with
paintings by Murillo and an outstanding **marble floor** with geometric design.

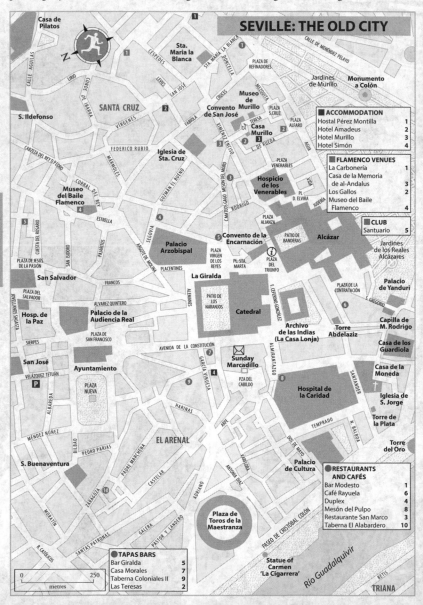

SEVILLE: THE OLD CITY

■ ACCOMMODATION

Hostal Pérez Montilla	1
Hotel Amadeus	2
Hotel Murillo	3
Hotel Simón	4

■ FLAMENCO VENUES

La Carbonería	1
Casa de la Memoria de al-Andalus	3
Los Gallos	2
Museo del Baile Flamenco	4

■ CLUB

Santuario	5

● RESTAURANTS AND CAFÉS

Bar Modesto	1
Café Rayuela	6
Duplex	4
Mesón del Pulpo	8
Restaurante San Marco	3
Taberna El Alabardero	10

● TAPAS BARS

Bar Giralda	5
Casa Morales	7
Taberna Coloniales II	2
Las Teresas	9

Puerta del Nacimiento

Continuing to the southwest corner and the **Puerta del Nacimiento** – the door through which pass all the *pasos* and penitents who take part in the Semana Santa processions – you then turn right (north) along the west wall, passing the Puerta Principal.

The Capilla de San Antonio

In the northwest corner, the **Capilla de San Antonio** has Murillo's *Vision of St Anthony* depicting the saint in ecstatic pose before an infant Christ. A magnificent work: try to spot where the restorers joined San Antonio back into place after he had been crudely hacked out of the picture by thieves in the nineteenth century. He was eventually discovered in New York – where art dealers recognized the work they were being asked to buy – and returned to the Catedral. *The Baptism of Jesus* above this is another fine work by the same artist.

The Capilla Real

The nave's north side leads to the Puerta de la Concepción, through which you will exit – but before doing so, continue to the northeast corner to view the domed Renaissance **Capilla Real**, built on the site of the original royal burial chapel and containing the body of Fernando III (El Santo) in a suitably rich, silver shrine in front of the altar. The large tombs on either side of the chapel are those of Fernando's wife, Beatrice of Swabia, and his son, Alfonso the Wise. The chapel is reserved for services and private prayer and may only be viewed via the entrance in Pza. Virgen de los Reyes (Mon–Sat 8am–2pm & 4–7pm; free). You are now close to the entry to the Giralda tower.

La Giralda

Same ticket as Catedral

The **entrance to the Giralda** lies to the left of the Capilla Real in the Catedral's northeast corner. Unquestionably the most beautiful building in Seville, the **Giralda**, named after the sixteenth-century *giraldillo*, or weather vane, on its summit, dominates the city skyline. From the entrance you can ascend to the **bell chamber** for a remarkable **view** of the city – and, equally remarkable, a glimpse of the Gothic details of the Catedral's buttresses and statuary. But most impressive of all is the tower's inner construction, a series of 35 gently inclined ramps wide enough to allow two mounted guards to pass.

The minaret

The Giralda tower, before it was embellished with Christian additions (see below), was the mosque's **minaret** and the artistic pinnacle of Almohad architecture. Such was its fame that it served as a model for other minarets at the imperial capitals of Rabat and Marrakesh. It was used by the Moors both for calling the faithful to prayer (the traditional function of a minaret) and as an observatory, and was so venerated that they wanted to destroy it before the Christian conquest of the city. This they were prevented from doing by the threat of Alfonso (later King Alfonso X) that "if they removed a single stone, they would all be put to the sword". Instead, it became the bell tower of the Christian Catedral.

The Giralda's construction

The Moorish structure took twelve years to build (1184–96) and derives its firm, simple beauty from the shadows formed by blocks of brick trelliswork (a style known as *sebka*), different on each side, and relieved by a succession of arched niches and windows. The original harmony has been somewhat spoiled by the Renaissance-era addition of balconies and, to a still greater extent, by the four diminishing storeys of the belfry – added, along with the Italian-sculpted bronze figure of "Faith" which surmounts them, in 1560–68, following the demolition by an earthquake of the

4

MOORISH SEVILLE

Seville was one of the earliest Moorish conquests (in 712) and, as part of the **Caliphate of Córdoba**, became the second city of al-Andalus. When the caliphate broke up in the early eleventh century it was by far the most powerful of the independent states (or *taifas*) to emerge, extending its power over the Algarve and eventually over Jaén, Murcia and Córdoba itself. This period, under a series of three Arabic rulers from the **Abbadid dynasty** (1023–91), was something of a golden age. The city's court was unrivalled in wealth and luxury and was sophisticated, too, developing a strong chivalric element and a flair for poetry – one of the most skilled exponents being the last ruler, al-Mu'tamid, the "poet-king". But with sophistication came decadence, and in 1091 Abbadid rule was overthrown by a new force, the **Almoravids**, a tribe of fanatical Berber Muslims from North Africa, to whom the Andalucians had appealed for help against the rising threat from the northern Christian kingdoms.

Despite initial military successes, the Almoravids failed to consolidate their gains in al-Andalus and attempted to rule through military governors from Marrakesh. In the middle of the twelfth century, they were in turn supplanted by a new Berber incursion, the **Almohads**, who by about 1170 had recaptured virtually all the former territories. Seville had accepted Almohad rule in 1147 and became the capital of this last real empire of the Moors in Spain. Almohad power was sustained until their disastrous defeat in 1212 by the combined Christian armies of the north, at Las Navas de Tolosa. In this brief and precarious period, Seville underwent a renaissance of public building, characterized by a new vigour and fluidity of style. The Almohads rebuilt the Alcázar, enlarged the principal mosque – later demolished to make room for the Christian Catedral – and erected a new and brilliant minaret, a tower over 100m tall, topped with four copper spheres that could be seen for miles around: the Giralda.

original copper spheres. Even so, it remains in its perfect synthesis of form and decoration one of the most important and beautiful monuments of the Islamic world.

The Patio de los Naranjos

To reach the Catedral's exit, move east along the nave's north side to reach the Puerta de la Concepción, passing through this to enter the **Patio de los Naranjos**. Along with the Giralda tower, this was the only feature to be spared from the original mosque. In Moorish times the mosque would have been entered via the Puerta del Pardon, now the visitor exit. Taking its modern name from the orange trees that now shade the patio, this was the former mosque's entrance courtyard. Although somewhat marred by Renaissance additions, the patio still incorporates a **Moorish fountain** where worshippers carried out ritual ablutions prior to worship. Interestingly, it incorporates a sixth-century font from an earlier Visigothic cathedral, which was in its turn levelled to make way for the mosque.

Archivo de las Indias

Mon–Sat 9.30am–4.45pm, Sun 10am–1.45pm; guided visits daily at noon and 1pm • Free

If the Columbus tomb has inspired you, or you have a keen interest in the navigator's travels, visit the sixteenth-century **Archivo de las Indias**, between the Catedral and the Alcázar. Originally called La Casa Lonja, it served as the city's old stock exchange (*lonja*). Built in the severe and uncompromising style of El Escorial near Madrid, and designed by the same architect, Juan de Herrera, in the eighteenth century it was turned into a storehouse for the archive of the Spanish empire – a purpose it served for almost three hundred years. In 2006, this mountain of documentation (of vital importance to scholars) was moved to another building around the corner and the Archivo was renovated, enabling visitors to enjoy Herrera's masterpiece in all its splendour once again. The exterior is defined by four identical facades, while corner pyramids supporting weather vanes are the main decorative feature. Inside, the sumptuous marble floors, bookcases in Cuban wood, arcaded central patio, and grand staircase in pink and black marble are a visual feast. The upper floor houses temporary **exhibitions** of interesting documents from the archive; these frequently include items such as Columbus' log and a letter from a penurious Cervantes (pre-*Don Quixote*) petitioning the king for a position in the Americas – fortunately for world literature, he was turned down.

The Ayuntamiento

Pza. de San Francisco • Guided visits Mon–Thurs 4.30pm & 7.30pm, Sat 10am; closed Aug • Free • ☎ 902 559 386

Another building worth a look and sited slightly to the north of the Catedral is the sixteenth-century **Ayuntamiento**, with a richly ornamented Plateresque facade by Diego de Riaño. The equally impressive interior – with Riaño's star-vaulted entrance hall and council chamber with gilded coffered ceiling – is open for guided visits.

The Alcázar

April–Sept Tues–Sat 9.30am–7pm; Oct–March Tues–Sat 9.30am–5pm; during busy periods a flow control system operates whereby 750 people are allowed to enter every 20–30min • €9.50 • ⓦ patronato-alcazarsevilla.es

Rulers of Seville have occupied the site of the **Alcázar** from the time of the Romans. Here was built the great court of the **Abbadids**, which reached a peak of sophistication and exaggerated sensuality under the cruel and ruthless al-Mu'tadid – a ruler who enlarged the palace in order to house a harem of eight hundred women, and who decorated the terraces with flowers planted in the skulls of his decapitated enemies. Later, under the **Almohads**, the complex was turned into a citadel, forming the heart of the town's fortifications. Its extent was enormous, stretching to the Torre del Oro on the bank of the Guadalquivir.

Parts of the Almohad walls survive, but the present structure of the palace dates almost entirely from the Christian period. Seville was a favoured residence of the Spanish kings for some four centuries after the Reconquest – most particularly of **Pedro the Cruel** (Pedro I; 1350–69) who, with his mistress María de Padilla, lived in and ruled from the Alcázar. Pedro embarked upon a complete rebuilding of the palace, employing workmen from Granada and utilizing fragments of earlier Moorish buildings in Seville, Córdoba and Valencia. Pedro's works form the nucleus of the Alcázar as it is today and, despite numerous restorations necessitated by fires and earth tremors, it offers some of the best surviving examples of **Mudéjar architecture** – the style developed by Moors working under Christian rule. Later monarchs, however, have left all too many traces and additions. Isabel built a new wing in which to organize expeditions to the Americas and control the new territories; Carlos V married a Portuguese princess in the palace, adding huge apartments for the occasion; and under Felipe IV (c.1624) extensive renovations were carried out to the existing rooms. On a more mundane level, kitchens were installed to provide for General Franco, who stayed in the royal apartments whenever he visited Seville.

Entry to the Alcázar and the Patio de la Montería

The Alcázar is entered from the Pza. del Triunfo, adjacent to the Catedral. The gateway, flanked by original Almohad walls, opens onto a courtyard where Pedro I (who was known as "the Just" as well as "the Cruel", depending on one's fortunes) used to give judgement; to the left is his **Sala de Justicia** and beyond this the **Patio del Yeso**, the only surviving remnant of the Almohads' Alcázar. The main facade of the palace stands at the end of an inner court, the **Patio de la Montería**; on either side are galleried buildings erected by Isabel. This principal facade is pure fourteenth-century Mudéjar and, with its delicate, marble-columned windows, stalactite frieze and overhanging roof, is one of the finest things in the whole Alcázar.

The Salón del Almirante

As you will exit on the other side of the complex, it's probably better to look round the **Salón del Almirante** (or Casa de Contración de Indias), the sixteenth-century building on the right, before entering the main palace. Founded by Isabel in 1503, this gives you a standard against which to assess the Moorish forms. Here most of the rooms seem too heavy, their decoration ceasing to be an integral part of the design. The only notable exception is the **Sala de Audiencias** (or Capilla de los Navigantes, Chapel of the Navigators) with its magnificent *artesonado* ceiling inlaid with golden rosettes; within is a fine sixteenth-century *retablo* by Alejo Fernández depicting Columbus (in gold) and Carlos V (in a red cloak) sheltering beneath the Virgin. In the rear, to the left, are portrayed the kneeling figures of the Indians to whom the dubious blessings of Christianity had been brought by the Spanish conquest.

The royal apartments

Daily 10am–1.30pm; guided tours last 30min and take place every 30min • €4.50 extra

The **royal apartments**, known as the **Palacio Real Alto**, are open for visits when not in use, and a temporary desk located in front of the Salón del Almirante sells tickets for a guided tour. This takes in the **royal chapel**, with its fine early sixteenth-century *retablo* by Nicola Pisano; the so-called **bedroom of Pedro I**, with fine early Mudéjar plasterwork; and the equally splendid **Sala de Audiencias** – with more stunning plaster and tile decoration – which is still used by the royal family when receiving visitors in Seville.

Palacio de Pedro I

As you enter the main palace, the **Palacio de Pedro I**, the "domestic" nature of Moorish and Mudéjar architecture is immediately striking. This involves no loss of grandeur but simply a shift in scale: the apartments are remarkably small, shaped to human needs, and take their beauty from the exuberance of the decoration and the imaginative use of space and light. There is, too, a deliberate disorientation in the layout of the rooms, which makes the palace seem infinitely larger and more open than it really is. From the entrance court a narrow passage leads straight into the central courtyard, the **Patio de las Doncellas** (Patio of the Maidens), its name recalling the Christians' tribute of one hundred virgins presented annually to the Moorish kings. The heart of the patio has recently been restored to its fourteenth-century original state after having been buried under a tiled pavement for four centuries. Archeologists have replanted the six orange trees that once grew in sunken gardens to either side of a central pool. The pool is now filled with goldfish – as it was in the time of Pedro I – a medieval way of eliminating mosquitoes in summer. The court's stuccowork, *azulejos* and doors are all of the finest Granada craftsmanship. Interestingly, it's also the only part of the palace where Renaissance restorations are successfully fused – the double columns and upper storey were built by Carlos V, whose *Plus Ultra* ("yet still farther") motto recurs in the decorations here and elsewhere.

Salons de Carlos V and Embajadores

Past the **Salón de Carlos V**, distinguished by a superb ceiling, are three rooms from the original fourteenth-century design built for María de Padilla (who was popularly thought to use magic in order to maintain her hold over Pedro – and perhaps over other gallants at court, too, who used to drink her bath water). These open onto the **Salón de Embajadores** (Salon of the Ambassadors), the most brilliant room of the Alcázar, with a stupendous *media naranja* (half-orange) wooden dome of red, green and gold cells, and horseshoe arcades inspired by the great palace of Medina Azahara outside Córdoba. Although restored, for the worse, by Carlos V – who added balconies and an incongruous frieze of royal portraits to commemorate his marriage to Isabel of

Portugal here – the salon stands comparison with the great rooms of Granada's Alhambra. Adjoining are a long dining hall (*comedor*) and a small apartment installed in the late sixteenth century for Felipe II.

Patio de las Muñecas

The last great room of the palace – the **Patio de las Muñecas** (Patio of the Dolls), takes its curious name from two tiny faces decorating the inner side of one of the smaller arches. It's thought to be the site of the harem in the original palace. In this room, Pedro is reputed to have murdered his brother Don Fadrique in 1358; another of his royal guests, Abu Said of Granada, was murdered here for his jewels (one of which, an immense ruby that Pedro later gave to Edward, the "Black Prince", now figures in the British crown jewels). The upper storey of the court is a much later, nineteenth-century restoration. On the other sides of the patio are the **bedrooms** of Isabel and of her son Don Juan, and the arbitrarily named **Dormitorio del los Reyes Moros** (Bedroom of the Moorish Kings).

Palacio de Carlos V

To the left of the main palace loom the large and soulless apartments of the **Palacio de Carlos V** – something of an endurance test, with endless tapestries (eighteenth-century copies of the sixteenth-century originals now in Madrid) and pink, orange or yellow paintwork. Their classical style asserts a different and inferior mood.

The gardens

It's best to hurry through to the beautiful and rambling **Jardines de los Reales Alcázares** (gardens), the confused but enticing product of several eras, where you can take a well-earned rest from your exertions. Here you'll find the vaulted baths in which María de Padilla is supposed to have bathed (in reality, an auxiliary water supply for the palace), and the **Estanque de Mercurio** with a bronze figure of the messenger of the gods at its centre. This pool was specially constructed for Felipe V in 1733, who whiled away two solitary years at the Alcázar fishing here and preparing himself for death through religious flagellation. Just to the left of the pool a path beyond the Puerta de Marchena leads to a pleasant **cafetería** with a terrace overlooking the gardens. South of here towards the centre of the gardens there's an unusual and entertaining **maze** of myrtle bushes and, nearby, the **pavilion** (*pabellón*) **of Carlos V**, the only survivor of several he built for relaxation.

Antigua Fábrica de Tabacos

Sept–June Mon–Sat 10am–6pm • Free

Immediately south of the Alcázar and fronting Avda. San Fernando lies the old tobacco factory and the setting for Bizet's *Carmen*. Now part of the university, the massive **Antigua Fábrica de Tabacos** was built in the 1750s and retains its position as the largest building in Spain after El Escorial. At its peak in the following century, it was also the country's largest single employer, with a workforce of some four thousand women, *cigarreras* – "a class in themselves", according to Richard Ford, who were forced to undergo "an ingeniously minute search on leaving their work, for they sometimes carry off the filthy weed in a manner her most Catholic majesty never dreamt of." Open when the university is in session, you are free to wander through the public areas and use the *cafetería*.

Parque María Luisa and Plaza de España

Ten minutes' walk to the south of the Alcázar, lies the **Parque de María Luisa** and the adjoining **Plaza de España**. These are wonderfully relaxing places to get away from the city bustle and are among the most pleasant – and impressive – public spaces in Spain.

The Parque de María Luisa used to form part of the vast grounds of the Palacio de San Telmo. The palace's nineteenth-century owner, the dowager duchess María Luisa, donated the park to the city in 1893 which then named it after her. Amid the ornamental pools and tree-shaded avenues lie various pavilions from the ill-fated Spanish Americas Fair. The Plaza de España was designed as the centrepiece of the fair, which was somewhat scuppered by the 1929 Wall Street crash. A vast semicircular complex, with its fountains, monumental stairways and mass of tile work, it would seem strange in most Spanish cities, but here it looks entirely natural, carrying on the tradition of civic display. At the fair, the plaza was used for the Spanish exhibit of industry and crafts, and around the crescent are *azulejo* scenes representing each of the provinces – an interesting record of the country at the tail end of a moneyed era. The buildings here fell into a terrible state in the latter part of the twentieth century, but have now been superbly restored and refurbished. The tiny strip of canal fronting the plaza has been refilled with water and *sevillanos* can be seen once again pottering about in the little rented boats.

Museo Arqueológico and Museo de Costumbres Populares

Pza. de América s/n • June–Sept Tues–Sat 9am–3.30pm, Sun 10am–5pm; Oct–May Tues–Sat 10am–8.30pm, Sun 10am–5pm • €1.50, free with EU passport • ☎ 955 120 632

Many of the buildings from the 1929 Spanish Americas Fair, some of them amazingly opulent, were put to use as public buildings after the event. Two of the grandest mansions – facing each other across an ornamental garden – are sited at the southern end of the Parque de María Luisa and have been pressed into service to house the city's archeological and folk museums.

The farthest south is the city's **Museo Arqueológico**, the most important archeology collection in Andalucía. The main exhibits include the **Carambolo Treasure**, a hoard of prehistoric gold jewellery found in the Seville suburb of Camas in 1958, and attributed to the land of Tartessus (the Biblical Tarshish) which, although not yet identified, probably lay in the region between Seville and the mineral-rich hills of Huelva. The treasure is now displayed in its own section – with background information on the Tartessian culture – on the second floor. The remainder of the collection displays Roman mosaics and artefacts from nearby Itálica and a unique Phoenician statuette of Astarte-Tanit, the virgin goddess once worshipped throughout the Mediterranean.

Opposite is the fabulous-looking **Museo de Costumbres Populares** (Popular Arts Museum), with an equally fine patio. The museum has displays of costumes, implements, furniture, textiles, photos and posters from times past, with interesting displays relating to traditional arts and crafts and the April *feria*. The basement ceramic display – illustrating the regional developments of this craft inherited from the Moors – is a highlight.

Barrio Santa Cruz

The **Barrio Santa Cruz** is very much in character with the city's romantic image, its streets narrow and tortuous to keep out the sun, the houses brilliantly whitewashed and festooned with flowering plants. Many of the windows are barricaded with *rejas* (iron grilles), behind which girls once kept chaste evening rendezvous with their *novios* who were forced to *comer hierro* ("eat iron") as passion mounted.

Casa de Pilatos

Pza. de Pilatos 1 • Daily: March–Sept 9am–7pm; Oct–Feb 9am–6pm • €6 ground floor only, both floors €8 (including audio-guide); Wed 3–7pm free for EU citizens with passport or ID card • ☎ 954 225 298

Of the numerous mansions, by far the finest is the so-called **Casa de Pilatos**, built by the Marqués de Tarifa on his return from a pilgrimage to Jerusalem in 1519 and popularly thought to have been in imitation of the house of Pontius Pilate. In fact, it's an interesting and harmonious mixture of Mudéjar, Gothic and Renaissance styles, featuring brilliant *azulejos*, a tremendous sixteenth-century stairway and one of the most elegant domestic patios in the city.

Hospicio de los Venerables Sacerdotes

Pza. de los Venerables 8 • Daily 10am–2pm & 4–8pm; guided visits every 30min • €5.50, Sun 4–7.30pm free • ☎ 954 562 696

Patios are a feature of almost all the houses in Santa Cruz: they are often surprisingly large and in summer they become the principal family living room. One of the most beautiful is within the Baroque **Hospicio de los Venerables Sacerdotes**, near the centre in a plaza of the same name – one of the few buildings in the *barrio* worth actively seeking out. The former hospice also displays some outstanding artworks including **sculptures** by Martínez Montañés and a painting of the *Last Supper* by Roelas, plus some wonderfully restored **frescoes** by Lucás Valdés and Valdés Leal in addition to a *Fray Pedro de Oña* by Zurbarán displaying the artist's special gift for portraying white draperies. The museum has recently added a Centro Velázquez which – in addition to other works by the Spanish master – displays a fine *Santa Rufina* and a spectacular *Inmaculada Concepción*.

Museo del Baile Flamenco

C/Manuel Rojas Marcos 3 • Daily 10am–7pm • €10 • ⓦ www.museoflamenco.com

The **Museo del Baile Flamenco** is an innovative and entertaining museum dedicated to the history and evolution of this emblematic *andaluz* art form. Set up in collaboration with celebrated flamenco dancer Cristina Hoyos, the museum is interactive (and multilingual), employing the latest sound and image technology to familiarize visitors with the origins of flamenco and the range of dance styles or "*palos*", which can all be seen at the touch of a button. The museum also stages concerts of flamenco.

Plaza de la Encarnación and Las Setas

Mirador and rooftop walkway Sun–Thurs 10.30am–11.45pm, Fri–Sat 10.30am–12.45am • €3 • **Museum** Tues–Sat 10am 8pm, Sun10am–2pm • €2.10 or free with a Real Alcázar entry ticket • ⓦ setasdesevilla.com

Almost at the geographical centre of the former walled city of Seville, the **Plaza de la Encarnación** was created in 1819 after Napoleon's invading forces demolished the convent of the same name that stood on the spot. Long criticized for its bleakness, at the start of the new millennium the city government decided to spectacularly raise its profile with a breathtaking piece of modern architecture.

Taking seven years to build, **Las Setas** or Metropol Parasol (as it is officially dubbed) is a 30m-high, 150m-long structure comprising a series of undulating wood-waffle flat-topped mushroom structures on giant concrete pillars. Claimed by its German architect, Jürgen Mayer, to be the world's largest timber construction, it incorporates a market, shopping mall, restaurant and a **basement museum** that imaginatively displays the ruins of Roman Sevilla – complete with mosaics – encountered during the preliminary exacavations. The structure's high point (in all senses) is a spectacular undulating **walkway** across the roof to a sky deck with stunning views over the city. When unveiled in 2011 the structure attracted much criticism and its official name did not last more than a couple of days – *sevillano* residents took one look and tagged it Las Setas (the mushrooms), the name everyone uses today.

Río Guadalquivir and around

Down by the **Río Guadalquivir** are pedal-boats for idling away the afternoons, and at night a surprising density of local couples. The main riverside landmark here is the twelve-sided **Torre del Oro**, built by the Almohads in 1220 as part of the Alcázar fortifications. It was connected to another small fort across the river by a chain that had to be broken by the Castilian fleet before their conquest of the city in 1248. The tower was later used as a repository for the gold brought back from the Americas – hence its name.

Hospital de la Caridad

Entry on C/Temprado 3 • Mon–Sat 9am–1pm & 3.30–7pm, Sun 9am–12.30pm • €5 including audio-guide • ⓦ www.santa-caridad.es

The **Hospital de la Caridad** was founded in 1676 by Don Miguel de Mañara, the inspiration for Byron's *Don Juan*. According to the testimony of one of Don Miguel's friends, "There was no folly which he did not commit, no youthful indulgence into which he did not plunge … (until) what occurred to him in the street of the coffin." What occurred was that Don Miguel, returning from a reckless orgy, had a vision in which he was confronted by a funeral procession carrying his own corpse. He repented his past life, joined the Brotherhood of Charity (whose task was to bury the bodies of vagrants and criminals), and later set up this hospital for the relief of the dying and destitute, for which purpose it is still used. Don Miguel commissioned a series of eleven paintings by Murillo for the chapel; seven remain (the French stole the others during the Napoleonic occupation), including a superlative image of *San Juan de Dios* for which Mañara himself posed as the model. Alongside them hang two *Triumph of Death* pictures by Valdés Leal. One, depicting a decomposing bishop being eaten by worms (beneath the scales of justice labelled *Ni más, Ni menos* – No More, No Less), is so powerfully repulsive that Murillo declared that "you have to hold your nose to look at it". The mood of both works may owe a lot to the vivid memory of the 1649 plague that killed almost half the population of the city.

Museo de Bellas Artes

Pza. del Museo 9 • June–Sept Tues–Sat 9am–3.30pm, Sun 10am–5.30pm; Oct–May Tues–Sat 10am–8.30pm, Sun 9am–5pm • €1.50, free with EU passport • ⓦ museodebellasartesdesevilla.es

Near the Pza. de Armas bus station is one of Spain's most impressive art galleries, the **Museo de Bellas Artes**, housed in a beautiful former convent. The collection is frequently rotated, so not all the works mentioned here may be on show.

Room 1

Among the highlights is a wonderful late fifteenth-century sculpture in painted terracotta in Room 1, *Lamentation over the Dead Christ*, by the Andalucian **Pedro Millán**, the founding father of the Seville school of sculpture. A marriage of Gothic and expressive naturalism, this style was the starting point for the outstanding seventeenth-century period of religious iconography in Seville.

Rooms 2 to 4

A later example, in Room 2, is a magnificent *San Jerónimo* by the Italian **Pietro Torrigiano**, who spent the latter years of his life in the city. Room 3 has a *retablo* of the *Redemption* (c.1562), with fine woodcarving by Juan Giralte. Here also is displayed the grisly terracotta sculpture of the severed head of John the Baptist by Nuñez Delgado, not something you want to see too soon after lunch.

Room 5

Beyond a serene patio and cloister, Room 5 is located in the monastery's former church, where the recently restored paintings on the vault and dome by the eighteenth-century *sevillano*, Domingo Martínez, are spectacular. In addition to a monumental *Last Supper* by Alonso Vázquez, here also is the nucleus of the collection: **Zurbarán**'s *Apotheosis of St Thomas Aquinas*, as well as a clutch of works by **Murillo** in the apse, crowned by the great *Immaculate Conception* – known as "*La Colosal*" to distinguish it from the other work here with the same name. Below this is displayed the same artist's *Virgin and Child*; popularly known as *La Servilleta* because it was said to have been painted on a dinner napkin, the work is one of Murillo's greatest.

Rooms 6 to 10

Upstairs, Room 6 (quadrated around the patio) displays works from the Baroque period, among which a moving *Santa Teresa* by **Ribera** – Spain's master of *tenebrismo* (darkness penetrated by light) – and a stark *Crucifixion* by Zurbarán stand out. Room 10 contains more imposing canvases by Zurbarán, including *St Hugo visiting the Carthusian Monks at Supper* and another almost sculptural *Crucifixion* to compare with the one in Room 6. Here also are sculptures by **Martínez Montañés**, the sixteenth-century "Andalucian Lysippus", whose early *St Dominic in Penitence* and *San Bruno* from his mature period display mastery of technique.

Rooms 11 to 14

The collection ends with works from the Romantic and Modern eras. In Room 11, an austere late canvas by **Goya** of the octogenarian *Don José Duaso* compensates for some not terribly inspiring works accompanying it. In Room 12, Gonzalo Bilbao's *Las Cigarreras* is a vivid portrayal of the wretched life of women in the tobacco factory during the early years of the last century. Also here is a monumental canvas by nineteenth-century *sevillano* artist José Villegas Cordero, *La Muerte del Maestro*, depicting the death of a *torero*, which was purchased by the Junta de Andalucía in 1996. Room 13 has an evocative image of *Sevilla en Fiestas* dated 1915 by Gustavo Bacarisas and finally, in Room 14 there's *Juan Centeño y su cuadrilla* by Huelvan artist Daniel Vásquez Díaz, who worked in Paris and was a friend of Picasso. This stirring image of the *torero* and his team provides an appropriately *andaluz* conclusion to a memorable museum.

Triana

Over the Río Guadalquivir is the **Triana** *barrio*, scruffy, lively and well away from the tourist trails. This was once the heart of the city's *gitano* community and, more specifically, home of the great flamenco dynasties of Seville who were kicked out by developers early last century and are now scattered throughout the city. The *gitanos* lived in extended families in tiny, immaculate communal houses called *corrales* around courtyards glutted with flowers; today, only a handful remain intact. Triana is still, however, the starting point for the annual pilgrimage to El Rocío (end of May), when a myriad painted wagons leave town, drawn by oxen. It houses, too, the city's oldest working **ceramics factory**, Santa Ana, where the tiles, many still in the traditional, geometric Arabic designs, are hand-painted in the adjoining shop.

La Cartuja

Tues–Sat 11am–9pm, Sun 11am–3pm • €3, free Tues–Fri 7–9pm & Sat 11am–9pm with EU passport • ⓦ caac.es

At Triana's northern edge lies **La Cartuja**, a fourteenth-century former Carthusian monastery expensively restored as part of the Expo '92 World's Fair. Part of the complex is now given over to the **Centro Andaluz de Arte Contemporáneo** (same hours and ticket) which stages rotating exhibitions from a large and interesting collection of contemporary work by *andaluz* artists, including canvases by Antonio Rodríguez Luna, Joaquín Peinado, Guillermo Pérez Villalta, José Guerrero and Daniel Vásquez Díaz. Two other galleries stage temporary exhibitions by international artists and photographers (see website for details).

Isla Mágica

April–Nov daily 11am–7.30pm; closes 11pm July & Aug • €29, kids €21; evening-only tickets €20, kids €15; extra €7 (no reductions) to enter Aquapark • ⓦ islamagica.es

The remnants of much of the **Expo '92 site** itself have been incorporated into the **Isla Mágica**, an amusement park based on the theme of sixteenth-century Spain, with water and roller-coaster rides, shows and period street animations (included in ticket price). The recently added Aquapark has the usual water chutes and slides but requires a supplementary ticket (and you must enter the main park first).

Pabellón de la Navegación and Schindler Torre Mirador

Camino de los Descubrimientos 2 • May–Oct Tues–Sat 11am–8.30pm, Sun 11am–3pm; Nov–April 10am–7.30pm • €4.90 • ⓦ www.pabellondelanavegacion.es

Another remnant of **Expo '92**, the **Pabellón de la Navegación** has been turned into an exhibition space dedicated to the history of Spanish navigation and discovery with lots of interactive gadgetry. The museum is divided into four sections: navigators, the history of navigation, shipboard life and the history of Seville, and the English translations are well done. Your entry ticket also allows you to ascend the 65m high **Schindler Torre Mirador** (taking its name from the Swiss company who built it), another Expo leftover, from where there are stunning views over the river and the old city.

Itálica and around

April–Sept Tues–Sat 9am–8.30pm, Sun 10am–4pm; Oct–March Tues–Sat 9am–5.30pm, Sun 10am–4pm • €1.50, free with EU passport

The Roman ruins and remarkable mosaics of **Itálica** and the exceptional Gothic **Monasterio San Isidoro del Campo** lie some 9km to the north of Seville, just outside the village of **Santiponce**, where also lie the well-preserved remains of a Roman theatre.

Itálica was the birthplace of two emperors (Trajan and Hadrian) and one of the earliest Roman settlements in Spain, founded in 206 BC by Scipio Africanus as a home for his veterans. It rose to considerable military importance in the second and third centuries AD, was richly endowed during the reign of Hadrian (117–138) and declined as an urban centre only under the Visigoths, who preferred Seville, then known as *Hispalis*. Eventually, the city was deserted by the Moors after the river changed its course, disrupting the surrounding terrain.

Throughout the Middle Ages, the ruins were used as a source of stone for Seville, but somehow the shell of its enormous **amphitheatre** – the third largest in the Roman world – has survived. Today, it's crumbling perilously, but you can clearly detect the rows of seats, the corridors and the dens for wild beasts. Beyond, within a rambling and unkempt grid of **streets** and **villas**, about twenty **mosaics** have been uncovered. Most are complete, including excellent coloured floors depicting birds, Neptune and the seasons, and several fine black-and-white geometric patterns.

Monasterio San Isidoro del Campo

April–Sept Wed & Thurs 10am–2pm, Fri & Sat 10am–2pm & 5.30–8.30pm, Sun 10am–3pm; Oct–March Wed & Thurs 10am–2pm, Fri & Sat 10am–2pm & 4–7pm, Sun 10am–3pm • €2

A little over 1km to the south of Santiponce on the road back to Seville lies the former Cistercian **Monasterio San Isidoro del Campo**. Closed for many years, it has now been painstakingly and gloriously restored and shouldn't be missed.

Founded by the thirteenth-century monarch Guzmán El Bueno of Tarifa, the monastery is a masterpiece of Gothic architecture, which, prior to its confiscation during the nineteenth-century Disentailment, was occupied by a number of religious orders. Among these were the *ermitaños jerónimos* (Hieronymites) who, in the fifteenth century, decorated the central cloister and the Patio de los Evangelistas with a remarkable series of **mural paintings** depicting images of the saints – including scenes from the life of San Jerónimo – as well as astonishingly beautiful floral and Mudéjar-influenced geometric designs. In the seventeenth century, the monastery employed the great *sevillano* sculptor Martínez Montañés to create the magnificent **retablo mayor** in the larger of the complex's twin churches.

ARRIVAL AND DEPARTURE

BY PLANE

The airport bus (daily and roughly hourly between 5am–1am; €4 or €6 return), takes 45min to the centre and terminates at the central Pza. de Armas bus station, stopping at the train station en route. A taxi from the airport into the centre currently costs €25 (officially regulated fare for up to four people) plus €1/bag (slightly more Sun and after 10pm). The current fare can be obtained from the taxi authority ☎ 954 505 840 or any *turismo*.

BY TRAIN

Points of arrival are straightforward, though the train station, Santa Justa, is a fair way out on Avda. Kansas City, the airport road. Bus #32 will take you from here to Pza. del Duque (near the El Corte Inglés store), from where all sights are within easy walking distance; alternatively, bus #C1 will take you to the Prado de San Sebastián bus station. A bus map detailing all routes is available from the *turismo*. For timetables and ticket information, consult RENFE ☎ 902 240 202, ⓦ renfe.es.

Destinations Algeciras (7 daily, change at Antequera or Bobadilla; 3hr 30min); Almería (4 daily; 5hr 40min); Badajoz (3 daily, change at Puertollano; 5hr 15min); Cádiz (15 daily; 1hr 45min); Córdoba (AVE 19 daily, 45min; 6 *cercanías* daily, 1hr 20min); Granada (4 daily; 3hr 15min); Huelva (3 daily; 1hr 35min); Madrid (AVE 14 daily; 3hr 20min); Málaga (11 daily; 2hr 30min); Mérida (daily; 4hr 20min).

BY BUS

The city has two bus stations. The Prado de San Sebastián (☎ 954 417 111), station handles most connections within Andalucía (except Huelva province). The larger Pza. de Armas (☎ 954 908 040) station is located on the square of the same name by the Puente del Cachorro on the river. This has services to and from Badajoz, Extremadura (the provinces of Cáceres and Badajoz), Huelva, Madrid and international destinations. Buses for Itálica also leave from here.

Destinations Albufeira, Portuguese Algarve (via Ayamonte and Faro; 4 daily; 2hr 30min); Algeciras (4 daily; 3hr 50min); Almería (3 daily; 3hr 30min); Aracena (2 daily; 1hr 20min); Badajoz (4 daily; 3hr 30min); Cádiz (10 daily; 1hr 45min); Carmona (16 daily; 45min); Córdoba (8 daily; 1hr 45min); Écija (9 daily; 1hr 15min); El Rocío (2 daily; 1hr 30min); Granada (8 daily; 3hr); Huelva (20 daily; 1hr 15min); Jerez de la Frontera (7 daily; 1hr 15min); Madrid (8 daily; 6hr); Málaga (8 daily; 2hr 45min); Matalascañas (4 daily; 2hr); Mérida (5 daily; 1hr 15min); Ronda (7 daily; 2hr 30min).

BY CAR

Driving in Seville is an ordeal, especially in the narrow streets of *barrios* such as Santa Cruz, and on-street parking spaces are almost impossible to find. Your best bet for parking is to find a pay **car park** (they are signed all around the central zone), or to choose accommodation with a garage (for which you will be charged extra).

GETTING AROUND

By bus All bus journeys have a flat fare of €1.40. Tussam (Seville's bus company, ⓦ tussam.es) also sells one-day (€5) or three-day (€10) *tarjetas turísticas* with unlimited journeys. These are available from the Tussam offices above or at the airport and the Santa Justa train station. To visit Itálica and Monasterio San Isidoro del Campo, take bus #M172 from the Pza. de Armas station (every 30min, Sun every hour; 20min). The easiest way to see both monuments is to ask the bus to drop you at the monastery stop ("Parada Monasterio") on the outward journey. You can then cover the 1.5km (15min walk or take a later bus) through Santiponce to the Itálica site entrance (from where buses return to the city).

By metro The city is engaged in constructing a metro system that will eventually criss-cross Seville. The first sections linking the southern suburbs to the Puerto de Jerez and Triana opened in 2009. This is not very useful for visitors and the system is unlikely to be extended before 2017.

By tram A new tram system will also be expanded in the years to come but presently runs only from Pza. Nueva to the San Bernardo train station to the southeast of the centre, passing the Prado de San Sebastián bus station en route.

By open-top bus tour Good if you're pressed for time, this hop-on, hop-off service is operated by City Sightseeing Sevilla (☎ 902 101 081, ⓦ city-sightseeing.com); buses leave half-hourly from the riverside Torre del Oro, stopping at or near the main sites (24hr ticket €18, reductions for kids). Information is provided by earphone commentary in sixteen languages.

By taxi The main central ranks are in Pza. Nueva, the Alameda de Hércules and the Pza. de Armas and Prado de San Sebastián bus stations. The basic charge for a short journey is around €5 but rates rise at night and weekends. A reliable taxi service, Radio Taxi, will come and collect you if you ring them on ☎ 954 580 000.

INFORMATION

Turismo is at Pza. del Triunfo 1 close to the exit from the Alcázar (Mon–Fri 9am–7.30pm, Sat & Sun 9.30am–7.30pm; ☎ 954 210 005). This office tends to be overwhelmed in peak periods, but they have accommodation lists and can give you a copy of the very useful free listings magazine *El Giraldillo*.

Municipal tourist office Less chaotic, and therefore much more helpful, this office is inside the Castillo de San Jorge, across the Puente de Triana (aka Isabel II) on the west bank of the river (Mon–Fri 9.30am–1.30pm & 3.30–7.30pm, Sat & Sun 10am–1.30pm; ☎954 332 240, ⓦturismosevilla.org), with a sub-office at Santa Justa train station.

ACCOMMODATION

Seville has some of the finest **hotels** in Andalucía. The most attractive area to stay is undoubtedly the **Barrio Santa Cruz**, though this is reflected in the prices, particularly during high season (April–June). Slightly farther out, another promising area is to the north of the Pza. Nueva, and especially over towards the river and the Pza. de Armas bus station. The once drab **Alameda de Hércules** is now one of the city's foremost up-and-coming zones.

If you're arriving during any of the major **festivals**, particularly Semana Santa or the Feria de Abril (April fair), you're strongly advised to book ahead – be aware also that this is when hotel rates are at their highest. The rates quoted below are for high season which is the price point below "*temporada extra*" (extra high season) charged during Semana Santa and the Feria de Abril.

BARRIO SANTA CRUZ AND CATEDRAL AREA

★**Las Casas del Rey de Baeza** Pza. Jesús de la Redención 2 ☎954 561 496, ⓦhospes.com; map pp.264–265. Wonderful hotel with rooms arranged around an eighteenth-century *sevillano corral*. The plant-bedecked interior patio is a picture, and stylishly furnished pastel-shaded rooms come with traditional exterior *esparto* blinds, a neat finishing touch – and there's a rooftop pool to cool off in. €175

Hostal Pérez Montilla Pza. Curtidores 13 ☎954 421 854, ⓦpensionperezmontilla.com; map p.268. Spotless *hostal* on a tranquil square with economically priced rooms. A few cheaper rooms come without bath; those with have a/c and (most) TV. Ask for an exterior room as these have more light. €25

Hostal Puerta Carmona Pza. de San Agustín 5 ☎954 988 310, ⓦhostalpuertacarmona.es; map pp.264–265. Very pleasant *hostal* with good-value modern en-suite rooms with a/c and TV; they will advise on where to park nearby. €55

★**Hotel Amadeus** C/Farnesio 6 ☎954 501 443, ⓦhotelamadeussevilla.com; map p.268. Welcoming hotel housed in an eighteenth-century *casa señorial* and owned by an aficionada of the great composer. There's a *sala de música*, and the soundproofed and stylish rooms come with a/c, satellite TV, wi-fi and free internet access. There's a grand piano in the patio and they even loan guests musical instruments. The house is topped off with a stunning roof terrace (with telescope) for breakfasting. €115

Hotel Murillo C/Lope de Rueda 7 ☎954 216 095, ⓦhotelmurillo.com; map p.268. Traditional hotel in a restored mansion close to Pza. Santa Cruz with all facilities plus amusingly kitsch features, including suits of armour and paint-palette key rings. Also rents out fully equipped apartments nearby (see website). €115

Hotel Simón C/García de Vinuesa 19 ☎954 226 660, ⓦhotelsimonsevilla.com; map p.268. Well-restored mansion in an excellent position across from the Catedral. All rooms are en suite and a/c, and this can be a bargain out of high season. €115

Oasis Backpackers Palace C/Almirante Ulloa 1 ☎955 262 696, ⓦoasisseville.com; map pp.264–265. New privately run hostel in a superbly refurbished mansion with neat rooms and six to fourteen bed dormitories. The rooms are en suite and have a/c; the dorms have personal property lockers with their own keys. The range of facilities in communal areas include a cafetería, internet screens, guest kitchen, rooftop pool and solarium. Dorms €18, doubles €63

SANTA CATALINA, SAN PEDRO, ALAMEDA DE HÉRCULES

Hostal Alameda Alameda de Hércules 31 ☎954 900 191, ⓦhostalalameda.es; map pp.264–265. Modern, pleasant and very friendly *hostal* overlooking the tree-lined Alameda. En-suite rooms are all exterior-facing with small balconies and come with a/c and a TV. €45

Hostal Parladó C/Jesus del Gran Poder 130 ☎954 371 430, ⓦhostalparlade.com; map pp.264–265. At the northern end of the atmospheric Alameda de Hércules this is a very pleasant (and economically priced) small *hostal* with cosy en-suite rooms equipped with a/c and TV. €55

★**Hotel Sacristía de Santa Ana** Alameda de Hércules 22 ☎954 915 722, ⓦhotelsacristia.com; map pp.264–265. Beautiful hotel with delightful rooms – the external ones have Alameda views – inside a seventeenth-century *casa señorial* with many original features. Facilities include minibar, room safe, plasma TV and DVD players for rent. €90

YOUTH HOSTELS AND CAMPING

Albergue Juvenil Sevilla C/Isaac Peral 2 ☎955 035 886; map pp.264–265. Leafy, if often crowded, youth hostel some way out in the university district; take bus #34 from the Prado de San Sebastián bus station to get there. Rooms are doubles, triples or quadruples and the price is per person. Under-26 €22, over-26 €26

Camping Villsom 10km out of town on the main Cádiz road ☎954 720 828. Recently overhauled campsite with a pool. Half-hourly buses from Avda. de Portugal (near the Prado de San Sebastián bus station) take 20min – the M132 signed "Dos Hermanas por Barriadas" will drop you outside. €22.50

EATING AND DRINKING

Seville is packed with lively and enjoyable **bars and restaurants**, and you'll find somewhere to eat and drink at just about any hour. With few exceptions, anywhere around the major sights and the **Barrio Santa Cruz** will be expensive. The two most promising central areas are down **towards the bullring** and north of here towards the Pza. de Armas bus station. The **Pza. de Armas** area is slightly seedier but has the cheapest *comidas* this side of the river. Wander down C/Marqués de Parades, and up C/Canalejas and C/San Eloy, and find out what's available. Across the river in **Triana**, C/Betis and C /Pureza are also good hunting grounds.

RESTAURANTS AND CAFÉS

BARRIO SANTA CRUZ AND AROUND THE CATEDRAL

Bar Modesto C/Cano y Cueto 5 ☎954 416 811, ⓦmodestorestaurantes.com; map p.268. At the north end of Santa Cruz, this mid-priced bar-restaurant is one of the city's most noted. House specials include *punta de solomillo* (pork tenderloin) and *coquinas* (clams). It offers a range of *menús de degustación* ranging from €35–50 and has an attractive terrace. Main dishes €15–19. *Modesto* built its reputation on its tapas and it has now opened a separate tapas bar opposite the restaurant. In both venues the kitchen continues throughout the day. Daily 12.30pm–1am.

Café Rayuela C/Miguel de Mañara 9 ☎954 225 762; map p.268. Pleasant lunchtime venue serving value-for-money *raciones* at outdoor tables in a pedestrianized street near the Alcázar. They offer a range of salads and a paella for €6.50 making it an ideal lunch stop. There's also a menu for under €10. Mon–Fri 7am–midnight; Sat 11am–5pm.

Duplex C/Don Remondo 1 ☎954 225 762; map p.268. Cosy and friendly little diner, typical of many now opening up across the city, with a nonstop kitchen serving up a series of two-course menus for €8–12.50 plus a range of *platos combinados*, curries, and a dozen varieties of salad. Daily noon–5pm & 7pm–midnight.

Mesón del Pulpo C/Tomás Ibarra 10 ☎654 979 735; map p.268. Excellent little Galician restaurant popular with locals. Specializes (as its name implies) in *pulpo a la gallega* (octopus), and there's a decent menu for around €10. Daily 11.30am–4pm & 8.30pm–midnight.

Restaurante San Marco C/Mesón del Moro 4 ☎954 214 390; map p.268. Good Italian pasta, risotto and pizzas served inside a remarkable twelfth-century Moorish bathhouse which has attracted the likes of Tom Cruise and Madonna. Main dishes €9–18. Daily 1–4pm & 7.30pm–midnight.

TRIANA AND THE RÍO GUADALQUIVIR

Bar-Restaurante Casa Manolo C/San Jorge 16 ☎954 334 792; map pp.264–265. Buzzing Triana bar-restaurant with tapas and *raciones* (or breakfast) in the bar or economical *platos combinados* in a dining room just off it. Their fish arrives fresh daily from Isla Cristina in Huelva and there's a menu for €10. Tues–Sat 9am–6pm & 8pm–midnight; Sun noon–6pm & 8pm–midnight; closed Mon.

El Faro de Triana Puente de Triana ☎954 331 251; map pp.264–265. Sitting atop the western end of the Puente de Triana (aka Puente de Isabel II), the dining room and roof terrace here give amazing river views. Tapas at the bar and *raciones* at the tables consist of fish, meat and seafood. Daily 8am–1am.

Kiosko de las Flores C/Betis s/n ☎954 274 576, ⓦkioskodelasflores.com; map pp.264–265. Wonderful riverside location for this mid-priced restaurant specializing in fish and seafood. Their terrace has great views over the river to the Torre del Oro. Tapas are served at the bar and there's a menu for around €20. Main dishes €10–22. Tues–Sat noon–4pm & 8pm–midnight, Sun noon–4pm.

La Primera del Puente C/Betis 66 ☎954 276 918; map pp.264–265. The riverside terrace of the restaurant over the road has one of the city's best vistas; soft-talk a waiter to get a frontline table. You can enjoy low-priced, generous *raciones* or *media raciones* of fish, meat and seafood. Paella is a daily special and there's a reasonably priced wine list. Daily noon–4.30pm & 8.30pm–midnight.

Restaurante Salas C/Almansa 15 ☎954 217 796, ⓦhosteriasalas.com; map pp.264–265. The impeccable table linen and elegant, light and airy scoured brick and tiled interior suggest that this is a quality restaurant. But prices are not high and the specialities of the house include grilled fish and meat dishes. There's a bar area serving tapas and two spacious dining rooms with efficient service. Main dishes €8–18. Daily noon–1am.

★Taberna El Alabardero C/Zaragoza 20 ☎954 502 721, ⓦwww.tabernadelalabardero.com; map p.268. Elegant nineteenth-century *casa-palacio sevillana* with attractive decor and an upmarket clientele. Pricey – and outstanding – cutting-edge restaurant upstairs where the *menú de degustación* costs around €70 with wine; a cheaper 4-course *menú ejecutivo* costs €33. However, a daily bargain €12.90 lunchtime menu (€17.50 Sat–Sun lunch, €19.90 dinner) in the patio bar below comes from the same kitchen. They also offer a tapas menu in the bar. Daily 1–4.30pm & 8pm–midnight; closed Aug.

CENTRO, LA MACARENA, ALAMEDA AND SANTA JUSTA

Contenedor C/San Luís 50 ☎954 916 333; map pp.264–265. Relaxed and friendly diner with daily specials such as *arroz con setas y pato* (duck and mushroom rice) as well as curries and fish and meat dishes. There's a piano for

4

any customers inclined to tinkle the ivories and they stage art exhibitions on the walls. Tapas are on offer from Tuesday to Friday at lunch and there's live acoustic music on Tuesday and Wednesday evenings. Main dishes €8–20. Mon 8.30–11pm, Tues–Sun 1.30–4pm & 8.30–11pm; closed Aug.

Mesón Serranito Alfonso XII 9 ☎954 218 299, ⓦmesonserranito.com; map pp.264–265. Cosy little restaurant beyond a lively tapas bar out front, with excellent fish and meat dishes and a menu for around €9. The kitchen is non-stop and it also does breakfasts. Daily 8am–midnight.

Pando C/San Eloy 47 ☎954 221 625; map pp.264–265. Lively, stylish tapas and *raciones* restaurant, which also does salads. Wide range of meat and fish dishes: try their *merluza en sidre* (hake in cider). An ideal lunch stop. Main dishes €9–20. Mon–Sat 8am–4.30pm & 8pm–midnight, Sun 9am–4.30pm.

Restaurante Los Gallegos C/Capataz Franco 1 ☎954 214 011; map pp.264–265. Friendly and inexpensive Galician restaurant in a tiny alley off C/Martín Villa, serving *gallego* specialities (try their *tarta de Santiago* dessert). Menu for €14. Daily 11am–midnight; closed Sun eve.

Zarabanda C/Padre Tarín 6 ☎954 903 080; map pp.264–265. Economical and friendly little family restaurant cooking pizzas and Mediterranean dishes to a high standard. They work with the market so it's worth checking the blackboard for daily specials. Also offers a variety of tapas as well as risottos and there are veggie options. Just the place for a lunch stop. Main dishes €8–14. Mon & Sun 2–4pm, Tues–Sat 2–4pm & 9pm–midnight.

TAPAS BARS

For casual eating and drinking and taking tapas – Seville's great speciality – there are bars all over town. The tapas venues all serve barrelled sherries from nearby Jerez and Sanlúcar (the locals drink the cold, dry *fino* with their tapas, especially *camarones*, or shrimps); a *tinto de verano* is the local version of *sangría* – wine with lemonade, a great summer drink. Outside the centre, you'll find lively bars in the Pza. Alfalfa area, and across the river in Triana – particularly in and around C/Castilla and C/Betis. Over recent years, a zone that has emerged as a focus for artistic, student and gay bar-hoppers is the Alameda (de Hércules).

BARRIO SANTA CRUZ AND AROUND THE CATEDRAL

★**Bar Europa** Junction of C/Alcaicería de Loza and C/Siete Revueltas ☎954 217 908, ⓦbareuropa.info; map pp.264–265. Approaching its centenary, this is a fine old watering hole with lots of cool tiled walls, plus excellent *manzanilla* and a variety of tapas served on marble-topped tables. Try their outstanding *croquetas de jamón ibérico* (jamón croquettes) or *risotto de cola de toro* (oxtail risotto). Has an outdoor terrace and also does breakfasts. Daily 8.30am–12.30am.

Bar Giralda C/Mateus Gago 1 ☎954 228 250, ⓦbargiralda.es; map p.268. Excellent and popular bar in a converted ancient Moorish bathhouse, with a wide selection of tapas. House specials include *calabacín al horno* (baked courgette). Daily 1pm–midnight.

Casa Morales C/García de Vinuesa 11 ☎954 221 242; map p.268. Earthy, traditional bar (founded 1850) with barrelled wine and a few *tablas* (tapas served on wooden boards). Specials include *morcilla* (blood pudding) and *salchichón* (salami). Mon–Sat noon–4pm & 8pm–midnight, Sun noon–4pm.

★**Taberna Coloniales II** C/Fernández y González 36 ☎954 229 381; map p.268. Offspring of the similarly named establishment in Pza. Cristo de Burgos, this is up to the same high standard. Tapas are served at the bar, but cornering a table (not always easy) will allow you to feast on a wide range including *solomillo al whisky* (pork loin in grog) and *papas a la brava* (potatoes in a spicy sauce); the *raciones* are meal-sized portions, and as they let you round things off with coffee and *desserts de la casa* why bother with a restaurant? Varied (and fair-priced) wine list, too. Daily 1.30–4.15pm & 8.15pm–midnight.

★**Las Teresas** C/Santa Teresa 2 ☎954 213 069; map p.268. Good beer and sherry are served in this atmospheric L-shaped bar with hanging cured hams and tiled walls lined with faded *corrida* photos. It's also worth stopping here for breakfast the morning after. Try the *pulpo a la gallega* (Galician octopus) and their traditional *arroz dominical* ("Sunday rice") served only on the Sabbath. Daily 9am–midnight.

TRIANA AND THE RÍO GUADALQUIVIR

★ **Bar Bistec** C/Pelay y Correa 34 ☎954 274 759, ⓦbarbistec.com; map pp.264–265. Excellent, ancient and hearty Triana hostelry, with a sparkling Triana-tiled interior and outdoor tables in summer fronting the church of Santa Ana. Specials include *cabrillas* (spicy snails), *codorniz en salsa* (quail) and *pan de mi pueblo* (cod gazpacho). They also do *raciones* and sell wine by the bottle, tempting you to make a meal of it. Mon, Tues & Thurs–Sun 11.30am–4pm & 7.30pm–midnight.

Bodega Siglo XVIII C/Pelay y Correa 32 ☎954 274 113, ⓦwww.sigloxviii.com; map pp.264–265. The neighbour of Bar Bistec and another great Triana bar. Things to try here are *ajo blanco* (white gazpacho) and *cordero en salsa de frutos secos* (lamb in dried fruit sauce). Tues–Sun 12.30–4pm & 8pm–midnight.

CENTRO, LA MACARENA, ALMEDA AND SANTA JUSTA

Bar Caracoles C/Pérez Galdos ☎954 213 172; map pp.264–265. Classic tapas bar in the vibrant Alfalfa *barrio* just off its main square. There's a spacious bar for winter dining but in summer everyone sits out on their terrace. House specials include (you've guessed it) *caracoles* as well as *solomillo al whisky* and *bacalao a la Bilbaina* (cod in chilli sauce). Daily noon–4pm & 8pm–midnight.

Bar Eslava C/Eslava 3–5 ☎954 906 568, Ⓦespacioeslava.com; map pp.264–265. Very good and extremely popular bar – which often means you can't get through the door – with a mouthwatering range of tapas. Try their *strudel de verduras* (pastry with veggie filling) or *pimiento relleno de merluza* (pepper stuffed with hake). Tues–Sat 12.30pm–1am, Sun 12.30–5pm.

La Giganta C/Alhondiga 6 (facing the walls of the church of Santa Catalina) ☎954 210 975, Ⓦlagigantabar.com; map pp.264–265. Taking its name ("The Big Lady") from the figure of Faith atop the Giralda tower, the bar has had a makeover and is now startlingly modern inside with lots of bare brick and stripped pine surfaces. House special is *tablas* (boards of cheese or meat) and there's also a wide tapas range including *tempura de verduras*, *costillas* (ribs) and *carrillada* (stewed pork cheeks). Also has a pleasant street terrace. Daily noon–midnight; kitchen noon–4pm & 8pm–midnight.

★**El Rinconcillo** C/Gerona 32 ☎954 223 183, Ⓦelrinconcillo.es; map pp.264–265. Seville's oldest bar (founded in 1670) does a fair tapas selection as well as providing a hang-out for the city's literati. Renowned for its *espinacas con garbanzos* (spinach with chickpeas), one of the city's most popular tapas, you could also try a tasty *bacalao a la roteña* (cod in onion sauce). Its dining rooms also function as a very good mid-priced restaurant. Daily 1pm–1.30am.

NIGHTLIFE

Seville is a wonderfully late-night city, and in summer and during fiestas, the streets around the central areas – particularly the Pza. de Alfalfa, Alameda de Hércules and Triana riverfront zones – are often packed out until the small hours. Throughout the summer, the Alcázar, the Prado de San Sebastián gardens and other squares host occasional **free concerts**. Information on these should be available from the *turismo*, the local press and the *El Giraldillo* listings magazine.

FLAMENCO

Flamenco music and dance is on offer at dozens of places in the city, some of them extremely tacky and expensive. Unless you've heard otherwise, avoid the fixed "shows", or *tablaos* (many of which are a travesty, even using recorded music) – the spontaneous nature of flamenco makes it almost impossible to timetable into the two-shows-a-night cabaret demanded by impresarios.

Bar Quita Pesares Pza. Jerónimo de Córdoba; map pp.264–265. Owned and run by a flamenco singer, this is a chaotic place where there's often impromptu music, especially at weekends (Fri–Sat), when things get lively around midnight. Mon–Sat noon–4pm & 8pm–2am; closed July & Aug.

La Carbonería C/Levies 18 ☎954 563 749; map p.268. An excellent bar that often has spontaneous flamenco (try Thurs after 10pm). It used to be the coal merchants' building (hence the name) and is a rambling and welcoming place. They also do tapas and *raciones*. Tricky to find, but well worth the effort. Daily noon–late.

Casa de la Memoria de al-Andalus C/Jiménez de Enciso 28 ☎954 560 670, Ⓦcasadelamemoria.es; map p.268. This cultural centre is dedicated to promoting the art of flamenco and features up-and-coming talent – many flamenco luminaries made their first appearances here. It stages nightly flamenco performances at 7.30pm and 9pm with occasional extra concerts at 10.30pm (ring or stop by for details). Space is limited and tickets must be booked in advance – in person or by phone or email. €18 or €15 for students with ID.

Los Gallos Pza. Santa Cruz ☎954 216 981, Ⓦtablaolosgallos.com; map p.268. Along with the *Casa de la Memoria* (see above) and the *Museo del Baile Flamenco* (see below) this is the nearest you'll get to the real thing in a commercial setting. Professional *cantantes* do their best to create some *duende* (magic) and sometimes succeed. However, it's pricey (€35 including one drink). Daily shows at 8.15pm and 10.30pm.

Museo del Baile Flamenco ☎954 340 311, Ⓦwww.museoflamenco.com; map p.268. Regular concerts are staged at the Museo del Baile Flamenco (see p.275). Visit their website for details.

LIVE MUSIC AND CLUBS

Earlier on in the evening, Seville's *discotecas* attract a very young crowd; the serious action starts after midnight and often lasts till well beyond dawn. For rock and pop music the bars around Pza. Alfalfa and Alameda de Hércules have the best of the action.

Abril C/Luís Montoto 118 ☎954 571 072, Ⓦabril-sevilla.com; map pp.264–265. Cavernous and loud, this is the ultimate in trendy *sevillano* nightlife often featuring well-known international DJs. If you're in the mood to dance, this is the place. Wed–Sat 11.30pm–dawn.

Antique Avda. Matemáticos Rey Pastor y Castro s/n ☎954 462 207, Ⓦantiquetheatro.com; map pp.264–265. Popular with Seville's fancier dancers, this place comes with a transparent dancefloor, a summer terrace ("Rosso"), and sounds that range from Latin pop to heavier stuff. Thurs–Sat midnight–late.

Azucar de Cuba Paseo de las Delicias 3 ☎672 093 296, Ⓦazucardecuba.com; map pp.264–265. A corner of Cuba in Seville where the proprietors (from Havana) play salsa sounds accompanied by authentic nibbles. Live music on Thurs & Sun. Tues–Sun 5pm–late.

Bulebar Alameda de Hércules 83 ☎954 901 954, Ⓦcafebulebar.com; map pp.264–265. Late-opening bar with a plant-filled terrace facing the Alameda. Often stages theatre, music (from classical to jazz) or other events. Daily 7pm–3am.

La Caja Negra C/Fresa 15 ☎606 909 828, Ⓦconciertoslacajanegra.com; map pp.264–265. On the way to the Barqueta bridge, this is a cosy little music bar where you can join a packed audience enjoying beer while listening to live alternative music, anything from flamenco to rock. Check website for details and tickets. Mon–Wed Flamenco from 9.45pm; Thurs–Sat live music from 9.45pm; Sun gigs by their own rock band from 9.30pm.

Fun Club Alameda de Hércules 86 ☎636 669 023, Ⓦfunclubsevilla.com; map pp.264–265. Popular weekends-only music and dance bar – favouring rock, reggae, hip-hop and salsa – with live bands. Thurs–Sat

from 9pm (if there's live music) or 11pm–dawn.

Kudeta Pza. Legión 8 inside the Pza. de Armas shopping mall ☎954 651 011, Ⓦkudetasevilla.es; map pp.264–265. Three-storey Asian-fusion resto-lounge-*discoteca* where you can follow a meal by smoking a hookah on terrace loungers or take a drink in the *discoteca*. Club daily 11pm–7am; bar daily 3pm–late.

Santuario Cuesta del Rosario s/n ☎667 796 972, Ⓦsantuariosevilla.com; map p.268. Attractive and upmarket smaller club playing techno, funk, soul and hip-hop to a predominantly over-30s clientele. Sometimes hosts live bands. Mon–Thurs 10pm–late, Fri–Sun 4pm–late.

Urbano Comix C/Matahacas 5 ☎954 210 387; map pp.264–265. Popular student bar – with hippy overtones – featuring zany urban decor. Sounds include grunge metal, rock, punk and R&B, often with live bands. Daily 9.30am–late.

SHOPPING

Casa del Libro C/Velázquez 8 ☎954 222 496; map pp.264–265. Central bookshop that stocks a range of books in English (and other languages) as well as maps. Mon–Sat 9.30am–9.30pm, Sun 11am–3pm & 5–9pm.

El Corte Inglés Pza. Duque de la Victoria ☎954 597 000; map pp.264–265. Seville's branch of Spain's major department store chain has designer fashions as well as an excellent supermarket and bookstore. It also stocks the international press. Mon–Sat 10am–10pm.

Kiosko La Campana La Campana s/n; map pp.264–265. The city's best news kiosk with a comprehensive range of international newspapers. It's located in front of the *pastelería La Campana* at the northern end of C/Sierpes. Daily 8am–2pm & 5–9pm.

Risko Avda. Kansas City 26, close to Santa Justa train

station ☎954 570 849, Ⓦrisko.es; map pp.264–265. Stocks maps and a range of outdoor clothing and equipment. Mon–Fri 10am–2pm & 6–8.30pm, Sat 10am–2pm.

Vértice C/San Fernando 33 ☎954 211 654; map pp.264–265. Another very good bookshop with a broad selection of titles in English. Mon–Fri 9.30am–2pm & 5–8.30pm, Sat 10.30am–2pm.

Markets Entertaining Sunday *mercadillos* (roughly 10am–2pm depending on weather) take place on Pza. del Cabildo opposite the Catedral (stamps, coins, pins, ancient artefacts), and on Pza. del Museo in front of the Museo de las Bellas Artes (various art, tiles and woodcarvings). C/Feria's long-standing and vibrant El Jueves (Thursday market) with secondhand bric-a-brac and antiques, east of the Alameda de Hércules, is another good one.

DIRECTORY

Airport For flight information, call ☎954 449 000.

Currency exchange Bureaux de change can be found on Avda. de la Constitución, Pza. Duque de la Victoria and Pza. Nueva.

Bullfights The main *corridas* are staged during the April *feria*, but not regularly outside this month. Details and tickets – costing between €25 and €150 depending on seat and *toreros* – from the Pza. de Toros (☎902 223 506) on fight days from 4.30pm or in advance (with commission) from the Impresa Pagés ticket office at C/Adriano 37.

Football Seville has two major Primera Division teams: Sevilla CF (who finished fifth in La Liga in 2014) plays at the Sánchez Pizjuán stadium (☎954 535 353, Ⓦsevillafc.es) and Real Betis – promoted to the First Division of La Liga in 2011 and relegated back to the Second Division in 2014 – uses the Manuel Ruiz de Lopera stadium (☎902 191 907, Ⓦrealbetisbalompie.es), in the southern suburbs. Match

schedules are in the local or national press, and tickets are surprisingly easy to get hold of for many matches (check the stadium or *turismos*).

Hospital English-speaking doctors are available at Hospital Universitario Virgen Macarena, C/Dr Marañon s/n (☎955 008 000), behind the Andalucía parliament building to the north of the centre. For emergencies, dial ☎061.

Left luggage There are coin-operated lockers (ask for the *consigna*) at the Santa Justa train station in a basement (to the right as you enter; 6am–12.30am). There are left luggage offices at the Prado de San Sebastián (daily 5.30am–midnight), and Pza. de Armas (9.30am–1.30pm & 3–6pm) bus stations; note that the latter one is not inside the bus station but around the right side of the building where there are taxis.

Lost property Oficina de Objetos Perdidos, C/Manuel V. Sagastizábal 3, next to the Prado de San Sebastián bus

station (Mon–Fri 9.30am–1.30pm; ☎ 954 420 703).
Police Central local police stations are at C/Arenal 1
(☎ 954 275 509) and C/Credito 11 (☎ 954 289 555), off the
north end of the Alameda de Hércules. Dial ☎ 092 or ☎ 112

(local police) or ☎ 091 (national) in an emergency.
Post office Avda. de la Constitución 32, by the Catedral;
Lista de Correos (poste restante) Mon–Fri 8.30am–8.30pm,
Sat 9.30am–1pm.

The Sierra Morena

The longest of Spain's mountain ranges, the **Sierra Morena** extends almost the whole
way across Andalucía – from Rosal on the Portuguese frontier to the dramatic pass of
Despeñaperros, north of Linares in the province of Jaén. Its hill towns marked the
northern boundary of the old Moorish Caliphate of Córdoba, and in many ways the
region still signals a break, with a shift from the climate and mentality of the south to
the bleak plains and villages of Extremadura and Castilla-La Mancha. The range is not
widely known – with its highest point a mere 1110m, it's not a dramatic sierra – and
even Andalucians can have trouble placing it.

Aracena and around

Some 90km northwest of Seville, **ARACENA** is the highest town in the Sierra Morena
with sharp, clear air, all the more noticeable after the heat of the city. A substantial but
pretty place, it rambles partly up the side of a hill topped by the **Iglesia del Castillo**, a
Gothic-Mudéjar church built by the Knights Templar around the remains of a Moorish
castle. The town is flanked to the south and west by a small offshoot of the Sierra
Morena – the **Sierra de Aracena** – a wonderfully verdant corner of Andalucía with
wooded hills and villages with cobbled streets, which is perfect for hiking (see p.286).

Gruta de las Maravillas

Daily 10.30am–1.30pm & 3–6.30pm; guided hourly visits, half-hourly at weekends • €8.50

Aracena's principal attraction is the **Gruta de las Maravillas**, the largest and arguably the
most impressive cave in Spain. Supposedly discovered by a local boy in search of a lost
pig, the cave is now illuminated and there are guided tours as soon as a couple of dozen

---

SIERRA MORENA PRACTICALITIES

The Morena's **climate** is mild – sunny in spring, hot but fresh in summer – but it can be very
cold in the mornings and evenings. A good **time to visit** is between March and June, when
the flowers, perhaps the most varied in the country, are at their best. You may get caught in
the odd thunderstorm, but it's usually bright and hot enough to swim in the reservoirs or
splash about in the clear springs and streams, all of which are good to drink. If your way takes
you along a river, you'll be entertained by armies of frogs and turtles plopping into the water
as you approach, by lizards, dragonflies, bees, hares and foxes peering discreetly from their
holes – and, usually, no humans for miles around.

GETTING AROUND

East–west **transport** in the sierra is very limited. Most of the bus services are radial and
north–south, with Seville as the hub, and this leads to ridiculous situations where, for instance,
to travel from Aracena to Cazalla de la Sierra, a distance of some 80km, you must take a bus to
Seville, 70km away, and then another up to Cazalla – a full day's journey of nearly 150km.

   Buses from Seville to the sierra leave from the Plaza de Armas station. If you just want to
make a quick foray into the hills, **Aracena** is probably the best target (and the most regularly
served town). If you're planning on some walking, it's also a good starting point: before you
leave Seville, however, be sure to get yourself a decent **map** (see p.286) which, though it will
probably be crammed with misleading information, should point you in the right direction to
get lost somewhere interesting.

THE KING OF HAMS

Surrounding Aracena is a scattering of attractive but economically depressed villages, most of them dependent on the **jamón industry** and its curing factory at Jabugo. *Jamón serrano* (mountain ham) is a *tapa* or *bocadillo* standard throughout Spain, and some of the best, *jamón de bellota* (acorn-fed ham), comes from the Sierra de Aracena, where herds of sleek black pigs grazing beneath oak trees are a constant feature. In October, the acorns drop and the pigs, waiting patiently below, gorge themselves, become fat and are promptly whisked off to be slaughtered then cured in the dry mountain air. The meat of these black pigs is exceptionally fatty when eaten as pork but the same fat that marbles the meat adds to the tenderness during the curing process. This entails first of all covering the hams in coarse rock or sea salt to "sweat", after which they are removed to cool cellars to mature for up to two years. *Jamón serrano* from mass-produced white pigs is matured for only a few weeks, hence the incomparable difference in taste. At Jabugo the best of the best is then further graded from one to five *jotas* (the letter "J" for Jabugo) depending on its quality. A whole leg of *cinco jotas jamón* will set you back anything from €250 to €350. The *turismo* can provide details of where to sample and buy.

or so people have assembled; to protect the cave there's now a strict limit of 35 persons per visit. At weekends and holiday periods, try to visit before noon – coach parties with advance bookings tend to fill up the afternoon allocation. On Sunday, there's a constant procession, but usually plenty of time to gaze and wonder. The cave is astonishingly beautiful, and funny, too – the last chamber of the tour is known as the Sala de los Culos (Room of the Buttocks), its walls and ceiling an outrageous, naturally sculpted exhibition, tinged in a pinkish-orange light.

ARRIVAL AND DEPARTURE

ARACENA

By bus The station, Avda. de Sevilla s/n, lies on the southeast side of town close to the Parque Municipal and operates services to and from Seville as well as throughout the Sierra de Aracena.

INFORMATION AND ACTIVITIES

Turismo At the Gruta (daily 10am–2pm & 4–6pm; ☎ 663 937 877, ⓦ www.aracena.es).

Hiking You can get useful information (including maps and leaflets) on the surrounding Parque Natural Sierra de Aracena y Picos de Aroche from an information centre in the ancient *cabildo* (town hall), Pza. Alta 5 (June–Sept 8am–2pm; Oct–May Tues–Sun 10am–2pm & 4–6pm). You should also ask at the Aracena *turismo* for the free *Senderos de la Sierra de Aracena y Picos de Aroche* map listing 23 waymarked routes, and they also sell a more detailed *Mapa Guía de la Sierra de Aracena y Picos de Aroche*. A good hiking guide, *Sierra de Aracena* by David & Ros Brawn, details 27 clearly described walks in the sierra ranging between four and fourteen kilometres. An accompanying map for the book is sold separately, and all walks have GPS waypoints identifying key locations en route.

ACCOMMODATION

Camping Aracena, Ctra. N-433, km83 ☎ 699 768 167, ⓦ www.campingaracena.es. Campsite with pool and plenty of shade plus a bar, but no shop or restaurant. It's located about 3km out of town along the Seville road (N433), then left for 500m on the road towards Corteconcepción. **€21**

Casa Manolo C/Barberos 6 ☎ 959 128 014. The best of a limited choice of places to stay, and at the bottom end of the scale for rooms sharing bath. **€22**

Hospedería Reina de los Angeles Avda. Reina de los Angeles s/n, near the Gruta de las Maravillas ☎ 959 128 367, ⓦ hospederiaaracena.com. A rather institutional-looking place that betrays its origins as a former student hostel. However, redecorated and refitted, its ninety en-suite and rather Spartan rooms (some single) are nevertheless clean, bright and good value. Easy street parking. **€41**

Hotel Convento de Aracena C/Jesús María 19 ☎ 959 126 899, ⓦ hotelconventoaracena.es. The town's four-star luxury option is located inside a tastefully restored sixteenth-to-eighteenth-century former Dominican convent. Rooms overlook the cloisters and quadrangle now planted with trees and aromatic herbs. Facilities include a pool and spa. A former convent herb garden now stands outside the hotel's top-notch restaurant, *Huerto*. See website for offers. **€102**

Hotel Sierra de Aracena Gran Vía 21 ☎ 959 126 175, ⓦ hotelsierradearacena.com. This traditional hotel has pleasant, decent-sized rooms (including ten singles), some with views. Public areas include a bar-cafetería. **€68**

EATING AND DRINKING

Aracena is at the heart of a prestigious *jamón*-producing area, so try to sample some, and, when they're available, the delicious wild asparagus, and local snails – in the fields in spring and summer, respectively. *Setas* (wild mushrooms) are another prized delicacy.

Café-Bar Manzano Pza. del Marqués de Aracena ☏ 959 128 123. One of Aracena's most popular bars has now added a restaurant just around the corner. The bar serves a range of well-prepared tapas and *raciones* and has a terrace on the square. The restaurant serves up economical sierra cuisine and has a menu for around €15. Mon & Wed–Sun 8am–midnight.

Casas Pozo La Nieve 40 ☏ 959 128 212. One of the town's top three restaurants, this is sited near the Gruta de las Maravillas and is only open lunchtimes. All the pork-based dishes are excellent, as is the *jamón* and *salchichón* (salami). Wine prices are reasonable, there's a menu for around €15 (including wine) and an outdoor terrace. Main dishes €11–20. Daily 11.30am–5pm.

★ **Restaurante José Vicente** Avda. Andalucía 51 ☏ 959 128 455. For a memorable splurge this is the place to come. Arguably the town's best restaurant, patrons gather to savour the five grades of Jabugo *jamón ibérico* (black-pig ham) under the approving gaze of owner/chef José Vicente Sousa. The €25 menu, which often includes a mouthwatering *solomillo ibérico* (black-pig loin), is recommended. The *costillas de cerdo ibérico* (ribs) are also mouthwatering and the *helado de castañas* (chestnut ice cream) makes a perfect end to a feast. Main dishes €14–20. Daily 12.30–4.30pm; evenings by prior reservation only.

La Serrana Pozo de la Nieve s/n ☏ 959 127 613. The third of the triumvirate of Aracena's best restaurants, and located opposite *Casas* (see above), this is another place where sierra cooking is at its best. All the pork dishes are recommended and there's a menu for €15. Has a pleasant street terrace. Main dishes €16–20. Daily noon–5pm.

Almonaster La Real

The **sierra villages** – Jabugo, Aguafría, Almonaster La Real – all make rewarding bases for walks, though all are equally ill-served by public transport (details from the Aracena *turismo*). The most interesting is **ALMONASTER LA REAL**, whose castle encloses a tiny ninth-century mosque, **La Mezquita** (daily 10am–7pm; free), with what is said to be the oldest *mihrab* in Spain. Tacked onto the mosque is the village bullring, which sees action once a year in August during the annual *feria*.

ACCOMMODATION AND EATING   ALMONASTER LA REAL

Hotel Casa García ☏ 959 143 109. At the entrance to the village, this a comfortable place to stay, with balcony rooms, many with views. It also has a good restaurant below, with tasty *jamón* and sierra specialities. **€45**

Las Palmeras C/Carretera s/n ☏ 609 232 078. This is another option for food – it has a plant-bedecked terrace and is on the road into the village before *Casa García*. Sierra specialities are served and they also do tapas. Main dishes €10–20. Mon–Wed & Fri–Sun noon–5pm & 8–11pm.

The Costa de la Luz

Stumbling on the villages along the **Costa de la Luz**, between Algeciras and Cádiz, is like entering a new land after the parade of flashy high-rise resorts along the Costa del Sol. The journey west from Algeciras seems in itself a relief, the road climbing almost immediately into rolling green hills, offering fantastic views down to Gibraltar and across the Strait to the just-discernible white houses and tapering minarets of Moroccan villages. Beyond, the Rif mountains hover mysteriously in the background, and on a clear day, as you approach **Tarifa**, you can distinguish Tangier on the edge of its crescent-shaped bay. Beyond Tarifa lies a string of excellent golden-sand beaches washed by Atlantic breakers and backed by a clutch of low-key resorts such as **Conil**. Inland, the haunting Moorish hill town of **Vejer de la Frontera** beckons, while set back from the sea at Bolonia is the ancient Roman settlement of **Baelo Claudia**.

Tarifa

TARIFA, spreading out beyond its Moorish walls, was until the mid-1980s a quiet village, known in Spain, if at all, for its abnormally high suicide rate – a result, it is said, of the unremitting winds that blow across the town and its environs. Today, it's a prosperous, popular and, at times, very crowded resort, following its discovery as Europe's prime **windsurfing** and **kitesurfing** spot. There are equipment-rental shops along the length of the main street, and regular competitions are held year-round. Development is moving ahead fast as a result of this new-found popularity, but for the time being it remains an attractive place for a stopover.

San Mateo
Daily 8.30am–1pm & 5.30–9pm • Free

If windsurfing is not your motive for visiting Tarifa, there can still be an appeal in wandering the crumbling ramparts, gazing out to sea or down into the network of lanes that surround the fifteenth-century, Baroque-fronted church of **San Mateo**, which has a beautiful late Gothic interior.

Castillo de Guzmán
Tues–Sun 11am–2pm & 4–7pm • €2

Worth a look is the **Castillo de Guzmán**, the site of many a struggle for this strategic foothold into Spain. It's named after Guzmán el Bueno (the Good), Tarifa's infamous commander during the Moorish siege of 1292, who earned his tag for a superlative piece of tragic drama. Guzmán's 9-year-old son had been taken hostage by a Spanish traitor, and surrender of the garrison was demanded as the price of the boy's life. Choosing "honour without a son, to a son with dishonour", Guzmán threw down his own dagger for the execution. The story – a famous piece of heroic resistance in Spain – had echoes in the Civil War siege of the Alcázar at Toledo, when the Nationalist commander defied similar threats, an echo much exploited for propaganda purposes.

ARRIVAL AND INFORMATION   TARIFA

By bus Frequent services to Seville, Málaga, Cádiz and points in between. The station's at the northern end of town near the *gasolinera* (petrol station) from where the main Algeciras–Cádiz road (C/Batalla del Salado) leads to the walled old town, a 5–10min walk. Along here there's a supermarket, fried-fish and *churro* stalls, and windsurfing-equipment shops.

By ferry Tarifa offers the tempting opportunity for a trip to Morocco – a day-trip by catamaran to Tangier is feasible.

Information on schedules and fares is available from the *turismo* or the friendly travel agency Viajes Baelo Tour, Avda. Constitución 5 (☎ 956 681 242, ✉ viajes-baelo @hotmail.com), near the *turismo*. A useful site for checking the latest ferry schedules is ⊕ directferries.co.uk.

Turismo The welcoming *turismo*, on the central Paseo la Alameda (Mon–Fri 10am–2pm & 4–6pm, Sat & Sun 10am–2pm; ☎ 956 680 993, ⊕ aytotarifa.com), can help with maps and accommodation.

WHALE- AND DOLPHIN-WATCHING TRIPS

Tarifa is home to **whale- and dolphin-watching** excursions in the Strait of Gibraltar, which leave daily from the harbour. The two-hour trip is a fairly steep €30 (reductions for under-14s), but this includes another trip free of charge if there are no sightings. Places must be booked in advance from either of two non-profit-making organizations: **Whale Watch**, Avda. de la Constitución 6, close to the *turismo* (☎ 956 682 247, reservations ☎ 639 476 544, ⊕ whalewatchtarifa.net), and **FIRMM** (Foundation for Information and Research on Marine Mammals), C/Pedro Cortés 3, slightly west of the church of San Mateo (☎ 956 627 008, ⊕ firmm.org). The latter also offers a more specialized tour in summer for spotting Orca whales (€45/3hr). A more commercial operation, **Turmares**, with an office on the beach road near the foot of the Paseo de la Alameda (☎ 956 680 741, ⊕ turmares.com), also runs whale-spotting trips (€30, kids €20) with a glass-bottomed boat.

ACCOMMODATION

Tarifa has plenty of **places to stay**, though finding a bed in summer (or when there's a surfing tournament) can often be a struggle, with crowds of windsurfers cornering every available room. The town also sets a premium on its undoubted charms and room rates tend to be higher here than in other resorts along this coast. A little way out of town to the west, there are six **campsites** and the *turismo* can provide a list of these or visit 🌐 campingsandalucia.es. You should be aware that we quote the high-season tariff which in Tarifa can fall by up to sixty percent outside July and August.

Casa Facundo C/Batalla del Salado 47 ☎ 956 684 298, 🌐 hostalfacundo.com. Reliable and friendly family *hostal* on the main road into town just outside the walls, offering dorm beds, rooms sharing bath and en-suite rooms with TV (€70). They have constructed *Hostal Tarifa* an impressive new *hostal* across the road (see below). Dorms €35, doubles €60

★ **Hostal Africa** C/María Antonia Toledo 12 ☎ 956 680 220, 🌐 hostalafrica.com. Charming, small *hostal* with clean and simple rooms with and without bathrooms (en suites costs €65) and spectacular sea views from a communal terrace. €50

Hostal La Calzada C/Justina Pertiñez 7 ☎ 956 680 366. Popular and friendly *hostal* in the centre of the old town,

close by the church of San Mateo, offering a/c en-suite rooms with TV. Wi-fi zone. €105

Hostal Tarifa C/Batalla del Salado 40 ☎ 608 428 211, 🌐 hostaltarifa.com. This impressive new *hostal* belonging to the proprietors of *Casa Facundo* is a hotel in all but name. Pristine rooms come with all facilities a/c, TV and sparkling bathrooms and most have sit-out balconies. The welcome is warm and the price we quote (July–Aug) halves during the rest of the year. Own garage. €135

Hotel Misiana C/Sancho IV El Bravo 18 ☎ 956 627 083, 🌐 misiana.com. Central, stylish place in the heart of the old town with arty decor whose rooms are decorated with modern art and Moroccan furnishings. €135

EATING AND DRINKING

Tarifa has a wide range of **places to eat**, divided between the old town inside the walls and the new town beyond this. This is another place to try Cádiz's tasty *urta* (sea bream), available all over town. In summer the council erects *carpas* (**disco tents**) on the Playa de los Lances beach.

★ **Bar El Francés** Paseo C/Sancho IV El Bravo 21 ☎ 685 857 005. A highly popular French tapas and *raciones* bar adding a subtly Gallic touch to such staples as *calamares*, *rabo de toro* and *tortilla de camarones* and *pulpo braseado* (octopus), besides adding a few more exotic dishes such as *picaña* (Brazilian beefsteak). Has a small street terrace. Mon–Wed & Fri–Sun 1pm–midnight.

Bar Morilla C/Sancho IV El Bravo 2 ☎ 956 681 757. Central bar where *tarifeños* gather to breakfast or munch early-evening tapas while contemplating the ancient stones of nearby San Mateo. Later, cloths are thrown over the tables as the restaurant hits its stride. *Urta* is frequently on the menu, but the bar also offers meat dishes and there's a *menú del día* for €12. Daily 8.30am–midnight.

★ **Mandragora** C/Independencia 3 ☎ 956 681 291. One of a number of restaurants and tapas bars in town

offering dishes from both sides of the straits. But this is a cut above the rest and in addition to Moroccan couscous and *berenjenas bereber* (aubergine), it does excellent *raciones*, including *boquerones rellenos* (stuffed anchovies) and tasty dishes like *rape con crema de erizos y setas* (monkfish with wild mushrooms in a sea urchin sauce). Also offers a range of vegetarian options. Main dishes €12–20. Mon–Sat 6.30pm–midnight; closed Jan & Feb.

Tarifa Eco Center C/San Sebastián 4, outside the walls ☎ 956 627 220, 🌐 tarifaecocenter.com. This interesting complex has an organic vegetarian restaurant (pasta, pizzas, quiches, *tabouli* etc) out front, eco-shop at the rear and a chill-out zone serving herbal and other teas to the side. Off a courtyard terrace are rooms offering yoga, pilates and other courses. Restaurant Tues–Sun 10am–midnight; shop Mon–Sat 10am–midnight.

Tarifa Beach

Heading northwest from Tarifa, you find the most spectacular **beaches** of the whole of the Costa de la Luz – wide stretches of yellow or silvery-white sand, washed by some magical rollers. The same winds that have created such perfect conditions for windsurfing can, however, sometimes be a problem for more casual enjoyment, sandblasting those attempting to relax on towels or mats and whipping the water into whitecaps.

The beaches lie immediately west of town. They get better as you move past the tidal flats and the mosquito-ridden estuary – until the dunes start and the first campervans lurk among the bushes. At **TARIFA BEACH**, a little bay 9km from town, there are restaurants, a windsurfing school, campsites and a string of pricey hotels, including the exclusive *Hurricane Hotel*.

ACCOMMODATION	**TARIFA BEACH**

Tarifa's six campsites all lie to the west of the town and are served (July–Aug only) by a bus service (roughly every 90min) from the bus station daily between 7.50am–11pm.

Camping Río Jara On the N340 road 4km northwest of town ☎ 956 680 570, ⓦ campingriojara.com. The nearest campsite to the town fronts the beach and has plenty of shade; facilities include supermarket and bar-restaurant and there's access for disabled campers. **€31**

Camping Torre de la Peña On the N340 7km northwest of town ☎ 956 684 903, ⓦ campingtp.com. A decent campsite close to the sea with plenty of shade;

facilities include pool, supermarket, laundry and a decent restaurant. **€26.60**

Hurricane Hotel Carretera Cádiz s/n ☎ 956 68 49 19, ⓦ hotelhurricane.com. Set in dense gardens 7km west of Tarifa at the ocean's edge, this luxurious California-style hotel has tastefully decorated a/c rooms, fully equipped gym, two pools, stables, windsurfing school and its own restaurant. Rooms with sea view carry a supplement. B&B. **€170**

Bolonia

April–June Tues–Sat 10am–8.30pm, Sun 10am–5pm; July–Sept Tues–Sun 10am–5pm; Oct–March Tues–Sat 10am–6.30pm, Sun 10am–5pm • Free guided visit all year Wed at noon • €1.50, free with EU passport

At the Roman town of **BOLONIA**, or *Baelo Claudia* as the Romans knew it, beyond a new visitor centre and museum you can make out the remains of three temples and a theatre, as well as a forum, numerous houses, and a fascinating factory for making *garum* fish sauce, a Roman culinary passion. The ticket office provides you with a detailed site plan. Bolonia can be reached down a small side road that turns off the main Cádiz road 15km after Tarifa.

ARRIVAL AND DEPARTURE	**BOLONIA**

There's a bus service in July and August (3 daily) from Tarifa to the site. If you don't have your own transport take a taxi (up to four people one-way), which will cost approximately €30. Details on both from the Tarifa *turismo*.

ACCOMMODATION AND EATING	

Bolonia has a fine **beach** with bars and eating places and a few **places to stay**. There are a couple of *chiringuitos* on the beach serving grilled fish – otherwise most of the places to eat are in the small village of Bolonia itself.

★**Hostal La Hormiga Voladora** C/El Lentiscal 15 ☎ 956 688 562. This delightful retreat with en-suite garden rooms close to the beach is the best choice should you wish to stay. It's located at the eastern end of the village next to the *Panadería Beatriz*. Breakfast (extra) is served on a patio shaded by a prodigious mulberry tree. **€70**

Las Rejas Close to the Hostal La Hormiga Voladora, ☎ 956 688 546. *Las Rejas* is perhaps Bolonia's best restaurant. All the fish and *mariscos* are fresh – as is of course the tuna in season – and they can rustle up a decent lunchtime paella if you're looking for a beach snack. May–Sept daily 1–4pm & 8–11pm; Oct–April Sat 1–4pm & 8–11pm, Sun 1–5pm.

Vejer de la Frontera

While you're on the Costa de la Luz, be sure to take time to visit **VEJER DE LA FRONTERA**, a classically white, Moorish-looking hill town set in a cleft between great protective hills that rear high above the road from Tarifa to Cádiz. The drama of Vejer is in its isolation and elevated position, both easily appreciated from an approach road that winds upwards for a dizzying 4km. This eventually arrives at the Parque de los Remedios and a **car park**, which, given Vejer's tortuously narrow streets, one-way system and traffic congestion, you'd be strongly advised to make use of if you've arrived by car; this is also where the **bus** drops you. From here you'll need to ascend a further 300m along C/Los Remedios to reach La Plazuela, the effective centre of town.

Vejer has a remoteness and Moorish feel as explicit as anywhere in Spain. There's a castle and a church of curiously mixed styles (mainly Gothic and Mudéjar), but the main fascination lies in exploring the brilliant white and labyrinthine alleyways, wandering past iron-grilled windows, balconies and patios, and slipping into a succession of bars.

INFORMATION
VEJER DE LA FRONTERA

Turismo In the Parque de los Remedios, Avda. de los Remedios 2 (April–Sept Mon–Sat 10am–2pm & 6–9pm, Sun 11am–3pm; Oct–March Mon–Sat 10am–2pm & 4–6pm, Sun 10am–2pm; 📞956 451 736, 🌐www.turismovejer.es); it can provide a useful town map.

ACCOMMODATION

★**La Casa del Califa** Pza. de España 16 📞956 447 730, 🌐lacasadelcalifa.com. One of Vejer's most striking hotels is *La Casa del Califa*, occupying a refurbished, rambling house, parts of which date back to Moorish times; the stylish rooms are decorated with Moroccan fittings and guests have use of two patios with fine views and a library. Also has a charming *casa rural* next door with rooms and suites around a pool. *Rough Guide* readers with this guide can claim (at check-in) a ten percent reduction. Both B&B. Doubles €100, *casa rural* €121
Casa Rural Leonor C/Rosario 25, near the Castillo 📞956 451 085, 🌐casaleonor.com. A charming *casa rural* in a converted Moorish dwelling with comfortable en-suite rooms, friendly proprietors, and fabulous views towards Morocco from a roof terrace. They also have apartments nearby sleeping up to four. Doubles €50, apartments €70
Camping Vejer Ctra. N-340, Km 39.5 📞956 450 988, 🌐campingvejer.es. Vejer's campsite lies below town on the main N340 Málaga-to-Cádiz road. There's decent shade, and facilities include a pool, bar and supermarket. Closed October to May. €22
★**El Cobijo de Vejer** C/ San Filmo 7 📞956 45 50 23, 🌐elcobijo.com. Excellent *hostal* inside a traditional house with delightful flower filled patio and individual rooms on various levels. The higher-priced *Zahara* and *Xauen* (the latter has two fabulous terraces) with their own kitchens are the ones to go for. All rooms are a/c, and have fridges and satellite TV. A lavish breakfast (extra) is also available. €85
Hotel Convento de San Francisco La Plazuela 📞956 451 001, 🌐tugasa.com. Housed in a converted seventeenth-century convent on the smaller of the town's two main squares, this is a very pleasant hotel where the former monastic cells – with exposed stone walls – have been turned into attractive a/c rooms. Also has its own bar (see below) and restaurant. €89

EATING AND DRINKING

Vejer has plenty of places for **eating and drinking** scattered all around the old town. Besides tapas bars and budget restaurants there are a couple of places worth paying a bit extra for.

Bar Peneque Pza. de España 27 📞956 450 209. Traditional and entertaining local bar built into a cave with tables at the back for munching *raciones* should you not feel like joining in the domino games favoured by regulars. Mon–Sat 6am–midnight.
El Jardín del Califa Pza. de España 16. The mid-priced Michelin-recommended restaurant attached to the hotel of the same name has a Moroccan chef and serves up a variety of Moroccan and Middle Eastern-inspired dishes on a tree-shaded courtyard terrace. Specialities include tagines and spicy fish dishes. An adjacent and stylish bar-*tetería* offers stunning views from its roof terrace. Main dishes €12–20. Daily 1–3.30pm & 8–11pm.
Mesón Pepe Julián C/Juan Relinque 7 📞956 451 098. Popular local bar with *azulejo*-lined walls serving up decent tapas – specials include *chorizo ibérico* and *calamares* (squid). Mon, Tues & Thurs–Sun noon–4.30pm & 8pm–midnight; closed Nov.
El Refectorio La Plazuela 📞956 451 001. Comprising the *Hotel Convento de San Francisco's* mid-priced restaurant (housed in the ancient convent's former chapel) and *cafetería* (aka Bar Pza.) in its former refectory (with fresco remnants), with an entrance on the square. The latter is a good place for a leisurely breakfast or an early evening *tapa* and offers a weekday lunchtime *menú turistico* for €10. The restaurant offers a selection of well-prepared regional specialities. Main dishes €11–17. Daily 1.30–4pm & 8.30–11pm; bar daily 8am–midnight.

Conil

Some 10km northwest of Vejer, lies the increasingly popular resort of **CONIL**. Outside July and August, though, it's still a good place to relax, and in mid-season the only real drawback is trying to find a room. Conil Town, once a poor fishing village, now seems entirely modern as you look back from the beach, though when you're actually in the streets you find many older buildings, too. The majority of the tourists are Spanish, so there's an enjoyable atmosphere, and, if you are here in mid-season, a very lively nightlife.

The **beach**, Conil's *raison d'être*, is a wide bay of brilliant yellow sand stretching for many kilometres to either side of town and lapped by an amazingly, not to say disarmingly, gentle Atlantic – you have to walk a long way before it reaches waist height. The area immediately in front of town is the family beach; up to the northwest you can walk to some more sheltered coves, while across the river to the southeast is a topless and nudist area. If you walk along the coast in this direction, you'll see that the beach is virtually unbroken until it reaches the cape, the familiar-sounding **Cabo de Trafalgar**, off which Lord Nelson achieved victory and met his death on October 21, 1805. When the winds are blowing, this is one of the most sheltered beaches in the area. It can be reached by road, save for the last 400m across the sands to the rock.

ARRIVAL AND INFORMATION   CONIL

By bus Most buses use the Transportes Comes station (☎ 956 442 916) on C/Carretera; walk towards the sea and you'll find yourself in the centre of town.

Turismo Just south of the bus station at the junction of C/Carretera and C/Menéndez Pidal (daily: June–Sept 9am–2pm & 6–9pm; Oct–May 8.30am–2.30pm; ☎ 956 440 501, ⓦ conil.org); it's worth picking up a copy of their useful free booklet *Conil en su Bolsillo*, which details all the town's tapas bars, restaurants and much more.

ACCOMMODATION AND EATING

Accommodation needs are served by numerous hotels and *hostales,* augmented in high season by a multitude of private rooms for rent; full details on all of these are available from the *turismo*. As with other resorts in this zone room rates fall sharply outside of July and August. Seafood is king here and Conil has lots of good **restaurants** along the front; try the *ortiguillas* – deep-fried sea anemones – which you see only in the Cádiz area.

Camping Fuente del Gallo Urbanización Fuente de Gallo s/n ☎ 956 440 137, ⓦ www.camping fuentedelgallo.com. The nearest campsite to the town lies a stiff 3km walk (or easy taxi ride) north of the centre and is sited 400m inland from the superb Playa la Fontanilla. There are good facilities including a bar-restaurant and a pool. **€25.50**

★**Casa Alborada** C/G. Gabino Aranda 5 ☎ 956 443 911, ⓦ alboradaconil.com. Delightful small boutique hotel with flamboyantly decorated and individually styled bedrooms and bathrooms – the bathroom of room 10 gets the star prize. Also has a stunning roof terrace/solarium with loungers and sofas offering spectacular views of the coast. Outside July and August rates halve. **€90**

Hostal La Posada C/Quevedo s/n ☎ 956 444 171,

ⓦ laposadadeconil.com. Dapper *hostal* with clean and tidy en-suite a/c rooms with TV – many with sea views – above a good restaurant with terrace. Also has a garden pool. High-season rate applies August only. B&B. **€80**

Hostal La Villa Pza. de España 6 ☎ 956 44 10 53. Economical en-suite rooms above a bar-restaurant on a central square. Open May–Oct. **€45**

Hotel Flamenco Playa Fuente de Gallos ☎ 956 440 711, ⓦ hipotels.com. Fronting the Fuente del Gallo beach, this elegant four-star one-hundred roomer is one of the resort's older luxury places, and is set in a tranquil location. Well-appointed rooms have balcony terraces and sea views and there's a bar-restaurant, two garden pools and steps down to a fine strand. In July and August there's a minimum stay of two to four nights (see website for details). **€150**

Cádiz

CÁDIZ is among the oldest settlements in Spain, founded about 1100 BC by the Phoenicians and one of the country's principal ports ever since. Its greatest period, however, and the era from which the central part of town takes most of its present appearance, was the eighteenth century. Then, with the silting up of the river to Seville, the port enjoyed a virtual monopoly on the Spanish–American trade in gold and silver, and on its proceeds were built the Catedral – itself golden-domed (in colour at least) and almost Oriental when seen from the sea – grand mansions, public buildings, dockyards, warehouses and the smaller churches.

Inner Cádiz, built on a peninsula-island, remains much as it must have looked in those days, with its grand, open squares, sailors' alleyways and high, turreted houses. Literally crumbling from the effect of the sea air on its soft limestone, it has a tremendous atmosphere – slightly seedy, definitely in decline, but still full of mystique.

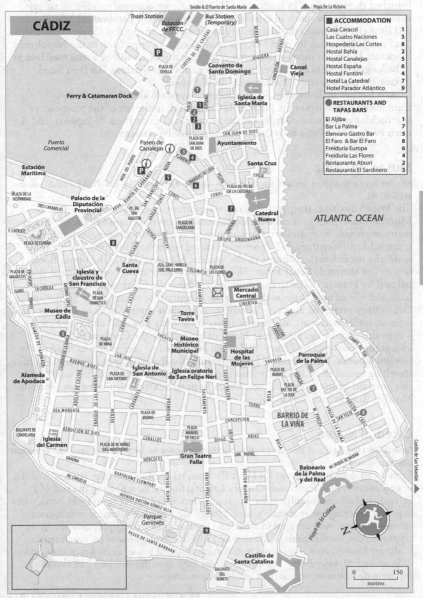

CÁDIZ

ACCOMMODATION	
Casa Caracol	1
Las Cuatro Naciones	3
Hospedería Las Cortes	8
Hostal Bahía	2
Hostal Canalejas	5
Hostal España	6
Hostal Fantoni	4
Hotel La Catedral	7
Hotel Parador Atlántico	9

RESTAURANTS AND TAPAS BARS	
El Aljibe	1
Bar La Palma	7
Elenvaro Gastro Bar	5
El Faro & Bar El Faro	8
Freiduría Europa	6
Freiduría Las Flores	4
Restaurante Atxuri	2
Restaurante El Sardinero	3

ATLANTIC OCEAN

Unlike most other ports of its size, Cádiz seems immediately relaxed, easy-going and not at all threatening, even at night. Perhaps this is due to its reassuring shape and compactness, the presence of the sea, and the striking **sea fortifications** and waterside **alamedas** making it impossible to get lost for more than a few blocks. But it probably owes this tone as much to the town's tradition of liberalism and tolerance – one maintained through the years of Franco's dictatorship even though this was one of the first towns to fall to his forces, and was the port through which the Nationalist armies launched their invasion. In particular, Cádiz has always accepted its substantial gay community, who are much in evidence at the city's brilliant **Carnaval** celebrations. In 2012 the city celebrated the bicentenary of the 1812 Constitution (Spain's first, called "La Pepa") and setting up of the Cortes (parliament), in opposition to the Napoleonic blockade. The major monument commemorating this event will be a **new road bridge** – the longest in Spain and currently under construction – named "La Pepa", and linking Puerto Real across the bay with the old town.

Cádiz has two main **beaches** – the excellent **Playa de la Victoria** (and its less commercial continuation the Playa de la Cortadura), to the left of the promontory approaching town (reached from the centre on bus #1 from Plaza de España), and the often overcrowded **Playa de la Caleta** on the peninsula's western tip.

Museo de Cádiz

June–Sept Tues–Sat 9am–3.30pm, Sun 10am–5pm; Oct–May Tues–Sat 10am–8.30pm, Sun 10am–5pm • €1.50, free with EU passport • ☎ 856 105 023

The **Museo de Cádiz**, the province's most important, overlooks the leafy Pza. de Mina and incorporates the **archeological museum** on the ground floor, which has many important finds and artefacts from the city's lengthy history, including two remarkable fifth-century-BC Phoenician carved sarcophagi in white marble (one male, the other female), unique to the western Mediterranean. The upper floor houses the **Museo de Bellas Artes**. This contains a quite exceptional series of saints painted by Francisco Zurbarán, brought here from the Carthusian monastery at Jerez and one of only three such sets in the country (the others are at Seville and Guadalupe) preserved intact, or nearly so. With their sharply defined shadows and intense, introspective air, Zurbarán's saints are at once powerful and very Spanish – even the English figures such as Hugh of Lincoln, or the Carthusian John Houghton, martyred by Henry VIII when he refused to accept him as head of the English Church. Perhaps this is not surprising, for the artist spent much of his life travelling round the Carthusian monasteries of Spain and many of his saints are in fact portraits of the monks he met. Other important artists displayed here include Murillo, Rubens and Alonso Cano.

Catedral Nueva

Catedral Nueva Mon–Sat 10am–6.30pm, Sun 1.30–6.30pm • €5 including museum, free Sun 11.30am–12.30pm • **Torre de Poniente** Daily 10am–6pm • €4

Even if you don't normally go for High Baroque, it's hard to resist the attraction of the huge and crumbling eighteenth-century **Catedral Nueva**, now nearing the end of a belated (and astronomically expensive) restoration. Once this is completed, work will begin on restoring the roof and "gilded" dome. The Catedral's interior is decorated entirely in stone, with no gold in sight, and in absolutely perfect proportions. In the crypt, you can see the tomb of Manuel de Falla, the great *gaditano* (as inhabitants of Cádiz are known) composer of such Andalucía-inspired works as *Nights in the Gardens of Spain* and *El Amor Brujo*. For a magnificent view over the city, you can also climb the **Torre de Poniente**, one of the Catedral's twin towers.

Santa Cruz

Mon 5.30–7.30pm, Tues–Sat 9.45am–12.45pm & 5.30–7.30pm, Sun 10am–12pm & 6–7.30pm • Free

East of the Catedral on the edge of the Barrio del Populo, the city's oldest quarter dating from the Middle Ages, lies the "old" or original Catedral, **Santa Cruz**. This was one of the buildings severely knocked about by the Earl of Essex during the English assault on Cádiz in 1596, causing the thirteenth-century church to be substantially rebuilt. A fine Gothic entry portal survived, and inside there's a magnificent seventeenth-century *retablo* with sculptures by Martínez Montañés. A first-century-BC **Roman theatre** (daily 10am–2.30pm; free) has been excavated behind, close to the sea.

Torre Tavira

C/Marqués del Real Tesoro 10 • Daily: June–Sept 10am–8pm; Oct–May 10am–6pm • €6 • ☎ 956 212 910

North of the Catedral along C/Sacramento is the **Torre Tavira**, an eighteenth-century mansion with the tallest tower in the city, from where there are great **views** over the rooftops to the sea beyond; it also houses an entertaining **camera obscura**.

Hospital de las Mujeres

C/Hospital de Mujeres 26 • Mon–Fri 10am–1.30pm & 5.30–8pm, Sat 10am–1.30pm • €1.50; ask the porter for admission

One of the most impressive Baroque buildings in the city, the chapel of the **Hospital de las Mujeres**, houses a brilliant **El Greco**, *St Francis in Ecstasy*. It's one of the Cretan artist's finest portrayals of the saint, although it's a rather sombre study using copious shades of grey.

Santa Cueva

C/Rosario s/n • Mon–Fri 10.30am–2pm & 4.30–8pm, Sat 10.30am–2pm, Sun 10am–1pm • €3

A short walk southeast from the Museo de Cádiz is the eighteenth-century **Oratorio de Santa Cueva**, which houses three fine Goya frescoes. The church is divided into two dramatically contrasting parts. In the elliptical **upper oratory** beneath an elegant dome are three frescoes representing the *Miracle of the Loaves and Fishes*, the *Bridal Feast* (either side of the main altar) and the *Last Supper* (above the entrance), an unexpected depiction of Christ and the disciples dining sprawled on the floor, Roman style. The other works here are depictions of biblical scenes by minor artists.

In sharp contrast to the chapel above is the **subterranean chapel**, containing a sculpture of the Crucifixion whose manifest pathos adds a sombre note. An eighteenth-century work of the Genoa school, the image is said to have inspired visiting composer Joseph Haydn to write his *Seven Last Words* (of Christ) oratorio. A small museum has been added between the two chapels giving background information on the building's history and includes a display of Haydn's original score.

Plaza de las Flores and Mercado Central

Head west from the Catedral and it's a couple of blocks to the **Plaza de las Flores** (aka Pza. Topete), one of the city's most emblematic squares. Fronted by the striking early twentieth-century *Correos*, the square is a riot of colour most days due to the many flower sellers that have their stalls here. Adjoining the plaza to the west is the Pza. de la Libertad, the whole of which is taken up by the nineteenth-century **Mercado Central**, an elegant Neoclassical construction with a colonnade of Doric pillars enclosing the central area. Following a five-year refurbishment the building has been restored to its former glory, with vendors' stalls modernized to comply with current hygiene requirements. On weekday mornings it's a beehive of activity and not to be missed. In addition to the usual fish, meat, fruit and veg the new building has attracted a kaleidoscopic multitude of stalls selling everything from herbs and spices to exotic teas and world beers.

ARRIVAL AND DEPARTURE   CÁDIZ

By train The station is on the periphery of the old town, close to Pza. de San Juan de Dios, busiest of the city's many squares. For current timetables and ticket information, consult RENFE ☎ 902 240 202, ⟱ renfe.es.

Destinations Córdoba (3 daily; 2hr 30min–3hr 30min); El Puerto de Santa María (16 daily; 30min); Granada (1 daily, change at Seville; 5hr); Jerez (16 daily; 35min); Madrid (15 daily; 4hr 15min–5hr 30min); Seville (15 daily; 1hr 45min).

By bus Currently all buses arrive and depart from a temporary bus station to the side of the train station. The nearby port area of the Puerto Comercial is being redeveloped and the city's plan at the time of writing is to relocate a new bus station here which is planned to happen in 2015. Either *turismo* will be able to provide information on this.

Destinations Algeciras (8 daily; 2hr 30min); Arcos de la Frontera (4 daily; 1hr 30min); Chipiona (9 daily; 1hr 15min); Conil (13 daily; 1hr); El Puerto de Santa María (20 daily; 35min); Granada (4 daily; 5hr 15min); Jerez de la Frontera (13 daily; 45min); Málaga (4 daily; 4hr); Sanlúcar de Barrameda (5–9 daily; 1hr); Seville (8 daily; 1hr 45min); Tarifa (6 daily; 2hr); Vejer de la Frontera (6 daily; 1hr).

By car Coming by car, you'll soon discover sea-locked Cádiz's acute lack of parking space, and if you don't want to spend an age searching you'd be best off taking accommodation with a garage (all the hotels will assist with parking) or heading for a car park – two of the most central inside the city walls are by the train station and along Paseo de Canalejas near the port.

By ferry Today the only long-distance ferry services from Cádiz are to the Canary Islands. Trasmediterranea, Estación Marítima (☎ 956 227 421, ⟱ trasmediterranea.es), currently operates a weekly sailing (Tues 5pm) to Las Palmas and Tenerife. Local ferries sail across the bay to El Puerto de Santa María and the beach resort of Rota. The service to El Puerto is by catamaran (information/ timetables in Spanish only: ⟱ cmtbc.es). All three services including the boat to Rota sail from the same dock on the south side of the Puerto Comercial. A useful site for checking the latest ferry schedules is ⟱ directferries.co.uk.

Destinations Las Palmas (1 weekly; 39hr); El Puerto de Santa María (catamaran: weekdays every 30min between 7.45am–10pm; weekends reduced sailings ending at 8.30pm; 50min; €5.30 return); Rota (weekdays 7 daily; 50min; €10.10 return); Tenerife (1 weekly; 48hr).

INFORMATION AND TOURS

Turismo Avda. Ramón de Carranza (Mon–Fri 9am–7.30pm, Sat & Sun 10am–2.30pm; ☎ 956 203 191) near to Pza. San Juan de Dios; there's also a useful *turismo municipal* on the Paseo de Canalejas (July–Sept Mon–Fri 8.30am–6.30pm, Sat–Sun 9am–5pm; Oct–June Mon–Fri 9am–7pm, Sat & Sun 9am–5pm; ☎ 956 241 001).

Open-top bus tour City Sightseeing Cádiz (☎ 956 105 650, ⟱ www.city-sightseeing.com) runs a hop-on, hop-off clockwise route around the peninsula and has stops at or near Pza. San Juan de Dios, the Catedral, Parque Genovés, Playa de la Victoria and places in between. Tickets cost €17, are valid for 24hr and include earphone commentary.

ACCOMMODATION

In tune with the city itself, much of Cádiz's budget **accommodation** has seen better days. Although things are slowly improving, there's still a shortage of good-quality accommodation in all categories. Radiating out from the Pza. San Juan de Dios is a dense network of alleyways crammed with **hostales** and **fondas** and a few less inviting options. More salubrious places to stay are to be found a couple of blocks away, towards the Catedral or Pza. de Candelaria.

★**Casa Caracol** C/Suárez de Salazar 4 ☎ 956 261 166, ⟱ hostel-casacaracol.com. Friendly backpackers' place with dorm beds in a large house near Pza. San Juan de Dios. Also has some double rooms sharing bathrooms and pricier en-suite rooms in a new *hostal* nearby. Guests have use of a communal kitchen and the proprietors hire out cycles and surfboards. Dorms €18, doubles €45

Las Cuatro Naciones C/Plocia 3 ☎ 956 255 539. Clean, unpretentious place with low-priced rooms sharing bathrooms, close to Pza. San Juan de Dios. €42

★**Hospedería Las Cortes** C/San Francisco 9 ☎ 956 212 668, ⟱ hotellascortes.com. Splendid newish hotel in

a stylishly restored *casa señorial*. Elegant rooms are well equipped and include a minibar. Facilities include sauna and gym, and there's a *cafetería* and restaurant. Can advise on parking. High-season price August only. B&B. €151

Hostal Bahía C/Plocia 5 ☎ 956 259 061, ⟱ hostal bahiacadiz.com. Reasonable-value and conveniently located *hostal*, offering a/c rooms with baths. Request their more attractive balcony rooms. €79

Hostal Canalejas C/Cristóbal Colón 5 ☎ 956 264 113, ⟱ www.hostalcanalejas.com. Pleasant two-star *hostal* in completely restored townhouse. En-suite rooms come with a/c and TV, and there's a wi-fi zone plus car park

4

A FEAST MADE IN HEAVEN

Takeaway **fried fish** was invented in Cádiz (despite English claims to the contrary), and there are numerous *freidurías* (fried-fish shops) around the town, as well as stands along the beach in season. Few eating experiences here can beat strolling the city streets while dipping into a *cartucho* (paper funnel) of *pescado frito*. In the bars, *tortilla de camarones* (shrimp fritter) is another superb local speciality. Worth seeking out are:

Freiduría Europa C/Hospital de Mujeres 21 ☎ 956 227 305, ⓦ freiduriaeuropa.es. Excellent fried-fish shop, similar and near to *Freiduría Las Flores*. Typical *cartucho* €3–5. Daily 11.30am–5pm & 7.30pm–midnight.

★ **Freiduría Las Flores** Plaza de las Flores 4 ☎ 956 226 112. Outstanding fried fish is cooked up here and if you buy a takeaway you can carry your *cartucho* to the terrace tables of the nearby bar *La Marina*, fronting the post office. Order a glass (or bottle) of chilled white wine to wash it down with, and you've got a feast made in heaven. Typical *cartucho* €3–5. Daily 9am–midnight.

nearby. Avoid the windowless interior rooms though. **€80**

Hostal España Marqués de Cádiz 9 ☎ 956 285 500, ⓦ pensionespana.com. Pleasant *hostal* inside a restored *casa palacio* offering reasonable rooms (some sharing bath for €60) with fans ranged around a patio. **€45**

Hostal Fantoni C/Flamenco 5 ☎ 956 282 704 ⓦ hostalfantoni.es. Good-value *hostal* in a renovated townhouse with lots of *azulejos* and cool marble, offering simple and en-suite rooms, the latter with a/c and TV. **€70**

★ **Hotel La Catedral** Pza. de la Catedral 9 ☎ 956 291 142, ⓦ hotellacatedral.com. Charming new small hotel 50m from the Catedral's front door. Comfortable rooms are well equipped and all have balconies where you can feast your eyes on the Catedral's imposing facade. Add an infinity rooftop pool – where you seem to swim almost within touching distance of the Catedral's bell tower – and you have a perfect place to stay. They can advise on parking. Ring reception for the best available rate. B&B. **€132**

Hotel Parador Atlántico Parque Genovés 9 ☎ 956 226 905, ⓦ www.parador.es. Opened in 2012, this state-of-the-art rectilinear construction fronting the sea replaced the old parador which was razed to make way for it. Beyond an austere exterior lie 124 rooms and suites filled with five-star comforts, all with terrace balcony and sea view. Features include full-size rooftop pool, solarium, bars, restaurant and gardens. **€290**

EATING AND DRINKING

There are great **places to eat** all over town and the streets around Pza. San Juan de Dios, Pza. de las Flores and Pza. de la Libertad (containing the market) are all places where you'll find good bars and restaurants. In sea-girthed Cádiz, of course, fish is king and nowhere more so than in the old fishermans' quarter, the Barrio de la Viña. Here in the streets surrounding a tiny square named Pza. Tío de la Tiza – particularly along C/Virgen de la Palma – *gaditanos* gather to stuff themselves at economical *marisquerías*.

El Aljibe C/Plocia 25 ☎ 956 266 656. A very good restaurant serving up a range of traditional dishes. House specials include *almejas a la marinera* (clams in garlic sauce). Also serves tasty tapas in its bar. *Menú de degustación* €42 including wine. Main dishes €10–18. Daily noon–4pm & 7.30–11.30pm.

★ **Bar El Faro** C/San Félix 15. Tapas bar of the renowned restaurant (see below), and probably the best in town. A stand-up place where the *finos* are first-rate, the service is slick and the seafood tapas are mouthwateringly delicious. House specials include *tortillitas de camarones* (shrimp fritters) and *tostaditas de pan con bacalao* (cod on toast). Daily 12.30–4.30pm & 8.30pm–midnight.

Bar La Palma C/de la Palma 7 ☎ 956 228 587. In the old fishing quarter of the Barrio de la Viña, this is one of a number of good fried-fish restaurants along this street. There's a pleasant terrace and a great atmosphere as this street is one big terrace at weekends. Main dishes €7–15.

Daily 11.30am–midnight.

Elenvaro Gastro Bar C/Zorilla 1 ☎ 956 223 852. New gastro tapas bar serving up very good tapas and *raciones* with a creative edge. You could try their *pulpo a la brasa* (grilled octopus) and on Saturday and Sunday there's paella. Tapas €4–7. Daily noon–5pm & 8pm–midnight.

★ **El Faro** C/San Félix 15 ☎ 956 211 068, ⓦ elfarodecadiz.com. In the heart of the Barrio de la Viña, this is one of the best fish restaurants in Andalucía. House specialities include *pulpo* (octopus), *merluza* (hake), *urta* (sea bream), and a delicious *arroz marinero* (Andalucian paella). There's a *menú de degustación* for €37 (excluding wine) and a menu for around €25 (Mon–Fri) which you may need to ask for. Their excellent tapas bar is also well worth a visit. Daily 12.30–4.30pm & 8.30–11.30pm.

★ **Restaurante Atxuri** C/Plocia 7 ☎ 956 253 613, ⓦ atxuri.es. This is an outstanding and highly popular Basque fish restaurant offering excellent Basque- and *andaluz*-inspired fish dishes at reasonable prices. Also has an excellent tapas bar and they offer meal-sized *media raciones* (€6–10) in the bar or on a pleasant outdoor terrace. Main dishes €10–19. Booking advisable for restaurant. Daily 1.15–5.30pm & 9pm–midnight;

closed eve Sun–Wed (except July–Sept).
Restaurante El Sardinero Pza. San Juan de Dios 4. Traditional *gaditano* fish restaurant offering good-quality fish dishes served on a pleasant terrace. Main dishes €8–18. Daily 11am–midnight.

El Puerto de Santa María

Just 10km across the bay, **EL PUERTO DE SANTA MARÍA** is the obvious choice for a day-trip from Cádiz, a traditional family resort for both *gaditanos* and *sevillanos* – many of whom have built villas and chalets along the fine **Playa Puntillo**. This strand is a little way out from town (10–15min walk or local bus ride), a pleasant place to while away an afternoon; there are friendly beach bars where for ridiculously little you can nurse a litre of *sangría* while munching *mariscos*.

ARRIVAL AND INFORMATION   EL PUERTO DE SANTA MARÍA

By catamaran The catamaran from Cádiz (operated by Consorcio de Transportes (☎ 902 450 550) is quicker and cheaper than the bus (€2.65 one-way, €5.30 return); the 40min trip across the bay departs from the Muelle Reina Victoria jetty (near the train station) roughly half-hourly between 7.45am and 10pm. The return timetable is similar, with sailings roughly half-hourly between 7am and 8.45pm. Check all return times when you board on the

outward journey if you don't want to be stranded.
Turismo Housed in the splendid Baroque Palacio de Aranibar, Pza. del Castillo facing the Castillo de San Marcos (daily: May–Sept 9am–2pm & 6–8pm; Oct–April 10am–2pm & 5.30–7.30pm; ☎ 956 542 475, ⓦ turismoelpuerto.com). Here you can pick up a detailed street map as well as a *Ruta del Tapeo* leaflet to help find the best tapas bars.

4

ACCOMMODATION AND EATING

The best areas in town for **places to eat** are the Ribera del Marisco, a street upstream from the ferry dock, lined with a variety of seafood restaurants and bars serving tapas and *raciones*, and the nearby Pza. de la Herrería.

Bar La Dorada Avda. de la Bajamar 26 ☎ 956 855 214. Inexpensive meal-sized raciones are served up at this friendly bar with a terrace overlooking the river. The *pescado frito* is superb, and house specials include *choco a la plancha* (cuttlefish) and *tortillitas de camarones* (shrimp fritters). Tues–Sun 1–4pm & 8pm–midnight.
Camping Playa Las Dunas Paseo Marítimo Playa de la Puntilla ☎ 956 872 210, ⓦ lasdunascamping.com. Large campsite near the beach with plenty of shade plus pool, restaurant and supermarket. Bus #2 from the Pza. de las Galeras Reales (ferry quay) will take you there. **€21.20**
Hostal Loreto C/Ganado 17 ☎ 956 542 410,

ⓦ pensionloreto.com. Pleasant *hostal* with a delightful patio. Rooms come with or without bath; en suites (€48) have ceiling fans, fridge and TV. **€42**
Hotel Santa María Avda. Bajamar s/n ☎ 956 873 211, ⓦ hotelsantamaria.es. Good-value three-star riverfront hotel in a converted eighteenth-century *palacio* with a/c balcony rooms, restaurant, garage (or there's an easy access pay car park fronting the hotel) and rooftop pool. **€133**
★**Pensión Santa María** C/Pedro Múñoz Seco 38 ☎ 956 853 631. Very welcoming family *pensión*, for spotless rooms with and without bath (en suites cost €65), run by an ebullient *dueña andaluza* (female proprietor). She'll even do

---

VISITING SANTA MARÍA'S SHERRY BODEGAS

Santa María's principal attraction is a series of **sherry bodegas** – long, whitewashed warehouses flanking the streets and the banks of the river. Until the train was extended to Cádiz, all shipments of sherry from Jerez came through Santa María, and its port is still used to some extent. Many of the firms offer tours and tastings to visitors – the most worthwhile tours are offered by two of the town's major producers, Osborne, C/Los Moros 7 (visits: in English daily at 10.30am; in Spanish daily at 11am and midday; ☎ 956 869 100; €8; booking required), and Gutierrez Colosía, Avda. Bajamar 40 (Mon–Fri 1pm, Sat 12.30pm & 1.30pm; €6; ☎ 956 852 852; no booking required) who let you taste five *finos* and an *aperitivo*. The *turismo* can provide details of visits to smaller *bodegas*.

a bit of washing for you. There's a guests' kitchen and if you want to practice your Spanish, here's the place to stay. **€45**

★**Romerijo** Ribera del Marisco ☎956 541 254, ⓦromerijo.com. This enormous, economical and justifiably popular seafood bar dominates the strip here. You can get a takeaway of *mariscos* in a *cartucho* (paper funnel) from their shop and eat it at outdoor tables where buckets are provided for debris and waiters serve beer; the *cóctel de mariscos* (seafood cocktail) or any of the six types of *langostinos* (prawns) are delicious. Typical *cartucho*

€3–6. The same firm's *freiduría* restaurant over the road is equally excellent. Daily 11am–midnight.

Sol y Sombra Pza. de Ahuja, facing the bullring ☎956 874 703. Taking its name from the nearby bullring's seating arrangements, this is often a lively venue – especially on fight days – and prepares good and cheap tapas. House specials include *fideos con almejas* (vermicelli with clams) and paella. Its restaurant is also recommended and does a lunchtime menu for €10. Mon, Tues & Thurs– Sun 8am–midnight.

Sanlúcar de Barrameda

Like its neighbour El Puerto, **SANLÚCAR DE BARRAMEDA**, 15km to the northwest, also has its sherry connections. Nine kilometres east of Chipiona and set at the mouth of the Guadalquivir, it's the main depot for **manzanilla** wine, a pale, dry variety much in evidence in the bars, which you can also sample during visits to the town's **bodegas**. Sanlúcar is also the setting for some exciting **horse races** along the beach in the first and third weeks of August (check with the *turismo* for exact dates), a great time to be here.

Bodega Antonio Barbadillo

C/Sevilla 25 • Visits in English Tues–Sat 11am • €3 • ☎956 385 500, ⓦbarbadillo.com

The town's major producer, **Bodega Antonio Barbadillo**, in the *barrio alto* near the castle, is one of the most interesting *bodegas* to visit, with a stop at their shop and museum thrown in at the end. A list of Sanlúcar's seven other *bodegas* offering visits is available from the *turismo* (see opposite).

Barrio Alto

There's not a great deal to see in Sanlúcar, although the attractive old quarter in the upper town, or **Barrio Alto**, is worth taking time to explore. The town's port was the scene of a number of important maritime exploits: Magellan set out from here to circumnavigate the globe; Pizarro embarked to conquer Peru; and 4km upriver, from the fishing harbour of Bonanza, Columbus sailed on his third voyage to the Americas. The few buildings of interest in the town are all located in the Barrio Alto, reached by following the Cuesta de Belén uphill from the lower town.

A CRUISE INTO PARQUE NACIONAL COTO DE DOÑANA

One of the best things about Sanlúcar is its shell-encrusted **river beach** and warm waters, a couple of kilometres' walk from the town centre and usually quite deserted. This is flanked, on the opposite shore, by the beginnings of the **Parque Nacional Coto de Doñana** (see p.306), whose vast marshy expanses (strictly regulated access) signal the end of the coast road to the west. Visits to the park from Sanlúcar are possible with a boat cruise, which, while it doesn't allow for serious exploration, is nevertheless a wonderful introduction to this remarkable area. The trip lasts approximately three hours and allows two short, guided walks inside the park to spot wildlife. The **Real Fernando** – which has a cafetería on board – leaves daily from the Bajo de Guía quay (May–Sept Mon–Sat 10am & 5pm; Oct–April daily 10am & 5pm; €17.27, under-12s half-price; booking essential on ☎956 363 813, ⓦwww.visitasdonana.com). Tickets should be collected (at least 30min before sailing) from the Fábrica de Hielo, Bajo de Guía s/n, the national park's **exhibition centre** (daily 9am–8pm) opposite the *Real Fernando's* jetty. Also note that binoculars are pretty essential, and, while they can be hired on board, having your own is a distinct advantage.

Palacio de los Duques de Medina Sidonia

Visits Tues–Fri 12.30pm, Sun 11.30am & 12.30pm • €5; book in advance • ☎ 956 360 161, ⊕ fcmedinasidonia.com

The most significant of the upper *barrio*'s buildings, this is the magnificent sixteenth- to eighteenth-century ducal palace of **Medina Sidonia**, stuffed with paintings by Spanish masters, including Goya. Until her death in 2008 the duchess of Medina Sidonia (last in a family line going back to the Middle Ages) lived here and had been an inveterate opponent of the Franco regime (her nickname was La Duquesa Roja, "the Red Duchess"). The palace and family estate is now in the care of the foundation she created. The guided tour of the house and its beautiful gardens takes an hour. Part of the palace now houses a *hospedería* (hotel) and very pleasant *cafetería*.

Nuestro Señora de la O

Mon–Thurs & Sat 11am–1.30pm • €1 with audio-guide

Alongside the ducal palace, the thirteenth-century church (with later additions) of **Nuestro Señora de la O** was founded by the family of Guzmán El Bueno (see p.278). The impressive exterior has a fine Gothic-Mudéjar portal depicting, above an elegant arched doorway with archivolt molding, lions bearing the coats of arms of the Guzmáns. Inside there is a superb *artesonado* ceiling.

Castillo de Santiago

C/Eguilaz • Tues–Sun 11am–2.30pm • €6, kids €4 including audio-guide • ☎ 956 923 500

The **Castillo de Santiago** was constructed by the second duke of Medina Sidonia in the fifteenth century. Fernando and Isabel once put up here when visiting the dukes, and it served as a barracks for the invading French army in the early nineteenth century and later as a prison. A ruin for most of the last century, it has recently been renovated and the audio-guided visits enable you to see the castle's barbicans and hexagonal tower as well as the Pza. de Armas and towers with stunning views over the town and the river towards the Parque Nacional Coto de Doñana.

INFORMATION

SANLÚCAR DE BARRAMEDA

Turismo Calzada de la Duquesa (July & Aug Mon–Fri 10am–2pm & 6–8pm, Sat & Sun 10am–2pm; March–June & Sept–Nov Mon–Fri 10am–2pm & 5–7pm, Sat & Sun 10am–2pm; Dec–Feb Mon–Fri 10am–2pm & 4–6pm, Sat & Sun 10am–2pm; ☎ 956 366 110, ⊕ sanlucardebarrameda.es), near the start of the avenue leading to the river estuary. They can also inform about a number of free wi-fi zones in the centre of town.

ACCOMMODATION AND EATING

There's a shortage of budget accommodation in Sanlúcar, and in August you'll be pushed to find anything at all. This is when a number of *casas particulares* open to mop up the overflow. Enquire at the *turismo* for information about these. For **tapas** you shouldn't miss *Casa Balbino* (see p.302). For more elaborate fare, head to the Bajo de Guía – a river beach backed by a line of great seafood restaurants. You can take a taxi or walk there by continuing past the *turismo* to the end of the Calzada de la Duquesa and turning right (east) when you hit the river, about 1km from the town centre.

★ **Bar-Restaurante El Bigote** Bajo de Guía 10 ☎ 956 362 696. Celebrated establishment and one of the "big two" on the waterfront which has recently edged in front of its neighbour. You can eat outstanding tapas in their lively bar next door or more formally in the restaurant, where the fish and the house *arroz de marisco* (seafood paella) are outstanding. An upstairs dining room offers panoramic views across the river towards the Doñana national park. Main dishes €10–20; reservation advised. Mon–Sat 1–4pm & 7.30–11.30pm.

★ **Casa Balbino** Pza. del Cabildo 11. Behind an unassuming facade lies one of the best tapas bars in Andalucía. Long established, its walls are hung with faded photos and the obligatory bulls' heads, and the smoothly efficient bar staff will guide you through a daunting tapas menu. To kick-off your session you could try their celebrated *tortilla de camarones* (shrimp fritters) or *caracolas* (whelks). There is a (self-service) terrace on the square. Daily noon–5pm & 7.30pm–midnight; closed Jan.

★**Hostal Gadir** C/Caballeros 19 ☎956 366 078, ⓦhostalgadir.com. Wonderful and friendly, family-run *hostal* with sparkling a/c rooms, some with terraces others with Jacuzzis. Rooms 3, 4, 5 & 10 (with Jacuzzi) have a superb view of the gardens of the Palacio de Orleáns y Borbón opposite. All rooms come with a/c and TV. A bargain in high season, it's a steal at other times of the year. Also offers single rooms (€35). **€50**

Hotel Barrameda C/Ancha 10 ☎956 385 878, ⓦhotelbarrameda.com. A newish, central and welcome addition to the town's accommodation options offering light and airy a/c rooms with plasma TV, some with balconies. Also has a pleasant patio, solarium roof terrace and a *cafetería*. **€89**

Mirador Doñana Bajo de Guía s/n ☎956 364 205, ⓦmiradordonana.com. The second of the Bajo de Guía's

"big two" is under new management – but with the same head chef – and has had a makeover, with a redesigned bar and upstairs restaurant with views towards Doñana. There's also a very pleasant outdoor terrace overlooking the river. House specials include *corvina a la plancha con tártara* (meagre with a tartar sauce) and the whole gamut of *Sanluqueño* shellfish – *langostinos, gambas, cigales* (scampi) and *bogovante* (lobster). Main dishes €9–20. Tues–Sun noon–5pm & 8pm–midnight.

Pensión Blanca Paloma Pza. de San Roque ☎956 380 981, ⓔhostal_blanca_paloma@yahoo.es. Good-value and friendly *pensión* with simple rooms (shared) bathrooms in a central position on this small plaza. **€31**

★**Posada de Palacio** C/Caballeros 11 ☎956 36 48 40, ⓦposadadepalacio.com. An elegant converted eighteenth-century *casa palacio* in the Barrio Alto with a delightful patio and tastefully furnished rooms with character. Rooftop terraces, bar and an intimate atmosphere together make this rather special. **€109**

Jerez de la Frontera

4

JEREZ DE LA FRONTERA, 30km inland towards Seville, is the home and heartland of sherry (itself an English corruption of the town's Moorish name – *Xerez*) and also of Spanish brandy. An elegant and prosperous town, it's a tempting place to stop, arrayed as it is round the scores of *bodegas*, with plenty of sights to visit in between.

Life is lived at a fairly sedate pace for most of the year here, although things liven up considerably when Jerez launches into one or other of its two big **festivals** – the May Horse Fair (perhaps the most snooty of the Andalucian *ferias*), or the celebration of the vintage towards the end of September.

VISITING JEREZ DE LA FRONTERA'S BODEGAS

The **tours of the sherry and brandy processes** can be interesting – almost as much as the sampling that follows – and, provided you don't arrive in August when much of the industry closes down, there are a great many firms to choose from. The visits are conducted either in English (very much the second language of the sherry world) or a combination of English and Spanish and last for about an hour. Many of these *bodegas* were founded by British Catholic refugees, barred from careers at home by the sixteenth-century Supremacy Act, and even now they form a kind of Anglo-Andalucian tweed-wearing, polo-playing aristocracy (on display, most conspicuously, at the Horse Fair). The González cellars – the *soleras* – are perhaps the oldest in Jerez and, though it's no longer used, preserve an old circular chamber designed by Eiffel (of the tower fame). If you feel you need comparisons, you can pick up a list of locations and opening times of the other *bodegas* from the *turismo*.

JEREZ'S "BIG TWO": THE BODEGAS

González Byass C/María González ☎956 357 016, ⓦwww.bodegastiopepe.com. Makers of the famous Tio Pepe brand and also a major brandy producer. Visits with wine tasting cost €12.50, for tapas and wine tasting the price is €16.50. Visits in English daily at noon, 1pm and 2pm.

Pedro Domecq C/San Ildefonso 3 ☎956 151 500, ⓦbodegasfundadorpedrodomecq.com. Producers of the well-known La Ina brand. Besides manufacturing sherry, they are also a major brandy producer. A visit with wine tasting costs €8. Reservation required. Mon–Fri hourly visits on the hour 10am–4pm, Sat noon, 1pm and 2pm.

Centro Andaluz de Flamenco

Pza. de San Juan • Mon–Fri 9am–2pm • Free • ⓦ centroandaluzdeflamenco.es

Jerez is famous throughout Spain for a long and distinguished **flamenco** tradition, and if you're interested in finding out more about Andalucía's great folk art, then a visit to the **Centro Andaluz de Flamenco** in the atmospheric *gitano* quarter, the Barrio de Santiago, is a must. There's an audiovisual introduction to *El Arte Flamenco* (hourly on the half-hour), plus videos of past greats and information on flamenco venues in the town.

The Alcázar

July–Sept Mon–Fri 10am–7.30pm, Sat & Sun 9.30am–3pm; Oct & Feb–June Mon–Fri 9.30am–6pm, Sat & Sun 9.30am–3pm; Nov–Jan daily 10am–2.30pm • €5 or €7 including camera obscura

The substantial **Alcázar** lies just to the south of the focal Pza. del Arenal. To reach the entrance, take a right off the southern end of Pza. del Arenal into Pza. Monti, at the end of which you turn left into C/M. María González. The entrance lies uphill on the left. Constructed in the twelfth century by the Almohads, though much altered since, the Alcázar has been extensively excavated and restored in recent years. The **gardens** have received particular attention: the plants and arrangements have been modelled as closely as possible – using historical research – on the original. The interior contains a well-preserved mosque complete with *mihrab* from the original structure, now sensitively restored to its original state after having been used as a church for many centuries. The eighteenth-century **Palacio de Villavicencio** constructed on the west side of the Alcázar's Patio de las Armas (parade ground) houses a **camera obscura** (same hours) offering views of the major landmarks of the town as well as the sherry vineyards and the sea beyond.

Catedral de San Salvador

Mon 10am–9pm, Tues–Sat 10am–6.30pm, Sun 10am–noon • €5, free Mon 7–9pm & Sun

The eighteenth-century **Catedral de San Salvador** was rather harshly dismissed by British hispanist Richard Ford as "vile Churrigueresque" because of its mixture of Gothic and Renaissance styles, but an elegant facade – largely the work of Vincente Acero – is not without merit. Inside, over-obvious pointing gives the building an unfinished, breeze-block aspect, while, in the sacristy, there's a fine, little-known painting by Zurbarán – *The Sleeping Girl*. The most exciting time to be here is September, when on the broad steps of the Catedral, below the free-standing bell tower – actually part of an earlier, fifteenth-century Mudéjar castle – the wine harvest celebrations begin with the crushing of grapes.

Archeological Museum

Pza. del Mercado • July–Aug Tues–Sun 10am–2pm; Sept–June Tues–Fri 10am–2pm & 4–7pm, Sat & Sun 10am–2pm • €5 including useful audio-guide which you may need; exhibit information is in Spanish only

Following years of closure for refurbishment, the excellent **Archeological Museum** has reopened; it lies five minutes north of the centre on the edge of the Barrio de Santiago. The itinerary opens with Jerez's impressive prehistoric past (look out for some four-thousand-year-old cylinder-shaped idols with starburst eyes from Cerro de las Vacas). Star exhibits in the Greek and Roman sections include a seventh-century-BC Greek military helmet, Roman amphorae – many stamped with the maker's name – and in the Visigothic section a fine sarcophagus carved with curious vegetable, animal and human symbols. The museum has added an expanded Moorish section with some fine ceramics – look out for an exquisite caliphal bottle vase – and interesting displays (with artefacts) relating to daily life in this period. Another new section dealing with the Christian Middle Ages features an exquisite fifteenth-century alabaster relief carved in England, and depicting the Resurrection of Christ; this is one of a number of similar works found in the town and underlines the importance of trade – not only in wine – between Jerez and the British Isles in this period.

Real Escuela Andaluz del Arte Ecuestre

Avda. Duque de Abrantes s/n • **Performances** Tues & Thurs noon, plus Fri noon in Aug • €21–27 • **Visits** non-performance days 10am–2pm • €11 • Information & reservations ✆ 956 319 635, ⊕ realescuela.org

Evidence of Jerez's great enthusiasm for horses can be seen at the **Real Escuela Andaluz del Arte Ecuestre** (Royal Andalucian School of Equestrian Art), which offers the chance to watch them performing to music. Training, rehearsals (without music) and visits to the stables and museum take place on other weekdays.

ARRIVAL AND INFORMATION   JEREZ DE LA FRONTERA

By plane From Jerez airport (7km out of town on the NIV; ✆ 956 150 000), there are daily buses to the centre between 6.30am and 9.45pm (€1.10) with a less frequent service from the bus station in the reverse direction and at weekends. The airport also has a **train station** (on the opposite side of the airport car park) which connects with Jerez station, a 10min journey. There are currently 8 daily trains between 7.30am and 10.40pm, but it would be wise to confirm times with the airport's *turismo* or general information desk. A taxi from the airport costs approximately €16–20 depending on traffic and time of day.

By train The train station, Estación de Ferrocarril, is at Pza. de Estación s/n (✆ 902 240 202), is eight blocks (10min walk) east of the town's central square, Pza. del Arenal. Frequent trains link Jerez with Cádiz, Seville and Córdoba. To reach the centre, take #10 urban bus from outside the station.

By bus The bus station, Estación de Autobuses, is at Pza. Estación s/n (✆ 956 149 990), which is next to the train station. To reach the centre, take #10 urban bus from outside the station.

Destinations Algeciras (2 daily; 2hr 30min); Arcos de la Frontera (17 daily; 35min); Cádiz (17 daily; 45min); Chipiona (10 daily; 40min); Córdoba (3 daily; 3hr 30min); El Puerto de Santa María (15 daily; 30min); Málaga (3 daily; 5hr); Ronda (7 daily; 2hr 30min); Sanlúcar de Barrameda (12 daily; 30min); Seville (7 daily; 1hr 30min); Vejer de la Frontera (1 daily via Cádiz; 1hr 30min).

By car Coming by car, you'll meet the familiar problem of finding a place to park; to avoid being clamped or towed, use the pay car parks signed in the centre or park farther out and walk in. There is a huge underground car park beneath Pza. del Arenal.

Turismo Pza. del Arenal, in the northwest corner of Jerez's main square (June–Sept Mon–Fri 9am–3pm & 5–7pm, Sat & Sun 9.30am–2.30pm; Aug Sat–Sun 8am–4pm; Oct–May Mon–Fri 9am–3pm & 4.30–6.30pm, Sat & Sun 9.30am–2.30pm; ✆ 956 341 711, ⊕ turismojerez.com); it's well stocked with information about the town and the area and can supply a detailed town map.

ACCOMMODATION

There's usually no problem finding **rooms** in Jerez except during April and May, when Semana Santa, the Festival de Jerez, the World Motorcycle Championship (held at the town's Formula 1 racing circuit) and the Feria del Caballo (May Horse Fair) come one after the other and fill the town to bursting point. During these events ("*temporada extra*") prices can double or even treble; we have quoted the normal high-season price.

Albergue Juvenil Avda. Blas Infante 30 ✆ 856 814 001. Good-value seven-storey hostel with double a/c en-suite rooms and a pool; but out in the suburbs. Take bus #9 from outside the bus station. Under-26 **€22**, over-26 **€26**

Hostal Las Palomas C/Higueras 17 ✆ 956 343 773, ⊕ www.pension-las-palomas.es. The most central budget option, with clean and simple rooms, some en suite (€30). **€25**

Hotel El Ancla C/Mamelón 15 ✆ 956 321 297, ⊕ www. hotel-el-ancla8.webnode.es. Welcoming and good-value place, fronting the upper end of the Alameda Cristina on the north side of the centre. Some rooms overlooking the noisy street (not so at night) are compensated for by views of square and fountains. **€39**

Hotel Al Andalus C/Arcos 29 ✆ 956 323 400, ⊕ hotelalandalusjerez.com. Comfortable hotel with two pretty patios. Recently refurbished rooms – the better ones lie off the inner patio – are equipped with a/c and TV. **€40**

Hotel Bellas Artes Pza. del Arroyo 45, facing the Catedral, ✆ 956 348 430, ⊕ hotelbellasartes.org. Charming and good-value small hotel inside a refurbished *casa palacio* on the Catedral square. Individually styled rooms are well-equipped with minibar and plasma TV, and the public areas include a library and roof terrace (with

loungers) for having breakfast or enjoying a fine view of the Catedral and surrounding town. Also has a couple of suites. Doubles €56, suites €70
Hotel Doña Blanca C/Bodegas 11 ☎ 956 348 761, ⓦ hoteldonablanca.com. One of the most central and intimate of the upper-range places, with well-equipped a/c balcony rooms with minibar and satellite TV, in a quiet

street. Own garage (€11/day). €70
★ **Hotel-Hostal San Andrés** C/Morenos 12 ☎ 956 340 983, ⓦ hotel-sanandres.com. Excellent and friendly hotel-*hostal* offering (in the *hostal*) both en-suite (€45) and rooms sharing bath; the hotel's rooms are all en suite with a/c and TV. There's also a charming patio below. Hostal €40, hotel €45

EATING AND DRINKING

Jerez's booming sherry trade ensures that the town's **restaurants** are kept busy, and a few of these are very good indeed. Befitting the capital of sherry production Jerez also has a range of great bars where *fino* – the perfect partner for tapas – can be sampled on its own turf.

★ **Bar Juanito** C/Pescadería Vieja 4 ⓦ bar-juanito .com. In a small passage off the west side of Pza. del Arenal, this is one of the most celebrated tapas bars in town, with a menu as endless as the number of excellent *finos* on offer. Specials include *berza jerezano* (chickpea stew). They have now added a restaurant should you wish to make a meal of it. Main dishes €13–16. Mon–Sat noon–5pm & 8pm–midnight, Sun noon–5pm; July–Aug closed Sun.
Cafetería Bar La Once C/Gaitán s/n ☎ 690 960 456. The spotless a/c bar-café of Spain's powerful charity for the blind serves up one of the cheapest three-course meals in town for €6.50 (including wine) – an excellent deal. Daily 7am–9pm.
La Carboná C/San Francisco de Paula 2 ☎ 956 347 475, ⓦ lacarbona.com. Cavernous but wonderfully atmospheric mid-priced restaurant inside an old *bodega*, specializing in charcoal-grilled fish and meat and – in season – fresh tuna. Their *maridajes con vino de jerez* (€32) presents three courses, each accompanied by the

appropriate Jerez wine. Main dishes €12–20. Mon & Wed–Sun 12.30–4.30pm & 8pm–12.30am.
La Condesa Pza. Rafael Rivero, C/Tornería 24 ☎ 956 326 700. The Michelin-recommended restaurant of the *Hotel Palacio Garvey* is an excellent place for a meal, especially on their attractive terrace. A three-course menu (€14 including wine) is recommended and often features *solomillo en salsa oloroso* (pork loin in sherry sauce). House specials include a tasty *salmorejo de remolacha con mojama y feta* (beetroot gazpacho with tuna and feta cheese). Main dishes €8–15. Daily 1–4pm & 8.30–11pm.
Restaurante Gaitán C/Gaitán 3 ☎ 956 345 859. One of Jerez's oldest traditional restaurants has had a makeover and a tapas bar now stands out front with the restaurant behind. A range of *jerezano* dishes are on offer including *cordero confitado con miel y brandy de jerez* (lamb with a honey and brandy sauce). It also has a range of menus from €12–20 (including wine). Main dishes €10–16. Mon–Fri noon–4.30pm & 8–11.30pm; Sat noon–4.30pm.

4

Huelva province

The **province of Huelva** stretches between Seville and Portugal, but aside from its scenic section of the Sierra Morena to the north and a chain of fine **beaches** to the west of the provincial capital, it's a pretty dull part of Andalucía, laced with large areas of swamp – the *marismas* – and notorious for mosquitoes. This distinctive habitat is, however, particularly suited to a great variety of wildlife, especially birds, and over 60,000 acres of the delta of the Río Guadalquivir (the largest roadless area in western Europe) have been fenced off to form the **Parque Nacional Coto de Doñana**. Here, amid sand dunes,

CROSSING THE BORDER TO PORTUGAL

From Huelva you can head straight **along the coast to Portugal**. There are a number of good beaches and some low-key resorts noted for their seafood, such as **Isla Cristina**, along the stretch of coastline between Huelva and the frontier town of **Ayamonte**, but not much more to detain you. A good bus service along this route and a new road suspension bridge across the Río Guadiana estuary and border, linking Ayamonte and **Vila Real de Santo Antonio** in Portugal, make for a relatively painless crossing of the country border. From this approach, a good first night's target in Portugal is **Tavira**, on the Algarve train line. Note that Portugal is an hour behind Spain throughout the year.

VISITING PARQUE NACIONAL COTO DE DOÑANA

Visiting Doñana involves (perhaps understandably) a certain amount of frustration. At present, it's open only to a **boat cruise** from Sanlúcar (see p.300) and to brief, organized **tours** (May–Sept daily 8.30am & 5pm; Oct–April Tues–Sun 8.30am & 3pm; €29.50) by all-terrain 24-seater buses – four hours at a time along one of five charted, 80km routes. The starting point for the tours (run by the Cooperativa Marismas del Rocío, ⊛ donanavisitas.es) and the place to book them (essential, and as far ahead as possible in high season), is at the Centro de Recepción de Acebuche, 4km north of Matalascañas towards El Rocío and Almonte (daily April–Sept 8am–3pm & 4–9pm, Oct–March 8am–3pm & 4–7pm). The number for phone bookings is ☎959 430 432 (English spoken) or at the Cooperativa's office, Pza. del Acebuchal 16, El Rocío ☎671 596 550. The tours are quite tourist-oriented and point out only spectacular species such as flamingos, imperial eagles, deer and wild boar (binoculars are pretty essential). If you're a serious ornithologist, enquire instead at the *centro* about organizing a private group tour.

There are excellent birdwatching **hides** (daily 8am–8pm) at the El Acebuche, La Rocina and El Acebron reception centres, as well as a 1.5km footpath from El Acebuche, which creates a mini-trek through typical *cotos*, or terrains, to be found in the reserve. Although binoculars are on hire, they sometimes run out, and you're advised to bring your own. All three centres have exhibitions and displays covering the species to be seen in the park and the history of human activity within its boundaries.

pine woods, marshes and freshwater lagoons, live scores of flamingos, along with rare birds of prey, around thirty pairs of the endangered Spanish lynx, mongooses and a startling variety of migratory birds.

Parque Nacional Coto de Doñana

The seasonal pattern of its delta waters, which flood in winter and then drop in the spring, leaving rich deposits of silt, raised sandbanks and islands, gives **Coto de Doñana** its uniqueness. Conditions are perfect in winter for ducks and geese, but spring is more exciting; the exposed mud draws hundreds of flocks of breeding birds. In the marshes and amid the cork-oak forests behind, you've a good chance of seeing squacco herons, black-winged stilts, whiskered terns, pratincoles and sand grouse, as well as flamingos, egrets and vultures. There are, too, occasional sightings of the Spanish imperial eagle, now reduced to a score of breeding pairs. Conditions are not so good in late summer and early autumn, when the *marismas* dry out and support far less birdlife.

It is no Iberian Arcadia, however, and given the region's parlous economic state the park is under constant threat from development. Even at current levels the drain on the water supply is severe, and made worse by **pollution** of the Guadalquivir by farming pesticides, Seville's industry and Huelva's mines. The seemingly inevitable disaster finally occurred in 1998 when an upriver mining dam used for storing toxic waste burst, unleashing millions of litres of pollutants into the Guadiamar, which flows through the park. The noxious tide was stopped just 2km from the park's boundary, but catastrophic damage was done to surrounding farmland, with nesting birds decimated and fish poisoned. What is even more worrying is that the mining dams have not been removed (the mines are a major local employer) but merely repaired.

Equally disturbing are the proposals for a huge new tourist centre to be known as the Costa Doñana, on the very fringes of the park. Campaigning by national and international environmental bodies resulted in this project being shelved, but the threat remains, much of the pressure stemming from local people who see much-needed jobs in this or similar proposals.

El Rocío

Set on the northwestern tip of the *marismas*, **EL ROCÍO** is a tiny village of white cottages and a church stockade where perhaps the most famous pilgrimage-fair of the south takes place annually at Pentecost. This, the **Romería del Rocío**, is an extraordinary spectacle, with whole village communities and local "brotherhoods" from Huelva, Seville and even Málaga converging in lavishly decorated ox carts and on horseback. Throughout the procession, which climaxes on the Saturday evening, there is dancing and partying, while by the time the carts arrive at El Rocío they've been joined by busloads of pilgrims swelling numbers in recent years to over half a million. The fair commemorates the miracle of Nuestra Señora del Rocío (Our Lady of the Dew), a statue found in the thirteenth century – so it is said – on this spot and resistant to all attempts to move it elsewhere. The image, credited with all kinds of magic and fertility powers, is paraded before the faithful early on the Sunday morning.

In spring, as far as **birdwatching** goes, the town is probably the best base in the area. The adjacent *marismas* and pine woods are teeming with birds, and following tracks east and southeast of El Rocío, along the edge of the reserve itself, you'll see many species (up to a hundred if you're lucky).

ACCOMMODATION   **EL ROCÍO**

The village makes a nice **place to stay**, with wide, sandy streets, cowboy-hatted horseriding farmers and a frontier-like feeling, and prices for most of the year are reasonable. That said, don't even think about getting a room during the *romería* as they not only cost over ten times normal prices, but are booked up years ahead. All the accommodation options listed below (except the *Hospedería*) have their own decent restaurants.

Camping La Aldea ☎ 959 442 677, ⊛ campinglaaldea .com. El Rocío's campsite lies on the village's northern edge along the Almonte road (A483), and offers good facilities and a reasonable amount of shade. **€23.60**

Hospedería Puente del Rey Avda. Canaliega 1 ☎ 959 442 575. A ringer for the hotel in the film *The Shining*, this huge and rather incongruous hotel has gone through a series of owners, name changes and makeovers. Rooms come with a/c, fridge and TV. **€70**

Hostal Cristina C/Real 32 ☎ 959 406 513. One of

El Rocío's oldest budget establishments, this is a welcoming place with en-suite a/c rooms (some with *marismas* views) and its own restaurant. **€50**

★ **Hotel Toruño** Pza. Acebuchal 22 ☎ 959 442 323, ⊛ toruno.es. This is the best of the more expensive places, with comfortable rooms overlooking the *marismas*. The best view is from Room 225 but some of the ground-floor rooms (109, 111 & 115) also allow you to spot flamingos, herons, avocets and lots more while lying in bed. B&B. **€64**

The Columbus Trail

It has to be said that the city of **Huelva** is perhaps the least attractive and least interesting of Andalucía's provincial capitals. However, nearby – and easily reached by buses from Huelva or with your own transport – is the Columbus Trail: a clutch of locations associated with the fifteenth-century **voyages of Christopher Columbus**.

Across the Río Tinto estuary from Huelva, the monastery of **La Rábida** and the villages of **Palos** and **Moguer** are all places connected with the voyages of Columbus (Cristóbal Colón in Spanish) to the New World.

La Rábida

8km from Huelva • April–Sept Tues–Sat guided tours hourly 10am–1pm & 4–7pm, Sun 10.45am–1pm & 4–7pm; Oct–March Tues–Sat 10am–1pm & 4–6.15pm, Sun 10.45am–1pm & 4–6.15pm • €3 • ⊛ monasteriodelarabida.com • Easily reached by bus from Huelva's bus terminal, Avda. Dr. Rubio s/n

La Rábida, is a charming and tranquil fourteenth-century Franciscan monastery whose fifteenth-century abbot was instrumental in securing funds for the voyage from the monarchs Fernando and Isabel. The guided tour includes the Sala Capitular (chapterhouse) where the final plans for the voyage were made, and the monastery's fourteenth-century church where Columbus and his crew prayed before setting sail.

Muelle de la Carabelas

June–Sept Tues–Sun 10.30am–10pm; Oct–May Tues–Sun 9.30am–8pm • €3.55

Just behind the monastery of La Rábida, on the Río Tinto estuary, the **Muelle de la Carabelas** (Harbour of the Caravels) has impressive full-size replicas of the three caravels that made the epic voyage to the New World, while an adjoining museum features among its displays facsimiles of Columbus' geography books annotated in his surprisingly delicate hand.

San Jorge

C/Fray Juan Peréz 19 • Mon–Fri 10am–noon & 6–7.30pm

The church of **San Jorge** in the village of **Palos** is where, in August 1492, Columbus and his crew heard Mass before setting sail from the now silted-up harbour. The church's southern Mudéjar portal through which Columbus – flanked by his captains – left the church, can be seen as well as the nearby La Fontanilla, a medieval well from which the ships took on water for the voyage.

Convento de Santa Clara

Hourly guided tours Tues–Sat 10.30am–6.30pm, Sun 10.30am–12.30pm • €3

At the whitewashed town of **MOGUER** is the fourteenth-century **Convento de Santa Clara**, in whose church Columbus spent a whole night in prayer as thanksgiving for his safe return. The tour also takes in some notable artworks and the ancient monastery's cloister and refectory.

4

GETTING AROUND   THE COLUMBUS TRAIL

Frequent buses from **Huelva's main bus station** at Avda. Dr Rubio s/n (☎902 114 492) link La Rábida, Palos and Moguer, and both Palos and Moguer have accommodation.

ACCOMMODATION

Hostal Platero C/Aceña 4 Niño, Moguer 13 ☎959 372 159. For overnight rooms in Moguer this central *hostal* fits the bill and has good-value en-suite rooms with a/c and TV. **€30**

Hotel La Pinta C/Rábida 79, Palos ☎959 530 164, ⓦhotellapinta.com. This pleasant two-star hotel is a good bet for a/c en-suite rooms and there's a decent restaurant, *El Paraiso*, a few doors away. **€67**

Seville to Córdoba

The direct route from **Seville to Córdoba**, 135km along the valley of Guadalquivir, followed by the train and some of the buses, is a flat and rather unexciting journey. There's far more to see following the route just to the south of this, via **Carmona** and **Écija**, both interesting towns, and more still if you detour further south to take in **Osuna** as well. There are plenty of buses along these roads, making travel between the villages easy. Overnighting, too, is possible, with plenty of places to stay – although Carmona is an easy day-trip from Seville.

Carmona

Set on a low hill overlooking a fertile plain, **CARMONA** is a small, picturesque town made recognizable by the fifteenth-century tower of the Iglesia de San Pedro, built in imitation of the Giralda. The tower is the first thing you catch sight of and it sets the tone for the place – an appropriate one, since the town shares a similar history to Seville, less than 30km distant. It was an important Roman city (from which era it preserves a fascinating subterranean necropolis), and under the Moors was often governed by a brother of the Sevillan ruler. Later, Pedro the Cruel built a palace within its castle, which he used as a "provincial" royal residence.

To get your bearings, it's helpful to know that the town consists of the *casco antiguo* (old town) inside the walls entered through the impressive Puerta de Sevilla, and the more modern town to the west of this. The heart of the old quarter is the **Plaza de San Fernando** (often referred to as the "Plaza Mayor") which, though modest in size, is dominated by splendid Moorish-style buildings. Behind it, and just to the south, there's a bustling fruit and vegetable **market** most mornings in the porticoed Plaza del Mercado.

Iglesia de San Pedro

C/San Pedro s/n • Mon & Thurs–Sun 11am–2pm plus Wed–Mon service at 8.30pm • €1.20

The **Iglesia de San Pedro** is a good place to start exploring the town; its soaring tower, built in imitation of the Giralda and added a century later, dominates Carmona's main thoroughfare, C/San Pedro. Inside there's a splendid Baroque *sagrario* (sacristy) by Figueroa.

Puerta de Sevilla

Guided tours July–Aug Mon–Fri 10am–3pm & 4.30–6pm, Sat & Sun 10am–3pm; Sept–June Mon–Sat 10am–6pm, Sun 10am–3pm • €2, Mon free

From the Paseo del Estatuto, the modern town's main thoroughfare, looking east, you get a view of the magnificent Moorish **Puerta de Sevilla**, a grand, fortified Roman double gateway (with substantial Carthaginian and Moorish elements) to the old town. It now houses the *turismo*, which organizes guided tours of the gate's upper ramparts. The **old town** is circled by 4km of ancient walls, inside which narrow streets wind up past Mudéjar churches and Renaissance mansions.

Santa María la Mayor

Mon–Sat 9am–2pm & 5–7pm, Sat 9–2pm, Sun 9–11.30am; closed second half Aug, first half Sept • €3

To the east of Pza. San Fernando, is **Santa María la Mayor**, a fine Gothic church built over the former Almohad Friday (main) mosque, whose elegant patio it retains, complete with orange trees and horseshoe arches. Like many of Carmona's churches, it is capped by a Mudéjar tower, possibly utilizing part of the old minaret.

Museo de la Ciudad

Mon 11am–2pm, Tues–Sat 11am–7pm, Sun 9.30am–2pm • €3, Tues free

To the east of Pza. San Fernando, and housed in the graceful eighteenth-century Casa del Marqués de las Torres, is the **Museo de la Ciudad**, which documents the history of the town with mildly interesting displays of artefacts from the prehistoric, Iberian, Carthaginian, Roman, Moorish and Christian epochs. The museum has a *cafetería*, open to all.

Pedro's Alcázar

Parador bars, restaurants and public areas open to nonguests

Dominating the ridge of the town are the massive ruins of **Pedro's Alcázar**, an Almohad fortress transformed into a lavish residence by the fourteenth-century king. He employed the same Mudéjar craftsmen who worked on the Alcázar in Seville. The fortress was destroyed by an earthquake in 1504 and partly rebuilt by Fernando (after Isabel's death) but then fell into ruin. What remains has now been incorporated into a remarkably tasteful parador.

Puerta de Córdoba

Following C/Martín López and its continuations east from Pza. de San Fernando for 500m will bring you to an imposing Roman gateway, the **Puerta de Córdoba**, where the town comes to an abrupt and romantic halt. This was the start of the ancient Córdoba road (once the mighty Via Augusta heading north to Zaragoza, Gaul and finally Rome itself, now a dirt track) which dropped down from here to cross the vast plain below. Following the road for a few kilometres will lead you to a five-arched Roman bridge, just visible on the plain below.

Roman necropolis

July–Aug Mon–Sat, 10am–3pm, Sun 10am–3pm; Sept–June Mon–Sat 10am–6pm, Sun 10am–3pm • €2, free Mon • ☏ 600 143 632

The extraordinary **Roman necropolis** lies on a low hill at the opposite end of Carmona; if you're walking out of town from San Pedro, take C/Enmedio, the middle street (parallel to the main Seville road) of three that leave the western end of Paseo del Estatuto and follow this for about 450m. Here, amid the cypress trees, more than nine hundred family tombs dating from the second century BC to the fourth century AD can be found. Enclosed in subterranean chambers hewn from the rock, the tombs are often frescoed and contain a series of niches in which many of the funeral urns remain intact. Some of the larger tombs have vestibules with stone benches for funeral banquets, and several retain carved family emblems (one is of an elephant, perhaps symbolic of long life). Most spectacular is the **Tumba de Servilia** – a huge colonnaded temple with vaulted side chambers. Opposite the site is a partly excavated **amphitheatre**.

ARRIVAL AND INFORMATION   CARMONA

By bus Buses from Seville stop on the central Paseo del Estatuto in sight of the landmark ancient gateway, the Puerta de Sevilla.
By car Your best bet is to use the reasonably priced car park beneath the Paseo de Estatuto.
Turismo The Puerta de Sevilla also houses an efficient

turismo (July–Aug Mon–Fri 10am–3pm & 4.30–6pm, Sat & Sun 10am–3pm; Sept–June Mon–Sat 10am–6pm, Sun 10am–3pm; ☏ 954 190 955, ⊛ turismo.carmona .org), which is well stocked with information, and can provide a town map.

ACCOMMODATION

Carmona has a shortage of **places to stay**, especially in the budget category; particularly in spring and high summer, it's worth ringing ahead. The cheaper places lie outside the walls, while a clutch of more upmarket options all occupy scenic locations in the old town.

Hostal Comercio C/Torre del Oro 56 ☏ 954 140 018. Built into the Puerta de Sevilla gateway this is a charming small and friendly family-run *hostal* that celebrated its centenary in 2014. Offers compact a/c en-suite rooms (without TV) around a pretty patio. **€50**
Hotel San Pedro C/San Pedro 3 ☏ 95 419 00 87. Near the church of San Pedro this is a central and pleasant budget option for a/c en-suite rooms with TVs. **€49**
★ **Parador Nacional** Alcázar Rey Don Pedro ☏ 954 141 010, ⊛ www.parador.es. Despite more recent competition

at this end of the market, a superb location, patios and swimming pool ensure that this is still the nicest – and best value – of the luxury places in town. Pay a few euros extra for a room with a balcony. It's worth calling in for a drink at the bar, to enjoy the fabulous views from the terrace. **€188**
Posada San Fernando Pza. San Fernando 8 ☏ 954 141 408, ⊛ posadasanfernando.com. Newish and attractive small hotel with friendly proprietors on the old town's focal square. Rooms are individually styled and come with a/c, minibars and plasma TVs. **€65**

EATING AND DRINKING

There are plenty of places to eat both in the old and new towns, and you don't need to spend a fortune to eat well.

Bar Goya C/Prim 42 ☏ 954 143 060. This lively tapas bar is housed in a fifteenth-century edifice off the west side of Pza. de San Fernando in the old town. There's also a pleasant terrace and house specials include *alboronía* (ratatouille) and *chipirón plancha en salsa verde* (fried squid in green sauce). June–Sept Mon–Fri 8am–5pm & 8pm– midnight, Sat & Sun noon–midnight; Oct–May Mon–

Fri 8am–midnight, Sat & Sun noon–midnight.
Mingalario Pza. Cristo del Rey 1 ☏ 954 143 893. In the old town, facing the church of El Salvador, this is another fine old bar with excellent tapas. House specials include *gambas al ajillo* (shrimps in garlic). Daily 9am–5pm & 7pm–midnight.
★ **Molino de la Romera** C/Pedro s/n ☏ 954 142 000.

With a great terrace view across the *campiña* and housed in a sixteenth-century Moorish oil mill, this pleasant restaurant serves up regional dishes, has a good-value menu for around €12 and also does *raciones*. Its *dulces* are prepared by the nuns of the nearby Convento de Santa Clara. Main dishes €10–16. Tues, Wed & Sun 1–4pm, Thurs–Sat 1–4pm & 8–11pm.

Parador Nacional Alcázar Rey Don Pedro ☎ 95 414 10 10. The restaurant of the parador is a model of baronial splendour which can be experienced on a *menú del día* for €33 that includes many local dishes; they also offer vegetarian and diabetic menus. Daily 1–4pm & 8–11pm.

El Tapeo C/Prim 9 ☎ 640 212 773. Tapas bar-restaurant offering a decent tapas selection – try the *espinacas con garbanzos* (spinach with chickpeas) or *berenjenas fritas* (aubergine). Aside from a range of meat and fish dishes, the restaurant also offers a good-value menu for €10. Mon–Sat 8am–midnight.

Écija

Lying midway between Seville and Córdoba in a basin of low sandy hills, **ÉCIJA** is known, with no hint of exaggeration, as *la sartenilla de Andalucía* ("the frying pan of Andalucía"). In mid-August, it's so hot that the only possible strategy is to slink from one tiny shaded plaza to another, or with a burst of energy to make for the riverbank.

The heat is worth enduring, since this is one of the most distinctive and individual towns of the south, with eleven superb, decaying church towers, each glistening with brilliantly coloured tiles. It has a unique domestic architecture, too – a flamboyant style of twisted and florid forms, best displayed on C/Castellar, where the magnificent painted and curved frontage of the huge **Palacio de Peñaflor** (interior currently closed; enquire at the *turismo*) runs along the length of the street; the building has a fine patio and until recently housed Écija's public library. Other sights not to be missed are the beautiful polychromatic tower of the church of **Santa María**, overshadowing the main Pza. de España, and the **Palacio de Benamejí**, a stunning eighteenth-century palace on C/Castillo, south of Pza. de España, that has a beautiful interior patio and has now been declared a national monument.

Museo Histórico Municipal

Palacio de Benamejí, C/Canovas de Castillo • June–Sept Tues–Fri 10am–2.30pm, Sat 10am–2.30pm & 8–10pm, Sun 10am–3pm; Oct–May Tues–Fri 10am–1.30pm & 4.30–6.30pm, Sat 10am–2pm & 5.30–8pm, Sun 10am–3pm • Free • ⓦ museo.ecija.es

The magnificent eighteenth-century Palacio de Benamejí, a short walk southwest of Pza. de España, is now home to the **Museo Histórico Municipal**, the town museum, which displays archeological finds from all periods. There is a particularly interesting section on Astigi's (the town's Roman name) role in the olive-oil trade – Spanish oil was prized in Imperial Rome. One sensational recent addition is the **Amazona de Écija**, a stunning, almost totally intact first-century-AD Roman statue accidentally discovered in the 2002 excavations to build a car park beneath the main square, Pza. de España. Two metres tall and depicting an Amazon resting against a pillar, it is of the highest craftsmanship and still bears traces of ochre paint. The statue has now become the town's civic icon. The museum has been expanded to include a whole upper floor dedicated to displaying a marvellous collection of **Roman mosaic pavements** which have been unearthed in excavations in and around the town.

Plaza Mayor

The town's focal **Plaza Mayor** (Pza. de España) was a building site for seven years during the construction of a controversial subterranean car park. Following this upheaval, the revamped square has been turned into a rather desolate, modernistic space jarring with the Baroque splendours surrounding it. A **Roman bath** discovered in the course of these works – just one of many archeological discoveries – can now be viewed under a canopy in the plaza's southeast corner.

INFORMATION ÉCIJA

Turismo Located at the Museo Histórico Municipal (see p.311) inside the Palacio de Benamejí (June–Sept daily 10am–2pm; Oct–May daily 10am–2pm & Tues, Thurs, Fri, Sat 5–7pm; ☎955 902 933, ⓦturismoecija.com).

ACCOMMODATION AND EATING

Bar La Reja C/Garcilopez 1 ☎954 833 012. Next door to the *Hotel Platería*, this bar has a wide choice of tapas and *raciones*. Specialities include fish and *mariscos*. Tues–Sat 12–6pm & 9pm–midnight.

Cafetería Pasareli Pasaje Virgen del Rocío 2 ☎955 904 383. Tucked away in a cul-de-sac off the east side of the Pza. de España, this place serves up a range of fish and meat dishes – including *atún fresco de almadraba* (fresh tuna) in season – and has a budget menu for €10. Also has a small terrace. Tues–Sat 9.30am–midnight, Sun noon–5pm.

Casa Emilio On the south side of the Pza. Mayor. A decent stop for tapas and *raciones*; try their local cheeses and *charcutería* (cured pork). Fri–Wed 8.30am–midnight, Thurs 8.30am–2pm.

Hotel Palacio de los Granados C/Emilio Castelar 42

☎955 905 344, ⓦwww.palaciogranados.com. To the east of the Pza. de España, this is a beautifully restored eighteenth-century mansion with delightful patios, a small pool, and rooms decorated with original contemporary artworks. €140

Hotel Platería C/Garcilópez 1 ☎955 902 754, ⓦhotelplateria.net. Off the east side of the Pza. Mayor, this comfortable hotel has modern a/c rooms. The restaurant is reliable and serves a bargain weekday menu for €9. House specials include *solomillo ibérico* (pork loin). Main dishes €8–12. Daily noon–4pm & 8pm–midnight. €60

Hotel Sol Pirula C/Miguel de Cervantes 50 ☎954 830 300, ⓦwww.hotelpirula.com. South of the centre, this three-star modern hotel has decent a/c rooms above its ground-floor restaurant. Own garage. €72

Osuna

OSUNA (like Carmona and Écija) is one of those small Andalucian towns that are great to explore in the early evening: slow in pace and quietly enjoyable, with elegant streets of tiled, whitewashed houses interspersed with fine **Renaissance mansions**. The best of these are off the main street, C/Carrera, which runs down from the central Pza. Mayor, and in particular on C/San Pedro, which intersects it; at no. 16, the **Cilla del Cabildo** has a superb geometric relief round a carving of the Giralda, and, farther along, the eighteenth-century **Palacio de El Marqués de la Gomera** – now a hotel and restaurant (see opposite) – is a stunning Baroque extravaganza. There's also a marvellous **casino** on Pza. Mayor, with 1920s Mudéjar-style decor and a grandly bizarre ceiling, which is open to all visitors and makes an ideal place for a cool drink.

The old university and Colegiata

May–Sept Tues–Sun 10am–1.30pm & 4–7pm, July & Aug closed Sun pm; Oct–April Tues–Fri 10am–1.30pm & 3.30–6.30pm • Colegiata with guided tour €3, La Encarnación €2.50, old university patio open during term time except July & Aug (free)

Two huge stone buildings stand on the hilltop: the **old university** (suppressed by reactionary Fernando VII in 1820) and the lavish sixteenth-century **Colegiata**, which contains the gloomy but impressive pantheon and chapel of the dukes of Osuna, descendants of the kings of León and once "the lords of Andalucía", as well as a museum displaying some fine artworks, including imposing canvases by Ribera. Opposite the entrance to the Colegiata is the Baroque convent of La Encarnación (same hours as Colegiata), which has a fine plinth of Sevillan *azulejos* round its cloister and gallery.

INFORMATION OSUNA

Turismo Housed in the town museum, Museo de Osuna, C/Sevilla 37, west of the main square (July–Aug Tues–Sat 10am–2pm & 5–8pm, Sun 10am–2pm; Sept–June Tues–Sat 10am–2pm & 5–8pm, Sun 10am–2pm; ☎954 815 732, ⓦwww.turismosuna.es) the *turismo* has information on the town and can provide a map.

ACCOMMODATION AND EATING

In Osuna **accommodation** is not plentiful, but outside of national holiday periods and the local *fería* (third or fourth week in May) there's usually no great problem finding a place to stay. All the same, it's worth ringing ahead. There are **food and drink** possibilities all over town and many of the accommodation options also have restaurants of their own. Osuna also has some fine tapas bars and the three we've listed below are all top-notch and well worth seeking out.

★**Casa Curro** Pza. Salitre 5 ✆955 820 758. The town's best (and liveliest) tapas and *raciones* bar cooks up a tasty range of seafood and meat dishes, many with a creative slant. Choose from the specials chalked up on the numerous blackboards covering the walls. There's a superb restaurant in the back, too. Main dishes (restaurant) €9–15. Tues–Sun noon–1am.

Hostal Caballo Blanco C/Granada 1 ✆954 810 184. Welcoming and comfortable *hostal* with en-suite a/c rooms with TV in a remodelled old coaching inn. It has a large car park at the back. The *hostal's* restaurant is very good for *comida casera*, serving up dishes such as *redondillo guisado* (beef stew) and *gachas de osuna* (local "gruel") as well as the usual standards. Main dishes €6–14. Daily 1–4pm & 7–10pm. €50

Hostal Granadino Pza. Salitre 1 ✆954 810 000. Slightly further away from the centre and southwest of the Pza. Mayor, this is a friendly place offering a/c en-suite rooms above a restaurant. €42

Hotel Esmeralda C/Tesorero 7 ✆955 821 073, ⓦhotelesmeralda.es. After a complete refit this is a transformed hotel with elegant a/c en-suite rooms with minibars, TVs and safes. Stunning rooftop terrace with plunge pool. Has own restaurant and (free) parking which should be reserved in advance. €55

★**Hotel Palacio Marqués de la Gomera** C/San Pedro 20 ✆954 81 22 23, ⓦhotelpalaciodelmarques.es. The town's four-star option, set inside one of the most beautiful *casa palacios* in the country, is a dream. A national monument in its own right, this eighteenth-century mansion has a breathtakingly beautiful patio with a Baroque chapel just off it and all rooms are tastefully and individually furnished. Room 7 was used by Franco Zeffirelli when here making a film about the life of María Callas and has a spectacular exterior balcony, while the irresistibly romantic Room 10 is situated in the palace's tower. There's a restaurant on-site too. Rates increase by 15 percent Fridays and Saturdays. €78

Taberna Jicales C/Esparteros 11 ✆954 810 423. Excellent tapas bar with an outdoor terrace. There's a mouthwateringly long tapas *carta*, and house specials include *boquerones fritos* (anchovies), *tortillitas de camarones* (shrimp fritters) and *manitas de cerdo* (pig's trotters in sauce). They also offer tasty desserts and are open for breakfast. Mon, Tues & Thurs–Sun 7am–1am.

★**Torresvera** C/Alfonso XII ✆630 467 883. Another of Osuna's outstanding tapas bars, with a wide (and often creative) range of tapas. Try their *tempura de verduras* (vegetable tempura) or *solomillo de cerdo con miel de caña* (pork loin with molasses). Their *raciones* are a good size and as they also offer desserts it's easy to make a meal of it on their pleasant outdoor terrace. Menu for €8. Daily 12.30–5pm & 8pm–1am; closed Nov.

Córdoba

CÓRDOBA lies upstream from Seville beside a loop of the Guadalquivir, which was once navigable as far as here. It is today a minor provincial capital, prosperous in a modest sort of way. Once, however, it was the largest city of Roman Spain, and for three centuries it formed the heart of the western Islamic empire, the great medieval caliphate of the Moors.

It is from this era that the city's major monument dates: the **Mezquita**, the grandest and most beautiful mosque ever constructed by the Moors in Spain. It stands right in the centre of the city, surrounded by the old Jewish and Moorish quarters, and is a building of extraordinary mystical and aesthetic power. Make for it on arrival and keep returning as long as you stay; you'll find its beauty increases with each visit, as, of course, is proper, since the mosque was intended for daily attendance.

The Mezquita apart, Córdoba itself is a place of considerable charm. It has few grand squares or mansions, tending instead to introverted architecture, calling your attention to the tremendous and often wildly extravagant **patios**. These have long been acclaimed, and they are actively encouraged and maintained by the local council, which runs a "Festival of the Patios" in May. Away from the Mezquita,

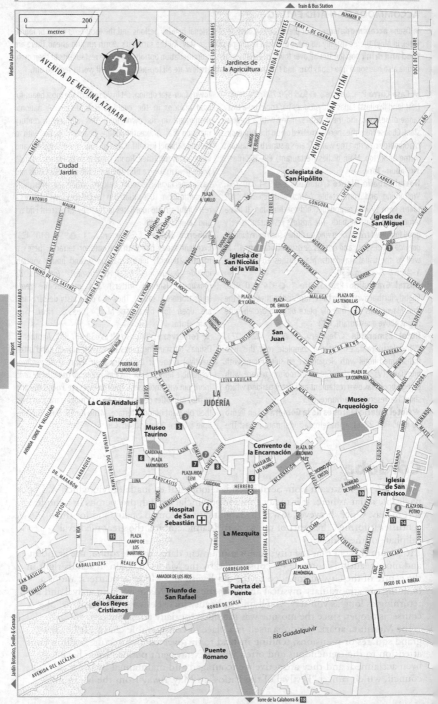

Train & Bus Station

0 — 200
metres

N

Medina Azahara

AVENIDA DE MEDINA AZAHARA

Ciudad
Jardín

Jardines de
la Agricultura

AVENIDA DEL GRAN CAPITAN

Colegiata de
San Hipólito

Iglesia de
San Miguel

Jardines de
la Victoria

Iglesia de
San Nicolás
de la Villa

PLAZA DE
LAS TENDILLAS

San
Juan

Museo
Arqueológico

LA
JUDERÍA

La Casa Andalusí

Sinagoga

Museo
Taurino

Convento de
la Encarnación

Iglesia
de San
Francisco

PLAZA DEL
POTRO

PUERTA DE
ALMODÓBAR

Hospital
de San
Sebastián

La Mezquita

PLAZA
CAMPO DE
LOS
MARTIRES

Alcázar
de los Reyes
Cristianos

Triunfo de
San Rafael

Puerta del
Puente

PLAZA
ALHÓNDIGA

PASEO DE LA RIBERA

Airport

Jardín Botánico, Seville & Granada

Puente
Romano

Río Guadalquivir

RONDA DE ISASA

AVENIDA DEL ALCÁZAR

Torre de la Calahorra & 18

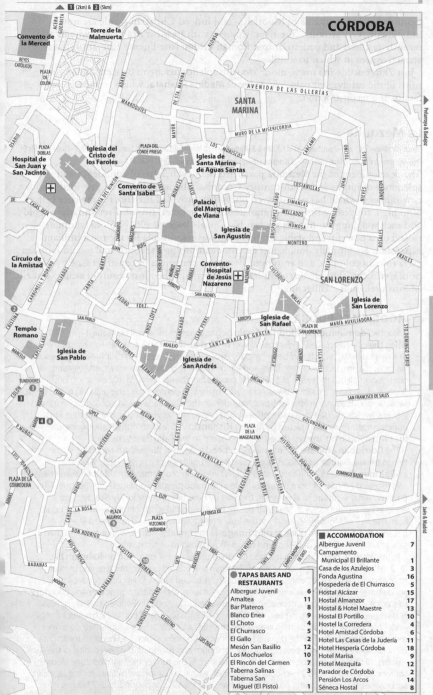

CÓRDOBA

■ (2km) & ■ (5km)

Convento de la Merced
Torre de la Malmuerta
REYES CATÓLICOS
PLAZA DE COLÓN
ADARVE
MARROQUIES
DE STA. MARINA
ALONSO
AVENIDA DE LAS OLLERÍAS
SANTA MARINA
Peñarroya & Badajoz
OSARIO
PLAZA DOBLAS
Iglesia del Cristo de los Faroles
PLAZA DEL CONDE PRIEGO
MAYOR
LOS MORISCOS
MURO DE LA MISERICORDIA
CARCAMO
Iglesia de Santa Marina de Aguas Santas
TOCINO
VIEJAS
REQUENA
Hospital de San Juan y San Jacinto
DE R. CASAS DEZA
PUERTA DEL RINCÓN
MORALES
STAS.
DAIRY
Convento de Santa Isabel
TERRES
COSTANILLAS
SIMANCAS
OBISPO LOPEZ CRIADO
MELLADOS
HUMOSA
JUAN
MICANILLO
NIEVES
ROSALES
Palacio del Marqués de Viana
CHAPARRO
MAGENES
RIFO
JUAN
Iglesia de San Agustín
MONTERO
FRAILES
Círculo de la Amistad
CARBONELL Y MORAND
ALVAROS
SANTA
MARTA
ENRIQUE REDEL
MUÑOZ CAPILLA
PARRAS
NAZARENO
CUSTODIO
VELASCO
Convento-Hospital de Jesús Nazareno
SAN LORENZO
CRISTINA
PEDRO FDEZ.
SAN ANDRÉS
ROELAS
Iglesia de San Lorenzo
Templo Romano
MARCELO
CAPITULARES
SAN PABLO
HNOS. LOPEZ
MANCHADO
ISAK PERU
ARROYO
Iglesia de San Rafael
PLAZA DE SAN LORENZO
MARÍA AUXILIADORA
STO. DOMINGO SABIO
Iglesia de San Pablo
VILLALONES
REALEJO
BLAMEJO
SANTA MARÍA DE GRACIA
Iglesia de San Andrés
P. ERDIGO
SAN LORENZO
ESCALUELA
MUÑICES
ABÉJAR
TUNDIDORES
COLON
RODRIGUEZ
PEDRO
D. VICTORIA
D. MÉNDEZ
SAN FRANCISCO DE SALES
P. MUÑOZ
MADRID
LOPEZ
GUTIERREZ DE LOS
REGINA
E. AGUSTINA
GOLONDRINA
CERRO
LUIS TOMÁS
RIDRI
PLAZA DE LA MAGDALENA
HISTORIADOR DOMÍNGUEZ ORTIZ
DOMINGO BADÍA
PLAZA DE LA CORREDERA
ALCAHARA
LA RAYURA
ARENILLAS
C. DE ISABEL II.
MAGDALENA
FRANCISCO BORJA
RONDA PE ANDUJAR
Jaén & Madrid
ARMAS
CARLOS
LA ROSA
PLAZA AGUAYOS
S. ELOY
ALFONSO XII
DON RODRIGO
PLAZA VIZCONDE MIRANDA
AGUSTÍN MORENO
SIETE
BEZVEDRAS
FRIAS
CRUZ VERDE
THILE MARHONUYO
CAMPO MADRE DE DIOS
BADANAS
MUÑIO TRIGO
VALDERRAMA
NOQUES
RONQUILLO BRICEÑO
CLAUSTRO
RAFE
LUIS DÍAZ

4

● **TAPAS BARS AND RESTAURANTS**
Albergue Juvenil — 6
Amaltea — 11
Bar Plateros — 8
Blanco Enea — 9
El Choto — 4
El Churrasco — 5
El Gallo — 2
Mesón San Basilio — 12
Los Mochuelos — 10
El Rincón del Carmen — 7
Taberna Salinas — 3
Taberna San Miguel (El Pisto) — 1

■ **ACCOMMODATION**
Albergue Juvenil — 7
Campamento Municipal El Brillante — 1
Casa de los Azulejos — 3
Fonda Agustina — 16
Hospedería de El Churrasco — 5
Hostal Alcázar — 15
Hostal Almanzor — 17
Hostal & Hotel Maestre — 13
Hostal El Portillo — 10
Hostel la Corredera — 4
Hotel Amistad Córdoba — 6
Hotel Las Casas de la Judería — 11
Hotel Hesperia Córdoba — 18
Hotel Marisa — 9
Hotel Mezquita — 12
Parador de Córdoba — 2
Pensión Los Arcos — 14
Séneca Hostal — 8

Córdoba's other remnants of Moorish – and indeed Christian – rule are not individually very striking. The river, though, with its great **Arab water wheels** and recently restored and pedestrianized **Roman bridge** (the Puente Romano), is an attractive area in which to wander.

Just 7km outside the town, more Moorish splendours are to be seen among the ruins of the extravagant palace complex of **Medina Azahara**, which is undergoing fascinating reconstruction.

La Mezquita

March–Oct Mon–Sat 10am–7pm, Sun 8.30–11.30am & 3–7pm; Nov–Feb Mon–Sat 10am–6pm, Sun 8.30–11.30 & 3–6pm • €8, kids €4; Free entrance at side doors Mon–Sat 8.30–9.20am for services but without lighting • ☎ 957 470 512

The development of the **Mezquita** paralleled the new heights of confidence and splendour of ninth- and tenth-century Córdoba. Abd ar-Rahman III provided it with a new minaret (which has not survived but which provided the core for the later belfry), 80m high, topped by three pomegranate-shaped spheres, two of silver and one of gold and each weighing a tonne. But it was his son, **al-Hakam II** (961–76), to whom he passed on a peaceful and stable empire, who was responsible for the most brilliant expansion. He virtually doubled its extent, demolishing the south wall to add fourteen extra rows of columns, and employed Byzantine craftsmen to construct a new *mihrab*, or prayer niche; this remains complete and is perhaps the most beautiful example of all Moorish religious architecture.

4

MOORISH CÓRDOBA

Córdoba's **domination of Moorish Spain** began thirty years after its conquest – in 756, when the city was placed under the control of **Abd ar-Rahman I**, the sole survivor of the Umayyad dynasty, which had been bloodily expelled from the eastern caliphate of Damascus. He proved a firm but moderate ruler, and a remarkable military campaigner, establishing control over all but the north of Spain and proclaiming himself emir, a title meaning both "king" and "son of the caliph". It was Abd ar-Rahman who commenced the building of the Great Mosque (La Mezquita, in Spanish), purchasing from the Christians the site of the cathedral of St Vincent (which, divided by a partition wall, had previously served both communities). This original mosque was completed by his son **Hisham** in 796 and comprises about one-fifth of the present building, the first dozen aisles adjacent to the Patio de los Naranjos.

The **Cordoban emirate**, maintaining independence from the eastern caliphate, soon began to rival Damascus both in power and in the brilliance of its civilization. **Abd ar-Rahman II** (822–52) initiated sophisticated irrigation programmes, minted his own coinage and received embassies from Byzantium. He in turn substantially enlarged the mosque. A focal point within the culture of al-Andalus, this was by now being consciously directed and enriched as an alternative to Mecca; it possessed an original script of the Koran and a bone from the arm of Mohammed and, for the Spanish Muslim who could not get to Mecca, it became the most sacred place of **pilgrimage**. In the broader Islamic world, it ranked third in sanctity after the Kaaba of Mecca and the al-Alqsa mosque of Jerusalem.

In the tenth century, Córdoba reached its zenith under a new emir, **Abd ar-Rahman III** (912–61), one of the great rulers of Islamic history. He assumed power after a period of internal strife and, according to a contemporary historian, "subdued rebels, built palaces, gave impetus to agriculture, immortalized ancient deeds and monuments, and inflicted great damage on infidels to a point where no opponent or contender remained in al-Andalus. People obeyed en masse and wished to live with him in peace." In 929, with Muslim Spain and part of North Africa firmly under his control, Abd ar-Rahman III adopted the title of "caliph". It was a supremely confident move and was reflected in the growing splendour of Córdoba, which had become the largest, most prosperous city of Europe, outshining Byzantium and Baghdad (the new capital of the eastern caliphate) in science, culture and scholarship. At the turn of the tenth century, Moorish sources boast of the city's 27 schools, 50 hospitals (with the first separate clinics for the leprous and insane), 900 public baths, 60,300 noble mansions, 80,455 shops and 213,077 houses.

Al-Hakam had extended the mosque as far to the south as was possible. The final enlargement of the building, under the chamberlain-usurper **al-Mansur** (977–1002), involved adding seven rows of columns to the whole east side. This spoiled the symmetry of the mosque, depriving the *mihrab* of its central position, but Arab historians observed that it meant there were now "as many bays as there are days of the year". They also delighted in describing the rich interior, with its 1293 marble columns, 280 chandeliers and 1445 lamps. Hanging inverted among the lamps were the bells of the pilgrimage Catedral of Santiago de Compostela. Al-Mansur made his Christian captives carry them on their shoulders from Galicia – a process that was to be observed in reverse after Córdoba was captured by Fernando el Santo (the Saint) in 1236.

Entering the Mezquita

As in Moorish times, the **Mezquita** is approached through the **Patio de los Naranjos**, a classic Islamic ablutions court that preserves its orange trees, although the fountains for ritual purification before prayer are now purely decorative. Originally, when in use for the Friday prayers, all nineteen naves of the mosque were open to this court, allowing the rows of interior columns to appear an extension of the trees with brilliant shafts of sunlight filtering through. Today, all but one of the entrance gates is locked and sealed, and the mood of the building has been distorted from the open and vigorous simplicity of the mosque to the mysterious half-light of a cathedral.

Nonetheless, a first glimpse inside the Mezquita is immensely exciting. "So near the desert in its tentlike forest of supporting pillars," Jan Morris found it, "so faithful to Mahomet's tenets of cleanliness, abstinence and regularity." The mass of supporting pillars was, in fact, an early and sophisticated innovation to gain height. The original architect had at his disposal columns from the old Visigothic cathedral and from numerous Roman buildings; they could bear great weight but were not tall enough, even when arched, to reach the intended height of the ceiling. His solution (which may have been inspired by Roman aqueduct designs) was to place a second row of square columns on the apex of the lower ones, serving as a base for the semicircular arches that support the roof. For extra strength and stability (and perhaps also deliberately to echo the shape of a date palm, much revered by the early Spanish Arabs), the architect introduced another, horseshoe-shaped arch above the lower pillars. A second and purely aesthetic innovation was to alternate brick and stone in the arches, creating the red-and-white-striped pattern that gives a unity and distinctive character to the whole design.

The mihrab

The uniformity was broken only at the culminating point of the mosque – the domed cluster of pillars surrounding the sacred **mihrab**, erected under al-Hakam II. The *mihrab* has two functions in Islamic worship: it indicates the direction of Mecca (and hence of prayer) and it amplifies the words of the imam, or prayer leader. At Córdoba, it is also of supreme beauty.

The inner vestibule of the niche (frustratingly fenced off) is quite simple in comparison, with a shell-shaped ceiling carved from a single block of marble. The chambers to either side – decorated with exquisite Byzantine mosaics of gold, rust red, turquoise and green – constitute the *maksura*, where the caliph and his retinue would pray.

The Catedral

Originally, the whole design of the mosque would have directed worshippers naturally towards the *mihrab*. Today, though, you almost stumble upon it, for in the centre of the mosque squats a Renaissance **Catedral coro**. This was built in 1523 – nearly three centuries of enlightened restraint after the Reconquest – and in spite of fierce opposition from the town council. The erection of a *coro* and *capilla mayor*, however, had long been the "Christianizing" dream of the Catedral chapter and at last they had found a monarch – predictably Carlos V – who was willing to sanction the work. Carlos, to his credit, realized the mistake (though it did not stop him from destroying parts of the Alhambra and Seville's Alcázar); on seeing the work completed, he told the chapter, "You have built what you or others might have built anywhere, but you have destroyed something that was unique in the world." To the left of the *coro* stands an earlier and happier Christian addition – the Mudéjar **Capilla de Villaviciosa**, built by Moorish craftsmen in 1371 (and now partly sealed up). Beside it are the dome and pillars of the **earlier mihrab**, constructed under Abd ar-Rahman II.

The belfry and outer walls

The **belfry**, the **Torre del Alminar** at the corner of the Patio de los Naranjos, is contemporary with the Catedral addition. Close by, the **Puerta del Perdón**, the main entrance to the patio, was rebuilt in Moorish style in 1377. It's worth making a tour of the Mezquita's **outer walls** before leaving; parts of the original "caliphal" decoration surrounding the portals (in particular, some exquisite lattice work) are stunning.

Torre de la Calahorra

Puente Romano s/n • Daily: May–Sept 10am–8.30pm; Oct–April 10am–6pm • €4.50 • ☎ 957 293 929

At the eastern end of the Roman bridge over the Guadalquivir, the medieval **Torre de la Calahorra** houses a gimmicky, high-tech museum containing models of the pre-cathedral Mezquita, weird talking tableaux and a rather incongruous multimedia presentation on the history of man; there's a great panoramic **view**, though, from the top of the tower towards the city. As you cross the bridge you can see, near the western riverbank, the wheels and the ruined mills that were in use for several centuries after the fall of the Muslim city, grinding flour and pumping water up to the fountains of the Alcázar.

Alcázar de los Reyes Cristianos

Pza. Campo Santo de los Mártires s/n • June 16–Sept 15 Tues–Sun 8.30am–2pm; Sept 16–June 15 Tues–Fri 8.30am–8.15pm, Sat 8.30am–4pm, Sun 8.30am–2pm • €4.50, free Tues–Fri 8.30–9.30am • ☎ 957 420 151

After the Christian conquest, the Alcázar was rebuilt a little to the west by Fernando and Isabel, hence its name, **Alcázar de los Reyes Cristianos**. The buildings are a bit dreary, having served as the residence of the Inquisition from 1428 to 1821, and later as a prison until 1951. However, they display some fine mosaics and other relics from Roman Córdoba, among which is one of the largest complete Roman mosaics in existence, and the wonderful **gardens** are a great place to get your breath back.

Plaza de la Corredera

To the northeast of the Mezquita, near the Museo Arqueológico and in an area that was once the *plateros* or silversmiths' quarter, you'll find **Plaza de la Corredera**, a once ramshackle but now wonderfully refurbished colonnaded square, much resembling Madrid's or Salamanca's Pza. Mayor. Unique in Andalucía, the square's complete enclosure occurred in the seventeenth century and presented the city with a suitable space for all kinds of spectacles. These included burnings by the Inquisition as well as bullfights, from which event the tiny Callejón Toril (Bull Pen) on the square's eastern side takes its name. Now bars and restaurants line the square, and their terraces are popular places to sit out on summer evenings.

La Judería

Between the Mezquita and the beginning of Avda. del Gran Capitán lies **La Judería**, Córdoba's old Jewish quarter, and a fascinating network of lanes – more atmospheric and less commercialized than Seville's Barrio Santa Cruz, though tacky souvenir shops are beginning to gain ground.

Sinagoga

C/Judíos 20 • Tues–Sun 9am–2.45pm & 3.30–5.30pm • €0.30, free with EU passport • ☎ 957 202 928

Near the heart of La Judería is a **sinagoga**, one of only three synagogues in Spain – the other two are in Toledo – that survived the Jewish expulsion of 1492. This one, built in 1316, is minute, particularly in comparison with the great Santa María in Toledo, but it has some fine stuccowork elaborating on a Solomon's-seal motif and retains its women's gallery. Outside is a statue of Maimónides, the Jewish philosopher, physician and Talmudic jurist, born in Córdoba in 1135.

Museo Taurino

Pza. de Maimónides s/n • June 15–Sept 15 Tues–Sat 8.30am–3pm, Sun 8.30am–2.30pm; Sept 16–June 14 Tues–Fri 8.30am–8.45pm, Sat 8.30am–4.30pm, Sun 8.30am–2.30pm • €4.50, free Tues–Fri 8.30–9.30am

The small **Museo Taurino** (Bullfighting Museum) warrants a look, if only for the kitschy nature of its exhibits: row upon row of bulls' heads, two of them given this "honour" for having killed matadors. Beside a copy of the tomb of Manolete – most famous of the city's *toreros* – is exhibited the hide of his taurine nemesis, Islero.

Museo Arqueológico

Pza. de Jerónimo Páez • June 16–Sept 15 Tues–Sun 10am–5pm; Sept 16–June 15 Tues–Sat 10am–8.30pm, Sun 10am–5pm • €1.50, free with EU passport • ☎ 957 355 517

The **Museo Arqueológico** is now in two buildings, one completely new and the other its first refurbished home, the beautiful sixteenth-century mansion of Casa Páez, which has a basement viewing area that incorporates the *grados* (seats) of the Roman theatre both it and the mansion are built on top of. The museum exhibits an extensive Moorish collection, and well-presented Iberian and Roman sculptures as well as Caliphal ceramics and *azulejos*.

Plaza del Potro

Near the river is **Plaza del Potro**, a fine old square named after the colt (*potro*) that adorns its restored fountain. This, as a wall plaque proudly points out, is mentioned in *Don Quixote*, and indeed Cervantes himself is reputed to have stayed at the inn opposite, the **Posada del Potro**, which has an atmospheric cattle yard within. The restored building is currently used as a centre for the study of flamenco and stages exhibitions and sporadic concerts (details from the *turismo*).

Palacio del Marqués de Viana

Pza. de Don Gome 2 • Guided tours (45min) July 1–Aug 31 Tues–Sun 9am–2pm & 5–10pm; Sept 1–June 30 Tues Sat 10am–7pm, Sun 10am–3pm • €8, patios only €5 • ☎ 957 496 741

In the north of town, towards the train station, are numerous Renaissance churches – some converted from mosques, others showing obvious influence in their minarets – and a handful of convents and palaces. The best of these, still privately owned although not by the family, is the **Palacio del Marqués de Viana**, whose main attraction for many visitors is its twelve flower-filled patios. The house itself – an ongoing work started in the fourteenth century – is mildly interesting and the guided tour (in Spanish only) leads you through drawing rooms, gaudy bedrooms (one with a telling

Franco portrait), kitchens and galleries while pointing out furniture, paintings, weapons and top-drawer junk the family amassed over the centuries.

ARRIVAL AND DEPARTURE

CÓRDOBA

By train From the splendid combined train and bus station on Pza. de las Tres Culturas, on Avda. de América at the northern end of town, head east to the junction with broad Avda. del Gran Capitán; this leads down to the old quarters and the Mezquita (15min walk or bus #3 from outside the station).

Destinations Algeciras (2 daily; 3hr 10min); Cádiz (2 daily; 2hr 20min); Granada (2 daily; 2hr 25min); Jaén (4 daily; 1hr 45min); Madrid (22 AVE daily; 1hr 50min); Málaga (10 AVE daily; 50min); Ronda (2 daily; 1hr 40min); Seville (26 AVE daily; 45min).

By bus Buses arrive at the combined train and bus station on Pza. de las Tres Culturas. See train information above for details on getting to the centre.

Destinations Badajoz (1 daily; 4hr 30min); Écija (5 daily;

55min); Granada (10 daily; 2hr 45min); Jaén (6 daily; 2hr); Madrid (7 daily; 4hr 45min); Málaga (4 daily; 2hr); Seville (7 daily; 2hr).

By car Arriving by car can be a pain, especially during rush hour in the narrow streets around the Mezquita. Parking in the centre is also a major headache, and it's worth considering staying somewhere that doesn't require traversing the old quarter. Better still is if you park up for the duration of your stay – Avda. de la República Argentina bordering the Jardines de la Victoria on the western edge of the old quarter, and across the river in the streets either side of the *Hotel Hesperia Córdoba* are possible places – and get around the city on foot, which is both easy and enjoyable.

INFORMATION AND TOURS

Turismo At the Palacio de Congresos y Exposiciones at C/Torrijos 10 (Mon–Fri 9am–7.30pm, Sat & Sun 9.30am–3pm; ☎ 957 355 179), alongside the Mezquita.

Municipal tourist office Córdoba's municipal tourist office (ⓦ turismodecordoba.org) has joined forces with a private company to provide tourist information from three central kiosks: at Pza. Campo de los Martires, almost facing the Alcázar (daily June 16–Sept 15 9am–2pm & 5–7.30pm; Sept 16–June 15 9am–2pm & 4–7pm); in Pza. de las Tendillas in the centre of the modern town (daily

10am–2pm & 5–7.30pm); and on the main concourse of the train station (daily 9am–2pm & 5–7.30pm).

Guided walks Several companies including Córdoba Visión and Konexión Tours offer guided walks around the old city (English spoken; 2–3hr; €20–35); tickets available at any of the tourist offices.

Opening hours Córdoba changes its monument timetables more than any other town in Andalucía – it's wise to check with one of the tourist offices for the latest information.

ACCOMMODATION

The majority of **places to stay** are concentrated in the narrow maze of streets to the north and east of the Mezquita. Finding a room at any time of the year – except during Semana Santa and the May festivals (the city's busiest month) – isn't usually a problem. It's also worth bearing in mind that Córdoba's high season (the price we quote) is April to June, while July and August are the hotel trade's low-season months when the more upmarket places often drop their prices dramatically.

Albergue Juvenil Pza. Judá Levi ☎ 957 355 040, reservations ☎ 955 035 886, ⓦ inturjoven.com. Excellent and superbly located modern youth hostel (with twin, triple and four-person en-suite rooms), which also serves meals. It's a prime destination for budget travellers, so you may need to book ahead at busy periods. Under-26 €21, over-26 €25

Casa de los Azulejos C/Fernando Colón 5 ☎ 957 470 000, ⓦ casadelosazulejos.com. Stylish, small boutique hotel with distinctively furnished rooms, featuring iron bedsteads and artworks, ranged around a leafy patio, itself used for art shows. Has own car park. B&B. €78

Campamento Municipal El Brillante Avda. El Brillante 50 ☎ 957 403 836, ⓦ campingelbrillante.com. Córdoba's local campsite (with restaurant and pool)

is 2km north of the centre in the El Brillante *barrio*, and served by bus #10 or #11 from the bus station. Tents and equipment for hire. €28

Fonda Agustina C/Zapatería Vieja 5 ☎ 957 470 872. Charming and spotlessly clean little *fonda*, with basic rooms in a tranquil location. €50

Hospedería de El Churrasco C/Romero 38 ☎ 957 294 808, ⓦ www.elchurrasco.com. Elegant and welcoming nine-room hotel in La Judería belonging to the restaurant of the same name. Entry is through a double patio, and rooms are classically furnished with chintz drapes and bedcovers, and some have terraces. Facilities include minibar, in-room internet and rooftop terrace/solarium. €178

★**Hostal Alcázar** C/San Basilio 2 ☎ 957 202 561, ⓦ hostalalcazar.com. Comfortable and welcoming family-run *hostal* with a nice patio and a range of rooms (most en suite) with a/c and TV. Also has some good-value apartments opposite. Has a car park. B&B. Doubles €45, apartments (up to four people) €80

Hostal Almanzor Corredidor Luís de la Cerda 10 ☎ 957 485 400, ⊛ hostal-almanzor.es. East of the Mezquita, a pleasant refurbished *hostal*, with a/c, en-suite rooms with TV. Free use of car park. €60

★**Hostal & Hotel Maestre** C/Romero Barros 4 & 16 ☎ 957 475 395 for the hostal, ☎ 957 472 410 for the hotel, ⊛ hotelmaestre.com. Excellent *hostal* between C/ San Fernando and the Pza. del Potro and neighbouring hotel with attractive a/c en-suite rooms with TV. Also has some good-value two-person apartments. *Rough Guide* readers with this guide get free underground parking (excluding April & May). *Hostal* €46, hotel €56, apartments €60

Hostal El Portillo C/Cabezas 2 ☎ 957 472 091, ⊛ hostalelportillo.com. Beautiful, refurbished and friendly old *hostal* with elegant patio, offering en-suite a/c singles and doubles. €45

Hostel La Corredera C/Rodríguez Marín 15 ☎ 957 470 581, ⊛ www.hostellacorredera.com. Clean and friendly refurbished place with rooms sharing bath, and great views over the plaza from some rooms. €50

Hotel Amistad Córdoba Pza. de Maimónides 3 ☎ 957 420 335, ⊛ nh-hoteles.com. Stylish upmarket hotel with comfortable rooms incorporating three eighteenth-century mansions, near the old wall in La Judería. Car park available. Frequently runs special offers (see website). €135

Hotel Las Casas de la Judería C/Tomás Conde 10 ☎ 957 202 095, ⊛ casasypalacios.com. This five-star hotel is an exquisitely charming restoration of an ancient *casa palacio* and rooms are arranged around patios with

tinkling fountains and scented flowers. The elegant rooms are decorated with period furnishings and artworks and come with satellite TV and all the five-star frills. Also has a spa, restaurant and garage. €315

Hotel Hespería Córdoba Avda. de la Confederación s/n ☎ 957 421 042, ⊛ hoteles-hesperia.es. Luxurious four-star hotel with great views across the river towards the Mezquita and city from rooms at the front. Features include restaurant, *cafetería*, pool and rooftop bar (with the same view) and easy access to the town across the pedestrianized Puente Romano. Own car park or easy parking nearby. Runs frequent special offers (see website). €195

Hotel Marisa C/Cardenal Herrero 6 ☎ 957 473 142, ⊛ www.hotelmarisa.es. Two-star hotel with a superb position immediately outside the Mezquita. Rooms come with a/c and TV. Own garage. €85

Hotel Mezquita Pza. Santa Catalina 1 ☎ 957 475 585, ⊛ hotelmezquita.com. Atmospheric and central hotel in a converted sixteenth-century mansion with excellent a/c rooms. €125

Parador de Córdoba Avda. de la Arruzafa s/n, off Avda. El Brillante ☎ 957 275 900, ⊛ www.parador.es. Córdoba's modern parador is located on the outskirts of the city 5km to the north of the Mezquita, but compensates with pleasant gardens, a pool and every other amenity (including a shooting range). €164

Pensión Los Arcos C/Romero Barros 14 ☎ 957 485 643, ⊛ pensionlosarcos.com. Excellent *hostal* with simple rooms (some en suite) around a delightful patio. €55

★**Séneca Hostal** C/Conde y Luque 7 ☎ 957 491 544, ⊛ senecahostel.com. Wonderful place to stay, with simple and en-suite rooms around a stunning patio with Moorish pavement where you can take breakfast. Very popular, so book ahead. €70

EATING AND DRINKING

Bars and **restaurants** are on the whole reasonably priced – you need only to avoid the touristy places around the Mezquita. There are lots of good places to eat in La Judería and in the old quarters off to the east, above Paseo de la Ribera. Two celebrated specialities worth trying here are *rabo de toro* (slow-stewed bull's tail) and *salmorejo*, the delicious *cordobés* variant of gazpacho, made with bread, tomatoes, oil and chopped *jamón* often topped off with sliced hard-boiled eggs.

Albergue Juvenil Pza. Judá Levi s/n. The youth hostel's *cafetería* (open to all) has some of the cheapest food in town, with hearty three-course lunch and dinner menus a bargain €8. Daily 2–3pm & 8.30–9.30pm.

★**Amaltea** C/Ronda de Isasa 10 ☎ 957 491 968. Excellent organic restaurant with special veggie and celiac menus, run by a charming Wolverhampton-educated *cordobesa*. Specialities of the house include *couscous con verduras* (vegetables). Plenty of organic wines and a few special beers, too – try the Alhambra 1925. Main dishes €10–16. Mon–Sat 1–4pm & 7.30pm–midnight, Sun 1–4pm.

★**Bar Plateros** C/San Francisco 6 ☎ 957 470 304. Headquarters of the Plateros chain of tapas bars in a

converted former convent. What started in 1868 as a mutual benefit society for the workers in Córdoba's silversmith trade eventually branched out into the *bodega* business, presently owning three excellent bars around the city. Now over a century old and serving a wide range of tapas – house specials include *arroz con bacalao* (cod paella) and *perdiz en escabeche* (marinated partridge). The bar is light and airy with a glass-covered patio complemented by hanging plants and *azulejos*. Mon–Sun 8am–4pm & 8pm–midnight; closed Sun July & Aug.

Blanco Enea Pza. San Pedro 1 ☎ 957 100 675. Located in a tiny square a couple of blocks south of Pza. de la Corredera. Choose from informal eating downstairs and on the terrace with *raciones* to share, or finer dining upstairs where signature dishes include *ostrón gallego con jugo de rabo de toro* (large oyster in oxtail sauce) and *tataki de solomillo* (beef). Main dishes €8–21. Tues–Sat 12.30–4.30pm & 8.30–11.30pm, Sun 1.30–4.30pm.

El Choto C/Almanzor 10 ☎957 760 115. Attractive, small and serious restaurant with a little outdoor terrace offering a range of well-prepared fish and meat dishes including its signature dish *choto asado* (roast kid). There's a four-course *menú de degustación* for €70 for two (including wine) and a *menú de la casa* for around €22 (both Tues–Fri). Main dishes €14–28. Tues–Sat 1–5pm & 7.30pm–midnight, Sun 1–5pm.

★**El Churrasco** C/Romero 16 (not C/Romero Barros) ☎957 290 819. This renowned restaurant has attractive rooms and patio is famous for its *churrasco* (a grilled pork dish, served with pepper sauces) and Cordoban local dish *salmorejo*. Main dishes cost €15–28. Daily 1–4pm & 8pm–midnight; closed Aug.

★**El Gallo** C/María Cristina 6 ☎957 471 780. A classic old *cordobés* drinking hole, which has changed little since it opened at the turn of the twentieth century; try their *gambas rebozadas* (fried prawns) washed down with outstanding *amargoso montilla* from their own *bodega*. Tues–Sun 11am–5pm & 8pm–midnight.

Mesón San Basilio C/San Basilio 19 ☎957 297 007. Good, unpretentious and busy local restaurant offering well-prepared fish and meat *raciones* and *platos*

combinados, plus weekday menus for €12 (lunch) and €18 (dinner). Mon–Sat 1–4pm & 8–11.30pm, Sun 1–4pm.

Los Mochuelos C/Agustín Moreno 51 ☎957 251 749. Traditional tapas and *raciones* restaurant with large variety of dishes including *revuelto de setas con salmón* (scrambled eggs with wild mushrooms and salmon) and *mochuelitos* (spicy meat); plenty of atmosphere, stacked sherry butts, bullfight posters and a pleasant patio. *Raciones* €7–15. Mon noon–3pm, Tues–Fri 8am–4pm & 7pm–midnight, Sat & Sun 9am–midnight.

El Rincón del Carmen C/Romero 4 ☎957 291 055. Small, pleasant café-restaurant with a charming patio terrace below and restaurant upstairs, serving reasonably priced *raciones* and *media raciones*. Menu for €18. Daily 10am–midnight.

★**Taberna Salinas** C/Tundidores 3 ☎957 480 135. Reasonably priced *taberna* established in 1879, with dining rooms around a charming patio. Good *raciones* place – try their *naranjas con bacalao* (cod with oranges) – and serves a great *salmorejo*. Main dishes €7–17. Mon–Sat 12.30–4pm & 8–11.30pm; closed Aug.

Taberna San Miguel (El Pisto) Pza. San Miguel 1 ☎957 470 166. Known to all as *El Pisto* (the ratatouille), this is one of the city's legendary bars – over a century old – and not to be missed. Wonderful *montilla* and tapas: *rabo de toro, potaje de garbanzos con manitas* (chickpea stew with trotters) and ratatouille are house specials. *Raciones* €7–18. Mon–Sat noon–4pm & 8.30pm–12.30am; closed Aug.

Medina Azahara

April–Sept Tues–Sat 10am–8.30pm, Sun 10am–2pm; Oct–March Tues–Sat 10am–2pm & 5–6.30pm, Sun 10am–2pm; confirm winter hours with site ☎957 355 506 · €1.50, free with EU passport but a ticket still needs to be collected · ☎957 104 933

Seven kilometres to the northwest of Córdoba lie the vast and rambling ruins of **Medina Azahara**, a palace complex built on a dream scale by **Caliph Abd**

THE RISE AND FALL OF MEDINA AZAHARA

Medina Azahara was a perfect symbol of the western caliphate's extent and greatness, but it was to last for less than a century. Al-Hakam II, who succeeded Abd ar-Rahman, lived in the palace, continued to endow it, and enjoyed a stable reign. However, distanced from the city, he delegated more and more authority, particularly to his vizier Ibn Abi Amir, later known as **al-Mansur** (the Victor). In 976, al-Hakam was succeeded by his 11-year-old son Hisham II and, after a series of sharp moves, al-Mansur assumed the full powers of government, keeping Hisham virtually imprisoned at Medina Azahara, to the extent of blocking up connecting passageways between the palace buildings.

Al-Mansur was equally skilful and manipulative in his wider dealings as a dictator, retaking large tracts of central Spain and raiding as far afield as Galicia and Catalunya; consequently, Córdoba rose to new heights of prosperity. But with his death in 1002 came swift decline, as his role and function were assumed in turn by his two sons. The first died in 1008; the second, Sanchol, showed open disrespect for the caliphate by forcing Hisham to appoint him as his successor. At this, a popular revolt broke out and the caliphate disintegrated into civil war and a series of feudal kingdoms. Medina Azahara was looted by a mob at the outset, and in 1010 was plundered and burned by retreating Berber mercenaries.

ar-Rahman III. Naming it after a favourite, az-Zahra (the Radiant), he spent one-third of the annual state budget on its construction each year from 936 until his death in 961. Ten thousand workers and 1500 mules and camels were employed on the project, and the site, almost 2km long by 900m wide, stretched over three descending terraces. In addition to the palace buildings, it had a zoo, an aviary, four fishponds, three hundred baths, four hundred houses, weapons factories and two barracks for the royal guard. Visitors, so the chronicles record, were stunned by its wealth and brilliance: one conference room was decorated with pure crystals, creating a rainbow when lit by the sun; another was built round a huge pool of mercury.

The Royal House

For centuries following its downfall the Medina Azahara continued to be looted for building materials; parts, for instance, were used in the Seville Alcázar. But in 1944 excavations unearthed the remains of a crucial part of the palace – the **Royal House**, where guests were received and meetings of ministers held. This has been meticulously reconstructed and, though still fragmentary, its main hall must rank among the greatest of all Moorish rooms. It has a different kind of stuccowork from that at Granada or Seville – closer to natural and animal forms in its intricate Syrian *Hom* (Tree of Life) motifs. Unlike the later Spanish Arab dynasties, the Berber Almoravids and the Almohads of Seville, the caliphal Andalucians were little worried by Islamic strictures on the portrayal of nature, animals or even men – the beautiful hind in the Córdoba museum is a good example – and it may well have been this aspect of the palace that led to such zealous destruction during the civil war.

The reconstruction of the palace gives a scale and focus to the site. Elsewhere, you have little more than foundations to fuel your imaginings, amid an awesome area of ruins, hidden beneath bougainvillea and rustling with cicadas. Perhaps the most obvious of the outbuildings yet excavated is the Aljama mosque, just beyond the Royal House, which sits at an angle to the rest of the buildings in order to face Mecca.

The gardens

After an extensive study of soil samples by biologists from Córdoba University to ascertain which plants and flowers would have originally been cultivated in the extensive **gardens**, reconstructive planting took place and the trees, shrubs and herbs are now maturing into a delightful and aromatic garden the caliphs would recognize.

ARRIVAL AND DEPARTURE   MEDINA AZAHARA

By car To reach the Centro de Interpretación, follow Avda. de Medina Azahara west out of town, onto the road to Villarubia and Posadas. About 4km down this road, make a right turn (signed for the site), after which it's another 1km to the Centro de Interpretación. Note that you are now obliged to park your car here and take the dedicated bus service to the site. If you continue up the road to the site car park (now for staff only) you will arrive at a locked gate forcing you to turn around and go back.

By bus City bus #01 from a stop on the Avda. de la República Argentina (at the northern end, near a petrol station) will drop you off at the intersection from where it's a 1km walk to the Centro de Interpretación. Ask the driver for "El Cruce de Medina Azahara". A dedicated bus service also links the city with the site (April–Sept Tues–Sat 10.15am & 5pm, Sun 9.30am & 10.15am; Oct–March Tues–Sun 9.30am & 10.15am; €7 return). The bus departs

from a signed stop on the Glorieta (roundabout) Cruz Roja at the southern end of Paseo de la Victoria (confirm this at the tourist office), but tickets must be purchased in advance from any municipal tourist office kiosk (see p.320). Tickets cannot be purchased on the bus.

By taxi A taxi will cost you about €25 one-way for up to five people, or there's a special round-trip deal ("Taxi-Tour Córdoba") for €45, which includes a 1hr wait at the site while you visit. A convenient taxi rank is located outside the *turismo* on the west side of the Mezquita.

Guided trips Córdoba Vision runs guided trips to the site (Tues–Sun 11am; €20; ☎957 299 777, English spoken); buses leave from the same stop on Avda. del Alcázar as the bus service. The tour bus will park at the Centro de Interpretación and both you and the guide will use the bus service to the site.

Visiting the site Visitors must arrive at the Centro de

Interpretación, a complex incorporating a museum, shop and *cafetería*; from here take a bus (every 10–20min; €2.10 return)

from the car park for the 2km journey to the site; once you have your ticket you can walk to the site but it is all uphill.

Jaén province

There are said to be over 150 million olive trees in the province of Jaén. They dominate the landscape as infinite rows of green against the orange-red earth, occasionally interspersed with stark white farm buildings. It's beautiful on a grand, sweeping scale, though it conceals a bitter and entrenched economic reality. The majority of the olive groves are owned by a mere handful of families, and for most residents this is a very poor area.

Sights may not be as plentiful here as in other parts of Andalucía, but there are a few gems worth going out of your way to take in. Fairly dull in itself, the provincial capital of **Jaén** merits a visit for its fine Catedral and Moorish baths, while farther to the northwest **Baeza** and **Úbeda** are two remarkable Renaissance towns jam-packed with architectural gems such as exuberant Renassiance palaces, richly endowed churches and fine public squares. Both were captured from the Moors by Fernando el Santo and stood for two centuries at the frontiers of the reconquered lands facing the Moorish kingdom of Granada. Extending northeast from the town of Cazorla, **Parque Natural de Cazorla**, Andalucía's biggest natural park, is a vast expanse of dense woodlands, lakes and spectacular crags.

Jaén

JAÉN, the provincial capital and by far the largest town, is an uneventful sort of place but there are traces of its Moorish past in the winding, narrow streets of the old quarter and in the largest surviving Moorish baths in Spain. Activity is centred on Pza. de la Constitución and its two arterial streets, Paseo de la Estación and Avda. de Madrid. The town is overlooked by the Cerro de Santa Catalina, a wooded hill topped by a restored Moorish fort, now partly transformed into a spectacular parador.

Catedral

Pza. de Santa María s/n • **Church** Mon–Sat 10am–2pm & 4–7pm, Sun 10am–noon & 4–7pm • €5 • **Museum** Daily 11am–2pm & 6–8pm • Free • ☎ 953 234 233

West of the focal Pza. de la Constitución is the imposing seventeenth-century Renaissance **Catedral**, by the great local architect Andrés de Vandelvira, whose design had the most influence over the building as it looks today. The spectacular **west facade**, flanked by twin sixty-metre-high towers framing Corinthian pillars and statuary by the seventeenth-century master Pedro Roldán, is one of the masterpieces of Andalucian Renaissance architecture.

Baños Árabes

Pza. Santa Luisa de Marillac • Tues–Sat 9am–2.30pm & 4–9.30pm, Sun 9am–2.30pm • Free • ☎ 953 248 068

To the north of the Catedral, between the churches of San Andrés and Santo Domingo, you'll find the painstakingly restored Moorish *hammam* in the **Baños Árabes**. Among the finest of their kind in Spain, the baths were originally part of an eleventh-century Moorish palace, and are now located inside the sixteenth-century Palacio de Villardompardo, which was constructed over it. On view are the various rooms (containing hot, tepid and cold baths), with pillars supporting elegant horseshoe arches and brickwork ceilings pierced with distinctive star-shaped windows.

By train The train station (☎ 902 434 323) is on Paseo de la Estación (bus #4 or #8 from the centre).
Destinations Cádiz (4 daily; 4hr 50min); Córdoba (4 daily;

1hr 40min); Madrid (4 daily Mon–Sat, 3 daily Sun; 4hr); Seville (4 daily; 2hr 55min).
By bus The bus station (☎ 953 232 300) is at Pza. Coca de

la Pinera, 300m northeast of Pza. de la Constitución.

Destinations Almería (2 daily; 4hr); Baeza/Úbeda (14 daily; 1hr 25min); Cazorla (3 daily; 2hr 30min); Córdoba (7 daily; 2hr); Granada (14 daily; 1hr 10min); Madrid (5 daily; 4hr 20min); Málaga (3 daily; 3hr 15min); Seville (daily; 4hr).

Turismo To the north of the Catedral on C/Maestra 8 (Mon–Fri 9am–7.30pm, Sat & Sun 9.30am–3pm; ☏ 953 190 455, ⓦ www.turjaen.org).

ACCOMMODATION

Places to stay in town are limited and – with the exception of *Albergue Inturjoven* – relatively expensive. There's usually no problem in finding accommodation at any time of the year and there are no seasonal rate changes. Mosquitoes can be a real problem in the town during the summer when places with a/c come into their own.

★**Albergue Inturjoven** C/Borja s/n ☏ 955 035 886, ⓦ inturjoven.com. Behind the imposing facade of a former eighteenth-century hospital lies the youth hostel's excellent modern, if minimalist in style, en-suite a/c rooms and "apartments" (which add a *salón* but no kitchen). There's also a pool. Somewhat incongruously the *albergue* also houses a full-blown spa with a variety of detox and anti-*edad* (ageing) cures costing much more than the rooms. Under-25 **€22**, over-25 **€26**

Hostal Estación RENFE Pza. Jaén por la Paz ☏ 953 27 46 14, ⓦ hostalestacionferrocarriljaen.com. RENFE's own *hostal* at the front of the station is a rather swish affair with comfortable a/c rooms with TVs and a car park. B&B. **€45**

Hotel Europa Pza. de Belén 1 ☏ 953 22 27 00, ⓦ hoteleuropajaen.es. Perhaps the best of the more upmarket places in the centre, where attractive a/c rooms come with safes and satellite TVs. B&B. **€66**

★**Parador Castillo de Santa Catalina** Castillo, sited on a hill 3km from town ☏ 953 23 00 00, ⓦ www .parador.es. For a truly memorable experience you could stay at this most spectacularly sited hotel. The comfortable rooms have fine balcony views with a sheer drop to the valley below; facilities include a pool, restaurant, bar and ample parking. **€169**

EATING AND DRINKING

Off the east side of Pza. Constitución, C/Nueva has a clutch of **places to eat** and there is a bunch of tapas bars in the streets to the north of the Catedral.

Café del Pósito Pza. del Pósito s/n. Above the west side of the focal Pza. de la Constitución, you'll find this busy café-bar which serves tapas and *raciones* until late; also has a terrace with outdoor tables. *Raciones* €6–13. Daily 11.30am–midnight.

El Tostón C/Bernardo López 11 ☏ 953 872 311. A reliable choice for tapas and *raciones*. Serves a good *revuelto de bacalao y gambas* (scrambled eggs with cod and prawns). Main dishes €10–15. Tues–Sun 9am–4pm & 8pm–midnight.

El Zurito C/Rastro 6 ☏ 605 988 016. One of Jaén's oldest (and smallest) bars and best eateries. Dishes depend on chef Juan Ramón's fancy but red tuna, steaks and tapas are staples. Arrive early to get one of the two tables. Main dishes €13–24. Mon–Sat 10am–5pm & 8.30pm–midnight.

La Loggia C/Carrera de Jesús 5 ☏ 953 331 074. This basement restaurant is decked in green stripes and serves stylish tapas and main dishes – try the *cochinillo confitado* (glazed suckling pig) – and has a pleasant street terrace next to the Catedral. Main dishes €6–13. Tues–Sun 12.30–4pm & 8.30pm–midnight.

Mesón Río Chico C/Nueva 12 ☏ 953 240 802. Popular tapas bar and *marisquería*. House specials include *almejas al ajillo* (clams in garlic) and the signature *rabo de toro*. Main dishes €8–15. Daily 1–4pm & 8pm–midnight.

Baeza

BAEZA is tiny, compact and provincial, with a perpetual Sunday air about it. At its heart is the Pza. Mayor – comprised of two linked plazas, Pza. de la Constitucíon at the southern end with a garden, and smaller Pza. de España to the north – flanked by cafés and very much the hub of the town's limited animation.

There are no charges to enter most of Baeza's monuments, but you may offer the guardian a small *propina* (tip).

Plaza de Leones

The **Plaza de Leones**, an appealing cobbled square enclosed by Renaissance buildings, stands slightly back at the southern end of Pza. de la Constitución. There's an ancient central fountain, while at its eastern flank is the former Audiencia (court house), now housing the *turismo*. Here, on a rounded balcony, the first Mass of the Reconquest is reputed to have been celebrated. The adjoining gate, the Puerta de Jaén, was a memento (or rebuke) left by Carlos V to the town that had opposed him and commemorates the Germanic ruler's procession through here in 1526, en route to marry Isabel of Portugal.

Palacio de Jabalquinto

Patio open Mon–Fri 9am–2pm • ☎ 953 742 775

The finest of Baeza's mansions is the **Palacio de Jabalquinto**, now a seminary, with an elaborate Gothic Hispano-Flemish (Isabelline) front (showing marked Moorish influence in its stalactite decoration). Built in the fifteenth century by the Benavides family, the tranquil interior patio has a double tier of arcades around a central fountain and a superb Baroque **staircase** with fine carving.

Catedral de Santa María

Mon–Fri 10.30am–2pm & 4–7pm, Sat 10am–7pm, Sun 10am–6pm • €4 • ☎ 953 742 188

The rather squat sixteenth-century **Catedral de Santa María**, is another design by Vandelvira. Like many of Baeza and Úbeda's churches, it has brilliant painted *rejas* (iron screens) created in the sixteenth century by Maestro Bartolomé, the Spanish master of this craft. His work enclosing the choir, with depictions of a Virgin and Child accompanied by angels and cherubs, is stunning. In the cloister, part of the old mosque (which the church replaced) has been uncovered, but the Catedral's real novelty is a huge silver *custodia* – cunningly hidden behind a painting of St Peter, which whirls aside for a €1 coin.

ARRIVAL AND INFORMATION   BAEZA

By bus The bus station (☎ 953 740 469) is at the end of C/San Pablo and along C/Julio Burell.

By train The nearest train station is Linares-Baeza, 14km from Baeza and served by frequent trains from Seville, Córdoba and Granada (there's a connecting bus for most trains, except Sat & Sun; €15 taxi ride). Most bus connections are via Úbeda.

INFORMATION AND ACTIVITIES

Turismo On Pza. de Leones, in the former Audiencia or court building (Mon–Fri 9am–7.30pm, Sat & Sun 9.30am–3pm; ☎ 953 779 982); you can pick up a map here, and they can also provide details of daily guided tours of the town.

Hiking There are some good walks around town; wandering up through the Puerta de Jaén on Pza. de los Leones and along the Paseo de las Muralla (aka Paseo de Don Antonio Machado) takes you round the edge of Baeza with fine views over the surrounding plains. You can cut back to Pza. Mayor via the network of narrow stone-walled alleys – with the occasional arch – that lies behind the Catedral.

ACCOMMODATION AND EATING

The town has a decent range of **places to stay**, some of which are architectural gems. There's usually no problem finding rooms in Baeza except during the summer *fería* in mid-August and even then you should have no trouble if you ring ahead. It's worth noting that many hotels have a weekend surcharge policy so if you can avoid a Friday-to-Saturday stay prices often fall considerably.

Los Aliatares Pza. de España s/n ☎ 953 740 193. This modern, airy bar is a great place to kick off your day with a lazy breakfast on the town's best terrace. Later in the day it serves good *tapas de autor* (signature tapas) such as *tortilla de gula* (eel omelette), *raciones* and *tostas* – try the partidge pâté toast with anchovies. Daily 7.30am–1am.

La Almazara C/Benavides 15 ☎ 953 741 650. The pleasant terrace of this mid-priced restaurant is a good place for alfresco dining. The bonus of a terrace table is also being able to feast your eyes on Baeza's magnificent sixteenth-century *ayuntamiento* opposite. Serves well-prepared meat, fish and game dishes and there's a weekday menu for €11 or €15 on weekends. Main dishes €7–18. Daily 12.30–4pm & 8pm–midnight.

★**Aznaitin** C/Cabreros 2 ☎ 953 740 788, ⓦ hostalaznaitin.com. Splendid *hostal* in the old quarter with stylishly decorated en-suite rooms. Friendly service, attractive pool and breakfast included adds up to an outstanding deal. Easy parking nearby or use their garage. Reduced rates Sun–Thurs. €53

Hotel Palacio de los Salcedo C/San Pablo 18 ☎953 747 200, ⌨palaciodelossalcedo.com. Lovely converted sixteenth-century palace with slightly over-the-top Louis XV-style rooms with a/c, TVs, minibars and safes. Interior rooms are gloomy but come with Jacuzzi. Reduced rates Sun–Thurs. B&B. €70

★**Hotel Puerta de la Luna** C/Pintada Alta s/n ☎953 74 70 19, ⌨hotelpuertadelaluna.com. Beautiful four-star hotel situated in a refurbished seventeenth-century *casa palacio*. Facilities include two delightful patios, a restaurant, a library and a small pool. The comfortably

furnished tiled-floor rooms are airy and well equipped, and it has its own car park. €142

Hotel TRH Ciudad de Baeza C/Concepción 3 ☎953 748 130, ⌨trhhoteles.com. Well-equipped a/c rooms partly housed in a stylishly converted Renaissance monastery with a glassed-in patio. They do frequent cut-price deals so it's worth giving them a ring or checking the website. €160

El Sarmiento Pza. del Ardeciano 10 ☎953 740 323. Specializing in *carnes asados* (roasted meat dishes) this is an excellent restaurant with a pleasant terrace on this attractive square behind the Catedral; there's a daily menu for €15. Main dishes €9–21. Tues–Sun 1.30–4pm & 8.30–11.30pm.

Úbeda

ÚBEDA, 9km east of Baeza and built on the same escarpment overlooking the valley of the Guadalquivir, looks less promising when you reach it. Don't be put off by the modern suburbs, though, for hidden away in the old quarter is one of the finest architectural jewels in the whole of Spain, and perhaps even Europe. Follow the signs to the Zona Monumental and you'll eventually reach the **Plaza de Vázquez de Molina**, a tremendous Renaissance square and one of the most impressive of its kind on the peninsula. Most of the buildings around the square are the late sixteenth-century work of Andrés de Vandelvira, the architect of Baeza's Catedral and numerous churches in both towns. One of these buildings, the **Palacio de las Cadenas**, originally a palace for Felipe II's secretary, houses Úbeda's *ayuntamiento* and features a magnificent facade fronted by monumental lions.

Capilla del Salvador

Pza. de Vázquez de Molina • Mon–Sat 9.30am–2pm & 4.30–6.30pm, Sun 11.30am–2pm & 4.30–7.30pm • €5 • ☎609 279 905

At the eastern end of Pza. de Vázquez de Molina, the **Capilla del Salvador**, erected by Vandelvira, though actually designed by Diego de Siloé, architect of the Málaga and Granada Catedrals, is the finest church in Úbeda. It's a masterpiece of Spanish Renaissance architecture with a dazzling Plateresque facade, its highlight a carving of the Transfiguration of Christ flanked by statues of San Pedro and San Andrés. Inside, the Transfiguration theme is repeated in a brilliantly animated *retablo* by Alonso de Berruguete, who studied under Michelangelo. Entry to the church is via a doorway on the south side.

San Pablo

Pza. del Primero de Mayo • Tues–Fri 11am–1pm & 6–7.30pm, Sat 11am–1pm, Sun noon–1.30pm • Free • ☎953 750 637

The lovely square, Pza. del Primero de Mayo, is home to a bandstand and the superb arcaded sixteenth-century Ayuntamiento Viejo (Old Town Hall) from where councillors once watched heretics – denounced by the Inquisition – burn in fires located on the site of the modern bandstand. Here also is the idiosyncratic church of **San Pablo**, incorporating various Romanesque, Gothic and Renaissance additions and crowned by a Plateresque tower. It also boasts a thirteenth-century exterior and a superb portal.

INFORMATION	**ÚBEDA**

Turismo Housed in its own Renaissance mansion, the Palacio del Marqués de Contadero, C/Baja Marqués 4, just to the west of the Pza. de Vázquez de Molina (Mon–Fri 9am–7.30pm, Sat & Sun 9.30am–3pm; ☎953 779 204); they can provide a town map.

ACCOMMODATION

You'll find the only budget **places to stay** within walking distance of the bus station, in the modern part of town. The *casco antiguo* (old quarter) now has a choice of more upmarket places, some in stunning ancient palaces and mansions. Úbeda's high season is in April and May and thus hotel (but not *hostal*) rooms tend to be significantly cheaper in July and August. As in Baeza, many hotels apply a Friday-to-Saturday surcharge.

Hostal Victoria C/Alaminos 5 ☎ 953 791 718. A 5min walk east of the bus station, this is a comfortable, welcoming *hostal* offering pleasant, a/c en-suite rooms with TVs. It has its own car park, too. €38

Hotel María de Molina Pza. del Ayuntamiento s/n ☎ 953 795 356, ⓦ hotelmariademolina.es. In the heart of the old quarter, this hotel is housed in a magnificent sixteenth-century *casa palacio* with a superb patio. Rooms come with a/c, safe and satellite TVs, and some have balconies. €70

Hotel El Postigo C/Postigo 5 ☎ 953 750 000, ⓦ hotelelpostigo.com. In the old quarter, this modern three-star hotel offers well-equipped rooms with satellite TVs, and a small pool in their terrace gardens with olive trees. Has own library and huge log fire for winter days. €70

★ **Parador Condestable Dávalos** Pza. de Vázquez de Molina 1 ☎ 953 750 345, ⓦ www.parador.es. On arguably the most beautiful *plaza* in Andalucía, Úbeda's parador is housed in a fabulous sixteenth-century Renaissance mansion, with some of the well-appointed rooms overlooking the square. Call in for a drink if you're not staying. €188

EATING AND DRINKING

There are plenty of **places to eat** around Avda. Ramón y Cajal in the new town.

Asador Al-Andalus C/Los Canos 28, north of the old quarter ☎ 953 791 862. Just south of the bullring, this is a popular weekend venue combining local cuisine with a Moorish touch. House specialities include *rape a la brasa estilo mozárabe* (chargrilled monkfish Moorish style) and *lomo de orza* (marinated pork loin). Main dishes €8–15.

Tues–Sun 1.30–4.30pm & 8.30pm–midnight.

El Seco C/Corazón de Jesús 8 ☎ 953 791 452. Close to the Pza. del Ayuntamiento, this mid-priced restaurant is a cut above the norm; it is noted for its tasty *potaje carmelitano* (chickpea, leek and cod soup) but also does excellent meat and game dishes and there's a weekday menu. Main dishes

PARQUE NATURAL DE LAS SIERRAS DE SEGURA Y CAZORLA

Even casual visitors to **Parque Natural de las Sierras de Segura y Cazorla** are likely to see a good variety of wildlife, including *Capra hispanica* (Spanish mountain goat), deer, wild pig, birds and butterflies. Ironically, though, much of the best viewing will be at the periphery, or even outside the park, since the wildlife is most successfully stalked on foot, and walking opportunities within the park itself are surprisingly limited.

The main **information centre** inside the park is the Torre del Vinagre Centro de Interpretación (April–June daily 10am–2pm & 4–7pm; July–Sept daily 10am–2pm & 6–8pm; Oct–March Tues–Sun 10am–2pm & 4–6pm; ☎ 953 721 351). It's worth getting hold of a good **map** from here: the 1:100,000 map, *Parque Natural de las Sierras de Cazorla y Segura*, and the 1:50,000 version, *Cazorla*, are recommended, but best of all is the 1:40,000 set of map and guide packs to the Sierras de Cazorla and Segura (divided into two zones), published by Editorial Alpina, which are the most accurate maps available, detailing *senderos* (footpaths), mountain-bike routes, refuges, campsites and hotels. In addition to the hiking routes marked on the maps above, Guy Hunter-Watts' *Walking in Andalucía* details six clearly described walks in the park of between 5km and 19km.

Two daily **buses** link Cazorla with **Coto Ríos** (Mon & Fri only depart 7.15am & 2.30pm, return 9am & 4.15pm; 1hr 15min) in the middle of the park (confirm these with the bus company Carcesa on ☎ 953 721 142). Distances between points are enormous, so to explore the park well you'll need a car and be prepared for long treks.

There are six official **campsites** plus seven designated camping areas throughout the park, which are accurately marked on the Editorial Alpina map. There's more accommodation at Coto Ríos, with three privately run campsites and a succession of *hostales*. Before setting out, you can also get the latest update on transport, campsites and accommodation from the *turismo* in Cazorla.

OPPOSITE THE ALHAMBRA (P.332) >

€12–20. Mon–Thurs & Sun 1–4pm, Fri & Sat 1–4pm & 8–11pm.

Parador Condestable Dávalos Pza. de Vázquez de Molina 1 ☎ 953 750 345. If you want to dine in style in the old quarter, try the parador's expensive restaurant, which serves superbly prepared regional dishes such as *andrajos de Úbeda* (stew of cod, meat and vegetables) and *pierna de cabrito con tomillo* (kid goat baked with thyme) that are available on a weekday menu (€30). Daily 1.30–4pm & 8–11pm.

Taberna Misa de 12 Pza. del 1ª de mayo 7 ☎ 953 828 197. A square up from the Pza. del Ayuntamiento, this small bar serves tapas and *raciones* inside and on its pleasant shady terrace. Chargrilled meat is a speciality. Main dishes €7–33. Wed–Sun noon–4pm & 8pm–midnight.

Úbeda Kapital C/María de Molina 13 ☎ 953 828 205. Just north of the *Ayuntamiento*, this bar with a cool patio serves a reliable weekday menu for €12 featuring *andrajos* and *rabo de toro*. Tapas and *raciones* are also available. Daily noon–4pm & 7–11.30pm.

Cazorla

During the Reconquest of Andalucía, **CAZORLA** acted as an outpost for Christian troops, and the two castles that still dominate the town testify to its turbulent past – both were originally Moorish but later altered and restored by their Christian conquerors. Today, it's the main base for visits to the **Parque Natural de las Sierras de Segura y Cazorla**, a vast protected area of magnificent river gorges and forests. Cazorla also hosts the **Fiesta de Cristo del Consuelo**, with fairgrounds, fireworks and religious processions on September 16 to 21.

Cazorla itself is constructed around three main squares. Buses arrive in the busy, commercial **Pza. de la Constitución**, linked by the main C/Muñoz to the second square, **Pza. de la Corredera** (or *del Huevo*, "of the Egg", because of its shape). The *ayuntamiento* is here, a fine Moorish-style palace at the far end of the plaza. Beyond, a labyrinth of narrow, twisting streets descends to Cazorla's liveliest square, **Pza. de Santa María**, which takes its name from the old Catedral that, damaged by floods in the seventeenth century, was later torched by Napoleonic troops. Its ruins, now preserved, and the fine open square form a natural amphitheatre for concerts and local events as well as being a popular meeting place.

Museo de Artes y Costumbres

Pza. de Santa María • June to mid-Sept Tues–Sat 9.30am–3.30pm, Sun 10am–5pm; mid-Sept to May Tues–Sat 10am–8.30pm, Sun 10am–5pm • €1.50, free with EU passport

Cazorla's lower square, Pza. de Santa María, is dominated by **La Yedra**, an austere, reconstructed castle tower, which houses the **Museo de Artes y Costumbres**, an interesting folklore museum displaying domestic utensils, clothing, textiles and furniture from bygone times.

INFORMATION   CAZORLA

Turismo The *turismo* is at Pza. de Santa María s/n, (Tues–Sun 10am–1pm & 4–8pm; ☎ 953 710 102, ⊛ www.cazorla.es), and can provide a useful town map.

ACCOMMODATION

Outside August, finding a **place to stay** is usually no problem, as most visitors are either en route to, or leaving, the park. It's worth noting that outside the high summer months it can get quite chilly here in the evenings and while all the hotel rooms have heating, not all the *hostales* do, so enquire if you think this may be a problem.

Albergue Juvenil Pza. Mauricio Martínez 6 ☎ 955 035 886, ⊛ inturjoven.com. Cazorla's tidy youth hostel, housed in a former convent, has some double rooms and a pool, and is reached by following C/Juan Domingo (reached via steps) from Pza. de la Constitución. Under-26 **€22**, over-26 **€26**

Camping Cortijo ☎ 953 721 280, ⊛ campingcortijo. com. Cazorla's campsite, with its stunning views of the town and surrounding mountains and plenty of shade, is located beyond the Castillo de la Yedra, 1km from the centre; to get there, follow the Camino San Isicio from Pza. de Santa María. **€15.70**

Hotel Guadalquivir C/Nueva 6 ☎ 953 720 268, ⊛ hguadalquivir.com. Central, charming and friendly small hotel offering comfy en-suite a/c rooms with TV. **€56**

Hotel Puerta de Cazorla Avda. del Guadalquivir 49 ☎ 953 724 342, ⓦ puertadecazorla.es. Just outside the centre (reached up a steep hill), this new hotel comes with spotless en-suite rooms with a/c and TVs. Friendly proprietor can give handy local advice. **€45**

Hotel Sierra de Cazorla 2km outside Cazorla, in the village of La Iruela ☎ 953 720 015, ⓦ hotelsierra decazorla.com. Modern complex comprising three- and four-star hotels plus a spa. The three-star option is particularly good value, with balcony rooms (best views from A10–A17) and scenic surroundings; there's also a restaurant, bar and great pool. Produces its own walks guide for guests. There is a surcharge in August. **€66**

Parador El Adelantado 25km away in the park ☎ 953 727 075, ⓦ www.parador.es. Somewhat featureless modern building made attractive by its wonderful woodland setting and a swimming pool. Make sure to get a room with a view (rooms 4–11 and 18–22 are the ones to go for). Also has its own bar and restaurant. Closed mid-Nov to Feb. **€125**

Pensión Taxi Travesía de San Antón 7 ☎ 953 720 525. Up steps opposite the bus stop in Pza. de la Constitución, this is a friendly budget option with a good-value *comedor* (dining room). En-suite rooms have a/c, heating and TVs. **€40**

EATING AND DRINKING

★ **Bar Mesón La Montería** Pza. de la Corredera 20 ☎ 953 720 542. This place, one of the most popular of Cazorla's tapas bars, specializes in local game. *Patatas a lo pobre* (sautéed potatoes with garlic) is a house special or you could try their noted *venado a la brasa* (chargrilled venison). Main dishes €12–14. Thurs–Tues 12.30–4pm & 8–11pm.

Bar Rincón Serrano Pza. de la Corredera 12 ☎ 953 721 004. This good bar is usually packed due to its custom of giving a free *tapa* (which is chosen for you) with every drink. Daily noon–4pm & 8–11pm.

★ **Gastrobar La Sarga** Pza. del Mercado 13 ☎ 953 721 507. One of Cazorla's top restaurants reinvented itself in 2013 with designer decor and gastro tapas. The *caldereta de gamo con patatas a lo pobre* (fallow deer venison stew with potatoes) is one of the excellent game options (only available as *raciones*) and the *milhojas de queso con frutos secos y miel* (cheese millefeuille with dried fruit and honey) one of the most popular tapas. Main dishes €5–12. Fri Wed noon–4pm & 8–11pm.

Leandro C/Hoz 3 ☎ 953 720 632. Atmospheric and rustic restaurant offering mountain game such as venison and wild boar. The house specialities include venison grilled on a wood-fired range and local dish *rin ran* (cream of potatoes and red pepper with cod). Expect to pay €8–22 for a main dish. Wed–Mon 1.30–4.30pm & 8.30–11pm.

Mesón Don Chema Escaleras del Mercado 2 ☎ 953 710 529. Down steps off C/Muñoz, this is an economical restaurant specializing in *carnes de monte* (mountain game). Other specialities include *jamón ibérico* and *queso curado* (cured cheese). Also has a menu for €12. Main dishes €7–15. Mon–Sat 1–4pm & 8.30–11pm, Sun 1–4pm.

4

Granada

If you see only one town in Spain, it should be **GRANADA**. For here, extraordinarily well preserved and in a tremendous natural setting, stands the **Alhambra** – the most exciting, sensual and romantic of all European monuments. It was the palace fortress of the Nasrid sultans, rulers of the last Spanish Moorish kingdom, and in its construction Moorish art reached a spectacular and serene climax. But the building seems to go further than this, revealing something of the whole brilliance and spirit of Moorish life and culture. There's a haunting passage in Jan Morris' book, *Spain*, which the palace embodies:

"Life itself, which was seen elsewhere in Europe as a kind of probationary preparation for death, was interpreted [by the Moors] as something glorious in itself, to be ennobled by learning and enlivened by every kind of pleasure."

Built on the slopes of three hills, the rest of the city basks in the Alhambra's reflected glory. Because the Moorish influence here was so ruthlessly extinguished following capitulation to the Catholic monarchs Fernando and Isabel, Granada tends to be more sober in character and austere in its architecture than Andalucía's other provincial capitals. Many visitors, once they've viewed the Alhambra, are too jaded or can't be fussed to take in the city's other sights, which is a pity, for Granada has much to offer. The hilltop **Albaicín**, the former Moorish town, is a fascinating quarter full of narrow alleyways and small squares, and a great place for an hour's stroll. Not far away, too, is the Catedral with the gem of the **Capilla Real** attached to it, the final resting place of the Catholic monarchs who ended Moorish rule in Spain. Add in an **archeological museum**, **Moorish baths** and some fine churches, including a spectacular **La Cartuja** monastery, and you have more than enough to start you thinking about extending your stay.

The Alhambra

Daily: mid-March to mid–Oct 8.30am–8pm, mid-Oct to mid-March 8.30am–6pm; last admission 1hr before closing time • €14 • ☎ 958 027 971

The **Alhambra**, a treasure of Moorish Spain, is one of Spain's architectural wonders and its most-visited monument. There are three distinct groups of buildings on the Alhambra hill: the **Palacios Nazaríes** (Royal Palace, or Nasrid Palaces), the palace gardens of the **Generalife** and the **Alcazaba**.

Brief history

This Alcazaba, the fortress of the eleventh-century Ziridian rulers, was all that existed when the Nasrid ruler Ibn al-Ahmar made Granada his capital, but from its reddish walls the hilltop had already taken its name: *Al Qal'a al-Hamra* in Arabic means literally "the red fort". Ibn al-Ahmar rebuilt the Alcazaba and added to it the huge circuit of walls and towers that forms your first view of the castle. Within the walls he began a palace, which he supplied with running water by diverting the River Darro nearly 8km to the foot of the hill; water is an integral part of the Alhambra and this engineering feat was Ibn al-Ahmar's greatest contribution. The Palacios Nazaríes was essentially the product of his fourteenth-century successors, particularly Yusuf I and Mohammed V, who built and redecorated many of its rooms in celebration of his accession to the throne (in 1354) and the taking of Algeciras (in 1369).

Following their conquest of the city in 1492, **Fernando and Isabel** lived for a while in the Alhambra. They restored some rooms and converted the mosque but left the palace structure unaltered. As at Córdoba and Seville, it was **Emperor Carlos V**, their grandson, who wreaked the most insensitive destruction, demolishing a whole wing of rooms in order to build a Renaissance palace. This and the Alhambra itself were simply ignored by his successors, and by the eighteenth century the Palacios Nazaríes was in use as a prison. In 1812, it was taken and occupied by **Napoleon's forces**, who looted and damaged whole sections of the palace, and on their retreat from the city tried to blow up the entire complex. Their attempt was thwarted only by the action of a crippled

---

A WALK TO THE ALHAMBRA

The standard approach to the Alhambra is along the **Cuesta de Gomérez**, the semi-pedestrianized road that climbs uphill from Granada's central Pza. Nueva. The only traffic allowed to use this road are taxis and residents' vehicles. Should you decide to **walk** up the hill along the Cuesta de Gomérez (a pleasant 20min stroll from Pza. Nueva), after a few hundred metres you reach the **Puerta de las Granadas**, a massive Renaissance gateway erected by Carlos V. Here two paths diverge to either side of the road: the one on the right climbs up towards a group of fortified towers, the **Torres Bermejas**, which may date from as early as the eighth century. The left-hand path leads through the woods past a huge terrace fountain (again courtesy of Carlos V) to the main gateway – and former entrance – of the Alhambra. This is the **Puerta de la Justicia**, a magnificent tower that forced three changes of direction, making intruders hopelessly vulnerable. It was built by Yusuf I in 1340 and preserves above its outer arch the Koranic symbol of a key (for Allah the Opener) and an outstretched hand, whose five fingers represent the five Islamic precepts: prayer, fasting, alms-giving, pilgrimage to Mecca and the oneness of God. Enter here if you've got your ticket and want to visit the Alcazaba and Palacios Nazaríes. If you need to collect tickets or want to visit the Generalife first, the **entrance and ticket office** – at the eastern end, near to the Generalife – lie a further five-minute walk uphill, reached by following the wall to your left.

MOORISH GRANADA

Granada's glory was always precarious. It was established as an independent kingdom in 1238 by **Ibn al-Ahmar**, a prince of the Arab Nasrid tribe that had been driven south from Zaragoza. He proved a just and capable ruler, but all over Spain the Christian kingdoms were in the ascendant. The Moors of Granada survived only through paying tribute and allegiance to Fernando III of Castile – whom they were forced to assist in the conquest of Muslim Seville – and by the time of Ibn Ahmar's death in 1275 theirs was the only surviving Spanish Muslim kingdom. It had, however, consolidated its territory (stretching from just north of the city down to a coastal strip between Tarifa and Almería) and, stimulated by refugees, developed a flourishing commerce, industry and culture.

By a series of shrewd manoeuvres Granada maintained its autonomy for two and a half centuries, its rulers turning for protection, in turn as it suited them, to the Christian kingdoms of Aragón and Castile and to the Merinid Muslims of Morocco. The city-state enjoyed a particularly confident and prosperous period under **Yusuf I** (1334–54) and **Mohammed V** (1354–91), the sultans responsible for much of the existing Alhambra palace. But by the mid-fifteenth century, a pattern of coups and internal strife became established and a rapid succession of rulers did little to stem Christian inroads. In 1479, the kingdoms of Aragón and Castile were united by the marriage of Fernando and Isabel, and within ten years they had conquered Ronda, Málaga and Almería. The city of Granada now stood completely alone, tragically preoccupied in a civil war between supporters of the sultan's two favourite wives. The Reyes Católicos made escalating and finally untenable demands upon it, and in 1490 war broke out. **Boabdil**, the last Moorish king, appealed in vain for help from his fellow Muslims in Morocco, Egypt and Ottoman Turkey, and in the following year **Fernando and Isabel** marched on Granada with an army said to total 150,000 troops. For seven months, through the winter of 1491, they laid siege to the city, and on January 2, 1492, Boabdil formally surrendered its keys. The Christian Reconquest of Spain was complete.

soldier (José García) who remained behind and removed the fuses; a plaque honouring his valour has been placed in the Pza. de los Aljibes.

Two decades later, the Alhambra's "rediscovery" began, given impetus by the American writer **Washington Irving**, who set up his study in the empty palace rooms and began to write his marvellously romantic *Tales of the Alhambra* (on sale all over Granada – and good reading amid the gardens and courts). Shortly after its publication, the Spaniards made the Alhambra a **national monument** and set aside funds for its restoration. This continues to the present day and is now a highly sophisticated project, scientifically removing the accretions of later ages in order to expose and meticulously restore the Moorish creations.

The citadel

Within the **citadel** stood a complete "government city" of mansions, smaller houses, baths, schools, mosques, barracks and gardens. Of this only the **Alcazaba** and the **Palacios Nazaríes** remain; they face each other across a broad terrace (constructed in the sixteenth century over a dividing gully), flanked by the majestic though incongruous **Palacio de Carlos V**.

The Alcazaba

The entrance to the Alhambra brings you into the complex at the eastern end, near to the Generalife gardens. However, as you will have a time slot for entering the Palacios Nazaríes (usually up to an hour ahead), it makes sense chronologically and practically to start your visit with the **Alcazaba** at the Alhambra's opposite, or western, end, entered through the **Puerta del Vino** – named from its use in the sixteenth century as a wine cellar.

The Alcazaba is the earliest and most ruined part of the fortress. At its summit is the **Torre de la Vela**, named after a huge bell on its turret, which until recent years was rung to mark the irrigation hours for workers in the *vega*, Granada's vast and fertile plain. It

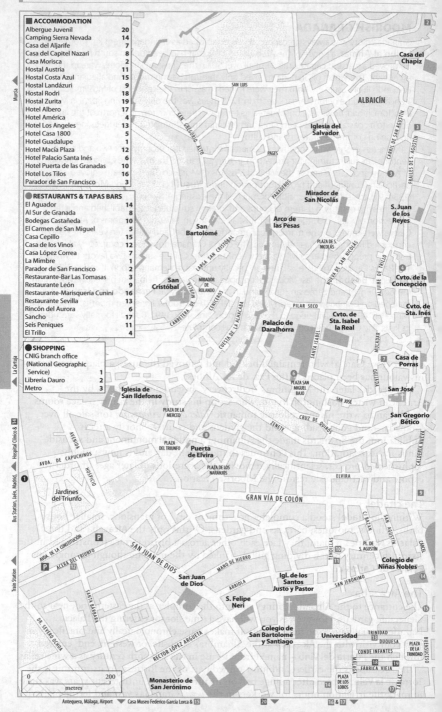

■ **ACCOMMODATION**

Albergue Juvenil	20
Camping Sierra Nevada	14
Casa del Aljarife	7
Casa del Capitel Nazari	8
Casa Morisca	2
Hostal Austria	11
Hostal Costa Azul	15
Hostal Landázuri	9
Hostal Rodri	18
Hostal Zurita	19
Hotel Albero	17
Hotel América	4
Hotel Los Angeles	13
Hotel Casa 1800	5
Hotel Guadalupe	1
Hotel Macía Plaza	12
Hotel Palacio Santa Inés	6
Hotel Puerta de las Granadas	10
Hotel Los Tilos	16
Parador de San Francisco	3

● **RESTAURANTS & TAPAS BARS**

El Aguador	14
Al Sur de Granada	8
Bodegas Castañeda	10
El Carmen de San Miguel	5
Casa Cepillo	15
Casa de los Vinos	12
Casa López Correa	7
La Mimbre	1
Parador de San Francisco	2
Restaurante-Bar Las Tomasas	3
Restaurante León	9
Restaurante-Marisquería Cunini	16
Restaurante Sevilla	13
Rincón del Aurora	6
Sancho	17
Seis Peniques	11
El Trillo	4

● **SHOPPING**

CNIG branch office (National Geographic Service)	1
Librería Dauro	2
Metro	3

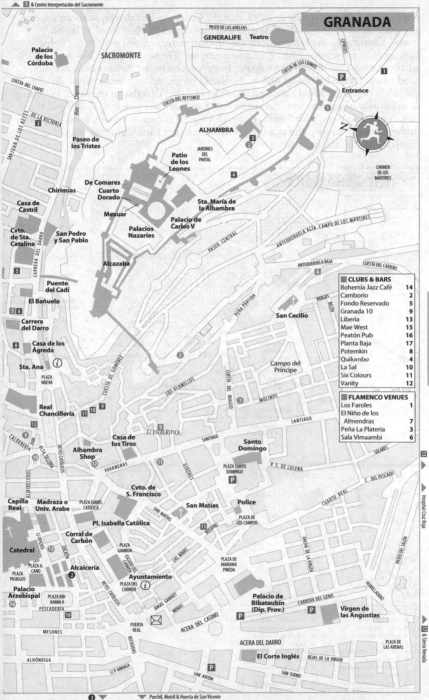

▲ ⓵ & Centro Interpretación del Sacromonte

GRANADA

PASEO DE LAS ADELFAS

GENERALIFE Teatro

CUESTA DE LOS CHINOS

P

SACROMONTE

Entrance

CUESTA DEL CHAPIZ

Palacio
de los
Córdoba

Río Darro

CUESTA DEL REY CHICO

SANTIAGUN DE LOS REYES

DE LA VICTORIA
2

ALHAMBRA

3
2

Z

Paseo de
los Tristes

JARDÍNES
DEL
PARTAL

Patio
de los
Leones

4

CARMEN
DE LOS
MÁRTIRES

Chirimías

De Comares
Cuarto Dorado

Casa de
Castril

Sta. María de
la Alhambra

Mexuar

Cvto.
de Sta.
Catalina

San Pedro
y San Pablo

Palacios
Nazaríes

Palacio de
Carlos V

CARRERA DEL DARRO

ANTEQUERUELA ALTA CAMPO DE LOS MÁRTIRES

Alcazaba

PASEO CENTRAL

5

ANTEQUERUELA BAJA

CUESTA DEL CAIDERO

Puente
del Cadí

4

El Bañuelo

5 6

PEÑA PARTIDA

VARGAS BELÉN

CLUBS & BARS

Bohemia Jazz Café	14
Camborio	2
Fondo Reservado	5
Granada 10	9
Libería	13
Mae West	15
Peatón Pub	16
Planta Baja	17
Potemkin	8
Quilombo	4
La Sal	10
Six Colours	11
Vanity	12

Carrera
del Darro

San Cecilio

Casa de
los Ágreda

8

Sta. Ana

ⓘ

PLAZA
NUEVA

Campo del
Príncipe

LOS ALAMILLOS

MOLINOS

SANTIAGO

FLAMENCO VENUES

Los Faroles	1
El Niño de los	
Almendras	7
Peña La Plateria	3
Sala Vimaambi	6

Real
Chancillería

11 10

CALDERERÍA

9

10

REYES CATÓLICOS

C/ ESCOLÁSTICA

Casa de
los Tiros

SANTIAGO

**Santo
Domingo**

SOLARES

C. DEL PESCADO

Alhambra
Shop

PAVANERAS

GIRONES

PLAZA SANTO
DOMINGO

P

P. S. DE LUCENA

Cvto. de
S. Francisco

PLAZA ISABEL
CATÓLICA

CUARTO REAL

**Capilla
Real**

Madraza o
Univ. Arabe

SAN MATÍAS

San Matías

Police

Pl. Isabella Católica

PLAZA DE
LOS CAMPOS

ROSARIO

ANCHA DE LA VIRGEN

PASEO DE SALÓN

Corral de
Carbón

PLAZA
GAMBOA

LAS MINAS

Catedral

Alcaicería

PLAZA A.
CANO

2

Ayuntamiento
ⓘ

PLAZA DEL
CARMEN

PLAZA DE
MARIANA
PINEDA

Palacio
Arzobispal

PLAZA BIB-
RAMBLA

PESCADERÍA

16

ANGEL GANIVET

MORAS

**Palacio de
Bibataubín**
(Dip. Prov.)

CARRERA DEL GENIL

P

HUMILLADERO

**Virgen de
las Angustias**

MÉSONES

PUERTA
REAL

ACERA DEL CASINO

P

PLAZA DE
LAS ARENAS

ALHÓNDIGA

El Corte Inglés

ACERA DEL DARRO

REJAS DE LA VIRGEN

SAN ISIDRO

C/ P. ARRAGA

SAN ANTÓN

P

❸ ▼ ▼ Purchil, Motril & Huerta de San Vicente

4

was here, at 3pm on January 2, 1492, that the Cross was first displayed above the city, alongside the royal standards of Aragón and Castile and the banner of St James. Boabdil, leaving Granada for exile in the Alpujarras, turned and wept at the sight, earning from his mother Aisha the famous rebuke: "Do not weep like a woman for what you could not defend like a man." To gain access to the Palacios Nazaríes you need to recross the **Pza. de los Aljibes**. In Nasrid times, this area was a ravine dividing the hill between the Royal Palace on one side, and the Alcazaba on the other. Following *la reconquista*, the ravine was filled in to hold two rainwater cisterns (*aljibes*) and the surface above laid out with fortifications. During the construction of Carlos V's palace in the sixteenth century, the area was cleared to create a parade ground, the rather desolate form it retains today.

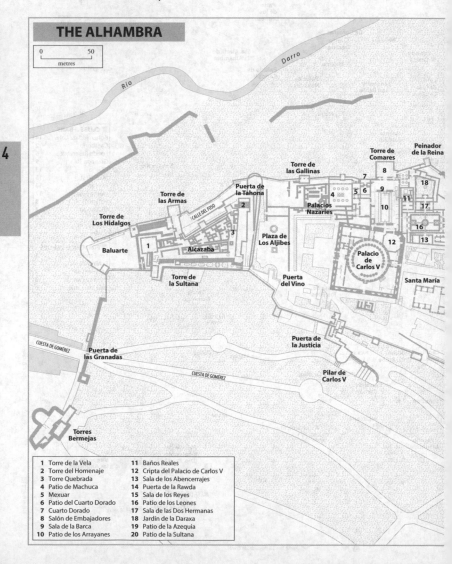

1 Torre de la Vela	11 Baños Reales
2 Torre del Homenaje	12 Cripta del Palacio de Carlos V
3 Torre Quebrada	13 Sala de los Abencerrajes
4 Patio de Machuca	14 Puerta de la Rawda
5 Mexuar	15 Sala de los Reyes
6 Patio del Cuarto Dorado	16 Patio de los Leones
7 Cuarto Dorado	17 Sala de las Dos Hermanas
8 Salón de Embajadores	18 Jardín de la Daraxa
9 Sala de la Barca	19 Patio de la Azequia
10 Patio de los Arrayanes	20 Patio de la Sultana

The Palacios Nazaríes

It is amazing that the **Palacios Nazaríes** has survived, for it stands in utter contrast to the strength of the Alcazaba and the encircling walls and towers. It was built lightly and often crudely from wood, brick and adobe, and was designed not to last but to be renewed and redecorated by succeeding rulers. Its buildings show a brilliant use of light and space, but they are principally a vehicle for ornamental stucco decoration.

Arabic inscriptions feature prominently in the ornamentation. Some are poetic eulogies to the buildings and builders, others to various sultans (notably Mohammed V). Most, however, are taken from the Koran, and among them the phrase *Wa-la ghaliba illa-Llah* (There is no Conqueror but God) is tirelessly repeated. This became the battle cry (and family motto) of the Nasrids upon Ibn al-Ahmar's return in 1248

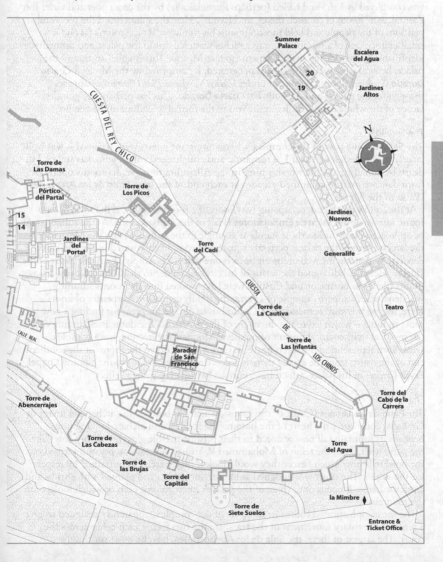

from aiding the Castilian war of Fernando III against Muslim Seville; it was his reply to the customary, though bitterly ironic, greetings of Mansur (Victor), ridiculing his role as a feudal puppet of the Christian enemy.

The palace is structured in three parts, each arrayed round an interior court and with a specific function. The sultans used the **Mexuar**, the first series of rooms, for business and judicial purposes. In the **Serallo**, beyond, they received embassies and distinguished guests. The last section, the **Harem**, formed their private living quarters and would have been entered by no one but their family or servants.

The Mexuar

The council chamber, the main reception hall of the **Mexuar**, is the first room you enter. It was completed in 1365 and hailed (perhaps formulaically) by the court poet and vizier Ibn Zamrak as a "haven of counsel, mercy, and favour". Here the sultan heard the pleas and petitions of the people and held meetings with his ministers. At the room's far end is a small oratory, one of a number of prayer niches scattered round the palace and immediately identifiable by their distinctive alignment (to face Mecca). This "public" section of the palace, beyond which few would have penetrated, is completed by the Mudéjar **Cuarto Dorado** (Golden Room), decorated under Carlos V, whose *Plus Ultra* motif appears throughout the palace, and the **Patio del Cuarto Dorado**. This has perhaps the grandest facade of the whole palace, for it admits you to the formal splendour of the Serallo.

The Serallo

The **Serallo** – the part of the complex where important guests were received – was built largely to the design of Yusuf I, a romantic and enlightened sultan who was stabbed to death by a madman while worshipping in the Alhambra mosque. Its rooms open out from delicate marble-columned arcades at each end of the long **Patio de los Arrayanes** (Patio of the Myrtles).

At the court's north end, occupying two floors of a fortified tower, is the royal throne room, known as the **Salón de Embajadores** (Hall of the Ambassadors). As the sultan could be approached only indirectly, it stands at an angle to the entrance from the Mexuar. It is the largest room of the palace, perfectly square and completely covered in tile and stucco decoration. Among the web of inscriptions is one that states simply "I am the Heart of the Palace." Here Boabdil signed the terms of his city's surrender to the Catholic kings, whose motifs (the arms of Aragón and Castile) were later worked into the room's stunning wooden dome, a superb example of *lacería*, the rigidly geometric "carpentry of knots". Here, too, so it is said, Fernando met Columbus to discuss his plans for finding a new sea route to India – which led to the discovery of the Americas. The dome itself, in line with the mystical-mathematical pursuit of medieval Moorish architecture, has a complex symbolism representing the seven heavens. Carlos V tore down the rooms at the southern end of the court; from the arcade there is access (frequently closed) to the gloomy **Chapel Crypt** (*cripta*) of his palace, which has a curious "whispering gallery" effect.

The Harem

The **Patio de los Leones** (Court of the Lions), which has become the archetypal image of Granada, constitutes the heart of the **harem**. The stylized and archaic-looking lions beneath its fountain (all now restored to their pristine marble glory) probably date, like the patio itself, from the reign of Mohammed V, Yusuf's successor; a poem inscribed on the bowl tells how much fiercer they would look if they weren't so restrained by respect for the sultan. The court was designed as an interior garden and planted with shrubs and aromatic herbs; it opens onto three of the palace's finest rooms, each of which looks onto the fountain.

The most sophisticated rooms in this part of the complex, apparently designed to give a sense of the rotary movement of the stars, are the two facing each other across the court. The largest of these, the **Sala de los Abencerrajes**, has the most startlingly beautiful ceiling in the Alhambra: sixteen-sided, supported by niches of stalactite vaulting, lit by windows in the dome and reflected in a fountain on the floor. This light and airy quality stands at odds with its name and history, for here Abu'l-Hasan (Boabdil's father) murdered sixteen princes of the Abencerraje family, whose chief had fallen in love with his favourite, Zoraya; the crimson stains in the fountain are popularly supposed to be the indelible traces of their blood, but are more likely to be from rust.

At the far end is the **Sala de los Reyes** (Hall of the Kings), whose dormitory alcoves preserve a series of unique paintings on leather. These, in defiance of Koranic law, represent human scenes; it's believed that they were painted by a Christian artist in the last decades of Moorish rule. The second of the two facing chambers on the court's north side, the **Sala de las Dos Hermanas** (Hall of the Two Sisters), is more mundanely named – from two huge slabs of marble in its floor – but just as spectacularly decorated, with a dome of over five thousand "honeycomb cells". It was the principal room of the sultan's favourite, opening onto an inner apartment and balcony, the **Mirador de Daraxa** (known in English as the "Eyes of the Sultana"); the romantic garden patio below was added after the Reconquest.

Beyond, you are directed along a circuitous route through **apartments** redecorated by Carlos V (as at Seville, the northern-reared emperor installed fireplaces) and later used by Washington Irving. Eventually you emerge at the **Peinador de la Reina**, or Queen's Tower, a pavilion that served as an oratory for the sultanas and as a dressing room for the wife of Carlos V; perfumes were burned beneath its floor and wafted up through a marble slab in one corner.

From here, passing the **Patio de la Lindaraja** (added in the sixteenth century – though the basin of its marble fountain was taken from outside the Mexuar), you reach the **Baños Reales** (Royal Baths). These are tremendous, decorated in rich tile mosaics and lit by pierced stars and rosettes once covered by coloured glass. The central chamber was used for reclining and retains the balconies where singers and musicians – reputedly blind to keep the royal women from being seen – would entertain the bathers. At present, entry is not permitted to the baths, though you can make out most of the features through the doorways. The visit route exits via the exquisite **Pórtico del Partal**, with the **Torre de las Damas** (Ladies' Tower) and elegant portico overlooking a serene pool. What appears no more than a garden pavilion today is in fact the surviving remnant of the early fourteenth-century Palace of the Partal, a four-winged structure originally surrounding the pool, the Alhambra's largest expanse of water. The **Jardines del Partal** lie beyond this, and the nearby gate brings you out close to the entrance to the Palacio de Carlos V.

Palacio de Carlos V

The grandiose **Palacio de Carlos V** seems totally out of place here, its austere stone-built architecture jarring with the delicate Oriental style and materials of the Moorish palace. Begun in 1526 it was never finished – the coffered ceilings of the colonnade were added only in the 1960s before which the Ionic columns had projected into open sky – as shortly after commissioning it, Carlos V left Granada never to return. Despite its incongruity the edifice is, however, a distinguished piece of Renaissance design in its own right – the only surviving work of Pedro Machucha, a former pupil of Michelangelo.

Museo de Bellas Artes

Mid-March to mid-Oct Tues 2.30–8pm, Wed–Sat 9am–8pm, Sun 9am–2.30pm; mid-Oct to mid-March Tues–Sat until 6pm • €1.50, free with EU passport

On the palace's upper floor – reached by steps from a circular central courtyard where bullfights were once held – is a mildly interesting **Museo de Bellas Artes**. Here are displayed some notable examples of *andaluz* wood sculpture by seventeenth-century *granadino* Alonso Cano among others, as well as some vibrantly coloured abstract works by twentieth-century artist José Guerrero, who spent part of his life in New York and was influenced by American Expressionism.

Museo de la Alhambra

Mid-March to mid-Oct Tues & Sun 8.30am–2.30pm, Wed–Sat 8.30am–8pm; mid-Oct to mid-March Tues & Sun 8.30am–2.30pm, Wed–Sat 8.30am–6pm • Free

The lower floor holds the **Museo de la Alhambra** (aka Museo Hispano-Musulman), a small but fascinating collection of Hispano-Moorish art, displaying many items discovered during the Alhambra restoration including fine woodcarving and tile work. The star exhibit is a beautiful fifteenth-century metre-and-a-half-high **Alhambra vase** (Jarrón de las Gacelas), made from local red clay enamelled in blue and gold and decorated with leaping gazelles.

The Generalife

Paradise is described in the Koran as a shaded, leafy garden refreshed by running water where the "fortunate ones" may take their rest. It is an image that perfectly describes the **Generalife**, the gardens and summer palace of the sultans. Its name means literally "Garden of the Architect", and the grounds consist of a luxuriantly imaginative series of patios, enclosed gardens and walkways.

By chance, an account of the gardens during Moorish times, written rather poetically by the fourteenth-century court vizier and historian Ibn Zamrak, survives. The descriptions that he gives aren't all entirely believable, but they are a wonderful basis for musing as you wander around the patios and fountains. There were, he wrote, celebrations with horses darting about in the dusk at speeds that made the spectators rub their eyes (a form of festival still indulged in at Moroccan *fantasías*); rockets shot into the air to be attacked by the stars for their audacity; tightrope walkers flying through the air like birds; and men bowled along in a great wooden hoop, shaped like an astronomical sphere.

Today, devoid of such amusements, the gardens are still evocative – above all, perhaps, the **Patio de los Cipreses** (aka Patio de la Sultana), a dark and secretive walled garden of sculpted junipers where the Sultana Zoraya was suspected of meeting her lover Hamet, chief of the unfortunate Abencerrajes. Nearby, too, is the inspired flight of fantasy of the **Escalera del Agua**, a staircase with water flowing down its stone balustrades. From here you can look down on the wonderful old Arab quarter of the Albaicín.

ARRIVAL AND DEPARTURE
THE ALHAMBRA

By bus A dedicated minibus service, the Alhambrabus (line #C3; daily 7am–11pm, every 10min; €1.20), departs from Pza. Isabel La Católica near the Catedral. This will drop you outside the Alhambra's entrance and ticket office.

By car To approach the Alhambra by car, use the signed route from the Puerta Real along the Paseo del Salón and the Paseo de la Bomba to the Alhambra's car park, close to the entrance and ticket office on the eastern edge of the complex.

On foot The standard approach to the Alhambra is along the Cuesta de Gomérez, the semi-pedestrianized road that climbs uphill from Granada's central Pza. Nueva (see box, p.334).

INFORMATION AND TICKETS

Information To check any changes to opening times, admission charges or booking procedures, visit the Alhambra's website ⓦ alhambra-patronato.es.

TICKETS

Buying tickets in person To protect the Alhambra, only 6600 daily admissions are allowed. If you're buying tickets in person, you have three options: you can buy them at the Alhambra shop in town (C/Reyes Católicos 40; daily 9.30am–8.30pm), at the entrance (ticket office opens at 8am), where queues can be long, or by credit card from any ServiCaixa machine (several are located in a small building signed off the car park near the ticket office); insert your card into the machine and request a day and time. All

tickets will state whether they are for morning (8.30am–2pm) or afternoon (mid-March to mid-Oct 2–8pm, mid-Oct to mid-March 2–6pm) sessions, and you must enter between the stated times (once inside, you may stay as long as you wish). However, you should bear in mind that tickets put on sale in the manners above are only what remain after pre-booked ticket sales (see below), which could well mean in high season that no tickets are on sale at the entrance.

Buying tickets in advance Alternatively, and this is the method strongly recommended by the Alhambra to guarantee entry on a specific day, you can book in advance, either online (ⓦ alhambra-tickets.es; €1.40 booking fee) or by phone on (from Spain) ☎ 902 888 001 or (from abroad) ☎958 926 031 (24hr service). Tickets should then be collected at least 1hr before your time slot for the Palacios Nazaríes, allocated when booking, (see below) from a ServiCaixa machine or the Alhambra ticket office. You will need your credit card and passport for identification. If you've bought concessionary tickets, they can only be collected from the Alhambra ticket office.

VISITING THE ALHAMBRA
The tickets have sections for each part of the complex – Alcazaba, Palacios Nazaríes, Generalife – which must be used on the same day. Note that you will not be allowed to enter the complex (even with pre-booked tickets) less than an hour before closing time. To alleviate the severe overcrowding that used to occur, tickets are stamped with a half-hour time slot during which you must enter the Palacios Nazaríes. You will not be allowed to enter before or after this time, but once inside the palace you can stay as long as you like: any waiting time can be spent in the Alcazaba, museums or the Generalife. Note, too, that the Museo de la Alhambra and the Museo de las Bellas Artes, both in the Palacio de Carlos V, have different hours and admission fees to those of the Alhambra. If you're planning to spend the day at the Alhambra, book a slot for the Palacios Nazaríes between 11.30am and 1.30pm. This allows you entry to the Alcazaba and Generalife at any time afterwards. An earlier or later time slot limits your access to the Alcazaba and Generalife to before 2pm or after 2pm respectively.

SPECIAL EVENTS
The Alhambra is also open for floodlit visits, limited to the Palacios Nazaríes (mid-March to mid-Oct Tues–Sat 10–11.30pm, ticket office open 9.45–10.15pm only; mid-Oct to mid-March Fri & Sat 8–9.30pm, ticket office open 7.45–8.15pm only; €8), and occasional concerts are held in its courts (details from the *turismo*). Availability of tickets (which can be pre-booked) is subject to the same terms as for daytime visits.

The Albaicín

Declared a UNESCO World Heritage Site in 1994, the **Albaicín** stretches across a fist-shaped area bordered by the river, the Sacromonte hill, the old town walls and the winding C/Elvira (parallel to the Gran Vía de Colón). The best approach is along Carrera del Darro, beside the river. Coming from the Alhambra, you can make your way down the Cuesta de los Chinos – a beautiful path and a short cut.

Baños Árabes Al Andalus
C/Santa Ana 16 · Daily 10am–midnight, reservation required · Bath only €24 · ☎958 229 978, ⓦ hammamalandalus.com

Just to the east of Pza. Nueva behind the church of Santa Ana, the **Baños Árabes Al Andalus** gives you some idea of what a **Moorish bathhouse** would have been like when functioning. Here you can wallow in the graded temperatures of the re-created traditional baths – decorated with mosaics and plaster arabesques – or take tea in the peaceful *tetería* (tearoom) upstairs.

Casa de Castril
Carrera del Darro 43

On Carrera del Darro, the **Casa de Castril**, a Renaissance mansion, houses the town's **archeological museum**. Due to reopen sometime in 2015 after extensive restoration, it exhibits some remarkable finds from the Neolithic Cueva de los Murciélagos (Cave of

---

PERSONAL SAFETY IN THE ALBAICÍN

Although you certainly shouldn't let it put you off visiting the atmospheric Albaicín quarter, it's worth bearing in mind that the area has been the scene of repeated **thefts** from tourists. To ensure your visit is a happy one, take all the usual precautions: avoid carrying around large amounts of money or valuables (including airline tickets and passports – a photocopy of the latter will satisfy museums), and keep what you have in safe pockets instead of shoulder bags. If you do get something snatched, don't offer resistance; crime in these streets rarely involves attacks to the person, but thieves will be firm in getting what they want. Finally, try not to look like an obvious tourist (map/guidebook in hand is a dead giveaway) or flaunt expensive-looking photographic equipment or mobile phones, and keep to the streets where there are other people about, particularly at night.

the Bats) in the Alpujarras; there are also exhibits from Granada's Phoenician, Roman, Visigothic and Moorish periods. Beside the museum, C/Zafra ascends to the church of **San Juan** (which has an intact thirteenth-century minaret) and then, following a series of convoluted turnings the church of **San Nicolás**, whose square offers a stunning **view of the Alhambra**, considered the best in town.

El Bañuelo

Carrera del Darro 31 • Daily: mid-March to mid-Oct 10am–8pm; mid-Oct to mid-March 10am–6pm • Free • ☎ 958 229 738

On Carrera del Darro are the remains of the **Bañuelo**, a marvellous and little-visited Moorish public bath complex. Built in the eleventh century, the sensitively restored building consists of a series of brick-vaulted rooms with typical star-shaped skylights (originally glazed) and columns incorporating Visigothic and Roman capitals.

Sacromonte

To the east of the Albaicín is the gypsy cave-quarter of **Sacromonte**. Like many cities in Andalucía, Granada has an ancient and still considerable *gitano* population, from whose clans many of Spain's best flamenco guitarists, dancers and singers have emerged. They have traditionally lived in caves in this area, although these days the *barrio* is better known for its nightlife. If you wander up here in the daytime, take a look at the old **caves** on the far side of the old Moorish wall – most of them deserted after severe floods in 1962. There are fantastic views from the top. Sacromonte now has its own museum, the **Centro Interpretación del Sacromonte** (Barranco de los Negros s/n; daily: mid-March to mid-Oct 10am–8pm; mid-Oct to mid-March 10am–7pm; €5; ☎958 215 120) depicting the life and times of the *barrio.*

The Capilla Real

Mid-March to mid-Oct Mon–Sat 10.15am–1.15pm & 4.30–7.15pm; mid-Oct to mid-March Mon–Sat 10.15am–11.15pm & 4.30–6.15pm; Sun 11am–1.15pm & 2.30–6.15pm • €4 • ☎ 958 227 848

In addition to Granada's Moorish legacy, it's worth the distinct readjustment and effort of will to appreciate the city's later Christian monuments, notably the **Capilla Real** (Royal Chapel), in the centre of town adjoining the Catedral at the southern end of Gran Vía de Colón. It's an impressive building, flamboyant late Gothic in style and built ad hoc in the first decades of Christian rule as a mausoleum for Los Reyes Católicos, the city's "liberators".

The tombs

The monarchs' **tombs** are as simple as could be imagined: Fernando (marked with a not-easily-spotted "F" on the left of the central pair) and Isabel, flanked by their daughter Joana ("the Mad") and her husband Felipe ("the Handsome"), resting in lead coffins placed in a plain crypt. But above them – the response of their grandson Carlos V to what he found "too small a room for so great a glory" – is a fabulously elaborate **monument** carved in Carrara marble by Florentine Domenico Fancelli in 1517, with sculpted Renaissance effigies of the two monarchs; the tomb of Joana and Felipe alongside is a much inferior work by Ordóñez. In front of the monument is an equally magnificent **reja**, the work of Maestro Bartolomé of Jaén, and a splendid **retablo** behind depicts Boabdil surrendering the keys of Granada.

Isabel, in accordance with her will, was originally buried on the Alhambra hill (in the church of San Francisco, now part of the parador), but her wealth and power proved no safeguard of her wishes. The queen's final indignity occurred during the 1980s when the candle that she asked should perpetually illuminate her tomb was replaced by an electric bulb – it was restored in 1999 following numerous protests.

The Sacristy

In the Capilla's **Sacristy** is displayed the sword of Fernando, the crown of Isabel and her outstanding personal collection of **medieval Flemish paintings** – including important works by Memling, Bouts and van der Weyden – and various Italian and Spanish paintings, including panels by Botticelli, Perugino and Pedro Berruguete.

The Catedral

April–Oct Mon–Sat 10.45am–1.15pm & 4–7.45pm, Sun 4–7.45pm; Nov–March Mon–Sat 10.45am–1.15pm & 4–6.45pm, Sun 4–6.45pm • €4 • ☎ 958 222 959

For all its stark Renaissance bulk, Granada's **Catedral**, adjoining the Capilla Real and entered from the door beside it, is a disappointment. It was begun in 1521, just as the chapel was finished, but was then left incomplete well into the eighteenth century. At least it's light and airy inside, though, and it's fun to go round putting coins in the slots to light up the chapels, where an El Greco *St Francis* and sculptures by Pedro de Mena and Martínez Montañés will be revealed.

San Juan de Dios

Northwest of the Catedral, ten minutes' walk along C/San Jerónimo, the Hospital of **San Juan de Dios**, with a pair of spectacular Renaissance patios, lies beyond a majestic portal. The inner patio has wonderful but sadly deteriorating frescoes depicting the San Juan's miracles. The hospital is still in use, but the porter will allow you a brief look. Next door, the hospital's church, a Baroque addition, has a Churrigueresque *retablo* – a glittering, gold extravaganza by Guerrero.

4

LORCA'S GRANADA

One of the ghosts that walks Granada's streets and plazas is that of Andalucía's greatest poet and dramatist **Federico García Lorca** who was born in 1898 in Fuente Vaqueros, a village in the *vega*, the fertile plain to the west of the city. In the summer months the family – Lorca's father was a wealthy landowner – moved to the Huerta de San Vicente, now in the city suburbs but then a tranquil rural plot on the city's edge. Both sites can be visited.

HUERTA DE SAN VICENTE

Mid-March to mid-Oct Tues–Sun 9.30am–1.30pm & 5–7.30pm; mid-Oct to mid-March Tues–Sun 9.30am–1.30pm & 5–6.30pm (guided tours every 45min only) • €3 • ☎ 958 258 466 • Southbound bus #C5 from Pza. Isabel La Católica or a taxi

Southwest of the centre, the **Huerta de San Vicente** comprises the house – with Lorca's bedroom – where he composed many of his best-known poems. The visit enables you to see the light and airy rooms and – in the poet's room – some original furniture including his work desk, bed and a poster of the Barraca theatre company which he helped to set up. When the Lorcas had it the house was surrounded by five acres of fruit trees and vegetable plots. Today it sits in the centre of what is claimed to be Europe's largest rose garden, Parque Federico García Lorca, the city's belated tribute.

CASA MUSEO FEDERICO GARCÍA LORCA

April, May, June & Sept Tues–Sat 10am–1pm & 5–6pm, Sun 10am–1pm; July & Aug Tues–Sun 10am–2pm; Oct–March Tues–Sat 10am–1pm & 4–5pm, Sun 10am–1pm; guided visits on the hour • €1.80 • ☎ 958 516 453, ⓦ www.museogarcialorca.org • Buses (hourly from 9am, last bus returns 9pm; 20min) leave from Avda. de Andaluces, fronting the train station

To the west of the city, in pleasant **Fuente Vaqueros**, Lorca's birthplace, has been transformed into a museum, the **Casa Museo Federico García Lorca**, and contains an evocative collection of Lorca memorabilia.

La Cartuja

Daily: April–Oct 10am–1pm & 4–8pm, Nov–March 10am–1pm & 4–6pm • €4 • ☏ 958 161 932 • The monastery is a 10–15min walk from the Hospital of San Juan de Dios; bus line #C2, going north along the Gran Vía, also passes by

On the northern outskirts of town, **La Cartuja** is perhaps the grandest and most outrageously decorated of all the country's lavish Carthusian monasteries. It was constructed at the height of Baroque extravagance – some say to rival the Alhambra – and has a chapel of staggering wealth, surmounted by an altar of twisted and coloured marble.

Monasterio de San Jerónimo

Mid-March to mid-Oct Mon–Fri 10am–1.30pm & 4–7.30pm, Sat & Sun 10am–2.30pm & 4–7.30pm; mid-Oct to mid-March Mon–Fri 10am–1.30pm & 4–6.30pm, Sat & Sun 10am–2.30pm & 4–6.30pm • €3.50 • ☏ 958 279 337

The elegant Renaissance **Monasterio de San Jerónimo** was founded by the Catholic monarchs, though built after their death, with two imposing patios and a wonderful frescoed church. The largest of the patios (or cloisters in this context) is an elegant work by Diego de Siloé with two tiers of 36 arches. The church, also by Siloé, has been wonderfully restored after use as a cavalry barracks and has fabulous eighteenth-century frescoes.

ARRIVAL AND DEPARTURE   GRANADA

BY PLANE

The airport is 17km west of the city on the A92 *autovía*; buses connect with Pza. Isabel La Católica in the centre of town (11 daily; 30min; €3 one-way). Buses run out to the airport from a stop on the east side of Gran Vía opposite the Catedral. Check with the operator (Gonzalez S.L.; ☏ 958 490 164, ⌨ autocaresjosegonzalez.com) for the latest timetable. Alternatively, a taxi costs about €25–30.

BY TRAIN

The train station (☏ 902 240 202) is 1km or so out on Avda. de Andaluces, off Avda. de la Constitución; to get into town, take bus #LAC, which runs direct to Gran Vía de Colón and the centre every 5min (€1.20). The most central stop is by the Catedral on the Gran Vía. Note that if you're travelling to Málaga the bus is much quicker and easier.

Destinations Algeciras (3 daily, 4hr 15min); Almería (4 daily; 2hr 20min); Antequera (9 daily; 1hr 30min); Córdoba (2 daily; 2hr 25); Linares-Baeza (daily; 2hr 10min); Madrid (daily; 4hr 25min); Málaga (8 daily, change at Antequera; 2hr 40min); Ronda (3 daily; 2hr 40min); Seville (4 daily; 3hr 10min).

BY BUS

The city's main **bus station** is on Carretera de Jaén (☏ 958 185 480), some way out of the centre in the northern suburbs – bus #3 or #33 from outside will drop you near the Catedral (15min) – and handles all services except those to the Lorca museum at Fuente Vaqueros (see p.343). For departure information, check with the individual companies: Alsa (serving practically all destinations; ☏ 902 422 242, ⌨ alsa.es) and Empresa Bonal (serving the north

side of the Sierra Nevada. (☏ 958 465 022). All terminals are on bus routes #SN1, #SN2 and #N5.

Destinations Alicante (5 daily; 5hr); Almería (8 daily; 2hr 15min); Cádiz (4 daily; 5hr); Cazorla (2 daily; 4hr); Córdoba (8 daily; 2hr 30min); Jaén (16 daily; 1hr 15min); Madrid (9 daily; 5hr); Málaga (12 daily; 1hr 45min); Mojácar (Daily; 4hr 30min); Motril (11 daily; 1hr 10min); Seville (5 daily; 3hr); Sierra Nevada (daily; 45min); Lanjarón & Órgiva (6 daily; 1hr 30min; 2 daily to other villages in the Alpujarras); Pradollano (3–4 daily in winter, daily in summer; 45min); Valencia (3 daily; 7hr 45min); Úbeda/Baeza (7 daily; 2hr 20min).

BY CAR

Arriving by car you'll face the usual snarl-ups in the centre of town (try to time your arrival with the siesta) and the near-impossibility of finding on-street parking. You must also be careful not to enter the restricted-access central streets such as the Gran Vía, Recogidas and Reyes Católicos. If you ignore warning signs and enter these streets your numberplate will be photographed and you will be fined at least €60 (unless your hotel is actually in one of these streets – no exceptions are allowed).

Car parks (*parking subterráneo*) are located at Puerta Real (down the right-hand side of the post office); La Caleta, near the train station; and on C/San Agustín, beneath the municipal market off the west side of Gran Vía near the Catedral. Long-term free street parking places are often to be found along Carrera del Genil and the Paseo del Salón, slightly southwest of the centre or across the bridges over the Genil to the southeast.

INFORMATION AND TOURS

Turismo The city's best and most efficient tourist office is the municipal tourist office at Pza. del Carmen s/n, inside the *Ayuntamiento* (mid-March to mid-Oct Mon–Sat 10am–8pm, Sun 10am–2pm; mid-Oct to mid-March

Mon–Sat 10am–7pm, Sun 10am–2pm; ☎958 248 280, Ⓦgranadatur.com). They also have a sub-office in the Alhambra's ticket office (open same hours as the monument). The city's rather lethargic Junta de Andalucía *turismo*, C/Santa Ana 2 (Mon–Fri 9am–7.30pm, Sat & Sun 9.30am–3pm; ☎958 575 202), is up steps to the right of the church of Santa Ana off Pza. Nueva.

Guided walks Cicerone Granada's tour (daily 10.30am, 11am Nov–Feb; 2hr; English & Spanish; €12, under-14s

free; book in high season; ☎600 412 051, Ⓦciceronegranada.com) starts at the green and white "Meeting Point" kiosk in the northeast corner of Pza. Bib Rambla and takes in the city's major sights (but not the Alhambra).

Listings The online *Guía del Ocio* (Ⓦguiadelocio.com /granada) details most of what's happening on the cultural and entertainment front, as does the city's daily paper, *Ideal*, which is particularly good in its weekend editions.

ACCOMMODATION

Granada has some of the most beautiful **hotels** in Spain, most noticeably in the atmospheric Albaicín but also along the Gran Vía, C/Reyes Católicos, in and around Pza. Nueva and Puerta Real and off Pza. del Carmen. In the university zone, Pza. de la Trinidad (and east of here) is another good place to look, along with the semi-pedestrianized (taxis and residents only) Cuesta de Gomérez, which leads up from Pza. Nueva towards the Alhambra. In high season (April–June & Sept) and especially during Semana Santa (Easter Week), you should book as far ahead as possible.

All hotels have either their own **car park** or garage (€10–20/vehicle/day) or can advise on finding a parking place for your vehicle. The main problem, almost anywhere, is **noise**, though the recently built road to the Alhambra, diverting traffic away from the centre, has made a big difference.

Albergue Juvenil Camino de Ronda 171 ☎955 035 886, Ⓦwww.inturjoven.com. Granada's youth hostel is conveniently close to the train station: turn left onto Avda. de la Constitución and left again onto Camino de Ronda. From the bus station, take bus #SN2 and get off at the stop after the railway bridge. It's efficiently run with facilities such as a laundry, lockers and towel hire, and all rooms are en-suite doubles; the staff are friendly but the food is institutional; it can also be booked up for days ahead in summer. Under-26 €21, over-26 €26

Camping Reina Isabel 4km along the Zubia road to the southwest of the city ☎958 590 041, Ⓦcamping reinaisabel.es. This site, which has a pool, is less noisy and shadier than the *Sierra Nevada*, making a pleasant rural alternative; can be reached by the Zubia-bound bus from the bus station, but with your own transport the city is still in easy reach. €21

Camping Sierra Nevada Avda. de Madrid 107 ☎958 150 062, Ⓦcampingsierranevada.com. The closest campsite to the centre (bus #SN1 from the centre or 3min walk south from the bus station), and with a welcome pool. Closed Nov–Feb. €25.80

★**Casa del Aljarife** Placeta de la Cruz Verde 2 ☎958 222 425, Ⓦcasadelaljarife.com. This welcoming upmarket Albaicín *hostal*, which occupies a restored sixteenth-century mansion near the heart of the *barrio*, has four lovely en-suite a/c rooms (two with Alhambra views) around a patio. The owner will meet you in nearby Pza. Nueva to guide you to the *hostal*. €95

★**Casa del Capitel Nazari** Cuesta de Aceituneros 6 ☎958 215 260, Ⓦhotelcasacapitel.com. A beautiful sixteenth-century *palacio* transformed into an enchanting small hotel with elegant rooms overlooking a triple-tiered patio; superior doubles have an Alhambra view. Special

offers in July, Aug, and Nov–Feb can cut prices significantly. Parking nearby. €125

★**Casa Morisca** Cuesta de la Victoria 9 ☎958 215 796, Ⓦhotelcasamorisca.com. Stunningly romantic small Albaicín hotel inside an immaculately renovated fifteenth-century Moorish mansion with exquisite patio; there are re-created Moorish furnishings throughout, and room 15 (with Alhambra views) is the one to go for. Exterior rooms cost more. Free street parking. €127

Hostal Austria Cuesta de Gomérez 4 ☎958 227 075, Ⓦpensionaustria.com. Efficient, Austrian-run *hostal* offering compact en-suite a/c rooms (with no TV). Own garage. €48

★**Hostal Costa Azul** C/Virgen del Rosario 5 ☎958 222 298, Ⓦhostalcostaazul.com. Friendly, central, small *hostal* for pleasant a/c en-suite rooms. Has own restaurant next door. Also rents out some luxurious apartments nearby. *Rough Guide* readers with this guide can claim a fifteen percent discount on apartments. Doubles €55, apartments €75

Hostal Landázuri Cuesta de Gomérez 24 ☎958 221 406, Ⓦwww.hostallandazuri.com. Pleasant, good-value rooms, some en suite (€59), plus its own bar and a roof terrace with a view of the Alhambra. Own parking. Some singles. €45

Hostal Rodri C/Laurel de las Tablas 9 ☎958 288 043, Ⓦhostalrodri.com. Very comfortable, clean and quiet *hostal*, just off Pza. de la Trinidad near the Catedral. Owners can help with tourist information. €48

Hostal Zurita Pza. de la Trinidad 7 ☎958 275 020, Ⓦpensionzurita.es. Pleasant place where immaculate rooms come with and without baths (en-suite rooms €42), and all have TVs and a/c. Has own garage. €34

Hotel Albero Avda. Santa María de la Alhambra 6

958 226 725, hotelalbero.com. Excellent-value small hotel on the access road to the Alhambra to the south of the centre. Sparkling a/c rooms come with TV and some with balconies, and there's easy street parking. Ring if you have problems finding them (English spoken). €41

Hotel América Real de la Alhambra 53 958 227 471, hotelamericagranada.com. Charming one-star hotel in the Alhambra grounds; however, you're paying for location rather than creature comforts (a/c but no TVs) and prices are unjustifiably high. Booking essential. €99

Hotel Los Angeles Cuesta Escoriaza 17 958 221 423, hotellosangeles.net. Pleasant and good-value four-star hotel on a leafy, quiet avenue within easy walking distance of the Alhambra. All rooms come with a minibar and some with terrace balconies, and there's a garden, pool and car park. €85

Hotel Casa 1800 C/Benalúa 11 958 210 700, hotelcasa1800.com. A stone's throw from the Paseo de los Tristes, this seventeenth-century restored mansion has a fine tiered patio. Romantic spacious rooms and deluxe suites have balconies with exceptional views of the Alhambra. Complimentary afternoon tea. €190

Hotel Guadalupe Paseo de la Sabica s/n 958 225 730, hotelguadalupe.es. Comfortable and well-appointed hotel a stone's throw from the Alhambra's entrance – some of the a/c rooms have partial Alhambra views. Clients get reduced-rate parking in Alhambra car park, or the Alhambra bus from Pza. Nueva drops you nearby. Does frequent offers, and outside high season, rates drop by fifty percent. €85

Hotel Macía Plaza Pza. Nueva 4 958 227 536, maciahoteles.com. Centrally located hotel, with pleasant rooms overlooking an atmospheric square. Does frequent discounts and special offers. If full, they have a couple of other same-standard hotels nearby (see website for details). Exterior rooms cost more. Ten percent discount for *Rough Guide* readers with this guide. €130

★**Hotel Palacio Santa Inés** Cuesta de Santa Inés 9 958 222 362, palaciosantaines.com. Sumptuous six-room hotel in a restored sixteenth-century Mudéjar mansion on the edge of the Albaicín, with views of the Alhambra. €120

Hotel Los Tilos Pza. de Bib-Rambla 4 958 266 712, www.hotellostilos.com. Pleasant, two-star hotel well located near the Catedral on an atmospheric square; make sure you request an exterior room if you don't want to overlook a gloomy light well. All rooms a/c, and some higher ones (try 301 & 302 or 401 & 402) have great Alhambra views. *Rough Guide* readers with this guide booking by the hotel website can claim a five percent discount. B&B. €80

Hotel Puerta de las Granadas Cuesta de Gomérez 14 958 216 230, hotelpuertadelasgranadas.com. Small, modern hotel on the way to the Alhambra with a/c en-suite rooms, the top one has Alhambra views. *Rough Guide* readers with this guide booking by phone can claim a ten percent discount. €64

Parador de San Francisco Real de la Alhambra 958 221 440, www.parador.es. Without question the most desirable – and most expensive – place to stay in Granada; a fifteenth-century converted monastery (where Isabel was originally buried) in the Alhambra grounds. We quote the cheapest standard room but suites (costing double this) have the best views. Booking (at least three months ahead) is essential. If you aren't staying, call in for a drink at the attractive terrace bar. €336

EATING

When it comes to **restaurants**, Granada certainly isn't one of the gastronomic centres of Spain, possibly due in part to the *granadino* **tapas bars** that tempt away potential diners by giving out some of the most generous tapas in Andalucía – one comes "free" with every drink. A flavour of North Africa is to be found along **C/Calderería Nueva** and its surrounds in "Little Morocco", where you'll find health-food stores, as well as numerous Moroccan tearooms and eating places. This street is useful for assembling picnics for Alhambra visits, as is the revamped ultramodern **Mercado Municipal** in Pza. San Agustín just north of the Catedral (Mon–Sat 8.30am–2pm). The warren of streets between **Pza. Nueva** and the **Gran Vía** has plenty of good-value places, particularly tapas bars, as does the area around **Plaza del Carmen** (near the *ayuntamiento*) and along C/Navas. Another good location is the **Campo del Príncipe**, a pleasant square below the south side of the Alhambra hill, with a line of open-air restaurant terraces, highly popular on summer nights.

RESTAURANTS

CITY CENTRE AND ALBAICÍN

El Aguador Pza. Romanilla 12 958 523 889. This family-run restaurant has a large outside terrace and atmospheric *bodega* for inside dining. Specialities include *carnes a la brasa* (charcoal grilled meats) and rice dishes. Main dishes €9–22. Daily noon–midnight.

Casa Cepillo C/Pescadería 8. Cheap and cheerful *comedor* with an excellent-value menu for around €10; the soups are especially good. Mon–Fri noon–4pm.

El Trillo Callejón del Aljibe del Trillo 3 958 225 182. Enchanting little mid-priced restaurant in an Albaicín *carmen* offering Basque-influenced cuisine: *arroz con jabalí y setas* (rice with wild boar and mushrooms) is a signature dish. Has outdoor tables on a delightful garden patio shaded by pear and quince trees. Main dishes €8–18. Daily 1–4pm & 7–11pm; eve only in July & Aug.

★**Restaurante-Bar Las Tomasas** Carril de San Agustín 4 958 224 108. Pricey restaurant with an international menu in a huge and beautiful *carmen* with a stunning terrace view of the floodlit Alhambra at night. *Rodaballo a la bilbaína* (skate Bilbao-style) is a speciality. You can also nurse a *tinto de verano* and try the tapas if you don't want a full meal. Main dishes €12–24. Wed–Sun 1.30–4pm & 8–11.30pm, Tues 8–11.30pm.

Restaurante León C/Pan 3. Long-established restaurant and serving many *carne de monte* (game) dishes, with a good-value menu for €10. Main dishes €7–15. Mon & Thurs–Sun 1–4pm & 8–11.30pm, Tues 1–4pm.

★**Restaurante-Marisquería Cunini** C/Pescadería 9 ☎ 958 250 777. One of Granada's most established and outstanding upmarket restaurants serving mainly fish. Also has a superb tapas bar attached. Despite having recently expanded its dining area, booking is still advised. Main dishes €10–24. Tues–Sat 12–4pm & 8pm–midnight, Sun noon–4pm.

Restaurante Sevilla C/Oficios 12 ☎ 958 221 223. One of the few surviving prewar restaurants, and once a haunt of Lorca, this is a pleasant restaurant with a tourist menu for €11 and €18, plus an outdoor terrace – beneath the walls of the Capilla Real – in summer evenings. Main dishes €6–18. Mon–Sat 11am–midnight, Sun 11am–4pm.

Rincón del Aurora Pza. San Miguel Bajo 7 ☎ 958 205 657. This popular bar-restaurant is probably the best of the bunch on this atmospheric square. House specials include *lomo al Pedro Ximénez* (pork in sweet wine) and *albóndigas* (meatballs). Main dishes €6–13. Tues–Sun 11am–midnight.

AROUND TOWN

★**El Carmen de San Miguel** Pza. Torres Bermejas 3 ☎ 958 226 723. One of Granada's noted places to eat, with a fabulous terrace looking out over the city (book a frontline table). One of the restaurant's signature dishes, *cochinillo confitado a la vainilla* (suckling pig with vanilla), typifies its innovative approach (occasionally overdone) to *andaluz* cuisine. *Menús de degustación* for €32 and €55. Mon–Sat 1.30–4pm & 8.30–11.30pm.

★**Casa López Correa** C/los Molinos 5 ☎ 958 223 775. Wonderfully cosy and atmospheric English-run neighbourhood café. An eclectic menu includes excellent salads and pastas and lots more – try their chilli con carne or curries. There's a menu for €10 and Thursday-night quiz sessions. Signature cocktails are on offer nightly after 10pm. Main dishes €5–19. Mon–Fri noon–4pm & 8pm–1am, Sat 8pm–1am.

La Mimbre Paseo del Generalife s/n. With a delightful terrace shaded by willows (*mimbres*), this is one of the best of the restaurants on the Alhambra hill. The food is good, but they are sometimes overwhelmed in high season. There are decent menus for €15.50 and €17.50, which you may need to ask for. Main dishes €11–18. Daily May–Sept noon–4pm & 8–11.30pm; Oct–April noon–5pm.

Parador de San Francisco Alhambra ☎ 958 221 440. The parador's restaurant is one of the best in an upmarket chain often noted for its blandness. There's a pleasant dining room plus a terrace with fine views, and regional specialities appear on a varied and not-too-bank-breaking menu (€34). Daily 1–4pm & 8–11.30pm.

Sancho C/Tablas 16 ☎ 958 254 654. Reliable restaurant near Pza. de la Trinidad and popular with locals. Serving hearty breakfasts and then grilled meat and salads later on. Pleasant street terrace. Main dishes €7–22. Mon–Sat 8am–midnight.

Seis Peniques Pza. de Padre Suárez ☎ 958 226 256. A very good little bar-restaurant with a large terrace facing the Casa de los Tiros. Offers great tapas in the bar and serves a decent menu in the restaurant for €9. Main dishes €5–19. Daily 8am–midnight.

TAPAS BARS

Al Sur de Granada C/Elvira 150 ☎ 958 270 245. A thoroughly modern and very friendly bar-shop serving mostly organic breakfasts (from €6), sandwiches and salads (from €8). They stock over fifty local *granadino* wines and stage tastings plus exhibitions of work by local artists. Great stop for organic picnic food. Daily 9am–11.30pm.

Bodegas Castañeda C/Almericeros 1. Enjoyable – if slightly touristy these days – century-old tapas institution. Has some outdoor tables. Recommended tapas include paté and cheese *tablas* ("boards" – on which they're served, from €8), *montaditos* (tapas on bread) and baked potatoes. Mon–Fri 11am–4.30pm & 7pm–1am, Sat & Sun 11pm–2am.

Casa de los Vinos C/Monjas del Carmen 2 ☎ 958 222 595. Also known as "La Brujidera", this tiny establishment has one of Granada's best selection of Spanish wines. Sip your pick from over 150 while you sit in the all-wood interior or on the tiny outside terrace. *Tablas* of cold meat, cheese and paté cost €8–15. Daily 12.30–4pm & 8.30pm–1am.

DRINKING AND NIGHTLIFE

Bohemia Jazz Café Santa Teresa 17 🌐 facebook.com /bohemiajazzcafe. Relaxed jazz bar with cool sounds, and walls lined with photos and memorabilia. Daily 3pm–2am.

Camborio Camino del Sacromonte s/n 🌐 facebook .com/El-Camborio. Fashionable *discobar* housed in a cave, which is especially popular with Erasmus students. Be alert for bag-snatchers in this area. Tues–Sat 11pm–late.

Fondo Reservado C/Santa Ines 4. Funky gay and straight bar with a hilarious drag show every weekend. Daily 10.30pm–4am.

Granada 10 C/Carcél Baja 10 ⓦfacebook.com /granada-10. Small and popular central *discoteca* inside a beautifully restored old retro cinema. Daily midnight–late.

Librería C/Duquesa 8. Busy blues bar with live acts on Thursday evenings. Also has good pool tables. Daily 4pm–4am.

Mae West C/Arabial s/n ⓦibribones.com. Nightclub in the Centro Comercial Neptuno with live gigs, stand-up comedians and disco music. Daily 4pm–late.

Pub Peatón C/Socrates 25 ⓦfacebook.com/PeatonPub. *Discobar* popular with a wide age group, hosting regular sixties and seventies nights. Daily 9pm–late.

Planta Baja Horno de Abad ⓦfacebook.com /salaplantabaja. Long-established *discobar* – garage and lounge are big here – now in a new home with plenty of live gigs. Wed–Sat 10pm–late.

★**Potemkin** Pza. Hospicio Viejo s/n. Great pint-sized *copas* bar with cool sounds (mainly first half of twentieth-century jazz) which also stages art exhibitions on its walls. A great feature here are the Japanese tapas and sushi nights (Wed & Sat). Mon–Fri 8.15am–4pm & 8pm–midnight, Sat & Sun 8pm–1am.

Quilombo C/Carril de San Cecilio 21. This place has a pool table and big dancefloor that starts humming around 3am. Sometimes stages live music. Wed–Thurs midnight–6am, Fri & Sat midnight–7am.

La Sal C/Santa Paula 11. Originally a lipstick lesbian dance bar, this place is now attracting gay men too. Tues–Sun 11pm–3am.

Six Colours C/Tendillas de Santa Paula 11. With lots of action this is probably the hottest gay venue in town, attracting a younger crowd than many of the other gay bars. 10pm–late.

Vanity C/Santa Barbara 3. Located (incongruously) next to *Hacienda* tax office, this is a huge dance venue where you can watch yourself on the giant screens while the DJs play salsa, reggae and house. Daily midnight–late.

FLAMENCO

When it comes to **flamenco**, finding anything near the real thing in Granada is not as easy as you might think. Shows in Sacromonte, traditionally the home of the city's flamenco performers, are generally shameless rip-offs and – unless you've heard otherwise from a knowledgeable source – to be avoided.

Los Faroles Sacromonte. An exception to our warning given in the above, this is sited almost at the very end of the line of "caves" – ask anyone for directions as it's well known. This is also a good place for a lunch time or evening drink, with a view of the Alhambra from its terrace. The genial owner is a fount of information on flamenco and the impromptu real thing often happens here after dark. Daily 11am–late.

El Niño de los Almendras C/Muladar de Doña Sancha, Albaicín. This tiny, unsigned bar – done up inside to resemble a cave – was owned by the flamenco singer of the same name who died in 2013, but unforgettable flamenco still happens here. Fri midnight–late.

Peña La Platería Plazoleta de Toqueros 7, Albaicín

ⓣ958 210 650, ⓦlaplateria.org.es. Private club devoted to the celebration of Andalucía's great folk art. There are frequent flamenco performances (Thurs or Sat are your best chances – check the club's Facebook page ⓦfacebook .com/plateriaflamenco; entry €8), and visitors are generally welcomed so long as they show a genuine interest. You'll need to arrive between 9–10pm, speak some Spanish and use a bit of charm.

Sala Vimaambi Cuesta de San Gregorio 30, Albaicín ⓣ958 227 334, ⓦvimaambi.com. A cultural and craft centre with frequent presentations of flamenco and *raices* (roots) music from North Africa and South America. Concerts usually take place on Fri & Sat at 10pm, but not all are open to non-members. Ring or check their website for the current programme.

SHOPPING

CNIG branch office (National Geographic Service) Avda. Divina Pastora 7. Sells a specialist selection of 1:500,000 and 1:25,000 maps. Mon–Fri 9am–2pm.

Librería Dauro C/Zacatín 3. This bookshop also sells maps of Granada and the surrounding area. Mon–Fri 9.45am–1.30pm & 5.30–8.30pm, Sat 10am–2pm.

Metro C/Gracia 31, off C/Alhóndiga. Granada's best international bookshop, with a wide selection of books on the Alhambra, Granada and Lorca, plus walking maps. Mon–Fri 10am–2pm & 5–8pm, Sat 11am–2pm.

DIRECTORY

Hospital Cruz Roja (Red Cross), C/Escoriaza 8 ⓣ958 222 222; Hospital Clinico San Cecilio, Avda. del Doctor Olóriz, near the Pza. de Toros ⓣ958 023 000.

Police For emergencies, dial ⓣ091 (national) or ⓣ092 (local). The Policía Local station is at Pza. de Campos 3

ⓣ958 808 502. There's also a property lost-and-found section in the *ayuntamiento* building on Pza. del Carmen (ⓣ958 248 103).

Post office Puerta Real (Mon–Fri 8.30am–8.30pm, Sat 9.30am–1pm).

Parque Nacional Sierra Nevada

The mountains of the **Sierra Nevada**, designated Andalucía's second **national park** in 1999, rise to the south of Granada, a startling backdrop to the city, snowcapped for much of the year and offering good trekking and also skiing from late November until late April. The ski slopes are at **Pradollano**, an unimaginative, developed resort just 28km away from the city centre. From here, you can make the two- to three-hour trek up to **Veleta** (3400m), the second-highest peak of the range (and of the Iberian Peninsula); this is a perfectly feasible day-trip from Granada by bus.

The Sierra Nevada is particularly rich in **wild flowers**, with fifty varieties unique to these mountains. **Wildlife** abounds away from the roads; one of the most exciting sights is the *Cabra hispanica*, a wild horned goat that (with luck) you'll see standing on pinnacles, silhouetted against the sky. Birdwatching is also superb, with the colourful hoopoe – a bird with a stark, haunting cry – a common sight.

The Veleta ascent

From the *Albergue Universitario*, the Capileira road (closed to vehicles) runs past the **Pico Veleta**; now asphalted, it is perfectly – and tediously – walkable. With your own transport, it's possible to shave a couple of kilometres off the walk to the summit by ignoring the no-entry signs at the car park near the *Albergue* and continuing on to a second car park farther up the mountain, from which point the road is then barred. Although the peak of the mountain looks deceptively close from here, you should allow two to three hours up to the summit and two hours down. There is no water en route so you'd be advised to take some along; the summit makes a great place for a picnic. Weather permitting, the **views** beyond the depressing trappings of the ski resort are fabulous: the Sierra Subbética of Córdoba and the Sierra de Guadix to the north, the Mediterranean and Rif mountains of Morocco to the south, and nearby to the southeast, the towering mass of **Mulhacén** (3483m), the Spanish peninsula's highest peak.

Pradollano

PRADOLLANO (aka Solynieve "Sun and Snow"), which lies outside the boundaries of the national park, is a hideous-looking ski resort regarded by serious alpine skiers as something of a joke, but with snow lingering so late in the year, it does have obvious attractions.

ARRIVAL AND DEPARTURE — PARQUE NACIONAL SIERRA NEVADA

By car To reach the *parque nacional* with your own transport, take the Acera del Darro and follow signs for the Sierra Nevada. Beyond the visitor centre, the route into the park continues for a further 10km to pass the Pradollano ski resort.

By bus Buses from Granada are operated by Autocares Bonal (☎ 958 465 022) with a daily service to Pradollano (€9 return, departs 9am, returns from Pradollano 5pm) and the *Albergue Universitario*, where the bus terminates. Tickets should be bought in advance at the bus station, although you can pay on board if the bus isn't full. For the winter service (Oct–March), ring the bus company or check with the *turismo*.

INFORMATION

El Dornajo Paque Nacional Sierra Nevada Visitor Centre Ctra. de Sierra Nevada km 23 (daily 10am–2pm & 5–7pm, Oct–March 4–6pm; ☎ 958 340 625, ⓦ magrama. gob.es). Signposted just off the road, the main information centre sells guidebooks, maps and hats (sun protection is vital at this altitude), and has a permanent exhibition on the park's flora and fauna. They can provide hiking information (English spoken) and rent out horses and mountain bikes. The centre also has a *cafetería* with a stunning terrace view.

Maps The best map of the Sierra Nevada including the lower slopes of the Alpujarras is the one co-produced by the Instituto Geográfico Nacional and the Federación Española de Montañismo (1:50,000), generally available in

4

THE MOORS AND AFTER

When they came to occupy the Alpujarras, the **Moors** set about improving agricultural techniques and modified the terracing and irrigation in their inimitable way. They transformed the Alpujarras into an earthly paradise, and here they retired to bewail the loss of their beloved lands in **al-Andalus**, resisting a series of royal edicts demanding their forced conversion to Christianity. In 1568, they rose up in a final, short-lived revolt, which led to the expulsion of all Spanish Moors. Even then, however, two Moorish families were required to stay in each village to show the new Christian peasants, who had been marched down from Galicia and Asturias to repopulate the valleys, how to operate the intricate irrigation systems.

Through the following centuries, the land fell into the hands of a few wealthy families, and the general population became impoverished labourers. The Civil War passed lightly over the Alpujarras: the occasional truckload of Nationalist youth trundled in from Granada, rounded up a few bewildered locals and shot them for "crimes" of which they were wholly ignorant; Republican youths came up in their trucks from Almería and did the same thing. Under Franco, the stranglehold of the landlords increased and there was real hardship and suffering. Today, the population has one of the lowest per capita incomes in Andalucía, with – as one report put it – "a level of literacy bordering on that of the Third World, alarming problems of desertification, poor communications and a high degree of underemployment".

Ironically, the land itself is still very fertile – oranges, chestnuts, bananas, apples and avocados grow here – while the recent influx of **tourism** is bringing limited wealth to the region. The so-called "High" Alpujarras have become popular with Spanish tourists and also with migrants from northern Europe who have purchased property here; Pampaneira, Bubión and Capileira, all within half an hour's drive from Lanjarón, have been scrubbed and whitewashed. Though a little over-prettified, they're far from spoilt, and have acquired shops, lively bars, good, unpretentious restaurants and small, family-run **pensiones**. Other villages, less picturesque or less accessible, have little employment, and are sustained only by farming.

Granada. A 1:40,000 map and guide set, *Sierra Nevada and La Alpujarra*, published in English by Editorial Alpina, is also good and comes with a booklet describing walks in the park and information on flora and fauna.

ACCOMMODATION

Albergue Juvenil C/Peñones 22 ☎ 955 035 886, ⓦ inturjoven.com. For budget accommodation, try the modern and comfortable *Albergue Juvenil*, on the edge of the ski resort, where you can get great-value (outside the Nov–March ski season) double and four-bed rooms, all en suite. They also rent out skis and equipment. Under-26 **€22**, over-26 **€26**

Albergue Universitario Ctra de Sierra Nevada km 36 ☎ 958 481 003, ⓦ alberguesierranevada.com. In isolated Peñones de San Francisco lies one more option:

the *Albergue Universitario*, which has bunk rooms, doubles sharing bathrooms, and a restaurant. Ski and equipment hire also available. B&B. **€22**

Camping Las Lomas ☎ 958 484 742, ⓦ camping laslomas.com. The only campsite in the area is at the Ruta del Purche, 15km out of Granada and halfway to Pradollano, with a supermarket and restaurant. The bus will drop you at the road leading to the site, from where it's a good 1km walk. **€27**

Las Alpujarras

Beyond the mountains, farther south from Granada, lie the great **valleys of the Alpujarras**, first settled in the twelfth century by Berber refugees from Seville, and later the Moors' last stronghold in Spain.

The valleys are bounded to the north by the Sierra Nevada, and to the south by the lesser sierras of Lujar, La Contraviesa and Gador. The eternal snows of the high sierras keep the valleys and their seventy or so villages well watered all summer long. Rivers have cut deep gorges in the soft mica and shale of the upper mountains, and over the centuries have deposited silt and fertile soil on the lower hills and in the

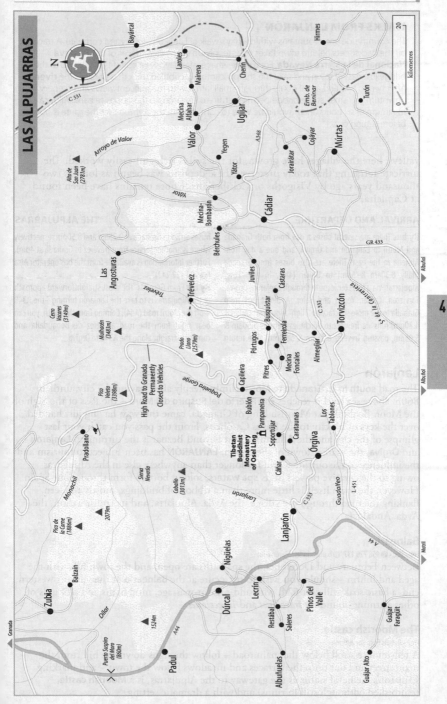

LAS ALPUJARRAS

WALKS FROM LANJARÓN

The countryside and mountains within a day's walk of Lanjarón are beyond compare. A track off the backstreets behind town takes you steeply up to the vast spaces of the **Reserva Nacional de la Sierra Nevada**. For a somewhat easier day's walk out of Lanjarón, go to the bridge just east of town and take the sharply climbing, cobbled track that parallels the **river**. After two to two and a half hours through small farms, with magnificent views and scenery, a downturn to a small stone bridge permits return to Lanjarón on the opposite bank. Allow a minimum of six hours and it would be wise to confirm with the *turismo* that the route is open before setting out.

---

valleys; here the villages have grown, for the soil is rich and easily worked. The intricate terracing that today preserves these deposits was begun as long as two thousand years ago by Visigoths or Celtiberians, whose remains have been found at Capileira.

ARRIVAL AND DEPARTURE

THE ALPUJARRAS

By bus There are several buses a day from both Granada and Motril to Lanjarón and Órgiva, and one a day from Almería in the east. There are also buses from Granada (daily 8.30am & 5pm) to Ugíjar (4hr), in the "Low" Alpujarras, via a less scenic route through Lanjarón, Órgiva, Torvizcón, Cadiar, Yegen and Valor. A direct bus from Granada to the more spectacular "High" Alpujarras (noon & 4.30pm) runs via Trevélez to Bérchules (returns 5.50am & 5.05pm, passing Trevélez 6.15am & 5.30pm). The return

buses arrive in Granada at 9.25am and 8.50pm respectively (there is another service from Trevélez to Granada at 4pm). Further information is available from the bus operator Alsa (☎ 902 422 242).

By car From Granada, the most straightforward approach to the Alpujarras is to take the Lanjarón turning –the A348 – off the Motril road (A44). Coming from the south, you can bear right from the road at Vélez de Benaudalla and continue straight along the A346 to Órgiva.

Lanjarón

The road **south from Granada to Motril** climbs steeply after leaving the city, until at 860m above sea level it reaches the **Puerto del Suspiro del Moro** – the Pass of the Sigh of the Moor. Boabdil, last Moorish king of Granada, came this way, having just handed over the keys of his city to the Reyes Católicos. From the pass you catch your last glimpse of the city and the Alhambra. Just beyond Béznar is the turning to **Lanjarón** and **Órgiva**, the market town of the region. **LANJARÓN** has been subject to tourism and the influence of the outside world for longer than anywhere else in the Alpujarras owing to the curative powers of its **spa waters**, sold in bottled form throughout Spain. However, the town itself is little more than a ribbon of buildings, mostly modern, flanking the road through the village, the Avda. Alpujarra, and its continuation, the Avda. Andalucía

Balneario

Feb–Dec • ☎ 958 770 137, ⓦ balneariodelanjaron.com

Between February and December, the spa baths are open, and the town fills with the aged and infirm – should you wish to try a cure at the **Balneario** at the village's western end, a basic soak will cost €24, with add-ons for massage, mud baths and all kinds of other alarming-sounding *tracciónes* and *inyecciónes*.

The Moorish castle

Free • Details from the *turismo*

A ten-minute stroll below the main road – follow the signs down the hill from the main street and out onto the terraces and meadows below the town – and marking Lanjarón's medieval status as the gateway to the Alpujarras, is a **Moorish castle**, refurbished (although still in ruins) and with a dramatic setting.

ARRIVAL AND INFORMATION

LANJARÓN

By bus Buses stop at the two roundabouts at either end of the town and you can buy tickets on board or online from Alsa.

Turismo Opposite the Balneario, Avda. Andalucía s/n (Mon–Sat 10am–2pm & 4.30–8.30pm, Sun 10–2pm; ☎ 958 770 462).

ACCOMMODATION AND EATING

Lanjarón has a good choice of **restaurants** and tapas bars, many attached to the hotels, which often offer good-value menus.

Bar Galvez C/Real 95 ☎ 958 770 702. Popular and economical bar-restaurant serving up tapas and *raciones* as well as *platos combinados*. A good choice if you're on a tighter budget with a menu for €12. Daily 7am–11pm.

★**Hotel Alcadima** C/Francisco Tarrega 3 ☎ 958 770 809, ⓦ alcadima.com. The excellent *Hotel Alcadima* has the best pool and restaurant terrace in town, and many of the comfortable rooms boast stunning balcony views towards the castle. **€85**

Hotel Castillo Alcadima C/Francisco Tarrega 3 ☎ 958 770 809. Perhaps the best choice for dining out is the terrace restaurant of the hotel of the same name, which is a pretty perfect place to while away a summer evening with

a superb terrace view of the castle. Specialities include meat dishes of the sierra but also fish and some vegetarian possibilities including an *ensalada alpujarreña* and a menu for €15. Daily 1– 4pm & 8–11pm.

Hotel España Avda. Alpujarra 42 ☎ 958 771 386, ⓦ lanjaronh.com. The grand-looking *Hotel España*, next door to the Balneario, has played host to Lorca and Manuel de Falla in its time. Slightly past its prime, it is nevertheless good value, very friendly and has a pool. B&B. **€40**

Hotel Paris Avda. Alpujarra 23 ☎ 958 770 556, ⓦ hotelparislanjaron.com. A charming and very good value hotel on the main street. Rooms come with TVs and there's a decent restaurant and large pool. B&B. **€44**

Órgiva

Heading east out of Lanjarón brings you after 11km to **ÓRGIVA** (also spelled Órjiva), the "capital" and market centre of the western Alpujarras. It is closer to the heart of the valley but is still really only a starting point; if the bus goes on to Capileira, you may want to stay on it. If you're **driving**, it's worth noting that petrol stations become scarcer from this point on.

Órgiva is a lively enough town, though, with plenty of bars and hotels and an animated **Thursday market** that draws in shoppers from far and wide. On the main street is an over-restored Mudéjar palace, now housing the *ayuntamiento*, and the sixteenth-century church of **Nuestra Señora de la Expectación**, whose towers add a touch of fancy to the townscape.

ACCOMMODATION AND EATING

ÓRGIVA

Agua Viva in C/Yáñez 27 ☎ 958 785 157. Órgiva's best fusion restaurant has a very pleasant rustic-modern dining room plus a small terrace. Signature dishes include a traditional Sunday roast (including vegan option), dhal soup and teriyaki pork spring rolls. Daily menu is €10, main dishes cost €9–17. Tues–Sat 1–4pm & 7.30–11.30pm, Sun 1–4pm.

Alma Alpujarreña C/González Robles 49 ☎ 958 784 085. For budget accommodation, one of the nicest places is the pretty *Alma Alpujarreña*, a little beyond the traffic lights at the town's main (and solitary) intersection, with simple and en-suite rooms. The *hostal* has a decent and economical terrace restaurant with a good-value menu for €10. House specials include a tasty *sopa de ajo* (garlic soup) and a *paella vegetal* (vegetarian). Main dishes €7–15. Daily noon–midnight. **€40**

La Almazara C/González Robles 53. Offers a range of hearty mountain dishes as well as excellent freshly made

pizzas. Also has a pleasant garden terrace. Main dishes €8–15. Tues & Thurs–Mon 2.30–4pm & 8–11pm.

Baraka C/Estación 12. An economical place worth seeking out in the upper town near the market, this is a pleasant small Moroccan-style café and *tetería* serving falafel, couscous, tagines and a variety of teas. Main dishes €5–13. Mon–Wed, Sat & Sun noon–10.30pm, Thurs & Fri noon–4.30pm.

Camping Órgiva Ctra. A348 km 18.9 ☎ 958 784 307, ⓦ campingorgiva.com. Órgiva's campsite, with ample shade plus a pool, bar and restaurant, lies 2km south of town, reached by continuing along the road where the bus drops you. It also rents out cabins and bungalows, has its own restaurant and pool and can advise on walking routes and renting horses in the nearby Sierra de Lújar. **€20**

Hotel El Semáforo Avda. González Robles 14 ☎ 958 784 309, ⓦ elsemaforo.es. Close to the main traffic junction (its name means "traffic lights"), this is a decent place for clean and tidy a/c en-suite rooms with TVs. **€40**

4

The High (western) Alpujarras

The so-called High Alpujarras include the villages of Pampaneira, Bubión and Capileira, all picture-postcard places and hugely popular with Spanish and foreign visitors. The best way to experience the **High Alpujarras** (and get off the tourist track) is to walk, and there are a number of paths between Órgiva and Cadiar, at the farthest reaches of the western valleys. Equip yourself with a compass and the Instituto Geográfico Nacional/Federación Española de Montañismo 1:50,000 map or the Editorial Alpina map, which cover all the territory from Órgiva up to Bérchules (Alpina) and Berja (IGN/FEM) respectively. Alternatively, take a bus from Lanjarón (daily 1pm), which winds through all the upper Alpujarran villages. There are some excellent **Walkers' guides** to the Alpujarras (see p.921).

Cáñar, Soportújar and Carataunas

From Órgiva, the first settlements you reach, almost directly above the town, are **CÁÑAR** and **SOPORTÚJAR**, the latter a maze of sinuous white-walled alleys. Like many of the High Alpujarran villages, they congregate on the neatly terraced mountainside, planted with poplars and laced with irrigation channels. Both villages are perched precariously on the steep hillside with a rather sombre view of Órgiva in the valley below, and the mountains of Africa over the ranges to the south.

Just below the two villages, the tiny hamlet of **CARATAUNAS** is particularly pretty and puts on a lively start to its Semana Santa on Palm Sunday, when an effigy of Judas is tossed on a bonfire.

Poqueira Gorge and around

Shortly after Carataunas the road swings to the north, and you have your first view of the **Poqueira Gorge**, a huge, sheer gash into the heights of the Sierra Nevada. Trickling deep in the bed of the cleft is the Río Poqueira, which has its source near the peak of Mulhacén. The steep walls of the gorge are terraced and wooded from top to bottom, and dotted with little stone farmhouses. Much of the surrounding country looks barren from a distance, but close up you'll find it's rich with flowers, woods, springs and streams.

A trio of villages – three of the most spectacular and popular in the Alpujarras – teeters on the steep edge of the gorge. The first is neat, prosperous and pretty **Pampaneira**. Nearby **Bubión** is backed for much of the year by snowcapped peaks. The village has a private **museum**, the Casa Alpujarreña (Wed–Mon 11am–2pm, Fri, Sat & Sun also 5–7pm; €1.80), just off Pza. de la Iglesia, the main square, displaying aspects of the folklore, daily life and architecture of the Alpujarras in a traditional house. Two kilometres north of Bubión, **Capileira** is the highest of the three villages and the terminus of the road – Europe's highest, but now closed to traffic – across the heart of the Sierra Nevada from Granada. The village's interesting **museum** (just downhill from the information kiosk; open only on public holidays; €1.50), contains displays of regional dress and handicrafts, as well as various bits and pieces belonging to, or produced by, Pedro Alarcón, the nineteenth-century Spanish writer who made a trip through the Alpujarras and wrote a (not very good) book about it.

Tibetan Buddhist Monastery of Osel Ling

Daily 3.30–6pm • ☏ 958 343 185 • 2km from Carataunas turn left (signed "Camino Forestal") and drive up the track for 6km

Above Pampaneira, on the very peak of the western flank of the Poqueira gorge, is the **Tibetan Buddhist Monastery of Osel Ling** ("Place of Clear Light"), founded in 1982 by a Tibetan monk on land donated by the communities of Pampaneira and Bubión. The simple, stone-built monastery, is complete with stupas and stunning **views** across the Alpujarras. Lectures on Buddhism are held regularly and facilities exist for those who want to visit for periods of retreat in cabins dotted around the site.

The Taha villages

Pitres and **Pórtugos**, 6km east of Pampaneira, are perhaps more "authentic" and less polished villages than in the High Alpujarras. Down below the main road (GR421) linking Pitres and Pórtugos are the three villages of Mecina Fondales (and its offshoot, Mecinilla), Ferreirola and Busquístar; along with Pitres, these formed a league of villages known as the *Taha* under the Moors. **Ferreirola** and **Busquístar** are especially attractive, as is the path between the two, clinging to the north side of the valley of the Río Trevélez. You're out of tourist country here and the villages display their genuine characteristics to better effect, while all around you is some of the best Alpujarran walking country.

Trevélez

TREVÉLEZ, at the end of an austere ravine carved by the Río Trevélez, is purportedly Spain's highest permanent settlement, with cooler temperatures year-round than its neighbours. In traditional Alpujarran style, it has lower, middle and upper quarters (*barrios bajo*, *medio* and *alto*) overlooking a grassy, poplar-lined valley where the river starts its long descent.

Bérchules

Heading east from Trevélez, you come to **Juviles**, an attractive village straddling the road, followed, 5km further on, by **BÉRCHULES**, a high village of grassy streams and chestnut woods, also famous for its *jamón*. It is a large, abruptly demarcated settlement, three streets wide, on a sharp slope overlooking yet another canyon.

Cádiar

Just below Bérchules is **CÁDIAR**, the central town – or "navel" as Gerald Brenan termed it – of the Alpujarras, more attractive than it seems from a distance, and a place that springs into life when a colourful **produce market** is held on the 3rd and 18th of every month. The annual **Fuente del Vino** wine and cattle fair (Oct 5–9) turns the waters of the fountain literally to wine.

ARRIVAL AND DEPARTURE

THE HIGH (WESTERN) ALPUJARRAS

By bus There are three daily buses to Capileira from Granada. In addition to this, anything going to Ugíjar and Berja will come very close to Capileira; buses to Granada and Órgiva pass by in the early morning with two in the late afternoon.

INFORMATION AND ACTIVITIES

PAMPANEIRA

Information and tours On its leafy main square, Pza. de la Libertad, is Nevadensis, an information centre for the Natural and National Parks of the Sierra Nevada (Sun & Mon 10am–3pm, Tues–Sat 10am–2pm & 4–6pm; ☎958 763 127, ☻nevadensis.com); they also sell large-scale topographical maps of the zone, and offer horseriding tours and guided treks, including an ascent of Mulhacén. Other activities on offer include mountain biking, climbing, canyoning and cross-country skiing. If you're thinking of a longer stay, this is also where you can pick up a list of hostels, village houses and farmhouses for rent throughout the Alpujarras.

BUBIÓN

Information Rustic Blue (☎958 763 381, ☻rusticblue .com), a privately run information office on the main road to the right as you enter the village, can also book horseriding and walking tours and help with accommodation in fully equipped houses across the Alpujarras.

Horseriding For trips of five to seven days, contact the friendly Rancho Rafael Belmonte (☎958 763 135, ☻ridingandalucia.com), at the bottom of the village near Rustic Blue, or the long-established Dallas Love (☎608 453 802, ☻spain-horse-riding.com).

CAPILEIRA

Information A kiosk for the national park is at the centre of the village (daily 10am–2pm & 5–8pm), near where the bus drops you. It hands out a village map and acts as an information office.

Hiking If you're thinking of doing any walking in this zone, this is probably the best village in which to base yourself.

Maps In addition to the information in the various villages, more fine walking routes are detailed in *34 Alpujarras Walks* by Charles Davis, *Landscapes of Andalucía* by John and Christine Oldfield, *Walking in Andalucía* by Guy Hunter-Watts and *Holiday Walks in the Alpujarra* by Jeremy Rabjohns.

4

ACCOMMODATION

There are plenty of places to stay in the High Alpujarras but outside high summer make sure that the room heating is adequate as nights can be chilly.

SOPORTÚJAR

Bar Correillo C/Real, Soportújar ☏958 787 578. Behind the church, this bar can provide excellent-value en-suite rooms. **€44**

PAMPANEIRA

Hostal Pampaneira C/José Antonio 1 ☏958 763 002, ⓦhostalpampaneira.com. Homely *hostal* above a bar-restaurant with functional en-suite rooms with TV and heating. B&B. **€42**

Hotel Estrella de Las Nieves C/Huertos 21, 200m along the road climbing above the village ☏958 763 981, ⓦestrelladelasnieves.com. This plush hotel has well-equipped en-suite rooms, many with their own terrace balcony and spectacular views. Facilities include a garden pool and garage. B&B. **€70**

BUBIÓN

Las Terrazas Pza. del Sol 7 ☏958 763 034, ⓦwww .terrazasalpujarra.com. This is a comfortable and welcoming *hostal* with rustic tile-floored en-suite rooms with heating, many with views. It also rents out some apartments and does a good-value breakfast for €2.75. Doubles **€36**, apartments **€45**

Los Tinaos C/Parras s/n ☏958 763 217, ⓦwww .lostinaos.com. This option offers some excellent heated apartments that come with garden terraces, kitchens, satellite TVs and fine views. **€55**

CAPILEIRA

El Cascapeñas Carretera de la Sierra 5 ☏958 763 011, ⓦelcascapeñas.com. This place, near the bus stop, has good-value en-suite rooms with TVs, split between a *hostal* and hotel. Hostal **€36**, hotel **€50**

Finca Los Llanos Carretera Sierra Nevada s/n ☏958 763 071, ⓦhotelfincalosllanos.com. This is a relatively luxurious option with spacious rooms with terraces; facilities include a pool (at 1560m altitude) and good restaurant. B&B. **€77**

Hostal Atalaya C/Perchel 3 ☏958 763 025, ⓦhostalatalaya.com. To the right as you enter the village, this is a pleasant little place with en-suite rooms with TVs and terrific views from those at the front. **€36**

Mesón-Hostal Poqueira C/Dr Castilla 11 ☏958 763 048, ⓦhotelpoqueira.com. Near the bus stop, this is a welcoming option for en-suite heated rooms, some with terraces and views, and there's also a pool and good restaurant with a menu for around €10. It also has some attractive apartments sleeping up to four (€50–80) for longer stays. **€40**

PITRES

Balcón de Pitres Carretera Órgiva–Ugíjar km 51 ☏958 766 111, ⓦbalcondepitres.com. Pitres' campsite with restaurant and pool, is located in a stunning position 1km west of the village, with fine views. Closed Jan & Feb. **€18**

Hotel San Roque C/Cruz 1 ☏958 857 528. On the east side of the village, the *Hotel San Roque* has decent rooms with (on the south side) mountain views. B&B. **€58**

Refugio de los Albergues Carretera A4132 s/n, Pitres ☏958 343 176. On the village's eastern edge, the *Refugio de los Albergues* is an old Civil War hostel with dormitory beds and one double room sharing a bathroom. Also has a communal kitchen. Dorms **€10**, doubles **€30**

BUSQUÍSTAR

Casa Sonia C/San Francisco 5 ☏958 857 503, ⓦcasasoniaenbusquistar.com. This is a charming *casa rural* in the heart of the village near the church, with elegant en-suite a/c rooms, some with great views. B&B. **€60**

FERREIROLA

★**Sierra y Mar** C/Albaycin 3 ☏958 766 171, ⓦsierraymar.com. A delightful Scandinavian-run guesthouse in a traditional mountain dwelling, with fine views and where the owners – enthusiastic walkers – will advise on routes in the area. B&B. **€62**

MECINA FONDALES

Hotel de Mecina Fondales C/La Fuente s/n, Mecina Fondales ☏958 766 241, ⓦwww.hoteldemecina.com. A delightful and comfortable hideaway, where many rooms come with terrace balconies and fine views. Also has an excellent garden pool and can provide useful information about the area and on renting horses and mountain bikes. *Rough Guide* readers with this guide get twenty percent off. **€88**

TREVÉLEZ

Camping Trevélez ☏958 858 735, ⓦcampingtrevelez .net. Trevélez's campsite lies 1km out along the Órgiva road; conditions are arctic in midwinter, but it also rents out some heated cabins (€26–70). **€17.75**

Hostal Fernando C/Pista del Barrio Medio s/n ☏958 858 565. Located in the *barrio medio*, this is a friendly place with good-value heated (useful outside July & Aug) en-suite rooms. **€30**

★**Hotel La Fragua I** C/Antonio 4, barrio alto ☏958 858 626, ⓦhotellafragua.com. With its pine-furnished en-suite heated rooms, with TV and many with fine views, this is probably the most pleasant place to stay in the village. It's popular with hiking groups; thus you may be better off ringing ahead to be sure of a room. The proprietors can provide information on walking and other mountain pursuits such as horseriding and mountain biking. They also own a superb and justly popular restaurant (with veggie options) and *Hotel La Fragua II* nearby (see website for details). **€50**

BÉRCHULES

Hotel Los Bérchules C/Bérchules ☎958 852 530, ⓦhotelberchules.com. On the main road into the village, this two-star hotel has comfortable rooms above its own restaurant and there's also a pool. **€60**

El Mirador de Berchules Pza. de Zapata 1 ☎958 769 090, ⓦmiradordeberchules.com. In the upper village (ask for directions), this is an attractive option for studios and apartments with terraces and views. Also has its own good tapas bar, restaurant and pool. Studio **€55**, apartment **€60**

EATING AND DRINKING

PAMPANEIRA

Bar Belezmín Pza. Libertad 11 ☎958 763 102. On Pampaneira's main square, this is one of the village's best places to eat, with a menu filled with hearty *alpujarreña* dishes such as *jabalí* (wild boar) and *perdiz* (partridge). Main dishes €9–17. Tues–Sun 10.30am–11pm.

Casa Julio Avda. de la Alpujarra 9 ☎958 763 322. Another place offering solid mountain fare accompanied with vegetables from its own *huerta* (vegetable garden). House specials include *potaje de hinojos* (fennel stew) and there's an €8 menu. Main dishes €5–12. Wed–Mon 1.30–4pm & 8.30–11pm.

Hostal Pampaneira C/José Antonio 1 ☎958 763 002. The *hostal*'s restaurant is also worth a try and cooks up many local dishes with style. Try the *potaje de garbanzos* (a warming chickpea soup). There's a menu for €9. Daily 1–4pm & 8–11pm.

BUBIÓN

The two best places to eat in the village feature *alpujarreño* specialities such as *migas* (breadcrumbs fried in garlic) and *plato alpujarreño* (a hefty fry-up) on their menus.

La Artesa C/Carretera s/n ☎958 763 082. A good option for solid mountain cooking with a menu for €9. Main dishes €6–13. Thurs–Tues 10am–5pm & 7–11pm.

Teide C/Carretera s/n ☎958 763 037. This is the better of the two restaurants on opposite sides of the road here and has a leafy terrace and a good-value weekday menu for €9. Main dishes €6–17. Daily noon–4pm & 8–11pm.

El Vergel de Bércules C/Baja de la Iglesia 5 y 14 ☎958 852 608. This new addition is just below the church (as the street name implies) and offers comfortable studios and apartments with kitchens, *salóns*, TVs and woodstoves. One-night stays are possible outside July & Aug. **€40**

CÁDIAR

★**Alquería de Morayma** 2km from Cádiar ☎958 343 303, ⓦalqueriamorayma.com. The most tempting place to stay here is an out-of-town option, 2km away along the A348 towards Torvizcón, where this excellent-value aparthotel is housed in a converted *alpujarran cortijo* (farmhouse) sited in 86 acres of farmland. There are charmingly rustic rooms and apartments (almost same price), many with patio terraces, and it has its own good restaurant (open to nonguests). Guests can go mountain biking and horseriding, and there are also plenty of hiking trails. The *Morayma*'s own organic farm and vineyard on the estate, the *bodega* of which is open to visitors, also supplies the restaurant and provides its virgin olive oil and bottled wine. **€62**

CAPILEIRA

Bar El Tilo C/Calvario 1 ☎958 763 181. On the focal Pza. Calvario in the lower village, this is a decent place for *bocadillos* or *chacinería* (cured pork products) or simply for watching-the-world-go-by drinks on its tranquil terrace shaded by a lime tree. Daily noon–4pm & 7–11pm.

Bodega La Alacena C/Trocadero 1 ☎958 763 407. Downhill from *Bar El Tilo*, this is a popular option for *jamón* and cheese tapas and its shop also sells local products such as honey, wine, cheese and hams. Main dishes €7–14. Fri–Wed 11am–3pm & 5–10pm.

El Fogón de Raquel Pza. del Tilo s/n, ☎679 554 879. Reliable home cooking with local dishes such as *sopa alpujarreña* (with egg, ham and almonds) and home-made desserts. Tues–Sat noon–4pm & 7.30–11pm, Sun noon–4pm.

La Casa de Paco y Pilar Carretera Sierra Nevada 16 ☎958 763 142. Cosy restaurant with well-prepared *alpurrajeño* specialities (with some vegetarian options). Has a pleasant garden terrace and a €10 menu. Main dishes €8–17. Mon, Tues & Thurs–Sun 11am–4.30pm & 7–11pm.

Mesón Rural Panjuila C/Carretera 24 ☎958 763 294. This is a pleasant and economical rustic place for *alpujarreño* specialities with a €10 menu. Daily noon–4pm & 8–11pm.

MECINA FONDALES

L'Atelier C/Alberca s/n ☎958 857 501. Arguably the best place for food here is this French-run restaurant specializing in vegetarian/vegan cuisine, and located in the old village bakery in Mecinilla. Booking is advised at weekends. Also lets a few rooms, should you fancy staying after dinner. Daily 1–4pm & 7.30–10pm.

Hotel de Mecina Fondales C/La Fuente s/n ☎ 958 766 241. The hotel has its own decent restaurant offering well-prepared Alpujarran cuisine. Its bar is also open for breakfast. Daily 1–4pm & 8–11pm.

TREVÉLEZ

Mesón La Fragua C/San Antonio s/n ☎ 958 858 573. The hotel restaurant is Trevélez's best place to eat, serving well-prepared dishes in a rustic two-storey bar-restaurant. *Venao en salsa* (venison) and *cordero a la moruna* (lamb) feature among a wide range of specialities, and there is a range of salads and vegetarian dishes, too. Mains €8–14. Daily 12.30–4pm & 8–10.30pm.

Mesón Haraicel C/Real s/n just above the barrio bajo's main square, Pza. Francisco Abellán ☎ 958 308 530. Economical restaurant serving meat and fish dishes as well as salads; also offers tapas and *raciones* in its bar. Small outdoor terrace. Main dishes €9–19. Daily 9.30am–10pm.

Mesón del Jamón C/Carcel 13 ☎ 958 858 679. Trevélez's *jamón serrano* is a prized speciality and an obsession throughout eastern Andalucía and this is a good place to try it. Also serves *platos combinados*. Main dishes €7–11. Daily 1–4pm & 7.30–11pm

Mesón Joaquín C/Puente s/n. In the lower *barrio*, this is another good place to try the local *jamón*, which you can also purchase in larger quantities from its *jamón* store opposite. The restaurant also does *platos combinados* and *solomillo de cerdo* (pork loin) is a house special. There's also a menu for €11. Daily 9am–7pm.

BÉRCHULES

Bar Vaquero Pza. de Abastos s/n ☎ 958 852 549. This earthy bar on the village's main square is a good place to stop for breakfast or, later in the day, tapas and *raciones*. Daily 8am–10pm.

Eastern Alpujarras

Cádiar and Bérchules mark the end of the western Alpujarras, and a striking change in the landscape; the dramatic, severe but relatively green terrain of the Guadalfeo and Cádiar valleys gives way to open rolling and much more arid land. The villages of the eastern Alpujarras display many of the characteristics of those to the west, but as a rule they are poorer and much less visited by tourists. There are attractive places to visit nonetheless, among them **Yegen**, which Brenan wrote about, and the market centre of **Ugíjar**.

Yegen

In **YEGEN**, made famous by **Gerald Brenan**, some 7km northeast of Cádiar, there's a plaque on the house (just along from the central fountain) where the author lived during his ten or so years of Alpujarran residence. His autobiography of these times, *South from Granada*, is the best account of rural life in Spain between the wars, and describes the visits made here by Virginia Woolf, Bertrand Russell and the arch-complainer Lytton Strachey. Disillusioned with the strictures of middle-class life in England after World War I, Brenan rented a house in Yegen and shipped out a library of two thousand books, from which he was to spend the next eight years educating himself. He later moved to the hills behind Torremolinos, where he died in 1987, a writer better known and respected in Spain (he made an important study of St John of the Cross) than in his native England.

Brenan connections aside, Yegen is one of the most characteristic Alpujarran villages, with its two distinct quarters, cobbled paths and cold-water springs.

ACCOMMODATION AND EATING   YEGEN

Bar Pensión La Fuente Pza. de Fuente s/n ☎ 958 851 067, ⊛ pensionlafuente.com. Opposite the fountain in the square, this is a small *hostal* offering rooms with bathrooms and whose bar is decorated with some old photos of Brenan. B&B. The restaurant is a good breakfast option for nonguests too and later in the day serves tapas and *raciones* as well as *platos combinados* and a daily menu for €10. Main dishes €9–12. Mon & Tues–Thurs 8am–10.30pm. €40

El Rincón de Yegen Camino de Gerald Brenan s/n ☎ 667 964 010, ⊛ elrincondeyegen.com. Heading east out of Yegen, you'll find more upmarket accommodation at this pleasant country hotel where heated rooms come with TVs. There are also apartments for longer stays, as well as a pool and a good, inexpensive restaurant. **€50**

El Tinao C/Carretera 12 ☎ 958 851 212. Bright and airy en-suite rooms are on offer at this *hostal* located on the main road, it also rents a couple of fully equipped houses in the village (three nights minimum). If you fancy eating here, Irish-born Loranne can cook whatever you fancy if you pre-order, but she specializes in local dishes, steaks with all the trimmings and home-made pizzas. There's a good-value menu for €10. Main dishes €6–15. Tues–Sun noon–midnight. Doubles **€35**, house from **€45**

From the Alpujarras to Almería province

One way of entering Almería province from the Alpujarras is to take the A337 minor mountain road from Laroles (some 17k east of Yegen), which climbs dizzily and scenically to the **Puerto de la Ragua**, at 1993m Andalucía's highest all-weather pass. If you keep going straight on the **A92 autovía**, you'll meet the Almería–Sorbas road at what has become known as **Mini Hollywood** (see p.363), the preserved film set of *A Fistful of Dollars*. Alternatives are the winding A348 that eventually arrives at Almería city or the most straightforward route from Granada – and that followed by buses – via the *autovía*.

La Calahorra

Above La Calahorra • Wed 10am–1pm & 4–6pm • €3

The main landmark, 16km beyond the town of Guadix, famous for its cave dwellings, is a magnificent sixteenth-century castle on a hill (15min hike) above the village of **La Calahorra**, one of the finest in Spain, with a remarkable Renaissance patio within. It's a private property and only available for viewing on Wednesday, but if you call the guardian the day before (avoiding siesta time, C/los Claveles 2 ☎ 958 677 098; Spanish only), he may be able to let you in.

ACCOMMODATION AND EATING	**LA CALAHORRA**
Hostal-Restaurante La Bella Carretera de Aldeire 1 ☎ 958 677 000. For rooms, try the central *Hostal-Restaurante La Bella*, which, in addition to en-suite rooms,	also has a decent restaurant with a good weekday €10 menu. Daily 6.30pm–1am. **€40**

Almería province

The **province of Almería** is a strange corner of Spain. Inland, it has an almost **lunar landscape** of desert, sandstone cones and dried-up riverbeds. The coast to the east of the provincial **capital** is still largely unspoilt; lack of water and roads frustrated development in the 1960s and 1970s and even now, development is limited to small areas. This allowed the creation in the 1980s of the **Parque Natural de Cabo de Gata**, a haven for flora and fauna. To the west of Almería is another story, though, with a sea of plastic greenhouses spreading in a broad swathe for a good 30km across the Campo de Dalías, the source of much of Almería's new-found wealth.

A number of **good beaches** are accessible by bus, and in this hottest province of Spain they're worth considering during what would be the off season elsewhere, since Almería's summers start well before Easter and last into November. In midsummer, it's incredibly hot (frequently touching 38°C/100°F in the shade and often well above), while all year round there's an intense, almost luminous, sunlight. This and the weird scenery have made Almería one of the most popular **film locations** in Europe – much of *Lawrence of Arabia* was shot here, along with scores of spaghetti Westerns.

4

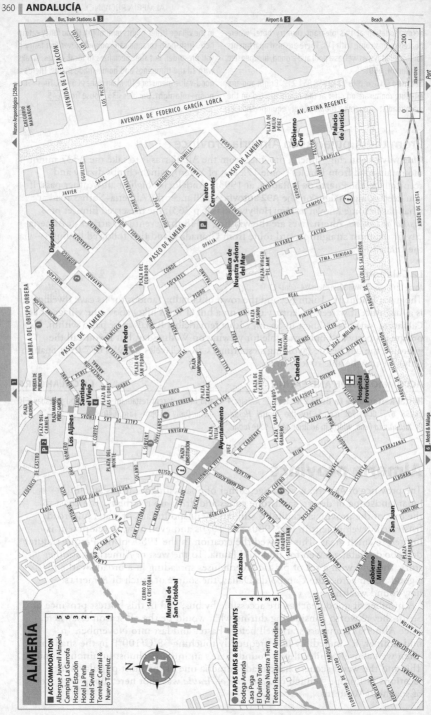

ALMERÍA

■ ACCOMMODATION

Albergue Juvenil Almería	5
Camping La Garrofa	6
Hostal Estación	3
Hotel La Perla	2
Hotel Sevilla	1
Torreluz Central & Nuevo Torreluz	4

● TAPAS BARS & RESTAURANTS

Bodega Aranda	1
Casa Puga	4
El Quinto Toro	3
Taberna Nuestra Tierra	2
Tetería Restaurante Almedina	5

Museo Arqueológico (250m)

Gregorio Marañón

0   200
metres

Port

AVENIDA DE LA ESTACIÓN

LOS PICOS

AVENIDA DE FEDERICO GARCÍA LORCA

Av. REINA REGENTE

Gobierno Civil

Palacio de Justicia

PLAZA DE EMILIO PÉREZ

PASEO DE ALMERÍA

ANDÉN DE COSTA

Teatro Cervantes

MARTÍNEZ CAMPOS

Diputación

Basílica de Nuestra Señora del Mar

PLAZA VIRGEN DEL MAR

STMA. TRINIDAD

PASEO DE ALMERÍA

RAMBLA DEL OBISPO ORBERA

San Pedro

PLAZA DE SAN PEDRO

Catedral

PLAZA DE LA CATEDRAL

Hospital Provincial

Santiago el Viejo

Los Aljibes

Ayuntamiento

PLAZA VIEJA

PLAZA CONSTITUCIÓN

San Juan

Alcazaba

PLAZA DE ISAGESTEBAN

Gobierno Militar

PLAZA CHAFARINAS

Muralla de San Cristóbal

CERRO DE SAN CRISTÓBAL

N

Madrid & Málaga

Motril & Málaga

Almería

ALMERÍA is a pleasant, modern city, spread at the foot of a stark grey mountain in the heart of Almería province. Once you've seen the stunning Moorish Alcazaba, an austere Catedral and a wonderfully presented archeological museum there's not a lot left to do. Any time left over is probably best devoted to sampling the cafés, tapas bars and terrazas in the streets circling the Puerta de Purchena, the focal junction of the modern town, or strolling along the main Paseo de Almería down towards the harbour and taking day-trips out to the beaches along the coast. The city's own **beach**, southeast of the centre beyond the train lines, is long but nothing special.

The Alcazaba

April to mid-June Tues–Sat 10am–8.30pm, Sun 10am–5pm; mid-June to mid-Sept Tues–Sun 10am–5pm; mid-Sept to March Tues–Sat 10am–6.30pm, Sun 10am–5pm • €1.50, free with EU passport • ☎ 950 801 008

At the summit of the stark, grey hill overlooking the city is a tremendous **Alcazaba**, probably the best surviving example of Moorish military fortification in Spain, with three huge walled enclosures, in the second of which are the remains of a mosque, converted to a chapel by the Reyes Católicos. In the eleventh century, when Almería was an independent kingdom and the wealthiest, most commercially active city of Spain, this citadel contained immense gardens and palaces and some twenty thousand people. Its grandeur was reputed to rival the court of Granada, but comparisons are impossible since little beyond the walls and towers remains, the last remnants of its stuccowork having been sold off by the locals in the eighteenth century.

From the Alcazaba, you get a good view of the coast, of Almería's **cave quarter** – the Barrio de la Chanca on a low hill to the left – and of the city's strange, fortified **Catedral**.

The Catedral

Mon–Fri 10am–1.30pm & 4–5pm, Sat 10am–1.30pm • €5 • ☎ 669 913 628

Like the Alcazaba, the **Catedral**, in the heart of the old quarter, also has a fortress look about it. Begun in 1524 on the site of the great mosque – conveniently destroyed by the 1522 earthquake – it was designed in the late Gothic style by Diego de Siloé, the architect of the Catedral at Granada. Inside, the sober Gothic **interior** is distinguished by some superb sixteenth-century choir stalls carved in walnut by Juan de Orea and a stunning eighteenth-century altar. The church also contains a number of fine **pasos** of the Passion carried in the Semana Santa processions at Easter; among these, *El Prendimiento* (the Arrest of Christ) is outstanding.

Museo Arqueológico

Carretera de Ronda 91 • Mid-June to mid-Sept Tues–Sun 10am–5pm; mid-Sept to mid-June Tues–Sat 10am–8.30pm, Sun 10am–5pm • €1.50, free with EU passport • ☎ 950 100 409

Almería's splendid and recently constructed **Museo Arqueológico** is worth a visit for its impressive collection of important artefacts from the prehistoric site of Los Millares, as well as interesting Roman and Moorish collections, including some fine Moorish ceramics.

ARRIVAL AND INFORMATION   ALMERÍA

By air Almería's international airport is 8km out of town with a connecting bus service (#22, labelled "El Alquián") every 1hr 10min (between 6.45am–9.45pm) from the junction of Avda. Federico García Lorca and C/Gregorio Marañón.

By train Almería's bus and train stations (☎ 902 320 320) have been combined into a striking Estación Intermodal, on Carretera de Ronda, a couple of blocks east of Avda. de Federico García Lorca, with the bus terminals and train platforms side by side.

Destinations Granada (4 daily; 2hr 20min); Seville (4 daily; 5hr 40min).

By bus Almería's bus station (☎ 950 170 050) has frequent connections with provincial and regional destinations.

Destinations Agua Amarga (1 daily; 1hr 30min); Cabo de Gata/San José (3 daily; 55min); Carboneras (3 daily Mon–Fri, 1 daily weekends; 1hr 15min); Córdoba (1 daily; 5hr); Granada (5 daily; 2hr); Jaén (3 daily; 3hr); Madrid (19 daily; 7hr 30min); Málaga (7 daily; 3hr 15min); Mojácar (5 daily; 1hr 15min); Nijar (5 daily Mon–Fri, 2 daily weekends; 35min); Seville (3 daily; 5hr 30min); Tabernas (7 daily; 40min); Ugíjar (1 daily; 2hr 45min).

By ferry There are boats to Melilla and Nador on the Moroccan coast throughout summer (fewer out of season), a journey that can pay dividends in both time and money Algeciras (in comparison to) if you're driving (daily; 8hr 30min Melilla, 5hr Nador). For information and tickets, contact Compañía Trasmediterránea, Parque Nicolás Salmerón 19, near the port (☎ 902 454 645, ⊛ trasmediterranea.es). A useful site for checking the latest ferry schedules is ⊛ directferries.co.uk.

Turismo On C/Parque de Nicolás Salmerón (Mon–Fri 9am–7.30pm, Oct–May 8.30am–2pm, Sat & Sun 9.30am–3pm; ☎ 950 175 220). They have local and regional information plus a list of most buses out of Almería, as well as train and boat schedules.

ACCOMMODATION

Albergue Juvenil Almería C/Isla de Fuerteventura s/n ☎ 955 035 886, ⊛ inturjoven.com. A swish 150-double-room affair on the east side of town next to the Estadio Juventud sports arena; take bus #1 from the junction of Avda. Federico García Lorca and C/Gregorio Marañon. Under-26 **€22**, over-26 **€26**

Camping La Garrofa Carretera Nacional 340 km 435 ☎ 950 235 770, ⊛ lagarrofa.com. The city's nearest campsite is sited on the coast at La Garrofa, some 5km west, easily reached by the buses to Aguadulce and Roquetas de Mar. **€25**

Hostal Estación C/Calzada de Castro 37 ☎ 950 267 239, ⊛ hostalestacion.com. Situated close to the train and bus stations, and offering decently furnished en-suite rooms and garage parking. **€40**

Hotel La Perla Pza. del Carmen 7 ☎ 950 238 877, ⊛ www.hotellaperla.es. The city's oldest hotel once played host to big-name stars making Westerns at Mini Hollywood. Offers pleasant a/c rooms with satellite TV; some at the rear can be rather cramped, so check what you're offered. **€56**

Hotel Sevilla C/Granada 25 ☎ 950 230 009, ⊛ hotelsevillaalmeria.com. Welcoming, modern, small hotel with en-suite rooms equipped with a/c and TV. **€42**

Torreluz Central & Nuevo Torreluz Pza. Flores 8 & 10 ☎ 950 234 399, ⊛ torreluz.es. One of the town's leading hotels contains good-value two- and four-star (€54) options in the same complex. Aimed at the corporate sector, the rather staidly furnished rooms underline this. **€40**

EATING AND DRINKING

Almería has a surprising number of interesting and good-value places to **eat and drink**, and you get a **free tapa with every drink**. Most of the best are around the Puerta de Purchena and in the web of narrow streets lying between the Paseo de Almería and the Catedral.

Bodega Aranda Rambla del Obispo Orbera 8 ☎ 950 237 597. Great tapas bar which fairly hums at lunch times when local professionals come to grab a bite. In former days this was the "sordid" *pensión* where a penurious Gerald Brenan put up in 1921 (sleeping six to a room) while waiting for a letter with money from England – which never came. Main dishes €8–14. Mon–Thurs, Sat & Sun 9am–4.30pm, Fri 9am–11pm.

★**Casa Puga** Corner of C/Lope de Vega and C/Jovellanos ⊛ barcasapuga.es. With hams hanging from the ceiling, marble-topped tables and walls covered with *azulejos*, this is an outstanding tapas bar – founded in 1870 – with a great atmosphere and loyal clientele; try the *atún en escabeche* (marinated tuna) or *boquerones en vinagre* (fresh anchovies in vinegar). Main dishes €8–15. Mon–Sat noon–4pm & 8.30pm–midnight.

★**El Quinto Toro** C/Reyes Católicos 6 ☎ 950 239 135.

Top-notch atmospheric tapas bar taking its name from the fifth bull in the *corrida* (reputed to always be the best). Friendly service and mouthwatering *patatas a lo pobre con huevo* (potatoes with fried egg). Main dishes €8–21. Mon–Sat 1.30am–4pm & 8pm–midnight.

Taberna Nuestra Tierra C/Jovellanos 16 ☎ 679 897 432. Great tapas and *raciones* made with local ingredients only; house specials are *ventresca de atún con ajoblanco* (tuna) and *revuelto de morcilla con piñones* (black pudding with pine nuts). Main dishes €5–18. Daily 7.30am–4pm & 8pm–midnight.

★**Tetería-Restaurante Almedína** C/Paz 2 ☎ 629 277 827. Very friendly little Moroccan-run *tetería* which serves full meals later in the day, including couscous and chicken and lamb tagines. Stages live concerts of flamenco and North African music on Saturdays. Main dishes €10–15. Tues–Sun 1–11pm.

Mini Hollywood

Daily: April–Oct 10am–6pm; May–June & Sept 10am–7pm; July & Aug 10am–9pm • €22, under-12s €12.50 • ☎ 902 533 532,
Ⓦ www.oasysparquetematico.com • Buses from Almería's Intermodal bus-train station to Tabernas stop at Mini Hollywood on the
outward journey, but not on the return so you need to get a taxi to Tabernas from Mini Hollywood (about €6)

The N340a northwest from Almería towards Tabernas follows the Andarax riverbed
before forking right into the badlands, an area resembling Arizona, which looks as if it
should be the backdrop for a Hollywood Western. Just beyond the fork, at **Oasys Mini
Hollywood**, you discover that someone else had the same idea first. This is a full-blown
Western movie set, and a visit here is hard to resist – especially if you're travelling with
kids – although it's probably better value if you time your arrival to coincide with one
of the shows. Once inside you can walk around the set of *A Fistful of Dollars* and
various other spaghetti Westerns that were filmed here, and wander down Main Street
into the *Tombstone Gulch* saloon for a drink. The fantasy is carried a step further with
acted-out "shows" (11am, 3pm & 6pm), when actors in full cowboy rig blast off
six-guns during a mock bank raid or re-enact the "capture, escape and final shooting of
Jesse James". The complex has also added a somewhat incongruous **zoo**, featuring birds
and reptiles, as well as rhinos, lions and other big cats prowling around depressingly
small cages. Further along the same road is another movie location, Fort Bravo (aka
Texas Hollywood where an episode of *Doctor Who* was filmed in 2012), with similar
features (plus an Indian tepee village and Mexican town), opening hours and prices.

Níjar

Following the A7 east from Almería brings you, after 24km, to the turn-off for **NÍJAR**,
famed throughout Andalucía for its pottery. A neat, white and typically Almerian town,
with – in the upper *barrio* – narrow streets designed to give maximum shade, it makes for
an interesting visit inland from the coast and Parque Natural de Cabo de Gata to the south.

Níjar is firmly on the tourist trail owing to the inexpensive **handmade pottery**
manufactured in workshops and sold in the shops along the broad main street – Avda.
García Lorca – and C/Real to the west, where many of the potters have their
workshops. The more authentic potters, however, are located in the **barrio alfarero**,
along C/Real running parallel to the main street, where the workshops of Granados, El
Oficio and the friendly and cheaper Angel y Loli (at no. 54) are located; also, in a tiny
street off the southern end of C/Real, is the studio-shop (named "La Tienda de los
Milagros") of talented English ceramic artist Matthew Weir. Níjar is known, too, for its
jarapas: quilts, curtains and rugs made from rags, and widely on sale around the town.

INFORMATION	NÍJAR
Turismo At the junction of C/Real with Avda. García Lorca (June–Sept Mon–Sun 10am–2pm & 4–8pm; Oct–May	Mon–Sat 10am–2pm & 4–8pm; ☎ 950 612 243, Ⓦwww .nijar.es); it can provide literature on the town and region.

ACCOMMODATION AND EATING

Cortijo La Alberca North of the town, Camino del Huebro ☎ 619 665 931, Ⓦ cortijolaalberca.com. Homely en-suite rooms with mountains views. B&B. **€80** **La Mandila** On the bend to the upper square at no. 17 ☎ 950 106 299. Spanish meets Venezuelan cuisine at this new arrival, which has a terrace overlooking the mountains.	Main dishes €7–19. Daily 11am–midnight. **El Pipa** Pza. La Glorieta ☎ 627 313 679. The best of the bunch of the tapas and *raciones* bars in the upper square, Pza. La Glorieta, beyond the church. Main dishes €5–12. Mon–Thurs 7.15am–5pm, Fri–Sun 7.15am–midnight; closed Nov.

The Costa de Almería

Almería's best **beaches** lie along its eastern coast, the Costa de Almería. Those to the
west of the city, particularly surrounding the "ugly sisters" resorts of Aguadulce and

Roquetas de Mar, have already been exploited, and what remains is rapidly being covered with *invernaderos*, or plastic tents, for fruit and vegetable production. In stark contrast, the eastern stretch of the Almerian coastline offers some of the most relaxing beaches left in Spain: half-abandoned fishing communities that have only begun to be promoted for tourists relatively recently. Outside the centres of **Mojácar** and **San José** development is low-key, and with a short walk along the coast you should be able to find plenty of relatively secluded spots to lay your towel.

El Cabo de Gata

The closest resort with any appeal is the modest **EL CABO DE GATA**, inside the **Parque Natural de Cabo de Gata**, where there is a long expanse of coarse sand. Six buses a day run between here and Almería. Arriving at El Cabo, you pass a lake, the **Laguna de Rosa**, protected by a conservation society and home to flamingos and other waders throughout the summer. Around the resort are plentiful bars, cafés and shops, plus a fish market. The beach gets windy in the afternoons, and it's a deceptively long walk eastwards to **Las Salinas** (The Salt Pans) for a couple of bar-restaurants and a café.

A few kilometres south of here, the **Faro de Cabo de Gata** (lighthouse) marks the cape's southern tip. There's also a **mirador** here from where you can get a great view of the rock cliffs and – on clear days – Morocco's Rif mountains.

INFORMATION   EL CABO DE GATA

Information In the lighthouse car park an information cabin (June–Sept daily 11am–3pm & 6–8pm, August daily 11am–3pm & 6–9pm; March–May & Oct–Dec Sat & Sun 11am–3pm & 4–6pm) has maps and information on the natural park.

ACCOMMODATION

Camping Cabo de Gata Carretera Cabo de Gata s/n, on the coast 2km northwest of the village ☎ 950 160 443, ⓦ campingcabodegata.com. Decent campsite with reasonable, if not plentiful, shade and where facilities include a pool and restaurant. **€25.50**

Hostal Las Dunas C/Barrio Nuevo 58 ☎ 950 370 072, ⓦ hostallasdunas.es. Some 100m inland from the seafront, this friendly option has functional a/c en-suite rooms with TVs. **€55**

San José

SAN JOSÉ is an established and popular family resort, set back from a sandy beach in a small cove, with shallow water. More fine **beaches** lie within easy walking distance and one of the best – Playa de los Genoveses – a kilometre-long golden strand, can be reached by a track to the southwest.

ARRIVAL AND INFORMATION   SAN JOSÉ

By bus San José is served by three daily buses to and from Almería, with a journey time of 55min.
By road Although it's possible to hike to the resort along a coastal track from the Faro de Cabo de Gata (lighthouse), this is now closed to vehicles. Going by road entails retracing your route to the resort of El Cabo de Gata and then following the inland road via the village of El Pozo de los Frailes.
Information On the main street, Avda. de San José, near the centre of the village, you'll find a Centro de Información for El Cabo de Gata natural park (Mon–Sat 10am–2pm & 5.30–8.30pm, Sun 10am–2pm; ☎ 950 380 299), which has lots of information on guided walks and horse treks, plus a complete list of accommodation.

ACCOMMODATION

Accommodation can be hard to come by in summer, but outside high season (July & Aug only and the rate we quote) prices fall sharply.

Albergue Juvenil C/Montemar s/n ☎ 950 380 353, ⓦ alberguesanjose.com. This privately run youth hostel has 86 places divided between rooms sleeping from two to six persons. It is usually booked solid at

Easter and in August. €14

Cortijo El Sotillo Carretera San José s/n ☎ 950 61 11 00, ⓦ cortijoelsotillo.es. A kilometre from the centre, this refurbished eighteenth-century ranch-house converted into a four-star country hotel has elegant rustically furnished rooms, an excellent mid-priced restaurant, bar, pool, tennis courts, and stables with horses for hire. €158

Hostal Aloha C/Cala Higuera s/n ☎ 950 611 050, ⓦ hostalaloha.com. Refurbished *hostal* with excellent a/c en-suite rooms and the bonus of a fine palm-fringed pool at the rear; they also have a very good restaurant and tapas bar below. €85

Hostal Brisa Mar C/Ancla s/n ☎ 950 380 431, ⓦ hostalbrisamar.com. To the left of the main road as you come in, this is a bright and airy option with a/c en-suite balcony rooms with TVs and a pretty garden. €73

Hostal Sol Bahía C/Correos 5 ☎ 950 380 306, ⓦ solbahiasanjose.es. Near the main junction in the centre of the village, this is one of the better-value central places, offering spacious a/c en-suite balcony rooms with TV. €70

Hotel Agades Agidir C/Córdoba s/n ☎ 950 380 390, ⓦ hotelagades.com. Very pleasant option with a/c en-suite balcony rooms with satellite TVs, plus garden pool, bar and restaurant. Sited on the right-hand side of the main road as you enter San José and a 5min walk from the village. €95

EATING AND DRINKING

There are numerous **places to eat** around the beach and harbour zones, plus some well-stocked supermarkets. For fresh fish, try the restaurants overlooking the harbour.

4 Nudos Puerto Deportivo ☎ 620 938 160. This is a harbourside restaurant where rice dishes (e.g. *arroz meloso con bogavante* – rice with lobster) and fresh fish are house specials. It also does meat dishes and has a pleasant terrace. Main dishes €12–22. April–Oct daily 9am–midnight; Nov–March Tues–Fri 11am–8pm, Sat & Sun 9am–5pm & 7pm–midnight.

Bar-Restaurante El Emigrante C/Correo s/n ☎ 950 380 307. Near the village's main junction, this is a friendly and good-value place facing the *Hostal Sol Bahía*; it offers a variety of fish and meat *platos combinados*, also does tapas and has a menu for €12. Main dishes €6–16. Daily 9am–4pm & 7pm–midnight.

Restaurante Mediterráneo Puerto Deportivo ☎ 950 380 093. Also on the harbourside and with an inviting terrace, this is another reliable fish restaurant which also does tasty rice dishes, salads and couscous. Main dishes €7–16. Daily noon–5pm & 7–11pm.

Los Escullos, La Isleta and Las Negras

The isolated and peaceful resort of **LOS ESCULLOS**, has a reasonable sandy beach fronted by a formidable eighteenth-century fort, the refurbished **Castillo de San Felipe**.

Two kilometres farther east is **LA ISLETA**, another fishing hamlet, with a sleepy atmosphere and bags of charm. There's a rather scruffy village beach but a much better one a few minutes' walk away in the next bay to the east – the Playa la Ola.

LAS NEGRAS, 5km farther on, is another place with a decidedly Spanish feel, where there's a cove with a pebbly beach and a few bars and restaurants.

ACCOMMODATION   LOS ESCULLOS, LA ISLETA AND LAS NEGRAS

Arrecife C/Bahía 6, Las Negras ☎ 950 388 140. This is an attractive and good-value *hostal* with a/c en-suite sea-view rooms with terrace balconies. €51

La Caleta Las Negras ☎ 950 525 237, ⓦ camping lacaleta.com. A campsite set in a tranquil location with its own bay, reached via a signed 1km road just outside the village. Facilities include minimarket, pool and bar-restaurant. €24.80

Camping Los Escullos Los Escullos ☎ 950 389 811, ⓦ losescullossanjose.com. Campsite set back from the sea with limited shade; facilities include bar-restaurant, pool and games courts. €25.70

Casa Emilio Los Escullos ☎ 950 389 761, ⓦ hostal casaemilio.es. Close to the beach, this is a pleasant *hostal-restaurante* offering a/c en-suite rooms with terrace balcony above a decent restaurant. B&B. €60

Hostal Isleta de Moro La Isleta ☎ 951 389 713. Overlooking the harbour, this *hostal* has reasonably priced en-suite balcony rooms with sea views, plus a popular bar-restaurant below for tapas and good fish meals. €50

Agua Amarga

There's no road from Las Negras to Agua Amarga (10km north as the crow flies); to reach it by road you'll need to head 5km inland to the village of Fernan Pérez from where a narrow road heads east for 11km to reach the small resort. Agua Amarga is served by just one daily direct **bus** from Almería.

AGUA AMARGA is a one-time fishing hamlet that has transformed itself into a pleasant and easy-going resort. A fine sand EU-blue-flagged beach is the main attraction, and this is backed by a tasteful crop of villas.

ACCOMMODATION AND EATING	AGUA AMARGA

Apartamentos Caparrós C/Aguada 13 ☎ 950 138 246, ⓦ costamarga2002.es. This proprietor has a variety of fully equipped apartments, sleeping up to four, around the resort, most only a few metres from the beach. **€90**

Hotel Family C/La Lomilla 6 ☎ 950 138 014, ⓦ hotelfamily.es. The best-value place to stay is this welcoming French-run *hostal*, set back from the south end of the beach. It has comfortable tile-floored rooms, a pool and a very good French–Spanish restaurant with an excellent-value menu for €23. B&B. **€89**

Hotel El Tío Kiko C/Embarque 12 ☎ 950 138 080, ⓦ eltiokiko.com. One of a clutch of luxury places here, this is a boutique, adult-only hotel with terrace sea-view rooms arranged around a pool. B&B. **€175**

Hotel las Calas C/Desagüe 1a ☎ 950 138 016, near Hotel Family. The restaurant of this hotel offers a selection of reasonably priced fish and rice-based dishes such as *arroz con bogavante* (lobster). Main dishes €10–20. Daily 1.30–4pm & 8pm–midnight.

Restaurante La Palmera C/Aguada 4 ☎ 950 138 208. With its terrace fronting the beach this is another popular seafood restaurant where paella features as a house special. Main dishes €11–20. Daily 9am–11pm.

Los Tarahis C/Desagüe s/n ☎ 950 138 235. With a sea-view terrace, this is a decent place serving fish and *arroces* (such as paellas) as well as salads. Main dishes €9–19. May–Oct daily 10am–11pm.

Mojácar

MOJÁCAR is eastern Almería's main resort, hugely popular with Spaniards and foreign visitors throughout summer. The coastal strip takes its name from the ancient hill village that lies a couple of kilometres back from the sea – Mojácar Pueblo – a striking agglomeration of white cubist houses wrapped round a harsh outcrop of rock. In the 1960s, when the main Spanish *costas* were being developed, this was virtually a ghost town, its inhabitants having long since taken the only logical step and emigrated. The town's fortunes suddenly revived, however, when the local mayor, using the popularity of other equally barren spots in Spain as an example, offered free land to anyone willing to build within a year. The scheme was a modest success, attracting one of the decade's multifarious "artist colonies", now long supplanted by package-holiday companies and second-homers. The long and sandy **beach**, down at the development known as Mojácar Playa, is excellent and the waters (like all in Almería) are warm and brilliantly clear.

Mojácar Pueblo

MOJÁCAR PUEBLO is linked to the coastal resort 2km below by a road that climbs from a prominent seafront junction called "El Cruce"; hourly **buses** also make the climb from here until 11.30pm, after which it's a punishing hike or a taxi. The village is more about atmosphere than sights, and once you've cast an eye over the heavily restored fifteenth-century church of **Santa María**, the main diversion is to wander the narrow streets with their flower-decked balconies and cascading bougainvillea, and call in at the numerous boutiques and bars.

INFORMATION	MOJÁCAR

Turismo Pza. Fronton, opposite the church of Santa María (June–Sept Mon–Fri 10am–2pm & 5–7pm, Sat & Sun 10am–1pm; Oct–May Mon–Fri 10am–2pm & 4–6pm, Sat & Sun 10am–1pm; ☎ 902 575 130, ⓦ mojacar.es). You'll need their free map to negotiate the maze of narrow streets.

ACCOMMODATION AND EATING

Casa Minguito Pza. del Ayuntamiento s/n ☎ 950 478 614. This long-standing restaurant, with its pleasant terrace, serves meat and fish dishes as well as a tasty paella for two for €26 or a menu for €15. Main dishes €9–20. Daily noon–4pm & 7pm–midnight;

Oct–May closed Thurs.

Hostal Arco Plaza Edificio Plaza, just off the main square ☎ 950 472 777, ⓦ hostalarcoplaza.es. Pleasant small *hostal* and a reasonable deal for a/c en-suite rooms with TV. **€45**

Hostal El Olivar C/Estación Nueva 11 ☎ 950 472 022, ⓦ hostalelolivar.es. Clean and comfortable *hostal* just round the corner from the *turismo* offering en-suite rooms with a/c and TV. The owners are friendly and helpful. B&B. €55

Rincón de Embrujo C/Alcalde Jacinto s/n ☎ 600 531 270. With a terrace on the *plazuela* fronting the church, this is a handy and economical place for *platos combinados* and *raciones* of seafood like *boquerones fritos* (fried anchovies) or *chipirones* (baby squid). Expect to pay €6–22 for a main dish. Daily 10.30am–4pm & 7pm–midnight; mid-Sept to June closed Thurs.

La Taberna Pza. del Cano s/n ☎ 950 615 106. This place, tucked under the arch, is a well-established favourite with locals and visitors, offering tapas, *raciones* and fresh fish. The *pincho cristiano* (tuna and dogfish kebab) is definitely worth trying. Expect to pay €6–15 for a main dish. Mon–Sat 1–4pm & 8–11pm, Sun 1–4pm.

Mojácar Playa

The beach resort of **MOJÁCAR PLAYA** is a refreshingly brash alternative to the upper village and caters to a mix of mainly Spanish tourists who fill its four-kilometre-long beach all summer. The busy road behind the strand is lined with hotels, restaurants and bars stretching north and south of the main junction, El Cruce, marked by a large *centro comercial*.

INFORMATION

MOJÁCAR PLAYA

Punto de información Small tourist office on the beach on El Cruce (June–Sept Mon–Fri 5–7pm, Sat 10am–1pm; Oct–May Mon Mon–Fri 10am–2pm Sat 10am–1pm; ☎ 902 575 130, ⓦ mojacar.es). The *turismo*'s map also covers the coastal strip and is a useful aid to getting your bearings.

ACCOMMODATION AND EATING

There are plenty of *hostales* and hotels lining the seafront of Mojácar Playa and outside July and August (the resort's only high-season months) prices fall by up to forty percent.

Albatros Avda. del Mediterráneo s/n, 1km south of the El Cruce junction. A beachfront *chiringuito* opposite (and owned by) the *Hotel El Puntazo*, this is a reliable place for fresh fish and *mariscos*. Main dishes €7–24. Daily 11am–midnight.

El Cantal de Mojácar Paseo Mediterráneo s/n ☎ 950 478 204. A kilometre or so south of El Cruce, this is a good campsite and not too far from the beach. €31.50

Casa Egea C/Las Ventanicas 127, 2km south of El Cruce ☎ 950 472 190. On the seafront, this is a long-established and reliable restaurant specializing in fresh fish, seafood and local specialities such as *caracoles* (snails) and stews. Main dishes €8–22. Daily 10.30am–4.30pm & 7.30–11.30pm.

Hotel El Puntazo ☎ 951 478 229, ⓦ hotelelpuntazo .com. One of the more established upmarket places for a/c sea-view terrace rooms, with minibars and safes. €99

Hotel Río Abajo ☎ 950 478 928, ⓦ rioabajomojacar .com. Some 2km north of El Cruce where the Río de Aguas meets the sea, this is a pleasant, leafy complex, extensively refurbished in 2014, with en-suite rooms actually on the beach. Has own pool and breakfast is available. €60

Hotel Sal Marina Avda. del Mediterráneo 261 ☎ 950 472 404, ⓦ hotelsalmarina.com. South of El Cruce, this is a seafront hotel with very pleasant a/c balcony rooms with sea views; drops prices by thirty percent outside July and Aug. €80

Restaurante Sal Marina Avda. del Mediterráneo 261 ☎ 950 472 404. On the landward side of the road, and attached to the hotel of the same name, this is a decent restaurant specializing in fish and seafood cuisine. Has a pleasant sea-view terrace. Main dishes €7–19. Daily 1–4pm & 7–11pm.

4

Castilla y León and La Rioja

VINEYARDS NEAR SAN VICENTE, LA RIOJA

5

Castilla y León and La Rioja

The foundations of modern Spain were laid in the kingdom of Castile. Stretching north from Madrid, and incorporated within the modern *comunidad* of Castilla y León, it's a land of frontier fortresses – the *castillos* from which it takes its name – and a vast, fertile central plateau, the 700 to 1000m-high *meseta* that is given over almost entirely to grain. Beyond the historic cities, huge areas stretch to the horizon without a single landmark, not even a tree, though each spring a vivid red carpet of poppies decorates fields and verges. The Río Duero runs right across the province and into Portugal, with the river at the heart of one of Spain's great wine-producing regions, Ribera del Duero; another, more famous wine region lies to the north in the autonomous *comunidad* of La Rioja, whose vineyards line the banks of the Río Ebro.

It was Castile that became the most powerful force of the Reconquest, extending its domination through military gains and marriage alliances. By the eleventh century, Castile had merged with and swallowed León; through Isabel's marriage to Fernando in 1469 it encompassed Aragón, Catalunya and eventually the entire peninsula. The monarchs of this triumphant age were enthusiastic patrons of the arts, endowing their cities with superlative monuments, above which, quite literally, tower the great Gothic cathedrals of **Salamanca**, **León** and **Burgos**. These three cities are the major draws of the region, though in **Valladolid**, **Zamora** and even unsung **Palencia** and **Soria** you'll find outstanding reminders of the glory days of Old Castile. But equally in many lesser towns – notably **Ciudad Rodrigo**, **El Burgo de Osma** and **Covarrubias** – you'll be struck by a wealth of art and architecture that's completely at odds with their current status.

Outside the main population centres, the sporadic and depopulated villages, bitterly cold in winter, burning hot in summer, are rarely of interest. That said, there are a few enclaves of mountain scenery, from the **Sierra de Francia** in the deep southwest to the lakeland of the **Sierra de Urbión** in the east. Moreover, the **wine region** of La Rioja has charms that go way beyond its famous product – the likeable provincial capital of **Logroño** is known for its lively tapas bars, while high in the Riojan hills are unsung mountain villages and monasteries that reward the intrepid driver.

The final feature of the region is the host of Romanesque churches, monasteries and hermitages, a legacy of the **Camino de Santiago**, the great pilgrim route from the Pyrenees to Santiago de Compostela. It cuts through La Rioja and then heads west across the upper half of Castilla y León, taking in the great cathedral cities of Burgos and León, but also many minor places of great interest, from **Frómista** in the central plains to **Astorga** and **Villafranca del Bierzo**.

LAS MÉDULAS

Highlights

❶ Universidad de Salamanca The graceful university buildings of Salamanca are an essential first stop in this most captivating of cities. **See p.378**

❷ Museo Nacional de Escultura, Valladolid The finest collection of Renaissance sculpture in Spain – housed in a magnificently restored monastic church. **See p.395**

❸ La Rioja's monasteries Take a fantastic mountain drive to the wine region's peerless monasteries. **See p.415**

❹ Dinosaur-hunting, Enciso Set out on the trail of La Rioja's 120-million-year-old dinosaurs. **See p.418**

❺ Burgos Catedral The tourist crowds can't dull the appeal of this extraordinary masterpiece of Gothic art. **See p.419**

❻ Covarrubias The Gothic church, white half-timbered houses and numerous flower boxes make this small town quaint and very charming. **See p.424**

❼ Parador Hostal de San Marcos, León A sumptuous monastery on the Santiago pilgrim route is now one of Spain's finest paradores. **See p.437**

❽ Las Médulas The devastation wreaked by Roman gold mining created an eerily captivating landscape. **See p.442**

HIGHLIGHTS ARE MARKED ON THE MAP ON PP.372–373

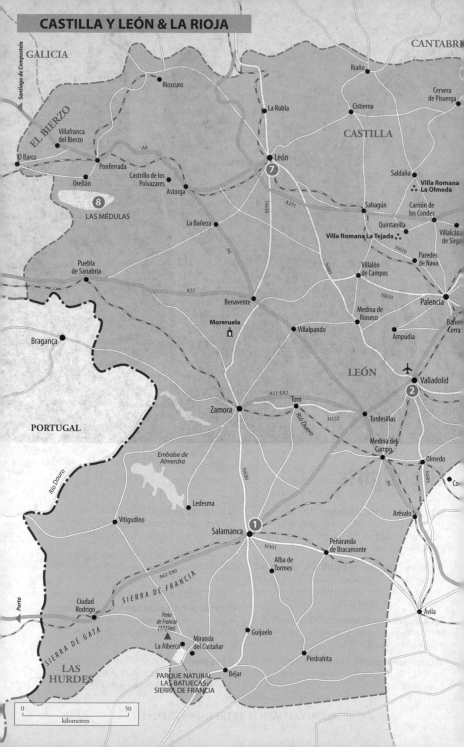

CASTILLA Y LEÓN & LA RIOJA

GALICIA

Santiago de Compostela

CANTABRI

Riaño

Cervera
de Pisuerga

EL BIERZO

Rioscuro

La Robla

Cistierna

CASTILLA

Villafranca
del Bierzo

O Barco

Ponferrada

A6

León

Saldaña

Villa Romana
La Olmeda

Orellán

Castrillo de los
Polvazares

Astorga

A231

N630

Sahagún

Carrión de
los Condes

Quintanilla

8
LAS MÉDULAS

La Bañeza

A6

Villa Romana La Tejada

N610

Villalcázar
de Sirga

Paredes
de Nava

Puebla
de Sanabria

A52

N601

Villalón
de Campos

N610

Palencia

Benavente

Medina de
Rioseco

Baños
Cerra

Bragança

Moreruela

Villalpando

Ampudia

PORTUGAL

LEÓN

Valladolid

A11-E82

Toro

2

Zamora

Río Duero

N122

Tordesillas

Embalse de
Almerdra

Medina del
Campo

Olmedo

N630

Río Douro

Ledesma

A6

N601

Co

Vitigudino

Arévalo

Porto

Salamanca

1

Peñaranda
de Bracamonte

A62-E80

SIERRA DE FRANCIA

N501

Alba de
Tormes

Ciudad
Rodrigo

Peña
de Francia
(1723m)

Guijuelo

Ávila

SIERRA DE GATA

La Alberca

Miranda
del Castañar

Piedrahita

LAS
HURDES

PARQUE NATURAL
LAS BATUECAS-
SIERRA DE FRANCIA

Béjar

0   50
kilometres

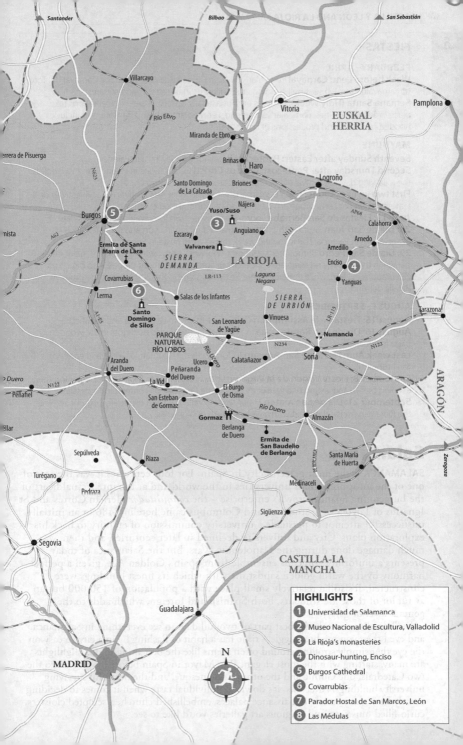

HIGHLIGHTS

1. Universidad de Salamanca
2. Museo Nacional de Escultura, Valladolid
3. La Rioja's monasteries
4. Dinosaur-hunting, Enciso
5. Burgos Cathedral
6. Covarrubias
7. Parador Hostal de San Marcos, León
8. Las Médulas

5

FIESTAS

FEBRUARY– APRIL

Week before Lent: Carnaval Particularly lively in Ciudad Rodrigo, when the Carnaval del Toro (Ⓦ carnavaldeltoro.es) sees bull-running and bullfights in the streets and squares.

Semana Santa (Holy Week): Easter is enthusiastically observed here – celebrations take place in all the big cities, particularly Valladolid, León, Salamanca and Zamora, and include hooded penitents and processions of holy statues.

MAY/JUNE

Seventh Sunday after Easter: Pentecost Week-long Feria Chica in Palencia.

Second Thursday after Pentecost: Corpus Christi Celebrations in Palencia and Valladolid; the following day, the festival of El Curpillos is celebrated in Burgos.

First two weeks of June: FACYL Salamanca's International Arts Festival (Ⓦ facyl-festival.com) features street concerts, urban art, DJ sets and neighbourhood events.

June 11: Fiestas de San Bernabé Logroño's festivities run for a week around this date.

24: Día de San Juan Fiesta with bullfighting and dancing in León and more religious observances in Palencia. The following week there's a big fiesta in Soria.

29: Día de San Pedro Burgos starts a vibrant two-week fiesta, when *gigantillos* (giant effigies) parade in the streets, and there are concerts, bullfights and all-night parties. Also big celebrations in León, while in Haro (where festivities start on the 24th) there's the drunken Batalla del Vino.

AUGUST– SEPTEMBER

August 15: Fiesta de la Assumption Colourful festivals in La Alberca and Peñafiel.

August 16: Día de San Roque Fiesta in El Burgo de Osma; also bullfights in the wooden plaza in Peñafiel.

Last week Aug: Fiesta de San Agustín In Toro, with the "fountain of wine" and *encierros* (bull-running).

September 8: Fiesta Virgen de la Vega First day of the fiesta in Salamanca, beginning the evening before and lasting two weeks, as well as the famous bull-running in Tordesillas.

September 21: Día de San Mateo Major *ferias* in Valladolid and especially Logroño, where the Rioja harvest is celebrated with a week's worth of high jinks.

Salamanca

SALAMANCA is the most graceful city in Spain. For four centuries it was the seat of one of the most prestigious universities in the world and at the intellectual heart of the burgeoning Spanish crown's enterprise – the *conquistador* Hernán Cortés and St Ignatius of Loyola were students, and Columbus came here in 1486 in an initially unsuccessful attempt to persuade a university commission of enquiry to back his exploration plans. City and university declined in later centuries, and there was much damage done during the Napoleonic Wars, but the Salamanca of today presents a uniformly gorgeous ensemble from Spain's Golden Age, given a perfect harmony by the warm golden sandstone with which its finest buildings were constructed. It's still a relatively small place with a population of 150,000 but an awful lot of those are students, both Spanish and foreign, which adds to the general level of gaiety.

You'll need to set aside the best part of two full days to see everything in Salamanca, and even then you might struggle – time has a habit of flashing by in a city so easy on the eye that simply strolling around often seems like the best thing to do. Highlights are many, starting with the most elegant Pza. Mayor in Spain before moving on to the two Catedrals, one Gothic and the other Romanesque, and the beautiful surviving university buildings. After this, it's down to individual taste when it comes to deciding exactly how many stately Renaissance palaces, embellished churches, sculpted cloisters, curio-filled museums and religious art galleries you'd like to see.

Plaza Mayor

The grand **Plaza Mayor** is the hub of Salamantine life. Its vast central expanse is enclosed by a continuous four-storey building, broken only by the grand *ayuntamiento* (city hall) on its northern side. The building was the work of Andrea García Quiñones and of Alberto Churriguera, younger brother of José, and nowhere is the Churrigueras' inspired variation of Baroque (see box, p.380) so refined as here. Cafés, restaurants and small shops ring the arcades, and some *pensiones* and hotels occupy parts of the upper storeys, but signs, advertising, lights and other modern clutter are not allowed to intrude upon the harmonious facades. Right around the arcades, facing out into the square, are medallion portraits of Spain's nobility and royalty through the ages, including the current king and queen and, a more surprising survivor, that of "Franco, Caudillo de España" (northeast corner, above *Confitería Madrileña*).

Mercado Central

Pza. del Mercado • Daily 8am–2pm

Arches from Pza. Mayor lead out into the surrounding shopping streets, including, on the east side, to Pza. del Mercado and the red-brick-and-iron **Mercado Central**. The city's small two-tier market is a good place for picnic provisions, and it's surrounded on all sides by lively restaurants and tapas bars.

Convento y Museo de las Úrsulas

C/Las Úrsulas, entrance near Campo de San Francisco • Tues–Sun 11am–1pm & 4.30–6pm; closed last Sun of month • €2 • ☎ 923 219 877

The unusual open-topped tower of the **Convento y Museo de las Úrsulas** rises above a charming quarter west of Pza. Mayor. Inside, sitting in the dark, cheery Franciscan nuns scrabble for change for the rare visitor and then turn on the lights so that you can inspect the primitive artworks, including the portrait of Úrsula herself – a Romano-British princess of the fourth century AD, martyred by the Huns while on pilgrimage to Rome. Look up for the greater treasure – the impressive, decorated, coffered ceiling – and on the way out examine the superb marble **tomb of Archbishop Alonso Fonseca**, founder of the convent.

Casa de las Muertes

C/Bordadores • No public access

Facing the east wall of the Convento de las Úrsulas is the impressive Plateresque facade of the **Casa de las Muertes** (House of the Dead), the mansion of leading Salamantine architect Juan de Álava, named for the four small skulls at the base of the upper windows.

CASTILIAN CUISINE

It often seems like there's part of a pig, sheep or a cow on every plate in **Castile** – steaks can be gargantuan, the traditional roast meats, found everywhere, are *cochinillo* (suckling pig), *lechazo* (lamb) and *cabrito* (kid), while hearty Castilian appetites think nothing of limbering up first with a thick *sopa castellano*, usually containing chickpeas or white haricot beans, both staple crops from the *meseta*. In **Salamanca province**, *jamones* (hams) and *embutidos* (sausages) are at their best; in **Burgos** it's *morcilla* (black pudding) that's king. If you're feeling faint at the thought of so much meat – and Castilian menus can, truth be told, get a little monotonous – then the legendary tapas bars of **León** and **Logroño** ride to the rescue, where bite-sized morsels, from cuttlefish to mushrooms, offer a change of pace and diet. Only really in **La Rioja** does the traditional, heavy Castilian diet give way to something lighter and more varied. The rivers that irrigate the vines also mean freshwater fish, particularly trout, while La Rioja is the one part of the region where the contemporary Spanish foodie buzz has secured a real foothold.

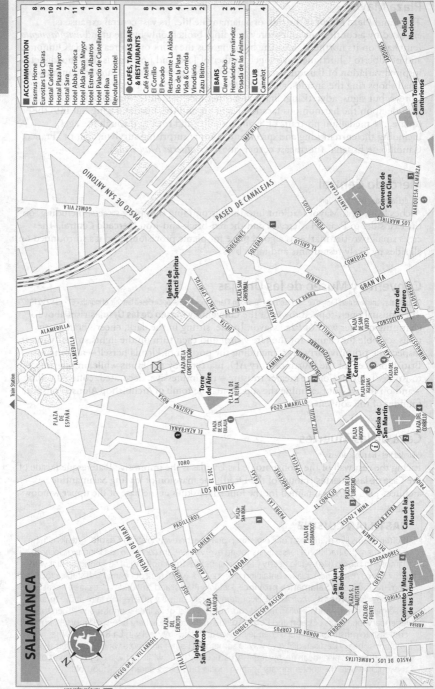

SALAMANCA

ACCOMMODATION	
Erasmus Home	8
Eurostars Las Claras	3
Hostal Catedral	10
Hostal Plaza Mayor	2
Hostal Sara	7
Hotel Abba Fonseca	11
Hotel Alda Plaza Mayor	4
Hotel Estrella Albatros	1
Hotel Palacio de Castellanos	9
Hotel Rua	6
Revolutum Hostel	5

CAFÉS, TAPAS BARS & RESTAURANTS	
Café Atelier	8
El Corrillo	7
El Pecado	3
Restaurante La Aldaba	6
Río de la Plata	4
Vida & Comida	5
Zazu Bistro	2

BARS	
Clavel Ocho	2
Hernández y Fernández	3
Posada de las Ánimas	1

CLUB	
Camelot	4

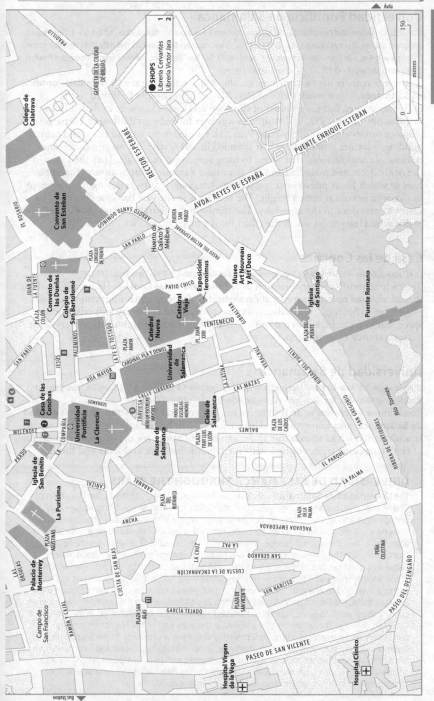

▲ Ávila

● SHOPS
1 Librería Cervantes
2 Librería Víctor Jara

0   150
metres

5

Universidad Pontifícia de Salamanca

C/La Compañía • **Universidad Pontifícia** Mon–Fri 10.30am–12.45pm & 5–6.30pm, Sat–Sun 10.30am–1.30pm & 5–7.15pm; Spanish-only guided tours set off every 45 minutes • €3 • ☎ 923 277 100, 🖳 www.upsa.es • **Scala Coeli** Dec–Feb daily 10am–6pm (last entrance 5.15pm), March–Nov daily 10am–8pm (last entrance 7.15pm) • €3.75, free Tues 10am–noon, combined ticket to Universidad Pontifícia, Clerecía and Scala Coeli €6 • ☎ 923 277 174, 🖳 torresdelaclerecia.com

Salamanca actually has two universities, the minor one being the **Universidad Pontifícia de Salamanca**, a short walk south of Pza. Mayor. It was originally linked to the university proper, but the faculties of theology and canon law were excluded from the main institution in 1852, and Pontificía was later formally established as a separate religious university in 1940 by Pope Pius XII. Guided tours around the grand central building, a former Jesuit college first founded in 1617, start at a magnificent stone staircase, *la escalera noble*, that seems to hang suspended in the air. They then take in the richly decorated main hall and the grandiose Baroque cloister, around the upper level of which Jesuit priests once walked meditational circuits, believing themselves to be closer to heaven at such a height. The tour ends in the vast Baroque church of **La Clerecía**, next door to the university. The climb up the church towers – **Scala Coeli**, or Stairway to Heaven – is worth the effort for the magnificent views of the city.

Casa de las Conchas

C/La Compañía 2 • Mon–Fri 9am–9pm, Sat 9am–2pm & 4–7pm, Sun 10am–2pm & 4–7pm • Free • ☎ 923 269 317

The early sixteenth-century mansion called the **Casa de las Conchas** (House of Shells) is named after the rows of carved scallop shells that decorate its facade, symbol of the pilgrimage to Santiago. The building is now partly a public library and exhibition space, but you can look into the courtyard and enjoy a good view of the towers of La Clerecía church from the upper storey.

Universidad de Salamanca

C/Libreros • April–June Mon–Sat 10am–8pm, Sun 10am–2pm; July–Sept Mon–Sat 10am–2pm & 5–8.30pm, Sun 10am–2pm; Oct–March Mon–Sat 10am–7pm, Sun 10am–2pm • €10, free for under-12s • ☎ 923 294 400, 🖳 usal.es

You'll know when you've arrived at Salamanca's central honey-trap, the **Universidad de Salamanca**, also known as the Universidad Civil, by the milling tour groups, all straining their necks to examine the magnificent facade. It's the ultimate expression of the Plateresque style, covered with medallions, heraldic emblems and floral

UNIVERSIDAD DE SALAMANCA THROUGH THE YEARS

The **Universidad de Salamanca** was founded by Alfonso IX in 1218, and, after the union of Castile and León, became the most important in Spain. Its rise to international stature was phenomenal, and within forty years Pope Alexander IV proclaimed it equal to the greatest universities of the day. As at Oxford, Paris and Bologna, theories formulated here were later accepted as fact throughout Europe. The university continued to flourish under the Reyes Católicos, and in the sixteenth century it was powerful enough to resist the orthodoxy of Felipe II's Inquisition, but eventually, freedom of thought was stifled by the extreme clericalism of the seventeenth and eighteenth centuries. Books were banned for being a threat to the Catholic faith, and mathematics and medicine disappeared from the curriculum. During the Peninsular War, the French demolished 20 of the 25 colleges, and by the end of the nineteenth century there were no more than three hundred students (compared to 6500 in the late sixteenth century). The university saw a revival in the early part of the twentieth century, particularly under the rectorship of celebrated philosopher and man of letters Miguel de Unamuno. Today, numbers are higher than ever (around 30,000 students) and Salamanca Uni has a certain social cachet, though academically it ranks well behind Madrid, Barcelona and Seville. It does, however, run the highly successful Cursos Internacionales language school – nowhere else in Spain will you find so many young foreigners.

decorations, amid which lurks a hidden frog said to bring good luck and marriage within the year to anyone who spots it unaided. The centre of the facade is occupied by a portrait of Isabel and Fernando, surrounded by a Greek inscription commemorating their devotion to the university. There are several sections to visit, though the fee paid at the main entrance covers just the tour of the main building's lecture rooms and library.

Aula Fray Luís de León and library

The university's old lecture rooms are arranged around a courtyard. The **Aula Fray Luís de León** preserves the rugged original benches and the pulpit where this celebrated professor lectured. In 1572, the Inquisition muscled its way into the room and arrested Fray Luís for alleged subversion of the faith; four years of torture and imprisonment followed, but upon his release he calmly resumed his lecture with the words, "As we were saying yesterday..."

An elegant Plateresque stairway leads to the upper storey, where you'll find the old university **library**, stuffed with thousands of antiquated books on wooden shelves and huge globes of the world. There's a faded magnificence here, which gives some idea of Renaissance Salamanca's academic splendour.

Museo de Salamanca

Patio de las Escuelas 2 • July–Sept Tues–Sat 5–8pm, Sun 10am–2pm; Oct–June Tues–Sat 10am–2pm & 4–7pm, Sun 10am–2pm • €1.20, free weekends

Across from the university entrance is a small, enclosed square housing the **Museo de Salamanca**. This occupies an exquisite fifteenth-century mansion – originally the home of Isabel's personal physician – which is at least as interesting as the collection of Spanish religious paintings and sculpture contained within.

Cielo de Salamanca

Patio de Escuelas Menores • April–Sept Mon–Sat 10am–2pm & 4–8pm; Oct–March Mon–Sat 10am–2pm & 4–7pm • Free

At the back of the Patio de Escuelas, a beautifully sculpted double arch leads through to the cloistered Renaissance courtyard of the **Escuelas Menores**, which served as a kind of preparatory school for the university proper. A succession of weekend newlyweds pose here for photographs while, on the far side of the courtyard is the entrance to the **Cielo de Salamanca**, a remarkable zodiacal ceiling that was once housed in the university chapel. As your eyes adjust to the light, centaurs, serpents and the Grim Reaper all come into focus amid the twinkling stars.

Catedral Nueva

Entrance on C/Cardenal Pla y Deniel • April–Sept daily 9am–7.15pm; Oct–March daily 10am–5.15pm • €4.75 (for both Catedral Vieja & Nueva) • ☎ 923 217 476, ⓦ catedralsalamanca.org

You can't really tell from the outside, but Salamanca has two Catedrals – the earlier, Romanesque **Catedral Vieja**, or "old cathedral", is dwarfed by its **Catedral Nueva** ("new cathedral") neighbour. The latter, begun in 1513, was a glorious last-minute assertion of Gothic architecture. However, for financial reasons, construction eventually spanned two centuries and thus the building incorporates a range of styles. The main entrance on C/Cardenal Pla y Deniel is contemporary with that of the university and equally dazzling in its wealth of ornamental detail. Inside, when you stand under the dome, you can clearly see the transition from plain Gothic at the bottom to colourful, exuberant late Baroque at the top. Alberto Churriguera and his brother José both worked here – the former on the choir stalls (fenced off, but lit by enough natural light to appreciate their beauty), the latter on the majestic dome.

5

Outside, **Pza. Anaya** is one of *the* great meeting places for Salamanca students, who lounge in the grass beds of the rose gardens; while from the slightly raised Catedral terrace you get a classic city view of domes, spires and sandstone facades.

Catedral Vieja

C/Cardenal Pla y Deniel, enter through Catedral Nueva • Entrance and ticket kiosk inside Catedral Nueva • Daily: April–Oct 10am–7.15pm; Nov–March 10am–5.15pm • €4.75 (for both Catedral Vieja & Nueva) • ☎ 923 217 476, ⓦ catedralsalamanca.org

The chapels opening off the cloisters of **Catedral Vieja** were used as university lecture rooms until the sixteenth century and one, the **Capilla de Obispo Diego de Anaya**, contains the oldest organ in Europe (mid-fourteenth century). Otherwise, the old Catedral's most distinctive feature is its dome, known as the **Torre de Gallo** (Cock Tower) on account of its rooster-shaped weather vane. Fashioned like the segments of an orange, the dome derives from Byzantine models and is similar to those at Zamora and Toro; there's a good view of it from Patio Chico, the courtyard at the back of the Catedrals.

Exposición Ieronimus

Pza. Juan XXIII • Daily 10am–7pm • €3.75, free Tues 10am–noon

At the rear of the Catedral Vieja is the entrance to the **Exposición Ieronimus**, primarily a collection of rare documents relating to the Catedral and named after the first bishop of Salamanca. This may not tempt you in, though the exhibition occupies the medieval **Torre Mocha**. Be warned: there are 200 steps to the top of the tower but you'll be rewarded with outstanding views of the city.

Museo Art Nouveau y Art Deco

C/Gibraltar 14 • April to mid-Oct Tues–Fri 11am–2pm & 4–8pm, Sat & Sun 11am–8pm; mid-Oct to March Tues–Fri 11am–2pm & 4–7pm, Sat & Sun 11am–8pm • €4, free for under-14s and Thurs 11am–2pm • ☎ 923 121 425, ⓦ museocasalis.org

Explore the alleys behind the Catedral Vieja and you'll stumble upon Salamanca's quirkiest museum, the **Museo Art Nouveau y Art Deco**, contained within the Casa Lis. The mansion was built for an Art Nouveau enthusiast at the beginning of the twentieth century and is partly constructed from vibrantly painted glass (the best views of the house are actually from the ring road below). There's a terrific miscellany of objects inside, from bronze statues and porcelain figures to jewellery and furniture, with notable exhibits including the famous scent bottles René Lalique designed for Guerlain and Worth.

Convento de San Esteban

Pza. del Concilio de Trento • Daily 10am–1.30pm & 4–7.15pm • €3 • ☎ 923 215 000

On the eastern edge of the historic quarter stands the vast **Convento de San Esteban**, whose facade portrays yet another faultless example of Plateresque art – the graphic

---

SALAMANCA STYLE

Two great architectural styles were developed, and see their finest expression, in Salamanca. **Plateresque** is a decorative technique of shallow relief and intricate detail, named for its resemblance to the art of the silversmith (*platero*); Salamanca's native sandstone, soft and easy to carve, played a significant role in its development. Plateresque art cuts across Gothic and Renaissance frontiers – the decorative motifs of the university, for example, are taken from the Italian Renaissance but the facade of the Catedral Nueva is Gothic in inspiration. The later **Churrigueresque** style, an especially ornate form of Baroque, takes its name from **José Churriguera** (1665–1725), the dominant member of a prodigiously creative family, best known for their huge, flamboyant altarpieces.

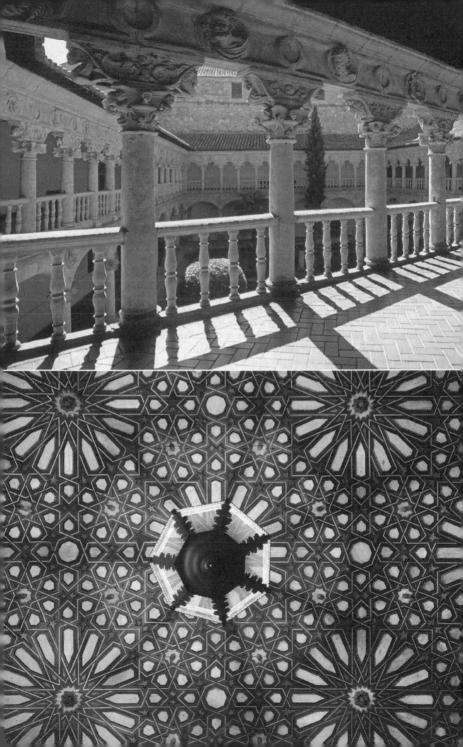

5

central panel depicts the stoning of its patron saint, St Stephen. Paying for entry also allows you to see the lavish Baroque *retablo* by José Churriguera – a mighty 27m high, and one of the artist's first commissioned works in Salamanca – as well as the choir, the handsome cloister and the museum of sacred art.

Convento de las Dueñas

Pza. del Concilio de Trento • Mon–Sat: Summer 10.30am–12.45pm & 4.30–7.30pm; winter 11am–12.45pm & 4.30–5.30pm • €2 • ☎ 923 215 442

The most beautiful cloisters in the city are at the **Convento de las Dueñas**, across the road from the Convento de San Esteban. Built in the sixteenth century on an irregular pentagonal plan, the imaginative upper-storey capitals are wildly carved with rams' heads, scallop shells, winged cherubs, mythical beasts and an extraordinary range of human faces. The nuns here sell boxes of delicious crumbly almond pastries (known as *amarguillos*) from a booth next to the entrance.

Convento de Santa Clara

C/Santa Clara 2 • Mon–Fri 9.30am–12.45pm & 4.25–6.10pm, Sat & Sun 9.30am–2.10pm • €3 • ☎ 660 108 314

The thirteenth-century **Convento de Santa Clara** was found to be concealing unsuspected treasure when the whitewash was taken off the chapel walls in 1976. Underneath was an important series of frescoes from the thirteenth to the eighteenth century, while Romanesque and Gothic columns and a stunning sixteenth-century polychrome ceiling were also uncovered in the cloister. But the most incredible discovery was made in the church, where the Baroque ceiling was found to be false; rising above this, you can see the original fourteenth-century beams, decorated with heraldic motifs of the kingdoms of Castile and León.

The Puente Romano

For a terrific city view up to the walls and spires of Salamanca, walk down below the Catedrals to the **Río Tormes** and cross the arched **Puente Romano**, built in the first century AD – try not to look back until you're most of the way across.

ARRIVAL AND DEPARTURE   **SALAMANCA**

The compact *casco histórico*, with the Pza. Mayor at its heart, spreads back from the Río Tormes, bounded by a loop of avenues. The main bus and train stations are on opposite sides of the city, each about a 15min walk or a €5 taxi ride from the centre.

By train From the main train station on Paseo de la Estación, go left to Pza. de España, from where C/Azafranal or C/Toro lead directly to the Pza. Mayor. Salamanca's other train station – Salamanca-La Almedilla – is closer to the centre but is for arrivals only. RENFE ☎ 902 240 202, ⓦ renfe.com.
Destinations Ávila (10 daily; 1hr); Burgos (4 daily; 2hr 30min); Madrid (8 daily; 2hr 30min); Valladolid (10 daily; 1hr 15min–1hr 30min).
By bus The bus station is on Avda. Filiberto Villalobos (☎ 923 236 717, ⓦ estacionautobusessalamanca.es). From here turn right and keep straight for 15mins until you reach Pza. Mayor. Companies with ticket offices here include Alsa (Burgos and Portugal; ☎ 923 258 205, ⓦ alsa.es); Auto-Res/Avanza (Valladolid/Madrid and Ávila; ☎ 923 232 266, ⓦ avanzabus.com); El Pilar (Ciudad Rodrigo; ☎ 923 222 608, ⓦ elpilar-arribesbus.com); Vivas (for León and

Astorga/Ponferrada; ☎ 923 223 587, ⓦ autocaresvivas.es); and Zamora-Salamanca (Zamora/León ☎ 923 223 587, ⓦ zamorasalamanca.es).
Destinations Astorga/Ponferrada (1–2 daily; 2hr 40min/3hr 30min); Ávila (4 daily; 1hr 30min); Burgos (4 daily; 3hr 30min); Cáceres (up to 9 daily; 3hr); Ciudad Rodrigo (up to 11 daily; 1hr); León (up to 3 daily; 3hr 30min); Madrid (every 30 mins–1hr; 2hr 30min); Palencia (up to 4 daily; 2hr 15min); Porto/Lisbon, Portugal (1–2 daily; 6hr/10hr); Valladolid (8 daily; 1hr 15min–2hr); Zamora (up to 17 daily; 1hr 10min).
By car As you drive into the centre, all the main hotels and car parks are clearly signposted. You can unload outside most hotels (though not on every street in the old centre), but street parking is usually restricted to 2hr, so it's best to use one of the garages or car parks (€16–20/day).

INFORMATION

Turismo The *turismo* is on Pza. Mayor 32 (Mon–Fri 9am–2pm & 4.30–8pm, Sat 10am–8pm, Sun 10am–2pm; winter Mon–Sat closes 6.30pm; ☎ 923 218 342, ⓦ salamanca.es). There is also a seasonal office (July–Sept, variable hours) situated inside the train station.

ACCOMMODATION

All the places reviewed below are in the *casco histórico*, and you'll be able to walk to everything in 5min or so. There are some splendid boutique and classy lodgings, but many budget *pensiones* are more or less permanently occupied by students during the academic year. You may be approached at the train or bus station and offered private rooms, but these are best avoided.

Erasmus Home C/Jesús 18 ☎ 923 710 257, ⓦ erasmushome.com. A friendly dutch-run hostel on a peaceful side street near the Casa de Conchas with bright, shared dorms. A simple coffee-and-toast breakfast is served in the *Erasmus Café*, a relaxed backpacker bar that's a 2min walk away on C/Meléndez. Dorms €17, doubles €34

Eurostars Las Claras C/Marquesa Almarza s/n ☎ 923 128 500, ⓦ eurostarshotels.com. Very comfortable, contemporary four-star hotel in a quiet corner of town – it's easy to find by car and has garage parking (€15/day); free street parking is sometimes available in the "white zone". Spacious rooms in muted colours provide a tranquil base, the buffet breakfast is excellent (€14 for two people), and there's a good restaurant. Good rates are available online. €69

Hostal Catedral Rúa Mayor 46, 1º ☎ 923 270 614, ⓦ hostalcatedralsalamanca.com. Clean, bright, budget *hostal* with pretty, traditionally furnished rooms and a charming welcome. It's in a great location overlooking busy Pza. Anaya and most rooms have Catedral views. Breakfast is not included. €50

Hostal Plaza Mayor Pza. del Corillo 20 ☎ 923 262 020, ⓦ hplazamayor.com. Despite the central location right next door to the Pza. Mayor, this is a surprisingly quiet and appealing budget option. The basic rooms have private bathrooms and a/c, and there's a garage on-site. €40

Hostal Sara C/Meléndez 11 ☎ 923 281 140, ⓦ hostalsara.org. The best – and friendliest – budget option on this busy street, 100m from Pza. Mayor. Its eighteen rooms are comfortably furnished, and feature wood floors and tiled bathrooms. Internal rooms are nice and quiet. Six of the rooms have a kitchen and cost €5 extra. €45

Hotel Abba Fonseca Pza. San Blas 2 ☎ 923 011 010, ⓦ abbafonsecahotel.com. A contemporary four-star hotel on a tranquil square a 10min walk from Pza. Mayor. Many rooms have lovely views across the city (though there are cheaper rooms without the views). €65

★ **Hotel Alda Plaza Mayor** C/Quintana 6 ☎ 622 111 597, ⓦ aldaplazamayor.es. This recently refurbished hotel in a historic building near the Pza. Mayor offers astonishingly good value. Rooms are modern and neutral, all with private bathrooms. Breakfast is available in the café-bar on the ground floor (€2.80/person), which also serves tapas until midnight. €30

★ **Hotel Estrella Albatros** C/Grillo 18 ☎ 923 266 033, ⓦ estrellaalbatros.com. The secret at this terrific four-star boutique hotel, a few minutes' walk from the old centre, is the sweeping city-view from the roof. Spacious, contemporary rooms are in soft colours, while classy bathrooms have smoked-glass sinks and Jacuzzi-baths. There's garage parking (€13.20/day). €49

Hotel Palacio de Castellanos C/San Pablo 58–64 ☎ 923 261 818, ⓦ nh-hotels.com. The glassed-in Renaissance cloister converted into a lobby lounge sets the tone in this lovely, marbled four-star hotel on the site of a former palace. Rooms are smart, rather than luxurious, but there's a fine restaurant, *Trento*. Book online in advance for some very good rates. €69

★ **Hotel Rua** C/Sánchez Barbero 11 ☎ 923 272 272, ⓦ hotelrua.com. The sparkling reception area, complete with chandeliers, is an attractive introduction to this four-star hotel. Although just a few steps away from Pza. Mayor, double glazing in the rooms does an excellent job of keeping out street noise. A breakfast buffet is included and there's discounted parking a 5min walk away. €75

Revolutum Hostel C/Sánchez Barbero 7 ☎ 923 217 656, ⓦ revolutumhostel.com. There's nothing understated about this funky hostel that mixes 1960s retro style with antique furnishing but the atmosphere is relaxed and inviting. Upstairs, there are double rooms as well as four- to five-bed dorms. The sleek glass bar serves flamboyant cocktails (noise can travel to some rooms at night). Dorms €19, doubles €45

EATING AND DRINKING

Salamanca is a great place for hanging out in bars and cafés. There are also many superb restaurants where you can eat really well for very little, although sitting outside to eat in the Pza. Mayor can attract a hefty mark-up. Just south of Pza. Mayor, the adjacent C/Meléndez and more touristy Rúa Mayor are packed with bars and restaurants, with enticing tables set out in the pedestrianized streets. There's another bunch of popular restaurants and tapas places near the market

5

(around Pza. del Mercado and up C/Pozo Amarillo), but the best (and cheapest) **tapas bars** in the city are a 15min walk north of the old centre, along C/Van Dyck (follow Paseo Doctor Torres Villarroel, cross Avda. Portugal, and Van Dyck is two streets up on the right).

CAFÉS AND RESTAURANTS

Café Atelier C/Serrano 33 ☎ 625 868 357. At this delightful café-bar near the university, the vegetarian dishes really hit the spot with their light, fresh ingredients. The kitchen is only open 11am–4pm, with *raciones* and a good-value menu (three courses for €10) plus soups, tortillas, croquettes, and salads and soya burgers on the main menu. Mon–Sat 11.30am–11.30pm.

★**El Corrillo** C/Meléndez 18 ☎ 923 271 917, ⓦ cafecorrillo.com. This arty café-bar and restaurant is great for a long lunch (from 1.30pm) or lazy dinner (from 9pm) in the pretty square out back; be sure to reserve in advance. The big menu (mains €8–22) mixes traditional dishes (fillet steak or grilled cuttlefish) with flashier, *vanguardista* (avant-garde) cooking (say, tempered tuna tataki with ginger foam). Otherwise there's breakfast for €6. Every Thursday and Sunday nights the café morphs into a hip jazz club, with live acts from 10pm. Daily 8.30am–3am.

★**El Pecado** Pza. Poeta Iglesias 12 ☎ 923 266 558, ⓦ elpecadorestaurante.es. The funky townhouse interior of leopardskin banquettes and deep pink walls is the backdrop for some equally adventurous regional cuisine – the spicy *patatas bravas* are given their kick with wasabi oil, or you can try things like *chipirones* (baby squid) stuffed with olives and cinnamon rice. Dishes cost €10–20, though there's an excellent-value €15 menu, served day and night, of simpler food like pasta, home-made burgers or grilled tuna. Daily 1.30–3.45pm & 8–11.30pm.

Restaurante La Aldaba C/Felipe Espino 6 ☎ 923 219 642. Traditional Spanish restaurant that serves hearty regional dishes (main €16–20), such as *rabo del toro* (ox-tail stew) and *merluza a la romana* (battered hake). Choose either the formal dining area at the back or order *pintxos* in the lively bar full of locals at the front. Daily

1–4pm & 8pm–midnight.

Río de la Plata Pza. Peso 1 ☎ 923 219 005, ⓦ restauranteriodelaplata.es. The well-regarded regional Castilian cuisine here is a real step up in quality from most places in the area – as are the prices. Hearty rustic dishes (mostly €14–25) range from rabbit stew to hake casserole; fish is a speciality, as are seasonal *horta* (countryside) dishes using ingredients like asparagus, beans and mushrooms. Tues–Sun 1.30–3.30pm & 8.30pm–midnight; closed 2 weeks in July & 2 weeks in Feb.

★**Vida & Comida** Pza. de Santa Eulalia ☎ 923 282 346, ⓦ vidaycomida.com. It's best to reserve a table at this popular restaurant, which serves *vanguardista* tapas. Choose from three *menús del día*: two tapas (€11.95), three tapas (€15.95) or four tapas (€19.95) plus water, bread and a dessert. Dishes include a delicate octopus carparccio and a cheesecake sprinkled with grated gran padano cheese. Tues–Sat 2–4pm and 9pm–midnight, Sun 2–4pm.

★**Vinodiario** Pza. de los Basilios 1 ☎ 923 614 925. Terrific contemporary wine bar with food, just off the main tourist track in a nice square with outdoor tables. There are some great wines by the glass, plus superior tapas and *raciones*, including warm goats' cheese salad and a ground-beef-and-herb hamburger (most dishes €5–15) and a cheesecake that's quite possibly worth the flight to Spain alone. Daily 10am–late.

Zazu Bistro Pza. de la Libertad 8 ☎ 923 261 690, ⓦ restaurantezazu.com. A classy French bistro that has outside tables in an attractive plaza adjacent to Pza. Mayor. Inside, the restaurant serves French classics, such as *boeuf bourguignon* and cassoulet, and dishes with a Spanish twist, including Iberian pork ribs, plus Italian pastas and risottos. The *menú del día* (€15) changes weekly. Daily 2–4pm & 9pm–midnight.

NIGHTLIFE

There's a whole host of student-oriented **bars and clubs** on the southeast edge of the *casco histórico*, particularly in the arcades of the Gran Vía, in Pza. de San Justo and near the market (near C/Varillas and C/Clavel). Another area for bars and clubs is around the Convento de las Úrsulas, though if you're looking for quantity over quality try the infamous **bars de litros** just to the north of here around Pza. de San Juan de Bautista, which sell drinks in litre "buckets". The café-bars in C/La Latina near the university are always bustling with students, day and night.

BARS

Clavel Ocho C/Clavel 8 ⓦ clavelocho.com. One of several amenable bars that put out tables in two interlinked squares just below the market, underneath the San Julian church walls. A good place to start the evening, while DJ sessions kick off after midnight most nights of the week. Sun–Fri 6pm–2am, Sat 4pm–4.30am.

★**Hernández y Fernández** Pza. de la Libertad. This

tasteful Tintin-themed café-bar is a dark and cosy place on a peaceful square just north of the Pza. Mayor. Stop for a coffee during the afternoon and you may find that you're still here late at night. Mon–Fri & Sun 3pm–1.30am, Sat 3pm–3am.

Posada de las Ánimas Pza. San Boal 7 ⓦ posada delasanimas.com. The shared *terraza* is a bit hidden away from the main drag, and don't miss the weird interior of cherubs, chandeliers and dolls' houses. Mon–Thurs & Sun 6pm–3am, Fri & Sat 6pm–4.30am.

CLUBS

Camelot C/Bordadores 3 ☎ 923 212 182, ⓦ camelot.es. Everyone in town knows this fun bar and *discoteca*, housed in part of the Convento de las Úrsulas. The interior, an ex-pilgrim's house, is a mix of medieval and industrial decor, with a bar on the first floor, above the dancefloor, and there are terraza seats outside. Mon–Thurs & Sun 6pm–4.30am, Fri & Sat 6pm–6.30am (opens at 4pm in summer).

DIRECTORY

Bookshop Librería Cervantes, C/Azafranal 25–27 and Librería Victor Jara, C/Melendez 21, have a reasonable selection of English-language books.

Hospitals Hospital Clínico, Paseo San Vicente 182 (☎ 923 291 100); Hospital Virgen de la Vega, Paseo San Vicente 58 (☎ 923 291 100).

Language courses Spanish-language courses offered by the Universidad de Salamanca (ⓦ cursosinternacionales. usal.es) are heavily subscribed, but there are loads of other schools – see ⓦ espanolensalamanca.com.

Laundry At Avda. De Villamayor 91, C/Gómez Ulla 40 and Paseo San Antonio 13.

Police Oficina de Denuncias y Atención al Ciudadano (ODAC), C/Jardines ☎ 923 127 700. Report an incident at the ODAC office, then non-Spanish citizens must take their police report to the relevant embassy. Report lost property at Avda. De la Aldehueva ☎ 923 279 195.

Post office Gran Vía 25 (Mon–Fri 8.30am–8.30pm, Sat 9.30am–1pm).

Ciudad Rodrigo

The unspoiled frontier town of **CIUDAD RODRIGO** – 90km southwest of Salamanca, astride the road to Portugal – is worth a detour even if you don't plan to cross the border. It's an endearingly sleepy place which, despite an orgy of destruction during the Peninsular War, preserves a rather austere castle (now a parador), a handsome Pza. Mayor and quiet old-town streets full of Renaissance mansions. It remains completely encircled by impressive walls and ramparts, and the thirty-minute walk around (and on top of) them is the best way to get an overview of the whole town. Given its history, it's perhaps surprising that there's much left to see at all. Ciudad Rodrigo was a crucial border point in the **Peninsular War**, guarding the route between Spain and Portugal. The town fell to the French after a fierce fight in 1810, but was later re-taken by the British in 1812 following a devastatingly rapid siege (cannonball dents are still visible above the doorway on one side of the Catedral). A triumphant rampage of looting followed, and when order was restored, the troops paraded out dressed in a ragbag of stolen French finery. A bemused Wellington muttered to his staff, "Who the devil are those fellows?"

ARRIVAL AND DEPARTURE

CIUDAD RODRIGO

By train There is a train station, a fair walk north of the centre, though there's only one train a day to Lisbon (currently at 2.07am) and another to Hendaye in France (3.59am; via Salamanca, Medina del Campo and Valladolid, all in the dead of night).

By bus From Salamanca, the bus is easily the most convenient way to get to Ciudad Rodrigo; the bus station is a 5min walk north of the old town.

By car Salamanca is under an hour's drive away. You can easily park outside the town walls, or try your luck with the limited spaces on Pza. Mayor.

INFORMATION

Turismo Pza. Mayor 27 (opening times vary; ☎ 923 498 400, ⓦ aytociudadrodrigo.es).

Centro de Recepción de Visitantes Av. Sefarad (opening times vary; ☎ 923 163 373, ⓦ ciudadrodrigo.net).

Online There's useful tourist information on ⓦ turismo ciudadrodrigo.com.

ACCOMMODATION

Hostal Puerta del Sol C/Rúa del Sol 33 ☎ 923 460 671, ⓦ hostalesenciudadrodrigo.com. Trim little en-suite rooms by the Puerta del Sol gate, and a cosy feel throughout.

Public parking 1min away through the gate. **€55**

★ **Hotel Conde Rodrigo I** Pza. de San Salvador 9 ☎ 923 461 404, ⓦ conderodrigo.com. An old mansion

5

loaded with character – check out the period-piece panelled bar. The rooms are nothing flashy, but perfectly decent and with good bathrooms, and it's very quiet at the rear. There's also private garage parking nearby (you can unload outside). **€66**

Parador de Ciudad Rodrigo Pza. Castillo 1 ☎ 923 460 150, Ⓦ parador.es. The main historic hotel has an unrivalled location in the old castle, which has been beautifully restored. There are views to all sides, and some very grand rooms and public spaces, as well as a restaurant and a car park. Advance online bookings can shave around €40 off the room rate. **€100**

EATING AND DRINKING

★**Estoril** C/General Pando 11 ☎ 923 460 550, Ⓦ restaurante-estoril.com. The best place in town for modern interpretations of regional cuisine – grilled baby octopus, *rabo de toro*, apple and foie gras timbal, etc. Meals are served in the formal, but unstuffy, restaurant to the rear (mains €13–20); otherwise there's a terrace at the front for tapas and *raciones*. Daily: terrace noon–midnight; restaurant: 1–4pm & 8–11pm.

El Rodeo C/Gigantes 10 ☎ 923 482 017. Simple, old-fashioned restaurant offering hearty local specialities, such as scrambled eggs with *farinato* (pork and bread sausage) and milk-fed lamb. There's a menu for €10, and you can eat in the evening for around €20. Daily 1–4.30pm & 7–11pm.

El Sanatorio Pza. Mayor 14 ☎ 923 461 054. Atmospheric little bar-restaurant whose walls are covered in bullfighting photos from decades of *corridas* and fiestas. Dishes €5–10. Daily 9am–midnight.

Sierra de Francia

The protected mountain region of the **Sierra de Francia** marks the southern region of Salamanca province, with captivating **La Alberca** the most obvious target. It's one of five "national monument" villages, along with the equally venerable **Mogarraz**, **Miranda del Castañar**, **San Martín del Castañar** and **Sequeros**. La Alberca makes a good walking base for the surrounding hills and valleys, notably the stunning **Valle de Las Batuecas**, with its isolated monastery and ancient rock art. The area is best explored by car, in particular the stunning route along the Río Alagón: from the Monasterio San José de Las Batuecas, skirt the eastern edge of the *parque natural* to the viewpoint Riomalo de Abajo (just over the border in Extramadura) for a glorious view of the **Meandro Melero** – an almost complete oxbow lake. Complete the circuit by following the river east to the pretty village of **Sotoserrano**.

La Alberca

Seventy-three kilometres southwest of Salamanca, **LA ALBERCA** sits in the middle of the **Parque Natural Las Batuecas-Sierra de Francia**. The historic town is ringed by the trappings of mass tourism these days. However the centre still maintains an extraordinary collection of late medieval, half-timbered houses. It's very pretty, and an obvious honeytrap for weekenders and coach parties who trawl the rather-too-clean cobbled lanes shopping for basketware and other souvenirs. The smell and dirt of the farmyard may be long gone, but La Alberca is still known for its *embutidos* and *jamones*, and every second shop displays the rich, nutty hams, smoked pork and cured sausages. A granite porker stands outside the church, while the most elegant houses are found in the arcaded **Pza. Mayor**, which is dominated by a stone cross.

ARRIVAL AND INFORMATION

LA ALBERCA

By bus Cosme buses (Ⓦ autocarescosme.com) run to La Alberca once daily from Salamanca, stopping on the edge of the old quarter. Departure times don't suit a day-trip except on Sunday, when you can get there and back in a day.

By car You should find somewhere to park on the main through-roads, though there's also a large car park a few hundred metres out on the Batuecas road, just past the *Hotel Antiguas Eras* and right next to the Casa del Parque information office.

Turismo C/La Puente 9 (Tues–Fri 10am–2pm & 4.30–6.30pm, Sat 10.30am–2pm & 4.30–6.30pm, Sun

10.30–2pm; ☎923 415 291 ⓦturismosierradefrancia .es); for information about walks in the region, visit Casa del Parque, Carretera Las Batuecas (Feb to mid-June & Oct–Dec Fri–Sat 10am–2.30pm & 3.30–7pm, Sun 10am–2pm, Mon–Thurs by appointment; mid-July to Sept Fri–Sat 10am–2.30pm & 3.30–7pm, Tues, Thurs & Sun 10am–2pm ☎923 415 421, ⓦmiespacionatural.es, ⓦpatrimonionatural.org).

Online The local town hall has a useful tourist website, ⓦlaalberca.com.

ACCOMMODATION AND EATING

Accommodation can be expensive for what you get, but there are some good deals around, both in the centre of town and on the Batuecas road, a few minutes' walk from the centre. There's also a terrific boutique hotel in nearby Mogarraz. Half a dozen **bars and restaurants** ring Pza. Mayor, and there are a few more down neighbouring streets serving tapas and meals: none particularly cheap, all agreeably rustic.

Al-Bereka 2km out on the Salamanca road (Km 76) ☎923 415 195, ⓦalbereka.com. The local campsite is more of a holiday complex, with rustic cabins and apartments to rent (from €55), as well as separate pools for adults and children, plus café and restaurant. Closed mid-Oct to mid-March. Camping **€20**, apartments **€55**

Hostal El Castillo Carretera Mogarraz ☎923 415 001, ⓦhostalelcastillo.com. This simple hotel next door to its sister hotel, *Hotel Doña Teresa* is a pleasant retreat away from La Alberca's touristy town centre. Good budget rooms have great views of the sierra; there's a bar on the ground floor with a pool table. **€39**

Hostal del Rincon de Trillo C/El Chorrito 11 ☎923 415 429, ⓦhostalelrincondeltrillo.com. The six simple rooms above a small, friendly bar on a quiet street in one of La Alberca's medieval buildings are tastefully presented with dark-wood furniture, white bedding and modern bathrooms. Price includes breakfast. **€40**

Hotel Antiguas Eras Carretera Batuecas ☎923 415 113, ⓦantiguaseras.com. Agreeable three-star hotel with spacious rooms, distant hill views, a peaceful garden and a family-friendly welcome. They have a recycling policy and serve Fairtrade coffee, which is unusual in Spain. Guests with a Rough Guide get a ten percent discount; other offers are available. **€70**

Hotel Doña Teresa Carretera Mogarraz ☎923 415 308, ⓦhoteldeteresa.com. The smartest choice in town is this four-star hotel, which also has a good restaurant. Weekend offers are available from €55 for a double room with breakfast, dinner and use of the amazing spa facilities at *Abadia de los Templarios* – a luxury hotel 1.5km along the Salamanca road (at km 76). Restaurant 1–4pm & 9–11pm. **€90**

★ **Villa de Mogarraz** C/Miguel Angel Maillo 54, Mogarraz, 7km east of La Alberca ☎923 418 080, ⓦhotelspamogarraz.com. For the finest lodgings in the area, drive the short distance east to the equally ancient village of Mogarraz, where this restored mansion offers wonderfully stylish bedrooms featuring plenty of exposed stone, reclaimed wood and antique colonial furniture. The best rooms have Jacuzzis. There are hip spa facilities and a good restaurant too, known for its grilled meats (meals around €35). Restaurant 1.30–4pm & 9–11.30pm. **€70**

Parque Natural Las Batuecas-Sierra de Francia

The rolling hills, craggy peaks, deep valleys and dense forests of the **PARQUE NATURAL LAS BATUECAS-SIERRA DE FRANCIA** are a big draw for hikers and naturalists alike. Along the network of trails that criss-cross the protected conservation area, walkers pass through a diverse landscape that teems with wildlife, where they may spot black vultures, owls, snakes, lizards and mountain goats. La Alberca is the obvious starting point for hikers: stop at the Casa del Parque information office to pick up maps to well-signposted trails of varying difficulty.

Peña de Francia

The most obvious route on a clear day is up to the summit of **Peña de Francia** (1728m), not quite the highest point in the range but the most panoramic. The trail is signposted a couple of hundred metres outside La Alberca on the Batuecas road, by the Cooperativa Chacinera (across from the *Hotel Antiguas Eras*); it's a very specific 8.3km on foot (6hr round trip) or 17km by road. There's the church and sanctuary of Our Lady of the Peña de Francia at the windswept summit, and there are even lodgings at the *Hospedería del Santuario Peña de Francia*, which has a welcome cafeteria (closed in winter).

5

Valle de Las Batuecas

The Batuecas road out of La Alberca climbs in 3.5km to the pass of **El Portillo** (1247m), surrounded by rugged hills. From here, the road drops sharply for another 9km, via a series of hairpin bends, into the **Valle de Las Batuecas**, where a signpost points you up a short track to a parking area outside the **Monasterio San José de Las Batuecas**. There's also a more direct 7km path (3hr 30min each way) from La Alberca, over the pass and down to the monastery. This sylvan retreat in a hidden valley was founded at the beginning of the seventeenth century, and is a closed Carmelite order (no public access). However, a signposted path around the side of the monastery leads along the babbling river to a series of three **rock-art** sites dating from between 5000 and 2500 BC, depicting hunting and pastoral scenes of goats and deer, and even human figures. The closest site, Cabras Pintadas, is an enjoyable half-hour's walk and scramble from the monastery gate.

Zamora and around

ZAMORA, 62km north of Salamanca and only 50km from the Portuguese border, is the quietest of the great Castilian cities, with a population of just 65,000. In medieval romances, it was known as *la bien cercada* (the well-enclosed) on account of its strong fortifications; one siege here lasted seven months. Its old quarters, still walled and medieval in appearance, are spread out along the top of a ridge that slopes down to the banks of the Río Duero, crossed at it widest point by a lovely sixteen-arched bridge and flanked by some restored medieval water mills, the Aceñas de Olivares. The city's Romanesque churches are its most distinctive feature, while the old town's streets and squares make for an attractive overnight stay. When it's time to move on, head east to Valladolid, with a stop in the small town of **Toro**, or north to León, via **Benavente**; Bragança, the first main town over the border in Portugal, is just over 100km away on a good road.

Romanesque churches

Opening times vary, consult tourist offices • Free

The joy of Zamora lies in its quiet, western old-town quarter – looking decidedly spruce and scrubbed these days – and, above all, in its 22 pale-stone **Romanesque churches**, with their unassumingly beautiful architecture, and towers populated by colonies of storks. The majority date from the twelfth century and reflect Castile's sense of security following the victorious campaigns against the Moors by Alfonso VI and El Cid. All are worthy of a closer look, though **San Juan de Puerta Nueva** (Pza. Mayor; closed Tues), **La Magdalena** (Rúa de los Francos; closed Mon) and **Santiago del Burgo** (C/Santa Clara; closed Mon) are considered the highlights.

Museo de la Semana Santa

Pza. de Santa María La Nueva • Tues–Sat 10am–2pm & 5–8pm, Sun 10am–2pm • €4 (€1 to take photographs)

One of several interesting museums in Zamora, the **Museo de la Semana Santa** is probably the most dramatic. One large room is lined with *pasos* – elaborate statues and floats depicting the Passion of Christ – which are paraded through the streets during Zamora's famous Holy Week processions (w semanasantadezamora.es).

Catedral

Pza. de la Catedral • Daily: April–Sept 10am–8pm; Oct 10am–6.45pm; Nov–March 10am–2pm & 4.30–7pm • €4, free Mon afternoons and for under-12s

The **Catedral**, enclosed within the ruined citadel at the far end of town, is now shining very brightly after restoration. Begun in 1151, its mainly Romanesque body is largely

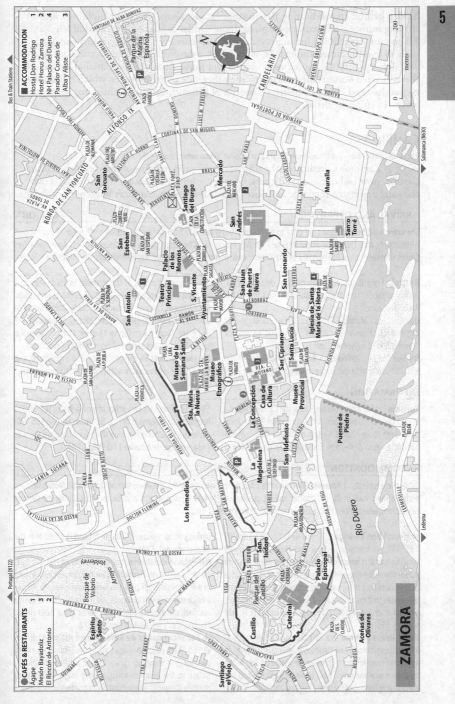

ZAMORA

■ **ACCOMMODATION**
Hostal Don Rodrigo	1
Hotel Horus Zamora	2
NH Palacio del Duero	4
Parador Condes de Alba y Aliste	3

● **CAFÉS & RESTAURANTS**
Agape	1
Mesón Bayadoliz	3
El Rincón de Antonio	2

Bus & Train Stations ◀

Portugal (N122) ◀

Salamanca (N630) ▶

Ledesma ▶

5

hidden behind an overbearing Renaissance facade, above which the building's most striking feature – a Byzantine-inspired dome similar to that of the Catedral Vieja at Salamanca – perches in incongruous splendour. However, it springs a surprise inside, with its famous carved **choir stalls**, which depict devout scenes and mystical animals as well as lusty carryings-on between monks and nuns. Access to the Catedral is through the associated **Museo Catedralicio**, on the other side of the cloisters, which houses the city's celebrated "Black Tapestries", a series of fifteenth-century Flemish masterpieces woven in stunning detail.

Castillo

Parque del Castillo • Tues–Sun 10am–2pm & 5–8pm (last entrance 20mins before close) • Free

Next to Zamora's Catedral are the impressive moated remains of the eleventh-century **Castillo**, now laid out as a shady park; wander round the back for majestic views over the surrounding countryside and Río Duero, along with Zamora's burgeoning suburbs.

ARRIVAL AND DEPARTURE   ZAMORA

The **train and bus stations** are close to each other, but a fair way from the centre, 30min walk north of Pza. Mayor. Alternatively, it's a 10min ride on bus #4 (every 20min), which leaves from outside the bus station and runs down Avda. Tres Cruces, dropping you at Pza. Sagasta by Pza. Mayor; note that the return bus departs from outside the market.

By train From the train station on Ctra. de la Estación, walk straight out over the roundabout in front to join the Avda. Tres Cruces.
Destinations Madrid (3 daily; 2hr); Santiago de Compostela (2 daily; 3hr 30min); Valladolid (daily; 1hr 10min); Vigo (2 daily; 4hr 30min).
By bus The bus station is on Avda. Alfonso Peña (☏ 980 521 282); turn right out of the main entrance, then right again around the side of the terminal to reach the main road; turn left here and follow Avda. Tres Cruces into town.
Destinations León via Benavente (6 daily; 2hr); Madrid (6 daily; 3hr); Palencia (3 daily; 2hr 20min); Salamanca (17 daily; 1hr 10min); Toro (up to 14 daily; 30min); Valladolid (up to 13 daily; 1hr 30min), Burgos (3 daily; 4hr 15min).
By car Car parks in the centre are well signposted, but some of the old town is residents-only access and parking.

INFORMATION

Turismo Pza. de Arias Gonzalo 5, near the Catedral (April–May Mon–Fri 10am–2pm & 5–8pm, Sun 9am–3pm; June–Sept 10am–2pm & 5–8pm daily; Oct–March Mon–Sat 10am–2pm & 4–7pm, Sun 10am–5pm; ☏ 980 533 694, ⓦ c). There are two other offices in town: the Oficina Patronato de Turismo is at Pza. de Viriato (☏ 980 536 495) while the regional office is on the edge of the old town at Avda. Príncipe de Asturias 1 (☏ 980 531 845).

ACCOMMODATION

While there is plenty of **accommodation** in Zamora, decent budget places to stay are thin on the ground. Most hotels are within a short walk of the old quarter and it's usually easy to find a room, except over Easter week during the famous processions, when prices double and accommodation is booked solid.

★ **Hostal Don Rodrigo** C/Virgen de la Concha 5 ☏ 980 535 123, ⓦ hostaldonrodrigo.es. This super-friendly two-star hostal is hands-down the best mid-range place to stay in town. The spic-and-span rooms have all the facilities that you'd expect at a good hotel, including memory-foam mattresses that make for a blissful night's sleep. Guests get a breakfast discount at the café around the corner (€3). Free parking. **€55**
Hotel Horus Zamora Pza. del Mercado 20 ☏ 980 508 282, ⓦ hotelhorus.com. Handsome boutique lodgings in a restored mansion right opposite the market. Most of the rooms are nice and quiet, with some set in the eaves, and there's a good contemporary restaurant and garage parking (there's also restricted street parking outside in the market square). **€70**
NH Palacio del Duero Pza. de la Horta ☏ 980 508 262, ⓦ nh-hotels.com. Housed in a former convent and winery in a quiet residential area, this large hotel is easy to spot as a brick chimney still looms beside it. Some of its 49 rooms overlook the attractive Iglesia de Santa Maria de la Horta. Cheaper deals are available online. **€72**
★ **Parador Condes de Alba y Aliste** Pza. de Viriato 5 ☏ 980 514 497, ⓦ www.parador.es. Zamora's classy parador is a stunning conversion of a fifteenth-century palace in the heart of town, mixing lovely rooms with princely trappings throughout, from the heroic medallions

surmounting the internal courtyard to the idly positioned suits of armour. An elevated garden terrace and open-air summer pool have city views, while a fine restaurant serves updated regional cuisine (mains around €20). Special room rates are available online. **€105**

EATING AND DRINKING

Zamora's most celebrated dishes are hearty affairs like *sopas de ajo* (garlic soup), *arroz de la Zamorana* (rice flavoured with pigs' trotters), and *habones Sanabreses* (broad beans cooked in a meaty paprika broth). **Restaurants, cafés** and superb **tapas bars** are found in three main zones. In **Los Lobos**, there's a cluster of no-nonsense **tapas bars** in the alleys around Pza. del Maestro; bars line the streets around the **Pza. Mayor** and there's a lively run of music, tapas and drinking **bars** in the narrow C/los Herreros; the **New Zone** is an up-and-coming, tapas district located east of Los Lobos, on C/Cervantes, C/Santa Teresa, C/Lope de Vega and C/Pablo Morillo.

Ágape Pza. de San Miguel 3 ☎980 536 962, ⓦagaperestaurante.com. An Italian restaurant with tables on the Pza. Mayor that serves pasta and pizza, as well as a *menú del día* (€12). The tapas creations, such as a smoked cod and orange salad and squid with aubergine ratatouille, are artistically presented. Daily 1.30–4pm & 7–11.30pm.

Mesón Bayadoliz C/Los Herreros. At this hole-in-the-wall place, delicious morsels are created with love over a hot, smoky grill, reminiscent of a Turkish mangal. At €1.50 per dish, you can have a feast. Try the chargrilled *brochettes*

(kebabs) and *lomo* (pork fillet in a ciabatta roll). Daily 6.30pm–late.

★**El Rincón de Antonio** Rúa de los Francos 6 ☎980 535 370, ⓦelrincondeantonio.com. The town's most inventive restaurant takes creative Castilian cuisine to a different level. With classy mains at €25 or so, and the *menú degustación* at €55, it's a special-occasion place, but you can always just drop in for fancy tapas at the bar (what they call *cocina en miniatura*). Mon–Sat 1.30–4pm & 8.30–11.30pm.

North of Zamora

To the north of Zamora, the baking wheat fields of the *meseta* extend to the horizon across the Tierra del Pan (The Land of Bread), historically one of Spain's key flour-producing regions. It's 140km from Zamora to León (or a 2hr bus ride) on a fast road (N630 then A66) and drivers can break the journey at a couple of interesting places.

Monasterio de Moreruela

Around 40km north of Zamora, look for a marked turn-off from the N630 (on the left) at the dusty roadside village of Granja de Moreruela. "Granja" means farm, meaning the village was originally an outlying property of the medieval **Monasterio de Moreruela**, which lies 3.7km from the highway down a paved country lane. It's now in ruins, and home to a large colony of storks, but is an evocative sight nonetheless, under a carpet of daisies and poppies, with rolling farmland to all sides.

Benavente

Thirty kilometres to the north of Monasterio de Moreruela, the town of **BENAVENTE** is rather charming once you penetrate the outskirts, with busy shopping streets set around two honey-coloured stone churches. A broad landscaped *paseo* offers extensive views over the surrounding countryside, while at the end of the gardens, the *Parador de Benavente* occupies the remains of the town's impressive castle.

Toro

TORO, 30km east of Zamora, looks dramatic seen from below: "an ancient, eroded, red-walled town spread along the top of a huge flat boulder", as Laurie Lee described it in *As I Walked Out One Midsummer Morning*. At closer quarters it turns out to be a rather ordinary provincial town, though embellished with one outstanding Romanesque reminder of past glory. Toro is also increasingly well known for its gutsy red **wines**, and the local tourist office can point you in the direction of local wineries open to the public.

5

THE BATTLE OF TORO

Toro – a historic military stronghold – played a role of vital significance in both Spanish and Portuguese history. The **Battle of Toro** in 1476, effectively ended Portugal's interest in Spanish affairs and laid the basis for the unification of Spain. On the death of Enrique IV in 1474, the Castilian throne was disputed: almost certainly his daughter Juana la Beltraneja was the rightful heiress, but rumours of illegitimacy were stirred up and Enrique's sister Isabel seized the throne. Alfonso V of Portugal saw his opportunity and supported Juana. At Toro, in 1476 the armies clashed and the Reyes Católicos – Isabel and her husband Fernando – defeated their rivals to embark upon one of the most glorious periods in Spanish history.

Colegiata de Santa María la Mayor

Off Pza. Mayor • Opening times vary, check at *turismo* for latest hours • €2

Toro's pride and joy is the **Colegiata de Santa María la Mayor**, whose west portal (c.1240), inside the church, is one of the most beautiful examples of Romanesque art in the region. Its seven recessed arches carved with royal and biblical themes still retain much of their colourful original paint. Also inspect *The Virgin of the Fly*, a notable fifteenth-century painting hanging in the sacristy – the eponymous insect perches on the Virgin's robes. Around the back of the church is a wide terrace with a famous view over the *meseta*, with the Río Duero far below.

ARRIVAL AND INFORMATION   TORO

By bus and car Buses to Toro are reasonably frequent (Zamora–Valladolid route; hourly service, fewer at weekends) and stop at the bus station. It's best to park outside town – walk through the big arch and straight on for about 5min, through the clock tower, to reach Pza. Mayor, with the Colegiata immediately behind.

Turismo Pza. Mayor 6 (Mon–Sun 10am–2pm & 4–7pm; ☎ 980 694 747, ⓦ toroayto.es).

ACCOMMODATION AND EATING

You're unlikely to want to stay the night, given the superior charms of nearby Zamora or Valladolid. Toro's a more realistic coffee or lunch stop – its Pza. Mayor is lined with characteristic red-brick houses and stone arcades, with many enticing **tapas bars** and **restaurants**.

Valladolid and around

VALLADOLID, at the centre of the *meseta* and capital of the Castilla y León region, ought to be dramatic and exciting. Many of the greatest figures of Spain's Golden Age – Fernando and Isabel, Columbus, Cervantes, Torquemada, Felipe II – lived in the city at various times, and for five years at the turn of the seventeenth century it vied with Madrid as the royal capital. It had wealth and prestige, yet modern Valladolid – a busy, working city of 310,000 – lost much that was irreplaceable, as many of its finest palaces and grandest streets were destroyed during the Peninsular War with France (1808–14). Nonetheless, much that remains is appealing in a city centre of restored squares and gleaming churches, with a series of excellent art museums including the Museo Nacional de Escultura, which holds the finest collection of religious sculpture anywhere in Spain. While it doesn't have the overriding beauty of Salamanca or the standout monumental presence of Burgos or León, Valladolid is an easy city to like – whether it's the pretty shaded gardens of the Campo Grande or the student bars lined up in the shadow of the majestic Santa María de la Antigua church. The best time to get a sense of the city's historic traditions is **Semana Santa** (Holy Week), when Valladolid is host to some of the most extravagant and solemn processions in Spain.

Outside the city, there are easy side trips to the historic towns of **Tordesillas** and **Medina del Campo**.

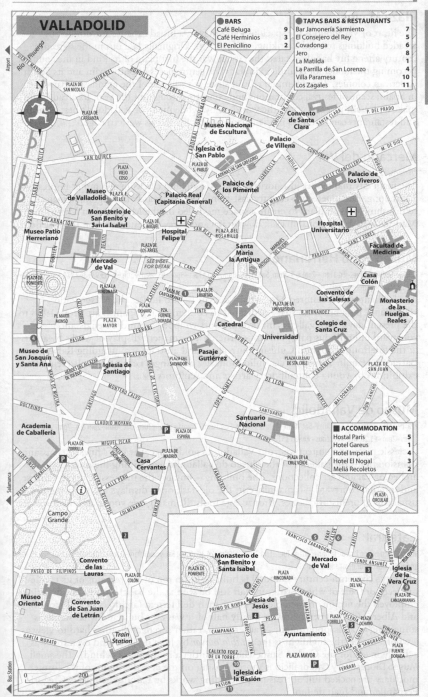

VALLADOLID

● BARS	
Café Beluga	9
Café Herminios	3
El Penicilino	2

● TAPAS BARS & RESTAURANTS	
Bar Jamonería Sarmiento	7
El Consejero del Rey	5
Covadonga	6
Jero	8
La Matilda	1
La Parrilla de San Lorenzo	4
Villa Paramesa	10
Los Zagales	11

■ ACCOMMODATION	
Hostal París	5
Hotel Gareus	1
Hotel Imperial	4
Hotel El Nogal	3
Meliá Recoletos	2

5

Plaza Mayor

The heart of Valladolid is the spacious **Plaza Mayor**, a broad expanse surrounded by arcaded buildings painted a striking, uniform red. Originally laid out in the sixteenth century after a fire had devastated the city, it was the first plaza of its kind in the country, becoming the model for countless similar civic centrepieces in both Spain and its South American colonies. Though much rebuilt since, it's still one of the grandest urban spaces in Spain, scene of festival celebrations and concerts throughout the year. Its arcade cafés make a pleasant place to watch the world go by, while many of Valladolid's best tapas bars and restaurants can be found in the narrow streets just off its western edge.

Mercado del Val

C/Francisco Zarandona

The main city **market** lies just north of Pza. Mayor, and clocks in at a rather impressive 112m long. The nineteenth-century cast-iron shed is currently undergoing a major refurbishment, with plans to create a space modelled on the Mercado San Miguel in Madrid, with a traditional market downstairs and bars and restaurants on the first floor.

Museo Patio Herreriano

C/Jorge Guillén 6 • Tues–Fri 11am–2pm & 5–8pm, Sat 11am–8pm, Sun 11am–3pm • €3, Wed & Sun €1 • ☎ 983 362 771, ⓦ museopatioherreriano.org

The brilliant-white, restored Monasterio de San Benito houses the **Museo Patio Herreriano**. It's a beautiful space dedicated to contemporary Spanish art (from 1918 to the present day), with galleries on several floors wrapped around a Renaissance courtyard of luminous pale gold stone. There's a permanent display of works by artists at the forefront of Spanish Cubism, Surrealism and abstract art, including Rafael Barradas, Joaquin Torres-García, Julio González and Ángel Ferrant, but also temporary exhibitions by young contemporary artists and sculptors.

Museo de Valladolid

Pza. de Fabio Nelli • July–Sept Tues–Sat 10am–2pm & 5–8pm, Sun 10am–2pm; Oct–June Tues–Sat 10am–2pm & 4–7pm, Sun 10am–2pm • €1.20, free weekends • ☎ 983 351 389

A classic piece of architecture from Valladolid's golden age, the city's finest Renaissance mansion holds the galleries of the **Museo de Valladolid**, containing the municipal archeological and art collections. The building – notably the impressive main staircase and internal courtyard – is magnificent; the old-fashioned displays less so, being the usual run of prehistoric bones, Bronze Age tools, Roman grave goods and medieval art.

Catedral

Visitors' entrance on Pza. de la Universidad • Tues–Fri 10am–1.30pm & 4.30–7pm, Sat & Sun 10am–2pm • Catedral free, museum €3 (free under-9s) • ⓦ catedral-valladolid.com

The city's sixteenth-century **Catedral** is built right on top of the remains of its medieval predecessor (part of whose structure can still be seen at the back), and its construction employed the not inconsiderable talents of Juan de Herrera (architect of El Escorial) and Alberto Churriguera. However, only half of it was ever built and what stands is something of a disappointment – rather plain, rather severe and rather hard to view as a whole. Inside, the highlight is the *retablo mayor* by Juan de Juni (and even this was actually made for the Gothic Santa María la Antigua in the plaza behind). The small **Museo Diocesano y Catedralicio** is more pleasing on the eye: the rooms of the former mortuary are packed full of treasures, including works by Baroque sculptors Gregorio Fernández and Juan de Juni.

FOOTSTEPS OF THE FAMOUS

Felipe II was born (1527) in Valladolid, and in other circumstances perhaps his home city, and not Madrid might have become the permanent Spanish capital. As it was, Valladolid was only briefly the capital (1601–06), but Felipe's birthplace, the Palacio de los Pimentel (C/Angustias), has a memorial plaque, and his statue is over the way in Pza. San Pablo. Another surviving palace, Palacio de los Viveros (C/Ramon y Cajal), is where the royal teenagers **Fernando and Isabel** married in 1469, later to be the "Catholic Monarchs" of a new, triumphant Spain. The widely travelled **Miguel Cervantes** spent a few years in the city, too – what's thought to have been his house (Casa Cervantes, just off C/Miguel Iscar) is now a small museum. However, the city is perhaps proudest of **Christopher Columbus** (Cristóbal Colón), who died here in 1506 – Valladolid devoted an entire year in 2006, and spruced up the old town, to celebrate the five-hundredth anniversary of the old mercenary's demise, and there's a replica of the house he died in, known as Casa Colón, on C/Colón.

Iglesia de San Pablo

Pza. de San Pablo • Open during services

If Valladolid's Catedral is no looker, you don't have to walk far to find a church that delivers. Protected by fourteen lions on pedestals brandishing heraldic plaques, the exuberant **Iglesia de San Pablo** – the sole surviving part of a Dominican convent destroyed in the nineteenth century – has an amazing facade that combines a wild mixture of styles in a froth of sculpted columns, expressive figures, and star and floral motifs. Added to by various regal and noble sponsors over a century or so, it's actually in two different styles, the lower part a lavish form of late Gothic known as Hispano-Flemish Gothic, the upper a confection of more classical style similar to the Catedral Nueva in Salamanca.

Museo Nacional de Escultura

C/Cadenas de San Gregorio 1–3 • Tues–Sat 10am–2pm & 4–7.30pm, Sun 10am–2pm • €3, free Sat afternoon & Sun • ☎ 983 250 375, ⓦ museoescultura.mcu.es

The most extraordinary sculpted facade of all in Valladolid is that of the **Colegio de San Gregorio**, adorned not just with coats of arms and crowned lions, but sculpted twigs, naked children clambering in the branches of a pomegranate tree and long-haired men carrying maces. Considered to be from the workshop of master sculptor Gil de Siloé, it's very much like icing on a cake – the Welsh historian Jan Morris, for one, was convinced that the flamboyant facade must be edible. The building was constructed as a theological college by the Bishop of Palencia, Fray Alonso de Burgos – the Chancellor of Castile and confessor to Queen Isabel – and was richly endowed with Gothic Hispano-Flemish architecture, most obviously with a gleaming two-tier courtyard of twisted stone columns and an upper gallery that's a sculpted flight of fancy of heraldic, mythic and regal symbols. Inside, too, the building has been majestically restored and now contains the unmissable religious art and sculpture collection of the **Museo Nacional de Escultura**.

The stunningly presented collection from the thirteenth to eighteenth centuries includes some of the most brilliant works of the Spanish Renaissance and Baroque eras. Set in majestic galleries on two floors, arranged around the San Gregorio courtyard, the hugely expressive statues, sculptures, *retablos* and other artworks were often commissioned directly for churches and monasteries, and it's rare to see such vibrant pieces at these close quarters – while if you look up, almost every gallery has its own antique coffered ceiling of gilt and painted wood.

The magnificent Renaissance works of sixteenth-century artists, such as **Alonso Berruguete** (1490–1561) and the Frenchman **Juan de Juni** (1507–77), are quite beautifully brutal: weeping crucifixion wounds, severed heads, cadaverous bodies, agonized faces and rapt expressions fill the building. The dissolved Valladolid monastery of San Benito el Real provides two pieces that are typical of the richness and power on

5

display: Berruguete's *retablo mayor* has a life-sized St Benedict almost striding out from the surrounding scenes of his miracles, while in an upper gallery sit the intricately carved and painted choir stalls, preserved in their jaw-dropping entirety. The lower level houses some of the best examples of *pasos processionals* in northern Spain, with seventeenth-century masterpieces by Gregorio Fernández and Francisco de Rincón. The melodramatic – often comical – figures on floats, depicting scenes from The Passion, continue to be paraded through the streets of Valladolid every Easter to celebrate Semana Santa.

Palacio de Villena

C/Cadenas de San Gregorio 2 • Tues–Sat 10am–2pm & 4–7.30pm, Sun 10am–2pm (only open for exhibitions, otherwise by appointment) • Free • ☎ 983 250 375

Across the street from the San Gregorio facade stands the Renaissance **Palacio de Villena**, used as the **Museo Nacional de Escultura**'s centre for temporary exhibitions and public events. It also contains one final, and extraordinary, flourish, namely the so-called **Belén Napolitano** or Nativity tableau – in an eighteenth-century Neapolitan street, between the hanging laundry, itinerant musicians and fruit sellers, the three Wise Men troop towards the manger on camels.

ARRIVAL AND DEPARTURE
VALLADOLID

Arrival points are centred around Campo Grande park: the **train station** is at the foot of the park, and the **bus station** a few minutes' walk west.

By plane There's a small airport (☎ 983 415 500, ⊛ aena.es) 10km outside the city, served by domestic flights only. Buses (€3) run to the centre, while a taxi should cost €20–25.

By train The train station is on C/Norte Recondo. It's a 15min walk up to town from the train station, or there are taxis outside – it's a €5 ride to Pza. Mayor. The AVE high-speed train service (reservations recommended) makes Valladolid just over an hour's jump from Madrid. It's also convenient by train from Valladolid to Palencia, Burgos, León and Medina del Campo. For information, consult RENFE ☎ 902 320 320, ⊛ renfe.com.

Destinations Burgos (up to 11 daily; 1hr–1hr 40min); León (up to 14 daily; 1hr 30min–2hr); Madrid (at least hourly, 1hr–2hr 45min); Medina del Campo (hourly; 25–35min); Palencia (at least hourly; 30–50mins); Salamanca (6 daily;

1hr 30min); Zamora (2 daily; 1hr 20min–2hr 20min).

By bus The Estación de Autobuses is at C/Puente Colgante 2 (☎ 938 236 308). Bus companies include Auto Res/Avanza to Tordesillas/Salamanca (☎ 983 220 274, ⊛ avanzabus. com) and La Regional to Tordesillas, Toro, Zamora, Palencia, Peñafiel (☎ 983 271 587, ⊛ laregionalvsa.com).

Destinations El Burgo de Osma (4 daily; 2hr); Burgos (5 daily; 2hr); León (up to 14 daily; 2hr); Madrid (hourly; 2hr 30min); Palencia (Mon–Fri hourly, Sat 6 daily, Sun 3 daily; 1hr); Peñafiel (up to 7 daily; 1hr); Salamanca (up to 8 daily; 1hr 40min); Segovia (hourly; 2hr); Soria (4 daily; 3hr); Zamora (Mon–Fri hourly, Sat & Sun 4–6 daily; 1hr 30min).

By car Some of the signposted car parks offer all-day parking for only €3/day, such as the one opposite the bus station.

INFORMATION

Turismo Acera de Recoletos, near the top of the Campo Grande (Easter week & July to mid-Sept Mon–Sat 9am–2pm & 5–8pm, Sun 9.30–3pm; rest of the year

Mon–Sat 9am–2pm & 4–7pm, Sun 9.30am–3pm; ☎ 983 219 310, ⊛ info.valladolid.es).

ACCOMMODATION

The main concentration of **accommodation** – in all price ranges – is in the pleasant area around Pza. Mayor, though there are also some places down the east side of Campo Grande.

★**Hostal París** C/Especería 2 ☎ 983 370 625, ⊛ hostalparis.com. The best mid-range place, with very agreeable rooms for the price. Some of the front ones have glassed-in street-facing balconies, though it's quieter at the back. Two cafés downstairs have good breakfast deals. **€45**

★**Hotel Gareus** C/Colmenares 2 ☎ 983 214 334, ⊛ hotelgareus.com. Stepping into the lobby at this terrific

four-star boutique hotel is like entering a wonderful library, with a wall lined with books, marble floors, Chesterfield-style armchairs and ethnographic sculptures. The elegant style continues in the spacious bedrooms and there's a fancy cocktail bar. **€65**

Hotel Imperial C/Peso 4 ☎ 983 330 300, ⊛ hotel imperial.com. Old-fashioned hotel in a beautiful

Renaissance mansion right by Pza. Mayor. Everything is a bit on the fussy side, and the columned bar is certainly a talking point. **€60**

Hotel El Nogal C/Conde Ansúrez 12–14 **☎** 983 340 333, **@** hotelelnogal.com. A smart three-star, offering tasteful rooms with crimson drapes and wood floors, and up-to-date bathrooms (the single rooms are a bit on the pokey side). There's a bar and restaurant too, with tables on Pza.

del Val around the back. **€60**

Meliá Recoletos C/Acera de Recoletos 13 **☎** 983 216 200, **@** solmelia.com. The city's finest boutique lodgings, opposite Campo Grande and not far from the train station, in a handsomely restored mansion. Upper-storey "loft" rooms have particularly good views. The same chain also has a cheaper city-centre hotel. **€110**

EATING AND DRINKING

Pza. Mayor has the best outdoor **cafés** for a drink with views, while the streets around C/Correos, just to the west, are lined with largely upscale **tapas bars and restaurants** (though you'll still get a *menú del día* here for €15). There are two good areas for late-opening **bars**: either in the Zona Coca – around the Pza. Marti y Monso – or anywhere around the Catedral and the nearby Santa María de la Antigua church.

TAPAS BARS

Bar Jamonería Sarmiento C/Conde Ansúrez 11 **☎** 983 355 514. A cross between a deli and a bar, this great little tapas bar presents a choice of cold cuts and simple tapas, from *morcilla* or *jamón* to *ventresca* tuna salad, accompanied by some fine regional wines from €1.50 a glass. Mon–Sat 11am–3pm & 7.30pm–midnight, Sun 12.30pm–midnight.

★ **Jero** C/Correos 11 **☎** 983 353 508. Valladolid has an annual creative tapas competition and *Jero* often comes out on top, with its remarkable sculpted canapés called things like "Matrix", "Galactico" or "Mission Impossible" (this last, for example, a *bacalao*-and-mushroom *montadito* topped with tomato confit, prawn and almond crunch), sold at a couple of euros a pop. Bar Mon & Wed–Sun noon–4pm & 8pm–midnight; restaurant Mon & Wed–Sun 1.30–4pm & 9.30pm–midnight.

La Matilda C/Ebanistería 16–18 **☎** 983 307 433, **@** factoriamatilda.wordpress.com. This friendly café overlooking the regenerated Pza. de Cantarranas is a treat for anyone in need of a good dose of healthy vegetarian food. The menu features salads, roasted vegetables, and pasta dishes, each for under €10. Tues–Thurs 12.30pm–11pm, Fri–Sat 12.30pm–midnight.

Villa Paramesa C/Calixto Fernadez de la Torre 5 **☎** 983 357 936, **@** villaparamesa.com. This well-regarded place, just off the Pza. Mayor, turns tapas-making into an artisanal craft, with elves in the kitchen turning out exquisite creations while the sommelier chooses wine from an extensive range. Daily 12.30–4pm and 8pm–midnight.

RESTAURANTS

El Consejero del Rey C/Francisco Zarandona 6 **☎** 983 660 889, **@** restaurantelconsejerodelrey valladolid.blogspot.co.uk. One of Valladolid's best restaurants, *El Consejero del Rey* serves beautifully presented mains, such as duck *magret* or red tuna with rosemary and Ribera wine, for around €17 each. Mon–Sat noon–5pm & 8pm–late, Sun noon–5pm.

★ **Covadonga** C/Fray Antonio Alcalde 8 1 **☎** 983 330 798. For a straightforward meal try this family-run place near the market, which dishes up home-cooked food at bargain prices, with nothing much over €7 or €8 and lots for considerably less (only a huge *chuletón*, or T-bone steak, at €15 might break the budget). Mon–Sat 1–4pm & 9–11.30pm.

★ **La Parrilla de San Lorenzo** Pza. Pedro Niño 1 **☎** 983 335 088, **@** parrilladesanlorenzo.es. To dine beneath the steady gaze of a Templar Knight in the cellar of a former convent is a unique experience. At this grandiose restaurant, you can admire the rich collection of gilt-framed art and museum pieces while tucking into the famous regional dish *lechazo* (suckling lamb). Mains cost around €17. Daily 11.45am–4.30pm & 9–11pm.

Los Zagales C/Pasión 13 **☎** 983 380 892, **@** loszagales .com. This Valladolid institution, traditionally decked out with Spanish tiles, timber beams and barrels, has won numerous awards for its tapas, such as "Obama en la Casa Blanca" – poached egg *en cocotte* with porcini. Mains €7–20; *menú del día* €19–24. Daily 11.30am–5.30pm & 7.30pm–12.30am.

BARS

Café Beluga C/Ramón Nuñez 1 This arty café-bar is one of a collective of businesses that has given the once down-at-heel Pza. de Cantarranas a face-lift in recent years. The square now hosts cultural activities and festivals, while the café has regular theatre, concerts and DJ nights. Mon–Fri noon–midnight, Sat noon–12.30am and Sun 5pm–midnight.

Café Herminios Pza. de la Universidad **☎** 628 008 217. Opens late afternoon for terraza drinks and cocktails, but becomes more of a thumping jazz bar as the night wears on, with DJs and live acts pumping out acid jazz, blues, Latin, Cuban and Brazilian sounds. Daily 5pm–3am.

★ **El Penicilino** Pza. de la Libertad. Studenty, yes, but a fine bar, with a bit more about it than many around the Catedral area. You'll be lucky to score an outdoor table, but it's nice and pub-like inside. Mon–Fri 10am–1.30pm & noon–2.30am.

5

Tordesillas

The quiet riverside town of **TORDESILLAS**, 30km southwest of Valladolid, boasts an important place in Spain's (indeed, the world's) history. It was here, with papal authority, that the **Treaty of Tordesillas** (1494) divided "All Lands Discovered, or Hereafter to be Discovered in the West, towards the Indies or the Ocean Seas" between Spain and Portugal, along a line 370 leagues west of the Cape Verde Islands. Brazil, allegedly discovered six years later, went to Portugal – though it was claimed that the Portuguese already knew of its existence but had kept silent to gain better terms. The rest of the New World, including Mexico and Peru, became Spanish, with the consequences to play out across the generations.

Today's town is a low-key delight of faded red-brick buildings set around a charming, arcaded Pza. Mayor. There's a museum or two, and several timeworn churches, while a long medieval bridge extends across the wide Río Duero. There's a small beach on the other side, although swimming is not recommended, and a summer bar (June–Sept) that's handily sited for an evening breeze off the river.

Real Monasterio de Santa Clara

Santa Clara • Tues–Sat 10am–2pm & 4–6.30pm, Sun 10am–3pm (last entrance 1hr before closing) • €6 • ☎ 983 770 071, ⓦ patrimonionacional.es

The town's most significant monument is the **Real Monasterio de Santa Clara**, which was originally built as a royal palace. It overlooks the Duero and is known as "The Alhambra of Castile" for its delightful Mudéjar architecture. The highlights here include the golden roof of the chancel and an organ that is thought to have belonged to the unfortunate **Juana la Loca** (Joanna the Mad), daughter of Fernando and Isabel. She spent 46 years locked up in a windowless cell within a palace that once stood in the centre of Tordesillas. After Isabel's death, she ruled Castile jointly with her husband Felipe I from 1504–06 but was devastated by his early death, and for three years afterwards toured the monasteries of Spain, keeping the coffin perpetually by her side and stopping from time to time to inspect the corpse. In 1509, she reached Tordesillas, where first Fernando and, later, her son, Carlos V, declared her insane, imprisoning her for half a century and assuming the throne of Castile for themselves.

Several of the Convento's rooms and spaces are open to the public, including the pretty patio, with its horseshoe arches and Moorish decoration, while the former palace's fourteenth-century **Baños Árabes** (Arab baths) can also be visited – though they're closed during wet weather to protect the Mudéjar wall paintings from humidity damage.

ARRIVAL AND DEPARTURE

TORDESILLAS

By bus There are departures to Valladolid (up to 7 daily; 30min) and Zamora (6 daily; 50min) with La Regional (ⓦ laregionalvsa.com). The bus station is situated outside the old town centre.

By car Parking is easy near the bridge, beneath the old town.

INFORMATION

Turismo Casas del Tratado, overlooking the river and signposted from the Pza. Mayor (June–Sept Tues–Sat 10am–1.30pm & 5–7.30pm, Sun 10am–2pm; Oct–May Tues–Sat 10am–1.30pm & 4–6.30pm, Sun 10am–2pm; ☎ 983 771 067, ⓦ tordesillas.net).

ACCOMMODATION AND EATING

Hostal San Antolín C/San Antolín 8 ☎ 983 796 771, ⓦ hostalsanantolin.com. The best of the town's accommodation options, on a quiet old street in the centre. Rooms are nicely furnished, in vibrant colours, and non-guests are welcome at the decent grill-restaurant (*menú del día* €12 weekdays, weekends €18, otherwise meals around €35). Restaurant 1–4pm & 9–11pm. **€45**

Parador de Tordesillas Carretera Salamanca 5, 1km out on the Salamanca road ☎ 983 770 051, ⓦ parador .es. This tranquil parador is almost country club in feel, with shaded grounds, a sizeable outdoor pool and comfortable, rustic-style rooms. The regional Castilian restaurant is a treat (*menú del día* €29, mains around €20). Restaurant 8–11am, 1.30–4pm & 8.30–11pm. **€95**

Medina del Campo

MEDINA DEL CAMPO, 23km south of Tordesillas and around 55km from Valladolid, stands below one of the region's great castles, the Moorish, brick-built Castillo de la Mota. The castle sits on one side of the train line, the town on the other, and it's also worth walking into the centre to see what's left of Renaissance Medina del Campo (Market of the Field), which in the fifteenth and sixteenth centuries was one of the most important market towns in Europe. Merchants came from as far afield as Italy and Germany to attend its *ferias* (fairs), and the handsome **Pza. Mayor de la Hispanidad** – ringed by cafés and restaurants – is still evocative of the days when the town's bankers determined the value of European currencies.

Castillo de la Mota

Avda. del Castillo • April–Sept Mon–Sat 11am–2pm & 4–7pm, Sun 11am–2pm; Oct–March Mon–Sat 11am–2pm & 4–6pm • €4, tours €6 (free entry to ground floor) • ☎ 983 812 724, ⓦ castillodelamota.es

A classic child's design if there ever was one – four square towers, battlements and a deep moat – the **Castillo de la Mota** often housed Queen Isabel's army, and later served as both prison and girls' boarding school. A visitor centre throws light on the castle's history, while areas open to the public include the main courtyard and lower rooms, including the impressive brick-vaulted chapel.

Museo de las Ferias

C/San Martín 26, near Pza. Mayor • Tues–Sat 10am–1.30pm & 4–7pm, Sun 11am–2pm • €2 (under-10s free) • ☎ 983 837 527, ⓦ museoferias.net

For the story of Medina's fifteenth- and sixteenth-century fairs, visit the **Museo de las Ferias**, which traces the history from their origins as simple trade gatherings to their later role as essential European money markets. Exhibits – from Flemish textiles to Italian silver – demonstrate the wealth that once poured into this now small town.

ARRIVAL AND DEPARTURE   **MEDINA DEL CAMPO**

By train The quickest way here is by train from Valladolid; there's an hourly service and the journey takes 20–30min. Turn right out of the station and keep walking for the castle and underpass to town.

Palencia and around

PALENCIA, 47km north of Valladolid, is Castile's least-known city, and capital of a small and equally unheralded province of the same name. Its outstanding Catedral hints at its rich past, especially in Roman and medieval times – Spain's oldest university was founded here in 1208, although it was later swallowed up by that of Salamanca – but today's city of 80,000 is a more modest place. There are pretty riverside gardens, famous Semana Santa processions and numerous restored plazas, most dominated by white-stone churches. In the wider province, Palencia also reveals its charms, especially in the north in the so-called Montaña Palentina – a region of peaks, lakes and Romanesque churches – but also along the Palencian section of the Santiago pilgrimage route (see p.426).

Catedral San Antolín

Pza. de la Inmaculada • May–Oct Mon–Fri 10am–1.30pm & 4.30–7.30pm, Sat 10am–2pm & 4–5.30pm, Sun 4.30–8pm; Nov–April Mon–Fri 10am–1.30pm & 4–7pm, Sat 10am–1.30pm & 4–5.30pm, Sun 4–7pm • €2, including museum €3 • ⓦ diocesispalencia.org/catedral

The older part of the city centre is at its most attractive near the Gothic **Catedral San Antolín**, which faces a large open square surrounded by restored buildings. The exterior is plain by Spanish standards; and as Palencia fell into decline soon after the Catedral's completion in 1219, there's an almost complete absence of Baroque trappings inside.

5

However, this simply focuses attention on the highlights within, notably the stunning *retablo mayor*, which contains twelve beautiful little panels, ten of them painted by Juan de Flandes, court painter to Isabel – it's the best collection of his work anywhere. A staircase leads down into the atmospheric crypt, containing the worn, carved columns of the earlier Visigothic and Romanesque churches on this site, and an ancient well. The ticket also includes entry to the enclosed cloisters, but to see the treasures of the on-site **Museo Catedralicio** (including an early El Greco and some Flemish tapestries), you'll have to pay another euro.

There are charming **riverside gardens** behind the Catedral, with two old stone bridges, while following the river further up, at the top of town, leads to more extensive parkland.

Plaza Mayor and around

Halfway along the main pedestrianized street of C/Mayor lies Palencia's principal square, **Plaza Mayor**, arcaded against the fierce Castilian summer sun and the biting winter winds. It's modest but attractive, like Palencia itself, with the old cast-iron market hall just visible off one side of the square and the thirteenth-century church of **San Francisco** off the other. If the church pricks your interest, then, with a map from the *turismo*, you can track down the other Romanesque and Gothic churches, all signposted on a walking route through town.

ARRIVAL AND DEPARTURE   PALENCIA

Palencia's adjacent **bus and train stations** are located at the north end of the city centre. The roundabout of Pza. León is over on the far side of the gardens to your left as you leave either terminal; from here the long, pedestrianized C/Mayor – the main shopping street – runs up to the Pza. Mayor (10min walk).

By train The train station is on Pza. de los Jardinillos.
Destinations Burgos (7 daily; 45min–1hr); León (up to 18 daily; 1hr–1hr 30min); Valladolid (hourly; 40min).
By bus The Estación de Autobuses is on C/Pedro Berruguete (☏ 979 743 222, ⓦ autobuses-palencia.es).
Destinations Burgos (up to 3 daily; 1hr 15min); Carrión de los Condes (3 daily; 45min); Frómista (Mon–Sat 3–4 daily;

30min); Madrid (6 daily; 3hr); Salamanca (up to 5 daily; 2hr 15min); Valladolid (hourly; 1hr); Zamora (up to 2 daily; 2hr 15min).
By car Short-term street parking is easy, or head for one of the signposted car parks, like that at the Estación de Pequeña Velocidad on C/Juan Ramón Jiménez just east of the market (overnight parking €1.50).

INFORMATION

Turismo C/Mayor 31 (July to mid-Sept Mon–Sat 9.30am–2pm & 5–8pm, Sun 9.30am–5pm; mid-Sept to June Mon–Sat 9.30am–2pm & 4–7pm, Sun 9.30am–5pm; ☏ 979 706 523, ⓦ palenciaturismo.es).

ACCOMMODATION

There aren't many exciting **accommodation** options in Palencia but hotels are at least reasonably priced and rarely full. If you prefer to see Palencia by day and stay outside the city, look no further than *Casa del Abad* in nearby Ampudia (see opposite).

Diana Palace Avda. de Santander 12 ☏ 979 018 050, ⓦ eurostarshotels.com. For a comfortable night in a four-star business hotel, try the *Diana Palace*, opposite the train station – there are really good web deals often available. **€50**
Hotel Don Rodrigo C/Los Gatos ☏ 979 700 937,

ⓦ hotelessuco.com. This two-star hotel near the Catedral is a good budget choice for a night or two in Palencia. The white-tiled rooms have everything you need, although they could do with updating. A simple buffet breakfast is included. **€35**

EATING AND DRINKING

Pza. Mayor comes into its own in the early evening, as families come out for a stroll and a drink. Later on, head for the tapas bars and restaurants on **Plaza Seminario** (off C/Cardenal Almaraz), C/Don Sancho and C/Los Soldados or to the bars on Paseo del Salón and Pza. San Pablo.

La Traserilla C/San Marcos 12 ☏ 979 745 421, ⊚ latraserilla.es. There's a buzz about this place as diners arrive, anticipating good food. The restaurant upstairs presents imaginative dishes, such as sardines with apple cream (mains €10–18, *menú del día* €29), while downstairs, the bar stocks superb wines and cheaper tapas bites. Daily 1–5pm & 8am–1am.

Basílica de San Juan de Baños

Baños de Cerrato, near Venta de Baños, 7km south of Palencia • April–Sept Tues–Sun 10.30am–2pm & 5–8pm; Oct–March Tues–Sun 11am–2pm & 4–8pm • €2, free Wed • Roughly hourly buses from Palencia bus station (only three or four at weekends) run out to Baños in around 15min

A tucked-away village just outside Palencia contains the oldest church in the entire peninsula. The seventh-century **Basílica de San Juan de Baños**, established by the Visigoth King Recesvinto in 661, has tiny lattice windows and horseshoe arches, and incorporates materials from Roman buildings.

Ampudia

28km southwest of Palencia, along the P 901

For a complete change of pace from the Castilian cities to all sides, make the quick drive from Palencia up onto the high farming plain, where the industrial suburbs soon give way to shimmering meadows, rippling cornfields and scores of wind turbines. The tiny town of **AMPUDIA**, with a population of well under a thousand, is a quiet gem, boasting two long porticoed streets whose seventeenth-century houses are supported by tree-trunk columns, some of which are several hundred years old. Once a serious feudal stronghold, Ampudia has a huge castle set on higher, grassy ground, with sweeping views, and an equally majestic Gothic church, though the somnolent streets, shuttered houses and dung-spattered farms at the town's edge are a more reliable indicator of its current status. That said, there is one magnificent place to stay here, ideal for a luxurious night out in the sticks.

ACCOMMODATION AND EATING   AMPUDIA

★ **Posada Real la Casa del Abad de Ampudia** ☏ 979 768 008, ⊚ rusticae.es. The former abbot's house is now a remarkable rustic-chic hotel. A bright sun mural shines down from the entrance cupola, while gorgeous rooms feature bold colour washes on rough plaster walls, reclaimed-wood furniture and designer bathrooms. Exposed stone and ancient beams abound, there's a retractable roof over the lounge-bar patio, while the classy restaurant – serving grilled hake to *chuletón* (mains €20–24) – occupies the old wine press. There's also a pool and some very elegant spa facilities (doubles with spa facilities is €105). Restaurant daily 1–4pm & 9–11pm. **€75**

The Ribera del Duero

The **Río Duero** long marked the frontier between Christian and Arab territory. It meanders right across central Castile, between Zamora and Soria, with the eastern section in particular, from Valladolid, marked by a series of spectacular castles and old market towns, some restored as tourist attractions, others crumbling to dust. This part of the river is also at the heart of one of Spain's greatest wine-producing areas, the **Ribera del Duero** (see box, p.402). It's a fine route to follow by car (N122), stopping off for lunch in rustic *posadas* and for walks in the beautiful surroundings. You can make the trip by bus, but if you do, realistically, you'll only be able to see the major towns of Peñafiel and El Burgo de Osma.

Peñafiel

The first stop along the Rio Duero from Valladolid is **PEÑAFIEL**, 60km to the east, whose fabulous castle is visible long before you reach the town. Standing on a narrow ridge, and at 210m long but only 23m across, it bears an astonishing resemblance to a huge ship run

5

THE WINES OF THE RIBERA DEL DUERO

Some of Spain's most celebrated red wine comes from the demarcated region of **Ribera del Duero** (W rutadelvinoriberadelduero.es), including the country's best-known and most expensive wine, Vega Sicilia. Around 170 wineries are found along the Duero, with many of the *bogedas* concentrated between Peñafiel and Aranda del Duero, 40km to the east. If you'd like to make winery visits (not all are open for tours), the comprehensive website is a good place to start – some wineries require advance reservations, though many have shops that are open to casual buyers mornings and afternoons. **Bodegas Alejandro Fernandez** (W grupopesquera.com) makes its fabulous Tinto Pesquera at Pesquera de Duero, 4km north of Peñafiel, while the acclaimed **Señorio de Nava** (W senoriodenava.es) is based at Nava de Roa, 13km to the east.

aground. At the edge of town and entirely surrounded by balconied wooden buildings, the other extraordinary sight is Pza. del Coso, which doubles as perhaps the most spectacular bullring in Spain during Peñafiel's Día de San Roque festival every August.

Castillo de Peñafiel

April–Sept Tues–Sun 11am–2.30pm & 4.30–8.30pm; Oct–March Tues–Sun 11.30am–2pm & 4–7pm • Castle €3.30, combined ticket with Museo Provincial del Vino €6.60, or €9.20 wine-tasting tour • ☎ 938 881 199, W provinciadevalladolid.com

It's quite a hike up to the **Castillo de Peñafiel** – it's far easier to drive – which was built in the mid-fifteenth century out of the region's distinctive white stone. Guided visits around the castle take around forty minutes or so, after which you're encouraged to explore the **Museo Provincial del Vino**, where you can learn all about the Ribera del Duero wines – and even taste a few if you wish.

ARRIVAL AND DEPARTURE   PEÑAFIEL

By bus From Valladolid, buses drop you on the west side of the Río Duratón – walk down to the river and cross the bridge, then turn right and walk up to the central Pza. de España. The street off the top of this square leads in 5min to Pza. del Coso.

By car Parking's not usually a problem, but if the town centre proves tricky, use the massive free car park a little way out on the road up to the castle.

ACCOMMODATION AND EATING

There are a couple of cheapish places to stay in the centre, but Peñafiel probably only warrants a night if you can run to one of the grander choices.

Hotel Convento Las Claras Pza. Adolfo Muñoz Alonso ☎938 878 168, W hotelconventolasclaras.com. This restored seventeenth-century convent by the bridge, now a four-star riverside hotel, retains its erstwhile elegance, with its cloister-lobby, tree-shaded terrace and garden pool. There's a good restaurant as well as a terrace café with a lunchtime *menú del día*. Restaurant daily 2–4pm & 9–11pm. **€105**

Hotel Ribera del Duero Avda. Escalona 17 ☎983 881 720, W hotelriberadelduero.com. A contemporary three-star hotel set in a rather fine old flour mill on the edge of town (Soria road), whose stylish rooms almost all have castle views. *Menú del día* €11 + IVA. Restaurant Mon–Fri 1.30–4pm & 9–11pm, Sat–Sun 2–4.30pm & 9–11pm. **€70**

Peñaranda del Duero

Whichever direction you come from you'll pass through rolling vineyards to reach the gorgeous, honey-toned town of **PEÑARANDA DEL DUERO**, whose restored historic kernel sits beneath a battlemented castle. It's a popular weekend getaway, hence the rather upmarket accommodation and pristine houses, but nothing detracts from the first view of the picture-perfect Pza. Mayor – Renaissance palace on one side, bulky church on the other and flower-decked wooden houses in the lanes beyond.

With a day to spare, you might want to take the signposted local **walk** (21km) that leads up hill and down dale from Peñaranda, through the woods. Back at La Vid by the highway, marvel at how such a small village with such a small name has quite such a large monastery.

El Burgo de Osma and around

There's absurdly picturesque Río Duero scenery at **EL BURGO DE OSMA**, once a very grand place boasting both Catedral and university. Today, there are gleaming town walls, a lovely riverside promenade and ancient colonnaded streets overhung by houses supported on precarious wooden props. It's quaint and gorgeous in equal measure, and while the dominant Catedral is the only actual sight, the town rewards a leisurely stroll up the arcaded main street to Pza. Mayor. On summer nights, as the temperature drops, the families of El Burgo use the main square, with its cafés and tree-shaded benches, as a playground, exercise yard and social club. Out of town, there are easy drives to all sorts of fascinating destinations, from canyon park to mighty fortress, which makes El Burgo well worth a night's stay.

ARRIVAL AND INFORMATION
EL BURGO DE OSMA

By bus and car El Burgo is 60km east of Aranda del Duero, and around 150km from Valladolid. The bus station is on the main Valladolid–Soria road through town, with free street parking along the road here, and Pza. Mayor just a minute or two's walk away.

Turismo Pza. Mayor, inside the former Hospital de San Agustín (Mon & Thurs–Sun 10am–2pm & 4–7pm, July & Aug daily, same hours; ☎ 975 360 116, ⓦ burgosma.es).

ACCOMMODATION

There is plenty of accommodation and at all three hotels below you can park virtually outside.

Hospedería El Fielato Avda. Juan Carlos I, 1º, at C/Mayor ☎ 975 368 236, ⓦ hospederiaelfielato.es. Decent rooms, if nothing glam, at a very reasonable hotel located in an old buiding right next door to the *Hotel II Virrey*. **€55**

Hotel II Virrey C/Mayor 2 ☎ 975 341 311, ⓦ virrey palafox.com. The town's best hotel comes complete with baronial fittings that are virtually tourist attractions in their own right. The rooms are rather more modern, with contemporary fabrics and furnishings. There's a café at the hotel (which is entered from either the main road through town or Pza. Mayor); the restaurant (see below) is further up the main road, and website deals often include dinner. **€50**

Posada del Canónigo C/San Pedro de Osma 19 ☎ 975 360 362, ⓦ posadadelcanonigo.es. At the bottom of the Catedral square, one of the former canons' houses – built right next to the town wall – is now atmospheric *Posada del Canónigo*, with a pretty courtyard and rustic rooms with carved wooden headboards. **€80**

EATING AND DRINKING

El Burgo is a pork and steak town, and you can eat big, meaty meals at a number of *asadores*, including a couple of places along C/Mayor. The *Restaurante Virrey* is the local pig specialist – it even has a "pork museum" and an annual spring pig slaughter (*matanza*).

Casa Engracia C/Ruiz Zorrilla 3 ☎ 975 340 155. Good for a meal at modest prices – there's tapas and drinks in the bar or meals in the small *comedor* at the back, where straightforward meat and fish grills go for €9–14, accompanied by decent local wine from ceramic jugs. Daily 10am–midnight, kitchen open 1–4pm & 9–11pm.

Restaurante Virrey C/Universidad 7 ☎ 975 340 222. In an undistinguished building on the main road, this is the best restaurant in town, renowned for its regional cuisine (mains €12–20). Pork in all guises is the *raison d'être* – especially at *matanza* weekends, when 24-dish tasting menus celebrate every cut of pork imaginable (€25). Tues–Sat 1.30–4pm & 9–11pm, Sun 1.30–4pm.

Parque Natural del Cañón del Río Lobos

Visitor centre: April–Sept daily 10am–8pm; Oct–March Mon–Fri 10am–2pm & 5–8pm, Sat & Sun 10am–8pm • ☎ 975 363 564

Don't miss the excursion north of El Burgo de Osma to the dramatically rocky landscape of **Parque Natural del Cañón del Río Lobos**. It's a quick 14km drive on a ruler-straight road to the small village of Ucero, just outside which (under the ruined castle) is the Casa del Parque **visitor centre**. From the visitor centre, the main road runs another kilometre or so up to the stone bridge over the source of the Río Ucero, where you've a choice. The signposted left turn here runs along the valley floor towards the Romanesque **Ermita de San Bartolomé**. There's a bar-restaurant near the turn, and plenty of parking and picnic places further in among the trees, from where paths run into the spectacular gorge – one of the walks from the visitor centre runs to the hermitage and back. The main road, meanwhile, twists up for 3km to the top of the canyon and the **Mirador de la Galiana** (1122m), affording mesmerizing views of the canyon walls and the circling eagles and vultures. It's worth noting that everything in the park is very busy in August, at Easter and on bank holidays, when it's not particularly *tranquilo* anywhere – the size of the car parks gives the game away.

Calatañazor

Halfway between El Burgo de Osma and Soria, just off the N122, lies tiny **CALATAÑAZOR**, a sleepy medieval village overseen by skimpy castle ruins and some remarkable old houses, with their distinctive conical chimneys, decorative coats of arms and wooden balconies. It often seems deserted, though there's enough weekend and holiday trade to warrant several shops selling local honey, dried wild mushrooms and cheese.

ACCOMMODATION AND EATING   CALATAÑAZOR

Casa del Cura ☎ 975 183 642, ⊛ posadarealcasa delcura.com. If you fancy a very quiet night, these rustic-chic lodgings make for a comfortable stay. There's also a rather fancy restaurant (meals around €30; daily 1–4pm & 9–11pm), with an outdoor terrace overlooking the gorge. Restaurant open 1–4pm & 9–11pm. **€75**

Fortaleza de Gormaz

15km southeast of El Burgo de Osma, near Gormaz • Always open • Free

You'll see the stupendous **Fortaleza de Gormaz** fortress long before you climb to it, passing the nondescript village of Gormaz. It was originally built by the Moors in the tenth century, and two of their keyhole doorways survive, as well as a later medieval tower dating from after the castle was captured and modified by the Christians. The fortress was once one of the largest fortified buildings in Spain – the inside is now a shell, albeit an enormous one, hundreds of metres across, and there are 28 towers in all, ruined but still mightily impressive. There are magnificent panoramas from here, down to the snaking Río Duero and the giant patchwork of fields in the cultivated plains below.

Berlanga de Duero

BERLANGA DE DUERO lies south of the N122 (Soria road), and a fair way south of the Río Duero as well, although it still takes the river's name. It's a quiet backwater that was rather more important in times past – the main sight is a **castle**, whose massive cylindrical towers and older double curtain-wall, reminiscent of Ávila, loom above the town. The way up is through a doorway in a ruined Renaissance palace, just a few minutes' walk from the centre. The **Pza. Mayor** is arcaded by precarious wooden posts sitting on stone pillars, while the other dominant monument is the **Colegiata de Nuestra Señora del Mercado**, one of the last flowerings of the Gothic style. Its unusually uniform design is a consequence of rapid construction – it was built in just four years. Berlanga also has several fine mansions, some pretty arcaded streets and **La Picota**, a "pillar of justice" to which offenders were tied (it's just outside the old town, on the El Burgo road). There are a few small hotels and restaurants, but little reason to stay overnight. The main square has a nice old café for coffee.

ARRIVAL AND DEPARTURE   BERLANGA DE DUERO

By bus and car There's a bus service to Berlanga de Duero on Mondays and Fridays from Soria, which stops just out of the old centre, on the El Burgo road. The town stands just off the CL116 between El Burgo de Osma and Almazán (25km from the former); coming from Gormaz (17km), follow the signs for Recuerda and then Morales.

Ermita de San Baudelio de Berlanga

Casillas de Berlanga, 8km south of Berlanga de Duero; follow the pink signs from town • April–Sept Wed–Sat 10am–2pm & 4–8pm, Sun 10am–2pm; Oct–March Wed–Sat 10am–2pm & 4–6pm, Sun 10am–2pm; hols 10am–2pm • €0.60, free Sat & Sun

The thousand-year-old **Ermita de San Baudelio de Berlanga** is the best-preserved and most important example of Mozarabic style in Spain. Five years after being declared a national monument, in the 1920s, its marvellous cycle of frescoes was acquired by an international art dealer and exported to the US. After much fuss, the Spanish government got some of them back on indefinite loan, but they are now kept in the Prado in Madrid (see p.77). In spite of this loss, the simple hillside hermitage remains a beauty. Its eight-ribbed interior vault springs from a central pillar, while much of the space is taken up by the tribune gallery of horseshoe arches. Some original frescoes do remain, including two bulls from the great sequence of animals and hunting scenes.

Soria and around

SORIA is a modest provincial capital of around 40,000 – an attractive place, despite encroaching suburbs, and the inspiration behind much of Antonio Machado's best-loved verse (the Seville-born poet lived here from 1907 to 1912). It stands between a ridgeback of hills on the banks of the Duero, with a castle ruin above and a medieval centre dotted with mansions and Romanesque churches. You can see all the sights easily in a day, but a quiet night or two has its attractions, especially if you use the city as a base to explore some of Castile's loveliest countryside. The Roman site of **Numancia**, in particular, is an easy side trip, while to the northwest rises the **Sierra de Urbión**, the weekend getaway of choice for Soria's inhabitants.

Parque Alameda de Cervantes

Always open • Free

For once, it isn't the Pza. Mayor – quiet and handsome though that is – that's the focal point of town; instead Soria's best feature is its central botanical gardens, the **Parque Alameda de Cervantes**. In early evening, the whole of Soria seems to decamp here for strolls, games and chats, and there are occasional concerts in the extremely curious bandstand, the so-called "Tree of Music", which is wrapped entirely around a large tree, and far above head height; the musicians have to wind their way up a metal staircase to perform.

Museo Numantino

Paseo del Espolón 8 • July–Sept 10am–2pm & 5–8pm, Sun 10am–2pm; Oct–June Tues–Sat 10am–2pm & 4–7pm, Sun 10am–2pm; hols 10am–2pm • €1.20, free Sat & Sun • ☎ 975 221 397

Just back from the Parque Alameda de Cervantes you'll find the excellent **Museo Numantino**, which gathers together the region's major archeological finds, from Neolithic bones to medieval ceramics. The Celtiberian and Roman displays do much to illuminate a visit to the nearby site of Numancia.

Iglesia de Santo Domingo

C/Santo Tomé, main entrance on Pza. del Vergell • Open only for services

Of all Soria's central churches, the highlight is the rose-coloured facade of the twelfth-century convent church of **Santo Domingo**, a few minutes' walk north of the main pedestrianized street. The recessed arches of the main portal are magnificently sculpted with scenes from the Life of Christ, surrounded by a wonderful gallery of heavily bearded musicians who resemble the lost medieval ancestors of ZZ Top – look out, in particular, for the fetching three-in-a-bed scene.

5

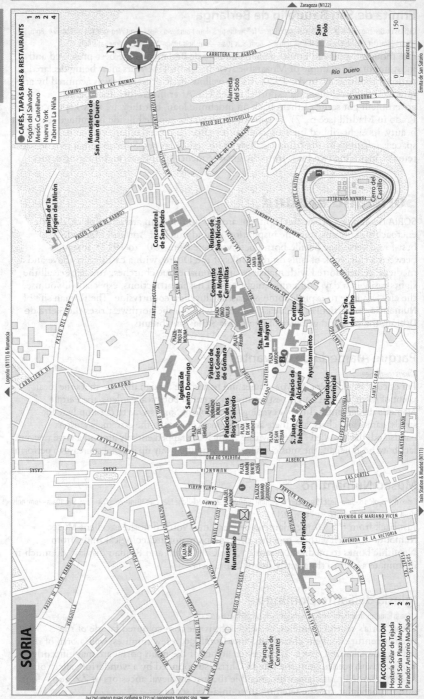

SORIA

CAFÉS, TAPAS BARS & RESTAURANTS

Fogón del Salvador	1
Mesón Castellano	3
Nueva York	2
Taberna La Niña	4

ACCOMMODATION

Hostería Solar de Tejada	1
Hotel Soria Plaza Mayor	2
Parador Antonio Machado	3

Zaragoza (N122)

Río Duero

San Polo

Cerro del Castillo

Ermita de San Saturio

S. PRUDENCIO

Alameda del Soto

CARRETERA DE AGREDA

CAMINO MONTE DE LAS ÁNIMAS

PASEO DEL POSTIGUILLO

Monasterio de San Juan de Duero

PUENTE MEDIEVAL

Ermita de la Virgen del Mirón

PASEO S. JUAN DE BARRIOS

PASEO DEL MIRÓN

Concatedral de San Pedro

Ruinas de San Nicolás

Convento de Monjas Carmelitas

STMA. TRINIDAD

SANTA APOLONIA

PLAZA SANTA CATALINA

LAS POSTAS

MARTÍN DE S. CLEMENTE

FERNÁN GONZÁLEZ

PRÍNCIPE CAUTIVO

NTRA.-SRA.-DE CALATAÑAZOR

Centro Cultural

Ntra. Sra. del Espino

Sta. María la Mayor

Palacio de los Condes de Gómara

Iglesia de Santo Domingo

Palacio de los Ríos y Salcedo

Ayuntamiento

Palacio de Alcántara

Diputación Provincial

S. Juan de Rabanera

LOGROÑO

CARRETERA DE

Logroño (N111) & Numancia

SANTO TOMÉ

CLEMENTE SÁENZ

CASAS

CASAS

PLAZA DEL VERGEL

PLAZA BERNARDO ROBLES

PLAZA DE SAN CLEMENTE

PLAZA MAYOR

PLAZA DE SAN ESTEBAN

PLAZA FUNCO MOLINA

PLAZA DE ARRIBA

COLLADO ZAPATERÍA

AGUIRRE

CABALLEROS

ALBERCA

LAS CORTES

NUMANCIA

SANTA MARÍA

RUTA DE CABALLEROS

PLAZA DE TOROS

PASEO DEL ESPOLÓN

PASEO DE SANTA BÁRBARA

STO. ÁNGEL DE LA GUARDA

VENUQUILLA

NICOLÁS RABAL

GARCÍA SOLIER

AVENIDA DE VALLADOLID

Parque Alameda de Cervantes

Museo Numantino

San Francisco

PLAZA MARIANO GRANADOS

PLAZA RAMÓN BENITO ACEÑA

PUERTAS DE PRO

MANUEL VICENTE

AVENIDA DE MARIANO VICEN

AVENIDA DE LA VICTORIA

MEDINACELI

ALFÉREZ PROVISIONAL

SANTA CLARA

JUAN ANTONIO GIMÓN

STA. TERESA DE JESÚS

LOS TILOS

Train Station & Madrid (N111)

Bus Station, Valladolid (N122) & Burgos/Sierra Urbión (N234)

N

0 150 metres

Concatedral de San Pedro

Pza. de San Pedro • July–Sept Tues–Sun 11am–2pm & 5–7pm; Oct–June, weekdays open for services, Sat 11am–2pm & 4–8pm, Sun 11am–2pm • Church free, cloisters €1

Down towards the river is Soria's now rather isolated Catedral, the **Concatedral de San Pedro**, whose interior takes the Spanish penchant for darkness to a ridiculous extreme. However, light and harmony are restored in the three bays of a superb Romanesque cloister, which belonged to the Catedral's predecessor. The fourth side of the cloister is glassed in and contains the Catedral's best-preserved sculpture, a magnificent late twelfth-century work showing Christ's entry into Jerusalem.

Monasterio de San Juan de Duero

Paseo de las Ánimas • July–Sept Tues–Sat 10am–2pm & 5–8pm, Sun & hols 10am–2pm; Oct–June Tues–Sat 10am–2pm & 4–7pm, Sun & hols 10am–2pm • €0.60, free Sat & Sun • ☎ 975 230 218

Standing on the old bridge over the Duero, at the foot of town, you suddenly realize that you're out of Soria and in the country. Just over the bridge stands the **Monasterio de San Juan de Duero**, whose ruined cloister is one of the most striking medieval monuments you'll ever see. Built in the thirteenth century by Mudéjar masons, each of the four sides of the cloister is in a different style, mixing Moorish, Romanesque and Gothic elements, with keyhole doorways and beautifully interlinked arches. The bare church, meanwhile, is now a museum, with two unusual freestanding temples inside boasting vivid, carved capitals.

ARRIVAL AND DEPARTURE   SORIA

By train The train station (☎ 902 432 343) is at the extreme southwest of the city, but limited services mean you're far more likely to arrive by bus.

By bus The bus station is on Avda. de Valladolid (☎ 975 225 160) at the western side of the city, a 15min walk from the centre.

Destinations Burgos (1–3 daily; 2hr–2hr 30min); El Burgo de Osma (Mon–Sat 2 daily, Sun daily; 1hr); Logroño (up to

5 daily; 1hr 30min); Madrid (8 daily; 2hr 30min); Medinaceli (2 daily; 1hr); Pamplona (5 daily; 2hr); Valladolid via Peñafiel (3 daily; 3hr); Vinuesa (2–3 daily; 35min); Zaragoza (9 daily; 2hr).

By car Street parking is easy to find, but is limited to 2hr in metered zones, so follow the signs to central car parks for overnight parking.

INFORMATION

Turismo C/Medinaceli 2, near Parque Alameda de Cervantes (July to mid-Sept daily 9am–8pm; mid-Sept to

June Mon–Sat 9.30am–2pm & 4–7pm, Sun 9.30am–5pm; ☎ 975 212 052, ⓦ www.sorianitelaimaginas.com).

ACCOMMODATION

Soria's tourists are rarely great in number, so finding a place to **stay** shouldn't be a problem. There are plenty of centrally located budget options, and a reasonable choice of mid-range and four-star hotels.

Hostería Solar de Tejada C/Claustrilla 1 ☎ 975 230 054, ⓦ hosteriasolardetejada.es. With its exposed wood and old stone walls, and charmingly decorated rooms all painted in different colours with coordinated fabrics, this is the best mid-range option in the city. **€56**

Hotel Soria Plaza Mayor Pza. Mayor 10 ☎ 975 240 864, ⓦ hotelsoriaplazamayor.com. This small boutique two-star townhouse has pride of place in Soria's prettiest old-town square. Some rooms in the eaves retain their old beams, while decor, fabrics, bathrooms and public areas are all in the best contemporary style. **€71**

★ **Parador Antonio Machado** Parque del Castillo ☎ 975 240 800, ⓦ www.parador.es. Soria's modern red-brick and glass parador has a beautiful hilltop location in the grounds of the ruined castle – there are steps down the hillside into the town centre (15min). Rooms are very spacious, with wooden floors and glassed-in balconies, and have stunning countryside views. Breakfast comes with the same glorious outlook, and the restaurant is a good choice for regional dishes (menu €34). You'll get a room much of the time for €95–110; check online for the best rates. **€160**

EATING AND DRINKING

Good **tapas** is the norm in Soria, while **restaurant** menus – here on the edge of Castile – show welcome Basque and Riojan influences, with fish and vegetables suddenly much more in evidence. The best selection of tapas bars is in Pza. Ramón Benito Aceña, at the end of the main drag, where the locals stand around outside at high circular tables and big wooden barrels. There's a grungier set of **bars** in nearby Pza. de San Clemente (just behind Citibank, off C/El Collado), while C/Manuel Vicente Tutot, behind the Museo Numatino, has a line of old-fashioned bars for Soria's cheapest eats. There are kiosk cafés in the Parque Alameda de Cervantes, nice for an early evening drink.

★ **Fogón del Salvador** Pza. del Salvador 1 ☎ 975 230 194, ⊛ fogonsalvador.com. An excellent *asador*, with tapas bar at the front and a more formal restaurant at the back, dominated by a huge wood-fired beehive oven and two mounted bulls' heads. The cuisine is typically meat-oriented – the steaks and chops are *buey* (ox) rather than *vaca* (beef), thus are hung longer, are darker in colour and richer tasting, or there are things like roast *cabrito*, a leg of lamb big enough for two, plus platters of smoked meats. Mains cost €14–21. Daily 1–4pm & 9pm–midnight.

Mesón Castellano Pza. Mayor 2 ☎ 975 213 045, ⊛ mesoncastellanosoria.com. Located in a cosy building of warm brick, with hams hanging from the wooden beams. You can hang out at the front with a cold beer, eat tapas at the bar or settle down for big meals in the *comedor*, where meat and fish dishes (including trout from the Río Ucero) run between €11 and €26. Daily 1–4pm & 9–11pm.

Nueva York C/Collado 18 ☎ 975 212 784, ⊛ pastelerianuevayork.es. The city's best pastry and cake place, also nice for breakfast, with tables outside on old-town square Pza. San Blas y el Rosel. Daily 8am–10pm.

Taberna La Niña Pza. Mayor 11 ☎ 686 938 179. The "Little Girl Tavern" is rather more old-school than the name suggests, a nice tiled place that's good for an early evening drink on Soria's most handsome square. Specialities are sandwiches (from €4) and cheese and meat platters to share (€14–18), and there's good regional wine by the glass. Daily 11am–midnight.

Numancia

Off the N111 to Logroño, just outside the village of Garray, 7km north of Soria • April–Sept Tues–Sat 10am–2pm & 4–8pm, Sun 10am–2pm; Oct–March Tues–Sat 10am–2pm & 4–6pm, Sun 10am–2pm • €0.60, free weekends

Around 7km north of Soria lie the evocative ruins of **Numancia**, a hilltop Celtiberian (third to second century BC) and later Roman settlement. Numancia was one of the last towns to hold out against the Romans, falling to Scipio in 133 BC; its long and fierce resistance was turned into a tragic play by Cervantes and dubbed "a sort of Vietnam for Rome" by novelist Carlos Fuentes. It's a stunningly sited spot, with extensive remains of streets, drains, courtyards and public baths, some reconstructed houses and a stretch of wall. There's a good English-language interpretive leaflet available.

Sierra de Urbión

Summer weekends and holidays see locals flock to the tranquil slopes of the **Sierra de Urbión**, northwest of Soria, with its network of hiking and cycling trails, and even skiing at Santa Inés. Nearest Soria, the lower section of what is a protected *reserva nacional* is focused on the shores of an enormous reservoir, the Embalse de la Cuerda del Pozo, which has pine-wood and beachside picnic areas and plenty of watersports facilities. Just to the north is the main village of Vinuesa, while the real highlight of the range lies further north still – the lovely alpine glacial lake of Laguna Negra.

Vinuesa

VINUESA makes the most obvious base for the Sierra de Urbión. It's a pleasant village, attuned to tourists, with many restored old houses, a church adopted by nesting storks, a number of banks and ATMs, and even a late-night bar or two.

ARRIVAL AND DEPARTURE   **VINUESA**

By bus The village is 33km from Soria (N234), and there are daily buses from Soria or Burgos.

ACCOMMODATION AND EATING

Half a dozen moderate **accommodation** options (mostly two-star-*hostal* standard) line the main road that leads down to the Laguna Negara turn-off. Nearly all the *hostales* have their own restaurants.

Camping Cobijo 2km along the Laguna Negara road ☎ 975 378 331, ⓦ campingcobijo.com. The local campsite is a large pine-shaded resort-style affair, with swimming pool, bikes for rent, a restaurant and a little supermarket. It also has basic rooms (sleeps two) and bungalows (sleeps three to six). Closed Nov–Easter. Camping **€20.80**, doubles **€53**, bungalows **€95**

Virginia C/Castillo de Vinuesa 21 ☎ 975 378 555, ⓦ virginiarh.net. Easily the pick of the local hotels, close to the bridge near the turn-off, with handsome rooms and a good-value restaurant of the same name just across the road (lunch around €12, dinner €20). Restaurant 1–4pm & 9–11pm. **€60**

Laguna Negara

It's definitely worth the drive up to the **Laguna Negara**, a shining body of water hemmed in by a dramatic amphitheatre of granite cliffs. There's a lakeside boardwalk and several hiking trails, including the serious ascent from the lake to the summit of **Pico Urbión** (2229m), just over the border in La Rioja. To reach the lake follow the signs (18km) from Vinuesa until you reach a small upper car park just 300m from the *laguna*; at busy times, or if the barrier is closed, you'll have to park at the much larger car park, 1km back down the road (20min walk), near the seasonal café-restaurant.

La Rioja province

One of Spain's most famous wine regions, La Rioja takes its name from the Río Oja, which flows from the mountains down to the Río Ebro, the latter marking the northern border of **La Rioja province** (ⓦ lariojaturismo.com). Confusingly, the demarcated wine region and province are not quite the same thing, since many of the best vineyards are on the north bank of the Ebro, in the Basque province of Araba – Alava in Castilian, the so-called Rioja Alavesa (see p.482). Nevertheless, the main wine towns are all in La Rioja proper, starting with the enjoyable provincial capital, **Logroño**, which is a great place to spend a couple of days eating and drinking. The province is traditionally divided further into two parts, with the busy little wine town of **Haro** being the mainstay of the **Rioja Alta**. This makes the best base for any serious wine touring, though there are *casas rurales* in many of the surrounding villages, too. It's also here, west of Logroño, that the Camino de Santiago winds on towards Burgos. East of Logroño is the **Rioja Baja**, the southeastern part of La Rioja province, which has quite a different feel – there are vineyards, but the main attraction is following in the footsteps of La Rioja's ancient dinosaurs.

Logroño is the hub for all local bus and train services, but if you want to do any more than see the towns of Nájera, Haro and Calahorra, it's far better to have your own transport, as connections to the smaller villages are rarely convenient for day-trips.

Logroño

LOGROÑO, lying on the Río Ebro, is a prosperous city of around 153,000 – a pleasant place of elegant streets, open squares and riverside parkland. The wine trade is not as immediately apparent here as in, say, Haro, and there are few cultural attractions that demand attention. But the big draw is the city's lively old quarter, the so-called *casco viejo*, with its unparalleled selection of excellent tapas bars, for which it's worth making a considerable detour. The two main annual events – each fuelled by copious wine-drinking – are the **Fiestas San Bernabé** (June), a week's worth of enjoyably rowdy local festivities, from street fairs and *pelota* tournaments to folk concerts and costumed processions, and the even more exuberant **Fiesta de San Mateo** (September), which coincides with the annual *vendimia* (grape harvest).

5

● CAFÉS, TAPAS BARS & RESTAURANTS		■ ACCOMMODATION	
Café Moderno	1	Hotel Marqués de Vallejo	3
Casa Pali	9	Hotel Portales	2
Las Cubanas	4	Pensión La Bilbaina	1
La Cueva	3		
Mesón del Abuelo	6	◆ SHOPS	
Paganos	7	Felix Barbero	1
Pata Negra	8	Vinos El Peso	2
La Taberna de Baco	2		
La Taberna del Laurel	10		
Vinissimo	5		

LOGROÑO

Museo de la Rioja

Pza. de San Agustín • Tues–Sat 10am–2pm & 4–9pm, Sun & hols 10am–2pm • Free • ☎ 941 291 259, ⓦ culturaderioja.org

Located across Espartero Palace, a Baroque beauty dating from the eighteenth century, and in a brand new purpose-built building, the engaging **Museo de la Rioja** tells the story of the La Rioja region – without the wine. Displays run from prehistory to the twentieth century and include religious and daily artefacts, Renaissance paintings and Roman murals. For anyone interested in the history of the area, this is a must-see.

Sala Amos Salvador

C/Once de Junio • Tues–Sat 11am–1pm & 6–9pm, Sun & hols noon–2pm & 6–9pm • Exhibitions usually free • ☎ 941 259 202, ⓦ larioja.org

Located in a former medieval convent, the seat of the regional government – the **Parlamento de la Rioja** – faces a cobbled square which has several late-night cafés. There's no public access to the government offices, but part of the building also once served as a nineteenth-century tobacco factory, the **Fabrica de Tabacos**, and is now used as a contemporary art and exhibition centre, the **Sala Amos Salvador**; the tall red-brick factory chimney still stands around the back on C/Portales.

Iglesia de Santiago el Real

C/Barriocepo 6 • Daily 8.15am–1.15pm & 6.30–8pm • Free

Before the wine trade brought prosperity to Logroño, the town owed its importance for some six centuries to the Camino de Santiago, hence the church dedicated to the saint, which stands close to the iron bridge over the Río Ebro. High on the south side (ie not the side facing the river) of the lofty sixteenth-century church of **Santiago el Real**, above the main entrance, is a magnificent eighteenth-century Baroque equestrian statue of St James, mounted on a stallion that Edwin Mullins (in *The Pilgrimage to Santiago*) describes as "equipped with the most heroic genitals in all Spain, a sight to make any surviving Moor feel inadequate and run for cover". On the other side of the church is the landscaped Parque del Ebro gardens, which are good for a stroll.

Concatedral Santa María de la Redonda

C/Portales 14 • Mon–Sat 8am–1pm & 6–9pm, Sun 8.30am–2pm & 6–8.45pm • Free • ⓦ laredonda.org

Logroño has many fine churches, principal among which is the mouthful of a Catedral, the **Concatedral Santa María de la Redonda**, which faces the old market square. The Catedral was originally a late Gothic hall church with a lovely, sweeping elevation that was extended at both ends in the eighteenth century – the twin-towered facade is a beautiful example of the Churrigueresque style. The evening *paseo*, meanwhile, fills the adjacent main street, C/Portales, packing out the bars and cafés under the arcades.

ARRIVAL AND DEPARTURE

LOGROÑO

Logroño is some 100km north of Soria, and 115km east of Burgos. The bus and train stations lie in the modern part of town, south of the central gardens of the **Paseo del Espolón**.

By train The train station is 400m south of the bus station, down Avda. de España.
Destinations Burgos (4 daily; 2hr 15min); Haro (2 daily; 40min); Madrid (daily; 3hr 15min); Palencia (daily; 3hr); Valladolid (daily; 3hr 45min); Vitoria (daily; 1hr 30min); Zaragoza (6 daily; 2hr).

By bus Logroño bus station, Avda. España 1 (☎ 941 235 983), is a 500m (10min) walk from the centre along C/ General Vara de Rey.
Destinations Bilbao (4–6 daily; 2hr 30min); Burgos

(Mon–Fri 7 daily, Sat & Sun 3–4 daily; 2hr); Calahorra (Mon–Sat 6–7 daily, Sun 3 daily; 1hr); Haro (Mon–Fri 7 daily, Sat & Sun 3–4 daily; 1hr); Nájera (Mon–Fri every 30–60min, Sat & Sun roughly hourly; 30min); Pamplona (up to 6 daily; 2hr); Soria (up to 5 daily; 1hr 30min); Vitoria (6–7 daily; 1hr).

By car Metered street parking and signposted garages are easy to find, though there's a large, free car park just opposite the surviving bit of medieval wall known as Murallas del Revellín, on the edge of the old town.

INFORMATION

Turismo The *turismo* at C/Portales 50 (Oct–May Mon–Fri 9am–2pm & 4–7pm, Sat 10am–2pm & 5–7pm, Sun 10am–2pm; June also Sun 5–7pm; July–Sept Mon–Fri 9am–2pm & 5–8pm, Sat 10am–2pm & 5–8pm; Sun 10am–2pm & 5–7pm; ☎ 941 291 260,

ⓦ lariojaturismo.com), provides a free map of town and information on the whole Rioja region.
Online Cultural news and events are covered on ⓦ culturalrioja.org.

ACCOMMODATION

You shouldn't have trouble finding **accommodation**, except during the week-long Fiesta de San Mateo, which starts on September 21, for which rooms are booked months in advance. The lowest-priced accommodation is in the old town; business-class three- and four-star places line the avenues in the more modern parts of town.

WHAT'S YOURS?

Cosecha (which literally means "harvest"), when used on its own, refers to young wines in their first or second year, which tend to have a fresh and fruity flavour – you'll also see these wines advertised as the *vino de año*. **Crianzas** are wines that are at least in their third year, having spent at least one year in an oak cask and several months in the bottle. **Reservas** are vintages that have been aged for three years with at least one year in oak; and **gran reservas** have spent at least two years in oak casks and three years in the bottle.

5

Hotel Marqués de Vallejo C/Marqués de Vallejo 8 ☎941 248 333, ⓦhotelmarquesdevallejo.com. This old-town hotel has been treated to a thorough makeover, giving it something of a boutique feel. Soundproofed rooms have polished wood floors and contemporary furnishings, and bathrooms are very swish. There's also adjacent private parking. Outside peak periods, rooms often go for a lot less. **€100**

Hotel Portales C/Portales 85 ☎941 502 794, ⓦhotelportales.es. Smart three-star hotel in contemporary style, right on the edge of the old town. Has garage parking. The website usually has some good deals. **€65**

Pensión La Bilbaina C/Capitán Gallarza 10 ☎941 254 226. Very smart en-suite rooms (including singles) at excellent prices. Everything is freshly painted and squeaky clean, though furnishings are a bit ascetic (bed, wardrobe, chair). Street-facing rooms are apt to be noisy at weekends. **€50**

EATING AND DRINKING

Logroño's old town is thick with bars and restaurants, and the local **cuisine** is celebrated for its potato and bean dishes, seasonal vegetables (particularly peppers, asparagus and mushrooms) and thick steaks. But Logroño's masterpieces are its **tapas bars**, clustered in the bar-run alleys of **C/Laurel** and **Travesía de Laurel**, and the similar **C/San Juan**. In these two locales alone are dozens of different bars, each with their own advertised speciality, from grilled mushrooms to octopus. Punters spill out in the alleys at the drop of a hat, washing it all down with a glass of the superb local Rioja wine. There are useful detailed bar guides on ⓦlogropincho.com.

Café Moderno C/Francisco Martínez Zaporta 9 ☎941 220 042, ⓦcafemoderno.com. A gloriously ornate café, established in 1916, with an antique bar full of old photographs, and locals playing board games inside. It's a good spot for breakfast, or a glass of *tinto* in the evening; there are reasonably priced meals (around €15). Daily 9am–midnight.

Casa Pali C/Laurel 11 ☎941 256 795. An old-town classic, knocking out tapas treats such as fried asparagus or *berenjena con queso* (aubergine with melted cheese). Mon & Wed–Sun 12.30–3pm & 8.30pm–midnight.

Las Cubanas C/San Agustín 17 ☎941 220 050, ⓦlascubanas.net. Best choice for a more refined night out, this classy restaurant dates from the 1920s, but the interior is sleek and contemporary. There's a choice of dishes from a modish Riojan menu (mains €14–23), for example ravioli of shrimp and *bacalao* followed by grilled monkfish or wild halibut. There's also a degustation menu. Mon–Sat 1–4pm & 9pm–midnight.

La Cueva C/San Juan 13 ☎675 671 388. A few of Logroño's tapas bars claim the mantle of mushroom king but this is the place for grilled mushroom *pinchos* par excellence. Daily 12.30–3pm & 8.30pm–midnight.

★**Mesón del Abuelo** C/Laurel 12 ☎941 224 663. At bright, bustling "Grandad's House", the tapas specialities are *chipirones* (baby squid), *sepia* (cuttlefish strips) and thin pork steaks, plonked on the grill and then doused in garlic sauce, for a couple of euros a time. Sit at the counter and order by pointing at dishes that take your fancy, perhaps langoustine or stuffed peppers (dishes €7–15). There's also a good wine list with plenty of decent Riojas at value-for-money prices. Daily 12.30–3pm & 8pm–midnight.

Paganos C/Laurel 22 ☎941 220 074. A no-nonsense, stand-up place specializing in *pinchos morunos* (mini pork kebabs), which come on a long skewer handed across the bar or out of the open window by the grill-maestro. Their other star dish is creamy tortilla, stuffed with potato or chorizo, cut into wedges and served on a slice of bread. Daily 12.30–3pm & 8pm–midnight.

Pata Negra C/Laurel 24 ☎941 213 645. The mural of acorn-rooting pigs on the wall is the clue, and this renowned *jamonera* (ham specialist) serves big cured meat platters at a price (up to €18) – or you can snack on mini-sandwiches (all under €3) mixing things like *jamón* and blue cheese or tuna and hot peppers, washed down with various grades of Rioja wine, which are all absurdly cheap. Daily 12.30–3pm & 8.30pm–midnight.

La Taberna de Baco C/San Agustín 10 ☎941 213 544. A truly excellent tapas bar, with a range of delicious specialities: try the *bombita* (potato-and-mushroom ball) or the *migas* (garlic and breadcrumb mixture with a fried egg) and brilliant fried green tomatoes. There are a few tables if you want to make a meal of it. Daily 1–4pm & 8pm–midnight.

La Taberna del Laurel C/Laurel 9 ☎941 220 143. Often bursting at the seams with patrons eagerly stuffing themselves with the house speciality, *patatas bravas*. Daily 12.30–3pm & 8.30pm–midnight.

★**Vinissimo** C/San Juan 23 ☎941 258 828. Fantastically creative tapas (*brochetas* of chicken, prawn or even wild boar are a speciality), plus a carefully selected wine list add up to a more refined tapas bar than usual. A small dining room offers a good-value menu (€10, weekends €12) and various à la carte options. Mon, Tues & Fri–Sun 12.30–4pm & 7.30pm–midnight, Thurs 7.30pm–midnight.

SHOPPING

Felix Barbero Botas Rioja C/Sagasta 8. Felix Barbero makes by hand the traditional *botas de vino* (leather flagons filled with wine) that farmers used to carry their daily ration of wine out into the fields. Mon–Sat 10am–2pm & 4–8pm.

Mercado de Abastos C/Sagasta 1. The daily market, the Mercado de Abastos, is definitely worth a visit for its traditional atmosphere and wide range of local produce. It's also right by many of the best tapas bars. Mon–Fri 7.30am–2pm & 4–8pm, Sat 7.30am–2pm.

Vinos El Peso C/Peso 1. On the corner of the Mercado de Abastos, Vinos El Peso is a wine shop with a decent selection of regional wines and helpful staff who can help you to select from the dizzying array on offer. Mon–Sat 10am–2pm & 5–8pm.

Haro and around

The capital of Rioja Alta is **HARO**, a modern, working town 44km northwest of Logroño. It's entirely devoted to the wine trade, but also has some lovely reminders of a grand past in an old centre that's worth at least a short stop – perhaps even overnight if the winery visits take their toll. Apart from harvest time (Sept), when everything shifts up a gear, the best time to be in Haro is in June, starting with the **Semana del Vino** (Wine Week, usually second week), when the bars and restaurants come together to offer *crianza* and *reserva* wine-tastings at bargain prices. There's more of the same during the continuous **fiestas** of San Juan, San Felices (the town's patron saint) and San Pedro (June 24–29), when there are outdoor concerts, street parades and the climactic **Batalla del Vino** (June 29), when thousands of people climb the Riscos de Bilibio (a small mountain near the town) to be drenched from head to foot in wine.

Plaza de la Paz and around

At the centre of Haro is **Plaza de la Paz**, a sloping square whose glass-balconied mansions overlook an archaic bandstand. An antique sign on the arcade at the top of the square is entirely in keeping with the prevailing sepia tone, prohibiting carriages from entering the narrow streets beyond and threatening a one-peseta fine for transgressors. The very small old quarter off the square is attractive in a faded kind of way, with parallel lanes leading up to the landmark Renaissance church of **Santo Tomás**, with its 68m-high wedding-cake tower and richly carved portal.

TOURING BODEGAS IN LA RIOJA

Wine is at the very heart of La Rioja's identity (Ⓦ riojawine.com), and few people will pass through without visiting a *bodega* and tasting a few *vinos*. If you can only visit one, make it Bodega Dinastía Vivanco in Briones (see p.414). In **Haro**, there are a dozen other *bodegas* within walking distance of town, most clustered around the train station – they offer daily tours (usually in English in the mornings), but you have to make a reservation (Haro *turismo* can advise about current tour times). Some are free, some charge €5–15 for tours and tastings lasting from ninety minutes to two hours. Scores of other wineries lie within half an hour's drive of Haro or Logroño, and tend to be open for drop-in visits without appointment. They've all got wine shops attached, and some have excellent restaurants. A good target is the striking village of **San Vicente de la Sonsierra** which has no fewer than sixteen wineries in the vicinity, while some of the most celebrated vineyards lie close to the town of **Laguardia** (see p.483), 19km northwest of Logroño or 26km east of Haro, in the Basque **Rioja Alavesa** region. **Cenicero** is also a good bet, with numerous big-name wineries located around the town.

Bodegas Bilbaínas ☏ 941 310 147, Ⓦ www .bodegasbilbainas.com. One of the oldest *bodegas* in Haro, established in 1901, home of the classic Viña Pomal wines and their flagship contemporary label, La Vicalanda. The 90min informative tour costs €5. Visits by appointment.

Bodegas Muga ☏ 941 311 825, Ⓦ bodegasmuga. com. Muga has a good visitor centre in Haro where you can learn about its painstaking traditional methods,

such as using egg whites to clean the wine of impurities. On the €6 tour you'll also get to taste two wines. Mon–Thurs 8am–2pm and 3.30–6pm, Fri 8am–2pm.

López de Heredia ☏ 941 310 244, Ⓦ www .lopezdeheredia.com. Standout attraction at this Haro winery is the eye-catching modernist wine shop designed by Zaha Hadid. Tours are free of charge. Visits by appointment.

5

Centro de Interpretación del Vino de la Rioja

C/Breton de los Herreros 4 • Fri & Sat 10am–2.30pm & 3.30–6pm, Sun 10am–2pm • €3 • ☎ 941 305 719, ⓦ vinodelarioja.org

The **Centro de Interpretación del Vino de la Rioja**, behind Haro's bus station, is the regional government's formal showcase for its wine production – hugely informative (there's an English audio-guide available) but unfortunately closed for most of the week. They also offer weekend wine-tasting courses, though visitors with a more casual interest, who just want to taste a wine or two, are better served by visiting one of the local *bodegas* (see box, p.413).

Museo de la Cultura del Vino

Bodega Dinastía Vivanco, Briones, 6km southeast of Haro on the N232 • Hours vary but roughly Aug–Sept Tues–Sat 10am–8pm, Sun 10am–6pm; Oct & April–July Tues–Fri & Sun 10am–6pm, Sat 10am–8pm; Nov Wed–Fri & Sun 10am–6pm; Dec & March Wed–Fri & Sun 11am–3pm, Sat 10am–6pm; Feb Sat 10am–6pm, Sun 11am–3pm; closed Jan; last entry 1hr 30min before closing • Museum €8, *bodega* tour €9 (reservations required), combination ticket €15 • ☎ 941 322 340 or ☎ 902 320 001, ⓦ www.dinastiavivanco.com

The best single visit for anyone interested in Rioja wine is the impressive **Museo de la Cultura del Vino** at the Dinastía Vivanco family *bodega* just outside Haro (you'll pass by on the drive from Logroño). It's a slick operation all round, with a comprehensive museum that covers every aspect of wine production, and guided tours of the associated winery that set off several times daily, taking you out into the vineyard and then down into the underground bowels of the operation. Add in a "tasting bar", with its automatic wine-dispensers, a well-stocked shop, café with vineyard views, fancy restaurant and vine-planted gardens, and you could easily spend half a day here.

ARRIVAL AND DEPARTURE   HARO

By train The train station is a 15min walk from the centre, down over the bridge on the other side of the river, at Barrio de la Estación 1.

By bus Services from Logroño by bus are far more frequent than those by train and the bus station is slightly closer in, at Pza Castañares de Rioja 4, a 10min walk from the centre of town.

By car Haro is only small, and finding free on-street parking isn't usually a problem.

INFORMATION

Turismo Pza. de la Paz (Tues–Fri 10.30am–2pm & 5–8pm, Sun 10.30am–2pm; ☎ 941 303 580, ⓦ haroturismo.org).

ACCOMMODATION

★**Hospedería Señorío de Briñas** C/Travesía de la C/Real 3, Briñas, 6km north of Haro ☎ 941 304 224, ⓦ hotelesconencantodelarioja.com. Magnificent baronial mansion in a charming riverside village. Rooms use the exposed stone and archaic features to ravishing effect, and there's a spa in the old wine cellar. A winery visit is also included. **€119**

Hotel Los Agustinos C/San Agustín 2 ☎ 941 311 308, ⓦ hotellosagustinos.com. This converted Augustinian convent founded in 1373, whose centrepiece is a magnificent glass-covered cloister, has rooms that mix traditional furnishings with up-to-date comforts. If you're staying, you're unlikely to eat anywhere other than the fine restaurant, *Las Duelas* (closed Jan), a contemporary Spanish place (mains from around €25) with dining in the hotel cloister. **€92**

Pensión La Peña C/Virgen de La Vega 1 ☎ 941 310 022. The best budget accommodation in town, with cosy, well-kept rooms, some of them en suite and many with balconies overlooking Pza. de la Paz. **€35**

EATING AND DRINKING

Even the humblest *tapa* is transformed by a glass of Rioja, and you'll get plenty – and very cheaply – in the dozen or so **bars and restaurants** that lie the short distance between Pza. de la Paz and Santo Tomás church.

Meson Los Berones C/Santo Tomás 23 ☎ 941 310 707. There's traditional Riojan tapas and good-value meals, day and night, in this rustic bar with a few wooden tables at the back. The €14 menu runs from grilled lamb chops to salt cod drenched in a spicy tomato sauce. Daily noon–midnight.

El Portillo Pza. San Martín 3 ☎ 941 898 050. This place, in a cute little square below the church, is less rustic and more contemporary than most, with fancy tapas (including a carpaccio of artichoke and *bacalao*), a good lunchtime menu for €13 and à la carte meals for around €30. Tues–Sun noon–4.30pm & 7–11.30pm.

Nájera

The Camino de Santiago sweeps through Logroño and on towards Burgos, passing to the south of Haro. At the small riverside town of **NÁJERA**, 15km south of Haro, dramatically sited below a pink, cave-riddled rock formation, you're ostentatiously welcomed to the "Capital of Furniture" (Nájera is known for its fixtures and fittings). Old and modern Nájera are separated by the grassy riverbanks of rippling Río Najerilla – there's plenty of free parking on either side – while just across the footbridge from the charming old town, there's a riverside **market** every Thursday.

Monasterio Santa María la Real

Pza. de Santa María • May–Sept Tues–Sat 10am–1pm & 4–7pm, Sun 10am–12.30pm & 4–6pm; Oct–April Tues–Sat 10am–1pm & 4–5.30pm, Sun 10am–12.30pm & 4–5.30pm • €3 • ☎ 941 361 083, ⊚ santamarialareal.net

Dominating the old town is the stork-topped Gothic **Monasterio Santa María la Real**. This contains a royal pantheon of ancient monarchs of Castile, León and Navarra, though best of all is the attractive sixteenth-century cloister of rose-coloured stone and elaborate tracery.

ACCOMMODATION	NÁJERA
Hotel San Fernando Paseo San Julián 1 ☎ 941 363 700. Reasonable rooms – nothing striking, but good for a	comfortable night – plus a rather unexpected traditional red English phone box in the lobby. **€80**

Santo Domingo de la Calzada

The small town of **SANTO DOMINGO DE LA CALZADA**, 20km west of Nájera, owes its history and much of its livelihood to the Santiago pilgrim route, which it is a stop on. The Catedral, with its fourteenth-century Mudéjar cloister, is dedicated to town founder Domingo de la Calzada, and since the earliest days of the pilgrimage there has been a welcome here for wayfarers, a steady stream of whom still pick their way though town; and there are plenty of inexpensive *menús del día* on offer at local restaurants to raise strength and spirits. The former medieval pilgrims' hospital is now a fine parador but, for all this, only the very centre of town around the Catedral is particularly attractive and, unless you're a foot-weary pilgrim or staying at the parador, there's no pressing need to stay long in town – Ezcaray to the south (see p.416) is a better overnight stop.

ACCOMMODATION AND EATING	SANTO DOMINGO DE LA CALZADA
★**Parador Santo Domingo de Bernardo de Fresneda** Pza. del Santo 3 ☎ 941 340 300, ⊚ www.parador.es. Only the wealthier sort of pilgrim gets to enjoy the luxurious comforts of the parador these days, in light rooms that occupy a modern annexe, grafted on to the old pilgrims' hospital. It's all nicely – if traditionally – done, though rooms are smaller than you'll get at some other paradors. A substantial breakfast is served in the lovely old restaurant until late morning. **€120**	★**Restaurante La Cancela** C/Mayor 51 ☎ 941 343 238, ⊚ restaurantelacancela.com. This fabulously friendly restaurant run by a father and son team serves up a delicious menu of high-quality Spanish dishes. Start with *jamón Ibérico de bellota* (€18) or local asparagus (€10.50) before ordering juicy *entrecot* (€17.90) or *bacalao* (€18.50) and take advice on the extensive wine list – there are too many excellent vintages here to choose from. Mon & Wed–Sun 1.30–3.30pm & 8–10.30pm.

The mountain monasteries of Suso, Yuso and Valvanera

Around 18km from Nájera (a little further from Santo Domingo), the stone village of **San Millán de la Cogolla** serves as gateway to the magnificent twin mountain monasteries known as **Yuso** and **Suso**. You can see these easily as a half-day diversion

5

from the main Rioja route, while a third monastery, **Valvanera**, lies further south, off the **LR113**, the trans-mountain road that provides a dramatic journey south and west between Nájera and Salas de los Infantes (90km; 2hr drive). This twists ever higher up the glorious, lush valley of the Río Najerilla, hugging the sides of the huge hydroelectric Mansilla dam, before careering across the bare uplands of the **Sierra de la Demanda** to cross into Castilla y León. The route makes a great roundabout approach to Burgos, and you'll emerge close to the equally magnificent monastery of Santo Domingo de Silos (see p.425).

Monasterio de Yuso

Easter–Sept Tues–Sun 10am–1.30pm & 4–6.30pm, plus Mon in Aug; Oct–Easter Tues–Sat 10am–1pm & 3.30–5.30pm, Sun 10am–1pm • Guided 50min visits €6 • ☎ 941 373 049, ⓦ monasteriodeyuso.org

The immense lower **Monasterio de Yuso**, which dominates the valley, was built in the sixteenth and seventeenth centuries to house the relics of the crowd-pulling sixth-century saint, San Millán. It's at the centre of some fairly big tourist business, with one wing of the monastery housing a four-star hotel, a couple of big restaurants and enough parking to accommodate the entire Spanish nation, should it choose to all come at once.

ACCOMMODATION   **MONASTERIO DE YUSO**

Hostería del Monasterio Monasterio de Yuso ☎ 941 373 277, ⓦ sanmillan.com. Situated in one wing of the monastery, this is rather a grand place to spend the night – and many of the rooms have Jacuzzi baths. **€135**

Posada de San Millán C/Prestiño, 5 ☎ 941 373 161, ⓦ lapoasadadesanmillan.es. Located in front of the Yuso complex, this simpler, rustic residence has just half a dozen inexpensive rooms. **€48**

Monasterio de Suso

Tues–Sun 9.30am–1.30pm & 3.30–6.30pm • Half-hourly tours from 9.55am–1.25pm & 3.55–5.55pm; reservations required at the lower ticket office at Yuso (access from the hotel courtyard) • €4 • ☎ 941 373 082, ⓦ monasteriodeyuso.org

Much older than Monasterio de Yuso, the **Monasterio de Suso** lies a few hundred metres up in the hills, hidden from public view. You're taken up by shuttle bus to see the beautiful, haunting building, the original site of Millán's burial before he was sanctified in 1030 and later transferred down the hill into surroundings more in keeping with a patron saint.

Monasterio de Valvanera

No public access to monastery buildings • ☎ 941 377 044, ⓦ valvanera.com

The wonderfully sited monastery, the **Monasterio de Valvanera**, is 35km further south of San Millán de la Cogolla (and a 5km detour off the LR113 mountain road). If anything, the location is even more dramatic than that of Yuso and Suso – it's situated 1000m above a steep-sided valley, with the tidy terraces of the Benedictine monks' vegetable gardens below. It's worth stopping briefly for the views – there's a bar and restaurant and some simple accommodation here – and to experience a monastic retreat with none of the crowds of its more renowned counterparts.

Ezcaray

For summer and winter escapes – hiking in the wooded valley of the Río Oja, skiing on the heights above – locals make a beeline up the LR111 to the pretty resort of **EZCARAY**, 15km south of Santo Domingo de la Calzada. This was a thriving textile centre in earlier centuries, which explains the mammoth former "royal factory" and dye shop you pass on the way into town (now partly converted into lodgings), while the ruined sixteenth-century bridge (destroyed by a flash flood in 1881) and the fortified medieval church in the centre also speak of former grandeur. Tourism has led to a smartening-up of Ezcaray's landscaped riverside gardens, porticoed streets and ancient squares, and its big, solid stone houses, many supported on gnarled wooden pillars, have small, deep-set windows to help keep out the winter chill. Ezcaray is an attractive place to spend the night, particularly as it has acquired a reputation as a foodie destination, with some excellent local restaurants, including one of Spain's finest regional gastro-hotels.

ACCOMMODATION AND EATING

EZCARAY

Echaurren C/Padre José García 19 ☎ 941 354 047, ⓦ rusticae.es. Opposite the main church, this family-run place, now in its fifth generation, features some very comfortable guest rooms above two restaurants *Echaurren* and *El Portal*. €135

Echaurren C/Padre José García 19. The seasonal menu here is based on traditional Riojan recipes from the current chef's mother (mains €17–23, *menú del día* €22).

Mon–Sat 1.30–3.30pm & 9.15–11pm, Sun 1.30–3.30pm; also open Sun 9.15–11pm in July & Aug.

El Portal C/Padre José García 19. Expect the finest seasonally led cuisine at this contemporary, creative and Michelin-starred restaurant (tasting menus at €60 and €85). Mon–Sat 1.30–3.30pm & 9.15–11pm, Sun 1.30–3.30pm; closed Mon July–Dec, & Mon–Tues Jan–June.

La Rioja Baja

Forty kilometres from Logroño, Calahorra is the main town of **La Rioja Baja**, the southeastern part of the province. After the wine towns of the Rioja Alta it's a bit of a disappointment, and there's not really a pressing need to stop, though it does have an appealing old town. Calahorra also offers an attractive back-country route to Soria, via Arnedo, 12km southwest of town, where the scenery suddenly changes from cultivated flatland to vivid red rock, punctured by hundreds of caves, both natural and man-made, used in the past as houses and hermitages. From here – past attractive riverside **Arnedillo**, until reaching the tiny valley-bottom village of Yanguas, 30km southwest – the LR115 makes a twisting journey through the narrow Río Cidacos gorge, before climbing up over the bare tops for the sweeping run into Soria, another 50km to the south. It takes a couple of hours all told from Calahorra to Soria, though it's much the best idea to break in the middle at **Enciso** for a spot of dinosaur-hunting. A hundred and twenty million years ago (in the early Cretaceous period), the southeastern part of La Rioja was a steamy marshland where dinosaurs roamed, leaving their footprints in mud that later fossilized, and you can spend an enjoyable day in the area following the tracks.

Calahorra

CALAHORRA, on the Cidacos river, was one of the most important cities in Roman Spain (known then as Calagurris) and today is known as the "city of vegetables" thanks to its fertile flood plains. Some remains from the Roman period can still be seen, including part of the original Roman walls, the remnants of a first-century villa called La Clínica and evidence of the Roman circus. A pleasant half-day can be spent strolling the old town, where you will also find the seventeenth-century Gothic Catedral of Santa María.

ACCOMMODATION AND EATING

CALAHORRA

Parador de Calahorra Paseo del Mercadal, 26500 ☎ 941 130 358, ⓦ www.parador.es. Comfortable red-brick hotel with simple wooden-floored rooms and an on-site bar and restaurant. €115

★ **Restaurante la Taberna de la Cuarta Esquina** Avda. del Cidacos 23 ☎ 941 134 355. Top-quality

restaurant in the heart of the old town, serving hearty local meat dishes and excellent calamari (€13.50), all washed down with an almost bewildering selection of Riojas. Very popular with locals; reservations recommended at weekends. Thurs–Mon 1–5pm & 8pm–midnight, Tues 1–5pm.

Arnedillo

ARNEDILLO, 24km southwest of Calahorra, is a pretty spot, a minor spa set in a deep river valley beneath spiky crags, with its church at the very bottom by the river. From

5

here it's an easy stroll off into the lovely surroundings, along the river and up the side valleys, past ruined water mills, restored hermitages and waterside allotments.

ACCOMMODATION AND EATING ARNEDILLO

Casa Cañas Avda. del Cidacos 23 ☏ 941 394 022, ⓦ restaurantecasacanas.com. At *Casa Cañas* they are very proud of their "century at your service", and so they should be – the food is excellent, with succulent grills the speciality, alongside Riojan staples like *pochas* (stewed white beans) and vegetable *minestra*. The menu is €12, or eat à la carte for around €20. Mon, Tues & Thurs–Sat

1–4pm & 9–11pm.
Hospederia Las Pedrolas ☏ 941 394 401, ⓦ laspedrolas.com. Although there's a *hostal* or two up on the main through-road, above the village, the best place to rest your head is this charming rustic house right outside the village church. Breakfast is also included. **€90**

Enciso

The village of **ENCISO**, 11km from Arnedillo and 35km southwest of Calahorra, is La Rioja's main dinosaur centre and the easiest place to see some preserved footprints. You can either drive out to the main sites, or take the well-signposted 6km circular **walk** from Enciso's El Barranco Perdido. There are lots of other signposted dinosaur sites in the vicinity, at Munilla or Préjano, for example, though many are on 4WD dirt tracks. A mountain bike would be ideal, or pack your hiking boots.

El Barranco Perdido

Hours vary but broadly daily June–Sept 11am–6.30pm, July & Aug 11am–8pm; Oct–May Sat & Sun 11am–8pm • €23.75 • ☏ 941 396 080, ⓦ barrancoperdido.com

Once just a small **Centre Paleontológico** giving information about the region's dinosaur sites, today Enciso is home to a greatly expanded and Disneyesque dinosaur-themed **El Barranco Perdido**. Rides, attractions and shows combine to make a full family-friendly day out, though those seeking an informative experience may be disappointed with its child-focused antics. For something quieter, follow the brown signposts from here which point you to the nearby sites of **Virgen del Campo** and **Valdecevillo**, both featuring lots of visible tracks in the stone as well as huge replica dinos to thrill the kids.

Burgos

BURGOS was the capital of Old Castile for almost five hundred years, the home of El Cid in the eleventh century, and the base, two centuries later, of Fernando III, the reconqueror of Murcia, Córdoba and Seville. It was Fernando who began the city's famous Gothic Catedral, one of the greatest in all Spain, and Burgos is a firm station on the pilgrim route. During the Civil War, Franco temporarily installed his Fascist government in the city and Burgos owes much of its modern expansion to Franco's "Industrial Development Plan", a strategy to shift the country's wealth away from Catalunya and the Basque Country and into Castile.

Burgos has been much scrubbed and restored over the last few years due to its (unsuccessful) candidature for European City of Culture for 2016. Every paving stone in the centre looks to have been relaid, and while it's no longer a clearly medieval city, the handsome buildings, squares and riverfront of the old town are an attractive prospect for a night's stay. Despite the encroaching suburban sprawl and a population of almost 200,000, when it comes down to it, Burgos really isn't that big. The Río Arlanzón bisects the city and neatly delimits the *casco histórico*, or old quarter, on the north bank. You can easily see everything here in a day, and while its lesser churches inevitably tend to be eclipsed by the Catedral, the two wonderful monasteries on the outskirts are by no means overshadowed.

Catedral

Pza. del Rey San Fernando • March–Oct 9.30am–7.30pm, last entrance at 6.30pm; Nov to mid-March 10am–7pm • €7 • ☎ 947 204 712,
🖰 www.catedraldeburgos.es

The *casco histórico* is totally dominated by the **Catedral**, one of the most extraordinary
achievements of Gothic art. Its spires can be seen above the rooftops from all over
town, and it's an essential first stop in Burgos. The Catedral has emerged from a
lengthy period of restoration, looking cleaner than it has for centuries, though visiting
it has been reduced to something of a production line, with a separate visitor centre,
well-stocked gift shop and one-way flow inside to keep tourists from worshippers.

The interior

Moorish influences can be seen in the Catedral's central **dome** (1568), supported on
four thick piers that fan out into remarkably delicate buttresses – a worthy setting for
the **tomb of El Cid** and his wife Jimena, marked by a simple slab of pink veined marble
in the floor below. Otherwise, perhaps the most striking thing about the vast interior is
the size and number of its side chapels, with the octagonal **Capilla del Condestable**,
behind the high altar, possibly the most splendid of all, featuring a ceiling designed to
form two concentric eight-pointed stars. In the **Capilla de Santa Ana**, the magnificent
retablo is by Gil de Siloé, a Flanders-born craftsman whose son Diego crafted the
adjacent double stairway, the glorious **Escalera Dorada**.

IT'S A MIRACLE

The most highly venerated place of worship inside the Catedral is the **Capilla del Santísimo Cristo de Burgos**, which contains a cloyingly realistic image of Christ (c.1300), endowed with real human hair and nails and covered with the withered hide of a water buffalo, still popularly believed to be human skin. Legend has it that the icon was modelled directly from the scene at the Crucifixion and that – miracle of miracles – it requires a shave and a manicure every eighth day. The chapel, however, is closed to anyone clutching a Catedral visitor's ticket – worshippers enter instead via the Puerta de Santa María outside.

Cloisters and Museo Catedralicio

The tourist route through the church leads out of the main body of the Catedral and into the spacious two-storey **cloisters**, and beyond this to a series of chapels that house the **Museo Catedralicio,** with its collection of religious treasures and two El Cid mementoes, namely his marriage contract and a wooden trunk. The light-filled lower cloister also has an audio-visual history of the church and its architecture, including a look at the various restoration projects.

Arco de Santa María

Tues–Sat 11am–2pm & 5–9pm, Sun 11am–2pm • Free • ☎ 947 288 868

The main approach to the old town and Catedral is across the **Puenta de Santa María**, where you're confronted by the **Arco de Santa María**, a gateway that originally formed part of the town walls. There are temporary art exhibitions held inside, and you can also view its exquisite Mudéjar ceiling, but it's the exterior that really catches the eye. It was embellished with statues in 1534–36 in order to appease Carlos V after Burgos' involvement in a revolt by Spanish noblemen against their new Flemish-born king. Carlos' statue is glorified here in the context of the greatest Burgalese heroes: Diego Porcelos, founder of the city in the late ninth century; Nuño Rasura and Laín Calvo, two early magistrates; Fernán González, founder of the Countship of Castile in 932; and, above all, **El Cid Campeador**, who is surpassed in popular sentiment only by St James in his legendary exploits against the Moors.

Museo de la Evolución Humana

Paseo Sierra de Atapuerca • Tues–Fri 10am–2.30pm & 4.30–8pm, Sat, Sun & daily in July & Aug 10am–8pm • €6; €11 including bus tour to archeological site • ☎ 902 024 246, ⓦ museoevolucionhumana.com

Burgos' main new cultural addition is the modernist riverfront cube housing the **Museo de la Evolución Humana**. This takes the important fossil finds and early human archeological sites at the local Atapuerca mountains as the starting point for an entertaining and informative tour through the history of human evolution. Wide-ranging displays cover subjects from the first use of fire to Darwin's expeditions aboard the *Beagle*, with the whole museum – and indeed human evolution itself – rooted in the idea of the connective ecosystems that have allowed *Homo sapiens* and their ancestors to develop over millions of years. The museum also runs daily bus tours out to the Atapuerca archeological sites, where fossils and tools have been found dating back well over a million years – some of the earliest such finds in Europe.

Centro de Arte Caja de Burgos (CAB)

C/Saldaña • Tues–Fri noon–2pm & 5.30–8pm, Sat 11.30am–2.30pm & 5.30–9pm, Sun 11.30am–2.30pm • Free • ☎ 947 256 550, ⓦ cabdeburgos.com

CAB, the city's newest arts centre, sits in a striking modern building right at the top of the steps by the church of San Esteban – it's a convenient stop on the way up to the castle. There are usually a couple of free exhibitions on at any one time – contemporary Spanish art and installations are its bread and butter – while CAB also puts on all sorts of other shows, events and workshops.

Castillo de Burgos

June–Sept daily 11am–8pm; Oct–May Sat & Sun 11am–2.30pm • €3.70 • ☎ 947 203 857

The highest point of town is marked by the **Castillo de Burgos**, a huge fortress that was largely destroyed by the French in 1813 – there are steps from opposite the church of San Esteban, which you can reach up C/Pozo Seco, behind the Catedral. The walls, battlements and staircases have been restored, and there's also a museum covering the history of the town, but even if you don't plan to go inside it's worth the short climb up the hill anyway, for the views from the *mirador* over the Catedral and town.

Monasterio de las Huelgas

Tues–Sat 10am–1pm & 3.45–5.30pm, Sun 10.30am–2pm • €5, free Wed • ☎ 947 201 630, ⓦ monasteriodelashuelgas.org • Around 1.5km west of the city centre (20min walk): cross Puente de Santa María, turn right and follow the signs along the riverbank

The Cistercian **Monasterio de las Huelgas** is remarkable for its wealth of Mudéjar craftsmanship. Founded in 1187 as the future mausoleum of Alfonso VIII (who died in 1214) and his wife Eleanor, daughter of Henry II of England, it became one of the most powerful convents in Spain. It was popularly observed that "If the pope were to marry, only the abbess of Las Huelgas would be eligible!" A community of nuns still lives here (making pottery that's for sale), and though you can enter through the gatehouse into the impressive courtyard, you have to pay to go any further.

It's very definitely worth it. The main **church**, with its typically excessive Churrigueresque *retablo*, contains the tombs of no fewer than sixteen Castilian monarchs and nobles, including Eleanor and Alfonso. Napoleon's troops paid their usual violent courtesy visit, and robbed the convent of its valuables, but remarkably, when the surviving tombs were later opened, many were found to contain regal clothes, embroidery and jewellery, now on display in a small **museum**. Other highlights include a set of delicate Romanesque cloisters, **Las Claustrillas**, and the ceiling of the main Gothic cloisters, which is adorned with patches of Mudéjar decoration. The **Capilla de**

EL CID CAMPEADOR

Principal landmark along the leafy Burgos riverfront – right on the Puente de San Pablo – is the magnificent equestrian **statue of El Cid**, complete with flying cloak, flowing beard and raised sword. The city lays full claim to the Castilian nobleman, soldier and mercenary, born Rodrigo Díaz in the nearby village of Vivar in 1040 or thereabouts. Actually, his most significant military exploits took place around Valencia, the city he took back briefly from the Moors after a long siege in 1094, but no matter – El Cid (from the Arabic *sidi* or lord) is a local boy, whose heroic feats (not all strictly historically accurate) have been celebrated in Spain since the twelfth century. His honorific title, **Campeador** ("Supreme in Valour"), is some indication of the esteem in which he's always been held, though there's generally a veil drawn over his avarice and political ambition, not to mention the fact that, as an exiled sword-for-hire in the 1080s, El Cid turned out for Moorish princes as easily as for Christian kings. He died in Valencia in 1099, and the city fell again to the Moors in 1102, after which his wife Jimena took El Cid's body to the monastery of San Pedro de Cardeña, south of Burgos, where it rested for centuries. The body disappeared to France after the ravages of the Peninsular War, but husband and wife were reburied together in Burgos Catedral in 1921.

5

Santiago also has a fine Mudéjar ceiling and pointed horseshoe archway. Its cult statue of St James has an articulated right arm, which enabled him to dub knights of the Order of Santiago (motto: "The Sword is Red with the Blood of Islam") and on occasion even to crown kings.

Cartuja de Miraflores

Mon–Sat 10.15am–3pm & 4–6pm, Sun 11am–3pm & 4–6pm • €1 • ☎ 947 252 586, ⓦ www.cartuja.org • Around 4km east of the centre – follow the path along the south bank of the river (towards *Camping Fuentes Blancas*), bear right up the hill at the Fuente del Prior park (45min) and cross the road for the monastery; it's well signposted by road all the way from town

The second of the town's two notable monasteries, the **Cartuja de Miraflores**, famous for its three dazzling masterpieces by sculptor Gil de Siloé, lies in a secluded spot, a very pleasant hour's walk from the centre. The monastery buildings are still in use and you can only visit the **church** (1454–1488), which is divided, in accordance with Carthusian practice, into three sections: for the public, the lay brothers and the monks. In front of the high altar lies the star-shaped carved alabaster tomb of Juan II of Castile (1405–1454) and Isabel of Portugal, of such perfection that it forced Felipe II and Juan de Herrera to admit "We did not achieve very much with our Escorial". Isabel la Católica, a great patron of the arts, commissioned it from Gil de Siloé in 1489 as a memorial to her parents. The same sculptor carved the magnificent altarpiece, plated with the first gold shipped back from the Americas and featuring scores of figures with expressive faces, so delicately carved that even the open pages of a Bible and parchment rolls are depicted. Finally comes the smaller but no less intricate tomb of the Infante (Crown Prince) Alfonso, brother of Queen Isabel, through whose untimely death in 1468 she was later able to claim the throne of Castile.

ARRIVAL AND DEPARTURE   BURGOS

By train Burgos Rosa de Lima station is on Avda. Príncipe de Asturias, 5km northeast of the centre, but bus #25 runs from right outside the entrance every 30min to Pza. España, a 20min journey. For current timetables and ticket information, consult RENFE (☎ 902 320 320, ⓦ renfe.com).
Destinations Bilbao (5 daily; 2hr 30min–4hr 30min); León (4 daily; 2hr); Logroño (4 daily; 2hr 15min); Madrid (7 daily; 2hr 30min–4hr 15min); Palencia (9 daily; 45min–1hr); Salamanca (4 daily; 2hr 30min); Valladolid (up to 13 daily; 1hr–1hr 20min); Vitoria (10 daily; 1hr 15min–1hr 30min); Zaragoza (4 daily; 4hr).

By bus The bus station is on C/Miranda (☎ 947 288 855) on the south side of the river – it's a short walk up to cross the bridges into town.
Destinations Bilbao (8 daily; 2hr); Carrión de los Condes

(daily; 1hr 20min); Covarrubias (Mon–Fri 2 daily, Sat daily; 1hr); Frómista (daily; 1hr); León (4–5 daily; 2hr direct, otherwise up to 3hr); Logroño via Nájera (Mon–Fri 7 daily, Sat & Sun 3–4 daily; 2hr); Madrid (10 daily; 2hr 45min); Palencia (up to 3 daily; 1hr 15min); Pamplona (4 daily; 3hr 30min); Salamanca (3 daily; 3hr 30min); San Sebastián (7 daily; 3hr 30min); Santander (4 daily; 3hr); Soria (up to 3 daily; 2hr–2hr 30min); Santo Domingo de Silos (Mon–Sat daily; 1hr 30min); Valladolid (5 daily; 2hr 30min); Vinuesa (2–3 daily; 2hr 15min); Zaragoza (4 daily; 4hr).

By car Short-term parking is available out of the centre along the river, though there are large central signposted car parks, including under Pza. Mayor, at Pza. de Vega (near the bus station), and at Pza. de España. Overnight parking costs around €20.

INFORMATION AND TOURS

Turismo C/Nuño Rasura 7, down an alley in a building off Pza. del Rey San Fernando, near the Catedral (Mon–Fri 9.30am–2pm & 4–7pm, Sat–Sun 9am–8pm; ☎ 947 288 874, ⓦ aytoburgos.es).
Trén Turístico A trolley-train rumbles around town

(hourly departures 3–7pm, weekends and holidays 11am–7pm), departing from outside the Catedral – it's €4, though the evening, floodlit tours (Fri–Sun plus hols departs 9.15pm, €5) might be the better choice.

ACCOMMODATION

It's generally nicest to stay over the river, closer to the old town, though many of the new three- and four-star hotels are on the outskirts or even further out.

Camping Fuentes Blancas Parque de Fuentes Blancas ☎ 947 486 016, ⓦ campingburgos.com. Out along the river, a 45min walk or a bus ride from the centre (catch it from Avda. del Arlanzón, along the river by the Cid statue). Facilities are excellent, including a large sunny pool, a restaurant and café, bikes for rent, mini golf and bungalows. Closed Oct–March. Camping **€25.19**, bungalows **€36**

Hotel Jacobeo C/San Juan 24 ☎ 947 260 102, ⓦ hoteljacobeo.com. Snazzy one-star outfit that offers small, trim rooms in muted, contemporary colours. There's a breakfast bar downstairs, though you're very close to all the cafés and restaurants. There are some dorms, and a parking garage. Dorms **€23.50**, doubles **€50**

Hotel Mesón del Cid Pza. de Santa María 8 ☎ 947 208 715, ⓦ mesondelcid.es. The best rooms to get here have balconies with great Catedral views. It's the most traditional hotel in the old town and has its own parking and a restaurant set apart from the main building. **€65**

Hotel Norte y Londres Pza. Alonzo Martínez 10 ☎ 947 264 125, ⓦ hotelnorteylondres.com. A two-star hotel in a very attractive *belle époque* house, right in the centre. There's a traditional feel throughout, and rooms reflect the period but are cosy and comfortable; a fair few triples offer a bit more space and flexibility. Book online for the best rates. **€45**

Hotel La Puebla C/Puebla 20 ☎ 947 200 011, ⓦ hotellapuebla.com. This elegant townhouse is the best boutique choice in the city. Huge beds and striking wall-coverings dominate the nineteen rooms, and while space is tight you can't fault black-marble designer bathrooms featuring his-and-her sinks and rain showers. Helpful staff can organize bike rental, and advise about parking. **€85**

Pensión Peña C/Puebla 18 ☎ 947 206 323. The top budget option in Burgos, this is a welcoming and immaculate *pensión*. It's right in the old town and popular with *camino* hikers, so advance reservations are essential. **€40**

EATING, DRINKING AND NIGHTLIFE

You'll find plenty of **restaurants** in Burgos serving traditional Castilian dishes, including the local speciality, *morcilla* (a kind of black pudding or blood sausage, mixed with rice). Good **tapas bars** are legion, especially down the narrow bar-run of C/San Lorenzo (off Pza. Mayor), but also along C/Avellanos, and near the Catedral around C/la Paloma. Burgos **nightlife**, meanwhile, is mainly generated by the local students, who hang out in the lively "pubs" and music bars in the open spaces of C/Huerto del Rey and C/Llana de Afuera, behind the Catedral – just follow the crowds. There's a more stylish scene over on C/Puebla and C/San Juan, where some fancier *copas* places hide behind smoked glass. After 3am, check out the late-night bars and **clubs** around the modern courtyard known as Pza. de Las Bernardas, just off C/Las Calzadas, east of the *casco histórico*, which are usually open till 7am.

CAFÉS

Juarreño Pza. Mayor 25 ☎ 947 213 490, ⓦ juarreno .com. The best address in town for cakes, sweets and pastries – beautifully concocted, artisan-made chocs, *bombóns*, croissants and cakes from a masterful *pastelería*. There are seats on the main square too. Mon–Thurs 9.30am–9.30pm, Fri 9.30am–10.30pm, Sat 10am– 10.30pm, Sun 10am–9.30pm.

TAPAS BARS AND RESTAURANTS

Bar Gaona Jardín C/Sombrerería 29 ☎ 947 206 191, ⓦ gaonajardin.com. Pick your way into the interior, modelled on an *andaluz* garden, where beautifully sculpted bite-sized *pinchos* (from €2) line the bar (specialities include the signature foie gras with apple purée). It can be hard to find the first time – it's tucked down a dead-end alley, around the block from C/la Paloma (and is not to be mistaken for the *Gaonas*, a more mainstream tapas bar and restaurant on that street). Tues–Sun 11am–3.30pm & 7pm–midnight.

La Cantina del Tenorio C/Arco del Pilar 10 ☎ 947 269 781, ⓦ lacantinadeltenorio.es. Atmospheric stone tavern with a nice line in creative fish *pinchos*, including anchovy and pickled peppers, smoked salmon and cherry tomatoes,

and razor clams and olives. Tapas and *raciones* €2–12. Tues–Sat 1pm–midnight, Sun 1–4pm.

Casa Ojeda C/Vitoria 5 ☎ 947 209 052, ⓦ restauranteojeda.com. One of the oldest and grandest places in town, dividing its efforts between deli, café, beer-house and restaurant. It's an ornately decorated space, with a smart Castilian restaurant upstairs and cheaper eats in the *comedor* or at the bar, though you're looking at *platos combinados* from €12.50 and à la carte dishes in the restaurant from around €20. Ask for wine recommendations to match your meal. Mon–Sat 1–4pm & 9–11pm, Sun 1–4pm.

★**Cervecería Morito** C/Diego Porcelos 1, cnr C/Sombrerería ☎ 947 267 555. The best budget dining spot in town, permanently rammed with locals at meal times. It's a no-nonsense bar serving huge freshly cooked, meal-in-one platters for around €10 (tuna *tortilla*, calamari and salad, say), or big stuffed sandwiches, *raciones*, salads and egg dishes (all €4–9), plus cheap-as-chips drinks. Daily noon–midnight.

La Esencia C/Peubla 18 ☎ 947 263 296, ⓦ restaurantelaesencia.es. Fine dining with a contemporary edge – think wild mushroom and king prawn salad or black pudding lasagne with red pepper

5

sauce, followed by seared tuna or fillet of sea bass. It's all beautifully presented, and fairly reasonably priced, with dishes at €14–23 and good-value tasting menus at €21 and €25. Gluten-free options are also available. Daily 1.30–4pm & 8.15–11.30pm.

La Favorita C/Avellanos 8 ☏947 205 949, ⓦlafavoritaburgos.com. The self-professed "urban tavern" reboots the genre, offering classic tapas and pinchos – croquetas to grilled foie gras, egg scrambles to tuna and chilli brochettes – but in a rustic-chic city bar setting. Pinchos start at €2, but dishes can cost as much as €18 for a plate of bellota ham. Daily noon–midnight.

★**Mesón los Herreros** C/San Lorenzo 20 ☏947 202 448, ⓦmesonlosherreros.es. At busy times, you have to perch around the barrel table-tops outside on the street at

this classic old-town tapas bar. There's a famously wide range of tapas and raciones (snails to stuffed mussels, €1.50–8) and, like the other places along here, there's also an upstairs comedor for meals – the excellent menú del día is €12 (€15 at weekends). Daily noon–midnight; restaurant 1–4pm & 8–11pm.

El Soportal C/Sombrerería 5 ☏947 277 574, ⓦelsoportal.es. A rare find indeed – a tapas bar that is open for breakfast. Start your day with tortillas and bocadillos from €2 and come back later to feast on tapas and raciones from mini hamburgers to huevos rotos. The wine list is high quality and their other speciality is gin and tonic. Mon–Fri 8.30am–11.30pm, Sat–Sun 12.30–11.30pm.

South and east of Burgos

South and east of Burgos lies a quartet of renowned sights – ancient hermitage, lavish abbey cloister and two very different restored towns – that are all easy excursions by car. They would make a fine, if busy, day's tour from Burgos, or can be seen en route to Soria, down the N234, though for an alternative overnight stop it's a hard choice between the dramatic parador at Lerma and the small-town charms of Covarrubias.

Ermita de Santa María de Lara

Quintanilla de las Viñas • May–Sept Wed–Sun 10am–2pm & 4–8pm; Oct–April Wed–Sun 10am–5pm; closed last weekend in each month • Free

Down the N234 from Burgos towards Soria, past the first signposted turn-off for Covarrubias, there's a detour after 34km to the dusty village of Quintanilla de las Viñas, which retains a rare Visigothic church and hermitage, the **Ermita de Santa María de Lara**. It's a remarkable survivor, a simple stone building on a bare hillock outside the village, dating back to around 700 AD. Only a third of its original size (the ground plan is still shown in the stone foundations outside), it nonetheless packs an emotive punch, not least in the delicately carved exterior friezes depicting grapes, animals, birds and a scallop shell over the door – centuries of pilgrims have left cruder scratched crosses on the walls. Inside, there's a stone arch with capitals representing the sun and moon, and a block that is believed to be the earliest representation of Christ in Spanish art. There's a custodian on site during opening hours, but outside official visiting times you'll only be able to see the exterior.

Covarrubias

The small town – village really – of **COVARRUBIAS**, 40km south of Burgos, is superbly preserved, with many white half-timbered houses and an air of sleepy gentility throughout. Set by an old bridge overlooking the Río Arlanza, the casco histórico is arranged around three adjacent plazas of ever increasing prettiness. The late Gothic **Colegiata de San Cosme y San Damián** is the main church, crammed with tombs that give an idea of the grandeur of the town in earlier times. The whole ensemble is studiously quaint, and attracts weekend tourists in numbers, but it's not yet overwhelmed – there's an antiques shop and a classy butcher-deli or two, but there are also locals tending to brimming flower boxes and children playing around the worn stone crosses.

ARRIVAL AND DEPARTURE

By bus and car It's easiest to come by car, since the limited bus service from Burgos means you'll probably have to stay the night. There's plenty of parking outside the village – you're not supposed to drive inside – and everything is within 2–3min walk, and easy to find.

ACCOMMODATION AND EATING

Hotel Nuevo Arlanza Pza. Mayor ☎ 947 400 511, ⓦ hotelnuevoarlanza.com. For views over the main square, ask for a front-facing room at the three-star *Nuevo Arlanza*; it also has its own restaurant, serving classic country Castilian cuisine, from *morcilla* to grilled trout. **€85**

Hotel Rey Chindasvinto Pza. del Rey Chindasvinto 5 ☎ 947 406 560, ⓦ hotelreychindasvinto.com. This place, right next to the main church, this is the town's best-value hotel, with charming owners and rustic wood-trimmed rooms. Hearty breakfasts are included. **€56**

Pension Casa Galín Pza. Mayor ☎ 947 406 552, ⓦ casagalin.com. Brightly furnished budget rooms in the main square, above a rustic tapas bar and restaurant where you'll get a straightforward meal at a reasonable price. The *menú del día* (€12) is usually available at night, too. Breakfast is an additional €3. Restaurant Mon & Wed–Sat 1–4pm & 9–11pm, Sun 1–4pm. **€40**

Santo Domingo de Silos

The Benedictine abbey of **Santo Domingo de Silos**, 18km southeast of Covarrubias, is one of Spain's greatest Christian monuments. It's surrounded by the fawn stone buildings of a small village of the same name, which has half a dozen small hotels and a few cafés and restaurants, all rather overpriced – indeed, having seen the abbey, there's no great reason to stay, as nearby Covarrubias is a far better overnight option.

Abadía de Santo Domingo de Silos

C/Santo Domingo • **Abbey** Tues–Sat 10am–1pm & 4.30–6pm, Sun & hols noon–1pm & 4–6pm • €3.50 • **Services** Mon–Sat 9am, Sun noon, plus daily 7pm, and others • ☎ 947 390 049, ⓦ abadiadesilos.es

The defining feature of the **Abadía de Santo Domingo de Silos** is a double-storey, eleventh-century **Romanesque cloister**, with eight graphic sculpted reliefs on the corner pillars. They include *Christ on the Road to Emmaus*, dressed as a pilgrim to Santiago (complete with scallop shell), in solidarity with pilgrims who make a hefty detour from the main route to see the tomb of Santo Domingo, the eleventh-century abbot after whom the monastery is named. The same sculptor was responsible for about half of the **capitals**, which besides a famous bestiary include many Moorish motifs, giving rise to speculation that he may have been a Moor. Whatever the case, it is an early example of the effective mix of Arab and Christian cultures, which was continued in the fourteenth century with the vivid, painted Mudéjar wood-beamed ceiling. A quite different sculptor carved many of the remaining capitals, including the two that ingeniously tell the stories of the Nativity and the Passion in a very restricted space. Visits to the monastery also usually include entry to the eighteenth-century **pharmacy**, which has been reconstructed in a room off the cloister. The monks who sing at the abbey are considered one of the top three **Gregorian choirs** in the world – you may remember their 1994 platinum-selling CD *Chant* – and many visitors make a point to attend a service to hear the singing.

Lerma

The upper town of **LERMA**, high above the Río Arlanza, takes some beating as a piece of vanity building, constructed almost entirely between 1606 and 1617 at the behest of the Duke of Lerma, court favourite of the weak Felipe III. A pious man, Lerma established no fewer than six monasteries and convents in town, while on the site of the former castle he erected an enormous ducal palace, fronted by a sweeping, arcaded plaza. This is now a magnificent parador – well worth planning an itinerary around – while the restored town lends itself to a half-day visit in any case, particularly if you coincide with the weekly Wednesday market that takes up the entire main square.

5

ARRIVAL AND DEPARTURE

LERMA

By bus and car There are daily buses from Burgos, 39km to the north, but realistically Lerma is a stop for drivers, overnight or otherwise, in combination with Covarrubias, 23km to the east, and Santo Domingo de Silos beyond. You can park in the vast square, except during the day on Wednesdays (market day).

ACCOMMODATION

Parador de Lerma Pza. Mayor ✆ 947 177 110, ⊛ www .parador.es. Everything is quite lovely in this beautifully restored ducal palace, with the tone set by the stunning central courtyard around which are the public areas and restaurant. Rooms are palatial and look out over the burned countryside far below. **€140**

EATING AND DRINKING

The pricey **restaurants** around the plaza all specialize in *lechazo asado* (roast suckling lamb), cooked in wood-fired ovens – around €35 or so for a serving for two people. For cheaper meals, walk straight down the steep hill from the main plaza and out through the town gate to the main road, where there's a handful of less rarefied restaurants and *hostales*.

The Camino de Santiago: Burgos to León

The central section of the great pilgrim route, the **Camino de Santiago**, cuts across the northern plains of Castilla y León, with the stretch from Burgos to León seen as one of the most rewarding – not for the walking, which can be flat and dull, but in terms of the art and architecture encountered along the way. From Burgos the *camino* runs south of the main road, via Castrojeriz and, more importantly, **Frómista**, before running up to **Carrión de los Condes** and **Sahagún**, the latter two towns both on the A231 Burgos–León road. With a car, rather than a rucksack and boots, there are also a couple of possible short detours off the main road to see the **Roman remains** on either side of Carrión de los Condes.

Frómista

FRÓMISTA still trades on the *camino*, but today's small crossroads of a town has only a fraction of the population of medieval times. Its undisputed highlight is the **church of San Martín**, which was originally part of an abbey that no longer exists. Carved representations of monsters, human figures and animals run right around the roof of

---

THE CAMINO DE SANTIAGO IN CASTILLA Y LEÓN

With the vineyards and well-watered countryside of La Rioja behind you, the **Camino de Santiago** arrives at Burgos and the start of the plains of Castile. Pilgrims are sharply divided about the *meseta*. Fans praise the big skies and the contemplative nature of the unchanging views, while detractors bemoan the bone-chilling wind that blows for nine months of the year, and the depressing way that you can see your destination hours before you reach it. It's certainly the flattest, driest part of the path and, if it's cold in winter, the lack of shade makes it uncomfortably hot in summer. The route often shadows the main road along a purpose-built gravel track, but there are many well-marked detours along isolated tracks crunchy with wild thyme.

Highlights are, of course, the glorious Gothic Catedrals of Burgos and León, after which the *meseta* ends at the town of Astorga, 50km southwest of León. From here you'll climb to the highest pass of the *camino* (1439m), where mist and fog can descend year-round and snow makes winter travel difficult. Good planning is therefore essential (see p.556). Traditionally, pilgrims bring a stone from home to leave on a massive pile at Cruz de Hierro, just before the pass. Things warm up considerably as you descend through gorgeous scenery to the Bierzo valley, 50km from Astorga, where the charming riverside town of Villafranca del Bierzo is an ideal place to rest before heading uphill into Galicia.

5

the eleventh-century church, which was built in a Romanesque style unusually pure for Spain, with no traces of later additions. A couple of other churches in Frómista are also associated with the *camino*, and there's usually a steady trail of walkers and cyclists passing through, taking advantage of the simple accommodation here.

Villalcázar de Sirga

Thirteen kilometres along the *camino* from Frómista (the route shadows the road), **VILLALCÁZAR DE SIRGA** has a notable church, Santa María la Blanca, built by the Knights Templar in the heart of the village. The Gothic style here begins to assert itself over the Romanesque, as witnessed by the figure sculpture on the two portals and the elegant pointed arches inside. Meanwhile, as pilgrims strike onwards past the village they are confronted by surely one of the most depressing signposts along the whole route – "Carrión de los Condes, 6km" (oh good), "Santiago de Compostela, 463km" (oh heck).

Carrión de los Condes and around

If the myths are to be believed, quiet, conservative **CARRIÓN DE LOS CONDES**, 80km west of Burgos and 40km north of Palencia, has a sensational past. In typically inflammatory fashion, it was reputed to be the place where, before the Reconquest, Christians had to surrender one hundred virgins annually to the Moorish overlords – a scene depicted on the badly worn portal of the church of Santa María del Camino, situated at the edge of the old town (where the *camino* comes into Carrión). Its pilgrim days have bestowed another dozen churches and monasteries upon Carrión, including the vast bulk of the Monasterio de San Zoilo – across the sixteenth-century bridge on the far side of town – whose cloister contains the tombs of the counts (*condes*) of Carrión, from whom the town's name comes. The pilgrim route picks its way through the centre, crossing the main square, Pza. del Generalisimo, still named for Franco after all these years. On hot days, it's the riverside park that is most tempting, especially if you've just walked here, while quick onward car journeys take you away from town to the region's remarkable Roman treasures. Come on a Thursday morning (market day) and Carrión's generally somnolent pulse is raised a little.

ARRIVAL AND DEPARTURE   CARRIÓN DE LOS CONDES

By bus and car Buses from Burgos and León stop outside the *Bar España* on the main road near the church of Santa María del Camino. Palencia buses stop in the square opposite. Ask in *Bar España* for tickets and times. There's plenty of free parking nearby.

INFORMATION

Punto de Información Callejón de Santiago (Mon–Fri 9am–2pm, Sat 11am–2pm & 5–7pm, Sun 11am–2pm; ☎ 979 880 932, ⊛ carriondeloscondes.es), is inside the Museo Contemporaneo – it's up the passage by the church of Santiago, facing the main square.

ACCOMMODATION AND EATING

There are several simple *pensiones* and pilgrim-only *albergues* in town, and some lovely rural accommodation in the nearby countryside. Most cafés and restaurants – including one or two overlooking the main square – are aimed firmly at the passing pilgrim trade, so prices everywhere are reasonable.

★**Estrella del Bajo Carrión** C/Mayor 32, Villoldo, CL615, 11km south of Carrión ☎ 979 827 005, ⊛ rusticae .es. The glam choice hereabouts is this delightful gastro-retreat in a nearby village. Spacious, all-in-white rooms are heavy with designer flair (larger studios cost €130), and there's a sun deck outside under a spreading tree. Breakfast is really good, while the handsome restaurant (open to non-guests; mains €20–30) serves creative regional cuisine using seasonal ingredients, from grilled veg with a slug of estate-bottled olive oil to wood-grilled venison. Restaurant 1.30–3.45pm & 9.45–10.45pm. **€90**

Hostal La Corte C/Santa María 34 ☎ 979 880 138,

ⓦhostallacorte.com. If you're on a budget, try these straightforward rooms right opposite Santa María del Camino church. The restaurant below is the place for good-value meals, from trout to *chuletón* (€3 pilgrim's breakfast; €11 menu; mains €10–18). Restaurant daily 6–10am, 1–4pm & 9–11pm. **€45**

Hotel Real Monasterio San Zoilo C/San Zoilo ☎979 880 049, ⓦsanzoilo.com. By far the most historic accommodation in town is this resolutely traditional four-star hotel converted from part of the monastery – follow the signs, over the bridge, to find it. It also has Carrión's most notable restaurant (*menú del día* €20, otherwise mains €13–25), serving fancied-up regional cuisine, from lamb to fish. Restaurant daily 1–4pm & 8.30–10.30pm. **€90**

Villa Romana La Olmeda

Pedrosa de la Vega, signposted 3km south of Saldaña, off CL615 • Tues–Sun 10.30am–6.30pm, last entry 6.15pm • €5, joint ticket with Villa Romana La Tejada €6, free Tues after 3pm • ☎979 119 997, ⓦvillaromanalaolmeda.com

It's a quick 19km drive northwest of Carrión on a ruler-straight road to the well-signposted **Villa Romana La Olmeda**, which is considered one of the most important domestic Roman sites in Spain, boasting more than 1500 square metres of well-preserved mosaics. Founded as a country estate in the first century AD, but extensively remodelled on palatial lines in the fourth century AD, La Olmeda was more than a mere villa – rather a thriving centre of local agriculture and industry. But faced with the slow collapse of the Roman Empire, the estate gradually fell into disrepair, its buildings demolished, the villa's mosaic floors buried under farmland and its very existence forgotten. It was rediscovered in 1968 and has since been fully excavated, with the entire complex of buildings and the surviving mosaics now sheltered under a dramatic, modernist steel hangar standing in open countryside. Raised walkways lead you around the complex, past reception and dining rooms, bedrooms, offices, storerooms, kitchens and baths, all radiating out from a central patio garden. Touch-screen monitors with computer-generated graphics show how the rooms might have looked, while the mosaics themselves are an impressive tour de force of polychromatic geometric designs, hunting scenes and more elaborate mythological sequences.

Saldaña and the Museo de La Olmeda

Iglesia de San Pedro • Tues–Sun 11am–2pm & 5–7pm • Free entrance with ticket for Villa Romana La Olmeda

For the archeological finds from Villa Romana La Olmeda, you have to continue 3km further north up the CL615 to the small town of **SALDAÑA**, whose medieval church of San Pedro has been pressed into service as the **Museo de La Olmeda**; follow the "Museo Archeológico" signs from the central Pza. Mayor. Glass cases in the church nave present a snapshot of Roman country life 1600 years ago, with displays of coins, lamps, belt buckles, rings, necklaces, hunting weapons and cooking utensils, recovered from the site excavations. Saldaña itself has a charming *casco histórico* of timber and brick houses ranged around its central square, near which you'll be able to park, and there are several cafés.

Villa Romana La Tejada

Quintanilla de la Cueza, 17km southwest of Carrión, off the N120 • April–Sept Tues–Sun 10am–2pm & 5–8pm; Oct & March Tues–Sun 10.30am–1.30pm & 4–6pm; closed Nov–Feb • €3 (€1 March & Oct), joint ticket with La Olmeda €6 • ☎650 410 913

The other Roman villa site near Carrión is a bit harder to find than Villa Romana La Olmeda, and nowhere near as impressive, though it is just as rewarding in its own way. The **Villa Romana La Tejada** is just past the dead-end hamlet of Quintanilla de la Cueza; there's an easy-to-miss sign off the highway (on the left, coming from Carrión), from where a narrow 1km road leads to a parking area surrounded by a high green hedge. The villa itself is hidden within a vast, unsightly shed, and is much less visited than La Olmeda, with which it is contemporary. But the surviving mosaics are another extraordinary reminder of the wealth that once characterized this now rather remote rural area, while La Tejada also shows off the hypocaust heating system that was de rigueur for any self-respecting Roman villa of the period.

Sahagún

From Carrión de los Condes the direct *camino* route west continues 35km to the small town of **SAHAGÚN**, once the seat of the most powerful monastery in all Spain. Although this is now little more than a ruined shell, several other churches in Sahagún repay the trip into town, particularly as the most interesting are built of red brick in characteristic Mudéjar style. A steady stream of pilgrims trudges into and out of Sahagún most days, but otherwise it really only warrants a quick stop for coffee and a tour of the churches before heading on to León.

Iglesia de San Tirso

C/San Tirso, by Parque San Benito, signposted through town • April–Sept Wed–Sat 10am–2pm & 4–8pm, Sun 10am–2pm; Oct–March Wed–Sat 10.40am–2pm & 3–5.50pm, Sun 10.40am–2pm • Free

The most delicate of Sahagún's churches is the beautifully restored twelfth-century **San Tirso**, a Mudéjar brick construction of great grace. If the beauty is all on the outside, it's still worth coinciding with the opening times, because inside the simple interior is a fascinating series of scale wooden models of all the town's famous churches – complete with doors that open and roofs that lift off to display minutely constructed interiors, complete with altars and pews.

Ruins of San Benito

Parque San Benito

Adjacent to San Tirso church is all that's left of the mighty twelfth-century monastery of **San Benito**, once without compare in Spain (there's a model of the original inside San Tirso). Originally dedicated to San Facundo and San Primitivo, only one ruined, fenced-off chapel remains of the medieval complex – the more prominent bell tower and the freestanding arched gateway across the road, the so-called **Arco de San Benito**, both also in ruins, were much later additions.

Iglesia de San Lorenzo

Pza. San Lorenzo, signposted off Pza. Mayor • **Church** open for mass only • **Museo de Semana Santa** Tues–Sun 11am–2pm & 5–8pm • Free (or donation)

Most imposing of the Mudéjar brick churches is thirteenth-century **San Lorenzo**, with its squat, square campanile – the church is currently propped up as the intricate brickwork has sagged over the centuries. In the adjacent building the small **Museo de Semana Santa** presents a fairly gory collection of life-sized, blood-spattered Christs either being led to the cross or crucified upon it. The museum is run by volunteers, so the hours are not always reliable.

ARRIVAL AND DEPARTURE   SAHAGÚN

By train Sahagún is an easy side trip from either Palencia or León (around 40min by train from either). The train station is a 10min walk from Pza. Mayor, down Avda. Constitución.

By bus Buses to León (1–2 daily; 1hr), Burgos (1 daily; 2hr 15min) and Carrión de Los Condes (1 daily; 50min) stop outside the *Hotel Puerta de Sahagún* on Carretera de Burgos (ⓦ alsa.es), a 10min walk from the train station.

By car Signs through town lead you to San Tirso and San Benito, and there's convenient parking near the San Benito ruins.

León

Even if they stood alone, the stained glass in the Catedral of **LEÓN** and the Romanesque wall paintings in its Panteón Real would merit a very considerable journey, but there's much more to the city than this. An attractive provincial capital that welcomes *camino* pilgrims by the thousand, it also presents itself as a lively university town with one of the best tapas bar scenes in Spain. Handsome old- and new-town areas, set back from extensive riverside gardens, complement each other, and, while the city's major

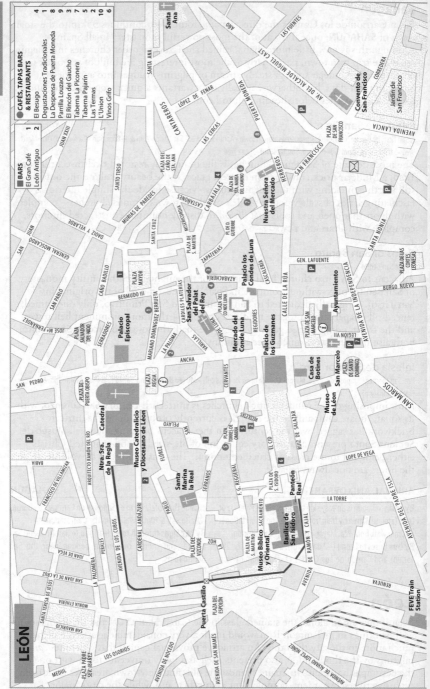

LEÓN

BARS
El Gran Café ... 1
León Antiguo ... 2

● CAFÉS, TAPAS BARS & RESTAURANTS
El Besugo ... 4
Degustaciones Tradicionales ... 1
La Despensa de Puerta Moneda ... 8
Parrilla Louzao ... 9
El Rincón del Gaucho ... 3
Taberna La Piconera ... 7
Taberna Pajarín ... 5
Las Termas ... 2
L'Union ... 10
Vinos Grifo ... 6

Santa Ana
Convento de San Francisco
Jardín de San Francisco
Nuestra Señora del Mercado
Palacio los Condes de Luna
Ayuntamiento
Palacio Episcopal
San Salvador del Palat del Rey
Mercado del Conde Luna
Palacio de los Guzmanes
Casa de Botines
San Marcelo
Museo de León
Catedral
Ntra.-Sra. de la Regla
Museo Catedralicio y Diocesano de León
Santa Marina la Real
Panteón Real
Basílica de San Isidoro
Museo Bíblico y Oriental
Puerta Castillo
FEVE Train Station

Hospital & Asturias

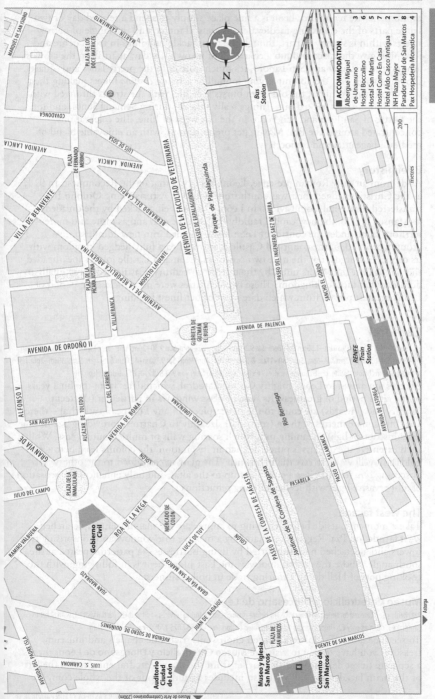

N

Bus Station

RENFE Train Station

Río Bernesga

ACCOMMODATION

Albergue Miguel de Unamuno	3
Hostal Boccalino	6
Hostal San Martín	5
Hostel Como En Casa	7
Hotel Aldo Casco Antigua	2
NH Plaza Mayor	1
Parador Hostal de San Marcos	8
Pax Hospedería Monástica	4

0   200
metres

MARQUÉS DE SAN ISIDRO
MARTÍN SARMIENTO
PLAZA DE LOS DOCE MÁRTIRES
COVADONGA
AVENIDA LANCIA
PLAZA DE FERNANDO MERINO
AVENIDA LANCIA
LUIS DE SOSA
VILLA DE BENAVENTE
BERNARDO DEL CARPIO
AVENIDA DE LA FACULTAD DE VETERINARIA
PASEO DE EXPALAGUINDA
Parque de Papalaguinda
PASEO DEL INGENIERO SÁEZ DE MIERA
PLAZA DE LA PÍCARA JUSTINA
C. VILLAFRANCA
AVENIDA DE LA REPÚBLICA ARGENTINA
CARD. LORENZANA
SANCHO EL GORDO
AVENIDA DE ORDOÑO II
GLORIETA DE GUZMÁN EL BUENO
AVENIDA DE PALENCIA
ALFONSO V
C. DEL CARMEN
ALCÁZAR DE TOLEDO
SAN AGUSTÍN
AVENIDA DE ROMA
COLÓN
GRAN VÍA DE
JULIO DEL CAMPO
PLAZA DE LA INMACULADA
MERCADO DE COLÓN
LUCAS DE TUY
COLÓN
AVENIDA DE ASTORGA
RAMIRO VALBUENA
Gobierno Civil
ROA DE LA VEGA
PASEO DE LA CONDESA DE SAGASTA
Jardines de la Condesa de Sagasta
PASEO DE SALAMANCA
PASARELA
JUAN MADRAZO
GRAN VÍA DE SAN MARCOS
JUAN DE BADAJOZ
AVENIDA DE SUERO DE QUIÑONES
LUIS S. CARMONA
AVENIDA DEL PADRE ISLA
Auditorio Ciudad de León
PLAZA DE SAN MARCOS
Museo de Iglesia San Marcos
PUENTE DE SAN MARCOS
Convento de San Marcos
Astorga
Museo de Arte Contemporáneo (200m)

5

monuments are renowned, León is a fine place simply to spend a relaxed day or two. Large parts of the encircling medieval walls are still intact, and the tangle of narrow streets within is shabby in part, though the ramshackle buildings in faded ochre and rose pink give the **casco antiguo** a charm all of its own. By day, apart from the crowds around the Catedral and San Isidoro, it's much quieter in the pretty lanes and squares, though always with the accompanying footfall of arriving *camino* hikers making their way into town. At night, the old town bursts into life, with the streets thronged with people and the bars packed out. Things really take off during **Semana Santa**, and for the **fiestas** of San Juan and San Pedro in the last week of June. The celebrations, concentrated around the Pza. Mayor, get pretty riotous, with an enjoyable blend of medieval pageantry and buffoonery.

Brief history

Aside from an early Roman presence, León's history is that of the Reconquest. In 914, as the Christians edged their way south from Asturias, Asturian king Ordoño II transferred his capital from Oviedo to León. Despite being sacked by the dreaded al-Mansur in 996, the new capital rapidly eclipsed the old, and as more and more territory came under the control of León it was divided into new administrative groupings: in 1035, the county of Castile matured into a fully fledged kingdom with its capital at Burgos. For the next two centuries, León and Castile jointly spearheaded the war against the Moors until, by the thirteenth century, Castile had come finally to dominate her mother kingdom. These two centuries were nevertheless the period of León's greatest power, from which date most of her finest buildings.

Catedral

Pza. Regia • May Mon–Fri 9.30am–1.30pm & 4–8pm, Sat 9.30am–12pm & 2–6pm, Sun 9.30–2pm; June–Sept Mon–Fri 9.30am–1.30pm & 4–8pm, Sat 9.30am–12pm & 2–6pm, Sun 9.30–11am & 2–8pm; Oct–April Mon–Sat 9.30am–1.30pm & 4–7pm, Sun 9.30am–2pm, last entrance 30mins before closing; closed during services • €5 (includes audio tour) • ☎ 987 875 770, ⓦ catedraldeleon.org

All eyes are drawn to León's mighty Gothic **Catedral**, which dates from the final years of the city's period of greatness. Its stained-glass **windows** in particular (thirteenth-century and onwards) are equal to the masterpieces in any European cathedral – there are 2000 square metres of them (second in size only to Chartres), providing a stunning kaleidoscope of light streaming in through soaring walls of multicoloured glass. While such extensive use of glass is purely French in inspiration, the colours used here – reds, golds and yellows – are essentially Spanish. The glass screen added to the otherwise obscuring *coro* (choir) gives a clear view up to the altar, and only enhances the sensation of all-pervasive light with its bewildering refractions.

The west facade

Take a moment outside before entering to appreciate the magnificent triple-arched **west facade** (on Pza. Regia), dominated by a massive rose window and comprising two towers and a detached nave supported by flying buttresses – a pattern repeated at the south angle. Above the central doorway, the Last Judgement is in full swing, with the cooking pots of Hell doing a roaring trade in boiled sinners.

Museo Catedralicio y Diocesano de Léon

Pza. Regia • See Catedral for times, last entrance 1hr before closing; closed during services • Full visit €5, partial visit €3, with ticket to Catedral €3, cloisters only €2, children under 12 and disabled visitors free • ☎ 987 875 770, ⓦ catedraldeleon.org

To see the Catedral's cloisters, carved choir stalls, rich side chapels and museum treasures you have to pay to visit the **Museo Catedralicio y Diocesano de Léon**; there's a separate ticket desk around the corner from the main Catedral entrance to the left of the main facade. The full visit also includes a guided tour of the whole complex

5

(in Spanish). You can opt for a partial visit, which includes the cloister and a selection of chapels and rooms of religious art, or simply visit the **cloister** alone. This is definitely worth doing: it's magnificently carved, and there's just enough left of the faded wall murals and coloured detail between the delicate ribbed arches to indicate how expressively rich and vibrant the cloisters once were. At the entrance to the museum (through a door off the cloister), there's also an impressive sixteenth-century staircase by sculptor Juan Badajoz el Mozo – one of the most important Renaissance works in León.

Plaza Mayor and around

A couple of minutes' walk south of Leon's Catedral lies the elegant, arcaded **Plaza Mayor**, for once not the absolute focus of attention in town and all the quieter for it, during the day at least. It's on the edge of the nightlife zone, which spills out from nearby **Pza. de San Martín**, also rather charming, though every building here is a bar or restaurant. Come the evening, and out come the beggars, cigarette bums and dodgy DVD merchants, mingling with the crowds.

Plaza de Santa María del Camino

Hands-down plaza winner in León is **Plaza de Santa María del Camino**, a gorgeous cobbled square with two big shady trees, a surviving wooden arcade and the pretty Romanesque church of Nuestra Señora del Mercado – the name a reminder that the square was once the site of the city's grain market (it's still known as Plaza del Grano). The squat church tower (facing C/Herreros) is flanked by two dinky, if regal, stone lions.

Palacio de los Condes de Luna

Pza. del Conde Luna • Mon–Fri 10am–8pm, Sat 10am–2pm & 5–9pm • Free • ☎ 987 216 794

Facing the Mercado del Conde Luna, the square's most historic building is the sixteenth-century **Palacio de los Condes de Luna**, former home of the counts (*condes*) of Luna, with its elegant facade and blind window arcade. It's now owned by the regional government, who in 2010 installed a permanent exhibition celebrating the 1100-year anniversary of the kingdom of León (which lasted from 910 to 1230), a period much vaunted in these parts. The palace has been beautifully restored and is open for temporary exhibitions and concerts.

Iglesia de San Salvador del Palat del Rey

C/Conde Luna, just off Pza. del Conde Luna • Hours vary according to exhibitions • Free

Possibly the oldest church in the city, **San Salvador** was founded by Ramiro II in the tenth century and served as an early pantheon for the Asturian kings (hence the "Palat del Rey" tag), until superseded by that of San Isidoro. There's virtually nothing left of the original church, or its Mozarabic successor, but this is another building that has been lovingly restored to serve as an exhibition hall, focusing on art, architecture and photography.

Plaza de Santo Domingo

The foot of the old town is marked by a series of striking buildings ranged around the traffic circle of **Plaza de Santo Domingo**. The modest **Ayuntamiento** sits back in its own square, across the road from the Renaissance **Palacio de los Guzmanes**. But it's the mock-Gothic, exuberantly turreted **Casa de Botines** that steals the show, an early (1892–93) work of *modernista* architect Antoni Gaudí, now an exhibition space and

Caja España bank building. Saint George (the Catalan patron saint) is doing his best to subdue a dragon above the entrance, while sitting on a bench opposite is a bronze statue of Gaudí himself, examining his plans for the building.

Basílica de San Isidoro

Pza. de San Isidoro • Daily 7.30am–11pm • Free

Founded by Fernando I, who united the two kingdoms of León and Castile in 1037, the mighty **Basílica de San Isidoro** was commissioned both as a shrine for the bones of San Isidoro and as a mausoleum for Fernando and his successors. Backing into the very walls of the city, it's a beautiful construction, dating mainly from the mid-twelfth century and thus one of the earliest Romanesque buildings in Spain. Two adjacent doorways show fine sculpted reliefs, of the Descent from the Cross (right) and the Sacrifice of Abraham (left), the latter surmounted by a later Renaissance pediment topped by the horseriding San Isidoro himself. Inside, the saint's bones lie in a reliquary on the high altar.

Panteón Real

Basílica de San Isidoro, entrance on Pza. de San Isidoro • May–June Mon–Thurs 10am–2pm & 4–7pm, Fri–Sat 10am–2pm & 4–8pm, Sun 10am–3pm; July –Sept Mon–Sat 9am–9pm, Sun 9am–3pm; Oct–April Mon–Sat 10am–2pm & 4–7pm, Sun 10am–2pm • €5, €1 Thurs from 4pm; free last Thurs from 4pm of each month • ☎ 987 876 161, ⓦ museosanisidorodeleon.com

The royal bones (of eleven kings and twelve queens) were laid to rest in tombs in the adjacent **Panteón Real** (signposted "Museo"), essentially two crypt-like chambers constructed between 1054 and 1063 as a portico of the church. It's a deeply atmospheric space, with two squat columns in the middle of the Panteón carved with thick foliage, rooted in Visigothic tradition. Moreover, towards the end of the twelfth century, these extraordinarily well-preserved vaults were then covered in some of the most significant **frescoes** in Spanish Romanesque art. These present a vivid splash of colour, depicting not just biblical scenes and stories but also an agricultural calendar, for example (on the underside of one entire arch). The central dome is occupied by Christ Pantocrator surrounded by the four Evangelists depicted with animal heads – allegorical portraits that stem from the apocalyptic visions in the Bible's Book of Revelation. Your ticket also allows you to visit the cloister, as well as the small museum of glittering church treasures and the impressive library.

Museo Bíblico y Oriental

Basílica de San Isidoro, entrance at Pza. de San Martino • Tues–Fri 11am–2pm & 5–9pm, Sat 10am–2pm & 5–9pm • €2 • ☎ 987 213 200, ⓦ biblicoyoriental.es

To the side of San Isidoro in the collegiate church buildings is the **Museo Bíblico y Oriental**, an unsung gem of a museum, home to some fascinating early manuscripts and objects relating to the history, archeology and languages of the Bible and the Orient. In essence, this means an exceptional – and ravishingly displayed – collection of pages from ancient Bibles and liturgical works (with texts in Hebrew, Aramaic, Greek and Coptic), finely worked carvings and crosses from the first few centuries after Christ, and an entire series of Mesopotamian writing tablets dating back to 3500 BC. There's also a rather splendid eighteenth-century Neapolitan Nativity panorama, alive with expressive, rustic figurines.

Convento de San Marcos and around

Pza. de San Marcos • 15min walk from the old town

The pilgrim route on to Astorga lies across the old bridge on the west side of town. Here, at the opulent **Convento de San Marcos**, and on presentation of the relevant documents, pilgrims were allowed to regain their strength before the gruelling Bierzo mountains west of León. The original pilgrims' hospital and hostel was built in 1168

5

for the Knights of Santiago, one of several chivalric orders founded in the twelfth century to protect pilgrims and lead the Reconquest. In the sixteenth century, it was rebuilt as a kind of palatial headquarters, its massive 100m-long facade lavishly embellished with Plateresque appliqué designs: over the main entrance, Santiago is depicted swatting Moors with ease. The monastery is now a parador, and is strictly off limits to nonguests beyond its foyer, bar and restaurant, but there are fine views of the building from the square and the nearby riverside gardens.

Museo y Iglesia San Marcos

Pza. de San Marcos • July–Sept Tues–Sat 10am–2pm & 5–8pm, Sun 10am–2pm; Oct–June Tues–Sat 10am–2pm & 4–7pm, Sun 10am–2pm • Guided visits to the choir stalls: Tues, Wed & Fri 1pm, Thurs 5.30pm • €0.60, free Sat & Sun • ☎ 987 245 061, ⊚ museodeleon.com

There's unimpeded access to the adjacent monastery church, the **Iglesia San Marcos**, which is vigorously speckled with the scallop-shell motif of the pilgrimage. However, the celebrated *coro alto* of the church, which has a fine set of carved stalls by Renaissance sculptor Juan de Juni, is out of bounds except on guided visits. Inside the church, there's a three-room annex of the **Museo de León**, which tells the story of the monastery. Portraits of the Knights of Santiago hang from the old sacristy walls, while the Cloister Room contains sarcophagi of the bishops who lived in the monastery.

Museo de León

Edificio Pallares, Pza. de Santo Domingo 8 • July–Sept Tues–Sat 10am–2pm & 5–8pm, Sun 10am–2pm; Oct–June Tues–Sat 10am–2pm & 4–7pm, Sun 10am–2pm • €1.20, free Sat & Sun • ☎ 987 221 602, ⊚ museodeleon.com

The new headquarters of the **Museo de León** – the Edificio Pallares – was built in 2007 to provide a more spacious home to the large collection that had been displayed in the Iglesia San Marcos since 1869. The collection is dedicated to the history of the province of León, from prehistory via the Roman Conquest and the Middle Ages to the present day and contains archeological artefacts galore and church treasures, including a fourteenth-century processional cross made of rock crystal and the Cristo de Carrizo – a 33cm-high ivory figure of Christ on the cross. Despite the excellent facilities at this new exhibition space, it's hard not to feel that the grand statues would have been more impressive to see back in their atmospheric old home.

Museo de Arte Contemporáneo

Avda. de los Reyes Leoneses 24 • Tues–Sun 10am–3pm & 4–9pm • €3, free Sun afternoon & Tues–Thurs 7–8pm • ☎ 987 090 000, ⊚ musac.es • 15min walk north of San Marcos

The city's main centre for contemporary art and culture is the dazzling **Museo de Arte Contemporáneo**. The multicoloured glass facade was inspired by the stained-glass windows in the Catedral, and regularly changing exhibitions feature works and installations by Spanish and international artists.

ARRIVAL AND DEPARTURE   LEÓN

León's *casco antiguo*, with most of the historic sights and best bars and restaurants, lies east of the Río Bernesga, with the modern part of the city laid out in between. The main **train and bus stations** are on the river's west bank, from where it's a 20min walk up to the Catedral or a 5min taxi journey.

BY TRAIN

Renfe train station Mainline train services are from the Renfe station, Avda. de Astorga on the west bank of the river (Renfe ☎ 902 320 320, ⊚ renfe.com).

FEVE train station León also has a second station, at Avda. de Padre Isla on the north side of town, from where FEVE trains (FEVE ☎ 987 271 210, ⊚ feve.es) run a long

daily route to and from Bilbao.

Destinations Astorga (up to 11 daily; 40min); Bilbao (daily; 5hr); Burgos (4 daily; 2hr); Logroño (1 daily; 4hr); Madrid (up to 13 daily; 3–5hr); Oviedo (up to 7 daily; 2hr); Palencia via Sahagún (up to 16 daily; 1hr–1hr 30min); Ponferrada (up to 11 daily; 1hr 30min–2hr); Valladolid (up to 14 daily; 1hr 30min–2hr); Vigo (up to 8 daily; 6hr 30min).

BY BUS

Estación de Autobuses Paseo del Ingenero Saenz de Miera (☏ 987 211 000). Alsa (ⓦ alsa.es) has services to Astorga, Burgos, Madrid, Carrion de los Condes and Sahagún; Vivas (ⓦ autocaresvivas.es) and Zamora–Salamanca (zamorasalamanca.es) to Zamora/Salamanca. Destinations Astorga/Ponferrada (at least hourly; 50min/1hr 30min); Burgos (4–5 daily; 2hr direct, otherwise up to 3hr); Carrión de los Condes (daily; 2hr); Madrid (12 daily; 3–4hr 30min); Oviedo (13 daily; 1hr 30min); Sahagún (1 daily; 1hr); Salamanca (4–5 daily; 2hr); Valladolid (up to 11 daily; 2hr); Zamora (up to 17 daily; 2hr).

BY CAR

Parking is much easier in the modern district than the old town. The car park behind the Catedral costs only €2.80/day (C/Babia ó Arquitecto Ramón Cañas del Río).

GETTING AROUND AND INFORMATION

Turismo Pza. Regia, opposite the Catedral (July to mid-Sept Mon–Sat 9.30am–2pm & 5–8pm, Sun 9.30am–5pm; mid-Sept to June Mon–Sat 9.30am–2pm & 4–7pm, Sun 9.30am–5pm; ☏ 987 237 082, ⓦ turismocastillayleon.com); Pza. San Marcelo (Mon–Sun 9.30am–2pm & 5–7.30pm; ☏ 987 878 336, ⓦ turismocastillayleon.com). **By taxi** Radio Taxi León (☏ 987 261 415); Taxi Villaquilambe (☏ 987 285 355).

ACCOMMODATION

In the **casco antiguo**, there's a cluster of budget places around the atmospheric Pza. Mayor, though anything without double-glazing close to the bars and restaurants can be very noisy at night. If you're on a bigger budget, you might prefer one of the decent mid-range options nearby. The quieter **new town** also offers some good cheap options, as well as the luxurious parador, and you're only ever a 15min walk or less from all the action.

CASCO ANTIGUO

★ **Albergue Miguel de Unamuno** C/San Pelayo 15 ☏ 987 233 010, ⓦ alberguunamuno.com. Just a few steps from one of the best tapas areas (around C/Cervantes) is this remarkably low-priced youth hostel, which doubles as a university halls of residence. As well as private and three- to four-bed dorm rooms, there's a self-service laundry, garden and restaurant. Dorms €10, doubles €15
Hostal Boccalino Pza. de San Isidoro 1 ☏ 987 223 060, ⓦ hostalboccalino.com. Sits on a lovely square overlooking San Isidoro church. The rooms are above a café-bar, and have parquet floors, good bathrooms with decent showers, double-glazing and church views; across the square is the associated restaurant, a good-value pizza and pasta place. €55
Hostal San Martín Pza. Torres de Omaña 1, 2º ☏ 987 875 187, ⓦ sanmartinhostales.com. An excellent *hostal* with simple but stylish rooms painted in pastel shades – though you can expect some noise from nearby bars if you're at the front. There's a fair choice of rooms, and you can pay as little as €20 single or €28 double if you're prepared to share bathroom facilities. €40
★ **Hotel Aldo Casco Antigua** C/Cardenal Landázuri 11 ☏ 987 074 000, ⓦ aldacascoantiguo.es. This fantastic little secret is tucked away behind the Catedral, with super rooms – all wood floors and rustic furnishings – that offer great value for money. The four-bed mixed dorms have en-suite bathrooms while each junior suite has its own terrace. Dorms €18, doubles €40
NH Plaza Mayor Pza. Mayor 15 ☏ 987 344 357, ⓦ nh-hotels.com. Chic boutique style in a classy refit of one of the square's handsome arcaded buildings. Facilities and services are four-star standard, and include one of super-chef Ferran Adrià's *Nhube* contemporary bistro-style restaurants. Best rates are online. €90
★ **Pax Hospedería Monastica** Pza. Santa María del Camino 11 ☏ 987 344 493, ⓦ hospederiapax.com. The monastic, yet luxurious, rooms and the wonderful location overlooking the loveliest plaza in Léon make this a special place to stay. With a convent (and pilgrim-only *albergue*) right next door, it's more than likely that you'll see a nun wandering around the hotel building on her way to Mass. Note that there's only one double bedroom (€90); all others are twin. €60

NEW TOWN

Hostel Como En Casa C/Legión VII, 6–2º Izda. ☏ 685 508 958, ⓦ hostelcomoencasa.com. Opened in Spring 2014, this new hostel is gorgeously decorated with wood-panelled walls and parquet floors. Breakfast is included and every room has a TV. The only downside is that all seven rooms – both private and dorms – have to share three bathrooms. Dorms €18, doubles €48
★ **Parador Hostal de San Marcos** Pza. San Marcos 7 ☏ 987 237 300, ⓦ www.parador.es. This sensational parador occupies one of León's most dramatic buildings. Bedrooms are of the antiques, four-poster and chandelier kind, though with all mod cons, and the best throw open windows right onto the vast square below. There's a sense of calm and majesty throughout – an enormous two-tier cloister sits at the centre of the building, and long, hushed corridors are lined with imperial rugs, ancient chests, iron tables and oil paintings. There's a good restaurant (mains from €23), and some sheltered garden seating in a quiet spot above the river. Web offers go as low as €120. €169

EATING, DRINKING AND NIGHTLIFE

The daily **Mercado del Conde Luna** sits in the middle of Pza. del Conde Luna, and offers a crash-course in Leonese cuisine, especially the meats which you'll see on every menu – not just the familiar chorizo, lamb and steak, but tripe and trotters, *morcilla* (blood sausage) and *costilla de cerdo* (smoked pork ribs). The liveliest **tapas bars and restaurants** are found around Pza. de San Martín – an area known as the **Barrio Húmedo** (the Wet Quarter) for the amount of liquid sloshing around. Bars here will give you a free *pincho* with every drink, so you can eat pretty well if you hop from bar to bar ordering *cortos* – small tumblers of beer for around €1.50 or so a pop. The other good area for bars is along C/Cervantes and in the surrounding little squares, where there's a mix of traditional tapas places and more contemporary *copas* and music bars. Music **bars and clubs** tend to open Thursday to Saturday, between 11pm and 5am.

TAPAS BARS

★Degustaciones Tradicionales (La Pitanza) C/Mariano Domínguez Berrueta 6 ⓣ987 214 732, ⓦdegustacionestradicionales.com. The "traditional tastes" in this fancily refurbished antique bar near Pza. Mayor are mainly regional cured meats and cheese, and the wine selection is excellent. Daily noon–4pm & 8pm–midnight.

La Despensa de Puerta Moneda C/Puerta Moneda 1 ⓣ987 170 317. A lovely little upscale grocery store that doubles as a cosy bar – *pintxos* of ham or chorizo are carved right off the counter, you pick a bargain glass of regional Bierzo wine and then find a place to perch amid the boxes of tomatoes, preserved vegetables and tins of peas. Mon–Fri 10.30am–4pm & 6.30–10.30pm, Sat 10.30am–3.30pm.

El Rincón del Gaucho C/Azabachería 1. Tucked in a back alley off San Martín, this classic old-town tapas bar is best known for its delicious variations of *patatas* served with every drink. Daily 12.30pm–3.30pm & 7.30pm–1am.

★Taberna Pajarín Pza. Torres de Omaña ⓣ676 066 899. Vie for position at the busy bar and order a traditional Léonese *tapa*, such as the knockout *morcilla* (a rich, garlicky purée of blood pudding) slathered onto crusty white bread, washed down with a great local wine. Daily noon–4.30pm and 7.30pm–midnight.

★Vinos Grifo Pza. Santa María del Camino 9 ⓣ987 177 428, ⓦvinosgrifo.com. Sitting outside this relaxed café/bar beside a convent in the pretty "Plaza del Grano" is a memorable experience. You pay for the location with the slightly pricey menu but *platos combinados* (€6.50) are available and you get a free *pintxo* with every drink. Daily noon–late.

RESTAURANTS

El Besugo C/Azabacheria 10 ⓣ987 256 995. A good choice for a well-priced meal in the Barrio Húmedo – look beyond the spit-and-sawdust bar and head upstairs to the old-fashioned *comedor*, where hoary old waiters dispense a large range of *raciones* and simple meat and fish grills, with plenty of choice for under €10 (otherwise dishes up to €15, *menú del día* €10.50). Mon 1.20–3.45pm, Wed–Sun 1.20–3.45pm & 8.20–11.45pm.

Parrilla Louzao C/Juan Madrazo 4 ⓣ987 271 432, ⓦparrillalouzao.com. Fine-dining restaurant specializing in regional meat dishes, such as cured meats and melt-off-the-bone *costillas de cerdo* (pork ribs), alongside other provincial favourites, such as Sahagún-style grilled leeks. Mains €10–20. Sept–June Mon–Sat noon–4pm & 8pm–midnight, July & Aug Mon–Fri noon–4pm & 8pm–midnight.

Taberna La Piconera Pza. Santa María del Camino 2 ⓣ987 263 456. Lunch here on the pretty cobbled square is a treat, enjoying a simple but tasty €10 menu that pulls in the passing pilgrims. It's a contemporary place inside, with *raciones* to share – prawns to carpaccio – and a good line in Leonese grilled meats (dishes €13–27). Summer 1pm–midnight, winter Tues–Sun 1–4pm & 9–11.30pm.

★Las Termas C/Paloma 13 ⓣ987 264 600, ⓦrestaurantelastermas.es. A sleek little number serving creative regional cuisine (*menú del dia* €13, or €15 at night Mon–Thurs, otherwise dishes €10–22; vegetarian menu €13). Menus change regularly, but seasonal salads and gutsy mains (like fresh anchovies with caramelized garlic and *Padrón* peppers) are typical. Their café next door has Catedral views, good cakes and home-made ice cream. Summer daily 1–11.30pm, winter daily 1–3.30pm & 8–11.30pm.

L'Union C/Flórez de Lemos 3 ⓣ987 261 710, ⓦrestaurantelaunion.es. A vegetarian gem in the new town. Wholesome mains (€9–14) include tasty salads, a hearty lasagne or the intriguingly named "biodynamic" pizza. *Menú del día* €12.50. Mon–Thurs 1.30–4pm, Fri & Sat 1.30–4pm & 8.30–11.30pm.

BARS

El Gran Café C/Cervantes 9 ⓣ987 272 301, ⓦelgrancafeleon.com. Rock-and-roll bar with a regular diet of indie and rock gigs, plus a free Tuesday night jam session (from 9pm) that's a city stalwart. Daily 4pm–4am.

León Antiguo Pza. Ordoño IV. A rather more civilized place than many to start the night, with an outdoor terrace overlooking the El Cid gardens and the Gaudí towers. Daily 6pm–2am.

NO ONE SHALL PASS

En route to Astorga, romantics will want to make the slight diversion off the highway to the small town of **Hospital de Órbigo**, 36km southwest of León. It was here, legend has it, that in 1434 Don Suero de Quiñones, a jilted knight, defeated three hundred men in a jousting tournament at the town's famous twenty-arched medieval bridge. Standing on the beautifully restored bridge today, it's easily imagined – astride a horse, furious at the world, picking off all-comers with a whacking great lance. And as only foot traffic is allowed, the long, cobbled bridge is still one of those places where the Camino de Santiago really reaches back into history, with knots of hiking pilgrims crossing all day, falling gratefully into one of the small cafés at the Astorga end of the bridge.

DIRECTORY

Concerts Main city concert hall is the Auditorio Ciudad de León, Avda. Reyes Leonese (☎ 987 244 663, ⌨ auditoriociudaddeleon.es), for everything from symphony orchestras to Gregorian choirs.
Hospital Hospital de Léon, C/Altos de Navas (☎ 987 237 400).

Laundry Lavandería La Paloma, C/Paloma 6.
Police Policía Nacional, Villa Benavente 6 (☎ 987 218 900); Policía Local, Pza. San Marcelo (☎ 987 878 354).
Post office Main branch at the southern end of Avda. de Independencia, by Pza. de San Francisco (Mon–Fri 8.30am–8.30pm, Sat 9.30am–1pm).

Astorga

For the very fittest of the pilgrims, it's one day's walk (50km) southwest of León to the next major stop at **ASTORGA**. The town has a long history – originally settled by the Romans (of whom many traces remain), sacked by the Moors in the eleventh century, then rebuilt and endowed with the usual hospices and monasteries, but as the pilgrimage lost popularity in the late Middle Ages, Astorga fell into decline. These days it's a bustling, if small, provincial capital that once again places much emphasis on the pilgrimage, and is full of footsore hikers and Santiago souvenir shops, not to mention an incongruously grand Catedral and an even more out-of-place *modernista* bishop's palace, the latter now used as a museum dedicated to the *camino*.

Catedral de Santa María

Pza. Catedral · **Catedral** Mon–Sat 9–10.30am, Sun 11am–1pm · Free · **Museo Catedralicio** March–Sept Tues–Sat 10am–2pm & 4–8pm, Sun 10am–2pm; Oct–Feb Tues–Sat 11am–2pm & 4–6pm, Sun 11am–2pm · €2.50, joint ticket with Museo de los Caminos €5 · ☎ 987 615 820

Astorga's **Catedral de Santa María** looks better than it has in centuries after a thorough restoration. Built between 1471 and 1693 (though on the site of a much older church), it has notable twin towers either side of the majestically carved main door, one in pink-tinged stone, one in green, colours that are repeated inside the nave on the soaring fluted columns. You can join worshippers and see the Catedral for free in the morning, but sightseers are encouraged to buy a ticket for the **Museo Catedralicio**, which in any case includes a visit to the church. Even if you're not normally interested in ecclesiastical treasures, the beautifully presented series of museum rooms is worth seeing. As well as the usual cases of robes, capes, mitres, crosses and chalices, there are some remarkable pieces here, including the Arcón de Carrizo – a beautiful painted twelfth-century wooden reliquary.

Museo de los Caminos

Pza. Eduardo del Castro · March–Sept Tues–Sat 10am–2pm & 4–8pm, Sun 10am–2pm; Oct–Feb Tues–Sat 11am–2pm & 4–6pm, Sun 11am–2pm · €3, joint ticket with Museo Catedralicio €5

Standing across from the Catedral – and to many minds, upstaging it – is the **Palacio Episcopal**, or Bishop's Palace, which was commissioned by a Catalan bishop from his

5

architect countryman Antoni Gaudí in 1886. It's a quite extraordinary building, more so inside than out, though even the exterior resembles some kind of Disney castle. Gaudí took the Gothic style as his inspiration and ran with it, resulting in a building of soaring brick and tile arches, intricate decorative work and luminous stained glass, culminating in an exquisite chapel that beats anything in the next-door Catedral hands down. The spectacular palace rooms now house the **Museo de los Caminos**, which traces the story of the pilgrimage through statues and artworks dating from its medieval origins, as well as examples of the documents issued at Santiago to certify that pilgrims had "travelled, confessed and obtained absolution". There's also a basement full of Roman altars and funerary statues and an attic devoted to contemporary regional art – together with a bird's-eye view down into the shining chapel.

Museo Romano

Pza. de San Bartolomé • July–Sept Tues–Sat 10am–2pm & 5–7.30pm, Sun 10.30am–2pm; Oct–June Tues–Sat 10.30am–2pm & 4–6pm, Sun 10am–2pm • €3, under-10s free • ☏ 987 616 937

Astorga's Roman past is covered in the fascinating **Museo Romano**, which displays local archeological finds alongside changing exhibitions on various themes. However, the town also preserves a rich set of excavated remains, including a surviving "Bear and Birds" mosaic in a wealthy private Roman house, the **Casa Romana** – located just a few steps along the road from the museum.

Jardín de la Sinagoga

Pza. San Francisco • Always open • Free

Astorga is ringed by an almost complete circuit of **walls**, late Roman in origin and reconstructed over the centuries. It's only a short walk from the Roman museum to the **Jardín de la Sinagoga**, which retains a section of the old Roman sewer system and is also the best place for a view from the walls out over the plains to the Sierra de Teleno.

ARRIVAL AND DEPARTURE

ASTORGA

By train The train station is a 15min walk from the town centre at Pza. de la Estación (RENFE ☏ 902 240 202, ⓦ renfe.com).
Destinations León (up to 11 daily; 40min); Ponferrada (up to 11 daily; 1hr); Madrid (2–4 daily; 4–6hr).
By bus The bus station on Avda. de la Murallas (☏ 987 619 100) is right opposite the Palacio Episcopal; frequent services from León and Ponferrada (Alsa ☏ 987 619 100 ⓦ alsa.es).
Destinations León (hourly; 50min); Ponferrada (hourly; 1hr); Villafranca del Bierzo (3–4 daily; 1hr 40min).
By car Free parking is easy outside of the old town, either along the bus station road opposite the Palacio Episcopal, or in the large car park further down under the town walls.

INFORMATION

Turismo Pza. Eduardo de Castro 5, across from the Palacio Episcopal (Tues–Sat 10am–2pm & 4–6.30pm, Sun 10am–2pm; ☏ 987 618 222, ⓦ ayuntamientodeastorga .com).

THE MARAGATOS

Astorga is the traditional market town of the **Maragatos**, a distinct ethnic group of unknown origin, possibly descended from the Berbers of North Africa, who crossed into Spain with the first Moorish incursions of the early eighth century. For several centuries, they dominated the Spanish carrying trade with their mule trains. Marrying only among themselves, they maintained their traditions and individuality well into recent decades. However, apart from the locally famous Maragato *cocido* – a typically hearty stew made with up to seven types of meat and sausage, plus chickpeas and cabbage – their only obvious legacy to Astorga is the pair of colourful clockwork figures dressed in traditional costume who jerk into action to strike the hour on the town-hall clock in Pza. Mayor.

ACCOMMODATION AND EATING

Astorga is an easy day-trip from León, but there's plenty of agreeable central accommodation if you fancied staying the night. Local **restaurants**, meanwhile, all advertise the delights of the *cocido maragato* (see box, opposite) for around €18/head – you eat the meats first, then the veg, then drink the broth, and good luck in finishing what tend to be gigantic portions. Astorga also has a reputation for its chocolate, production of which flourished here in the eighteenth and nineteenth centuries; there's even a chocolate museum in town and plenty of shops to buy the stuff in. The nicest places for a drink and a bite of tapas are the **cafés** and **bars** around Astorga's finest square, Pza. Mayor.

Aizkorri Pza. Mayor ☎ 987 618 611, ⓦ aizkorri.es. A fast-paced bar right on Astorga's main square serving outstanding Basque-style *pintxos*, such as a small but perfectly formed *bacalao* on toast with ratatouille and *alioli*. There are various menu options and mains for €10–15. Daily noon–4pm & 7pm–midnight.

★**Casa de Tepa** C/Santiago 2 ☎ 987 603 299, ⓦ casadetepa.com. The most atmospheric lodging in town is this handsome eighteenth-century townhouse with ten quiet, refined rooms (traditionally furnished, though with marble rain-shower bathrooms), and a sunny terrace garden where you can eat breakfast in summer. For

a suite add €15–30; private parking costs €11. **€108**

La Peseta Pza. de San Bartolomé 3 ☎ 987 617 275, ⓦ restaurantelapeseta.com. There's no quibbling among the locals when it comes to the town's best regional restaurant. Located just off Pza. Mayor, this restaurant has been in the hands of the same family for five generations (founded 1871). Specialities include the ubiquitous *cocido maragato* and anything from stewed veal to *bacalao confitado* (cod in garlic sauce) with mains in the entirely-reasonable-for-the-quality €11–20 range. There are also fifteen *hostal* rooms upstairs. Restaurant Mon 1–4.30pm & 8.30–11pm. **€60**

Castrillo de los Polvazares

A fascinating side trip from Astorga takes in the improbably pretty village of **Castrillo de los Polvazares**, considered to be an archetypal Maragato settlement (see box opposite), and now zealously preserved as a local heritage showpiece. There's basically one long main cobbled street, and a small, stork-topped church, with the rest being a charming collection of eighteenth-century, russet-coloured stone cottages flaunting window boxes and signs advertising honey (*miel*) for sale. Only residents can drive in (there's a car park by the bridge at the entrance to the village), so catch Castrillo at the right time – traffic-free, and only the cobbled footfall of pilgrims to disturb the timeless scene – and it resembles nothing so much as a Hardyesque Wessex village.

ARRIVAL AND DEPARTURE

By car Castrillo de los Polvazares is 5km west of Astorga on road LE142; by car, follow signs to Santa Colomba de

CASTRILLO DE LOS POLVAZARES

Somoza out of Astorga, or on foot follow any backpacking pilgrim – the *camino* runs close to the village.

ACCOMMODATION AND EATING

Hostería Casa Coscolo C/La Magdalena 1☎ 987 691 984, ⓦ casacoscolo.com. Not just hiking pilgrims will fall gratefully into this little hotel on Pza. de la Iglesia. The restored stone and wood house has four simple rooms,

brightly furnished in different seasonal colours, and a restaurant on hand to introduce you to the *cocido maragato* and other regional dishes. Restaurant 1–4pm & 9–11pm, winter hours can vary. **€50**

Ponferrada

At first sight, the heavily industrialized, bowl-shaped valley centred on the large town of **PONFERRADA** seems to have little to offer, but the mountainous terrain of the Bierzo has scenery as picturesque as any in Spain. The town itself sums up this dichotomy, dominated by its outlying industrial concerns and spreading suburbs, yet with a charming, unspoiled old quarter, through which trudge weary pilgrims girding their

5

loins for the mountains to come. Old and new towns are separated by the Río Sil, spanned by the iron bridge that gave Ponferrada its name, above which loom the high walls of the impressive castle. From the main square in the old town, **Pza. del Ayuntamiento**, pass through the quaint **Puerta del Reloj** (Clock Gateway) down to pretty **Pza. Virgen de la Encina**, which is overlooked by the town's finest Renaissance church and the curtain wall of the castle.

Castillo de los Templarios

Avda. del Castillo • Jan–Feb & mid-Oct to Dec Tues–Sat 11am–2pm & 4–6pm, Sun 11am–2pm; March Tues–Sat 11am–2pm & 4–7pm, Sun 11am–2pm; April to mid-Oct Tues–Sat 10am–2pm & 4.30–8.30pm, Sun 10am–2pm • €6 • ☎ 987 402 244

There are a couple of local museums in Ponferrada, but the only essential sight is the one you can hardly miss – the **Castillo de los Templarios**, which stands high above the river. Established by the Knights Templars in the thirteenth century, it's a textbook castle with fancy turrets and battlements, all gleaming after a handsome restoration.

ARRIVAL AND DEPARTURE
PONFERRADA

By train and bus The train and bus stations are in the new town. Train connections include Léon, Madrid and Santiago de Compostela. The bus station is a 20min walk from the old town along C/General Gómez Nuñez (subsequently Avda. Pérez Colino) or 5min by taxi (Radio Taxi ☎ 987 087 087). Alsa routes include Villafranca del Bierzo and Astorga (ⓦalsa.es).

By car If you're driving from Astorga, you'll hit the old town first and can avoid the new section altogether. There's parking on the edge of the old town, as well as under Pza. del Ayuntamiento, or free street parking on the bridge, below the castle.

INFORMATION

Turismo C/Gil y Carrasco 4, by the castle (mid-Sept to April Mon–Sat 10am–2pm & 4–7pm, Sun 10am–2pm; May to mid-Sept Mon–Sat 10am–2pm & 5–8.30pm, Sun 10am–2pm; ☎ 987 424 236, ⓦ ponferrada.org/turismo).

ACCOMMODATION, EATING AND DRINKING

There are plenty of **hotels** and *hostales* in the new town, all signposted as you drive in (and detailed on the tourist office website). But it's nicest to stay in the old quarter, where there's a simple choice.

La Capricciosa C/Paraisín 1 ☎ 987 111 603, ⓦ lacapricciosa.es. Prime position, with views over the pretty Pza. Virgen de la Encina, church and castle walls. It's an Italian place, with pizzas (€7–9) from the wood-fired oven – though they also use the traditional oven for pricier roast lamb and suckling pig dishes. Mon & Wed–Sun noon–4pm & 7pm–midnight.

Hotel Aroi Bierzo Plaza Pza. del Ayuntamiento 4 ☎ 987 409 001, ⓦ aroihoteles.com. Charming warm-toned rooms in a converted townhouse on the main square, with nice views from the windows. You can also grab an outdoor table for tapas and drinks from *La Taberna* (the former wine cellar), and there's contemporary regional cuisine in the hotel's *La Violeta* restaurant (mains €15–21). Restaurant 1–4pm & 9pm–midnight (winter: closed from 4pm). €80

Hotel Los Templarios C/Flórez Osorio 3 ☎ 987 411 484, ⓦ hotellostemplarios.info. Straightforward rooms in a small hotel with its own restaurant (*menú del día* €12). You'll find it just through the Clock Gateway from the main square. Restaurant 1–4pm & 9–11pm. €55

Las Médulas

Twenty-four kilometres southwest of Ponferrada lie **Las Médulas**, the jagged remains of hills ravaged by Roman strip-mining. Five tonnes of gold were ripped from the hillsides using specially constructed canals, leaving an eerie, mesmerizing landscape reminiscent of Arizona, peppered with caves and needles of red rock. Just outside Carucedo (on the N536), the road splits, with the right fork leading 3km up to the village of Las Médulas.

5

Las Médulas village

Aula April–Sept daily 10am–1.30pm & 4–8pm; Oct–March Mon–Fri 10am–2pm, Sat 10am–1.30pm & 3.30–6pm, Sun 10am–2pm •
€1.50 • ☎ 987 422 848 **Centro de Recepción** Daily March–Oct 11am–2pm & afternoon times vary; Nov–Feb 10.45am–3pm • Guided
walks €3 • ☎ 987 420 708, ⓦ ccbierzo.com

This is a pretty place of restored stone houses, climbing roses and spreading chestnut
trees set behind the largest rock outcrops, with a gaggle of studiously rustic cafés
and bars that caters for day-trippers. There's information on the region's archeology
in the museum – the **Aula Arqueológica** – outside which you'll have to park as cars
aren't allowed into the village. Guided walks depart from outside the **Centro de
Recepción de Visitantes de Las Médulas**, located 400 metres along the main street
by the church, which has a visitor information centre, bike hire and a shop. From
here, various signposted **trails** lead into the dramatic mine workings, the shortest
being the hike to Somido lake (3km return; 50min), for great views of the outcrops,
and the Las Valiñas trail (4km; 1hr 15min), which takes you partly inside the old
mines themselves.

Mirador de Orellán

The **Mirador de Orellán** offers the most spectacular panorama over the whole area
of crumbling peaks. A detour of the Las Valiñas trail leads up here, or you can
drive directly by taking the left fork out of Carucedo and winding up for 4.5km,
through the village of Orellán. It's a steep 600m walk from the car park to the
viewing platforms.

Villafranca del Bierzo

The last halt before the climb into Galicia, **VILLAFRANCA DEL BIERZO**, 22km from
Ponferrada, was where pilgrims on their last legs could chicken out of the final trudge.
Those who arrived at the Puerta del Perdón (Door of Forgiveness) at the simple
Romanesque **church of Santiago** could receive the same benefits of exemption of years
in Purgatory as in Santiago de Compostela itself. The town itself is quietly enchanting,
with a jumble of old-town streets, slate-roofed houses, encircling hills, cool mountain
air and the clear Río Burbia providing a setting vaguely reminiscent of the English Lake
District. The historic pilgrim connection makes it a great place to stop for the night,
with plenty of reasonably priced accommodation and a multitude of restaurants
offering good-value pilgrim menus.

ARRIVAL AND DEPARTURE   **VILLAFRANCA DEL BIERZO**

By bus and car Regular buses from Ponferrada stop
outside the tourist information centre on Avda. Díez

Ovelar, where there are also some parking spaces.

ACCOMMODATION AND EATING

Hostal Puerta del Perdón C/Pza. de Prim 4 ☎ 987 540
614, ⓦ lapuertadelperdon.com. The family-run "micro-
hostel" beside the Puerta del Perdón and its fine restaurant
both have a reputation for outstanding quality. There's a
pilgrim menu (€11); non-pilgrims can choose local
specialities from the à la carte menu (mains €12–18), such
as the chef's great-grandmother's recipe for *rabo de toro*.
Restaurant Mon–Thurs 1–4pm; Fri & Sat 1–4pm and
8–9.45pm. **€65**

Hotel Las Doñas del Portazgo C/Ribadeo 2 ☎ 987 542

742, ⓦ elportazgo.es. Probably Villafranca's most
upmarket accommodation, this boutique luxury hotel has
seventeen rooms with country chic decor. Located close to
the tourist information centre. **€82**

La Pedrera C/La Pedrera 9 ☎ 652 865 002, ⓦ lapedrera
.biz. Tucked away in a tiny street, this bistro has a lovely
garden, a creative menu, and a superb local wine list. Mains
cost €12–18. Try the dramatic *milhoja del la huerta*
(millefeuille with goats' cheese). Fri–Sat 1–4pm & 9–11pm,
Mon & Sun 1–4pm, Tues–Thurs by appointment.

Euskal Herria: the País Vasco and Navarra

PLAYA DE LA CONCHA, SAN SEBASTIÁN

Euskal Herria: the País Vasco and Navarra

The name the Basque people give to their own land, Euskal Herria, covers the three Basque provinces that today form the *Comunidad Autónoma del País Vasco* (in Basque, "Euskadi") – Gipuzkoa, Bizkaia and Araba – as well as Navarra (Nafarroa) and part of southwestern France. Much of this region is immensely beautiful, and especially so along the coast, where green and thickly forested mountains, interspersed with stark individual hills, seem in places to emerge from the sea itself. Yes, it often rains, and much of the time the countryside is shrouded in a fine mist, but so long as you don't mind the occasional shower, summer here offers a glorious escape from the unrelenting heat of the south.

Despite the heavy industrialization that has helped to make this one of the wealthiest areas in Spain, **Euskal Herria** is remarkably unspoiled – neat and quiet inland, rugged and wild along the coast. **San Sebastián** is a major resort city, with superb if crowded beaches and wonderful food, but lesser-known, similarly attractive villages line the coast all the way to **Bilbao**, home to the magnificent Museo Guggenheim. Inland, **Pamplona** boasts its exuberant Fiestas de San Fermín, while many other destinations have charms of their own, from the drama of the **Pyrenees** to the laidback elegance of **Vitoria-Gasteiz**.

Look out especially for quiet rural **accommodation** options, here in abundance thanks to the Basque government's **nekazalturismoa** (*agroturismo*) programme, which offers the opportunity to stay in traditional farmhouses and private homes, usually in areas of outstanding beauty, at very reasonable cost (€50–75). In Navarra, as in much of the country, these are known as **casas rurales**, or *landa exteak*. You can get details from the region's many excellent local **tourist offices** (which also handle bookings), or online at ⓦnekatur.net, and, for Navarra, ⓦcasasruralesnavarra.com.

While a reasonable **bus** network connects all the sizeable towns, the easiest way to get around the Basque Country is by car. In particular, if you want to follow the coast, the dramatic hills and cliffs mean there isn't always a shoreline road; with public transport especially you have to keep returning to the main roads way inland. **Train** services are relatively poor. San Sebastián lies on a major route to and from France, which also passes through Vitoria-Gasteiz, but Bilbao is off the main line on a minor spur, and direct trains between Bilbao and San Sebastián are much slower than the equivalent buses. Bilbao is, however, the eastern terminus of a separate narrow-gauge railway, formerly known as FEVE but now part of the national RENFE system, which follows the Atlantic coast west to Santander, Oviedo and beyond.

Brief history

When the **Romans** invaded, they defeated the Aquitani, who inhabited large areas of southwestern Gaul and northern Iberia, and spoke an ancestral version of Basque. However, they allowed the wild tribes known as the Vascones, who lived in the

Highlights

❶ Playa de La Concha, San Sebastián This graceful crescent strand, curving away from the delightful old town, has to count as one of the greatest urban beaches in the world. **See p.453**

❷ Pintxos The Basques prepare their tapas with a real gourmet flair, so snacking is an irresistible treat – especially in San Sebastián. **See p.458**

❸ Mundaka estuary Sublime scenery; world-class surfing; the beautiful seaside village of Mundaka; and Gernika, the Basque spiritual capital. **See p.465**

❹ Museo Guggenheim, Bilbao This swirling titanium edifice has become the symbol of the regenerated city. **See p.469**

❺ Bodegas Ysios An architectural extravaganza, designed to celebrate the rich red wines of Rioja. **See p.483**

❻ Fiestas de San Fermín Pamplona's famous fiesta is rowdy, dirty and lunatic, but for once the bulls get a fair shot. **See p.486**

❼ Olite Delightful village of ochre-coloured stone mansions on the edge of the Navarran plains. **See p.493**

❽ Bardenas Reales This eerie Wild-West desertscape is perhaps the last thing you'd expect to find in the Basque Country. **See p.495**

HIGHLIGHTS ARE MARKED ON THE MAP ON PP.448–449

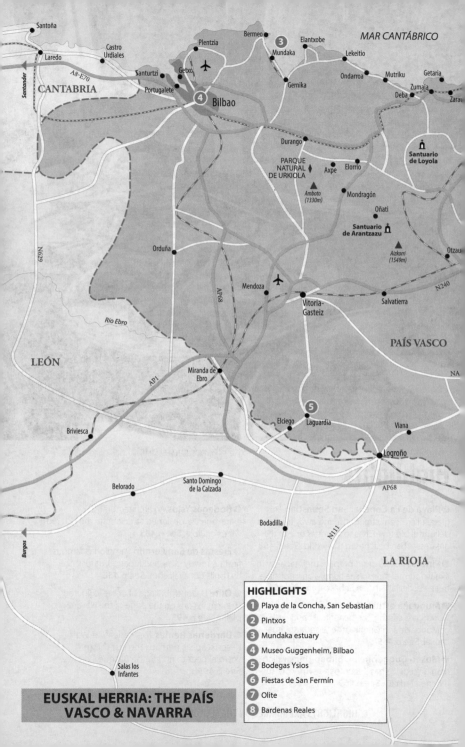

MAR CANTÁBRICO

Santoña
Laredo
Castro Urdiales
CANTABRIA
Santurtzi
Portugalete
A8-E70
Santander

Plentzia
Getxo
4 Bilbao

Bermeo
3 Mundaka
Elantxobe
Gernika
Lekeitio
Ondarroa
Mutriku
Getaria
Deba
Zumaia
Zarau

Durango
PARQUE NATURAL DE URKIOLA
Axpe
Elorrio
Ambeto (1330m)
Mondragón
Oñati
Santuario de Arantzazu
Aizkorri (1549m)
Otzau

Santuario de Loyola

Orduña
N629
Río Ebro
Mendoza
Vitoria-Gasteiz
Salvatierra
AP68
N240

LEÓN
PAÍS VASCO
NA

Miranda de Ebro
AP1
Briviesca
Elciego
5 Laguardia
Viana
Logroño

Belorado
Santo Domingo de la Calzada
AP68

Bodadilla
N111

LA RIOJA

Burgos

Salas los Infantes

HIGHLIGHTS

1. Playa de la Concha, San Sebastían
2. Pintxos
3. Mundaka estuary
4. Museo Guggenheim, Bilbao
5. Bodegas Ysios
6. Fiestas de San Fermín
7. Olite
8. Bardenas Reales

EUSKAL HERRIA: THE PAÍS VASCO & NAVARRA

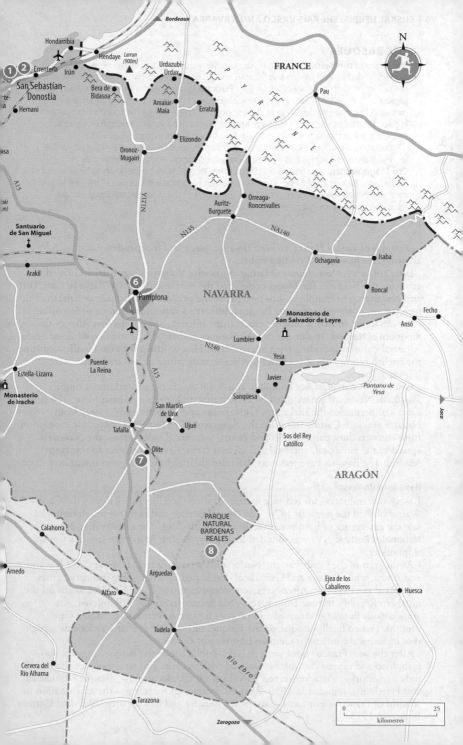

6

THE BASQUES

The origins of **the Basques** remain mysterious. They are a distinct people, generally with a different build from the French and Spanish and a different blood-group distribution from the rest of Europe. Their language, the complex **Euskara**, is unrelated to any other, and was already spoken in Spain when Indo-European languages such as Celtic and Latin began to arrive three thousand years ago. Written records were scarce until the first books in Euskara were published in the mid-sixteenth century. Language and culture survived instead through oral traditions, including that of the *bertsolariak* – popular poets specializing in improvised verse.

Archeological and genetic evidence suggests the Basque people may be the last surviving representatives of Europe's first modern human population, commonly known as **Cro-Magnon man**. Skull fragments dating from 9000 BC have been shown to be identical to present-day Basque cranial formation. Much anthropological work, above all by José Miguel de Barandiarán (who died in 1991, aged 101), lends itself to the view that the Basques have inhabited the western Pyrenees for thousands of years.

mountains of Euskal Herria, to keep their language and independence in return for allowing free passage and trading rights.

Later rulers were less accommodating. Successive **Visigoth** kings tried and failed to eradicate the Basques. The **Moors** conquered the lowlands of Araba (Alava in Castilian) and Navarra up to Pamplona, but never gained a grip on the mountainous north. This new enemy, however, forced the Basques, hitherto a collection of more or less allied tribes, to unite. In 818, a Basque leader, Iñigo Iñiguez, became the first ruler of the **Kingdom of Navarre**. In due course, the Basques embraced Christianity, while retaining ancestral customs including their ancient laws. First written down (in Castilian) during the twelfth century, these laws and privileges, maintained as oral traditions, were known as **fueros**.

Once the Reconquest was complete and Spain was being welded into a single kingdom, Navarre (by now ruled by French monarchs) was a missing piece. The Reyes Católicos persuaded the Bizkaians, Gipuzkoans and Arabans to split away from Navarre and join Castile. In return the *fueros* would be respected, including exemption from customs duty, conscription and central taxation. Under duress, the Navarrese agreed to the same deal, and by 1512 all four territories were subject to rule from Madrid. The Basques have jealously defended their right to self-government ever since.

Basque nationalism

Basque determination for self-rule increased when the Liberals, victors in the Carlist War, abolished the *fueros* in 1876. The late nineteenth and early twentieth centuries saw the emergence of Basque nationalism as an ideology. The conservative **Basque Nationalist Party** (PNV) was founded in 1895 by Sabino Arana, the son of a Carlist shipbuilder.

At the start of the Civil War, the Nationalists seized control of conservative Navarra and Araba, while Bizkaia and Gipuzkoa, dominated by left-leaning industrial cities, supported the Republic. After Navarrese troops captured Irun in 1936 and cut off the northern Republican zone from France, San Sebastián rapidly surrendered. An autonomous Basque government, in practice limited to Bizkaia, lasted just nine months. Franco finally conquered the Basques in June 1937, after a vicious campaign that included the infamous German bombing of **Gernika**.

After the war, Franco's boot went in hard. Public use of the Basque language was forbidden and central control was asserted with the gun. But state violence succeeded only in nurturing a new resistance, **ETA** (Euskadi ta Askatasuna – "Basque Homeland and Freedom"), founded in 1959. Its most spectacular success was the assassination in Madrid of Franco's right-hand man, prime minster and heir apparent, Admiral Carrero Blanco in 1973.

Separatism today

Things started to change following the **transition to democracy**. The new constitution granted the Basques limited autonomy, with their own parliament and tax collection. Today, there's a regional police force, the red-bereted *ertzaintza*, and the Basque language is taught in schools and universities. The Basque flag (*ikurriña*) flies everywhere. Basque demands for independence have not ended, however, and the violence has continued. Since 1968, ETA is estimated to have killed around 850 people, with targets ranging from members of the Spanish police and armed forces to Basque businessmen and politicians, academics, journalists, the tourist industry and random civilians. At the time of writing, however, the latest in a long succession of ceasefires, announced in 2010 and declared "permanent" in 2011, was continuing to hold. ETA further announced its willingness to negotiate a "definite end" to all its activities in 2012, and made a public start to decommissioning its arsenal in 2014. Currently, two-thirds of the elected Basque

6

FIESTAS

JANUARY

19–20: Festividad de San Sebastián Twenty-four hours of festivities, including a *tamborrada*, a march with pipes and drums.

FEBRUARY

Weekend before Ash Wednesday: *Carnaval* Throughout the region, but especially in Bilbao, San Sebastián and Tolosa.

MARCH/APRIL

March 4–12: A series of pilgrimages to the castle at Javier, birthplace of San Francisco Javier.
Semana Santa (Holy Week) Extensive Easter celebrations in Vitoria; also in Segura.
Easter Sunday: Aberri Eguna The Basque National Day celebrated, particularly in Bilbao.
April 28: Fiesta de San Prudencio Celebrated with *tamborradas* in Vitoria.

JUNE

24: Fiestas de San Juan In Lekeitio, Laguardia and Tolosa.
Last week: Fiesta de San Pedro In Mundaka, with Basque dancing.

JULY

First week: Fiesta at Zumaia with dancing, Basque sports and an *encierro* on the beach.
7–14: Fiestas de San Fermín In Pamplona, featuring the famous Running of the Bulls.
22: Fiesta de la Magdalena In Bermeo, with torch-lit processions of fishing boats and Basque sports.
24–28: *Encierro* in Tudela.

AUGUST

First weekend: Patron saint's celebration in Estella-Lizarra.
4–9: Fiesta de la Virgen Blanca In Vitoria, with bullfights, fireworks and *gigantones*.
Second weekend: Medieval festival in Olite.
14–17: Fiestas de Andra Mari In Ondarroa.
15: Semana Grande An explosion of celebration, notably in Bilbao, with Basque games and races, and San Sebastián, where the highlight is an International Fireworks Competition.

SEPTEMBER

First week: Euskal Jaiak Basque games in San Sebastián.
4: Fiesta de San Antolín In Lekeitio, where the local youth attempt to knock the head off a (dead) goose.
9: Día del Pescador In Bermeo.
12: *Encierro* in Sangüesa.
14: Patron saint's day in Olite, with yet more bulls.
Last two weeks: International Film Festival In San Sebastián.

parliament could broadly be considered as separatists, with half of those belonging to the left-wing Bildu coalition, but despite the new era of peace, the Spanish government has so far shown no willingness to negotiate over Basque self-determination.

San Sebastián

6

Making the most of its glorious location, curving languidly around a magnificent semicircular bay lined with golden sand, **SAN SEBASTIÁN** ranks among the great resort cities of Europe. Although it's the capital of its region, Gipuzkoa, and has a reputation as a hotbed of Basque nationalism, it has never been a major port, or much of an industrial centre. Instead its primary identity, ever since the Spanish royal family first decamped here for the summer in 1845, has been as a summer playground. In July and August especially, it tends to be packed out, and its hotels are among the most expensive in Spain.

While the superb sheltered **beach** on its very doorstep is the biggest attraction of all, San Sebastián also boasts a charming old-town core, the **Casco Viejo**, squeezed up against the foot of verdant Monte Urgull and renowned for its high-quality **food**. The new town to the south, known as **Centro** and the city's commercial hub, holds a fine crop of *belle époque* edifices, though they're interspersed between rather too many dreary newer buildings.

The official name of the city, **Donostia-San Sebastián**, is a tautology, in that Donostia is a Basque name for Saint Sebastian. Some say Sebastian was martyred in the Roman port of Ostia, and is thus the Don (saint) of Ostia; others that Ostia (or Osti) is simply an abbrevation of Sebastian.

Casco Viejo

Although San Sebastián's old town, or **Casco Viejo**, stands on the site where the city first developed, almost nothing predates the disastrous fire, set by British troops, that devastated the town in 1813. With little trace of its original walls surviving either, it's a formal grid far removed from the typical old quarters of other Spanish cities. Nonetheless, it's a delight, its narrow streets and occasional pretty squares thronged in the daytime with shoppers and sightseers, and at night with revellers eager to sample its legendary *pintxos* bars and restaurants.

Plaza de la Constitución

At the heart of the Casco Viejo, the **Plaza de la Constitución** makes a great arena for festivals. It even served as a bullring in the past; hence the numbers painted on the balconies to all sides. Amazingly, each window originally belonged to a separate apartment, each barely wider than a corridor; many dividing walls have now been removed, however, to make larger living spaces.

Museo San Telmo

Pza. Zuloaga 1 • Tues–Sun 10am–8pm • €6 • ☎ 943 481 580, ⒲ santelmomuseoa.com

Remodelled and expanded into a spectacular new extension in 2011, the **Museo San Telmo** is set below Monte Urgell at the northeast edge of the Casco Viejo. Its overall brief is to trace Basque history, and San Sebastián in particular, but many visitors find

---

THE FESTIVALS OF SAN SEBASTIÁN

San Sebastián's busy annual calendar of fiestas and festivals kicks off on the stroke of midnight at the start of January 20, the feast day of its namesake saint. Carnival too is celebrated in style, but the two biggest events of the year are the five-day **Jazz Festival** in late July (⒲ jazzaldia .com), which attracts well-known performers, not exclusively jazz, from all over the world, and the week-long **Film Festival** in the second half of September (⒲ sansebastianfestival.com).

it disjointed and confusing, with numerous themes and topics covered in its maze of buildings. The original core, a deconsecrated convent, displays vast monochromatic canvases by Catalan muralist Josep Maria Sert; exhibits elsewhere cover everything from whaling to 1960s' Basque pop music, with an astonishing crude wooden wolf trap as the highlight of the section on rural life. Several galleries hold the museum's fine art collection, with three El Greco paintings on the uppermost floor.

Basílica de Santa María
C/31 de Agosto 46 • Mon–Sat 8am–2pm & 4–8pm • Free • ☎ 943 423 124

The Baroque facade of the Basílica de Santa María is visible along the slender, arrow-straight C/Mayor, the main artery of the old town, all the way from the unremarkable Catedral in the new town. Although it dates from the eighteenth century, it only became a basilica following a papal visit in 1966; the pope's coat of arms can be seen along with a caravel of the kind used by Columbus, and an image of San Sebastián himself. You enter the main door to find that, thanks to the church's squashed-up position below Monte Urgull, the nave unexpectedly stretches not straight ahead of you but from side to side, with a huge altarpiece to your right and an alabaster Greek cross by Eduardo Chillida above the font to your left.

Monte Urgull

San Sebastián was originally a fishing settlement at the foot of the wooded **Monte Urgull**, a steep headland that until the connecting spit was built over was virtually an island in its own right. It takes barely twenty minutes to walk around the base of the hill, along a level path that offers tremendous sunset views, or a little longer to climb to its summit via the trails and stairways that lead up from the Casco Viejo. Topped by a massive statue of Christ, which towers over the Castillo de la Mota, the hillside intersperses formal gardens and wilder stretches, one of which, on the far side, cradles a small **cemetery** devoted to English soldiers who died during the First Carlist War, in the 1830s.

Castillo de la Mota
Monte Urgell • May–Sept daily 11am–8pm; Oct–April Tues–Fri 10am–2pm & 3–5.30pm, Sat & Sun 10am–5.30pm • €1 • ☎ 943 428 417

The **Castillo de la Mota** atop Monte Urgull would be worth entering simply to enjoy the magnificent views across the city and bay, but this castle also holds an enjoyable **museum**. Its entertaining romp through local history begins with the eleventh century, but focuses especially on the growth of tourism, with some great photos and film footage from the 1920s and 1930s.

Aquarium
Pza. de Carlos Blasco Imaz 1 • April–June & Sept Mon–Fri 10am–8pm, Sat & Sun 10am–9pm; July & Aug daily 10am–9pm; Oct–March Mon–Fri 10am–7pm, Sat & Sun 10am–8pm • €13, under-13s €6.50 • ☎ 943 440 099, ⊚ aquariumss.com

San Sebastián's modern **aquarium** occupies a large concrete building on the harbourfront below Monte Urgull. As much museum as aquarium, it traces the Basque relationship with the sea, and includes an entire whale skeleton. Nonetheless, it does hold tanks filled with live fish, the largest of which enables you to walk through a glass tunnel while fearsome sharks swim overhead.

Playa de La Concha
Ferries to Santa Clara: every 30min in summer, daily 10am–8pm • €4

The glorious crescent of sand that curves all the way west from the old town to the pleasant but unremarkable suburb of Ondarreta, the **Playa de La Concha**, must rank among the finest city beaches in the world. If you happen to see it for the first time at high tide, you may wonder what all the fuss is about, but as the sea withdraws its full

6

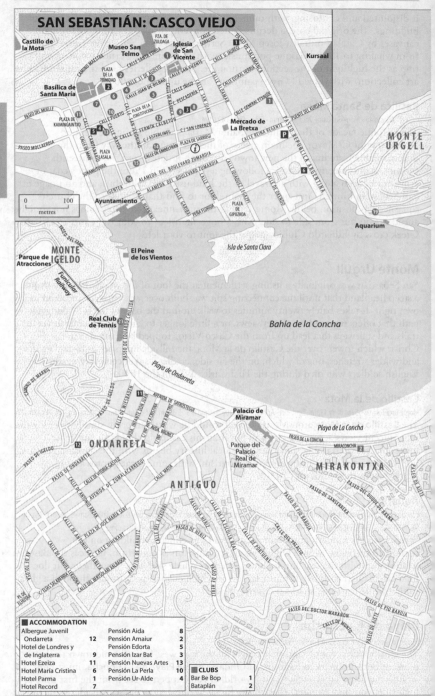

SAN SEBASTIÁN: CASCO VIEJO

Castillo de la Mota

Museo San Telmo

PZA. DE ZULOAGA

Iglesia de San Vicente

Kursaal

Basílica de Santa María

PLAZA DE LA TRINIDAD

Mercado de La Bretxa

Isla de Santa Clara

Ayuntamiento

Aquarium

MONTE URGELL

0   100
metres

MONTE IGELDO

Parque de Atracciones

El Peine de los Vientos

Funicular Railway

Real Club de Tennis

Bahía de la Concha

Playa de Ondarreta

Palacio de Miramar

Playa de La Concha

Parque del Palacio Real de Miramar

MIRAKONTXA

ONDARRETA

ANTIGUO

■ ACCOMMODATION			
Albergue Juvenil		Pensión Aida	8
Ondarreta	12	Pensión Amaiur	2
Hotel de Londres y		Pensión Edorta	5
de Inglaterra	9	Pensión Izar Bat	3
Hotel Ezeiza	11	Pensión Nuevas Artes	13
Hotel María Cristina	6	Pensión La Perla	10
Hotel Parma	1	Pensión Ur-Alde	4
Hotel Record	7		

■ CLUBS	
Bar Be Bop	1
Bataplán	2

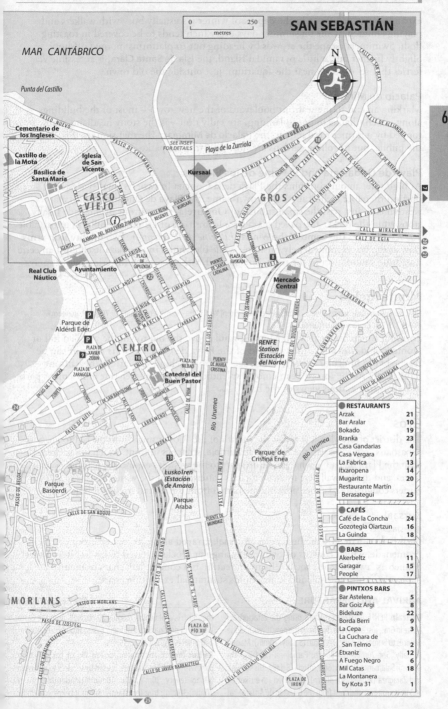

SAN SEBASTIÁN

MAR CANTÁBRICO

Punta del Castillo

Cementerio de los Ingleses

Castillo de la Mota

Basílica de Santa María

Iglesia de San Vicente

CASCO VIEJO

Kursaal

Playa de la Zurriola

GROS

Real Club Náutico

Ayuntamiento

Parque de Aldérdi Eder

CENTRO

Plaza de Xavier Zubiri

Plaza de Zaragoza

Catedral del Buen Pastor

Mercado Central

RENFE Station (Estación del Norte)

Río Urumea

EuskoTren (Estación de Amara)

Parque Araba

Parque Basoerdi

Parque de Cristina Enea

Río Urumea

MORLANS

Plaza de Pío XII

Plaza de Irún

RESTAURANTS	
Arzak	21
Bar Aralar	10
Bokado	19
Branka	23
Casa Gandarias	4
Casa Vergara	7
La Fabrica	13
Itxaropena	14
Mugaritz	20
Restaurante Martín Berasategui	25

CAFÉS	
Café de la Concha	24
Gozotegia Oiartzun	16
La Guinda	18

BARS	
Akerbeltz	11
Garagar	15
People	17

PINTXOS BARS	
Bar Astelena	5
Bar Goiz Argi	8
Bideluze	22
Borda Berri	9
La Cepa	3
La Cuchara de San Telmo	2
Etxaniz	12
A Fuego Negro	6
Mil Catas	18
La Montanera by Kota 31	1

6

expanse is revealed. Even in the depths of winter it's usually busy with walkers and playing children, while on summer days every inch tends to be covered in roasting flesh. Swimmers escape the crowds by heading out to platforms moored offshore. Slightly further out, a little pyramidal island, the **Isla de Santa Clara**, is accessible via ferries that set off from near the aquarium, just outside the old town.

Palacio de Miramar

Marking an end to the seafront boulevard of the new town – most of the buildings along which, thanks to poor planning, are sadly dull – is the stony headland that's topped by a former royal retreat, the **Palacio de Miramar**. The mansion itself is closed to the public, but its rolling gardens are now an attractive park.

Playa de Ondarreta and El Peine de los Vientos

At high tide, an outcrop splits the Playa de la Concha in two; its smaller western portion therefore technically has its own name, the **Playa de Ondarreta**. At its far western end, just past the small suburb of Ondarreta, the seafront promenade finally stops amid the rocks. The paved plaza here forms part of Eduardo Chillida's unmissable 1977 sculpture, **The Comb of the Winds** (*El Peine de los Vientos*). Two mighty iron arms claw at the waves immediately offshore, while blowholes in the plaza itself emit an eerie breathing sound most of the time, interspersed with occasional towering jets of spray.

Monte Igeldo

Funicular railway: daily summer 10am–10pm; winter daily except Wed 11am–6pm; every 15min • €1.70, or €3.10 return • ☎ 943 213 525, ⓦ www.monteigueldo.es

Forming a matching pair with Monte Urgull above the old town, the wooded hill of **Monte Igeldo** rises above the west end of the Playa de Ondarreta. Its summit can be reached via a **funicular railway**, which sets off from behind Ondarreta's beachfront tennis club. At the top you can enjoy a splendidly fading pay-per-ride amusement park as well as tremendous views of the bay.

Gros

The district of **Gros** lies just across the mouth of the Río Urumea from the old town. San Sebastián's "other" beach, the **Playa de la Zurriola**, stretches in front. Much less sheltered than the Playa de La Concha, its counterpart to the west, it's exposed to fearsome ocean waves, and the sea wall here took a ferocious battering from the winter storms of 2014. Surfers congregate to either side, but are barred from the central stretch of beach.

Kursaal

ⓦ kursaal.com.es

Gros is dominated by the huge, glass **Kursaal**, arrayed along its own seafront promenade, which consists of two starkly angular blocks referred to by architect Rafael Moneo as "two beached rocks". Its main feature is a concert hall that's home to September's film festival, and it also holds substantial exhibition space.

ARRIVAL AND DEPARTURE   SAN SEBASTIÁN

By train RENFE (ⓦ renfe.es) trains using the Estación del Norte in Gros, just across the river from the new town, include services to Burgos (6 daily; 3hr); Irún (8 daily; 20min); Madrid (6 daily; 5hr 20min–7hr 30min; Pamplona (2 daily; 1hr 40min); Salamanca (5 daily; 6hr); Vitoria (8 daily; 1hr 40min); and Zaragoza (2 daily; 3hr 40min). EuskoTren (ⓦ euskotren .es) trains run east and west from the Estación de Amara – at the south end of Centro, roughly 20min walk from the Casco Viejo – to destinations including Bilbao (hourly; 2hr 40min) and Irún (every half-hour; 35min).

By bus The main bus station, on Pza. Pio XII, basically a car park with a few bus shelters, is used by services to and from Bilbao (every 30min; 1hr 10min); Hondarribia (every 20min; 30min); Irún (constantly; 30min); Lekeitio (4 daily;

1hr 20min); Bera (Vera) de Bidasoa (2 daily; 50min); and Vitoria (6 daily; 2hr 30min).

By car You can't drive into San Sebastián's Casco Viejo.

Parking can be extremely problematic. If your hotel doesn't have its own car park – and very few do – head straight for the underground garages nearby.

INFORMATION

Turismo Boulevard 8, on the edge of the Casco Viejo (Mon–Thurs 9am–1.30pm & 3.30–7pm, Fri & Sat 10am–7pm, Sun 10am–2pm; ☎983 481 166, ⓦsansebastianturismo.com).

ACCOMMODATION

San Sebastián offers a fine crop of hotels, from *belle époque* beachfront palaces to charming old-town houses, but be warned that it has some of the highest rates in Spain. For a summer stay, or the film festival in September, you can expect to pay over €100 even for a run-of-the-mill room, and you'll need to book as far in advance as possible.

CASCO VIEJO

Hotel Parma Paseo de Salamanca 10 ☎943 428 893, ⓦhotelparma.com. It would be hard to pick a better location, handy for the heach at the edge of the old town. The rooms, though, are bland and faded and it can be noisy at night. The cheapest face an internal courtyard, but those on the upper level enjoy great sea views. Friendly, helpful staff make a big difference. **€157**

Pensión Amaiur C/31 de Agosto 44, 2º ☎943 429 654, ⓦpensionamaiur.com. Classic old-style budget hotel, in a venerable house deep in the warren-like streets of the old town. Rooms differ in size – some sleep four – and are decorated in widely varying styles. Some have en-suite bathrooms and private balconies, others share bathrooms, and there are two communal kitchens. **€70**

★Pensión Edorta C/Puerto 15, 1º ☎943 423 773, ⓦwww.pensionedorta.com. Welcoming family-run hotel, upstairs in a historic house in the heart of the old town, just up from the harbour. Bright, attractive rooms abound in period charm, with exposed stonework and ancient beams. The cheapest share bathrooms and lack even washbasins; book ahead, and pay up to €30 extra, for your own top-quality bathroom. **€70**

Pensión Izar Bat C/Fermin Calbetón 6, 1º ☎943 431 573, ⓦpensionizarbat.com. Six small, clean rooms, with comfortable beds and tiny en-suite bathrooms, but little else; you can also expect little help from the management. Considering its location in the prime nightlife district, it's reasonably quiet. **€70**

Pensión Ur-Alde C/Puerto 17, 2º ☎943 422 581, ⓦur-alde.com. Despite being in one of San Sebastián's older houses, this old-town hotel could be almost anywhere, but for its modern en-suite bathrooms, spotless decor, and central location, it's not bad value. Its ten guest rooms are decorated in widely varying (but generally uninspiring) styles. **€119**

CENTRO

Hotel de Londres y de Inglaterra C/Zubieta 2 ☎943 440 770, ⓦhlondres.com. The very welcoming *grande dame* of San Sebastián hotels, this impressive white nineteenth-century edifice commands a superb position overlooking the beach, a short walk from the old town. Live it up in style in a spacious, very comfortable room with huge seafront windows. Look for good low-season offers. **€318**

Hotel María Cristina Paseo Republica Argentina 4 ☎943 437 600, ⓦhotel-mariacristina.com. Landmark hotel, dominating the river mouth near the edge of the old town, that's the epicentre of September's film festival. Refurbished to mark its centenary in 2012, its sumptuous *belle époque* rooms are the last word in old-style luxury, boasting huge beds and opulent bathrooms. **€385**

Pensión Nuevas Artes C/Urbieta 64, 1ºB ☎943 474 905, ⓦpension-nuevasartes.com. Welcoming upscale *pensión*, run by an exceptionally hospitable, English-speaking mother-and-daughter team. Large comfortable rooms with exposed brickwork, glassed-in balconies, and good en-suite facilities. **€95**

★Pensión La Perla C/Loiola 10, 1º ☎943 428 123, ⓦpensionlaperla.com. Great-value new-town *pensión*, handy for bus and train stations as well as the old town and beach. Friendly service and simple but spacious rooms, all en suite and some with balconies. **€72**

GROS

Hotel Record Calzada Vieja de Ategorrieta 35 ☎943 271 255, ⓦhotelrecord.com. Somewhat incongruous little stand-alone hotel in a quiet residential corner of Gros a short walk from the beach, within easy reach of the old town. The fourteen rooms are far from fancy, but there's on-site parking, decent breakfasts, and scope to accommodate family groups. **€112**

Pensión Aida Iztueta 9, 1º ☎943 327 800, ⓦpensionesconencanto.com. This welcoming nine-room *pensión* stands in a relatively quiet location near the main train station, Zurriola beach, and old town. All rooms are newly and brightly decorated, with exposed stone and en-suite facilities. For maximum peace, opt for an "interior" room, though those facing out are equipped with balconies (and only cost a few euros more). **€84**

ONDARRETA

Albergue Juvenil Ondarreta Paseo de Igeldo 25

6

☎943 310 268, ⊛www.donostialbergues.org. The city's busy youth hostel is about as far as it could be from the old town, in a large pink mansion up the hill above the very far end of Ondarreta beach (bus #5, #16 or #25). Room capacities range from two to eighteen. There's a 2am curfew and 11pm "quiet" rule, while rates depend on the number of beds in your dorm, and your age. For an under-30 in a two- or four-bunk room, **€16.80**

Hotel Ezeiza Avda. Satrústegui 13, Playa de Ondarreta ☎943 214 311, ⊛hotelezeiza.com. This friendly hotel, facing the smaller of the bay's beaches, a long walk from the city centre, makes a good-value base for families looking for lower-key pleasures than the full-on city experience. All rooms are en suite and well maintained, with bright modern furnishings; most have lovely sea views. **€110**

EATING, DRINKING AND NIGHTLIFE

As the epicentre of the Basque culinary revolution, San Sebastián is a paradise for anyone who loves to eat. What's more, in addition to its world-famous gourmet restaurants it also has an astonishing profusion of bars that serve the latest concoctions in the form of **pintxos**. While it's very easy to sniff out your own favourites as you explore the Casco Viejo, it's worth joining one of the tourist board's guided tours, **Pintxos de San Sebastián** (11.30am: July & Aug Mon–Fri, June & Sept every Sat, Oct–May alternate Sats; ☎983 481 166, ⊛sansebastianturismo.com), which for €18 buys you drinks and *pintxos* in three old-town bars.

CAFÉS

Café de la Concha Paseo de La Concha s/n ☎943 473 600, ⊛cafedelaconcha.com. Don't come to this café-restaurant for the food, which is indifferent at best, and even the coffee's pretty poor, but come nevertheless, for the unmissable panorama of La Concha beach and the entire bay beyond. Daily 9am–11pm.

Gozotegia Oiartzun C/Igentia 2 ☎943 426 209, ⊛pasteleriaoiartzun.com. Most customers drop in at this *pastelería*, facing from the edge of the Casco Viejo across to the ornate town hall, just to pick up one of the superb cakes – try the little almond concoction known as a "Pastel Vasco" – but it also serves great coffee, and has a few pavement tables if you don't mind paying a little extra to linger. Daily 8am–9pm.

La Guinda C/Zabaleta 55 ☎843 981 715. With its whitewashed-wood aesthetic, this relaxed coffee bar/deli, a block back from the sea in Gros, wouldn't look out of place beside a New England beach. Drop in for breakfast or a substantial lunchtime salad, or linger over the €13 daily menu. Mon 8am–7pm, Tues–Thurs 8am–11pm, Fri 8am–midnight, Sat 9am–midnight, Sun 9am–7pm.

PINTXOS BARS

Bar Astelena C/Iñigo 1 ☎943 425 245. Tapas bar in a great location, at the edge of the main old-town square. The mouthwatering selection of *pintxos*, cold at one end of the bar and hot at the other, includes all sorts of ham and shellfish delights, and delicious pistachio croquettes for vegetarians. Daily noon–4pm & 7pm–midnight.

Bar Goiz Argi C/Fermín Calbetón 4 ☎943 425 204. Hugely popular Casco Viejo *pintxos* bar with a contemporary edge and no seating whatsoever. It's deservedly renowned for its €2.50 prawn brochettes, but everything's good, with a fine mixture of hot and cold snacks. The restaurant in the basement is good too, but entirely separate. Mon 10am–3.15pm, Wed–Sun 10am–3.15pm & 6.15–11.15pm.

Bideluze Pza. de Gipuzkoa 14 ☎943 422 880, ⊛bideluzebarkafe.multiespaciosweb.com. Classy café-bar,

in the new town facing an open garden square, attracting an arty crowd with its gleaming wooden railway-carriage seats and general feel of an old apothecary. Highly creative *pintxos*, with plenty of eggy treats at breakfast time, and abundant hammy sandwiches; in the evening it attracts a mixed crowd of drinkers. Daily 24hrs.

Borda Berri C/Fermín Calbetón 12 ☎943 430 342. Rustic, inviting old-town *pintxos* place, with yellow walls, almost no seating, and usually eager crowds of in-the-know tourists. There's no food on display; everything on the changing blackboard menu is cooked to order, in substantial starter-size portions that cost around €3. Fabulously tasty treats include a black-ink risotto with baby squid, though you'll need a strong stomach to sample the cod tripe in lurid green sauce (*kallos de bacalao al pil-pil*). Tues–Sun noon–3.30pm & 7–11pm.

La Cepa C/31 de Agosto 7 ☎943 426 394, ⊛barlacepa .com. Bustling, old-fashioned tapas bar in the heart of the old town, with hams festooning the ceiling and glass-topped tables holding tiny trinkets such as casino chips and sweets. Inexpensive *pintxos* are listed on the blackboard, along with more substantial *raciones*, like the succulent ham, *jamón jabugo*, costing €10.50 for a half *ración*. Mon & Wed–Sun 11am–midnight.

La Cuchara de San Telmo C/31 de Agosto 28 ☎943 435 446, ⊛lacucharadesantelmo.com. Long, narrow bar, squeezed into the far edge of the old town at the foot of Monte Urgull. Decorated in splashy colours, it attracts an alternative crowd, who usually spill out into the square outside. The *pintxos* are superb, with chunky meat and fish options and irresistible *tortilla*. Tues 8.30–11pm, Wed–Sun 1–3.30pm & 8.30–11pm.

★ **Etxaniz** C/Fermín Calbetón 24 ☎943 426 259. Tiny little hole-in-the-wall bar in the Casco Viejo, with bright green walls and no seats – there's not even a shelf to put down your food or drink – but a buzzy atmosphere. The counter is spread with a great selection of pungent (lots of garlic), delicious snacks, generally priced at just €1.60, and still available late

BASQUE CUISINE

Basque cuisine has established a reputation as the finest in Spain. Cutting-edge chefs such as Martín Berasetegui, Juan Mari Arzak, and Andoni Aduriz, the stars of the **nueva cocina vasca** (new Basque cuisine), delight in creating inventive new combinations and preparations, and restaurants throughout the region are crowded with eager diners happy to pay premium prices for superb food.

That said, Basque food doesn't have to be expensive. For visitors, the perfect way to sample it is in the form of **pintxos**, the Basque equivalent of tapas. Bar counters throughout the region, and above all in San Sebastián, are piled high with fabulously enticing and utterly delectable goodies, freshly cooked, priced as a rule at €2–3, and almost invariably excellent. Most also prepare more substantial or complicated *pintxos* and *raciones* to order. They're so irresistible that you may find you never quite make it to a restaurant for a sit-down meal – but you'll still come away raving about the Basque Country as one of the greatest foodie destinations on earth.

Seafood is a major ingredient of many Basque signature dishes. Look out especially for *bacalao* (cod) *a la vizcaina* or *al pil-pil, merluza* (hake) *a la vasca, txipirones en su tinta* (squid cooked in its ink) or *txangurro* (spider crab).

6

into the evening. Daily 11.30am–midnight.

★**A Fuego Negro** C/31 de Agosto 31 ☎650 135 373, ⊛afuegonegro.com. Hip, ultramodern old-town bar, decked out in crisp red and white, with an extensive menu of cocktails, wines and shots, and a staggering array of beautiful and succulent *pintxos*, many with a distinct molecular edge, for around €4. "Taste" (€35) and "Super Taste" (€50) menus, as well as various combination plates, allow you to sample several, but it's simplest to try whatever catches your eye – like the trio of crab, avocado and liquorice balls, a tiny meal in itself. Daily except Mon 12.30–4pm & 8–11pm.

Mil Catas C/Zabaleta 55 ☎943 321 656. This pared-down bar, a block back from Zurriola beach, is a great place to enjoy *pintxos* and *raciones* of meat and fish alike, plus simpler toast or egg-based plates. Tues–Sat 1–3.30pm & 8–11pm, Sun 1–3.30pm.

La Montanera by Kota 31 C/31 de Agosto 22 ☎943 429 936, ⊛kota31.es. Large, bright modern place that's rather the antithesis of most San Sebastián *pintxos* bars, and has a disconcerting soundtrack of 1980s' disco classics, but it serves consistently excellent snacks – be sure to try the meltingly soft liver with hummus and parmesan (€4.10) – plus staples like octopus and mussels, and has a sit-down dining room at the rear. Daily 10am–11pm.

RESTAURANTS

★**Arzak** Avda. Alcalde Elosegui 273 ☎943 285 593, ⊛arzak.es. What might look like a typical family-owned *taberna*, on the lower slopes of Monte Ulia 3km east of the centre beyond Gros, is in fact the crucible of Basque *nueva cocina*, triple-starred by Michelin. Father-and-daughter team Juan Mari and Elena Arzak prepare a different selection of stunningly creative dishes each day, with the set menu priced at €189 – look out especially for pigeon or lamb. Behind the scenes, a fully-fledged research lab is hard at work developing new concoctions. Tues–Sat

1–3.15pm & 5.45–11pm; closed mid-June to early July and last 3 weeks in Nov.

Bar Aralar C/Puerto 10 ☎943 426 378, ⊛bararalar .com. The pleasant little dining room of this unpretentious old-town place, at the far end of a tapas bar that offers a spectacular array of *pintxos*, is a good place to come when you simply feel like eating a substantial plate of good food – such as prawns with garlic, or clams – for around €10. Daily 10am–midnight.

Bokado Pza. Jacques Cousteau 1 ☎943 431 842, ⊛www .bokadomikelsantamaria.com. Stylish contemporary restaurant in an unbeatable setting – on the concrete roof of the aquarium, below Monte Urgull at the mouth of the bay – with tables both indoors and outside. As well as set menus at €40 and €55 they also offer *pintxos*, such as spider crab and leek ravioli. Tues & Sun 1.30–3.30pm, Wed–Sat 1.30–3.30pm & 9–11pm.

Branka Paseo de Eduardo Chillida 13 ☎943 317 096, ⊛branka-tenis.com. In a magnificent spot at the far west end of the bay – and appended to an exclusive tennis club – this modern structure holds an expensive restaurant upstairs and a less formal café downstairs. The latter makes an ideal lunchtime break in a day's stroll, offering ham, seafood or vegetable *raciones* at around €14 for a full portion, €8 for half. Café daily 9am–midnight, restaurant Mon–Sat 1.30–4pm & 8.30–11pm.

Casa Gandarias C/31 de Agosto 23 ☎943 426 362, ⊛restaurantegandarias.com. Very popular old-town restaurant, for once with as much of an emphasis on meat – from the cured hams hanging from the ceiling to chunky €20 steaks – as fish. As usual, there's a big selection of *pintxos*, but head for a table at the back and settle down for a solid, well-cooked meal. Daily 11am–midnight.

Casa Vergara C/Mayor 21 ☎943 431 073 ⊛restaurantecasavergara.com. Tucked away below the church at far end of C/Mayor in the old town, this fine old

6

bar-restaurant makes a dependable option whatever your appetite, with an excellent spread of interesting *pintxos*, but also good-value *raciones* and full meals, with a €22 set menu and a cider-house menu at €58 for two diners. Daily except Thurs 11am–4pm & 7pm–midnight.

La Fabrica C/Puerto 17 ☎943 432 110, ⓦrestaurantelafabrica.es. One of the best-value modern restaurants in the city, housed in a bare-bones former brewery in the Casco Viejo. Chef Inigo Bozai specializes above all in delicious fish dishes, available on a wide selection of set menus, ranging from €25 for a weekday lunch up to €37 and €39 for dinner (Fri & Sat). Mon–Sat 1–3.30pm & 8.30–11pm.

Itxaropena C/Embeltrán 16 ☎943 424 576. Charming, cosy old-town cider-house restaurant that serves hearty, high-quality traditional cuisine on menus ranging from €14 – which can get you paella, squid in ink, and dessert, plus cider – up to €75 for two people. Tues–Sat 1–3.30pm & 8–11pm, Sun 1–3.30pm.

Mugaritz Aldura Aldea 20, Errenteria ☎943 522 455, ⓦmugaritz.com. Consistently hailed as one of the top ten restaurants in the world and helmed by Andoni Aduriz, one of the great masters of molecular cuisine, *Mugaritz* represents contemporary Basque cuisine at its most outré. Inevitably, some ordinary diners find it pretentious, but visit with an open mind and you may well be blown away. The two main drawbacks are the location, in a rural hillside cottage 12km southeast of the centre, and the price – the only option is the changing daily menu of up to 24 dishes, costing €180. Mid-April to mid-Dec only: Tues 8–9.30pm, Wed–Sat 12.30–2pm & 8–9.30pm, Sun 12.30–2pm.

Restaurante Martín Berasategui C/Loidi 4, Lasarte-Oria ☎943 366 471 ⓦmartinberasategui.com. Contemporary rather than molecular, this three-star Michelin restaurant is housed in a bright modern structure in the hills 10km southwest of the city. Its eponymous chef remains rooted in traditional Spanish cuisine, while adding

his own subtle twists. À la carte prices are in the region of €70 for a main course, while the full tasting menu is €195. Wed–Sat 1–2.45pm & 8.30–10.15pm, Sun 1–2.45pm.

BARS

Akerbeltz C/de Mari 19 ☎943 451 452. Tiny little bar overlooking the harbour from the western side of the Casco Viejo, with a kitsch Stone Age theme. Crowds of drinkers tumble out onto the steps outside; stay indoors for pounding music and a gay-friendly vibe. Daily 4pm–2.30am.

Garagar Boulevard 22 ☎943 422 840. Big old pub on the inland edge of the Casco Viejo, with an authentic wood-panelled interior and plenty of draught beers, plus extensive café seating on the pavement outside. Daily 9am–3am.

People Avda. de Zurriola 41 ☎943 297 853, ⓦpeopledisco.com. This modern bar, in prime position directly above Zurriola beach, comes into its own around sunset, when its huge plate-glass windows offer spectacular views out to sea, and it segues bit by bit from restaurant to lounge to dance club. Attracting a mixed but generally youthful crowd, it serves cocktails, drinks, *pintxos* and *raciones*, plus breakfast goodies, sandwiches and fuller meals, and also has lots of outdoor seating. Daily 24hr.

CLUBS

Bar Be Bop Paseo de Salamanca 3 ☎943 429 869, ⓦbarbebop.com. Despite the name, this long-established club, facing the river at the east end of the Casco Viejo, treats punters not only to live cool jazz, but also has frequent DJ nights, with funk, soul and Latin on the playlist too. Late at night, when it's often the last old-town bar to remain open, it can get very full. Mon–Fri 3.30pm–4.30am, Sat & Sun 3.30pm–3.30am.

Bataplán Paseo de La Concha 10 ☎943 473 601, ⓦbataplandisco.com. Very glitzy dance club overlooking the main beach, with a fabulous outdoor terrace for hot nights. Daily 11pm–6am.

Hondarribia

Just under 40km east of San Sebastián, the frontier town of **HONDARRIBIA**, immediately across the mouth of the Bidasoa river from Hendaye in France, makes an appealing stopover. Down at water level, where the broad boulevards just back from the pretty harbour are lined with pavement cafés, it feels like a resort, but its fortified **Casco Antiguo**, a delightful little enclave higher up, offers a real sense of history. Filled with sturdily attractive medieval mansions, it centres on the **Pza. de Armas**, where the **Castille de Carlos V**, dating back to the tenth century, now houses an irresistible parador. The local beach, **Playa Hondartza**, lies a short walk north of the newer part of town.

ARRIVAL AND INFORMATION HONDARRIBIA

By bus There are regular buses from San Sebastián (every 20min; 30min), via the nearest train station at Irún.

Turismo Pza. de Armas 9 (July to mid-Sept daily

10am–1.30pm & 3.30–8pm; mid-Sept to June Tues–Sat 10am–1.30pm & 3.30–7pm, Sun 10am–2pm; ☎943 643 677, ⓦbidasoaturismo.com).

ACCOMMODATION

Hotel Obispo Pza. del Obispo ☎ 943 645 400, ⓦ hotelobispo.com. Fourteenth-century palace with long-range sea views from the edge of the old town, converted into a hotel that offers a blend of modern furnishings and traditional rooms with balconies, plus free use of bicycles. €168

Hotel Palacete Pza. de Gipuzkoa 5 ☎ 943 640 813, ⓦ hotelpalacete.net. Pleasant little medieval mansion in the heart of the old town, with a nice little courtyard and tasteful modern rooms. Good rates in low season. €115

Hotel San Nikolas Pza. de Armas 6 ☎ 943 644 278, ⓦ hotelsannikolas.es. Pretty townhouse in the Casco Antiguo, with pastel-blue balconies. Its sixteen en-suite rooms are relatively plain, but they have comfortable beds, and some enjoy sea views. €98

Parador de Hondarribia Pza. de Armas 14 ☎ 943 645 500, ⓦ www.parador.es. While the entrance to the magnificent Castille de Carlos V is on the Casco Antiguo's main square, the lavishly appointed rooms of the so-called *Emperador* offer tremendous hilltop views across to France, and there's also an excellent restaurant. €248

EATING AND DRINKING

While the Casco Antiguo is very short of restaurants and bars, the streets parallel to the waterfront down in the harbour are packed with so many *pintxos* bars and restaurants that you can simply browse in search of whatever takes your fancy.

Hermandad de Pescadores C/Zuloaga 12 ☎ 943 642 738. Hondarribia's finest seafood restaurant is in a 750-year-old building set just back from the harbour in the lower part of town. Crowds of eager diners squeeze onto wooden benches in its no-nonsense dining room to enjoy fresh fish at very reasonable prices. July–Sept daily except Mon noon–11pm; Oct–June Wed noon–4pm, Thurs–Sun noon–11pm.

Inland from San Sebastián: Gipuzkoa

Gipuzkoa, the smallest province in Spain, is in many ways the heartland of Basque language and culture. Medieval towns such as **Tolosa**, with its traditional *Carnaval*, and Oñati, famous for its ancient university, are set in spectacular mountain scenery. In the nearby Sierra de Urkilla, the **Santuario de Arantzazu** is a prime pilgrimage destination for Basques.

Tolosa

TOLOSA, 24km south of San Sebastián, is famous for its **carnival**, celebrated with fervour over six days in February. Considered by Basques as superior to the carnival in San Sebastián, it was the only one whose tradition was maintained throughout the Franco era. Although fairly industrialized, Tolosa has an extensive **Casco Histórico** with an impressive square, Pza. Euskal Herria, and is also well known for its *pintxos*: be sure to try the *guindillas de Ibarra* (pickled green chilli peppers), and the *alubias de Tolosa* (kidney beans, served with blood sausage, cabbage and pork).

Tolosa has the largest **market** in the Basque Country, held on Saturday; activity centres on the distinctive, partly covered, Pza. Berdura in the old town. Nearby, at Pza. Zaharra 3, not far from the *turismo*, is Gorrotxategi, a famous **chocolate** and sweet shop.

ARRIVAL AND INFORMATION   TOLOSA

By bus Tolosa is served by direct buses from San Sebastián (10 daily; 30min) and Vitoria (2 daily; 2hr 30min).
Turismo Pza. Santa María 1, near the river in the old town (mid-June to mid-Sept daily 10am–2pm & 3–7pm; mid-Sept to mid-June Tues–Sat 11am–2pm & 3–6pm, Sun 10am–2pm; ☎ 943 697 413, ⓦ tolosaldea.net).

ACCOMMODATION

Hotel Oria C/Oria 2 ☎ 943 654 688, ⓦ hoteloria.com. Plush, business-oriented modern hotel, 500m south of the old town, with smart and very comfortable rooms, plus its own restaurant and *asador*, offering a recommended cider-house set menu (closed Sun). €72

6

EATING AND DRINKING

Astelena Pza. Euskal Herria 4 ☎ 943 650 996, ⓦ astelena.com. Good-value restaurant on the main arcaded square in Tolosa's old town. There's some outdoor seating, but it's cosier inside. The changing €11.50 lunch menu, featuring for example lentils and anchovies, is recommended. Daily noon–4pm & 7.30–10.30pm.

★ **Beti Alai** C/Arrostegieta ☎ 943 673 381. The pick of the crop on the narrow alleyway that is old Tolosa's main nightlife area. Very good *pintxos* in the bar downstairs, including delicious *pastel de bacalao*, and full meals in the dining room upstairs, with lunch from €12. Tues, Wed & Fri–Sun 1–3.30pm & 8.30–11pm.

Oñati and around

Without doubt the most interesting inland town in Gipuzkoa, **OÑATI**, 65km southwest of San Sebastián, was described by the Basque painter Zuloaga as the "Basque Toledo". Its many historic buildings include such fine Baroque specimens as, at opposite ends of the arcaded Foruen Enparantz, the Baroque town hall and the parish church of **San Miguel**. Every count of Oñati from 988 until 1890 lies buried in the latter's crypt, while its cloister is unusual for being built over the river.

Look out for various Navarran-style *casas torres*, as well as private family mansions, and the Plateresque-style sixteenth-century monastery of **Bidaurreta**.

University of Sancti Spiritus

Mon–Fri 9am–5pm, Sat & Sun 11am–2pm • Free

The **University of Sancti Spiritus**, which dominates Oñati, was for many centuries the only functioning university in Euskal Herria. Open from 1548 until 1901, it remains intact. You are free to wander around the complex; the main facade, with its four pilasters adorned with figures, and the serene courtyard, are particularly impressive.

Santuario de Arantzazu

Daily 9.30am–9.30pm • Free • ⓦ arantzazukosantutegia.org • Hourly buses from Oñati

Clinging spectacularly to the mountainside above a gorge 9km south of Oñati, the **Santuario de Arantzazu** is a prime pilgrimage site for Basques, venerating **Our Lady of Arantzazu** (Santa María), the patron saint of Gipuzkoa. Built in 1950, its spiky monastery features contemporary work by the sculptors Chillida (the doors) and Sáenz de Oteiza (part of the facade). The severe modernist architecture might not be to everyone's taste, but it's worth looking inside for the soaring stained-glass windows.

ARRIVAL AND INFORMATION   OÑATI AND AROUND

Turismo C/San Juan 14, opposite Sancti Spiritus (April–Sept Mon–Fri 10am–2pm & 3.30–7.30pm, Sat 10am–2pm & 4.30–6.30pm, Sun 10am–2pm; Oct–March Mon–Fri 10am–1pm & 4–7pm, Sat & Sun 11am–2pm; ☎ 943 783 453, ⓦ www.oinati.org). Oñati's helpful *turismo* can arrange guided visits to the university and church.

ACCOMMODATION AND EATING

Arregi C/Garagaltza 21 ☎ 943 783 657, ⓦ casaruralarregi .es. A rural *agriturismo*, run by a friendly family, located 2km northwest of town, and holding chunkily furnished, good-value rooms as well as its own restaurant (closed Sat). **€44**

Hotel Ongi C/Zaharra 19 ☎ 943 718 285, ⓦ hotelongi .com. Simple but perfectly adequate lodging, just behind the university. Rates for the eighteen en-suite rooms drop significantly at weekends. **€56**

The Costa Vasca

West from San Sebastián, both road and rail run inland, following the Río Oria, then towards the coast at sprawling, overdeveloped Zarautz, some 20km from San Sebastián. From here on, the **Costa Vasca** is glorious – a rocky and wild coastline, with long stretches of road hugging the edge of the cliffs – all the way to Bilbao. The hillsides, particularly around Getaria, are famous for the production of fizzy *txakoli* wine. The farther you go, the less developed the resorts become.

Getaria

The tiny fishing port of **GETARIA**, 25km west of San Sebastián, lies not far beyond Zarautz. Founded in 1209, and sheltered by the humpbacked islet of **El Ratón** (The Mouse), it later became a major whaling centre. These days it's much more of a resort, with a crescent beach thronged in summer with surfers and holiday-makers, and overlooked by fancy fish restaurants arrayed along terraces high above the harbour. Cheaper bars and cafés lurk in the lanes just inland, while the village preserves the magnificent fourteenth-century church of **San Salvador**.

The first man to sail around the world, **Juan Sebastián Elcano**, was born in Getaria around 1487 – his ship was the only one of Magellan's fleet to make it back home. Every four years, during the village's **fiestas** on August 7, 2018, 2022, and so on, Elcano's landing is re-enacted on the beach.

Museo Cristóbal Balenciaga

Aldamar Parkea 6 • March–May & Oct Tues–Fri & Sun 10am–5pm, Sat 10am–7pm; June & Sept Tues–Sun 10am–7pm; July & Aug daily 10am–7pm; Nov–Feb Tues–Fri 10am–3pm, Sat & Sun 10am–5pm • €10 • ☎ 943 008 840, ⊕ cristobalbalenciagamuseoa.com

After many years of languishing incomplete on the hillside above Getaria, a quite extraordinary new museum dedicated to the life and work of the locally born fashion designer **Cristóbal Balenciaga** (1895–1972) finally opened in 2011. It's a classic example of Spain's twenty-first-century breed of overblown architectural projects, consisting of a vast black-glass extension tacked on the hollowed-out nineteenth-century Palacio Aldamar. The displays inside are on a much smaller scale, with a few dozen of Balenciaga's cocktail and wedding dresses displayed reverentially behind glass, each in its own dimly lit cage, rotating endlessly like a kebab on a spit.

ARRIVAL AND INFORMATION

GETARIA

By bus Getaria is served by direct buses from San Sebastián (daily, every 20–30min; 40min), which continue to Zumaia (15min).

Turismo The *turismo* is at Aldamar Parkea 2, immediately below the Balenciaga museum (Easter to mid-Sept Tues–Sun 10am–2pm & 4.30–7.30pm; ☎ 943 140 957, ⊕ getaria.net).

ACCOMMODATION

Casa Rural Itsas-Lore C/Eitzaga Auzoa 14 ☎ 943 140 619, ⊕ itsaslore.com. Charming rural house, built in 1995 2km up the hillside from Getaria on the way towards Santa Bárbara, with great views of the sea and the mountains. Each bathroom is shared by two of the comfortable guest rooms. One-night stays incur a hefty surcharge; rates are for multi-day stays. **€75**

★ Saiaz Getaria C/Roke Deuna 25 ☎ 943 140 143, ⊕ saiazgetaria.com. Magnificent fifteenth-century mansion, topped by formidable stone towers, now stylishly converted to hold seventeen exceptionally comfortable bedrooms; pay around €20 extra to secure a full-on sea view. **€109**

EATING AND DRINKING

Elkano C/Herrerieta 2 ☎ 943 140 024, ⊕ restaurante elkano.com. At his attractive restaurant in the heart of the old town, chef Aitor Arregui prepares truly excellent fresh fish and seafood meals for around €60 a head. Mid-July to Aug daily 1–3pm & 8–11pm; Sept to mid-July Mon & Sun 1–3pm, Wed–Sat 1–3pm & 8–11pm.

Mayflower Katrapuna 4 ☎ 943 140 658. Traditional grill with tables spreading across the harbour-view terrace, offering such delights as superb sardines, barbecued chicken, and *chipirones a lo Pelayo* (tiny cuttlefish with onion). Main dishes cost anything from €11 to €40, with octopus at €15. Daily 12.30–3.30pm & 8–11pm.

Politena C/Nagusia 9 ☎ 943 140 113. Like several bars along Getaria's very pretty principal lane, this friendly spot sets out *pintxos* on the bar and serves full meals in a dining room further back, and also has a couple of outdoor tables. Its €10.60 set menu is much better value than you'll find along the seafront. Mon & Wed–Sun 10am–11pm.

Ondarroa

The easternmost coastal town in Bizkaia, **ONDARROA** looks very different to the small resorts farther east towards San Sebastián. Squeezed in on either side of the mouth of a narrow, steep-sided river, it's quite a workaday place, with its seaward end dominated by a no-nonsense **fishing port** filled with an eclectic set of trawlers. However, it does make an interesting stopover, redeemed by an attractive **beach** within very easy walking distance east of the harbour, and the more substantial beach of **Saturrarán** around the headland beyond that.

ARRIVAL AND INFORMATION   ONDARROA

By bus Regular buses connect Ondarroa with the nearest train station at Deba, 8km east (5 daily; 10min).
Turismo On the port at Kofradi Zaharra-Erribera 9 (mid-June to mid-Sept daily 10.30am–2pm & 4.30–7.30pm; mid-Sept to mid-June Mon–Sat 10.30am–1.30pm & 5–7.30pm, Sun 10.30am–2pm; ☎946 831 951, ⓦ ondarroa.eu).

ACCOMMODATION

Camping Saturraran Saturraran ☎943 603 847, ⓦ www.campingseuskadi.com/saturraran. Summer-only campsite, 1km east of Ondarroa and set a short walk back from the glorious sheltered beach at Saturraran. Closed Oct–May. **€15**

Pensión Patxi C/Artabide 2 ☎609 986 446. Ondarroa's only accommodation option, a simple but good-value *pensión* a couple of streets back from the fray near the harbour. **€45**

Lekeitio

As one of the nicest seafront towns in the Basque Country, the lovely old port of **LEKEITIO**, on the west side of a broad river-mouth 10km west from Ondarroa, now welcomes plenty of pleasure boats to complement its active fishing fleet. Like many seafront towns hereabouts, it was hit hard by the storms of early 2014, and the sea wall bears the scars of being patched up in a hurry.

Well worth visiting for a day or overnight, Lekeitio is blessed with two fine **beaches** – one beside the harbour in the heart of town, and the other, better, across the river to the east. The little wooded island in the middle of the bay can be reached on foot at low tide.

Church of Santa María

Mon–Sat 8am–6pm • ☎946 840 954, ⓦ www.basilicadelekeitio.com

The **church of Santa María**, dominating Lekeito from a high perch above the harbour, contains a magnificent sixteenth-century Flemish Gothic altarpiece, the third largest on the peninsula after those of the cathedrals of Seville and Toledo.

Santa Catalina Lighthouse

Wed–Sun 11.30am–1pm & 4.30–6pm • €6 • ☎946 844 017, ⓦ lekeitio.org

The region's only lighthouse that's open to the public faces the open sea from a headland 2km north of the harbour. Displays inside the photogenic **Santa Catalina Lighthouse** explain the history of navigation along this stretch of coast, and allow visitors to pilot a virtual "boat" between Elantxobe and Lekeitio.

ARRIVAL AND INFORMATION   LEKEITIO

By bus Lekeitio is served by direct buses from the nearest station at Deba, 25km east (4 daily; 45min), as well as to Bilbao (hourly; 1hr) and San Sebastián (2–4 daily; 1hr).
By car Not only is there no parking east of the town centre, there's not even anywhere to turn around; park by the harbour if at all possible.
Turismo On the main waterfront square, Independentziaren Enparantza (daily 10am–3pm & 4–7pm; ☎946 844 017, ⓦ lekeitio.org).

ACCOMMODATION

Aisia Lekeitio Santa Elena s/n ☎946 842 655, ⓦaisiahoteles.com. This undeniably faded grand hotel occupies a great position facing the harbourfront beach, a short walk east of the town centre. Half of its 42 en-suite rooms enjoy superb sea views, for just a few euros extra, and there's also a restaurant and sea-water therapy centre. **€101**

★**Hotel Palacio Oxangoiti** C/Gamarra 2 ☎944 650 555, ⓦoxangoiti.net. Very central hotel, in a fine townhouse a few steps from the harbour. Seven comfortable en-suite rooms, several of which have balconies facing the church. **€110**

Hotel Zubieta Portal de Atea s/n ☎946 843 030, ⓦhotelzubieta.com. Charming, very elegant hotel, set in the gardens of an old palace on the inland side of town, not far from the harbour. Bright, well-furnished en-suite rooms and excellent breakfasts. **€109**

EATING AND DRINKING

Bar Marina Muelle Txatxo Kaia 1 ☎946 840 658. Lekeitio is teeming with places to eat and drink, with a long line of harbourfront restaurants and *pintxos* bars. This large, bare-bones bar on the corner of the quayside nearest the church has a few harbourfront tables, a surprisingly green interior with murals of the old town, and a good selection of inexpensive tapas. Daily 9am–11pm.

Elantxobe

The well-preserved fishing village of **ELANTXOBE**, 10km west of Lekeitio, merits a detour back to the coast from the main road west. When the access road forks just before town, head left for the main village, or right to drop down to the harbour. From the tiny central square (so small that buses have to park on a turntable and be manually spun around before they can leave), an incredibly steep cobbled street lined with attractive fishermen's houses, C/Nagusia, connects the village to the harbour below. In the other direction, it continues 2km up to the cemetery from where a signposted track leads to **Mount Ogoño**, at 280m the highest cliff on the Basque coast.

ARRIVAL AND DEPARTURE   ELANTXOBE

By bus Buses stop in the main square.

By car There is limited parking just before the harbour.

ACCOMMODATION

Caserio Arboliz C/Arboliz 12 ☎946 276 283, ⓦarboliz.com. This conspicuous white-painted house, perched on the clifftop in Ibarrangelu, 1km southeast of Elantxobe, has been converted into a comfortable rural *agroturismo*, with kitchen facilities available, and a lovely sea-view garden. **€65**

Itsasmin Ostatua C/Nagusia 32 ☎946 276 174, ⓦitsasmin.com. Simple *pensión* in the heart of Elantxobe. All its twelve rooms are en suite; half have little street-side balconies with harbour views. **€65**

EATING AND DRINKING

Makues C/Bide 1 ☎946 276 127. The best of Elantxobe's small crop of restaurants, just below the main square, and offering good dinner set menus from €20. Daily except Tues 1–3pm & 8–10.30pm.

Gernika

GERNIKA, beside the Río Oka 25km northeast of Bilbao, is the traditional heart of Basque nationalism. It was here that the Basque parliament met until 1876, and here, under the **Tree of Gernika**, that their rights were reconfirmed by successive rulers. For the Basques, a visit to Gernika is more of a pilgrimage than a tourist trip. The parliament, church and tree remained miraculously unscathed by the infamous bombing of 1937, but the rest of the town was destroyed and has been rebuilt. It's now rather nondescript, and not really a place to spend much time on a holiday, though the arcaded main street, **Artekalea**, has a certain appeal.

6

THE BOMBING OF GERNIKA

The name of Gernika is famous the world over thanks to the nightmare painting by **Pablo Picasso**, which commemorated its **saturation bombing** during the Spanish Civil War. In one of the first such raids ever perpetrated on a civilian centre, on April 27, 1937, planes from the Condor Legion, which had been lent to Franco by Hitler and had taken off from Vitoria-Gasteiz, took just three hours to obliterate 71 percent of the buildings in Gernika. The town had been chosen as the target largely for its symbolic importance. Around 250 people died, many of whom were attending the weekly market that's still held every Monday in the Pza. de Gernika. The nearby town of Durango had been bombed a few days earlier, but because there were no foreign observers, the reports were simply not believed. While the German government acknowledged its involvement in the bombing in 1997, to this day the Spanish government has never admitted its role.

Picasso started work on his painting the day that news of the bombing reached him in Paris. Finally brought "home" to Spain after the death of Franco, it is now exhibited in the Centro de Arte Reina Sofía in Madrid.

Gernika Peace Museum

Foru Pza., C/Artekalea • March–Sept Tues–Sat 10am–7pm, Sun 10am–2pm; Oct–Feb Tues–Sat 10am–2pm & 4–6pm, Sun 10am–2pm • €5 • ☎ 946 270 213, ⓦ www.museodelapaz.org

On the small open plaza across from the *turismo*, the **Gernika Peace Museum** sets out to commemorate the town's own tragedy and explore the very concept of peace. A reconstructed living room of a typical local house enables visitors to live through the bombing raid, complete with sound effects, while an extended section honours all the victims of the Basque conflict, listed according to whether they were killed by ETA, the security forces, or other groups.

Museo Euskal Herria

C/Allendesalazar 5 • July & Aug Tues–Sat 10am–2pm & 4–7pm, Sun 10.30am–2.30pm & 4–7.30pm, Sept–June closed Sun afternoon • €3, free on Sat • ☎ 946 255 451, ⓦ bizkaia.net/euskalherriamuseoa

Housed in an eighteenth-century mansion near the Basque parliament building, the **Museo Euskal Herria** traces the history of the Basque Country from its earliest prehistoric inhabitants. Each of its component regions, including the Kingdom of Navarre and the areas now belonging to France, is examined in systematic detail. There's some interesting material, but with captions in Basque and Spanish only, it's liable to fall rather flat for English-speaking visitors.

The Batzarretxea and the Tree of Gernika

C/Allendesalazar • Daily: summer 10am–2pm & 4–7pm; winter 10am–2pm & 4–6pm • Free • ⓦ jjggbizkaia.net

Although the government of the Basque Country as a whole is in Vitoria-Gasteiz, the **Batzarretxea**, or Casa de las Juntas, a short walk from the centre of Gernika, is home to the parliament of Bizkaia, which was reactivated in 1979. Visitors can enter the building itself, but the real attraction is what's left of the **Tree of Gernika** (Gernikako Arbola), the traditional meeting place of the Basque people. Now just a stump, protected in a little columned pavilion, it stands in the adjacent grounds, close to a replacement oak planted in 2005.

Europa Park and around

Stretching behind both the Batzarretxea and the Museo Euskal Herria, **Europa Park** contains ornamental gardens, a fast-flowing stream, and peace sculptures by Henry Moore and Eduardo Chillida. The Gothic church of **Santa María la Antigua** alongside is adorned with portraits of the various nobles of Bizkaia who pledged allegiance to the *fueros*.

ARRIVAL AND INFORMATION   GERNIKA

By bus Frequent buses from Bilbao stop in the town centre at C/ Iparraguirre 16.

By train Gernika's central station is a stop on the EuskoTren line between Bilbao (every 30min; 45min)

and Bermeo (every 30min; 20min).

Turismo C/Artekalea 8 (July & Aug Mon–Sat 10am–7pm, Sun 10am–2pm; Sept–June Mon–Sat 10am–2pm & 4–7pm, Sun 10am–2pm; ☎ 946 255 892, ⓦ gernika-lumo.net).

ACCOMMODATION

Hotel Gernika C/Carlos Gangoiti 17 ☎ 946 250 350, ⓦ hotel-gernika.com. Gernika's largest and most comfortable hotel is north of the centre, 500m on the road towards Bermeo. There's nothing remarkable about its forty en-suite rooms, but they're reasonably well kept and quiet, and there's a decent tapas bar next door. **€84**

Pensión Akelarre Ostatua C/Barrenkale 5 ☎ 946 270 197, ⓦ hotelakelarre.com. Cheap central *pensión*, right behind the *turismo*, with seventeen plain but brightly painted rooms equipped with showers. The front desk is closed 1–6pm, and after 9pm, but you can check in by inserting a credit card next to the door. **€55**

EATING AND DRINKING

★ **Baserri Maitea** C/Atzondoa, Forua ☎ 946 253 408, ⓦ baserrimaitea.com. Whether you eat in the spacious dining room inside this beautiful 300-year-old Basque farmhouse, a couple of kilometres north of Gernika, or outdoors in the garden, it's a great spot to enjoy traditional dishes roasted in a wood-fired oven. Typical meat and fish main courses cost €20–25, while set menus range from €48 to €60. May–Oct Mon–Sat 1–3.30pm & 9–11pm, Sun 1–3.30pm; Nov–April Mon–Thurs 1–3.30pm, Fri & Sat 1–3.30pm & 9–11pm.

Boliña C/Barrenkale 3 ☎ 946 250 300, ⓦ hotelbolina.net.

Behind the tourist office, this is the best-value restaurant in the centre of Gernika, and it also has a handful of cheap rooms. There's a €10 lunch menu, while the full evening tasting menu, with a good range of meat and fish, costs €35. Daily 12.30–3pm & 8–10.30pm.

Zallo Barri C/Juan Kaltzada 79 ☎ 946 251 800, ⓦ zallobarri.com. Smart restaurant, 500m south of the centre, that's home to highly acclaimed chef Iñigo Ordorica. Individual dishes for around €20, set menus from €28 upwards. Mon–Thurs & Sun 12.30–3.30pm, Fri & Sat 12.30–3.30pm & 8–11pm.

Mundaka

Flowing north from Gernika, the Río Oka broadens into an estuary that's fringed by hilly pinewoods and dotted with islets. A succession of sandy coves offer great swimming, but the best spots are at Sukarrieta and especially **MUNDAKA**. This lovely little village remains amazingly unspoiled, despite having achieved legendary status for its magnificent **surfing**, which includes what's claimed to be the longest left break in the world. Although Mundaka has frequently hosted world championship events, conditions tend to vary considerably from year to year. In good years, during the peak winter season, it's often possible to watch the surfers battle its trademark "Wave" from the plaza next to the church.

Playa de Laída

Ferry: June–Sept 10am–8pm; every 20min • €1.50

In summer, swimmers leap into the water from all along the shoreline and quayside in Mundaka. The nearest proper beach, however, lies across the river. From the inlet slightly south of the port, a passenger ferry makes frequent trips to **Playa de Laída**, an enormous area of white sand, which at low tide stretches across the mouth of the bay in an unbroken crescent.

ARRIVAL, INFORMATION AND ACTIVITIES   MUNDAKA

By train Mundaka is on the EuskoTren line between Bilbao (every 30min; 50min), Gernika (every 30min; 15min), and Bermeo (every 30min; 5min).

Turismo Next to the harbour on C/Kepa Deuna (mid-June to mid-Sept daily 10am–2pm & 3–7pm, mid-Sept to mid-June Wed–Sun 10.30am–2pm; ☎ 946 177 201,

ⓦ mundakaturismo.com).

Surfing The Mundaka Surf Shop, close to the port (Mon–Sat 10.30am–2pm & 5–8pm, Sun 11am–2pm; ☎ 946 876 721, ⓦ mundakasurfshop.com), sells and rents equipment (surfboards from €15 per half-day) and offers surf lessons (five 2hr lessons with board rental €120).

ACCOMMODATION AND EATING

Bar Los Txopos C/Devnaren 4 ☎ 946 876 482. Tapas bar with a full menu of *raciones* as well as everything from *tortillas* to burgers. In truth the food isn't exceptional, and the prices are relatively high, but the seafront location and expansive terrace seating make it all but irresistible anyway, even if just for a morning coffee. Daily 8am–11pm.

Hotel Mundaka C/Florentino Larriñaga 9 ☎ 946 876 700, ⓦ hotelmundaka.com. Attractive, surfer-friendly hotel, just off Mundaka's main square. Clean, comfortable rooms and a friendly welcome. **€85**

★**Hotel El Puerto** C/Portu 1 ☎ 946 876 725, ⓦ hotelelpuerto.com. This delightful hotel faces out to sea from right beside the fishing port, and has a lovely shaded terrace. Several of its en-suite rooms have great sea views. Be warned that it's liable to be noisy at night in summer. **€90**

Portuondo ☎ 946 877 701, ⓦ campingportuondo .com. This appealing campsite, popular with surfers, is perched high above the water a short walk south of town, with steps leading down to a rocky beach. There's a decent restaurant on site (closed Mon), and rental bungalow-style cabins are also available (€100). **€25.60**

Bermeo

BERMEO, 3km north of Mundaka, is a venerable old port with a large fishing fleet. Apart from the riot of red, green and blue boats in the harbour, there's very little to see – and surprisingly enough, neither are there any tapas bars or restaurants worth recommending. However, Bermeo makes a good base for the estuary beaches nearby, and it's also worth driving 8km west to the remarkable island shrine of **San Juan de Gaztelugatxe**, reached by crossing a little causeway and climbing two hundred steep steps.

ARRIVAL AND INFORMATION   BERMEO

By train Bermeo lies at the end of the EuskoTren line from Bilbao (every 30min; 1hr 15min), Gernika (every 30min; 20min) and Mundaka (every 30min; 5min).

Turismo Parque de Lamera, on the waterfront (summer

Mon–Fri 10am–7pm, Sat 10am–2pm & 4–7pm, Sun 10am–2pm; winter Mon–Sat 10am–2pm & 4–7pm, Sun 10am–2pm; ☎ 946 179 154, ⓦ www.bermeo.org).

ACCOMMODATION

★**Hostal Torre Ercilla** Talaranzko 14, 1° ☎ 946 187 598, ⓦ hoteltxaraka.com. Top-notch inexpensive accommodation a few streets up from the port behind Santa María church. Ask for the spacious corner room, with a balcony and glassed-in gallery as well as en-suite bathroom. **€63**

★**Lurdeia** Artike auzoa, s/n ☎ 946 477 001, ⓦ lurdeia .com. Lovely rural *agriturismo*, attached to a hilltop organic farm, with large, tastefully decorated and very comfortable rooms with magnificent long-distance ocean views. It's reached by a convoluted but clearly signposted 9km drive south from the centre of Bermeo. **€65**

Bilbao

Stretching for some 14km beside the Río Nervión, **BILBAO** (Bilbo) is a large city but seldom feels like one. Even though its urban sprawl now fills the narrow valley, you can always see the green slopes of the mountains to either side, beyond the high-rise buildings of the city centre. Bilbao's great achievement has been to reinvent itself since the collapse of its traditional industrial base at the end of the last century. The dramatic success since 1997 of the **Museo Guggenheim**, which transformed a postindustrial wasteland right in the city centre into a major tourist attraction, in turn triggered further visionary redevelopments including the construction of a new metro and airport.

With around 350,000 people in its urban core, and a total fast approaching one million in the metropolitan district, modern Bilbao is much the biggest city in the Basque Country, and serves as the capital of Bizkaia province. While it can't match San Sebastián for beaches or sheer prettiness, Bilbao still has plenty to offer, from its exuberant cutting-edge architecture and stimulating museums to the lively alleyways of its old town, the **Casco Viejo**, and its friendly inhabitants.

From the compact old town, on the river's right bank at the eastern edge of the city centre, an easy and pleasant stroll leads all the way to the Guggenheim, crossed by way of the showpiece **Zubizuri** footbridge. Only when Bilbao industrialized in the nineteenth century did it expand back onto the left bank, to create the much larger new town, or **Ensanche**. All but encircled by a huge loop in the river, this remains the commercial heart of the city, with its broad avenues radiating from the central Pza. Moyúa.

The Casco Viejo

What's now known as the "old town", the **Casco Viejo**, is not in fact the oldest part of Bilbao. The city started out as a cluster of small fishing villages on the left bank of the river, whereas the Casco Viejo grew up across the river between the fourteenth and nineteenth centuries. All the oldest buildings that still survive, however, are now concentrated here, and it's the most enjoyable area to explore on foot. A tight-knit labyrinth of old stone lanes, filled with bars and restaurants and cradling the delightful arcaded main square, the Pza. Nueva, it also holds some worthwhile museums.

Euskal Museoa Bilbao

Pza. Unamuno 4 • Tues–Sat 11am–5pm, Sun 11am–2pm • €3, free Thurs • ☎ 944 155 423, ⓦ euskalmuseoak.com

Devoted to Basque ethnology and history, the somewhat dour, old-school **Euskal Museoa Bilbao** is housed in the former Colegio de San Andrés. The cloister at its heart is a lovely retreat from the city bustle, and holds a stylized Iron Age statue known as the *Mikeldi*, depicting a hog with a disc in its belly, that's thought to have been used in ancient rituals. Displays in the museum itself trace Basque fishing traditions back over ten thousand years, follow local shepherds as far as the western US, and explain the growth of Bilbao. There's also a huge relief model of the whole of Bizkaia. No captions are in English.

Arkeologi Museoa

Calzadas de Mallona 2, Pza. Unamuno • Tues–Sat 10am–2pm & 4–7.30pm • €3 • ☎ 944 040 990, ⓦ euskalmuseoak.com

Hived off from the Euskal Museoa, Bilbao's small **archeology museum** stands across the same old-town square in a former train station that's been converted to the point of being unrecognizable. Galleries on its three floors cover specific eras of human history in Bizkaia, from the Neanderthals onwards, with eye-catching displays but little detail. Exhibits include a surprising number of actual skeletons, plus a small shipwrecked fishing vessel from the fifteenth century.

Mercado de la Ribera

C/de la Ribera • Mon & Sat 8am–3pm, Tues–Fri 8am–2.30pm & 5–8pm

Seven centuries after a daily food market was first established on the right bank of the Río Nervión, the **Mercado de la Ribera** remains the epicentre of life in Bilbao's old town. In its current form, it's an amalgam of a superbly elegant Art Nouveau building from 1929 with a modern revamp that has given it huge new windows, more space, and greater ease of access. Be sure to venture in to relish its vast array of fresh produce and seafood.

Museo Guggenheim

July & Aug daily 10am–8pm; Sept–June Tues–Sun daily 10am–8pm • €13, under-12s free • Free guided tour at 5pm • ☎ 944 359 090, ⓦ guggenheim-bilbao.es

Frank Gehry's astounding **Museo Guggenheim** looms over the left bank of the Río Nervión, ten minutes' walk west of the Casco Viejo. Completed in 1997, it was hailed by architect Philip Johnson as "the greatest building of our time". The construction of

BILBAO

ACCOMMODATION

Arriaga Suites	12
Bilbao Akelarre Hostel	5
Ganbara Hostel	11
Hesperia Bilbao	1
Hostal Begoña	9
Hostal-Residencia Ría de Bilbao	7
Hotel Carlton	10
Hotel Iturrienea Ostatua	14
Hotel López de Haro	6
Meliá Bilbao	3
Miró	4
Pensión Mardones	13
Pensión Mendez I & II	15
Pensión Zubia	8
Silken Gran Domine Bilbao	2

such a showpiece project on a derelict industrial site represented a colossal gamble by the Basque government, which hoped to stimulate the revitalization of Bilbao. Amazingly enough, it worked. A gargantuan sculpture, whose sensual titanium curves glimmer like running water in the sun, it has inevitably overshadowed the artworks it contains.

The best way to approach the museum is along the river, either along the quayside, or by crossing the high Puente de la Salve road bridge from Deusto on the north

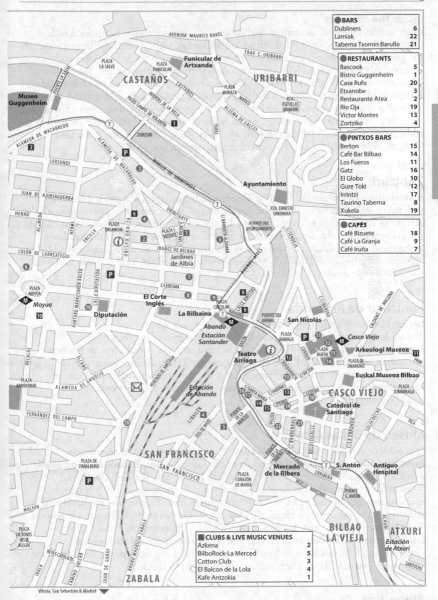

● BARS

Dubliners	6
Lamiak	22
Taberna Txomin Barullo	21

● RESTAURANTS

Bascook	5
Bistro Guggenheim	1
Casa Rufo	20
Etxanobe	3
Restaurante Atea	2
Río Oja	19
Victor Montes	13
Zortziko	4

● PINTXOS BARS

Berton	15
Café Bar Bilbao	14
Los Fueros	11
Gatz	16
El Globo	10
Gure Tokí	12
Irrintzi	17
Taurino Taberna	8
Xukela	19

● CAFÉS

Café Bizuete	18
Café La Granja	9
Café Iruña	7

■ CLUBS & LIVE MUSIC VENUES

Azkena	2
BilboRock-La Merced	5
Cotton Club	3
El Balcon de la Lola	4
Kafe Antzokia	1

bank. One of Louise Bourgeois' fearsome spindle-legged spiders, *Maman*, patrols the water's edge, while Anish Kapoor's column of glittering silver bubbles, *Tall Tree and the Eye*, stands in a reflecting pool alongside the building. The actual entrance, however, is via a walkway that descends from the structure's city side. Jeff Koons' enormous *Puppy* here, clad in colourful living flowers, was originally installed as a temporary exhibit for the opening ceremony, but became a permanent fixture after *bilbainos* clamoured for it to stay.

Inside the museum

Once inside, visitors flow seamlessly through the various galleries in no fixed order, crisscrossing the vast, light-filled atrium on walkways. Gehry called the largest room on the ground floor his "fish gallery"; stretching away beneath the road bridge, it's permanently given over to Richard Serra's disorienting sculpture series, *The Matter of Time*, consisting of eight enormous shapes of weathered steel, coiled and labyrinthine.

The rest of the museum hosts top-flight temporary exhibitions, and depending on space also displays a rotating selection from the Guggenheim Foundation's unparalleled collection of twentieth-century art, which features works by all the major modern and contemporary figures, including Kandinsky, Klee, Mondrian, Picasso, Cézanne, Chagall, Warhol, Calder and Rauschenberg, to name a few.

Zubizuri

Resembling a vast white sail filled by a fresh wind, Santiago Calatrava's spectacular pedestrian-only **Zubizuri** – the name simply means "white bridge" – curves majestically across the Río Nervión a few minutes' walk west of the old town. When it first opened, the bridge only provided access on the left bank to the Muelle de Uribitarte, down along the quayside. Calatrava was so angered when an extended walkway was added to connect with the higher Alameda Mazarredo that he sued the local council, and won €30,000 compensation.

Funicular de Artxanda

Daily every 10min: Mon–Fri 7.15am–11pm, Sat & Sun 8.15am–11pm; Oct–May until 10pm • €1

Three blocks north of the river, the Pza. Funicular marks the foot of the **Funicular de Artxanda**, an inclined railway built to serve commuters to the newer residential suburbs in 1931. It sweeps passengers 770m up the mountainside in less than five minutes. There are no views along the way, but a circular park at the top offers fabulous panoramas over the city and across into the verdant neighbouring valley.

Museo de Bellas Artes

Parque de Doña Casilda de Iturriza • Mon & Wed–Sun 10am–8pm • €7, free on Wed • ☎ 944 396 060, Ⓦ museobilbao.com

Inevitably doomed to play second fiddle to the Guggenheim, Bilbao's **Museo de Bellas Artes**, a short walk southwest in a very pleasant green park, is a high-quality art museum in its own right. Its sizeable permanent collection, housed in a bright, spacious modern annexe to its original core, ranges from anonymous medieval religious artworks to the present day. Highlights include El Greco's stark *St Francis*, Gauguin's *Washerwomen in Arles*, and Anish Kapoor's *Pool*, an impenetrable dish of reflective black lacquered steel. Basque artists are much better represented than in the Guggenheim; look out for Anselmo Guinea's 1899 Art Nouveau panel *Back From the Pilgrimage*, and José Arrue's later depictions of idyllic village life.

Alhóndiga

Pza. Arriquabar 4 • No fixed hours • Free • ☎ 944 014 014, Ⓦ www.alhondigabilbao.com

Entering the **Alhóndiga**, a former wine warehouse in the centre of the new town, you encounter a baffling space. The low ceiling is supported by 43 squat Philippe Starck-designed pillars in wildly differing styles and materials, while a fiery red sun hangs in the centre. Elements beyond include cafés and restaurants, a cinema down in the basement, assorted performance and exhibition spaces, and a gym.

FROM TOP MUSEO GUGGENHEIM (P.469); BODEGAS YSIOS (P.483) >

Museo Marítimo Ría de Bilbao

Muelle Ramón de la Sota • June–Sept Tues–Sun 10am–8pm; Oct–May Tues–Fri 10am–6pm, Sat & Sun 10am–8pm • €6, free on Tues Sept–June • ☎ 946 085 500, ⓦ www.museomaritimobilbao.org

The fancy **Museo Marítimo Ría de Bilbao** is at quayside level just west of the **Euskalduna** (an impressive edifice of rusty iron, glass, steel and concrete that hosts conferences and classical performances). The museum itself explains in intricate detail exactly how the *ría* between the city and the sea has been cleared over the centuries to deal with ever larger marine traffic. It's all very worthy, and you can clamber aboard assorted vessels in the old docks of the Euskalduna Shipyard outside. Sadly, however, hardly anyone seems to bother to visit.

Sopelana and Plentzia

For Sopelana, use Ⓜ Larrabasterra; for Plentzia use Ⓜ Plentzia

Bilbao is well provided with **beaches** along the mouth of the estuary and around both headlands. Metro Line 1 makes it easier to reach those on the east bank, for example at **Sopelana**, home to the nudist Playa de Arrietara. The beach at **Plentzia**, at the far end of the line, 15km out, is generally cleaner and not quite so crowded.

Getxo

For Getxo use Ⓜ Algorta; for Portugalete use Ⓜ Aleeta

Getxo, 10km downstream at the head of the port and consisting of several distinct communities, makes a particularly nice excursion. Its ancient fishing-port core, set on a hilltop not far east of the river-mouth, remains pretty and lively, and stands just above two nice beaches, Ereaga and Arrigunaga. Just before the river widens into the port, Getxo is connected with **Portugalete** on the west bank via the remarkable Vizcaya Bridge. The little gondola that dangles from this preposterous late nineteenth-century "**transporter bridge**" carries passengers (€0.30), and even half a dozen cars at a time (€1.25), across the river every few minutes.

ARRIVAL AND DEPARTURE BILBAO

BY AIR

Aeropuerto de Bilbao Bilbao's airport (ⓦ aeropuertodebilbao.net) is 12km north of town. A taxi into town costs around €30. Bizkaiabus services (every 30min; €1.40) takes 20min to reach Pza. Moyúa in the centre of the new town (Ensanche), and continues to the Termibús station (Ⓜ San Mamés); there are also hourly buses straight to Zarautz (€14.25) and San Sebastián (€16.50).

BY FERRY

Bilbao's ferry port is at Zierbena, 21km northwest of the city centre, on the western side of the river-mouth. Brittany Ferries (ⓦ brittany-ferries.co.uk) sail here from Portsmouth in the UK on Wed & Sat, and sail back from Bilbao on Tues & Thurs. Regular buses and trains run from the docks to the centre.

BY TRAIN

Estación de Abando The main RENFE train station, on Pza. Circular, across the river from the Casco Viejo, sees services to Barcelona (2 daily; 6hr 40min); Logroño (2 daily; 2hr 20min); Madrid (4 daily; 5hr–6hr 30min); and Salamanca (2 daily; 5hr 30min).

Estación de Santander Services along a separate narrow-gauge line, formerly known as FEVE but now also run by RENFE, head west along the coast from this highly decorative station, on the riverbank right below the Estación de Abando, to Santander (2 daily; 3hr) and beyond.

Estación de Atxuri South of the Casco Viejo on the right bank of the river, the Estación de Atxuri is used by frequent EuskoTren (ⓦ euskotren.es) trains to San Sebastián (2hr 40min), Gernika (45min), Mundaka (1hr 10min), and Bermeo (1hr 15min). Note that if you're heading for San Sebastián, the bus is much quicker.

BY BUS

Termibús station Most long-distance and international bus companies use the Termibús station, which fills an entire block between Luis Briñas and Gurtubay. To reach the town centre, change onto a local bus, head a block north to the San Mamés metro station or simply walk.

Destinations Barcelona (3 daily; 7hr 15min); Bermeo, via Gernika and Mundaka (30 daily; 1hr 10min); Burgos (11 daily; 3hr); Castro Urdiales (5 daily; 1hr); Elantxobe (3 daily; 1hr 30min); Lekeitio (5 daily; 1hr 30min); León (1 daily; 5hr

30min); Madrid (14 daily; 4hr 45min); Oñati (2 daily; 1hr 10min); Ondarroa (20 daily; 1hr 20min); Pamplona (6 daily; 2hr 15min); San Sebastián (every 30min; 1hr 10min); Santander (every 30min; 1hr 10min–1hr 30min); Santiago (4 daily; 10hr); Vitoria (every 30min; 1hr 15min); Zaragoza (7 daily; 4hr).

INFORMATION

Turismo Bilbao has tourist offices (☎944 795 760, ⓦbilbaoturismo.net) at Pza. Circular 1, across the river from the old town (daily 9am–9pm), and next to the

BY CAR

Driving If you're driving into Bilbao, you'll find the motorways very efficient at delivering you to the centre, but once there traffic is consistently dreadful; you're better off parking straight away in the car park nearest your accommodation, and walking from there.

Museo Guggenheim (July & Aug daily 10am–7pm; Sept– June Mon–Sat 10am–7pm, Sun 10am–3pm).

6

GETTING AROUND

By foot Central Bilbao is small enough to walk around comfortably; indeed, the riverside stroll between the Casco Viejo and the Guggenheim is a highlight for many visitors.
By taxi TeleTaxi (☎944 102 121, ⓦteletaxibilbao.com), Radio Taxi Bilbao ☎944 448 888, ⓦtaxibilbao.com.
By metro An easy, efficient service on the modern Metro Bilbao (ⓦmetrobilbao.net) runs every 4min from Plentzia (northeast of Getxo) to Extebarri, south of the city centre; a second line runs out to Santurtzi on the western side of the river-mouth. While the network is divided into three zones, all journeys in the city centre (including the Casco Viejo) lie within the same zone (€1.50, day pass €4.60).

By bus For parts the metro doesn't reach, there are red municipal buses (€1.25) with route maps at the green bus shelters, or for longer journeys (including to the airport) the blue-and-yellow Bizkiabuses.
By tram Green trams (€1.25) run along a single line, linking the Casco Viejo and the Museo Guggenheim with San Mamés and the bus station.
Tickets The BilbaoCard, available from any *turismo* or online (€6/10/12 for 1/2/3 days, ⓦbilbaoturismo.net), provides unlimited travel on the metro, tram, municipal and provincial buses and Artxanda funicular, and offers discounts of ten to fifty percent at various museums and shops.

ACCOMMODATION

The nicest area to stay has to be the **Casco Viejo**, though that's dominated by budget hotels and *pensiones*, and everywhere is liable to be very noisy at night. Bilbao's luxury hotels tend to be scattered across **Ensanche**; many feature hip, contemporary architecture and highly regarded restaurants, and can offer amazingly good value. Staying in **Deusto** or **Castaños**, on the north bank of the river, makes a good alternative. For help with bookings, try the *turismo*'s central **reservation** service (☎902 877 298, ⓦbilbaoreservas.com).

CASCO VIEJO

★**Arriaga Suites** C/Bidebarrieta 3 ☎635 707 247, ⓦarriagasuites.com. Six large, pleasantly furnished, and great-value suites, in prime position at the main approach to the Casco Viejo. Each is named after a Basque musician associated with the nearby theatre, and offers a fridge and microwave. **€79**
Ganbara Hostel C/Prim 13 ☎944 053 930, ⓦganbarahostel.com. Modern hostel on the edge of the old town, with accommodation in four-, six- and eight-person dorms. The spacious communal areas make up for the somewhat cramped dorms. Rates (€1.50 more on Fri & Sat) include free breakfast plus all-day tea and coffee, and there's a laundry and kitchen. Eight-bed dorm **€16**
Hotel Iturrienea Ostatua C/Santa María 14 ☎944 161 500, ⓦiturrieneaostatua.com. Clean, very friendly hotel, tucked away near the river in the Casco Viejo, with the feel of a B&B (breakfast is served until 11.30pm daily). There's exposed stonework and antique furniture throughout, while the walls are hung with original art and moody photos of Bilbao's industrial past. All rooms are en

suite; many have plants trailing over balconies, and double-glazing to cut down noise from the nearby bars. **€70**
Pensión Mardones C/Jardines 4, 2º & 4º ☎944 153 105, ⓦhostalmardones.com. Clean, functional rooms, not all of them en suite, with uninspiring but decent furnishings and dark wood floors; the fourth floor is preferable to the second-floor annexe. The *Amboto* restaurant alongside is recommended. **€60**
Pensión Mendez I & II C/Santa María 13, 1º & 4º ☎944 160 364, ⓦpensionmendez.com. Comfortable and clean rooms, simply but adequately furnished; they're hardly luxurious, but good value for anyone simply looking for a place to sleep. Those in *Mendez II* are slightly better, with en-suite bathrooms. Cash only. *Mendez I* **€35**, *Mendez II* **€50**

ENSANCHE
Hostal Begoña C/Amistad 2, 1º ☎944 230 134, ⓦhostalbegona.com. Solid mid-range option, near the narrow-gauge station and just a couple of minutes' walk over the bridge from the Casco Viejo. The colourful rooms

6

have lino floors, good en-suite facilities, and comfortable beds, but no views. **€66**

Hotel Carlton Pza. Moyúa 2 ☎944 162 200, ⊚hotel carlton.es. The *grande dame* of Bilbao's hotels, built in 1919 and still an atmospheric place to stay, with its abundant marble and dramatic stained-glass cupola. The rooms are tasteful and extremely comfortable, and several boast huge arched windows. Look for bargain rates online. **€83**

Hotel López de Haro Obispo Orueta 2 ☎944 235 500, ⊚hotellopezdeharo.com. Luxury five-star hotel built in 1890, with comfortable, modern rooms and bathrooms, but retaining nineteenth-century touches. Great location, and extremely tranquil. **€95**

★**Meliá Bilbao** C/Lehendakari Leizaola 29 ☎944 280 000, ⊚melia.com. This is one of Bilbao's most distinctive buildings, a bold, creative design inspired by Eduardo Chillida, utilizing Iranian pink marble and rusty garnet tones for the exterior, and green and white marble in the bathrooms. The stylish rooms are luxurious, with huge, incredibly comfy beds; there's also a pool. **€80**

Miró Alameda de Mazarredo 77 ☎946 611 880, ⊚mirohotelbilbao.com. Attractive fifty-room hotel, with minimalist decor, bathrooms finished in black marble (separated from the chic, white-coloured rooms by a curtain), and a decent spa. **€127**

Pensión Zubia C/Amistad 5 ☎944 248 566, ⊚pensionzubia.com. Simple, old-fashioned hotel, near the left bank of the river across from the Casco Viejo, where the plain modern rooms share bathrooms. The friendly staff are happy to share their local expertise; pets are welcome. **€40**

★**Silken Gran Domine Bilbao** Alameda de Mazarredo 61 ☎944 253 300, ⊚granhotel dominebilbao.com. The work of designer Javier Mariscal, this is a wonderfully inspiring five-star hotel, appropriately close to the Guggenheim and sporting one of the most creative lobbies you'll ever see. Each floor has a unique design, while the luxurious rooms have bathrooms with transparent glass, and tubs designed by Philippe Starck. Reserve ahead for the best rates. **€110**

CASTAÑOS AND DEUSTO

Bilbao Akelarre Hostel C/Morgan 4–6 ☎944 057 713, ⊚bilbaoakelarrehostel.com. Modern, well-run and well-equipped hostel near the university, a short walk from the Guggenheim. Some double rooms – albeit with individual bunks – plus dorms sleeping from four to twelve. Rates include free breakfast, coffee and tea. Twelve-bed dorm (per person) **€17.50**, doubles **€42**

Hesperia Bilbao Paseo Campo de Volantín 28 ☎944 051 100, ⊚hesperia-bilbao.com. Smart, modern riverfront hotel, in a funky, contemporary building lined with pastel-coloured glassed-in balconies, near the Zubizuri bridge. Rooms come with sleek, minimalist furnishings and there's on-site parking. **€82**

Hostal-Residencia Ría de Bilbao Ribera de Deusto 32 ☎944 765 060, ⊚riabilbao.com. A quiet place overlooking the river, 10min walk from the Euskalduna. Garden and cooking facilities; apartments for longer stays. Highly recommended if you don't mind staying well away from the action. **€50**

EATING AND DRINKING

While not quite on a par with San Sebastián, Bilbao ranks among the culinary capitals of Spain. **Innovative restaurants** and Michelin-star winners knock out everything from traditional Basque fare to high-class *nueva cocina vasca* meals that can cost as much as a five-star hotel room, while the **pintxos bars** are equally mouthwatering. Taking a high-speed *txikiteo* (*pintxos* crawl) through the Casco Viejo is an essential part of any visit – the best targets tend to be clustered in the *siete calles* (seven streets), bordered by C/de la Ronda and C/Pelota, but there are also some good options on C/Diputación in Ensanche. Bilbao's most famous dish is undoubtedly **cod** (*bacalao*), traditionally served with *salsa vizcaina* (a sauce of red onions and peppers) or *al pil-pil* (a garlic-based sauce). **Bars** (most serving *pintxos*) can be found all through the Casco Viejo; C/Barrenkale is the heart of the madness, but the outdoor tables in the beautiful Pza. Nueva make a great place for a more relaxed drink in the early evening. Ensanche, too, has plenty of pubs and bars.

CAFÉS

Café Bizuete Pza. Santiago 6b ☎944 794 278, ⊚cafeteriabizuete.multiespaciosweb.com. The nicest spot for coffee in the Casco Viejo, this old-fashioned café faces the Catedral across a small square. Breakfast deals at €2.50 and €4 are served until noon, with *pintxos* and sandwiches available later on; most locals, however, simply drop in for coffee and a cake, or the €3.50 *chocolate con churros*. Mon–Sat 8am–10pm.

Café La Granja Pza. Circular 3 ☎944 230 813, ⊚grupoiruna.net. This spacious and slightly faded Art Nouveau café features iron columns and beautiful lamps.

Drinks and *pintxos* are served all day, with a €13.75 menu of the day, and there's live traditional music some evenings. A popular rendezvous for commuters at either end of the working day. Mon–Fri 7.30am–midnight, Sat 10.30am–1.30am.

★**Café Iruña** Colón de Larreategui ☎944 237 021, ⊚cafesdebilbao.net. Historic café and bar, facing the little Jardines de Albia park, and established in 1903. Elaborate murals and ornate Mudéjar decor and traditional grocery-style tiling make its three sections – a bar, a café, and a dining room – marvellously atmospheric. It's busy around breakfast time; later on it serves set, menus at €14 and €28, and it's also a great spot for a drink or a few *pintxos* – the €2.30 *pinchos morunos*, or mini-kebabs, are especially worth trying. Mon–Thurs 7.30am–midnight, Fri 7.30am–1am, Sat 10am–2am, Sun 10am–midnight.

PINTXOS BARS

Berton C/Jardines 11 ☎ 944 167 035, ⊛ pintxozpintxo .com. This friendly Casco Viejo bar, a warm inviting space with some outside tables and lots of drinking space inside, has been such a success that it now has three neighbouring offshoots, including a recommended restaurant. Fresh modern *pintxos* for around €2.70, including quails' eggs with prawns and mushrooms, and lots of ham options, plus *raciones* of ham, anchovies and the like. Tues–Sun 11am until late.

★**Café Bar Bilbao** Pza. Nueva 6 ☎ 944 151 671, ⊛ bilbao-cafebar.com. Exceptional anchovy, ham and *bacalao al pil-pil pintxos*, served by *simpático* staff, with everything labelled on the counter in the stylish old blue-tiled café, and some tables on the Casco Viejo's lovely main square. Daily 9am–11pm.

Los Fueros C/Fueros 6 ☎ 944 150 614. If you fancy getting away from the old-town crowds, nip behind the back of Pza. Nueva and try this small bar, specializing in grilled prawns (*gambas*) and barnacles (*percebes*). Mon, Tues & Thurs–Sat 11am–3pm & 6.30–10pm, Sun 10.30am–3pm.

Gatz C/Santa María 10 ☎ 944 154 861, ⊛ bargatz.com. Cosy late-night tapas bar in the old town, serving exquisite *pintxos* such as delicious cod, or the Basque equivalent of ratatouille in a tiny tart, to a mixed younger crowd. Good selection of wines and beers. Mon–Thurs 1–3pm & 7–11pm, Fri 1–3pm & 7pm–midnight, Sat 1pm–midnight, Sun 1–3pm.

El Globo C/Diputación 8 ☎ 944 154 221, ⊛ barelglobo .com. Creative, high-quality *pintxos* near Pza. Moyúa in the central Abando district. The interior decor is part wine bar, part upscale sandwich bar, and there's also outdoor seating – order through the hatch in the wall. Plentiful seafood options include baby squid with caramelized onions, or you can opt for goats' cheese. Mon–Thurs 8am–11pm, Fri & Sat 8am–midnight.

Gure Toki Pza. Nueva 12 ☎ 944 158 037. Tiny tapas bar, tucked in the corner of the Casco Viejo's main square. Irresistible, eye-catching *pintxos ornamentales* include lovely langoustine and squid concoctions, or you can buy a more substantial salad to eat at the barrels in the square itself. Mon, Tues & Thurs 9am–10.30pm, Fri & Sat 9am–11pm, Sun 9am–3.30pm.

Irrintzi C/Santa María 8 ☎ 944 167 616, ⊛ irrintzi.es. Hip, buzzing old-town tapas bar, with groovy murals and an indie soundtrack, plus some of Bilbao's most creative *pintxos*, such as a monkfish lollipop served with strawberry gazpacho in a glass. Mon–Thurs 9.30am–11pm, Fri 9.30am–midnight, Sat noon–midnight, Sun noon–10pm.

Taurino Taberna C/Ledesma 5 ☎ 944 240 723. A much-loved throwback to bygone Bilbao days, this hole-in-the-wall place, on the appealing, bar-filled, pedestrianized C/Ledesma in the new town, stands out from the crowd for its wall-to-ceiling bullfighting-themed decor. Besides its sheer atmosphere, however, it also serves a great range of snacks, from *tortilla* to grilled-vegetable sandwiches. Mon–Fri 10am–10pm, Sat 10am–11pm.

Xukela C/El Perro 2 ☎ 944 159 772, ⊛ xukela.com. With its red panelling and check tablecloths, this perennially popular Casco Viejo tapas bar is oddly reminiscent of a French bistro, and serves substantial enough *raciones* to make a hearty meal; but it's best known for its wide range of snacks and top-class wine list. There's plenty of open space for drinkers who prefer to stand. Daily 1.30–11.30pm.

RESTAURANTS

Bascook C/Barroeta Aldamar 8 ☎ 944 009 977, ⊛ bascook.com. Among Bilbao's most popular new restaurants of recent years, *Bascook* is the brainchild of chef Aitor Elizegi. His playful ideas include having a menu that's also a magazine, and offering three separate cuisines – world, vegetarian and, for those with time to linger, slow food. Take your pick from all three, with mains at €12–20 and set menus from €24 for lunch and €50 for dinner. Daily 1–3pm & 8.30–11.30pm.

Bistro Guggenheim Guggenheim Museum ☎ 944 239 333, ⊛ bistroguggenheimbilbao.com. The Guggenheim's in-house bistro serves a great-value set lunch menu (€19.80) of zestful modern Basque cuisine, and dinner menus at €28 and €40, while its café section sells simpler snacks all day. Either one makes a perfect complement to a few hours in the museum itself. Café Tues–Sun 9am–8.30pm; restaurant Tues–Wed & Sun 1–3.15pm, Thurs–Sat 1–3.15pm & 8.30–10.30pm.

Casa Rufo C/Hurtado de Amézaga 5 ☎ 944 432 172, ⊛ casarufo.com. Deservedly popular *cocina* in the Abando district, with three cosy, themed dining rooms specializing in three main items: cod and two types of unbelievably succulent steak (*chuleton*, priced by the kilo), the main reason you'll need a reservation. Count on spending close to €50 per person. Mon–Sat 1.30–4pm & 8.30–11pm.

Etxanobe Euskalduna, Avda. Abandoibarra 4 ☎ 944 421 071, ⊛ en.etxanobe.com. Enjoying tremendous views of the city from its open-air terrace, the Michelin-starred Euskalduna restaurant is run by celebrated Basque chef Fernando Canales. His innovative contemporary cuisine is available on several set menus, with €70 alternatives including a vegetarian option, and ranging up to €120. Mon–Sat 1–4pm & 7.45pm–midnight; closed first 3 weeks of Aug.

Restaurante Atea Paseo de Uribitarte 4 ☎ 944 005 869, ⊛ atearestaurante.com. Good-value, central restaurant south of the river near the Zubizuri bridge, where the modern

6

dining room lurks behind the facade of a former customs warehouse, and there are also outdoor tables. With the emphasis on a quick turnaround, the €18 set lunch is a tray holding three *pintxos* plus main course, salad and dessert. Tues–Sat 1.30–4pm & 8.30–11pm, Sun 1.30–4pm.

★ **Río Oja** C/El Perro 6 ☎ 944 150 871, ⓦ www.rio-oja .com. Cosy, old-fashioned, much-loved and exceptionally inexpensive Casco Viejo restaurant with an unusual emphasis on hearty stews (*cazuelas*) and sauces, arrayed along the bar for diners' inspection. With clams in green sauce for €12, or quail stew for just €8, this is a place to experiment a little; they also serve *raciones*. Tues–Sun 9am–11pm.

Victor Montes Pza. Nueva 8 ☎ 944 157 067, ⓦ victormontes.com. Atmospheric bar and dining room, lined with a collection of over 1600 wines, on the attractive main square of the old town. Traditional grills, special hams and fresh fish are served in the main, very popular dining room, or sumptuous *pintxos* in the bar; there are tables on the square in summer. Mon–Sat 1.30–4pm & 8–11pm, Sun 1.30–4pm.

Zortziko C/Alameda de Manzarredo 17 ☎ 944 239 743,

ⓦ zortziko.es. Effortlessly classy, highly acclaimed restaurant, with classic French decor and an array of fine *nueva cocina* dishes. Chef Daniel García's creations are best sampled on the set tasting menus, and especially the eleven-course €85 option. Mon 1–3.30pm, Tues–Sat 1–3.30pm & 8.30–11pm.

BARS

Dubliners Pza. Moyúa 6 ☎ 944 236 214, ⓦ dublinersbilbao.com. Bilbao is full of Irish pubs and this is one of the best, with pints of Guinness and Murphy's going for little over €5, and hearty set menus for under €20. Mon–Thurs 8am–midnight, Fri 8am–3am, Sat noon–3am, Sun 2–11pm.

Lamiak C/Pelota 8 ☎ 944 159 642. Large, gay-friendly café-bar with a cool gallery packed with tables upstairs, and a fashionable crowd at the weekends. Mon–Thurs & Sun 4pm–midnight, Fri & Sat 4pm–2am.

Taberna Txomin Barullo C/Barrencalle 40 ☎ 944 152 788. A great, laidback café-bar in the old town, with nationalist murals and a friendly alternative crowd. Daily noon–midnight.

NIGHTLIFE AND ENTERTAINMENT

The city has a pulsating **nightlife**, especially at the weekends – and goes totally wild during the August **fiesta**, with scores of open-air bars, live music and impromptu dancing everywhere and a truly festive atmosphere. Bilbao also has a vibrant **club** scene, with the edgier San Francisco district south of the Casco Viejo, across the river and home to Bilbao's West African and Moroccan population, a hot area for dancing till dawn. Hard rock and punk fans tend to congregate in the grungy bars along C/ Iturribide, northeast of the Casco Viejo. For **live music** listings, check the local newspaper *El Correo* (ⓦ elcorreo.com).

CLUBS AND LIVE MUSIC VENUES

Azkena C/Ibañez de Bilbao 26 ☎ 944 240 890, ⓦ azkena.com. Popular live music space and bar, with simple, minimalist decor and a dancefloor that tends to get busy late in the evenings. Mon–Thurs 3–11pm, Fri & Sat 6pm–3.30am.

El Balcon de la Lola C/Bailén 10 ☎ 635 757 763. Dance club, a short walk across the river from the Casco Viejo, which attracts an excited and very friendly mixed gay-straight crowd. Thurs 11.45pm–5.15am, Fri 11.45pm–6.15am, Sat noon–3.30pm & 11.45pm–6.15am, Sun noon–4.30pm.

BilboRock-La Merced Muelle de la Merced 1 ⓦ bilbao.net/bilborock. Large, retro-styled converted church, just across the Puente La Merced from the Casco Viejo, that's among the city's best live venues for rock and alternative music. Irregular hours; depends on schedules.

Cotton Club C/Gregorio de la Revilla 25 ☎ 944 104 951, ⓦ cottonclubbilbao.es. Popular live music and disco venue, entered on C/Simón Bolívar, featuring everything from jazz and blues to rock and house. For most of the year, but not July and August, there's live music nightly except Monday. Beer starts at €4, and

there's no cover. Mon–Thurs 4.30pm–3am, Fri & Sat 6.30pm–6.30am, Sun 6.30pm–3am.

Kafe Antzokia C/San Vicente 2 ☎ 944 246 107, ⓦ kafeantzokia.com. This cinema-turned-nightclub has an emphasis on live shows, and attracts big names, from world music and reggae to folk- and punk-influenced groups and Basque musicians. Resident DJs spin an eclectic mix Saturday nights, with plenty of local sounds. The restaurant is open at lunchtimes for drinks and light meals; set menu €12.50. Mon–Wed 9.30am–10pm & 11pm–1am, Thurs 9.30am–10pm & 11pm–4.30am, Fri 9.30am–10pm & 11pm–5.30am, Sat noon–5.30am, Sun 6pm–midnight.

MUSIC AND THEATRE VENUES

Euskalduna Avda. Abondoibarra ☎ 944 035 000, ⓦ www.euskalduna.net. Ultramodern structure, built on the ruins of the city's last shipyard, which serves as home to the Bilbao Symphony Orchestra, with a programme of opera and classical music, and theatrical performances. Box office Mon–Fri 9am–2pm & 4–7pm.

Teatro Arriaga Pza. Arriaga ☎ 944 163 333, ⓦ www .teatroarriaga.com. This magnificent old-town landmark hosts dance and music events, as well as theatre.

DIRECTORY

Football Athletico Bilbao (w athletic-club.net), known for their red-and-white-striped shirts as *Rojiblancos*, are famous for only fielding Basque players or products of their own youth system, and have never been relegated from the Primera División. Watch them play at the Campo de San Mamés, at the western edge of the new town.

Hospital Hospital de Basurto, Avda. de Montevideo 18 ☎ 944 006 000 (M San Mamés). Call ambulances on ☎ 944 410 081 or ☎ 944 100 000 (24hr).

Post office Alameda Urquijo 19 (Mon–Fri 8am–9pm, Sat 9am–2pm; M Abando or Moyúa). There's another post office near the Guggenheim main entrance, Alameda Mazarredo 13 (same hours).

6

Vitoria-Gasteiz

The capital of the entire País Vasco, as well as of Araba (Alava), **VITORIA-GASTEIZ** is a fascinating and exceptionally friendly old city, all the better for lying off the tourist circuit, and well worth a couple of days' visit. Sancho el Sabio, King of Navarre, built a fortress here in 1181, on the site of the Basque village of **Gasteiz**. He renamed it **Vitoria** to celebrate his victories over Alfonso VIII of Castille, who promptly captured it back in 1200. Stretching along a low ridge in the heart of a fertile plain, Vitoria subsequently prospered as a trading centre for wool and iron, and still boasts an unusual concentration of Renaissance palaces and fine churches.

The streets of the city's Romanesque old town, the **Casco Medieval**, still wrap themselves like a spider's web around either side of the central hill, while a neater grid of later developments, **Ensanche**, lies below on the plain. All Vitoria's graceful mansions and churches are built from the same greyish-gold stone, and many of the medieval buildings are amazingly well preserved. The pick of the bunch, on C/Fray Zacarías near the Catedral, include the **Palacio de Escoriaza-Esquibel**, with its sixteenth-century Plateresque portal, and the **Palacio de Montehermoso**, now run as a cultural and exhibition space. On the southern edge of the old town, the porticoed **Pza. de España** is a gem, while the neighbouring **Pza. de la Virgen Blanca** is more elegant, with glassed-in balconies. If you find the hill itself a bit of a challenge, note that Vitoria offers a remarkable feature: **moving stairways** climb it from both the east (Cantón de San Francisco Javier) and west (Cantón de la Soledad) sides.

Catedral de Santa María

Catedral Guided tours: daily 11am–2pm & 5–8pm; booking essential • €8.50, with tour of city walls €10, with tower €10.50 • ☎ 945 255 135, w catedralvitoria.com • **Visitor centre** Daily 10.30am–2pm & 4.30–8pm • Free

After nine centuries of tottering precariously at the highest point of Vitoria's old town, at the north end of the ridge, the venerable **Catedral de Santa María** had to be closed for reconstruction in 1994. It has now finally reopened, although the work is still ongoing. A **visitor centre** off Pza. de la Burullería holds displays on the project, and

---

VITORIA'S FESTIVALS

Vitoria's largest annual festival, the **Fiesta de la Virgen Blanca**, is celebrated from August 4 to August 9 each year. On the first day, head for the Pza. de la Virgen Blanca with a blue-and-white festival scarf, a bottle of champagne (or cava) and a cigar, and wearing old clothes. At 6pm, in the "Bajada del Celedón", an umbrella-toting life-size doll dressed in traditional costume appears from the church tower and flies through the air over the plaza. This is the signal to spray champagne everywhere (hence the old clothes), light the cigar and put on your scarf – which the hard core don't take off until midnight on August 9, when Celedón returns to his tower, signalling the end of the fiesta. In between, the town is engulfed in a continuous party.

During the third week of July, the city also hosts a **jazz festival** that attracts big-name performers (w jazzvitoria.com), while it's also the scene of parades and celebrations in the days leading up to **Mardi Gras**.

6

■ ACCOMMODATION
La Casa de los Arquillos	2
Hotel Ciudad de Vitoria	3
Hotel Dato	5
Hotel Desiderio	1
NH Canciller Ayala	4
Pensión Araba 2	6

● PINTXOS BARS & RESTAURANTS
Asador Sagartoki	6
Ikea	7
La Malquerida	3
El Portalón	2
Saburdi	8
Toloño	5
El Tulipan de Oro	1
Virgen Blanca	4

VITORIA-GASTEIZ

serves as the starting point for **tours** not only of the site, but also the Catedral's tower and the city walls. During the last tour each evening, coloured lights are projected onto the superbly carved fourteenth-century west doorway, to reveal how it has changed in appearance over the centuries.

Museo Bibat de Naipes y Arqueología

C/Cuchillería 54 • Tues–Fri 10am–2pm & 4–6.30pm, Sat 10am–2pm, Sun 11am–2pm • €3, free first Sat of month • ☎ 945 203 707

The word "Bibat" translates as "two in one", to denote the fact that this complex consists not only of two buildings fused together, but two distinct museums. The first and more unusual, housed in a grand medieval mansion, is devoted to **playing cards** (*naipes*). While many are rather beautiful, by their very nature they're also small and repetitive, and in the absence of much contextual material it's not as interesting as you might hope.

The modern interconnected annexe holds well-presented **archeological artefacts** found locally, ranging through prehistoric, Roman and early medieval times. One skull, dating from 2500 BC, has a neatly chipped stone arrowhead embedded in its base.

Artium

C/Francia 24 • Tues–Fri 11am–2pm & 5–8pm, Sat & Sun 11am–9pm • €6, Wed by donation • ☎ 945 209 000, ⓦ artium.org

East of the old town and not far from the bus station, the **Artium** is an attractive museum of contemporary art. Its subterranean galleries concentrate largely on temporary exhibitions of Basque and Spanish artists, for which the Artium is able to draw on the city's permanent collection of more than three thousand works.

Museo de Bellas Artes

Paseo de Fray Francisco de Vitoria • Tues–Fri 10am–2pm & 4–6.30pm, Sat 10am–2pm & 5–8pm, Sun 11am–2pm • €3, free first Sat of month • ☎ 945 181 918

A magnificent mansion on an attractive pedestrianized avenue in the Senda district, southwest of Vitoria's centre, holds the regional **Museo de Bellas Artes**. Its fine collection centres on the period from 1700 to 1950; highlights include *costumbrista* paintings, depicting Basque cultural and folk practices.

ARRIVAL AND INFORMATION   VITORIA-GASTEIZ

By train Vitoria's RENFE train station is in the commercial district, a 10min walk south of the old town along the pedestrianized C/Dato. Services include to Madrid (5 daily; 3hr 45min–5hr 30min); Miranda del Ebro (14 daily; 20min); and Pamplona (5 daily; 1hr).

By bus As this book went to press, Vitoria was about to open a new bus station, at Pza. America Latina, a mile

northwest of the old town. Services run to: Bilbao (every 30min; 1hr 10min); Laguardia (4 daily; 1hr 45 min); Logroño (8 daily; 2hr); and Pamplona (10 daily; 1hr 30min).

Turismo Pza. de España 1 (July–Sept daily 10am–8pm; Oct–June Mon–Sat 10am–7pm, Sun 11am–2pm; ☎ 945 161 598, ⓦ turismo.vitoria-gasteiz.org).

ACCOMMODATION

As Vitoria is not a major tourist destination, there's little accommodation within the old town; on the plus side, rates are generally remarkably cheap. Budget hotels are concentrated near the train and bus stations, while more expensive options tend to be in Ensanche, south of the Casco Medieval.

★ **La Casa de los Arquillos** C/los Arquillos 1 ☎ 945 151 259, ⓦ lacasadelosarquillos.com. Lovely little boutique hotel (which calls itself a B&B) in a superb central location in a medieval building that's been converted to hold eight stylish en-suite bedrooms. The one snag is that this spot can get a little noisy, especially at weekends. Two-night minimum stay. **€76**

Hotel Ciudad de Vitoria Portal de Castilla 8 ☎ 945 141 100, ⓦ hoteles-silken.com. Opulently *belle époque*, this beautifully restored historic hotel, a short walk from the old town, opens to a vast central atrium, and offers comfortable, lavishly appointed rooms with immaculate marble-clad bathrooms. Extras include a fitness centre, cocktail bar, good buffet breakfasts, and free street parking outside. **€62**

Hotel Dato C/Dato 28 ☎ 945 147 230, ⓦ hoteldato .com. Beyond the gaudy mix of classical statues and gilded mirrors in the stairwells, this cosy hotel, close to the station, has super-helpful staff and tastefully decorated rooms with colourful batik bedspreads. All rooms have

baths; pay a little extra for an enclosed balcony. **€54**

Hotel Desiderio C/Colegio San Prudencia 2 ☎ 945 251 700, ⓦ hoteldesiderio.es. Welcoming hotel in a good location just below, and immediately east of, the old centre. The rooms are spruce and simple rather than fancy – those at the front have better views – with comfortable beds, and there's a café downstairs. **€50**

NH Canciller Ayala C/Ramón y Cajal 5 ☎ 945 130 000, ⓦ nh-hotels.com. Modern, business-oriented hotel in a convenient and pleasant location on the edge of the Parque de la Florida. The super-comfortable rooms come with polished wood floors and smart, contemporary furniture and fittings. **€72**

Pensión Araba 2 C/Florida 25 ☎ 945 232 588, ⓦ pensionaraba.com. An excellent-value *pensión* in an immaculately kept family home near the station, offering four clean en-suite rooms, each capable of sleeping up to four guests. **€50**

EATING AND DRINKING

Vitoria-Gasteiz has a solid selection of quality **restaurants** and **cafés**, aimed principally at a no-nonsense local clientele – plazas de España and Virgen Blanca hold particularly appealing arrays of outdoor cafés – while **pintxos bars** are spread throughout both Ensanche and the edges of the Casco Medieval. Look out for such regional specialities as potatoes with chorizo, *porrusalda* (leek soup) and *perretxikos* (wild mushrooms with egg). The city's dynamic **nightlife** is primarily

---

CHOCS AWAY

Vitoria is famous for its attachment to **chocolates**. *Trufas, bombones* and *vasquitos y neskitos* can be purchased, along with cakes such as *chuchitos de Vitoria* (a bit like profiteroles) and other sugary delights, at **Goya**, C/Dato 6.

---

fuelled by its student population. The main areas are the streets off C/Dato in Ensanche, and the pubs on the eastern side of the Casco Medieval, particularly on C/Cuchillería.

PINTXOS BARS AND RESTAURANTS

★**Asador Sagartoki** C/Prado 18 ☎945 288 676, ⓦsagartoki.com. Far and away the best *pintxos* in the city – beautiful to look at, and delicious to eat. Be sure to try the amazing egg-yolk parcels, or the foie gras cornets. On weekdays, you can sample five, plus a glass of wine, for just €10.80. Mon–Fri 10am–midnight, Sat & Sun 11am–midnight.

Ikea Portal de Castilla 27 ☎945 144 747, ⓦrestauranteikea.com. Don't be misled by the Scandinavian-sounding name; this is Vitoria's most acclaimed restaurant, a chic and expensive dining room in a stone townhouse transformed by architect Javier Mariscal. It serves good Basque food with a contemporary spin; mains from around €25, and set menus from €49. The liver pâté is highly recommended. Tues–Sat 1–3.30pm & 8.30–11.30pm, Sun 1–3.30pm; closed last 3 weeks of Aug.

La Malquerida C/Correría 10 ☎945 257 068, ⓦlamalquerida.com.es. Hugely popular, hip, tapas bar, a few steps away from the Pza. de la Virgen Blanca. A chalked-up menu of innovative snacks and *raciones* is to be enjoyed both indoors and out, with crowds spilling out into the adjoining alleyways. Daily 11am–midnight.

El Portalón C/Correría 150 ☎945 142 755, ⓦrestauranteelportalon.com. Vitoria's most beautiful sixteenth-century house makes an atmospheric setting for this pricey restaurant specializing in traditional Basque cooking. It's very dependable, if not exceptional, with a €35 weekday lunch menu and dinner menus from €46, or €65 for the "theatrical" option with costumed staff. Mon–Sat 1.30–3.30pm & 8.30–11pm, Sun 1.30–3.30pm.

Saburdi C/Dato 32 ☎945 147 016, ⓦsaburdi.com. Busy, friendly tapas bar, with outdoor tables on the main pedestrian road up from the station, which serves great-value *pintxos* from €1.60 – try the cod with squash, or quail's egg with ham – and more substantial *raciones*. Daily 9am–11pm.

Toloño Cuesta San Francisco 3 ☎945 233 336, ⓦtolonobar.com. Determinedly modern tapas bar on the edge of the old town, with bright coloured lighting and brisk service, free nibbles with each drink, and a good changing menu of €3 *pintxos*. Late-night DJs at weekends. Sun–Thurs noon–1am, Fri & Sat noon–3am.

El Tulipan de Oro C/Correría 157 ☎945 142 043. Cosy tapas bar in an aged wood-beamed house, serving chorizo flambéed at the bar over pig-shaped alcohol burners, with a €10 weekday set menu. Mon–Thurs 11.30am–4pm & 7–11pm, Fri & Sat 11.30pm–midnight, Sun 11.30am–11pm.

Virgen Blanca Pza. de la Virgen Blanca 3 ☎945 286 199. Restaurant/bar with the feel of a British gastropub, in a great location with a terrace perched at the top end of the plaza, plus an atmospheric dining room with exposed brick walls and wooden tables. *Raciones* and sandwiches, or set lunch and dinner menus. Mon 6pm–2am, Tues–Sun 9am–2am.

Rioja Alavesa

Forty kilometres south of Vitoria-Gasteiz, across a range of high, little-populated hills, the wine-growing district of **Rioja Alavesa** feels a rather incongruous appendage to the Basque Country. The north side of the Ebro valley does, however, belong to **Araba**, the same province as Vitoria-Gasteiz. As a result, so too do several of the richest and most famous Rioja wineries, even though the province of La Rioja, as well as the largest town hereabouts, Logroño (see p.409), lies immediately across the river.

Assuming you have your own transport, exploring the picturesque villages and **bodegas** of Rioja Alavesa makes a wonderful way to spend a day. The pick of the towns is lovely old **Laguardia**, while competition between the wineries is so fierce that several have invested quite astonishing amounts of money to attract attention, most notably **Bodegas Ysios** with its Santiago Calatrava-designed headquarters, and **Marqués de Riscal**, where Frank Gehry has created an amazing showpiece hotel.

If you drive down from Vitoria-Gasteiz, be sure to stop after 35km at the **Balcon de la Rioja**, a staggering hillside viewpoint that offers a panorama over the plains below.

Laguardia

Though little more than a village, **LAGUARDIA**, 15km northwest of Logroño, is the largest community in Rioja Alavesa. Known to the Basques as Biasteri, it's a gorgeous spot, stretching along the crest of a low ridge overlooking the vineyards, and still surrounded by its medieval walls.

Within its stout gateways, a couple of slender cobbled lanes, lined with ancient mansions, connect the churches at either end. The finer of the two, **Santa María de los Reyes** to the north, boasts an ornately carved Gothic doorway. Much of the town itself is actually concealed from view; beneath the surface, the hilltop is riddled with subterranean cellars, hollowed out to store the wine on which its prosperity is based.

6

Bodegas Ysios

Tours Mon–Fri 11am, 1pm & 4pm, Sat & Sun 10am, 11am & 1pm, plus English tour at 4pm; €12; reserve ahead • ☎ 902 239 373, ⓦ ysios.com

Framed by the hills that rise to the north, the mesmerizing **Bodegas Ysios** undulates through the vineyards 2km north of Laguardia, off the Vitoria-Gasteiz road. Its resemblance to an ancient temple is entirely deliberate; the name Ysios honours twin Egyptian deities Isis and Osiris, and no expense was spared when architect Santiago Calatrava, also responsible for Bilbao airport, was commissioned to construct a new winery in 2001. The aluminium roof surmounts a wooden structure that on a more mundane level looks like a row of wine barrels.

Bodegas Marqués de Riscal

Daily Tours, times vary; €10.25; must be reserved in advance • ☎ 945 180 888, ⓦ marquesderiscal.com

Just outside the appealing village of **ELCIEGO**, 5km southwest of Laguardia, is the **Bodegas Marqués de Riscal**, one of the oldest and largest of the Rioja vineyards. Several tours each day provide the opportunity to learn all about its history, and explore every stage of manufacture, from pressing to bottling. After seeing the cellars, used to store every vintage since 1858, you also get to taste a white and a red.

Although the *bodega* forms part of the so-called City of Wine, the major component of which is the extraordinary **hotel**, tours do not go into the hotel itself, but simply admire it from a distance of around 50m.

ARRIVAL AND INFORMATION

RIOJA ALAVESA

By bus Laguardia is served by regular buses from Vitoria-Gasteiz (4 daily; 1hr 45min).
Turismo C/Mayor 52, Laguardia (Mon–Sat 10am–2pm

& 4–7pm, Sun 10.45am–2pm; ☎ 945 600 845, ⓦ laguardia-alava.com). Detailed information on the many local *bodegas*.

ACCOMMODATION AND EATING

LAGUARDIA

★ **Castillo el Collado** Bodegas Palacio ☎ 945 621 200, ⓦ hotelcollado.com. Elegant B&B inn, just south of town on the road to Elciego, with a dozen antique-furnished rooms, individually styled on such themes as "Love and Madness", and an intimate, top-notch restaurant. **€125**
Hospedería Los Parajes Pza. Mayor 46–48 ☎ 945 621 130, ⓦ hospederiadelosparajes.com. One of two fancy restaurants in a luxury hotel in the very heart of town, serving main courses like loin of venison or turbot with couscous for around €20, or a set menu for €55. Daily 8.30–11pm.
Hostal/Bar Biazteri C/Berberana 2 ☎ 945 600 026, ⓦ biazteri.com. Simple good-value en-suite rooms at the

south end of town, above a bar that serves €10 weekday lunches including a glass of Rioja, and also excellent tapas. **€54**
Hotel Villa de Laguardia Paseo San Raimundo 15 ☎ 945 600 560, ⓦ hotelvilladelaguardia.com. Large country-house hotel a short walk south of the town wall, with light, spacious rooms and a good restaurant. **€77**

ELCIEGO

Hotel Marqués de Riscal C/Torrea 1, Elciego ☎ 945 180 880, ⓦ hotel-marquesderiscal.com. Designed by Frank Gehry and echoing his Guggenheim Museum, this extraordinary hotel, swaddled in a baffling tangle of colossal multicoloured titanium ribbons, is an amazing structure to find in such a tiny place. Laid out to offer beautiful views of the ancient village nearby, it's absolutely breathtaking, but it's also smaller than you might expect. The 43 rooms themselves are large and opulent, but only half of them are in the main structure; the rest are set into the adjacent hillside, connected via a walkway. There are also two very classy restaurants. €304

Pamplona

6

A prosperous city of just under 200,000 inhabitants, **PAMPLONA** (Iruña) is a robust, visceral place, with a rough-hewn edge and a strong streak of macho self-confidence. Having started out as a powerful fortress town defending the northern approaches to Spain at the foothills of the Pyrenees (the city takes its name from the Roman general Pompey), it later became capital of Navarra – often a semi-autonomous state – and an important stop on the Camino de Santiago. With plenty to offer around its Casco Antiguo – enticing churches, a beautiful park and the massive citadel – Pamplona makes an appealing year-round destination, though for anyone who has been here during the thrilling week of the **Fiestas de San Fermín** a visit at any other time can only be an anticlimax.

Everything you're likely to want to see in Pamplona lies within its remarkably compact **Casco Antiguo**. Centred on the **Pza. del Castillo**, and ringed with fashionable cafés, it's a glorious and very much lived-in jumble of buildings from all eras, where every twisting stone lane is worth exploring and intriguingly tatty old shops and bars lie concealed behind medieval shutters.

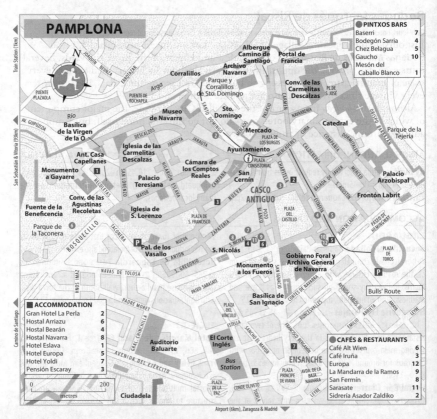

PAMPLONA

● **PINTXOS BARS**

Baserri	7
Bodegón Sarria	4
Chez Belagua	5
Gaucho	10
Mesón del Caballo Blanco	1

Bulls' Route ——

■ **ACCOMMODATION**

Gran Hotel La Perla	2
Hostal Arriazu	6
Hostal Bearán	4
Hostal Navarra	8
Hotel Eslava	1
Hotel Europa	5
Hotel Yoldi	7
Pensión Escaray	3

● **CAFÉS & RESTAURANTS**

Café Alt Wien	6
Café Iruña	3
Europa	12
La Mandarra de la Ramos	9
San Fermín	8
Sarasate	11
Sidrería Asador Zaldiko	2

Airport (6km), Zaragoza & Madrid ▼

Catedral de Santa María

C/Curia s/n • **Catedral** Mon–Sat 9–10.30am & 7–8.30pm, Sun 10am–2pm • **Museum** Mon–Sat 10.30am–5pm • €5 • ☎ 948 212 594, ⓦ catedraldepamplona.com

Built between the late fourteenth and the early sixteenth centuries, the **Catedral de Santa María** is basically Gothic. While it may not look promising at first, thanks to an unattractive facade added in the eighteenth century, it's worth paying to go inside. In the Catedral itself, the tomb of the recumbent Carlos III and his queen Eleanor, in the centre of the nave, dates from 1413. The fee also admits you to the appealing cloisters beyond, where you'll find several superbly sculpted doorways. The finest, the Puerta de la Preciosa, leads to what were originally the sleeping quarters, now home to an exhibition celebrating the Catedral's musical heritage. Another opens onto a chapel with a lovely star vault, and another into the **Museo Diocesano**, a collection of Navarran sacred art.

6

The city walls

Behind the Catedral, in one of the oldest parts of Pamplona, the most substantial remaining section of the **city walls** looks down over a loop of the Río Arga. If you head out through the gate here, the Portal de Zumalacárregui (or de Francia), you can follow paths down to the river, the perfect vantage point from which to admire the impregnability of these defences.

Museo de Navarra

C/Santo Domingo 47 • Tues–Sat 9.30am–2pm & 5–7pm, Sun & public hols 11am–2pm • €2, free Sat eve & Sun • ☎ 848 428 926, ⓦ www.cfnavarra.es/cultura/museo

Although a magnificent medieval hospital just inside Pamplona's city walls serves as the entrance to the **Museo de Navarra**, most of its consistently beautiful treasures are displayed in the light, uncluttered galleries of a modern annexe. Prehistoric relics in the basement include a dyed-green skull found in (or near) an ancient copper mine; higher up is a large mosaic floor taken from a Roman villa in Tudela. Other highlights include an ornately carved Muslim casket from 1004; a thirteenth-century ceiling fresco from a chapel in Olite; and fourteenth-century Gothic murals from Pamplona's own Catedral; and, amid the extensive collection of paintings, Goya's full-length portrait of the Marqués de San Adrián, from 1804.

ARRIVAL AND DEPARTURE
PAMPLONA

By train Pamplona's train station is 1.5km northwest of the old city on Avda. San Jorge, served by local bus #9. RENFE trains connect the city with Barcelona (6 daily; 4hr); Madrid (10 daily; 3–5hr); San Sebastián (2 daily; 1hr 45min); Vitoria (6 daily; 1hr); and Zaragoza (8 daily; 2hr).
By bus The bus station is 250m south of the old town on C/

Yanguas y Mirando. Connections include: Bilbao (6 daily; 2hr 15min); Irún (3 daily; 2hr); Ochagavía (daily except Sun; 2hr); Roncal (daily; 1hr 45min); San Sebastián (9 daily; 1–3hr); Zaragoza (2–3 daily; 4hr).
By car Drivers should leave their cars in the car parks at Pza. del Castillo, the bus station, or the bullring.

INFORMATION

Turismo Pamplona's main *turismo* is at C/ San Saturnino 2, adjoining Pza. Consistorial in the old town (June–Sept Mon–Sat 9am–7pm, Sun 10am–2pm; Sept–May

Mon–Fri 10am–5pm, Sun 10am–2pm; ☎ 848 420 100, ⓦ turismodepamplona.es).

ACCOMMODATION

Much the most enjoyable area of Pamplona in which to stay is the Casco Antiguo, which has a reasonable selection of accommodation. The rates below refer to the peak summer season but *not* San Fermín, when they double or even triple.

Gran Hotel La Perla Pza. del Castillo 1 ☎ 948 223 000, ⓦ granhotellaperla.com. You simply can't beat

Pamplona's grandest hotel for location, right on the main old-town square, or history – past guests include

6

FIESTAS DE SAN FERMÍN

Famous worldwide, thanks to Ernest Hemingway's 1926 *The Sun Also Rises*, as the **Running of the Bulls**, Pamplona's legendary **Fiestas de San Fermín**, or Sanfermines, lasts from noon on July 6 until midnight on July 14. The daily early-morning bull-run, or **encierro**, is just one component of nine days of riotous celebration, which also features bands, parades – the largest are on July 7 and July 10 – and 24-hour dancing in the streets. For details, see ⓦ sanfermin.com.

At the end of the week (midnight July 14), the festivities are officially wound up for another year with a mournful candlelit procession, the **Pobre De Mi** (Poor Me).

ACCOMMODATION AND SECURITY

Accommodation during the fiesta should be booked in advance – and be warned that many hotels triple their rates. If you arrive without a reservation, head for the *turismo*, where locals offer **rooms** at exorbitant prices. Many revellers simply sleep outdoors, on the ramparts, in the park or plaza. **Petty crime** soars, but valuables and luggage can be left at the bus station.

The **campsite**, *Ezcaba*, 7km east (☎ 948 330 315, ⓦ campingezcaba.com), can be reserved in advance, and is connected by regular buses, as well as a straightforward cycle lane. Security is tight – admission is by pass only and a guard patrols all night. **ATMs** frequently run out of money during the festival, while **banks** are closed over the weekend.

EL ENCIERRO

The **encierro**, the Running of the Bulls, takes place every morning from July 7 onwards. Six bulls are released at 8am, to run from the Corralillos near Pza. Santo Domingo to the bullring, where they will fight that evening. They take around four minutes to race a fenced-off course of just over 800m, through Pza. Consistorial and along C/Estafeta; official *pastores* (shepherds) armed with sticks make sure they keep going. In front, around and occasionally beneath the bulls run the hundreds of locals and tourists who are foolish or drunk enough to test their daring against the horns.

To **watch** the *encierro*, arrive early, by 6am. The best vantage points are near the start, or on the wall leading to the bullring. Try to get a spot on the outer of the two barriers – don't worry when the one in front fills up and blocks your view, as all these people will be moved on by police before the run.

The event divides into two parts. First comes the actual running of the bulls, when the object is to run with the bull or whack it with a rolled-up newspaper. Even if you don't see the bulls amid the runners, you'll sense the terror and excitement down on the ground; occasionally, if a bull manages to breach the wooden safety barriers, this spreads to the watching crowd.

Hemingway and Chaplin. Spacious, well-restored rooms overlook either the square or lively C/Estafeta behind, with bargain rates for advance bookings. **€139**

Hostal Arriazu C/Comedias 14 ☎ 948 210 202, ⓦ hostalarriazu.com. Conveniently central and surprisingly quiet *hostal*, offering comfortable en-suite rooms just a few steps from the main square. **€55**

Hostal Bearán C/San Nicolás 25 ☎ 948 223 428, ⓦ hostalbearan.es. A clean *hostal* in the heart of the old town, whose simple en-suite rooms are perfectly acceptable for budget travellers who don't mind a bit of late-night noise so long as they're close to all the action. **€50**

Hostal Navarra C/Tudela 9, 2° ☎ 948 225 164, ⓦ hostalnavarra.com. Well-established *hostal* near the bus station. All its clean if slightly small rooms, accessible by stairs only, have en-suite facilities and have been pleasantly refurbished, and there's a laundry. **€55**

Hotel Eslava Pza. Virgen de la O 7 ☎ 948 222 270, ⓦ hotel-eslava.com. Cosy, welcoming hotel in a quiet corner of the old town, run by the Eslava family. Rooms are bright and en suite, albeit rather anonymous; some have balcony views overlooking the gardens to the south. There are fifteen doubles and thirteen particularly well-priced singles, with a bar in the basement. **€70**

Hotel Europa C/Espoz y Miña 11 ☎ 948 221 800, ⓦ hoteleuropapamplona.com. Smart modern hotel just off the main square, offering compact, well-equipped rooms above one of the city's best restaurants. Breakfast works out much cheaper if reserved with the room. **€82**

Hotel Yoldi Avda. de San Ignacio 11 ☎ 948 224 800, ⓦ hotelyoldi.com. Old hotel with smart, stylish rooms, a few hundred metres south of the Casco Viejo, near the bus station and not far from the bullring – this is where the bullfighters stay during San Fermín. Discounts on parking in nearby garages. **€78**

Pensión Escaray C/Nueva 24, 1° ☎ 948 227 825. Ageing but friendly place in a charming building in the old town. Rooms are small but clean, with wooden floors and shared bathrooms. **€45**

Next, bullocks with padded horns are let loose on the crowd in the bullring. By then, the bullring is already too crowded for anyone who has watched the running to get in there; to see both, you'll have to go on two separate mornings. Buy tickets for the bullring from the office outside, not from the touts inside.

TAKING PART

If you decide to **run** in the *encierro* – and we strongly advise you not to – remember that although it's generally less dangerous than it looks, at least one person gets seriously injured every year, while a total of fifteen have been killed in the last hundred years. Find someone who knows the ropes to guide you through the first time, and don't try any heroics. Don't get trapped hiding in a doorway, or come between a scared bull and the rest of the pack. Traditionally, women don't take part, though more and more do so. Under-18s are barred.

The only official way in is at the **starting point**, Pza. Santo Domingo, entered via Pza. San Saturnino. Shortly before the start, the rest of the course is cleared. Then, shortly before 8am, you're allowed to make your way to your own preferred starting point. To mark the start, two rockets are fired: one when the bulls are released, and the second when they are all out. As soon as the first goes, you can start to run, though if you do so you'll probably reach the ring well before the bulls and be booed for your trouble, if you wait a while, you're more likely to get close to the bulls. No one is allowed to stop altogether. There are plenty of **escape points**, but they're only for use in emergency – try to get out prematurely, and you'll be shoved back. A third rocket is fired when all the bulls are in the bullring, and a final fourth once they've all entered the corral within.

OTHER SAN FERMÍN EVENTS

Fireworks go off every evening in the Ciudadela park (about 11pm), and there's a **funfair** on the open ground alongside. Competing **bands** stagger through the streets all day playing to anyone who'll listen, and there's live **music** nightly from midnight in the bars and at Pza. del Castillo.

Bullfights take place daily at 6.30pm. Tickets (€15–75) can be bought at the Pza. de Toros, or online at ⓦferiadeltoro.es. Spain's main **opposition to bullfighting** is organized by ADDA (Asociación Defensa Derechos Animal ⓦaddaong.org), whose website has information (in English) about international campaigns and current actions.

Among the best of the **other Basque towns** where fiestas involve some form of *encierro* are Tudela (July 24–28), Estella-Lizarra (first weekend of Aug, with no official ban on women participants), and Tafalla (mid-Aug)

EATING AND DRINKING

The greatest number of **restaurants** and raucous little **bars** are on C/San Nicolás and its continuation, C/San Gregorio, and also along C/Estafeta on the *encierro* route. For good, inexpensive set menus and a wide range of **pintxos** and bocadillos, head for the streets around C/Mayor, in particular C/San Lorenzo. Navarra is noted for its fine asparagus, red peppers and red wines.

PINTXOS BARS

Baserri C/San Nicolás 32 ☎948 222 021, ⓦrestaurantebaserri.com. Highly acclaimed tapas bar, with a huge wine list and an innovative panoply of snacks, with various special deals on multiple *pintxos*, including five "creative" ones for €14, plus a set menu in the restaurant at the back, including wine, for €13.50 at lunchtime, or €24 at weekends. Sun–Thurs 1–4pm & 8–11pm, Fri & Sat 1–4pm & 8.30–11.15pm.

Bodegón Sarria C/Estafeta 50–52 ☎948 227 713, ⓦbodegonsarria.com. Tapas bar and restaurant, where the *pintxos* taste as good as they look – try the artichoke plate – hams hang from the beams, and the glossy brick walls make an appealing backdrop. Daily 9am–2am.

Chez Belagua C/Estafeta 49–51 ☎948 210 970, ⓦchezbelagua.com. Stylish, albeit intensely green-coloured, bar serving a mouthwatering array of *pintxos*, such as foie gras with caramelized apple; baby eels; squid with onion; and black pudding, as well as a €12 daily menu and an excellent wine selection. Daily 9.30am–midnight.

★**Gaucho** Traversa de Espoz y Mina 1 ☎948 225 073, ⓦcafebargaucho.com. Excellent tapas bar, just off Pza. del Castillo, where a tremendous range of *pintxos*, using ingredients like sea urchin roe or foie gras, attracts a mixed crowd that spills out across the street at weekends. Daily 8am–2am.

★**Mesón del Caballo Blanco** C/Redín ☎948 211 504. Perhaps the most atmospheric bar in town, well away from the bustle in a converted medieval church, with a tree-shaded terrace at the top of the city walls giving fantastic views of Pamplona and the mountains beyond. Snacks range from nachos with guacamole for €4.50 up to *jamón ibérico* for €15, plus a long list of *tostadas*. Mon–Thurs noon–11.30pm, Fri–Sun Thurs noon–1am.

CAFÉS AND RESTAURANTS

Café Alt Wien Parque de la Taconera ☎650 486 569, ⓦ cafevienes.com. Also known as *El Vienés*, this park café is a great place to eat a simple breakfast and relax in peaceful surroundings, though it can get crowded with families in the afternoon. Daily 9am–10pm, weekends only Oct–April.

★**Café Iruña** Pza. del Castillo 44 ☎948 222 064, ⓦ cafeiruna.com. Elegant *belle époque* café and bar, with fine *pintxos* and a €13.90 set menu. There's seating on the plaza or inside the grand old nineteenth-century dining room, with its huge mirrors and decorative pillars, and for once the TV is tiny, and dwarfed by its surroundings. Mon–Thurs & Sun 8am–10pm, Fri & Sat 9am–2am.

Europa C/Espoz y Mina 11 ☎948 221 800, ⓦ hreuropa .com. This hotel restaurant is considered one of the best dining rooms in Navarra, under the direction of local culinary star Pilar Idoate, who knocks out a carefully crafted seasonal menu featuring traditional and *nouvelle* dishes. Tasting menus €48 and €60, plus a €33 version for guests only. Mon–Sat 1–3.30pm & 8–11pm.

La Mandarra de la Ramos C/San Nicolás 9 58 ☎948 212 654, ⓦ lamandarradelaramos.es. There's a definite emphasis on meat and substance in this gleaming bar/restaurant, where the €23.50 set menu bursts with hearty options like peppers stuffed with mince, plus abundant jams and cheeses. Most dishes are also available as *raciones*, and there's a long list of salads as well. Tues–Thurs & Sun 10am–midnight, Fri & Sat 10am–2.45am.

San Fermín C/San Nicolás 44 ☎948 222 191, ⓦ www .restaurantesanfermin.com. Simple, first-floor dining room serving up classics such as *ajoarriero*, a tasty cod dish, seasonal vegetables and sumptuous desserts. Meat for fish mains at €15–20, and seasonal set menus from €25. Tues–Thurs & Sun 1–4pm, Fri & Sat 1–4pm & 9–11pm.

Sarasate C/San Nicolás 19–21 ☎948 225 727, ⓦ restaurantesarasate.com. This great vegetarian restaurant, hidden away upstairs on a lively old-town street, was established in the 1950s, and has a set menu for €11 plus a good list of organic wines. Mon–Thurs & Sun 1–4pm, Fri & Sat 1–4pm & 8.30–11pm.

Sidrería Asador Zaldiko C/Santo Domingo 39 ☎948 222 277, ⓦ zaldiko.com. Close to the Museo Navarra, this typical Navarran grill and cider house knocks out excellent grilled steaks and lamb for around €20, cooked over a wood-fired *parilla*. Mon–Sat 1–3pm & 9pm–midnight.

Southwest of Pamplona

Pamplona having long served as a gateway city to Spain, it's no surprise that the main route southwest towards the heart of the peninsula – by way of Logroño – holds some impressive medieval towns, including **Puente La Reina** and **Estella-Lizarra**.

Puente La Reina

Few towns so perfectly evoke the days of the great medieval pilgrimages as **PUENTE LA REINA** (Gares), 20km southwest of Pamplona. This is the meeting place of the two main Spanish routes: the Navarrese trail, via Roncesvalles and Pamplona, and the Aragonese one, via Jaca, Leyre and Sangüesa. From here on, all pilgrims followed the same path to Santiago.

The main historic thoroughfare through town, C/Mayor, is lined by tall buildings decorated with their original coats of arms. At its western end, the town's namesake **bridge**, among the finest in Spain, crosses the Río Arga. Built by royal command at the end of the eleventh century, it's still in use, though now by pedestrians and animals only.

At the eastern edge of town is a twelfth-century Templar church, the **Iglesia del Crucifijo** (open for services only), which contains an unusual Y-shaped crucifix.

INFORMATION   PUENTE LA REINA

Turismo C/Mayor 105, right by the bridge (Tues–Fri 9.30am–4.30pm, Sat 10am–2pm, Sun 11am–2pm; ☎948 341 301, ⓦ puentelareina-gares.es).

ACCOMMODATION AND EATING

★**Hotel Bidean** C/Mayor 20 ☎948 341 156, ⓦ bidean .com. Charming hotel in a seventeenth-century mansion in the very heart of town, with a high standard of comfort in its modernized rooms, and a good restaurant in its

cavernous cellars, with a €6 set menu. Twenty percent reductions for pilgrims. **€69**
Joaquin C/Mayor 48 ☎ 948 340 931. The nicest place to eat in town, on the ground floor of one of its finest old houses. Serves traditional Navarran cuisine, including *alubias* (kidney beans) at reasonable prices and a menu of the day at €9.50. Daily 1–3.30pm & 8–11pm.

Estella-Lizarra

The old town of **ESTELLA–LIZARRA**, 20km west of Puente La Reina, boasts a fine crop of monuments. While most of the old quarter, centred on **Pza. de los Fueros**, lies cradled within a loop of the Río Ega, many of its most interesting buildings are across the river in Barrio San Pedro. The whole place is small enough to be explored thoroughly on foot; be sure to seek out such churches as the fortified **San Pedro de la Rúa**, just up the hill from the *turismo*, and long-abandoned **Santo Sepulcro**.

Palacio de los Reyes de Navarra

C/San Nicolás 1, Barrio San Pedro • Tues–Fri 9.30am–1pm, Sat, Sun & hols 11am–2pm • Free • ☎ 948 546 161, ⓦ museogustavodemaeztu.com

Navarra's only large-scale Romanesque civil edifice, the twelfth-century **Palacio de los Reyes de Navarra**, is now open as an art gallery devoted to the Basque painter Gustavo de Maeztu (1887–1947).

INFORMATION	ESTELLA-LIZARRA
Turismo C/San Nicolás 3 (Easter to mid-Oct Mon–Sat 10am–2pm & 4–7pm, Sun 10am–2pm; mid-Oct to Easter Mon–Fri 10am–5pm, Sat & Sun 10am–2pm; ☎ 948 556 301,	ⓦ turismotierraestella.com). The well-stocked *turismo*, next door to the Palacio de los Reyes de Navarra, can advise on all Camino-related issues.

ACCOMMODATION	
Hospedería Chapitel C/Chapitel 1 ☎ 948 551 090. Comfortable and very friendly upscale hotel, in a seventeenth-century building in the heart of the old town that has been beautifully and inventively restored, and offers good buffet breakfasts. **€90** **Hotel Tximista** C/Zaldu 15 ☎ 948 555 870, ⓦ hotel tximista.com. Striking modern hotel 1km northwest of	the old town, imaginatively welded around a nineteenth-century industrial complex, but offering very bright upscale rooms in a verdant garden setting. **€90** **Pensión San Andrés** Pza. Santiago 58, 1° ☎ 948 554 158. Estella's cheapest accommodation is in an unbeatably central location, right on the main square in the old town. Assorted simple rooms, both with and without en-suite facilities. **€40**

EATING AND DRINKING	
Asador Astarriaga Pza. de los Fueros 12 ☎ 948 550 802, ⓦ asadorastarriaga.com. Decent and very central restaurant, with extensive terrace seating out on the square as well as a stylish dining room, where the set menu	costs €27. Mon–Sat 1–4pm & 8–10.30pm, Sun 1–4pm. **La Moderna** C/Mayor 54 ☎ 948 550 007. Central café-bar that opens early for breakfast, and serves a good array of *pintxos* later on. Daily 8am–11pm.

The Navarran Pyrenees

East of Pamplona, the **Navarran Pyrenees** bite a hundred-kilometre-wide chunk out of France. While the frontier itself is lined with jagged 2000-metre peaks, most of this area consists of lush green uplands rather than impenetrable mountain fastnesses. For travellers, it's most readily explored as a driving day-trip from Pamplona, though several of the pretty and fundamentally similar villages along the way also make appealing overnight stops. Each tends to have at least one little hotel in order to cope with the steady trickle of **pilgrims** en route to Santiago.

Ever since the Middle Ages, the obvious route between Navarra and France has been to follow the **Roncesvalles** pass. As immortalized in the *Song of Roland*, Charlemagne was retreating this way in 778, after laying Pamplona to waste, when Basque warriors ambushed his forces and killed the noblest of his French knights, Roland himself.

Auritz-Burguete

Once it manages to break free from Pamplona's infuriatingly labyrinthine ring road, the N135 climbs steeply northeast along the Valle de Erro. With no need to huddle against the elements, each successive village straggles alongside the road and river. The first place it's worth pausing is **AURITZ-BURGUETE**, just after the road makes a sharp northwards turn to climb towards the pass. With their ornate gingerbread trimmings, the traditional houses here epitomize the local architectural style.

6

ACCOMMODATION AND EATING   AURITZ-BURGUETE

Hostal Burguete C/Única 51 ☎948 760 005, ⓦhotelburguete.com. After a century as the focal point for the village – Ernest Hemingway stayed here while writing *Fiesta* – this old-fashioned hotel is still very presentable, with its large, plain and shiny-floored en-suite rooms and a simple, good-value dining room. **€50**

Loizu C/San Nicolás 13 ☎948 760 008, ⓦloizu.com. Large gabled house at the south end of town, that has 27 very pleasant, modernized en-suite rooms. Its fine restaurant serves good-value contemporary cuisine on set menus starting at €20. Discounts for pilgrims. **€85**

Orreaga-Roncesvalles

Despite its fame as the traditional Spanish starting point of the Pilgrim Route to Santiago – road signs make it clear that the Gallego city lies a leg-aching 790km west – **ORREAGA-RONCESVALLES** is no more than a small cluster of buildings beside the N135. As you approach from Spain, neither the avenue of trees lining the 2km road from Auritz-Burguete nor the sloping hillside meadows around the hamlet itself hint at the peaks that soar to the east.

Colegiata de Santa María

Feb, March, Nov & Dec daily 10am–2pm & 3.30–6pm; April–Oct daily 10am–2pm & 3.30–7pm; closed Jan • Church free; cloister €2.80, with museum €4.50 • ☎948 790 480, ⓦwww.roncesvalles.es

Orreaga-Roncesvalles centres on a venerable monastery complex that stretches northwards away from the road. Its various elements can be visited in different combinations, with free access to the brooding church known as the **Colegiata de Santa María**. You have to pay to see its elegant Gothic cloisters, however, while to learn more about the history of the pilgrimage, visit the small adjoining museum.

Silo de Carlomagno

A roadside chapel near the Colegiata de Santa María, named the **Silo de Carlomagno** for its resemblance to a granary, is said to mark the spot decreed by Charlemagne for the burial of Roland and his other fallen heroes. This site, however, only rose to prominence after the bishop of Pamplona built a pilgrimage hospital here in 1127.

INFORMATION   ORREAGA-RONCESVALLES

Turismo The *turismo* is located inside the monastery complex (Mon–Sat 10am–2pm & 4–7pm, Sun

10am–2pm; ☎948 760 301, ⓦwww.roncesvalles.es).

ACCOMMODATION AND EATING

Hostal Casa Sabina ☎948 760 012, ⓦcasasabina .es. Four rather spartan but clean en-suite rooms, above a welcoming little mountain restaurant/bar just in front of the tourist office. On weekdays, a €9 set menu for pilgrims is served at 7pm & 8.30pm; the price for others is €14, or you can buy a plate of pasta and a glass of wine for €7. **€55**

La Posada de Roncesvalles ☎948 760 225, ⓦlaposadaderoncesvalles.com. Large hostel run under the auspices of the monastery, with comfortable en-suite rooms; those that sleep four cost a little extra. The usual dinner menu costs €17.60, but there's a €9 version for pilgrims, who can also get discounted accommodation. **€61**

THE CAMINO DE SANTIAGO IN NAVARRA

The **Camino de Santiago** crosses into Navarra from France via the foothills of the Pyrenees, descending steeply to the historic monastery at **Orreaga-Roncesvalles**. As the mountains peter out, the path passes alongside trout-filled rivers lined with beech trees and through traditional whitewashed Basque villages graced with Romanesque churches.

Navarra has invested considerably in this section of the route, and its twenty or so *albergues* – all with comfortable, if basic, facilities – are among the best along the *camino* (see box, p.556). The path mainly follows dirt farm-tracks, although some stretches have been paved, which makes the walking less messy but leaves pilgrims prone to blisters.

Traces of Charlemagne's tenth-century foray into Spain are everywhere in Navarra, from the pass before Roncesvalles by which he entered the country to a stone monument some 20km farther on that depicts the massive Stride of Roland, his favourite knight. The region also contains some of Hemingway's much-loved haunts; the *camino* passes through his trout-fishing base at **Auritz-Burguete**, just 3km from Roncesvalles, and lively **Pamplona**, another 40km into the walk.

There are a couple of stiff climbs, notably the 300m up to the **Alto de Perdón**, just outside Pamplona. Here, legend tells of an exhausted medieval pilgrim who stood firm against the Devil's offer of water in exchange for a renunciation of his Christian faith. The pilgrim was rewarded when Santiago himself appeared, and led him to a secret fountain.

Navarra boasts some fine Romanesque architecture, including the octagonal church at **Eunate**, 20km from Pamplona, thought to be the work of the Knights Templar, and the graceful bridge that gave its name to **Puente La Reina**, 4km farther on. The architectural highlight is undoubtedly the small town of **Estella-Lizarra**, where it's worth spending an afternoon exploring the Palacio de los Reyes de Navarra and the many lovely churches. The route from Estella-Lizarra is lined with vineyards, and Bodegas de Irache's free Fuente del Vino (wine fountain), just outside town, is said to fortify pilgrims for the journey on through the Rioja region to Santiago de Compostela.

Ochagavía

If, rather than heading north into France from Orreaga-Roncesvalles, you retrace your steps to Auritz-Burguete and then turn east on to the NA140, you'll find yourself on a remote and rather lovely road that repeatedly undulates from valley to valley. Though each is separated from the next by steep and densely wooded hills, the road never climbs above the treeline.

Just over 30km along, at the confluence of the Zatoia and Anduña rivers, the ancient settlement of **OCHAGAVÍA** makes the ideal spot to break a day-trip from Pamplona. The Anduña cuts a broad swathe through the heart of town, with a pleasant promenade stroll along both its banks, forested slopes looming to either end, and a fine old church on the hillside just above. For details of longer hikes hereabouts – especially in the **Irati Forest** immediately north – pick up a trail map from the tourist office.

INFORMATION   **OCHAGAVÍA**

Turismo C/de Izalzu, on the north bank of the river (mid-June to mid-Sept Mon–Sat 10am–2pm & 4.30–8.30pm, Sun 10am–2pm; mid-Sept to mid-June Mon–Sat 10am–2pm & 4.30–7.30pm, Sun 10am–2pm; ☎ 948 890 641, ⓦ otsagabia.net).

ACCOMMODATION AND EATING

Hostal Orialde C/Urrutia 6 ☎ 948 890 270, ⓦ hostalorialde.com. Sturdy farmhouse, facing a footbridge on the river's south bank, that's now a hotel with ten antique-furnished, en-suite rooms. €65

Hotel Rural Auñamendi Pza. Gúrpide ☎ 948 890 189, ⓦ hotelruralauniamendi.com. Slightly pricey but comfortable en-suite rooms, on an open square set slightly back south of the river. The pub-like restaurant on the ground floor (closed Sat eve & Sun) serves main courses from around €10, including local trout with ham. €81

Roncal

Twenty kilometres southeast of Ochagavía, the **Valle de Roncal** is arguably the prettiest in the Navarran Pyrenees. In high summer it can get a bit too busy for comfort, but come spring or autumn its villages and meadows, wild flowers and trees, are a delight. The nicest place to get your bearings and grab a meal is the little community of **RONCAL** itself, clustered beside the NA137, 6km south of its junction with the NA140 at Isaba.

INFORMATION   RONCAL

Turismo C/Julian Gayarre (mid-June to mid-Sept Mon–Sat 10am–2pm & 4.30–8pm, Sun 10am–2pm; mid-Sept to mid-June Mon–Thurs & Sun 10am–2pm, Fri & Sat 10am–2pm & 4.30–8pm; ☎ 948 475 317, ⊚ valledoroncal .es). Doubles as a Nature Interpretation Centre, with details of hiking and other activities in the surrounding countryside.

ACCOMMODATION AND EATING

Hostal Zaltúa C/ Castilla 3 ☎ 948 475 008, ⊚ zaltua .com. Large white hotel, where the main road crosses the river, with eleven well-priced en-suite rooms. There's also a decent restaurant, on a raised terrace with river views. **€55**

Monasterio de San Salvador de Leyre

Daily: March–May & Oct 10.15am–7pm, June–Sept 10am–7.30pm, Nov–Feb 10.30am–6.30pm • Services 5 daily 6am–9.10pm • €2.75, or €3 for guided tours, in Spanish only, every 45min • ☎ 948 884 150, ⊚ monasteriodeleyre.com

The **Monasterio de San Salvador de Leyre**, 50km southwest of Roncal, grew as the first stop in Navarra on one of the many different routes used by pilgrims heading from France to Santiago. To reach it from Roncal, you have to briefly dip southwards into the province of Aragón, then head west back into Navarra on the A21, the main road between Pamplona and Jaca.

The monastery itself stands amid mountainous country 4km northeast of **YESA**. Although the convent buildings date from the sixteenth to eighteenth centuries, the church is largely Romanesque; its tall, severe apses and belfry perched on the south apsidal roof are particularly impressive. After languishing in ruins for over a century, it was restored and reoccupied by the Benedictines in the 1950s and is now in immaculate condition. The crypt, with its sturdy little columns, is the highlight. You can also access the church by attending **services**, at most of which the twenty or so white-habited monks employ Gregorian chant.

ACCOMMODATION AND EATING   MONASTERIO DE SAN SALVADOR DE LEYRE

Hospedería de Leyre ☎ 948 884 100, ⊚ monasteriodeleyre.com. Housed in the monastery's former hospice, this smart hotel has a roughly equal mix of double and single (half-rate) rooms, all en suite, as well as a handful capable of accommodating three or four guests. Its restaurant serves a good-value €17.60 dinner menu. **€77**

Javier

Although tiny **JAVIER**, 5km south of Yesa, never had anything to do with the Pilgrim Route, it's a place of pilgrimage in its own right, as St Francis Xavier was born in its redoubtable **castle** in 1506. Javier itself, 500m beyond the castle, is predominantly modern, and holds nothing of interest.

Castillo de Javier

Daily 10am–1.30pm & 3.30–6.30pm • €2.75 • ☎ 948 884 024

The patron saint of Navarra, St Francis Xavier, ranks among the most famous Jesuits. He travelled all over the Far East, dying in China in 1552. The restored **castle** that was his birthplace, originally built as a Moorish stronghold in the ninth century, now serves as an absorbing **museum** dedicated to the saint's life; labels are in Spanish only.

Coachloads of pilgrims arrive here daily, and the castle is surrounded by spacious grounds that hold a large cafeteria as well as plenty of room for picnics.

ACCOMMODATION AND EATING   JAVIER

Hotel Xabier ☎948 884 006, ⓦhotelxabier.com. Rather grand but nonetheless relaxing hotel, facing the main entrance to Javier's castle, with rooms and a restaurant that serves a good-value €19 set menu. **€88**

Sangüesa

Once a major stop on the Pilgrim Route, the rather run-down little town of **SANGÜESA**, 8km southwest of Javier, can still boast a number of significant monuments, including several churches from the fourteenth century and earlier. Many of its streets can have changed little in centuries, and still hold some handsome mansions, the remains of a royal palace and a medieval hospital, as well as the seventeenth-century Palacio de Ongay Vallesantoro.

Santa María La Real

C/Mayor 1 • June & Sept Mon–Thurs 10am–2pm, Fri & Sat 10am–2pm & 4–6.30pm; July & Aug Mon–Sat 10am–2pm & 4–6.30pm, Sun 4–6.30pm; irregular hours in low season • €2.30 • ☎948 870 132

The Romanesque church of **Santa María La Real**, pressed up against the Río Aragón at the west end of Sangüesa, dates from the twelfth century. Its finest feature is its southern facade, with a richly carved doorway and sculpted buttresses: God, the Virgin and the Apostles are depicted amid a chaotic company of warriors, musicians, craftsmen, wrestlers and animals.

Southern Navarra

South of Pamplona, the country changes rapidly; the mountains are left behind and the monotonous plains of central Spain begin to open out. The people are different, too – more akin to their southern neighbours than to the Basques. Regular buses and trains run south to **Tudela**, Navarra's second city, passing through Tafalla and **Olite**, while attractive smaller towns and villages dot the area.

Olite

OLITE, 42km south of Pamplona, is as gorgeous a small town as you could ever hope to stumble across, all the more unexpected a pleasure in that its larger neighbour Tafalla is quite unremarkable, and the town itself is surrounded by ugly modern developments. Its dominant feature is a former royal palace, the **Palacio Real de Olite**, but it also has a couple of fine old churches, Romanesque **San Pedro** and Gothic **Santa María**.

Olite's exuberant **Fiesta del Patronales** takes place from September 13 to 19, and there's a **medieval festival** on the second weekend in August leading up to the saint's day of Olite's patron, the "Virgin of the Cholera" on August 26, which commemorates the town's salvation from the cholera epidemic of 1885.

Palacio Real de Olite

March & second half of Oct Mon–Fri 10am–6pm, Sat & Sun 10am–6.30pm; April & first half of Oct daily 10am–7pm; May, June & Sept Mon–Fri 10am–7pm, Sat & Sun 10am–8pm; July & Aug daily 10am–8pm; Nov–Feb daily 10am–6pm • €3.50, or €4.90 with guided tour • ☎948 740 035, ⓦwww.palaciorealdeolite.com

The magnificent **Palacio Real de Olite**, which rambles along most of Olite's eastern flank, was commissioned in 1387 by Carlos III, the French-born king of Navarre. All fairy-tale turrets and grand halls, keeps and dungeons, it's such a colossal structure that it takes a couple of hours to explore properly – and that's despite the fact that only its so-called "New Palace" section is open to visitors, as the oldest parts now house the local parador. The entire complex was originally sumptuously decorated and painted in bright colours, but few fixtures and trappings now remain; the appeal instead is largely architectural, supplemented by the tremendous views over the old town.

Galerías Medievales

Pza. Carlos III • June & Sept Mon–Thurs 10am–2pm, Fri & Sat 10am–2pm & 4–6.30pm; July & Aug Mon–Sat 10am–2pm & 4–6.30pm, Sun 4–6.30pm; irregular hours rest of year • €1.75 • ☎ 948 741 885

Olite's central square, Pza. Carlos III, sits atop a series of impressive **Medieval Galleries**, unearthed in the 1980s. Their original purpose is a mystery; they could have been a market or crypt, or even part of a secret tunnel linking Olite with Tafalla. Now accessed via a spiral stairway that drops from the square, they now hold displays on the costumes and cuisine of the Navarran court, aimed largely at schoolchildren.

Museo del Vino

Pza. de los Teobaldos 10 • April to mid-Oct Mon–Sat 10am–2pm & 4–7pm, Sun 10am–2pm; mid-Oct to March Mon–Sat 10am–2pm & 3–6pm, Sun 10am–2pm • €3.50, or €2.50 if you visit palace as well • ☎ 948 741 273, ⓦ guiartenavarra.com

Housed, along with the *turismo*, in one of Olite's abundant spare seventeenth-century palaces, the well-presented **Museo del Vino** celebrates the town's central role in the Navarran wine industry. Visitors who make their way through its three floors of high-tech displays are rewarded with a complimentary glass of wine.

ARRIVAL AND INFORMATION   OLITE

By bus Buses to Pamplona (12 daily; 50min) and Tudela (5 daily; 50min).
By train Three daily trains connect Olite with Pamplona to the north (40min) and Tudela to the south (45min).

Turismo Pza. de los Teobaldos 10, opposite the parador (Easter–Sept Mon–Sat 10am–2pm & 4–7pm, Sun 10am–2pm; Oct–Easter Fri 4.30–6.30pm, Sat 10am–2pm & 4.30–6.30pm, Sun 11am–2pm; ☎ 948 741 703, ⓦ www.olite.es).

ACCOMMODATION AND EATING

★ **Casa Zanito** C/Mayor 16 ☎ 948 740 002, ⓦ hotelolite .com. Atmospheric townhouse hotel, with quiet, well-appointed rooms and a very good restaurant serving a great €23 dinner menu. **€65**
Hotel Merindad de Olite Rúa de la Judería 11 ☎ 948 740 735, ⓦ www.merindaddeolitehoteles.com. Cosy hotel in a reconstructed house kitted out in medieval style. Ten individually themed rooms with balconies and en-suite

facilities, plus a reasonable restaurant. **€68**
Parador de Olite Pza. de los Teobaldos 2 ☎ 948 740 000, ⓦ www.parador.es. Olite's fabulous parador makes the most of its superb setting inside the Palacio Viejo, with stone staircases and ancient hallways leading to lavishly comfortable rooms, some of which are in a newer wing and have glassed-in balconies. The modern, street-level dining room has a €33 set menu. **€120**

Ujué

Twenty kilometres northeast of Olite, a lonesome road winds off eastwards from San Martín de Unx to bring you, after 8km, to tiny, hilltop **UJUÉ**. This perfect medieval defensive village perches high on the terraced hillside above the harsh, arid landscape; it's inconceivably narrow to drive into, and all but impossible to park once you're in.

Ujué is dominated by the thirteenth-century Romanesque church of **Santa María**, where the heart of King Carlos II of Navarra is supposedly preserved inside the altar. Views from its balconied exterior extend over the whole region of La Ribera. It's also the destination of a notable **romería** (pilgrimage), on the first Sunday after St Mark's Day (April 25), when half the populace of Tafalla walk through the night to celebrate Mass here to commemorate their town's reconquest from the Moors in 1043.

From Ujué's main square, a couple of pedestrianized cobbled streets plunge down to the beautiful little Pza. Mayor, which holds a ramshackle old bar with a balcony terrace.

Parque Natural Bardenas Reales

Free • Information centre daily: mid-April to Aug 9am–2pm & 4–7pm; Sept to mid-April 9am–2pm & 3–5pm • ☎ 946 830 308, ⓦ bardenasreales.es

The further south you travel in Navarra, the drier the landscape becomes, until it's hard to believe you're still in the Basque Country. Indeed, the extraordinary **Parque Natural Bardenas Reales** (Bardenas Reales Natural Park), 70km south of Pamplona, looks more like the deserts of the Wild West than anything you'd expect to find in Spain.

To reach these desolate, eerily beautiful badlands, detour east of the main north–south roads to reach the village of Arguedas, 20km north of Tudela, then follow the signs east. Entrance is free, but it's worth stopping to pick up maps and advice at the **information centre**, 6km along. With an hour to spare, drivers can complete a short dirt-road loop to admire some of the most spectacular formations, including stark mesas, jagged striated hills, and bizarre isolated rock columns. If you have more time you can venture further off the beaten track, or explore the various clearly marked hiking trails.

Tudela

Thousand-year-old **TUDELA**, on the banks of the Ebro 90km south of Pamplona, lies at the heart of the region known as La Ribera. Its old town, stretching north of the richly decorated **Pza. de los Fueros**, is a jumble of cobbled lanes little changed since Alfonso I of Aragón ended the Moorish occupation of the city in 1119. The thirteenth-century **Puente Sobre** over the Ebro looks as if it could never have carried the weight of an ox cart, let alone seven centuries of traffic on the main road to Zaragoza.

The Catedral and the Museo de Tudela

C/Roso • Mon–Fri 10am–1.30pm & 4–7pm, Sat 10am–1.30pm • €4 • ☎ 948 402 161, ⓦ museodetudela.com

The main doorway of Tudela's sturdy twelfth-century Gothic **Catedral** only offers access to a small portion of the interior. To see the rest, pay for admission to the adjoining **Museo de Tudela**, in the former dean's palace, where the various polychrome statues, paintings and altarpieces are nicely displayed without being all that interesting. This leads to some impressive Romanesque cloisters, adorned on all sides with deft primitive carvings, and there are large placards explaining the city's Muslim and Jewish traditions.

ARRIVAL AND INFORMATION   TUDELA

By bus Tudela is connected regularly by bus with Pamplona (9 daily; 1hr 30min).
By train Trains from Tudela run to Madrid (13 daily; 2hr 15min), Pamplona (11 daily; 1hr 10min) and Zaragoza (14 daily; 45min).

Turismo Pza. de los Fueros 5–6 (Mon–Fri 9.30am–2pm & 4–8pm, Sat 10am–2pm & 4–8pm, Sun 10am–2pm; ☎ 948 848 058, ⓦ tudela.com).

ACCOMMODATION AND EATING

AC Ciudad de Tudela C/Misericordia ☎ 948 402 440, ⓦ ac-hotels.com. Tudela's classiest accommodation, in an imposing eighteenth-century mansion at the edge of the old town, has smart, plushly furnished rooms, aimed primarily at business travellers, plus a restaurant. **€92**
Hostal Remigio C/Gaztambide Carrera 4 ☎ 948 820 850, ⓦ hostalremigio.com. Plain, light, en-suite rooms at reasonable prices, just off Pza. de los Fueros close to the old town, with a good modern restaurant downstairs. **€60**
Rancho Grande C/San Nicolás s/n ☎ 948 822 780. Simple, friendly little bar, with lots of appetizing tapas spread out on the counter, and more substantial *raciones*, like stuffed onions or artichokes with *jámon*, for around €10. Daily except Wed noon–midnight.

Cantabria and Asturias

NARANJO DE BULNES, PICOS DE EUROPA

Cantabria and Asturias

While the northern provinces of Cantabria and Asturias are popular holiday terrain for Spaniards and the French, they remain hardly touched by the mass tourism of the Mediterranean coast, mostly because of the somewhat unreliable weather. But the sea is warm enough for swimming in summer, and the sun does shine, if not every day; it's the warm, moist climate, too, that's responsible for the forests and rich vegetation that give the region its nickname, Costa Verde, or the Green Coast. The provinces also boast old and elegant seaside towns, and a dramatic landscape that features tiny, isolated coves along the coast and, inland, the fabulous Picos de Europa, with peaks, sheer gorges and some of Europe's most spectacular montane wildlife.

7

Cantabria, centred on the city of Santander and formerly part of Old Castile, was long a conservative bastion amid the separatist leanings of its coastal neighbours. **Santander** itself, the modern capital, is an elegant if highly conventional resort, linked by ferry to Plymouth and Portsmouth in Britain. Either side lie attractive, lower-key resorts, crowded and expensive in August especially, but quieter during the rest of the year. The best are **Castro Urdiales**, to the east, and **Comillas** and **San Vicente de la Barquera** to the west. Perhaps the pick of the province's towns, though, is the beautiful **Santillana del Mar**, overloaded with honey-coloured mansions and, at times, with tourists, too. Inland lies a series of **prehistoric caves**: the most famous, **Altamira**, is no longer open to the public but is explained by a great museum, while another can be seen at **Puente Viesgo**, near Santander.

To the west lie the towering cliffs and rugged coves of **Asturias**, a land with its own idiosyncratic traditions, which include status as a principality (the heir to the Spanish throne is known as the Príncipe de Asturias), and a distinctive culture that incorporates bagpipes and cider (*sidra* – served from above head-height to add fizz). Asturias has a base of heavy industry, especially mining and steelworks – and a long-time radical workforce – but for the most part, the coastline is a delight, with wide, rolling meadows leading down to the sea. Tourism here is largely local, with a succession of old-fashioned and very enjoyable **seaside towns** such as **Ribadesella**, **Llanes** and **Cudillero**. Asturias also holds three sizeable cities: **Oviedo**, a delightful regional capital with a recently restored old centre; **Avilés**, at its best during the wild *Carnaval* celebrations; and nearby **Gijón**, which enjoys a vibrant nightlife and cultural scene as well as good beaches.

Inland, everything is dominated by the **Picos de Europa**, which take in parts of León, as well as Cantabria and Asturias, though for simplicity the whole national park is covered in this chapter. A quiet pleasure on the peripheries of the mountains, as in Cantabria, is the wealth of Romanesque, and even rare pre-Romanesque, churches found in odd corners of the hills. These reflect the history of the old Asturian kingdom – the embryonic kingdom of Christian Spain – which had its first stronghold in the mountain fortress of **Covadonga**, and spread slowly south with the Reconquest.

SANTILLANA DEL MAR

Highlights

❶ Playas From El Sardinero in Santander all the way west through Asturias, the region has over two hundred beaches to choose from. **See p.503**

❷ Santillana del Mar Wander the narrow streets of this chocolate-box village, with its picturesque houses and stunning Romanesque church. **See p.509**

❸ Picos de Europa With its soaring peaks, verdant hillsides, remote villages and medieval towns, all within a few kilometres of the coast, this compact mountain range should not be missed. **See p.514**

❹ Cares Gorge The finest hiking trail in the Picos: a horizontal walk through the vertical world of the Desfiladero de Cares. **See p.524**

❺ Sidra Asturias' national drink must be poured from a great height to attain optimum fizz. **See p.529**

❻ Avilés Carnaval Experience Spain at its most vibrant during the Mardi Gras celebrations. **See p.535**

❼ Santa María del Naranco, Oviedo An enigmatic, jewel-like pre-Romanesque church. **See p.538**

❽ Cudillero This lovely little fishing port might have been airlifted straight from a Greek island. **See p.540**

HIGHLIGHTS ARE MARKED ON THE MAP ON PP.500–501

THE NARROW-GAUGE RAILWAY

Communications in Cantabria and Asturias are generally slow, with the one main road following the coast through the foothills to the north of the Picos de Europa. If you're not in a hurry, try using the narrow-gauge **rail line** which until recently was known as **FEVE**. You'll probably still see that name, but the network is now run by the main national RENFE; you'll find timetables in a separate section of the RENFE website (ⓦrenfe.es).

The line can be broadly split into three routes: Bilbao in the Basque Country to Santander; Santander to Oviedo (where local services serve the triangle of Gijón, Avilés and Oviedo); and Oviedo to Ferrol in Galicia. The route is, on the whole, breathtakingly beautiful, skirting beaches, crossing *rías* and snaking through a succession of limestone gorges, but you will need several days to see it in its entirety.

Santander

7

Much the largest city in Cantabria, with a population approaching 200,000, **SANTANDER** is an elegant, refined resort with excellent transport connections. While its setting on the narrow Bahía de Santander is beautiful – from the heart of the city, you can enjoy clear views across the bay to rolling green hills and high mountains that seem to glow at sunset, and superb sandy **beaches** line much of the shorefront – the city centre lost most of its finest buildings to a massive fire in 1941. Nonetheless, the narrow lanes of the **old town**, running parallel to the waterfront, still abound in atmospheric bars and restaurants. The local beaches – the best is sandy **El Sardinero**, facing the open sea a couple of kilometres east – are broad and clean enough for Santander to rival Biarritz and San Sebastián as a favourite summer retreat for

CANTABRIA & ASTURIAS

HIGHLIGHTS

1. Playas
2. Santillana del Mar
3. Picos de Europa
4. Cares Gorge
5. Sidra
6. Avilés Carnaval
7. Santa Mariá del Naranco, Oviedo
8. Cudillero

sophisticated holiday-makers from the interior. Santander may have a much more bourgeois identity than many of its earthier northern neighbours – and away from the beaches there's not all that much to see or do – but it's not a bad place to while away a day or two.

Old Town Santander

Most of what's known as the **old town** in Santander, a compact grid of streets that stretches along the shoreline of the bay, is actually not very old at all, as the area had to be entirely rebuilt after the fire of 1941 destroyed its medieval core. It doesn't look particularly modern, though, just slightly faded and dull. As you stroll around, the only area that holds any great appeal lies a block back from the waterfront, along the parallel lanes that connect the colonnaded **Pza. Porticada** in the west to the **Pza. de Pombo** and the **Pza. Montero**.

Museo de Prehistória y Arqueologia de Cantabria (MUPAC)

C/Hernán Cortés 4 • Mid-June to mid-Sept Wed–Sun 10.30am–2pm & 5–8.30pm, mid Sept to mid June Wed–Sun 10am–2pm & 5–8pm • €5 • ☎ 942 209 922, ⓦ museosdecantabria.es/prehistoria

The basement of the attractive Mercado del Este, in the heart of the old town, has been imaginatively transformed to house the **Museo de Prehistória y Arqueologia de Cantabria (MUPAC)**. This cavernous modern space follows a timeline though the history of the region from its earliest human inhabitants up to the Roman occupation. When you first enter, it feels oddly empty, but once you get used to the tiny scale of its most ancient artefacts, such as complex bone tools and knapped flints, you'll see that they're absolutely exquisite. The real standout is an ibex head carved during the Magdalenian

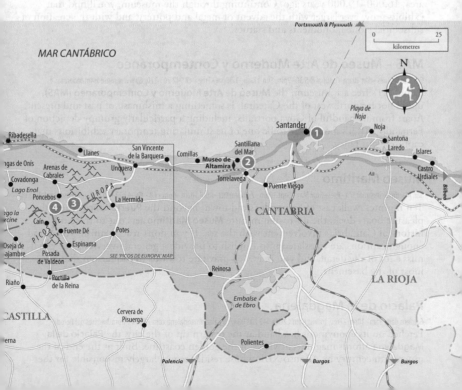

FIESTAS

JANUARY

22: Saint's day fiesta at San Vicente de la Barquera.

FEBRUARY–APRIL

Start of Lent: Carnaval Week-long festivities in Avilés, Gijón, Oviedo, Mieres, Santoña – fireworks, fancy dress and live music.
Good Friday: Re-enactment of the Passion at Castro Urdiales.
Easter Sunday and Monday: Bollo Cake festival at Avilés.
First weekend after Easter: La Folia Torch-lit procession at San Vicente de la Barquera; a statue of the Virgin Mary is carried through town on a fishing boat.

JUNE/JULY

June 29: La Amuravela Cudillero enacts an ironic review of the year – and then proceeds to obliterate memories.
Throughout July: Weekly fiestas in Llanes, with Asturian dancers balancing pine trees on their shoulders and swerving through the streets. Also, tightrope walking and live bands down at the harbour.
First Friday: Coso Blanco Nocturnal parade at Castro Urdiales.
Mid-July: Festival de Folk Cultural fiesta at San Vicente de la Barquera.
July 15: Traditional festival at Comillas, with greased-pole climbs, goose chases and other such events.
July 25: Festival of St James Cangas de Onis.

area, 16,000–19,000 years ago. Continuing through the museum, you'll find that exhibits grow ever larger with the advent of metal and pottery, and with the creation of substantial stone monuments and statues.

MAS – Museo de Arte Moderno y Contemporáneo

C/Rubio 6 • Tues– Sat 10am–1.30pm & 5.30–9pm, Sun 11am–1.30pm • Free • ☎ 942 203 120, ⓦ www.museosantandermas.es

Santander's free art museum, the **Museo de Arte Moderno y Contemporáneo (MAS)**, uphill not far northwest of the Catedral, is something a mishmash of past and present. Apart from its handful of Goya portraits, including a particularly grumpy depiction of Fernando VII, it's most likely to be one of its stimulating temporary exhibitions that captures your fancy.

Museo Marítimo

San Martín de Bajamar s/n • Tues–Sun: May–Sept 10am–7.30pm; Oct–April 10am–6pm • €8 • ☎ 942 274 962, ⓦ museosdecantabria.es

Ten minutes' walk east of Santander's old town, beyond the **Puerto Chico** where the pleasure boats dock, the up-to-the-minute **Museo Marítimo** sets out to trace the history of Cantabria's involvement with the sea. If you don't read Spanish, you'll find enough captions are translated into English to provide a general overview, but you'll miss a lot of the detail, and you may well gravitate towards the aquarium that fills most of the basement.

Palacio de la Magdalena

Gardens daily 8am–10pm • Free, tourist train €2 • ☎ 942 203 084, ⓦ palaciomagdalena.com • Bus #1 from Jardines del Pereda

Perched on its eponymous headland at the eastern tip of the city, the **Palacio de la Magdalena** affords magnificent views of the golden coastline. Built at the end of the nineteenth century by Alfonso XIII, whose residence was largely responsible for the

AUGUST

Throughout August: Festival Internacional Music and cultural festival, featuring prestigious performers, at Santander.

First or second weekend: Descenso Internacional del Sella Mass canoe races from Arriondas to Ribadesella down the Río Sella, with fairs and festivities in both towns.

First Sunday: Asturias Day Celebrated above all at Gijón.

12: Fiesta at Llanes.

15: El Rosario The fishermen's fiesta at Luarca, when the Virgin is taken to the sea.

Last Friday: Battle of the Flowers At Laredo.

Last week: San Timoteo Fairly riotous festivities at Luarca: best on the final weekend of the month, with fireworks over the sea, people being thrown into the river and a Sunday *romería*.

SEPTEMBER

7–9: Running of the bulls at Ampuero (Santander).

19: Americas Day In Asturias, celebrating the thousands of local emigrants in Latin America; at Oviedo, there are floats, bands and groups representing every Latin American country. The exact date for this can vary.

21: Fiesta de San Mateo At Oviedo, usually a continuation of the above festival.

Last Sunday: Campoo Day Held at Reinosa, and featuring a parade in traditional dress.

29: Romería de San Miguel At Puente Viesgo.

NOVEMBER

First or second weekend: Orujo Local-liquor festival in Potes.

30: San Andrés Saint's day fiesta, celebrated with a small regatta at Castro Urdiales. The tradition is to sample sea bream and snails.

town's fashionable status, the grounds now make a popular retreat for families keen to escape the crowded beaches.

The beaches

The first of Santander's beaches, **Playa de la Magdalena**, lies on the southern side of Magdalena headland. A beautiful yellow strand, sheltered by cliffs and flanked by a summer **windsurfing** school, it is deservedly popular. Around the headland to the north, two smaller and often slightly quieter beaches, **Camello** and **La Concha**, precede the main event, **El Sardinero**, which stretches for two magnificent kilometres, and is itself divided at high tide into two sections, Primera to the south and Segunda to the north.

Somo

Water taxi departs Puerto Chico every 20min • €4 return

If you find all the city beaches too crowded, catch a **water taxi** across the bay to the long stretches of dunes at **Somo** – a major **surfing** destination where you'll find boards to rent and a summer **campsite** – and **Pedreña**.

ARRIVAL, DEPARTURE AND GETTING AROUND   SANTANDER

By plane Ryanair flights from London Stansted, as well as domestic flights, land at the Aeropuerto de Santander, 4km south at Parayas on the Bilbao road, across the bay in full view of the city. Several car rental companies have outlets; a taxi into town costs around €20, and buses run nonstop to the bus station (6.30am–10.45pm; €2).

By train The RENFE and narrow-gauge (formerly FEVE) train stations stand side by side on the Pza. Estaciónes, just back from the waterside 500m west of the old town. Mainline trains run directly to Madrid (3 daily; 4hr 40min);

change at Palencia for east–west routes including León. Narrow gauge services run east to Bilbao (2 daily; 3hr) and west towards Oviedo (1 daily; 4hr 45min).

By bus A largely subterranean bus station (☎942 211 995) faces the train stations across Pza. Estaciónes. An extensive network of city buses covers all areas; routes #1, #3, #4, #7 and #E shuttle between the centre and El Sardinero. Routes further afield are listed on ⓦtransportedecantabria.es.

Destinations Barcelona (3 daily; 6hr 30min–9hr); Bilbao

7

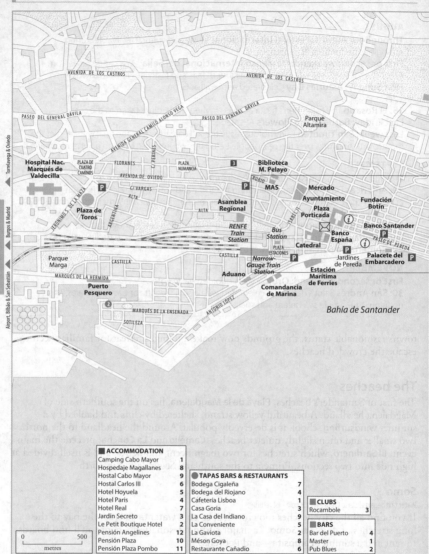

Torrelavega & Oviedo ◀

Burgos & Madrid ◀

Airport, Bilbao & San Sebastián ◀

■ ACCOMMODATION	
Camping Cabo Mayor	1
Hospedaje Magallanes	8
Hostal Cabo Mayor	9
Hostal Carlos III	6
Hotel Hoyuela	5
Hotel Paris	4
Hotel Real	7
Jardin Secreto	3
Le Petit Boutique Hotel	2
Pensión Angelines	12
Pensión Plaza	10
Pensión Plaza Pombo	11

● TAPAS BARS & RESTAURANTS	
Bodega Cigaleña	7
Bodega del Riojano	4
Cafetería Lisboa	1
Casa Goria	3
La Casa del Indiano	9
La Conveniente	5
La Gaviota	2
Méson Goya	8
Restaurante Cañadio	6

■ CLUBS	
Rocambole	3

■ BARS	
Bar del Puerto	4
Master	1
Pub Blues	2

(every 30min; 1hr 30min); Oviedo (14 daily; 2hr 15min); Potes via San Vicente and Unquera (3 daily; 2hr 30min); Santillana (7 daily; 40min).

By ferry Brittany Ferries (ⓦ brittany-ferries.co.uk) from England dock right in the heart of the city, a short walk from either the old town or the train and bus stations.

INFORMATION

Santander tourist office The municipal *turismo* stands in the Jardines de Pereda near the ferry port (mid-June to mid-Sept daily 9am–9pm; mid-Sept to mid-June Mon–Fri 9am–7pm, Sat 10am–7pm, Sun 10am–2pm; ☎ 942 203 000, ⓦ www.santander.es).

Cantabria tourist office Mercado del Este 4, C/Hernán Cortés (daily 9am–9pm; ☎ 901 111 112, ⓦ turismodecantabria.com).

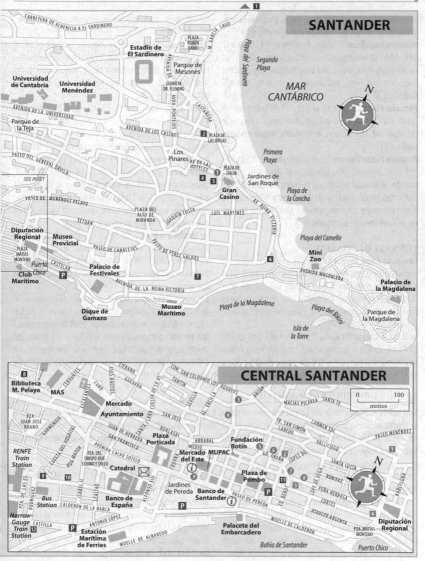

SANTANDER

CENTRAL SANTANDER

ACCOMMODATION

July and August aside, Santander usually has enough **accommodation** to go round. The fundamental choice lies in whether you want to stay in the **old town** or near **El Sardinero** beach; they're too far apart for either district to make a good base for visiting the other.

CENTRAL SANTANDER

★**Hospedaje Magallanes** C/Magallanes 22 ☎942 371 421, ⊚hospedajemagallanes.com. Plain, neat rooms at bargain prices in an anonymous modernized block, with a lift, a 15min walk north of the train and bus stations. The staff are exceptionally helpful. The cheapest options share bathrooms; pay €20 extra for en-suite facilities. **€49**

Hostal Cabo Mayor C/Cádiz 1, 2° ☎942 211 181, ⊚hcabomayor.com. Six spotless little en-suite rooms

7

across from the train stations, decorated in a modern palette of blacks and whites, with friendly management. **€65**

Pensión Angelines C/Atilano Rodríguez 9, 1° 25 ☎ 942 312 584, ⓦ www.pensionangelines.com. Basic but scrupulously clean rooms, in a busy location very near the train, bus and ferry, and sharing all washing and WC facilities. **€40**

Pensión Plaza C/Cádiz 13 ☎ 942 212 967, ⓦ pension -plaza.com. Small, good-value modern *pensión* very near the train and bus stations, with eleven simple en-suite rooms. **€61**

Pensión Plaza Pombo C/Hernán Cortés 25, 3° ☎ 942 212 950, ⓦ pensionplazapombo.com. Attractive central *pensión*, in an ideal position for enjoying Santander's bars and restaurants. Behind the old-fashioned public areas, the actual rooms are surprisingly modern and bright, though not all have en-suite bathrooms. **€68**

THE REST OF THE CITY

Camping Cabo Mayor ☎ 942 391 542, ⓦ cabomayor .com. Well-equipped site with a swimming pool, 2km north of the casino on a bluff known as Cabo Mayor, a 10min walk from Sardinero beach. Take bus #9 to Cueto from opposite the *ayuntamiento*. Closed mid-Oct to mid-April. **€30.30**, bungalow **€65**

★ **Hostal Carlos III** Avda. Reina Victoria 135 ☎ 942 271 616, ⓦ www.hostalcarlos3.com. Well-run *hostal* in a wonderful turreted old mansion overlooking Playa de la Magdalena. Some rooms have sea-view balconies,

others their own private courtyards. Closed Nov–March. **€79**

Hotel Hoyuela Avda. de los Hoteles 7 ☎ 942 282 628, ⓦ gruposardinero.com. Traditional, stately and expensive hotel, perfect for El Sardinero beach. Huge rooms, many with sea views, and good service. Rates drop enormously out of season. **€169**

Hotel Paris Avda. de los Hoteles 6 ☎ 942 272 350, ⓦ hotelparissantander.es. An imposing nineteenth-century hotel, ageing gracefully and very near El Sardinero beach; some of its large, bright rooms have stylish sea-view balconies. Closed mid-Oct to mid-May. **€125**

Hotel Real Paseo Pérez Galdós 28 ☎ 942 932 424, ⓦ hotelreal.es. Elegant, upmarket hotel, a 10min walk from the centre near Playa de la Magdalena; huge rooms with sea views, and a sea-water spa. Expect old-fashioned grandeur, not every modern amenity. **€200**

★ **Jardín Secreto** C/Cardenal Cisneros 37 ☎ 942 070 714, ⓦ jardinsecretosantander.com. Small and very welcoming B&B, with six stylish rooms featuring exposed brickwork and attractive bed linens, and sharing use of the eponymous secret garden. **€75**

Le Petit Boutique Hotel Avda. de los Castros 10 ☎ 942 075 768, ⓦ lepetithotelsantander.com. Rather exquisite B&B, housed in an unexpected little cottage just a few metres up from the centre of El Sardinero beach. The seven tastefully decorated bedrooms are named for different world cities, and vary considerably in size; the breakfasts are excellent. **€129**

EATING, DRINKING AND NIGHTLIFE

Santander's old town holds the largest selection of **cafés**, **bars** and **restaurants**, though plenty more lie close to El Sardinero. As both a university town and an upscale resort, Santander also offers lively **nightlife**, especially on summer weekends. In the summer, the city hosts an international university, augmented by a **music and cultural festival** throughout August (ⓦ festivalsantander.com).

TAPAS BARS AND RESTAURANTS

Bodega Cigaleña C/Daoiz y Velaverde 19 ☎ 942 213 062. Beyond its gorgeous tiled exterior, this atmospheric, museum-like bar, decorated with old bottles, is a lovely spot to enjoy tapas and a glass of wine, or linger over the traditional €38.50 set dinner menu. The €20 set lunch menu is not very good value, however. Mon 9pm–midnight, Tues–Sat 1–4pm & 9pm–midnight; closed last week in May & Nov and first week in June & Dec.

Bodega del Riojano C/Río de la Pila 5 ☎ 942 216 750. Traditional *bodega* in a sixteenth-century wine cellar, serving good *raciones* at €8–14, with a flagstone floor, beautifully painted casks and antique furniture. Mon–Sat 1.30–4pm & 8.30pm–midnight, Sun 1.30–4pm.

Cafetería Lisboa Pza. Italia, Sardinero ☎ 942 271 020. Of the clutch of restaurants in front of the casino, all with summer *terrazas*, this serves the best food, with a €18.50 lunch menu. Daily 9am–1am.

Casa Goria Travesía la Pila ☎ 942 222 286. Traditional tiled tapas bar, just off C/Río de la Pila, where the ceiling is adorned with hanging Cantabrian hams. Wonderful *empanadas* and *pinchos*, with a dining room at the back serving a €13 set-lunch menu, should the popular bar get claustrophobic. Daily 1–4pm & 8pm–midnight.

La Casa del Indiano Mercado del Este, C/Hernán Cortés 4 ☎ 942 074 660, ⓦ casadelindiano.com. Popular South American-style sit-down bar inside the flagstone-floored former market. Open from breakfast onwards for drinks and snacks, with seating in the central patio as well as along the fine old counter, and a full restaurant menu (mains €10–17, €22 set menu) plus a fine spread of *pintxos*. There always seems to be a special deal of some kind, like the €1 offer on *pintxos* on Thursdays. Daily 8am–midnight.

★ **La Conveniente** C/Gómez Oreña 19 ☎ 942 212 887. Very old-fashioned and very atmospheric nineteenth-century *bodega* serving fried fish and other delicious, but pricey, snacks. Live piano music, too. Mon–Sat 7pm–1am.

La Gaviota C/Marqués de la Ensanada 32, Barrio de Puerto Pesquero ☎ 942 361 871, ⓦ lagaviota.es. The best of several similarly busy, unpretentious seafood restaurants down by the port, featuring a street barbecue of spectacular, freshly caught seafood. You can spend anything, from a few euros for a set menu or plate of sardines, to a small fortune for fishy exotica. Daily 12.30–4.15pm & 7pm–midnight.

Méson Goya C/Daoiz y Velaverde 25 ☎ 942 213 966, ⓦ mesongoya.com. Restaurant in a fine old house in the heart of the old town, serving a good range of traditional Spanish dishes, as €9–15 *raciones* or on set menus priced at €40 and €60 for two diners. Daily except Wed 11am–5pm & 7pm–12.30am.

Restaurante Cañadio Pza. Cañadio ☎ 942 314 149, ⓦ restaurantecanadio.com. The city's most famous restaurant, known far and wide for the sublime fish and regional cooking of Paco Quirós. Typical main dishes cost €18–24, or you can simply join the foodies at the tables in the more modest bar, snacking on delicious *raciones* (€8.50–14), the €9 dish of the day (on weekdays only), or the even cheaper *pintxos*. Daily 1–4pm & 9pm–midnight.

BARS AND CLUBS

Bar del Puerto C/Hernán Cortés 63 ☎ 942 213 001, ⓦ bardelpuerto.com. Swish bar and restaurant popular with the sailing set. Mon–Sat 1–4pm & 9pm–midnight, Sun 1–4pm.

Master C/Sol 57, ☎ 942 217 501. Very fancy cocktail bar, where the latest spur-of-the-moment concoctions cost around €10. Daily 7pm–3am.

Pub Blues Pza. Cañadio 15 ☎ 942 314 305. Popular blues and jazz music bar, with an expensive restaurant attached. Mon–Wed 7.30pm–3.30am Thurs–Sat 7.30pm–4.30am.

Rocambole C/Hernán Cortés 35 ☎ 942 364 025, ⓦ salarocambole.com. Late-night club attracting a young and trendy crowd; Motown music and expensive drinks. Things tend not to get going before 3am. Daily 9pm until dawn.

East to Castro Urdiales

Easily accessible by car but still appealingly rural, the coast east of Santander is becoming ever more developed for tourism. The best-known resort is **Laredo**, with its enormous beach, but lower-key alternatives include the fishing ports of **Santoña** and **Castro Urdiales**.

Laredo

From its old core, sheltered behind a rocky promontory, **LAREDO**, poised 50km both east of Santander and west of Bilbao, has expanded westwards along the sandspit at the mouth of the Río Asón to become one of Cantabria's most popular resorts. In summer, the beaches and profusion of pubs, clubs and discos attract a young crowd, while there's enough of interest during the rest of the year to keep most of the hotels and restaurants open.

Laredo was Cantabria's capital for a spell in the nineteenth century. Set well back from the overdeveloped beachfront, the village-like old town, the **Puebla Vieja**, stills retains the odd trace of its former walls and gates, climbing up towards a splendid thirteenth-century parish church, **Santa María de la Asunción** (daily 10am–1pm & 4–7.30pm). Beyond that, you can climb quickly to the cliffs and grand open countryside.

A five-minute walk from the old town leads down to the best **beach** this side of San Sebastián, the **Playa de Salvé**. A gently shelving crescent of sand, well protected from the wind, it stretches for a full 5km.

INFORMATION AND ACTIVITIES   **LAREDO**

Turismo Laredo's well-stocked *turismo* is housed in a former radio station on Alameda Miramar at the west end of the old town, close to the bus terminal (daily: July to mid-Sept 9am–9pm; mid-Sept to June 9.30am–1.30pm & 4–7pm; ☎ 942 611 096, ⓦ laredo.es).

Scuba diving Mundo Submarino, based in Laredo (☎ 942 611 861, ⓦ mundosubmarino.es) runs scuba-diving courses across the Cantabrian Sea.

Boat trips Boats from the end of the harbour nearest the old town cross to Santoña (March–Oct; €3 return), and set out on hour-long sea cruises (mid-June to mid-Sept; €10; ☎ 942 605 903, ⓦ excursionesmaritimas.com).

7

ACCOMMODATION

Camping Laredo C/República de Filipinas 2 ☎942 605 035, ⓦwww.campinglaredo.com. Conveniently located just back from the beach, not far west of the town centre, with separate adults' and kids' pools and some wooden "eco-bungalows". Closed mid-Sept to May. **€34.50**, bungalow **€95**

Hotel Cortijo C/González Gallego 3 ☎942 605 600, ⓦwww.hotelcortijo.com. Clean, simple hotel, a block back from the beach, a short walk from the old town. Nothing fancy, but great value for such a central location. **€45**

EATING AND DRINKING

Guti C/Mayor 7 ☎942 605 674, ⓦrestauranteguti .com. The pick of several options along the main street of the old town, serving good-value local cooking in a little dining room; mixed grills are the house speciality. The special weekend set menu costs €25. Daily except Wed 1.30–4pm & 8.30pm–midnight.

El Pescador Avda. Cantabria 2 ☎942 606 638, ⓦrestaurantepescador.es. Good seafood restaurant, with a prime position on the beachfront not far from the old town; their catch of the day, costing around €20, is always excellent, and there's a €22 daily set menu. Daily noon–3pm & 7.30–11pm.

Santoña

West across the mouth of the estuary from Laredo, the compact little town of **SANTOÑA** is still a working fishing port, shielded from the open ocean by the mighty wooded hill of Monte Ganzo, and famous for its **anchovies**. You can watch the catch being unloaded before sampling it in the tiny bars grouped around the streets leading up from the port, particularly C/General Salinas.

Turismo Santoña's *turismo* is in the central Palacio Manzanedo (Mon–Sat 10am–2pm & 5–8pm, Sun 11am–2pm; ☎942 660 066, ⓦturismosantona.es).

ACCOMMODATION, EATING AND DRINKING

Hotel Juan de la Cosa Playa de Berria 14 ☎942 661 238, ⓦhoteljuandelacosa.com. Modern hotel with large sea-view rooms and apartments, on the ocean side of the headland 2km west of central Santoña straight across from Berria beach. **€92**

Napoleon C/Alfonso XII 34 ☎942 662 347. This good fish restaurant on the eastern edge of old-town Santoña is a great place to try the succulent local anchovies, on set menus from €25. Daily noon–4pm & 8–11pm.

Castro Urdiales

The congenial, handsome resort of **CASTRO URDIALES**, 20km east of Laredo, is only a short drive west from the huge conglomeration of Bilbao, and both hotel rooms and space on the beaches are at a premium in high season and at weekends.

Castro Urdiales retains a considerable fishing fleet, gathered around a beautiful natural **harbour**. Above this looms a massively buttressed Gothic church, **Santa María**, and a lighthouse, built within the shell of a Knights Templar castle. These are linked to the remains of an old hermitage by a dramatic reconstructed medieval **bridge**, known locally as the Puente Romano, under which the sea roars at high tide. The old quarter, the **Mediavilla**, is relatively well preserved, with arcaded streets and tall, glass-balconied houses.

Flaviobriga

C/Ardigales 5–7 • July & Aug Tues–Sun 11am–2pm & 5–8pm • Free • ⓦturismocastrourdiales.net

Castro Urdiales stands on the site of the Roman town of **Flaviobriga**, and a short stretch of ancient Roman street has been unearthed on C/Ardigales. You can simply admire it from the pavement outside, or enter to take a closer look at the foundations of assorted buildings.

The beaches

In high season, the main "town beach", **Playa del Brazomar**, a small strip of sand hemmed in by a cement esplanade, can be very busy. However, the crowds can be left behind by heading farther east to more secluded coves, or west to **Playa Ostende**, with its rough, dark sand. From this latter beach, there's an unusual walk back to town along the cliffs, with the sea pounding the rocks beneath you. In a tiny bay en route, the sea comes in under a spectacular overhang.

ARRIVAL AND INFORMATION — CASTRO URDIALES

By bus The local bus terminal is a good half-hour walk east of the centre on C/Leonardo Rucabado, but town buses, and services to Bilbao, stop outside *Café-Bar Ronda* on Paseo Menendez Pelayo.

By car Finding a parking space in Castro Urdiales is appallingly difficult in season; you'll spare yourself a lot of hassle if you settle for the first roadside space you see.

Turismo In the castellated old town hall, at the head of the harbour (Mon–Sat 9am–2pm & 5–7pm; ⓣ 942 871 512, ⓦ turismocastrourdiales.net).

ACCOMMODATION

Castro Urdiales' best-value **accommodation** is scattered through the narrow, pedestrianized streets of the old town.

Hotel Las Rocas C/Flaviobriga 1 ⓣ 942 860 400, ⓦ lasrocashotel.com. Imposing, classy, pastel-yellow hotel, facing the beach in the newer part of the town. Comfortable upscale rooms with sea views, plus private parking; a real bargain for the price. €93

Pensión La Mar C/La Mar 27 ⓣ 942 870 524, ⓦ lamarcastro.es. Clean and presentable, if far from distinguished, en-suite rooms, on a little shopping street just back from the sea in the heart of town. €60

EATING AND DRINKING

Places to **eat** are clustered beneath the arches at the castle end of the harbour. Lively **C/Ardigales**, a block inland from the Paseo del Mar and packed with *mesones* and *tabernas*, is the centre of the nightlife scene.

La Cierbanata C/La Correría 15 ⓣ 942 781 195, ⓦ lacierbanata.com. The pick of the row of old-fashioned tapas bars under the arcades just back from the harbour, with a colourful tiled interior and a few wooden benches outside. *Pintxos* for just €1 and *raciones* of mussels, razor-shell clams and the like from just €4. Daily noon–midnight.

★ **Mesón Marinero** C/La Correría 23 ⓣ 942 860 005, ⓦ mesonmarinero.com. Top-notch fish restaurant, with harbour-facing tables beneath the arches of a huge white waterfront building. Main courses cost upwards of €20, and there's a €28 set menu, but you can dine well and cheaply on the *pintxos* set out along the bar. Daily 9am–midnight.

Sidrería Marcelo C/Ardigales 12 ⓣ 942 867 058. Traditional cider-house across from the Roman ruins, with standing room at the barrels outside as well as great snacks or a good set menu for €27.40 inside – and fresh cider. Tues–Sun 10.30am–4pm & 7.30pm–midnight.

Santillana del Mar and around

The picturesque village of **SANTILLANA DEL MAR** is the first major tourist destination west of Santander. No less an authority than Jean-Paul Sartre, in *Nausea*, hailed Santillana as "*le plus joli village d'Espagne*". The crowds that flock here in summer have unquestionably diminished its appeal, but on a quiet day it remains as beautiful as ever. Its cobbled lanes abound in gorgeous sandstone churches and mansions with flowery overhanging balconies, while the farms and fields that climb the adjacent hillsides give it a lovely rural atmosphere. Strolling is a delight, even if most of the ochre-coloured buildings now hold restaurants, hotels or souvenir shops.

Despite consisting of little more than two pedestrianized streets and a couple of plazas, Santillana feels more like a sizeable medieval town that never grew beyond its original core than a village.

Many of the fifteenth- to eighteenth-century **mansions** clustered close to the Pza. Mayor still belong to the original families, but their noble owners have rarely visited in the last couple of centuries. Among the finest is the **Casa de los Hombrones**, on C/Cantón, named after the two moustached figures that flank its grandly sculpted escutcheon.

La Colegiata

Pza. Las Arenas • Tues–Sun: June–Sept 10am–1.30pm & 4–7.30pm; Oct–May 10am–1.30pm & 4–6.30pm • €3 with Museo Diocesano • ☎ 942 840 317, ⓦ www.santillanamuseodiocesano.com

Jutting out into the fields at the north end of the village, Santillana's elegantly proportioned village church, **La Colegiata**, is dedicated to Santa Juliana. Her recumbent tomb is in the central aisle of the church itself, which also holds a magnificent *retablo*. The most outstanding feature of the complex, however, is its ivy-drenched twelfth-century **Romanesque cloister**, where the squat, paired columns and lively capitals are carved with images of animals and hunting, as well as ornate patterns and religious scenes.

Museo Diocesano Regina Coeli

El Cruce • Tues–Sun: June–Sept 10am–1.30pm & 4–7.30pm; Oct–May 10am–1.30pm & 4–6.30pm • €3 with La Colegiata • ☎ 942 840 317, ⓦ www.santillanamuseodiocesano.com

On the main road just across from the village entrance is the seventeenth-century **Altamira Convento de Regina Coeli**, which houses the **Museo Diocesano Regina Coeli**, an exceptional museum of painted wooden figures and other religious art: pieces brilliantly restored by the nuns and displayed with great imagination to show the stylistic development of certain images, particularly of San Roque, a healing saint always depicted with his companion, a dog who licks the plague sore on his thigh.

The Caves of Altamira

Museum May–Oct Tues–Sat 9.30am–8pm, Sun 9.30am–3pm; Nov–April Tues–Sat 9.30am–6pm, Sun 9.30am–3pm • €3 • ☎ 942 818 815, ⓦ museodealtamira.mcu.es

The **Caves of Altamira**, which burrow into the hillside 2km west of Santillana, consist of an extraordinary series of caverns, adorned by prehistoric human inhabitants around fourteen thousand years ago with paintings of bulls, bison, boars and other animals. Etched in red and black with confident and impressionistic strokes, and sealed by a roof collapse a thousand years later, the murals were in near-perfect condition when rediscovered in the 1870s, their colours striking and vigorous; as Picasso put it, "After Altamira, everything is decadence". During the 1950s and 1960s, however, they seriously deteriorated due to the moisture released in the breath of visitors, and the caves are now **closed** to prevent further damage.

Alongside the site, the fascinating **Museo de Altamira** centres on a "Neocave", a large and very convincing replica of a portion of the caverns that gives a spine-tingling sense of how the paintings look *in situ*. Comprehensive displays in the adjoining galleries trace human history all the way back to Africa, with three-dimensional replicas and authentic finds from Altamira and other Spanish sites, and plentiful captions in English. No one knows exactly why the Paleolithic art at Altamira was created, but archeologists say it was not primarily related to hunting; the specific animals depicted were not eaten any more than other species.

ARRIVAL AND INFORMATION   SANTILLANA DEL MAR

By bus Local buses stop on the main road near the tourist office; services include Santander (7 daily; 40min), and the nearest train station, 9km southeast in Torrelavega (20 daily; 20min).

Turismo C/Jesús Otero 20, just off the main road and adjoining the village's largest car park (daily: June–Sept 9am–9pm; Oct–May 9.30am–2pm & 4–7pm; ☎ 942 818 812, ⓦ santillana-del-mar.com).

ACCOMMODATION

Santillana is not really a destination for budget travellers. If you're going to spend a night here, it's worth paying to stay in one of its many gorgeous luxury **hotels**, which uniquely include two **paradores**.

Camping Santillana Carretera Comillas km 6 ☎ 942 818 250, ⓦ campingsantillana.com. Santillana's large campsite, with a pool and good facilities, is located 1km northwest of the village along the Comillas road. Open all year, it also offers bungalows and studios for rent. €24, studio €60, bungalow €80

Casa del Marqués C/Canton 26 ☎ 942 818 888, ⓦ turismosantillanadelmar.com. Grand and very luxurious historic hotel, with sumptuous public spaces and tasteful, well-appointed rooms. €115

Casa del Organista C/Los Hornos 4 ☎ 942 840 452, ⓦ casadelorganista.com. This beautiful eighteenth-century B&B, just up from the central square, has very comfortable rooms, some with balconies, as well as nice public spaces, and also serves great breakfasts. Highest rates apply three weeks in August only. €93

Hotel Altamira C/Canton 1 ☎ 942 818 025, ⓦ hotelaltamira.com. Fine hotel opening off the corner of the main square, with 32 plush antique-furnished rooms

and suites, lots of wood panelling, and several dining rooms. The front courtyard makes a delightful breakfast venue. €100

★**Parador Gil Blas** Pza. Ramón Pelayo 11 ☎ 942 028 028, ⓦ www.parador.es. Housed in a splendid mansion adjoining the main square, this definitive parador features a delightful terrace restaurant. €188

Parador Santillana Pza. Ramón Pelayo ☎ 942 818 000, ⓦ www.parador.es. Santillana's second luxury parador stands in a tasteful building that's set slightly back from, and higher than, the central square. When demand is low, in winter, it's liable to shut its doors, in which case reservations are honoured by the *Gil Blas* instead. €125

Santa Juliana C/Carrera 19 ☎ 942 840 106, ⓦ santillanadelmar.com. While ranking among Santillana's cheaper *posadas*, this still maintains high standards, and offers six attractive, beamed en-suite B&B rooms. Three-night minimum stay in summer. €60

EATING AND DRINKING

Santillana is disappointingly short on tapas bars, and although it holds plenty of conventional **restaurants**, most tend to be expensive and relatively ordinary.

Los Blasones Pza. de la Gandara 8 ☎ 942 818 070, ⓦ restlosblasones.restaurantesok.com. Reliable restaurant, in a fine old building near the main car park, with set menus from €18; the good-value €30 option features clams followed by steak or duck. Daily except Thurs 1–4pm & 8–11.30pm; closed mid-Dec to mid-March.

El Jardín del Marqués C/Canton 24 ☎ 942 840 363. Whether you want a coffee or a substantial salad, this relaxed café, sprawling along one side of surprisingly large

walled gardens across from the *Casa del Marqués* hotel, makes a great retreat in summer from the heat and bustle of the village. Daily noon–11.30pm.

Restaurante Castillo Pza. Mayor ☎ 942 818 377. Well located on the main square, with a couple of stone benches for soaking up the early-morning sun, this place is busy with locals year-round. It acts as a *sidrería* near the front and a more formal restaurant further back, with a great-value daily set menu at €17.50. Daily 10am–4pm & 8–11pm.

Puente Viesgo: prehistoric caves

Las Monedas & El Castillo: April to mid-June & mid-Sept to Oct Wed–Sun 9.30am–2.30pm & 3.30–6.30pm; mid-June to mid-Sept Tues–Sun 9.30am–2.30pm & 3.30–7.30pm; Nov–March Wed–Fri 9.30am–3.30pm, Sat & Sun 9.30am–2.30pm & 3.30–5.30pm • €3 • ☎ 942 598 425, ⓦ cuevas.culturadecantabria.com

The attractive village of **PUENTE VIESGO**, set in a river gorge amid forested escarpments on the N623 to Burgos, 15km southeast of Santillana or 24km southwest of Santander, stands close to some remarkable **prehistoric caves**. Guided tours (in Spanish only) depart from an informative visitor centre located 1.5km up a winding mountain road from the village bus stop (served by SA Continental buses from the main station in Santander). Two of the four caves, 700m apart, are open to the public, **Las Monedas** and the slightly better **El Castillo**, but places are limited, and in summer it's best to book at least 24 hours in advance. The caves are magnificent, with weirdly shaped stalactites and stalagmites, and bizarre organ-like lithophones, natural features used by

Paleolithic peoples to produce music, while the astonishing paintings, depicting animals from mammoths to dogs, are clear precursors to the later developments at Altamira. The visitor centre has an excellent digital exhibit enabling 360-degree views and interactive "tours".

ACCOMMODATION PUENTE VIESGO

La Anjana Corrobarceno 8 ☎942 598 526, ⓦposadalaanjana.es. Spacious, well-equipped rooms at the south end of Puente Viesgo, where the price includes breakfast in the excellent restaurant. €75

Gran Hotel Balneario C/Manuel Pérez Mazo ☎942 598 061, ⓦbalneariodepuenteviesgo.com. Luxurious four-star hotel with its own lavish spa, set in superb

grounds overlooking the glorious valley, and very close to the caves. €120

Pensión La Terraza C/General 49 ☎942 598 102, ⓦlaterrazadepuenteviesgo.es. Squat little yellow-painted hotel, typical of several cheaper alternatives in Puente Viesgo, where the simple but attractive rooms share bathrooms. Closed Oct–June. €77

7 South of Santander: Reinosa and the Ebro

South of Santander, a large area of quiet Cantabrian countryside is dominated by an extensive reservoir, the Pantano del Ebro. The N611 to Palencia brushes its shores en route to the pleasant old town of **Reinosa**. To the east, the **Río Ebro** trails a lovely valley, past a succession of unspoiled villages, Romanesque architecture and cave churches.

Reinosa

REINOSA is a pretty, characteristically Cantabrian town with glass-fronted balconies and *casonas* – seventeenth-century townhouses – that display the coats of arms of their original owners.

On the last Sunday in September – "**Campoo Day**" – the people of the Alto Campoo region, of which Reinosa is the capital, celebrate their unique folklore and traditions. Locals parade in distinctive alpine-style costume, complete with the unusual stilted clogs known as *albarcas*, and enjoy displays of traditional dance, typical foods and the usual late-night festivities.

INFORMATION REINOSA

Turismo Avda. Puente Carlos III 25 (mid-June to mid-Sept Mon–Fri 9.30am–2.30pm & 5–8pm, Sat & Sun 9.30am–2.30pm; mid-Sept to mid-June Mon–Fri 9.30am–2.30pm; ☎942 755 215, ⓦaytoreinosa.es).

ACCOMMODATION

Hotel San Roque Avda. Cantabria 3 ☎942 754 788, ⓦwww.hotelsanroque.eu. Simple but comfortable en-suite rooms in an appealing restored building, a short walk from the liveliest part of town; it also has a decent restaurant. €69

Posada Fontibre El Molino 23, Fontibre ☎942 779 655, ⓦposadafontibre.com. Rambling old mill, full of bizarre knick-knacks, near the source of the Ebro in a pretty little valley 5km west of Reinosa, with six quirky, rather lovely bedrooms; breakfast costs €5.50 extra. €84

EATING AND DRINKING

For a small town, Reinosa has a wide range of traditional **bodegas** and **mesones**, concentrated around the central Pza. de la Constitución.

El Molino C/Deltebre 2 ☎942 771 077, ⓦelmolino reinosa.com. Cosy, split-level, rural-themed restaurant, where the excellent home-made food attracts diners from miles around. On weekdays, there's a €16 lunch menu; otherwise expect to pay €12–19 for a main course. Daily

except Wed 1.30–3.30pm & 9–11pm.

Pepe el de los Vinos Avda. Puente Carlos III 29 ☎942 750 588. Central bar that makes a good venue for a glass of wine and a snack, and also offers more substantial meals. Daily noon–11pm.

The western Cantabrian coast

West of Santillana, the coast is dotted with a succession of small, low-key resorts as far as drab little **Unquera** on the border with Asturias. Both the main towns, **Comillas** and **San Vicente de la Barquera**, are worth a visit, having retained a traditional, earthy feel long since abandoned elsewhere in a flood of high-rise hotels and apartments. The narrow-gauge rail line runs inland along this stretch, but the towns are linked by regular bus services.

Comillas

COMILLAS, 16km west of Santillana del Mar, is a curious rural town with pretty cobbled streets and squares, which in its centre seems almost oblivious to the proximity of the sea. It nonetheless boasts a pair of superb beaches: **Playa de Comillas**, the closest, has a little anchorage for pleasure boats and a few beach cafés, while the longer and less developed **Playa de Oyambre** is 4km west out of town towards the cape.

El Capricho

Barrio de Sobrellano • Daily: March–June & Oct 10.30am–8pm, July–Sept 10.30am–9pm, Nov–Feb 10.30am–5.30pm • €5 • ☎ 942 720 365, ⓦ elcaprichodegaudi.com

Comillas is the unlikely location of the first house ever designed by architect **Antoni Gaudí**. Built in 1883, the villa known as **El Capricho** stands an easy walk from the centre. With its whimsical tower, adorned like most of the exterior with glazed handmade sunflower tiles, it has the incongruous air of a Hansel and Gretel gingerbread house. Visitors wander at will through both the gardens and the house itself, which curves around a greenhouse that may well predate Gaudí's commission.

Palacio de Sobrellano

Daily: April to mid-June & mid-Sept to Oct Tues–Sun 9.30am–2.30pm & 3.30–6.30pm; mid-June to mid-Sept Tues–Sun 9.30am–2.30pm & 3.30–7.30pm; Nov–March Tues–Fri 9.30am–3.30pm, Sat & Sun 9.30am–2.30pm & 3.30–5.30pm • Gardens free, palace €4, guided tour only • ☎ 942 720 339, ⓦ centros.culturadecantabria.com

The enormous **Palacio de Sobrellano**, which stands all but next door to El Capricho but can only be accessed from the main road below, is another nineteenth-century *modernista* extravaganza. Designed by Gaudí's associate, Juan Martorell, it was home to the Marqués de Comillas, whose statue overlooks the beach from a nearby hillside.

ARRIVAL AND INFORMATION   COMILLAS

By bus Frequent buses use the main coast road through Comillas. Destinations San Vicente (7 daily; 15min); Santander (7 daily; 45min); Santillana (4 daily; 35min).

Turismo C/La Aldea 2 (summer Mon–Sat 9am–9pm, Sun 11am–1pm & 5–8pm; winter Mon–Sat 9am–2pm & 4–6pm, Sun 9am–2pm; ☎ 942 722 591, ⓦ comillas.es).

ACCOMMODATION

The basic choice in Comillas is between paying a bit extra to stay right by the **beach**, or settling for the cheaper options up in **town**, which is where you'll probably choose to spend the evening anyway.

Camping Comillas ☎ 942 720 074, ⓦ campingcomillas .com. Attractive campsite in a great position, right above the beach on the headland at the east side of town. Closed Oct–May, except Easter. **€25.50**

Hostal Esmeralda C/Antonio López 7 ☎ 942 720 097, ⓦ hostalesmeralda.com. Beautifully furnished place in a fine old building, with breathtaking sea views, though it's on a rather unattractive street at the east end of the old town. **€80**

Hotel Josein C/Manuel Noriega 27 ☎ 942 720 225, ⓦ www.hoteljosein.com. Custard-yellow hotel spilling down the hillside immediately above the Playa de Comillas; the lovely rooms have floor-to-ceiling sea-view windows and galleries that literally overhang the beach. The old town is an easy 10min walk away. Rates include breakfast. Closed Oct–April. **€120**

Hotel Marina de Campios C/General Pielagos 14 ☎ 942 722 754, ⓦ marinadecampios.com. Very charming hotel in a nineteenth-century house just south of the old centre, with twenty antique-furnished rooms. A/c costs €10 extra. Closed mid-Nov to March. **€120**

7

EATING AND DRINKING

Bar El Siglo Pza. de la Constitucíon 11 ☎ 646 374 424. Lovely *mesón*, with tables on the square beside a huge, very plain church, and a cosy interior where you can enjoy hearty portions of ham and cheese, or seafood *raciones* such as squid for €6 or clams for €12. Daily noon–11pm; closed Mon–Wed in winter.

Gurea C/Ignacio Fernández de Castro 11 ☎ 942 722 446. Good local cuisine in a large indoor dining room, with set menus from €14 for lunch, €22 for dinner. Mon–Sat 11am–4pm & 7.30–11pm, Sun 11am–4pm.

San Vicente de la Barquera

The approach to **SAN VICENTE DE LA BARQUERA**, marooned on both sides by the sea 12km west of Comillas, is dramatic. If you're following the coast road, you reach the town via a long causeway across the Río Escudo, the Puente de la Maza. Local lore maintains that if you manage to hold your breath all the way across the bridge, your wish will come true. Inland, dark green, forested hills rise towards the Picos de Europa, strikingly silhouetted as the sun goes down.

The town itself is functional rather than pretty, with little left of its historic core. On the other hand, it's a thriving fishing port with a string of locally famed seafood restaurants – San Vicente is usually packed with day-trippers in summer, here to spend serious money on eating and drinking. If you're looking for a **beach**, you'll find a good sweep of sand fifteen minutes' walk away, across the causeway on the east side of the river and flanked by a small forest.

A hot climb up from the modern town soon brings you to the remnants of the hilltop medieval town, which despite its intriguing setting and spectacular views turns out to be somewhat humdrum. At either end of the ridge, you'll find an impressive Renaissance **ducal palace** (Tues–Sun 11am–2pm & 5–8pm; €1.40) and a sturdy Romanesque-Gothic church, **Santa María de los Ángeles**.

ARRIVAL AND INFORMATION	**SAN VINCENTE DE LA BARQUERA**

By train The nearest station on the narrow-gauge railway is 4km south at La Alcebasa.

By bus Buses stop 100m south of the old centre, at the bottom of Avda. Miramar near the west end of the causeway.

Destinations Comillas (7 daily; 15min); Potes (3 daily; 1hr 20min); Santander (16 daily; 1hr 10min).

Turismo Avda. Generalísimo 20, in the heart of town (Tues–Sat 10am–2pm & 4–7pm, Sun 10am–2pm; ☎ 942 710 797, ⓦ sanvicentedelabarquera.es).

ACCOMMODATION AND EATING

Hotel Luzón Avda. Miramar 1 ☎ 942 710 050, ⓦ hotelluzon.net. A refined hotel close to the seafront, alongside the main square, with 36 pleasant rooms with large windows. **€70**

Pensión del Corro C/Corro 1 ☎ 942 712 613, ⓦ pension elcorro.com. On the steps leading from the back of the main square, this homely place, where the brightly painted rooms have slightly run-down bathrooms, is the cheapest central option. **€45**

★ **El Pescador** Avda. Generalísimo 26 ☎ 942 710 005. It's not immediately obvious when you peer into its cavernous interior from this street, but this large, rough-and-ready tapas-bar-cum-restaurant also offers waterfront open-air tables on the quayside around the back. There's something to suit every budget, with a wonderful-value €10 set lunch menu; a plate of anchovies, the big local speciality, for under €10; a fabulous array of seafood specialities at more like €10–20; and all sorts of pricier seafood platters and paella-type feasts. Daily noon–11pm.

The Picos de Europa

The **PICOS DE EUROPA** may not be the highest mountains in Spain, but they're the favourite of many walkers, trekkers and climbers. Designated a national park in its entirety, the range is a miniature masterpiece: a mere 40km across in either direction, shoehorned in between three great **river gorges**, and straddling the provinces of Asturias, León and Cantabria. Asturians see the mountains as a symbol of their national identity, and celebrate a cave-shrine at **Covadonga** in the west as the birthplace of Christian Spain.

Hikes in the Picos are amazingly diverse, with trails to suit all levels, from a casual morning's stroll to two- or three-day treks. Although the most spectacular and popular routes are along the 12km **Cares Gorge**, and around the high peaks reached from the cable car at Fuente Dé and the subterranean funicular railway at Poncebos, dozens of other paths explore the river valleys or climb into the mountains. Take care if you go off the marked trails: the Picos can pose extreme challenges, with unstable weather and treacherous, unforgiving terrain.

As road access has opened up, the Picos have been brought increasingly into the mainstream of tourism, and the most accessible areas get very crowded in July and August. If you have the choice, and are content with lower-level walks, spring is best, when the valleys are gorgeous and the peaks still snowcapped, although the changing colours of the beech forests in autumn give some competition.

You can **approach** – and leave – the Picos along half a dozen roads: from León, to the south; from Santander and the coast, to the north and northeast; and from Oviedo and Cangas de Onís, to the northwest. Public transport serves much of the park, but services are generally infrequent, even in summer.

The east: the Cantabrian Picos

If you're driving along the coast and want to dip briefly into the Picos, the Asturian portion of the range (see p.522) is the most readily accessible. It takes little more effort, however, to reach the **Cantabrian** section of the mountains, where following the valley of the Río Deva from **Potes** to **Fuente Dé** takes you into the very heart of the Picos. Villages such as **Espinama** make superb overnight stops, and the opportunities for **hiking** are endless.

From the coast to Potes

The N621 heads inland from the coast at **Unquera**, at the mouth of the Deva on the Cantabria–Asturias border. Decision time comes 12km along, at sleepy little **PANES**, where the C6312 forks west into Asturias, towards Arenas de Cabrales and Cangas de Onís, while the N621 continues south towards Potes.

Immediately south of Panes, you enter the eerily impressive gorge of the Río Deva, the **Desfiladero de La Hermida**, whose sheer sides are so high that they deny the village of **LA HERMIDA** any sunlight from November to April. From nearby **Urdón**, a path leads west to Sotres (see p.525); it's a pleasant few hours' walk, with mountains looming up around you.

Around 6km south of La Hermida, the village of **Lebeña** lies amid beautiful countryside, a very short detour east of the main road. Its church, **Santa María** (Tues–Sun 10am–1.30pm & 4–7.30pm; €1), built in the early tenth century by "Arabized" Christian craftsmen, is considered the supreme example of Mozarabic

---

WILDLIFE IN THE PICOS

Wildlife is a major attraction in the Picos de Europa. In the **Cares Gorge**, you may well see griffon vultures, black redstarts and ravens, while birdwatchers will want to keep a special eye out for the butterfly-like flight of the tiny, red-winged wallcreeper, named for the mouse-like way it creeps along the vertical cliff faces. Wild and domestic goats abound, with some unbelievably inaccessible high mountain pastures. **Wolves** are easy to imagine in the grey boulders of the passes, but **bears**, despite local gossip and their picturesque appearances on the tourist-board maps, are very seldom spotted. An inbred population of about a hundred specimens of *Ursus arctos pyrenaicus* (Cantabrian brown bear) remains in the southern Picos, most of them tagged with radio transmitters; another isolated group survives in western Asturias.

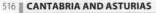

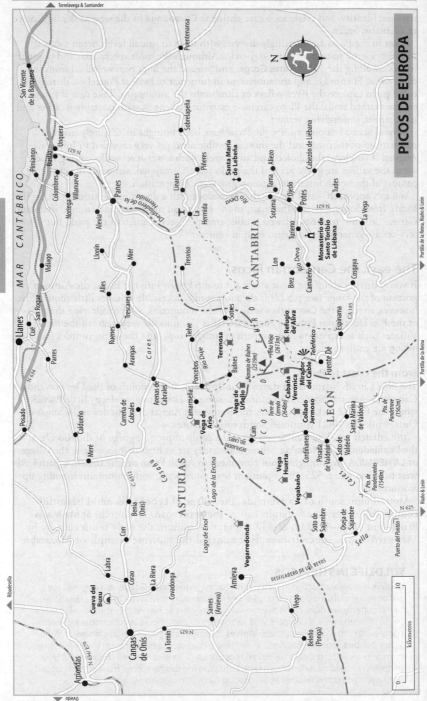

PICOS DE EUROPA

architecture, with its thoroughly Islamic geometric motifs and repetition of abstract forms.

Potes

POTES, the main road junction and travellers' base on the east side of the Picos, is still just 500m above sea level, but it's beautifully situated, at the confluence of the Deva and Quiviesa rivers in the shadow of tall white peaks. Once past its unpromising outskirts, at its core it's a lovely medieval village, tumbling down to the Río Deva in higgledy-piggledy abandon.

While Potes can get very clogged indeed with traffic and sightseers in summer, don't let that put you off visiting. Away from the main road, the central lanes and riverbanks are truly attractive, and it's well worth taking a stroll along its roughly cobbled alleyways, which are lined with good little shops and bars as well as plenty of tourist tat. Several impressive timbered mansions stand hung with vines and geraniums. The **Casa de Cultura** on C/Sol 20 (March–Oct Tues–Sun 11.30am–2pm & 5.30–8pm; €5) holds an interesting **map museum**.

Torre del Infantado

Tues–Sun: July to mid-Sept 10am–2pm & 4–8pm, mid-Sept to June 10am–2pm & 4–6pm • €3 • ☎ 942 738 107, ⓦ centros.culturadecantabria.com

The thirteenth-century **Torre del Infantado**, the landmark tower in the centre of Potes, has been beautifully converted to hold a permanent exhibition called **Beato de Liébana y Los Beatos**. While the subject matter may seem arcane – the illuminated edition of the Apocalypse of St John that was produced by a ninth-century monk called Beato in the nearby monastery of Liébana – it's actually hugely enjoyable, learned and lurid at the same time, and gloriously colourful.

ARRIVAL AND INFORMATION

POTES

By bus Potes' bus station is in the Pza. de la Independencia at the west end of town. Palomera buses run to Santander (2–3 daily, 2hr 30min) via San Vicente (1hr 30min); in summer, there are also connections to Fuente Dé (Mon–Fri 3 daily, Sat & Sun daily).

Turismo In the bus station (daily 10am–2pm & 4–6pm; ☎ 942 738 126).

ACCOMMODATION

Albergue el Portalón Vega de Liébana ☎ 942 736 048, ⓦ albergue-el-portalon.com. Private hostel, in a fine seventeenth-century building 8km south of Potes. Activities range from paragliding and mountain biking to climbing and trekking. Rates include breakfast; full board also available for €9 extra. Dorms **€15**

★ **Casa Cayo** C/Cántabra 6 ☎ 942 730 150, ⓦ casacayo .com. Very friendly and welcoming little hotel in Potes' most atmospheric old street, enjoying lovely river views, with a lively bar and excellent restaurant downstairs. Some rooms are tucked into the attic. **€60**

★ **La Casa de las Chimeneas** Tudes ☎ 942 736 300, ⓦ lacasadelaschimeneas.es. Gorgeous complex of holiday apartments, in a converted farmstead in the lovely little hilltop village of Tudes, 9km south of Potes. The English owners also run a tiny bar/café opposite, *La Taberna del Inglés*. One-night stays are not available from mid-July to mid-August, when apartments are only rented by the week. **€95**

Casa Gustavo Guesthouse Aliezo, 3km east of Potes ☎ 942 732 010, ⓦ picos-accommodation.co.uk. English-owned farmhouse B&B, which arranges skiing and canoeing. A useful resource for help and advice on making the most of the Picos for visitors who don't speak Spanish. **€60**

Hostería Antigua C/Cántabra 9 ☎ 942 730 037, ⓔ hosteriaaantigua@hotmail.com. Fine and very central old inn, with nice wooden balconies, on a narrow medieval lane. **€70**

EATING AND DRINKING

Asador Llorente C/San Roque 1 ☎ 942 738 165. The wooden balcony of this busy bar/grill, renowned for its good, cheap *raciones* and substantial cheese platters, hangs high above the Quiviesa. Daily noon–3.30pm & 8–11pm.

Casa Cayo C/Cántabra 6 ☎ 942 730 150, ⓦ casacayo.com.

7

PICOS PRACTICALITIES

ACCOMMODATION

While options of all kinds abound in the more popular villages, it's essential to book accommodation in advance, especially in summer. Alpine **refugios**, high in the mountains, range from organized hostels to free, unstaffed huts where you'll need to bring your own food. They provide blankets or hire out sleeping bags for around €1. In many places, guests have to leave their rucksacks outside the dorm, so bring a small padlock. **Camping** beside the *refugios* is accepted, and about half a dozen more campsites are scattered around the villages. Camping outside these sites is officially prohibited below 1600m, and subject to on-the-spot fines, but unofficially you won't be disturbed once away from populated areas.

ACTIVITY OPERATORS

Companies arranging activities of all kinds in the Picos, from canoeing and canyoneering to horseriding and mountain biking, include:

Cangas Aventura ☎ 985 849 261, ⓦ cangasaventura .com; offices at Avda. Covadonga 17, Cangas de Onís, and Finca La Dehesa, Arriondas.

Jaire Aventura Avda. Covadonga 14, Cangas de Onís ☎ 985 841 464, ⓦ jairecanoas.com.

Montañas del Norte El Muelle 26, Ribadesella, ☎ 985 841 035, ⓦ montanasdelnorte.com.

Picos Tour C/San Roque 6, Potes ☎ 942 730 005, ⓦ picostour.com.

Torretours Arenas de Cabrales ☎ 985 846 640, ⓦ picosadventure.com.

Turaventura Caso de la Villa 50, Ribadesella ☎ 985 860 267, ⓦ turaventura.com.

CLIMATE

Good days for walking in the valleys come along even in the depths of winter, but at high altitudes the **walking season** lasts from late June to September, varying according to the preceding winter's snowfall. All year round, the weather is unstable, with brilliant sunshine rapidly turning to clouds, cold rain or dense mist; in summer, cloud often descends on the valleys, while higher up it remains bright and clear.

EQUIPMENT

Most trails in the Picos are stony, rugged and steep; **hiking boots** are necessary on all but the easiest routes. Safe, reliable water sources are sporadic, so carry your own. The routes given in this guide, unless mentioned otherwise, are straightforward and well marked; for walks at high altitude or off the marked trails, proper equipment and experience are essential.

Very nice hotel restaurant with a river-view dining room; portions are healthy and prices are reasonable, with starters at €6–10 and mains at €11–16. The €15 *Lebaniego* stew is a huge meal in itself. Daily except Thurs 1–4pm & 8–11pm.
Casa Susa C/Cántabra 5 ☎ 942 731 014. Lively, central tapas bar with a broad selection of tasty, well-priced

raciones, and a set menu for €10. Daily noon–midnight.
Sidrería La Majada C/Independencia ☎ 629 434 627. Attractive little bar/restaurant, in an old cottage down by the river, with lots of outdoor tables. Snacks, main dishes such as chicken with apple for €11, and an €11 set menu. Daily 12.30–4pm & 7–11pm.

The Deva valley

A lovely little road, the CA185, heads west into the mountains from Potes, running beside the Río Deva below a grand sierra of peaks known as the Macizo Oriental. En route to the cliff-walled natural amphitheatre at Fuente Dé, it passes through several delightful villages.

Monasterio de Santo Toribio de Liébana

Daily : May–Sept 10am–1pm & 4–7pm, Oct–April 10am–1pm & 4–6pm • Free • ☎ 942 730 550, ⓦ santotoribiodeliebana.org

Close by Turieno, on the south bank of the river above the main road from Potes, the much-reconstructed eighth-century **Monasterio de Santo Toribio de Liébana** preserves fine Romanesque and Gothic details, and the largest claimed piece of the True Cross. It was here during the ninth century that one monk, Beato, produced illustrations of the

GUIDED WALKS

Between July and September, the national park service operates a weekly rota of free daily **guided walks** of easy to moderate standard, lasting 3–5hr and leaving from various points around the park's perimeter. These are an excellent way for novice walkers to get to know the Picos, although guides don't necessarily speak any English. The national park offices also have lists of **guiding companies** operating in each province.

MAPS

Best are the **Adrados** editions, in two 1:25,000 sheets, one covering the western massif, the other the central and eastern massifs. Adrados also publish good walking and climbing guides.

MOUNTAIN FEDERATIONS

For further information on trekking and climbing in the Picos, contact:

Federacíon de Montañismo de Asturias Oviedo ☎ 985 252 362, ⓦ fempa.net.

Federacíon de Deportes de Montaña de Castilla

y León Valladolid ☎ 983 360 295, ⓦ fclm.com.
Federacíon Cántabra de Montaña y Escalada
Reinosa ☎ 942 755 294, ⓦ fcdme.es.

NATIONAL PARK OFFICES

For **online information** on the Picos, see ⓦ reddeparquesnacionales.mma.es. The huge **visitor centre** (daily 9am–6pm; ☎ 942 738 109) at **Sotama**, 6km south of **Lebeña** in Cantabria, offers comprehensive audiovisual displays and exhibitions, plus information on guided walks. Two additional **provincial offices** provide information on routes, activities and wildlife within the park, although each tends to be short of information on the other regions: Casa Dago, Avda. Covadonga 43, Cangas de Onís, Asturias (see p.528), and Posada de Valdeón, León (see p.522). **Information centres** also operate in summer in Poncebos, Fuente Dé, Los Lagos, and Panes, while the park headquarters is at C/Arquitecto Reguera 13, Oviedo (Mon–Fri 8am–3pm; ☎ 985 241 412).

TRANSPORT

There are no drivable **roads** cross the Picos (except the 4WD track from Espinama to Sotres), and circuits by road are long and slow; if you plan to trek across the range, make sure you allow sufficient time to get back to your starting point. **Bus** services along the main roads are limited to one or two a day, and are very sketchy out of season. **Bikes** can be rented in Potes and other main towns.

Apocalypse that were so influential that they inspired the creation of similar works – all known as "Beatos" – all over medieval Europe. A few reproductions of Beato's works are on show, but there's a much better exhibition in Potes (see p.517).

Turieno

TURIENO, across the river from the main road 3km west of Potes, is a quiet village where, once you're off the highway, you're as likely to share the road with a donkey as a car. Narrow mule tracks run to nearby hamlets that scarcely see a tourist from one year to the next; the walk to **Lon** and **Brez** is especially worthwhile, through a profusion of wild flowers and butterflies.

Cosgaya

The quiet and pretty village of **COSGAYA** lies 13km southwest of Potes and 6km east of Espinama. No more than a brief riverside strip, it remains idyllic despite the presence of two large hotels, one either side of the road.

Espinama

Twenty kilometres from Potes – far enough to feel that you're deep into the heart of the mountains – **ESPINAMA** is a charming little village, spilling down the hillside at the mouth of a slender gorge cut by the little Río Nevandi. Like Cosgaya, it straddles a busy road, but when the traffic dies down after dark it's a magical spot, and in the daytime there are plenty of walks (see box opposite) in the nearby woods and meadows.

Fuente Dé

Teleférico June & Sept Mon–Fri 10am–6pm, Sat & Sun 9am–7pm; July & Aug daily 9am–8pm; shorter hours in winter • €10 one-way, €16 return • ☎ 942 736 610

The road comes to a halt 4km past Espinama, hemmed in on three sides by towering sheer-sided walls of rock. This is the source of the Río Deva; debate as to whether its name should be Fuente de Deva or Fuente de Eva has left it called simply **FUENTE DÉ**. Most visitors to this lonely spot are here to ride the **teleférico**, a cable car that climbs almost vertically up 753m of cliff. It's an extremely popular excursion throughout the year, and though the cars set off every twenty minutes, carrying twenty passengers each time and taking under five minutes for the trip, you may well have a long wait to ascend, especially in the middle of the day. If that's the case, then you'll probably find yourself queuing again to come down, which in the mountain chill, 1900m above sea level, is not nearly so congenial.

The cable car provides easy access to an extraordinary mountainscape, well worth seeing even if you don't have time to **hike** any distance from the top. Many day-trippers simply wander around close to the upper station, known as **El Cable**, where they make an incongruous spectacle with their bathing suits and toddlers in tow. The views back down to the valley are amazing, while an enticing track immediately sets off higher into the wilderness. Within a few minutes' walk there may not be another soul around, and it's easy to tailor a walk to your energy levels, or the prevailing weather conditions.

There's a simple café at the upper station, and the restaurant at the *Refugio de Aliva* (see box opposite) is less than 4km along the main trail.

ACCOMMODATION AND EATING
DEVA VALLEY

Camping La Isla Turieno ☎ 942 730 896, ⓦ campinglaislapicosdeeuropa.com. Very attractive campsite, tucked close to the river behind an orchard in Turieno, with a swimming pool and pony trekking. Closed Nov–March. **€21.30**, four-person bungalow **€76**

Camping El Redondo Fuente Dé ☎ 942 736 699, ⓦ elredondopicosdeeuropa.com. A 240-place campsite hidden away in a lovely wooded spot on the slopes above the road, with a shop and bar. Closed Oct–May. **€20**

Camping San Pelayo Baró ☎ 942 733 087, ⓦ campingsanpelayo.com. Pleasant family-oriented campsite, in a tiny village 10km up the valley west of Potes, with its own restaurant and a sizeable pool. Closed Nov–Easter. **€18.70**

Hostal Nevandi Espinama ☎ 942 736 608, ⓦ apartamentosnevandi.com. In the heart of Espinama village, the *hostal* has ten plain but comfortable en-suite doubles, with large beds; the owners also offer several larger self-catering apartments in the ravishing, even smaller hamlet of Pido just across the valley. **€50**, apartments **€66**

Hotel Cosgaya Cosgaya ☎ 942 733 230, ⓦ hotel cosgaya.es. The smaller of Cosgaya's two roadside hotels, housed in a sturdy alpine-looking stone-built mansion, offers 24 tasteful en-suite doubles, all with views, plus a pool. **€75**

★ **Hotel del Oso** Cosgaya ☎ 942 733 018, ⓦ hoteldeloso .com. Rather grand but extremely welcoming hotel, in a fine old house beside both road and river. The spacious terrace is a great place to lounge over a coffee or drink. Fifty spacious well-furnished rooms, plus a good dining room and an outdoor pool surrounded by lawns. **€85**

Hotel Rebeco Fuente Dé ☎ 942 736 600, ⓦ hotelrebeco.com. Perched at road's end in Fuente Dé, this modern hotel resembles a mountain lodge. Eleven of its thirty en-suite rooms are family-sized, and its good-value restaurant stretches onto a nice mountain-view terrace. **€65**

Parador de Fuente Dé ☎ 942 736 651, ⓦ www .paradores.es. Modern parador set in a stunning mountain amphitheatre, near the foot of the cable car. The comfort inside belies the uninspiring exterior, there's a good restaurant, and bargain off-season rates are frequently available. **€85**

Posada Javier Turieno ☎ 942 732 122, ⓦ posadajavier .com. Pretty little rural hotel, set well away from the main road amid the fields, and equipped with eight very pleasantly decorated (and centrally heated) en-suite rooms. **€60**

★ **Puente Deva** Espinama ☎ 942 736 658, ⓦ hostalpuentedeva.com. The en-suite rooms belonging to this inviting little inn are actually in a separate building,

HIKING IN THE EASTERN PICOS: FROM ESPINAMA AND FUENTE DÉ

The best starting point for hikes into the mountains from the Picos' eastern side has to be **Espinama**, though if you're at all pressed for time, taking the cable car up from **Fuente Dé** and then hiking back down to Espinama (10km; 3–4hr) makes a quick and relatively pain-free alternative.

A superb trek (12.5km; 5hr) follows a dirt track (passable in 4WD vehicles) from Espinama to **Sotres**, 8km east of Poncebos. Setting off north from Espinama, it climbs stiffly, winding past hay fields, until tall cliffs on either side form a natural gateway, and you enter a landscape of rocky summer pasture and small streams. Near the highest point, 4.5km along, the track divides; the left-hand path leads up to the *Refugio de Aliva* and the top of the cable car, but for Sotres continue straight ahead, up to the ridge forming the pass.

Over the divide the scenery changes again, into a mass of crumbling limestone. In spring and winter, the downhill stretch of track here is slippery and treacherous. Next you climb slightly once again to the east, to reach Sotres itself, which has a grim, almost fortified feel, clinging to a cliff edge above a stark green valley. A zigzag climb to the west leads in 5km (around 2hr) to the more appealing village of **Bulnes** (see p.525).

Accommodation is available in both Sotres and Bulnes, but you can also stay higher up in the mountains in the hotel-like rooms of the remote *Refugio de Aliva* (☎ 942 730 999; closed Oct–April; €50), which has a restaurant and its own fiesta, on July 2. That stands 3.5km northeast of the top of the Fuente Dé cable car, along the clearly signposted PR 24 trail, which then continues down another 2km to meet the track up from Espinama at the junction described above.

7

50m away; they're clean and correct, with valley views, but can get very cold out of season. The *Vicente Campo* restaurant in the inn itself serves absolutely delicious food year-round, with set menus from €12, fabulous steaks, and specials such as succulent roast kid for €21. Restaurant daily 8–10pm. **€42**

Remoña Espinama ☎ 942 736 605, ⓦ turismoruralremona.es. Cosy en-suite rooms above an old tavern on the main road, where the dining room serves a decent traditional set menu for €13, as well as self-contained apartments in a newly built structure nearby. Restaurant daily 8–10pm. **€49**

The south: the Leonese Picos

Although the southern flanks of the Picos de Europa lie in the region of **León**, visitors naturally experience the national park, and the mountains themselves, as a single unit. Exploring the southern side of the Picos from the north coast requires considerable time and effort, but those who do make the journey, or approach from the south, are rewarded with some of the mountains' most attractive little towns and villages, which also make a great approach to the hike along the **Cares Gorge**.

Posada de Valdeón

Whether you're approaching from León, or simply touring the perimeter of the mountains, only one route leads into the heart of the Picos from the south. It starts from the village of **POSADA DE VALDEÓN**, which stands at the junction of two minor roads. The village itself enjoys a delightful setting, surrounded by soaring mountain slopes, and makes an ideal base for hikers.

Coming **from the east**, you'll get here by way of tiny **Portilla de la Reina**, a hamlet on the N621 that's served by León–Potes buses and lies 10km southeast of the high mountain pass known as the **Puerto de San Glorio**, a total of 38km southeast of Potes. The minor and quite enchanting LE243 runs 20km north from Portilla de la Reina to Posada, its last three ravishing kilometres as a narrow single-lane track. Coming **from the west**, LE244 leaves the N625 just south of another pass, the **Puerto del Pontón**, and a total of 45km south of Cangas de Onís; it remains broad and easy for its entire 23km run to Posada. Finally, it's also possible to reach the village **on foot** from Fuente Dé, in about four hours, over a mix of dirt tracks and footpaths.

Cordiñanes and Caín

The **Río Cares** runs through Posada del Valdeón, and its gorge begins just north of the village. Over its first section, as far as Caín, it remains relatively wide, running past brilliant green meadows at the base of the cliffs, and paralleled on its eastern side by a narrow paved road. The village of **CORDIÑANES**, 2km along – and also accessible on foot, via a dirt track on the western side of the river – makes for an especially peaceful night's stop. In summer, **CAÍN** itself, 6km further north, is a pretty village where the one main street can get uncomfortably full of hikers and day-trippers; a grocery sells basic supplies.

INFORMATION
THE LEONESE PICOS

National Park office A short way up a side road just south of the centre in Posada del Valdeón (July–Sept Mon–Fri 8am–3pm, Sat & Sun 9am–2pm & 4–6.30pm; Oct–June Mon–Fri 8am–3pm; ☎ 987 740 549).

ACCOMMODATION AND EATING

Albergue Cuesta-Valdeón C/San Sebastián, Los Llanos de Valdeón ☎ 633 682 365, ⓦ alberguelacuesta .org. Simple, clean hostel just north of Posada, offering dorm beds with shared kitchen and bathrooms. Dorms **€10**

Casa Cuevas Travesía del Cares, Caín ☎ 987 740 500, ⓦ casacuevas.es. Friendly hotel/café/grill, facing the river at the final bend in the road in the centre of Caín, serving grilled meats, like a succulent chicken for €8, plus an €11 set menu, on its large terrace, and also offering decent en-suite rooms. **€42**

Cumbrés Valdeón Travesía de Soto, Posada de Valdeón ☎ 987 742 710, ⓦ cumbresvaldeon.es. Smart modern inn on the western edge of the village, where several of the comfortable rooms have mountain-view balconies. Closed mid-Dec to mid-Feb. **€60**

★ **Desván Valdeón** Travesía de Prada 10, Posada de Valdeón ☎ 987 742 733, ⓦ desvanvaldeon.com. Stylish, top-quality restaurant that serves exceptional food at affordable prices, including great salads and desserts, and delicious, delicate blue-cheese croquettes for under €10. All seating is indoors, in a well-lit upstairs dining room that also has a mountain-view balcony. The opening hours can

be erratic outside summer. Daily 1–3pm & 8–10.30pm; closed Dec–Feb.

Hostal La Ruta Travesía del Cares 15, Caín ☎ 987 742 702. Right at the opening of the gorge path, this simple modern *hostal* offers rooms with and without en-suite bathrooms. Its inexpensive restaurant serves an €11 set menu on a pleasant covered terrace. Closed mid-Oct to mid-March, restaurant open for all meals daily. **€40**

★ **Pensión Begoña** Pza. Cortina El Concejo 8, Posada de Valdeón ☎ 987 740 516. Very friendly, clean and homely place in the centre of the village, with simple shared-bath rooms in the main building, and slightly smarter en-suite rooms in an annexe at the back; prices for both are exceptionally good value. The downstairs restaurant, open for all meals daily, has outdoor tables, and serves inexpensive local food like wild boar stew and ultra-strong cheese. **€40**

La Posada del Montañero Caín ☎ 985 742 711, ⓦ asturjoven.com/posada-montanero.html. Imposing cream-coloured hotel, right at the end of the road, with decent en-suite rooms and a good terrace restaurant, open for all meals daily and serving an €11 daily set menu. Three-night minimum in Aug; closed Dec–Feb. **€56**

The Sella valley

The road running along the western end of the Picos, the N625 between Riaño and Cangas de Onís, is arguably as spectacular as the Cares Gorge. Mountains rear to all sides and for much of the way the road traces the gorge of the **Río Sella**. The central section of this, the **Desfiladero de los Beyos**, is said to be the narrowest motorable gorge in Europe – a feat of engineering rivalling anything in the Alps, and remarkable for the 1930s.

Not far south of the road's highest pass, the frequently foggy 1290-metre **Puerto del Pontón**, the exceptionally pretty village of **OSEJA DE SAJAMBRE** stands high on the steep slope of a broad and twisting valley.

The north: the Asturian Picos

The most striking thing about the northern flanks of the Picos de Europa is just how near the mountains are to the sea. There's spectacular scenery to be enjoyed barely a

7

HIKING IN THE SOUTHERN PICOS: THE CARES GORGE

Deservedly the most popular walk in the Picos takes hikers into the heart of the central massif, along the **Cares Gorge** (**Desfiladero de Cares**). Its most enclosed section, between Caín and Poncebos – a massive cleft more than 1000m deep and 12km long – bores through awesome terrain along an amazing footpath hacked out of, and at times right through, the cliff face. Maintained in excellent condition by the water authorities, it's perfectly safe. Many day-trippers simply get a taste of it by walking as far as they choose to and from Caín, but with reasonable energy, it's perfectly possible to hike its full length – in both directions – in well under a day.

The **gorge** proper begins immediately north of Caín, where the valley briefly opens out, before suddenly disappearing as a solid mountain wall blocks all but a thin vertical cleft. In its early stages, the trail burrows through the rock, before emerging onto a broad footpath. During busy periods, the first few kilometres are thronged with day-trippers thrilling at the dripping tunnels and walkways. If you're prone to a fear of heights, you may not get more than a kilometre or so from Caín, but that in itself makes a lovely walk.

Around 4km out from Caín, the crowds usually thin out. The mountains rise pale and jagged to either side, with griffon vultures circling the crags. The river drops steeply, some 150m below you at the first bridge, but closer to 300m by the end. Just over halfway along, the canyon bends to the right and widens to descend to Poncebos. Enterprising individuals run makeshift, summer-only refreshments stands. For its final 3km, the main route climbs a dry, exposed hillside.

It is, of course, equally possible to walk all or part of the gorge from the north, starting at Poncebos (see opposite).

dozen kilometres inland from resorts such as Ribadasella and Llanes. The AS114 highway runs parallel to the coast through the foothill area known as **Cabrales**, providing easy access to the mountain fastnesses that lie to the south, beyond **Poncebos** and **Covadonga**.

Arenas de Cabrales

The main village of this region, **ARENAS DE CABRALES** (shown on some maps as Las Arenas), might seem unremarkable if you simply scoot through, but stop for a while and you'll find it a cheerful, friendly little place. Not too commercialized, it holds a good selection of restaurants and inexpensive accommodation. On the last Sunday in August, Arenas hosts the **Asturian Cheese Festival**, an excuse for plenty of dancing and music but, oddly enough, not all that much cheese.

Cueva el Cares

Summer daily 10am–2pm & 4–8pm • 45min guided tour in Spanish €4.50 • ☎ 985 846 702, ⊕ fundacioncabrales.com

The Cabrales area is famed for its exceptionally strong cheese. Gastronomes will want to check out the **Cueva el Cares**, a cheese-making museum beside the river a short way down the road towards Poncebos. Guided tours lead visitors into a series of natural caves, with pungent cheeses sedately fermenting in every nook and cranny.

ARRIVAL AND INFORMATION

ARENAS DE CABRALES

By bus Three daily buses run from outside the *turismo* towards Cangas del Onís and Oviedo.

Turismo There's a helpful booth on the main street near the bridge (June–Sept Mon 9am–2pm & 4–9pm, Tues–Sun 9am–9pm; May & Oct Tues–Thurs 10am–2pm & 4–8pm, Fri–Sun 9am–9pm; ☎ 985 846 484, ⊕ cabrales.org).

ACCOMMODATION

Camping Naranjo de Bulnes ☎ 985 846 578, ⊕ campingnaranjodebulnes.com. Decently equipped campsite, with nicely shaded pitches set amid the woods and meadows 1km east of town. Closed mid-Oct to March. **€25.60**

Picos de Europa C/Mayor s/n ☎ 985 846 491, ⊕ hotelpicosdeeuropa.com. Large hotel, right by the river in the middle of town, painted an unmissable shade of orange, and offering well-equipped en-suite rooms plus a pool and a pleasant mountain-view terraza. **€70**

Torrecerredo Barrio de Vega s/n ☎ 985 846 640, ⓦ picosadventure.com. Cheerful hotel with an appealing hostel-like atmosphere, enjoying great mountain views from its perch amid the fields on the hillside a few hundred metres along a narrow lane from the west end of town. The English owners can arrange a wide range of mountain activities, including all-inclusive walking weeks. **€70**

Villa de Cabrales C/Mayor s/n ☎ 985 846 719, ⓦ hotelvilladecabrales.com. Prices at this elegant hotel, at the west end of town, drop considerably out of season, but it's good value even in summer. En-suite rooms (no. 31 is the best), a good bar, and a garden terrace with mountain views. **€75**

EATING AND DRINKING

Chigre el Orbayu C/Pedro Niembro ☎ 646 396 252. Funky little *sidrería* and café, with outdoor tables on a cobbled backstreet and an inexpensive daily set menu. They even offer a cider-based *sangría*. Daily noon–3pm & 6–11pm.

Restaurante La Panera C/Sublayende 1 ☎ 985 846 810. Garden restaurant, a short climb up from the highway just east of the main intersection. Enjoy a €15 lunchtime *menú del día*, or dinner for €23 32, while admiring the mountain views; the local beans, *fabadas Asturianas*, are the speciality. Daily 1–3pm & 7.30–10pm; closed Jan.

★ **Sidrería Calluenga** Pza. Castañedo ☎ 985 846 719. Wonderful village restaurant, on a little square set well back from the main road and open on one side to a little stream. Fabulous local dishes include clams with wild mushrooms for €12, cod with potatoes for €9, or *cazuela de arroz*, a huge casserole of rice with Cabrales cheese for €13. There's also a €15 set lunch menu. Daily 9.30am–midnight.

Poncebos

The dead end AS264 branches south off AS114 at Arenas, climbing alongside the Cares river into the mountains. Most visitors simply go the first five, easy, kilometres to **PONCEBOS**, a gloomy little spot, too small to be considered even a village, that's home to an antiquated power plant and three unattractive and somewhat institutional hotels.

If you have your own transport, you're better off staying in Arenas or further afield, but for hikers Poncebos offers the twin advantages of lying at the northern end of the **Cares Gorge**, which ranks among the Picos' very best trails, as well as at the foot of the steep, hour-and-a-half trek up the gorge of the Tejo stream to lovely little **Bulnes**.

Funicular de Bulnes

Daily: Easter & July–Sept 10am–8pm; rest of year 10am–12.30pm & 2–6pm; additional train Mon–Fri 8.30am • Adults one-way €17.10, round-trip €21.50; under-13s one-way €4.20, round-trip €6.50 • ☎ 902 422 242, ⓦ alsa.es

A bizarre **funicular railway** takes around twelve minutes to burrow 2km upwards through a long round hole in the rock from Poncebos, and emerge at a point 400m higher, just below **Bulnes**. You don't have to be a die-hard mountaineer to feel there's something not quite right about an underground railway that tunnels through a beautiful mountain landscape without so much as a glimpse of light. For the casual visitor, however, it provides easy access to the inner recesses of the Picos massif, in a much less forbidding, and more picturesque, spot than the desolation encountered at the top of the Fuente Dé cable car.

Bulnes and Sotres

The tiny but delightful stone-built mountain village of **BULNES** nestles in a cleft cut by the Río Tejo between two high peaks. Long the exclusive preserve of hardy hikers, it now also handles a daily influx of nonchalant sightseers on the funicular from Poncebos – when you emerge from the railway tunnel, it lies just a couple of hundred metres up and to the left, along an easy footpath. Many visitors now bring baby-buggies, and romping infants contrast strangely with exhausted trekkers in the two streamside cafés in the heart of the village.

SOTRES, 5km east of Bulnes on foot and also accessible by road, 9km east of Poncebos along the narrow CA1, is not one of the more attractive Picos villages. As the trailhead for a number of particularly notable hikes, however (see box, p.526), it's a well-established walkers' base.

7

HIKING IN THE NORTHERN PICOS: FROM PONCEBOS AND SOTRES

The best starting points for hikes on the northern flanks of the Picos are Poncebos and Sotres. Besides being the northern trailhead for the Cares Gorge, **Poncebos** lies at the foot of the path up to Bulnes. Allow 1hr 30min for that climb, which branches east from the gorge trail 1km south of Poncebos, across the medieval bridge of Jaya. If you have problems with vertigo, you're better off taking the funicular.

Sotres, 9km east of Poncebos along the narrow CA1, is not especially attractive, but it marks the northern end of the ravishing 12.5-kilometre hike from Espinama (see p.521), and makes a good overnight halt for walkers heading across the central Picos. A direct trail connects Sotres with Bulnes in 5km, by way of the broad, windy pass of **Pandébano**. An old, steep, cobbled path leads down to Bulnes itself.

From both Bulnes village and the pass at Pandébano, well-used paths lead up to the **Vega de Urriello**, the high pasture at the base of the **Naranjo de Bulnes** (2519m). An immense slab of orange-hued rock, the Picos' trademark peak stands aloof from the jagged grey sierras around it. The approach from Pandébano is easier, a two- to three-hour hike along a track that passes the small *refugio* of **Terenosa** (☎ 985 252 362; no food; closed Oct–April). The direct path up from Bulnes is heavy going, and takes up to six hours in bad conditions, with a slippery scree surface that's dangerous when wet. Once up on the plateau, you'll find another *refugio*, the **Vega de Urriello**, at 1953m (☎ 984 090 981), and a permanent spring, as well as large numbers of campers and rock climbers.

Experienced trekkers only, equipped with the appropriate maps and gear, can stay the night in the *Vega de Urriello* before continuing across the central massif, through an unforgiving roller-coaster landscape, to the **Cabaña Veronica** *refugio*, which is for emergency use only, and has just three bunks. An easy descent from there brings you to the top of the **Fuente Dé** cable car. Alternatively, you can continue west through further challenging terrain to another *refugio* at **Collado Jermoso** (☎ 636 998 727, ✇ www.colladojermoso.com) before dropping down the ravine of Asotín takes you finally to Cordiñanes at the top of the **Cares Gorge**.

ACCOMMODATION   BULNES AND SOTRES

★**La Casa del Chiflon** Bulnes ☎ 985 845 943, ✇ casadelchiflon.com. Lovely little B&B, offering simple en-suite rooms for two, three or four guests, a few metres from a cosy streamside bar and restaurant in the middle of Bulnes, where the owners serve hearty and very tasty mountain food. **€60**

Hotel Peña Castil Sotres ☎ 985 945 070, ✇ www .hotelpenacastil.com. Stone-built inn, in a dramatic mountain setting on the edge of Sotres, where one of the en-suite rooms can sleep a family group of up to five people. Hiking and 4WD trips available. Closed Dec–March. **€60**

Pensión Casa Cipriano Sotres ☎ 985 945 024, ✇ www.casacipriano.com. Good-value little village hotel, with fourteen en-suite B&B rooms. They can also arrange hiking and 4WD expeditions, while the dining room is open for all meals daily. **€65**

Covadonga

Cave Mon–Fri 10am–6pm, Sat 9am–6pm; free • **Museum** daily 10.30am–2pm & 4–7.30pm; €2.50 • ☎ 985 846 035, ✇ santuariodecovadonga.com

High in the northern Picos, the pilgrimage site of **COVADONGA** is renowned as the place where the **Reconquest of Spain** began. Squeezed between enormously steep slopes, it's a stupendous spot, centring on a cave set into a high cliff face, from immediately below which a powerful waterfall spurts forth. It lies 5km up a spur road that parallels the Río Reinazo south into the mountains, 4km east of Cangas de Onís.

According to Christian chronicles, in 718, the Visigothic King Pelayo and a small group of followers repelled the Moorish armies here outnumbered 31 to 400,000. While the reality was slightly less dramatic, the Moors being little more than a weary and isolated expeditionary force, the symbolism of the event lies at the heart of Asturian, and Spanish, national history, and the defeat allowed the Visigoths to regroup, slowly expanding Christian influence over the northern mountains of Spain and Portugal.

Although overwhelmed with tourists in summer, Covadonga remains a serious religious shrine. There's no village here, just a cluster of buildings dominated by a grandiose nineteenth-century pink-granite **basilica** that's more impressive from the outside than in. Alongside, the **Museo de Covadonga** displays assorted paintings and engravings.

A short walk leads through cliff-face shrines to the **cave** itself. Daily Mass is celebrated in the stone chapel at the far end, next to Pelayo's sarcophagus.

ACCOMMODATION AND EATING	COVADONGA

Gran Hotel Pelayo ☎985 846 061, ⓦgran hotelpelayo.com. In truth this large hotel, next to the cave, is something of an eyesore, but once you're inside the views are tremendous, and the rooms are generally very comfortable. **€70**

Hospedería del Peregrino ☎985 846 047, ⓦpicosdeeuropa.net/peregrino. Cheap and cosy little *fonda* on the main road below the cave town, with an excellent restaurant, open for lunch and dinner daily, that specializes in *fabada asturiana*. Closed Nov to mid-March. **€40**

Lago de Enol and Lago de la Ercina

Beyond Covadonga, the road climbs sharply to reach the placid **mountain lakes** of Enol and **La Ercina** after 12km. To no specific schedule, however, it's often closed to all private traffic in summer, at which times visitors have to catch shuttle buses from Cangas de Onís.

The **Mirador de la Reina**, a short way before the lakes, gives an inspiring view of the assembled peaks. From the higher Lago de la Ercina, a good path leads east–southeast within three hours to the **Vega de Ario**, where there's a **refugio** (☎650 092 000, ⓦrefugiovegadeario.es; closed Nov–April), camping on the meadow, and unsurpassed **views** across the Cares Gorge to the highest peaks in the central Picos.

Most walkers, however, trek south from the lakes to the **Vegarredonda** *refugio* (☎985 922 952, ⓦvegarredonda.com). This popular route initially follows a dirt track but later becomes an actual path through a curious landscape of stunted oaks and turf. Vegarredonda, about three hours' walk, overlooks the very last patches of green on the Asturias side of the Cornión massif. From here the path continues west for another hour up to the viewing point, the **Mirador de Ordiales**.

Cangas de Onís

The busy market town of **CANGAS DE ONÍS** stands at the junction of the main routes between the Picos and central Asturias. The surrounding peaks provide a magnificent if distant backdrop to its big sight – the so-called **Puente Romano** (Roman Bridge), splashed across the front of many local tourist brochures. Although this high-arched bridge, with its cross dangling beneath, has been rebuilt many times, it retains a good deal of charm.

As an early residence of the fugitive Asturian-Visigothic kings, Cangas lays claim to the title of "First Capital of Christian Spain". Today, however, it belies such history; only a small area of town, well east of the river, retains any of its medieval architecture. Instead it's a somewhat scruffy, workaday place, specializing in activity tourism, that's nonetheless ideal for a comfortable night, a drink in a nice little bar, and a solid meal after a spell in the mountains. It also abounds in stores selling souvenir packages of delicious local drinks and food products, such as Cabrales cheese, cured meats, cider and multicoloured *fabadas* (beans).

Capilla de Santa Cruz

Mon–Fri 10am–2pm & 4–7pm, Sat 10am–2pm & 4–7.30pm • Free

The curious little **Capilla de Santa Cruz** is a fifteenth-century rebuilding of an eighth-century chapel that counts as one of the earliest Christian sites in Spain. It was founded over a Celtic dolmen, now visible through an opening in the floor. To get there from the bridge, take the first left off the main road eastwards, the Avenida de Covadonga, and cross Río Güeña.

By bus Alsa buses (ⓦalsa.es) connect Cangas with Arenas de Cabrales (5 daily; 35min); Covadonga (5 daily; 15min); Llanes (1 daily in Aug; 50min); Posada de Valdeón (2 daily in summer; 2hr 30min); and Ribadesella (1 daily; 30min).
Turismo Avda. de Covadonga 1, immediately east of the bridge (July–Sept daily 10am–10pm; Oct–June Mon–Sat 10am–2pm & 4–7pm, Sun 10am–2pm; ☎985 848 043, ⓦcangasdeonis.com).
National Park office Casa Dago, Avda. de Covadonga 43

(July–Sept Mon–Fri 8am–3pm, Sat & Sun 9am–2pm & 4–7pm; Oct–June Mon–Fri 8am–3pm; ☎985 848 614, ⓦreddeparquesnacionales.mma.es).
Tours The many activity operators in Cangas (see p.518) can arrange tours and adventures of all kinds. Jaire Aventura, Avda. Covadonga 14 (☎985 841 464, ⓦjairecanoas.com) offers a €40 day-trip that drops hikers off at Caín and picks them up in Poncebos after walking the Cares Gorge.

Hotel Covadonga Avda. de Castilla 38 ☎985 848 135, ⓦhotel-covadonga.com. Simple but friendly hotel, a 5min walk south of the centre, offering plain, good-value rooms with river views. **€60**
Hotel Nochendi Constantino González 4 ☎985 849 513, ⓦhotelnochendi.com. Much the fanciest hotel in the middle of Cangas, with crisp, neat, modern rooms with stylish bathrooms, and its own good restaurant. Closed Jan. **€99**
Hotel Puente Romano Puente Romano 8 ☎985 849 339, ⓦhotelpuenteromanocangas.com. Ochre-coloured

villa in a great location beside the bridge on the west bank of the river, holding 27 sizeable, comfortable rooms. **€75**
Parador de Cangas de Onís Villanueva, Cangas de Onís ☎985 849 402, ⓦwww.parador.es. Spacious and fancy parador, in the sumptuously restored monastery of La Vega, 2km north of town towards Arriondas. **€150**
Pensión Labra Avda. de Castilla 1, 1° B ☎985 849 047, ⓦpensionlabra.com. Inexpensive en-suite rooms, very close to the bridge, in an apartment in a modern block above the main-street shops. Not all rooms have windows. **€50**

El Corcho C/Ángel Tarano 5 ☎985 849 477, ⓦsidreriacangasdeonis.com. The pick of several classic *sidrerías* in this small alleyway, just east of Pza. Ayuntamiento. Lots of outdoor tables (equipped with nifty cider-pouring devices), and a great range of snacks, like *patatas con Cabrales* for €5 or peppers stuffed with prawns and cod for €9. Daily except Tues 11am–4pm & 6pm–midnight.
La Golosa Avda. de Covadonga 4 ☎985 849 007. This stylish café-bakery, close to the bridge, is an elegant breakfast option with a good array of pastries. Tues–

Sun 8am–10pm.
★**La Sifonería** C/San Pelayo 28 ☎985 849 055, ⓦlasifoneria.net. Small *sidrería* and tapas bar, kitted out with a great collection of antique soda siphons, not far south of Avda. de Covadonga. With its attractive tiled decor and hearty mountain food, it's always packed with locals; be sure to try a delicious €12 *sartén*, a single-pan melange of, for example, ham, eggs and potatoes. The same owners run a fully fledged restaurant two doors away. Mon & Wed–Sun noon–4pm & 7pm–midnight.

The Asturian coast: Llanes to Lastres

Once you get into Asturias, the coast becomes wilder and more rugged, as it parallels the **Picos de Europa** just 20km inland. The **narrow-gauge (FEVE) line** hugs the shoreline as far as **Ribadesella**, an attractive little fishing port, before turning inland towards Oviedo. Beyond Ribadesella, towards Gijón, there are fewer appealing towns, though the fishing village of **Lastres** makes a pretty stop.

Llanes

Asturias's easternmost resort, **LLANES**, is a delightful seaside town, crammed between the foothills of the Picos and a particularly majestic stretch of the coast. To the east and west stretch sheer cliffs, little-known beaches and a series of beautiful coves, yours for the walking. The three town beaches are small but pleasant and very central, while the excellent **Playa Ballota** is only 3km to the east, with its own supply of spring water down on the sand (and a nudist stretch). A long *rambla*, the **Paseo de San Pedro**, runs along the top of the dramatic cliffs above the western town beach, the little **Playa del Sablón**.

In the centre of town, a tidal stream lined with cafés and seafood restaurants runs down into a small harbour. In the **old town** itself, a tangle of lanes twists around a small hill to the west and tall medieval walls shelter a number of impressive buildings in various stages of restoration or decay, which include the **Torre Medieval**; the semi-ruined and overgrown Renaissance palaces of the **Duques de Estrada** and the **Casa del Cercau** (both closed to the public); and the **Basílica de Santa María**, built in the plain Gothic style imported from southern France.

ARRIVAL AND INFORMATION
LLANES

By train Llanes' narrow-gauge railway station is a short walk southwest of the centre.
Destinations Oviedo (4 daily; 2hr 30min); Ribadesella (4 daily; 35min); Santander (2 daily; 2hr 5min).
By bus The bus terminal is at the bottom end of C/Pidal, not far southeast of the stream.

Destinations Gijón (5 daily; 1hr 40min); Ribadesella (8 daily; 30min); San Vicente (4 daily; 30min).
Turismo C/Posada Herrera (mid-June to mid-Sept daily 10am–2pm & 5–9pm; mid-Sept to mid-June Mon–Sat 10am–2pm & 4–6.30pm, Sun 10am–2pm; ☎ 985 400 164, ⊛ llanes.com).

ACCOMMODATION

Camping La Paz Playa de Vidiago ☎ 985 411 235, ⊛ campinglapaz.com. Wonderful ocean-view campsite, located on a dramatic headland overlooking a lovely, undeveloped sandy beach, 5km east of Llanes and a 10min walk from Vidiago station. Closed mid-Oct to mid-April. **€29**
El Habana Hotel de Campo La Pereda s/n, Llanes ☎ 985 402 526, ⊛ www.elhabana.net. Large, very welcoming country-house hotel in a peaceful little village just 3km inland from Llanes, set against the foothills of the Picos. Spacious and nicely furnished rooms, plus a pool and a dining room for guests only. Closed Nov–March. **€129**

Hotel Sablón Playa del Sablón 1 ☎ 985 401 987, ⊛ www.hotelsablon.com. Slightly fading red-brick hotel in an irresistible location, perched on the bluff just above the Playa del Sablón, a short walk west of the old town. Most, but not quite all, of the spacious tiled-floor rooms have large sea-view windows. **€120**
Posada del Rey C/Mayor 11 ☎ 985 401 332, ⊛ laposadadelrey.es. This attractive little hotel, in a lively and thus potentially noisy lane in the heart of old Llanes, offers comfortable, pleasantly furnished en-suite rooms. **€113**

EATING AND DRINKING

El Almacén C/Posada Herrera s/n ☎ 985 403 007, ⊛ sidreria-el-almacen.com. Cosy *sidrería*, tucked away in a very quiet spot just inside the walls near the *turismo*, with outdoor tables and a wide selection of tapas and small plates, including all sorts of mushrooms, as well as €6 bottles of wine. Daily 1–3pm & 6–11pm.

★ **El Bodegón** Pza. de Siete Puertas ☎ 985 400 185. This characterful old-style tavern, spilling out onto benches in a pretty tree-shaded square near the harbour, is good for *sidra* and Asturian *raciones*, with its seafood specialities typically costing €7.50 to €11. Daily except Thurs noon–4pm & 7.30pm–midnight.

ASTURIAN FOOD AND DRINK

Asturian food is not for the faint-hearted, and it's certainly not for vegetarians. The signature dish is **fabada**, a dense haricot-bean stew floating with pungent chunks of meat: black pudding, chorizo and ham. It's served in a round terracotta dish, and you mop up the juice with the ubiquitous hunk of solid bread. **Seafood** is another feature, from sea urchins – particularly popular in Gijón – to sea bream and squid. The region produces a huge variety of **handmade cheeses**, most notably the blue-veined, pungent and totally delicious *cabrales*, which, in its purest form, is made with cow, sheep, and goats' milk combined. Another variety is a small cone-shaped cheese, known as *afuega'l pitu*, which sometimes has a wrinkled exterior owing to its having been hung in cloth.

Everywhere you go, you're bound to see waiters and punters pouring **sidra** (cider) – which you can only order by the bottle – from above their heads into wide-rimmed glasses. The idea is that you knock back the frothing brew in one go. Since it's a point of honour for the waiters to stare straight ahead rather than look at the glasses, and any residue that you don't drink within a minute or two is summarily discarded on the floor, it's hardly surprising the region seems to reek of stale cider.

Confitería Vega C/Mercaderes 8 ☎985 400 822, ☻confiteriavegallanes.com. This old-fashioned bakery and cake shop is a great place for takeaway goodies. Daily 8am–3pm & 4.30–9pm.

La Covadonga C/Manuel Cué 8 ☎985 400 891.

White-tablecloth restaurant with some outdoor seating on an alley just up from the harbour, serving a great-value €11 set menu that includes three courses plus wine. Tues–Sun 12.30–3.30pm & 7.30–10.30pm.

Ribadesella

The unaffected old port of **RIBADESELLA**, 18km west of Llanes, at the mouth of the Sella river, is linked by a bridge to a sedate resort area that faces one of the finest **beaches** in Asturias. The attractive **old town**, crammed up against the hillside to the east, consists of successive, long stone alleyways, running parallel to the **fishing harbour** and bursting with great little bars and *comedores*. In the seafood joints lining the harbour you can sample delicacies such as *centolla* (spider crab) and *lubina* (sea bass), as well as Asturian specialities.

Across the bridge to the west, ten minutes' walk from the old town, the excellent town beach, **Playa Santa Marina**, is lined with the impressive nineteenth-century mansions built by returning emigrants who'd prospered in the Americas. The seafront itself is a pleasant pedestrian promenade.

Cueva Tito Bustillo

Cave mid-April to Oct Wed–Sun first tour 10.15am, last 5pm • **Museum** Feb–June & mid-Sept to Dec Wed–Fri 10am–2.30pm & 3.30–6pm, Sat & Sun 10am–2.30pm & 4–7pm; July to mid-Sept Wed–Sun 10am–7pm; cave and museum closed for several days in early Aug, exact dates vary • Cave and museum €7.20, no children under 7; museum only €5.20; both free Wed • ☎985 185 860, ☻centrotitobustillo.com

Sealed by a landslide around 12,000 years ago, and only rediscovered in the late 1960s, the **Cueva Tito Bustillo** on the west side of the river is adorned with a remarkable collection of **prehistoric paintings**, created between 25,000 BC and 10,000 BC. Best known for its vivid depictions of horses, it's also quite a natural wonder, with mighty stalactites hanging from the ceiling.

The cave is located a short walk from the old town – turn left along the riverbank from the west end of the bridge. Tickets are sold in a modern **museum** a couple of minutes' further walk from the cave entrance, but you can only see the cave itself on guided tours, restricted to 350 visitors per day; it's necessary to **reserve** far in advance, by phone or online. Otherwise, barring last-minute no-shows, you're unlikely to get inside, and will have to settle for the museum's excellent displays on ancient art and artefacts from all over the region.

If you are lucky enough to join a cave tour, you'll encounter an experience more akin to entering a long tunnel than a cave, particularly since the current entrance is a man-made passageway. There's no elevation change, you simply penetrate for around half a mile further into the hillside to reach the main chamber. A quick-fire Spanish guide points out the intricacies of the paintings, many of which are superimposed one atop the other and thus hard for the uninitiated to decipher.

ARRIVAL AND INFORMATION   RIBADESELLA

By train Ribadesella's narrow-gauge railway station is a stiff climb up from the old town on C/Santander. Destinations Llanes (4 daily; 35min); Oviedo (4 daily; 3hr); Santander (2 daily; 1hr 30min).

By bus The bus station is near the tourist office, at the east end of the bridge.

Turismo In the old town, on Paseo Princesa Letizia at the east end of the bridge (May, June & mid-Sept to Oct Mon–Sat 10am–2pm & 5–8pm, Sun 11am–2pm; July to mid-Sept daily 10am–10pm; Nov–April Tues–Sat 10am–2pm & 4–6.30pm, Sun 11am–2pm; ☎985 860 038, ☻ribadesella.es).

ACCOMMODATION

Albergue Ribadesella C/Ricardo Cangas 1 ☎985 861 105, ☻albergueribadesella.com. Not surprisingly, this

gorgeous hostel, set in a beachfront mansion facing the Playa Santa Marina, is often booked out by groups. Rates include breakfast; over-25s pay €2 extra. Closed Nov. Dorms €13

Camping Ribadesella C/Sebreño ☎985 858 293, ⓦcamping-ribadesella.com. Ribadesella's best campsite is a few hundred metres from the sea, just south of the main road, beyond the west end of the beach, but has a great outdoor pool and a covered indoor one. Closed Oct–June except Easter. €26, bungalow €77

Hotel Ribadesella Playa C/Ricardo Cangas 3 ☎985 860 715, ⓦhotelribadesellaplaya.com. While it's not the most spectacular of the beachside villas, this affordable option offers pleasant rooms – many with great sea views – for reasonable rates, as well as buffet breakfasts. The old town is within easy walking distance. €125

Hotel Villa Rosario C/Dionisio Ruizsánchez 6 ☎985 860 090, ⓦgranhoteldelsella.com. A gingerbread confection of pyramidal turrets and enamelled chrome tiles, this grand seafront mansion includes a wooden-decked terrace and a covered beach-view restaurant. The lovely light rooms in the villa proper, also known as "El Palacete", are preferable to those in the modern extension alongside, *Villa Rosario II*. €185

Pensión Arbidel C/Escura 1 ☎985 860 141, ⓦarbidelpension.com. Inexpensive, cheerful little option, back from the sea at the south end of the old town, offering pleasant en-suite rooms above the town's best restaurant (see below). €60

Puente del Pilar C/Puente del Pilar ☎985 860 446, ⓦdesdeasturias.com/puentedelpilar. The best-value hotel on the west side of the bridge, albeit set 200m back from the sea beside a muddy stream. Sixteen very tasteful rooms, peaceful gardens, and a restaurant serving traditional Asturian food. Closed Oct–Easter. €80

EATING AND DRINKING

★**Arbidel** C/Escura 1 ☎985 861 440, ⓦarbidel.com. Lovely little restaurant in the old town, tucked into a backstreet, with indoor and outdoor tables. The best way to sample its Michelin-starred modern cuisine, which places an emphasis on light, zestful seafood dishes, is on the €30 tasting menu. Tues–Sat 1.30–3.45pm & 8.30–11.45pm, Sun 1.30–3.45pm.

Casa Gaspar C/López Muñiz 6 ☎985 857 663. Popular cider-house restaurant, with lots of outdoor tables on a pedestrian square in the heart of the old town, a few blocks inland. The great-value €10 set lunch menu offers *fabadas asturianas* followed by a substantial meat or fish main course; set dinner menus start at €15. Daily 11am–midnight.

Sidrería La Marina C/Manuel Caso de la Villa ☎985 861 219. Big, buzzy place, facing the port on a busy road and offering anything from full meals to €12 steaks and tasty snacks. Kitchen Tues–Sun 11.30am–4pm & 7.30pm–midnight.

Lastres

LASTRES, off the Santander–Gijón highway 25km west of Ribadesella, below larger **Colunga**, is a tiny fishing village built dramatically on a steep and very verdant cliffside. Day-trippers huff and puff their way along its precipitous pedestrian lanes, down to the modern harbour, but it's a nice enough place to consider spending a night or two, with the bonus of a couple of good beaches on its outskirts.

ACCOMMODATION AND EATING   **LASTRES**

Casa Eutimio C/San Antonio s/n ☎985 850 012, ⓦcasaeutimio.com. Very nice en-suite rooms comfortably furnished in warm colours, in a great location above the port. Good seafood restaurant, serving all meals daily. €66

Costa Verde Playa la Griega ☎985 856 373. Large, well-maintained campsite, with grassy pitches set close to an excellent beach, 2km east of Llastres. Closed Oct–Easter. €25

Gijón

With 275,000 inhabitants, the port of **GIJÓN** (Xixón) is the largest city in Asturias. Despite its industrial reputation, it remains largely surrounded by open green countryside, and it's a genuinely enjoyable place to visit, with its dynamic old core flanked either side by a huge curving **beach** and a vibrant pleasure port. Much of the city had to be rebuilt after the intensive bombardment it suffered during the Civil War; when miners armed with sticks of dynamite stormed the barracks of the Nationalist-declared army, the beleaguered colonel asked ships from his own side, anchored offshore, to bomb his men rather than let them be captured.

7

Gijón fans back along the coast in both directions from the stark rocky headland known as **Cimadevilla**, with the modern marina of the pretty **Puerto Deportivo** to the west (and the commercial port out of sight beyond that), and the town beach to the east. War damage has left little to see on Cimadevilla itself, though high up at the tip of the promontory a grassy park enjoys great views of the Cantabrian Sea, framed by Eduardo Chillida's sculpture *Elogio del Horizonte* (Eulogy to the Horizon). The epicentre of today's city lies at the narrow "neck" of the peninsula, immediately south of Cimadevilla. On its western side, the **Pza. del Marqués** holds a statue of Pelayo, the eighth-century king who began the Reconquest.

In the second week of July, the city hosts the **Semana Negra** (ⓦsemananegra.org), an arts festival that centres on the El Moliñón football stadium in Parque Isabel La

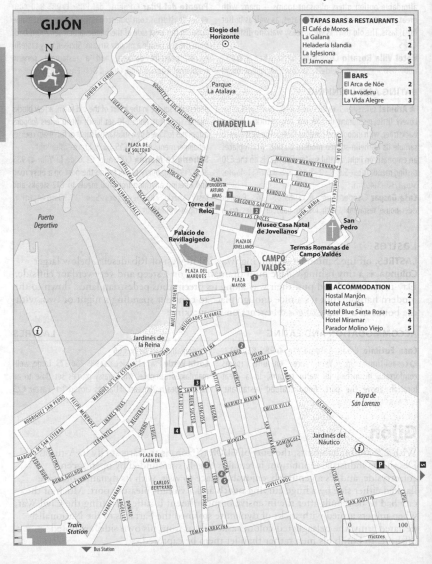

GIJÓN

N

● TAPAS BARS & RESTAURANTS
El Café de Moros	3
La Galana	1
Heladería Islandia	2
La Iglesiona	4
El Jamonar	5

■ BARS
El Arca de Nöe	2
El Lavaderu	1
La Vida Alegre	3

■ ACCOMMODATION
Hostal Manjón	2
Hotel Asturias	1
Hotel Blue Santa Rosa	3
Hotel Miramar	4
Parador Molino Viejo	5

Elogio del Horizonte

Parque La Atalaya

CIMADEVILLA

PLAZA DE LA SOLEDAD

Puerto Deportivo

MAXIMINO MARINO FERNANDEZ

BATERIA

PLAZA PERIODISTA ARTURO ARIAS

SANTA CANDIDA

MARIA BANDUJO

GREGORIO GARCIA JOVE

Torre del Reloj

ROSARIO LAS CRUCES

San Pedro

Museo Casa Natal de Jovellanos

Palacio de Revillagigedo

PLAZA DE JOVELLANOS

Termas Romanas de Campo Valdés

CAMPO VALDÉS

PLAZA DEL MARQUÉS

PLAZA MAYOR

MUELLE DE ORIENTE

MELQUIADES ÁLVAREZ

Jardínes de la Reina

TRINIDAD

SANTA ELENA

SAN ANTONIO

JULIO SOMOZA

LE MERCED

INSTITUTO

SANTA ROSA

RÍURA SUCESO

ESPACIOSA

BEGONA

MARTÍNEZ MARINA

EMILIO VILLA

SAN BERNARDO

DOMÍNGUEZ GIL

CABRALES

ELCURIDA

Playa de San Lorenzo

Jardínes del Náutico

RODRIGUEZ SAN PEDRO

FELIPE MENENDEZ

MARQUÉS DE SAN ESTEBAN

CERVANTES

LINARES RIVAS

SANTA LUCIA

HUONU

LERUEL

S. REGUERAL

PLAZA DEL CARMEN

BEGONA

LEON

MUNUZA

AGUA

LOS MOROS

JOVELLANOS

SAN AGUSTÍN

JACOBO OLAÑETA

MARQUÉS DE SAN ESTEBAN

PEDRO DURO

ZARACONDEGUI

NUMA GUILHOU

EL CARMEN

ÁLVAREZ GARAYA

DONATO ARGÜELLES

CARLOS BERTRAND

TOMÁS ZARRACINA

P

Train Station

Bus Station

0 ___ 100
metres

5

Católica, and incorporates poetry recitals, art displays and cultural performances amid much general partying.

Palacio de Revillagigedo

Pza. del Marqués 2 • June–Aug Tues–Fri 6–9pm, Sat & Sun 11.30am–2.30pm & 6–9pm; Sept–May irregular hours • Free • ☎ 985 346 921

Dominating the seafront Pza. del Marqués, the **Palacio de Revillagigedo** is a splendid mix of neo-Baroque and neo-Renaissance styles, and, in its own way, its light modern interior is every bit as striking as the eighteenth-century facade. The complex is used for annual exhibitions, and also hosts music, theatre and other cultural events.

Museo Casa Natal de Jovellanos

Pza. de Jovellanos Tues–Fri 9.30am–2pm & 5–7.30pm, Sat & Sun 10am–2 & 5–7.30pm • Free • ☎ 985 185 152, ⊛ museos.gijon.es

While few non-Spanish visitors may be familiar with the politician and writer Gaspar Melchor de Jovellanos (1744–1811), it's well worth dropping into the spacious and very central house where he was born. As well as exhibits on the man himself, the **Museo Casa Natal de Jovellanos** holds an enjoyable collection of Asturian art, including a fascinating self-portrait by the stylish Julia Alcayde (1885–1939), and the glossy hardwood sculptures of José María Navascués (1934–79), blending human figures with machines.

Termas Romanas de Campo Valdés

Tues–Fri 9.30am–2pm & 5–7.30pm, Sat & Sun 10am–2pm & 5–7.30pm • €2.50, free Sun • ☎ 985 185 151, ⊛ museos.gijon.es

An inconspicuous entrance from the seafront promenade just north of the end of the San Lorenzo beach, on the east side of the peninsula, leads to the remarkable **Termas Romanas** (Roman Baths) of ancient Gigia. Uncovered during an aborted attempt to build an underground car park, they lie beneath an open park in front of the San Pedro church. A subterranean museum displays their history and use, while walkways allow you to crisscross the actual ruins.

Playa de San Lorenzo

The sands of the **Playa de San Lorenzo**, a lengthy golden beach reminiscent of the one at San Sebastián, curve 2km westwards from Campo Valdés. In the summer, the whole city seems to descend here on afternoons and weekends, which makes things pretty crowded when the strand dwindles at high tide. All year round, it's the focus of the evening *paseo*, and even on the gloomiest winter day some hardy surfer is usually braving the waves. At the far end of the beach, the tranquil Parque Isabel La Católica stretches back along the east bank of the Río Piles.

ARRIVAL AND INFORMATION	GIJÓN

By boat LD Lines (⊛ ldlines.co.uk) connect Gijón by ferry services with Poole in England (1 weekly; crossing time 25hr) and Ste-Nazaire in France (3 weekly; crossing time 15hr).

By train Local RENFE trains use the station on Pza. El Humedal, 300m south of the *turismo*; these include services on the narrow-gauge line formerly known as FEVE, on which passengers using coastal services both east and west have to change at El Berrón. Long-distance RENFE services arrive at a separate station on Avda. de Juan Carlos I, another 300m west. Destinations Narrow-gauge: Oviedo (every half-hour; 30min); RENFE; León (6 daily; 2hr 30min); Madrid (5 daily; 5hr 15min–7hr 30min); Oviedo (5 daily; 25min).

By bus The wonderful Art Deco bus station is just south of the narrow-gauge station, between C/Ribadesella and C/Llanes. The express bus from Asturias airport costs €8 (7am–11.20pm; 45min).

Turismo Gijón's *turismo* is on a broad jetty in the middle of the marina (daily 10am–2.30pm & 4.30–7.30pm; ☎ 985 341 771, ⊛ www.gijon.info). There's a summer-only office in the Jardines del Náutico (May to mid-July & Sept–Oct daily 10am–8pm, mid-July to Aug daily 10am–10pm). Both sell the Gijón Card, which gives free admission to the city's museums, free use of public transport, and many other discounts (€10/12/15 for 1/2/3 days; half-price on Tues).

ACCOMMODATION

Hostal Manjón Pza. del Marqués 1 ☏ 985 352 378, ⓦ hostalmanjon.com. This large modern block offers adequate en-suite rooms at good prices, in a convenient location for both the old town and the harbour; the best rooms have sea views. €50

Hotel Asturias Pza. Mayor 11 ☏ 985 350 600, ⓦ hotelasturiasgijon.com. Friendly but pricey hotel on the attractive main square between the beach and port, with a choice between "modern" or "classic" rooms. The somewhat aseptic on-site café serves a €10 lunch menu. €110

Hotel Blue Santa Rosa C/Santa Rosa 4 ☏ 985 091 919, ⓦ bluehoteles.es. Modern hotel in very central location near the old town, which rather extraordinarily manages to have its own underground car park, as well as a little café and street-level terrace. The bedrooms are small, but they're dazzlingly bright and clean, with a/c and blue bed linens; some have galleried windows. €97

Hotel Miramar C/Santa Lucía 9 ☏ 985 351 108, ⓦ www.hotelmiramargijon.com. Tastefully restored hotel, close to the action immediately south of the old town, with presentable rooms that are better value in low season. €80

Parador Molino Viejo Parque de Isabel La Católica ☏ 985 370 511, ⓦ www.parador.es. The usual luxurious standard of parador accommodation, set in a converted water mill in an attractive park 500m inland from the east end of the beach. €150

EATING AND DRINKING

The streets around the seafront and immediately behind contain a mass of little **café-restaurants**, all reasonably priced and most with a set menu. If in doubt, head to any of the *sidrerías* around Pza. Mayor.

El Café de Moros C/de los Moros 13. Spacious, old-fashioned, wooden-floored café, with a real homely feeling, set in a high-ceilinged former sewing-machine shop and using old sewing tables. Especially good for breakfast and strong coffee; no outdoor seating. Mon–Fri 8.30am–10pm, Sat & Sun 9.30am–3pm & 6–10pm.

La Galana Pza. Mayor 10 ☏ 985 172 429, ⓦ restauranteasturianolagalana.es. This great big bar/restaurant on the central square is Gijón's best-known rendezvous for cider and food, from snacks to full meals. Packed out every night, it's very friendly and welcoming, with tapas portions for €5–7, *raciones* for more like €10, a daily set menu for €12, and a big selection of *cazuelina* stews. Daily noon–4pm & 7pm–1.30am.

Heladería Islandia C/San Antonio 4 ☏ 985 350 747, ⓦ heladeriaislandia.com. Inventive ice-cream joint offering (among other flavours) *sidra*, *fabada* and *cabrales* cheese. Daily 10am–2.30pm & 5–11pm.

La Iglesiona C/Begoña 34 ☏ 985 171 417, ⓦ laiglesiona.com. Among the larger of the enticing tapas bars that line "La Ruta", with a fine array of hams hanging from the ceiling. Order a glass of wine and you'll be given some free snacks, or pay €17 for a plate of melt-in-your mouth *jamón iberico*. They also do a great line in €10–13 *tortillas*, including *tortilla de bacalao* (cod). Tues–Sat 11am–4pm & 8pm–midnight, Sun 11am–4pm.

El Jamonar C/Begoña 38 ☏ 985 342 844. Atmospheric old-school tapas bar, serving *raciones* and good fish dishes, with a great-value three-course €8.50 menu on weekdays, plus various set menus for two, including Gallego, Gourmet and Grill options, priced at €28–40. Daily noon–2.30pm & 8pm–midnight.

NIGHTLIFE

At the weekend, a lively **nightlife** scene kicks off around the area known as **La Ruta**, a grid enclosed by C/Santa Lucía, C/Buen Suceso and C/Santa Rosa, a few hundred yards east of Pza. del Carmen. People also head to Cimadevilla, whose bars are crammed in summer, C/Rufo Rendueles and its extensions along the beach. The main **clubbing** area is focused around **El Náutico** farther north, and along the streets nearby, especially lively C/Jacobo Olañeta and C/San Agustín.

BARS

El Arca de Nöe C/Esculto Sebastián Miranda 1 ☏ 985 351 437. When you've had your fill of raucous *sidrerías*, get a cool taste of Montmartre at this arty jazz bar, with its open shuttered windows and fine wines; there's no food, though. Daily 6pm–1am.

El Lavaderu Pza. Periodista Arturo Arias 1 ☏ 985 359 380, ⓦ ellavaderu.wordpress.com. On summer evenings, youthful crowds – and copious quantities of cider – spill out from this charming old-fashioned bar, just up from the port, to fill the wide square outside, which as well as large tables holds a broad staircase ideal for soaking up the sun. Come at a quieter moment, though, and it's a great spot for an outdoor meal, with all the usual *raciones* at €9–19, and a daily €11 set lunch menu. Daily except Tues 11am–1am.

La Vida Alegre C/Buen Suceso 8. The most laidback bar on La Ruta, with fairy lights and exposed brick walls and a cool mambo soundtrack. Mon–Fri 1–3pm & 7pm until late, Sat & Sun 7pm until late.

Avilés

Determined to consign its gritty industrial reputation to the past, the city of **AVILÉS**, 23km west from Gijón, has greatly cleaned up its act in recent years. While its arcaded **old town**, on the west bank of the namesake Ría de Avilés, is looking spruce, the futuristic **Centro Niemeyer**, immediately across the river, is an architectural showpiece that sadly seems unlikely to survive.

The old town

Strewn with fourteenth- and fifteenth-century churches and palaces, Avilés' likeable **old town** is home to most of the city's shops, bars and places to stay, as well as the pretty, walled **Parque de Ferrera**.

Churches worth a closer look include the Romanesque **San Nicolás de Bari**, on C/San Francisco, and the thirteenth-century **Santo Tomás**. La Iglesia de los Padres Franciscanos contains the tomb of Don Pedro Menéndez de Avilés, the first governor of Spanish Florida, who founded the first European city in what is now the United States, St Augustine, in 1565.

There are also some superb palaces, especially the Baroque **Camposagrado**, in Pza. Camposagrado, built in 1663 and now serving as an art school, and the seventeenth-century **Palacio de Marqués de Ferrera** in Pza. de España, now an expensive hotel. Around the corner on C/San Francisco is the city's most distinctive monument, the seventeenth-century **Fuente de los Caños**, with its six grotesque heads spouting water.

Centro Niemeyer

☏ 984 835 031, ⓦ niemeyercenter.org

Great hopes for Avilés' twenty-first-century regeneration project were pinned on the **Centro Niemeyer**, a multipurpose cultural complex constructed on a former industrial site directly across the river from the old town. Designed by Brazilian architect Oscar Niemeyer, it opened on his 103rd birthday in 2010. Consisting of three stark geometric buildings – a dome, a tower encircled by a spiral staircase, and a long sinuous S-curve – set atop an enormous dazzling-white platform that's ideal for public events, it was intended to host a wide range of performances and temporary exhibitions. By the time Niemeyer himself passed away in 2012, however, his creation was deep in financial and political trouble. The open air platform is used for occasional events, and the occasional exhibition is open in summer, but otherwise it looks like becoming one of the most embarrassing white elephants in a land of pallid pachyderms. Check the website to see whether things have changed.

CARNAVAL IN ASTURIAS

Carnaval, the Mardi Gras week of drinking, dancing and excess, usually takes place over late February and early March. Spanish celebrations are reckoned to be at their wildest in Tenerife, Cádiz and Asturias – and, in particular, **Avilés**. Events begin in Avilés on the **Saturday before Ash Wednesday**, when virtually the entire city dons fancy dress and takes to the streets. Many costumes are veritable works of art, ranging from toothbrushes to mattresses and packets of sweets. By nightfall, anyone without a costume is likely to be drenched in some form of liquid.

The festivities, which include live music and fireworks competitions, last till dawn. It's virtually impossible to find accommodation, but the celebrations continue throughout Asturias during the following week. Sunday is, in fact, a rest day before *Carnaval* continues in **Gijón** on the **Monday** night. On **Tuesday** night, the scene shifts to **Oviedo**, where the crowds tend to be smaller and the events less frantic. Finally, on the **Friday after Ash Wednesday**, **Mieres**, a mining town just southeast of Oviedo, plays host to celebrations in an area known as C/Vicio.

ARRIVAL AND INFORMATION

By plane Asturias airport, 14km west of Avilés, has all the usual car-rental outlets, and is connected to the city by express buses (7am–11.20pm; €4; 20min).

By train Mainline and narrow-gauge RENFE trains use the same station on Avda. Telares, a short walk north of the old town, across Parque Muelle.

By bus The bus terminus is alongside the train station on Avda. Telares, just north of the centre.

Turismo C/Ruiz Gómez 21, off Pza. de España (July to mid-Sept daily 10am–8pm; mid-Sept to June Mon–Fri 9am–2pm & 4.30–6.30pm, Sat & Sun 10am–2pm; ☎ 985 544 325, ⊛ avilescomarca.info).

ACCOMMODATION

Hotel Don Pedro C/Fruta 22 ☎ 985 512 288, ⊛ hdonpedro.com. On a central pedestrian street, with 25 rather sumptuous, warm-toned rooms, many featuring exposed stone walls. The one potential drawback is late-night noise from the nearby bars. **€80**

Palacio de Ferrera Pza. de España 9 ☎ 985 129 080, ⊛ hotelpalaciodeferrera.es. This smart, central hotel, housed in a grand seventeenth-century mansion, is the most luxurious option in town, with spacious modernized rooms. Look for weekend discounts. **€125**

Palacio Valdes C/Ponte Llano 4 ☎ 984 112 111, ⊛ hotelpalaciovaldes.com. Pleasant, good-value renovated hotel, at the edge of the old town facing the bridge to the Centro Niemeyer, and offering tasteful modern bedrooms, some of which have turquoise balconies. **€88**

Pensión Puente Azud C/Acero 5 ☎ 985 550 177, ⊛ hostalpuenteazud.com. In truth, the small en-suite rooms of this simple *pensión*, 500m southeast of the centre, are no more exciting than its drab blue exterior, but the rates are absolutely unbeatable. **€30**

EATING AND DRINKING

Casa Alvarin C/las Alas 2 ☎ 985 540 113, ⊛ casaalvarin.com. Good old-fashioned *sidrería*, tucked down an alleyway just off the main square, with a full range of hearty *raciones*, from beans with clams to octopus or succulent ham, and a €15 set menu. Daily 1.30–4pm & 8pm–midnight; closed second half June & first half Oct.

Casa Tataguyo Pza. Carbayedo 6 ☎ 985 564 815, ⊛ tataguyo.com. This very charming 1840s *mesón*, one of several on the same square, is the oldest in town. Dependable local cuisine, at €15–20 for a main course. Daily noon–3.30pm & 8pm–midnight; closed mid-April to mid-May.

Oviedo

The bourgeois culture of **OVIEDO** contrasts sharply with the working-class ethos of its neighbours. As the Asturian capital, it has long been relatively wealthy. That history can be traced through the grand, lovingly restored administrative and religious buildings that render the city among the most attractive in the north. The old quarter, all the better for being largely pedestrianized, is a knot of squares and narrow streets built in warm yellow stone, while the newer part is redeemed by a huge public park right in its centre. Throughout the city are excellent bars and restaurants, many aimed at the lively student population.

Around the Catedral, enclosed by scattered sections of the medieval town walls, a compact, attractive quarter preserves the remains of **Old Oviedo**. Much was destroyed in the Civil War when Republican Asturian miners laid siege to the Nationalist garrison; the defenders were relieved by a Gallego detachment when on the brink of surrender.

Three small **churches** in Oviedo, built in a style unique to Asturias, rank among the most remarkable in Spain. All date from the first half of the ninth century, a period of almost total isolation for the Asturian kingdom, which then extended just 65km by 50km, and was the only part of Spain under Christian rule. Oviedo became the centre of this outpost in 810, as the base for King Alfonso II, son of the victorious Pelayo.

The Catedral

Mon–Sat 10am–2pm & 4–7pm • €7 for entire complex, €3.50 for Cámara Santa & diocesan museum

In the ninth century, King Alfonso II built a chapel, the **Cámara Santa** (Holy Chamber), to house the holy relics rescued from Toledo when it fell to the Moors. Remodelled in the twelfth century, it now forms the inner sanctuary of Oviedo's unusually uncluttered Gothic **Catedral**. With its primitive capitals, the innermost of the Cámara Santa's pair of interconnecting chapels is thought to be Alfonso's original building. The antechapel is a quiet little triumph of Spanish Romanesque; each of the six columns supporting the vault is sculpted with a pair of superbly humanized Apostles.

Built around the attractive Gothic cloister, itself built on pre-Romanesque foundations, the **diocesan museum** holds a high-quality collection of devotional art and artefacts.

Museo de Bellas Artes

C/Santa Ana 1 • July & Aug Tues–Sat 10.30am–2pm & 4–8pm, Sun 10.30am–2.30pm; Sept–June Tues–Fri 10.30am–2pm & 4.30–8.30pm, Sat 11.30am–2pm & 5–8pm, Sun 11.30am–2.30pm • Free • ☎ 985 213 061, ⊛ museobbaa.com

The eighteenth-century Palacio de Velarde, immediately south of the Catedral, houses the **Museo de Bellas Artes**. The highlights of its bold collection of contemporary Spanish art are on the top floor: Picasso's *Mosquetero con Espada y Amorcillo* is a gleeful take on historical portraiture, while Dalí's lyrical *Metamorfosis de Ángeles* has an unusually muted palette of browns and blues. The C/Santa Ana entrance brings you

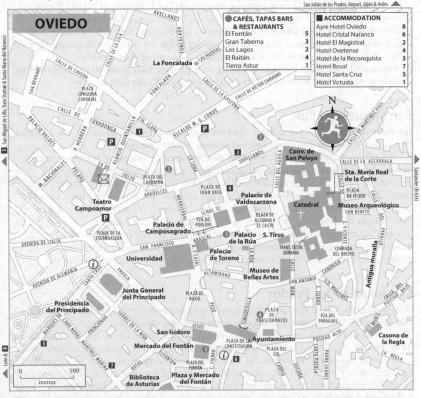

7

OVIEDO

☐ CAFÉS, TAPAS BARS & RESTAURANTS	
El Fontán	5
Gran Taberna	3
Los Lagos	2
El Raitán	4
Tierra Astur	1

■ ACCOMMODATION	
Ayre Hotel Oviedo	8
Hotel Cristal Naranco	6
Hotel El Magistral	2
Hotel Ovetense	4
Hotel de la Reconquista	3
Hotel Rosal	7
Hotel Santa Cruz	5
Hotel Vetusta	1

directly to another gem of the collection: El Greco's sombre portraits of the twelve Apostles (1585–90), which favour psychological depth over symbolism.

Museo Arqueológico

Pza. Alfonso II • Wed–Fri 9.30am–8pm, Sat 9.30am–2pm & 5–8pm, Sun 9.30am–3pm • Free • ⓦ museoarqueologicodeasturias.com

Oviedo's **Museo Arqueológico** occupies an impressively revamped modern structure behind the Catedral, built around the former convent of San Vicente and affording views of otherwise inaccessible parts of the building. Its comprehensive run-through of several thousand years of Asturian history is of most interest to locals, but it does hold some beautiful ancient artefacts. Ask for a booklet of translations, as few captions are in English. The section on the region's prehistoric caves is especially interesting.

Santa María del Naranco

April–Sept Mon & Sun 9.30am–1pm, Tues–Sat 9.30am–1pm & 3.30–7pm; Oct–March Mon 10am–1pm, Tues–Sat 10am–2.30pm, Sun 10am–12.30pm • €3 guided tour in Spanish, with San Miguel de Lillo; free on Mon with no guide

The greatest Asturian church, **Santa María del Naranco**, stands majestically amid the fields on a wooded slope 3km above the city. It's an easy signposted drive, or a 45-minute walk from the train station through the quiet suburb of Ciudad Naranco. The one drawback is that its impact is inevitably diminished by the huge tour groups that descend upon it in summer.

The initial glimpses of the warm stone and simple bold outline, in perfect harmony with its surroundings, led Jan Morris to describe it as "formidable beyond its scale". If you think it doesn't look like a church, there's a good reason for that – it wasn't built as one. Instead it was designed as a palatial hunting lodge for Alfonso's successor, Ramiro I (842–52), and only converted into a church at the end of that century. Architecturally, the open porticoes at both ends predate later innovations in Byzantine churches, while thirty or so distinctive decorative medallions skirt the roof.

San Miguel de Lillo

April–Sept Mon & Sun 9.30am–1pm, Tues–Sat 9.30am–1pm & 3.30–7pm; Oct–March Mon 10am–1pm, Tues–Sat 10am–2.30pm, Sun 10am–12.30pm • €3 guided tour in Spanish, with Santa María del Naranco; free on Mon with no guide

King Ramiro's palace chapel, **San Miguel de Lillo**, stands a couple of hundred metres beyond Santa María. Built with soft golden sandstone and red tiles, it's generally assumed to be by the same architect – Tiodo – but its design is quite different. Less than half of the original ninth-century church remains, the rest having been swept away by a landslide and clumsily rebuilt in the thirteenth century. The altar sits in Santa María del Naranco, and much of the interior sculpture has been removed to the Museo Arqueológico, but look for the window grilles carved from single slabs of limestone, and the superb Byzantine-style carved door frames depicting, incongruously enough, the investiture of a Roman consul, complete with circus-style festivities.

San Julián de los Prados

C/Gijón • May–Sept Mon 10am–12.30pm, Tues–Fri 10am–12.30pm & 4–5.30pm, Sat 9.30am–noon & 3.30–5pm; Oct–April Mon 10am–12.30pm, Tues–Sat 9.30–11.30am • €1.20 guided tour in Spanish, free on Mon with no guide

The nearest of Oviedo's remarkable "Asturian-Visigoth" churches to the city, **San Julián de los Prados**, also known as **Santullano**, stands alongside a highway ten minutes' walk northeast of the centre. Built around 830, it is large and spacious, with an unusual "secret chamber" built into the outer wall. The original frescoes inside, still remarkably colourful, are executed in similar style to those of Roman villas – along with architectural motifs, you'll see two Latin crosses hung with the letters alpha and omega.

ARRIVAL AND DEPARTURE

OVIEDO

By plane Asturias airport is 50km northwest of the city; express buses to and from Oviedo cost €8 (7am–11.20pm; 45min).

By train Both the RENFE and narrow-gauge (FEVE) train stations are in the same building on Avda. de Santander, northeast of the city centre.

Destinations Barcelona (2 daily; 10hr 20min); Ferrol (2 daily; 6hr 20min); León (6 daily; 2–3hr); Madrid (5 daily; 5–7hr); Ribadesella (4 daily; 2hr); Santander (2 daily; 4hr 40min).

By bus Oviedo's bus terminal (☎985 969 696, ⓦwww .estaciondeautobusesdeoviedo.com) is a short walk northeast of the train stations, on C/Pepe Cosmen.

Destinations Avilés (every 30min; 30min–1hr); Cangas de Onís (10–14 daily; 1hr 20min); A Coruña via Betanzos (6 daily; 4hr–6hr 15min); Covadonga (2 daily; 1hr 45min); Cudillero (1–2 daily; 1hr 10min); Gijón (every 15min; 30min–1hr); León (11 daily; 1hr 30min–2hr); Lugo (3 daily; 4hr 15min–5hr); Madrid (14 daily; 5–7hr); Pontevedra (2 daily; 7hr 30min); Ribadeo via Luarca (5 daily; 3hr); Ribadesella (8 daily; 1hr 10min–1hr 40min); Santander (10 daily; 2hr 15min–3hr 45min); Santiago (4 daily; 4hr 30min–6hr 50min); Valladolid (5 daily; 3hr 15min–4hr); Vigo (2 daily; 6hr 45min–8hr); Villaviciosa (12 daily; 30min–1hr).

INFORMATION

Turismo Oviedo's *turismo* is at Pza. de la Constitución 4 (mid-June to mid-Sept daily 9.30am–7pm; mid-Sept to mid-June Mon–Fri 9.30am–6pm, Sat 10am–6pm;

☎985 300 202, ⓦturismoviedo.es); there's also a booth at Marqués de Santa Cruz 1 (daily 10am 7pm; ☎985 227 586).

ACCOMMODATION

Oviedo has a good supply of **accommodation**, with cheaper *hostales* concentrated along C/Uría, opposite the train station, and along C/Nueve de Mayo and its continuation, C/de Caveda.

Ayre Hotel Oviedo C/Policarpo Herrero s/n ☎985 964 777, ⓦayrehoteles.com. This gleaming architectural showpiece, 1km southwest of the old town, forms part of a complex designed by Santiago Calatrava that also includes the city's conference centre and a high-end shopping centre. While not the greatest of locations, it does mean you'll pay astonishingly low prices for what you get. High-tech features in the bright ultramodern rooms include "chromotherapy systems" built into the beds, to adjust the colour and strength of the lighting. **€65**

Hotel Cristal Naranco C/Carta Puebla 6 ☎985 220 012. Well-appointed, very modern little hotel with surprisingly large rooms, tucked down an alleyway at the south end of the old town. **€60**

Hotel El Magistral C/Jovellanos 3 ☎902 305 902, ⓦelmagistral.com. Comfortable modern hotel in a very central location near the Catedral; the rooms themselves are less stylish than the flamboyant public spaces. **€83**

Hotel Ovetense C/San Juan 6 ☎985 220 840, ⓦhotelovetense.com. Plain but great-value en-suite rooms in the old town, above a lively bar-restaurant

– which is where you have your breakfast – near the Catedral and cider lanes. **€50**

Hotel de la Reconquista Gil de Jaz 16 ☎985 241 100, ⓦhoteldelareconquista.com. Very comfortable accommodation with top-notch service and a price tag to match, in a magnificent eighteenth-century hospital near Parque de San Francisco and the train station. **€125**

Hotel Rosal C/Cabo Noval 2 ☎985 202 984, ⓦhotelrosal.es. Restored nineteenth-century building, a short walk south of the old town, offering twelve bright, sizeable en-suite rooms and exceptionally helpful staff. **€45**

Hotel Santa Cruz C/Marqués de Santa Cruz 6 ☎985 215 333, ⓦsantacruzoviedo.com. Friendly place in a great location, with en-suite rooms overlooking Parque de San Francisco. Not as fancy as the website might suggest, but not bad for the price. **€66**

Hotel Vetusta C/Covadonga 2 ☎985 222 229, ⓦhotelvetusta.com. Stylish modern hotel, with galleried upper storeys, on the northern edge of the old town near the cider lanes. Sixteen pleasant rooms, half of which have mini-saunas. **€56**

EATING, DRINKING AND NIGHTLIFE

Oviedo's most renowned area for **eating and drinking** lies immediately north of the Catedral, just outside the pedestrian district, where lively **C/Gascona** is festooned with a large neon sign proclaiming it "El Bulevar de la Sidra"; the area is known for its spit-and-sawdust *sidrerías*, or **cider bars**. On weekend nights, the city is liable to fill up with huge crowds of teenage revellers, who commandeer many of its public spaces. If you prefer a less raucous atmosphere, head for the graceful arcaded **Pza. de Fontán** near the old market, ringed by Asturian restaurants and excellent speciality food shops.

El Fontán C/Fierro 2 ☎985 222 360. This café-restaurant on the upper floor of the market, with large windows

overlooking the square outside but also the stalls within, makes an excellent breakfast or lunch spot, with everything

7

from *chocolate con churros* to a substantial €11 set menu, and meat or fish mains for €11–23. Sun–Thurs 6am–1.30pm, Fri & Sat 6am–2.30pm.

Gran Taberna Pza. Porlier 1 ☎985 220 006, ☜lagrantaberna.com. This classy place, on a pedestrian street leading west from the Catedral and offering some tables outside on the square, makes a welcome retreat on Oviedo's more hectic nights. There's a carte menu of tapas for €7–12, great-value €10 and €15 ("Asturia", featuring *fabada*) set menus, and solid grilled meat and fish for €20 and up, or you can just sip on a glass of wine in peace. Daily 8.30am–12.30am.

Los Lagos Pza. del Carbayón 4 ☎985 200 697. Excellent *sidrería*, beside a busy road near the cider lanes, and filled with the heady smell of strong Asturian foods, cider and sawdust. Good-value €9.50 set menu. There's another branch at C/Cervantes 7. Mon–Sat 11am–midnight.

El Raitán Pza. Trascorrales 6 ☎985 206 764,

☜elraitan.es. Superb, atmospheric restaurant in a delightful square off Pza. Mayor. The wide selection of set menus ranges from €18 for a vegetarian meal to the huge *menú degustación de cocina asturiana* for €36, which includes crab soup, *fabada*, and onion-stuffed boar. Mon & Wed–Sat 1–3pm & 7pm–midnight, Sun 1–3pm.

★**Tierra Astur** C/Gascona 1 ☎985 202 502, ☜tierra-astur.com. At the top of "El Bulevar de la Sidra", this bustling place is the best and most salubrious *sidrería* hereabouts, with a large indoor dining room and an enclosed wooden terrace as well as its own large deli. Run by the best known local food distributor, it's unbeatable for quality. Enormous platters of local cheeses and meats – starting at €5, they range upwards to phenomenal sizes – rich Asturian cuisine, and, of course, large quantities of cider. While there's a €10 lunch menu, the all-day, seasonally changing set menu at €15, with three courses plus drinks, is superb. Live music Thurs & Fri. Daily 11am–1am.

West to Galicia

The coast west of Avilés, as far as the Río Navia, is rugged, with scarcely more than a handful of resorts carved out from the cliffs. The most appealing are the old port and resort of **Luarca**, and pretty little **Cudillero**. West again from the Río Navia, the coast becomes marshy and largely unexceptional.

Cudillero

CUDILLERO is a delightful, picturesque little fishing port, squeezed so tightly into a narrow, corkscrewing valley 25km west of Avilés that none of its buildings manage to face directly out to sea. Nonetheless, the brightly coloured arcaded houses that rise, one above the other, up the steep horseshoe of cliffs that surround the port give it the feel, and appeal, of a Greek island village, and it's usually thronged with visitors in summer. As you climb the twisting main street away from the water, the architecture becomes grittier, but the whole town still oozes character. There's no beach here, however – the nearest is the lovely cove at **Playa Aguilar**, 3km east – so the most obvious attractions are the **fish tavernas** in the cobbled plaza just above the seafront.

ARRIVAL AND INFORMATION   CUDILLERO

By train The narrow-gauge station is atop the cliffs, well above town.
Destinations: Avilés (14 daily; 50min); Gijón (14 daily; 1hr 40min), Oviedo (9 daily, via Pravia; 1hr 20min), and Viveiro (2 daily; 3hr 15min).
By bus Cudillero is connected with Avilés (8 daily; 50min) and Gijón (8 daily; 1hr 15min).
By car The most direct route down into Cudillero is a precipitous and very narrow road that twists its way down the cliffs from the narrow-gauge station, a stiff 25min walk

or a hair-raising drive. Motorists would do better to follow the longer road that leaves the N632 a couple of kilometres further west, and approaches the village along the coast; the only sizeable car park is by the sea, a couple of hundred metres west of the centre.
Turismo In a modern building facing the harbour, just west of the village centre (Tues–Fri 10am–2pm & 5–7pm, Sat 11am–2pm & 5–7pm, Sun 11am–2pm; ☎985 591 377, ☜cudillero.org).

ACCOMMODATION

Camping Cudillero C/Playa Aguilar ☎985 590 663, ☜campingcudillero.com. Rural campsite, set well back

from the clifftops east of town, a steep 1.4km walk above gorgeous Aguilar beach, with a snack bar and shop, plus rental bungalows and a heated pool. Closed mid-Sept to mid-April. **€23**, bungalow **€70**

★**La Casona de Pio** C/Riofrío 3 ☏ 985 591 512, ⓦ lacasonadepio.com. Cudillero's nicest hotel, set just back from the main seafront square. Lovely, very comfortably furnished en-suite rooms with galleried windows (though not quite sea views), room service and a

good restaurant downstairs. The excellent breakfast costs €7 extra. Closed Jan. **€92**

Hotel Sol de la Blanca C/Suárez Inclán 84 ☏ 985 591 268, ⓦ hotelsoldelablanca.es. Simple little *pensión*, halfway up the hill on the main street up from the port, and offering good-value en-suite doubles. Closed Oct–Easter. **€70**

EATING AND DRINKING

Los Arcos C/Fuente de Abajo 2 ☏ 985 590 086. While the restaurants that squeeze cheek-by-jowl into Cudillero's pretty seafront plaza look universally irresistible, the actual food can vary widely in quality. This is the most dependable option, with a €25 set menu, seafood tapas at €13–20 and fish mains at €19–26. Daily: June–Sept 1–4pm & 8–11pm; Oct–May 1–4pm.

Rincón Pixueto Pza. Principal ☏ 650 112 032. This friendly little place, right at the start of the hill as you leave the seafront, has several outdoor tables, and offers much more affordable prices than the main square, with a good-value €10 set menu and decent *raciones*. Daily noon–11pm.

7

Luarca

Beyond Cudillero, the N632 leaps over viaducts spanning deep, pine-wooded gorges. About 50km west, the attractive port of **LUARCA** is accessed from the N632 by a road that dips down steeply to the coast. A mellow place, it's built around an S-shaped cove surrounded by sheer cliffs. Down below, the town is bisected by a small, winding river, and knitted together by numerous narrow bridges.

Luarca is a seaside resort in a modest, faded sort of way, which has defiantly retained its traditional character, including a few *chigres* – old-fashioned Asturian taverns – where you can be initiated into the art of *sidra* drinking. The fishing-harbour area is the heartbeat of the town: cross the bridge from the plaza, and follow the river. The town **beach** is divided in two: the closer strip is narrower but more protected, while the broader one beyond the jetty is subject to seaweed litter.

From the *turismo*, C/de la Carril leads up to the cliffs overlooking the port, which has an unusual decorative cemetery, a hermitage chapel and a lighthouse.

ARRIVAL AND INFORMATION   LUARCA

By train The narrow-gauge station is 2km east of town.

By bus The bus station, just off C/Crucero on the river, is connected with Oviedo (4 daily; 1hr 30min) and Ribadeo (4 daily; 1hr 25min).

By car Central Luarca is very short on parking; it's best to

park on the edge of town as soon as you arrive.

Turismo Palacio de Gamoneda, Pza. Alfonso X (daily 10.30am–1.45pm & 4–7pm; ☏ 985 640 083, ⓦ turismoluarca.com).

ACCOMMODATION AND EATING

Camping Los Cantiles Valdes ☏ 985 640 938, ⓦ campingloscantiles.com. A year-round campsite, facing the lighthouse across a rocky cove from the clifftop east of town, with facilities to match its superb setting, including a shop and summer-only café. **€18**

Hotel Rico Pza. Alfonso X 6 ☏ 985 470 559, ⓦ hotelrico .com. Small, modern, good-value hotel in the very centre of town, where the rather minimal en-suite rooms do at least have large galleried windows. **€75**

Villa La Argentina Villar s/n ☏ 985 640 102, ⓦ www .villalaargentina.com. Grand and very comfortable

rooms, in a sumptuous *belle époque* mansion, with spacious formal gardens, a 15min walk east of the centre in the hillside Villar district. **€98**

Villa Blanca Avda. de Galicia 25–27 ☏ 985 641 035, ⓦ villablancaluarca.es. Smart, formal gourmet restaurant in the heart of town, with a hard-earned reputation for serving the best in traditional Asturian cuisine; the emphasis, naturally, is on seafood. The €11 weekday lunch menu is a real bargain. Daily 1–3pm & 8–11pm; closed Mon in winter.

Galicia

SANTUARIO DA VIRXE DA BARCA, MUXÍA

Galicia

Passionately entangled with the Atlantic Ocean at the northwest corner of the Iberian Peninsula, Galicia feels far removed from the rest of Spain. Everywhere is green, from the high forested hills to the rolling fields, a patchwork of tiny plots still farmed by hand. Indeed, with its craggy coast and mild, wet climate, Galicia is more like Ireland than Andalucía. Its people take pride in their Celtic heritage, and cherish the survival of their language, Galego. It's hardly off the beaten track, however. Santiago de Compostela ranked during the Middle Ages as the third city of Christendom, and pilgrims have been making their way here along the Camino de Santiago for well over a thousand years.

Santiago itself remains the chief attraction for visitors. Still focused around its unspoiled medieval core, an enticing labyrinth of ancient arcades and alleyways, it should be on every itinerary. Galicia's other major selling point is its endlessly indented **shoreline**, slashed by the powerful sea into the deep, narrow estuaries known here as *rías*, and framed by steep green hillsides. Sadly, a lack of planning controls has meant that much of the coast is depressingly overbuilt, albeit with dreary villas and apartments rather than high-rise hotels. With each town tending to merge into the next, those few resorts that remain recognizable as sturdy little medieval fishing villages, such as **Cambados**, **Muros** and **Baiona**, come as welcome highlights. Pretty, secluded sandy beaches do exist, but they take a bit of finding these days, and often require a drive away from the built-up areas.

Broadly speaking, of the distinct coastal stretches, the **Rías Altas** in the north are wilder and emptier, while the picturesque **Rías Baixas**, neighbouring Portugal, are warmer and more developed, and consequently attract many more visitors. In between the two lie the dunes and headlands of the more rugged **Costa da Morte**. Only a couple of the seafront towns have grown to become cities: the modern ports of **A Coruña**, with its elegant glass-encased balconies, and **Vigo**, perched alongside a magnificent bay. Further inland, the settlements are more spread out, and the river valleys of the Miño and the Sil remain beautifully unspoiled, while the attractive provincial capitals of **Pontevedra**, **Ourense** and **Lugo** seem little changed since the Middle Ages.

The Galegos are renowned for having **emigrated** all over the world. Between 1836 and 1960, around two million Galegos – roughly half the total population – left the region, thanks largely to the demographic pressure on agricultural land. Half of them ended up in Argentina, where Buenos Aires is often called the largest city in Galicia. An untranslatable Galego word, *morriña*, describes the exiles' particular sense of homesick, nostalgic longing. That Celtic melancholy has its counterpart in the exuberant devotion to the land, its culture and its produce that you'll encounter in Galicia itself, as evinced in its music – they even play the bagpipes (or *gaita galega*) – literature and festivals. Above all, Galegos view their **food** and **wine** almost as sacraments; share in a feast of the fresh local seafood, washed down with a crisp white Albariño, and you may find the *morriña* gets a hold on you, too.

ILLA DO FARO, ILLAS CÍES

Highlights

❶ Santiago de Compostela The goal of pilgrims for over a thousand years, this ravishing cathedral city is a labyrinth of ancient lanes and dramatic squares. **See p.546**

❷ Sunset at Fisterra Fantastic views over the Atlantic, from the very edge of the world. **See p.571**

❸ Pimientos de Padrón Once tasted, these randomly piquant green peppers, fried in hot oil and sprinkled with sea salt, are never forgotten. **See p.573**

❹ Seafood and white wine Galicia is renowned for its delicious *mariscos* and unique Ribeiro and Albariño wines. **See p.574**

❺ Pontevedra Pontevedra's sleepy *zona monumental* metamorphoses into a lively party zone after dark. **See p.579**

❻ The Illas Cíes The pristine sands of these three islets make for an irresistible day-trip. **See p.585**

❼ The parador at Baiona This fabulous hotel enjoys an unsurpassable setting; look out for special offers on room rates. **See p.586**

❽ Cañón de Río Sil A truly staggering gorge, carved by the Romans into still-functioning vine-growing terraces. **See p.590**

HIGHLIGHTS ARE MARKED ON THE MAP ON P.546

Santiago de Compostela

The ancient pilgrimage centre of **SANTIAGO DE COMPOSTELA** ranks among the most beautiful cities in all Spain. A superb ensemble of twisting stone lanes, majestic squares and ancient churches, interspersed with countless hidden nooks and crannies, its medieval core remains a remarkably integrated whole, all the better for being very largely pedestrianized. Hewn from time-weathered granite, splashed with gold and silver lichen and sprouting vegetation from the unlikeliest crevices, the buildings and plazas, arcades and flagstones seem to blend imperceptibly one into the other. Warrens of honey-coloured streets wind their way past a succession of beautiful monasteries and convents, culminating in the approach to the immense **Pza. do Obradoiro**, flanked by the magnificent **Catedral**, the supposed resting place of the remains of St James. To enjoy an overall impression of the whole ensemble, take a walk along the promenade of the **Paseo da Ferradura**, in the spacious **Alameda** just southwest of the old quarter.

To this day, locals and visitors alike continue to flock to the old quarter for its round-the-clock vitality, making it far more than a mere historical curiosity. Modern tourists

HIGHLIGHTS

1. Santiago de Compostela
2. Sunset at Fisterra
3. Pimientos de Padrón
4. Seafood and white wine
5. Pontevedra
6. The Illas Cíes
7. The Parador at Baiona
8. Cañon de Río Sil

GALICIA

GALEGO FOOD

Galegos boast that their **seafood** is the best in the world, and for quality and sheer diversity it's certainly hard to match. Local wonders to look out for include *vieiras* (the scallops whose shells became the symbol of St James), *mejillones* (the rich orange mussels from the *rías*), *cigallas* (Dublin Bay prawns, though often inadequately translated as shrimp), *anguilas* (little eels from the Río Miño), *zamburiñas* (little scallops), *xoubas* (sardines), *navajas* (razor-shell clams), *percebes* (barnacles), *nécoras* (shore crabs) and *centollas* (spider crabs). *Pulpo* (octopus) is so much a part of Galego eating that there are special *pulperías* cooking it in the traditional copper pots, and it's a mainstay of local country fiestas. In the province of Pontevedra alone, Vilanova de Arousa has its own mussel festival (first Sun in Aug), Arcade has one devoted to oysters (first weekend in April), and O Grove goes all the way, with a generalized seafood fiesta. When eaten as tapas or *raciones*, seafood is not overly expensive, though always be wary of items like *percebes* that are sold by weight – a small plateful can cost as much as €50. Superb **markets** can be found everywhere; the coastal towns have their rows of seafront stalls with supremely fresh fish, while cities such as Santiago hold grand old arcaded market halls, piled high with farm produce from the surrounding countryside.

Another speciality, imported from the second Galego homeland of Argentina, is the **churrasquería** (grill house). Often unmarked and needing local assistance to find, these serve up immense *churrascos* – a term that in Galicia usually refers to huge portions of beef or pork ribs, cooked on a traditional open grill (*parrilla*). While Galegos don't normally like their food highly spiced, *churrascos* are usually served with a devastating garlic-based *salsa picante*.

Other common dishes are *caldo galego*, a thick stew of cabbage and potatoes in a meat-based broth; *caldeirada*, a filling fish soup; *lacon con grelos*, ham boiled with turnip greens; and the ubiquitous *empanada*, a flat light-crusted pie, often filled with tuna and tomato. Should you be around during the summer months, be sure to try *pimientos de Padrón*, sweet green peppers fried in oil, served as a kind of lucky dip with a few memorably spicy ones in each serving.

may be as likely to be attracted by its food, drink and history as by religion, but pilgrims still arrive in large numbers, sporting their *vieira* (scallop shell) symbol. Each year at the **Festival of St James** on July 25, a ceremony at his shrine re-dedicates the country to the saint. Those years in which the saint's day falls on a Sunday are designated "Holy Years", and the activity becomes even more intense. The next will be in 2021.

For all its fame, however, Santiago remains surprisingly small. Its total population is estimated at around 100,000, of whom, amazingly, 40,000 are students at its venerable university. Almost everything of interest to visitors is contained within the densely packed historic core, known as the *zona monumental*, which takes roughly fifteen minutes to cross on foot but several days to explore thoroughly. Most of the commercial activities and infrastructure lie a short distance downhill to the south, in the less appealing modern quarter, which is also where the students tend to live. A high hillside 2km southeast is topped by the City of Culture, home to a museum and performance centre, but wander away from the *zona monumental* in most other directions, and you can quickly reach open countryside.

Uniquely, Santiago is a city at its best in the rain; situated in the wettest fold of the Galego hills, it suffers brief but frequent showers. Water glistens on the facades, gushes from the innumerable gargoyles and flows down the streets.

The Catedral

Daily 7am–8.30pm • ☎ 981 569 327, ⓦ catedraldesantiago.es

All roads in Santiago lead to the **Catedral**. You first appreciate its sheer grandeur upon venturing into the vast expanse of Pza. do Obradoiro. Directly ahead stands a fantastic Baroque pyramid of granite, flanked by immense bell towers and everywhere adorned with statues of St James in his familiar pilgrim guise with staff, broad hat and scallop-shell badge. This is the famous **Obradoiro facade**, built between 1738 and 1750 in the

FIESTAS

MARCH

1: San Rosendo Celanova's big festival, at the monastery.
Pre-Lent: *Carnavales* throughout the region.

APRIL/MAY

Semana Santa (Holy Week) Celebrations include a symbolic *descendimiento* (descent from the Cross) at Viveiro on Good Friday and a Resurrection procession at Fisterra. On Palm Sunday, there are Stations of the Cross at Monte San Tecla, near A Guarda.
Sunday after Easter: Fiesta de Angula Elver festival at Tui.
Second Monday after Easter: Fiesta San Telmo At Tui.
Late April to early May (dates vary) Festival at Ribadavia celebrating and promoting Ribeiro wines.
May 1: *Romería* at Pontevedra marks the start of a month-long festival.

JULY

First weekend: Rapa das Bestas The capture and breaking in of wild mountain horses at Viveiro.
11: Fiesta de San Benito At Pontevedra, with river processions, and folk groups, and a smaller *romería* at Cambados.
Second weekend: Medieval de Betanzos Three-day fair at Betanzos, reliving the town's time under Andrade rule.
Second weekend: International Festival of the Celtic World Galicia's most important music festival is held in Ortigueira (🌐festivaldeortigueira.com); pipe bands from all the Celtic lands perform, alongside musicians from around the world, and every event is free.
16: Virgen del Carmen Sea processions at Muros and Corcubión.
24–25: St James (Sant Yago) Two days of celebration in many places, with processions of bigheads and *gigantones* on the 24th and spectacular parades with fireworks and bands through the following evening.
25: Santiago Galicia's major fiesta, at its height in Santiago de Compostela. The evening before, there's a fireworks display and symbolic burning of a cardboard effigy of the mosque at Córdoba. Also designated "Galicia Day", the festival has become a nationalist event, with political and cultural events for about a week on either side.

AUGUST

First Sunday Albariño wine festival at Cambados; bagpipe festival at Ribadeo; Virgen de la Roca observances outside Baiona; pimiento festival at Padrón; Navaja (razor shell) festival at Fisterra.
16: Fiesta de San Roque Festivals at all churches that bear his name: at Betanzos, there's a Battle of the Flowers on the river and the launching of the Fiesta del Globo.
24: Fiesta (and bullfights) at Noia.
25: Fiesta de San Ginés At Sanxenxo.

SEPTEMBER

6–10: Fiestas del Portal At Ribadavia.

OCTOBER

First two weekends: Fiesta do Marisco Seafood festival at O Grove.

NOVEMBER

Early Nov: Magosto castaña Chestnut festival at Ourense.
11: Fiesta de San Martín At Bueu.

efflorescent style known as Churrigueresque by an obscure Santiago-born architect, Fernando de Casas. No other work of Spanish Baroque can compare with what Edwin Mullins sublimely called its "hat-in-the-air exuberance".

Behind the facade, the main body of the Catedral is Romanesque, rebuilt in the eleventh and twelfth centuries after a devastating raid by the Muslim vizier of Córdoba, al-Mansur, in 977. Although, perhaps not surprisingly, he failed to find the body of the saint, he forced the citizens to carry the bells of the tower to the mosque at Córdoba – a coup that was later dramatically reversed (see p.317).

Pórtico de Gloria

The acknowledged highlight of Santiago's Catedral – indeed, one of the great triumphs of medieval art – is the **Pórtico de Gloria**, the original west front, now installed just inside the main doors, immediately behind the Obradoiro facade.

Completed in 1188 under the supervision of Maestro Mateo, the Pórtico represented both the culmination of all Romanesque sculpture and a precursor of the new Gothic realism, each of its host of figures being strikingly relaxed and quietly humanized. The real mastery is in the assured marshalling of the ensemble. Above the side doors are representations of Purgatory and the Last Judgement, while Christ presides in glory over the main door, flanked by his Apostles, and surrounded by the 24 Elders of the Apocalypse playing celestial music.

So many millions of pilgrims have given thanks at journey's end, by praying with the fingers of one hand pressed into the roots of the Tree of Jesse below the saint, that five deep and shiny holes have been worn into the solid marble. Finally, for wisdom, they would lower their heads to touch the brow of Maestro Mateo, the humble squatting figure on the other side.

The High Altar

The spiritual climax of each pilgrimage to Santiago comes when pilgrims climb the steps that lead up behind the **High Altar** – an extraordinary gilded riot of eighteenth-century Churrigueresque – embrace the Most Sacred Image of Santiago, and kiss his bejewelled cape. The whole process is rounded off by making confession and attending a High Mass.

The Botafumeiro

Thanks to an elaborate pulley system in front of the altar, operated by eight priests (*tiraboleiros*), the Catedral's immense "**Botafumeiro**" (incense burner) is swung in a vast thirty-metre ceiling-to-ceiling arc across the transept. Originally designed to fumigate bedraggled pilgrims, it's now used only at certain services – ask whether there's one during your visit.

The crypt

A steady procession of pilgrims also visits the bones of St James, which are kept in a **crypt** beneath the altar. Lost for a second time in 1700, after being hidden before an English invasion, these relics were rediscovered during building work in 1879. In fact, the workers found three skeletons, which were naturally held to be those of St James and his two followers. The only problem was identifying which one was the Apostle. This was fortuitously resolved as a church in Tuscany possessed a piece of Santiago's skull that exactly fitted a gap in one of those here.

The Catedral museum

Daily: April–Oct 9am–8pm, Nov–March 10am–8pm • €6 museum only, various combination tickets including guided tours cost up to €15 • ☎ 981 557 812, ⓦ catedraldesantiago.es

Santiago's **Catedral museum** has its own entrance to the right of the main Catedral facade. Its ground floor holds archeological displays, while upstairs you'll find assorted relics of the cathedral's history, including the Botafumeiro itself when it's not in use. From there you can walk into the late Gothic cloisters, the courtyard of which offers a wonderful prospect of the riotous mixture of the exterior. Back inside, the tapestry rooms on the topmost floor include pieces based on Goya paintings, and open onto a long open-air gallery with similarly good views over the Pza. do Obradoiro.

Doors from both the cloisters and the cathedral itself lead into the **Treasury**, where the highlight is a huge carved altarpiece depicting the legend of St James.

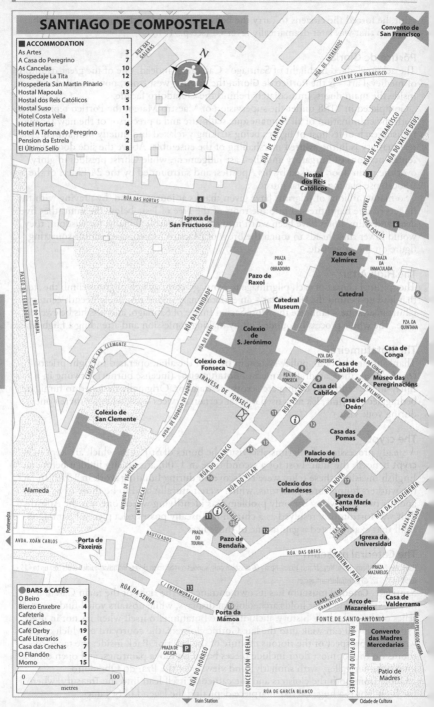

SANTIAGO DE COMPOSTELA

N

■ ACCOMMODATION	
As Artes	3
A Casa do Peregrino	7
As Cancelas	10
Hospedaje La Tita	12
Hospedería San Martin Pinario	6
Hostal Mapoula	13
Hostal dos Reis Católicos	5
Hostal Suso	11
Hotel Costa Vella	1
Hotel Hortas	4
Hotel A Tafona do Peregrino	9
Pension da Estrela	2
El Último Sello	8

● BARS & CAFÉS	
O Beiro	9
Bierzo Enxebre	4
Cafeteria	1
Café Casino	12
Café Derby	19
Café Literarios	6
Casa das Crechas	7
O Filandón	5
Momo	15

Convento de San Francisco

COSTA DE SAN FRANCISCO

RÚA DE ENTRERRIOS

RÚA DAS GALERAS

RÚA DE CARRETAS

RÚA DE SAN FRANCISCO

RÚA DO VAL DE DEUS

RÚA DAS HORTAS

Igrexa de San Fructuoso

Hostal dos Reis Católicos

TRAVESA DÚAS PORTAS

PRAZA DO OBRADOIRO

Pazo de Xelmírez

PRAZA DA INMACULADA

Pazo de Raxoi

Catedral Museum

Catedral

PASEO DA FERRADURA

RÚA DO POMBAL

RÚA DA TRINIDADE

RÚA DE RAXOI

Colexio de S. Jerónimo

PZA. DA QUINTANA

Colexio de Fonseca

CAMPO DE SAN CLEMENTE

PZA. DAS PRATERÍAS

Casa de Cabildo

Casa de Conga

RÚA DA CONGA

Museo das Peregrinacións

RÚA DE XELMÍREZ

TRAVESA DE FONSECA

PZA. DE FONSECA

Casa del Cabildo

Casa del Deán

Colexio de San Clemente

AVDA. DE RODRIGO DE PADRÓN

RÚA DA RAIÑA

Casa das Pomas

Palacio de Mondragón

Alameda

AVENIDA DE FIGUEROA

RÚA DO FRANCO

RÚA DO VILAR

Colexio dos Irlandeses

RÚA NOVA

Igrexa de Santa María Salomé

RÚA DA CALDEIRERÍA

ENTRECERCAS

ENTREMURALLAS

TRAV. SALOMÉ

PRAZA DA UNIVERSIDADE

Pontevedra

AVDA. XOÁN CARLOS

Porta de Faxeiras

BAUTIZADOS

PRAZA DO TOURAL

Pazo de Bendaña

Igrexa da Universidade

RÚA DAS ORFAS

CARDENAL PAYA

PRAZA MAZARELOS

C / ENTREMURALLAS

RÚA DA SENRA

Porta da Mámoa

TRANS. DOS GRAMÁTICOS

Arco de Mazarelos

Casa de Valderrama

FONTE DE SANTO ANTONIO

RÚA DO PASAXE DE ABSIRA

CONCEPCIÓN ARENAL

RÚA DO PATIO DE MADRES

Convento das Madres Mercedarias

Patio de Madres

PRAZA DE GALICIA

RÚA DO HORREO

RÚA DE GARCÍA BLANCO

0		100
	metres	

Train Station

Cidade de Cultura

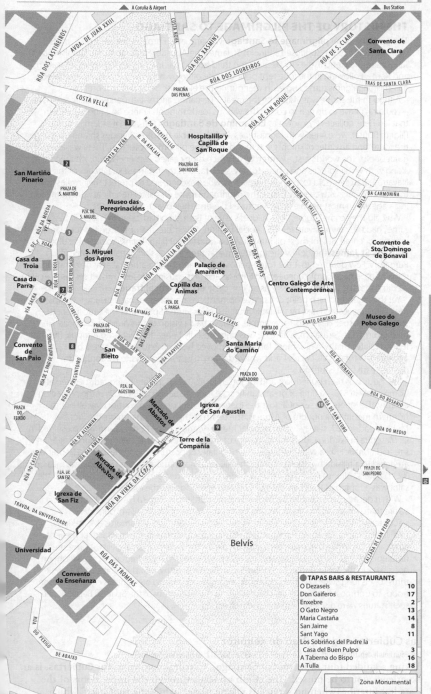

A Coruña & Airport

Bus Station

8

Convento de Santa Clara

RÚA DE S. CLARA

TRAS DE SANTA CLARA

AVDA. DE JUAN XXIII

RÚA DOS CASTIÑEIROS

RÚA DOS XASMÍNS

COSTA NOVA

RÚA DOS LOUREIROS

COSTA VELLA

PRACIÑA DAS PENAS

RÚA DE SAN ROQUE

1

R. DO HOSPITALILLO

R. DA ATALAIA

PORTA DA PENA

Hospitalillo y Capilla de San Roque

PRAZIÑA DE SAN ROQUE

DA CARMONIÑA

RUELA

RÚA DE RAMÓN DEL VALLE - INCLÁN

2

San Martiño Pinario

PRAZA DE S. MARTIÑO

Museo das Peregrinacións

PZA. DE S. MIGUEL

RÚA DE MOEDA VELLA

C. DE S. XOÁN

3

RÚA DA ALGALIA DE ABAIXO

RÚA DA ENTREMUROS

RÚA DAS RODAS

Convento de Sto. Domingo de Bonaval

4

S. Miguel dos Agros

RÚA DA ALGALIA DE ARRIBA

RÚA DA TROIA

RUELA DE REIS SALÉN

Palacio de Amarante

Centro Galego de Arte Contemporánea

Casa da Troia

Casa da Parra

5

6

RÚA DA AZUBECHERÍA

VÍA SACRA

7

RÚA DAS ÁNIMAS

Capilla das Ánimas

PZA. DE S. PARGA

R. DAS CASAS REAIS

SANTO DOMINGO

Museo do Pobo Galego

PRAZA DE CERVANTES

RÚA DE SAN BIEITO

R. VELLA DAS ÁNIMAS

PORTA DO CAMIÑO

RÚA DE S. PAIO DE ANTEALTARES

8

RÚA TRAVIESA

RÚA DO BONAVAL

Convento de San Paio

San Bieito

Santa María do Camiño

RÚA DO PRESINTORIO

PZA. DE AGOSTIÑO

PRAZA DO MATADOIRO

RÚA DO ROSARIO

PRAZA DO FEIXOO

R. DE S. AGOSTIÑO

RÚA DO MEDIO

RÚA DE ALTAMIRA

Mercado de Abastos

Igrexa de San Agustín

RÚA DE SAN PEDRO

10

RÚA DAS AMEAS

9

Torre de la Compañía

PRAZA DE SAN PEDRO

RÚA 'PO CASTRO

PZA. DE SAN FIZ

Mercado de Abastos

15

CALZADA DE SAN PEDRO

Igrexa de San Fiz

RÚA DA VIRXE DA CEPA

TRAVDA. DA UNIVERSIDADE

Belvís

Universidad

RÚA DAS TROMPAS

Convento da Enseñanza

VÍA DO PÁXIGO

DE ABAIXO

● TAPAS BARS & RESTAURANTS	
O Dezaseis	10
Don Gaiferos	17
Enxebre	2
O Gato Negro	13
María Castaña	14
San Jaime	8
Sant Yago	11
Los Sobriños del Padre la Casa del Buen Pulpo	3
A Taberna do Bispo	16
A Tulla	18

Zona Monumental

THE HISTORY OF THE PILGRIMAGE TO SANTIAGO

The great medieval **pilgrimage to Santiago** was arguably Europe's first exercise in mass tourism. Home to the supposed shrine of St James the Apostle (Santiago to the Spanish, Saint Jacques to the French), the city became the third holiest site in Christendom, after Jerusalem and Rome. Following in the footsteps of Godescale of Puy, who arrived in 951, an estimated half-million pilgrims turned up each year during the eleventh and twelfth centuries.

Although the shrine was visited by the great – Fernando and Isabel, Carlos V, Francis of Assisi – you didn't have to be rich to come. The various roads through France and northern Spain that led here, collectively known as **El Camino de Santiago** (The Way of St James, or the Pilgrim Route), were lined with monasteries and charitable hospices. Villages sprang up along the route, and an order of knights was founded for the pilgrims' protection. There was even a guidebook – the world's first – written by a French monk called Aymery Picaud, who recorded, along with water sources and places to stay, such facts as the bizarre sexual habits of the Navarrese Basques (said to expose themselves when excited, and to protect their mules from their neighbours with chastity belts). The pilgrimage route was an extraordinary phenomenon in an age when most people never ventured beyond their own town or village.

Why did they come? Some, like Chaucer's Wife of Bath, who had "been in Galicia at Seynt Jame", had their own private reasons: social fashion, adventure, the opportunities for marriage or even for crime. But for most pilgrims, it was a question of faith. Thanks to the miraculous power of **St James**, they knew the journey guaranteed a remission of half their time in Purgatory. Few doubted that the tomb beneath Santiago's high cathedral altar held the mortal remains of James, son of Zebedee and Salome and first cousin of Jesus Christ. It seems scarcely credible that the whole business was an immense **ecclesiastical fraud**.

Yet the legend, at each point of its development, has no apparent basis in fact. It begins with the claim, unsubstantiated by the Bible, that St James visited Spain after the Crucifixion, to spread the gospel. He is said, for example, to have had a vision of the Virgin in Zaragoza. He then returned to Jerusalem, where he was undoubtedly beheaded by Herod Agrippa. But the legend relates that two of James's followers removed his corpse to Jaffa, where a boat appeared, without sails or crew, and whisked them in just seven days to Padrón, 20km downstream from Santiago.

The body was then buried, lost and forgotten for 750 years, before being rediscovered at Compostela in 813 – a time of great significance for the Spanish Church. Over the preceding century, the Moors had swept across the Iberian Peninsula, gaining control over all but the northern mountain kingdom of Asturias. The death of their great champion, the Prophet Muhammad, in 632, still lay within popular memory, and a bone from his arm was preserved in La Mesquita in Córdoba. Thus the discovery of the bones of St James, under a buried altar on a site traditionally linked with his name, was singularly opportune. It occurred after a hermit was attracted to a hillside by visions of stars; the hill was known thereafter as Compostela, meaning "field of stars". Alfonso II, king of Asturias, came to pay his respects and built a chapel, and the saint was adopted as the champion of Christian Spain against the infidel.

Within decades, the saint had appeared on the battlefield. Ramiro I, Alfonso's successor, swore that James had fought alongside him at the Battle of Clavijo (844), personally slaughtering 60,000 Moors. Over the next six centuries Santiago Matamoros (Moor-killer) manifested himself at some forty battles, assisting, for example, in the massacre of the Inca armies in Peru. While that may seem an odd role for the fisherman-evangelist, it presented no problems to the Christian propagandists who portrayed him most frequently as a knight on horseback in the act of dispatching whole clutches of swarthy, bearded Arabs with a single thrust of his long sword. (With consummate irony, when Franco brought his crack Moroccan troops to Compostela to dedicate themselves to the overthrow of the Spanish Republic, all such statues were discreetly hidden under sheets.)

Las Cubiertas and the Pazo de Xelmírez

Tues–Sun hourly departures 10am–2pm & 4–8pm • €12 • ☎ 981 557 812, ⌨ catedraldesantiago.es

Taking a guided tour of its **roof** of Santiago's Catedral, known as **Las Cubiertas**, is an experience not to be missed. The climb up leads through the upper floors of the Catedral interior (when no service is taking place), while the roof itself, which consists of shallow granite steps, offers superb views over the rest of the city, as well, of course, as the Catedral's own towers and embellishments. Every way you turn, it's crawling with pagodas, pawns, domes, obelisks, battlements, scallop shells and cornucopias.

The tours start by visiting the **Pazo de Xelmírez** (Palacio Arzobispal Gelmírez), which adjoins the Catedral to the north and is entered to the left of the main stairs. Archbishop Xelmírez rebuilt the Catedral in the twelfth century, raised the see to an archbishopric and "discovered" a ninth-century deed that gave annual dues to St James's shrine of one bushel of corn from each acre of Spain reconquered from the Moors – a decree that was repealed only in 1834. His opulent palace features a vaulted twelfth-century kitchen and a thirteenth-century synodal hall, along with plenty of ancient statues.

Note that the standard tour features a quick-fire Spanish commentary that may well leave you floundering; to be sure of a place on an English-language tour, at no extra charge, contact them five days in advance in summer, or two days in low season.

Praza do Obradoiro

You could easily spend several hours exploring the squares around the Catedral. The **Praza do Obradoiro**, in front of the main facade, is Santiago's most formal and impressive public space. Its northern side is dominated by the elegant Renaissance **Hostal dos Reis Católicos** (Hostal de los Reyes Católicos). As late as the thirteenth century the Catedral was used to accommodate pilgrims, but slowly its place was taken by convents around the city. Fernando and Isabel, in gratitude for their conquest of Granada, added to these facilities by building this superb hostel for the poor and sick. Now a parador, it's very much *the* place to stay if you can afford it. Even if you're not staying here, stroll in to take a look at its four lovely courtyards or the chapel with magnificent Gothic stone carvings, or simply to have a drink or meal.

Praza da Quintana

Just as large as the Pza. do Obradoiro, but somehow more intimate, the **Praza da Quintana** holds a flight of broad steps that join the back of the Catedral to the high walls of the **Convento de San Paio**, and serve around the clock as impromptu benches for students and backpackers. The "Porta Santa" doorway here is only opened during Holy Years (see p.547).

Praza das Praterías

The **Praza das Praterías**, the Silversmiths' Square, centres on an ornate fountain of four horses with webbed feet, and features the seventy-metre-high Berenguela, or **clock tower**. On its west side is the extraordinarily narrow **Casa del Cabildo**, which was built in 1758 to fill the remaining gap and ornamentally complete the square – you'd never know to look at it, but it's little more than a facade.

San Martiño Pinario

Pza. San Martiño • Daily except Mon 11am–1.30pm & 4–6.30pm • €2.50 • ☎ 981 589 200, ⍩ museosanmartinpinario.com

The **Pza. da Inmaculada**, on the Catedral's northern side, is dominated by the grand Baroque frontage of the Benedictine monastery of **San Martiño Pinario**. At 20,000 square metres, this ranks among the largest religious buildings in Spain. Its left flank, as you face it, is now run as a hotel, while the monastery church to the right, entered via the nearby Pza. San Martiño, holds a quite extraordinary **museum**. The church itself is filled with magnificent Baroque altarpieces, while the various chapels and rooms to the side display bejewelled treasures and sculptures. Upstairs, things take a surprising twist: the monks' natural history collection includes a grotesque stuffed sloth, sharing space with an echidna and a pangolin, and there's also an apothecary they put together to treat pilgrims.

Museo das Peregrinacións

Rúa de San Miguel and Pza. das Praterías • Tues–Fri 10am–8pm, Sat 10.30am–1.30pm & 5–8pm, Sun 10.30am–1.30pm • €2.50 •
℡ 981 581 558, Ⓦ mdperegrinacions.com

Santiago's **Museo das Peregrinacións**, which relates the story of pilgrimage not only here but also to religious shrines the world over, has long been housed in the sixteenth-century Pazo de Don Pedro, a short way east of San Martiño Pinario. For several years it has also been due to move to new premises in the Pza. das Praterías. Strangely enough, at the time of research, both buildings were open. No one seems to know how that situation will resolve itself, but for the moment the museum's original incarnation still holds the bulk of the displays, including an intriguing room that explores how depictions of St James himself reflect his changing image over the centuries, while the newer version has superb models of both Catedral and town in the Middle Ages, and an interactive video game in which visitors use the avatar of a medieval pilgrim to explore the city.

Museo do Pobo Galego

C/San Domingos de Bonaval • Tues–Sat 10.30am–2pm & 4–7.30pm, Sun 11am–2pm • €3, free on Sun • ℡ 981 583 620,
Ⓦ museodopobo.es

Immediately northeast of the old quarter is the convent and church of **Santo Domingo**, which contains a unique seventeenth-century triple stairway, each spiral of which leads to different storeys of a single tower. If several of you set off up different flights, you may lose each other for hours. The convent houses the fascinating **Museo do Pobo Galego**, which features a diverse overview of Galego crafts and traditions, with a moving account of Galicia's history of emigration. Many aspects of the way of life displayed haven't yet entirely disappeared, though you're today unlikely to see *corozas*, straw suits worn into the last century by mountain shepherds. The convent chapel serves as the **Panteón de Galegos Ilustres**, home to the mortal remains of such local heroes as the poet Rosalía de Castro and the essayist and caricaturist Castelao. Gardens and orchards stretch up the hillside behind, offering a wonderful spot for a break from sightseeing.

Centro Galego de Arte Contemporánea

Rúa Valle Inclan • Tues–Sun 11am–8pm • Free • ℡ 981 546 619, Ⓦ www.cgac.org

The modern **Centro Galego de Arte Contemporánea**, opposite Santo Domingo convent, is a gloriously light and large exhibition space. It generally stages temporary shows of contemporary art and sculpture.

Cidade da Cultura

Monte Gaiás • Daily: April–Sept 8am–11pm, Oct–March 8am–8pm; museum closed Mon • Free • ℡ 881 997 565, Ⓦ cidadedacultura.org

Perched on a hillside overlooking the city, only 2km southeast of the centre but further than most visitors would choose to walk, the Cidade da Cultura (City of Culture) is an extravagant architectural showpiece that's yet another product of Spain's early twenty-first-century economic over-exuberance. Since its first sections, a museum and

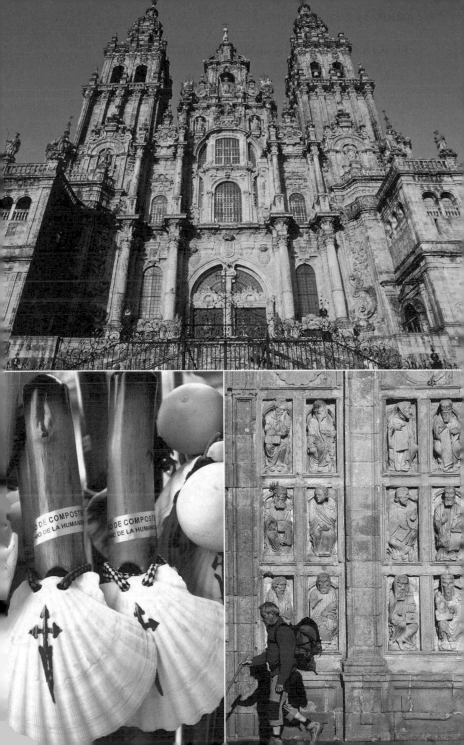

PRACTICALITIES OF THE CAMINO DE SANTIAGO

Most pilgrims heading for Santiago stay in hostels, called **albergues** or **refugios**. Conveniently spaced anywhere from 10 to 20km apart, these provide simple dormitory accommodation, are usually equipped with hot showers, sometimes have kitchen facilities and charge either a nominal fee of a few euros or ask for a donation. *Albergues* can get crowded in summer, so pilgrims sometimes have to sleep on mattresses on the floor. For those who crave a little more comfort, more upmarket choices are often available. As a pilgrim, you'll also receive special treatment at restaurants – most will have a pilgrim menu for about €8 – and meals are served earlier than the Spanish norm, at about 8pm.

To prove your pilgrim status at the *albergues*, you'll need a **credencial** (pilgrim passport); it's best to get one in advance from your local pilgrim association (see below), although you can also pick one up at the *albergue* in Roncesvalles. You can then collect *sellos* (stamps, as proof of your pilgrimage) from *albergues*, churches and even some enterprising cafés, and finally show your stamped *credencial* in Santiago in order to get a *compostela* (certificate of pilgrimage). According to the official rules, you need only walk the final 100km of the route, or cycle the last 200km, to be entitled to a *compostela*. If your motives are other than strictly religious, apply for a *certificado* rather than a *compostela*.

It's difficult to lose your way. The *camino* sticks to good tracks and minor roads, is clearly marked with yellow arrows, and mostly passes through populated areas where locals can steer you in the direction of Santiago. Spring and autumn are the **best seasons**: the route is quieter than in summer, most *albergues* are open, and you'll miss the weather extremes of the *meseta* and the mountains. If you're fit and healthy, you can walk from Roncesvalles to Santiago de Compostela in about a month, covering around 25km a day. Nevertheless, allow extra time for rest days, unforeseen injuries or just a whimsical decision to linger in one of the lovely towns en route.

The most useful website for information on the *camino* is ⓦ csj.org.uk. Run by the UK-based **Confraternity of St James**, it publishes route guides, maintains a busy online forum, and has links to similar organizations and **pilgrim associations** all over the world.

performance centre, opened in 2011, they've seen much less use, and far fewer visitors, than anticipated, and the future components of the plan have been quietly abandoned. Were the whole place to close down, it would come as no surprise.

CAMINO DE SANTIAGO

ARRIVAL AND DEPARTURE

By plane Santiago's airport is 13km east of the city in Lavacolla, on the road to Lugo, and is served by Ryanair flights from London Stansted. Frequent local buses (every half-hour; €3) connect the airport with the bus station and Rúa Doctour Teixeiro – the closest stop to the old town, just south of Pza. de Galicia. Taxis into town charge a flat rate of €22.

By train The train station is a 10min walk south of the old town at Rúa de Horreo 75.

Destinations A Coruña (16 daily; 35min); Burgos (daily; 8hr); Donostía/San Sebastian (daily; 10hr 30min); León (1–3 daily; 5hr); Madrid (3–7 daily; 5hr 30min–10hr 30min); Medina del Campo (3–7 daily; 4hr 20min–8hr); Ourense (10 daily; 40min–1hr 40min); Palencia (1–3 daily; 7hr); Pontevedra (15 daily; 1hr); Vigo (15 daily; 1hr 30min)

By bus Santiago's bus station is in an inconvenient and

SANTIAGO DE COMPOSTELA

very urbanized location, a 10min walk northeast of the old town. For schedules see ⓦ monbus.es.

Destinations A Coruña (hourly; 1hr 15min); Barcelona (daily; 17hr); Betanzos (7 daily; 1hr 30min); Camariñas (4 daily; 3hr); Cambados (5 daily; 2hr); Fisterra (4 daily; 3hr); León (daily; 6hr); Lugo (9 daily; 2hr); Madrid (3–6 daily; 9hr 30min); Muros (hourly; 1hr 30min); Muxía (2 daily; 2hr); Noia (hourly; 50min); Ourense (7 daily; 2hr); Padrón (every 30min; 45min); Pontevedra (hourly; 1hr); Vigo (hourly; 1hr 30min–2hr).

By car Drivers have little choice but to use one of the large car parks (ⓦ tussa.org) on the periphery, as almost all the streets in the old quarter are pedestrianized, and very few hotels offer parking facilities. The closest to the Catedral is the huge Xóan XXIII car park, a short distance north, which is also where all coach tours pull in.

INFORMATION

Turismo Rúa do Vilar 63 (June–Sept daily 9am–9pm; Oct–May Mon–Fri 9am–7pm, Sat & Sun 9am–2pm & 4–7pm; ☎ 981 555 129, ⓦ santiagoturismo.com) in the old town, also sells stamps. A separate office nearby at Rúa

do Vilar 30–32 (mid-April to mid-Oct Mon–Fri 9am–8pm, Sat 10am–8pm, Sun 10am–3pm; mid-Oct to mid-April Mon–Sat 10.3am–7pm; ☎ 981 584 081, ⓦ turgalicia.es) provides information on Galicia as a whole.

ACCOMMODATION

Santiago offers an enormous array of **accommodation** to suit all budgets, ranging from its gorgeous parador down to the many inexpensive *hostales* aimed at pilgrims and young travellers. Your priority should definitely be to stay in the old quarter, which is in any case where most places are concentrated. Even during the July festival, this is rarely a problem, as half the bars in the city rent out rooms. The city's tourist office offers discount bookings and last-minute availability online (ⓦ santiagoturismo.com).

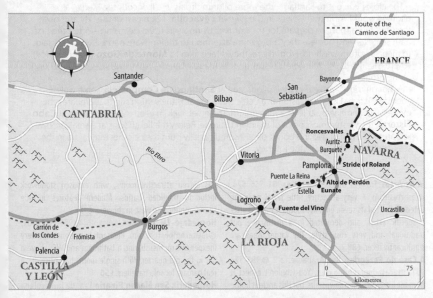

8

THE CAMINO DE SANTIAGO

The **Camino de Santiago**, or Pilgrim Route, is the longest-established "tourist" route in Europe. Its final section through Galicia provides echoes of the medieval pilgrimage to the thousands who walk it every year, armed with the traditional staff and the scallop-shell emblem of St James. Today's pilgrims seldom walk from their homes to Santiago de Compostela and back; most follow one of the half a dozen or so standard pilgrimage routes through Spain and France. The most popular, the 750-kilometre **Camino Francés**, heads westward from Roncesvalles (or Orreaga-Roncesvalles in Basque) in the Pyrenees across northern Spain. You don't have to be Christian, or even religious, to follow the route. For roughly half of all pilgrims, the journey to Santiago is prompted by their religious faith, while others want to experience their own spiritual quest, or simply to immerse themselves in Spanish history and culture. Whatever the motivation, the *camino*'s popularity has exploded in recent decades; while only a handful of people walked to Santiago in the 1960s, the route now attracts well over 100,000 pilgrims a year, half of whom are Spanish.

THE CAMINO DE SANTIAGO IN GALICIA

The Camino de Santiago in Galicia passes few tourist sights, meandering instead through countless tiny villages. Pilgrims work a little harder on this last leg as the route clambers up and down steep hills and valleys, but the scenery is gorgeous compensation: green with oak forests and patchworked fields. Galicia is green for a reason, however; the region gets a lot of rain, and you can get caught in a storm even in summer.

The Galician government has made a huge effort to promote the *camino*, maintaining an extensive network of pilgrim hostels along the eight separate routes that converge on Santiago – all are listed on the website ⓦxacobeo.es. The **Camino Francés** enters Galicia at the Pedrafita do Cebreiro pass, a desolate spot where hundreds of English soldiers froze or starved to death during Sir John Moore's retreat towards A Coruña in 1809. It's a fierce climb of 30km from Villafranca del Bierzo in León up cobbled paths often slick with mud and dung to the mountain village of **O Cebreiro**. There can be snow here in winter, and fog often obscures the spectacular views, but it's a magical place, with round, thatched-roof *pallozas* (stone huts) and intricate *horréos* (granaries).

The *camino* is naturally at its most crowded in Galicia. The volume of pilgrims peaks at **Sarría**, 115km from Santiago, which is the last major town where you can start walking and still earn a *compostela*.

The closer you get to Santiago, the more pilgrim rituals you'll encounter. Medieval pilgrims would wash themselves in the river at **Lavacolla**, 12km east of the city and now the site of its airport, to prepare for their arrival. During this ritual cleansing – often the first bath since leaving home – they'd pay extra attention to their private parts; *lavacolla* is said to mean scrotum-washing. From there, they'd race 5km to **Monte de Gozo** (Mount of Joy), where the first to cry "*mon joie*" on spotting Santiago's Catedral spires was declared the king of the group.

Although most people end their pilgrimage at **Santiago de Compostela**, some walk another 75km to Fisterra (Finisterra), a Celtic route towards the setting sun that predates the medieval pilgrimage by at least a millennium. The quiet, well-marked rural route ends at **Cabo Fisterra**, the westernmost point of mainland Europe. Below the lighthouse, at a small bronze sculpture of a pair of walking boots, pilgrims traditionally burn their clothes after a dip in the sea to celebrate the end of the journey.

★**As Artes** Travesa Dúas Portas 2 ☎981 555 524, ⓦasartes.com. A very attractive little hotel near the Catedral. Each of its seven en-suite rooms is named after a specific artist, and decorated in a distinctive but traditional and very cosy style. The larger ones are significantly nicer. **€88**

A Casa do Peregrino Rúa Azabachería 2 ☎981 573 931, ⓦacasadoperegrino.com. You wouldn't expect it from the ice-cream shop downstairs, but this ancient house has eleven attractive rooms, with exposed stonework including moulded basins. Modern features include soundproofing and walk-in showers. **€95**

Hospedaje La Tita Rúa Nova 46 ☎981 583 981, ⓦlatitacompostela.com. Pleasant, bare-bones and very inexpensive rooms, sharing a bathroom and WC, above a bar in the old quarter. With single rooms half-price, it's a real bargain for solo travellers. **€50**

Hospedería San Martín Pinario Pza. da Inmaculada

☎981 560 282, ⊛www.sanmartinpinario.eu. Stylish contemporary hotel, occupying part of a colossal and very central monastery. The rooms are still recognizably cells, with bathrooms, minimal furnishings and no TVs, but the beds are extremely comfortable, with luxurious linens. A hugely atmospheric and remarkably quiet location, it also offers all meals in its cavernous ancient dining rooms, open to non-guests as well. **€59**

Hostal Mapoula Rúa do Entremurallas 10 ☎981 580 124, ⊛mapoula.com. Clean, friendly, third-storey *hostal*, with spacious, en-suite rooms; some sleep three or four guests. It's close to the heart of the action, near good cafés and bars, so don't be put off by the slightly dingy alleyway. **€50**

★**Hostal dos Reis Católicos** Pza. do Obradoiro 1 ☎981 582 200, ⊛www.parador.es. Santiago's magnificent parador, facing the Catedral, is one of the world's most famous – and possibly oldest – hotels. Its 136 irresistibly luxurious rooms are arranged around four separate tranquil courtyards, and there are also two restaurants and a plush bar. It's worth every penny, especially if you get a multi-day discount. **€161**

Hostal Suso Rúa do Vilar 65 ☎981 586 611, ⊛hostalsuso.com. A neat, comfortable *hostal*, run by four friendly brothers, and consisting of ten en-suite rooms above a good bar-restaurant that stands alongside the *turismo* in a lively arcaded street. **€49**

★**Hotel Costa Vella** Rúa da Porta da Peña 17 ☎981 569 530, ⊛costavella.com. Welcoming, very comfortable and beautifully furnished hotel on the northern edge of the old quarter, with views over the rooftops. Paying a little extra gets you a larger room with a delightful balcony. Rates include breakfast, served in the small flower-filled garden in summer, which stays open as a bar all day. Nonguests are also welcome for breakfast – not a bad idea if you're staying somewhere plainer. **€81**

Hotel Hortas Rúa Hortas 30 ☎881 359 018. Tasteful conversion of a typical townhouse, a short walk from the Catedral down a quiet street, into a seven-room hotel. Sparkling modern bathrooms, plus a café downstairs. **€75**

Hotel A Tafona do Peregrino Rúa Virxe da Cerca 7 ☎981 568 923, ⊛atafonadoperegrino.com. Old house turned hip modern hotel, immediately east of the old quarter – across the road from the marketplace – featuring lots of exposed stonework and gleaming tiles. Smart bedrooms, two lounges, and a bar-café downstairs. **€70**

Pension da Estrela Plazuela de San Martín Pinario 5 ☎981 576 924, ⊛pensiondaestrela.com. Very welcoming little hotel, consisting of several spacious, simple en-suite rooms in private apartments facing a small and picturesque central square. There's also a shared kitchen, and the owners will wash a load of laundry for €6. **€45**

El Último Sello Rúa Preguntoiro 10 ☎981 563 525, ⊛thelaststamp.com. Named to signify the "last stamp" on the special passports carried by pilgrims, this new hostel is housed in a freshly converted historic building in the heart of town. Each guest gets a dorm bed, with its own lockable cupboard, but rooms can be configured to suit groups of two to eight guests, and there's a communal kitchen and laundry. Dorm **€18**

CAMPING

As Cancelas Rúa de 25 de Julio 35 ☎981 580 266, ⊛campingascancelas.com. Located well outside the old town, a half-hour walk uphill northeast from the Catedral, this year-round campsite has tent pitches and some four-person rental bungalows (€80). Served by buses #8 and #9, as well as the airport bus, it's reached via the road to A Coruña, branching off at the Avda. del Camino Francés. **€28.50**

EATING, DRINKING AND NIGHTLIFE

Santiago holds a plethora of great **places to eat**. The two main concentrations lie along the parallel rúas Franco and Raiña, which can get very busy in summer, and northeast of the Catedral on the quieter rúas da Troia and Porta da Peña, where there's much more outdoor seating. Traditional **tapas bars**, with small dishes spread out on the counter, are outnumbered by informal *mesones*, serving substantial and consistently superb seafood *raciones* for around €10. There are also plenty of more formal **restaurants**. With all those students to keep the city buzzing, countless bars remain alive with drinkers long into the night.

Santiago is also the best place in Galicia to hear Celtic **music**, played either by solo performers on *gaitas* (bagpipes), or by student ensembles known as *tunas,* who stroll the streets in historic garb at night, especially in summer, playing assorted guitars, mandolins and fiddles.

TAPAS BARS AND RESTAURANTS

O Dezaseis Rúa San Pedro 16 ☎981 564 880, ⊛dezaseis.com. Friendly rustic restaurant, near what was traditionally the main entry point for pilgrims reaching Santiago, where the good-value menu of local specialities includes a weekday set lunch for €12. Mon–Sat 2–4pm &

8.30pm–midnight.

Don Gaiferos Rúa Nova 23 ☎981 583 984, ⊛dongaiferos.com. Traditional restaurant, formal without being stuffy, in attractive cellar-like surroundings. The speciality is superb seafood cuisine, with simple but delicious fish dishes from around €20, and a set menu at

FOOD SHOPPING IN SANTIAGO

If you're shopping for your own food, don't miss the large covered **Mercado de Abastos**, held daily until 3pm in and around the venerable stone halls of the Pza. de Abastos, on the southeast edge of the old city. Thursday is the main market day, but it's also bustling on Saturdays. In addition, tiny delicatessens throughout town sell the traditional breast-shaped **cheese**, *queso de tetilla*, as well as flat *tarta de Santiago* almond cakes, adorned with crosses in honour of the Apostle; the *tartas* at *El Coral* at Dr Texeiro 32 are particularly renowned.

€22. Tues–Sat 1.15–3.45pm & 8.15–11.30pm, Sun 1.15–3.45pm.

Enxebre Hostal dos Reis Católicos, Pza. do Obradoiro 1 ☎ 981 582 200. The less formal of the parador's two restaurants, housed in the attractive former cellars and with its own entrance just off the square, serves tasty variations on traditional Galego cuisine, with tapas-sized portions as well as daily specials for around €15. Daily 1–4pm & 8–11.30pm.

O Gato Negro Rúa da Raiña s/n ☎ 981 583 105. Join the crowds jostling at the plain white bar, or push past to find a table in the back room, then settle down to enjoy classic Galego specialities such as *empanada* or peppers for around €3, or shellfish of all kinds. Tues–Sat 12.30–3pm & 7.30–11pm, Sun 12.30–3pm.

★**Maria Castaña** Rúa da Raiña 19 ☎ 981 560 137. This cosy bar/restaurant, with rough-hewn tables and exposed stone, serves delicious food at reasonable rather than rock-bottom prices, from simple seafood tapas or soft cheese wrapped in anchovies, via scrambled-eggy *revoltas*, with seaweed for example, for around €9, to paella-like fish *cazolos*, designed to share, at €29–45, plus affordable bottles of fine Galego wine. Daily 1–4pm & 8–11.30pm.

San Jaime Rúa da Raiña 4 ☎ 981 572 257, ⓦ restaurantesanjaime.com. All the usual *raciones* are available inside this little bar, and there's a limited-choice set-lunch menu for €12.90, but the best reason to come is to nab one of the few tables on the pretty Pza. de Fonseca, and enjoy the finest *chocolate con churros* in town. Daily 10am–11pm.

Sant Yago Rúa da Raiña 12 ☎ 981 582 444, ⓦ sant-yago.com. Smoked hams and cheese are the speciality at this friendly, stylish tapas bar, which also has an upstairs dining room, but the *tortillas* and seafood are every bit as good, and very well priced, with almost everything at or under €10, and a great-value three-course *menú del día* for €10.80 including wine. Daily noon–11pm; closed Mon in low season.

★**Los Sobriños del Padre la Casa del Buen Pulpo** Fonte de San Miguel 7 ☎ 981 583 566. The long-winded name belies the simplicity, and quality, of the *pulpo* (octopus), *tortilla* and other *raciones* at this very plain little local restaurant, which has pavement tables and serves

white china jugs full of wine for just €4. If you only eat *pulpo* once in your life, make it here. Mon–Sat noon–3pm & 7–11pm.

A Taberna do Bispo Rúa do Franco 37 ☎ 981 586 045, ⓦ atabernadobispo.com. This smart, busy tapas bar on the main tourist thoroughfare stands out for its brightly lit counter display of appetizing goodies, with lots of cheese and meat snacks as well as its €5–10 seafood offerings. Daily noon–midnight.

A Tulla Callejon de Entre Rúas 1 ☎ 981 580 889, ⓦ restauranteatulla.net. Small, very friendly bar-restaurant, shoehorned into a tiny square up an even tinier alley between rúas Nova and Vilar. Wonderful home cooking, from the bread and wide array of vegetables to the meat and seafood main dishes, almost all priced at €10 or less. Wed–Sat 1–4pm & 8.30pm–midnight, Mon, Tues & Sun 1–4pm; closed Tues in low season.

BARS AND CAFÉS

O Beiro Rúa da Raiña 3 ☎ 981 581 370, ⓦ obeiro.com. The back room in this *vinoteca*, very close to the Catedral, is a friendly and relaxing place to choose from a long list of fine local wines by the glass, or buy bottles to take home. There's also an upstairs dining room. Daily 11am–3.30pm & 6pm–1am.

Bierzo Enxebre Rúa do Troia 10 ☎ 981 581 909, ⓦ bierzoenxebre.es. Spilling out across an old stone alleyway, this ranks among the city's nicest places to drink outside on a sunny evening; there's also a decent, good-value but less exciting dining room indoors. Daily 1–3pm & 6pm–midnight.

Cafetería Hostal dos Reis Católicos, Pza. do Obradoiro 1. On a summer evening, the outdoor terrace at the parador, with views back towards the Catedral and out to the green hills, is the ideal spot to linger over a sunset cocktail. Daily 1pm–midnight.

Café Casino Rúa do Vilar 35 ☎ 981 577 503, ⓦ cafecasino.es. With its deep sofas and wood panelling, plus outdoor seating on the old stone lane, this venerable café/tearoom has a real old-world charm. Mon–Wed 8.30am–midnight, Thurs 8.30am–1am, Fri & Sat 11am–2am, Sun 9am–midnight.

★**Café Derby** Rúa das Orfas 29 ☎ 981 586 417. This

classic old café-bar facing the Pza. da Galicia from the edge of the old quarter, and kitted out with dark-wood panelling, green leather bar stools and bentwood chairs, has been a favourite local rendezvous for well over eighty years. Daily 8am–midnight.

Café Literarios Pza. da Quintana ☎981 882 912. The terrace of this popular café, perched at the top of the broad stairs in the square behind the Catedral, makes a perfect venue for peaceful people-watching. Daily 10am–1am.

Casa das Crechas Via Sacra 3 ☎981 576 108. Art Nouveau bar with a slightly boho edge just behind the Pza. da Quintana, with an emphasis on Galego, Breton and Celtic sounds, along with world music in general. Daily 4.30pm–4am.

O Filandón Rúa da Azabachería 6 ☎981 572 738. Thread your way through the simple cheese and wine shop to reach the narrow, bustling bar in the cave-like space at the back, where students and wine-lovers enjoy cheap, high-quality local *vinos* and free meaty morsels. Mon–Sat 8pm–1am.

Momo Virxe da Cerca 23 ☎981 565 580, ⊕pubmomo .com. A popular hangout with wide-ranging appeal, full of students during termtime. Fantastic and varied decor includes Parisian-style mini café-bars, an outdoor terrace and a jungle dancefloor. Daily 4pm–4am.

The Rías Altas

Galicia's north coast has been ravaged by the ocean into a series of dramatic bays and estuaries known as the **Rías Altas** (High Estuaries). As you head westward from Asturias, the coastline becomes noticeably more desolate, the road twisting around rocky inlets where wind-lashed villages cling to the shore, backed by eucalyptus forests and wild-looking hills. Driving is slow, though the final stretch of the **narrow-gauge railway**, from Luarca to Ferrol, is perhaps the most picturesque of the entire route.

Ribadeo

RIBADEO, the easternmost Galego town and *ría*, has little to offer beyond a certain crumbling charm. Its finest architecture is concentrated around the Pza. de España, where the **Palacio del Marqués de Sargadelos**, with its unusual decorative tower, is the town's main monument.

Thanks to its succession of fine beaches, the coast immediately west of Ribadeo has been subject to almost continuous low-level strip development. It's well worth stopping at the **Praia As Catedrais**, however, 6km along, where low tide reveals a procession of extraordinary natural arches, towering from a stark sandscape. The waves are usually too strong for swimming, but it's an unforgettable spot for coastal hiking, along a network of boardwalks.

ARRIVAL AND INFORMATION   RIBADEO

By train Ribadeo is served by trains along the coast, east towards Cudillero (2 daily; 2hr 10min) and west towards Viveiro (3 daily; 1 hr 5min).

Turismo Rúa Gamalo Fierros 7 (Mon–Fri 9am–4pm & 3–8pm, Sat & Sun 10am–2pm & 5–8pm; ☎982 128 689, ⊕ribadeoturismo.com), near the parador.

ACCOMMODATION, EATING AND DRINKING

Mediante Pza. de España 16 ☎982 130 453, ⊕hrmediante.com. The best-value alternative to the parador, on a pedestrian street in the centre of town. Several of its twenty rooms have balconies overlooking the main square. **€70**

Parador de Ribadeo Rúa Amador Fernández 7 ☎982 128 825, ⊕www.parador.es. Ribadeo's modern parador, a short way south of the centre, faces the green fields of Asturias across the Eo estuary. Its rooms spill down the riverbank in successive sunny tiers, each with its own glassed-in gallery. **€120**

★**San Miguel** Porto do Porcillán ☎982 129 717, ⊕restaurantesanmiguel.org. Superb, albeit expensive, seafood restaurant, immediately beneath the main road bridge across from Asturias, a short walk from Ribadeo's tiny and somewhat faded harbour. Fabulous views and great food, with huge paellas or *zarzuelas* priced at around €25 per person. Daily 1–4pm & 9pm–midnight.

8

Viveiro

Now much more of a tourist centre than a port, **VIVEIRO**, 60km west of the Asturian border, has holiday homes spreading up the hillsides of the *ría* and along its many **beaches**. The old town, however, remains protected by the vestiges of its Renaissance walls. Largely closed to traffic, its narrow streets are lined with glass-fronted houses in delicate wooden frames.

The large **Praia de Covas** is a good ten minutes' walk from town across a causeway, while the pick of several more peaceful beaches around the bay is the **Praia de Faro**, further up towards the open sea.

ARRIVAL AND INFORMATION VIVEIRO

By train and bus Both the bus station and the narrow-gauge railway station (2–3 trains daily in each direction to Ribadeo and Ferrol) are across the harbour from the old town, 5mins' walk apart.
Turismo Avda. Ramón Canosa (mid-June to mid-Sept

Mon–Fri 10.30am–2.30pm & 4.30–8pm, Sat 11am–2pm & 5–7pm, Sun 11am–1.30pm; mid-Sept to mid-June Mon–Wed & Fri 11am–2pm & 4.30–7.30pm, Thurs 11am–2pm; ☎ 982 560 879, ⓦ viveiro.es), on the edge of the old town on the waterfront.

ACCOMMODATION

With no hotels in the heart of the old town, there's something to be said for staying near the beaches, across the harbour.

Camping Vivero Praia de Covas ☎ 982 560 004, ⓔ campingdevivero@gmail.com. Viveiro's spacious, well-shaded campsite is located just behind the largest local beach. Closed Oct–May. **€20**
Hostal Vila Rúa Nicolás Montenegro 57 ☎ 982 561 331, ⓦ hotel-vila.es. Plain but clean and perfectly adequate

hotel, in a drab street just outside the walls at the Porta del Vallado. **€55**
Hotel As Areas Rúa Granxas 84 ☎ 982 560 605, ⓦ hotelesasareas.es. Comfortable hotel, set just back from the long Praia de Covas beach and a 20min walk from town. Free parking. **€64**

EATING AND DRINKING

O Asador Rúa Melitòn Cortiñas 15 ☎ 982 551 865, ⓦ oasador.com. Not far southwest of the main square in the old town, this formal restaurant offers excellent seafood, with fish mains for around €20 and a tasting menu for €40. Daily 1–3pm & 8–10.30pm.

O Muro Rúa Margarita Pardo de Cela 28 ☎ 982 560 823. This busy, functional *pulpería* and grill serves a wide menu of fish and meats, and even pizzas. Typical mains cost around €20, but there's a €9 *menú del día*. Tues–Sun 1–3.30pm & 7.30–10pm.

Porto do Barqueiro and Ortigueira

West of Viveiro, shorefront development finally thins out, and the scenery grows ever more dramatic. The next two *ría* villages (and train stops) are **PORTO DO BARQUEIRO**, 16km along, a tiny and very picturesque fishing port of slate-roofed houses near Spain's northernmost point, and the larger **ORTIGUEIRA**, 14km farther on, set amid a dark mass of pines and host to July's musical extravaganza, the International Festival of the Celtic World (ⓦ festivaldeortigueira.com).

ACCOMMODATION PORTO DO BARQUEIRO AND ORTIGUEIRA

★ **El Castaño Dormilón** 0 Baleo 15, Ortigueira ☎ 981 400 994, ⓦ elcastanodormilon.es. Former school, a short way inland 4km east of Ortigueira, which has been exquisitely converted into a bright, great-value and exceptionally comfortable rural inn. Rates include breakfast. **€89**

Hotel Porto do Barqueiro Porto do Barqueiro ☎ 981 414 098, ⓦ hotelportodobarqueiro.com. The best value among a handful of hotels dotted around the tiny harbour at Porto do Barqueiro; the rooms are undeniably plain, but the views are great, and €10 extra gets you a private balcony. **€50**

San Andrés de Teixido

While the narrow-gauge railway heads inland after Ortigueira, drivers can make a worthwhile side trip to the hermitage at **SAN ANDRÉS DE TEIXIDO**, the so-called

Mecca of the Galegos. The tortuous road up here leaves the main AC862 at **Mera**, 9km west of Ortigueira, and climbs for a magnificent 12km farther, high above the coast, threading in and out of the pine forests into rolling clifftop meadows and bare heathland. The cliffs at **Vixia de Herbeira**, just short of the sanctuary, are said to be the tallest in Europe, at over 600m, while the church itself perches high above the ocean. Like so many of Galicia's sanctuaries, it is based on a pre-Christian religious site, but a monastery was already in place by the twelfth century. It now welcomes coachloads of Galego pilgrims, so the adjoining hamlet holds a café as well as plenty of souvenir stalls.

Cedeira

CEDEIRA, 12km southwest of San Andrés in its own attractive little *ría*, is a graceful port where elegant houses and pleasant tapas bars line the shaded, canalized mouth of a little stream, while a huge beach sweeps south.

ACCOMMODATION
CEDEIRA

Hotel Herbeira Lugar de Cordobelas ☎ 981 492 167, ⓦ hotelherbeira.com. This startling modern hotel, on a hillside 1km south of town, looks like a stack of boxes; each holds a bright, beautifully equipped room with great views of both beach and town, and there's a large pool. **€93**

Betanzos

As the navy-dominated port of Ferrol, birthplace of General Franco, is best avoided, the final stop worth making in the Rías Altas is the ancient town of **BETANZOS**. Twenty kilometres southeast of A Coruña, at the head of the **Ría de Betanzos**, it's built on a pre-Roman site so old that what was once a steep seafront hill is now located well inland at the confluence of the Mendo and Mandeo rivers. The base of the hill is surrounded by fragments of medieval walls, now largely built over.

Betanzos' attractive main square, **Pza. dos Irmáns García Naveira**, is just below its appealing hilltop old quarter. A short walk up from here brings you to the much smaller Pza. da Constitución, home to the Gothic church of Santiago. Within the mass of twisting and tunnelling narrow streets immediately below stands the twelfth-century church of **Santa María do Azougue**, while the tomb of Conde Fernán Perez de Andrade "O Boo" (The Good), who commissioned its construction, lies in the Gothic **Iqrexa de San Francisco** opposite.

If you're in Betanzos on August 16, don't miss the **Fiesta del Globo**, the highlight of which is the midnight launch, from the Torre de Santo Domingo in the main square, of the world's largest paper balloon, daubed with political slogans. There is also a medieval **festival** in the second weekend of July, when the town is transported back to the times of the Andrade lords.

Museo das Mariñas

Rúa Emilio Romay 1 • June–Sept Mon–Fri 10am–1pm & 4–8pm, Sat 10.30am–1pm • €1.20 • ☎ 981 771 946

Just behind Betanzos' main square, the excellent **Museo das Mariñas** provides a fascinating insight into the history of the town and neighbouring *mariñas* (sea-facing villages), and includes a colourful collection of period costumes.

ARRIVAL AND DEPARTURE
BETANZOS

By train and bus The Betanzos Ciudad RENFE train station, a 10min walk south of the centre, is only used by the four daily trains between Ferrol and A Coruña. Other trains use the Betanzos Infesta station, 2.5km away at the top of a steep climb. Buses from A Coruña pull up just behind the square.

By car Driving in central Betanzos is all but impossible; park down by the river, and walk up from there.

INFORMATION

Turismo Pza. de Galicia 1, just off the main square (July to mid-Sept Mon–Fri 10am–2pm & 4.30–7.30pm, Sat & Sun 11am–2pm; mid-Sept to June Mon–Fri 10am–2pm & 4–7pm, Sat 10.30am–1pm; ☎ 981 776 666, ⓦ betanzos.net).

ACCOMMODATION

Hotel Garelos Rúa Afonso IX 8 ☎ 981 775 922, ⓦ hotelgarelos.com. A short walk west of the main square, just outside the hilltop centre, this jazzed-up town hotel offers smart, modernized en-suite rooms at slightly inflated prices. **€77**

EATING AND DRINKING

Eating and drinking possibilities in Betanzos centre on the row of attractive bars under the stone arcades of the main square, and the two tiny alleys that drop down between them.

★**Casa Carmen** Rúa da Fonte de Unta 12 ☎ 696 255 365. Delightful old *mesón*, with several tables beneath the venerable stone arches that lead down from the central square. There's a great range of seafood *raciones* and a €10.50 lunch menu; and the speciality is *tortilla de Betanzos*, an omelette that sandwiches layers of spinach and tomato. Mon & Wed–Sun 12.30–5pm & 8pm–1am.
O Pote Travesía do Progreso 9 ☎ 981 774 822, ⓦ mesonopote.com. Betanzos' finest tapas bar, tucked down a narrow alleyway, with a wide range of tasty snacks, a €16 menu of local specialties, and a buzzy atmosphere. Mon–Sat 1–4pm & 8–11.30pm, Sun 1–4pm.
Vinoteca Versailles Venela del Campo ☎ 981 772 910. Lovely modernist café, right on the main square, with decorative dark-wood panelling. Ideal for morning coffee, or fine wines later in the day. Thurs–Tues 10am–11pm.

A Coruña

The fine port of **A CORUÑA** centres on a narrow peninsula that juts from Galicia's northern coast, 64km north of Santiago. A broad headland curves in both directions from the end of that peninsula to create two large bays: one faces across to Ferrol, and shelters a large harbour, while the other lies open to the Atlantic, and is lined by a long sandy beach. In the dynamic city in between, a five-minute walk takes you from a bustling modern port to a relaxed resort, by way of old stone alleyways where tantalizing restaurants, tapas bars and nightspots jostle for attention.

The distinctive glass-fronted galleries of the sea-facing buildings, rising six storeys high along the Avenida da Marina in front of the port, form a magnificent ensemble. They were originally designed so local residents, whose lives were intertwined with the ocean, could watch the activity of the harbour in shelter.

Praza de María Pita

The heart of A Coruña, poised between the old city and its modern sprawl just inland from the port, is the colonnaded **Praza de María Pita**. The city's role as the departure point for the Spanish Armada in 1588 earned it a retaliatory visit from Sir Francis Drake the following year. His attack was only repelled when a humble local heroine, María Pita, killed the English standard-bearer; her spear-waving statue now dominates the square.

The old town

East of the Pza. de María Pita, the narrow and atmospheric streets of the **old town** wind around the Romanesque churches of **Santiago** and **Santa María del Campo**, and are shielded from the sea by a high wall. A small walled garden, the **Xardín de San Carlos**, holds the tomb of English general Sir John Moore, who died in battle near A Coruña in 1809 during the British retreat from the French during the Peninsular

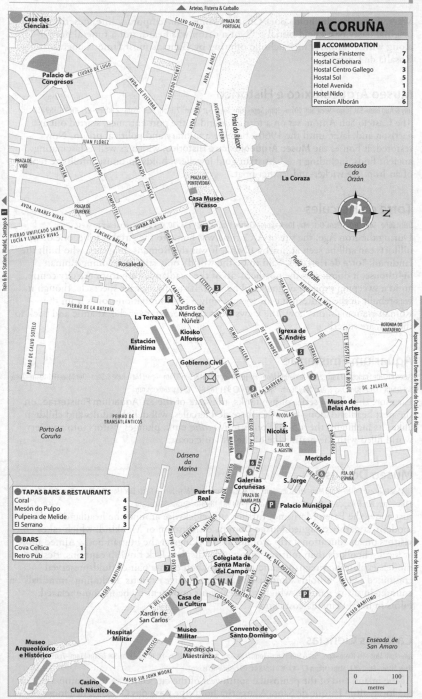

Arteixo, Fisterra & Carballo

A CORUÑA

Casa das Ciencias

Palacio de Congresos

CALVO SOTELO

PRAZA DE PORTUGAL

CIUDAD DE LUGO

ALFREDO VICENTI

AVDA. RUBINE

AVDA. B. AIRES

AVDA. DE FISTERRA

AVENIDA DE PEDRO

Praia do Riazor

JUAN FLÓREZ

PRAZA DE VIGO

FONTÁN

EL FERROL

BELANZOS

COMPOSTELA

FONSECA

PRAZA DE OURENSE

AVDA. LINARES RIVAS

C. JUANA DE VEGA

SÁNCHEZ BREGUA

DURAN LORIGA

PRAZA DE PONTEVEDRA

Casa Museo Picasso

La Coraza

Enseada do Orzán

N

PIERAO UNIFICADÓ SANTA LUCÍA Y LINARES RIVAS

Rosaleda

Praia do Orzán

PIERAO DE LA BATERÍA

LOS CANTONS

ESTRECA

RUA ALTA

JUAN CANALEJO

BARRIE DE LA MAZA

ROTONDA DO MATADERO

PEIRAO DE CALVO SOTELO

La Terraza

Xardins de Méndez Núñez

RUA NUEVA

Kiosko Alfonso

OLMOS

GALERA

DE SAN ANDRÉS

Igrexa de S. Andrés

DEL ORZÁN

SOL

C. DEL HOSPITAL SAN ROQUE

DE ZALAETA

Estación Marítima

Gobierno Civil

REAL

RUA DE LA BARRERA

CORRALÓN

Museo de Belas Artes

Porto da Coruña

PEIRAO DE TRANSATLÁNTICOS

Dársena da Marina

AVDA. DA MARINA

RIEGO DE AGUA

S. NICOLÁS

S. Nicolás

PZA. DE S. AGUSTÍN

FRANXA

PAN-ADEIRAS

PZA. DE ESPAÑA

Mercado

OLLOEIRA

Galerías Coruñesas

Puerta Real

PRAZA DE MARÍA PITA

S. Jorge

MERCADO

Palacio Municipal

TAREÑAS

SANTIAGO

PASEO DE LA DÁRSENA

Igrexa de Santiago

NTRA. SRA. DEL ROSARIO

M. ASTRAY

VERAMAR

PASEO MARÍTIMO

PASEO MARÍTIMO

Colegiata de Santa María del Campo

HERRERÍAS

ZAPATERÍA

CORTADURÍA

MAESTRANZA

OLD TOWN

P. DEL PARROTE

Casa de la Cultura

Xardín de San Carlos

Museo Militar

Hospital Militar

S. FRANCISCO

Convento de Santo Domingo

Xardins da Maestranza

Enseada de San Amaro

Museo Arqueolóxico e Histórico

Casino Club Náutico

PASEO SIR JOHN MOORE

0   100
metres

Train & Bus Stations, Madrid, Santiago

Aquarium, Museo Domus & Praias do Orzán & de Riazor

Torre de Hercules

8

Wars. A wall nearby holds poet Charles Wolfe's contemporary lines describing his original hasty battlefield burial – "Not a drum was heard, not a funeral note" – along with a similarly melancholic offering by Galicia's most famous poet, Rosalía de Castro.

Museo Arqueolóxico e Histórico

July & Aug Tues–Sat 10am–9pm, Sun 10am–3pm; Sept–June Tues–Sat 10am–7.30pm, Sun 10am–2.30pm • €2 • ☎ 981 189 850

The Castelo San Antón, set on a former island at the port entrance, started out as a garrison and, later, until the 1960s, became a military and political prison. Now restored, it houses the **Museo Arqueolóxico e Histórico**, which as well as fascinating ancient finds, including pre-Christian gold jewellery, holds an unusual full-size replica of an Iron Age wicker-and-leather boat.

Torre de Hercules

Daily: June–Sept 10am–9pm, Oct–May 10am–6pm • €3, free Mon • ☎ 981 223 730, ⓦ torredeherculesacoruna.es

During the Iron Age, the site of A Coruña was home to the Artabri tribe, one of whose hillforts can still be seen at nearby Elviña. It was the Romans, however, who built the landmark **Torre de Hercules**. Said to be the world's only still-functioning Roman lighthouse, it dominates the northern tip of the headland, 2km from the city centre, amid a sweeping expanse of grass and heather. It's an impressive spectacle, though it was rebuilt in the eighteenth century and only a few foundation stones from the Roman era remain on show. The views from the top, out over the Atlantic and back to the city, are superb.

Aquarium Finisterrae

Paseo Alcalde Francisco Vázquez 34 • Jan–April Mon–Fri 10am–6pm, Sat & Sun 11am–8pm; May, June & Sept–Dec Mon–Fri 10am–7pm, Sat & Sun 11am–8pm; July & Aug daily 10am–9pm • €10 • ☎ 981 189 842, ⓦ casaciencias.org

Far more than just a series of fish tanks, the state-of-the-art **Aquarium Finisterrae**, on the next headland along from the Torre de Hercules, will delight adults and children alike. Its highlight, the 4.5-million-litre *Nautilus* tank, plunges visitors into a watery world filled with the marine life of the Atlantic coast.

Museo Domus

Rúa Santa Teresa 1 • Jan–April Mon–Fri 10am–6pm, Sat & Sun 11am–7pm; May, June & Sept–Dec Mon–Fri 10am–7pm, Sat & Sun 11am–7pm; July & Aug daily 10am–8pm • €2, cinema €4 • ☎ 981 189 840, ⓦ casaciencias.org

Just above the Paseo Marítimo, further anti-clockwise around the headland, is the modern, superbly designed **Museo Domus**, or Museum of Mankind, which takes visitors on an educational trip around the workings of the human body. Aimed more at local schoolkids than tourists, many of its displays lack English captions. Besides models explaining pregnancy and childbirth, and even a pair of fluid-preserved conjoined twins, it holds some fascinating interactive exhibits, including "mindball", a counter-intuitive game in which you beat your opponent by being more relaxed. Films in its 3D cinema cost extra.

Casa das Ciencias

Jan–April Mon–Fri 10am–6pm, Sat & Sun 11am–7pm; May, June & Sept–Dec Mon–Fri 10am–7pm, Sat & Sun 11am–7pm; July & Aug daily 10am–8pm • €2, planetarium €2 • ☎ 981 189 844, ⓦ casaciencias.org

At the inland end of the peninsula, southwest of the city centre, a tower atop a hill in the lovely little Parque de Santa Margarita holds the **Casa das Ciencias**, or House of

Science. Filled with gadgets to play with, this enjoyable science museum is intended mainly for kids, and also features a planetarium.

Museo de Belas Artes

Rúa Zalaeta • Tues–Fri 10am–8pm, Sat 10am–2pm & 4.30–8pm, Sun 10am–2pm • €2.40, free Sat pm & all Sun • ☎ 881 881 700, ⓦ museobelasartescoruna.xunta.es

Conveniently located in a modern building in the old city core, A Coruña's fine arts museum, the **Museo de Belas Artes**, concentrates largely on religious art of the seventeenth and eighteenth centuries. Its pride and joy are a couple of small Rubens canvases, on themes taken from Greek mythology.

The beaches

The sweeping golden arc of the city's main beaches, **Praia do Orzán** and the contiguous **Praia de Riazor**, line the opposite side of the peninsula from the Dársena. Considering how very close they are to the city centre, they're surprisingly clean and unpolluted, and you need to arrive early in summer to grab a prime spot.

Casa Museo Picasso

Payó Gómez 14 • Wed & Sun 10.30am–2pm, Thurs–Sat 10.30am–2pm & 5.30–8pm• Free • ☎ 981 920 010

Pablo Picasso lived in A Coruña between the ages of 9 and 13, and produced his first oil paintings here. The **Casa Museo Picasso**, his former home just west of the city centre, is a typical galleried townhouse. It's of interest mainly for its authentic (but not original) period furnishings rather than the few reproduced paintings by both Pablo and his father.

ARRIVAL AND DEPARTURE

By train A Coruña's train station is south of the city, where Avda. Alcalde Alfonso Molina meets the ring road, Ronda de Outeiro; it's a half-hour walk to the centre, or you can take buses #5 or #11.

Destinations Barcelona (2 daily; 14hr); Betanzos (2 daily; 30min); Bilbao (daily; 11hr); Burgos (4 daily; 8–9hr); León (3 daily; 6hr); Lugo (4 daily; 1hr 45min); Madrid (2 daily; 8–10hr); Ourense (10 daily; 1hr 10min–3hr); Santiago de Compostela (16 daily; 35min); Vigo (15 daily; 2hr); Zaragoza (2 daily; 12hr).

By bus The bus station is 2km south of the centre at Rúa Cabelleros 21, a short walk from the train station.

Destinations Betanzos (every 30min; 45min); Camariñas

(3 daily; 2hr); Fisterra (5 daily; 2hr 10min); Laxe (3 daily; 1hr 50min); Lugo (8–14 daily; 1hr 15min); Madrid (8 daily; 7hr); Ourense (5 daily; 2hr 30min); Oviedo (4 daily; 3hr 45min–6hr); Pontevedra (10 daily; 1hr 45min); Santiago de Compostela (hourly; 1hr 15min); Vigo (9 daily; 2hr 15min); Viveiro (1 daily; 3hr 30min).

By car Driving in A Coruña is extremely difficult and unrewarding; no map could do justice to the tangle of dead-end and one-way streets in the old quarter. Drive out to the Torre de Hercules, but otherwise it's best to park as soon as possible, ideally in the central, underground Los Cantones car park.

INFORMATION

City turismo Pza. de María Pita 6 (Mon–Fri 9am–8.30pm, Sat 10am–2pm & 4–8pm, Sun 10am–3pm; ☎ 981 923 093,

ⓦ turismocoruna.com). You can also pick up tourist information at the Torre de Hercules.

ACCOMMODATION

Whatever your budget, the pedestrian streets that approach Pza. María Pita and the old town are the best hunting grounds for **accommodation**, though if you're driving you won't be able to park nearby.

Hesperia Finisterre Paseo del Parrote 2 ☎ 981 205 400, ⓦ hesperia-finisterre.com. The top option in town, this vast orange waterfront five-star, in easy reach of

everything, comes complete with tennis courts, Olympic-size swimming pool and every conceivable luxury. All rooms have sea views. **€125**

Hostal Carbonara Rúa Nueva 16 ☎981 225 251, ⓦhostalcarbonara.com. Simple en-suite rooms, some with balconies, in a friendly central location, with discounted parking in the nearby Orzan-Riazor car park. €60

Hostal Centro Gallego Rúa Estrella 2 ☎981 222 236, ⓦcentrogallegocoruna.com. The simple rooms at this budget hotel above a bar, several of which have balconies, are great value for such a central location. €57

Hostal Sol Rúa Sol 10 ☎981 210 362, ⓦhotelsol coruna.com. Behind the unprepossessing modern exterior, with its bordello-style flashing sign, the rooms in this central option, are stylish and comfortable. Rates include parking – a major plus for drivers. €75

Hotel Avenida Rúa Alvaro Cunqueiro 1 ☎981 249 466, ⓦhotelavenida.com. Stylish modern hotel, in a not especially attractive neighbourhood well south of the centre, but surprisingly quiet and offering a high standard for the price. €61

Hotel Nido Rúa San Andrés 146 ☎981 213 201, ⓦhotel-nido-coruna.com. On central A Coruña's main street, close to all the action, with fifty smart, shiny if unexciting rooms; for a quieter night, ask for one facing the courtyard. €60

Pensión Alborán Rúa Riego de Agua 14 ☎981 226 579, ⓦhostalalboran.es. Excellent location near Pza. María Pita, with thirty comfortable rooms, all with bath and some with balconies overlooking the attractive pedestrianized street. €50

EATING

The small streets leading west from Pza. de María Pita, from Rúa da Franxa through to Rúa La Galera, Rúa Los Olmos and Rúa Estrella, are crowded with bars that offer some of Spain's tastiest **seafood**.

Coral Rúa da Estacada 9 ☎981 200 569, ⓦrestaurantemarisqueriacoral.com. A Coruña's best formal restaurant, set very slightly back from the main portside boulevard in a tiny square. Typical meat main dishes cost €18–20, fish a little more. Daily 1–4pm & 8.30–11.30pm.

Mesón do Pulpo Rúa da Franxa 9 ☎981 202 444. In the cluster of *marisquerías* just off Pza. de María Pita, with no outside seating. Ultra-fresh seafood is the speciality; a full *ración* of its trademark octopus, sprinkled with paprika, costs €11.50, but half-portions are available. Mon–Sat 11am–3.30pm & 7.30pm–midnight.

Pulpeira de Melide Pza. de España 16 ☎981 152 197, ⓦpulpeirademelide.com. Enjoy the outdoor seating on the central square as you grapple with the eight-armed beauties at this classic Galego octopus restaurant, where a full *ración* costs €14; naturally they also offer a full range of regional specialities. Tues–Sat 11am–3.30pm & 7pm–midnight.

El Serrano Rúa la Galera 23 ☎981 220 353, ⓦelserrano. es. A cornucopia for carnivores, this fine old *jamonería* serves ham platters for €10 to €24, plus all kinds of sausage as well, and there's also a full menu of *raciones*, including excellent squid. Mon–11am–4pm & 7pm–midnight.

DRINKING AND NIGHTLIFE

In summer, the beachfront **bars** across the peninsula do a roaring trade, while bar-filled Rúa Orillamar is a good place to start the evening.

Cova Celtica Rúa do Orzan 82 ☎981 915 140. Celtic pub with exposed stone walls that's a popular rendezvous for folky students. Besides beers and a devastating coffee liqueur, it also serves snacks, and often has live Galego music. Mon–Thurs 7.30pm–2am,

Fri & Sat 7.30pm–3.30am.

Retro Pub Rúa do Orzan 19. Lively late-night pub in the heart of old-town A Coruña's busiest nightlife district, with a classic rock soundtrack and live bands at weekends. Daily 8pm–2am.

The Costa da Morte

Wild, windy and at times desolate, the **Costa da Morte**, west of A Coruña, is often passed over by tourists heading south to the beaches of the Rías Baixas. But while the Costa da Morte lacks both the climate and the infrastructure for large-scale tourism, it's not nearly as overdeveloped as the regions to the south, while boasting similarly beautiful coves, tiny fishing villages huddled against the headlands, and forested mountain slopes aplenty.

Its fearsome name – "Coast of Death" – stems from the constant buffeting the shoreline receives from the Atlantic waves. The most notorious of the countless

GETTING AROUND THE COSTA DA MORTE

While it's well worth following the coastal road west around the Costa da Morte all the way to Fisterra, you'll need to allow plenty of time. **Driving** is slow, and, with no train lines, **buses** offer the only public transport. They're predominantly operated by Monbus (w monbus.es), whose routes include Camariñas to Cée via Muxía (1 daily; 1hr), and Fisterra to Santiago via Cée, Carnota, Muros and Noia (6 daily; 3hr).

shipwrecks that litter the seabed is the oil tanker *Prestige*, which snapped in two following a ferocious storm in 2002. Although 77,000 tonnes of crude oil were released into the ocean, barely a trace of oil remained just twelve months later.

The coast from **Camariñas** to **Fisterra** is the most exposed and westerly stretch of all. Ever since a Roman expedition under Lucius Florus Brutus was brought up short by what seemed to be an endless sea, it has been known as *finis terrae* (the end of the world). This is prime territory, however, for hunting *percebes* (barnacles), one of Galicia's most popular and expensive seafood delicacies, which have to be scooped up from the very waterline. Collectors are commonly swept away by the dreaded "seventh wave", which can appear out of nowhere from a calm sea.

Even where the isolated coves do shelter fine beaches, you will rarely find resort facilities. While the beaches may look splendid, braving the water is recommended for only the strongest of swimmers, and the climate is significantly wetter and windier here than it is a mere 100km or so further south.

Malpica de Bergantiños

Few potential stopping points lie immediately west of A Coruña. If you're driving, take the toll motorway to its end at the busy inland road junction of **Carballo**. Heading north from there for 15km brings you to **MALPICA DE BERGANTIÑOS**, the first of a succession of tiny seaside ports. Crammed onto the neck of a narrow peninsula, Malpica consists of a harbour on one side and a marvellous – though exposed – beach hardly 100m away on the other.

The best local beach, the sheltered **Praia de Niñons**, is roughly 10km west. Follow signs for **Corme**, then turn right at the village of Niñons, from where narrow lanes thread through fields of maize to the sea. A granite church with a *fuente* (fountain) stands guard just above the beach itself, a crescent of thick sand that stretches out to either side of a little stream. Young Spaniards set up fireside campsites here in summer, but the solitary bar isn't open at night.

ACCOMMODATION, EATING AND DRINKING	**MALPICA DE BERGANTIÑOS**
Hostal Casa da Vasca Porto de Bariza 42 ☎ 981 721 960, w casadavasca.com. Seafront inn, on a gloriously isolated headland halfway between Malpica and the Niñons beach, with six comfortable modern rooms. **€65** **San Francisco** Rúa Eduardo Pondal 5 ☎ 981 720 489.	Good seafood restaurant in a tiny fishing village, where you can choose your dinner from a tankful of live sea creatures. Typical mains cost around €14, but watch out – a plate of *percebes* can easily work out at €100. Daily 12.30–3.30pm & 7.30–10.30pm.

Laxe

Some 24km southwest from Malpica, having crossed the River Anllóns via an ancient bridge at **Ponteceso**, the coast road reaches **LAXE** (pronounced "la-shay"), which offers the area's safest swimming. A formidable sea wall protects a small harbour, while the long sweep of fine, clean sand is backed by café-lined streets.

Just outside Laxe are two beaches, the deserted **Praia de Soesto**, which, though exposed, more than rivals the town beach; and a perfect cove, the **Praia de Arnado**.

There's another massively long beach, the **Praia de Traba**, 6km south; remote as anything, it's backed by sand dunes and a jigsaw of mini-fields.

ACCOMMODATION, EATING AND DRINKING	LAXE

Casa do Arco Pza. de Ramón Juega 1 ☎ 981 706 904, ⓦ casadoarco.es. This fine restaurant is housed in an ancient archway that leads off Laxe's attractive little seafront square. Most fish and meat dishes cost around €20, while there's a €20 set menu on weekdays, and a tasting menu at €40. They also run a cheaper *méson* and tapas bar, and offer simple rooms (€60). Daily except Tues 12.30–3.30pm & 7.30–11pm.

Hostal Bahía Avda Besugueira 24 ☎ 981 728 304, ⓦ bahialaxe.com. Laxe's most appealing hotel is right in the port, above a burger bar. Several of its en-suite rooms have spacious balconies with sea views, costing €20 extra. **€50**

Camariñas

Although the seafront buildings of **CAMARIÑAS**, 25km southwest of Laxe, are almost entirely modern, it's still an attractive village, curled around a harbour that holds a fishing fleet as well as the yachts of well-heeled visitors.

Camariñas marks the start of Galicia's wild west, at the region's westernmost extremity. A five-kilometre trek from town leads to the lighthouse at **Cabo Vilán**, guarding the treacherous shore on a rocky outcrop; climb the adjacent rocks for a stunning sea view. Winds whip viciously around the cape, and the huge, sci-fi propellers of the adjacent wind farm spin eerily, lit by the searchlight beam of the lighthouse once darkness falls.

ACCOMMODATION, EATING AND DRINKING	CAMARIÑAS

Café Bar Playa Avda. Ambrosio Feijoo 3 ☎ 635 523 002. This simple village bar, across from the harbour, serves great tapas and *raciones* at rock-bottom prices; even their bread is wonderful. Daily noon–3.30pm & 7–11pm.

Hostal Gaviota Rúa do Rio 15 ☎ 981 736 522, ⓦ hostalgaviota.en.eresmas.com. Modern hotel, set slightly back from the sea, with a dozen plain but reasonably pleasant rooms. **€50**

★ **Hotel Puerto Arnela** Pza. del Carmen 20 ☎ 981 705 477, ⓦ hotelpuertoarnela.es. This lovely little flower-bedecked hotel, in one of Camariñas' few ancient houses, faces the sea from the far end of the port. The nicest rooms have their own balconies; there's also a small restaurant, and the owners are exceptionally friendly. Rates include breakfast. **€60**

Muxía

On the tip of a rocky promontory, across the *ría* from Camariñas, the small fishing port of **MUXÍA** is nothing special. Make your way up to the Romanesque church on the hill above, though, and there's a fabulous view to either side of the headland. Paths lead down to the eighteenth-century **Santuario da Virxe da Barca**, where a massive sea-level church marks what was once an important site of Galicia's pre-Christian animist cult. The cult was centred around the strange granite rocks at the farthest point of the headland, some of which are precariously balanced and said to make wonderful sounds when struck correctly; others supposedly have healing power. In later times, the rocks were reinterpreted as being the remains of the stone ship that brought the Virgin to the aid of Santiago, an obvious echo of the saint's own landing at Padrón.

ACCOMMODATION AND EATING	MUXÍA

Casa de Lema Morpeguite ☎ 981 729 813, ⓦ casadelema.com. Lovely rural inn, inland 8km south of Muxía, with very comfortable exposed-stone rooms and nice gardens, and fresh home-cooked meals. **€70**

O' Coral Rúa Marina 22 ☎ 981 742 501, ⓦ restauranteocoral.com. Welcoming little restaurant in the town harbour, with outdoor seating overlooking the sea and good prices on seafood, with a €15 set menu, and paella for two costing €30. Daily 1–4.30pm & 8.30–11.30pm.

Fisterra

Famed, until Columbus told Europe differently, as the western limit of the world, the town of **FISTERRA** (**Finisterre**) still looks like it's about to drop off the end of the earth. On a misty, out-of-season day, it can feel like no more than a grey clump of houses wedged into the rocks, but it puts on a cheerier face in the summer sunshine.

Just beyond the southern end of Fisterra's long harbour wall, a tiny bay cradles an appealing beach, overlooked by the pretty little eighteenth-century **Castelo de San Carlos**. Originally an artillery post, this now holds a museum of fishing (May–Aug daily 11am–2.30pm & 4–8pm; Sept–April Tues–Sat 10.30am–1.30pm & 3.30–6.30pm, Sun 10.30am–1.30pm; €2). Beside the road south out of town is **Santa María das Areas**, is a small but atmospheric church. Its beautiful carved altar, like the strange weathered tombs left of the main door, is considerably older than the rest of the building.

ACCOMMODATION   FISTERRA

Albergue de Paz Rúa Victor Cardalda ☎ 981 740 332. Fisterra's cheapest accommodation, near the little castle at the south end of the port, with individual beds in two- to five-person dorms. **€10**

Casa Velay Pza. Cerca 1 ☎ 981 740 127, ⊛ casavelay.es. Poised above the northern end of Fisterra's little in-town beach, this friendly establishment offers bargain-priced rooms, and also has a good-value bar/restaurant, with outdoor sea-view tables. Restaurant daily 1–4pm & 8.30pm–midnight. **€40**

Hostal Praia de Estorde Praia de Estorde 217 ☎ 981 745 585, ⊛ restauranteplayadeestorde.wordpress.com.

Delightful if somewhat isolated *hostal*/restaurant, commanding a fine white-sand beach that nestles in a small cove 7km east of Fisterra, 1km beyond the village of Sardiñeiro. They also run a small summer-only campsite, *Ruta de Finisterre*, in the woods across the road. Tent plus car **€18**, *hostal* **€75**

Hotel Rural Prado da Viña Camino Barcia ☎ 981 740 326, ⊛ hotelruralpradodavina.com. Very comfortable little purpose-built B&B, on the hillside a short way north of central Fisterra, with nice en-suite rooms and a small swimming pool. Rates include breakfast. **€80**

Fisterra Lighthouse

Thanks to the shape of the headland, the **Fisterra Lighthouse**, which marks the final point of the Camino de Santiago, is actually 4km south of Fisterra itself. The road there leads first along a heather-clad mountainside, then through a pine-forest plantation; the squat, square lighthouse perches high above the waves at the tip of the cape. When, as so often, the whole place is shrouded in thick mist and the mournful foghorn wails across the sea, it's an eerie spot. Traditionally, this is where pilgrims would burn their clothes, signalling the end of the pilgrimage, and also collect their scallop shell; the wearing of a scallop throughout the journey is a relatively recent phenomenon.

ACCOMMODATION, EATING AND DRINKING   FISTERRA LIGHTHOUSE

★**Semaforo** Faro de Fisterra ☎ 981 725 869, ⊛ osemaforo.com. Small hotel/restaurant, a few metres before the lighthouse and the only place to stay right at the cape itself, which charges somewhat over the odds for its

five upscale guest rooms. The restaurant serves a €20 lunch menu, or you can get cheaper tapas at *O Refuxio*, the bar below. Closed Nov. Restaurant open daily 1.30–4pm & 8.30pm–midnight. **€110**

Ezaro, O Pindo and Carnota

Around **EZARO**, where the Río Xallas meets the sea 30km east of Fisterra, the scenery is marvellous. The rocks of the sheer escarpments above the road are so rich in minerals that they are multicoloured, and glisten beneath innumerable tiny waterfalls. Upstream there are warm, natural lagoons and more cascades. Another couple of kilometres on, the little (though far from picturesque) port of **O PINDO**, beneath a stony but thickly wooded hill dotted with old houses, also has a small beach.

Towards Carnota, another 12km south, the series of short beaches finally joins together into one long, unbroken line of dunes, swept by the Atlantic winds. The village of **CARNOTA** is a couple of kilometres from the shore, but its palm trees and old church are still thoroughly caked in salt. To get to the beach, you have to follow a long wooden boardwalk across the marshes.

ACCOMMODATION
O PINDO

Pensión Sol E Mar Praia do San Pedro, O Pindo ☎ 981 760 298. Good-value sea-view hotel on the main coast road, a short walk from the beach and with eight comfortable en-suite rooms. **€50**

Ría de Muros e Noia

The **Rías Baixas**, much the most touristed portion of Galicia's coastline, start in the north with the **Ría de Muros e Noia**. In truth, this *ría* is so close to the Costa da Morte that there's little difference in climate or appearance, and it remains relatively underdeveloped, but unspoiled little **Muros** is well worth visiting.

Muros

Some of the best traditional Galego architecture outside Pontevedra can be found in the old town of **MUROS**, enhanced by a marvellous natural setting at the widest point of the Ría de Muros, just before it meets the sea. The town rises in tiers of narrow streets from the curving waterfront, where fishing boats unload their catch, to the Romanesque **Iglesia de San Pedro**. Everywhere you look are squat granite columns and arches, flights of wide steps, and benches and stone porches built into the house fronts. There's also a nice – though small – **beach** on the edge of town next to the road to Fisterra.

ARRIVAL AND INFORMATION
MUROS

By bus Monbus services from Santiago (hourly; 1–2hr) stop across from the *Ría de Muros* hotel (see below).
Turismo The seasonal *turismo* is in the central square, where the coast road bends (July to mid-Sept Mon–Fri 10am–2pm & 4–7pm, Sat 10.30am–3pm, Sun 11am–2pm & 4–9pm; mid-Sept to June Mon–Fri 10am–3pm; ☎ 981 826 050, ⊛ muros.es).

ACCOMMODATION

★**Hostal Ría de Muros** Rúa Castelao 53 ☎ 981 826 056. A real unexpected gem; behind its unprepossessing exterior on the coast road through town, this eight-room hotel offers fantastic value. The six rooms away from the road are smart but unexceptional, but the seafront doubles on the top storey, which cost €10 extra, are breathtaking: spacious and tastefully furnished, with glorious balconies facing the harbour and bay. **€50**

★**Jallambau Rural** Lugar de Miraflores ☎ 981 826 083, ⊛ jallambaurural.com. Commanding a majestic panorama of the bay from the hillside above town, and reached via a ferociously steep, narrow road, this superbly equipped and positioned four-room B&B can also be rented in its entirety as a holiday home. Four-night minimum in high season. **€70**

EATING AND DRINKING

Pulpería Pachanga Rúa Castelao 29 ☎ 981 826 048. Right on the seafront, with outdoor seating in its own little precinct, this excellent *raciones* bar-restaurant has a stone-vaulted interior, and serves fresh seafood and grilled meats; you can eat well for €10 a head. Daily 11am–11pm.

Xamonería O Varadoiro Rúa A Canavala 2, Pza. da Pescadería ☎ 981 826 331. This cheap ham, cheese and tapas place is one of several good café-restaurants on a little inland square, a block back from the seafront behind the Ría de Muros. Daily noon–3pm & 7.30–11pm.

Noia

NOIA (Noya), 25km east of Muros near the head of the *ría*, is, according to a legend fanciful even by Galego standards, named after Noah, whose Ark is supposed to have struck land nearby. Scarcely less absurd is Noia's claim to be a "Little Florence", on the strength of a couple of nice churches and an arcaded street or two. Nonetheless, there is a lot to like about Noia. Developed in the Middle Ages to serve as Santiago's port, and now connected to it by a fast motorway, it recently experienced a major overhaul that reinvigorated its medieval core. The single most impressive building, the church of **San Martino**, dominates a delightful ancient square.

ACCOMMODATION, EATING AND DRINKING   NOIA

Hospederia Valadares Rúa Egás Móniz 1 ☎ 981 820 436, ⓦ hospederiavaladares.com. Clean modern hotel beside the main promenading square, at the edge of the old core, offering simple rooms plus a restaurant serving all meals. **€50**

Tasca Típica Rúa Cantón 15 ☎ 981 821 842. Hugely atmospheric tapas bar, spreading from a fourteenth-century mansion onto tables tucked beneath imposing stone arches, and serving, as promised, the typical array of Galego specialities. Daily 10.30am–3.30pm & 8–10.30pm.

Baroña

From Noia the AC301 heads inland through deep, lush gorges towards Padrón. To trace the southern side of the Ría da Noia, sometimes called the "Cockle Coast", follow the C550 as it winds past dunes that serve in good weather as excellent beaches.

From the roadside *Castro de Baroña* restaurant, just outside **BAROÑA** (Basonas) 18km along, a fifteen-minute walk down through the woods leads to a lovely little beach. Built on top of a rocky outcrop that juts from the sand into the sea, and somehow spared by the mighty Atlantic waves for the last two millennia, are the remains of the **Castro de Baroña** itself. This once-impregnable pre-Roman settlement consists of the circular stone foundations of several thatched dwellings – similar to those at A Guarda farther south – which were in turn enclosed behind a fortified wall.

Ría de Arousa

Tourism on a significant scale starts to make its presence felt in the next *ría* south, the **RÍA DE AROUSA**. The most popular destination is the old port of **O Grove** – linked by bridge to the island of **A Toxa**, which holds a very upscale enclave of luxury hotels – while much the nicest of the old towns hereabouts is **Cambados**, renowned for its beautiful central plaza.

Strip development mars much of the coast, but the hillsides just inland are a patchwork of tiny fields, primarily planted with the grapes that go into the delicious local **Albariño wine**. Gourmets will want to sample authentic *pimientos* in the village of **Padrón**.

Padrón

According to legend, St James completed his miraculous posthumous voyage to Galicia by sailing up the Ría de Arousa as far as **PADRÓN**. Accumulated silt from the Río Ulla having left it stranded 12km inland, Padrón is no longer even on the sea, and the old town now consists of a handful of narrow pedestrian lanes squeezed between two busy roads. There's surprisingly little to show for the years of pilgrimage, except an imposing seventeenth-century church of Santiago, where the actual *padrón* (mooring post) to which the vessel was tied supposedly resides under the high altar.

Padrón is best known as the source of the small green peppers known as **pimientos de Padrón**. Available in summer only, they're served whole, shallow-fried in oil and liberally sprinkled with sea salt. Most are sweet, but around one in ten is memorably hot.

Rosalía de Castro museum

A Matanza • June–Sept Tues–Sat 10am–2pm & 4–8pm, Sun 10am–1.30pm; Oct–May Tues–Sat 10am–1.30pm & 4–7pm, Sun 10am–1.30pm • €2 • ☎ 981 811 204, ⓦ rosaliadecastro.org

A short walk east of old Padrón, just across the tracks from the pink-painted RENFE station, the house of nineteenth-century Galego poet **Rosalía de Castro** is now a **museum**. Unless you're a devotee of her work, the jumble of texts, photographs and bric-a-brac may not hold much interest, but the low-ceilinged rooms furnished in period style have character, and the gardens are pleasant.

INFORMATION   PADRÓN

Turismo Avda. de Compostela (Tues–Sat 10am–2pm & 4.15–7pm, Sun 10am–1.30pm; ☎646 593 319, ⓦ concellodepadron.es).

ACCOMMODATION, EATING AND DRINKING

O Pementeiro Pza. do Castro 3 ☎981 810 641, ⓦ restauranteopementeiro.es. Though it serves a full regional menu, this central restaurant is especially renowned for its local peppers; sample a plateful for well under €10. Daily 12.30–2.30pm & 7–11pm.

Pensión Jardín Rúa Salgado Araújo 3 ☎981 810 950, ⓦ pensionjardin.com. The best-value place to stay in

Padrón; a beautiful eighteenth-century house, overlooking the park on the edge of the old town. **€60**

Pulpería Rial Pza. das Travesas 13 ☎981 811 624, ⓦ pulperiarial.com. Friendly and attractive octopus and seafood restaurant, on a tiny little square in the heart of the old town; a plate of their signature *pulpo* costs €10. Daily noon–3pm & 6–10.30pm.

THE WINES OF GALICIA

Thanks largely to the international success of its crisp, dry **Albariño**, now the best-known Spanish white wine, Galicia has become a premium wine-producing region. The Romans first introduced vines two thousand years ago, growing them on high terraces sculpted by slaves into the banks of rivers like the Miño and Sil. With its mild climate and high rainfall, Galicia is more akin to Portugal than to the rest of Spain – Galego wines, and especially Ribeiro, were much exported to Britain during the seventeenth and eighteenth centuries, before declining relations between Britain and Spain led the Portuguese to develop their own wineries, which produce similar wines to this day.

Technically, "Albariño" is the name of a grape variety, introduced to Galicia by monks who followed the Camino de Santiago all the way from the Rhine during the twelfth century – it translates literally as "white wine from the Rhine". Albariño cultivation centres around the **Rías Baixas** (ⓦ doriasbaixas.com), where around five thousand farmers grow grapes on tiny, scattered plots, often banding together to bottle and market their wine. The largest cooperative winery, **Condes de Albarei**, on the main road 2km south of Cambados, is open for guided tours and visits (☎986 543 535, ⓦ condesdealbarei.com).

The best-selling wine in Galicia itself is **Ribeiro**, produced around **Ribadavia** on the Río Miño. It comes in both white and red, from such grape varieties as Treixadura, Torrontés and Loureira. The recent success of Albariño having spurred greater quality control, white Ribeiro has lost its previous trademark cloudiness, and is seen as the closest Spanish approximation to the dry Muscadet of France. Ribadavia's tourist office (ⓦ ribadavia.net) organizes guided tours, and provides maps and listings for free, self-guided winery visits.

Only the **Ribeira Sacra** region, concentrated along the stunning canyon of the Río Sil (see p.590), produces more red than white wine. That it's not better known is largely because two-thirds of it never reaches the market but is drunk by the producers themselves. There are no large wineries or even cooperatives, but the three thousand or so farmers who create it have instigated a tourist route through the region and its vineyards (ⓦ ribeirasacrata.com).

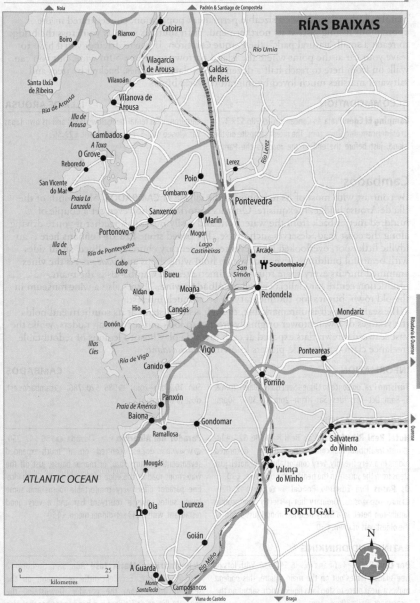

RÍAS BAIXAS

Noia

Padrón & Santiago de Compostela

Boiro

Rianxo

Catoira

Río Umia

Vilagarcía
de Arousa

Caldas
de Reis

Santa Uxía
de Ribeira

Vilaxoán

Ría de Arousa

Vilanova de
Arousa

*Illa de
Arousa*

Cambados

Río Lerez

A Toxa

O Grove

Lerez

Reboredo

Poio

San Vicente
do Mar

Combarro

Pontevedra

*Praia La
Lanzada*

Sanxenxo

Marín

Portonovo

Mogor

Arcade

*Illa de
Ons*

*Lago
Castiñeiras*

San
Simón

♨ Soutomaior

Ría de Pontevedra

*Cabo
Udra*

Bueu

Moaña

Redondela

Aldan

Mondariz

Hio

Cangas

Donón

Ponteareas

*Illas
Cíes*

Vigo

Ría de Vigo

Canido

Porriño

Panxón

Baiona

Salvaterra
do Minho

Praia de América

Gondomar

Tui

ATLANTIC OCEAN

Ramallosa

Valença
do Minho

Mougás

PORTUGAL

Oia

Loureza

N

Goián

Río Miño

0   25
kilometres

A Guarda

*Monte
SantaTecla*

Camposancos

Viana do Castelo

Braga

8

Ribadavia & Ourense ▶

Ourense ▶

Illa de Arousa

The first two towns on the southern shore of the Ría de Arousa, **Vilagarcía de
Arousa** and **Vilaxoán**, just over 20km southwest of Padrón, are too industrialized
to make worthwhile stops. A little further south, however, a 2km road bridge leads out
to the wooded **ILLA DE AROUSA**, which holds some great beaches. Effectively part of the

mainland, the island holds a sizeable permanent population, concentrated in the eponymous fishing port at its northern end. Turn south as soon as you cross the bridge to reach a small "natural park", the **Parque Carreirón**. If you're driving, you'll have to leave your car at the point where the island narrows to a mere 50m wide, but you can walk on from here to reach half a dozen fine, isolated beaches, backed by trees and saltwater marshes much loved by migratory water birds.

ACCOMMODATION   ILLA DE AROUSA

Camping El Edén Praia do Concerrado ☎ 986 527 378, ⓦ eledencampingplaya.com. The nicest campsite on the island, just before the end of the road to the Parque Carreirón, with rental bungalows (€50) and its own tapas bar. Closed mid-Sept to mid-April. **€23.30**

Cambados

By contrast with most of its neighbours, the village of **CAMBADOS**, 5km south of the Illa de Arousa bridge, is exquisite. Only its historic core, however, set a couple of hundred metres back from the waterfront and easily missed altogether if you're driving along the coast road, deserves such praise. The paved stone **Pza. de Fefiñáns** here is an idyllic little spot, overlooked by a seventeenth-century church and lined on all sides with beautiful buildings, several of which hold wine shops and *bodegas*. As the vines crammed into its every spare square centimetre testify, Cambados is the main production centre for Galicia's excellent **Albariño wine**. There's also a **wine museum** in the old town, but it's too rudimentary to be of much interest.

The seafront itself is unremarkable, though a small island at its southern end holds the vestiges of a watchtower originally erected to look out for Viking raiders, while the vast seaweed-strewn flats exposed at each low tide play host to legions of redoubtable freelance clam- and cockle-pickers known as *mariscadoras*.

INFORMATION   CAMBADOS

Turismo Pza. do Concello (June–Sept daily 10am–2pm & 5–8pm; Oct–May Tues–Sat 10am–2pm & 4.30–7.30pm, Sun 10.30am–2pm; ☎ 986 520 786, ⓦ cambados.es), close to the ocean.

ACCOMMODATION

Hotel Real Ribadomar Rúa Real 8 ☎ 986 524 404, ⓦ hotelrealribadomar.com. Thoughtfully decorated rooms in a very friendly, very comfortable little hotel, just steps from the square in the heart of the old town. **€90**

Os Pasos Rúa Eduardo Pondal 1 ☎ 986 542 020, ⓦ hotelospazos.es. Ordinary but perfectly comfortable family-run hotel, in a lively neighbourhood just south of the oldest part of town. **€50**

Parador del Albariño Pza. Clazada ☎ 986 542 250, ⓦ www.parador.es. Centred on a much-expanded seventeenth-century *pazo*, or manor house, just off the waterfront road at the edge of the old town, Cambados' fine parador offers very comfortable rooms and some lovely suites, plus a courtyard bar and a very good restaurant, with a €33 set-dinner menu. **€150**

EATING AND DRINKING

Bar Laya Pza. de Fefiñáns ☎ 986 542 436. With lots of tree-shaded tables out on the main square, this *bodega* makes a great place to stop for a liquid lunch, sampling the local wines. Daily 10am–1pm.

Pub Brothers Pza. Alfredo Brañas 2. On summer weekends, the old lanes just inland from Cambados' marketplace fill with young revellers; this pub, on a tiny square, is right in the thick of things, and often features late-night DJs and/or live music. Fri & Sat 4.30pm–4am, Sun 4.30pm–1am.

★**Restaurante María José** Rúa San Gregorio 2 ☎ 986 542 281. Excellent little restaurant, on the seafront across from the parador. Downstairs, the separate *Rincon de Tío Paco* is a good tapas bar that also sells ice cream. Up above, María José adds a creative twist to Galego staples, with a €12.50 lunch menu and set-dinner menus, including half a bottle of Albariño per person, at €15 and €20. Mon–Wed & Sun 1.30–4pm, Thurs–Sat 1.30–4pm & 9–11.30pm.

O Grove and A Toxa

At the northern tip of the peninsula that lies across the bay from Cambados, **O GROVE** exists primarily as a family resort. Inexpensive bars and restaurants compete for the attention of the summer influx of visitors, while hotels line the waterfront Rúa Teniente Domínguez and its continuation, Rúa Castelao. The town plays host to a huge Fiesta do Marisco, or Shellfish Festival, early in October.

Across the bridge, the pine-covered islet of **A TOXA** (La Toja) caters for a completely different clientele. It's very explicitly a playground for the wealthy, with luxury holiday homes and three huge and very expensive hotels set in the forest clearings, and a nine-hole golf course so guests can practise their swing.

Acuario de O Grove

Aquarium July & Aug daily 10am–9pm; Sept–June Mon–Fri 10am–6pm, Sat & Sun 10.30am–7.30pm • €12 **Glass-bottomed boats** April–June & Oct 2–4 daily; July–Sept every 30min 10.30am–7.30pm • €15 • ☎ 986 732 327, ⓦ acuariodeogrove.es

In the port area of Punta Moreiras, just before the village of **Reboredo** 3km southwest of O Grove, the **Acuario de O Grove** displays a huge selection of Atlantic marine life, and explains the various fishing traditions of Galicia.

INFORMATION
O GROVE AND A TOXA

Turismo There's a small kiosk by the port of O Grove (Mon–Sat 10am–8pm, Sun 11am–2pm; ☎ 986 731 415, ⓦ turismogrove.com).

ACCOMMODATION

Though **O Grove** has plenty of accommodation options, those along the seafront tend to be pricey in summer. Even more exclusive and expensive hotels lie across the bridge on **A Toxa**, while the pretty village of **San Vicente do Mar**, 8km southwest at the opposite end of the peninsula, offers cheaper and quieter alternatives.

Casa Angelina Rúa Torre Cacheiras 4, San Vicente ☎ 986 738 167, ⓦ casaangelina.com. This attractive modern house, close to the beach at the western tip of the peninsula, offers ten comfortable en-suite rooms, the nicest of which have sea-view balconies. **€45**

Hesperia Isla La Toja A Toxa ☎ 986 730 050, ⓦ hesperia.com. The most luxurious of A Toxa's three hotels, with extravagant sea-view rooms, two fine restaurants and two cafés. Spa facilities include a dazzling turquoise indoor pool with a cascading waterfall, while treatments on offer involve liberal use of mineral salts and mud. For a particularly decadent massage, you can even have yourself rubbed with chocolate oil, then given a chocolate body mask. **€170**

Hotel Puente de la Toja Rúa Castelao 206, O Grove ☎ 986 730 761, ⓦ hotelpuentedelatoja.com. The smartest waterfront hotel in O Grove, facing the bridge to the island, can be great value in low season. Rates include breakfast. **€89**

CAMPING

Moreiras Rúa Reboredo 26, Moreiras ☎ 986 731 691, ⓦ campingmoreiras.com. Well-shaded beachfront campsite near the tip of a little inlet 3km west of O Grove, close to the aquarium and with its own restaurant and shop. They also have bungalows, starting at €59 for two people. **€25**

Paisaxe II Praia de Area Grande ☎ 986 738 331, ⓦ campingplayapaisaxe.com. Large campsite, just back from the beach near San Vicente, 8km west of O Grove, with rental bungalows from €90 and a restaurant. Closed Nov–March. **€22**

EATING AND DRINKING

Although the waterfront by the port in O Grove is full of the inevitable *marisquerías*, it holds disappointingly few tapas places.

★ **Balcón** Pza. de Arriba 11, O Grove ☎ 610 569 021. Very friendly tapas bar/*meson*, with a few tables on a tiny square just up from the seafront, a cosy interior, and polka-dot flowerpots up on the balcony. As well as a great-value, all-day €10 set menu, they offer good sandwiches and

snacks. Daily noon–11pm.

O Lavandeiro Rúa Hospital 2, O Grove ☎ 986 731 956. Fancy fishy restaurant, set slightly back from the port, where a *mariscada* (seafood platter) for two costs €42. Tues–Sun 1–3.45pm & 8.15–11.15pm.

8

Ría de Pontevedra

Of all the Rías Baixas, the long, narrow **Ría de Pontevedra** is the archetype, its steep and forested sides closely resembling a Scandinavian fjord. **Pontevedra** itself is a lovely old city, set slightly back from the sea at the point where the Río Lérez begins to widen out into the bay. Though it lacks a beach of its own, it makes a good base for excursions along either shore of its *ría*. The **north coast** is the more popular with tourists, with Sanxenxo (Sanjenjo) as its best-known resort, but if you want to avoid the built-up sprawl, head for the **south coast**, which stretches out past secluded beaches towards the rugged headland, ideal for camping in privacy.

Praia La Lanzada and the north-shore beaches

The southern side of the narrow neck of the peninsula that holds O Grove is adorned with the region's largest beach, the vast golden arc of **PRAIA LA LANZADA**. Packed with sun worshippers in summer and a favourite of windsurfers in winter, the whole strand is best admired from the sloping hillside of the peninsula at its western end. The mainland to the east holds several more excellent **beaches**, often far less crowded than La Lanzada. Most have campsites nearby.

Sanxenxo

The coastal resort of **SANXENXO** (Sanjenjo) lies 10km southeast of La Lanzada, or 17km west of Pontevedra. Together with the barely distinguishable suburb of **Portonovo**, 3km west, it forms the heart for Galicia's one real exercise in mass tourism: not that there's any large-scale development, just a long succession of little beaches, each with its own crop of largely seasonal small **hotels**. Individually they tend to be nice enough, but cumulatively they're overwhelming; as the major attraction for Spanish visitors is the summer **nightlife**, they're interspersed with bars and clubs that keep going from 10pm until 8am nightly.

INFORMATION

SANXENXO

Turismo In the marina at the east end of the main Praia de Silgar beach (July to mid-Sept Mon–Sat 10am–2pm & 4–8.30pm, Sun 10am–2pm; mid-Sept to June Tues–Sat 9.30am–2pm & 4–7pm; ☎ 986 720 825, ⊛ sanxenxo.es).

ACCOMMODATION

Antiga Casa de Reis Lugar de Reis 39, Padriñan ☎ 986 690 550. This lovely B&B, set in a restored farmhouse up in the hills 2km northeast of Sanxenxo, offers a great change of pace. All its seven antique-furnished rooms (including one single at €75) have en-suite facilities, and are named for particular grape varieties; this is prime wine-growing territory. Closed Dec–March. **€119**

Hotel Farsund Praia de Areas 54 ☎ 986 729 000, ⊛ hotelfarsund.es. Friendly little hotel, with simple but perfectly adequate rooms, in a quiet area a very short walk from the beach west of central Sanxenxo. Closed Nov–April. **€60**

Illa de Ons

The beautiful **ILLA DE ONS** lies out on the ocean at the mouth of the Ría de Pontevedra. Wilder and more windswept than the nearby Illas Cíes, it's home to a community of fishermen and some interesting birdlife. Good walking tracks here provide terrific views of coast and sea; you can hike round the entire island in about three hours, or climb to the lighthouse and back in just over an hour.

Although you arrive at the pretty Praia das Dornas, the eastern shore is indented with half a dozen small but very sandy **beaches** so it's easy enough to escape the crowds and find your own patch of paradise. The best of the lot is the **Praia de Melide**, a gorgeous stretch of white sand near the northern tip. There are no hotels or other facilities, but it is possible to **camp** for free, within a designated area.

By ferry Several ferry companies serve Illa de Ons, for €14 return; broadly speaking, with individual variations, they run daily between June and early September, and on weekends only in May and late September. Naviera Mar de Ons sail from Sanxenxo, Portonovo and Bueu (☎986 225 272, ⓦmardeons.com); Cruceiros Rías Baixas from Sanxenxo and Portonovo (☎986 731 343, ⓦcrucerosriasbaixas.com); and Pirates de Nabia depart from Bueu (☎986 320 048, ⓦpiratasdenabia.com).

Combarro and Poio

The fishing village of **COMBARRO**, 7km west of Pontevedra, boasts the largest collection of *hórreos* (stone granaries) in Galicia, lining the waterfront and looking out across the *ría* to Marín. A path cut into the rocks leads from the main square behind the *hórreos*; it's littered with souvenir shops and poky but atmospheric bars and tavernas, several of which have outdoor tables. During Combarro's **sardine festival**, on June 23, the fish are grilled in the open air on the shore. Inland, the tight streets are lined with little houses, each with its Baroque stone balcony and gallery, winding claustrophobically towards the chapel of San Roque at the heart of town.

Monasterio de Poio

April–Oct Mon–Sat 10.30am–1.30pm & 4.30–8pm, Sun 4.30–8pm; Nov–March Mon–Sat 10am–1pm & 4–6pm, Sun 4–6pm • €1.50 • ☎ 986 770 000, ⓦmonasteriodepoio.com

Two kilometres east of Combarro, above the modern town of **POIO**, the seventeenth-century Benedictine **MONASTERIO DE POIO** is a haven of calm. Its cloister features a million-piece mosaic mural of the Camino de Santiago, created between 1989 and 1992 by Czech artist Anton Machourek, and there's also an eccentric little museum of tiny books.

Casa Solla Avda. Sineiro 7 ☎986 872 884, ⓦnove.biz /es/solla. Very fancy, expensive modern restaurant, on the main road through Poio, offering delicious gourmet food and good views over the fields. The set tasting menu costs €61, and there are gourmet versions at €78 and €98. Tues, Wed, Fri & Sat 1.30–3.45pm & 9–11.30pm, Thurs & Sun 1.30–3.45pm.

Monasterio de Poio ☎986 770 000, ⓦmercedarios .com. The stately monastery of Poio also contains a wonderful *hospedaría*, modern and efficient despite the age and beauty of its setting, and with a *cafetería* that serves all meals daily, 8am–8pm. **€50**

Pontevedra

Compact, charming and very tourist friendly, **PONTEVEDRA** is the quintessential old Galego town. Located just back from the open sea at the head of its namesake *ría*, at the last bend in the Río Lérez, it was supposedly founded by a Greek hero returning from the Trojan War, and later became a prosperous medieval fishing port. Although it has lost its ancient walls, it still centres on an attractive *zona monumental*. A maze of pedestrianized flagstoned alleyways, interspersed with colonnaded squares, granite crosses and squat stone houses with floral balconies, the old quarter is always lively, making it perfect for a night out enjoying the regional food and drink.

Prazas da Peregrina and da Ferrería

Two adjoining squares connect Pontevedra's old and new quarters. The **Praza da Peregrina** holds a pilgrim chapel, the **Santuario de la Peregrina**, a tall, eye-catching Baroque structure with a floor plan in the shape of a scallop shell, while the **Praza da Ferrería** is a paved square lined by arcades on one side and rose trees on the other. On its eastern side, the town's main church, **San Francisco**, is best admired from outside.

Amid the fountains, gardens, and open-air cafés that surround the Praza de Ferrería, all the daily rituals of life in a small town take place, especially during the Sunday *paseo*, when the entire population hits the streets. It's also the prime location for the city's many festivals, the busiest of which, **Os Maios**, lasts through the whole of May.

To reach the **zona monumental**, follow any of the narrow lanes that lead north from Praza da Ferrería. Rúa Figueroa swiftly reaches the attractive little complex of old stone houses adjoining the picture-postcard **Pza. da Leña**.

The Alameda and around

Leading down from Pza. de España towards the sea, the **Alameda** is a grand promenade watched over by magnificent buildings and dotted with monuments commemorating largely naval achievements. Slightly off the Alameda stands a **statue of Christopher Columbus**. Some locals even claim the navigator was a native son who decided to pass himself off as Genoese.

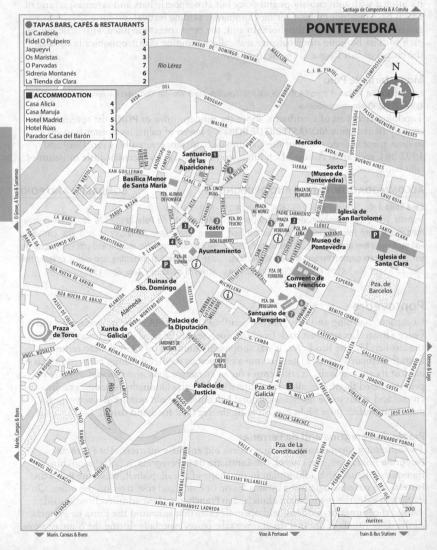

TAPAS BARS, CAFÉS & RESTAURANTS	
La Carabela	5
Fidel O Pulpeiro	1
Jaqueyvi	4
Os Maristas	3
O Parvadas	7
Sidreria Montanés	6
La Tienda da Clara	2

ACCOMMODATION	
Casa Alicia	4
Casa Maruja	3
Hotel Madrid	5
Hotel Rúas	2
Parador Casa del Barón	1

PONTEVEDRA

Museo de Pontevedra

Pza. da Leña • Tues–Sat 10am–9pm, Sun 11am–2pm • Free • ☎ 986 804 100, ⦿ museo.depo.es

Centering on a couple of old stone houses, linked by a little open-air bridge, in the gorgeous Pza. da Leña, the **Museo de Pontevedra** traces local history from megaliths and hand axes, via pre-Roman gold and silver, to the modern era. As well as a large model of Christopher Columbus' flagship, the *Santa María*, which was built in Pontevedra and is also known, here at any rate, as *La Galega*, there's also a strange underground chamber remodelled to evoke the officers' room of the *Numancia*, Spain's first ironclad warship, built in 1862.

In 2012, the museum expanded into a vast new complex 100m east, which consists of the new **Sexto** (Sixth) building and the converted Sarmento convent. Typical products of Spain's early twenty-first-century boom years, and now as a rule disconcertingly empty, the galleries here display an extensive collection of art and sculpture from the town and province. Pride of place goes to the artist and writer **Alfonso Castelao**, who was driven into exile under Franco, and died in Argentina in 1950. His beautifully observed paintings, drawings and cartoons, at their most moving when depicting prewar poverty and the horror of the Civil War, celebrate the strength and resilience of the Galego people.

ARRIVAL AND DEPARTURE
PONTEVEDRA

By train and bus Both stations are about 1km southeast of the centre, side by side, and connected to the town centre by half-hourly buses from the bus station (€1). At least one local bus hourly connects the bus station with each of Cambados, Cangas, O Grove and Vigo; each route

takes an hour or less.
By car If you're driving, you won't be able to penetrate the historic core; it's best to park on the fringes, in the big car parks under Rúa Santa Clara and Pza. de España.

INFORMATION

Turismo Pza. da Verdura, in the old town (summer daily 9am–2pm & 4–8pm; winter Mon–Sat 9.30am–2pm &

4.30–7.30pm, Sun 10am–2pm; ☎ 986 090 890, ⦿ visit-pontevedra.com).

ACCOMMODATION

Finding good **accommodation** in Pontevedra is a little challenging. While it's definitely preferable to stay in the winding streets of the **zona monumental**, where there is at least a good parador, that area holds very few mid-range options, so you may well have to settle for a plain, simple budget alternative. Hotels in the new town tend to be characterless and overpriced.

Casa Alicia Avda. de Santa María 5 ☎ 986 857 079, ⦿ habitacionescasaalicia.blogspot.fr. Four good-value, well-kept rooms, sharing bathrooms, in a pleasant house on the edge of the old quarter. **€40**
Casa Maruja Avda. de Santa María 12 ☎ 986 854 901, ✉ casamarujapontevedra@gmail.com. Very plain but clean and perfectly acceptable en-suite rooms, just inside the old quarter; the garish bathrooms are not exactly soothing, though. **€45**
Hotel Madrid Rúa Andrés Mellado 5 ☎ 986 865 180, ⦿ hotelmadrid.org. A somewhat anonymous hotel, a short walk south of La Peregrina in the newer part of town. Its standard modern rooms are light and spacious, making it a good-value alternative. **€46**

Hotel Rúas Rúa Figueroa 5 ☎ 986 846 416, ⦿ hotelruas.net. This welcoming central hotel is in an excellent location, in an attractive building near the museum and tourist office with entrances on two of Pontevedra's squares, and has its own good restaurant and café. Its en-suite rooms are good value, though they can get noisy on a summer night; choose one without an external window if that's a concern. **€55**
Parador Casa del Barón Rúa del Barón 19 ☎ 986 855 800, ⦿ www.parador.es. Elegant but delightfully cosy and well-priced parador, in a historic stone mansion tucked into a tiny square in the heart of the old quarter, with a little off-street parking. **€130**

EATING AND DRINKING

The twisting streets of old Pontevedra are packed with tiny **bars** and **restaurants**, and are especially jammed with late-night revellers at weekends. When it comes to **tapas bars**, the choice is almost overwhelming. Prime areas to start

8

exploring include the *zona's* prettiest squares: the tiny **Pza. da Cinco Rúas** is a central hub, from which five streets lined with bars run spoke-like in all directions; the arcaded **Pza. da Verdura** is a lively nightlife centre, where several bars have open-air tables; and the elegant **Pza. Teucro**, with its orange trees, holds some grown-up wine bars.

La Carabela Pza. da Ferraría ☎ 986 581 245. Named for Columbus' flagship, this handsome old café has been the favourite rendezvous on Pontevedra's central square for generations; huddle over a €3 breakfast at the picture windows inside, or savour evening drinks and free peanuts at the numerous outdoor tables, under the arcades and spilling into the flowery gardens. Daily 8am–1am.

Fidel O Pulpeiro Rúa San Nicolás 7 ☎ 986 851 234, ⓦ opulpeiro.es. Central, simple *mesón*, just off the Pza. da Cinco Rúas, with glaring lights and white tables but big helpings of fabulous fresh octopus and seafood for €10–12. Daily except Wed 11am–3pm & 7pm–3am.

Jaqueyvi Rúa Dona Tareixa 1 ☎ 986 861 820. When you've had your fill of seafood, come to this smart bar, in front of the Teátro Municipal, for traditional Galego hams and cheeses. Friendly and intimate, with the odd formal touch, it serves mixed platters at good prices, along with excellent local wines. Daily 11am–4pm & 6pm–12.30am.

★ **Os Maristas** Pza. da Verdura 5 ☎ 986 844 075. Busy bar with a lot of outdoor seating, that serves a full menu of *raciones* but is renowned for the astonishing liqueur, Tumba

Dios, an esoteric but fearsome blend of *aguardiente* (firewater) and *vino de pasas* (raisin wine), laced with coffee plus sundry secret herbs and spices. Daily 10am–3pm & 7pm–midnight.

★ **O Parvadas** Rúa González de Zúñiga 4 ☎ 986 864 710. Wonderfully atmospheric bar, tucked away in a little cottage behind the Peregrina church, and also known as *Casa Fernandes*. Besides serving delicious, ultra-cheap Ribeiro wine in white ceramic bowls, they offer a full menu of *raciones*. Join the local elders indoors, or head for the tiny vine-covered courtyard at the back. Mon–Sat noon–midnight.

Sidreria Montañés Rúa González de Zúñiga 6 ☎ 986 101 594. Asturian-style cider is something of a rarity in Galicia, but this lively bar, with an extensive outdoor patio, is a welcome exception, and it also serves great Asturian stews and cheeses. Mon–Sat noon–midnight.

La Tienda da Clara Pza. de Teucro 16 ☎ 986 102 071. Classy wine shop that also serves fine wines and beer, plus well-priced snacks, to be relished at outdoor tables that spread from under the arcades onto the attractive Pza. de Teucro. Daily 1–3.30pm & 7pm–2am.

The southern shore

Though the first stretch of the Ría de Pontevedra's southern side is extremely ugly, those who press on beyond the military town of **Marín**, 7km southwest of Pontevedra and also home to an exceptionally smelly paper factory, are rewarded with some gorgeous and largely deserted little bays. **Buses** from Pontevedra's Pza. de Galicia run right around the headland and along the southern shore of the *ría*.

Praia de Mogor

Beyond Marín the bay broadens into a series of breathtaking sandy coves. A narrow side road drops away from the main coast road immediately beyond the naval academy outside Marín, leading to three beaches. The second of these, the **Praia de Mogor**, is perfect, with fields of green corn as the backdrop to a crescent of fine, clean sand, one end of which is shielded by a thick headland of dark green pines. There are a couple of seasonal bar-cum-restaurants overgrown with vines, and the villagers' rowing boats are pulled up in the shade of the trees.

Ría de Vigo

The **Ría de Vigo** ranks among the most sublime natural harbours in the world. Its narrowest point is spanned by a vast suspension bridge that carries the Vigo–Pontevedra highway; you'll see its twin towers from all around the bay. On the inland side is what amounts to a saltwater lake, the inlet of **San Simón**. The road and railway from Pontevedra run beside it to **Redondela**, separated from the sea by just a thin strip of green fields, and pass close to the tiny San Martín islands, once a leper colony and used during the Civil War as an internment centre for Republicans. Beneath these waters lies a fleet of Spanish bullion galleons, sunk by a combined Anglo-Dutch force at the Battle of Rande in 1703.

The city of **Vigo** looks very appealing, spread along the waterfront, but although it makes a good base for trips along the south shore to **Baiona**, across the bay to **Cangas**, and, especially, out to the wonderful **Illas Cíes**, it has few attractions of its own.

Cangas

The prime reason to visit the ever-growing resort of **CANGAS**, facing Vigo across the *ría*, is to enjoy the superb twenty-minute **ferry** ride from Vigo. During the crossing, watch out for the *mexilloneiras* – ramshackle rafts used for cultivating mussels and perched on the bay like water-spiders; sometimes they are topped by little wooden huts.

Cangas is at its most lively during the Friday **market**, when the seafront gardens are filled with stalls. Otherwise, make for the **Praia de Rodeira**, a ten-minute walk from the ferry jetty (turn right as you get off, then follow the seafront); which is a beautiful five-hundred-metre sandy beach with majestic views.

The beaches and hills west of Cangas are stunning and all but deserted. The best target is the **Praia de Melide**, at the tip of the peninsula 2km beyond **Donón**. An isolated cove backed by woods and a lighthouse, it offers superb walks along the cape.

ARRIVAL AND INFORMATION   CANGAS

By bus and ferry Frequent ferry services between Cangas and Vigo operate daily (from Vigo 7.30am–10.30pm; from Cangas 7am–10pm; €4.45 return, €3.40 if the outbound trip is before 9am; wmardeons.com). Ferries to the Illas Cíes also leave from here in summer (May–Sept 4 daily;

1hr; €18.50), and there's a bus station alongside the jetty used by buses to and from Pontevedra and Vigo.
Turismo The *turismo* is right where the ferries dock (Mon–Fri 9am–3pm & 4.30–7.30pm, Sat & Sun 9am–2pm & 4.30–7.30pm; ☎986 392 023, wcangas.org).

ACCOMMODATION AND EATING

A considerable main cluster of **bars and restaurants** surrounds the port in Cangas.

Hostal Prado Viejo Rúa Ramón Cabanillas 16, Moaña ☎986 311 634, wpradoviejo.com. Pleasant hotel in Cangas' closest neighbour, Moana, 5km east; it has stylish en-suite rooms with floor-to-ceiling windows, a smart seafood restaurant and private parking. **€55**
Hotel Airiños Avda. Eugenio Sequeiros 30, Cangas ☎986 304 000, wairinos.com. This modern hotel offers comfortable sea-view rooms on the inland side of Cangas'

waterfront public park, and also has a decent restaurant. **€85**
Hotel Playa Avda. Ourense 78, Cangas ☎986 301 363, whotel-playa.com. Good-value hotel, right on the beach in the middle of the Praia de Rodeira, and open year-round. As well as tasteful, well-equipped rooms, they also offer self-catering apartments of various sizes. **€63**

Castillo de Soutomaior

Daily except Mon: summer 11am–2pm & 5–9pm, winter 11am–2pm & 4–7pm • €1.50 • ☎986 804 100, wcameliagalicia.com

A worthwhile detour 2km east of the village of Arcade, north of Vigo on the old road to Pontevedra, leads to the twelfth-century hilltop **castle of Soutomaior**. The rambling halls and towers of the castle itself are used for temporary exhibitions, while its superb landscaped grounds are planted with mighty sequoias and other exotic species. One former inhabitant travelled to Samarkand early in the fifteenth century, as ambassador to the court of Tamerlane the Great.

Vigo

Few cities enjoy such a superb natural setting as **VIGO**. Arrayed along the sloping southern shoreline of its namesake estuary, it enjoys superb views not only of the bay itself, surrounded by green forest ridges, but also out towards the ocean. While it's undeniably magnificent when seen from a ship entering the harbour, once you're ashore it fails to live up to that initial promise, and few visitors use it as anything more than an overnight stop.

Although Vigo is now the largest city in Galicia, home to some 300,000 people, Baiona, closer to the mouth of the *ría*, was the principal port hereabouts until the nineteenth century. Then the railways arrived, and Vigo became the first Galego town to industrialize, with the opening of several sardine canneries. It's now Spain's chief fishing port – indeed, some claim it's the largest in the world – with wharves and quays stretching almost 5km along the shore.

Pride of place in the middle still belongs to the passenger port where generations of Galego emigrants formerly embarked for the Americas. These days, cruise passengers mingle with tourists arriving at the **Estación Marítima de Ría** off the Cangas ferry, and set off to explore the steep, cobbled streets that climb up into the old city, known as **O Berbés** and crammed with shops, bars and restaurants.

Along the seafront early in the morning, kiosks revive fishermen with strong coffee, while there and in the lively daily market hall nearby, the **Mercado da Pedra**, their catch is sold. Immediately below, on the aptly named **Rúa da Pescadería**, women set out plates of fresh oysters on permanent granite tables to tempt passers-by. On **Rúa Carral**, shops sell kitsch marine souvenirs.

Castro hill

A stiff but enjoyable climb up from the old town, mostly along stone staircases, brings you to the top of the **Castro hill**. So named for the circular ancient ruins still visible on one side, and also the site of a seventeenth-century castle, the hill provides comprehensive views.

Museo Quiñones de León

Tues–Fri 10am–2pm, Sat 5–8pm, Sun 11am–2pm • Free • ☎ 986 295 070, ⓦ museodevigo.org

The **Museo Quiñones de León** is the focal point of the large **Parque de Castrelos**, the extensive formal gardens and woodlands which begin 2km southwest of Castro hill. Set in an attractive old manor house, it's one of Galicia's widest-ranging museums, covering both the archeology and history of Vigo and its region. It also boasts a fine collection of Galego art.

The beaches

Most of the **beaches** near Vigo are crowded and unappealing. Farther south, however, the beach at **Samil** is better, while those at **Vao** and **Canido**, further on, are also quite reasonable, and are equipped with campsites.

ARRIVAL AND DEPARTURE	VIGO

By plane Vigo's airport, currently served by internal Spanish flights only, is 9km east of the city on bus route #9A.

By train Vigo's RENFE station is 500m southeast of the old town.

Destinations A Coruña (15 daily; 2hr); Barcelona (2 daily; 14–15hr); Burgos (4 daily; 7–8hr); Irún (daily; 11hr 30min); León (5 daily; 6hr); Madrid (6 daily; 6hr 30min–11hr 15min); Ponferrada (6 daily; 4–5hr); Pontevedra (15–18 daily; 30min); Oporto (2 daily; 2hr 15min); Santiago de Compostela (15–18 daily; 1hr 30min).

By bus Vigo's bus station is 500m south of the RENFE station, making it 1km southeast of the old town. Local buses #12A and #12B (all €1.32; ⓦ vitrasa.es) run via the train station to the Porta do Sol in the old town.

Destinations A Coruña (9 daily; 2hr 15min); Baiona (every 15min; 1hr); Cangas (20 daily; 1hr); Lugo (5–6 daily; 3hr); Madrid (3 daily; 8hr); O Grove (2 daily; 1hr 15min); Oporto and Lisbon (3 weekly; 3hr 30min/6hr); Ourense (13 daily; 2hr); Oviedo (daily; 6hr 15min); Pontevedra (every 30min; 30min–1hr); Ribadavia (13 daily; 1hr 30min); Santiago de Compostela (hourly; 1hr 30min–2hr); Tui (every 30min; 45min).

By car The most convenient central car parks are on the seafront at Rúa das Avenidas – where a truly extraordinary elevator system whisks your car away from you – and beneath the Porta do Sol.

By boat Boats from the Estación Marítima, immediately below the old town, cross the *ría* to Cangas (see p.583), and head out in season to the Illas Cíes (see opposite).

INFORMATION

Turismo Avda. In the Estación Marítima, at Cánovas del Castillo 3 (April–Sept daily 10am–5pm, Oct–March Mon–Sat 8am–3pm; ☎ 986 224 757, ⓦ turismodevigo.org/en.

Vigo's **hotels** are concentrated in two main areas: around the old town, down by the port, which is close to the best restaurants and bars; and in the less atmospheric streets up by the train station.

Hostal Ancla Dorada Rúa Irmandiños 2 ☎ 986 223 403, ⓦ ancladorada.com. Welcoming family hotel, 200m west of the train station towards the old town, with clean, simple rooms, some with shared bathrooms and some sleeping up to four. **€40**

Hostal Casais Rúa Lepanto 16 ☎ 986 112 956, ⓦ hostalcasaisvigo.com. Simple and very friendly budget

hotel, offering small en-suite rooms in a surprisingly quiet location near the train station. Rates include breakfast. **€38**

★ **Hotel Puerta Gamboa** Rúa Gamboa 12 ☎ 986 228 674, ⓦ hotelpuertagamboa.com. Very friendly family-run hotel, set in a charming nineteenth-century house in the old town, just a few steps from the ferry port. All eleven rooms are en suite, with good facilities; some have large balconies. Rates include breakfast, and drop considerably in low season. **€105**

Hotel Puerta del Sol Rúa Porta do Sol 14 ☎ 986 222 364, ⓦ hotelpuertadelsol.es. Clean, very central hotel that offers small but pleasant en-suite rooms with TV, plus a couple of five-person apartments. Good off-season and weekend discounts. **€65**

EATING AND DRINKING

Virtually all the **bars** in Vigo's old quarter serve great tapas. Rúa da Pescadería is the liveliest place for **lunch**, at the outdoor tables among the oyster sellers.

Marisquería Bahía Rúa da Pescadería ☎ 986 449 655, ⓦ marisqueriabahia.com. Taking up most of one side of the so-called "street of oysters", this claims to be the largest seafood restaurant in Spain. Decorated with an odd mixture of underwater scenes and antelope heads, it serves consistently excellent seafood, and prices aren't too steep, starting at around €15. Daily except Wed 11am–5pm & 8.30pm–12.30am.

El Mosquito Pza. da Pedra 4 ☎ 986 433 570, ⓦ elmosquitovigo.com. Crowds flock to this intimate family-run restaurant immediately above the fish market,

for the city's finest Galego cuisine. Seafood is of course the speciality; just be prepared to pay significantly more than you would in a typical *raciones* place, with the set menu costing €35. Mon–Sat 1.30–4pm & 8pm–midnight; closed mid-Aug to mid-Sept.

Taverna da Curuxa Rúa dos Cesteiros 7 ☎ 986 438 857. Top-quality *raciones*, from *pimientos* to squid in all forms, in a deliberately rustic setting just off Pza. de Constitución in the heart of the old town. Daily except Tues 11.30am–12.30am.

The Illas Cíes

The most irresistible sands of the Ría de Vigo adorn the three islands of the **Illas Cíes**, which can be reached by boat from Vigo, and (less regularly) from Baiona and Cangas. Sprawling across the entrance to the *ría*, battered by the open Atlantic on one side but sheltering delightful sandy beaches where they face the mainland, the islands were long used by raiders such as Sir Francis Drake as hideouts from which to ambush Spanish shipping, but are now a nature reserve. The most southerly, **Illa de San Martiño**, is an off-limits bird sanctuary; the other two, **Illa do Monte Ayudo** and **Illa do Faro**, are joined by a narrow causeway of sand, which cradles a placid lagoon on its inland side.

Most visitors stay on the sands, where you'll find a sprinkling of bars and a campsite in the trees; if you want to escape the crowds, it's easy to find a deserted spot – particularly on the Atlantic side. From the beach, a long climb up a winding rocky path across desolate country leads to a lighthouse with a commanding ocean view. The islands' campsite has a small shop and restaurant, but if you're on a budget you're better off taking your own supplies.

ARRIVAL AND DEPARTURE   ILLAS CÍES

Ferries Mar de Ons ferries (40min; €18.50 return; ☎ 986 438 358, ⓦ mardeons.com) run from Estación Marítima in Vigo from July until the second Sunday of September (10 daily; first leaves Vigo at 9.15am, last leaves Cíes at

8pm), and less frequently from the last weekend in May to end of June, and during the second half of September (4 daily; first leaves Vigo at 10.15am, last leaves Cíes at 7.15pm). Services also operate from Cangas and Baiona, less frequently but following the same seasonal pattern; in summer, the first boat leaves Cangas at 9.45am, and the last Cangas boat leaves Cíes at 7.45pm, while the corresponding times for Baiona are 9.45am and 8.15pm. Only a certain number of visitors are allowed to visit the Cíes on any one day, so aim for an early boat.

ACCOMMODATION

Camping Islas Cíes ☎ 986 438 358, ⓦ campingislascies .com. This gloriously sited campsite is the only accommodation option on the islands; if you want to stay in mid-season, book ahead to make sure there's space. It has its own shop, café and restaurant, and tents are available for rent if you don't have your own. Closed Oct–May. Per person €8

Baiona

BAIONA (Bayona), 21km southwest of Vigo, is situated just before the open ocean at the head of a miniature *ría*, the smallest and southernmost in Galicia. This small and colourful port, which nowadays makes a healthy living from its upscale tourist trade, was the first place in Europe to hear of the discovery of the New World. On March 1, 1493, Columbus's *Pinta* made its triumphant return to Spain; the event is commemorated by numerous sculptures scattered around the town. An exact replica of the *Pinta* (daily 10am–8.30pm; €2) is moored in the harbour, which these days contains pleasure yachts rather than fishing boats.

The **medieval walls** that surround the wooded promontory adjoining Baiona enclose an idyllic parador (see below). It's definitely worth paying the €1 fee to walk around the parapet, which provides a series of changing, unobstructed views across the *ría* to the chain of rocky islets that leads to the Illas Cíes. Another hugely enjoyable footpath circles beneath the walls at sea level, and provides access to several diminutive beaches. These are not visible from the town proper, which despite its fine esplanade has only a small, if attractive, patch of sand.

Praia de América

Galicia's best-known **beach** lies 2km east of Baiona, across the mouth of the bay. The **Praia de América** is a superb, long curve of clean sand that remains surprisingly underdeveloped considering its reputation, lined at a discreet distance by imposing suburban villas, only a few of which hold hotels or other businesses. A coastal footpath leads north to the beach from the village of **Ramallosa**, on the seafront Vigo–Baiona highway, near the spot where a splendid little Roman bridge crosses the Río Miñor.

ARRIVAL AND INFORMATION   BAIONA

By bus Buses between Vigo and A Guarda stop near the seafront, close to the tourist office and parador.
Turismo Baiona's seafront *turismo* is alongside the gate that leads up to the parador (Mon–Sat 10.30am–2pm & 4–7.30pm, Sun 11am–2pm & 4–7pm; ☎ 986 687 067, ⓦ baiona.org).

ACCOMMODATION

Hotel Tres Carabelas Rúa Ventura Misa 61 ☎ 986 355 133, ⓦ www.hoteltrescarabelas.com. Good-value hotel on a narrow pedestrianized street one block inland, where each of the seventeen en-suite rooms honours a particular hero of the sea, from Robinson Crusoe to Moby Dick. **€93**
★ Parador Conde de Gondomar Monte Real ☎ 986 355 000, ⓦ www.parador.es. It's hard to imagine any better location than Baiona's gorgeous parador, which, though totally surrounded on the headland by genuine medieval walls, is actually a modern version of a traditional Galego manor house. The rooms are spacious and comfortable, with superb views, and as well as two restaurants, it has a couple of bars, both open to non-residents, one of which stands alone in the grounds. **€174**
Pazo de Mendoza Rúa Elduayen 1 ☎ 986 385 014, ⓦ pazodemendoza.com. Appealing eleven-room hotel in a converted manor house adjoining the Pza. Pedro de Castro on Baiona's seafront esplanade, with sea views. **€109**

CAMPING

Bayona Playa Praia Ladeira, Sabaris ☎ 986 350 035, ⓦ www.campingbayona.com. While the beach itself isn't as good as Praia de América, the waterfront setting of this year-round campsite, 1km east of town on a long spit of land with the sea to one side and an inland lagoon to the other, is magnificent, and it has a large waterslide too. Bungalows from €146, pitches with car €22.45

Playa América Nigran ☎ 986 365 404, ⓦ campingplayaamerica.com. Huge campsite beside Baiona's best beach, 2km across the bay, which has abundant rental bungalows as well as tent pitches. Closed mid-Oct to mid-March. Bungalows from €95, pitches with car €21.50

EATING AND DRINKING

Seafood **restaurants** abound on Pza. Pedro de Castro and along Rúa Ventura Misa, most with tanks stuffed full of doomed marine creatures. Ventura Misa is also the hub of the town's **nightlife**, with several bars and pubs staying open late.

Casa Rita Carabela La Pinta 17 ☎ 677 068 365. You have to trust your waiter at this top-notch seafood restaurant in the heart of the old town; there's no menu, he just brings you whatever his wife happens to have bought in the morning market. For a memorable meal, expect to pay around €40 per person. Daily: summer 1–4pm &

8.30pm–midnight, winter 1–4pm.

Jaqueyvi Rúa de Reloxo 2 ☎ 986 356 773. Smart little restaurant that specializes in rice with fish; expect to pay around €20 a head for a full meal. Daily 11am–4pm & 6pm–midnight.

Oia

The C550 highway continues due south for 30km from Baiona to the mouth of the Río Miño, which marks the frontier with **Portugal**. Once a windswept wilderness, this straight stretch of coastline is now scattered with *hostales* and hotels. There are no beaches, but the sight of the ocean foaming through the rocks is mightily impressive.

Immediately around the first curve from Baiona, a massive granite statue known as the **Virgen de la Roca** towers above the sea; on appropriately solemn religious occasions, devotees climb up inside it and onto the boat she holds in her right hand. Halfway between Baiona and A Guarda, beneath the town of **OIA** – itself little more than a very tight bend in the road – nestles a remarkable Baroque **monastery**, with its sheer stone facade surviving the constant battering of the ocean.

8

ACCOMMODATION OIA

Talaso Atlántico As Mariñas, Mougas ☎ 986 385 090, ⓦ talasoatlantico.com. Facing dramatically out to sea from the hillside above the monastery at Oia, this spa-hotel specializes in thalassotherapy, or sea-water treatment. Between relaxing in the large, heated indoor sea-water pool, with its huge picture windows and assorted high-pressure jets, guests can sample a wide range of seaweed wraps and beauty treatments. €150

A Guarda

The workaday port of **A GUARDA** (La Guardia), just short of the mouth of the Miño, is largely the modern creation of emigrants returned from Puerto Rico. However, this is an ancient site, and home to some remarkable prehistoric ruins.

Monte Santa Tecla

Archeological museum March–Nov daily 9.30am–11pm • €1

The extensive remains of a **celta** – a pre-Roman fortified hill settlement – set amid the thick pine woods of **Monte Santa Tecla**, can be reached by a stiff thirty-minute climb or an easy drive up from A Guarda. Occupied between around 600 and 200 BC, the *celta* was abandoned when the Romans established control over the north. The site consists of the foundations of well over a hundred circular dwellings, crammed tightly inside an encircling wall. A couple have been restored as full-size thatched huts; most are excavated to a metre or so, though some are still buried. On the north slope of the mountain there is also a large **cromlech**, or stone circle, and if you continue upwards you pass along an avenue of much more recent construction, lined with the Stations of the Cross, and best seen looming out of a mountain mist. Five minutes farther on, at the top, are a church, a small **archeological museum** of Celtic finds from the mountain, two restaurants and a hotel.

Camposancos

While A Guarda itself has a couple of small **beaches**, there's a better stretch of sand at the village of **Camposancos** about 4km south, facing Portugal and a small islet capped by the ruins of a fortified Franciscan monastery.

ARRIVAL AND INFORMATION A GUARDA

By bus ATSA buses (every 30min from Tui; 2 daily from Baiona) arrive at the small Pza. Avelino Vicente, well above the port.

By ferry Camposancos is connected by ferry across the Río Miño with Caminha in Portugal (daily: every 30min summer 9.30am–10.30pm, winter until 7.30pm; pedestrians €1, car & driver €3 one-way).

Turismo A Guarda has a *turismo* at Rúa Pza. do Reloxo 1 (Mon–Fri 9am–2pm; ☎ 986 614 546, ⊛ aguarda.es).

ACCOMMODATION, EATING AND DRINKING

Casa Chupa Ovos Rúa A Roda 24 58 ☎ 986 611 015. Cosy, friendly restaurant, a couple of streets up from the harbour, run by a local fishing family and specializing in fresh, inexpensive seafood, with typical *raciones* costing round €10. Daily except Wed 1–4pm & 7.30–11.30pm.

Hotel Convento de San Benito Pza. San Benito ☎ 986 611 166, ⊛ hotelsanbenito.es. Much the best hotel in A Guarda, in the beautiful old Benedictine convent right by the port, with a couple of dozen antique-furnished rooms that enjoy great sea views. €75

Hotel Pazo Santa Tecla Monte Santa Tecla ☎ 986 610 002, ⊛ hotelpazo.com. One-star hotel, poised above the *celta* at the top of Monte Santa Tecla, and boasting glorious views along the coast and the Río Miño; all rooms are en suite. Closed Jan. €55

Tui

TUI (Tuy, pronounced *twee*), 24km inland along the Miño from A Guarda and roughly the same distance south of Vigo, is the principal Galego frontier town on the river, staring across to the neat ramparts of Portuguese **Valença do Minho**. While Valença is a much more compelling destination – its old quarter is positively delightful – Tui does have its moments. The old town stands back from the river, tiered amid trees and stretches of ancient walls above the fertile riverbank. Sloping lanes, paved with huge slabs of granite, climb to the imposing fortress-like **Catedral** dedicated to San Telmo, patron saint of fishermen, while a pair of enticing little river beaches lie on the far side of the old town from the main street.

A fifteen-minute walk out of town leads to the Portuguese border, by way of an iron bridge designed by Gustave Eiffel (creator of the famous Parisian landmark). The ravishing little town of **VALENÇA DO MINHO**, dwarfed behind its mighty ramparts, lies a similar distance beyond. There's no border control at the bridge: just stroll (or drive) across and head up the hill to the centre.

ARRIVAL AND INFORMATION TUI

By train If you're coming by train from Ribadavia or Ourense, it's much quicker to go to Guillarei station, a taxi ride 3km east from the town, than to wait for a connection to Tui itself.

By bus Tui has regular buses to Vigo and A Guarda.

Turismo Pza. do San Fernando (April–Dec Mon–Fri 10am–8pm, Sat & Sun 10am–2.30pm & 3.30–7.30pm; ☎ 677 418 405).

ACCOMMODATION

Hotel Colón Rúa Colón 11 ☎ 986 600 223, ⊛ www.hotelcolontuy.com. Modern hotel with large, comfortable rooms, a good restaurant, a pool and great views across to Valença. Rates include breakfast. €91

Parador San Telmo Avda. Portugal s/n ☎ 986 600 309, ⊛ www.parador.es. Tui's imposing parador, out near the border with Portugal, features extensive landscaped grounds with a good swimming pool and tennis courts. Closed Dec–Feb. €110

EATING AND DRINKING

O Novo Cabalo Furado Pza. do Concello 3 ☎ 986 601 215, ⓦ onovocabalofurado.com. Next to the cathedral, the more formal offshoot of the *Vello Cabalo* is the best of Tui's surprisingly small handful of restaurants. If money's no object, this is the place to sample the local speciality, *angulas*,

baby eels from the river, a plate of which is liable to cost over €25. Mon & Sun noon–3.30pm, Tues–Sat noon–11pm.
O Vello Cabalo Furado Rúa Seixas 2 ☎ 986 603 800. Good and very affordable *raciones*, a block down from the cathedral. Daily noon–4pm & 8pm–midnight.

Inland Galicia

While most visitors to Galicia concentrate their attentions on Santiago and the coast, the interior of the region can be both spectacular and intriguing. The **Romans** were always more interested in mining gold from inland Galicia than they were in its coastline, and some remarkable vestiges of their ancient occupation still survive, including the terraced vineyards along the stupendous **canyon of the Río Sil**, and the intact walls of unspoiled **Lugo**. The obvious route for exploring the region is the one used by the Romans, following the beautiful **Río Miño** upstream, via towns such as **Ribadavia** and **Ourense**, and through the wine regions of **Ribeiro** and **Ribeira Sacra**.

Ribadavia

Roughly 60km east of either Vigo or Tui along the A52 motorway, but more pleasantly approached by following the N120 highway or the train line up the lovely valley of the Miño – which tends to fill with mist every morning – the riverside town of **RIBADAVIA** is a good deal grander than its size might promise. Centre for a thousand years of the Ribeiro wine industry, it's home to several fine churches and a sprawling **Dominican monastery.**

Ribadeo also has an interesting **Barrio Xudeo** (Jewish Quarter), dating back to the eleventh century, when the town's first Jewish immigrants arrived. By the fourteenth century, Jews constituted half the local population, and this ranked among the most important and prosperous Jewish communities in Spain. Many Jews, however, were forced to convert to Catholicism during the Inquisition.

Head for the tiny square behind the Iglesia de la Magdalena for a wonderful view of the hillside terraces. Immediately above the central Pza. Maior, which is home to several good bar-restaurants, look out for the remains of the small but quaint **Castillo de los Condes de Ribadavia.**

INFORMATION   **RIBADAVIA**

Turismo Ribadavia's *turismo* is in a Baroque former palace on the central Pza. Maior (Mon–Sat 10am–3pm &

5–8pm, Sun 10.30am–2.30pm; ☎ 988 471 275, ⓦ turismoribadavia.com).

ACCOMMODATION

Hostal Plaza Pza. Maior 15 ☎ 988 470 576, ⓦ hostalplazaribadavia.com. The only hotel in the old

town, this hostal has good en-suite rooms as well as its own restaurant. **€40**

Celanova

Monastery daily 9am–2pm & 4–7pm, tours hourly • €1.50 • ☎ 988 432 201

Little **CELANOVA**, 35km southeast of Ribadavia and best reached along the high and winding road that follows the south bank of the Miño, is hardly more than a village. Its long, narrow main square is appealingly overshadowed by a vast and palatial **Benedictine monastery**, officially known as the Monasterio de San Salvador. Felipe V retired into monastic life here, having spent much of his reign securing the throne in the War of the Spanish Succession (1701–13). The monastery is now a school, but you

8

can explore its two superb cloisters – one Renaissance, the other Baroque – and the cathedral-sized church. Most beautiful of all is the tiny, tenth-century Mozarabic chapel of **San Miguel** in the garden.

Ourense

Set slightly back from the Miño atop a low hill, the historic core of **OURENSE** (Orense), one of Galicia's four provincial capitals, is more engaging than you might expect from the dispiriting urban sprawl that surrounds it. While not a place to spend more than one night – and not a place to break a train or bus journey, as both stations are a considerable way out – across the river – the old quarter does at least offer a handsome and lovingly restored tangle of stepped streets, patrician mansions with escutcheoned doorways, and grand little churches squeezed into miniature arcaded squares. Its centrepiece is a squat, dark **Catedral**, an imitation of the one in Santiago, which contains a museum of religious odds and ends that's not really worth bothering with.

A bewildering number of bridges cross the River Miño as it curves extravagantly through Ourense. The oldest is the thirteenth-century **Ponte Romana**, but the most visually impressive is the modern **Ponte Milenio**, a futuristic road bridge with an undulating pedestrian loop that provides great views.

ARRIVAL AND INFORMATION OURENSE

By train Ourense's train station is north of the river, 2.5km from the old town and served by local buses.
Destinations A Coruña (10 daily; 1hr 10min–3hr); Burgos (4 daily; 5hr 30min); León (4 daily; 4hr); Madrid (6 daily; 5hr–9hr 30min); Monforte de Lemos (5 daily; 40min); Pontevedra (2 daily; 2hr 45min); Ribadavia (daily; 20min); Santiago de Compostela (10 daily; 40min); Vigo (8 daily; 2hr).

By bus The long-distance bus station is north of the river, 2.5km from the old town; change to a local bus to reach the centre.
Destinations A Coruña (5 daily; 2hr 30min); Celanova (8 daily; 1hr 30min); Lugo (5 daily; 2hr); Santiago de Compostela (7 daily; 2hr); Vigo (12 daily; 2hr).
Turismo Isabela la Católica 2 (Mon–Fri 9am–2pm & 4–8pm, Sat & Sun 11am–2pm; ☎988 366 064, Ⓦturismourense.com).

ACCOMMODATION

Gran Hotel San Martín Rúa Curras Enriquez 1 ☎988 371 811, Ⓦgh-hoteles.com. Ourense's most luxurious hotel is a smart modern high-rise near the river in an unexciting part of town, a few minutes' walk from the old quarter. Spacious and very comfortable rooms at exceptionally good rates. **€50**
Hostal Candido Rúa Hermanos Villar 15 ☎988 229 607,

Ⓦhostalcandido.es. Nine basic en-suite rooms, located above an old-fashioned *chocolatería* near the cathedral. **€36**
Hotel Zarampallo Rúa Hermanos Villar 19 ☎988 230 008, Ⓦzarampallo.com. Smart, modern little doubles, with either shower or bath, in the heart of the old town, plus a restaurant downstairs. **€50**

EATING AND DRINKING

Casa do Pulpo Rúa Juan de Austria 15 ☎988 238 308. This nice little tapas bar, facing the cathedral, sells all kinds of seafood and meat dishes as well as its signature octopus, and has a €10 lunch menu. Daily except Tues noon–midnight.

Casa María Andrea Rúa San Miguel 7 ☎988 277 045, Ⓦcasamariaandrea.com. Spacious, good-value old-town restaurant, with balcony seating above a pretty little square, and a €10 menu. Daily 1–4pm & 9pm–midnight.

Cañon de Río Sil

It's only practicable to explore the area northeast of Ourense by car – here you'll find inland Galicia's most spectacular scenery and you can expect the driving to be slow. Follow the N120 out of the city, alongside the Río Miño, and after 20km you'll reach the confluence of the Miño with the lesser **Río Sil**. For roughly 50km east from here, the final stretch of the Sil is quite extraordinarily picturesque and dramatic, flowing through a stunning canyon known as the **Gargantas del Sil**.

The gorge is the heartland of the **Ribeira Sacra wine** region, the only part of Galicia that produces more red than white wine. Even where they're all but vertical, the river cliffs are almost always terraced with grape vines. That phenomenal landscaping project was started by the Romans, and has continued for two millennia. A high mountain road climbs east from the N120 just before the confluence, then winds along the topmost ridge of the canyon's southern flank, passing through a succession of lovely villages.

Castro Caldelas
The village of **CASTRO CALDELAS** surmounts a small hilltop 50km northeast of Ourense, a few kilometres south of the canyon itself. The medieval castle at the very top (daily 10am–2pm & 4–8pm; free) gives tremendous views over the town and surrounding countryside.

Just before the village, a side road drops back down to the river, where a small jetty is the base for **boat trips** on the Sil (daily in summer, schedules vary; €13; ☎988 215 100, ⓦwww.riosil.com).

Doade
A steep and precipitous winding road, LU903, climbs 4km up the northern slopes of the Sil gorge from the boat jetty, to reach the village of **DOADE**. Shortly before the village, a dirt road leads an amazing viewpoint over the canyon and its ancient vineyards. A statue of a woman grape harvester, officially entitled the **Spatium Interpretationis Riveyra Sacrata**, commemorates nine centuries of viniculture.

INFORMATION   CAÑON DE RÍO SIL

Turismo Castro Caldelas has a useful *turismo* in the hilltop castle (daily 10am–2pm & 4–8pm; ☎988 203 358, ⓦwww.castrocaldelas.es).

ACCOMMODATION, EATING AND DRINKING

Casa da Eira Lugar Albuergería 31 ☎988 201 595, ⓦacasadaeira.com. An amply comfortable B&B in a Galego farmhouse 10km west of Parada do Sil, with extensive views out over the canyon and a couple of rental apartments too. Not only do they encourage you to explore on foot, but they also supply hiking maps and personal GPS systems. Room €64, apartment €96

Parador of Santo Estevo de Ribas de Sil Nogueira de Ramuín ☎988 010 110, ⓦwww.parador.es. One of the newest and nicest paradors in the country, 8km east of the main road, and housed within a magnificently converted tenth-century monastery. The ancient cloisters remain intact, but it also boasts ultramodern spa facilities, including a whirlpool bath set on an outdoor terrace, and a beautifully styled contemporary restaurant. Closed Dec–Feb. €110

Pousada Vicente Risco rúa Grande 4, Castro Caldelas ☎988 203 360, ⓦwww.pousadavicenterisco.com. A very pleasant little hotel in the heart of the village, with eight attractive and good-value en-suite rooms, and a good restaurant. Restaurant daily 1–3pm & 7.30–9.30pm. €55

★ **Reitoral de Chandrexa** Parada do Sil ☎988 208 099, ⓦwww.chandrexa.com. Higgledy-piggledy old farmhouse, with magnificently uneven oak floors and exposed beams, tucked away down a very rural lane 6km north of the village of A Teixeira. All its three delightful B&B rooms are similarly priced though only some have en-suite facilities. The friendly owner prepares fabulous dinners on demand, with produce from his own fields, and also offers canoe rental. €53

Monforte de Lemos
A dozen kilometres north of Doade, or 66km south of Lugo along the C546, the rail junction of **MONFORTE DE LEMOS** makes a satisfyingly unspoiled and ancient overnight stop. The town proper, which is home to an incongruously gigantic yet elegant Renaissance **Colegio**, encircles a hill of largely tumbledown old houses. The surprisingly rural area at the top of the hill holds a rambling ensemble which includes the **Torre de Homenaxe** and a 400-year-old monastery that's home to an imposing parador.

INFORMATION

Turismo Monforte's *turismo*, alongside the Colegio (Tues–Sun 10am–2pm & 5–9pm; ☎982 404 715, ⓦconcellodemonforte.com), can advise on tours of the Ribeira Sacra wine region and its Romanesque monuments.

ACCOMMODATION, EATING AND DRINKING

★**O Grelo** c/Campo de la Virgen s/n ☎982 404 701, ⓦresgrelo.com. This fabulous restaurant, a short way down the hillside from the parador, offers an inventive if expensive take on traditional Galego cuisine. You can normally expect to pay around €50 for a full meal, though on Friday evenings you can sample the food in the form of tapas. Mon–Sat 1–4pm & 8.30pm–midnight, Sun 1–4pm.

Hostal Puente Romano Paseo do Malecón 0 ☎982 403 551, ⓦhpuenteromano.com. Light, good-value

hotel, beside the river in the town proper, with large, nicely furnished en-suite rooms. **€45**

Parador de Monforte de Lemos Pza. Luis de Góngora y Argote ☎982 418 484, ⓦwww.parador.es. Stately parador, housed in a grand Benedictine monastery, on the highest point not only in town but for a considerable distance around. Fifty spacious rooms, with tiled floors and huge comfortable beds, plus a pool and restaurant. **€100**

Lugo

The oldest city in Galicia, and as "Lucus Augusti" the region's first capital, two thousand years ago, **LUGO** is, these days, a small town that's chiefly remarkable for its stout **Roman walls**. Rated as the finest late Roman military fortifications to survive anywhere in the world, the walls with which the Romans enclosed this hilltop, overlooking the Miño river, still form a complete loop around the old town. Few traces remain of the 71 semicircular towers that once punctuated the perimeter; instead, a broad footpath now runs atop the full 2.5-kilometre length of the ramparts, so a thirty-minute walk takes you all the way around, to admire the city core from every angle.

Sadly, insensitive building and a busy loop road make it impossible to appreciate the walls from any distance outside, but the road does at least keep traffic out of the centre, which maintains an enjoyable if slightly neglected medley of medieval and eighteenth-century buildings. The most dramatic of the old city gates, the **Porta de Santiago**, in the southwest, offers access to an especially impressive stretch of wall, leading past the **Catedral**.

Catedral de Santa María

Daily 8am–8.30pm • Free

The large and very mossy **Catedral de Santa María**, tucked into a corner of the walled city, was originally Romanesque when built in the twelfth century. Since then, it has been repeatedly rebuilt, with flamboyant Churrigueresque flourishes still conspicuous despite the more recent Neoclassical facade. The interior is remarkable for being entirely split down the middle, its two separate aisles running either side of a succession of chapels and altars.

Museo Provincial

Rúa Nova • Mon–Fri 9am–9pm, Sat 10.30am–2pm & 4.30–8pm, Sun 11am–2pm • Free • ☎982 242 112, ⓦmuseolugo.org

Partly housed in the old Convento de San Francisco, Lugo's excellent **Museo Provincial** holds a well-displayed collection of Galego art, contemporary Spanish work swiped from the Prado, and an early collection of Galicia's Sargadelos china, alongside the more predictable Roman remains and ecclesiastical knick-knacks.

ARRIVAL AND INFORMATION

By train Lugo's train station is 600m northeast of the old town.
Destinations A Coruña (4 daily; 1hr 40min); Madrid (2 daily; 7–9hr).

By bus The bus station is just south of the walls, on Pza. da Constitucíon.
Destinations A Coruña (hourly; 2hr); Ourense (5 daily; 2hr); Pontevedra (5 daily; 2hr); Santiago de Compostela

(9 daily; 2hr); Vigo (5 daily; 3hr); Viveiro (4 daily; 2–3hr).
Turismo Pza. do Campo 11, in the old town (Mon–Wed

11am–1.30pm & 5–7.30pm, Thurs–Sat 11am–7.30pm,
Sun 11am–6pm; ☎ 982 251 658, ⓦ lugoturismo.com).

ACCOMMODATION

Hotel España Rúa Vilalba 2 ☎ 982 816 062. Simple budget hotel, immediately outside the walls not far from the cathedral; the quietest of its decent en-suite rooms face a courtyard rather than the street. **€42**

Méndez Núñez Rúa Raiña 1 ☎ 982 230 711, ⓦ hotelmendeznunez.com. Upscale hotel, in a modern building with large balconies, within the walls immediately north of the central Pza. Maior. Crisply minimal furnishings but a good standard of comfort. **€54**

EATING AND DRINKING

Mesón de Alberto Rúa da Cruz 4 ☎ 982 228 310, ⓦ mesondealberto.es. Fancy old-town restaurant, which specializes in rice dishes to share – expect to pay around €40 per head for a full meal. There's also a good tapas bar at the front, where €15 buys you a full meal of 4 tapas plus dessert and wine. Mon, Wed & Thurs 1–4pm & 8–11pm, Tues & Sun 1–4pm, Fri & Sat 1–4pm & 8.30pm–midnight.

Mesón O Castelo Rúa Nova 23 ☎ 982 253 098, ⓦ pulperiaocastelo.com. One of the very best bar-restaurants on the old town's busiest lane, facing the provincial museum. A great range of inexpensive tapas and *raciones*: *pulpo* costs €9.80, while you can get a substantial meat dish for €7, or try a delicious local sausage for €2.30. Daily noon–3pm & 7pm–midnight.

Sobrado dos Monxes

Mon–Sat 10am–1pm & 4.30–7.30pm, Sun 12.15–1pm & 4.30–7pm • €1

The twelfth-century Cistercian monastery of **Sobrado dos Monxes** makes a highly worthwhile detour en route between Lugo and Santiago. The range of the abbey buildings proclaims past royal patronage, their scale emphasized by the tiny village below, while the huge church itself sprouts flowers and foliage from every niche and crevice, its honey-coloured stone blossoming with lichens and mosses. Within, all is immensely grand – long, uncluttered vistas, mannerist Baroque, and romantic gloom; there are superb, worm-endangered choir stalls (once in Santiago's cathedral) and, through an arch in the north transept, a tiny, ruined Romanesque chapel. A community of monks maintains the monastery and operates a small shop.

8

Aragón

BASÍLICA DE NUESTRA SEÑORA DEL PILAR, ZARAGOZA

9

Aragón

Politically and historically Aragón has close links with Catalunya, with which it formed a powerful alliance in medieval times, exerting influence over the Mediterranean as far away as Athens. Locked in on all sides by mountains, it has always had its own identity, with traditional *fueros* like the Basques and a written Aragonese language existing alongside Castilian. The modern *autonomía* – containing the provinces of Zaragoza, Teruel and Huesca – is well out of the Spanish political mainstream, especially in the rural south, where Teruel is Spain's least populated region. Coming from Catalunya or the Basque Country, you'll find that the Aragonese pace of life is noticeably slower.

It is the **Pyrenees** that draw most visitors to Aragón, with their sculpted valleys, stone-built farming villages and excellent trekking. Some valleys have been built up with expensive ski resorts, but they still reveal the stunning wilderness of the **Parque Nacional de Ordesa** and the **Parque Natural de Posets-Maladeta**, with their panoply of canyons, waterfalls and peaks. Aragón's Pyrenean towns are also renowned for their sacred architecture; **Jaca** has one of the country's oldest Romanesque cathedrals.

The most interesting monuments of central and southern Aragón are, by contrast, Mudéjar: a series of churches, towers and mansions built by Muslim workers in the early decades of Christian rule, which have been on UNESCO's World Heritage list since 2001. In addition to its absorbing Roman remains, **Zaragoza**, the Aragonese capital and the only place of any real size, sets the tone with its remarkable Aljafería palace.

Other examples are to be found in a string of smaller towns, in particular **Tarazona**, **Calatayud**, **Daroca** and – above all – the southern provincial capital of **Teruel**. This region is extremely remote and even its capital doesn't see too many passing visitors. It is unjustly neglected, considering its superb Mudéjar monuments, and there are some wonderful rural routes to explore. In southern Aragón, the captivating walled village of **Albarracín** is incredibly picturesque, while to the east lies the isolated region encompassing the **Sierra de Gúdar** and **El Maestrazgo**, a rugged countryside stamped with dark peaks and gorges. This area is largely untouched by tourism, so transport of your own is a big help, if not essential here.

The languid **Cinco Villas**, northwest of Zaragoza, make for an interesting and laidback couple of days of touring; the most interesting are **Sos del Rey Católico** and **Uncastillo**.

Zaragoza

The city of **ZARAGOZA** is home to almost half of Aragón's 1.5 million population and the majority of its industry. It's a sizeable but immensely enjoyable place, with a lively zone of bars and restaurants tucked in among remarkable monuments, and it's a handy transport nexus, too, for both Aragón and beyond. Its centre reflects an air of prosperity in its wide, modern boulevards, and stylish shops and bars. Highlights include the spectacular Moorish

LOS ARCOS AQUEDUCT, TERUEL

Highlights

❶ **Basílica de Nuestra Señora del Pilar, Zaragoza** The majestic shrine of one of the most revered patron saints of Spain. **See p.599**

❷ **The Aljafería, Zaragoza** Step into the Moorish past at this magnificent palace. **See p.604**

❸ **Cinco Villas** Experience small-town Aragón as it once was in these lovely "five villages", where you might go all day hearing nothing but pealing church bells in the mountain stillness. **See p.608**

❹ **Teruel** Not only does this historic provincial capital feature majestic Mudéjar architecture,

but you can often have it all to yourself – Teruel is refreshingly off the tourist trail. **See p.613**

❺ **Albarracín** Wander medieval lanes past balconied houses in this postcard town. **See p.617**

❻ **Monasterio de San Juan de la Peña** Built right into a craggy mountain, it's hard to tell where the rock face ends and the monastery begins. In a word – stunning. **See p.632**

❼ **Parque Nacional de Ordesa** Located in the Pyrenees, this dramatic, canyon-slashed landscape offers fine high-altitude hiking. **See p.639**

HIGHLIGHTS ARE MARKED ON THE MAP ON P.598

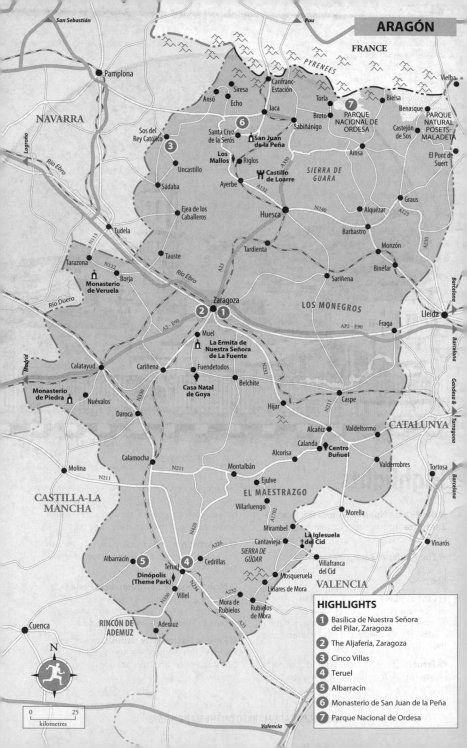

ARAGÓN

FRANCE

PYRENEES

San Sebastián

Pau

Pamplona

Vielha

NAVARRA

Canfranc-Estación

Torla

Bielsa

Benasque

PARQUE NATURAL POSETS-MALADETA

Ansó

Siresa

Echo

Jaca

Broto

Sabiñánigo

Santa Cruz de la Serós

San Juan de la Peña

Ainsa

El Pont de Suert

Sos del Rey Católico

Los Mallos

Riglos

Castillo de Loarre

Castejón de Sos

Logroño

Uncastillo

Ayerbe

SIERRA DE GUARA

Graus

Sádaba

Huesca

Alquézar

A123

Río Ebro

Ejea de los Caballeros

N240

Barbastro

Tardienta

Monzón

Tudela

Tauste

Binéfar

Río Ebro

A23

Sariñena

Tarazona

N122

LOS MONEGROS

Lleida

Monasterio de Veruela

Borja

Zaragoza

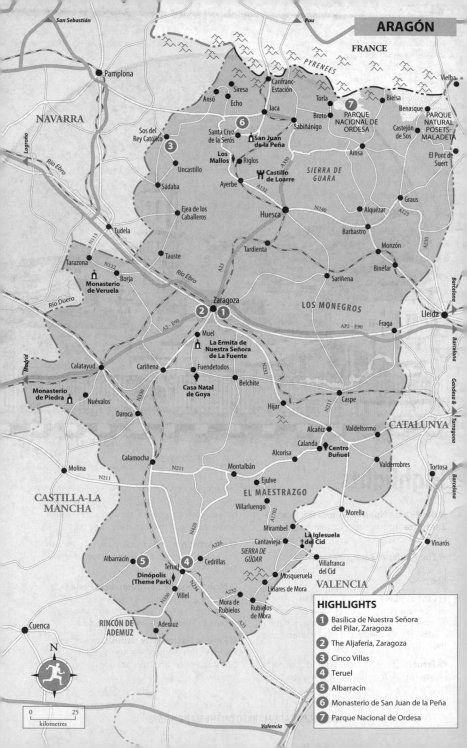

Barcelona

Río Duero

A2 - E90

AP2 - E90

Fraga

Barcelona

Muel

Madrid

La Ermita de Nuestra Señora de La Fuente

Calatayud

Cariñena

Fuendetodos

Belchite

N232

Gandesa & Tarragona

Monasterio de Piedra

Nuévalos

Casa Natal de Goya

N330

Hijar

N211

Caspe

CATALUNYA

Daroca

Alcañiz

Valdeltormo

Molina

Calamocha

N211

Montalbán

Alcorisa

Calanda

Centro Buñuel

Valderrobres

Tortosa

CASTILLA-LA MANCHA

Ejulve

EL MAESTRAZGO

Morella

Barcelona

Villarluengo

A1702

Mirambel

Vinarós

Cuenca

RINCÓN DE ADEMUZ

Albarracín

Teruel

Cedrillas

Cantavieja

La Iglesuela del Cid

SIERRA DE GÚDAR

Villafranca del Cid

VALENCIA

Dinópolis (Theme Park)

Villel

N234

Mosqueruela

Linares de Mora

Ademuz

Mora de Rubielos

Rubielos de Mora

A33

A232

N

0   25
kilometres

Valencia

HIGHLIGHTS

1. Basílica de Nuestra Señora del Pilar, Zaragoza
2. The Aljafería, Zaragoza
3. Cinco Villas
4. Teruel
5. Albarracín
6. Monasterio de San Juan de la Peña
7. Parque Nacional de Ordesa

Aljafería, an impressive collection of **Roman ruins** and an awesome basilica, devoted to one of Spain's most famous incarnations of the Virgin Mary, **Nuestra Señora del Pilar**.

The city's **fiestas** in honour of the revered saint Virgen del Pilar – which take place throughout the week closest to October 12 – are well worth planning a trip around, as long as you can find accommodation. In addition to the religious processions (which focus October 12), the local council lays on a brilliant programme of cultural events, featuring top rock, jazz and folk bands, floats, bullfights and traditional *jota* dancing.

The **Pza. del Pilar** is the obvious point to start exploring Zaragoza. The square, paved in a brilliant, pale stone, was remodelled in 1991, creating a vast, airy expanse from **La Seo**, past the great Basílica de Nuestra Señora del Pilar, and over to Avda. César Augusto. The plaza spans the city's entire history: Roman ruins at both ends; between the churches, a Renaissance exchange house, the **Lonja**; and, at the centre, some modern statuary and the **Fuente de la Hispanidad**, a giant waterfall shaped like a section of Central America and the Caribbean to commemorate the discovery of the Americas in 1492.

Basílica de Nuestra Señora del Pilar

Pza. del Pilar • Daily: summer 6.45am–9.30pm; winter 6.45am–8.30pm • Free • ⓦ cabildodezaragoza.org

Majestically fronting the Río Ebro, the **Basílica de Nuestra Señora del Pilar** is one of Spain's greatest and most revered religious buildings. It takes its name from a **pillar** – the centrepiece of the church – on which the Virgin Mary is said to have descended from heaven in an apparition before St James the Apostle. The structure around this shrine is truly monumental, with great corner towers and a central dome flanked by ten brightly tiled cupolas; it was designed in the late seventeenth century by Francisco Herrera el Mozo and built by Ventura Rodríguez in the 1750s and 1760s.

The pillar, encased in a marble surround and topped by a diminutive image of the Virgin, is constantly surrounded by pilgrims, lining up to touch an exposed (and thoroughly worn) section. Elsewhere, the main artistic treasure of the cathedral is a magnificent sixteenth-century alabaster reredos on the high altar.

Museo Pilarista and Torre

Museo Mon–Fri 9am–1.30pm & 4–5.30pm, Sat 9am–1.30pm • €2 • **Torre** Mon–Thurs & Sat: summer 9.30am–2pm & 4–7pm; winter 10am–1.30pm & 4–6.30pm • €3

Off the church's north aisle is the **Museo Pilarista**, where you can inspect at close quarters the original sketches for the decoration of the domes by Goya, Velázquez, and Francisco and Ramón Bayeu. Your ticket also admits you to the **Sacristía Mayor**, off the opposite aisle, which has a collection of religious paintings and tapestries. You'll have to pay extra, however, if you want to enjoy the panoramic views from the **Torre**, the tower at the northwest corner of the church.

Torreón de la Zuda

Glorieta de Pío XII • Mon–Sat 10am–1.30pm & 4.30–7.30pm, Sun 10am–1.30pm • Free

Near the basilica looms the **Torreón de la Zuda**, part of Zaragoza's impressive medieval fortifications. The tower was built atop the **Roman walls** and after the Reconquest it formed part of the stately residential palace of various Aragón monarchs, from Alfonso I el Batallador to Jaime I.

Lonja

Pza. del Pilar • Usually only open for art exhibitions and temporary shows • Free • ☎ 973 397 239

The sixteenth-century **Lonja**, the old exchange building, is a Florentine-influenced structure, with an interior of elegant Ionic columns and a soaring, vaulted ceiling. A recurring motif throughout the building is the Zaragoza city shield.

9

FIESTAS

MAY

First Friday: Battle of Vitoria Commemorated in Jaca with processions and folkloric events.
Monday of Pentecost: Romería Nuestra Señora de Calentuñana At Sos del Rey Católico.

JUNE

Nearest Sunday to the 19th: Fiesta de los Mozos Celebrated in Cantavieja with a serious religious event but also with dancing and the usual fairground activities.
25: Fiesta de Santa Orosia In Jaca.

JULY

First and second week: Vaquilla del Ángel One of Aragón's major festivals sees Teruel burst into ten days of festivities.
Last two weeks: Pireneos Sur World music festival at Sallent de Gallego and Lanuza (Ⓦ pirineos-sur.es).

AUGUST

Early August: Fiesta de San Lorenzo In Huesca.
14–15: Fiestas del Barrio Street markets and parties in Jaca.
27–28: *Encierros* – crazy local bull-running – at Cantavieja.

SEPTEMBER

Early September: Feria de Teruel Annual town fair.
4–8: Fiesta at Barbastro includes *jota* dancing, bullfights and sports competitions.
8: Virgin's birthday prompts fairs at Echo and Calatayud.
8–14: Bull-running and general celebrations at Albarracín.

OCTOBER

Week closest to October 12: Aragón's most important festival, in honour of the Virgen del Pilar. Much of the province closes down around the October 12, and at Zaragoza there are floats, bullfights and *jota* dancing.

La Seo

Pza. del Pilar • Summer Tues–Fri 10am–7pm, Sat 10am–1pm & 2pm–7pm; Sun 10am–noon & 1pm–7pm; winter Tues–Fri 10am–2pm & 4–6pm, Sat 10am–1pm & 4–6pm, Sun 10am–noon & 4–6pm; sometimes closed for special occasions; last entry 30min before closing • €4, includes Tapestry Museum

The old cathedral, Catedral de San Salvador, known as **La Seo**, stands at the far end of Pza. del Pilar. The gleaming exterior is essentially Gothic-Mudéjar with minor Baroque and Plateresque additions, while to the left of the main entrance is a Mudéjar wall with elaborate geometric patterns. Inside, the superb *retablo mayor* contains some recognizably Teutonic figures executed by the German Renaissance sculptor, Hans of Swabia. Also housed within La Seo is the **Museo de Tapices**, which features a formidable collection of Flemish and French tapestries from the fourteenth to seventeenth centuries.

The Roman Route

Ruta Romano ticket €7 • See Ⓦ zaragoza.es for up-to-date information on the Roman sites

Zaragoza has an impressive Roman history, which can be explored via a variety of museums and architectural remains. If you plan on visiting all the sights, consider buying a combined **Ruta Romano** ticket at the *turismo* or at any of the Roman sites.

Museo del Foro de Caesaraugusta

Pza. de la Seo 2 • Tues–Sat 10am–2pm & 5–9pm, Sun 10am–2.30pm • €3, or Ruta Romano ticket • ☎ 976 721 221

Just outside the Catedral, marked by a striking entrance portal lined with onyx, is the **Museo del Foro de Caesaraugusta** – Zaragoza's name derives from that of Caesar Augustus

(César Augusto in the Spanish form). The museum comprises the ruins (primarily foundations) of the old Roman forum, located in an impressive underground chamber beneath the plaza, as well as a small exhibition with displays of artefacts found on site.

Museo del Teatro de Caesaraugusta

C/San Jorge 12 • Tues–Sat 10am–2pm & 5–9pm, Sun 10am–2.30pm • €3.50, or Ruta Romano ticket • ☎ 976 726 075

Near Pza. de San Pedro Nolasco, a vast modern canopy covers the ruins of the Roman theatre, which are the highlight of the **Museo del Teatro de Caesaraugusta**. The exhibit features audiovisual displays, collections of archeological finds and a walk through the theatre and its vaulted galleries, which gives you a sense of its former glory and grandeur.

Museo de las Termas Públicas and Museo del Puerto Fluvial

Museo de las Termas Públicas C/San Juan y San Pedro 3–7 • Tues–Sat 10am–2pm & 5–9pm, Sun 10am–2.30pm • €3, or Ruta Romano ticket • ☎ 976 72 14 23 • **Museo del Puerto Fluvial** Pza. San Bruno 8 • Tues–Sat 10am–2pm & 5–9pm, Sun 10am–2.30pm • €2.50, or Ruta Romano ticket • ☎ 976 721 207

The **Museo de las Termas Públicas** displays the remains of the foundations of the city's Roman baths, along with a scale model. The **Museo del Puerto Fluvial** preserves the vestiges of the Roman river-port buildings and installations, and also features audiovisuals that delve into their history.

Museo Ibercaja Camón Aznar

C/Espoz y Mina 23 • Tues–Sat 10am–2pm & 5–9pm, Sun 10am–2pm • Free • ⓦ museo.ibercaja.es

A block south of the Pza. del Pilar, in the impeccably restored Palacio de los Pardo, is the **Museo Ibercaja Camón Aznar**, which houses the private collections of José Camón Aznar, one of the most distinguished scholars of Spanish art. Highlights include a permanent display of most of Goya's prints – the artist was born at nearby Fuendetodos (see p.607).

Museo Pablo Gargallo

Pza. San Felipe 3 • Tues–Sat 9am–9pm, Sun 9am–2pm • €4

On the western side of the *casco viejo* (old town), the **Museo Pablo Gargallo** is housed in the attractive Renaissance Palacio Argillo and features the work of the celebrated Aragonese sculptor, including striking sculptures, engravings and the moulds he used. Some of Gargallo's sculptures reveal hints of Cubism, while others are more traditional renderings in bronze and marble.

Santa María Magdalena

Pza. de Magdalena • Usually only open for exhibitions • ☎ 976 299 598

The handsome church of **Santa María Magdalena** features the finest of Zaragoza's several Mudéjar towers. It's considered the city's best remaining example of civil Mudéjar architecture from the fifteenth century. It occasionally hosts temporary exhibits on local history and cultures.

Centro de Historia de Zaragoza

Pza. San Agustín 2 • Tues–Sat 10am–2pm & 5–9pm, Sun 10am–2.30pm • Free • ☎ 976 721 885

The **Centro de Historia de Zaragoza**, housed in the old convent of San Agustín, has innovative galleries on Zaragoza's history, organized thematically, including on the city's rich array of lively festivals and its role as a bustling trade centre. The museum is also often used for contemporary art exhibitions, both local and international.

9

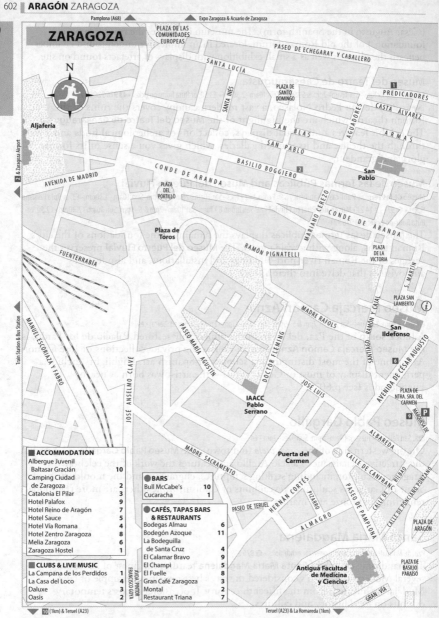

ZARAGOZA

PLAZA DE LAS
COMUNIDADES
EUROPEAS

PASEO DE ECHEGARAY Y CABALLERO

SANTA LUCÍA

SANTA INÉS

PLAZA DE
SANTO
DOMINGO

1 PREDICADORES

CASTA ÁLVAREZ

SAN BLAS

SAN PABLO

AGUADORES

ARMAS

BASILIO BOGGIERO **2**

San
Pablo

CONDE DE ARANDA

Aljafería

AVENIDA DE MADRID

PLAZA
DEL
PORTILLO

MARIANO CEREZO

CONDE DE ARANDA

Plaza de
Toros

RAMÓN PIGNATELLI

PLAZA
DE LA
VICTORIA

FUENTERRABÍA

S. MARTÍN

PLAZA SAN
LÁMBERTO **i**

MADRE RAFOLS

RAMÓN Y CAJAL

SANTIAGO

San
Ildefonso

PASEO MARÍA AGUSTÍN

DOCTOR FLEMING

JOSÉ LUIS

AVENIDA DE CÉSAR AUGUSTO

6

PLAZA DE
NTRA. SRA. DEL
CARMEN

JOSÉ ANSELMO CLAVÉ

IAACC
Pablo
Serrano

9

MARQUESA DE

P

ALBAREDA

MADRE SACRAMENTO

Puerta del
Carmen

CALLE DE CANFRANC

CALLE DE BILBAO

PASEO DE PAMPLONA

CALLE DE

CALLE DE PONCIANO PONZANO

HERNÁN CORTÉS

PIZARRO

PASEO DE TERUEL

ALMAGRO

PLAZA DE
ARAGÓN

ACCOMMODATION
Albergue Juvenil
  Baltasar Gracián   **10**
Camping Ciudad
  de Zaragoza   **2**
Catalonia El Pilar   **3**
Hotel Palafox   **9**
Hotel Reino de Aragón **7**
Hotel Sauce   **5**
Hotel Vía Romana   **4**
Hotel Zentro Zaragoza **8**
Melia Zaragoza   **6**
Zaragoza Hostel   **1**

CLUBS & LIVE MUSIC
La Campana de los Perdidos **1**
La Casa del Loco   **4**
Daluxe   **3**
Oasis   **2**

AVDA. PINTOR
FRANCISCO GOYA

BARS
Bull McCabe's   **10**
Cucaracha   **1**

**CAFÉS, TAPAS BARS
& RESTAURANTS**
Bodegas Almau   **6**
Bodegón Azoque   **11**
La Bodeguilla
  de Santa Cruz   **4**
El Calamar Bravo   **9**
El Champi   **5**
El Fuelle   **8**
Gran Café Zaragoza   **3**
Montal   **2**
Restaurant Triana   **7**

Antigua Facultad
de Medicina
y Ciencias

PLAZA DE
BASILIO
PARAÍSO

GRAN VÍA

10 (1km) & Teruel (A23) ▼   Teruel (A23) & La Romareda (1km) ▼

Train Station & Bus Station

MANUEL ESCORIAZA Y FABRO

2 & Zaragoza Airport

Museo de Zaragoza and around

Museum Pza. de los Sitios 6 • Tues–Sat 10am–2pm & 5–9pm, Sun 10am–2pm • Free • **San Miguel** C/San Miguel • **Santa Engracia** Pza. de Santa Engracia • Enquire at museum about church opening hours • ⓦ museodezaragoza.es

The well-curated **Museo de Zaragoza** features works by famous Aragonese artist Goya, along with other exhibits that span the city's Iberian, Roman and Moorish past. Nearby is a pair of interesting churches: **San Miguel**, which has a minor *retablo* by Forment and a Mudéjar tower, and **Santa Engracia**, with a splendid Plateresque portal.

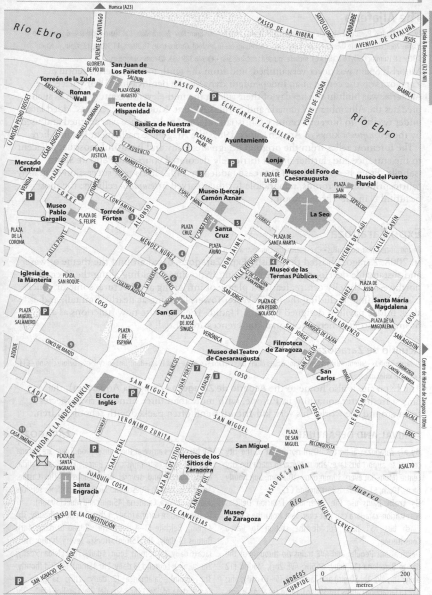

IAACC Pablo Serrano

Paseo María Agustín 20 • Tues–Sat 10am–2pm & 5–9pm, Sun 10am–2pm • Free • ☎ 976 280 659, ⓦ iaacc.es

The eye-catching **Aragonés de Arte y Cultura Contemporáneos Instituto** (Aragón Institute of Contemporary Arts and Cultures), or **IAACC**, has recently been expanded with a sleek design by acclaimed Aragonese architect José Manuel Pérez Latorre. A wide range of exhibits include contemporary art, architecture, design and sculpture. The centre is named after Pablo Serrano, a well-known Aragonese abstract sculptor whose works are also shown here.

9

The Aljafería

Avda. de Madrid, Parque de Aljafería • April–Oct daily 10am–2pm & 4.30–8pm; Nov–March Mon–Sat 10am–2pm & 4–6.30pm, Sun 10am–2pm; closed some Thurs & Fri mornings (when meetings are in session). Guided tours 10.30am, 11.30am, 12.30pm, 4.30pm, 5.30pm & (summer only) 6.30pm • €5, includes guided tour, free Sun • ☎ 976 289 683, ⓦ cortesaragon.es

Moorish Spain was never very unified, and from the tenth to the eleventh century Zaragoza was the centre of an independent dynasty, the Beni Kasim. Their palace, the **Aljafería**, was built in the heyday of their rule in the mid-eleventh century and, as such, predates the Alhambra in Granada and Seville's Alcázar. Much, however, was added later, under twelfth- to fifteenth-century Christian rule, when the palace was adapted and used by the *reconquista* kings of Aragón. Since 1987, the Aragonese parliament has met here.

The foremost relics from the original design are a tiny and beautiful **mosque**, adjacent to the entrance and, farther on, an intricately decorated court, the **Patio de Santa Isabella**. From here, the **Grand Staircase** (added in 1492) leads to a succession of mainly fourteenth-century rooms, remarkable for their carved *artesonado* ceilings; the most beautiful is in the Throne Room.

Expo Zaragoza

On and around Avda. de Ranillas • ⓦ expozaragozaempresarial.com

In 2008, Zaragoza hosted the splashy **Expo Zaragoza**, based around the theme of water and sustainable development. The gleaming Expo site, unfolding along the river just northwest of the city centre, featured plenty of intriguing architecture, some of which is still standing, including the iconic **Water Tower**, looming at nearly 76m tall; and a sleek bridge pavilion designed by Zaha Hadid. The Expo site now functions as a business district, where occasional conferences are hosted.

Acuario de Zaragoza

Avda. de Ranillas • Summer daily 10am–8pm; winter Mon–Thurs 11am–7pm, Fri–Sun 10am–8pm; last entry 45min before closing • €14 • ⓦ acuariodezaragoza.com

The Expo site is also home to the **Acuario de Zaragoza** (Zaragoza Aquarium), the largest freshwater aquarium in Europe, with more than three hundred river species from around the world. It's very kid-friendly, and often packed with schoolchildren.

ARRIVAL AND DEPARTURE   ZARAGOZA

By air Zaragoza's airport is 10km northwest of the city centre; an airport bus takes about 30min to reach the city centre (Mon–Sat every 30min 6am–10.30pm, Sun hourly 6am–10pm; €1.70). Taxis cost around €25.

By train Trains use the intermodal Estación Delicias (ⓦ estacion-zaragoza.es), just over 3km from the centre. Catch bus #51 from outside the station to Paseo Constitución.

Destinations Regular and AVE trains zip throughout the day to Barcelona (16 daily; 4–5hr; AVE 2hr), Madrid (12 daily; 3hr; AVE 1hr 50min) and Tarragona (5–10 daily; 3hr; AVE to Tarragona Camps 1hr 30min). There are also services to Bilbao (4 daily; 5hr); Burgos (5 daily; 4hr); Cáceres (daily; 7hr); Cádiz (daily; 9hr); Córdoba (2 daily; 6–8hr); Girona (daily; 6hr 30min); Huesca (4–7 daily; 50min–1hr); Jaca (daily; 3hr 20min); León (3 daily; 6hr); Lleida (10–12 daily; 1hr 40min); Logroño (9 daily; 2hr); Málaga (daily; 11hr); Pamplona (7 daily; 2–3hr); Salamanca (3 daily; 4hr 30min–8hr); San Sebastián (4 daily; 4hr); Seville (daily; 7hr); and Teruel (3 daily; 3hr).

By bus Buses arrive at the train station. There are Agreda and Alsa services from Asturias, Barcelona, Bilbao, Galicia, León, Madrid and several destinations in Old Castile; Agreda services to Huesca and Jaca; and Eurolines services south to Daroca, Cariñena (45min) and Muel (30min).

Destinations A Coruña (daily; 12hr); Barcelona (hourly; 3hr 45min); Belchite (3–4 daily; 1hr); Bilbao (9 daily; 4hr); Burgos (3 daily; 4hr 15min); Huesca (every 30min; 1hr); Jaca (6 daily; 2hr 15min); León (3 daily; 7hr); Lleida (5 daily; 2hr 30min); Logroño (3 daily; 2hr 15min); Madrid (hourly; 3hr 45min); Salamanca (2 daily; 7hr); Santiago de Compostela (daily; 13hr); Sos del Rey Católico (daily; 2hr 15min); Tarragona (7 daily; 2hr 45min); and Valladolid (5 daily; 5hr).

By car Car rental is available from Atesa, Avda. Alcalde Comex Laguna, 82 (☎ 976 352 805); Avis, Paseo Fernando el Católico 9 (☎ 976 489 236); and Hertz, Avda. de Goya 61–63 (☎ 976 320 400).

By taxi Radio-Taxi Aragón (☎ 976 380 099); Radio-Taxi Zaragoza (☎ 976 424 242).

INFORMATION AND TOURS

Turismo The main *turismo* is opposite the basilica on Pza. del Pilar (daily 10am–8pm; ☎ 976 201 200, ⊚ zaragoza.es /turismo). This caters for the city, while a well-equipped office on Avda. César Augusto 25 (Mon–Fri 10am–2pm & 5–8pm, Sat 10am–2pm & 5–8pm, Sun 10am–2pm; ☎ 976 282 181, ⊚ turismodearagon.com) has information on the Zaragoza province. There's also a *turismo* booth (daily 10am–8pm) at the train station, which can supply you with a map.

Tours The *turismo* offers several different walking tours around town from €5.50, including one in English (Saturdays). The Bus Turístico (Tourist Bus) travels between all the main sights every 35–40min, departing from C/Don Jaime, next to the Lonja (summer daily; winter weekends only; €8; ☎ 976 201 200). The full journey takes about 1hr 45min.

Discount card The *turismo* sells the Zaragoza Card (⊚ zaragozacard.com; 24hr €18, 48hr €21, 72hr €24), which offers access to the main sights around town, a certain number of free rides on public transport, discounts at hotels and restaurants, and a free ride on the Bus Turístico.

ACCOMMODATION

Zaragoza has a decent range of accommodation, from simple *pensiones* to well-appointed hotels. The central, atmospheric *casco viejo* houses many of the *pensiones,* both around Pza. del Pilar and the small streets off C/Méndez Núñez. You'll also find a good number of hotels dotted around the area east of Pza. de España.

Albergue Juvenil Baltasar Gracián C/Franco y López 4 ☎ 976 306 692, reservations ☎ 902 088 905, ⊚ reaj .com. This well-run hostel, about 500m from the train station, has basic but clean rooms sleeping two, four or eight people on bunk beds, and breakfast in the simple dining room included. Discount for under-26s. **€18.70**

Camping Ciudad de Zaragoza C/San Juan Bautista de la Salle, about 6km southwest of the city ☎ 976 753 870, ⊚ campingzaragoza.com. This well-tended campsite, on the city's outskirts, has good facilities, including a pool, organized kids' activities, bungalows (sleeps four) and a café/restaurant for campers with a €10 *menú del día* (€18 on weekends). **€22.45**, bungalow **€70**

Catalonia El Pilar C/Manifestación 16 ☎ 976 205 858, ⊚ hoteles-catalonia.es. Located inside a lovely *modernista* building on the edge of the old town, this hotel blends contemporary design with traditional features such as a wrought-iron lift. Rooms feature designer furnishings and a simple, understated colour scheme. **€84**

Hotel Palafox Marqués de Casa Jiménez ☎ 976 237 700, ⊚ palafoxhoteles.com. One of the closest five-stars to the *casco viejo*, this sleek spot sports a blend of contemporary, Aragonese and Mudéjar design by Pascua Ortega. Excellent facilities, including parking, a fine restaurant (closed Sun & Aug) and an outdoor pool. **€79**

Hotel Reino de Aragón C/Coso 80 ☎ 976 468 200, ⊚ hotelreinodearagon.com. Smart Silken chain hotel with a boutique feel. Rooms combine classical and contemporary style with satellite TV and marble-clad bathrooms. Sometimes offers good online deals in low season. **€76**

Hotel Sauce C/Espoz y Mina 33 ☎ 976 205 050, ⊚ hotelsauce.com. Along with its great name, this hotel has a central location – 100m from Pza. del Pilar – and well-maintained, attractively furnished rooms to offer. There's also a 24hr bar. The best prices are online. **€49**

Hotel Vía Romana C/Don Jaime I 54 ☎ 976 398 215, ⊚ hotelviaromana.com. Smart mid-range hotel, just off the Pza. del Pilar, in a well-restored building with neat, comfortable rooms, some with city views. There are cheap weekend deals and good online discounts. **€50**

Hotel Zentro Zaragoza C/Coso 86 ☎ 976 703 300, ⊚ hotelzentrozaragoza.com. This upmarket hotel, also from Silken, reveals a *modernista* facade and an elegant, cool-toned lobby (from which you can peer down at the underground Roman remains) that gives way to handsome rooms. Check the website for good last-minute or low-season offers. **€80**

★**Melia Zaragoza** Avda. Cesar Augusto, 13 ☎ 976 430100, ⊚ melia.com. Smart, centrally located hotel within a few minutes walk of El Tubo. Rooms are vast, with separate seating and desk areas and the plush decor exudes a homely feel. There's a decent gym and a buffet breakfast, plus complimentary access to a nearby swimming pool. **€98**

Zaragoza Hostel C/Predicadores 70 ☎ 976 282 043, ⊚ alberguezaragoza.com. Central, spacious, lively hostel built in a solid, medieval building near the banks of the Ebro. Doubles and dorm rooms, kitchen use and breakfast included. Dorms **€12.10**, doubles **€47**

EATING

The *casco viejo* features an array of economic restaurants, *comedores* and bars. As you'd expect in a place of this size, you'll also find upmarket restaurants scattered throughout the rest of the city. For tapas – and plenty of late-night drinking – head to **El Tubo**, the series of narrow streets near Pza. de España, particularly Estébanes, Cuatro de Agosto and La Libertad; also try the areas around Pza. de Santa Marta or Pza. de San Pedro Nolasco.

9

ARAGONESE CUISINE

Aragonese cuisine in many ways reflects the region: rugged, hearty, traditional. In a word: meat. Popular dishes include roast lamb (**ternasco**, derived from the word *tierno*, or tender); plump coils of pork sausages, such as **longaniza**; and, of course, **ham**, particularly from Teruel, whose dry but cold winds create an ideal climate for curing. The region is also known for its stews, such as **chilindrón**, which gets its name from the heavy pot in which it is cooked. Multiple varieties exist – the traditional version is a fragrant mix of bell peppers, chicken and cured ham. **Migas** ("breadcrumbs"), based on day-old bread cooked with garlic, peppers and other ingredients, is a popular dish throughout central Spain; the Aragón recipe calls for sausage and grapes. As for fish, fresh river **trout** from the Pyrenees often appears on menus, while sweets include the region's famous **frutas de Aragón**: candied fruits covered in chocolate. Aragón also has several **wine-growing regions**, including Somontano, Campo de Borja, Cariñena and Calatayud.

Bodegas Almau Estébanes 9 ☎976 299 834, ⊛bodegasalmau.es. Spirited tapas bar established in 1870, with a handsome, tiled interior that gives way to a bustling outdoor courtyard area strewn with pebbles and barrel-tables. A range of tasty tapas includes their speciality of *dulce de anchoa* (sweet anchovy) an award-winner. Mon–Sat 11am–2pm & 7pm–midnight.

Bodegón Azoque Casa Jiménez 6 ☎976 220 320, ⊛bodegonazoque.com. Upmarket tapas bar, catering to a smart business crowd sipping quality wine at the rustic, wood-encased bar. Barrels of wine stand at the door, while diners graze on sardines and the celebrated *jamón de Jabugo*. Mon–Sat 11.30am–4pm & 7.30pm–midnight, Sun 11.30am–4pm.

La Bodeguilla de Santa Cruz C/Santa Cruz 3 ☎976 200 018, ⊛bodeguillasantacruz.net. A traditional tapas bar that looks much like an old apothecary, serving a creative selection of beautifully presented tapas and *raciones*. Mon–Fri 7pm–midnight, Sat noon–midnight, Sun 7pm–midnight.

El Calamar Bravo C/Cinco de Marzo 14 ☎976 794 264. A popular and inexpensive tapas bar with outstanding *calamares* sandwiches and *patatas bravas* (€2.50–4.50), all smothered in mayonnaise and spicy salsa. A few tables line one side of the fish-and-chip-shop-esque interior. Daily 11am–3pm & 6–11pm.

★**El Champi** C/La Libertad 16 ☎976 204 645. Lively tapas joint that's known for its signature (and only) *tapa* – succulent mushrooms topped with one prawn and a powerful garlic sauce. Daily noon–late.

El Fuelle C/Mayor 59 ☎976 398 033, ⊛el-fuelle.com. Earthy local *cocina*, specializing in no-frills Aragonese cuisine, especially meat dishes. Great atmosphere and value for money. Mon–Sat 1–4pm & 8–11pm, Sun 1–4pm.

Gran Café Zaragoza C/Alfonso I 25 ☎976 394 125. Historic, genteel café; the nineteenth-century interior features dark-wood ceilings, a burnished wooden bar, and large windows overlooking the street. Serves simple *bocadillos*. Daily 8.30am–10pm.

Montal Torre Nueva 29 ☎976 298 998, ⊛montal.es. An old shop dating from 1919 that also has an alluring restaurant. Relax on a Renaissance balcony for an elegant dinner of regional cuisine (menu €59). Reservations essential. Mon–Sat 1.30–3pm & 9–10.30pm (or until last diner).

Restaurant Triana C/Estébanes 7 ☎976 293 082, ⊛restaurantetrianazaragoza.com. Friendly family-run restaurant and *taberna* serving a full range of tapas and traditional Aragonese mains such as *entrecot ternera* (veal steak) (€18). Good, locally focused wine list. Mon–Sat 1–4pm & 8pm–late.

DRINKING AND NIGHTLIFE

The *casco viejo* has several hopping *zonas* of music-and-tapas bars and nightclubs, including the area around C/Contamina and C/Temple, which hits its stride at the weekends after midnight.

BARS

Bull McCabe's C/Cádiz ☎976 225 016, ⊛bullmccabes .net. One of the most popular of Zaragoza's Irish bars, with two floors and reasonably priced pints of the black stuff. Mon–Fri 9.30am–12.30pm, Sat 2pm–2.30am, Sun 5pm–2am.

Cucaracha C/Temple 25. Raucous place in the heart of *casco viejo*'s bar district, especially popular for its range of

mind-numbing shots. Tends to get busy well after midnight. Wed–Sat 9pm–late.

CLUBS AND LIVE MUSIC

La Campana de los Perdidos C/Prudencio 9 ⊛campanadelosperdidos.com. Wonderfully unique bar with an old-time, traditional decor, a cave-like cellar and a great line-up of local performers, from jazz to folk music.

Check the website for what's on and timings. Wed & Sun 7pm–midnight, Thurs–Sat 9pm–3.15am.

La Casa del Loco C/Mayor 10 ☎976 396 771, ⓦlacasadelloco.com. Rock pub with plenty of live acts, and a mix of the latest English and Spanish sounds, along with the occasional Ibiza-style foam party. Cover €7–10 for live shows. Thurs–Sat 9.30pm–6am.

Daluxe Pza. del Pilar 12 ⓦdaluxe.es. Plush *discoteca*, home to the late-night party crowd, just behind the main *turismo*. Thurs 11am–5.30am, Fri 10pm–6.30am, Sat 8pm–6.30am.

Oasis C/Boggiero 28 ☎976 439 534, ⓦoasisclubteatro.com. A grand old concert hall with a glitzy disco and pub, and live shows that sometimes include drag acts. Fri & Sat 9pm–late.

DIRECTORY

Cinema Filmoteca de Zaragoza, Pza. de San Carlos 4 (ⓦfilmotecazaragoza.com), has an arts programme, including original-language movies.

Football Real Zaragoza (ⓦrealzaragoza.com) plays at La Romareda stadium in the south of the city.

Hospital Miguel Servet, Pza. Isabel la Católica 1–3 ☎976 765 500.

Post office The main *Correos* is at Paseo de la Independencia 33 (Mon–Fri 8.30am–8.30pm, Sat 8.30am–2pm).

Shops The big shopping street is Paseo de la Independencia, south of Pza. de España, and is lined with chain stores, including a branch of El Corte Inglés. Northwest of the city lies the Grancasa (ⓦgrancasa.es), one of Zaragoza's largest shopping centres.

South of Zaragoza

Few tourists spend much time exploring the sights and towns to the south of Zaragoza, and with the Pyrenees just a step to the north, it is perhaps no wonder. However, wine buffs might want to follow the **Ruta de los Vinos** through **Cariñena**. There are vineyards dotted all over Aragón, but some of the best wines – strong, throaty reds and good whites – come from this region, whose towns and villages are best explored with your own transport.

Goya enthusiasts will be interested in **Muel**, and his birthplace in **Fuendetodos**. Nearby lies **Belchite**, one of Spain's most poignant reminders of the Civil War. Buses travel from Zaragoza to several towns in this area, including Cariñena, Muel and Belchite.

Muel and La Ermita de Nuestra Señora de la Fuente

Hermitage: Mon–Sat 10am–2pm & 4–7pm, Sun 10am–2pm • Free

MUEL marks the northernmost point of the region and was once a renowned pottery centre. It has seen much better days, however, and few trains stop here any more. The town's interest lies in a Roman fountain and a hermitage, **La Ermita de Nuestra Señora de la Fuente**, which has some early frescoes of saints by Goya painted in 1772. It's signposted on the edge of town, with a small car park nearby.

Fuendetodos

Buses run 2 times daily (1 daily at weekends) from Zaragoza to Fuendetodos (55min)

Francisco Goya, who became court painter to Carlos IV, spent his early childhood in the quiet village of **FUENDETODOS**, 24km southeast of Muel. The small, pretty town, with stone houses and flowers sprouting on balconies, features Goya's home, which has been turned into a charming museum.

Casa Natal de Goya and Museo del Grabado de Goya

C/Zuloaga • Tues–Sun 11am–2pm & 4–7pm • €3 • ⓦfundacionfuendetodosgoya.org

The **Casa Natal de Goya** is the eighteenth-century labourer's house where Goya was born in 1746; it has been faithfully restored, complete with rustic, period decor. Entry is included with tickets to the **Museo del Grabado de Goya**, 100m farther along C/Zuloaga at no. 3, which exhibits four of the artist's print series: *Caprichos* (Caprices), *Desashres*

(Disasters), *Tauromaquia* (Bullfighting) and *Disparates* (Absurdities). *Caprichos* and *Disparates* represent a savage attack on the follies Goya perceived in Spanish society at the time, while *Tauromaquia* reflects the artist's genuine passion for bullfighting.

Belchite

Autocares Hife buses (☎ 902 119 814, ⓦ hife.es) run from Zaragoza (3–4 daily)

Of all the reminders of the Spanish Civil War, the war-torn town of **BELCHITE**, 20km east of Fuendetodos and 50km southeast of Zaragoza, is perhaps the most haunting. It's also the most unforgettable, which is why this casualty of war was left untouched after it was bombed by Franco's forces. Residents built a new Belchite 1km away from its ravaged sibling.

The sign at the entrance for the bombed-out Belchite reads simply "*Belchite, Pueblo Viejo*". Dusty streets are lined with abandoned houses, their twisted wrought-iron balconies dangling askew. Peeling shutters creak in the wind, while crumbling walls bear bullet holes. The church is especially affecting, with jagged holes in the ceiling gaping at the sky, and crushed rocks where the pews used to be. The only signs of life are the occasional shepherd and his flock, weaving through the silent ruins to the green fields beyond.

Cariñena

Twenty-seven kilometres west of Fuendetodos, just off the main A23 highway, **CARIÑENA** is the capital of the Campo de Borja *comarca*. The town was named after the Cariñena grape and is home to a small wine museum and a clutch of **bodegas**, where you can taste and buy wine. Buses arrive here twice a day from Zaragoza.

Museo del Vino

Camino de la Platero 1 • Tues–Fri 10am–2pm & 4–6pm, Sat 11am–2pm & 4–6pm, Sun 11am–2pm • €2 • ⓦ docarinena.com

This well-run **Museo del Vino** explores the Cariñena wine region through a variety of exhibits, including old wine-making instruments, photos of ancient *bodegas* and vineyards of the region, and audiovisual displays. The museum can also supply recommendations for touring the local vineyards.

Grandes Vinos y Viñedos

Shop usually Mon–Fri 8am–2pm & 4–6pm • Tours €6, includes a commemorative bottle of wine; call ahead (tours fixed when ten or more people sign up) • ☎ 976 621 261, ⓦ grandesvinos.com • To reach it, follow the N330 north towards Zaragoza and after 3km turn left at the sign for Santuario de Ntra. Sra. de Lagunas

A good place to taste and buy wine is the *tienda* at **Grandes Vinos y Viñedos**, one of the largest *bodegas* in Aragón. They offer tours, which includes a visit to the blending building, the modern bottling plant and the ageing section, as well as a tasting at the end. You can also visit the small on-site **museum**.

North of Zaragoza

For a real taste of rural Spanish life, head north from Zaragoza to the delightful **Cinco Villas**, a collection of hill towns which stretches for some 90km along the border with Navarra and comprises **Tauste, Ejea de los Caballeros, Sádaba, Uncastillo and Sos del Rey Católico**. Each of the towns has its own charm and the five are set in beautiful, scarcely visited countryside. The title of Cinco Villas is owed to Felipe V, who awarded it for their services in the War of the Spanish Succession (1701–14). For those en route to the Pyrenees (the road past Sos continues to Roncal in Navarra) or to Pamplona, the Cinco Villas make a pleasant stop-off. **Sos** and **Uncastillo** are the most interesting of the five and attract the majority of visitors – but you could easily still have the streets to yourself.

Tauste, Ejea de los Caballeros and Sádaba

TAUSTE, closest of the towns to Zaragoza, has an interesting parish church built in the Mudéjar style. Nearby **EJEA DE LOS CABALLEROS** retains elements of Romanesque architecture in its churches. Twenty kilometres northwest, remote, tranquil **SÁDABA** boasts an impressive thirteenth-century castle, as well as the remains of an early synagogue.

Uncastillo

As its name suggests, **UNCASTILLO**, 15km northwest of Sádaba, is arranged around an imposing castle. This dates from the twelfth century and houses the small **Museo de la Torre** (July to mid-Sept daily 11am–2pm & 5–8pm; mid-Sept to June Wed–Fri 11am–2pm, Sat & Sun 11am–2pm & 4–6pm; €2.50; ☎ 976 679 121, ⓦ fundacionuncastillo.com), which has simple exhibits on the castle and Uncastillo's history, including a short video that can be screened in English on request. The village is also home to the remains of an aqueduct and there are a few pleasant traditional bars on the main square.

Sos del Rey Católico

SOS DEL REY CATÓLICO, 120km from Zaragoza, derives its name from Fernando II, El Rey Católico, born here in 1452 and as powerful a local-boy-made-good as any Aragonese town could hope for. The narrow cobbled streets of the *centro histórico*, like so many in Aragón, are packed with marvellously grand mansions. Sos also features a lovely Romanesque **church** and the ruined **Castillo de la Peña Felizana**, which offers magnificent views over the village's terracotta rooftops and surrounding countryside. The excellent parador has memorable vistas and might entice you to spend at least one night.

Casa Palacio de Sada

Pza. Hispanidad 1 • June to mid-Sept daily 10am–2pm & 4–8pm; mid-Sept to May Wed–Fri 10am–1pm & 4–7pm, Sat & Sun 10am–2pm & 4–7pm • Tours daily at 10am, 11am & 1pm • €2.40

At the heart of the *centro histórico* is the stately **Casa Palacio de Sada**, where Fernando el Católico was reputedly born in 1452. The grand palace houses the *turismo*, and also has exhibits on the history of the impressive Aragonese monarchy.

Iglesia de San Esteban

Pza. de la Iglesia • Daily 10am–1pm & 3.30–5.30pm, call ☎ 948 888 203 for access if locked • €1

The Romanesque parish church of **San Esteban** in the centre of the town dates back to the eleventh century and has an impressive northern facade. Its unusual lower chapel, dedicated to Santa María del Perdón, features apses with beautifully preserved colourful fourteenth-century frescoes and detailed capitals. You may need to ask at the nearby caretaker's cottage for the church to be unlocked and there's a small charge for the lights to be switched on.

ARRIVAL, INFORMATION AND TOURS | NORTH OF ZARAGOZA

By bus Only one bus a day makes it up from Zaragoza to Sos (2hr 30min), leaving at 5pm from Monday to Friday and returning at 7am. You'll need your own transport if you want to explore this area in any depth.

Turismo Casa Palacio de Sada, Sos (June to mid-Sept daily 10am–2pm & 4–8pm; mid-Sept to May Wed–Fri 10am–1pm & 4–6pm, Sat & Sun 10am–2pm & 4–7pm; ☎ 948 888 524, ⓦ civitur.es); Iglesia de San Martin de Tours, Uncastillo (same hours, but until 7pm Wed–Fri in winter; ☎ 976 679 061).

Tours In addition to the tour of the Palacio de Sada, the Sos tourist office also offers a guided walk through the village (€5).

ACCOMMODATION AND EATING

The best base for the area is the parador in Sos, but the other villages have a few choices, while the surrounding countryside features a number of quaint *casas rurales*. The local turismos can help with recommendations.

9

UNCASTILLO

Bar Cindol Pza. del Ordinario 6 ☎976 679 296. The most popular bar on the main square serves local wines and small tapas dishes (around €2) such as prawns in garlic sauce and croquettes. At weekends it can feel like the whole village is here. Daily 10am–late.

★**Posada la Pastora** Behind the Santa María church ☎976 679 499, ⚓lapastora.net. This lovingly renovated, excellent-value *posada* has contemporary, country-house-style rooms and friendly owners who can help you explore the area. Some rooms have balconies and there's an excellent, hearty breakfast. **€70**

SOS DEL REY CATÓLICO

Albergue de Sos C/Meca ☎948 888 480, ⚓alberguedesos.com. The cheapest accommodation in town is the handsome, well-maintained *Albergue de Sos* in a medieval *torre*, with stone walls, brightly patterned furnishings and spacious, clean public areas.

Sheets and duvets are included, towel rental is an extra €3. Dorms **€17**

Hotel Triskel C/las Afueras 9 ☎948 888 570, ⚓hoteltriskel.com. This comfortable though otherwise characterless hotel overlooks the old town, with a lovely view – get one with a balcony. The cosy restaurant serves regional cuisine. **€80**

★**Parador Sos del Rey Católico** C/Arquitecto Sainz de Vicuña ☎948 888 011, ⚓www.parador.es. This superb hotel is well worth a splurge and makes a great base for touring the area. In the finest parador tradition, it's a lovely blend of historic and modern architecture – and also has spectacular panoramic views across the surrounding unspoilt countryside. Rooms have character and are reasonably spacious, while the elegant restaurant serves Aragonese specialities, such as *ternasco*, or young lamb, and wine from the Campo de Borja region. Service can be a little laidback, though. **€112**

West of Zaragoza

The Aragonese plains are dotted with reminders of the Moorish occupation, and nowhere more so than at **Tarazona**, an atmospheric old town loaded with Mudéjar architecture. If you're en route to Soria or Burgos, it's an ideal place to break the journey. Don't miss out, either, on the tranquil Cistercian monastery of **Veruela**, 15km southeast, and the magnificent **Monasterio de Piedra**, 20km south of the attractive Moorish town of **Calatayud**. Further south, **Daroca** is another imposing town well worth a visit.

Tarazona

TARAZONA's most absorbing sights lie in the old upper town, incorporating the **Judería** and **Morería** (Jewish and Moorish quarters, respectively), which stands on a hill overlooking the river, its medieval houses and mansions lining the *callejas* and *pasadizos* – the lanes and alleyways.

Ayuntamiento

Pza. de España

At the heart of the old town is **Pza. de España**, which is flanked by a magnificent sixteenth-century **ayuntamiento**, with a facade of coats of arms, sculpted heads and figures in high relief. A frieze, representing the triumphal procession of Carlos V after his coronation as Holy Roman Emperor in Bologna, runs the length of the building, while the large figures underneath represent Hercules and other classical heroes performing feats of mythological proportions.

Santa María Magdalena and around

C/Conde • Open for services only

The Mudéjar tower of the church of **Santa María Magdalena** dominates the town. Within the church, look for the interesting fifteenth-century wooden lectern, carved in a geometric pattern. From the entrance there are especially good views of the eighteenth-century **Pza. de Toros** below – an octagonal terrace of houses, with balconies from which spectators could view the *corrida*.

Catedral

C/la Verónica • Tues–Sat: mid-June to mid-Sept 4–6pm; mid-Sept to mid-June 11am–2pm & 4–7pm, Sun 11am–2pm & 4–6pm; sometimes closed Tues • €4 • ☎ 976 640 271, ☽ catedraldetarazona.es

In the lower town, the principal sight is the **Catedral**, which was built mainly in the fourteenth and fifteenth centuries. It's a typical example of the decorative use of brick in the Gothic-Mudéjar style, with a dome built to the same design as that of the old Catedral in Zaragoza, and Mudéjar cloisters. Parts of the interior may be closed for an extensive renovation, which has been in process since the 1980s.

Monasterio de Veruela

Daily: April–Sept 10.30am–8pm; Oct–March 10.30am–6pm • €1.80 • ☎ 976 644 640

The **Monasterio de Veruela**, isolated in a fold of the hills 15km to the southeast of Tarazona, and standing within a massively fortified perimeter, is one of Spain's great religious houses. The monastery is uninhabited now, but the magnificent church, built in the severe twelfth-century Transitional style of the Carthusians, is kept open. The monastery admission ticket also gives access to the fourteenth-century cloisters and convent buildings.

Museo del Vino

Mon & Wed–Sun: April–Sept 10.30am–8pm; Oct–March 10.30am–6pm • free with monastery ticket • ☽ docampodeborja.com

Housed within the monastery complex is a well-run **Museo del Vino**, which offers several floors of snazzy exhibits that trace Campo de Borja wine from grape to glass. You can also enjoy the wine tastings at high tables overlooking the ancient monastery and there's a well-stocked shop.

ARRIVAL AND INFORMATION   TARAZONA

By bus Regular daily buses travel between Zaragoza and Tarazona (1hr 15min).

Turismo Pza. de San Francisco (Mon–Fri 9.30am–1.30pm & 4–7pm; Sat 10am–2pm & 4–7pm, Sun 10am–2pm &

4–6pm; ☎ 976 640 074, ☽ turiaso.com). The *turismo*, in the main square below the Catedral, runs guided tours of the town (€3/1hr or €5/2hr) on Sat at 5pm (6pm June–Aug) and Sun at noon.

ACCOMMODATION

Condes de Visconti C/Visconti 15 ☎ 976 644 908, ☽ condesdevisconti.com. Lovely sixteenth-century *palacete* with individually decorated rooms, some with hardwood floors and wood-beam ceilings. **€90**

Hostal Palacete de los Arcedianos Pza. Arcedianos 1 ☎ 976 642 303, ☽ palacetearcedianos.com. Basic hotel near Pza. de España, with simple en-suite rooms in a refurbished sixteenth-century building. **€42**

Hostal Santa Agueda C/Visconti 26 ☎ 976 640 054, ☽ santaagueda.com. This welcoming *hostal* is set in a lovingly restored historical home, with lovely period

furnishings. A buffet breakfast is included and the *hostal* also houses a small exhibit on Tarazona 1920s singer and vaudeville performer Raquel Meller. **€55**

★ **La Merced de la Concordia** Pza. de la Merced 2 ☎ 976 199 344, ☽ lamerced.info. Handsome hotel in a 1501 *palacete* with modern flourishes that juxtapose nicely with the historical interior: pale-wood floors, recessed lights and sleek furnishings meet stone walls and restored rustic ceilings. Some of the rooms are suites and very spacious. Enjoy creatively prepared regional fare in the elegant, soft-toned restaurant (closed Sun dinner & Mon). **€70**

EATING AND DRINKING

El Caserón 2 Reino Aragón 2 ☎ 976 642 312. Located just north of the old town, this friendly bar has haunches of ham dangling over the bar, and serves up traditional cuisine. Mon–Sat 10am–11.30pm.

El Galeón Avda. La Paz 1 ☎ 976 642 965. In the lower town, this mid-priced restaurant serves good traditional food, including grilled *ternasco* (lamb) and seafood. Menu €9. Mon–Sat 1–4pm & 8pm–midnight, Sun 1–4pm.

Calatayud

Like Tarazona, **Calatayud** is a town of Moorish foundation. It's worth climbing up to the old upper town where, amid a maze of alleys, stand the church of **San Andrés** (generally closed; enquire at *turismo*) and **Colegiata de Santa María** (open most

9

Saturdays; enquire at *turismo)* both of which have ornate Mudéjar towers. Santa María, the collegiate church, also has a beautifully decorative Plateresque doorway, while towards the river, at C/Valentín Gómez 3, **San Juan el Real** (daily 10am–1pm & 4–8pm; free; ⓦsanjuanelreal.com) features paintings attributed to the young Goya. The ruins of a Moorish **castle** (open access; free) survive on high ground at the opposite end of town from the train station. The views from here are lovely, and you can walk around the evocative ruins and parts of the city wall.

Museo de Calatayud

Pza. de Santa Teresa 3 • Mon–Sat 9.30am–1.30pm & 4–8pm, Sun 9.30am–1.30pm • Free • ⓣ 976 897 816

The well-curated **Museo de Calatayud** is housed in the historic Convento de la Orden del Carmelo. The interior is a pleasing blend of classic and contemporary architecture, and exhibits and audiovisual displays explore Calatayud's culture and history, with a focus on archeological finds, including Roman remains and ceramics from the nearby site of Augusta Bilbilis.

ARRIVAL AND INFORMATION   CALATAYUD

By bus Regular daily buses travel between Zaragoza and Calatayud (1hr).
Turismo Museo del Calatayud, Pza. de Santa Teresa 3

(Mon–Sat 9.30am–1.30pm & 4–8pm; ⓣ 976 886 322, ⓦ turismocalatayud.com).

ACCOMMODATION

Hospedería Mesón la Dolores Pza. Mesones 4 ⓣ 976 889 055, ⓦ mesonladolores.com. Comfortable hotel in a rustic eighteenth-century building with stone arches, tiled floors and dark wood ceilings. The restaurant serves a hearty *menú del día* (€12.50, weekends €20), which includes gazpacho and grilled meats. **€81**
Hotel Castillo de Ayud Avda. de la Diputación 8 ⓣ 976 880 088, ⓦ hotelcastillodeayud.com. This stylish, luxury

belle époque complex has two adjoining places to stay – the beautifully renovated, traditional *Chalet de los Sánchez* and a contemporary three-star hotel, the *Castilo de Ayud* itself – as well as a soothing spa. The simple but good restaurant in the modern hotel has a surprisingly well-priced weekly lunch menu for €11 while there's also a more upmarket restaurant in the *Chalet*, with a tasting menu for €35. *Castilo de Ayud* **€70**, *Chalet de los Sánchez* **€75**

Monasterio de Piedra

Gardens: summer daily 9am–8pm; daily winter 9am–6pm • €15 • ⓣ 902 196 052, ⓦ monasteriopiedra.com

The **Monasterio de Piedra** – "The Stone Monastery" – lies 20km south of Calatayud, 4km from the village of **NUÉVALOS**. The monastic buildings, once part of a grand Cistercian complex, are a ruin, but they stand amid lush park-like **gardens**, which seem all the more verdant in this otherwise harsh, dry landscape. The entrance fee includes a guided tour of the monastery's cloisters, church, wine cellar, refectory and kitchens. Red arrows mark out a route through the park and take you past a series of waterfalls, grottoes and lakes.

ARRIVAL AND DEPARTURE   MONASTERIO DE PIEDRA

By bus In summer a daily bus generally runs from Zaragoza to Nuévalos (2hr 30min). In winter it usually only runs twice during the week and on the weekends.

ACCOMMODATION

Hotel Monasterio de Piedra Near the gardens' entrance ⓣ 976 849 011, ⓦ monasteriopiedra.com. This handsome abbey-turned-hotel is part of the Monasterio de Piedra and allows you to sleep in the Cisterian monks' rooms, which have been plushly renovated and have views of the cloisters, monastery or park. **€123**
Hotel Río Piedra Carretera del Monasterio de Piedra, Nuévalos ⓣ 976 849 007, ⓦ www

.hotelriopiedra.com. This family-run hotel, at the foot of the road up to the monastery, has a range of rooms, some with terraces. The restaurant serves well-prepared regional cuisine. **€80**
Hotel Las Truchas Carretera del Monasterio de Piedra, Nuévalos ⓣ 976 849 040, ⓦ hotellastruchas.com. This family-run, reasonably priced hotel has simply furnished but clean rooms, and a pool. **€70**

Daroca

DAROCA, 38km southeast of Calatayud, is a charming old town, set within an impressive run of **walls** that includes no fewer than 114 towers and encloses an area far greater than that needed by the present population of around 2300. The last major restoration of the walls was in the fifteenth century, but though largely in ruins today, they are still striking.

You enter the town through its original gates, the **Puerta Alta** or stout **Puerta Baja**, the latter decorated with the coat of arms of Carlos I. Within, C/Mayor runs between the two gates, past ancient streets dotted with Romanesque, Gothic and Mudéjar **churches**.

Colegial de Santa María

Pza. de España • Tues–Sun: summer 11am–1pm & 5.30–8pm; winter 11am–1pm & 5.30–7pm • Free

The appeal of Daroca lies more in the whole ensemble rather than any specific monuments, though the principal church, the Renaissance **Colegial de Santa María**, on the main street off Pza. de España, does have a small museum of religious artefacts, including robes, silverwork, *retablos* and paintings.

ARRIVAL AND INFORMATION · DAROCA

By bus Daroca is connected to Calatayud, Teruel and Cariñena/Zaragoza by a couple of daily bus services; buses pull in on the C/Mayor close to the Puerta Baja.

Turismo C/Mayor 44 (daily 10am–2pm & 4–7.30pm; ☎ 976 800 129). The small *turismo* offers tours for groups of two or more (Tues–Sun 11am, also 4.30pm or 6pm in summer; €4/person).

ACCOMMODATION AND EATING

Hotel Cien Balcones C/Mayor 88 ☎976 545 071, ⓦcienbalcones.com. As the name suggests, this welcoming hotel has balconies galore, many fronted by wrought-iron handiwork, and overlooking a breezy patio. Ask about their creative packages, one of which includes a horse ride into the countryside. The elegant *Ruejo* restaurant serves regional cuisine. Breakfast included. **€72**

La Posada del Almudí C/Grajera 7 ☎976 800 606, ⓦposadadelalmudi.es. Near Pza. Santiago, this place has two types of room: those in the restored fifteenth- to sixteenth-century mansion house; or those in a modern, stylish annexe across the street. There's also a bar and good restaurant (best to reserve; dinner for hotel guests only) at which breakfast is included. **€65**

Teruel

The provincial capital of **TERUEL** offers an appealing glimpse into this rugged and sparsely populated wedge of Aragón. Because it's often overlooked, the region came up with the playful slogan "*Teruel existe*" ("Teruel exists"). If you're looking for somewhere remote, you're in the right region, with its back-of-beyond villages and medieval sights that haven't been prettified. The land, too, is high and harsh, with the coldest winters in the country.

The town of Teruel is a likeable and impressively monumental place, with some of the finest **Mudéjar** work in Spain. Like Zaragoza, it was an important Moorish city and retained significant Muslim and Jewish communities after its Reconquest by Alfonso II in 1171. As you approach town, the Mudéjar towers, built by Moorish craftsmen over three centuries, are immediately apparent, and – like the fabulous Mudéjar ceiling in the cathedral – should not be missed.

The **centro histórico**, located on a hill above the Río Turia, has the Pza. del Torico at its heart and is enclosed by a few remains of fortified walls, with a viaduct linking it to the modern quarter to the south. Leading off to the north is a sixteenth-century aqueduct, **Los Arcos**, a slender and elegant piece of monumental engineering.

La Escalinata

From the train station, straight ahead of you is **La Escalinata**, a flight of steps decorated with bricks, tiles and turrets that is pure civic Mudéjar in style – note the iron gap in

9

the wall to the left, where a lift (free) shoots up to the *paseo*, part of the extensive redevelopment of the site in 2004 by British architect David Chipperfield.

Torre de El Salvador and Torre de San Martín

Torre de El Salvador C/El Salvador 5 • Summer Mon 10am–2pm, Tues–Sun 10am–2pm & 4–8pm; winter Mon 11am–2pm, Tues–Sun 11am–2pm & 4.30–7.30pm • €2.50 • **Torre de San Martín** C/San Martin • Not open to public • ⓦ teruelmudejar.com

The **Torre de El Salvador** is the finest of Teruel's four Mudéjar towers and is thought to have been built in the fourteenth century. It is covered with intricately patterned and proportioned coloured tiles to stunning effect, echoed closely in its more modest sister tower, **Torre de San Martín** (exterior only), which is best reached via C/los Amantes and said to predate it. A common feature of all the towers is that they stand separate from the main body of the church to which they belong, a design that was almost certainly influenced by the freestanding minarets seen in Muslim architecture.

Catedral de Santa María de Mediavilla

Pza. de la Catedral • Daily summer 11am–2pm & 4–8pm; winter 11am–2pm & 4–7pm • €3, joint ticket with Museo Diocesano • ☎ 978 618 016

The **Catedral de Santa María de Mediavilla**, built in the twelfth century but gracefully adapted over subsequent years, boasts a fine Mudéjar tower, incorporating Romanesque windows and a lantern with Renaissance and Mudéjar features. The interior follows a more standard Gothic-Mudéjar pattern and at first sight seems unremarkable, save for its brilliant Renaissance *retablo*. Climb the stairs by the door, however, and put money

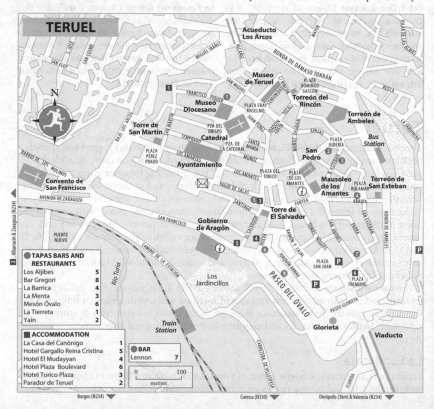

TERUEL

TAPAS BARS AND RESTAURANTS	
Los Aljibes	5
Bar Gregori	8
La Barrica	4
La Menta	3
Mesón Óvalo	6
La Tierreta	1
Yaín	2

ACCOMMODATION	
La Casa del Canónigo	1
Hotel Gargallo Reina Cristina	5
Hotel El Mudayyan	4
Hotel Plaza Boulevard	6
Hotel Torico Plaza	3
Parador de Teruel	2

BAR	
Lennon	7

0   100
metres

in the illuminations box, and the fabulous **artesonado ceiling** is revealed. Completed between 1260 and 1314 by Moorish craftsmen, it's a fascinating mix of geometric Islamic motifs and medieval painting of courtly life.

Museo Diocesano

Pza. de la Catedral • Daily 11am–2pm & 5–7pm; last entry 30min before closing • €3, joint ticket with Catedral • ☎ 978 61 99 50

Standing next to the Catedral, the sixteenth-century Palacio Episcopal houses the **Museo Diocesano**. Inside, look out for the *Calvario*, a beautiful woodcarving of Jesus (whose arms are missing), St John and the Virgin Mary, carved in the fifteenth century but for many years hidden behind a wall in a church in Sarrón, where it was discovered in 1946. Another highlight is the *Arbol de la Vida*, a striking seventeenth-century ivory carving of Christ.

Museo de Teruel

Pza. Fray Anselmo • Tues–Fri 10am–2pm & 4–7pm, Sat & Sun 10am–2pm • Free • ⓦ museo.deteruel.es

The well-run **Museo de Teruel** is worth a peek for its range of exhibits on local folklore and traditional rural life, including pottery, silverwork, clothing and a reconstructed interior of an eighteenth-century chemist shop. The museum also has interesting temporary exhibitions, including contemporary photography.

San Pedro and Mausoleo de los Amantes

Daily 10am–2pm & 4–8pm • **San Pedro** C/Matías Abad 3 • €2 • **Mausoleo de los Amantes** €4, combined ticket of church, tower and mausoleum €9 • ⓦ amantesdeteruel.es

Just beyond Pza. del Torico, which is flanked by a trio of *modernista* houses, is the church of **San Pedro**, endowed with a lovely thirteenth century Mudéjar tower that you can visit. Its claim to fame, however, relates to the nearby **Mausoleo de los Amantes**, a chapel containing the alabaster tomb of the Lovers of Teruel, Isabel de Segura and Juan Diego Martínez de Marcilla. This pair's tale of thwarted love is a legend throughout Spain. The story goes that Diego, ordered by his lover's family to go away and prove himself worthy, left Teruel for five years, returning only to find that Isabel was to be married that same day. He asked for a last kiss, was refused and died, heartbroken; Isabel, not to be outdone, arranged his funeral at San Pedro, kissed the corpse and died in its arms. The lovers' (reputed) bodies were exhumed in 1955 and now lie illuminated for all to see – a macabre yet popular pilgrimage for newlyweds.

Dinópolis

Hours vary but broadly April–June Thurs–Fri 10am–7pm & Sat–Sun 10am–8pm, July to mid-Sept daily 10am–8pm, mid-Sept to Dec & March to mid-April Sat–Sun 10am–8pm • €27, under-12s €21.50 • ⓦ dinopolis.com

Teruel is an important place for paleontology, as the location of the first Spanish dinosaur discovery, the Aragosaurus, and loosely based on this heritage is **Dinópolis**, a lively dinosaur theme park. Located on the outskirts of town, the park is replete with rides, guides dressed (and acting) like mad professors and oodles of dinosaur exhibits. Dinópolis also run a number of other similarly themed parks in the region, including the Bosque Pétreo (Petrified Forest); enquire at the ticket office for details.

ARRIVAL AND INFORMATION   TERUEL

By train Trains run regularly from Zaragoza (2hr 15min) and Valencia (2hr 30min). The station is on the fringes of the *centro histórico*; from the train station, walk up La Escalinata and C/Nueva into town.

By bus The bus station is also on the eastern edge of town;

walk north a short way up the ring road, taking the first left to Pza. Judería. There are a number of bus companies, so check the timetables in the windows before buying a ticket, as some buses are considerably slower than others. All services are reduced on Sundays.

9

Destinations Ademuz (Mon–Sat; 55min); Albarracín (Mon–Sat; 2hr); Barcelona (twice daily; 6hr 45min); Valencia (5 daily; 2hr 30min); Zaragoza (7 daily; 2hr 15min). **Turismo** Pza. de los Amantes 6 (daily 10am–2pm & 4–8pm;

Aug daily 10am–8pm; ☎ 978 624 105, ⊛ teruel.es).
Regional tourist office C/San Francisco, near the La Escalinata (Mon–Sat 9am–2pm & 4.30–8pm, Sun 10am–2pm & 4.30–8pm; ☎ 978 602 279).

ACCOMMODATION

La Casa del Canónigo C/San Martín ☎ 978 607 199, ⊛ casadelcanonigo.com. Well-preserved *casa* in the middle of the old town, set in a seventeenth-century mansion that was acquired by the *canónigo* (canon) of the Teruel Catedral in 1698. There are six well-furnished apartments (sleeps two), all with kitchens. Apartments **€70**
Hotel Gargallo Reina Cristina Paseo del Óvalo 1 ☎ 978 606 860, ⊛ gargallohotels.es. This attractive hotel by the Torre del Salvador has modern if unexciting rooms, as well as an excellent restaurant that serves regional cuisine, from the famous local ham to a dessert of *arroz con leche caramelizado* (rice with caramelized milk). A buffet breakfast is included. **€85**
Hotel El Mudayyan C/Nueva 18 ☎ 978 623 042, ⊛ elmudayyan.com. Lovely, petite hotel where you can – quite literally – explore underground Teruel: medieval tunnels, once used by priests to travel to and from the sacristy, extend below the hotel, and intrepid guests can venture into them (as far as they dare), led by the owners

who can expound on Teruel's history. *El Mudayyan*'s eight rooms are snug but individually and attractively decorated with Mudéjar touches, while a small Moroccan-style tearoom makes for a relaxing afternoon. Breakfast included. **€80**
Hotel Plaza Boulevard Pza. Tremedal 3 ☎ 978 608 817, ⊛ bacohoteles.com. This smart modern hotel near Pza. San Juan has contemporary rooms with wooden floors and king-size beds. There's a café, kids playroom and TV room. Breakfast included. **€85**
Hotel Torico Plaza C/Yagüe de Salas 5 ☎ 978 617 010, ⊛ bacohoteles.com. Centrally located contemporary hotel with understated, simple rooms and suites. A breakfast buffet is included and there's convenient parking close by. **€85**
Parador de Teruel Carretera Sagunto-Burgos, 2km out of town ☎ 978 601 800, ⊛ www.parador.es. This modern hotel, on a wooded hillside overlooking the town and towers, has a swimming pool, tennis courts and a large garden. Rooms are fresh and spacious and many have fine views over the countryside. **€133**

EATING AND DRINKING

The town's most celebrated gastronomic creation is **Jamón de Teruel**. You'll find the tasty, fat-streaked *jamón* in shops and served up in tapas bars and restaurants all over town and trying it is an experience not to be missed. The main areas for restaurants are on the eastern side of the old town, principally Pza. Judería, C/Bartolomé Esteban, C/Abadía and C/San Esteban, though you'll also find lively cafés on Pza. del Torico. For bars, check out the streets around Pza. Judería and Pza. Bolamar.

Los Aljíbes C/Yagüe de Salas 3. A buzzing café and *bodega* specializing in Aragonese and Navarran cuisine such as *migas a la Pastora* and juicy lamb (main courses €14–18), with a well-stocked tapas counter and an extensive wine list featuring local vintages. Daily 8am–11pm; closed Sun in Aug & Sept, plus last 2 weeks of July.

Bar Gregori Paseo del Óvalo 6 ☎ 978 600 580. This friendly tapas bar serves all the favourites, including Teruel's famous *jamón* and pigs' ears. Outside tables, plus good, keenly priced wine and *sangría* make for a chilled place to pass the evening. Daily late morning–1am.
La Barrica C/Abadia 5 ☎ 978 618 235. Cosy, inventive

EL RINCÓN DE ADEMUZ

El Rincón de Ademuz (⊛ rincondeademuz.com), 30km due south of Teruel, is a strange little region: a Valencian province enclosed within Aragonese territory. It's a very remote corner of Spain, with a bleak kind of grandeur, and sees scarcely a tourist from one year to the next.

The place to head for – and if you're bussing it, the only realistic place to get to from Teruel – is **ADEMUZ** itself, without doubt Spain's tiniest and least significant provincial capital. Strung along a craggy hill at the confluence of two long rivers, this could make a beautiful base for walking, and there's a fascination just in wandering the streets with their dark stone cottages and occasional Baroque towers.

For energetic **trekking** there's Torre Baja, which lies to the north along the Río Turia, and beyond it the beautiful village of Castielfabib. The most interesting of these little Ademuz hamlets, Puebla de San Miguel, is to the east, in the Sierra Tortajada, easily accessible by road from Valencia, but also from a minor road just out of Ademuz in the Teruel direction, east over the Río Turia bridge and signposted to Sabina, Sesga and Mas del Olmo.

tapas bar serving a variety of dishes and an extensive list of wines. Try the *patatas* with *jámon* and truffle mayonnaise. Wed–Fri & Mon 9.30am–3.30pm & 8–11pm, Sat–Sun noon–3.30pm & 8–11pm.

Lennon C/San Andrés 23 ☎ 978 601 970. A vast, laidback bar with several rooms, comfy chairs and sofas, occasional live music and a pool table. Tues–Sun 3pm–midnight, or later.

La Menta C/Bartolomé Esteban 10 ☎ 978 605 804, ⓦ restaurantelamenta.com. One of the city's top restaurants, with a carefully constructed menu that changes weekly, and sumptuous dishes of Aragonese classics (including local truffle) from around €20. Mon–Sat 1.30–3pm & 9–11pm.

Mesón Óvalo Paseo del Óvalo 2 ☎ 978 618 235, ⓦ mesonovalo.es. A very popular *mesón* with warm, tangerine-coloured walls, quality cooking (the trout dishes are excellent) and a range of Maestrazgo specialities from around €15. Tues–Sat 1–4.30pm & 8.30–11.15pm, Sun 1–4.30pm.

La Tierreta Francisco Piquer 6 ☎ 978 617 923, ⓦ latierreta.com. Tucked away behind the Catedral is this elegant restaurant with a modern wooden interior. The innovative dishes (€16–20) are rooted in regional produce, such as monkfish flavoured with saffron culled from the nearby Monreal del Campo and wild sea bass with seasonal mushrooms. Mon & Sun 1.30–4pm, Tues–Sat 1.30–4pm & 9–11pm.

★**Yaín** Pza. de la Judería 9 ☎ 978 624 076, ⓦ yain.es. Proof that creative, gourmet fare has a place in Teruel. The sleek restaurant (named after the Hebrew word for "wine", because of its location on Pza. de la Judería) reveals gleaming dark wood, alabaster lamps and an impressive wine cellar. Regional dishes (€13–19) with a twist include *pimiento del piquillo* (bright-red peppers shaped like a *piquillo*, or "little beak") stuffed with cod, and quail with a *garbanzo* puree. The three course Menu Yaín (€30) makes for a memorable splurge and includes a "surprise dessert". Tues & Sun 1.30–3.15pm, Wed–Sat 1.30–3.15pm & 9–11pm.

Albarracín

ALBARRACÍN, 38km west of Teruel, is one of the more accessible targets in rural southern Aragón – as well as one of the most picturesque towns in the province, poised above the Río Guadalaviar and retaining, virtually intact, its medieval streets and tall, balconied houses. There's a historical curiosity here, too, in that from 1165 to 1333, the town formed the centre of a small independent state, the kingdom of the Azagras.

Despite its growing appeal as a tourist destination, Albarracín's dark, enclosed lanes and ancient buildings adorned with splendid coats of arms still make for an intriguing wander. Approaching from Teruel, you may imagine (wrongly) that you're about to come upon a large town. The **medieval walls** swoop back over the hillside, protecting, within the loop of the river, a far greater area than the extent of the town, past or present.

Moving on from Albarracín, if you have transport, you could take a pleasant route west to Cuenca through beautiful countryside, by way of Frías de Albarracín and the source of the Río Tajo (see p.183).

Catedral and Museo Diocesano

C/Catedral • Daily 10.30am–noon & 4.30–6pm; sometimes closed for renovations • €3.50, includes entry to museum • ⓦ fundacionsantamariadealbarracin.com

The **Catedral**, a medieval building remodelled in the sixteenth to eighteenth centuries, rises over a small square, and features an eye-catching gilded altarpiece. The **Museo Diocesano**, housed in the attached Palacio Obispal, displays religious and sacred art from around the region, including painting, sculpture, metalwork and musical instruments. The cathedral is currently under extensive, long-term renovation so may sometimes be closed to visitors.

Museo de Albarracín

C/San Juan 18 • Mon–Fri 10.30am–1pm & 4.30–5.30pm, Sat 10.30am–1pm & 4.30–7pm, Sun 10.30am–1pm • €2.50 • ☎ 978 704 035

The well-curated **Museo de Albarracín** is housed in an eighteenth-century hospital that was also used as a prison after the Civil War. It features a range of exhibits and audiovisual displays on the history, art and culture of Albarracín, including rare archeological finds including a series of eleventh-century ceramics.

> ### ALBARRACÍN'S MUSEUMS
>
> If you plan on seeing most of Albarracín's sights, opt for a **joint ticket** for €7, that allows access to all the main sights, including the Catedral, Museo Diocesano, Museo de Albarracín, the castle and Torre Blanca. For an extra €2, your ticket includes a guided tour of town. Tickets are on sale at the Centro de información, and at all the sights.

Castillo de Albarracín

Tours: summer daily 11am, noon, 1pm, 5pm, 6pm & 7pm; less regular in winter • €2.50

The crumbling but atmospheric **castle**, in the southern part of town on an impressive clifftop, forms part of Albarracín's impressive early remains, and dates from the ninth century when the town was a fortified Islamic outpost. Among its remains are parts of a tenth-century Moorish palace, a hammam and various lookout points along the ancient walls as well as several murals from the Christian era.

Torre Blanca and Torre del Andador

Torre Blanca Daily: summer 10.30am–2pm & 5–8pm; winter usually daily 1–2pm & 7–8pm, but sometimes only open weekends • €1.50 • ☎ 978 704 035 • **Torre Andador** Open access • Free

The **Torre Blanca**, near Albarracín's castle, has been extensively renovated and houses temporary changing exhibitions on everything from portrait paintings to contemporary photography, arranged over three levels. You can also climb up to a lookout point for sweeping views over the surrounding landscape. The **Torre del Andador** looms over the northern part of town.

ARRIVAL AND INFORMATION

ALBARRACÍN

Bys bus Regular buses run from Teruel (45min).

Turismo C/San Antonio, next to the main bridge (Mon–Sat 10am–2pm & 4–8pm, Sun 10am–2pm & 4–7pm; ☎ 978 710 262, ⓦ comarcadelasierradealbarracin.es), has information on the town and the surrounding region.

Centro de Información C/Catedral, next to the Catedral (daily: summer 10am–2pm & 4–8pm; winter 10am–2pm & 4–6.30/7pm; ☎ 978 704 035, ⓦ fundacionsanta mariadealbarracin.com). The centre offers guided tours (1hr 30min; €2) of Albarracín that depart at various times of the day; enquire within.

ACCOMMODATION AND EATING

★ **Casa Santiago** Subida a las Torres 11 ☎ 978 700 316, ⓦ www.casadesantiago.net. This inviting, family-run hotel is set in a restored country house at the top of a stone staircase near the Pza. Mayor. The eight cosy, individually decorated rooms have colourful quilts and wood-beamed ceilings – some even have four-poster beds. There is also a sun-lit sitting room where you can look out over the brightly tiled roofs of Albarracín. The simple restaurant serves local cuisine. **€64**

El Hostal Los Palacios C/Los Palacios, beyond the

Portal de Molina ☎ 978 700 327, ⓦ montepalacios .com. This welcoming hotel features sixteen warm, well-cared-for rooms, some with rustic brick walls, and a casual terrace restaurant-bar serving hearty regional cuisine with a *menú del día* for €16. **€45**

Posada del Adarve C/Portal de Molina 23 ☎ 978 700 304, ⓦ posadadeladarve.com. Relax in handsome, carefully renovated rooms and suites, some with wood-beam ceilings, tiled floors and rustic wooden furniture, in a historic townhouse that is part of the town's medieval walls. **€60**

Sierra de Gúdar

The mountains of the **SIERRA DE GÚDAR** and nearby El Maestrazgo (see p.620), to the east and northeast of Teruel, are an area of great variety and striking, often wild, beauty, with severe peaks, deep gorges and lush meadows. Just over one hundred years ago, this now impoverished region had four times the number of inhabitants it does today. Defeated in their attempts to make a living from agriculture, many of them left to seek their fortunes in the cities, leaving behind the crumbling remains of the once grand, honey-hued farmhouses that dot the landscape and the stone-walled terraces etched into the steep-sided hills.

A landscape of sharp, rocky crags, Sierra de Gúdar is easy to access by following the N234 southeast from Teruel and then heading northeast into the mountains along the A232. This will bring you to the lovely medieval villages of **Mora de Rubielos**, 42km from Teruel, and its even lovelier twin, **Rubielos de Mora**. Head north from here for **Linares de Mora** and Mosqueruela, also charming and remote mountain villages. Your own transport is essential in this region.

Mora de Rubielos and Rubielos de Mora

These confusingly named villages both have fine collections of medieval houses, with small, wrought-iron balconies, bedecked with flowers. Both are lovely places to while away an afternoon. **MORA DE RUBIELOS** has an impressive castle, while **RUBIELOS DE MORA**, 14km from Mora de Rubielos, features handsome *palacios* with finely carved wooden eaves, a small art museum and the **Ex Colegiata de Santa María la Mayor**, on Pza. de Marqués de Tosos, which has an ostentatious tiered bell tower. If you want to see inside, enquire at the *turismo*.

Castillo de Mora de Rubielos

Mora de Rubielos • Mon–Fri 10am–2pm & 5–7.30pm, Sat 10am–2pm & 5–8pm, Sun 10am–2pm • €2

For such a small place, Mora de Rubielos has an extremely grand **castle**, built in a luminous pinkish-gold stone, which during the Middle Ages served as both defensive fort and noble residence, and was the heart of town life. Inside, several fairly nondescript rooms, squeezed between the castle's outer and inner walls, are set around a courtyard of pointed arches. One room hosts a small **Museo Etnológico**, a motley collection of rustic antiquities. If it's open, it's worth having a peek inside the bulky, Gothic **Ex Colegiata de Santa María** below the castle.

Fundación Museo Salvador Victoria

C/Hospital 13, Rubielos de Mora • Daily 10am–2pm & 5–8pm • Free • ☎ 978 804 034, ⊕ salvadorvictoria.com

Housed in the eighteenth-century Hospital de Gracia, the **Fundación Museo Salvador Victoria** features an in-depth collection of work by Salvador Victoria (1928–1994), from lithographs to luminous paintings. The museum also has a well-curated collection of contemporary Spanish art from the second half of the twentieth century, including works by Lucio Muñoz, Rafael Canogar, Manuel Rivera and Antonio Saura.

Linares de Mora

The vegetation becomes scrubbier and the views more dramatic as the road climbs north 25km from Rubielos to **LINARES DE MORA**, a beguiling place, with houses piled higgledy-piggledy up the mountainside and glorious views. Its ruined castle is situated, rather precariously, on a jutting rock above the village, while another promontory hosts a church.

ARRIVAL AND DEPARTURE   MORA DE RUBIELOS AND RUBIELOS DE MORA

By bus Buses are infrequent in this area, but most villages are connected with each other and/or Teruel once a day. A bus (Mon–Fri) leaves Teruel in the afternoon for Mosqueruela via Mora de Rubielos, Rubielos de Mora and Linares de Mora, returning in the early morning.

INFORMATION

Mora de Rubielos C/ Diputación 2 (Tues–Fri 10am–2pm & 5–7.30pm, Sat & Sun 5–8pm; ☎ 978 800 000, ⊕ moraderubielos.com).

Rubielos de Mora C/Hispanoamérica 1 (daily July–Sept 10am–2pm & 5–8pm; Oct–June 10am–2pm & 4–7pm; ☎ 978 804 001, ⊕ rubielosdemora.es).

9

ACCOMMODATION AND EATING

MORA DE RUBIELOS

Hotel Jaime I Pza. de la Villa ☎978 800 184, ⓦhoteljaime.com. This attractively restored hotel has 28 elegantly rustic rooms in an old mansion, some with wooden beams and large balconies. The restaurant serves good regional cuisine. Breakfast costs extra. **€79**

Hotel La Trufa Negra Avda. Ibañez Martín 10 ☎978 807 144, ⓦlatrufanegra.com. This swanky hotel has stylish rooms full of amenities, a luxurious spa and an upmarket restaurant serving excellent local cuisine. This area of the Maestrazgo is famous for its truffles and the hotel offers trips out into the countryside with truffle-hunters and their dogs, you can then enjoy the truffles on the tasting menu. Daily 1.30–3.30pm & 8.30–10.30pm. **€133**

RUBIELOS DE MORA

Hotel de la Villa Pza. del Carmen ☎978 804 640, ⓦdelavillahotel.es. This handsome hotel has a restored sixteenth-century facade, a stone-arch entrance, fourteen elegant rooms with wooden furnishings and beamed ceilings, and a fine restaurant with a €15 menú del día. **€90**

Los Leones Pza. Igual y Gil 3 ☎978 804 477, ⓦlosleones.info. A well-restored seventeenth-century palace near the church, complete with antique bedsteads and heavy wooden doors. Also has a smart restaurant serving an excellent array of regional specialities. **€70**

LINARES DE MORA

El Portalico C/Portalico ☎978 802 110, ⓦhostal elportalico.com. Situated on the edge of the old quarter, this basic but clean hostal is set in a historic mansion and has pleasant, simply furnished rooms with wrought-iron beds. Breakfast is included and there are also half- and full-board packages from €36/person. **€40**

El Maestrazgo

Unfolding northeast of Teruel, the **MAESTRAZGO** is dry, windswept, rugged terrain dominated (and named after) the Maestrazgo mountain range. In keeping with the rest of the region, the Maestrazgo is sparsely populated and can often seem to be stuck in time, particularly if you wander the quiet, cobbled streets of its ancient mountain villages. In the southern Maestrazgo, **Cantavieja** makes a useful base for exploring – or walking in – the region, while to the southeast lies the well-preserved **La Iglesuela del Cid**. The northern limits of the Maestrazgo edge into Tarragona province in Catalunya, and can be approached from Tarragona/Gandesa, or from Zaragoza via Alcañiz, where the N232 forks: east to the lovely town of **Valderrobres**, with its superb castle and elegant Gothic church, and south to **Calanda** and a centre dedicated to film-maker Luis Buñuel.

Cantavieja

CANTAVIEJA, dramatically situated by the edge of an escarpment at an altitude of 1300m, is a little livelier and larger than most Maestrazgo villages, though its population is still under a thousand. The beautiful, porticoed **Pza. de Cristo Rey**, halfway up C/Mayor from Pza. de España, is typical of the region, and the escutcheoned *ayuntamiento* bears a Latin inscription with suitably lofty sentiments: "This House hates wrongdoing, loves peace, punishes crimes, upholds the laws and honours the upright."

Museo de las Guerras Carlistas de Cantavieja

C/Mayor 15 • Mon 4–7.30pm, Tues–Wed 10am–1.30pm & 4–7.30pm, Thurs 10am–1pm & 4–7.30pm, Sat 10am–2pm & 4–7.30pm, Sun 10am–2pm • €1.50

The small but well-curated **Museo de las Guerras Carlistas de Cantavieja** documents the nineteenth-century Carlist Wars in Cantavieja via panels, scale models, old uniforms, newspaper clippings and weapons. There are also fascinating audiovisual displays on the theme of "El Maestrazgo en Tiempos de Cambio" ("Maestrazgo in Times of Change"), which covers the cultural and geographical evolution of this mountainous region, focusing on the Carlist Wars era.

Mirambel

The best views of Cantavieja can be found on the rough and narrow road to **MIRAMBEL**, 15km to the northeast and walkable in about four hours. The village preserves a timeless atmosphere, with its ancient walls, gateways and stone houses. It was temporarily thrown into a whirl of excitement when Ken Loach filmed *Land and Freedom* (1995) here, but these days it's back to its usual, sleepy self.

La Iglesuela del Cid

LA IGLESUELA DEL CID, 11km to the southeast of Cantavieja, is a fine walk along a rough country road. The village's name bears witness to the exploits of **El Cid Campeador**, who came charging through the Maestrazgo in his fight against the infidel. Other than the El Cid *romería*, a fiesta organized by the village forty days after Easter (usually in May), there's nothing else to commemorate the legendary hero.

The village's ochre-red, dry-stone walls, ubiquitous coats of arms and stream – now little more than a trickle – are picturesque, but there's not much else to see. The central, compact Pza. de la Iglesia is enclosed by the old *ayuntamiento*, the attractive **Iglesia Parroquial de la Purificacíon** and a restored eighteenth-century *palacio*, now an upmarket hotel (see p.622).

Villarluengo and beyond

A dramatic, almost alpine, route is in store if you head 30km northwest from Cantavieja, past Cañada de Benatanduz to **VILLARLUENGO**, an enchanting village of ancient houses stacked on a terraced hillside.

Continue 6km farther north on the A1702, over the Villarluengo Pass (1132m), and you'll come to the wonderfully atmospheric *Hostal de la Trucha*. A further 19km, over another pass and past the striking jagged limestone ridges known as **Los Órganos de Montoro**, the road drops down to the small village of **Ejulve**, and then 11km north to the N211 between Montalbán and Alcañiz.

Calanda and Centro Buñuel

C/Mayor 48, on the edge of town • Tues–Sun 10.30am–1.30pm & 4–8pm • €3.50 • ⓦ cbcvirtual.com

CALANDA is home to the excellent **Centro Buñuel**, dedicated to surrealist film-maker Luis Buñuel, who was born here in 1900. Buñuel left Spain in the 1930s, spending his most creative periods in France and then Mexico, where he died in 1983, but he remained fond of his hometown throughout his life. The centre houses a series of innovative displays on the man and his movies, and also has an extensive film library.

Valderrobres

VALDERROBRES is one of the Maestrazgo's most attractive towns. It stands 50km from Calanda, near the border with Catalunya and astride the Río Matarraña, whose crystal waters, flanked by lush valleys, teem with trout. The old quarter sits north of the river, connected to the new town by Avda. Hispanidad and the Puente de Piedra, with the unassuming seventeenth-century **ayuntamiento** on Pza. España just over the bridge – this was considered so characteristic of the region that it was reproduced in Barcelona's Poble Espanyol open-air museum in 1929.

Dominating the town is the **Castillo** (May–Sept Tues–Sat 10.30am–2pm & 5–8.30pm, Sun 10.30am–2pm, Oct–April Fri–Sat 11am–2pm & 4–6.30pm, Sun 11am–2pm; €4, audio-guide €1), once owned by the archbishops of Zaragoza and restored in the 1980s. Today it hosts cultural events and exhibitions. There is also a fourteenth-century church here, **Santa María La Mayor,** which has a fine rose

9

window and is one of the most impressive examples of Levantine Gothic architecture in the region.

ARRIVAL AND INFORMATION
EL MAESTRAZGO

By bus The main approaches to El Maestrazgo are from Teruel, and there are daily buses to Cantavieja and La Iglesuela del Cid, or from Morella in the province of Castellón. Bus schedules tend to vary widely, so it's best to confirm with the *turismo* in Teruel. The main bus route to northern Maestrazgo is between Valderrobres and Alcañiz (50min) and Tortosa (1hr); buses run Monday to Friday and stop next to the iron bridge in Valderrobres.

Turismos In Cantavieja the *turismo* is at C/Mayor 15 (mid-July to mid-Sept daily 10am–2pm & 4–7pm; mid-Sept to mid-July usually Sat & Sun only; ☎964 185 414, ⓦcantavieja.es). Valderrobres' *turismo* is at Avda. Cortes de Aragón 7, near the iron bridge (July & Aug Tues–Sun 9.30am–2pm & 5–7.30pm, Sun 9.30am–2pm; Sept–June Wed–Sat 10am–2pm & 4–6pm, Sun 10am–2pm; ☎978 890 886).

ACCOMMODATION AND EATING

CANTAVIEJA

★ **Hotel Balfagón** Avda. Maestrazgo 20 ☎964 185 076, ⓦhotelbalfagon.com. This stylish and modern hotel, on the main road at the southern edge of town, has comfortable rooms and a spa with sauna and Jacuzzi. There's also an excellent restaurant that serves traditional cuisine and more than eighty different wines, and a lounge bar with expansive terrace. **€73**

MIRAMBEL

Guimera C/Agustín Pastor 28 ☎964 178 269, ⓦhostalguimera.com. Excellent little *fonda* with cosy rooms, comfy beds and a good-quality, popular restaurant serving home-cooked dishes, such as *judías blancas con chorizo* (white beans with sausage) and a variety of good-priced menus. Breakfast is an extra €3. **€34**

LA IGLESUELA DEL CID

Casa Amada C/Fuente Nueva 10 ☎964 443 373. This simple *hostal*, on the main road through the village, has basic rooms and a restaurant serving well-priced, substantial country cooking. Restaurant closed Sun dinner. **€40**

Hospedería La Iglesuela del Cid C/Ondevilla 4 ☎964 443 476, ⓦwww.hospederiasdearagon.com. Elegant boutique hotel, set in the eighteenth-century Palacio Matutano-Daudén, with luxurious rooms. The restaurant serves regional cuisine and offers a *menú del día* for €15. Breakfast included. **€70**

VILLARLUENGO AND AROUND

Fonda Villarluengo C/Castel 1, Villarluengo ☎978 773 014. Friendly *hostal* with well-maintained rooms above a bar and a *comedor* serving simple meals. Restaurant closed Tues. **€35**

Hostal de la Trucha C/Las Fábricas, 6km north of Villarluengo ☎978 773 008, ⓦgargallo-hotels.com. Set in an old farmhouse on the banks of the tranquil Río Pitarque, this wonderfully atmospheric *hostal* has 54 simple rooms with Castilian furniture and tiled floors. There's also an outdoor swimming pool and a restaurant that serves trout caught in the fish farm a few metres away. **€50**

VALDERROBRES

Fonda La Plaza Pza. España 8, opposite the *ayuntamiento* ☎978 850 106, ⓦfondalaplaza.es. Longtime *fonda* in the old quarter, which has atmospheric, rustic rooms set in a medieval mansion. The restaurant serves a *menú del día* (€12, weekends €12–20). Breakfast is included. **€65**

Hostal Querol Just up Avda. Hispanidad from the bridge ☎978 850 192, ⓦhostalquerol.com. This plain but adequate *hostal* has simple, clean rooms and a bar and *comedor* serving local cuisine. Half- and full-board packages are available. Restaurant closed Sun. **€48**

El Salt Elvira Hidalgo 14 ☎978 890 865, ⓦhotelelsalt.com. In the new town, this is one of the more comfortable options. It's not far from the river, and has well-maintained rooms and a simple restaurant. **€50**

Huesca

HUESCA, the provincial capital, is a pleasant mix of urban and rustic, with modern apartment buildings lining its perimeter and a dark, atmospheric old quarter with outdoor cafés and drinking dens. Huesca's history is impressive: the Romans settled here first, calling it Osca, followed by the Moors who took Huesca in 718, just seven years after their arrival in Spain, and ruled it for almost four hundred years. In 1096, it became the capital of the Aragón kingdom until power was transferred to Zaragoza in the early twelfth century. Huesca is also a good jumping-off point for the splendid castle of **Loarre**.

Catedral and Museo Diocesano

Pza. de la Catedral • **Catedral and Museo** Mon–Fri 10.30am–2pm & 4–7pm, Sat 10.30am–2pm • €4 • **Catedral only** Services Mon–Sat 5–7pm, Sun 8.15am–1pm & 5–7pm • Free

The **Catedral**, standing majestically at the centre of the old town, beautifully reveals the city's past, featuring every architectural style from brick Mudéjar to soaring Gothic. It features a superb sixteenth-century alabaster *retablo* by the legendary Renaissance artist Damián Forment, with a triptych detailing scenes from the Crucifixion. A spiral staircase (180 steps) in one corner of the Catedral leads up the fourteenth-century bell tower to a terrace affording sweeping views over the city and to the Pyrenees beyond. The **Museo Diocesano** exhibits well-preserved religious works, including sacred art, from medieval to Baroque, culled from across the region.

Ayuntamiento

Pza. de la Catedral 1 • Contact *turismo* for opening times • €2

The **Ayuntamiento** features a Baroque staircase and a nineteenth-century painting, *The Bell of Huesca*, which depicts one of the more macabre moments in Huesca's history. As the legend goes, in the twelfth century King Ramiro II ordered the beheading of a group of noblemen who had apparently committed treason. He then had their heads laid out in a circle, forming the base of the bell, and suspended one of the heads on a rope over the circle, as the bell's clapper. It is this Ramiro II who is buried in San Pedro el Viejo.

Museo de Huesca

Pza. de la Universidad • Tues–Sat 10am–2pm & 5–8pm, Sun 10am–2pm • Free

The **Museo de Huesca** showcases a wide variety of archeological and artistic items from around the province, including the ruins of a Roman necropolis, lithographs by Goya, and paintings by Aragonese artists, including Huesca native Ramón Acín. The museum is built around the octagonal courtyard of the Palacio de los Reyes de Aragón.

San Pedro el Viejo

Pza. de San Pedro • Mon–Sat 10am–1.30pm & 4–6pm, Sun 11am–noon & 1–1.30pm • €2.50

Founded as a Benedictine monastery in the eleventh century, the church of San Pedro el Viejo houses the tombs of Aragonese royalty King Alfonso I and his son Ramiro II. It also features a lovely, well-maintained Romanesque cloister with beautifully carved capitals.

ARRIVAL AND INFORMATION   HUESCA

By train and bus The intermodal train and bus station is on C/Zaragoza, south of town. Huesca is well connected by bus and train to the region and beyond: regular Alosa buses (walosa.es) connect the town with Zaragoza (just over 1hr), Jaca (1hr 15min), Barbastro (50min), Lleida (2hr 30min) and Barcelona (4hr). Numerous trains run daily to Zaragoza (just over 1hr) and Teruel (3hr 15min). AVE trains also run to Zaragoza (40min) and Madrid (just over 2hr).

Turismo Pza. López Allué (daily 9am–2pm & 4–8pm; 974 292 170, whuescaturismo.com).

ACCOMMODATION

Hostal Joaquín Costa C/Joaquín Costa 20 974 241 774, whostaljoaquincosta.com. Central, amiable *hostal* with 23 diminutive rooms decorated in a white-and-grey colour scheme and with bathrooms revealing designer flair. **€50**

Hostal San Marcos C/San Orencio 10 974 222 931, whostalsanmarcos.es. Friendly *hostal* with no-frills but well-maintained en-suite rooms. Within easy walking distance of Huesca's main sights and just 500m from the bus and train station. **€37**

Hotel Sancho Abarca Coso Alto 52 974 220 650, whotelsanchoabarca.com. A notch above the other accommodation in town, this hotel has modern, crisp rooms with decently sized, modern bathrooms, a spa and fitness centre with a sauna, and a restaurant serving Aragonese cuisine. **€64**

La Posada de la Luna C/Joaquín Costa 10 974 240 857, wposadadelaluna.com. Petite, colourful, boutique-style hotel with cosy rooms and good bathrooms. **€55**

9

EATING AND DRINKING

Hervi C/Santa Paciencia 2 ☎974 240 333, ⓦrestaurantehervihuesca.com. A lively restaurant with a local crowd, hearty dishes, including grilled meats and seafood (mains from €26), and nicely priced regional wines. Wed & Fri–Tues 1.30–3.30pm & 8.30–10.30pm.

Meson Doña Taberna Avda Juan XIII 13, ☎974 21 44 74, ⓦwww.donataberna.es. This warm and welcoming restaurant serves a wide range of Aragonese produce, including delicious steaks, and grilled fish. The menu of the day is usually a good choice, featuring three courses for just €12, including bread and a drink. Tues–Sun noon–11pm.

★ **Restaurante Venta del Sotón** Ctra. A-132 Huesca ☎974 270 241, ⓦventadelsoton.com. This unusual restaurant is arranged around a circular fireplace that is not just a decorative feature, but also used for cooking. There are three tasting menus: the three-course regional menu (€31) of typical Aragonese dishes, the five-course Venta del Sotón menu (€45) and the decadent eight-course Lornezo

Acín menu (€125) which features caviar, lobster and local cheeses plus local Marboré wine and a glass of champagne. Tues–Sun 1.30–3.30pm & 9–11pm.

La Taberna de Lillas Pastia Pza. Navarra 4 ☎974 211 691, ⓦlillaspastia.es. Dine on gourmet Aragonese cuisine, from suckling pig to *arroz negro* (rice cooked in squid ink) topped with tender octopus. The speciality is truffle (*la trufa*) and the wine selection is chosen from local vineyards, including the Somontano region. Splurge on the four-course truffle menu (€65). Tues–Sat 1.30–3.30pm & 9.30–11pm, Sun 1.30–3.30pm.

Las Torres C/María Auxiliadora 3 ☎974 228 213, ⓦwww.lastorres-restaurante.com. Innovative cuisine finds inspiration in the local bounty, from freshwater fish to pig's trotters to aromatic herb sauces. The dining room is grandly elegant, with white linen tablecloths and sparkling crystal glasses. Expect to pay around €60/person. Usually daily lunch & dinner but call ahead.

Around Huesca

The mountainous terrain around Huesca reveals several eye-catching sights, including the imposing, eleventh-century **Castillo de Loarre** and **Los Mallos**, a surreal series of rock formations that jut into the sky.

Castillo de Loarre

36km northwest of Huesca and 4km beyond the village of Loarre • March to mid-June & mid-Sept to Oct & 10am–7pm; mid-June to mid-Sept daily 10am–8pm; Nov–Feb Tues–Sun 11am–5.30pm • €3.90, or €5.50 with guided tour • ☎974 342 161, ⓦcastillodeloarre.es

From afar, the scene looks like little more than rocky outcrops punctuating the Aragonese landscape but as you draw closer, the eleventh-century **Castillo de Loarre** comes into magnificent focus, glowering from its hilltop perch. The castle was constructed in the eleventh century by Sancho Ramírez, king of Aragón and Navarra and its dark and mysterious, mazelike interior makes for great exploring: tunnels lead down to dark cellars, and narrow stairs wind up to lookout towers that command wonderful views over the far-reaching fields. The castle's two main **towers** are the imposing Torre de la Reina, and the Torre del Homenaje, which features a huge fireplace. You can also peer into a quiet Romanesque **church**, which has detailed, carved capitals in the apse.

ARRIVAL AND DEPARTURE   CASTILLO DE LOARRE

By foot The castle is a 2km (1hr) walk from the village. Take the PR-HU105 footpath.

By bus During the week, two buses run daily from Huesca to Loarre (40min), with one service on Sat.

By train Ayerbe, 7km southwest of Loarre, has the closest train station, with services from Huesca (30min), though schedules vary; check ahead. A bus makes the 10min trip between Ayerbe and Loarre daily during the week.

ACCOMMODATION

Camping La Banera 1.5km out of Ayerbe on the road to Loarre ☎974 380 242, ⓦcampinglabanera.com. This decent, well-maintained campsite has hot water in the bathrooms, and a small bar-restaurant (open to campers only). **€14.40**

Hospedería de Loarre Pza. Miguel Moya ☎974 382 706, ⓦhospederiadeloarre.com. Restored seventeenth-century *hospedería* with warmly decorated, comfortable rooms and a respected restaurant serving Aragonese cuisine (menu from €17). Breakfast included. **€60**

PARQUE NACIONAL DE ORDESA (P.634) >

9

Los Mallos and Riglos

About 45km from Huesca, the village of Riglos is a good base for the otherworldly towering rock formations of **Los Mallos** (The Mallets), which are popular with rock climbers.

ACCOMMODATION   LOS MALLOS AND RIGLOS

Refugio de Riglos At the entrance to Riglos ☎ 974 383 051, ⊛ refugioderiglos.es. Catering to climbers and trekkers, this *refugio* has two-, six- and eight-bed rooms and a fitness room with a climbing wall, so you can warm up before doing the real thing. There's also a communal kitchen with fridge and microwave, and an on-site restaurant, *Bon Appétit*, serving hearty Aragonese food. Dorms **€16.40**

Sierra de Guara

The bird's-eye view of the relatively under-the-radar **SIERRA DE GUARA** shows an arid, almost desolate terrain cleaved by over two hundred sculpted canyons and gorges that look like giant, angry slashes in the earth. This is canyoning (*barranquismo*) country: the eastern half of Sierra de Guara is the most popular section for outdoor activities, and the pleasant town of **Alquézar**, in the southeastern corner, functions as the Guara's hub.

Alquézar

Tackling the great outdoors and brushing up your Aragonese history are prime draws in small but well-preserved **ALQUÉZAR**, which lies about 45km from Huesca and 20km northwest of Barbastro. In town the streets are dotted with outdoor operators and tour companies that specialize in canyoning, mountain climbing and hiking excursions (see box opposite).

Colegiata de Santa María del Mayor

April–Oct 11am–1.30pm & 4.30–7.30pm; Nov–March 11am–1.30pm & 4–6pm • €2.50, €3 includes Casa Fabián • ⊛ somontano.org/alquezar

Keeping watch over Alquézar is the imposing **Colegiata de Santa María del Mayor**, which was originally built as a Moorish citadel in the eighth century. It was later conquered by the Christians, who adapted it into a monastery and fortress complex in the twelfth century. Reflecting its long and varied history, the Colegiata reveals art and architecture from throughout the ages: the Romanesque cloister has detailed capitals and frescoes depicting the New Testament that were created in the fifteenth to eighteenth centuries, while the Gothic-Renaissance church is heavy on Baroque art, but also has a simple yet powerful wooden Crucifixion dating back to the thirteenth century.

ARRIVAL AND INFORMATION   ALQUÉZAR

By bus Buses generally run daily to Alquézar from Huesca (50min) and Barbastro (30min); times vary widely, so confirm in advance with the tourist office.

Turismo C/Arrabal, on the edge of the old town (daily 9am–1.30pm & 4.30–8pm; Aug daily 9am–8pm; sometimes limited hours in winter; ☎ 974 318 940, ⊛ alquezar.org).

ACCOMMODATION

Albergue Rural de Guara C/Pilaseras ☎ 974 318 956, ⊛ albergueruraldeguara.com. Sturdy, simple *refugio* above town with views over the countryside and simple rooms, some with bunk beds. Sometimes closed in winter. Dorms **€14.50**

Hotel Castillo C/Pedro Arnal Cavero 11 ☎ 974 942 565, ⊛ hotelcastilloalquezar.com. This traditional Aragonese farmhouse was converted into a hotel in 2013 and features stone walls, wooden beams and cool, modern decor. Rooms are spacious and many have private terraces overlooking the town. **€89**

Hotel Maribel C/Arrabal ☎ 974 318 979, ⊛ hotelmaribel.es. This colourful, quirky – and slightly kitsch – boutique hotel has nine opulent rooms, each one named (and individually decorated) after different types of grape. The Moscatel room has a canopied bed and

CANYONING IN THE SIERRA DE GUARA

Alquézar has a range of quality canyoning operators who cater to all levels, and offer everything from thrilling descents into dark, echoing caves to treks along gaping gorges to river rafting. Average cost is around €55–65 per person per day, with prices varying depending on the level of difficulty and size of tour group.

OUTDOOR OPERATORS IN ALQUÉZAR

Avalancha C/Arrabal s/n ☏ 974 318 299, ⓦ avalancha.org. This well-regarded operator organizes canyoning, rafting, hiking and skiing trips plus paintball and accommodation.

Guias Boira Paseo San Hipólito ☏ 974 318 974, ⓦ guiasboira.com. This friendly operator offers a wide range of guided trips, including canyoning, via ferrata, rafting and *escalada en hielo* (ice climbing). They can also help with accommodation.

Swarovski crystal lamp, while the Moristel features a forged-iron headboard and wallpaper in a colour "inspired by the tones in the water of the river Vero." They also have a smart, self-contained house in town (€350/night, €2100/week) and run a good restaurant, *Casa Gervasio* (see below). A locally sourced breakfast is included. **€150**

Hotel Villa de Alquézar C/Pedro Arnal Cavero 12 ☏ 974 318 416, ⓦ villadealquezar.com. A stone arch graces the front door at this artfully renovated hotel, which has wood-beam ceilings and a terrace with views of the Colegiata and the Río Vero canyon. Some rooms have their own private terraces; all have comfortable beds and en-suite bathrooms. **€69**

EATING AND DRINKING

Casa Gervasio C/Arnal Cavero 13 ☏ 974 318 282, ⓦ grupogervasio.com/restaurante-casa-gervasio. Decent restaurant with a breezy terrace with pots of flowers and stone walls. The menu is a creative take on local cuisine and might include *longaniza* (sausage), chickpeas with shellfish or rabbit in almond sauce and is arranged in two different tasting menus (€25). Daily 1.30–3.30pm & 8–11pm; more limited hours in winter.

Casa Pardina C/Medio ☏ 974 318 425, ⓦ casapardina .com. Handsome, rustic restaurant with modern touches,

and a lovely terrace that overlooks the Guara countryside. *Menú Casa Pardina* €27, *menú tradicional* €35. Easter–Oct Mon & Wed–Sun 1.30–3.30pm & 8.30–10.30pm; Nov–Easter usually open Fri–Sun only.

Restaurante Cueva Reina C/Baja 42 ☏ 974 318 182, ⓦ restaurantecuevareina.es. This contemporary restaurant has a comfortable dining room with views over the Río Vero and serves dishes such as pork in local Somontano wine and roast Aragonese lamb shoulder. Four-course menu €28.50. Daily 1.30–3.30pm & 8.30–10.30pm.

Barbastro

BARBASTRO's formidable history put it on the map, but it's the rich local wines that have given this small town its staying power as a tourist destination. For more than three centuries, the Moors ruled Barbastro as one of their chief outposts in the far north. In 1137, it was here that the marriage of Petronia, daughter of Ramiro of Aragón, to Count Ramón Berenguer IV of Barcelona established the union of Aragón and Catalunya. As for the *vino*: Barbastro is capital of the **Somontano** wine region, and makes for an ideal jumping-off point for tastings at the thirty-plus *bodegas* and vineyards clustered around town (see box, p.628).

Barbastro's old town exudes a certain faded glory and is presided over by a sturdy Gothic Catedral. In **Pza. de la Constitución** sits the fifteenth-century *ayuntamiento*. Nearby are the arcaded **Pza. del Mercado** and the shaded **Paseo del Coso**, where you can ease into the evening over a drink or three at the outdoor bars.

Catedral

Pza. Palacio • **Catedral** Tues–Sat 10.30am–1.30pm & 4.30–6.30pm • €2.50, €5 includes Museo Diocesano • **Museo** June–Sept Tues–Sat 5–8pm, Sun 11am–2pm; Oct–May Tues–Sat 4–7pm, Sun 11am–2pm • €4 • ⓦ museodiocesano.es

The handsome sixteenth-century **Catedral** features an alabaster *retablo* by Damián Forment. He left the work unfinished when he died in 1540, and the remainder was

9

completed by his student, Liceire, two decades later. The Catedral bell tower has been well preserved, while inside the building are elegant ribbed vaults and a nave with carved columns. The **Museo Diocesano** features a well-maintained collection of sacred art from Aragón's rural medieval churches, archeological remains from the Moorish era, and an array of Gothic and Romanesque murals, including several beautiful depictions of the Madonna and Child.

ARRIVAL AND INFORMATION

By bus Multiple daily buses operate to Huesca (50min), where you can make connections to Jaca and Zaragoza. Buses also travel to Lleida (1hr 30min), Benasque (1hr 45min) and Alquézar (40min).

BARBASTRO

Turismo Avda. de la Merced 64 (July & Aug Mon–Sat 10am–2pm & 4–7.30pm, Sun 10am–2pm & 5–7pm; Sept–June Tues–Sat 10am–2pm & 4–7.30pm; ☎974 308 350, ☻turismobarbastro.org).

ACCOMMODATION

La Alcoba de Baco C/Mayor ☎974 316 342, ☻viajesenoturismo.es. Next to the Palacio de los Argensola, these handsome, central apartments have full kitchens, and cater to those visiting Somontano for *enoturismo* (wine tourism). They often offer good weekend packages that include wine tastings and dinner. **€75**

Hostal Pirineos C/General Ricardos 13 ☎974 310 000. Simple *hostal* with basic, well-maintained rooms. The restaurant serves good food, with a menu starting at €14. **€35**

Hotel San Ramón del Somontano C/Academia Cerbuna 2 ☎974 312 825, ☻hotelsanramon somontano.com. This beautiful four-star hotel is set in a 1903 modernist *hostal* that has hosted everyone from George Orwell to Miguel de Unamuno. The elegant original design has been artfully incorporated into the modern hotel. There's a spa and some rooms have Jacuzzis. The restaurant (see below) serves Aragonese cuisine. **€125**

EATING AND DRINKING

Flor C/Goya 3 ☎974 311 056, ☻restauranteflor.com. Dine on creative cuisine, from hake and cod in fragrant sauces to suckling pig and beef fillet, at this elegant, well-regarded restaurant. Excellent Somontano wine list. Dishes €14–24. Tues–Sat 1.30–3.30pm & 9–11pm; Sun 1.30–3.30pm.

San Ramón del Somontano Hotel San Ramón del

Somontano ☎974 312 825, ☻hotelsanramon somontano.com. The well-appointed restaurant in this historic hotel serves tasty regional cuisine based on locally sourced ingredients, plus an array of Somontano wines. Veal fillet €18.50. Daily 1.30–3.30pm & 9–11pm.

The Aragonese Pyrenees

The **ARAGONESE PYRENEES** define all the superlatives associated with the soaring Pyrenean mountains: the peaks here are the highest, the wildest and, in the eyes of many, the most beautiful of the Spanish Pyrenees. From the snowy mountain tips

SOMONTANO WINE

Somontano has become one of Aragón's most distinguished D.O. – Denominación de Origen – wine regions, with more than thirty vineyards producing superb red, white and rosé wines from a variety of local and international grapes. The **Espacio del Vino** interpretation centre (Mon–Sat 10am–2pm & 4.30–7.30pm, ☻dosomontano.com/el espacio del vino) is in the same building as the Barbastro tourist office, and features a short film on the history of Somontano wine, along with a shop.

The organization **Ruta del Vinos Somontano** (Somontano Wine Routes; ☻rutadelvinos omontano.com) offers myriad tours, including the wine bus (€26), which runs every third Saturday of the month from Zaragoza and Huesca, taking in a range of wineries and including some free time in either Barbastro or Alquezar.

Many of the vineyards are also individually open to visitors (generally Mon–Sat, morning to early evening), and offer tours (ranging from free to €5). The Barbastro *turismo* has a wealth of information on routes, vineyards and itineraries.

9

piercing the deep blue sky to lushly forested valleys and thundering rivers, the Aragonese Pyrenees are one of the country's national treasures. So lace up your ski or hiking boots, and take to the verdant valleys or snow slopes – the mountains offer adventure throughout the seasons.

Jaca, the biggest city in the Aragonese Pyrenees, has plenty of bus connections into the mountains. It also boasts a formidable Catedral and a decent array of hotels and *hostales*, making it a popular base, particularly for the busy **ski resorts** to the north, including Astún and Candanchú. As for summer activities, hiking trails traverse the entire range, including in the gorgeous **Ansó** and **Hecho** valleys and the magnificent **Parque Nacional de Ordesa y Monte Perdido** – a real must-visit.

Jaca

The busy industrial town of **JACA** is one of the main crossroads and transport hubs of northern Aragón, and first impressions are not great. Venture into the city centre, however, and you'll find a bevy of sights that powerfully evoke the town's long history, including the magnificent Catedral. Extending south of the Catedral is Jaca's *casco antiguo*, which includes atmospheric plazas and streets, and the fifteenth-century Torre de Reloj (watchtower).

Jaca was founded by the Romans and then conquered by the Moors in the early eighth century. Later in the century it was won back by the Christians, in a victory that's celebrated annually on the first Friday in May. In an interesting twist, the Moorish armies were driven back thanks to an immense – and brave – effort by the town's women, and the festival includes a parade that pays homage to these brave Jaca ladies. In the eleventh century, Jaca became the first capital of the Aragón kingdom, though by the end of the century the power had shifted to Huesca.

Jaca makes for a good jumping-off point for outdoor adventure in the Pyrenees, including skiing at Astún and Candanchu, just 30km away (see box, p.631). During the **Festival Folklórico de los Pirineos** (⊕jaca.es/festival), held in late July and early August every odd-numbered year, people stream in from all over the Pyrenees to show off their cultural traditions with religious dances, performances and food. Also in August, over a

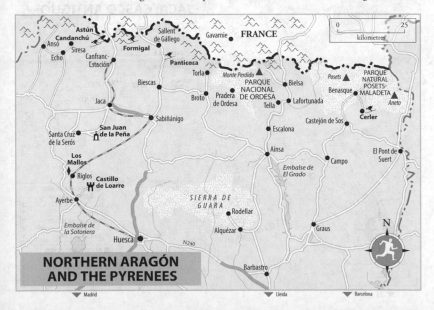

NORTHERN ARAGÓN AND THE PYRENEES

9

two-week period, is the annual **Festival Internacional en el Camino de Santiago** (⊕www. festivalcaminosantiago.com) featuring religious and classical music concerts at different venues, including the famous Catedral, as well as a medieval market in the city centre.

Catedral and Museo Diocesano

Pza. de San Pedro • **Catedral** Daily noon–1.30pm & 4–7pm • Free • ☎ 974 356 241 • **Museo Diocesano** July & Aug Tues–Sun 10am–1.30pm & 4–8pm; Sept–June Tues–Fri 10am–1.30pm & 4–7pm, Sat 10am–1.30pm & 4–8pm, Sun 10am–1.30pm • €6, €7.50 with guided tour • ⊕ diocesisdejaca.org

The jewel of Jaca is its eleventh-century **Catedral de San Pedro Apóstol**, one of the oldest in Spain, and perhaps the city's finest reminder of its years as the seat of the Aragonese kingdom. The Catedral's incredible history and staying power is revealed through its gorgeous amalgam of styles, from French Romanesque to Gothic. And, while the original Romanesque design has been largely built over – the original ceilings were in wood, which were replaced by double-barrel vaults – you can still find vestiges of it, such as the simple main door. Within the Catedral are elegant carvings gracing the capitals, a sixteenth-century statue of Santiago and a central apse painted in 1792 by Aragonese artist Manuel Bayeu, who was Francisco Goya's brother-in-law. A highlight is the shrine of Santa Orosía, the patron saint of Jaca. Adjoining the Catedral is the **Museo Diocesano**, which displays an extensive collection of religious art, artefacts and frescoes from mountain churches throughout the area.

Ciudadela

Avda. del Primer Viernes de Mayo • Tues–Sun 11am–2pm & 5–8pm, closed for part of Nov • €10, includes museum • ☎ 974 360 443, ⊕ ciudadeladejaca.es

The impressive star-shaped **Ciudadela** (also known as the Castillo de San Pedro) looms just east of the centre of town, and is still partly used by the military. Wander along the fortified walls for lovely views of the surrounding mountains and countryside. The **Museo de Miniatura Militares** (Museum of Military Miniatures) within is a remarkable – almost mesmerizing – collection of over 35,000 toy soldiers, dioramas, models and

HIT THE SLOPES IN ARAGÓN

Skiing in the Aragon Pyrenees matches that of Catalunya and, increasingly, of France. Overall, the **ski resorts** are well maintained and cater to all levels, from downhill daredevils to wobbly first-timers. Note that, as in the Catalan Pyrenees, some of the best discounts are via pre-trip package deals offered by hotels, agencies or the resorts themselves. But even if you don't book a package ahead of time, you can often find deals once you've arrived, offered by the *turismos* as well as the hotels and the resorts.

In the west are **Candanchú** (@candanchu.com), which has a well-known ski school, and **Astún** (@astun.com), with a wide range of pistes, including plenty for beginners. The main hub for accommodation and other services is **Jaca**.

Partly funded by the Aragón government, Aramón (@aramon.com) now manages a group of formerly independent ski resorts. Of these, **Formigal** is one of the largest, with 93 runs and 21 lifts, and caters to all levels. **Panticosa** is smaller but less crowded, with daily numbers limited to 3500 people. In the Pyrenees' easternmost section, sleek **Cerler** attracts seasoned skiers, with several ski centres totalling about 52km, altitudes up to 2630m, 61 runs and 18 lifts. Cerler also offers equipment rental and ski and snowboard schools. **Benasque** is a popular hub for Cerler.

more. The tiny lead soldiers, measuring 2cm in height, are depicted in historical battles from around the world, from the Crusades to the Crown of Aragón era.

Puente San Miguel

The fifteenth-century **Puente San Miguel** arches across the river west of the Ciudadela. It was the main entrance to Jaca used by pilgrims on the Camino Aragonés, a branch of the Camino de Santiago.

ARRIVAL AND INFORMATION
JACA

By bus Regular buses travel daily from the central bus station, on Pza. de Biscós, to Huesca (1hr 15min), Zaragoza (2hr 15min) and to Pamplona (1hr 45min).

By train The train station, on C/Ferrocarril, is about a 15min walk from the town centre. Regular trains run to Zaragoza (3hr 20min) and other regional towns.

Turismo Pza. de San Pedro (summer Mon–Sat 9am–9pm, Sun 9am–3pm; winter Mon–Fri 9am–1.30 & 4.30–7pm, Sat 10am–1pm & 5–7pm; @974 360 098, @jaca.es).

ACCOMMODATION

★**Barrose** C/Estiras 4, Barós @974 360 582, @barosse.com. This wonderfully unique adults-only *casa rural*, in a village 2km south of Jaca, blends designer style with rustic, romantic appeal. Each of the five rooms is named after traditional edifices, such as the Romanesque-style Ermita (hermitage), with stone, gleaming woods and elegant drapes, and there's a sauna and spa. **€130**

Hostal La Casa del Arco C/San Nicolás 4 @974 364 448, @lacasadelarco.net. Historic hotel located next to the Catedral, with simple but well-maintained rooms and, unusually for this part of Spain, a vegetarian restaurant. Some rooms share bathrooms and the hotel uses renewable energy and grows its own produce in an organic garden. **€30**

Hotel Conde Aznar Paseo de la Constitución 3 @974 361 050, @condeaznar.com. This welcoming family-run three-star hotel has rooms done up in elegant, old-fashioned decor. The restaurant serves tasty Aragonese cuisine with a Basque flourish. **€65**

Hotel Mur C/Santa Orosia 1 @974 360 100, @hotelmur.com. Famed writers and artists from Pío Baroja to Santiago Ramón y Cajal have warmed the beds at this large, historic hotel, which first opened its doors in 1875. Rooms are a bit dated in their decor, but are handsomely maintained. Breakfast is included. **€65**

EATING AND DRINKING

La Casa del Arco C/San Nicolás 4 @974 364 448, @lacasadelarco.net. This charmingly offbeat spot serves creative vegetarian cuisine, with a focus on organic products. The weekday three-course menu is a good deal at €14. Mon–Sat 1.30–3.30pm & 8.30–10.30pm.

Lilium Av. del Primer Viernes de Mayo 8 @974 355 356. This popular restaurant is spread over three levels and serves home-style Alto-Aragonese dishes such as lamb *al estilo de mi madre* (in the style of my mother), washed down with an extensive wine list of Somontanos and Riojas. Mon, Tues & Sun 11.30am–5pm, Wed–Sat 11.30am–5pm & 7.30pm–midnight.

Restaurante Biarritz Avda. Primer Viernes de Mayo 12 @974 361 632, @restaurantebiarritz.com. The

9

speciality at this welcoming restaurant is *carnes a la brasa* (grilled meats), from thick, juicy steaks to tender veal. Pair your meat with fresh salads of goat cheese and *bacalao* (cod). The menu starts at €15. Mon, Tues & Thurs–Sun 1–4pm & 7.30–11pm.

Restaurante Cobarcho Ramiro I 2 ☎974 363 643, ⓦrestaurantecobarcho.com. Aragón is meat country – and you can get a hearty taste of it at this friendly spot: grilled and roasted lamb chops and T-bone steaks, suckling pig, duck and more are on the menu at equally friendly prices, including a *menú del día* for €13.50. Tues–Sun 11.30am–4pm & 7.30–11.30pm.

La Tasca de Ana Ramiro I 3 ☎974 364 726, ⓦlatascadeana.com. It can get crowded and loud, but if you're going to do tapas in Jaca, this long-running spot is the place to go. It draws a healthy mix of locals and visitors, all here to chow on the delicious small bites, from grilled squid, pungent cheeses and cured hams to the perennially popular *langostinos* (prawns). Mon–Fri 7–11pm, Sat & Sun 12.30–3.30pm & 7–11.30pm.

San Juan de la Peña and around

March–May & Sept–Oct 10am–2pm & 3.30–7pm; June–Aug daily 10am–2pm & 3–8pm; Nov–Feb Mon–Fri & Sun 10am–2pm, Sat 10am–5pm • €7, or €8.50 for access to both interpretation centres; all admission includes Santa María church • ☎974 355 119, ⓦmonasteriosanjuan.com

The **Monasterio de San Juan de la Peña**, set amid protected natural parkland 21km south of Jaca, is one of the most stunning sacred buildings in Aragón, if not in Spain. Tucked protectively under the overhang of a massive boulder, it's built right into a rocky mountain: from certain angles, it's hard to tell where man-made structure ends and nature begins. Dating from the ninth century, the monastery is named after a hermit who lived in solitude atop the towering cliff (*peña*). The monastery features a Romanesque church with twelfth-century murals and the Gothic San Victorián chapel, but the real standout is the elegant twelfth-century cloister, shaded by the bulging rock face that looms over it. The cloister has ornate capitals, depicting Bible scenes.

In 1675, a fire in the monastery forced the monks to leave and build a newer one, which sits further up the hill. The **Monasterio Nuevo** (same hours as old monastery) features a helpful visitors' centre and two interpretation centres, which chronicle the history of the monastery and the eventful lives of Aragón's kings and queens.

Church of Santa María

Daily 10am–2pm & 3–8pm • €2, or included in admission to San Juan de la Peña

From San Juan de la Peña, a series of trails fans out through the forest, including a popular path to the nearest village, **Santa Cruz de la Serós**, 7km away, which is home to the elegant eleventh-century Romanesque church of **Santa María**, formerly a monastery. The trail is signposted from near the church.

ARRIVAL AND DEPARTURE   SAN JUAN DE LA PEÑA AND AROUND

By bus There is no scheduled bus from Jaca, but in high season a bus occasionally connects Santa Cruz de Serós to the monastery; call the monastery to confirm.

ACCOMMODATION

Hospedería Monasterio de San Juan de la Peña ☎974 374 422, ⓦwww.hospederiasdearagon.com. Forming part of the Monasterio Nuevo, this handsome four-star hotel features elegant rooms, lovely gardens, a rustic restaurant and a spa. **€150**

Valles de Echo and Ansó

Wild and beautiful, the **Ansó and Echo valleys**, northwest of Jaca, burrow deep into the Pyrenees. The terrain is by turns desolate and fecund and the tiny mountain villages are as quaint as they come. But perhaps the main allure is that this region gets fewer visitors than elsewhere in the Pyrenees and although the summer can get busy, in the off-season you can often have an entire trail (if not an entire valley) largely to yourself. In fact, if there is activity on the slopes, it's usually the local **wildlife** – the forested mountains, especially in the Valle de Echo, are home to creatures large and small, from chamois to red squirrels to a small population of brown bears. Keep an eye out too for all sorts of birds, including the lammergeier bearded vulture. The valley's main towns are the charming Echo and Ansó, while elsewhere, natural wonders abound, including **La Selva de Oza** (about 5km from Siresa), a spruce and pine forest crossed by the rushing Río Aragón Subordán, which is thick with Pyrenean trout.

Echo and around

Lovely **ECHO**, the main town of the valley of the same name, is the very definition of rustic Aragón. Stone houses with wrought-iron balconies cast shadows on cobbled streets, the scene framed by vivid green valleys and elegant peaks. The village made its mark in history as the *sede* (seat) of the young Aragonese kingdom, and is also where King Alfonso I was born. Here, locals speak "Cheso", a dialect of Aragonese.

Museo del Arte Contemporáneo al Aire Libre
Ctra. Oza • Open access • Free

Echo also has an arty angle: until the mid-1980s, the town hosted an annual symposium on contemporary sculpture, founded by artist Pedro Tramulas. One of its legacies is the **Museo del Arte Contemporáneo al Aire Libre**, an open-air sculpture park near the entrance to town, featuring striking contemporary stone pieces – the juxtaposition of modern art and historic town makes for a memorable scene.

ARRIVAL AND INFORMATION   ECHO AND AROUND

By bus Buses from Jaca service Echo and Siresa (both around 1hr) generally once a day Monday to Friday.
Turismo In the Museo de Arte Contemporáneo al Aire

Libre (July–Oct daily 10am–1.30pm & 5.30–8pm; usually closed mid-Oct to mid-June; ☎974 375 505, ⊛valledehecho.net).

ACCOMMODATION

Albergue Siresa C/Reclusa, Siresa, 2km north of Echo ☎974 375 385, ⊛alberguesiresa.com. This basic, friendly *albergue*, in the heart of small Siresa, has comfortable bunk-bedded dorms and plenty of information on exploring the surrounding mountains, including books and mountain gear rental; they can also arrange guided hikes. Breakfast included; half- and full-board packages are also available. Dorms **€16.50**
Borda Bisaltico Carretera Gabardito, 6km north of town ☎974 375 388 or 974 375 098, ⊛bordabisaltico .com. This well-tended complex features a campsite, an *albergue* with four-person dorms, and basic apartments. **€19**, dorms **€20**, apartments **€100**
Camping Valle de Hecho Carretera Puenta la Reina ☎974 375 361, ⊛www.campinghecho.com. This

well-run campground has a range of amenities, including an outdoor pool, a restaurant, a cafeteria and organized activities, including hiking excursions. They also have wooden bungalows. **€17.16**, bungalows **€97.27**
Casa Blasquico Pza. Palacio de la Fuente 1 ☎974 375 007, ⊛casablasquico.es. Lovingly cared for rooms, each named after a flower or herb, feature comfortable beds, hardwood floors and clean bathrooms. The hotel also has the acclaimed *Restaurante Gaby* where breakfast is served for an extra €6. **€40**
Hotel Castillo d'Acher Pza. Mayor, Siresa ☎974 375 313. Basic, well-maintained but somewhat dated rooms in the centre of the village. The restaurant serves decent regional cuisine, including *conejo con caracoles* (rabbit with snails), tripe with chickpeas and grilled meats. **€50**

EATING AND DRINKING

Restaurante Gaby Casa Blasquico ☎974 375 007, ⊛casablasquico.es. This lovely restaurant is a town institution – and for good reason. It's the model of mountain charm: low, wood-beamed ceilings; walls hanging with old photos; and excellent regional cuisine,

including grilled *conejo* (rabbit, €21), crêpes with mushrooms, and a superb wine list, with a particular focus on Aragón's Somontano wines. Daily 1.30–3.30pm & 8.30–10pm; may have limited hours in winter.

Ansó

ANSÓ rivals Echo for rustic, alpine appeal: red-roofed stone houses stand out against a backdrop of lush greenery, with the big, blue sky opening above. As with many

9

mountain villages in the Pyrenees, the pleasure here is to just wander the cobbled streets and Pza. Mayor, and perhaps to take some shade along the banks of the river, the Río Veral.

ARRIVAL AND INFORMATION

ANSÓ

By bus Buses from Jaca serve Ansó 1–2 times daily (just over 2hr).

Turismo Pza. Mayor (July–Aug Mon–Tues 10am–noon &

6–8pm, Wed–Sun 10am–1.15pm & 5–8pm; closed in winter; ☏ 974 370 225).

ACCOMMODATION

El Pajar de Pierra Avda. Pedro Cativiela 3a & 3b ☏ 619 224 539 or ☏ 660 836 220, ☏ elpajardepierra.com. Two side-by-side *casa rural*-style houses done up as an elegant farmhouse, featuring cosy interiors and lovely mountain views throughout, especially from the breezy garden. Groups and families can rent out the full house (each includes five bedrooms, three bathrooms, and a fully

equipped kitchen) by the day (€175) or week (€800). **€55**

Posada Magoria C/Milagro 32 ☏ 974 370 049, ☏ posadamagoria.com. This inviting *posada* has been beautifully restored, with wood-beam ceilings, solid furniture and comfortable beds. The restaurant (reserved for guests) serves organic vegetarian cuisine using vegetables grown in the garden, including squash and aubergine. **€55**

Parque Nacional de Ordesa y Monte Perdido and around

The best of Aragón's natural wonders all seem to converge with climactic glory in the **PARQUE NACIONAL DE ORDESA Y MONTE PERDIDO**. Presiding over the park's greenery is the Monte Perdido (Lost Mountain) range, the largest limestone chain in Western Europe. Verdant valleys blanketed in beech, fir and pine cut through the terrain, and clear blue streams and gushing waterfalls keep the fields lush and green. After the snow melts, honeysuckle, primroses and irises bloom in rocky crevices and on sun-speckled slopes. As for wildlife, the park is teeming with it: Egyptian vultures and golden eagles soar overhead; Pyrenean chamois scamper up hillsides; and trout dart through ice-cold streams.

Many of the deep valleys were created by massive glaciers, at the heads of which are cirques: basins shaped like an amphitheatre with steep walls of rock. Elsewhere, tiny alpine villages, with stone houses crowned with sandstone-tile roofs and conical chimneys, dot the mountainsides and make for pleasant stops along the many routes that meander through the park.

The park is divided roughly into three main sections: **Ordesa** (to the west), **Añisclo** (to the south) and **Escuaín** (to the east). The town of **Torla**, 3km south of the park's southwest border, is the most popular gateway.

Torla

TORLA in many ways exemplifies the modern-day Pyrenean town: turn down one cobbled street in the old town, and you're rewarded with the alluring sight of stone houses prettily framed by bright-green valleys and naked peaks; turn the other way, and you run smack into a high-rise hotel or a belching tour bus pulling into a car park. It is, however, this very mix of low-key village life and tourist-friendly amenities that makes Torla a good base for exploring the park.

Hikes in the park

The park offers a wide range of hikes, from half-day ambles to multi-day treks, all of which take you past natural wonders, including crashing waterfalls, gaping canyons and vivid-green valleys. You can access the park on foot from Torla on the well-marked GR15 path from town, which eventually links up with the GR11, a right fork of which goes to **Pradera de Ordesa**, entrance to the **Cañón de Ordesa** and the starting point for most of the popular hikes further into the park. The whole trek from Torla to Pradera takes about two hours.

Circo de Soaso

The **Circo de Soaso** trek is one of the park's main crowd-pleasers, and for good reason. It offers a lovely overview of the park's natural highlights – gorgeous greenery, tumbling waterfalls – but it's not too challenging, and it can be completed in a day. From Pradera de Ordesa the route leads through forest, followed by a steep climb up the **Senda de los Cazadores** (Hunters' Path), which then flattens out as the Faja de Pelay path to the beautiful **Cola de Caballo** (Horsetail Waterfall). The journey takes about three to four hours each way (around 6–7hr round trip).

Circo de Cotatuero

This trek has a lovely waterfall as a reward, and takes you along the northern crest of the impressive **Valle de Ordesa**. The full round-trip hike takes about 5 to 6 hours. Park officials warn that the hike should only be done in the summer or early autumn as in the winter and spring there is a risk of avalanches. From Pradera de Ordesa, the hike starts steeply and eventually leads to a lookout point below the thundering **Cascada de Cotatuero.** To return from the Cascada, head downhill and then continue on the Cotatuero *circo* back to the Pradera de Ordesa.

Refugio Góriz and Monte Perdido

From Pradera de Ordesa, trek along the GR11 to Circo de Soaso (about 3hr) and then up to the *Refugio Góriz* at 2169m (see p.637), the traditional jumping-off point to climb **Monte Perdido** (3355m). The trek up Monte Perdido (about 5hr) requires intermediate mountaineering skills, crampons and other professional equipment. It is not to be undertaken lightly.

Brecha de Rolando and Refuge des Sarradets

If you have a head for heights, try this memorable onward route from the Cascada de Cotatuero: from the waterfalls, on the Cotatuero cirque, you can climb, via a series of iron pegs in a wall, the **Clavijas de Cotatuero**. Note that you don't need any special climbing equipment but you should be fit and have the aforementioned affinity for heights. Once you've done the climb, it's about a two- to three-hour trek to the **Brecha de Rolando**, a large natural gap in the Cirque de Gavarnie on the French border. From the Brecha, it's then a steep climb (about 500m) to the *Refuge des Sarradets* at 2587m (see p.637), across the border in France.

Parc National des Pyrénées and Gavarnie village

The northern section of the park is adjacent to France's **Parc National des Pyrénées**, which in total runs for about 100km along the Spain–France border. The French side offers more of the same wild Pyrenean landscape, and a popular trek with hikers is to cross northwest into the French park and on to the pretty village of **Gavarnie**. Many will do this hike over the course of a couple of days. From Torla, hike along the GR15.2 to **Puente de los Navarros** and then continue on the GR11 to San Nicolás de Bujaruelo (roughly 7km from Torla), which is marked by a medieval bridge. Here you'll find the *Refugio Valle de Bujaruelo* (see p.637). From the San Nicolás bridge, you can trek over mountains and into France and Garvarnie – about a six- to eight-hour hike.

Cañón de Añisclo and Garganta de Escuaín

The canyons of **Añisclo** and **Escuaín** dramatically carve up the terrain in the southeast corner of Ordesa. These canyons draw considerably fewer tourists than the Cañón de Ordesa, in part because it can be a tough area to penetrate, with no public transport and minimal accommodation. With your own transport, it is well worth getting off the beaten track here.

9

Cañón de Anísclo

From the north, the **Cañón de Anísclo** – filled with jagged cliffs, quiet forests of looming trees and gurgling brooks – is a day-hike from *Refugio Góriz*. If you have your own transport, you can reach it from the south. About 13km from tiny **Escalona**, 10km north of Aínsa, in the direction of Sarvisé is a trail that leads into the canyon; it's a five-hour round-trip trek through the most verdant section of the gorge to the clearing, **La Ripareta**.

Garganta de Escuaín

Centro de Visitantes, Tella: late March to mid-Oct 9am–2pm & 4.15–7pm, late June to mid-Sept 9am–1pm & 4.15–8pm • ☎ 974 243 361

The **Garganta Escuaín**, in the Río Yaga valley, may be smaller than Anísclo but it is just as spectacular. It's best accessed from the village of **Lafortunada**, 20km north of Aínsa. From Lafortunada, you can trek the GR15 trail for the two-hour trip to the pretty village of **Tella**, which has a **park information office**. Just beyond the village, a trail leads to tiny **Escuaín**, from where it's about an hour into the gorge. With your own transport, you can also reach Escuaín from a small road off the Escalona–Sarvisé road.

Aínsa and around

In certain lights of day, the medieval stone village of **Aínsa** looks like it has sprouted from the earth itself, with its cobbled streets, rooftops in varying shades of rust and grey and tendrils of green hanging out of flowerpots on wrought-iron balconies. The village is perched on a hill and views of the surrounding looming mountains greet you around every turn. Aínsa also has a decent selection of accommodation and makes an ideal base for exploring the park, as it lies about 10km from the trail into the **Cañón de Anísclo**.

Iglesia de Santa María

Pza. Mayor • Generally daily 10am–2pm & 4–9pm • Belfry entry €1

The exceptional Romanesque **Iglesia de Santa María** rises over the Pza. Mayor, and features a simple entryway with four archivolts (decorative arches). Inside are a triangular cloister and a fortified four-storeyed belfry, which you can ascend for far-reaching views from the top.

Bielsa

Some 33km north of Aínsa lies the small town of **BIELSA**, west of which sits the gorgeous *Parador de Bielsa* (see p.638), the most comfortable jumping-off point for exploring the park. Bielsa sits at the confluence of the Cinca and Barrosa rivers, and northeast of town, in the park, unfolds the lush Valle de Pineta and the glassy Lago de Marboré. From the parador, which sits at the park's edge, you can trek – 4 to 5 hours one-way – through the valley to Marboré Lake, and there are numerous shorter walks in the area which provide an excellent introduction to the park.

ARRIVAL AND DEPARTURE

PARQUE NACIONAL DE ORDESA Y MONTE PERDIDO AND AROUND

By bus One bus every day (either early morning or mid-day) from Sabiñánigo, a transport hub for the area, to Aínsa stops at Torla (1hr) and Barbastro. There are additional weekday services in July and August between Sabiñánigo and Torla and three times a week (daily in summer) there's also a service to Bielsa (just under 1hr). Several daily buses operate from Jaca to Sabiñánigo. In the summer, a shuttle runs from Torla to the park entrance (every 15–30min: daily 6am–7pm; €3/€4.50 one-way/return) and no cars are allowed to drive in.

By car Outside of high season (Easter week and July to mid-Sept) you can drive to the park border, northwest from Torla. Otherwise you'll have to leave your vehicle in the Torla car park and board the shuttle to the park (see above).

INFORMATION

Centro de Visitantes The park is well served by tourist information offices, including a gleaming centre in the car park at Torla (daily: summer 9am–1pm & 4.15–8pm; winter 9am–2pm & 4–7pm; ☎ 974 486 472) with permanent displays on the ecology of the park and an ascending ramp that simulates climbing a mountain, featuring a different rock face on each floor. A lookout point at the top offers views of the Aragonese landscape.

Turismos There are tourist offices in several towns near the park. You can get info on park conditions, trails and maps here but don't expect English to be spoken. In Torla the *turismo* is on C/Fatás, in the old town (mid-June to mid-Sept Mon–Sat 9.30–1.30pm & 5–9pm; ☎ 974 486 378). Aínsa's *turismo* is at Avda. Ordesa 5 (daily 10am–2pm &

4–7.30pm; shorter hours in winter; ☎ 974 500 767), Bielsa's is on Pza. Mayor (daily 10am–2pm & 4–7.30pm, shorter hours in winter; ☎ 974 501 127).

Maps and guides Editorial Alpina (ⓦ editorialalpina .com) has good maps of the park. Cicerone (ⓦ cicerone .co.uk) publishes in-depth trekking guides, including one on the Spanish Pyrenees and the GR11 trail.

Online ⓦ ordesa.net has plenty of information on the park, including on accommodation and restaurants.

ACCOMMODATION AND EATING

The towns around the park have a decent mix of hotels and budget beds (book ahead in high season). The park has a number of basic stone refuges (€15–30/person), where you can stay when on longer treks. Note that refuges will often be closed for a part of the low season; enquire before setting out. Camping is prohibited inside the park.

TORLA

Camping Río Ara 300m from Torla, on the road to Ordesa, signposted from road ☎ 974 486 248, ⓦ campingrioara.com. Set in a verdant riverside area close to town, this leafy campsite has a café/bar, supermarket and wi-fi. There is also information on trekking into the park. Open Easter–Oct. **€16.40**

Camping y Refugio Valle de Bujaruelo 7km north of Torla, off the A-135, in the Valle de Bujaruelo ☎ 974 486 348, ⓦ campingvalledebujaruelo.com. Well-maintained alpine complex, surrounded by the leafy Valle de Bujaruelo, with a range of accommodation, including camping (most plots with electricity), dorms for two to five people in the refuge and bungalows with kitchenettes. Open Easter to October. **€18**, dorms **€14**, bungalows **€100**

Hotel Villa Russell C/Principal s/n ☎ 974 486 770, ⓦ hotelvillarussell.com. This established, amiable spot, on Torla's main drag, offers basic (and rather dated) but well-cared-for rooms with an alpine feel, wooden furnishings and cosy blankets. Some rooms come with a small kitchenette, so you can self-cater. **€104**

Refugio Luicen Briet C/Francia ☎ 974 486 221, ⓦ refugiolucienbriet.com. Long-running, stone-walled refuge-style hostel with well-maintained dorm rooms and double en suites. They also run the nearby restaurant, *La Brecha*, with simple, local cuisine from Navarran trout to grilled rabbit. Breakfast is an extra €5 and there are half-and full-board packages available. Dorms **€10**, doubles **€40**

Villa de Torla Pza. Aragón 1 ☎ 974 486 156, ⓦ hotelvilladetorla.com. This handsome alpine hotel has fairly straightforward rooms with the occasional rustic touch (hardwood floors, old-fashioned furniture) but it's the surprising discovery that there's an outdoor pool – surrounded by mountain greenery – that makes it a notch above the others. **€69**

REFUGES IN THE PARQUE NACIONAL DE ORDESA

Refugio Góriz ☎ 974 341 201, ⓦ goriz.es. This refuge

has a well-maintained interior, comfortable mattresses and a restaurant. It's always a good idea to book ahead in summer, though even if the refuge is full and you have a tent, you can camp nearby and eat at the hut. Note that if you're making reservations more than two days in advance of your stay, you can only reserve online; otherwise, you can call to book a space. **€16.60**

Refuge des Sarradets ☎ +33 06 83 38 13 24, ⓦ ffcam.fr. Simply furnished, well-run refuge on the French side of the mountains with great views that gets busy in summer. Generally staffed Easter–Oct only. **€19.10**

Refugio Valle de Bujaruelo ☎ 974 486 412, ⓦ mesondebujaruelo.com. Comfortable refuge with meal service and camping. There are dorms and simple private doubles. They can also arrange guided treks with the well-run Grupo Explora Casteret (ⓦ casteret grupoexplora.com). Open weekends from mid-March to the end of summer; limited opening times rest of year. **€18**, dorms **€15**, doubles **€31**

AÍNSA AND AROUND

Albergue Mora de Nuei Portal de Abajo 2, Aínsa ☎ 974 510 614, ⓦ alberguemoradenuei.com. Top-notch hostel, featuring well-maintained dorms with sturdy wooden bunks, clean bathrooms and a snack bar. They also have comfortable doubles. Dorms **€17**, doubles **€120**

Bodegas de Sobrarbe C/Mayor, Aínsa 2 ☎ 974 500 237. The area around the Pza. Mayor is dotted with restaurants and cafés, including this *bodega*, set in an ancient building and exuding a medieval feel – stone arches, wooden tables and hearty Aragonese meats (from €15). Daily 12.30–3.30pm & 8.30–10.30pm.

Hostal Matazueras Pza. Mayor, Bielsa ☎ 974 501 006, ⓦ matazueras.com. Located on the main square in Bielsa, this restaurant and bar has a pleasant outdoor terrace. The menu of the day features numerous options including a delicious home-made paella (€12). Daily noon–11pm.

9

Parador de Bielsa Valle de Pineta, 14km northwest of Bielsa ☎ 974 501 011, ⓦ www.parador.es. This inviting, rustic parador has handsome, spacious rooms with lovely mountain views. It sits on the eastern slopes of the park and makes a comfortable base for exploring the area, with numerous hikes starting from its front door. The restaurant serves regional cuisine, including Aragón's version of *migas*, with sausage and grapes. Note that there is no public transport between the parador and Bielsa, but taxis are available between the two (around €20 one-way). **€117**

Los Siete Reyes Pza. Mayor 27, Aínsa ☎ 974 500 681, ⓦ lossietereyes.com. Wonderfully rustic hotel right on the Pza. Mayor, with inviting rooms that blend old and new – stone walls, colourful art, crisp linens. **€90**

Benasque and around

East of Bielsa lies the small town of **BENASQUE**, spectacularly set in the spacious green Ésera valley and ringed by rocky mountains. Much of the surrounding area is protected as the **Parque Natural Posets-Maladeta**, and numerous trails snake through the valleys and up the mountains. A lively crossroads, the town of Benasque itself is hardly untouched – it's often crammed with adventure-seeking tourists in high season – but this also means that it has plenty of outdoor sports services and tours, mountaineer-friendly accommodation and decently priced restaurants where you can refuel over robust meals.

Benasque is especially popular with avid climbers and trekkers who wish to ascend the Pyrenees' highest peaks, **Aneto** (3404m) and **Posets** (3371m). To do this you'll need all the proper equipment: crampons, ice axe, rope and a helmet to guard against falling rocks. If you're less experienced, your best bet is to go on a trek with one of the many operators in town (see box below). Either way, the tourist office has simple maps and can update you on weather and trail conditions. There's a popular ski hub at **Cerler** (see box, p.631).

ARRIVAL AND INFORMATION

By bus Regular buses run from Barbastro (2hr) and Huesca (2hr 45min). Buses from other towns in the region, including Aínsa, also run to Benasque but via connections in Barbastro.

BENASQUE AND AROUND

Turismo C/San Sebastián, on the southeast edge of town (daily in summer 9.30am–1pm & 4.30–8pm; may have limited hours in winter; ☎ 974 551 289, ⓦ turismobenasque.com).

ACCOMMODATION

Hotel Aneto Carretera de Francia 4 ☎ 974 551 061, ⓦ hotelesvalero.com. One of the first four-star hotels in the area, *Hotel Aneto* has spacious, well-appointed rooms and fetching mountain views, plus both indoor and outdoor swimming pools. They can also help arrange hiking and ski trips. **€145**

Hotel Aragüells Avda. Los Tilos ☎ 974 551 619, ⓦ hotelaraguells.com. Well-maintained though simple

---

ADVENTURE ACTIVITIES IN BENASQUE

Benasque is filled with a wide variety of adventure operators and gear shops; the *turismo* can direct you to recommended outfits. The prices for guided outdoor trips, from mountain treks to snowboarding courses, are similar to other Pyrenean destinations, ranging from around €50 per person per day, with prices varying depending on the level of difficulty and size of tour group.

OUTDOOR OPERATORS

All Radical Mountain Avda. Francia ☎ 974 551 425, ⓦ allradicalmountain.com. This well-run outfit specializes in snowboarding and other winter sports; they rent out skis and snowboards and other gear and equipment, and offer ski and snowboard classes.

Barrabés Avda. Francia ☎ 974 551 351, ⓦ barrabes .com. Large, well-regarded adventure retailer that

rents out gear, guidebooks, maps and more. Keep an eye out for their ongoing *rebajas* (sales).

Compañía de Guías Valle de Benasque Based in the All Radical Mountain shop, Avda. Francia ☎ 974 551 425, ⓦ guiasbenasque.com. This long-running operator offers all manner of guided climbs, treks and hikes through all the seasons – and for all levels.

HIKES AND REFUGES AROUND BENASQUE

Benasque falls more or less in the middle of the trans-Pyrenean GR11 trail, making the town a popular resting spot for hikers, whether for one or more nights. One of the best ways of exploring the surrounding wilderness is to use the many refuges dotted around Benasque as your base.

One of the more popular treks is northwest of Benasque, along the Estós valley to the **Refugio de Estós**, a three-hour trek. You can then continue over the Puerto de Gistaín to the **Refugio de Viadós**, which takes another 5 hours. Viadós is a base for treks up Posets, but again, this is a serious undertaking, and you'll need all the proper equipment to do this climb.

An alternative to this route (though best if you're in tip-top shape, because it can be challenging) is northwest up the Eriste valley, 4km southwest of Benasque, and then over the **Collado de Eriste** before descending to Viadós. Along this route, you can stop at the **Refugio Ángel Órus**.

North of Benasque lies the lush **Upper Esera valley** and massive **Maladeta massif**. A small hub is **La Besurta**, about 16km northeast of Benasque (and linked by buses in summer), which has parking and a small hut/bar with food and supplies (summer only) and is a gateway to hikes in the area. A good base is *Hotel-Spa Hospital de Benasque* (see below), about 3km before you reach La Besurta. In the summer, buses connect Benasque to La Besurta (€12 round-trip) and also to Valle de Vallibierna and the **Refugio Pescadores**, 11km northwest of Benasque.

REFUGES AROUND BENASQUE

Refugio Ángel Órus ☎ 974 344 044, ⓦ refugioangelorus.com. Located in the Valle del Forcau at a height of 2148m. Open year-round. Breakfast €5. Dorms €16.60

Refugio Estós ☎ 974 344 515, ⓦ refugiodeestos .com. Beautifully situated hostel with lake and mountain views. Open year-round. Breakfast €5. Half-board €37.60. Dorms €16.30

Refugio de Viadós ☎ 974 506 163 or ☎ 974 506 082, ⓦ alberguesyrefugiosdearagon.com. Located in Chistau valley, with wonderful mountain views. Open at Easter, weekends between Easter and the summer, and daily from July to September. Breakfast is €7 extra. Dorms €11.50

rooms with wooden floors as well as a restaurant serving regional cuisine; they also offer nearby apartments (call ahead for prices). €75

Hotel Ciria Avda. Los Tilos ☎ 974 551 612 or 974 551 080, ⓦ hotelciria.com. Long-time, family-run hotel in the middle of town that has cosy rooms with sturdy furnishings. They can also arrange for guided treks into the mountains. The popular restaurant *El Fogaril* serves hearty mountain cuisine. Hotel closed two weeks around Easter (when ski season ends) and in mid-October. €112

Hotel-Spa Hospital de Benasque Camino Real de Francia, Los Llanos del Hospital, about 3km from La Besurta ☎ 974 552 012, ⓦ llanosdelhospital.com. Los Llanos del Hospital is a mountain resort anchored by a large, handsome alpine lodge with a wide range of rooms and services, including an excellent spa. The resort is a great jumping-off point for exploring the Parque Natural Posets-Maladeta, with a range of activities throughout the year, from skiing in winter to hiking in summer. Regular buses run from La Besurta. €86

EATING AND DRINKING

El Fogaril Hotel Ciria ☎ 974 551 612 or 974 551 080, ⓦ hotelciria.com. The Ciria brothers, who are avid hunters and fishermen, bring back their prey and catch to this well-regarded restaurant, which is known for serving game and meat dishes that you often won't find elsewhere, from wild boar to partridge to *sarrio* (Pyrenean mountain goat), all of which are sometimes roasted in a wood oven. Expect to pay €18–25/person. Daily 1.30–3.30pm & 8.30–10.30pm.

La Llardana Camino de San Anton, at the entrance to Benasque ☎ 974 551 687, ⓦ lospirineos.info/lallardana.

This amiable *casa rural* has a top-notch restaurant, with beautiful views, which features local cuisine with a modern twist, and may include ravioli with pine nuts, roast lamb with wild mushrooms, and quail. The tasting menu is around €30–35. They also have comfortable en-suite rooms. Daily 1–3.30pm & 8–11pm; sometimes closed Mon or Wed in winter.

Restaurante La Parrilla Ctra. Francia ☎ 974 551 134. Enjoy traditional mountain cuisine, from wild rice to rich Magret duck to grilled meats (from €14.50), at this friendly restaurant. Daily 1–4pm & 9–11.30pm.

Barcelona

PARC GÜELL

Barcelona

10

Barcelona – Spain's second city, and the self-confident capital of Catalunya – vibrates with life, and there's certainly not another city in the country to touch it for sheer style, looks or energy. It's long had the reputation of being the avant-garde capital of Spain, its art museums are world-class, its football team sublime, while its designer restaurants, bars, galleries and shops lead from the front. And in Antoni Gaudí's extraordinary church of the Sagrada Família, the winding alleys and ageing mansions of the picture-postcard Gothic Quarter, and the world-famous boulevard that is the Ramblas, you have three sights that are high up any Spanish sightseeing list. As a thriving port, prosperous commercial centre and buzzing cultural capital of 1.6 million people (metropolitan population 5 million), the city is almost impossible to exhaust – even in a lengthy visit you will likely only scrape the surface.

Everyone starts with the **Ramblas**, and then dives straight into the medieval nucleus of the city, the **Barri Gòtic** (Gothic Quarter), but there are plenty of other central old-town neighbourhoods to explore, from **La Ribera** – home to the celebrated **Museu Picasso** – to funky **El Raval**, where cool bars, restaurants and boutiques have mushroomed in the wake of the striking contemporary art museum, **MACBA**. Even if you think you know these heavily touristed neighbourhoods well, there's always something else to discover – tapas bars hidden down alleys little changed for a century or two, designer boutiques in gentrified old-town quarters, bargain lunches in workers' taverns, unmarked gourmet restaurants, craft outlets and workshops, *fin-de-siècle* cafés, restored medieval palaces and neighbourhood markets.

But endlessly fascinating as these districts are, Barcelona is so much more than just its old-town areas. The fortress-topped hill of **Montjuïc**, for example, contains the Olympic stadium used for the 1992 Games as well as some of the city's best art museums, notably **MNAC**, the Museu Nacional d'Art de Catalunya – note the word "nacional", which tells you all you need to know about Catalunya's strong sense of identity. Other museums too explore the work of internationally famous Catalan artists, from Joan Miró to Antoni Tàpies. In the nineteenth-century, uptown extension of the city – the **Eixample** – are found most of Barcelona's celebrated *modernista* architectural wonders, from private houses to Gaudí's peerless church, as well as modern creations such as the colour-changing **Torre Agbar** and cantilevering **Disseny Hub**, the city's applied art collections' new home.

MNAC

Highlights

❶ La Boqueria If you're not hungry when you visit the city's – some say Spain's – greatest market, you soon will be. **See p.650**

❷ MNAC A thousand years of Catalan art is contained within the superb Museu Nacional d'Art de Catalunya, the flagship gallery on the slopes of Montjuïc. **See p.666**

❸ Fundació Joan Miró The life's work of the iconic Catalan artist is housed in the city's best-looking gallery. **See p.667**

❹ Sagrada Família The *modernista* works of Antoni Gaudí define the city – his famous church is a virtuoso masterpiece. **See p.673**

❺ Parc Güell If you visit only one city park, make it Gaudí's extraordinary flight of fancy. See p.678

❻ FC Barcelona at Camp Nou The world's greatest football team? Only *madrileños* will argue with you. **See p.678**

❼ Las Golondrinas Jump on a sightseeing boat around the harbour and local coast to see Barcelona at its best. **See p.685**

❽ Bar hopping, El Raval Barcelona's coolest neighbourhood is the best place for a night on the tiles. **See p.694**

HIGHLIGHTS ARE MARKED ON THE MAP ON PP.644–645

If Barcelona sounds a bit too much like hard cultural work, then simply look instead for entertainment to the city's harbour, parks, gardens and beaches. Indeed, it's remarkably easy to forget you're in a big city at all sometimes – just to take one example, walking from the **Port Vell** harbour takes you along the marina, through the old fishing and restaurant quarter of **Barceloneta**, past the leafy **Parc de la Ciutadella**, and out along the beachside promenade to the bar-and-restaurant zone that is the **Port Olímpic**. Other easy city jaunts include a trip out to the **Diagonal Mar** conference and

exhibition district, where the Museu Blau holds the revamped natural science museum, or up to the distinctive neighbourhood of **Gràcia**, with its small squares, lively bars and Gaudí's amazing **Parc Güell**. If you're saving yourself for just one aerial view of Barcelona, wait for a clear day and head for **Tibidabo**, a mountain-top amusement park backed by the Collserola hills, while beyond the city limits the one day-trip everyone should make is to the mountain-top monastery of **Montserrat**, 40km northwest.

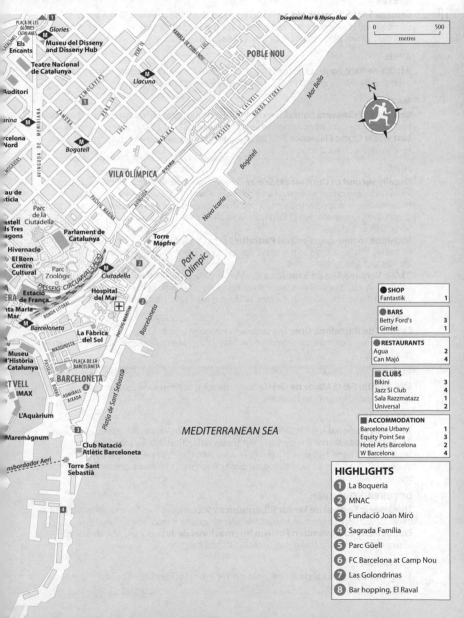

● SHOP	
Fantastik	1

● BARS	
Betty Ford's	3
Gimlet	1

● RESTAURANTS	
Agua	2
Can Majó	4

■ CLUBS	
Bikini	3
Jazz Sí Club	4
Sala Razzmatazz	1
Universal	2

■ ACCOMMODATION	
Barcelona Urbany	1
Equity Point Sea	3
Hotel Arts Barcelona	2
W Barcelona	4

HIGHLIGHTS

1. La Boqueria
2. MNAC
3. Fundació Joan Miró
4. Sagrada Família
5. Parc Güell
6. FC Barcelona at Camp Nou
7. Las Golondrinas
8. Bar hopping, El Raval

10

FIESTAS

FEBRUARY

Festes de Santa Eulàlia A week's worth of music, dances, parades of *gegants* (giants), *castellers* (human castle-builders) and fireworks in honour of one of Barcelona's patron saints – the saint's day falls on February 12.

EASTER

Semana Santa (Holy Week) There's a procession from the church of Sant Agustí on C/l'Hospital (El Raval) to La Seu and back, starting at 5pm on Good Friday, while Palm Sunday sees the blessing of the palms at La Seu and Sagrada Família.

APRIL

23: Día de Sant Jordi St George's Day, dedicated to Catalunya's dragon-slaying patron saint – the city fills with roses and books, exchanged by sweethearts as gifts.

MAY

Last week: Primavera Sound The city's hottest music festival heralds a massive three-day bash, attracting top names in rock, indie and electronica.

Last week: Ciutat Flamenco Four days of guitar recitals, singing and dancing, plus DJ sessions and a chill-out zone.

JUNE

Usually second or third week: Sónar Europe's most cutting-edge electronic music, multimedia and urban art festival attracts more than 120,000 visitors for three days of brilliant noise and spectacle. By day, the focus is on events at Fira Montjuïc; by night, the action shifts to out-of-town L'Hospitalet, with all-night buses running from the city to the Sónar bars and clubs.

Mid-June to mid-July: Festival Pedralbes Set in the lush Jardins del Palau Reial de Pedralbes, this newcomer to the music festival scene has drawn well-known acts such as Blondie and Julio Iglesias.

23/24: Verbena/Día de Sant Joan The "eve" and "day" of St John is the city's wildest annual celebration, with bonfires and fireworks (particularly on Montjuïc), drinking and dancing, and watching the sun come up on the beach. The day itself (24th) is a public holiday.

JULY

Festival de Barcelona Grec The summer's foremost arts and music festival spans the entire month, with main performances at Teatre Grec, Montjuïc's open-air Greek theatre (see p.667).

AUGUST

Mid-month: Festa Major de Gràcia Music, dancing, fireworks and *castellers* in the neighbourhood's streets and squares.

SEPTEMBER

11: Diada Nacional The Catalan national day is a public holiday in Barcelona.

24: Festes de la Mercè The city's biggest traditional festival lasts for a week around September 24 – the 24th itself is a public holiday (and there's free entry that day to city museums). Highlights include costumed giants, breathtaking firework displays and competing teams of *castellers*.

OCTOBER/NOVEMBER

Third week: Festival de Tardor Ribermúsica Wide-ranging five-day music festival held in the Born, with free concerts in historic and picturesque locations.

End October to November: Festival Internacional de Jazz The biggest annual jazz festival in town highlights big-name solo artists and bands.

DECEMBER

1–22: Fira de Santa Llúcia A Christmas market and crafts fair outside La Seu.

Along the Ramblas

It is a telling comment on Barcelona's character that one can recommend a single street – the **Ramblas** – as a highlight. No day in the city seems complete without a stroll down at least part of what, for Spanish poet Federico García Lorca, was "the only street in the world which I wish would never end". Lined with cafés, restaurants, souvenir shops, flower stalls and newspaper kiosks, it's at the heart of Barcelona's life and self-image.

The Ramblas splits the old-town areas of Barcelona in half, with the Barri Gòtic on the east flank of the avenue and El Raval on the west. It also actually comprises five separate sections strung head to tail – from north to south, Rambla Canaletes, Estudis, Sant Josep, Caputxins and Santa Mònica – though you'll rarely hear them referred to as such. Here, under the plane trees, you'll find flowers, plants, postcards, souvenirs, sweets and books. You can buy jewellery, have your portrait painted, play cards with a man on an upturned cardboard box (not a good idea), or while away time with the human statues.

10

Plaça de Catalunya

Ⓜ Catalunya

Plaça de Catalunya lies at the heart of the city, with the old town and port below it, and the planned Eixample district above and beyond. It was laid out in its present form in the 1920s, centred on a formal arrangement of statues, circular fountains and trees, and is the focal point for local events and demonstrations – notably the mass gathering here on New Year's Eve. It's the site of the main tourist office, while principal landmark is the massive **El Corte Inglés** department store, which has some stupendous views from its ninth-floor café. On the southwest side, over the road from the top of the Ramblas, is **El Triangle** shopping centre, whose ground-floor **Café Zurich** is a traditional Barcelona meeting place.

Església de Betlem and around

Ramblas 107 • Daily 8am–1.30pm & 6–9pm • Free • Ⓜ Liceu

The **Església de Betlem** was built in 1681 in Baroque style for the Jesuits, but was completely gutted in 1937 as anarchists sacked the city's churches at will. It seems hard to believe, but this part of the Ramblas was a war zone during the Spanish Civil War, when the city erupted into factionalism. As he recounted in *Homage to Catalonia*, **George Orwell** was caught in the crossfire between the nearby *Café Moka* (Ramblas 126) – the current café of the same name is a modern replacement – and the Poliorama cinema opposite, now the **Teatre Poliorama** (Ramblas 115).

Palau de la Virreina

Ramblas 99 • Tiquet Rambles office daily 10am–8.30pm; galleries Tues–Sun noon–8pm • Gallery admission usually free • ☎ 933 161 000, Ⓦ bcn.cat/virreinacentredelaimatge • Ⓜ Liceu

The graceful eighteenth-century **Palau de la Virreina** is used by the city council's culture

---

THE RAMBLAS STATUES

Time stands still for no man – not even for the human statues of the Ramblas, who make a living out of doing just that. A motley crew of figures once flanked the length of the street, but in 2012 – in an effort to keep pedestrian traffic moving and prevent pickpockets from preying on the gathering crowds – the city capped the number of human statues and relocated them to Rambla de Santa Mònica, the widest stretch of the Ramblas. Despite reductions in both territory and number, the remaining statues are still an attraction, and rightfully so. Day in and day out, these stalwarts of the Ramblas continue to climb upon their plinths and strike a pose. What else is a statue going to do?

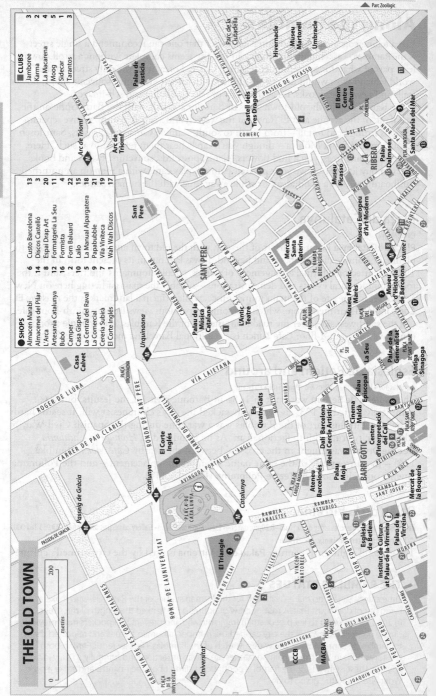

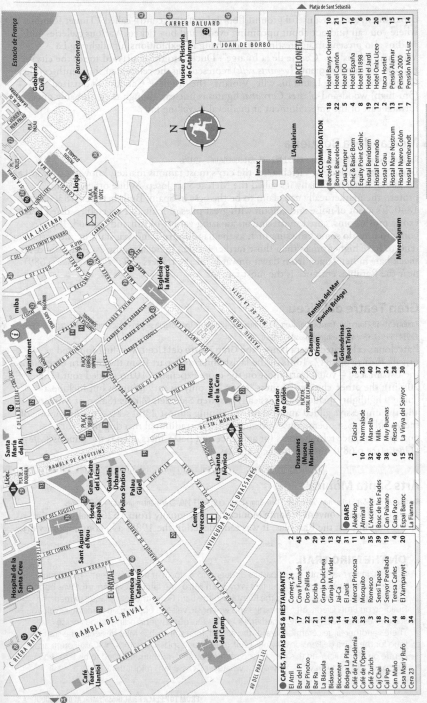

department, and has a useful ground-floor **information centre** called "Tiquet Rambles" where you can find out about upcoming events and buy tickets. Various galleries and studios also present an interesting mix of changing **exhibitions** highlighting La Virreina's role as the "Centre de la Imatge". Duck into the courtyard to see the city's two official **Carnival giants** (*gegants vells*) representing the celebrated thirteenth-century Catalan king, Jaume I, and his wife, Violant. The origin of Catalunya's outsized (5m-high) wood-and-plaster *Carnaval* figures is unclear, though they probably once formed part of the entertainment at medieval travelling fairs.

10

Mercat de la Boqueria

Ramblas 91 • Mon–Sat 8am–8.30pm • ☎ 933 182 584, ⓦ boqueria.info • Ⓜ Liceu

Beyond the Palau de la Virreina lies the city's most famous market, known locally as **La Boqueria**, though officially it's called the Mercat Sant Josep. While others might protest, the market really can claim to be the best in Spain. Built between 1836 and 1840, it's a riot of noise and colour, with great piles of fruit and vegetables, dried herbs, exotic mushrooms, cured meats and an amazing variety of fish and seafood. If you're going to buy, do some browsing first, as the flagship fruit and veg stalls by the entrance tend to have higher prices than those farther inside. There are some excellent stand-up snack bars in here, open from dawn onwards for the traders – *Bar Pinotxo* (see p.689) near the Ramblas entrance is the most famous.

Gran Teatre del Liceu

Ramblas 51–59 • Tours daily (except Aug) 10am, 11.30am, noon, 12.30pm & 1pm, English spoken • 10am tour €11.50, later tours €5.50 • ☎ 934 859 914, ⓦ www.liceubarcelona.cat • Ⓜ Liceu

Barcelona's celebrated opera house, the **Gran Teatre del Liceu**, was first founded as a private theatre in 1847. Tours of the lavish interior depart from the modern extension, the Espai Liceu – you'll learn most on the more expensive, 10am guided tour (1hr 20min); the other, cheaper "express" tours last only twenty minutes but include a guide. Highlights include the classically inspired **Saló dels Miralls** (Salon of Mirrors) and the impressive gilded auditorium containing almost 2300 seats – making it one of the world's largest opera houses. Meanwhile, the traditional meeting place for post-performance refreshments for audience and performers alike is the famous *Café de l'Òpera* (see p.689), just across the Ramblas.

Arts Santa Mònica

Ramblas 7 • Tues–Sat 11am–9pm, Sun & hols 11am–5pm • Free • ☎ 935 671 110, ⓦ artssantamonica.cat • Ⓜ Drassanes

The Augustinian **convent of Santa Mònica** dates originally from 1626, making it the oldest building on the Ramblas. It was remodelled in the 1980s as a contemporary **arts**

ON THE MIRÓ TRAIL

Halfway down the Ramblas, just past La Boqueria, look down at the pavement – that's right, the large circular mural under your feet is by **Joan Miró**. The famous Catalan artist was born just a couple of minutes' walk off the Ramblas in the Barri Gòtic (there's a plaque to mark the building on Ptge. Crèdit, off C/Ferran) – and when you've seen one Miró in Barcelona, well, you start to see them everywhere, whether it's T-shirts for tourists or branding for businesses. There's another large ceramic mural at the airport, for a start, while Miró designed the starfish logo for the Caixa de Pensions savings bank (there's one splashed across the CaixaForum arts centre on Montjuïc). And this is all on top of the Montjuïc museum devoted to his life's work (see p.667). In many ways, it's a Miró city, whatever Picasso fans might think.

centre, known as **Arts Santa Mònica**, and hosts regularly changing exhibitions in its grand, echoing galleries – it's an unusual space dedicated to "artistic creation, science, thought and communication" so there's usually something worth seeing.

Museu de la Cera

Ramblas 4–6, entrance on Ptge. de Banca 7 • July–Sept daily 10am–10pm; Oct–June Mon–Fri 10am–1.30pm & 4–7.30pm, Sat, Sun & hols 11am–2pm & 4.30–8.30pm • €15, under-11s €9 • ☎ 933 172 649, ⓦ museocerabcn.com • Ⓜ Drassanes

At the bottom of the Ramblas, housed in an impressive nineteenth-century bank building, is the city's wax museum, the **Museu de la Cera**. Needless to say, it's extremely ropey and enormously amusing, culminating in cheesy underwater and space capsules and an unpleasant "Terror" room. You also won't want to miss the museum's extraordinary grotto-bar, the *Bosc de les Fades* (see p.693).

Barri Gòtic

The **Barri Gòtic**, or Gothic Quarter, forms the very heart of the old town, spreading out from the east side of the Ramblas. It's a remarkable concentration of medieval buildings principally dating from the fourteenth and fifteenth centuries, when Barcelona reached the height of its commercial prosperity before being absorbed into the burgeoning kingdom of Castile. It takes the best part of a day to see everything here, with the Catedral – **La Seu** – a particular highlight, and you certainly won't want to miss the archeological remains at the **Museu d'Història de la Ciutat** or the eclectic collections of the **Museu Frederic Marès**. That said, sauntering through the atmospheric alleys or simply sitting at a café table in one of the lovely squares is just as much an attraction.

The picture-postcard images of the Barri Gòtic are largely based on the streets north of C/Ferran and C/Jaume I, where tourists throng the boutiques, bars, restaurants, museums and galleries. South of here – from Pza. Reial and C/d'Avinyó to the harbour – the Barri Gòtic is rather more traditional (or sometimes just plain run-down).

La Seu

Pza. de la Seu • Mon–Fri 8am–12.45pm & 5.15–7.30pm, Sat 8am–12.45pm & 5.15–7.30pm, Sun & hols 8am–1.45pm & 5.15–7.30pm (access to cloister until 12.30pm & 7pm) • Catedral and cloister free during general admission times, otherwise tourist admission charge obligatory 1–5pm, €6, but includes entrance to all sections • ☎ 933 428 262, ⓦ catedralbcn.org • Ⓜ Jaume I

Barcelona's Catedral, **La Seu**, is one of the great Gothic buildings of Spain. Located on a site previously occupied by a Roman temple and then an early Christian basilica, it was begun in 1298 and finished in 1448, save for the principal facade, which wasn't finally completed until the 1880s. The Catedral is dedicated to the city's co-patroness, **Santa Eulàlia**, martyred by the Romans for daring to prefer Christianity, and her tomb rests in a crypt beneath the high altar. The rest of the

---

BOHO BARCELONA AND THE FOUR CATS

There's not much to see in the shopping zone north of the Catedral, but a century or so ago a tavern called **Els Quatre Gats** (The Four Cats; C/Montsió 3, ⓦ 4gats.com) burned brightly as the heart of Barcelona's bohemian in-crowd. It was opened in 1897 as a gathering place for artists and literary types, with the building gloriously decorated in exuberant Catalan Art Nouveau style. *Els Quatre Gats* soon thrived as the scene of poetry readings and the venue for cultural debate, while a young Picasso designed the menu. Today, a modern restoration displays something of its former glory, with the – frankly overpriced – bar-restaurant overseen by a copy of Ramon Casas' famous wall painting of himself and café founder Pere Romeu on a tandem bicycle (the original is in MNAC).

interior is typically ornate, with no fewer than 29 side chapels, but the most magnificent part of the Catedral is its fourteenth-century **cloister**, which looks over a lush garden complete with soaring palm trees and – more unusually – a gaggle of honking geese. White geese have been kept here for over five hundred years, either (depending on which story you believe) to reflect the virginity of Santa Eulàlia or as a reminder of the erstwhile Roman splendour of Barcelona (geese having been kept on the Capitoline Hill in Rome).

Visit in the morning or late afternoon, and admission to the church interior and cloister is free. However, to see everything, it's better to visit between 1pm and 5pm when the obligatory admission charge includes entry to all sections of the Catedral, including the treasury and rooftop, as well as areas like the choir and various side chapels that are not open to the public during the general admission times.

Reial Cercle Artístic and Dalí Barcelona

C/Arcs 5 • Daily 10am–10pm • €10 • ☎ 933 181 774, ⓦ reialcercleartistic.cat • Ⓜ Jaume I

The handsome Gothic palace housing the **Reial Cercle Artístic** (Royal Artistic Circle) hosts various exhibitions and concerts, though the big draw is **Dalí Barcelona**, a collection of 44 wildly original bronze sculptures by Salvador Dalí, completed in the 1970s as a private commission for a wealthy Catalan businessman. The sculptures, large and small, are theatrically displayed under Gothic arches, behind swags of red velvet curtain, and depict various themes that fascinated Dalí throughout his life such as the sea, women, horses, mythology and religion.

Plaça del Rei

Ⓜ Jaume I

The harmonious enclosed square of **Plaça del Rei**, behind the Catedral apse, was once the courtyard of the palace of the counts of Barcelona, later the residence of the count-kings of Aragón. The palace buildings themselves are steeped in history, and include the romantic Renaissance **Torre del Rei Martí**, the main hall known as the **Saló del Tinell**, and the fourteenth-century **Santa Agata chapel** – there's no public access to the tower, though the interiors of both hall and chapel can usually be seen during a visit to the Museu d'Història de Barcelona (see below). The square itself, meanwhile, was the scene of one of Barcelona's greatest historic set pieces, since it was from the steps of the exterior stone staircase that Ferdinand and Isabella received Christopher Columbus on his triumphant return from his famous voyage of 1492.

Museu d'Història de Barcelona (MUHBA)

Pza. del Rei, entrance on C/Veguer • Tues–Sun 10am–8pm; Oct–March Tues–Sat 10am–2pm & 4–7pm, Sun 10am–8pm • €7, includes entry to other MUHBA sites, free Sun after 3pm • ☎ 932 562 100, ⓦ museuhistoria.bcn.cat • Ⓜ Jaume I

The **Museu d'Història de Barcelona** (Barcelona History Museum) comprises half a dozen sites across the city, though its crucial draw is its underground archeological section – nothing less than the extensive remains of the Roman city of Barcino, stretching under the surrounding streets as far as the Catedral. The remains date from the first to the sixth centuries AD and reflect the transition from Roman to Visigothic rule. Not much survives above chest height, but explanatory diagrams show the extent of the streets, walls and buildings, while models, mosaics, murals and displays of excavated goods help flesh out the reality of daily life in Barcino. Pza. del Rei's **Saló del Tinell** and the beautiful **Capella de Santa Agata** are also part of the history museum, and are usually open for visits with your museum ticket, though there's sometimes an extra charge for special exhibitions held in the Saló del Tinell.

Museu Frederic Marès

Pza. Sant Lu 5–6, off C/Comtes • Tues–Sat 10am–7pm, Sun & hols 11am–8pm • €4.20, free Sun after 3pm & first Sun of the month • ☎ 932 563 500, ⓦ www.museumares.bcn.cat • ⓂJaume I

One of the old town's most fascinating museums, the **Museu Frederic Marès** occupies a wing of the old royal palace, behind Pza. del Rei. It celebrates the diverse passions of sculptor, painter and restorer Frederic Marès (1893–1991), whose beautifully presented collection of ancient and medieval sculpture does little to prepare visitors for Marès' true obsession, namely a kaleidoscopic array of curios and collectibles. These present an incredible retrospective jumble gathered during fifty years of travel, with entire rooms devoted to keys and locks, cigarette cards and snuff boxes, fans, gloves and brooches, playing cards, walking sticks, dolls' houses, toy theatres and archaic bicycles, to name just a sample of what's on show. The museum's summer café (April–Sept; closed Mon) occupies the romantic courtyard, with seats under the orange trees.

Església de Santa María del Pi and around

Pza. Pi 7 • April–Oct Mon–Sat 10am–7pm, Sun & hols 4–8pm; Nov–March Mon–Sat 10am–6pm, Sun & hols 4–7pm • €4 • ☎ 933 184 743, ⓦ basilicadelpi.com • ⓂLiceu

The fourteenth-century **Església de Santa María del Pi** stands at the centre of three delightful little squares, five minutes' walk from the Catedral or just two minutes from the Ramblas. The church stands on the middle square, **Pza. Sant Josep Oriol**, the prettiest of the three, overhung with balconies and scattered with seats from the *Bar del Pi* (see p.689). This whole area becomes an **artists' market** at the weekend (Sat 11am–8pm, Sun 11am–2pm), while buskers and street performers often appear here, too. A **farmers' market** spills across Pza. del Pi on the first and third Friday, Saturday and Sunday of the month, selling honey, cheese, cakes and other produce, while the cafés of **Carrer de Petritxol** (off Pza. del Pi) are the place to come for a cup of hot chocolate – *Granja Dulcinea* (see p.689) at no. 2 is the traditional choice.

Palau de la Generalitat

Pza. Sant Jaume, entrance on C/Sant Honorat • 1hr tours on second & fourth weekend of the month (except Aug), hourly, 10am–12pm; advance bookings essential, by phone or through the website; public admitted April 23, and Sept 11 & 24 10am–6pm • Free, ID required • ☎ 934 024 600, ⓦ gencat.cat • ⓂJaume I

On the north side of **Pza. de Sant Jaume** – the square that marks the very centre of the Barri Gòtic – rises the **Palau de la Generalitat**, traditional home of the Catalan government, from where the short-lived Catalan Republic was proclaimed in April

---

A TOUR OF JEWISH BARCELONA

Barcelona's medieval Jewish quarter lay nestled in the shadow of the Catedral – under the Church's careful scrutiny. It was centred on C/Sant Domènec del Call, where you'll find the most notable surviving landmark, the **Antiga Sinagoga** (C/Marlet 5, corner with C/Sant Domènec del Call; June–Aug Mon–Fri 10.30am–6.30pm, Sat & Sun 10.30am–2.30pm, Sept–May Mon–Fri 11am–5.30pm, Sat & Sun 11am–3pm, sometimes closed Sat for ceremonies; €2.50; ☎933 170 790, ⓦcalldebarcelona.org; ⓂLiceu) – not many people stop by, and if you do, you'll get a personalized tour of the small room by a member of the local Jewish community. The prosperous settlement persisted until the pogrom and forced conversion of 1391, after which most of the buildings used by the Jews were torn down. However, a plaque further down C/Marlet (junction with C/Arc Sant Ramon del Call) marks the site of the former rabbi's house, while in nearby Plaçeta Manuel Ribé another house – originally belonging to a veil-maker – now serves as a small museum, the **Centre d'Interpretació del Call** (Pza. Manuel Ribé; Tues–Fri 11am–2pm, Sat & Sun 11am–7pm, Sun & hols 11am–2pm; free; ☎932 562 122, ⓦwww.museuhistoria.bcn.cat; ⓂLiceu).

10

1931. There's a beautiful cloister on the first floor, while opening off this is the chapel of Sant Jordi (St George, patron saint of Catalunya as well as England), and an upper courtyard planted with orange trees, overhung by gargoyles and peppered with presidential busts. Aside from the guided tours on alternate Sundays, the Generalitat is also traditionally open to the public on **Dia de Sant Jordi**, or Saint George's Day (April 23; expect a 2hr wait) – when the whole square is festooned with bookstalls and rose sellers – as well as **Diada Nacional de Catalunya** (National Day, September 11) and **La Mercè** (September 24).

10

Ajuntament de Barcelona

Pza. de Sant Jaume, entrance on C/Font de Sant Miquel • Public admitted Sun 10am–1.30pm • Free, English-language leaflet provided • 📞 934 027 000, 🌐 bcn.cat • Ⓜ Jaume I

On the south side of Pza. de Sant Jaume stands Barcelona's City Hall, the **Ajuntament**, parts of which date from as early as 1373, though the Neoclassical facade was added in the nineteenth century when the square was laid out. On Sundays you're allowed into the building for a self-guided tour around the rather splendid marble halls, galleries and staircases. The highlights are the magnificent restored fourteenth-century council chamber, known as the **Saló de Cent**, and the dramatic historical murals by Josep María Sert in the **Saló de les Cròniques** (Hall of Chronicles), while the ground-floor courtyard features sculptural works by some of the most famous Catalan artists.

Museu d'Idees i Invents de Barcelona (miba)

C/Ciutat 7 • Tues–Fri 10am–2pm & 4–7pm, Sat 10am–8pm, Sun & hols 10am–2pm • €8 • 📞 933 327 930, 🌐 mibamuseum.com • Ⓜ Jaume I

The impressive buildings of the Barri Gòtic have many grand entrances, from exterior stone staircases to courtyards into which you can drive a coach-and-four – but there's only one where you get to slide down an enclosed steel chute, water-park style, into the vaulted bowels of the building. That would be Catalan inventor Pep Torres' brain-boggling Barcelona Museum of Ideas and Inventions, known as **miba**, which presents a mixture of his own inventions and those of budding and established creative inventors worldwide.

Plaça Relal and around

Ⓜ Liceu

Of all the old-town squares, the most popular with visitors is the elegant nineteenth-century **Plaça Reial**, just off the Ramblas. It's studded with tall palm trees and decorated iron lamps (made by the young Antoni Gaudí), bordered by high, pastel-coloured arcaded buildings, and centred on a fountain depicting the Three Graces. It used to be a bit dodgy here, but most of the really unsavoury characters have been driven off over the years and predatory, menu-toting waiters are usually the biggest nuisance these days.

The alleys on the south side of Plaça Reial emerge on C/Escudellers – still with a late-night seediness about it, but teetering on the edge of respectability. Bars and restaurants around here attract a youthful crowd, nowhere more so than those flanking funky **Pza. de George Orwell**, at the eastern end of C/Escudellers. To the south, down **Carrer d'Avinyó**, is the harbourside neighbourhood known as **La Mercè**, formerly the home of merchants enriched by Barcelona's maritime trade. Carrer de la Mercè and the surrounding streets (particularly Ample, d'en Gignas and Regomir) are home to a series of old-style **taverns** that provide one of the old town's more authentic experiences.

Port Vell

Perhaps the greatest recent transformation in the city has been along the waterfront, where harbour and Mediterranean have once again been placed at the heart of Barcelona. The glistening harbourside merges seamlessly with the old town, with the tourist attractions of **Port Vell** (Old Port) just steps from the bottom of the Ramblas. Meanwhile, the pleasant walk around the harbour along the waterfront to Barceloneta takes you past the picturesque **marina**.

10

Mirador de Colón

Pza. del Portal de la Pau • Daily: March–Sept 8.30am–8.30pm; Oct–Feb 8.30am–7.30pm (last lift ride 30min prior to closing) • €4.50 • Ⓜ Drassanes

At the foot of the Ramblas, in the middle of swirling traffic, stands the striking **Mirador de Colón**, which commemorates the visit made by Christopher Columbus (known locally as Cristóbal Colón) to Barcelona in June 1493. A lift whisks you up to the enclosed *mirador* at Columbus' feet for terrific 360-degree city views.

Museu Marítim

Avgda. de les Drassanes • **Museum** daily 10am–8pm • Reduced museum admission during renovation works €2.50, free on Sun after 3pm • **Santa Eulàlia** Tues–Fri & Sun 10am–8.30pm, Sat 2–8.30pm (Nov–Match until 5.30pm) • €5, includes entry to temporary exhibits at the museum • ☎ 933 429 920, Ⓦ mmb.cat • Ⓜ Drassanes

Barcelona's medieval shipyards, or **Drassanes**, date from the thirteenth century, and were originally used as a dry dock to fit and arm Catalunya's war fleet in the days when the Catalan-Aragonese crown was vying with Venice and Genoa for control of the Mediterranean. The unique stone-vaulted buildings make a fitting home for the city's **Museu Marítim** (Maritime Museum), though a large-scale renovation project means access is restricted, probably until sometime in 2015. In the meantime, there's cut-price admission to one or two changing exhibitions that draw on the museum collections, and continued access to the shop and café. Your ticket also allows a quick tour of the **Santa Eulàlia**, moored over on the Moll de la Fusta, a three-masted ocean schooner that once made the run between Barcelona and Cuba.

Rambla del Mar and Maremàgnum

Moll d'Espanya 5 • Daily 10am–10pm • Free • ☎ 932 258 100, Ⓦ maremagnum.es • Ⓜ Drassanes

The old wharves and warehouses of the inner harbour have been replaced by an entertainment zone that is reached by the wooden **Rambla del Mar** swing bridge. This stretches across the harbour to **Maremàgnum**, two floors of restaurants, gift shops and boutiques plus outdoor seating and park areas that provide fantastic views back across the harbour to the city.

L'Aquàrium

Moll d'Espanya • July & Aug daily 9.30am–11pm; June & Sept daily 9.30am–9.30pm; Oct–May daily 9.30am–9pm • €20, under 1.4m €15, under 1.1m €5, under 90cm free, online discounts available • ☎ 932 217 474, Ⓦ aquariumbcn.com • Ⓜ Drassanes/Barceloneta

L'Aquàrium drags in families and school parties to see 11,000 fish and sea creatures in 35 themed tanks representing underwater caves, tidal areas, tropical reefs, the planet's oceans and other maritime habitats. It's vastly overpriced, and despite the claims of excellence it offers few new experiences, save perhaps the 80m-long walk-through underwater tunnel, which brings you face to face with rays and sharks.

Museu d'Història de Catalunya

Pza. de Pau Vila 3 • Tues, Thurs–Sat 10am–7pm, Wed 10am–8pm, Sun & hols 10am–2.30pm • €4.50, last Tues of the month free •
☎ 932 254 700, ⓦ mhcat.cat • Ⓜ Barceloneta

The only surviving warehouse on the Port Vell harbourside is known as the Palau de Mar, home to the **Museu d'Història de Catalunya**, which entertainingly traces the history of Catalunya from the Stone Age to the present day. On the fourth floor, the café-bar boasts a glorious view from its huge terrace.

El Raval

The old-town area west of the Ramblas is known as **El Raval** (from the Arabic word for "suburb"). In medieval times, it was the site of hospitals, churches and monasteries, but by the twentieth century it had acquired a reputation as the city's main red-light district, known to all as the Barri Xinès – China Town. Even today in the backstreets around C/Sant Pau and C/Nou de la Rambla are found pockets of sleaze, while a handful of old bars trade on their former reputations as bohemian hangouts. Over the last two decades, however, El Raval has changed markedly, particularly in the "upper Raval" around Barcelona's contemporary art museum, MACBA. Cutting-edge galleries, designer restaurants and fashionable bars are all part of the scene these days, although you'd hesitate to call El Raval gentrified, as it clearly still has its rough edges.

Museu d'Art Contemporani de Barcelona (MACBA)

Pza. dels Àngels 1 • Mon & Wed–Fri 11am–7.30pm, Sat 10am–9pm, Sun & hols 10am–3pm; tours in English vary, check website for schedule • €10; tour included in admission fee • ☎ 934 120 810, ⓦ macba.cat • Ⓜ Catalunya

Anchoring the upper Raval is the huge, luminous **Museu d'Art Contemporani de Barcelona**, known as **MACBA**. Once inside, a series of swooping ramps from the ground floor to the fourth floor afford continuous views of the square below – usually full of careering skateboarders. The collection represents the main movements in contemporary art since 1945, mainly in Catalunya and Spain but with a good smattering of foreign artists as well. The pieces are shown in rotating exhibitions, so you may catch works by Joan Miró, Antoni Tàpies, Eduardo Chillida, Alexander Calder, Robert Rauschenberg or Paul Klee. Joan Brossa, leading light of the Catalan avant-garde "Dau al Set" group, has work here, too, as do contemporary Catalan conceptual and abstract artists.

Centre de Cultura Contemporània de Barcelona (CCCB)

C/Montalegre 5 • CCCB Tues–Sun 11am–8pm; *C3* bar Mon–Fri 9am–9pm, Sat & Sun 11am–9pm • €6 • ☎ 933 064 100,
ⓦ cccb.org • Ⓜ Catalunya

Adjoining MACBA is the **Centre de Cultura Contemporània de Barcelona**, or **CCCB**, which hosts temporary art and city-related exhibitions as well as supporting a cinema and a varied concert and festival programme. At the back of the building, the *C3* café-bar has a sunny terraza on the modern square joining the CCCB to MACBA.

Filmoteca de Catalunya

Pza. Salvador Seguí 1–9 • Cinema Tues–Fri 5–10pm, Sat & Sun 4.30–10pm; Exhibition Hall Tues–Sun 4–9pm • €4 cinema or exhibition (exhibition entry includes a screening) • ☎ 935 671 070, ⓦ filmoteca.cat • Ⓜ Liceu

The Josep Lluís Mateo-designed **Filmoteca de Catalunya** marks yet another step in the revitalization of the Raval. Opened in early 2012, the building has two below-ground cinemas, as well as a film library, a bookshop and spaces for permanent and temporary cinema-related exhibitions. All the films are shown in their original language with Spanish or Catalan subtitles.

Hospital de la Santa Creu

Entrances on C/Carme and C/l'Hospital • Garden daily 10am–dusk • Free • La Capella, C/l'Hospital 56, exhibition information on
ⓦ lacapella.bcn.cat • Ⓜ Liceu

The **Hospital de la Santa Creu** occupies a large site between C/Carme and C/l'Hospital.
The attractive complex of Gothic buildings was founded as the city's main hospital in
1402, a role that it retained until 1930. The fifteenth-century hospital wards were
subsequently converted for cultural and educational use, and now hold the Royal
Academy of Medicine, an art and design school, and two libraries, including the
Catalan national library, the Biblioteca de Catalunya. Visitors can wander freely
through the charming medieval cloistered **garden** (access from either street), while the
hospital's former chapel, **La Capella** (entered separately from C/l'Hospital) is an
exhibition space for new contemporary artists. There's also the rather nice *El Jardí* **café**
in the garden at the C/l'Hospital side.

Rambla del Raval and around

Ⓜ Liceu

The most obvious manifestation of the changing character of El Raval is the **Rambla del
Raval**, a palm-lined boulevard that strikes through the centre of the district between
C/l'Hospital and C/Sant Pau. The *rambla* has a distinct character that's all its own – its
signature building, halfway down, is the glow-in-the-dark designer hotel *Barceló Raval*,
while on either side are kebab joints and grocery stores, and an increasing number of
fashionable cafés and bars. A weekend **street market** (selling anything from samosas to
hammocks) adds a bit more character, while the two extremes of the *rambla* offer a
snapshot of the changing neighbourhood. At the bottom end, off **C/Sant Pau**, the
barri's remaining prostitutes accost passers-by as they head back towards the Liceu and
the Ramblas. The top end, meanwhile, leads you straight into **C/Riera Baixa**, a narrow
street that's at the centre of the city's secondhand and vintage clothing scene.

Palau Güell

C/Nou de la Rambla 3–5 • April–Oct Tues–Sun & hols 10am–8pm; Nov–March Tues–Sun & hols 10am–5.30pm; last admission 1hr before
closing • €12 • ☎ 934 725 775, ⓦ palauguell.cat • Ⓜ Liceu

El Raval's outstanding building is the **Palau Güell**, an extraordinary townhouse designed
(1886–90) by the young Antoni Gaudí for wealthy ship-owner and industrialist Eusebi
Güell i Bacigalupi. At a time when architects sought to conceal the iron supports
within buildings, Gaudí turned them to his advantage, displaying them as decorative
features in the grand rooms on the **main floor**, which are lined with dark marble hewn
from the Güell family quarries. Meanwhile the famous **roof terrace** culminates in a
fantastical series of chimneys decorated with swirling patterns made from fragments of
glazed tile, glass and earthenware.

HIGH SOCIETY AT THE HOTEL ESPAÑA

There's a hidden gem tucked around the back of the Liceu opera house, on the otherwise fairly
shabby C/Sant Pau, where some of the most influential names in Catalan architecture and
design came together at the beginning of the twentieth century to transform the **Hotel
España** (see p.687) into one of the city's most lavish addresses. With a wonderfully tiled dining
room designed by Lluís Domènech i Montaner, a bar with an amazing marble fireplace by
Eusebi Arnau, and a bathing area with glass roof (now the breakfast room) whose marine
murals were executed by Ramon Casas, the hotel was the fashionable sensation of its day. A
century later it's back in vogue, following a remarkable contemporary restoration, and lunch or
dinner in the original *modernista* dining room (known as the *Fonda España*) is a real
in-the-know treat.

A painstaking restoration has returned the building to its original state and it's one of Barcelona's most popular attractions – numbers are limited and your ticket will be for a specific time-slot for a one-hour visit.

Sant Pere

The Barri Gòtic is bordered on its eastern side by Via Laietana, which was cut through the old town at the beginning of the twentieth century. Across it to the east stretches the quiet neighbourhood of **Sant Pere**, home to two remarkable buildings, the Palau de la Música Catalana concert hall and the restored neighbourhood market, Mercat Santa Caterina.

Palau de la Música Catalana

C/Sant Pere Més Alt • Guided tours (55min, every 30min) daily 10am–3.30pm, plus Easter week & July 10am–6pm; Aug 10am–8pm • €18; tour tickets available by phone, online, or at the box office, up to a week in advance • ☎ 902 442 882 or ☎ 932 957 200, Ⓦ palaumusica.org • Ⓜ Urquinaona

Lluís Domènech i Montaner's stupendous **Palau de la Música Catalana** barely seems to have enough space to breathe in the narrow C/Sant Pere Més Alt. Built in 1908, its bare brick structure is lined with tiles and mosaics, the highly elaborate facade resting on three great columns, like an elephant's legs. The stunning interior, meanwhile, incorporates a bulbous stained-glass skylight capping the second-storey auditorium – which contemporary critics claimed to be an engineering impossibility. Successive extensions and interior remodelling have opened up the original site – to the side, an enveloping glass facade provides the main public access to the box office, terrace restaurant and foyer bar. This is where you come to buy tickets for the **guided tours** of the original interior – as visitor numbers are limited you'll almost certainly have to book a day or two in advance.

Mercat Santa Caterina

Avgda. Francesc Cambó 16 • Mon 7.30am–2pm, Tues, Wed & Sat 7.30am–3.30pm, Thurs & Fri 7.30am–8.30pm, July & Aug open mornings only • ☎ 933 195 740, Ⓦ mercatsantacaterina.com • Ⓜ Jaume I

At the very heart of Sant Pere is the **Mercat Santa Caterina** whose splendid restoration has retained its nineteenth-century balustraded walls and added a dramatic multicoloured wave roof. During the renovation work, the foundations of a major medieval convent were discovered on the site – parts of the walls are visible behind glass at the rear of the market. Santa Caterina is one of the best places in the city to come and shop for food, and its market restaurant and bar is definitely worth a visit in any case.

La Ribera

South of Sant Pere, across C/Princesa, **La Ribera** sports Barcelona's biggest single tourist attraction, the **Museu Picasso**. The sheer number of visitors in this neighbourhood rivals the busiest streets of the Barri Gòtic, and this has had a knock-on effect in terms of the bars, shops and restaurants found here. La Ribera is at its most hip, and most enjoyable, in the area around the Passeig del Born, the elongated square leading from Santa María church to the **Borne Centre Cultural**, housed inside the stunningly restored iron-and-glass Antic Mercat del Born. This area – widely known as the Born – is one of the city's premier nightlife centres.

Museu Picasso

C/Montcada 15–23 • Tues, Wed, Fri–Sun & hols 9am–7pm; Thurs 9am–9.30pm; guided tours in English (Sun at 11am except Aug), advance bookings essential, by phone or by email through the website • €11, exhibitions €6.50, under-18s free, plus free Sun after 3pm & first Sun of month • ☎ 932 563 000, ⓦ www.museupicasso.bcn.cat • ⓜ Jaume I

The celebrated **Museu Picasso** is housed in a series of medieval palaces converted specifically for the museum. It's one of the most important collections of Picasso's work in the world, but even so, some visitors are disappointed: the museum contains none of his best-known works, and few in the Cubist style. But what is here provides a unique opportunity to trace Picasso's development from his early paintings as a young boy to the major works of later years.

The highlights

Particularly fascinating are the **early drawings**, in which Picasso – still signing with his full name, Pablo Ruíz Picasso – attempted to copy the nature paintings in which his father specialized. Paintings from his art-school days in Barcelona (1895–97) show tantalizing glimpses of the city that the young Picasso was beginning to know well – the Gothic old town, the cloisters of Sant Pau del Camp, Barceloneta beach – and even at the ages of 15 and 16 he was producing serious work. Later, there are paintings from the famous **Blue Period** (1901–04), the Pink Period (1904–06) and from his Cubist (1907–20) and Neoclassical (1920–25) stages. The large gaps in the main collection (for example, nothing from 1905 until the celebrated *Harlequin* of 1917) only underline Picasso's extraordinary changes of style and mood. This is best illustrated by the large jump to 1957, a year represented by his 44 interpretations of Velázquez's masterpiece **Las Meninas**, in which Picasso brilliantly deconstructed the individual portraits and compositions that make up Velázquez's work.

Museu Europeu d'Art Modern

C/Barra de Ferro 5 • Tues–Sun 10am–8pm • €7, €2 guided tour (Sat & Sun noon), under-12s free • ☎ 933 195 693, ⓦ meam.es • ⓜ Jaume I

Located in a renovated eighteenth-century palace – and just metres from the Museu Picasso – the **Museu Europeu d'Art Modern** focuses on modern and contemporary figurative art. It brims with haunting, humorous and sometimes disturbing works by the likes of Eduardo Naranjo, Paul Beel and Carlos Saura Riaza. It's also home to modern, Art Deco and Catalan sculptures.

Església de Santa María del Mar

Pza. de Santa María • Daily 9am–1pm & 5–8pm; tour 1–5pm • Free during general admission times, otherwise €5 (1–5pm); €10 guided tour • ☎ 933 102 390 • ⓜ Jaume I

La Ribera's flagship church of **Santa María del Mar** is the city's most exquisite example of pure Catalan-Gothic architecture. Conceived as thanks for the Catalan conquest of Sardinia in 1324, work on the church began in 1329 and was finished in just over half a century, which is pretty rapid for medieval church construction (and also explains its consistency of style). Its wide nave, narrow aisles, massive buttresses and octagonal, flat-topped towers are all typically Catalan-Gothic features, while its later Baroque trappings were destroyed during the Civil War, which is probably all to the good. Subsequent restoration work has concentrated on showing off the simple bare spaces of the interior and the stained glass, especially, is beautiful.

Passeig del Born

ⓜ Jaume I/Barceloneta

Fronting Santa María church is the fashionable **Passeig del Born**, an avenue lined with a parade of plane trees shading a host of classy bars, shops and delis. Shoppers scour the

PICASSO IN BARCELONA

Although born in Málaga, **Pablo Picasso** (1881–1973) spent much of his youth – from the age of 14 to 23 – in Barcelona, and there are echoes of the great artist at various sites throughout the old town. Not too far from the museum, you can still see many of the buildings in which Picasso lived and worked, notably the Escola de Belles Arts de Llotja (C/ Consolat del Mar, near Estació de França), where his father taught drawing and where Picasso himself absorbed an academic training. The apartments where the family lived when they first arrived in Barcelona – Ptge. d'Isabel II 4 and C/Reina Cristina 3, both opposite the Escola – can also be seen, though only from the outside. Less tangible is to take a walk down C/d'Avinyó, which cuts south from C/Ferran to C/Ample. Large houses along here were converted into brothels at the turn of the twentieth century, and Picasso used to haunt the street, sketching what he saw – women at one of the brothels inspired his seminal Cubist work, *Les Demoiselles d'Avignon*.

narrow, vaulted medieval alleys on either side for boutiques and craft workshops, while at night the Born becomes one of Barcelona's biggest bar scenes.

El Born Centre Cultural

Pza. Comercial 12, at Pg. del Born • Tues–Sun 10am–8pm • Free access to the centre, €6 exhibitions (includes audio-guide) • ☎ 932 564 190, ⓦ elborncentrecultural.cat • ⓜ Jaume I/Barceloneta

The handsome **Antic Mercat del Born** (1873–76) was the biggest of Barcelona's nineteenth-century market halls. It was the city's main wholesale fruit and veg market until 1971, and was then due to be demolished but was saved by local protest. It remained empty for decades, before finally reopening in 2013 as **El Born Centre Cultural**, where extensive archeological remains of eighteenth-century shops, factories, houses and taverns – all discovered underneath the market – are showcased inside the building's restored glass-and-cast iron frame.

Parc de la Ciutadella

Park entrances on Pg. de Picasso (ⓜ Barceloneta, or a short walk from La Ribera) and Pg. de Pujades (ⓜ Arc de Triomf); use ⓜ Ciutadella-Vila Olímpica for direct access to the zoo • Daily 10am–dusk • Park entrance free

East of La Ribera, across Passeig de Picasso, is the **Parc de la Ciutadella**, the largest green space in the city centre. It's also the meeting place of the Catalan parliament (no public access), occupying part of a fortress-like structure right at the centre of the park, the surviving portion of the star-shaped Bourbon citadel from which the park takes its name. In 1888, the park was chosen as the site of the Universal Exhibition, and the city's *modernista* architects left their mark here in a series of eye-catching buildings and monuments, not least the giant brick Arc de Triomf that dominates the avenue at the top of the park.

Cascada

Parc de la Ciutadella • ⓜ Arc de Triomf

The first of the major projects undertaken inside the park was the **Cascada**, the monumental fountain in the northeast corner. Assistant to the principal park architect was the young Antoni Gaudí, then a student, and the Baroque extravagance of the fountain is suggestive of the flamboyant decoration that was later to become Gaudí's trademark. Incidentally, Gaudí is also thought to have had a hand in the design of the Ciutadella's iron park gates.

Museu de Ciències Naturals

Pg. de Picasso • Under renovation at time of writing • ⓦ www.museuciencies.bcn.cat • ⓜ Arc de Triomf

The **Museu de Ciències Naturals**, the city's Natural Science Museum, has its public showcase, the Museu Blau, over at the Diagonal Mar Fòrum site (see p.664), but its genesis lies in two buildings in Parc de la Ciutadella that are currently undergoing major renovation (and will be for some time). The Neoclassical **Museu Martorell** formerly housed the city's geological collections, though the new permanent exhibition here will concentrate on the development of the natural sciences in Barcelona. The other building, a whimsical red-brick confection that was long the zoology museum, is universally known as the **Castell dels Tres Dragons** (Three Dragons Castle). It's going to become the research, study and conservation centre for the Natural Science Museum's geology and zoology collections. Meanwhile, the two real unsung glories of Ciutadella are its plant houses, the **Umbracle** (Palm House) and **Hivernacle** (Conservatory), which are arranged either side of the Museu Martorell, and are also closed for renovation.

10

Parc Zoològic

Main entrance on C/Wellington • Daily: Jan–March, Nov & Dec 10am–5pm; April to mid-May & mid-Sept to Oct 10am–6pm; mid-May to mid-Sept 10am–7pm • €17.90, under-12s €10.75, under-3s free • ☎ 902 457 545, ⓦ zoobarcelona.cat • Signposted from ⓜ Ciutadella-Vila Olímpica, or tram #T4 stops outside

The city zoo, the **Parc Zoològic**, takes up most of the southeastern part of Ciutadella park. It boasts over two thousand animals from over three hundred different species – a number seen by some as too high for a zoo that is still essentially nineteenth-century in character, confined to the formal grounds of a public park. Nonetheless, it's hugely popular with families, as there are mini-train and pony rides, a petting zoo and daily dolphin shows alongside the main animal attractions. The many endangered species on show include the Iberian wolf and big cats such as the Sri Lankan leopard and the Sumatran tiger. However, the zoo's days in its current form are numbered. Over the next few years its animal areas and habitats will be completely remodelled as the zoo attempts to expand its education, conservation and research facilities.

Barceloneta

There's no finer place for lunch on a sunny day than **Barceloneta**, an eighteenth-century neighbourhood of tightly packed streets with the harbour on one side and a **beach** on the other. It was laid out in 1755 – a classic eighteenth-century grid of streets where previously there had been mud flats – and the long, narrow streets are still very much as they were planned, broken at intervals by small squares and lined with multi-windowed houses. The local market, **Mercat de la Barceloneta**, was stylishly refurbished in 2007, and at Barceloneta's famous seafood restaurants – most characteristically lined along the harbourside **Passeig Joan de Borbó** – for most of the year you can enjoy your meal outside.

La Fàbrica del Sol

Pg. Salvat Papasseit 1 • Jan–July & Sept–Dec Tues–Fri 10am–2pm & 4.30–8pm, Sat 10am–2pm & 4–7pm; Aug Tues–Fri 10am–2pm only • Free • ☎ 932 564 430, ⓦ bcn.cat/lafabricadelsol • ⓜ Barceloneta

Inside the yellow-painted, red-brick building on the edge of the Parc de la Barceloneta – once the city's gas works – is the local council's **La Fàbrica del Sol**, a sustainable eco-centre that takes a close look at green living in all its guises, from recycling to transport. Although it's all in Catalan, the displays, gadgets and exhibits are all fairly

THE CROSS-HARBOUR CABLE CAR

The most thrilling ride in the city centre is **across the inner harbour on the cable car**, the Transbordador Aeri, which sweeps from the Torre Sant Sebastià, at the foot of Barceloneta, to the Torre Miramar in Montjuïc, with a stop in the middle at Torre de Jaume I (though this middle stop is currently closed for long-term repairs). Departures are every fifteen minutes (daily: March–May & Sept–Oct 11am–7pm; June–Aug 11am–8pm; Nov–Feb 11am–5.30pm), though in summer and at weekends you may have to wait for a while at the top of the towers for a ride, as the cars only carry about twenty people at a time. Tickets cost €11 one-way or €16.50 return.

10

self-explanatory – you've got to love the elevator that weighs its passengers in order to use the exact amount of energy required to lift them up to the roof terrace to see the building's garden and solar thermal system.

Platja de Sant Sebastià and Passeig Marítim

Ⓜ Barceloneta

Barceloneta's beach, **Platja de Sant Sebastià**, is the first in the series of sandy **city beaches** that stretches northeast from here along the coast. It curves out to the landmark, sail-shaped *W Barcelona* hotel (see p.687), which was designed by Catalan architect Ricardo Bofill. Meanwhile, at the Barceloneta end there are beach bars, outdoor cafés and public sculptures, while a double row of palms backs the **Passeig Marítim** esplanade that runs above the sands as far as the Port Olímpic (a 15min walk).

Port Olímpic

Ⓜ Ciutadella-Vila Olímpica

As you approach the **Port Olímpic** along the Passeig Marítim, the shimmering golden mirage above the promenade slowly reveals itself to be a **huge copper fish** (courtesy of Frank O. Gehry, architect of the Bilbao Guggenheim). It's the emblem of the huge seafront development constructed for the 1992 Olympics, and is backed by the city's two tallest buildings – the **Torre Mapfre** and the steel-framed **Hotel Arts Barcelona** – while the surrounding area has filled up with restaurants, cafés and bars. The whole zone turns into a full-on resort in summer, backed by a series of class-conscious clubs along Passeig Marítim that appeal to the local rich kids and A-list celebs.

Beyond the Port Olímpic, the **city beaches** are split into separate named sections (Nova Icària, Bogatell, Mar Bella, Nova Mar Bella and Llevant), each with showers, playgrounds and open-air café-bars. It's a pretty extraordinary leisure facility to find so close to a city centre – the sands are regularly swept and replenished, while joggers, cyclists and bladers have one of the Med's best views for company.

Diagonal Mar

Ⓜ El Maresme Fòrum, or tram #T4 to Fòrum via Glòries and Avgda. Diagonal

The waterfront convention and business district of **Diagonal Mar** was developed in the wake of the Universal Forum of Cultures Expo, held here in 2004. Everything is on a grand scale, starting with Jacques Herzog's dazzling blue biscuit-tin of a building hovering – seemingly unsupported – above the ground. This houses the main exhibitions of the Natural Science Museum (the **Museu Blau**), while the vast, landscaped area beyond is one of the city's showpiece urban leisure projects, the **Parc del Fòrum**.

Museu Blau

Pza. Leonardo da Vinci 4–5, Parc del Fòrum • Tues–Sat 10am–7pm, Sun & hols 10am–8pm • €7, includes entrance to Jardí Botànic at Montjuïc, under-16s free, plus free first Sun of the month & every Sun after 3pm • ☎ 932 566 002, ⓦ www.museuciencies.bcn.cat • Ⓜ El Maresme Fòrum, or tram #T4 to Fòrum

To unravel the mysteries of life, the universe and everything, you need travel no further than the Natural Science Museum's bold re-boot of its heritage collections, which were previously displayed in Parc de la Ciutadella. The million-strong collection of rocks, fossils, plants and animals have a state-of-the-art home in the visually stunning **Museu Blau** (Blue Museum), whose permanent exhibition – Planeta Vida (Planet Life) – plots a journey through the history of life on earth. It's heavily focused on evolutionary, whole-earth, Gaia principles, with plenty of interactive bells and whistles to guide you through topics as diverse as sex and reproduction and conservation of the environment.

Parc del Fòrum

Ⓜ El Maresme Fòrum, or tram #T4 to Fòrum via Glòries and Avgda. Diagonal

Diagonal Mar's main open space, the **Parc del Fòrum**, is an immense, undulating expanse that spreads towards the sea, culminating in a giant solar-panelled canopy that overlooks the marina, beach and park areas. The space can still seem a bit soulless at times – hot as Hades in summer, buffeted by biting winds in winter – but it's worth the metro ride if you're interested in heroic-scale public projects. In summer, temporary bars, dancefloors, open-air cinema and chill-out zones are established, while the city authorities have shifted some of the bigger annual music festivals and events down here to inject a bit of life outside convention time.

Montjuïc

You'll need to reserve at least a day to see **Montjuïc**, the steep hill and park rising over the city to the southwest. There's been a castle on the heights since the mid-seventeenth century, but since it was chosen as the site of the **International Exhibition** of 1929, Montjuïc has been firmly positioned as a cultural leisure park, anchored around the heavyweight art collections in the **Museu Nacional d'Art de Catalunya (MNAC)**. This unsurpassed national collection of Catalan art is supplemented by works in two other superb galleries, namely international contemporary art in the CaixaForum and that of the famous Catalan artist Joan Miró in the Fundació Joan Miró. In addition, there are several other minor museums, quite apart from the buildings and stadiums associated with the 1992 Olympics, which was centred on the heights of Montjuïc.

GETTING AROUND	MONTJUÏC

Metro The quickest way to Montjuïc is by metro (Ⓜ Espanya; follow exit signs for "Fira/Exposició"). From Pza. d'Espanya you can walk to CaixaForum, Poble Espanyol and MNAC – the Olympic area can then be reached by escalators behind MNAC.

Funicular The Funicular de Montjuïc (every 10min; Mon–Fri 7.30am–8pm, Sat, Sun & hols 9am–8pm, April–Oct daily until 10pm; €2.15, transport tickets and passes valid; ⓦ tmb.cat) departs from Ⓜ Paral.lel and takes a couple of minutes to ascend the hill. The upper station on Avgda. de Miramar is only a few minutes' walk from the Fundació Joan Miró, or you can switch to the Montjuïc cable car or bus services.

Cross-harbour cable car The Transbordador Aeri from Barceloneta (departures every 15min, daily: March–May, Sept & Oct 11am–7pm, June–Aug 11am–8pm, Nov–Feb

11am–5.30pm; €11 one-way/€16.50 return; ☎ 934 304 716) drops you by the Jardins de Miramar, from where it's a 10min walk to the Montjuïc cable car and funicular stations, and another 5min to the Fundació Joan Miró.

Montjuïc cable car The Telefèric de Montjuïc (daily: April, May & Oct 10am–7pm, June–Sept 10am–9pm, Nov–March 10am–6pm; €7.50 one-way/€10.80 return, under-12s €5.80 one-way/7.80 return, under-4s free; ⓦ tmb.cat), from Avgda. de Miramar whisks you up to the castle and back.

Bus services City bus #150 (transport tickets and passes valid) stops at the main Montjuïc attractions, departing from Avgda. de la Reina María Cristina, outside Ⓜ Espanya. The sightseeing, hop-on, hop-off Bus Turístic follows a similar route.

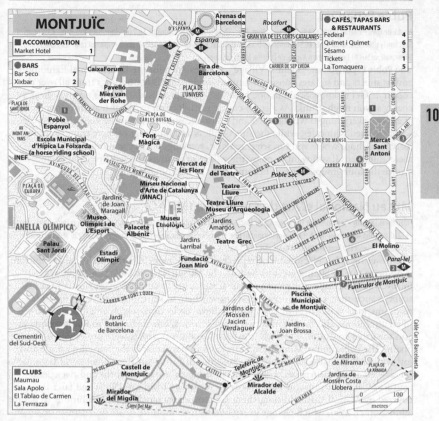

10

Font Màgica

Pza. de Carles Buïgas • April–Oct Thurs–Sun 9–11.30pm; Nov–March Fri & Sat only at 7pm, 7.30pm, 8pm & 8.30pm • Free • ⓜ Espanya

Walk up from the landmark Pza. d'Espanya, past the square's 47m-high twin towers and the vast exhibition halls, to the **Font Màgica** at the foot of the Montjuïc steps. On selected evenings, the "Magic Fountain" forms the centrepiece of an admittedly impressive, if slightly kitsch, sound-and-light show, with sprays and sheets of brightly coloured water dancing to the strains of Holst and Abba.

CaixaForum

Avgda. de Francesc Ferrer i Guàrdia 6–8 • Daily 10am–8pm; July & Aug Wed 10am–11pm • €4 • ☎ 934 768 600, ⓦ fundacio.lacaixa.es • ⓜ Espanya

CaixaForum is a terrific arts and cultural centre set within the old Casamarona textile factory, built in 1911. The undulating roof offers unique views, while the high Casamarona tower, etched in blue and yellow tiling, is as readily recognizable as the huge Miró starfish logos emblazoned across the building. The centre houses the Fundació La Caixa's celebrated contemporary art collection, focusing on the period from the 1980s to the present, with hundreds of artists represented, from Antoni Abad to Rachel Whiteread. Works are shown in partial rotation, along with an excellent programme of changing **exhibitions** across all aspects of the arts. The café occupies an airy converted space within the old factory walls.

10

Poble Espanyol

Avgda. de Francesc Ferrer i Guàrdia 13 • Mon 9am–8pm, Tues–Thurs & Sun 9am–midnight, Fri 9am–3am, Sat 9am–4am • €11, under-4s free, family ticket €30, night ticket €6.50, combined ticket with MNAC €18 • ☎ 935 086 300, ⓦ poble-espanyol.com • ⓜ Espanya and 800m walk, or bus #13 or #150 from Avgda. de la Reina María Cristina

The **Poble Espanyol**, or "Spanish Village", was designed for the International Exhibition, and its streets and squares consist of famous or characteristic buildings from all over the country. "Get to know Spain in one hour" is what's promised – and it's nowhere near as cheesy as you might think. As a crash-course introduction to Spanish architecture it's not at all bad: everything is well labelled and at least reasonably accurate. The echoing main square is lined with cafés, while the streets, alleys and buildings off here contain around forty workshops where you can see engraving, weaving, pottery and other crafts. Get there as it opens if you want to enjoy the village in relatively crowd-free circumstances – once the tour groups arrive, it becomes a bit of a scrum.

Museu Nacional d'Art de Catalunya (MNAC)

Palau Nacional • May–Sept Tues–Sat 10am–8pm, Sun 10am–3pm; Oct–April Tues–Sat 10am–6pm, Sun 10am–3pm; hols 10am–3pm • €12, ticket valid 48hr, under-16s & first Sun of the month free; special exhibitions, varied charges apply • ☎ 936 220 360, ⓦ mnac.cat • ⓜ Espanya, or bus #150 from Avgda. de la Reina María Cristina

The towering Palau Nacional, centrepiece of Barcelona's 1929 International Exhibition, is home to one of Spain's great museums, the **Museu Nacional d'Art de Catalunya (MNAC)**, showcasing a thousand years of Catalan art in stupendous surroundings. Its scope is such that it can be difficult to know where to start, but if time is limited it's recommended you concentrate on the medieval collection, which you'll be able to see in an afternoon. This is split into two main sections, one dedicated to **Romanesque** art and the other to **Gothic** – periods in which Catalunya's artists were pre-eminent in Spain. The collection of Romanesque frescoes in particular is the museum's pride and joy, while MNAC also has impressive holdings of European Renaissance and Baroque art, as well as an unsurpassed collection of "modern" (ie nineteenth- and twentieth-century) Catalan art up until the 1940s – everything from the 1950s and later is covered by MACBA. In addition, there are temporary blockbuster exhibitions (separate admission charge), which change every two to four months.

Romanesque collection

The **Romanesque collection** is the best of its kind in the world. From the eleventh century, the Catalan villagers of the high Pyrenees built sturdy stone churches, which were then lavishly painted in vibrantly coloured frescoes. To save them from degradation, the frescoes were moved to the museum and now are imaginatively presented in reconstructions of their original church settings. Still luminescent after eight hundred years, the frescoes have a vibrant, raw quality, best exemplified by those taken from churches in the Boí valley in the Catalan Pyrenees – such as the work of the anonymous "Master of Taüll" in the church of Sant Climent; look out for details such as the leper, to the left of the Sant Climent altar, patiently suffering a dog to lick his sores.

Gothic collection

The evolution from the Romanesque to the Gothic period was marked by a move from murals to painting on wood, and by the depiction of more naturalistic figures in scenes of the lives of saints and royalty. By the time of fifteenth-century Catalan artists like **Jaume Huguet** and **Lluís Dalmau**, works showed the strong influence of contemporary Flemish painting, in the use of denser colours, the depiction of crowd scenes and a concern for perspective. The last Catalan Gothic-era artist of note is the so-called **Master of La Seu d'Urgell**, who is responsible for a fine series of six paintings (Christ, the Virgin Mary, Saints Peter, Paul and Sebastian, and Mary Magdalene) that once formed the covers of an organ.

Renaissance and Baroque collections

Major European artists displayed include Rubens, Goya, El Greco, Zurbarán and Velázquez, though the museum is of course keen to play up Catalan works of the period, which largely absorbed the prevailing European influences – thus Barcelona artist **Antoni Viladomat** (1678–1755), whose twenty paintings of St Francis, executed for a monastery, are shown here in their entirety. However, more familiar to most will be the masterpieces of the Spanish Golden Age, notably Velázquez's *Saint Paul*.

10

Modern art collection

MNAC ends on a high note with its **modern Catalan art** collection, which is particularly good on *modernista* and *noucentista* painting and sculpture, the two dominant schools of the nineteenth and early twentieth centuries. Rooms highlight individual artists and genres, shedding light on the development of art in an exciting period of Catalunya's history, while there are fascinating diversions into *modernista* interior design (with some pieces by Gaudí), avant-garde sculpture and historical photography.

Fundació Joan Miró

Parc de Montjuïc • July–Sept Tues–Sat 10am–8pm, Thurs 10am–9.30pm, Sun & hols 10am–2.30pm; Oct–June Tues–Sat 10am–7pm, Thurs 10am–9.30pm, Sun & hols 10am–2.30pm • General admission €11, exhibitions €7, Espai 13 €2.50 • ☎ 934 439 470, ⓦ fundaciomiro-bcn.org • ⓜ Paral.lel, then Funicular de Montjuïc and 5min walk, or bus #13 or #150 from Avgda. de la Reina María Cristina

Montjuïc's highlight for many is the **Fundació Joan Miró**, Barcelona's most adventurous art museum, opened in 1975 and set among gardens overlooking the city. Joan Miró (1893–1983) was one of the greatest Catalan artists, establishing an international reputation while never severing his links with his homeland. He showed a childlike delight in colours and shapes and developed a free, highly decorative style – the paintings and drawings, in particular, are instantly recognizable, and are among the chief links between Surrealism and abstract art. Miró had his first exhibition in 1918, and after that spent his summers in Catalunya (and the rest of the time in France) before moving to Mallorca in 1956, where he died.

Inside the museum

Miró's friend, the architect Josep Lluís Sert, designed the beautiful building that now houses the museum, a permanent collection of paintings, graphics, tapestries and sculptures donated by Miró himself and covering the period from 1914 to 1978. For a rapid appraisal of Miró's entire *oeuvre*, look in on the museum's **Sala K**, whose 23 works are on long-term loan from a Japanese collector. Here, in a kind of potted retrospective, you can trace Miró's development as an artist, from his early Impressionist landscapes (1914) to the minimal renderings of the 1970s. Other exhibits include his enormous bright tapestries (he donated nine to the museum), pencil drawings and sculpture

---

TEATRE GREC AND THE BARCELONA FESTIVAL

Montjuïc takes centre stage each year during Barcelona's annual summer cultural festival (ⓦ grec.bcn.cat), known locally as the Grec, when arias soar from the open-air stage of the **Teatre Grec**, a Greek theatre cut into a former quarry on the Poble Sec side of the hill. Starting in late June (and running throughout July and sometimes into August), the festival incorporates drama, music and dance, with the opening sessions and some of the most atmospheric events staged in the theatre, from Shakespearean productions to shows by avant-garde performance artists. These can be magical nights – a true Barcelona experience – though you'll need to be quick off the mark for tickets, which usually go on sale in May.

10

THE OLYMPICS ON MONTJUÏC

The main road through Montjuïc climbs around the hill and up to the city's principal Olympic area, centred on the **Estadi Olímpic**. Built originally for the 1929 exhibition, the stadium was completely refitted to accommodate the 1992 opening and closing ceremonies, while to one side a vast terrace provides one of the finest vantage points in the city. Long water-fed troughs break the concrete and marble expanse, and the confident, space-age curve of Santiago Calatrava's **communications tower** dominates the skyline. Around the other side, just across the road from the stadium, the history of the Games themselves – and Barcelona's successful hosting – are covered in the **Museu Olímpic i de l'Esport** (Avgda. de l'Estadi 60; Tues–Sat 10am–6pm April–Sept until 8pm, Sun & hols 10am–2.30pm; €5.10; ☎932 925 379, ⓦmuseuolimpicbcn.com; ⓜEspanya then 25min walk, or bus #13 or #150 from Avgda. de la Reina María Cristina).

The 1992 Olympics were the second planned for Montjuïc's stadium. The first, in 1936 – the so-called "People's Olympics" – were organized as an alternative to the Nazis' infamous Berlin Games of that year, but the day before the official opening Franco's army revolt triggered the Civil War and scuppered the Barcelona Games. Some of the 25,000 athletes and spectators who had turned up stayed on to join the Republican forces.

outside in the gardens. Young experimental artists have their own space in the **Espai 13** gallery. There's also a bookshop, and a café-restaurant (10am–7pm) with outdoor tables on a sunny patio – you don't have to pay to get into the museum to use this.

Castell de Montjuïc

Carretera de Montjuïc • Daily: April–Sept 10am–8pm; Oct–March 10am–6pm • €5, free Sun after 3pm • ☎932 564 445, ⓦbcn.cat/castelldemontjuic • Direct access by Telefèric de Montjuïc, or bus #150 from Avgda. de la Reina María Cristina

Marking the top of Montjuïc and the end of the line is Barcelona's **castle** – and the best way up is by the **Telefèric de Montjuïc** (cable car), which tacks up the hillside, offering magnificent views on the way, before depositing you within the forbidding eighteenth-century walls. The fortress served as a military base and prison for decades, and was where the last president of the prewar Generalitat, **Lluís Companys i Jover**, was executed on Franco's orders on October 15, 1940.

In 2008 the castle was symbolically handed over to the city, and restoration work is now transforming the site into a combined peace museum, memorial space and Montjuïc interpretation centre. Something of its design and its brutal past are touched on in an exhibition in the Santa Amàlia bastion, in the inner keep, which also explains the future use to which the castle will be put. The cable-car ride and dramatic location merit a visit in any case.

Below the castle walls, a panoramic pathway – the **Camí del Mar** – has been cut from the cliff edge, providing scintillating views. The path is just over 1km long and ends at the back of the castle battlements near the **Mirador del Migdia**.

Jardí Botànic de Barcelona

C/Dr Font i Quer 2 • Daily: April–Sept 10am–7pm; Oct–March 10am–5pm • €3.50, or €7 combination ticket with Museu Blau, free Sun after 3pm & first Sun of month • ☎932 564 160, ⓦwww.museuciencies.bcn.cat • ⓜEspanya and 20min walk via escalators, or bus #13 or #150 from Avgda. de la Reina María Cristina

Principal among Montjuïc's many gardens is the city's botanical garden, the **Jardí Botànic de Barcelona**, which is laid out on terraced slopes that offer fine views across the city. The Montjuïc buses run here directly, or the entrance is just a five-minute walk around the back of the Olympic stadium. It's a beautifully kept contemporary garden, where wide, easy-to-follow paths wind through landscaped zones representing the flora of the Mediterranean, Canary Islands, California, Chile, North and South Africa and Australia.

The Eixample

The vast nineteenth-century street grid north of Pza. de Catalunya is the city's main shopping and business district. It was designed as part of a revolutionary urban plan – the **Eixample** in Catalan (pronounced aye-sham-pla, the "Extension" or "Widening") – that divided districts into regular blocks, whose characteristic wide streets and shaved corners survive today. It's not a neighbourhood as such – and, in fact, is further split into two distinct sections, namely the Dreta de l'Eixample (ie, the right-hand side) and Esquerra de l'Eixample (left-hand side), which fall either side of the two central parallel avenues, Passeig de Gràcia and Rambla de Catalunya. It's on and around Passeig de Gràcia, above all, that the bulk of the city's show-stopping *modernista* (Catalan Art Nouveau) buildings are found, along with an array of classy galleries and some of the city's most fashionable hotels, shops and boutiques.

10

Museu del Modernisme Català

C/Balmes 48 · Mon–Sat 10am–8pm, Sun & hols 10am–2pm · €10 · ☎ 932 722 896, ⓦ mmcat.cat · ⓜ Pg. de Gràcia

Barcelona's traditional "gallery district", around C/Consell de Cent, just off Rambla de Catalunya, is a fitting location for the stupendous *modernista* collection housed in the **Museu del Modernisme Català**. There are two exhibition floors in a restored building that was once a textile warehouse – the grand, vaulted basement contains paintings and sculpture while on the ground floor is *modernista* furniture, from screens to sofas. There are paintings and works by many famous names, whether oils by Ramon Casa i Carbó, or sinuous mirrors and tables by Antoni Gaudí (originally made for the *casas* Batlló and Calvet). But above all, this is a rare opportunity to examine extraordinary Art Nouveau fixtures, fittings and furniture – as a crash course in the varied facets of Catalan *modernisme*, beyond the iconic buildings themselves, it's invaluable.

Casa Amatller

Fundació Amatller, Pg. de Gràcia 41 · Check website for current guided tour details · €10, reservations essential, in person, by phone or email · ☎ 932 160 175, ⓦ www.amatller.org, ✉ amatller@amatller.org· ⓜ Pg. de Gràcia

First standout building on Passeig de Gràcia is Josep Puig i Cadafalch's striking **Casa Amatller** apartment block (1900), designed for Antoni Amatller, a Catalan chocolate manufacturer, art collector, photographer and traveller. The house has kept much of its original Art Nouveau furniture and interior design, and is currently being restored as a *modernista* cultural centre, but **guided tours** occasionally operate on various days, subject to the progress of the renovation works (the tours include a visit to Amatller's photographic studio and chocolate-tasting in the original kitchen).

Casa Batlló

Pg. de Gràcia 43 · Daily 9am–9pm, access occasionally restricted due to private events · €21.50, under-18s €18.50, under-6s free; advance-purchase tickets advised, in person, online or by phone · ☎ 932 160 306, ⓦ casabatllo.es · ⓜ Pg. de Gràcia

Perhaps the most extraordinary of all the private *modernista* mansions on Passeig de Gràcia stands right next door to Casa Amatller, namely the **Casa Batlló** – designed for the industrialist Josep Batlló – whose original construction was considered dull by contemporaries. Antoni Gaudí was hired to give it a facelift and created a naturalistic masterpiece: the stone facade hangs in folds, like skin, while on the rooftop sprout the celebrated mosaic chimneys and a little tower topped with a three-dimensional cross. The sinuous house interior also resembles some great organism, complete with window frames, doorways and staircases that display not a straight line between them. Self-guided audio tours show you the main floor, the patio and rear facade, the ribbed attic and the rooftop.

Fundació Antoni Tàpies

C/Aragó 255 • Tues–Sun 10am–7pm • €7 • ☎ 934 870 315, ⓦ fundaciotapies.org • Ⓜ Pg. de Gràcia

The definitive collection of the work of Catalan abstract artist **Antoni Tàpies** (1923–2012) is displayed in *modernista* architect Lluís Domènech i Montaner's first important building, the **Casa Montaner i Simon** (1880), which was converted in 1990 to house the **Fundació Antoni Tàpies**. The artist was born in the city in 1923 and was a founding member (1948) of the influential avant-garde grouping known as Dau al Set ("Die at Seven"). He was interested in collage and engraving techniques from an early age, and later developed an abstract style that matured during the 1950s. His large works are deceptively simple, though underlying messages and themes are signalled by the inclusion of everyday objects, unusual materials and symbols on the canvas. Tàpies' work is not immediately accessible (in the way of, say, Miró), and you're either going to love or hate the gallery: temporary exhibitions focus on selections of his work from every period, while special exhibitions highlight works and installations by other contemporary artists.

Museu Egipci de Barcelona

C/València 284 • Mon–Sat 10am–8pm, Sun 10am–2pm • €11 • ☎ 934 880 188, ⓦ museuegipci.com • Ⓜ Pg. de Gràcia

Half a block east of Passeig de Gràcia, the **Museu Egipci de Barcelona** is an exceptional collection of artefacts from ancient Egypt, ranging from the earliest kingdoms to the era of Cleopatra. The emphasis is on the shape and character of Egyptian society, and a serendipitous wander is a real pleasure, turning up items such as a wood and leather bed of the First and Second Dynasties (2920–2649 BC), some examples of cat mummies of the Late Period (715–332 BC), and a rare figurine of a spoonbill (ibis) representing an Egyptian god (though archeologists aren't yet sure which).

Palau Montaner

C/Mallorca 278 • Guided visits for groups only; reservations required • €6 • ☎ 933 177 652, ⓦ rutadelmodernisme.com • Ⓜ Pg. de Gràcia

The **Palau Montaner** was built in 1896 for a member of the Montaner i Simon publishing family. After the original architect quit, *modernista* architect Lluís

10

BUILDING A DESIGNER CITY

As Barcelona grew more prosperous throughout the nineteenth century, it was clear that the city had to expand beyond the Barri Gòtic. A contest was held to design the city's new quarters and the winning plan was that of utopian engineer and urban planner **Ildefons Cerdà i Sunyer**, who drew up a grid-shaped town marching off to the north, intersected by long, straight streets and cut by broad, angled avenues. Work started in 1859 and the Eixample immediately became the fashionable area in which to live, as the moneyed classes moved into luxurious apartments on the wide new avenues. As the money in the city moved north, so did a new class of architects who began to pepper the Eixample with ever more striking examples of their work, inspired by *modernisme*, the Catalan offshoot of Art Nouveau. Three **architects** in particular came to prominence in Barcelona and, in doing so, introduced a building style that has given the city a look like no other.

ANTONI GAUDÍ I CORNET

Born in Reus, near Tarragona, to a family of artisans, the work of **Antoni Gaudí i Cornet** (1852–1926) was never strictly *modernista* in style, but the imaginative impetus he provided was incalculable. Fantasy, spiritual symbolism and Catalan pride are evident in every building he designed, while his architectural influences were Moorish and Gothic, embellished with elements from the natural world. Gaudí rarely wrote a word about the theory of his art, preferring the buildings to demand reaction – no one stands mute in front of an Antoni Gaudí masterpiece.

LLUÍS DOMÈNECH I MONTANER

With Gaudí in a class of his own, it was **Lluís Domènech i Montaner** (1850–1923) who was perhaps the greatest pure *modernista* architect. Drawing on the rich Catalan Romanesque and Gothic traditions, his work combined traditional craft methods with modern technological experiments, seen to triumphant effect in his masterpiece, the Palau de la Música Catalana.

JOSEP PUIG I CADAFALCH

Like other *modernista* architects, the work of **Josep Puig i Cadafalch** (1867–1957) also contains a wildly inventive use of ceramic tiles, ironwork, stained glass and stone carving. His first commission, the Casa Martí, housed the famous *Els Quatre Gats* tavern for the city's avant-garde artists and hangers-on, while in various Eixample mansions Puig i Cadafalch brought to bear distinct Gothic and medieval influences.

Domènech i Montaner took over halfway through construction, and as a result the top half of the facade is clearly more elaborate than the lower part. Meanwhile, the period's most celebrated craftsmen were set to work on the interior, which sports rich mosaic floors, painted glass, carved woodwork and a monumental staircase. The building is now the seat of the Madrid government's delegation to Catalunya, but it is possible to arrange a **guided tour**.

La Pedrera

Pg. de Gràcia 92, tour entrance on C/Provença • **Self-guided visits** Daily: March–Nov 9am–8pm; Dec–Feb 9am–6.30pm, closed second week Jan • €16.50, under-6s free; audio-guide €4 • **Exhibitions** Daily 10am–8pm • €3 • **Nits d'Estiu** Thurs–Sat nights, mid-June to mid-Aug • €28 • Advance booking essential for self-guided visits and Nits d'Estiu, at the ticket office or online ☎ 902 101 212 or ☎ 902 202 138, ⓦ telentrada.com • ☎ 902 400 973, ⓦ lapedrera.com • Ⓜ Diagonal

Gaudí's weird and wonderful apartment building is simply not to be missed – though you can expect queues whenever you visit. Constructed as the Casa Milà between 1905 and 1911, and popularly known as **La Pedrera**, or the Stone Quarry, it was declared a UNESCO World Heritage Site in 1984. Its rippling facade, which curves around the street corner in one smooth sweep, is said to have been inspired by the mountain of Montserrat, and the apartments themselves, whose balconies of tangled metal drip over the facade, resemble eroded cave dwellings.

The self-guided visit includes a trip up to the extraordinary **roof terrace** (closed if it's raining) to see at close quarters the enigmatic chimneys, as well as an informative exhibition about Gaudí's work installed under the 270 curved brick arches of the attic. El Pis ("The Apartment") on the building's fourth floor re-creates the design and style of a *modernista*-era bourgeois apartment in a series of rooms that flow seamlessly from one to another. Casa Milà itself is still split into private apartments, while the whole building is administered by the Fundació Caixa de Catalunya. Through the main entrance on Passeig de Gràcia there's access to the Fundació's **exhibition hall** which hosts temporary art shows of works by major international artists.

Perhaps the best experience of all is the summer evening concert season known as **Nits d'Estiu** (summer nights), when you can enjoy the rooftop and night-time cityscape with a complimentary glass of cava and music from jazz groups and chamber ensembles.

Sagrada Família

C/Mallorca 401 • **Church** April–Sept daily 9am–8pm; Oct–March daily 9am–6pm; 50min guided tours in English April–Oct daily & Nov–March Sat & Sun 11.15am, 12.30pm, 1.45pm & 3pm; Nov March Mon Fri 10.15am, 12.15pm & 3pm • €14.80 (under 11s free) or €19.30 including guided tour or audio-guide; combination ticket with Casa Museu Gaudí at Parc Güell €18.30 • **Towers and museum** Daily 9am until 15–30min before church closes • Towers €4.50, timed elevator tickets available from main ticket office; museum free • ☎ 935 132 060, ⓦ sagradafamilia.cat • Ⓜ Sagrada Família, the metro drops you right outside

Nothing – really, nothing – prepares you for the impact of the **Temple Expiatori de la Sagrada Família** which occupies an entire city block between C/Mallorca and C/Provença, north of the Diagonal. In many ways the overpowering church of the "Sacred Family" has become a kind of symbol for the city. It is the most fantastic of the modern architectural creations in which Barcelona excels – even the coldest hearts will find the Sagrada Família inspirational in form and spirit.

Brief history

Although the church survived the Civil War, Gaudí's plans and models were destroyed in 1936 by the anarchists. Nonetheless, work restarted in the late 1950s amid great controversy, and has continued ever since – as have the arguments. On balance, it's probably safe enough to assume that Gaudí saw the struggle to finish the building as at least as important as the method and style. However, the current work has attracted criticism for infringing Gaudí's original spirit, while tunnelling under the temple for the high-speed AVE train line has kicked up a huge stink among critics who claim that the church will be put at risk (not so, say the tunnel engineers). All in all, though the project might be drawing inexorably towards completion (within the next twenty years, it's said), there's still plenty more time for argument.

ANTONI GAUDÍ: GOD'S ARCHITECT?

Begun in 1882 by public subscription, the Sagrada Família was originally intended as a modest, expiatory building that would atone for the city's increasingly revolutionary ideas. When **Antoni Gaudí** – only 31 years of age – took charge, he changed the direction and scale of the project almost immediately, seeing in the Sagrada Família an opportunity to reflect his own deepening spiritual and nationalist feelings. Indeed, after he finished the Parc Güell in 1911, Gaudí vowed never to work again on secular projects, but to devote himself solely to the **Sagrada Família**, which became perhaps the most daring creation in all Art Nouveau. Gaudí even ended up living in a workshop on site, and he was adapting the plans ceaselessly right up to his untimely death. Run over by a tram on the Gran Vía on June 7, 1926, he died in hospital three days later – his death was treated as a Catalan national disaster, and all of Barcelona turned out for his funeral procession. Following papal dispensation, he was buried in the Sagrada Família crypt, a fitting resting place for an architect whose masterpiece was designed (he said), to show "the religious realities of present and future life … man's origin, his end".

10

10

Visiting the building

The size alone is startling – Gaudí's original plan was to build a church to seat over 10,000 people, while the iconic **towers** rise to over 100m high. A precise symbolism pervades the facades, each of which is divided into three porches devoted to Faith, Hope and Charity. Gaudí made extensive use of human, plant and animal models in order to produce exactly the sculptural likenesses he sought – the spreading stone leaves of the roof in the church interior, for example, were inspired by the city's plane trees. Although parts of the interior still resemble a giant building site, and the **Glory facade** remains unfinished, the whole church will be roofed in due course, with a 170-metre-high central dome and tower to follow (which will then make the church the tallest building in Barcelona).

There are eight towers at the Sagrada Família, four on each current facade, though following Gaudí's design there will eventually be eighteen – twelve symbolizing the Apostles, four dedicated to the Evangelists and one each for Mary and Jesus. They have been likened to everything from perforated cigars to celestial billiard cues, and to see them at close quarters take one of the separate **elevators** that run up the Passion and Nativity facades. Your entrance ticket also gives you access to the **museum**, which traces the career of the architect and the history of the church.

Hospital de la Santa Creu i de Sant Pau

C/Sant Antoni María Claret 167, at c/Dos de Maig • Self-guided visits April–Oct Mon–Sat 10am–6.30pm; Nov–March Mon–Sat 10am–4.30pm; all year Sun & hols 10am–2.30pm • €8 • Tours daily in English April–Oct Mon–Sat at noon, 1pm, 4pm & 5pm; Nov–March Mon–Sat at noon, 1pm & 4pm; all year Sun & hols at noon & 1pm; there are also tours in Spanish/Catalan • €14 • ☎ 935 537 801, Ⓦ santpaubarcelona.org • Ⓜ Hospital de Sant Pau

Lluís Domènech i Montaner's *modernista* public hospital, the **Hospital de la Santa Creu i de Sant Pau**, is possibly the one building in town that can rival the Sagrada Família for size and invention. The hospital has its own metro stop, but it's far better to walk up the four-block-long Avinguda de Gaudí from the church, which gives terrific views back over the spires of the Sagrada Família.

Work started in 1902, the brief being to replace the city's medieval hospital buildings in the Raval. The architect spent ten years working on the project and left his trademarks all over it, notably the whimsical pavilions, turrets and towers covered with sculpture, mosaics, stained glass and ironwork. These days, the old buildings have been superseded by the modern hospital behind, though the fruits of the ongoing, painstaking restoration of the *modernista* property – including the ornate administration building, the Sant Rafael Pavilion and the breezy interior gardens – are now accessible to visitors. Informative **tours** of the site tell you more about the six-hundred-year history of the hospital as well as its future as a "campus of knowledge" populated by cultural, research and environmental organizations.

Plaça de les Glòries Catalanes

Ⓜ Glòries

Barcelona's major avenues all meet at the **Plaça de les Glòries Catalanes**, a glorified roundabout dedicated to the "Catalan glories", from architecture to literature. It's now at the centre of the city's latest bout of regeneration, which plans to tunnel the traffic underground. Signature buildings on the roundabout are Jean Nouvel's cigar-shaped **Torre Agbar** (142m), a highly distinctive aluminium-and-glass tower with no fewer than four thousand windows, housing the headquarters of the local water company and the sleek Disseny Hub, the new home of the city's applied art collections. The **Parc del Centre del Poble Nou** further down the Diagonal (10min walk from Glòries or tram stop Pere IV) is an eye-catching contemporary park set on another former industrial site – a surviving brick chimney stands in the centre, surrounded by willow trees.

CLOCKWISE FROM TOP LEFT PARC GÜELL (P.678); SAGRADA FAMÍLIA; CASA BATLLÓ (P.689); LA PEDRERA (P.672) >

Museu del Disseny and Disseny Hub

Pza. de les Glòries Catalanes 37–38 • **Museu del Disseny** check website for hours • Entrance fee for museum to be determined • ⓦ museudeldisseny.cat • **Disseny Hub** Tues–Sun 10am–8pm • Free • ☎ 932 566 713, ⓦ dhub.cat • ⓜ Glòries

The new **Museu del Dissney** brings together the collections of the **Museu de les Arts Decoratives** (Decorative Arts Museum), the **Museu de Cerámica** (Ceramics Museum), the **Museu Tèxtil i d'Indumentària** (Textile and Clothing Museum) and the **Gabinet de les Arts Gràfiques** (Department of Graphic Arts) in the **Disseny Hub** building. At the time of writing, the museum was still transitioning into its new home, so in the meantime, the zinc-plated building – nicknamed La Grapadora ("The Stapler") after its shape – is worth seeing. The Hub is also home to temporary exhibition spaces, a public library and the headquarters of local design institutions such as the Foment de les Arts i del Disseny (FAD).

Teatre Nacional de Catalunya

Pza. de les Arts 1 • Tours currently Wed & Thurs at 11am & 12.30pm • €8, reservations required • ☎ 933 065 700, ⓦ tnc.cat • ⓜ Glòries or tram #T4

Off to the southwest of Glòries, Catalunya's national theatre – the **Teatre Nacional de Catalunya** – presents the neighbourhood with a soaring glass box encased within a Greek temple on a raised dais, surrounded by manicured lawns. There are guided building and backstage **tours** for anyone interested in learning more, as well as a bar and restaurant that are open in the evening – a summer evening's drink on the open-air terraza is a nice way to take in the grandiose surroundings.

L'Auditori and the Museu de la Música

L'Auditori C/Lepant 150 • ⓦ auditori.cat • **Museu de la Música** C/Lepant 150 2a • Tues–Sat & hols 10am–6pm, Sun 10am–8pm • €5, free first Sun of the month & every Sun after 3pm • ☎ 932 563 650, ⓦ www.museumusica.bcn.cat • ⓜ Glòries/Marina

Forming a sort of cultural enclave, **L'Auditori** is the city's contemporary city concert hall, within which is housed the **Museu de la Música**. It's all very impressive, with soaring glass-walled display cases, and yet it struggles to engage, partly because of the sheer number and variety of instruments and partly because of the impenetrable commentary, with sections called things like "The humanist spirit and the predominance of polyphony". Make of that what you will, or the chronological "timeline" that runs from Pythagoras in the fifth century BC to 2007 when "the Rolling Stones continue to play".

Parc Joan Miró

C/Tarragona • Daily 10am–dusk • Free • ⓜ Tarragona

The main attraction on the left-hand side of the Eixample is the **Parc Joan Miró**, which features a raised piazza marked only by Joan Miró's gigantic mosaic sculpture *Dona i Ocell* ("Woman and Bird"), towering above a shallow reflecting pool. The rear of the park is given over to games areas and landscaped sections of palms and firs, with a kiosk café and some outdoor tables found in among the trees.

TREASURE-HUNTING AT ELS ENCANTS VELLS

A trove of dusty delights, the city's flea market, **El Encants Vells**, has a shiny new home. Now adjacent to the Teatre Nacional de Catalunya, the new site (Avgda. Meridiana 69; Mon, Wed, Fri & Sat 9am–8pm, plus public auctions 8–9.30am except Sat; ⓦ encantsbcn.com; ⓜ Glòries) sports multiple levels of open-air, treasure-hunting action – all protected by a large canopy whose metallic underside reflects the bustling market below. It's best in the early morning, and haggling for any "old charms" (*encants vells*) you might fancy is de rigueur, but you're up against experts.

Arenas de Barcelona

Gran Vía de les Corts Catalanes 373–385, at Pza. d'Espanya • Daily 10am–10pm • ☎ 932 890 244, ⊛ arenasdebarcelona.com • ⓂEspanya

The **Arenas de Barcelona**, the fabulous Moorish-style bullring, was originally built in 1900 but has been re-imagined as a swish shopping and leisure centre that opened in 2011. Conceived by architect Richard Rogers as a gateway to the city centre, and preserving the beautiful brick exterior, the various retail levels at Arenas are hung in sweeping, circular galleries, while right on top is a wide walk-around exterior promenade circling the dome, offering 360-degree views of the western side of the city.

10

Gràcia

Gràcia – the closest neighbourhood to the Eixample – was a village for much of its early existence before being annexed as a city suburb in the late nineteenth century. There's still a genuine small-town atmosphere here, very distinct from the old-town neighbourhoods, while Gràcia's vibrant cultural scene and nightlife counters the notion that Barcelona begins and ends on the Ramblas. That said, there's not that much to see, but wander the narrow, gridded streets, catch a film or hit one of the excellent local bars or restaurants, and you'll soon get the feel of a neighbourhood that – unlike some in Barcelona – still has a soul. Most of the boutiques, galleries, cinemas and cafés are near pretty **Pza. de la Virreina**, with **C/Verdi** in particular always worth a stroll. A short walk to the southwest, **Pza. del Sol** is the beating heart of much of the district's nightlife, while **Pza. Rius i Taulet**, the "clock-tower square", a couple of minutes to the south, is another popular place to meet for brunch. However, the one unmissable attraction is just on the neighbourhood fringe, namely the surreal Parc Güell, by architectural genius Antoni Gaudí.

Parc Güell

Main entrance C/d'Olot • Daily: April 8am–8pm; May–Oct 8am–9pm; Nov–March 8.30am–6pm • Monumental zone €7 online, €8 ticket office or ATM, under-6s free • ☎ 902 200 302, ⊕ parkguell.cat

Antoni Gaudí's extraordinary urban park on the outskirts of Gràcia, **Parc Güell** was originally planned as a private housing estate of sixty dwellings, furnished with ornamental paths, recreational areas and decorative monuments. Gaudí worked on the project between 1900 and 1914 but in the end only two houses were actually built, and the park was officially opened to the public instead in 1922. Laid out on a hill, which provides fabulous views back across the city, the park is an almost hallucinatory expression of the imagination. Pavilions of contorted stone, giant decorative lizards, a vast Hall of Columns (intended to be the estate's market), the meanderings of a huge ceramic bench – all combine in one manic swirl of ideas and excesses. Only eight hundred visitors are allowed inside the newly designated "monumental zone" – which comprises the park's most famous sites – per hour (once inside you can stay as long as you like), so it's best to book ahead.

Casa Museu Gaudí

Parc Güell (outside the monumental zone) • Daily: April–May 10am–8pm; June–Sept 9am–8pm; Oct–March 10am–6pm • €5.50, combination ticket with Sagrada Família €18.30 • ☎ 932 193 811, ⊕ casamuseugaudi.org

One of Gaudí's collaborators, Francesc Berenguer, designed and built a turreted house within the park for the architect. In the **Casa Museu Gaudí**, his ascetic study and bedroom have been kept much as they were in his day, while other rooms display a diverting collection of furniture he designed for other projects – a typical mixture of wild originality and brilliant engineering.

ARRIVAL AND DEPARTURE   GRÀCIA AND PARC GÜELL

By metro and train For Gràcia, the best metro stations are Ⓜ Diagonal (south), Ⓜ Fontana (north) or Ⓜ Joanic (east). For Parc Güell use Ⓜ Vallcarca; walk a few hundred metres down Avgda. de Vallcarca until you see the mechanical escalators on your left, ascending Baixada de la Glòria. Follow these right to the western-side park entrance (15min).

By bus Bus #24 from Pza. de Catalunya or Pg. de Gràcia stops on Carretera del Carmel at the eastern side gate of Parc Güell. The Bus Turístic stops at the bottom end of C/Larrard, on C/Mare de Deu de la Salut.

On foot Gràcia is a 30min walk from Pza. de Catalunya. From any of the neighbourhood stations, it's around a 500m walk to Gràcia's central squares. Walking to Parc Güell from Gràcia (Ⓜ Lesseps), turn right along Travessera de Dalt and then left up steep C/Larrard, which leads straight to the main entrance of the park on C/Olot (10min).

Les Corts and Pedralbes

To the northwest of the city centre, what was once the village of **Les Corts** is now largely indistinguishable from the rest of the modern city, save for the hallowed precincts of Camp Nou, FC Barcelona's stupendous football stadium. Nearby, across Avinguda Diagonal, the Palau Reial de Pedralbes is home to serene public gardens (the lush vegetation hides an early work by Gaudí), while a half-day's excursion can be made by walking from the palace, past the Gaudí dragon gate at Pavellons Güell to the calm cloister at the Gothic monastery of **Pedralbes**.

Camp Nou and FC Barcelona

Avgda. Arístides Maillol • ☎ 902 189 900 or ☎ 934 963 600, ⊕ fcbarcelona.com • Ⓜ Collblanc/María Cristina plus 10min walk

It's no exaggeration to say that football in Barcelona is a genuine obsession, with support for the local giants **FC (Futbol Club) Barcelona** raised to an art form. "More than just a club" is the proud boast, and certainly during the dictatorship years the club stood as a Catalan symbol around which people could rally. Arch-rivals, Real Madrid, on the other hand, were always seen as Franco's club. The swashbuckling players in the famous "blaugrana" (claret and blue) shirts have transcended national barriers to become every football fan's second favourite team; indeed, the four-times European champions (most recently in 2011) – mercurial masters of the elegant *tiki-taka*, pass-and-move style – are often hailed as the world's best team.

Museum and stadium tour

Museu del Futbol, entrance on Avgda. Arístides Maillol, through Gates (Accés) 7 and 9 • April & mid-Oct to Dec Mon–Sat 10am–6.30pm, Sun & hols 10am–2.30pm; May to mid-Oct daily 9.30am–7.30pm; last tour 45min before closing, no tours on match days • €23, under-13s €17, under-5s free • ☎ 902 189 900 or ☎ 934 963 600, ⓦ fcbarcelona.com/camp-nou

Together, the 98,000-seat stadium and museum – billed as the "Camp Nou Experience" – provide a magnificent celebration of Spain's national sport. The **self-guided tour**, complete with audio-guide, winds through the changing rooms and players' tunnel onto the pitch and up to the press gallery and directors' box for stunning views. The **museum** is jammed full of silverware and memorabilia, including the six cups won in 2009 alone, Barcelona's *annus mirabilis*, while a cracking multimedia zone profiles historic games and famous players and relives the match-day atmosphere. Finally, you're directed into the **FC Botiga** megastore, where you can buy anything from a replica shirt down to a branded bottle of wine.

Palau Reial de Pedralbes

Avgda. Diagonal 686 • Gardens daily 10am–dusk • Free • ⓜ Palau Reial or tram #T1, #T2 or #T3

Opposite the university on Avinguda Diagonal, the **Palau Reial de Pedralbes** is an Italianate palace set in formal grounds. Although the palace is closed to the public, the **gardens** – a breezy oasis of Himalaya cedars, strawberry trees and bougainvillea – are a lovely way to spend an afternoon. Hidden in a bamboo thicket, to the left-centre of the facade – is the "Hercules fountain" (1884), an early work by Antoni Gaudí. In late June, a music festival (ⓦ festivalpedralbes.com) takes place in the gardens.

Pavellons Güell

Avgda. de Pedralbes 7 • Tours Sat & Sun at 10.15am & 12.15pm in English, plus 11.15am & 1.15pm in Spanish/Catalan • €6 • ☎ 933 177 652, ⓦ rutadelmodernisme.com • ⓜ Palau Reial and 5min walk

As an early test of his capabilities, Antoni Gaudí was asked by his patron, Eusebi Güell, to rework the entrance, gatehouse and stables of the Güell summer residence, which was sited on a large working estate well away from the filth and the unruly mobs of downtown Barcelona. The brick-and-tile stables and outbuildings – known as the **Pavellons Güell** – survive as Gaudí created them, though it's the gateway that's the most famous element. An extraordinary winged dragon made of twisted iron snarls at the passers-by, its razor-toothed jaws spread wide in a fearsome roar.

Monestir de Pedralbes

Baixada del Monestir 9 • April–Sept Tues–Fri 10am–5pm, Sat 10am–7pm, Sun 10am–8pm; Oct–March Tues–Fri 10am–2pm, Sat & Sun 10am–5pm • €7, includes entry to other Museu d'Història de Barcelona sites • ☎ 932 563 434, ⓦ bcn.cat/monestirpedralbes • ⓜ Palau Reial and 20min walk; or FGC Reina Elisenda (frequent trains from Pza. de Catalunya) and 10min walk; or bus #64 from Pza. Universitat

Founded in 1326 for the nuns of the Order of St Clare, the Gothic **Monestir de Pedralbes** is, in effect, an entire monastic village preserved on the outskirts of the city, within medieval walls that completely shut out the clamour of the twenty-first century. After 600 years of isolation, the monastery was sequestered by the Generalitat during the Civil War and it later opened as a museum in 1983 – a new adjacent convent was built as part of the deal, where the Clare nuns still reside. The **cloisters** are the finest in the city, adorned by the slenderest of columns, with the only sound the tinkling water from the fountain. Side rooms and chambers give a clear impression of medieval convent life, from the chapterhouse and austere refectory to a fully equipped kitchen and infirmary. While the nuns themselves eschewed personal trappings, the monastery acquired valuable art and other possessions over the centuries – including pieces of Gothic furniture, paintings by Flemish artists, and some outstanding illuminated choir books. In the adjacent **church** the foundation's sponsor, **Elisenda de Montcada**, wife of Jaume II, lies in a superb, carved marble tomb.

10

Tibidabo and Parc de Collserola

The views from the heights of **Tibidabo** (550m), the peak that signals the northwestern boundary of the city, are legendary. On a clear day you can see across to the Pyrenees and out to sea even as far as Mallorca. However, while many make the tram and funicular ride up to Tibidabo's wonderfully old-fashioned amusement park, few realize that beyond stretches the **Parc de Collserola**, an area of peaks, wooded river valleys and hiking paths – one of Barcelona's best-kept secrets. Meanwhile, don't miss **CosmoCaixa**, the city's excellent science museum, which can easily be seen on the way to or from Tibidabo.

CosmoCaixa

C/Issac Newton 26 • Tues–Sun 10am–8pm • €4, under-16s €2, free children's activities & planetarium • ☎ 932 126 050, ⓦ obrasocial .lacaixa.es • FGC Avgda. del Tibidabo (trains from Pza. de Catalunya) and 10min walk, or Tramvia Blau stops close by

A dramatic refurbishment in 2005 transformed the city's science museum into **CosmoCaixa**, a must-see attraction, certainly if you've got children in tow – it's an easy place to spend a couple of hours. Hands-on experiments and displays investigate life, the universe and everything, "from bacteria to Shakespeare", with the two big draws being the 100 tonnes of "sliced" rock in the **Mur Geològic** (Geological Wall) and, best of all, the **Bosc Inundat** – nothing less than a thousand square metres of real Amazonian rainforest, complete with croc-filled mangroves, anacondas and giant catfish.

Parc d'Atraccions Tibidabo

Pza. del Tibidabo • Generally June–Sept & hols Wed–Sun, rest of the year Sat, Sun & hols only, closed Jan & Feb, park open from noon until 7–11pm depending on season • Skywalk ticket €12.70, full admission €28.50, plus family/discount tickets • ☎ 932 117 942, ⓦ tibidabo.es

Barcelona's self-styled "magic mountain" amusement park – the **Parc d'Atraccions** – has been thrilling the citizens for over a century. It's a mix of traditional rides, plus an influx of high-tech roller coasters and free-fall drops, laid out around several levels of the mountaintop and connected by landscaped paths and gardens. Some of the most famous historic attractions are grouped under the discounted "Skywalk" ticket, like the aeroplane – spinning since 1928 – the carousel, and the quirky Museu d'Autòmates, a collection of coin-operated antique fairground machines in full working order. Summer weekends finish with parades, concerts and a noisy *correfoc*, a theatrical fireworks display.

ARRIVAL AND DEPARTURE   TIBIDABO

By train, tram and funicular Take the FGC train (Tibidabo line 7) from Pza. de Catalunya station to Avgda. del Tibidabo (the last stop). From across the road an antique tram service, the Tramvia Blau (departures every 15–30min: Jan–April & mid-Oct to Dec Sat, Sun & hols 10am–6pm; May & June & mid-Sept to mid-Oct Sat, Sun & hols 10am–7.30pm; July to mid-Sept & Easter week daily 10am–7.30pm; €4.20 one-way) runs up the hill to Pza. del Doctor Andreu; there's a bus service instead out of season during the week. By the tram and bus stop on Pza. Doctor

Andreu (where there are several café-bars and restaurants), change to the Funicular del Tibidabo, with connections to Tibidabo at the top (every 15min, operates when the Parc d'Atraccions is open; €4.10 return, with park admission; €7.70 return, without park admission). The whole journey takes about 1hr.

By bus The Bus Turístic stops at Avda. del Tibidabo, where you can change for the Tramvia Blau. Alternatively, the special Tibibus (T2) runs direct to Tibidabo from Pza. de Catalunya (from 10.15am, every day the park is open; €2.95).

Parc de Collserola

Centre d'Informació • Daily 9.30am–3pm • ☎ 932 803 552, ⓦ parcnaturalcollserola.cat • FGC Baixada de Vallvidrera (on the Sabadell or Terrassa line from Pza. de Catalunya; 15min)

Given a half-decent day, local bikers, hikers and outdoors enthusiasts all make a beeline for the city's ring of wooded hills beyond Tibidabo, the **Parc de Collserola**. The **park information centre** lies in oak and pine woods, an easy, signposted ten-minute walk up through the trees from the FGC Baixada de Vallvidrera train station. There's a bar-restaurant here with an outdoor terrace, plus an exhibition on the park's history, flora and fauna, while the staff hand out English-language leaflets detailing the various walks, which range from a fifteen-minute stroll to the Vallvidrera dam to a couple of hours circling the hills.

10

ARRIVAL AND DEPARTURE

BARCELONA

Barcelona's main points of arrival are all fairly convenient, even the airport, and have useful train and metro stations for onward travel. In most cases, you can be off the plane, train, bus or ferry and in your hotel room within the hour. Note that some budget airline "Barcelona" flights are no such thing: for Ryanair arrivals at Girona airport (90km north of Barcelona), there's a connecting bus service (see p.738) to Barcelona Nord bus station, and there are also connecting buses from Reus airport, which is situated 110km south of Barcelona near Tarragona, (see p.782) to Barcelona Sants train station.

BY PLANE

Barcelona Airport Barcelona's airport (general information ☎ 902 404 704, ⓦ aena.es) is 18km southwest of the city at El Prat de Llobregat. A taxi to the city centre costs about €30, including the airport surcharge.

Airport train The airport train service (R2 Nord; daily 5.42am–11.38pm; journey time 20min; €4.10) runs every 30min to Barcelona Sants (the main train station), and continues on to Pg. de Gràcia (best stop for Eixample, Pza. de Catalunya and the Ramblas). It departs from Terminal T2, and there's a free shuttle bus to the station from T1 which takes around 10min. Trains back to the airport run from Barcelona Sants on a similar half-hourly schedule. City travel passes (*targetes*) and the Barcelona Card are valid.

Aerobus The Aerobus (daily 6am–1am; €5.90 one-way, €10.20 return; departures every 5–10min; ⓦ aerobusbcn .com) departs from both T1 and T2, stopping in the city at Pza. d'Espanya, Gran Via–Urgell, Pza. Universitat and Pza. de Catalunya. It takes 35–40min to reach Pza. de Catalunya, longer in the rush hour. Departures back to the airport from Pza. de Catalunya (in front of El Corte Inglés department store) – note that there are separate services to either Terminal T1 or T2.

BY TRAIN

Barcelona Sants The main station for national and international arrivals is Barcelona Sants (ⓜ Sants Estació), 3km west of the centre. From Sants, metro line 3 runs direct to Drassanes and Liceu (for the Ramblas), Catalunya (for Pza. de Catalunya) and Pg. de Gràcia (Eixample), while line 5 runs to Diagonal (Eixample and Gràcia).

AVE services The high-speed AVE line between Barcelona and Madrid (via Tarragona and Zaragoza) has cut journey times in half between the two cities (2hr 30min–3hr 10min, depending on the service). Arrivals and departures are at Barcelona Sants, though a second high-speed station is currently being built at La Sagrera, east of the centre beyond Glòries (completion date estimated 2016). Other high-speed services include Avant (medium distances) and Alvia (high-speed and normal rail network).

Estació de França Some inter-city services and regional trains also stop at Estació de França, 1km east of the Ramblas and close to ⓜ Barceloneta.

Regional and provincial trains Other possible arrival points by train are Pza. de Catalunya, at the top of the Ramblas (for trains from coastal towns north of the city, and towns on the Puigcerdà–Vic line), and Pg. de Gràcia (Catalunya provincial destinations).

Destinations Figueres (at least hourly; 1hr 50min–2hr 50min); Girona (Avant up to 22 daily, 40min; other services at least hourly 1hr 15min–2hr 10min); Lleida (Avant & Alvia at least hourly, 55min–1hr 5min; other services 9 daily; 2hr 20min–3hr 30min); Madrid (AVE up to 29 daily, every 25min at peak times, 2hr 30min–3hr 10min; other services 5 daily, 6–9hr); Portbou (hourly; 2hr 10min–2hr 50min); Puigcerdà (6 daily; 2hr 50min); Ripoll (up to 16 daily; 2hr); Sitges (every 10–30min; 25–35min); Tarragona (AVE & Avant up to 25 daily, 35min; other services every 15–30min, 1hr 20min); Valencia (up to 20 daily; 3hr 20min–5hr); Vic (hourly; 1hr 15min); Zaragoza (AVE & Alvia up to 30 daily, 1hr 20min–1hr 45min; other services up to 4 daily, 2hr 20min–5hr 20min).

BY BUS

Barcelona Nord The main bus terminal is on C/Ali-Bei (☎ 902 260 606, ⓦ barcelonanord.com; ⓜ Arc de Triomf), four blocks north of Parc de la Ciutadella. There's a bus information desk on the ground floor (daily 7am–9pm), with the ticket offices above at street level (advanced booking advised on long-distance routes). Some inter-city and international services also make a stop at the bus

10

terminal behind Barcelona Sants station on C/Viriat (Ⓜ Sants Estació). Either way, you're only a short metro ride from the city centre.

Destinations Andorra (8 daily; 3hr 15min–4hr); Cadaqués (1–2 daily; 2hr 45min); Girona (Mon–Sat 6–9 daily, Sun 3 daily; 1hr 30min); Lleida (Mon–Fri 14 daily, Sat 12 daily, Sun 7 daily; 2hr–3hr); Lloret de Mar (12 daily; 1hr); Madrid (15 daily; 8hr); Palafrugell (7 daily; 2hr 15min); Tarragona (7 daily; 1hr 30min); Tossa de Mar (8 daily; 1hr 20min); Valencia (7 daily; 5hr 30min); Zaragoza (16 daily; 3hr 45min).

BY FERRY

Estació Marítima Ferries from the Balearics dock at the terminal in Port Vell, at the bottom of Avgda. Paral.lel (Ⓜ Drassanes), not far from the Ramblas. There are ticket offices inside the terminal (July & Aug are very busy) for services to Palma de Mallorca, Mahón and Ibiza, with Trasmediterranea (Ⓦ trasmediterranea.es) and Balearia (Ⓦ balearia.net). Navi Grandi Veloci (Ⓦ www.gnv.it) runs services to Genoa, Italy, and Tangiers, Morocco. Grimaldi Ferries (Ⓦ www.grimaldi-ferries.com) serves Rome,

Livorno and Sardinia in Italy as well as Tangiers, Morocco.

BY CAR

Driving into Barcelona Head for the Ronda Litoral, the southern half of the city's ring road. Following signs for "Port Vell" takes you towards the main exit for the old town; exits for Gran Vía de les Corts Catalanes (C-31) and Avgda. Diagonal will suit better if uptown Barcelona is your destination.

Parking City-centre garages and car parks (1hr from €3, 24hr from €30) are linked to display boards that indicate where there are free spaces. There are cheaper BSM (Barcelona Serveis Municipals) **long-term car parks** for residents and visitors, best option being the large Pza. del Fòrum car park at Diagonal Mar (Ⓜ El Maresme-Fòrum), where parking for one to five days costs €38.90, plus €7.50 for each additional day. Closer to the centre, there's the 24-hour BSM car park at Barcelona Nord bus station (C/d'Ali-Bei 54; Ⓜ Arc de Triomf) which costs €18.35/day. Otherwise, the ubiquitous Área Verda meter-zones throughout the city allow pay-and-display parking for visitors (around €3/hr, 1 or 2hr maximum stay).

INFORMATION

The city tourist board, Turisme de Barcelona (☎ 932 853 834, Ⓦ barcelonaturisme.com), has a very useful English-language website, plus offices in the city centre as well as at the airport and Barcelona Sants station. There are also **staffed kiosks** in main tourist areas, such as on the Ramblas and outside the Sagrada Família, which sell discount passes and entrance tickets for popular attractions.

Turisme de Barcelona Main tourist office is at Pza. de Catalunya 17, opposite El Corte Inglés, Ⓜ Catalunya (daily 9.30am–9.30pm); also a Barri Gòtic office at Pza. de Sant Jaume, entrance at C/Ciutat 2, Ⓜ Jaume I (Mon–Fri 8.30am–8.30pm, Sat 9am–7pm, Sun & hols 9am–2pm). The main office is always busy – frustrating if you just want a quick answer to a question. There's also an accommodation desk, tour and ticket sales, and a gift shop.

Institut de Cultura Palau de la Virreina, Ramblas 99, Ⓜ Liceu (daily 10am–8.30pm; ☎ 933 161 000, Ⓦ bcn.cat /cultura). Cultural information office, for events, concerts, exhibitions and festivals; you can also buy tickets here.

Centre d'Informació de Catalunya Palau Robert, Pg.

de Gràcia 107, Eixample, Ⓜ Diagonal (Mon–Sat 10am–8pm, Sun & hols 10am–2.30pm; ☎ 932 388 091 or ☎ 012, Ⓦ gencat.cat/palaurobert). Information about travel in Catalunya, plus exhibitions and events relating to all matters Catalan.

City Information Service The Ajuntament (City Hall)'s 24-hour ☎ 010 telephone enquiries service (English-speaking staff available) can help with transport queries, public services and other matters, while their website (Ⓦ bcn.cat) and that of the regional government; (Generalitat, Ⓦ gencat.cat) are absolute mines of information about every aspect of cultural, social and working life in Barcelona; both have English-language versions.

GETTING AROUND

Much of what you'll want to see in the city centre can be reached on foot in under 20min from Pza. de Catalunya. But Barcelona also has an excellent integrated **public-transport system**, which comprises the metro, buses, trams, local trains and a network of funicular railways and cable cars. The local transport authority, **Transports Metropolitans de Barcelona** (TMB; Ⓦ tmb.cat, English-language version available), has a very useful website, while route and ticket information is posted at major bus stops and all metro and tram stations. A transit plan divides the province into six zones, but as the entire metropolitan area of Barcelona (including the airport) falls within Zone 1, that's the only one you'll normally need to worry about.

TICKETS AND TRAVEL PASSES

Tickets On all the city's public transport (including night buses and funiculars) you can buy a single ticket every time you ride (€2.15).

Targetes It's much cheaper to buy a *targeta* (discount ticket-strip), available at metro, train, tram and funicular stations, but not on the buses. The T-10 ("tay day-oo" in Catalan) gives you ten journeys for €8.25, and can be used by more than one

SIGHTSEEING DISCOUNT CARDS

If you're going to do a lot of sightseeing in a short amount of time, you can save yourself money by buying one of the widely available **discount cards**. Choose carefully, since some are targeted at very specific interests, or cover things like transport that you might already have paid for – and bear in mind that there's plenty to do in town for free.

Barcelona Card (2 days €34, 3 days €44, 4 days €52 or 5 days €58, full details on ⓦ barcelonaturisme.com). Free public transport, plus big discounts at museums (some with free admission), venues, shops and restaurants. It's available at points of arrival, tourist offices and kiosks, and other outlets, though there's a ten percent discount if you buy online.

Articket (€30, valid three months; ⓦ articketbcn.org). Free admission into six major art centres and galleries (MNAC, MACBA, CCCB, Museu Picasso, Fundació Antoni Tàpies and Fundació Joan Miró). Buy at participating galleries, at Barcelona tourist offices and kiosks, or online.

Ruta del Modernisme (€12, valid one year; ⓦ rutadelmodernisme.com). English-language guidebook, map and discount-voucher package that covers 116 *modernista* buildings in Barcelona and other Catalan towns. It's also packaged with *Let's Go Out*, a guide to *modernista* bars and restaurants (total package €18), with both available from the Centre del Modernisme desk at the main Pza. de Catalunya tourist office.

10

person at a time – just feed it through the barrier for each person travelling. Changing methods of transport within 1hr 15min counts as one journey with the T-10 (re-punch the ticket – it only registers once). There's also a single-person, one-day T-Día at €7.60 for unlimited travel within Zone 1, plus Hola BCN! combinations up to five days costing €30.50.
Out of town Heading for Sitges, Montserrat and other out-of-town destinations, you'll need to buy a specific ticket or relevant zoned *targeta*.

METRO, BUSES AND TRAMS
Metro The metro runs on eleven lines (with additional lines under construction or being planned). Hours of operation are Monday until Thursday, plus Sunday and public holidays 5am to midnight; Friday and the eves of public holidays 5am to 2am; Saturday and the day before a public holiday 24hr.
Buses Bus routes operate daily, roughly from 4/5am until 10.30pm, though some lines stop earlier and some run on until after midnight. Night buses (*Nit bus*) fill in the gaps on all main routes, with services every twenty minutes to an hour from around 10pm to 4am. Many bus routes (including all night buses) stop in or near Pza. de Catalunya.
Trams Lines #T1, #T2 and #T3 (daily 5am–midnight, Fri & Sat until 2am, every 8–20min) depart from Pza. Francesc Macià and run along the uptown part of Avda. Diagonal to suburban destinations in the northwest – useful tourist stops are at L'Illa shopping centre and the María Cristina and Palau Reial metro stations. There's also the handy Line #T4 from Ciutadella-Vila Olímpica (where there's also a metro station), up to Glòries and then down Avda. Diagonal to Diagonal Mar and the Parc del Fòrum.

TRAINS
FGC The city's commuter train line – Ferrocarrils de la Generalitat de Catalunya (FGC; ☏ 012, ⓦ fgc.cat) – has its main stations at Pza. de Catalunya and Pza. d'Espanya. You'll need this for Montserrat and Tibidabo.
Renfe The national rail service, Renfe (☏ 902 320 320, ⓦ renfe.com), runs all other services out of Barcelona, with local lines – north to the Costa Mareseme and south to Sitges – designated as *Rodiales/Cercanías*. The hub is Barcelona Sants, with services also passing through Pza. de Catalunya (heading north) and Pg. de Gràcia (south).

TAXIS
Black-and-yellow taxis have a green roof light on when available for hire – most short journeys across town run to around €9. There's a minimum charge of €2.60 and after that it's €1.03/km (€1.30–1.40 after 8pm, and on Sat, Sun & hols), with surcharges for baggage and picking up from Barcelona Sants station and the airport. Taxis have meters, so prices are transparent; asking for a receipt (*rebut*) should clear up any confusion. They can be called on the following numbers (though English is unlikely to be spoken): ☏ 933 222 222, ☏ 933 033 033, ☏ 933 300 300, ☏ 934 208 088.

CYCLING AND BIKE RENTAL
The city council's Bicing pick-up and drop-off scheme (ⓦ bicing.cat) is touted as Barcelona's new public transport system. You'll see the red bike and bike stations all over the city, but Bicing is not aimed at tourists, rather at locals who are encouraged to use the bikes for short trips. However, there are plenty of bike-rental outfits more geared to tourist requirements. Rental costs around €20, while many bike tour companies (see p.685) can also fix you up with a rental bike.
Bike rental outfits Biciclot, Pg. Marítim 33–35, Port Olímpic (ⓜ Ciutadella-Vila Olímpica), ☏ 932 219 778, ⓦ bikinginbarcelona.net; Un Coxte Menys/Bicicleta Barcelona, C/Esparteria 3, La Ribera (ⓜ Barceloneta), ☏ 932 682 105, ⓦ bicicletabarcelona.com.

10

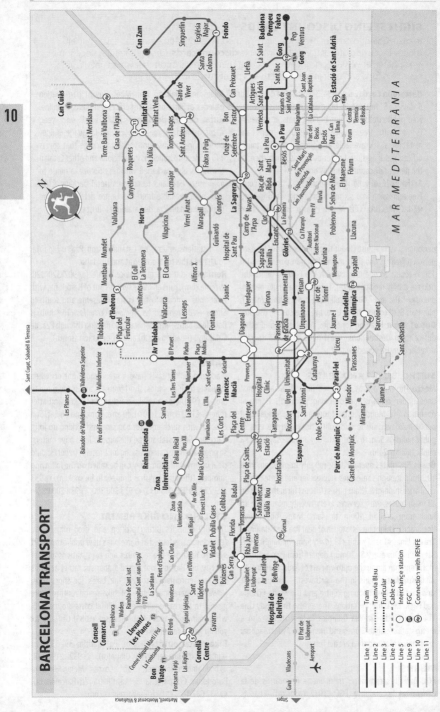

BARCELONA TRANSPORT

Legend:
- Line 1
- Line 2
- Line 3
- Line 4
- Line 5
- Line 9
- Line 10
- Line 11
- Tram
- Tramvia Blau
- Funicular
- Cable car
- Interchange station
- FGC
- Connection with RENFE

MAR MEDITERRÀNIA

TOURS

You can see the sights in Barcelona on anything from a Segway to a hot-air balloon. Walking tours and bike tours in particular are hugely popular, while other operators offer tapas-bar crawls, party nights and out-of-town excursions. Highest profile are the open-top sightseeing bus tours, whose board-at-will services stop outside every attraction in the city.

Barcelona Walking Tours ☏ 932 853 832, ⓦ barcelonaturisme.com. The tourist office coordinates a popular series of walks and tours, including a 2hr tour of the Barri Gòtic (daily 9.30am; €15.50), a 2hr Picasso tour (Tues, Thurs & Sat at 3pm; €21.50, includes entry to Picasso Museum), or a 2hr Modernisme tour (Fri & Sat, Oct–May at 3pm, June–Sept at 6pm; €15.50). Times given are for the current English-language tours, advance booking essential, ten percent discount if you buy online.

Bike Tours Barcelona ☏ 932 682 105, ⓦ biketoursbarcelona.com. Find the red-T-shirted guides in Pza. de Sant Jaume in the Barri Gòtic (top of C/Ciutat) – tours last 3hr (daily 11am, plus April–Sept Fri–Mon 4.30pm; €22), no reservations required.

Bus Turístic ⓦ barcelonabusturistic.cat. The main official sightseeing service (departures every 5–25min) with over forty stops on three combined routes, linking all the main tourist sights. Northern (red) and southern (blue) routes depart from Pza. de Catalunya (daily: April–Sept 9am–8pm; Oct–March 9am–7pm), and a full circuit on either route takes 2hr. The green Fòrum route (daily April–Sept 9.30am–8pm) runs from Port Olímpic to Diagonal Mar and back via the beaches, and takes 40min. Tickets available on board and online, at Sants station or at any

tourist office (€27 for one day, €35 for two days, children aged 4–12 €16/20 respectively, under-4s free).

Catamaran Orsom ☏ 934 410 537, ⓦ barcelona-orsom.com. Afternoon catamaran trips around the port (noon & 2.30pm; €15.50) and evening jazz cruises (6pm & 8pm; €17.50), with departures Easter week & June–Sept daily, May & Oct daily except Tues & Wed. There's a ticket kiosk at the quayside opposite the Columbus statue, but you should call in advance to be certain of departures.

Las Golondrinas ☏ 934 423 106, ⓦ lasgolondrinas.com. Daily sightseeing boats depart from Pza. Portal de la Pau, behind the Columbus monument – trips are either around the port (40min; €7.20, under-10s €2.80, under-4s free), or port and coast including the Port Olímpic and Diagonal Mar (90min; €15, under-10s €5.50, under-4s free). Departures are at least hourly June–Sept, less frequently Oct–May but still daily.

My Favourite Things ☏ 637 265 405, ⓦ myft.net. Highly individual tours – whether it's where and what the locals eat, Art Nouveau discoveries or forgotten neighbourhoods. Tours (in English) cost €26/person for groups of four or more and last around 4hr, advance bookings essential – call or email for latest information or tailor-made requests.

ACCOMMODATION

Finding a **hotel** vacancy in Barcelona can be very difficult, so it's always best to book in advance, especially at Easter, in summer and during festivals or trade fairs. Prices are high for Spain – absolute cheapest rooms in a simple family-run hotel, sharing a bathroom, cost around €50 (singles from €30), though for private facilities €70–80 a night is more realistic. Places with a bit of boutique styling start at around €100, while for Barcelona's most fashionable hotels, count on €250–400 a night. In youth hostels, or cheap hotels with dorms, a bed goes for €15–30 a night, depending on the season.

You can **reserve** hotel accommodation online with the city tourist board or make same-day bookings in person only at their **tourist offices** (see p.682). For apartments, try Barcelona On-Line (ⓦ barcelona-on-line.es) or Inside-BCN (ⓦ inside-bcn.com), while Barcelona-based **My Favourite Things** (ⓦ myft.net) has an eye for offbeat rooms and apartments in private houses.

THE RAMBLAS

★ **Hostal Benidorm** Ramblas 37 ☏ 933 022 054, ⓦ hostalbenidorm.com; ⓜ Drassanes; map pp.648–649. Refurbished *pensión* opposite Pza. Reial that offers real value for money. Plain rooms available for one to five people, all with bathtubs or showers, and a balcony and Ramblas view if you're prepared to pay a bit more. **€75**

Hostal Mare Nostrum Ramblas 67, entrance on C/Sant Pau 2 ☏ 933 185 340, ⓦ hostalmarenostrum.com; ⓜ Liceu; map pp.648–649. A cheery Ramblas *pensión* whose English-speaking management offers comfortable double, triple and family rooms with satellite TV and a/c.

The updated rooms – all are en suite – are modern and double-glazed against the noise, and some come with balconies and street views. **€100**

★ **Hotel H1898** Ramblas 109, entrance on C/Pintor Fortuny ☏ 935 529 552, ⓦ hotel1898.com; ⓜ Catalunya; map pp.648–649. The former HQ of the Philippines Tobacco Company has four grades of eye-popping boutique rooms (the standard is "Classic") in deep red, green or black. Public areas are similarly dramatic, like the neo-colonial lounge and bar, and the fanciest *Starbucks* in town. There are both outdoor and indoor pools and a glam spa, too. Special rates from €200. **€255**

10

10

WHAT'S THE NEIGHBOURHOOD LIKE?

First things first: if you hanker after a **Ramblas** view, you'll pay for the privilege – generally speaking, there are much better deals to be had either side of the famous boulevard, often just a minute's walk away. Most of Barcelona's cheapest accommodation (as well as some classy boutique choices) is found in the **Barri Gòtic** and **El Raval** neighbourhoods, which can both still have their rough edges – be careful (without being paranoid) when coming and going after dark. East of the Barri Gòtic, in **Sant Pere** and **La Ribera**, there are a number of safely sited budget, mid-range and boutique options, handy for the Picasso museum and Born nightlife area. North of Pza. de Catalunya, the **Eixample** has some of the city's most fashionable hotels, often housed in converted palaces and mansions and located just a few minutes' walk from the *modernista* architectural masterpieces. For waterfront views look at **Port Vell** at the end of the Ramblas, and at the **Port Olímpic** southeast of the old town. If you prefer neighbourhood living, then **Gràcia** is the best base, as you're only ever a short walk away from its bars, restaurants and clubs.

BARRI GÒTIC

Hostal Fernando C/Ferran 31 ☎ 933 017 993, ⊚ hfernando.com; Ⓜ Liceu; map pp.648–649. Light, modern rooms all with a/c and private bathroom (some cheaper singles share facilities). Straightforward dorm accommodation also available in en-suite rooms that sleep four to eight. Dorms €27, doubles €89

★ **Hostal Rembrandt** C/Portaferrissa 23 ☎ 933 181 011, ⊚ hostalrembrandt.com; Ⓜ Liceu; map pp.648–649. A safe, old-town budget *pensión*. Simple tile-floored rooms (a bit cheaper without private bathroom) have a street-side balcony or little patio, while larger rooms are more versatile and can sleep up to four. €65

Hotel Cantón C/Nou de Sant Francesc 40 ☎ 933 173 019, ⊚ hotelcanton-bcn.com; Ⓜ Drassanes; map pp.648–649. A modest one-star hotel that's only two blocks off the Ramblas and close to the harbour and Port Vell. Forty-seven rooms feature uniform blue-and-white trim curtains and bedspreads, central heating and a/c, fridge and wardrobe. €78

★ **Hotel DO** Pza. Reial 1 ☎ 934 813 666, ⊚ hoteldoreial .com; Ⓜ Liceu; map pp.648–649. Renowned Catalan architect Oriol Bohigas led the renovation of this nineteenth-century Neoclassical building on the city's emblematic Pza. Reial. The result is a gastronomic boutique hotel with eighteen impeccably appointed rooms, most overlooking the square, which seamlessly blends the contemporary with the timeless. On top of this, quite literally, is the rooftop lounge and blue-tiled plunge pool, plus spa with sauna, steam room and heated bench. It's not cheap, but the finer things in life rarely are. €230

Hotel el Jardí Pza. Sant Josep Oriol 1 ☎ 933 015 900, ⊚ eljardi-barcelona.com; Ⓜ Liceu; map pp.648–649. The hotel's location, overlooking the charming Pza. del Pi, is what sells this place – and explains the steepish prices for rooms that can seem a bit bare and poky. But the best (the top ones have terraces, from €10 extra) do look directly onto the square. €90

Itaca Hostel C/Ripoll 21 ☎ 933 019 751, ⊚ itacahostel .com; Ⓜ Jaume I; map pp.648–649. Bright and breezy converted house close to the Catedral, offering spacious hostel rooms (sleeping six, eight or ten) with balconies. Dorms are mixed, though you can also reserve a private room or apartment (sleeps up to six, €120). Dorms €27, doubles €70

Pensió Alamar C/Comtessa de Sobradiel 1 ☎ 933 025 012; ⊚ pensioalamar.com; Ⓜ Liceu/Jaume I; map pp.648–649. If you don't mind sharing a bathroom then this makes a convenient base. There are twelve rooms (including singles, doubles and triples), most with little balconies, and while space is tight, there's a friendly welcome, laundry service and use of a kitchen. No credit cards. €45

★ **Pensión Mari-Luz** C/Palau 4, 2º ☎ 933 173 463, ⊚ pensionmariluz.com; Ⓜ Jaume I/Liceu; map pp.648–649. This old mansion, on a quieter-than-usual Barri Gòtic street, offers inexpensive rooms (most share bathrooms), plus a more personal touch than many other places of its kind. It can be a tight squeeze when full, but a dozen apartments (sleeping two to six, €90–140) a few minutes' walk away in the Raval offer more space. €65

PORT VELL

★ **Bonic Barcelona** C/Josep Anselm Clavé 9 ☎ 626 053 434, ⊚ bonic-barcelona.com; Ⓜ Drassanes; map pp.648–649. Chic, charming and peaceful "urban guesthouse", just a few steps from the Ramblas. The eight rooms are simply furnished, and the three renovated bathrooms are shared. Advance reservations essential; minimum two-night stay required. €90

EL RAVAL

Barceló Raval Rambla del Raval 17–21 ☎ 933 201 490, ⊚ barcelo.com; Ⓜ Liceu/Sant Antoni; map pp.648–649. This glow-in-the-dark tower is a neighbourhood landmark and has sophisticated, open-plan rooms plus a 360-degree top-floor terrace with plunge pool and sensational city views. **€127**

Casa Camper C/d'Elisabets 11 ☏933 426 280, ⓦcasacamper.com; ⓜUniversitat/Liceu; map pp.648–649. Synonymous with creative, comfy shoes, Barcelona-based Camper has taken a bold step into the hospitality business with this sleek, minimalist hotel. The rooms are divided by a corridor: the "sleeping" side faces a six-storey-tall vertical garden; the other part is a "mini-lounge" with a flat-screen TV, hammock and street-facing balcony. **€215**

★**Hostal Grau** C/Ramelleres 27 ☏933 018 135, ⓦhostalgrau.com; ⓜCatalunya; map pp.648–649. A really friendly *pensión* with attractive rooms on several floors; you'll pay around €20 more for superior rooms with balconies, while two private apartments in the same building (sleeping two to six, available by the night, €150) offer a bit more independence. **€85**

★**Hotel España** C/Sant Pau 9–11 ☏935 500 000, ⓦhotelespanya.com; ⓜLiceu; map pp.648–649. The *modernista* icon has been sumptuously restored as a four-star-plus hotel, and the gem-like interior – colourful tiles, bright mosaics, sculpted marble, iron swirls and marine motifs – has no equal in Barcelona. Guest rooms are a perfectly judged boutique blend of earth tones and designer style, and there's a plunge pool and chill-out deck on the roof terrace. The handsome house restaurant – known as *Fonda España* – offers contemporary Catalan bistro dishes by hot chef Martín Berasategui. **€135**

Hotel Onix Liceo C/Nou de la Rambla 36 ☏934 816 441, ⓦonixliceohotel.com; ⓜLiceu/Drassanes; map pp.648–649. Steps from Palau Güell, this four-star hotel features minimalist decor that melds nicely with the building's older architectural elements. There's a tropical patio and big-for-Barcelona pool on the ground floor and an airy Mozarab-influenced lounge area. **€130**

★**Market Hotel** C/Comte Borrell 68, at Ptge. Sant Antoni Abat ☏933 251 205, ⓦmarkethotel.com.es; ⓜSant Antoni; map p.665. The designer-budget *Market* makes a definite splash with its part Japanese, part neo-colonial look. There's also an impressive restaurant, where the food is exceptionally good value, while the hotel's vintage Asian-style *Bar Rosso* is a bit of a local hipsters' haunt. **€100**

SANT PERE

★**Pensió 2000** C/Sant Pere Més Alt 6, 1° ☏933 107 466, ⓦpensio2000.com; ⓜUrquinaona; map pp.648–649. As close to a traditional, family-style B&B as Barcelona gets – seven en-suite rooms (some overlook the Palau de la Música Catalana, across the street) in a welcoming mansion apartment strewn with books, plants and pictures. A third person could easily share most rooms (€20 supplement). **€90**

LA RIBERA

★**Chic & Basic Born** C/Princesa 50 ☏932 954 652, ⓦchicandbasic.com; ⓜJaume I; map pp.648–649. Punchily boutique and in-your-face, from the open-plan, all-in-white decor to laugh-aloud conceits like adjustable mood-lighting, sashaying plastic curtains and mirrored walls. There are other Chic & Basic outlets in the city centre as well as apartments (details on the website). **€120**

Equity Point Gothic C/Vigatans 5, online bookings only ⓦequity-point.com, hostel information ☏932 687 808; ⓜJaume I; map pp.648–649. Of the three Equity Point hostels, this is the most backpacker-orientated, which might or might not be a good thing, depending on your view, age and capacity for company. Dorms **€25**

★**Hostal Nuevo Colón** Avgda. Marquès de l'Argentera 19, 1° ☏933 195 077, ⓦhostalnuevocolon.com; ⓜBarceloneta; map pp.648–649. Well-kept *pensión* sporting spacious rooms kitted out with directors' chairs and double glazing – you'll save around €15 if you forgo a private bathroom. Sunny front rooms, lounge and terrace all have side views to Parc de la Ciutadella. **€70**

Hotel Banys Orientals C/l'Argenteria 37 ☏932 688 460, ⓦhotelbanysorientals.com; ⓜJaume I; map pp.648–649. Funky boutique hotel with 43 minimalist rooms, plus some more spacious duplex suites (€140) in a nearby building. Hardwood floors, crisp white sheets, sharp marble bathrooms and urban-chic decor – not to mention bargain prices for this sort of style – make it a hugely popular choice. **€115**

BARCELONETA

Equity Point Sea Pza. del Mar 1–4, online bookings only ⓦequity-point.com, hostel information ☏932 312 045; ⓜBarceloneta; map pp.644–645. The budget beachside choice. Neat little en-suite bunk rooms sleep four to eight, while the attached café looks right out onto the boardwalk and palm trees. Dorms **€26**

★**W Barcelona** Pza. de la Rosa dels Vents 1 ☏932 952 800, ⓦw-barcelona.com; ⓜBarceloneta; map pp.644–645. The signature building on the Barceloneta seafront is the stupendously cool, wave-shaped *W Barcelona*. There's a hip, resort feel, with direct beach access, the open-plan designer rooms have fantastic views through floor-to-ceiling windows, and facilities are first-rate, from the iPod docks to infinity pool. Dining in hotel restaurant *Bravo 24* is courtesy of creative Barcelona chef Carles Abellan. **€260**

PORT OLÍMPIC

Hotel Arts Barcelona C/Marina 19–21, Port Olímpic ☏932 211 000, ⓦhotelartsbarcelona.com; ⓜCiutadella-Vila Olímpica; map pp.644–645. Thirty-three floors of five-star-plus designer luxury, with fabulous views of the port and sea. Service and standards are first-rate, and the rooms feature floor-to-ceiling

10

windows and enormous marble bathrooms. Seafront gardens encompass an open-air pool and hot tub, and there's a 43rd-floor spa. **€295**

EIXAMPLE

★**The5Rooms** C/Pau Claris 72, 1º ☎933 427 880, ⓦwww.thefiverooms.com; Ⓜ Urquinaona; map pp.670–671. The owner's impeccable taste and fashion background is evident in gorgeous contemporary-styled B&B rooms and apartments (from €175 for two people), where the feel is house party rather than hotel – breakfast is served whenever you like, and owner Jessica is happy to sit down and talk you through her favourite bars, restaurants and galleries. **€165**

★**BarcelonaBB** C/Mallorca ☎637 977 263, ⓦbarcelonabb.com; ⓂVerdaguer/Girona; map pp.670–671. Lovely rooms, amiable hosts and a tasty breakfast shared with other happy travellers – what's not to love about this cheery B&B? Four rooms share two large bathrooms, while the master suite has its own private bathroom. An en-suite room as well as three apartments (€100–140) in another building offer more privacy, but the communal, congenial atmosphere is part of the charm. Advanced reservations essential (contact for directions). **€80**

★**Barcelona Urbany** Avgda. Meridiana 97 ☎932 458 414, ⓦbarcelonaurbany.com; ⓂClot; map pp.644–645. Huge steel-and-glass four hundred-bed hostel that's on handy metro and airport train routes (it's an easy ride in to Pza. de Catalunya). The rooms are boxy en suites with pull-down beds (sleeping two to eight) that are just as viable for couples on a budget as backpackers. Rates vary according to season, but go as low as €10 for dorms and €50 for rooms. Bar and terrace, plus free health club and pool entry in the same building. Dorms **€32**, doubles **€68**

★**BCN Fashion House** C/Bruc 13 ☎637 904 044, ⓦbcnfashionhouse.com; ⓂUrquinaona; map pp.670–671. Italian owners have added a touch of chic flair to what was formerly an atelier in Barcelona's "garment district", and the seven spacious, high-ceilinged rooms (some with a veranda) are lightened with prints, sculptures and artefacts from their travels. **€94**

Casa de Billy Gran Via de les Corts Catalanes ☎934 263 048, ⓦcasabillybarcelona.com; ⓂRocafort; map pp.670–671. A welcoming guesthouse in a restored nineteenth-century building near Pza. d'Espanya with sixteen spotless rooms (singles and doubles; some en suite) elegantly decorated by Billy himself with antique mirrors, armoires and chandeliers. It's a rich, refined and utterly charming experience – for a reasonable price. Two-night minimum, advance reservations essential (contact for directions), over-18s only. **€90**

★**Equity Point Centric** Pg. de Gràcia 33, online bookings only ⓦequity-point.com, hostel information ☎932 312 045; ⓂPasseig de Gràcia; map pp.670–671.

Bills itself as "one of the most spectacular hostels in Europe" and it's hard to disagree, with around 450 beds spread across several storeys of a refurbished *modernista* building in a swish midtown location. Dorms sleep up to fourteen, while private rooms are also available (sleeping two to four, low-season rates from €90), all with lockers and en-suite shower rooms, and many with a balcony and views. Dorms **€22**, doubles **€130**

Hostal Girona C/Girona 24, 1º ☎932 650 259, ⓦhostalgirona.com; ⓂUrquinaona; map pp.670–671. Delightful, family-run *pensión* with a wide range of cosy, traditional rooms (not all en suite, from as low as €60), plus corridors laid with rugs, polished wooden doors, antique paintings and restored furniture throughout. **€85**

Hotel Axel C/d'Aribau 33 ☎933 239 393, ⓦaxelhotels. com; ⓂUniversitat; map pp.670–671. The *Axel's* snazzy "heterofriendly" boutique stylings are a real hit with gay visitors. It's a hip but relaxed space with designer rooms (featuring complimentary beauty products), a bar and restaurant that are part of the local scene, plus fabulous terrace pool and "Skybar". **€150**

Hotel Omm C/Rosselló 265 ☎934 454 000, ⓦhotelomm.es; ⓂDiagonal; map pp.670–671. The glam designer experience that is *Omm* means minimalist rooms, a studiously chic bar, Michelin-starred restaurant (closed Mon & Sun & Aug), plus terrace, pool and Spaciomm "relaxation centre", not to mention fearsomely handsome staff. **€200**

Mandarin Oriental Pg. de Gràcia 38–40 ☎931 518 888, ⓦmandarinoriental.com/barcelona; ⓂPasseig de Gràcia; map pp.670–671. The latest designer addition to Barcelona's most prestigious avenue fills the premises of a former bank building with a soaring white atrium and a serene selection of gorgeously light rooms. There's the obligatory superstar restaurant, *Moments*, while bar, spa, mimosa garden and rooftop "dipping pool" combine oriental tranquillity and Euro cool. **€400**

★**Somnio Barcelona** C/Diputació 251 2º ☎932 725 308, ⓦsomniohostels.com; ⓂPasseig de Gràcia; map pp.670–671. Simple but smart rooms with wood-block floors cater for singles, couples and friends. There are four spacious twin rooms, four double rooms (two are en suite) and a single room (some of the rooms have balconies). **€75**

GRÀCIA

★**Casa Gracia** Pg. de Gràcia 116 ☎931 874 497, ⓦcasagraciabcn.com; ⓂDiagonal; map p.677. A vibrant and stylish space spread over six floors in a *modernista* building. The crisply decorated rooms (from dorms to doubles to six-bed private rooms) are en suite, while the deluxe suite pampers with a spa bath, slippers and bathrobes. Though *Casa Gracia* is technically a hostel, you'll feel like you're staying in a (pretty good) hotel. Breakfast included. Dorms **€25**, doubles **€90**, deluxe suite **€135**

EATING

You'll probably do most of your **eating** where you do most of your sightseeing. However, if you venture no farther than the Ramblas, or the streets around La Seu, you are not going to experience the best of the city's cuisine – in the main tourist areas, food and service can be indifferent and prices high. Instead, explore the backstreets of neighbourhoods like Sant Pere, La Ribera, El Raval and Poble Sec, where you'll find excellent restaurants, some little more than hole-in-the-wall taverns, others surprisingly funky and chic. Most of the big-ticket, destination-dining restaurants are found in the Eixample, while Gràcia is a pleasant place to spend the evening, with plenty of good mid-range restaurants. For fish and seafood, you're best off in the harbourside Barceloneta district or at the Port Olímpic.

Most cafés are open from 7am or 8am until midnight, or much later – so whether it's coffee first thing or a late-night nibble, you'll find somewhere to cater for you. Restaurants generally open 1pm to 4pm and 8.30pm to 11pm, though in tourist zones like the Ramblas and Port Olímpic, restaurants tend to stay open all day.

RAMBLAS

CAFÉS

★**Cafè de l'Òpera** Ramblas 74 ☎933 177 585; ⓦcafeoperabcn.com; Ⓜ Liceu; map pp.648–649. If you're going to pay through the nose for a Ramblas seat, it may as well be at this famous old café-bar opposite the opera house (drinks and snacks from around €2), with its sought-after pavement tables. Daily 8.30am–2.30am.

Café Zurich Pza. Catalunya 1 ☎933 179 153; Ⓜ Catalunya; map pp.648–649. The most famous meet-and-greet café in town right at the top of the Ramblas underneath El Triangle shopping centre. Sit inside if you don't want to be bothered by endless rounds of buskers and beggars. Mon–Fri 8am–11pm, Sat 8am–midnight, Sun 9am–midnight.

Escribà Ramblas 83 ☎933 016 027, ⓦescriba.es; Ⓜ Liceu; map pp.648–649. Classy pastry shop in the historic *modernista* Antiga Casa Figueras building near the Boqueria market that many rate as the best bakery in Barcelona. The gorgeous individual-size cakes start at €4.50. Daily 9am–9pm.

TAPAS BARS

★**Bar Pinotxo** Mercat de la Boqueria, Ramblas 91 ☎933 171 731; ⓦpinotxobar.com; Ⓜ Liceu; map pp.648–649. The market's most renowned refuelling stop – just inside the main entrance on the right. Let the cheery staff steer you towards the tapas and daily specials (€5–15), anything from a slice of *tortilla* to fried baby squid. Mon–Sat 6.30am–4pm; closed Aug.

BARRI GÒTIC

CAFÉS

Bar del Pi Pza. Sant Josep Oriol 1 ☎933 022 123; ⓦbardelpi.com; Ⓜ Liceu; map pp.648–649. Best known for its terrace tables on one of Barcelona's prettiest squares. Linger over drinks, tapas (€1.50–10) and sandwiches (€4–6) as the old town reveals its charms, especially during the weekend artists' market. Tues–Fri 9am–11pm, Sat 9.30am–11pm, Sun 10am–10pm.

★**Caj Chai** C/Sant Domènec del Call 12 ☎933 019 592, ⓦcajchai.com; map pp.648–649. This refined backstreet boudoir with a lovely *terraza* offers a menu of painstakingly prepared teas (from €3), ranging from Moroccan mint to organic Nepalese *oolong*. Mon 3–10pm, Tues–Sun 10.30am–10pm.

Granja Dulcinea C/Petritxol 2 ☎933 026 824, ⓦgranjadulcinea.com; Ⓜ Liceu; map pp.648–649. One of the old town's age-old treats is to come here for a thick hot chocolate, slathered in cream (€3.10). It's a bygone-era kind of place, with dickie-bow-wearing waiters patrolling the beamed and panelled room. Daily 9am–1pm & 5–9pm; closed Aug.

TAPAS BARS

★**Bodega La Plata** C/Mercè 28 ☎933 151 009, ⓦbarlaplata.com; Ⓜ Drassanes; map pp.648–649. A classic taste of the old town, with a marble counter open to the street and dirt-cheap wine served straight from the barrel. For €5 or so you can get a couple of drinks and a dish of the speciality anchovies. Mon–Sat 9am–3pm & 6.30–11pm.

WHAT'S COOKING IN BARCELONA?

The minimalist, food-as-chemistry approach, pioneered by Catalan super-chef Ferran Adrià (of *El Bulli* fame), has Barcelona in a vice-like grip. The best local chefs continue to reinterpret classic Catalan dishes in innovative ways, and while prices in these gastro-temples are high there's a trend towards more economic, bistro-style dining even by the hottest chefs. The current fad is the fusion of Mediterranean and Asian flavours – a so-called **"Mediterrasian" cuisine**. It rears its head especially in the world of tapas, and in Barcelona these days, you're as likely to get shrimp tempura or a yucca chip as you are to get a garlic mushroom.

10

Sensi Tapas C/Ample 26 ☎ 932 956 588, ⓦ sensi.es; ⓜ Drassanes; map pp.648–649. Best to make reservations as this intimate space quickly fills with diners looking for tapas with an exotic spin. There are impeccably executed classics, but the stars of the show, such as the tender Iberian pork *tataki* and mussels steamed with heady red curry and basil, take their cues from further afield (€5–12). Daily 7pm–midnight.

RESTAURANTS

Bidasoa C/Serra 21 ☎ 933 818 063; ⓜ Drassanes; map pp.648–649. Tucked away on a narrow street in La Mercè, this third generation-owned restaurant offers simple and fresh Catalan and Basque-Navarre dishes – all of which are served by jocular staff in a bright, rustic dining room – at a good price (€5–€9). Tues–Thurs 1–5pm & 8–11pm, Fri & Sat 1–4pm & 8pm–midnight, Sun 1–5pm.

★**Café de l'Acadèmia** C/Lledó 1 ☎ 933 198 253; ⓜ Jaume I; map pp.648–649. Great for a date or a lazy lunch, with creative Catalan cooking served in a romantic stone-flagged restaurant or outside in the medieval square. Prices are pretty reasonable (mains €11–18) and it's always busy, so dinner reservations essential. Mon–Fri 1.30–4pm & 8.30–11.30pm; closed 2 weeks in Aug.

EL RAVAL
CAFÉS

★**Federal** C/Parlament 39 ☎ 931 873 607, ⓦ federalcafe.es; ⓜ Sant Antoni; map p.665. Effortlessly cool café, squished into a corner townhouse with a great little roof-garden on top. Australian owners have imported their own funky vibe, so whether you're looking for toast with Vegemite, a glass of New Zealand *sav blanc* or a dandelion soy latte, you can guarantee that there's nowhere else quite like this in Barcelona. Mon–Thurs 8am–11pm, Fri 8am–1am, Sat 9am–1am, Sun 9am–5.30pm.

Granja M. Viader C/Xuclà 4–6 ☎ 933 183 486, ⓦ granjaviader.cat; ⓜ Liceu; map pp.648–649. The oldest traditional *granja* (milk bar) in town has a pavement plaque outside for services to the city. Signature drink is their own invention "Cacaolat" (a popular chocolate drink), or try *mel i mató* (curd cheese and honey) or *llet Mallorquina* (fresh milk with cinnamon and lemon rind). Drinks and pastries from €3.50. Mon–Sat 9am–1.15pm & 5–9.15pm.

★**El Jardí** C/l'Hospital 56 ☎ 933 291 550, ⓦ eljardibarcelona.es; map pp.648–649. The "garden bar", hidden in the elegant courtyard of the Gothic Hospital de la Santa Creu is a real away-from-the-bustle find – drinks, snacks, salads and sandwiches (€2–10) during the day, plus a decent lunch menu (€12) and a changing list of market-fresh tapas. Mon–Fri 9am–midnight, Sat noon–midnight, Sun 11am–midnight.

TAPAS BARS

★**Dos Palillos** C/Elisabets 9 ☎ 933 040 513, ⓦ dospalillos.com; ⓜ Catalunya; map pp.648–649. This hipster hangout is a flag-waver for Asian fusion tapas, which offers à la carte *dim sum* in the front bar (Cantonese caramelized walnuts to steamed dumplings, mostly €5–7) and a back-room, counter-style Asian bar where tasting menus (€60, €70 and €85, reservations required) feature all the highlights. Tues & Wed 7.30–11.30pm, Thurs–Sat 1.30–3.30pm & 7.30–11.30pm; closed 2 weeks in Jan & 3 weeks in Aug.

RESTAURANTS

Bar Ra C/Carme 31 ☎ 615 959 872, ⓦ ratown.com; ⓜ Liceu; map pp.648–649. A hip little corner behind the Boqueria market, with a groove-ridden music policy, a funky feel and a sunny *terraza*. The menu is eclectic to say the least – veggie lasagne to tuna with wasabi and avocado – but it's all good stuff. A meal costs around €25. Mon–Thurs 7pm–2am, Fri & Sat 7pm–2.30am.

Cera 23 C/Cera 23 ☎ 934 420 808, ⓦ cera23.com; ⓜ Sant Antoni; map pp.648–649. Start your meal at this charming Galicia-meets-the-Mediterranean bistro with an effervescent blackberry mojito, and then tuck into market-fresh dishes like grilled duck with apples or a black rice-and-seafood "volcano" (mains €12–18). Daily 6.30pm–2am.

Romesco C/Sant Pau 28 ☎ 933 189 381; ⓦ restaurante-romesco.blogspot.co.uk; ⓜ Liceu; map pp.648–649. As long as you accept the limitations (dining under strip-lights, gruff waiters) you can hardly go wrong, as the most expensive dish on the menu in this simple diner is a €9 grilled sirloin and most dishes go for €6 or less. Mon–Fri 1–11.30pm, Sat 1–4.30pm & 8–11.30pm; closed Aug.

SANT PERE
TAPAS BARS

★**Mosquito** C/Carders 46 ☎ 932 687 569, ⓦ mosquitotapas.com; ⓜ Jaume I; map pp.648–649. A funky Asian tapas bar, festooned with hanging paper lanterns, which pours artisan beers and offers an authentic, made-to-order *dim sum* menu (dishes €3–5), from shrimp dumplings to tofu rolls. Mon 7.30pm–1am, Tues–Thurs & Sun 1pm–1am, Fri & Sat 1pm–2.30am.

RESTAURANTS

★**El Atril** C/Carders 23 ☎ 933 101 220, ⓦ atrilbarcelona.com; ⓜ Jaume I; map pp.648–649. Aussie-owned bistro-bar with a popular summer terraza – lunch is always a steal, with tapas served at other times, and dinner from 7pm. The changing menu ranges from *moules frites* to grilled kangaroo (mains €8–15). Mon 6pm–midnight, Tues–Sun noon–midnight.

Casa Mari y Rufo C/Freixures 11 ☎ 933 197 302;

ⓦ www.mariyrufo.com; ⓜ Jaume I; map pp.648–649. A great place for no-frills market cooking, with a busy family turning out quick-fried sardines, grilled Catalan sausage, steak and chips and the like – or ask what's good from the fish stalls that day. With lunch for an unbeatable €12 and dinner around €30, the locals know a good deal when they see one. Mon–Wed 1–6pm, Thurs & Fri 8pm–2am, Sat noon–2am.

Comerç 24 C/Comerc 24 ☎ 933 192 102, ⓦ carlesabellan.com; ⓜ Jaume I/Arc de Triomf; map pp.648–649. Chef Carles Abellan calls his cutting-edge cuisine "glocal" (ie, global plus local) and in the oh-so-cool interior you're presented with tapas-style dishes, mixing flavours and textures with seeming abandon but to calculated effect (such as foie gras and truffle hamburger, shot glasses of frothy soup, and tuna sashimi on pizza). Prices are around €80 a head. Tues–Sat 1.30–3.30pm & 8.30–11pm; closed 2 weeks in Aug.

LA RIBERA
TAPAS BARS

★**Cal Pep** Pza. de les Olles 8 ☎ 933 107 961, ⓦ calpep .com; ⓜ Barceloneta; map pp.648–649. You may have to queue for this famous tapas bar (there are no reservations), and prices are high for what's effectively a bar meal (up to €60 a head) but it's definitely worth it for the likes of impeccably fried squid, grilled monk fish, Catalan sausage and beans, and baby squid and chickpeas. Mon 7.30–11.30pm, Tues–Fri 1–3.45pm & 7.30–11.30pm, Sat 1.15–3.45pm; closed 3 weeks in Aug.

Mercat Princesa C/Flassaders 21, La Ribera ☎ 932 681 518, ⓦ mercatprincesa.com; ⓜ Jaume I; map pp.648–649. Enjoy food from more than a dozen gourmet stalls (think plump Chinese dumplings and artfully mounded montaditos; from €2.50) at communal tables inside a restored fourteenth-century palace's interior courtyard. It's a great option when your taste buds are pulling you in multiple directions. Mon–Wed & Sun 9am–midnight, Thurs–Sat 9am–1am.

El Xampanyet C/Montcada 22 ☎ 933 197 003; ⓜ Jaume I; map pp.648–649. Traditional blue-tiled bar doing a roaring trade in sparkling cava, cider and tapas (anchovies are the speciality, but there's also marinaded tuna, spicy mussels, sun-dried tomatoes, sliced meats and cheese). A drink and a couple of tapas will cost around €10. Tues–Sat noon–3.30pm & 7–11.30pm, Sun noon–4pm & 7–11.30pm; closed 2 weeks in Aug.

RESTAURANTS

Senyor Parellada C/Argenteria 37 ☎ 933 105 094, ⓦ senyorparellada.com; ⓜ Jaume I; map pp.648–649. An utterly gorgeous renovation of an eighteenth-century building is the mellow backdrop for genuine home-style Catalan cuisine – cuttlefish and cod, stuffed cabbage rolls,

duck with figs. Most dishes cost between €8 and €15. Daily 1–3.45pm & 8.30–11.30pm.

BARCELONETA
TAPAS BARS

★**Cova Fumada** C/Baluard 56 ☎ 932 214 061; ⓜ Barceloneta; map pp.648–649. Behind brown wooden doors on Barceloneta's market square (there's no sign), this rough-and-ready tavern may not look like much but the food's great –tapas made with ingredients fresh from the market (€2–10), from griddled sardines to the house speciality, the *bomba* (spicy potato-meatball). Mon–Wed 9am–3.20pm, Thurs & Fri 9am–3.20pm & 6–8.20pm, Sat 9am–1.20pm; closed Aug.

Jai-Ca C/Ginebra 9 & 13 ☎ 932 683 265; ⓜ Barceloneta; map pp.648–649. Always a winning choice for seafood tapas (dishes up to €10), with bundles of razor clams, plump anchovies, stuffed mussels and other platters piled high on the bar. Its new second location at no. 9 (Mon & Wed–Sun noon–midnight) serves the same menu. Tues–Sun 9am–midnight.

RESTAURANTS

Can Majó C/Almirall Aixada 23 ☎ 932 215 455, ⓦ canmajo.es; ⓜ Barceloneta; map pp.644–645. A lovely summer terraza by the beach promenade, where you can tuck into wonderful rice dishes, *fideuà* (noodles with seafood), *suquet* (fish stew) or grilled fish. Expect to pay €40–50 a head. Tues–Sat 1–4pm & 8–11.30pm, Sun 1–4pm.

★**Can Maño** C/Baluard 12 ☎ 933 193 082; ⓜ Barceloneta; map pp.648–649. This old-fashioned diner is packed with noisy locals around formica tables. Expect fried or grilled fish, roughhouse wine and absolutely no frills, but it's an authentic experience, which should cost around €15 a head. Mon 8–11pm, Tues–Fri 8.15–11am, 12.15–4pm & 8–11pm, Sat 8.15–11am & 12.15–4pm; closed Aug.

PORT OLÍMPIC
RESTAURANTS

Agua Pg. Marítim 30 ☎ 932 251 272, ⓦ grupotragaluz .com; ⓜ Ciutadella-Vila Olímpica; map pp.644–645. By far the nicest boardwalk restaurant on the beachfront strip, perfect for brunch, with a seasonal, contemporary Mediterranean menu – grills, *risotti*, pasta, salads and tapas (most dishes €9–23). Mon–Thurs 1–3.45pm & 8–11.30pm, Fri 1–3.45pm & 8–12.30am, Sat 1–4.30pm & 8–11.30pm & Sun 1–4.30pm.

POBLE SEC
TAPAS BARS

★**Quimet i Quimet** C/Poeta Cabanyes 25 ☎ 934 423 142; ⓜ Paral.lel; map p.665. In Poble Sec's cosiest tapas

10

bar, little plates of classy finger-food (mostly €3–10) are served reverently from the minuscule counter – things like roast onions, marinaded mushrooms, stuffed cherry tomatoes and anchovy-wrapped olives. Mon–Fri noon–4pm & 7–10.30pm, Sat noon–4pm; closed Aug.

Tickets Avgda. Paral.lel 164; online reservations only ⓦ ticketsbar.es/web; ⓜ Poble Sec; map p.665. Swanky tapas bar under the star-studded helm of pastry-chef supremo Albert Adrià and his *El Bulli*-famed brother Ferran Adrià. It's terrifically classy (dishes €5–20 each, expect to spend €70), but with only eighty covers a night, and online reservations up to two months in advance, you can't guarantee a table. Tues–Fri 7–11pm, Sat 1–3.30pm & 7–11.30pm; closed 2 weeks in Aug.

RESTAURANTS

★**La Tomaquera** C/Margarit 58, ☎ 675 902 389; ⓜ Poble Sec; map p.665. Chatter-filled tavern where the grilled chicken is sensational and the entrecôtes enormous (most mains €8–15). Locals limber up with an appetizer of pan-fried snails with chorizo and tomato. Tues–Sat 1–3.45pm & 8–11pm, Sun 1–3.45pm (closed Sun in June & July); closed Aug.

EIXAMPLE

CAFÉS

Fast Vínic C/Diputació 251 ☎ 934 873 241, ⓦ www .fastvinic.com; ⓜ Passeig de Gràcia; map pp.670–671. Designer sandwich bar with an emphasis on top-of-the-range ingredients from sustainable sources (sandwiches mostly €5–12), plus a range of more than twenty Catalan wines, starting at pocket-money prices. Mon–Sat noon–midnight.

TAPAS BARS

★**Tapas 24** C/Diputació 269 ☎ 934 880 977, ⓦ carlesabellan.com; ⓜ Passeig de Gràcia; map pp.670–671. Carles Abellan, king of pared-down designer cuisine at his famed restaurant *Comerç 24* (see p.691), offers a simpler tapas menu at this retro basement bar-diner, serving *patatas bravas*, Andalucian-style fried fish, oxtail, chorizo and fried eggs, croquettes and the like. Most tapas cost €4–16. Mon–Sat 9am–midnight.

RESTAURANTS

Casa Calvet C/Casp 48 ☎ 934 124 012, ⓦ casacalvet. es; ⓜ Catalunya/Urquinaona; map pp.670–671. The wonderfully decorated townhouse that a young Antoni Gaudí built for a Catalan industrialist makes for a truly glam night out. It offers a seasonally changing modern Catalan menu, with mains around the €30 mark, weekday lunch at €34 or tasting menus from €49 to €70. Mon–Sat 1–3.30pm & 8.30–11pm; closed Mon June–Aug.

Cinc Sentits C/d'Aribau 58 ☎ 933 239 490, ⓦ cincsentits .com; ⓜ Universitat; map pp.670–671. Contemporary Catalan cuisine that touches the "Five Senses" – the tasting menus (€65 and €80, matching wines available) use rigorously sourced ingredients (wild fish, mountain lamb, seasonal vegetables, farmhouse cheeses) in elegant, pared-down dishes that are all about flavour. Tues–Sat 1.30–3pm & 8.30–10pm; closed 2 weeks in Aug.

★**La Flauta** C/d'Aribau 23 ☎ 933 237 038; ⓜ Universitat; map pp.670–671. One of the city's best-value lunch menus (€13) sees diners queuing for tables early – get there before 2pm to avoid the rush. Meals are served tapas-style, day and night (dishes €4–10), based on seasonal market produce, from wild mushrooms to locally landed fish. Mon–Sat 8am–1am; closed 3 weeks in Aug.

★**Me** c/Paris 162 ☎ 934 194 933, ⓦ catarsiscuisine .com; ⓜ Diagonal; map pp.670–671. *Me* is all the rage for its clever fusion of cuisines from Vietnam and New Orleans by way of Barcelona – all places dear to owner Javier's heart. Expect fish steamed in banana leaves with coconut milk and spices or grilled Saigon rib-eye with lemongrass. Mains are €15–24, though lunch is a simpler, cheaper affair. Tues & Sat 8.45–11.30pm, Wed–Fri 1.45–3.30pm & 8.45–11.30pm.

GRÀCIA

TAPAS BARS

La Pepita c/Còrsega 343 ☎ 932 384 893, ⓦ lapepitabcn. com; ⓜ Diagonal/Verdaguer; map p.677. There's usually a queue out the door, and deservedly so. The tapas, like roasted chicken croquettes with romesco sauce (€4) or aubergine fritters with goat cheese, honey and apples (€8), are fantastic, and the atmosphere is chatty and convivial. Hundreds of "love notes" scrawled by customers on the white-tiled walls attest to its popularity. Mon 8pm–1.30am, Tues–Sat 9am–1.30am (kitchen open 1–4.30pm) & 7.30pm–midnight.

RESTAURANTS

★**Flash, Flash** C/Granada del Penedès 25 ☎ 932 370 990, ⓦ flashflashbarcelona.com; ⓜ Diagonal; map p.677. A classic 1970s' survivor, *Flash, Flash* does *tortillas* (€6–9) served any time you like, any way you like, from plain and simple to elaborately stuffed, with sweet ones for dessert. Chances are you'll love the original white leatherette booths and monotone "models-with-cameras" cutouts – very Austin Powers. Daily 1pm–1.30am, bar open 11am–2am.

Goliard C/Progrés ☎ 932 073 175, ⓦ restaurantegoliard.es; ⓜ Diagonal; map p.677. Smart but casual *Goliard* offers a pared-down dining experience in a contemporary foodie bistro that looks like it should cost three times as much. Although the menu is divided into starters and mains (most things €7–15), there

BARCELONA'S VEGETARIAN RESTAURANTS

Vegetarians will find themselves pleasantly surprised by the choice available in Barcelona if they've spent any time in other areas of Spain. The restaurants listed below are reliable places for a good veggie meal, but you'll also be able to do pretty well for yourself in tapas bars and modern Catalan brasseries and restaurants.

La Báscula C/Flassaders 30 ☎933 199 866; Ⓜ Jaume I; map pp.648–649. An old chocolate factory in the backstreets has been given a hippy-chic makeover by a local cooperative and serves up veggie pastas, turnovers, couscous, quiches and salads (dishes around €9). Wed–Sat 1pm–midnight, Sun 1–8pm.

Biocenter C/Pintor Fortuny 25 ☎933 014 583, ⓦ restaurantebiocenter.es; Ⓜ Liceu; map pp.648–649. One of the longest-running strictly veggie places in town, with a popular fixed-price lunch menu (€10.20, weekends €12.35). For dinner, they dim the lights, add candles and sounds, and turn out a few more exotic dishes, from seitan in a white wine reduction to ginger tofu (mains around €12). Mon–Sat 1–11pm, Sun 1–4pm.

Sésamo C/Sant Antoni Abat 52 ☎934 416 411; Ⓜ Sant Antoni; map p.665. Classy tapas place (bar at the front, restaurant tables at the back) that offers up a heavily vegetarian-orientated chalkboard menu of innovative dishes – think strawberry-basil gazpacho, slow-roast tomato tart, or a daily risotto and pasta dish, all in the range €7–15. Tues–Sun 7.30pm–midnight.

Teresa Carles c/Jovellanos 2 ☎933 171 829, ⓦ teresacarles.com; Ⓜ Catalunya; map pp.648–649. Stylish vegetarian and vegan cuisine served in a hip – but most certainly not "hippy" – space with soaring ceilings, exposed brick walls and soft, white lighting. The lunch menu (€9.50) is a great bargain, while à la carte offerings like artisanal pastas, a hearty seitan burger and vegan ceviche cost €9–12. Brunch is served until 2pm. Daily 9am–11.30pm.

are smaller portions available if you want to mix and match. Mon–Fri 1.30–3.30pm & 8.45–11.15pm, Sat 8.45–11.15pm.

La Singular C/Francesc Giner 50 ☎932 375 098; Ⓜ Diagonal; map p.677. The tiniest of kitchens turns out refined Mediterranean food at moderate prices – say, aubergine and smoked fish salad, or chicken stuffed with dates and ham, with most dishes costing €5–15. Mon–Thurs 1–4pm & 8.30–11.30pm, Fri 1–4pm & 8.30–12.30am, Sat 8.30pm–12.30am.

DRINKING AND NIGHTLIFE

Whatever you're looking for from a night out, you'll find it somewhere in Barcelona – bohemian boozer, underground club, cocktail bar, summer dance palace, techno temple, Irish pub or designer bar, you name it. Best known of the city's **nightlife haunts** are its hip designer **bars**, while there's a stylish **club and music scene** that goes from strength to strength fuelled by a potent mix of resident and guest DJs, local bands and visiting superstars. Local listings magazines *Guía del Ocio* (ⓦ enbarcelona.com) and *Time Out Barcelona* (ⓦ timeout.com/barcelona) cover up-to-date openings, hours and club nights, and most bars, cafés and music stores carry flyers and free magazines containing news and reviews. For the Barcelona music scene, check out the website ⓦ atiza.com.

ESSENTIALS

Opening hours and closing days Most bars stay open until 2am, or 3am at weekends, while clubs tend not to open much before midnight and stay open until 5am, or even later at weekends – fair enough, as they've often barely got started by 3am. Unlike restaurants, bars and clubs generally stay open throughout August.

Admission charges Some clubs are free before a certain time, usually around midnight. Otherwise, expect to pay €10–20, though this usually includes your first drink (if there is free entry, don't be surprised to find that there's a minimum drinks' charge of anything up to €10). Tickets for gigs run from €20 to €50, depending on the act though there are cheaper gigs (€5–20) almost every night of the year at a variety of smaller clubs and bars.

BARS

RAMBLAS

Bosc de les Fades Ptge. de la Banca 5 ☎933 172 649, ⓦ museocerabcn.com; Ⓜ Drassanes; map pp.648–649. Tucked away in an alley off the Ramblas, by the wax museum, the "Forest of the Fairies" is festooned with gnarled plaster tree trunks, fountains and stalactites. It's a cheesy location for a cocktail or two. Mon–Thurs 10am–1am, Fri 10am–1am, Sat 11am–2am, Sun 11am–1am.

BARRI GÒTIC

★ **L'Ascensor** C/Bellafila 3 ☎933 185 347; Ⓜ Jaume I; map pp.648–649. Sliding, antique wooden elevator doors announce the entrance to "The Lift", but it's no theme bar – just an easy-going local hangout that's great for a late-night drink. Daily 6pm–3am.

10

Glaciar Pza. Reial 3 ☎933 021 163; ⓦlareial.com; ⓜLiceu; map pp.648–649. At this traditional Barcelona meeting point the terrace seating is packed most sunny evenings and at weekends. Mon–Thurs noon–2.30am, Fri & Sat noon–3am, Sun 11am–2.30am.

★**Milk** C/Gignàs 21 ☎932 680 922, ⓦmilkbarcelona .com; ⓜJaume I; map pp.648–649. Irish-owned bar and bistro that's carved a real niche as a welcoming neighbourhood hangout. Get there early for the famously relaxed brunch (daily 9am–4.30pm); there's also dinner and cocktails every night to a funky soundtrack. Daily 9am–2am.

EL RAVAL

Almirall C/Joaquin Costa 33 ☎933 189 917; ⓦcasaalmirall.com; ⓜUniversitat; map pp.648–649. Dating from 1860, Barcelona's oldest bar is a *modernista* design classic – check out the doors, counter, and stupendous glittering bar. Mon–Thurs & Sun 6pm–2am, Fri & Sat 6pm–3am.

Betty Ford's C/Joaquin Costa 56 ☎933 041 368; ⓜUniversitat; map pp.644–645. With a vibe somewhere between a student lounge and a beach bar, *Betty's* is a bouncy place full of bouncy young things, sipping colourful cocktails and cold Australian beer. Mon–Thurs 5pm–2.30am, Fri & Sat 5pm–3am, Sun 7pm–2.30am.

Marmalade C/Riera Alta 4–6 ☎934 423 966, ⓦmarmaladebarcelona.com; ⓜSant Antoni; map pp.648–649. The hugely glam facelift for the old Muebles Navarro furniture store has gone for big, church-like spaces and a back-lit Art Deco bar that resembles a high altar. Cocktails, bistro meals and gourmet burgers pull in a relaxed dine-and-lounge crowd. There's a popular weekend brunch. Mon–Wed 6.30pm–2.30am, Thurs–Sun 10am–2.30am.

★**Marsella** C/Sant Pau 65 ☎934 427 263; ⓜLiceu; map pp.648–649. Authentic, atmospheric 1930s bar – named after the French port of Marseilles – that featured in Woody Allen's *Vicky Cristina Barcelona*, so expect a spirited mix of film fans, oddball locals and young dudes. Daily 10pm–2.30am.

Muy Buenas C/Carme 63 ☎645 309 671; ⓜLiceu; map pp.648–649. Arguably the Raval's nicest traditional watering hole, with a restored *modernista* interior and eager-to-please staff making things go with a swing. Mon–Thurs 9am–2am, Fri 9am–3am, Sat 10am–3am, Sun 6pm–2am.

★**Resolis** C/Riera Baixa 22 ☎934 412 948; ⓜSant Antoni; map pp.648–649. A cool hangout with decent tapas, where punters spill out of the door on to "secondhand clothes street" and a good time is had by all. Mon–Thurs 6pm–1am, Fri & Sat 6pm–3am.

SANT PERE

★**Ale&Hop** c/Basses de Sant Pere 10 ⓦaleandhop .com; ⓜUrquinaona; map pp.648–649. Ten rotating taps pour artisanal beers in all styles (porters, stouts, lagers, gluten-free) with names like "Dark Alliance" and "Sex-A-Pils". There's also a large selection of bottled beer, a crowd-pleasing vegetarian bar menu and a weekend brunch (served until 5pm). Mon–Wed noon–2.30pm, Fri noon–3am, Sat 11am–3am, Sun 11am–2.30am.

★**Casa Paco** C/d'Allada Vermell 10 ☎935 073 719; ⓜJaume I; map pp.648–649. The *barri's* signature bar is this cool music joint that's a hit on the weekend DJ scene – the tagline "not a disco, just a bar with good music" says it all. April–Sept Mon–Thurs & Sun 9am–2am, Fri & Sat 9am–3am; Oct–March Mon–Thurs 6pm–2am, Fri & Sat 6pm–3am.

LA RIBERA

Espai Barroc C/Montcada 20 ☎933 100 673; ⓦpalaudalmases.com; ⓜJaume I; map pp.648–649. Every evening the doors are thrown open at the Palau Dalmases for drinks and cocktails in a remodelled medieval mansion known as the *Espai Barroc*, or "Baroque Space". Come on Thursday and you'll catch singers belting out arias as you sip fine wines under the chandeliers (recital at 11pm, €20, first drink included). Daily 7pm–2am.

★**La Fianna** C/Manresa 4 ☎933 151 810, ⓦlafianna .com; ⓜJaume I; map pp.648–649. Flickering candelabras, parchment lampshades, rough plaster walls and deep colours set the Gothic mood in this stylish lounge bar that's "putting the beat in the Born". Daily 6pm–2am.

La Vinya del Senyor Pza. Santa María 5 ☎933 103 379; ⓜJaume I; map pp.648–649. A great wine bar with front-row seats onto the lovely church of Santa María del Mar. The wine list is really good and there's classy tapas available. Mon–Thurs noon–1am, Fri & Sat noon–2am, Sun noon–midnight.

THE GIN AND TONIC CRAZE

In Barcelona, they don't let anything come between their gin and their tonic – not even the word "and". The **gintonic**, as it's known, has always been a favourite drink. In recent years, however, there's been a surge in bars specializing in the classic cocktail and its star ingredient, **ginebra**, with spots such as *Bobby Gin* in Gràcia (see opposite), *Dry Martini* in Esquerra de L'Eixample (see opposite) and *Xixbar* in Poble Sec (see opposite) stocking a long list of brands. And the tonic component has not been forgotten, with bars pouring a dizzying array of premium varieties. It's a refreshing trend worthy of a glass-clinking *salut*.

10

PORT VELL

★**Can Paixano** C/Reina Cristina 7 ☎933 100 839, ⓦcanpaixano.com; ⓜBarceloneta; map pp.648–649. A must on everyone's itinerary is this crowded backstreet joint where the drink of choice – all right, the only drink – is cava (the Catalan answer to champagne). Don't go thinking sophistication – the drinks might come in traditional champagne saucers (the sort of thing Dean Martin used to stack in a pyramid and then pour wine over), but this is a counter-only joint where there's fizz, tapas and tapas-in-sandwiches and that's your lot. And who could want more? Mon–Sat 9am–10.30pm; closed Easter week.

POBLE SEC

★**Bar Seco** Pg. Montjuïc 74 ☎933 296 374, ⓦbar -seco.com; ⓜParal.lel; map p.665. The "Dry Bar" is a local hit, with its mellow vibe, freshly squeezed juices, Free Trade drinks and artisan beers. Mon–Wed 9am–5.30pm, Thurs 9am–1am, Fri 9am–2am, Sat 10am–2am, Sun 10am–6pm.

Xixbar C/Rocafort 19 ☎934 234 314, ⓦxixbar.com; ⓜPoble Sec; map p.665. "Chicks" is an old *granja* (milk bar) turned candlelit, but completely unstuffy, cocktail bar. Gin's the big drink here (they claim over one hundred varieties), and they even have their own specialist gin shop on site. Mon 6.30pm–2.30am, Tues–Sat 5pm–2.30am.

EIXAMPLE

Belchica C/Villaroel 60 ☎625 814 001, ⓦfacebook .com/belchica; ⓜUrgell; map pp.670–671. Barcelona's first Belgian beer bar guarantees a range of decent brews (including hard-to-find Trappist ales). It's also a muso's joint, playing electronica, new jazz, lounge, reggae and other left-field sounds. Mon–Thurs 6pm–2.30am, Fri 6pm–3am, Sat 7pm–3am, Sun 7pm–2.30am.

Dry Martini C/Aribau 166 ☎932 175 072, ⓦwww .drymartinibcn.com; ⓜDiagonal; map pp.670–671. White-jacketed bartenders, dark wood and brass fittings, a self-satisfied air – it could only be the city's legendary uptown cocktail bar. Best drink to order? The clue's in the bar's name. Mon–Fri 1pm–2.30am (open 6.30pm in Aug), Sat & Sun 6.30pm–3am.

★**Velódromo** C/Muntaner 213 ☎934 306 022; ⓜHospital Clínic; map pp.670–671. A glam Art Deco gem, with a lofty, Parisian feel, a swooping staircase and a gleaming bar. It's ideal for swish drinks and cocktails, though with fancy breakfasts, brunch and a tapas-and-bistro menu it's also made for early starts and later dinners. Mon–Thurs 6am–2.30am, Fri & Sat 6am–3am.

GRÀCIA

Bobby Gin c/Francisco Giner 47 ☎933 681 892, ⓦbobbygin.com; ⓜDiagonal; map p.677. A sign inside says "El gintonic perfecto no existe" (the perfect gin and

tonic does not exist). Perhaps. But the sizeable G&Ts (from €8) here come very, very close. Mon–Wed & Sun 7pm–2am, Thurs 7pm–2.30am, Fri–Sat 7pm–3am.

Cafè del Sol Pza. del Sol 16 ☎934 155 663; ⓦcafedelsol.cat; ⓜFontana; map p.677. The grandaddy of the Pza. del Sol scene sees action day and night. On summer evenings, when the square is packed, there's not an outdoor table to be had. Mon–Thurs 1pm–2.30am, Fri & Sat 1pm–3am.

★**Canigó** C/Verde 2, ☎932 133 049, ⓦbarcanigo.com; ⓜFontana; map p.677. Family-run neighbourhood bar now entering its third generation. It's not much to look at, but the drinks are cheap and it's a real Gràcia institution, packed out at weekends with a young, hip and largely local crowd. Mon–Thurs 10am–2am, Fri 10am–3am, Sat 8pm–3am.

Virreina Pza. de la Virreina 1 ☎932 379 880, ⓦvirreinabar.com; ⓜFontana; map p.677. On one of the neighbourhood's prettiest squares, with a very popular summer *terraza*. It's one of those places where you drop by for a quick drink and find yourself staying for hours. Daily 10am–2am.

LES CORTS, PEDRALBES AND SARRIÀ-SANT GERVASI

Gimlet C/Santaló 46 ☎932 015 306, ⓦwww .gimletbcn.com; FGC Muntaner; map pp.644–645. Especially popular in summertime, when the street-side tables offer a great vantage point for watching the party unfold. There are also two or three other late-opening bars on the same stretch. Mon–Wed & Sun 6pm–1am, Thurs 6pm–2.30am, Fri & Sat 6pm–3am.

CLUBS AND LIVE MUSIC

BARRI GÒTIC

Jamboree Pza. Reial 17 ☎933 191 789, ⓦmasimas .com; ⓜLiceu; map pp.648–649. Nightly jazz gigs (from €12) pull in the crowds, while the wild Monday-night WTF jazz, funk and hip-hop jam session (from 8pm, €5) is a city fixture. The club kicks off after midnight (entry €10) playing funky sounds until the small hours. Gigs daily at 8pm & 10pm, club daily midnight–5am.

Karma Pza. Reial 10 ☎933 025 680, ⓦkarmadisco .com; ⓜLiceu; map pp.648–649. Old-school studenty basement place spinning indie, Britpop and US college, while a lively crowd gathers at the square-side bar and terraza. Club admission around €12. Tues–Sun midnight–5.30am.

La Macarena C/Nou de Sant Francesc 5 ⓦmacarena club.com; ⓜDrassanes; map pp.648–649. Once a place where flamenco tunes were offered up to La Macarena, the Virgin of Seville – now a heaving temple to all things electro. Entry free until around 1am, then from €5. Mon–Thurs & Sun 11.45pm–5am, Fri & Sat 11.45pm–6am.

10

THE BEAT FROM THE STREET

The Barcelona sound – *mestiza* – is a cross-cultural musical fusion whose heartland is the immigrant melting-pot of the Raval. The local postcode – **08001** – lends a name to the sound's hippest flagbearers, while also typically "Raval" is the collective called **Cheb Balowski**, an Algerian-Catalan fusion band. The biggest star on the scene is the Parisian-born, Barcelona-resident **Manu Chao**, whose infectious, multi-million-selling album *Clandestino* (1998) kick-started the whole genre. He's widely known abroad, and influenced many Barcelona bands, including the world music festival favourites **Ojos de Brujo** (Eyes of the Wizard), who present a fusion reinvention of flamenco and Catalan rumba. Other hot sounds come from the Latin American dub and reggae band **Go Lem System**, and the fusion-freestyle merchants **La Kinky Beat**.

★**Sidecar** Pza. Reial 7 ☎933 177 666, ⊕sidecarfactoryclub.com; ⓜLiceu; map pp.648–649. The old town's hippest concert space has nightly gigs and DJs championing rock, indie, roots, electronica and fusion acts. Entry €7–10; gigs up to €20. Mon–Thurs 7pm–5am, Fri & Sat 7pm–6am, gigs usually at 10.30pm, DJs at 12.30am.

★**Tarantos** Pza. Reial 17, Barri Gòtic ☎933 191 789, ⊕masimas.com; ⓜLiceu; map pp.648–649. Some purists are sniffy about the experience, but for a cheap flamenco taster you can't beat this small bar in front of a stage where young performers appear three times a night (club is vacated after each session), plus an extra session in July & Aug. Entry €10. Its sister club *Jamboree* is at the same address. Performances daily 8.30pm, 9.30pm & 10.30pm.

EL RAVAL

★**Jazz Sí Club** C/Requesens 2 ☎933 290 020, ⊕tallerdemusics.com; ⓜSant Antoni; map pp.644–645. Great for inexpensive (€5–10) gigs, every night from around 7.45pm or 8pm there's something different, from rock, blues, jazz and jam sessions to the popular weekly Cuban (Thurs) and flamenco (Fri) nights. Daily 7.45–11.30pm.

★**Moog** C/Arc del Teatre 3 ☎933 017 282, ⊕masimas.com; ⓜDrassanes; map pp.648–649. One of the most influential clubs around for electronic sounds, playing techno, electro, drum'n'bass and trance to a cool but up-for-it crowd. Admission €10. Daily midnight–5am.

POBLE NOU

Sala Razzmatazz C/Pamplona 88 ☎933 208 200, ⊕salarazzmatazz.com; ⓜBogatell; map pp.644–645. *Razzmatazz* hosts the biggest in-town rock gigs, while at weekends the former warehouse turns into "five clubs in one", spinning indie, rock, pop, techno, electro, retro and more in variously named music bars like "The Loft", "Pop Bar" or "Lolita". Admission €17, gets you entrance to all the bars. Thurs (Razz Club only), Fri & Sat 1–6am.

MONTJUÏC

El Tablao de Carmen Avgda. Francesc Ferrer i Guàrdia,

Poble Espanyol, Montjuïc ☎933 256 895, ⊕tablaodecarmen.com; ⓜEspanya; map p.665. The long-standing flamenco club in the Poble Espanyol at least looks the real deal, sited in a replica Andalucian street. Prices start from €41 for the show and a drink, rising to €70 for the show plus dinner. Advance reservations essential. Tues–Sun, shows at 7pm & 9.30pm.

La Terrrazza Avgda. Francesc Ferrer i Guàrdia, Poble Espanyol ☎867 969 825, ⊕laterrrazza.com; ⓜEspanya; map p.665. Open-air summer club that's *the* place to be in Barcelona. Nonstop dance, house and techno, though don't get there until at least 3am, and be prepared for the style police. May–Oct Thurs–Sat 11.45pm–6am.

POBLE SEC

★**Maumau** C/Fontrodona 35 ☎934 418 015, ⊕maumaunderground.com; ⓜParal.lel; map p.665. A great underground lounge-club, cultural centre and chill-out space with nightly film and video projections, exhibitions, and a roster of guest DJs playing deep, soulful grooves. Strictly speaking it's a private club, but they tend to let foreign visitors in for free. Thurs–Sat 9pm–2.30am.

Sala Apolo C/Nou de la Rambla 113 ☎934 414 001, ⊕sala-apolo.com; ⓜParal.lel; map p.665. Old-time ballroom turned hip concert venue with gigs on two stages (local acts to big names) and an eclectic series of club nights with names to reckon with (Nasty Mondays, Crappy Tuesdays, etc). Gigs €10–35, club nights €10–15. Daily midnight–5am.

GRÀCIA

★**Heliogàbal** C/Ramon i Cajal 80 ⊕heliogabal.com; ⓜJoanic; map p.677. A cool, twenty-something crowd flocks here for the live poetry and music – expect something different every night (Catalan versifying, jazz jam sessions and earnest singer-songwriters), starting at 10pm. Admission €5–10. Wed–Sat 9.30pm–2am.

Otto Zutz C/Lincoln 15 ☎932 380 722, ⊕ottozutz.com; FGC Gràcia; map p.677. It first opened in 1985 and has since lost some of its glam cachet, but this three-storey former textile factory still has a shed-load of pretensions. Admission €15. Tues–Thurs 11pm–3am, Fri & Sat midnight–6am.

LES CORTS, PEDRALBES AND SARRIÀ-SANT GERVASI

★**Bikini** Avgda. Diagonal 547 ☎933 220 800, ⓦbikinibcn.com; ⓜLes Corts/María Cristina; map pp.644–645. This traditional landmark of Barcelona nightlife offers a regular diet of great indie, rock, roots and world gigs, followed by club sounds. Admission €15–25, though some gigs up to €40. Thurs–Sat midnight–5am.

Universal C/Marià Cubí 182 ☎934 146 362, ⓦuniversalbcn.com; FGC Muntaner; map pp.644–645. A classic designer music bar and dance club that's been at the cutting edge of Barcelona style since 1985 – and there are still queues. Admission charged at weekends, from €10. Mon–Thurs 11pm–3.30am, Fri & Sat 11pm–5am.

ARTS AND CULTURE

10

As you would expect from a city of its size, Barcelona has a busy entertainment calendar – throughout the year there'll be something worth catching, whether it's a contemporary dance performance, cabaret show or night at the opera. Classical and contemporary music, in particular, gets an airing in some stunning auditoriums, while the city boasts a long tradition of street and performance art, right down to the human statues plying their trade on the Ramblas. A useful first stop for tickets and information is the **Palau de la Virreina**, Ramblas 99 (daily 10am–8.30pm; ☎ 933 161 000, ⓦtiquetrambles .bcn.cat; ⓜLiceu). **Ticketmaster** (☎ 902 150 025, ⓦticketmaster.es) and **TelEntrada** (☎ 902 101 212, ⓦtelentrada .com) are the main advance booking agencies.

The city council's Institute of Culture website, ⓦ **barcelonacultura.bcn.cat**, covers every aspect of art and culture in the city. Otherwise, the best **listings magazines** are the weekly *Guía del Ocio* (ⓦenbarcelona .com) and *Time Out Barcelona* (ⓦtimeout.com/barcelona), online or from any newspaper stand.

GAY AND LESBIAN BARCELONA

There's a vibrant local **gay and lesbian** crowd in Barcelona, not to mention the lure of nearby Sitges (see p.775), mainland Spain's biggest gay resort. There's a particular concentration of bars, restaurants and clubs in the so-called **Gaixample**, the "Gay Eixample", an area of a few square blocks just northwest of the main university in the Eixample. The biggest event of the year is *Carnaval* in Sitges, while the main city party is Barcelona's annual LGBT **Pride** festival (ⓦpridebarcelona.org), which has events running over ten days each June, from street parades to Tibidabo fun-fair parties.

There's a **lesbian and gay city telephone hotline** on ☎900 601 601 (daily 6–10pm). You'll find weekly bar and club listings in *Guía del Ocio* and *Time Out Barcelona*. The single best English-language website is the excellent 60by80 (ⓦ60by80.com/Barcelona), which has its finger on the pulse of all things hot, from shopping to partying. Other online resources include ⓦgaybarcelona4u.com and ⓦguiagaybarcelona.es (Spanish only).

GAY BARS AND CLUBS

Aire Sala Diana C/Valencia 236, Eixample ☎934 878 342, ⓦarenadisco.com; ⓜPasseig de Gràcia; map pp.670–671. The hottest, most stylish lesbian bar in town is a relaxed place for a drink and a dance to pop, house and retro sounds. Thurs–Sat 11pm–2.30am, July & Aug also Tues & Wed.

Arena Madre C/Balmes 32, Eixample; Classic C/Diputació 233; VIP Grand Vía de les Corts Catalanes 593; Dandy Grand Vía de les Corts Catalanes 593; ☎934 878 342, ⓦarenadisco.com; ⓜPasseig de Gràcia; map pp.670–671. The *Madre* "mother" club sits at the helm of the Arena empire, all within a city block (pay for one, get in to all) – frenetic house at *Arena Madre*, high disco antics at *Arena Classic*, more of the same plus dance, r'n'b, pop and rock at the more mixed *Arena VIP*, and vintage chart hits at *Arena Dandy*. Madre daily 12.30–5.30am; Classic Fri & Sat 2.30–5.30am; VIP Fri & Sat 1–6am; Dandy Fri & Sat 1–6am.

Dietrich C/Consell de Cent 255, Eixample ☎934 517 707; ⓜUniversitat; map pp.670–671. Well-known music bar and "teatro-cafè" – *tranquilo* during the week, but ever more hedonistic as the weekend wears on, with drag shows, acrobats and dancers punctuating the DJ sets. Thurs 10pm–2.30am, Fri & Sat 10pm–3am.

Metro C/Sepúlveda 185, Eixample ☎933 235 227, ⓦmetrodiscobcn.com; ⓜUniversitat; map pp.670–671. A gay institution in Barcelona, with extremely crowded club nights at weekends, playing current dance, techno and retro disco. Mon–Thurs & Sun 12.15–5am, Fri & Sat 12.15–6.30am.

Punto BCN C/Muntaner 63–65, Eixample ☎934 878 342, ⓦarenadisco.com; ⓜUniversitat; map pp.670–671. A Gaixample classic that attracts a lively crowd for drinks, chat and music. Wednesday happy hour is a blast, while Friday night is party night. Daily 6pm–2.30am.

10

CLASSICAL MUSIC AND OPERA

Most of Barcelona's classical music concerts take place in the extravagantly decorated Palau de la Música Catalana or at the purpose-built, contemporary L'Auditori, while opera is performed at its traditional home, the Gran Teatre del Liceu on the Ramblas. Notable festivals include the Festival de Barcelona Grec (July), and there are free concerts in Barcelona's parks each summer, the so-called Música als Parcs.

★**Ateneu Barcelonès** C/Canuda 6, Barri Gòtic ☎ 933 426 121, ⓦ ateneubcn.org; ⓜ Catalunya. This 150-year-old cultural association presents a variety of intellectually stimulating events throughout the year, including conferences, film screenings and workshops, as well as concerts and recitals (from baroque to contemporary), some of which take place in its verdant garden.

L'Auditori C/Lepant 150, Glòries ☎ 932 479 300, ⓦ auditori.cat; ⓜ Marina/Glòries. The city's main concert hall is home to the Orquestra Simfònica de Barcelona i Nacional de Catalunya (OBC), whose weekend concert season runs from October to June. Also other orchestral and chamber works, jazz and world gigs, and music for families.

Gran Teatre del Liceu Ramblas 51–59 ☎ 934 859 900; box office C/Sant Pau 1 ☎ 934 859 913, ⓦ www.liceubarcelona.com; ⓜ Liceu. Hosts a wide-ranging programme of opera and dance productions, plus other concerts and recitals. The season runs from September to July – note that sales for the next season go on general sale in mid-May. Box office Mon–Fri 1.30–8pm, Sat & Sun 1hr before performance.

★**Palau de la Música Catalana** C/Palau de la Música 4–6, off C/Sant Pere Més Alt, Sant Pere ☎ 932 957 200 or 902 442 882, ⓦ palaumusica.org; ⓜ Urquinaona. Home to the Orfeó Català choral group, and venue for concerts by the Orquestra Ciutat de Barcelona among others, though throughout the year you can catch anything, from *sardanes* to pop concerts.

DANCE

Barcelona is very much a contemporary dance city, with its own dedicated dance venue, Mercat de les Flors, as well as regular performances by regional, national and international artists and companies at theatre venues like the TNC, Teatre Lliure and Institut del Teatre.

Mercat de les Flors C/Lleida 59, Montjuïc ☎ 932 562 600, ⓦ mercatflors.cat; ⓜ Poble Sec. The city's old flower market serves as the "national centre for movement arts", with dance the central focus of its varied programme – from Asian performance art to European contemporary dance.

FILM

At most of the larger cinemas and multiplexes films are usually shown dubbed into Spanish or Catalan, though several cinemas do screen mostly original-language ("*v.o.*") foreign films. Tickets cost around €8, and most cinemas have one night (usually Mon or Wed) when entry is discounted, usually to around €6. Many cinemas also feature late-night screenings (*madrugadas*) on Friday and Saturday nights, which begin at 12.30am or 1am.

Cinema Maldà C/Pi 5, Barri Gòtic ☎ 933 019 350, ⓦ cinemamalda.net; ⓜ Liceu. Hidden away in a little shopping centre, just up from Pza. del Pi, the Maldà is a great place for independent movies and festival winners, all in *v.o.*

FilmoTeca Pza. Salvador Seguí 1–9, El Raval ☎ 935 671 070, ⓦ filmoteca.cat; ⓜ Liceu. Run by the Catalan government, the FilmoTeca (now in its new location in El Raval) shows three to five different films (often foreign-language, and usually in *v.o.*) every day – the programme changes every couple of weeks. Tickets are just €4/film, and there's also a €45 pass allowing entry to thirty films.

Sala Montjuïc Castell de Montjuïc ☎ 933 023 553, ⓦ salamontjuic.org, ⓦ atrapalo.com; cable car (Telefèric de Montjuïc) or cinema bus (normal tickets and passes valid) from Pza. d'Espanya (ⓜ Espanya),

CELEBRATING CATALAN-STYLE

Catalunya's national folk dance, the **sardana**, is danced every week in front of La Seu, in Pza. de la Seu (every Sun at noon, plus every Sat at 6pm from Easter until the end of Nov). Mocked in the rest of Spain, the dance is, the Catalans claim very democratic. Participants (there's no limit on numbers) all hold hands in a circle, each puts something in the middle as a sign of community and sharing, and since it is not overly energetic (hence the jibes), old and young can join in equally.

The main event in a **traditional Catalan festival** is usually a parade, either promenading behind a revered holy image (as on saints' days or at Easter) or a more celebratory costumed affair that's the centrepiece of a neighbourhood festival. At the main Eulàlia (Feb), Gràcia (Aug) and Mercè (Sept) festivals, and others, you'll encounter parades of *gegants*, 5m-high giants with papier-mâché heads based on historical or traditional figures. Also typically Catalan is the **correfoc** ("fire-running"), where brigades of drummers, dragons and devils with spark-shooting flares fitted to pitchforks cavort in the streets. Perhaps most peculiar of all are the **castellers**, the human tower-builders who draw crowds at every traditional festival, piling person upon person, feet on shoulders, to see who can construct the highest, most aesthetically pleasing tower (ten human storeys is the record).

departures from 8.30pm, returns when film finishes. From late June to early August there's a giant-screen open-air cinema at Montjuïc castle (Mon, Wed & Fri night; live music from 8.45pm, films at 10.15pm, tickets €6) – bring a picnic or buy food there. Screenings are in the original language, with Spanish subtitles.

Verdi C/Verdi 32, and **Verdi Park** C/Torrijos 49, Gràcia ☎932 387 990, @cines-verdi.com; ⓜFontana. Sister cinemas in adjacent streets showing independent, art-house and *v.o.* movies.

THEATRE AND CABARET

The Teatre Nacional de Catalunya (Catalan National Theatre) was conceived as a venue to promote Catalan productions, and features a programme of translated classics (such as Shakespeare in Catalan), original works and productions by guest companies. The other big local theatrical project is the Ciutat del Teatre (Theatre City) on Montjuïc, which incorporates the progressive Teatre Lliure and the Institut del Teatre theatre and dance school. Some theatres draw on the city's strong cabaret tradition – more music-hall entertainment than stand-up comedy, and thus more accessible to non-Catalan/Spanish speakers. For last-minute tickets visit the Palau de la Virreina (Ramblas 99; daily 10am–8.30pm), which offers same-day half-price tickets from 3hr before the show.

L'Antic Teatre C/Verdaguer i Callis 12, Sant Pere ☎933 152 354, @lanticteatre.com; ⓜUrquinaona. Independent theatre with a wildly original programme of events, many free, from video shows to offbeat cabaret performances. In the end though, the best bit may just be the summer garden bar (daily 4pm–midnight).

★**Cafè Teatre Llantiol** C/Riereta 7, El Raval ☎933 299 009, @llantiol.com; ⓜSant Antoni. Idiosyncratic cabaret café-theatre offering a mix of mime, song, clowning, magic and dance. Shows (€10–15) normally at 9pm & 11pm (6pm & 9pm on Sundays).

El Molino C/Vila i Vilà 99, Avgda. Paral.lel, Poble Sec ☎932 055 111, @elmolinobcn.com; ⓜParal.lel. One of Barcelona's most famous old cabaret theatres – the self-styled "Little Moulin Rouge" – has a classy new look for its burlesque and music stage shows. Performances from Thursday to Saturday (two people, plus a bottle of cava €50).

Teatre Lliure Pza. Margarida Xirgu 1, Montjuïc ☎932 892 770, @www.teatrelliure.cat; ⓜPoble Sec. The "Free Theatre" performs the work of contemporary Catalan and Spanish playwrights, as well as re-workings of the classics, from Shakespeare to David Mamet (some productions have English subtitles).

Teatre Nacional de Catalunya (TNC) Pza. de les Arts 1, Glòries ☎933 065 700, @tnc.cat; ⓜGlòries. Features major productions by Catalan, Spanish and European companies, as well as smaller-scale plays, experimental works and dance productions.

SHOPPING

While not on a par with Paris or the world's other style capitals, Barcelona still leads the way in Spain when it comes to **shopping**. It's the country's fashion and publishing capital, and there's a long tradition of innovative *disseny* (design), from clothes and accessories to crafts and household goods. The annual sales (*rebaixes*; *rebajas* in Castilian) follow the main fashion seasons – mid-January until the end of February, and throughout July and August.

ANTIQUES, ARTS, CRAFTS AND GIFTS

The best area for antiques browsing is around C/Palla, between La Seu and Pza. del Pí, combined with the antique market on Thursdays in front of La Seu. The Tallers Oberts, or Open Workshops (@tallersobertsciutatvella.net), are usually held over the last two weekends of May, when there are studio visits, exhibitions and other events.

★**Almacen Marabi** C/Cirera 6, La Ribera @almacen marabi.blogspot.com; ⓜJaume I; map pp.648–649. Mariela Marabi makes handmade felt finger dolls, mobiles, puppets and animals of extraordinary invention. Her eye-popping workshop also has limited-edition pieces by other selected artists and designers. Mon–Sat noon–2.30pm & 5–8.30pm.

Almacenes del Pilar C/Boqueria 43, Barri Gòtic ☎933 177 984, @almacenesdelpilar.com; ⓜLiceu; map pp.648–649. A world of frills, lace, cloth and materials used in the making of Spain's traditional regional costumes – pick up a decorated fan for just a few euros. Mon–Sat 10am–2pm & 4.30–8pm; closed Aug.

L'Arca C/Banys Nous 20, Barri Gòtic ☎933 021 598, @larcadelavia.com; ⓜLiceu; map pp.648–649. Catalan brides used to fill up their nuptial trunk (*arca*) with embroidered bed linen and lace, and this shop is a treasure-trove of vintage and antique textiles. Mon–Sat 11am–2pm & 4.30–8.30pm.

Artesania Catalunya C/Banys Nous 11, Barri Gòtic ☎934 674 660, @artesania-catalunya.com; ⓜLiceu; map pp.648–649. Changing exhibitions in the showroom of the local government's arts and crafts promotion board, from contemporary basketwork to colourful glassware. Mon–Sat 10am–8pm, Sun 10am–2pm.

Cereria Subirà Bxda. Llibreteria 7, Barri Gòtic ☎933 152 606; ⓜJaume I; map pp.648–649. Barcelona's oldest shop (since 1760) has a beautiful interior, selling hand-crafted candles. Mon–Thurs 9.30am–1.30pm & 4–8pm, Fri 9.30am–8pm, Sat 10am–8pm.

★**Espai Drap Art** C/Groc 1, Barri Gòtic ☎932 684 889, @drapart.net; ⓜJaume I; map pp.648–649. The Drap Art creative recycling organization has a shop and

10

10

exhibition space for artists to show their wildly inventive wares, from trash-bangles to tin bags. Tues–Fri 11am–2pm & 5–8pm, Sat 6–9pm.

★ **Fantastik** C/Joaquin Costa 62, El Raval ☎ 933 013 068, ⍟ fantastik.es; Ⓜ Universitat; map pp.644–645. You'll never know how you lived without such beguiling gifts, whether it's Chinese robots, African baskets, Russian domino sets or Vietnamese kitchen scales. Mon–Fri 11am–2pm & 4–8.30pm, Sat noon–9pm.

BOOKS

You'll find English-language books, newspapers and magazines at the stalls along the Ramblas.

Altaïr Gran Vía de les Corts Catalanes 616, Eixample ☎ 933 427 171, ⍟ altair.es; Ⓜ Universitat; map pp.670–671. Europe's biggest travel superstore has a massive selection of travel books, guides, maps and world music, plus a programme of travel-related talks and exhibitions. Mon–Sat 10am–8.30pm.

★ **La Central del Raval** C/Elisabets 6, El Raval ☎ 900 802 109, ⍟ lacentral.com; Ⓜ Catalunya; map pp.648–649. Occupying a unique space in the former Misericordia chapel, La Central is a fantastically stocked arts and humanities treasure-trove, with books piled high in every nook and cranny. Mon–Fri 9.30am–9pm, Sat 10am–9pm.

Hibernian Books C/Montseny 17, Gràcia ☎ 932 174 796, ⍟ hibernian-books.com; Ⓜ Fontana; map p.677. Barcelona's best secondhand English bookstore has around 40,000 titles in stock –you can part-exchange, and there are always plenty of giveaway bargains available. Mon 4–8.30pm, Tues–Sat 10.30am–8.30pm.

CLOTHES, SHOES AND ACCESSORIES

New designers can be found in the medieval streets and alleys of La Ribera, around Pg. del Born, but also down C/d'Avinyó in the Barri Gòtic, between C/Carme and MACBA in El Raval, and along C/Verdi in Gràcia. For secondhand and vintage clothing, stores line the whole of C/Riera Baixa (El Raval), with others nearby on C/Carme and C/l'Hospital, and on Saturdays there's a street market there.

Antonio Miró C/Rambla de Catalunya 125, Eixample ☎ 932 389 942, ⍟ antoniomiro.es; Ⓜ Passeig de Grácia; map pp.670–671. Barcelona's most innovative designer, especially good for classy suits, though now also branding accessories and household design items. Mon–Sat 10.30am–8.30pm.

Camper C/Pelai 13–37, El Triangle, Eixample ☎ 933 024 124, ⍟ camper.com; Ⓜ Catalunya; map pp.648–649. Spain's favourite shoe store opened its first shop in Barcelona in 1981. Providing hip, well-made, casual city footwear at a good price has been the cornerstone of its success. Mon–Sat 10am–10pm.

La Comercial C/Rec 73, La Ribera ☎ 933 192 435, ⍟ lacomercial.info; Ⓜ Jaume I; map pp.648–649. Five

boutiques plus a showroom – all clustered around C/Rec – comprise the fabulous La Comercial, which carries a carefully curated selection of on-trend men's and women's fashion, fragrances and chic home decor. Mon–Thurs 11am–9pm, Fri & Sat 11am–9.30pm.

Custo Barcelona Pza. de les Olles 7, La Ribera ☎ 932 687 893, ⍟ custo-barcelona.com; Ⓜ Barceloneta; map pp.648–649. Where the stars get their T-shirts. Hugely colourful designer tops and sweaters for men and women. There are other branches around town. Mon–Sat 10am–9pm, Sun noon–8pm.

Formista C/Sagristans 9, Barri Gòtic ☎ 933 186 020, ⍟ formista.com; Ⓜ Jaume I; map pp.648–649. Gallery-shop hybrid selling unique handmade objects by international designers and artists. There are sleek leather handbags alongside porcelain jewellery, hand-printed textiles and more. Mon–Sat noon–9pm.

★ **Lailo** C/Riera Baixa 20, El Raval ☎ 934 413 749; Ⓜ Liceu; map pp.648–649. Secondhand and vintage clothes shop with a massively wide-ranging stock, plus fancy dress costumes, tuxes and gowns available for hire. If you don't find what you want, just move on down the street to the neighbouring stores and outlets. Mon–Fri 10.30am–2pm & 5–8pm, Sat 10.30am–2.30pm 5–8.30pm.

Mango Pg. de Gràcia 36, Eixample ☎ 932 151 543, ⍟ mango.com; Ⓜ Passeig de Gràcia; map pp.670–671. Mango, now available worldwide, began in Barcelona and prices here are generally a bit cheaper than in North America or other European countries. Mon–Sat 10.15am–9.30pm.

Mango Outlet C/Girona 37, Eixample ☎ 934 122 935, ⍟ mangooutlet.com; Ⓜ Girona; map pp.670–671. Last season's Mango gear at unbeatable prices, with items starting at just a few euros. The shop is in the city's "garment district" and there are other outlet stores in the same neighbourhood. Mon–Sat 10am–9pm.

★ **La Manual Alpargatera** C/d'Avinyó 7, Barri Gòtic ☎ 933 010 172, ⍟ lamanualalpargatera.com; Ⓜ Liceu; map pp.648–649. Traditional workshop making *alpargatas* (espadrilles) to order, as well as other straw, rope and basketwork. Mon–Fri 9.30am–1.30pm & 4.30–8pm, Sat 10am–1.30pm & 4.30–8pm.

DEPARTMENT STORES AND MALLS

Department stores and shopping malls are open Monday to Saturday 10am–10pm, though the cafés and leisure outlets in malls often open later, and on Sunday.

Arenas de Barcelona Gran Via de les Corts Catalanes 373–385, Eixample ☎ 932 890 244, ⍟ arenasdebarcelona.com; Ⓜ Espanya; map pp.670–671. This designer mall is a glam refit of a former bullring, and while it's bigger on leisure facilities than shops and boutiques, you won't want to miss the view from the circular rooftop promenade. Mon–Sat 10am–10pm.

El Corte Inglés Pza. de Catalunya 14, Eixample ☎933 063 800, ⓦelcorteingles.es; ⓜCatalunya; map pp.648–649. The city's largest department store has outlets all over the city – visit the flagship Pza. de Catalunya branch for nine storeys of clothes, accessories, cosmetics, household goods, toys and the top-floor café. Mon–Sat 9.30am–9.30pm.

L'illa Avgda. Diagonal 557, Les Corts ☎934 440 000, ⓦlilla.com; ⓜMaría Cristina; map pp.670–671. The landmark uptown shopping mall is stuffed full of designer fashion (including the local Custo), plus Camper (shoes), FNAC (music, film and books), Decathlon (sports), El Corte Inglés (department store), Caprabo (supermarket), gourmet food hall and much more. Mon–Sat 10am–9.30pm.

DESIGN AND STYLE

Cubiña C/Mallorca 291, Eixample ☎934 765 721, ⓦcubinya.es; ⓜVerdaguer; map pp.670–671. The building itself is stupendous – Domènech i Montaner's *modernista* Casa Thomas – while inside holds the very latest in household design, from slinky CD racks to €5000 dining tables. Mon–Sat 10am–2pm & 4.30–8.30pm.

★**Vinçon** Pg. de Gràcia 96, Eixample ☎932 156 050, ⓦvincon.com; ⓜPasseig de Gràcia; map pp.670–671. The grandaddy of household style, with various street entrances and separate sections for bedroom and kitchen stuff, plus temporary art and design exhibitions in La Sala Vinçon. Mon–Fri 10am–8.30pm, Sat 8.30am–9pm.

FOOD AND DRINK

The main local supermarket chain is Caprabo (ⓦcaprabo .es), which has a useful branch in the Mercat de la Barceloneta, though most other branches are located in residential neighbourhoods, away from the tourist sights. The most convenient downtown supermarket is that in the basement of El Corte Inglés (Pza. de Catalunya), and there's also a Carrefour Market at Ramblas 113.

Bubó C/Caputxes 10, La Ribera ☎932 687 224, ⓦbubo .ws; ⓜJaume I; map pp.648–649. There are chocolates and then there are Bubó chocolates – jewel-like creations and playful desserts by pastry maestro Carles Mampel. Mon–Thurs & Sun 10am–10pm, Fri & Sat 10am–midnight.

★**Casa Gispert** C/Sombrerers 23, La Ribera ☎933 197 535, ⓦcasagispert.com; ⓜJaume I; map pp.648–649. Roasters of nuts, coffee and spices for over 150 years. It's a truly delectable store of wooden boxes, baskets, stacked shelves and tantalizing smells. Tues–Fri 9.30am–2pm & 4–8.30pm (also Mon, same times, in Oct, Nov & Dec), Sat 10am–2pm & 5–8.30pm.

★**Formatgeria La Seu** C/Dagueria 16, Barri Gòtic ☎934 126 548, ⓦformatgerialaseu.com; ⓜJaume I; map pp.648–649. Chatty Scottish owner Katherine is usually on hand to advise about her best farmhouse cheeses, and you can try before you buy with a €2.80 tasting plate. Tues–Thurs 10am–2pm & 5–8pm, Fri & Sat 10am–3.30pm & 5–8pm; closed Aug.

Forn Baluard C/Baluard 38–40, Barceloneta ☎932 211 208, ⓦbaluardbarceloneta.com; ⓜBarceloneta; map pp.648–649. There are scores of bakeries in Barcelona, but when push comes to shove, foodies pick the Baluard, right next to Barceloneta market, whose passion for artisan bread, cakes and pastries knows no bounds. Mon–Sat 8am–9pm.

Papabubble C/Ample 28, Barri Gòtic ☎932 688 625, ⓦpapabubble.com; ⓜDrassanes; map pp.648–649. Groovy young things rolling out home-made candy to a chill-out soundtrack. Mon–Fri 10am–2pm & 4–8.30pm, Sat 10am–8.30pm; closed Aug.

Vila Viniteca C/Agullers 7 & 9, La Ribera ☎902 327 777, ⓦvilaviniteca.es; ⓜBarceloneta; map pp.648–649. A very knowledgeable specialist in Catalan and Spanish wines. Pick your vintage and then nip over the road for the gourmet deli part of the operation. Mon–Sat 8.30am–8.30pm (closes Sat at 2.30pm in July & Aug).

MUSIC

Independent music and CD stores are concentrated around C/Tallers (El Raval), off the Ramblas.

Discos Castelló C/Tallers 7, El Raval ☎933 025 946, ⓦcastellodiscos.es; ⓜCatalunya; map pp.648–649. You can track down pretty much anything you want here, including classical recordings, pop, rock, *mestiza*, electronica, hardcore and Spanish and Catalan sounds – and if not, other neighborhood specialists should do the job. Mon–Sat 10am–8.30pm.

★**Wah Wah Discos** c/Riera Baixa 14, El Raval ☎934 423 703, ⓦwww.wah-wahsupersonic.com; ⓜLiceu; map pp.648–649. Vinyl heaven for record collectors – rock, indie, garage, 70s punk, electronica, blues, folk, prog, jazz, soul and rarities of all kinds. Mon–Sat 11am–2pm & 5–8.30pm.

DIRECTORY

Banks and exchange For out-of-hours exchange offices, look down the Ramblas, or go to Barcelona Sants (daily 8am–8pm); El Corte Inglés, Pza. de Catalunya (Mon–Sat 9.30am–9.30pm); or Turisme de Catalunya tourist office, Pza. de Catalunya 17 (Mon–Sat 9am–9pm, Sun 9am–2pm).
Consulates Australia, Avgda. Diagonal 433, Esquerra de l'Eixample ☎933 623 792, ⓦspain.embassy.gov.au, ⓜDiagonal; Britain, Avgda. Diagonal 477, Eixample ☎933 666 200, ⓦukinspain.fco.gov.uk, ⓜHospital Clínic; Canada, Pza. de Catalunya 9, ☎932 703 614, ⓦcanadainternational .gc.ca/spain-espagne, ⓜCatalunya; Republic of Ireland, Gran Vía Carles III 94, Les Corts ☎934 915 021, ⓦirlanda.es, ⓜMaría Cristina/Les Corts; New Zealand, Travessera de Gràcia 64, ⓜGràcia ☎932 090 399, ⓦnzembassy.com, FGC

10

Gràcia; USA Pg. de la Reina Elisenda 23, Sarrià ☎ 932 802 227, ⓦ barcelona.usconsulate.gov, FGC Reina Elisenda.

Hospitals For emergency hospital treatment, call ☎ 061 or go to one of the following central hospitals, which have 24hr accident and emergency (*urgències*) services: Centre Perecamps, Avgda. Drassanes 13–15, El Raval ☎ 934 410 600, Ⓜ Drassanes; Hospital Clínic i Provincial, C/Villaroel 170, Eixample ☎ 932 275 400, Ⓜ Hospital Clínic; Hospital del Mar, Pg. Marítim 25–29, Vila Olímpica ☎ 932 483 000, Ⓜ Ciutadella-Vila Olímpica; Hospital de la Santa Creu i Sant Pau, C/Sant Quintí, Eixample ☎ 932 919 000, Ⓜ Hospital de Sant Pau.

Laundries Lavomatic, Pza. Joaquim Xirau 1, Barri Gòtic ☎ 933 425 119, Ⓜ Drassanes, and C/Consolat del Mar 43–45, Pza. del Palau, La Ribera ☎ 932 684 768, Ⓜ Barceloneta (both Mon–Sat 9am–9pm); and LavaXpres, at sixteen locations, including C/Ferlandina 34, El Raval ☎ 933 183 018, ⓦ lavaxpres.com, Ⓜ Universitat (daily 8am–11pm).

Left luggage Barcelona Sants station (daily 7am–11pm; €3–4.50/day). There are lockers at the Estació de França, Passeig de Gràcia station and Barcelona Nord (all 6am–11.30pm; €3–4.50).

Pharmacies Usual hours are weekdays 9am to 1pm and 4pm to 8pm. At least one in each neighbourhood is open daily 24hr (and marked as such) – Farmacia Clapies, Ramblas 98 ☎ 933 012 843, ⓦ farmaciaclapes.com, Ⓜ Liceu, is convenient.

Police Guàrdia Urbana station at Ramblas 43, opposite Pza. Reial ☎ 932 562 430, Ⓜ Liceu (24hr; English spoken). To get a police report for your insurance, go to the Mossos d'Esquadra (Catalan police force) station at C/Nou de la Rambla 76–80, El Raval ☎ 933 062 300, Ⓜ Paral.lel (take your passport). Contact the police on: Mossos d'Esquadra ☎ 112, Policía Nacional ☎ 091, Guàrdia Urbana ☎ 092.

Post offices The main post office (*Correus*) is on Pza. d'Antoni López, Barri Gòtic ☎ 934 868 302, ⓦ correos.es, Ⓜ Barceloneta/Jaume I (Mon–Fri 8.30am–9.30pm, Sat 8.30am–2pm).

Swimming pools The city's most spectacular pool is the open-air Piscina Municipal de Montjuïc, Avgda. Miramar 31, Montjuïc, Funicular de Montjuïc (mid-June to early Sept daily 11am–6.30pm; €5). Indoor and outdoor beachside pools at Club Natació Atlètic Barceloneta, Pza. del Mar, Ⓜ Barceloneta (Mon–Fri 6.30am–11pm, Sat 7am–11pm, Sun 8am–5pm, until 8pm mid-May to Sept; full-day €12).

Telephone offices *Locutorios*, which specialize in discounted overseas connections – are scattered through the old city, particularly in El Raval.

Montserrat

The mountain of **Montserrat**, with its strangely shaped crags of rock, its monastery and ruined hermitage caves, stands just 40km northwest of Barcelona, off the road to Lleida. It's the most popular day-trip from the city, reached in around ninety minutes by train and then cable car or rack railway for a thrilling ride up to the monastery. Once there, you can visit the basilica and monastery buildings, and complete your day with a walk around the woods and crags, using the two funicular railways that depart from the monastery complex. Inevitably, both monastery and mountain are ruthlessly exploited as a tourist trip from the city or the Costa Brava, while the main **pilgrimages** take place on April 27 and September 8, but don't be put off – the place itself is still magical and well worth a visit.

Monestir de Montserrat

Legends hang easily upon Montserrat. Fifty years after the birth of Christ, St Peter is said to have deposited an image of the Virgin carved by St Luke in one of the mountain caves. The so-called Black Virgin (La Moreneta) icon was subsequently lost in the early eighth century, after being hidden during the Muslim invasion, but reappeared in 880, accompanied by the customary visions and celestial music. A chapel was built to house it, superseded in 976 by a Benedictine monastery, the Monestir de Montserrat, set at an altitude of nearly 1000m. Miracles abounded and the Virgin of Montserrat soon became the chief cult image of Catalunya and a pilgrimage centre second in Spain only to Santiago de Compostela. Its fortunes declined in the nineteenth century, though in recent decades Montserrat's popularity has again become established. Today, in addition to the tourists, tens of thousands of newly married couples come here to seek La Moreneta's blessing.

The monastery's various outbuildings – including hotel and restaurant, post office, souvenir shop, self-service cafeteria and bar – fan out around an open square, and there are extraordinary mountain views from the terrace.

Basílica

Daily 7.30am–8pm, access to La Moreneta 8–10.30am & noon–6.30pm; boys' choir Mon–Fri at 1pm & 6.45pm, Sun at noon & 6.45pm; performance times may vary during school holidays at Christmas/New Year and from late June to mid-Aug • Free

Of the religious buildings, only the Renaissance **Basílica** is open to the public. **La Moreneta** stands above the high altar, and the approach to this beautiful icon reveals the enormous wealth of the monastery, as you queue along a corridor leading through the back of the basilica's rich side chapels. The best time to visit the basilica is when Montserrat's world-famous **boys' choir** sings. The boys belong to the Escolania, a choral school established in the fourteenth century and unchanged in musical style since its foundation.

10

Museu de Montserrat

Daily 10am–5.45pm • €7

The **Museu de Montserrat** presents a few archeological finds brought back by travelling monks, together with paintings and sculpture dating from as early as the thirteenth century, including works by Old Masters, French Impressionists and Catalan *modernistas*. There's also a collection of Byzantine icons, though other religious items are in short supply, as most of the monastery's valuables were carried off by Napoleon's troops, who sacked the complex in 1811.

Mountain walks

Funicular departures vary by season, but mostly every 20min, daily 10am–6pm • Santa Cova €3.50 return, Sant Joan €9 return, combination ticket €10

Following the mountain tracks to the nearby caves and hermitages, you can contemplate Goethe's observation of 1816: "Nowhere but in his own Montserrat will a man find happiness and peace." One funicular drops to the path for **Santa Cova**, a seventeenth-century chapel built where the La Moreneta icon is said to have been found. It's an easy walk there and back, which takes less than an hour. The other funicular rises steeply to the hermitage of **Sant Joan**, from where it's a tougher 45-minute walk to the **Sant Jeroni** hermitage, and another fifteen minutes to the **Sant Jeroni summit** at 1236m.

ARRIVAL AND INFORMATION   MONTSERRAT

There are two ways to reach Montserrat by public transport: either by cable car or mountain railway, but in the first instance you need to take the **FGC train** (line R5, direction Manresa), which leaves Barcelona's Pza. d'Espanya (Ⓜ Espanya) daily at hourly intervals from 8.36am.

By cable car Get off the train at Montserrat Aeri (50min) for the connecting cable car, the Aeri de Montserrat (departures every 15min, March–Oct daily 9.40am–2pm & 2.35–7pm, Nov–Feb daily 10.10am–2pm & 2.35–5.45pm; ☏ 938 350 005, ⓦ aeridemontserrat.com). You may have to queue for 15min or so, but then it's an exhilarating 5min swoop up the sheer mountainside to a terrace just below the monastery.

By mountain railway The Montserrat mountain railway, the Cremallera de Montserrat (departures hourly, daily 8.48am–5.38pm, until 7.38pm at weekends April–Oct plus daily July–Sept; ☏ 932 051 515, ⓦ cremallera demontserrat.cat), departs from Monistrol de Montserrat (the next stop after Montserrat Aeri, another 5min), and takes 20min to complete the climb.

Tickets Return through-tickets from Barcelona cost around €20, either for the train/cable car or train/mountain

railway. There are also two combination tickets available: the Trans Montserrat (€27.50), which includes all transport services, including unlimited use of the mountain funiculars, and entry to the audiovisual exhibit; and the Tot Montserrat (€43.70), which includes the same plus monastery museum entry and a cafeteria lunch.

By car Take the A2 motorway as far as the Martorell exit, and then follow the N11 and C55 to the Montserrat turn-off – or park at either the cable-car or the mountain-railway station and take the rides up instead. All-in cable-car/ *cremallera*/Montserrat attraction combo tickets are available at the station for drivers who park-and-ride.

Visitor Centre ☏ 938 777 701, ⓦ www.montserratvisita. com; daily 9am–5.30pm, Sat, Sun & July–Sept until 6.45pm. You can pick up maps of the complex and mountain here, and staff can also advise about the accommodation options.

Catalunya

TEATRE-MUSEU DALÍ, FIGUERES

Catalunya

Barcelona may make the biggest splash with visitors, but it's the rest of Catalunya that defines the region's distinct – and proud – identity. From the soaring Pyrenees to the Mediterranean-licked coast to tiny villages presided over by stone chapels, this is a region that, perhaps more than anywhere else in Spain, feels like a country unto itself. You'll hear Catalan – and only Catalan – on the streets of many inland communities. And, though Barcelona leads the way in Catalan dining, it's beyond the city where you'll find even purer (and dare we say better) versions of the cuisine, rooted in Catalunya's natural bounty, from wild mushrooms to sun-warmed tomatoes. Catalan towns are generally very well-maintained – and often surprisingly prosperous – a relic of the early industrial era when Catalunya developed more rapidly than most of Spain. There's a confidence in being Catalan that dates back to the fourteenth-century Golden Age, when it was a kingdom that ruled the Balearics, Valencia, the French border regions, and even Sardinia. Times have changed, of course, but Catalunya, regally waving its flag, continues to exert a certain power that you'll feel in all corners of the region.

Catalunya (Cataluña in Castilian Spanish, Catalonia in English) is, above all, a spectacular study in contrasts, from the snowy peaks of the Pyrenees to the sparkling blue water of the coast's shallow coves. The showy swagger of Costa Brava's mega-resorts, meanwhile, mixes alluringly with the stillness of ancient monasteries hidden in the heartland. Despite this diversity, however, Catalunya is relatively compact, so it's possible – as many a local will proudly point out – to ski in the morning and sunbathe on the beach in the afternoon.

On the whole everything is easily reached from Barcelona; the city is linked to most main centres by excellent bus and train services. The obvious targets are the **coasts** north and south of the city, and the various **provincial capitals** (Girona, Tarragona and

SITGES

Highlights

❶ Cadaqués Experience the Costa Brava as it once was at this lovely, quirky seaside town. **See p.730**

❷ Girona This beautiful, labyrinthine city boasts a two-thousand-year-old history, including one of the best-preserved medieval Jewish quarters in the country. **See p.734**

❸ El Celler de Can Roca Feast on elevated Catalan cuisine at this handsome restaurant helmed by the Roca brothers, which is consistently voted as one of the best in the world. **See p.739**

❹ Teatre-Museu Dalí Explore the life and work of the flamboyant artist at this shrine to Surrealism. **See p.741**

❺ Skiing Baqueira-Beret Grab the ski poles: This premiere ski resort offers the finest skiing in the Pyrenees, if not in Spain. **See p.768**

❻ Cava country Sip Spain's magnificent bubbly at one of the *modernista* vineyards around Sant Sadurní d'Anoia and Vilafranca del Penedès. **See p.771**

❼ Sitges Sample the frenetic nightlife or, better still, the *Carnaval*, of chic Sitges. **See p.772**

❽ Roman Tarragona This ancient city reveals some of the country's most important remains of the Roman occupation. **See p.776**

HIGHLIGHTS ARE MARKED ON THE MAP ON PP.708–709

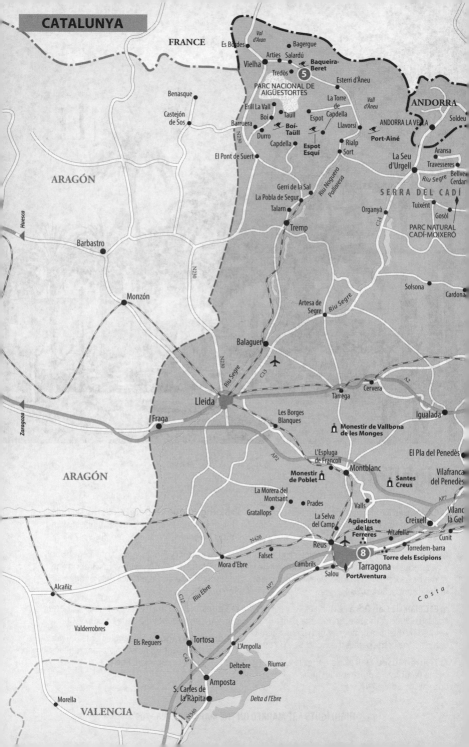

N

FRANCE

Perpignan

Latour de Carol

Llívia

uigcerdà

Alp

La Molina

Toses

La Masella

aga

des

Berga

Borredà

Núria

Queralbs

Ribes de Freser

Molló

Tregurà

Beget

Camprodon

Sant Martí d'Ogassa

Ripoll

GARROTXA

Sant Joan de les Abadesses

Olot

C26

Castellfollit

Santa Pau

PARC NATURAL DE LA ZONA VOLCÀNICA

Riu Freser

Banyoles

Riu Ter

Vic

Sant Hilari Sacalm

C25

Viladrau

Arbúcies

Santa Coloma de Farners

Hostalric

Maçanet

Sadernes

Darnius

Sant Llorenç

Besalú

GI 524

AP7

Siurana d'Empordà

La Jonquera

Rabós

Espolla

Mollet

Llançà

Portbou

El Port de la Selva

Cap de Creus

Sant Pere de Rodes

Figueres

Castelló d'Empúries

Empúries

L'Escala

Roses

Portlligat

Cadaqués

PARC NATURAL DELS AIGUAMOLLS DE L'EMPORDÀ

Costa Brava

Bordils

Púbol

Girona

C66

Torroella de Montgrí

Ullastret

Peratallada

La Bisbal

Pals

C66

Sa Riera

L'Estartit

Begur

Platja d'Aiguablava

Tamariu

Llafranc

Calella de Palafrugell

Palafrugell

Palamós

Platja d'Aro

S'Agaró

Sant Feliu de Guíxols

GI 682

Viladrau

Manresa

ontserrat

Terrassa

Sabadell

Granollers

C17

SERRA DEL MONTSENY

C32

Calella

Sant Pol de Mar

Tossa de Mar

N11

Blanes

Lloret de Mar

Costa Brava

Mataró

Barcelona

Costa Maresme

Castelldefels

Sitges

aurada

MEDITERRANEAN SEA

HIGHLIGHTS

1 Cadaqués

2 Girona

3 El Celler de Can Roca

4 Teatre-Museu Dalí

5 Skiing Baqueira-Beret

6 Cava country

7 Sitges

8 Roman Tarragona

0 ————————————— 25

kilometres

Lleida), destinations that make a series of comfortable day-trips. Even on a short trip, you can take in the medieval city of **Girona** and the surrounding area, which includes the extraordinary volcanic **Garrotxa** region, as well as the best of the beach towns on the **Costa Brava**, which runs up to the French border. This was one of the first stretches of Spanish coast to be developed for mass tourism, and though that's no great recommendation, the large, brash resorts are tempered by some more isolated beaches and lower-key holiday and fishing villages, such as **Cadaqués**. Just inland from the coast, **Figueres** contains the Teatre-Museu Dalí, Catalunya's biggest tourist attraction.

With more time, you can head for the **Catalan Pyrenees**, which offer magnificent and relatively isolated hiking territory, particularly in and around the **Parc Nacional de Aigüestortes**, and good skiing in winter. South of Barcelona, the **Costa Daurada** features a fine beach at **Sitges** and the attractive coastal town of **Tarragona**; inland, the appealing cava **vineyards** around Sant Sadurní d'Anoia or the romantic monastery of **Poblet** figure as approaches to the enjoyable provincial capital of **Lleida**.

Brief history

The **Catalan people** have an individual and deeply felt historical and cultural identity, seen most clearly in the language, which takes precedence over Castilian on street names and signs. Despite being banned for over thirty years during the Franco dictatorship, Catalan survived behind closed doors and has staged a dramatic comeback since the Generalísimo's death. As in the Basque Country, though, regionalism goes back much farther than this.

Early origins to the twentieth century

On the expulsion of the Moors in 874, Guifré el Pelós (Wilfred the Hairy) established himself as the first independent **Count of Barcelona**; his kingdom flourished and the region became famous for its seafaring, mercantile and commercial skills, characteristics that to some extent still set the region apart. In the twelfth century came union with Aragón, though the Catalans kept many of their traditional, hard-won rights (*usatges*).

CATALÀ

Learning a few phrases in Catalan will take you far in Catalunya. **Català** has more or less taken over from Castilian, a phenomenon known as the *venganza* (revenge), though few visitors realize how ingrained and widespread the language is and sometimes commit the error of calling it a dialect. On paper, Català looks like a cross between French and Spanish and is generally easy to understand if you know those two but, spoken, it has a distinct, rounded sound and is far harder to come to grips with, especially away from Barcelona, where accents are stronger.

When Franco came to power, publishing houses, bookshops and libraries were raided and Català books destroyed. While this was followed by a let-up in the mid-1940s, the language was still banned from the radio, TV, daily press and, most importantly, schools, which is why many older people today cannot necessarily write Català (even if they speak it all the time). As for Castilian, in Barcelona virtually everyone can speak it, while in country areas, many people can sometimes only understand it but not speak it.

Català is spoken in Catalunya proper, part of Aragón, much of Valencia, the Balearic Islands, the Principality of Andorra and in parts of the French Pyrenees, albeit with variations of dialect (it is thus much more widely spoken than several better-known languages such as Danish, Finnish and Norwegian). It is a Romance language, stemming from Latin and, more directly, from medieval Provençal and *lemosi*, the literary French of Occitania. Spaniards in the rest of the country tend to belittle it by saying that to get a Català word you just cut a Castilian one in half. In fact, the grammar is much more complicated than Castilian, and the language has eight vowel sounds (including three diphthongs). In the text we've tried to keep to Català names (with Castilian in parentheses where necessary) – not least because street signs and *turisme* maps are in Català. Either way, you're unlikely to get confused as the difference is usually only slight: ie Girona (Gerona) and Lleida (Lérida). There's a Catalan glossary to help you further (see p.927).

From then until the fourteenth century marked Catalunya's **Golden Age**, and in 1359 the Catalan Generalitat – Europe's first parliamentary government – was established.

In 1469, through the marriage of Fernando V (of Aragón) to Isabel I (of Castile), the region was added on to the rest of the emergent Spanish state. Throughout the following centuries the Catalans made various attempts to secede from the stifling grasp of central bureaucracy, which saw the Catalan enterprise as merely another means of filling the state coffers. Early industrialization, which was centred here and in the Basque Country, only intensified political disaffection, and in the 1920s and 1930s anarchist, communist and socialist parties all established major power bases in Catalunya.

The Civil War to the present day
In 1931, after the fall of the dictator General Primo de Rivera, a **Catalan Republic** was proclaimed and its autonomous powers guaranteed by the new Republican government. Any incipient separatism collapsed, however, with the outbreak of the Civil War, during which Catalunya was a bastion of the Republican cause, Barcelona holding out until January 1939. In revenge, Franco pursued a policy of harsh suppression, attempting to wipe out all evidence of Catalan cultural and economic primacy. Among his more subtle methods was the encouragement of immigration from other parts of Spain in order to dilute regional identity. Even so, Catalunya remained obstinate, the scene of protests and demonstrations throughout the dictatorship, and after Franco's death a **Catalan government** was formally reinstated in 1979. This, the semi-autonomous **Generalitat**, enjoys a high profile and continues to extend its power. In 2012, the pro-independence movement gained particular momentum, with a mass demonstration of 1.5 million people in Barcelona on September 11, Catalunya's national day. In 2013, hundreds of thousands formed a human chain, from the northern to southern borders of the region, to promote Catalan autonomy. And in December 2013, independence supporters defied the Spanish government by announcing that they planned to hold a referendum for Catalan independence in November 2014. Opinion poll numbers vary, but at the time of writing, many showed 55 percent of Catalans supporting independence, though this will likely fluctuate.

The Costa Brava

Stretching from Blanes, 60km north of Barcelona, to the French border, the unfairly maligned **Costa Brava** (Rugged Coast) boasts wooded coves, high cliffs, pretty beaches and deep blue water. Struggling under its image as the first developed package-tour coast in Spain, it is very determinedly shifting away from mass tourism. It is undeniable that the unharnessed tourist boom wreaked damage in some areas, but the old *sangría*-and-chips image is giving way to greater prominence for the area's natural beauty and fascinating cultural heritage.

Broadly, the coast is split into three areas: **La Selva** at the southern tip, clustered around brash **Lloret de Mar**, and the medieval walled town of **Tossa de Mar**; the stylish central area of **Baix Empordà** between Sant Feliu de Guíxols and Pals, popular with the chic Barcelona crowd, which boasts some wonderfully scenic stretches of rolling coastline around Palamós, the beaches and villages of inland Palafrugell and hilltop Begur; and the more rugged **Alt Empordà** in the north. This area is marked by the broad sweep of the Golf de Roses, site of a nature reserve, the Parc Natural dels Aiguamolls de l'Empordà, and the alluring peace of the ancient Greek and Roman settlement of Empúries, and extends to the bohemian Cadaqués, which attracts an arty crowd paying tribute to Salvador Dalí; the artist lived most of his life in the labyrinthine warren of converted fishermen's huts in a neighbouring cove, now a fabulous museum.

11

FIESTAS

FEBRUARY/MARCH/APRIL

Lent: Carnaval Sitges has Catalunya's best celebrations.
Easter: Semana Santa (Holy Week) Celebrations at Besalú, Girona and La Pobla de Segur.
April 23: Semana Medieval de Sant Jordi St George is celebrated throughout Catalunya, with a week of exhibitions, dances and medieval music in Montblanc, among other places (⚙ setmanamedieval.org).

MAY/JUNE

Throughout May and June: Festival de Jazz In Vic.
First fortnight of May: Festa de la Lana Annual wool fair in Ripoll.
Third week of May: Fires i Festes de la Santa Creu Processions and music in Figueres.
Corpus Christi (variable): Festa de Corpus Christi Big processions in Sitges, plus the massive **Patum** festival in Berga.
June 21–23: Festa de Sant Patllari In Camprodon.
June 24: Dia de Sant Joan Celebrated everywhere; watch out for things shutting down for a day on either side.

JULY/AUGUST

Early July to late August: Ripoll International Music Festival Classical music in Ripoll.
Third week of July: Festa de Santa Cristina At Lloret de Mar.
Mid-August: Festa de Sant Magí In Tarragona.
July/early August: Festival Internacional de Música In Torroella de Montgrí.
Mid-July to late August: Festival Jardins de Cap Roig In Calella de Palafrugell.
Late July: Festa del Renaixement (Renaissance Festival) in Taragona.
Late July to late August: Festival de Música de Begur In Begur.

SEPTEMBER

8: The Virgin's Birth celebrated in Cadaqués, Núria and L'Escala, among other towns.
22: Sant Maurici At his *ermita* in the national park above Espot.
Nearest weekend to 24th: Festa de Sant Primuns and Felician At Besalú.
Third week: Mercat de Música Viva festival in Vic.
Third week: Festa de Santa Tecla Human castles (*castells*) and processions of *gegants* (giant puppets) in Tarragona.

OCTOBER

8: Feria de Vielha Annual fair.
Last week: Fires i Festes de Sant Narcís In Girona.

NOVEMBER

1: Sant Ermengol Celebrations in La Seu d'Urgell.

DECEMBER

Early December: Mercat Medieval de Vic Re-creation of a medieval market in Vic.

GETTING AROUND   COSTA BRAVA

By car Driving is the easiest way to get around and gives you access to some of the more remote parts of the coast, though expect the smaller coastal roads to be very busy in summer and parking to be tricky in the major towns.

By bus Buses in the region are almost all operated by Sarfa (⚙ sarfa.com), which has offices in the bigger towns and offers an efficient service the length of the coast. Teisa (⚙ teisa-bus.com) also operates some routes in the area. You could consider using Girona or Figueres as a base for lateral trips to the coast, as both have big bus termini and are within an hour of the beach.

By train The train from Barcelona to the French border runs inland most of the time, serving Girona and Figueres, but emerging on the coast itself only at Llançà. The AVE train, which is faster but pricier, operates from Perpignan in France to Figueres and on to Barcelona. In December 2013, the AVE network reached a milestone when direct high-speed trains between Spain and France were launched for the first time, thereby connecting the Spanish high-speed rail system with the rest of Europe.

By boat Between Easter and September, there are daily boat services (*cruceros*), which cover short hops along the coast; there are generally services between Lloret de Mar, Tossa de Mar and Sant Feliu de Guíxols, among other coastal towns. Tourist offices have up-to-date information on companies and schedules; timetables and routes can vary yearly.

By foot You can access some of the lovelier coves by walking all or just parts of the fabulous Camí de Ronda necklace of footpaths that runs along almost all of the coastline.

Lloret de Mar

Brash, tourist-magnet **LLORET DE MAR**, some 66km northeast of Barcelona, is everything you've ever heard about it – and more. Yet underneath its undeniable beach-driven commercialism and gaudy nightlife is a centuries-old town trying to make itself known. The result is a mix of hedonism and history, with music-pumping disco clubs clustered around a delightful fifteenth-century church, high-rise monstrosities alongside genteel mansions and a packed main beach that belies some splendid rocky coves tucked away on either side of town. Lloret's main **beach** and neighbouring Fenals beach is where many of the hotels are grouped; the south end of Fenals, backed by pine woods, is much less crowded. Farther afield are a number of tiny **coves** favoured by local bathers. Cala Santa Cristina and the adjacent Cala Treumal are the best, while the lovely Cala Boadella is popular with nudists; all are off the Blanes road. Any sightseeing in Lloret is centred on the warren of streets in the **old town**, amid the hustle of T-shirt shops and tourist paraphernalia.

Church of Sant Romà and Capella del Santíssim

Pza. de l'Església • **Sant Romà** Open for services only • **Capella del Santíssim** Daily 10am–2pm & 5–8pm; confirm with *turisme*

Holding court over the old town is the colourful church of **Sant Romà**, originally built in Gothic style in 1522. A *modernista* renovation was begun in 1914, but much of this work was destroyed in the Civil War; only the adjacent **Capella del Santíssim**, with its Byzantine cupolas, Mudéjar and Renaissance influences, remains.

Museu del Mar

Pg. Camprodon i Arrieta • March–May, Oct & Nov Mon–Sat 9am–1pm & 4–7pm, Sun 10am–1pm & 4–7pm; June–Sept Mon–Sat 10am–1pm & 4–8pm, Sun 10am–1pm & 4–7pm; Dec–Feb Mon–Sat 9am–1.30pm & 3.30–6pm, Sun 9am–2pm; last admission usually 45min before closing time • €4 • ☎ 972 364 454, ✍ lloretdemar.org

Explore Lloret's maritime legacy – illustrated by ship models, a replica of an 1848 figurehead and photos and mementos – as well as other aspects of the town's history in the well-run **Museu del Mar**. The well-curated museum shares space with one of the town's *turisme* in Can Garriga, a beautifully restored nineteenth-century mansion on the town's stately promenade.

Jardins de Santa Clotilde

Daily: April–Sept 10am–8pm; Oct–March 10am–5pm; last admission 1hr before closing time; year-round guided tours Sun 10.30pm • €4

On a headland above the coast, southwest of town, are the surprisingly tranquil **Jardins de Santa Clotilde**, ornamental gardens laid out in *modernista* style in 1919 and offering fabulous views over the Mediterranean. Visitor numbers are limited to fifty at a time but you're most likely to find yourself alone, even in August. In spring and summer, you can sometimes catch live jazz on the weekends in the gardens; ask at the *turisme* for details.

Cementiri Modernista de Lloret de Mar

Camí del Repòs • Daily: April–Oct 8am–8pm, Nov–March 8am–6pm • ☎ 972 349 573

Head beyond the thronged beaches and noisy bars, and your reward is the quiet **Cementiri Modernista de Lloret de Mar** just west of the town centre. Created in 1901, this impressive cemetery features funerary art by an astonishing line-up of *modernista* greats, including Josep Puig y Cadafalch (see p.672), Antoni M. Gallisà i Soqué and Eusebi Arnau. Many of the lavish mausoleums were commissioned by *Indianos*, which is the term for locals who

11

left the Costa Brava in the 1800s to seek fortune in the Americas – mostly Cuba. While many didn't find riches abroad, those who did often returned to build grand mansions and, in the case of this cemetery, mausoleums.

ARRIVAL AND INFORMATION   LLORET DE MAR

By bus The bus station is north of the town centre, on Carretera de Blanes. As well as frequent services from nearby Tossa, there are regular buses from Barcelona (8–10 daily; 1hr 15min), Girona (5 daily; 1hr 20min), Palafrugell (2–3 daily; 1hr) and Platja d'Aro (2–4 daily; 50min), among others.

By boat *Cruceros* and other coastal boats dock at the beach, which is where the ticket offices are too. In summer there are around a dozen daily services up and down the coast.

Turisme The most central *turisme* is on the seafront at Pg. Camprodon i Arrieta 1 (March–May Mon–Sat 9am–1pm & 4–7pm, Sun 10am–1pm & 4–7pm; June–Sept Mon–Sat 9am–8pm, Sun 10am–1pm & 4–7pm; Oct & Nov daily 9am–1pm & 4–7pm; Dec–Feb daily 9am–1.30pm & 3.30–6pm, Sun 10am–3pm; ☏ 972 364 735, ⓦ lloretdemar.org).

ACCOMMODATION AND EATING

Many **hotels** in Lloret are block-booked by agents, so it's a good idea to book in advance, especially in the summer. As you'd expect, there are lots of high-rise hotels, but you'll also find some decent smaller spots in the old part of town, not far from the beach.

Though Lloret may be the domain of fast-food joints and fish and chips, there's still a reasonably good choice of places to **eat** in the old town. **Clubs** are mainly centred around Avgda. Just Marlés, the main road into town running perpendicular to the seafront, while lively **bars** dot the streets around Pza. d'Espanya and Pza. del Carme, just behind the beach.

Ca L'amic Carnisseria Vella 5 ☏ 972 367 857, ⓦ calamic.com. Feast on robust seafood dishes – such as *merluza*, or hake, with clams – and a good weekday lunch menu starting at €10 at this friendly, homespun restaurant. Tues & Wed 1–3.30pm, Thurs–Sun 1–3.30pm & 8–11pm.

Can Bolet Sant Mateu 6 972 371 237, ⓦ canbolet.com. With all the tourist restaurants that dominate Lloret, it's easy to forget that there are many family eateries with a long history – and *Can Bolet* is one of them. Founded in 1961, the welcoming restaurant serves classic Catalan dishes, including *fideuà* (a dish of traditional thin noodles) and grilled squid. Dishes €8–€16. Tues–Sat noon–4pm & 8–11.30pm, Sun noon–4pm.

Fergus Style Plaza Paris Pza. Paris 5 ☏ 972 364 558, ⓦ fergushotels.com. Fergus, which has a chain of well-maintained accommodation options on coastal Spain and in Mallorca, runs this comfortable hotel. Rooms come in a range of sizes, including quadruple rooms, which are ideal for families and groups of friends. After a day of sunning, enjoy the pleasant spa and outdoor Jacuzzi. **€65**

Hostal La Habana C/Les Taronges 11 ☏ 972 367 707, ⓦ lahabanalloret.com. Smart, family-run *pensió* on a narrow street leading from the beach to the old town, with bright, well-maintained rooms. **€40**

Hotel Santi Marta Platja de Santa Cristina ☏ 972 364 904, ⓦ hstamarta.com. A tranquil escape, this luxurious hotel sits above a quiet beach and the Ermita de Santa Cristina, between Lloret and Blanes, with elegant rooms and lovely views of the sea. **€180**

Tossa de Mar

Tossa de Mar is quite a sight upon arrival by boat: medieval walls and the turrets of the old quarter, **Vila Vella**, rise pale and shimmering on the hill above the modern town. Tossa has managed to escape the full-blown tourism of Lloret, 13km to the south, and balances comfortably between a restful holiday hub and working town. Founded originally by the Romans, the town has twelfth-century walls that surround the old quarter – a maze of cobbled streets, whitewashed houses and flower boxes – and climb the headland, offering terrific views over beach and bay.

Tossa's best beach is the **Platja de la Mar Menuda**, around the headland away from the old town and very popular with divers; look for a natural pink cross in the rock, supposedly marking where Sant Ramon de Penyafort gave a dying man his absolution in 1235. The central **Platja Gran**, though pleasant, gets crowded; if you have your own transport, make for the tiny coves north and south of the town, which are much more rewarding. Booths on the main beach sell tickets for **boat trips** (Easter–Oct) around the surrounding coastline, including to Sant Feliu.

CUINA CATALANA

"Catalunya has a fantastic climate, a rich plurality of products and diverse geography – the sea, the mountains, and the plains. There are few parts of the world this fertile."

Ferran Adrià

That's how the famous Catalan chef describes his home region's geographical bounty, source of its rich *cuina Catalana*. Culled from **"mar i muntanya"** (sea and mountain), Catalunya's cuisine matches fresh seafood on the coast with hearty meats (particularly sausages) inland, while fragrant fruits and vegetables provide ballast to every meal.

The **seafood** variety is impressive, and includes plump shrimp and langoustine; eel from the Ebro delta; trout from Pyrenean rivers; and the ever-present *bacallà* (cod). **Sausages**, most using pork as a base, include *botifarra*, *fuet* (a thin, dried sausage) and *llonganissa* (cured sausage). Catalunya has taken **mushrooms** to a high art, not least aromatic *bolets* (wild mushrooms), which are picked and prepared in autumn. In late winter and early spring, *calçots* (large, tender, sweet spring onions) are roasted over coals and dipped in a **romesco** sauce, which is made with tomatoes, peppers, onions, almonds, garlic and olive oil.

Perhaps Catalunya's best-loved export is **pa amb tomàquet**, bread rubbed with tomato and drizzled in olive oil, which is not only ubiquitous throughout the region, but in the rest of Spain. As for dessert: Catalunya's answer to crème brûlée is the custard-style **crema Catalana**. And when it comes time to celebrate, do so with **cava** (see p.771).

CATALAN CHEFS

Contemporary Catalan cuisine has become synonymous with **Ferran Adrià**, who transformed (and transfixed) the culinary world with his famous scented *espumas* (foams) and "molecular gastronomy" (or, as Ferran prefers to describe it, *cocina de vanguardia*). The effects have gone far beyond the dazzling laboratory of a kitchen in his former restaurant **El Bulli** on the Costa Brava. Ferran closed *El Bulli* in July 2011 to launch a nonprofit culinary foundation (see box, p.730). Chefs across the region have been inspired by Ferran, each adding their own spin, including (in Barcelona) Carles Abellán, as well as Albert Adrià who, with older brother Ferran, opened the excellent tapas bar *Tickets* (see p.692) in 2011, followed by several other restaurants in the city, adding to the Adrià empire. Elsewhere in the region, you'll find restaurants serving elevated Catalan cuisine, including at *Compartir* (see p.732) in Cadaques, helmed by three former *El Bulli* chefs; *El Motel* (see p.743), considered the birthplace of modern Catalan cuisine; and the legendary *Celler de Can Roca* (see p.739), voted best restaurant in the world in 2013.

Far de Tossa and around

Pq. de la Vila Vella • Tues–Sun 10am–5pm, sometimes open longer hours in summer • €3

Towering over the Vila Vella is the nineteenth-century **Far de Tossa**, home to an innovative exhibition on Mediterranean lighthouses. Just below here, not far from the ruins of the town's fifteenth-century Gothic church, stands a **statue of Ava Gardner**, who made the town famous in the 1950 film, *Pandora and the Flying Dutchman*.

Museu Municipal

Pza. Roig i Soler 1 • June–Sept Tues–Sat 10am–8pm, Mon & Sun 10am–2pm & 4–8pm; Oct–May Tues–Sat 10am–2pm & 4–8pm, Sun 10am–2pm • €3 • ☎ 972 340 709, Ⓦ www.tossademar.com/museu

Located in the old quarter, the **Museu Municipal** features a Roman mosaic and remnants, including ceramic vases, from a nearby excavated Roman villa, and a Chagall painting, *Celestial Violinist*. Chagall spent summers here for four decades, and evocatively called Tossa the "blue paradise".

ARRIVAL AND INFORMATION   TOSSA DE MAR

By bus The bus station is at Avgda. del Pelegrí, behind the *turisme*. To reach the centre, and the beaches, head straight down the road opposite the bus station and turn right along Avgda. Costa Brava. Tossa is an easy day-trip from Barcelona (up to 8 daily; 1hr 30min); Lloret (generally every 30min; 15min); and Girona (up to 2 daily; 1hr).

By boat *Crucero* boats stop right at the centre of the beach, with the ticket offices nearby. Boats travel to Sant Feliu (up to 5 daily; 45min), and Platja d'Aro/Sant Antoni de Calonge/ Palamós (up to 5 daily; 1hr 15min/1hr 25min/1hr 45min).

Turisme Avgda. del Pelegrí 25, in front of the bus station (April, May & Oct Mon–Sat 10am–2pm & 4–8pm; June–Sept Mon–Sat 10am–8pm; Nov–March Mon–Sat 10am–2pm & 4–7pm; ☎ 972 340 108, ⊕ infotossa.com).

ACCOMMODATION

There's plenty of accommodation in the warren of tiny streets around Sant Vicenç church and below the old city walls. There are also a handful of local campsites, all within 2–4km of the centre.

Cala Llevadó 3km out of town, off the road to Lloret ☎ 972 340 314, ⊕ calallevado.com. This is one of the better local campsites, with good facilities – swimming pool, bar-restaurant – plus plenty of outdoor activities, from wind-surfing to mini-golf. They also have bungalows (from €75), including raised-above-the-ground eco-friendly bungalows (€75), surrounded by pines. Closed Oct–April. **€49**

Gran Hotel Reymar Platja de Mar Menuda ☎ 972 340 312, ⊕ ghreymar.com. Sumptuous beachfront hotel across the bay from the Vila Vella. Modern rooms come with marble-clad bathrooms and terraces overlooking the sea. It has its own car park. Closed Nov–April. **€230**

Hotel Cap d'Or Pg. del Mar 1 ☎ 972 340 081, ⊕ capdor .com. Relaxed, friendly, ivy-clad *pensió* on the seafront – in the home of the family who has managed it since 1954 – nestled beneath the walls of the old town. Rates include breakfast. Closed Nov–April. **€85**

Hotel Delfin Avgda. Costa Brava 2 ☎ 972 340 250, ⊕ hotelesdante.com. Take in the sun from your balcony at this inviting hotel with spacious, modern rooms with marble bathrooms. The beach is just a 5min saunter away, and the generous buffet breakfast is included in the rate. **€75**

Hotel Diana Pza. d'Espanya 6 ☎ 972 341 886, ⊕ hotelesdante.com. Nicely located hotel in a *modernista* mansion on an attractive square, and with a bar on the seafront. Large rooms have sea or *plaça* (cheaper) views and tiled floors. Rates include breakfast. Closed Nov–Easter. **€140**

Hotel Sant March Avgda. del Pelegrí 2 ☎ 972 340 078, ⊕ hotelsantmarch.com. This amiable, family-run hotel has simple, clean rooms – many of which receive plenty of outdoor light – overlooking a breezy garden. They also have a small outdoor swimming pool. **€78**

Hotel Simeon C/Dr Trueta 1 ☎ 972 340 079, ⊕ hotelsimeon.com. Relax at this friendly hotel that's an easy stroll to the beach and the centre of town. Don't expect fancy; rooms are simple and spare, but well-maintained and have breezy balconies, plus breakfast is included. **€45**

Pola 4km north off the corniche road to Sant Feliu ☎ 972 341 050, ⊕ campingpola.es. This campsite sits in a pretty cove, has great facilities, from a pool to nearby tennis courts, and can organize outdoor activities, including kayaking and canoeing. Closed Oct–May. **€52**

EATING AND DRINKING

Tossa offers a range of restaurants, from top-notch seafood spots to simple *sangría*-and-tapas joints. Pg. del Mar and the road behind it, C/Portal, are brimming with alfresco options. Come evening, C/Sant Josep gets lively with revellers hitting the bars.

Bahía Pg. del Mar 19 ☎ 972 340 322, ⊕ restaurant bahiatossa.com. A welcoming interior and breezy terrace are the comfortable setting for tasty seafood meals (menus from €16–18 weekdays). Summer daily 1–3.30pm & 7.30–10.30pm; winter lunch only.

Castell Vell Pza. Pintor Roig i Soler ☎ 972 341 030, ⊕ castellvelltossa.es. In a tranquil corner of the old town, this spot serves tasty mid-priced fish, seafood and paella on a terrace shaded with vines. The hearty *menú del día* starts at €21. March–Oct Mon 8.30–10.30pm, Tues–Sun 1.30–3.30pm & 8.30–10.30pm.

★ **La Cuina de Can Simon** C/Portal 24 ☎ 972 341 269. This venerable joint turns out classic regional dishes in an elegant dining room of linen-topped tables, stone walls and oil paintings. The menu features a *mar i muntanya* (sea and mountain) section, including suckling lamb, oysters scented with green apple and lemon and lobster *suquet*, a local stew that originated on the Costa Brava. Main courses range €16–28. April to mid-Oct Wed–Sat 1–4pm & 8–11pm, Sun 1–4pm.

La lluna C/Abat Oliba 10 ☎ 972 342 523. Settle in to the outdoor garden patio at this small family-run tapas restaurant that's tucked into a quiet alley in the old town. The menu is rustically traditional – meatballs in cider, *patatas bravas*, garlic shrimp – along with fresh *sangría*. Tapas €5–11. April–Oct Mon–Wed & Fri–Sun 1–3pm & 7–10.30pm.

Baix Empordà

Baix Empordà, which unfolds north of La Selva, feels far less like a package-holiday hotspot than the rest of the coast, with more stylish towns and a greater local flavour. Known as the Triangle d'Or (Golden Triangle), as the ever-rising property prices and burgeoning number of upscale hotels will bear out, it is much favoured by chic Catalans and foreign visitors seeking less mass-tourism-oriented delights. **Platja d'Aro** is a smarter version of Lloret – with a particularly lively summer nightlife, popular with weekenders from Barcelona – while the working fishing ports of **Sant Feliu de Guíxols** and **Palamós** remain largely (and thankfully) aloof from their boisterous neighbours along the coast. Farther north, the area around **Palafrugell** boasts some fabulous cove towns, while hilltop **Begur** stands over a string of lovely little coves. **Inland** lures include the medieval towns of Pals and Peratallada, atmospheric Iberian ruins at Ullastret and the pottery industry of La Bisbal.

Sant Feliu de Guíxols and around

Separated from Tossa by 22km and, reputedly, 365 curves of stunning corniche, **SANT FELIU DE GUÍXOLS** is a bustling town with a decent beach and a cluster of handsome *modernista* buildings, evidence of its prosperous nineteenth-century cork industry. Its origins go back to the tenth century, when a settlement grew up around a Benedictine **monastery**, whose ruins, including the arched Porta Ferrada, still stand in Pza. Monestir.

Sant Feliu's old-world style is at its most apparent in the *modernista* **Casa Patxot** (built in 1917 and now home to the Chamber of Commerce) at Pg. del Mar 40, on the corner of Rambla Portalet, and the curious Moorish-style **Nou Casino La Constància** nearby at Pg. dels Guíxols 1–3, which was begun in 1851 and later adorned with *modernista* touches and brightly coloured swooping arches. The *passeig* follows the sweep of the coarse sand **beach** and yachting marina, while the streets back from the sea are great for a stroll past the shops and bars and the eighteenth-century **Pza. del Mercat**, with its bustling daily market.

Church of Sant Feliu es la Mare de Déu dels Àngels and Museu d'Història de la Ciutat

Pza. del Monestir • Museum: summer daily 11am–9pm; mid-Sept to summer Mon–Fri 10am–1pm & 4–7pm, Sat–Sun 10am–7pm • Free • ☎ 972 821 575, ⓦ guixols.cat

The **Church of Sant Feliu es la Mare de Déu dels Àngels** has a Romanesque facade and beautifully crafted crucifix dating from the same period as the Benedictine monastery, though it was rebuilt in Gothic style in the fourteenth century. The church is open for services only, while the rest of the complex is part of the **Museu d'Història de la Ciutat**, which contains absorbing exhibitions on the history of the town, including local archeological finds, as well as temporary exhibits on everything from local painters to photographers.

S'Agaró

On a headland north of Sant Feliu is the curious village of **S'AGARÓ**, created in the 1920s, where every house was built in the *modernista* style by Rafael Masó, a student of Antoni Gaudí. The short Camí de Ronda leading to the fabulous **Platja Sa Conca** is the best way to explore and take in a swim.

ARRIVAL AND INFORMATION	SANT FELIU DE GUÍXOLS

By bus Teisa bus services to and from Girona stop opposite the monastery, while the Sarfa bus station (for buses to and from Palafrugell, Girona and Barcelona) is a 5min walk north of the centre on the main Carretera de Girona, at the junction with C/Llibertat.
Destinations Barcelona (8 daily; 1hr 30min); Girona (July–Sept 11 daily; 2hr); Lloret de Mar (July & Aug 2–3 daily;

40min); Palafrugell (15 daily; 45min); Palamós (15 daily; 30min); Platja d'Aro (17 daily; 15min).
By boat *Cruceros* boats dock on the main beach, where you'll also find the various ticket offices.
Turisme Pza. del Monestir (June–Sept daily 10am–2pm & 4–8pm; Oct–May Mon–Sat 10am–1pm & 4–7pm, Sun 10am–2pm; ☎ 972 820 051, ⓦ guixols.cat).

ACCOMMODATION AND EATING

Cau del Pescador C/Sant Domènec 11 ☎ 972 324 052, ⓦ caudelpescador.com. This atmospheric spot has a generous choice of seafood, from Sant Feliu anchovies to

shrimp and squid, at mid-range prices. Daily 1–4pm & 8–11pm; Sept–June closed Mon dinner & Tues.
El Celler de Triton C/Sant Ramon 5 ☎ 972 327 531,

11

ⓦtritonsantfeliu.com. Eat well – but healthily – at this cosy café-restaurant where much of the menu is organic, from the grilled meats and fish to the beer. Even the cleaning products are eco-friendly. Plus, a top-notch array of vegetarian and vegan dishes includes grilled seasonal vegetables and rice, as well as gluten-free options. Mains €10–17. Mon & Wed–Sun 11am–midnight.

El Dorado Mar President Irla 15 ☎972 326 286, ⓦgrupoeldorado.com. The El Dorado mini-empire offers a range of dining in Sant Feliu. One of the best is this seaside spot, overlooking the harbour at the southern end of the beach. Feast on a menu of fresh seafood, from clams to cod. Menu starts at €20. Mon–Fri 1–4pm & 8–11pm, Sat–Sun 1–4.30pm & 8–11pm; closed Wed in winter.

Hostal de La Gavina Pujada de l'Hostal, S'Agaró ☎972 321 100, ⓦlagavina.com. Sitting in calm grounds overlooking Platja Sant Pol at the southern end of S'Agaró,

this five-star *hotel* features palatial, marble-floored rooms adorned with elegant hand-carved furniture and fine antique rugs and lamps; the luxury continues with wood-panelled dining rooms, bars, terraces, a saltwater pool and spa. **€320**

Hotel Hostal del Sol Carretera de Palamós 192 ☎972 320 193, ⓦhostaldelsol.cat. Take a breather from the beachside bustle at this colonial-style hotel, which rises up near S'Agaró, and has airy rooms that all face out, with lovely views. Plus, there are two pools, as well as a decent complimentary breakfast. **€80**

Hotel Plaça Pza. del Mercat 22 ☎972 325 155, ⓦhotelplaza.org. You'll find a score of family-run *hostals* and hotels in the old town, most within walking distance of the sea, and one of the better spots is this friendly, well-maintained hotel that's set back from the water in the market square. **€110**

Platja d'Aro and around

A few kilometres to the north of S'Agaró, **PLATJA D'ARO** is a neon strip of bars and shops running parallel to, but hidden from, a long sandy beach. It's by no means picturesque, but it does offer good **nightlife**, a great **beach** and some stylish **shopping**.

Beyond Platja d'Aro, the road leads to the more family-oriented but not terribly pretty town of **Sant Antoni de Calonge**; more enticing are the **coves** and beaches strung out between the two towns, all of which can be reached on foot by the serpentine and at times tricky **Camí de Ronda** or by a number of footpaths descending from the main road.

ARRIVAL AND INFORMATION — **PLATJA D'ARO AND AROUND**

By bus Regular Sarfa buses travel to Platja d'Aro from around the Costa Brava, including Girona (just under 2hr).

Turisme Cinto Verdaguer 4, on the junction with central Avgda. S'Agaró (July & Aug 8am–9pm, rest of year daily 9am–1pm & 4–7pm; ☎972 817 179, ⓦplatjadaro.com).

ACCOMMODATION

Platja d'Aro is filled with an array of hotels, from small family-run spots to larger tourist-driven resort hotels.

Hotel Bell Repòs C/Nostra Senora del Carme 18 ☎972 817 100, ⓦhotelbellrepos.com. This long-running hotel,

with clean, basic rooms, is near the main beach. A hearty buffet breakfast is included. **€96**

Palamós and around

Immediately northeast of Sant Antoni de Calonge, **Palamós** was founded· in 1277 and sacked by Barbarossa in 1543. The town's pleasant old quarter, set apart from the new on a promontory at the eastern end of the bay, makes for a pleasant afternoon wander and an evening at one of the breezy outdoor restaurant terraces.

Accessible from Palamós by road or along the Camí de Ronda are two fabulous **beaches**. The first, the idyllic **Cala S'Alguer**, is framed by nineteenth-century fishermen's huts, while the larger **Platja de Castell** was rescued from the clutches of property developers thanks to a local referendum. Perched on the headland at the northern tip of Platja de Castell are the tranquil ruins of an Iberian settlement.

Museu de la Pesca

Edifici del Tinglado, Port de Palamós • Mid-June to mid-Sept daily 10am–9pm; mid-Sept to mid-June Tues–Sat 10am–1.30pm & 3–7pm, Sun 10am–2pm & 4–7pm • €5 • ☎972 600 424, ⓦmuseudelapesca.org

The working fishing port here is home to the interesting **Museu de la Pesca**, chronicling the town's fishing and maritime history via audiovisual exhibits and historic fishing equipment and other archeological finds. The museum also organizes a variety of activities, many targeted at kids, including sailing and seafood cooking classes.

ARRIVAL AND INFORMATION   PALAMÓS AND AROUND

By bus Regular Sarfa buses travel to Palamós from around the Costa Brava, including Girona (1hr 30min).

Turisme Pg. del Mar (summer daily 9am–9pm; winter

Mon–Sat 10am–2pm & 4–7pm, Sun 10am–2pm; ☎972 600 550, ⓦ palamos.org).

EATING AND DRINKING

The town features a variety of good traditional restaurants. **Nightlife** is generally a fun and spontaneous affair; the best places are between the old town and the port in the La Planassa area (towards the end of the promontory).

Maria de Cadaqués C/Tauler i Servià 6 ☎972 314 009, ⓦ mariadecadaques.cat. This popular restaurant, just off the marina, has an impressive history: it was founded in 1936 as a fishermen's tavern, and continues to serve excellent shellfish and *calamares*. Dishes €12–25. Daily

2–4pm & 8–11pm; closed Sun eve.

La Plata Pza. San Pere 9–11, ☎635 234 246. Enjoy fruity cocktails, conversation and live music at this rocking spot, which also hosts theme nights. Thurs–Sat usually from 11pm; sometimes also open during the week.

11

Palafrugell

A cluster of streets and shops around a sixteenth-century church and the bustling Pza. Nova, **PALAFRUGELL**, lies seven kilometres north of Palamós, and 4km inland from the breezy coastline. It's at its liveliest during the morning produce market (Tues–Sun), which on Sunday expands to include clothing, toys and other items. In the summer (July to early Sept), Palafrugell hosts an evening handicrafts market (Thurs–Sat).

Fundació Vila Casas Can Mario

Pza. Can Mario 7 • Tues–Sun 5–9pm • €5 • ☎ 972 306 246, ⓦ fundaciovilacasas.com

Fundació Vila Casas Can Mario, a sleek modern art centre, set in an old cork factory, features temporary exhibits with a focus on contemporary sculpture by Catalan and Spanish artists. The well-curated centre is run by the nonprofit Fundació Vila Casas, headquartered in Barcelona, which has the primary goal of promoting contemporary Catalan art.

Fundació Josep Pla

C/Nou 51 • Summer Mon–Fri 9am–1pm & 5–8.30pm, Sat 10am–1pm & 5–8.30pm, Sun 10am–1pm; winter Mon–Fri 9am–2pm & 4–6.30pm, Sat 10.30am–2pm & 4–7pm, Sun 10.30am–2pm • €2.50 • ☎ 972 30 55 77, ⓦ fundaciojoseppla.cat

While relatively unknown beyond Catalunya, within the region Pla is considered one of the greatest writers in the Catalan language. Born in Palafrugell in 1897, Pla's literary opus was tremendous. As the *Paris Review* eloquently summed up his long career, "If Barça is more than just a football club, then Pla – a political and cultural journalist, travel writer, biographer, memoirist, essayist, novelist, and foodie, whose collected works clock in at more than thirty-thousand pages and thirty-eight volumes – was more than just a writer." The **Fundació Josep Pla**, which encompasses the house where Pla was born, features a permanent and temporary exhibits that chronicle Pla's life of letters, including photographs, books, clippings and more.

ARRIVAL AND INFORMATION   PALAFRUGELL

By bus Buses arrive at Palafrugell's Sarfa bus terminal at C/Luís Companys 2, a 10min walk from the town centre. Palafrugell is also well connected by bus to other cities in the region, including to Barcelona (6–8 daily; 2hr); Figueres (5 daily; 1hr 30min); Girona (15 daily; 1hr); L'Escala (4 daily; 35min); Lloret de Mar (2 daily; 1hr 30min); Palamós (15 daily; 15min); Pals (4 daily; 10min); and Sant Feliu (15 daily; 45min).

Turisme C/Carrilet 2, near the terminal (May, June & Sept Mon–Sat 10am–1pm & 5–8pm, Sun 10am–1pm; July & Aug Mon–Sat 9am–9pm, Sun 10am–1pm; Oct–April Mon–Sat 10am–1pm & 4–7pm, Sun 10am–1pm; ☎972 300 228, ⓦ visitpalafrugell.cat). There's also a *turisme* in the centre at C/Sta. Margarida 1 (Easter–Oct Mon–Sat 10am–1pm & 5–8pm, Sun 10am–1pm; same phone number).

ACCOMMODATION AND EATING

A wide range of accommodation is available in the surrounding beach towns (see opposite), including Llafranc and Tamariu, while in Palafrugell itself, the hotels are more basic – and accordingly a bit cheaper. Either way, it's wise to book ahead.

Arrels d'Empordà C/Torroella 3 ☎972 981 920, ⓦ novarahotels.com/en/arrels. This modern, well-appointed aparthotel has spacious apartments, decked out in contemporary furnishings, with full living rooms and kitchens, sleek bathrooms and balcony. Plus, there's a well-maintained pool. Apartments €110

Hostal L'Estrella C/les Quatre Cases 13 ☎972 300 005, ⓦ hostal-estrella.com. A decent budget choice, on a little street near the main Pza. Nova. The basic rooms are arranged around a cloistered courtyard dating from 1605. Rates include a generous buffet breakfast. €70

Mas Oliver Avgda. d'Espanya (outside town on the ring road) ☎972 301 041. Tuck into praised Catalan cuisine, including excellent grilled fish and meats. In warm weather dine on the outdoor terrace. The *menú del día* is a good deal, starting at €10. Mon & Wed–Sun 1.30–4pm & 8–11pm, Tues 8–11pm; closed usually Nov & Dec.

Orígens de l'Empordanet C/Botines ☎972 611 210, ⓦ origensdelempordanet.com. This casual eatery has a wide range of tapas and dishes, including ham-flecked croquettes, grilled meats, from chicken to the traditional Catalan *botifarra*, and warm crêpes folded with Roquefort cheese and walnuts. The menu also offers "*el raconet del vegetarià*" ("the vegetarian corner"), with a small but quality selection, like vegetable lasagne and spinach cannelonis. Mains €7–15. The weekday *menú del dia* is €11.50, and the restaurant also offers takeaway. Daily except Mon noon–10pm.

Pa i Raim C/Torres i Jonama 56 ☎972 304 572, ⓦ pairaim.com. Inviting, elegant restaurant featuring excellent Catalan cuisine with a twist, including monkfish with sautéed artichoke, and roast veal scented with vanilla. Mains €15–25. Tues–Sun 1.30–3pm & 8–10pm; closed Tues lunch in Aug and Sun in winter.

Around Palafrugell

The area around Palafrugell boasts tranquil, pine-covered slopes, which back three of the most alluring villages on the Costa Brava – **Calella**, **Llafranc** and **Tamariu** – each with a distinct character and all with scintillatingly turquoise waters. With no true coastal road, the beach development here has been generally mild – low-rise, whitewashed apartments and hotels – and although a fair number of foreign visitors come in season, it's also where many of the better-off Barcelonans have a villa for weekend and August escapes. All this makes for one of the most appealing (though hardly undiscovered) stretches of the Costa Brava.

Calella de Palafrugell

Captivating **Calella de Palafrugell** possesses a gloriously rocky coastline punctuated by several tiny sand and rocky **beaches** with a backdrop of whitewashed arches and *fin-de-siècle* villas. From the charming area around the minuscule main beaches, the town stretches southwards along a winding Camí de Ronda to the hidden **El Golfet** beach.

Jardí Botanic de Cap Roig

Daily: June–Sept 9am–8pm; Oct–May 9am–6pm • €6 • ⓦ jardins.caproig.cat

Above the El Golfet beach, the Cap Roig headland is home to the **Jardí Botanic de Cap**

CHEERS TO CREMAT

Catalan sailors returning from Cuba and the Antilles in the nineteenth century brought back more than soulful *havaneres* songs. They also brought back Caribbean rum, which forms the basis for **cremat**, a typical drink of the fishing villages in this region, particularly Calella and neighbouring Llafranc.

The potent concoction contains rum, sugar, lemon peel, coffee grounds and sometimes a cinnamon stick. The ritual of drinking *cremat* is a big part of the experience: it's brought out in an earthenware bowl and you have to set fire to it, occasionally stirring until (after a few minutes) it's ready to drink. Also part of the ritual is to sing *havaneres* while drinking.

Calella hosts a **Cantada de Havaneres** in July, with groups performing *havaneres* (tickets start at €30). Check in with the *turismes* in Palafrugell (see p.719) or Calella (see opposite).

Roig, a clifftop botanical garden and castle begun in 1927 by an exiled colonel from the tsar's army and his aristocrat English wife. This is also the site of the superb music event **Festival Jardins de Cap Roig** (mid-July to late Aug), which features everything from jazz to rock, and has hosted such big names as Bob Dylan, Diana Ross, Elvis Costello and Leonard Cohen.

Llafranc

A gentle, hilly twenty-minute walk from Calella de Palafrugell, high above the rocks along the Camí de Ronda, brings you to **Llaranc**, tucked into the next bay from Calella de Palafrugell, and with a good (if packed) stretch of **beach** and a glittering **marina**. A little more upmarket than Calella, it's a self-consciously opulent place with expensive beachside restaurants and hillside villas glinting in the sun. Steps lead up from the port for the winding climb through residential streets to the **Far de Sant Sebastià**, a lighthouse where you'll be rewarded with some terrific views.

Tamariu, Platja d'Aiguablava and Fornells

Tamariu, 4km north of Llafranc, is quieter and a great favourite with well-heeled Catalan families. The town's action is focused on the small seafront, and the **promenade** – lined with tamarind trees, the source of the town's name – has a hushed but inviting atmosphere, with small shops, pavement restaurants and neighbours sitting on their front porches. Geared more towards the summer-home crowd, the town has fewer hotels than other towns on the coast, but most are good.

It's a pleasant drive along the coast from here to Begur, passing **Platja d'Aiguablava**, the location of the lovely *Parador de Aiguablava* (see p.722). Just 1km north is the tiny and exclusive cove of **Fornells**, 3km from Begur.

11

ARRIVAL AND INFORMATION

AROUND PALAFRUGELL

By bus From June to Sept, buses run regularly from Palafrugell to Calella and then on to Llafranc (July & Aug every 30min; June & Sept roughly hourly), reducing to around four times daily from October to May. A less frequent service runs to the more distant beach at Tamariu (June–Sept; 3–4 daily).

Turisme C/les Voltes 6, Calella de Palafrugell (July & Aug daily 10am–8pm; Easter–June & Sept to mid-Oct Mon–Sat 10am–2pm & 5–8pm, Sun 10am–1pm; ☎972 614 475, ⓦ visitpalafrugell.cat).

ACCOMMODATION

CALELLA DE PALAFRUGELL

Hotel Garbi Pg. de les Roques 3–5 ☎937 690 858, ⓦ hotel-garbi.com. Take in the sea air from your balcony at this inviting hotel run by the Cardona family. Rooms are simple but pleasant and light-filled, with large windows, plus have comfy beds and well-equipped bathrooms. Splash in the outdoor pool or walk to the beach, which lies a 10min stroll away. **€95**

Hotel Sant Roc Pza. Atlàntic 2 ☎972 614 250, ⓦ santroc.com. This plush hotel sits perched over the sea, with superb views of the coves. The restaurant, *El Balcó del Calella*, serves tasty Mediterranean cuisine. **€140**

LLAFRANC

Hotel Casamar C/Nero 3 ☎972 300 104, ⓦ hotelcasamar.net. This friendly hotel has cool-toned rooms, and some have balconies that feature lovely views of the bay. The restaurant (see p.722) is a destination unto itself, serving signature Catalan cuisine. **€110**

Hotel El Far Far de Sant Sebastià ☎972 301 639, ⓦ elfar.net. This sumptuous hotel sits on a cliff, and the elegant rooms each have a balcony with panoramic views. The alluring restaurant serves fresh seafood and a good selection of paella, rice and *fideuà* (thin noodles) dishes. **€250**

Hotel Terramar Pg. Cipsela 1 ☎972 300 200, ⓦ hterramar.com. On the seafront, this comfortable hotel is run by the fourth generation of the same family, and has simple yet elegant rooms overlooking the beach. **€115**

TAMARIU

Hotel Hostalillo Bellavista 22 ☎972 620 228, ⓦ www .hotelhostalillo.com. Perched above the sea, and surrounded by pines, this inviting hotel features gorgeous views of the beach and bay. Relax in airy rooms, all with mini-fridges and most with balconies. **€115**

Hotel Tamariu Pg. del Mar 2 ☎972 620 031, ⓦ tamariu.com. The seafront *Tamariu*, originally a fishermen's tavern in the 1920s, has basic but comfortable rooms with terraces, as well as well-equipped apartments. Doubles **€150**, apartments **€200**

PLATJA D'AIGUABLAVA

Parador de Aiguablava ☎972 622 162, ⓦwww .parador.es. Set on a craggy headland jutting out into the sea, this modern hotel may lack the character of historic paradores, but has good facilities and large windows throughout to show off the magnificent views. The restaurant serves up a range of local dishes, including *anchoas* (anchovies) from L'Escala, and dishes rooted in Catalunya's *mar i muntanya* cuisine. **€150**

EATING AND DRINKING

CALELLA DE PALAFRUGELL

La Gavina C/Gravina 7 ☎972 614 554, ⓦlagavina calella.com. Dine on traditional Catalan cooking and a wide selection of fish and seafood for around €14–20; enjoy the sea breezes on the open, shaded terrace. Summer daily 8–11pm; usually closed Oct–March.

Tragamar Platja de Canadell ☎972 614 336, ⓦwww .tragamar.com. Run by Grupo Tragaluz of the perennially popular *Agua* in Barcelona (see p.691), this trendy restaurant focuses on fresh seafood, from monkfish to grilled lobster. Mains €15–25. Mid-June to mid-Sept daily 1–4.30pm & 8.30–11.30pm; rest of year closed Tues.

LLAFRANC

★**Casamar** Hotel Casamar C/Nero 3 ☎972 300 104, ⓦhotelcasamar.net. If you're going to splurge on your Costa Brava vacation, this is a place to do so. This classic restaurant, helmed by progressive chef Quim Casellas, overlooks the sea and features a seasonal menu of creative cuisine, including dishes like sauteed artichoke with quail's egg and filet of sole perfumed with passion fruit. Entrees €16–30. Tues–Sat 1.30–3.30pm & 8.30–11.30pm; usually closed Jan–March.

Llevant Hotel Llevant C/Francesc Blanes 5 ☎972 300 366, ⓦhotel-llevant.com. For good seafood, from shrimp to cod, dine at this welcoming restaurant where you can enjoy a hearty €20 menu. April to mid-Nov daily 1.30–3.30pm & 8.30–10.30pm; Jan–March Tues–Sat 1.30–3.30pm & 8.30–10.30pm, Sun closed 1.30–3.30pm.

Begur and around

In the lee of a ruined hilltop castle, chic **BEGUR**, about 7km from Palafrugell and slightly inland, stands at the centre of a web of winding roads leading down to its tranquil and equally stylish **beaches**. Narrow streets lead to the simple exterior and surprisingly ornate Gothic interior of the **Església Parroquial de Sant Pere**; most remarkable is the odd contrast between statuary and architecture, especially the simplicity of the alabaster *Madonna and Child* compared with the busy altarpiece. Watching over it all, the thrice-destroyed **Castell de Begur** offers fabulous perspectives of the rocky coves to the south and the curving swathe of the Golf de Roses to the north. The annual **Festival de Música de Begur**, generally from late July to late August, features everything from classical music to swing and jazz.

From here roads lead east to the **Cap de Begur**, with its spectacular *mirador*, the coves of **Sa Tuna** and **Aiguafreda**, linked by a scenic footpath (1km), and the pretty hamlet of **SA RIERA**, where you can walk to **Platja del Raco** and **Platja Illa Roja**, some of the best beaches on the coast.

ARRIVAL AND INFORMATION

BEGUR AND AROUND

By bus Sarfa buses travel to Begur from around the Costa Brava, including nearby Palafrugell (10min), and once a day from Girona (1hr 15min). The beaches are connected to the town by summer minibus services.

Turisme Avgda. Onze de Setembre 5, just south of Begur's main square, Pza. de la Villa (daily: spring and autumn 9am–2pm & 4–7pm; summer 9am–2pm & 4–9pm; winter 9am–2pm; ☎972 624 520, ⓦvisitbegur.cat).

ACCOMMODATION AND EATING

There are a few fairly expensive hotels at the beaches, while beyond the pleasant *Fonda Caner*, you'll find further options for a meal or a drink at plenty of beachside spots and in town around the Pza. del la Villa.

Aiguaclara Hotel Sant Miquel 2 ☎972 622 905, ⓦhotelaiguaclara.com. There's good reason this hotel receives so many accolades. Set in an 1866 colonial-style mansion, with just ten rooms, this is a wonderfully charming respite. The beautifully renovated rooms feature plump beds, tiled floors and balconies and terraces, with views of the village, castle and the Pyrenees rising far beyond. Closed Jan. **€110**

Fonda Caner C/Pi i Ralló 10 ☎972 622 391, ⓦhotel -rosa.com. The *Hotel Rosa* owners run this nearby, inviting restaurant, which has tiled floors and partially exposed stone walls. The menu of traditional Catalan dishes starts at €21.

April–Oct Mon–Fri 8–10.30pm, Sat & Sun 1–3.30pm & 8–10.30pm, also open lunch Mon–Fri in Aug.
Hotel Rosa C/Pi i Ralló 19 ☎972 623 015, ⓦhotel-rosa.com. This family-owned spot has comfortable rooms and a cheerful atmosphere. Ask about their off-season discounts. **€119**

Pals

Turisme: Pza. Major 7, in the old town (daily: June–Aug 10am–2pm & 5–8pm; rest of year 10am–2pm & 4–7pm; ☎972 637 380, ⓦpalsturisme.com).

The 7km journey north from Palafrugell to Torroella de Montgrí can be broken at **PALS**, also 7km from Begur. This fortified medieval village was long neglected until it was painstakingly restored by a local doctor after the Civil War, which has resulted in the rather unfortunate side effect of being invaded by scores of day-trippers. Even so, its fourteenth-century streets and hilltop setting make it an enjoyable place for a stroll. The golden-brown buildings cluster around a stark tower, all that remains of the town's Romanesque **castle**; below is the beautifully vaulted Gothic **Església de Sant Pere** and Romanesque **Torre de les Hores**.

La Bisbal

LA BISBAL, 12km northwest of Palafrugell on the main road to Girona, is a medieval market town in an attractive river setting. Since the seventeenth century, La Bisbal has specialized in the production of **ceramics**, and pottery shops line the main road through town (C/L'Aigüeta); these are great for browsing and picking up some terrific local pieces.

Ceramics apart, La Bisbal is a pleasant stop anyway, as its handsome old centre retains many impressive mansions, the architectural remnants of a once thriving Jewish quarter and the fortified medieval **Castell Palau de la Bisbal**.

Castell Palau de la Bisbal

Tues–Sat 11am–2pm & 5–8pm, Sun 11am–2pm • €2, guided tour €3

La Bisbal's most important historical building is the fortified **Castell Palau**, built for the bishops of Girona. The sturdy castle, which dates back to the eleventh and twelfth centuries, has been in continuous use since it was built, including a spell as a prison during the Spanish Civil War. Inside, you'll learn about medieval Catalunya while touring its various sections.

ACCOMMODATION AND EATING   LA BISBAL

Arcs de Monells C/Vilanova 1, Monells ☎972 630 304, ⓦhotelarcsmonells.com. This lovely hotel, set in a fourteenth-century hospital 3km northwest of town, is an elegant base for exploring the area. It has a beautifully renovated interior and comfortable rooms. **€185**
★**Hotel Castell d'Empordà** ☎972 646 254, ⓦcastelldemporda.com. This 800-year-old castle, perched on top of a hill 3km north of the town with beautiful views of the surrounding countryside, is now a sumptuous hotel. You're in good company: a captain for Christopher Columbus stayed here, and Dalí once tried to buy it. The restaurant celebrates the local bounty, and serves creative Catalan cuisine and excellent regional wines. Mains €14–28. Daily 1–2pm & 8–11pm. **€165**

Peratallada and Ullastret

Five kilometres northeast of La Bisbal is the medieval walled town of **PERATALLADA**, which has preserved a rustic feel, with the help of its tiny cobbled streets, stone arches and shaded squares. An influx of small hotels and restaurants has proved to be surprisingly in keeping with their thirteenth-century Romanesque setting, making it a fabulous base away from the beach. The focal point is the **Castell de Peratallada** (closed to visitors), whose origins have been dated to pre-Roman times.

Museu d'Arqueologia de Ullastret

Puig de Sant Andreu d'Ullastret • Summer Tues–Sun 10am–8pm; winter 10am–2pm & 3–6pm • €2.30

Six kilometres northeast lie the remains of the Iberian settlement of **Puig de Sant Andreu d'Ullastret**, a lovely, peaceful ruin with an archeological **museum**, with excavated artefacts from the area. The site is just north of the friendly, historic village of **Ullastret**, signposted off the main road.

INFORMATION   PERATALLADA AND ULLASTRET

Turisme The *turisme* is on Pza. del Castell, in front of the Castell de Peratallada (summer daily noon–2pm & 3–8pm; winter generally Sat & Sun only; ☎872 987 030, ⓦ visitlabisbal.cat).

ACCOMMODATION

Hostal Restaurant La Riera Pza. les Voltes 3, Peratallada ☎972 634 142, ⓦ lariera.es. Cosy *hostal*, comfortably housed in a seventeenth-century building – and one of the area's more economical options. Rate includes breakfast. The restaurant serves good Catalan cuisine. **€80**

Torroella de Montgrí

TORROELLA DE MONTGRÍ, 8km from Ullastret and 9km beyond Pals, was once an important medieval port, but today has been left high and dry by the receding Mediterranean. It now stands 5km inland, beneath the shell of the huge, crenellated **Castell de Montgrí** (at 302m, a stiff 30min walk away), built by King Jaime II between 1294 and 1301 but never completed. The town itself remains distinctly medieval in appearance with its narrow streets, fine mansions and fourteenth-century parish church of **Sant Genís** (daily 4–6pm; sometimes open in mornings as well). The town is probably best known for its **Festival Internacional de Música** (ⓦ en.festivaldetorroella.com), held each July and August in the main square and church, which features an excellent line-up of classical music.

ARRIVAL AND INFORMATION   TORROELLA DE MONTGRÍ

By bus Regular buses travel between Torroella and Barcelona (just under 2hr), as well as to L'Estartit (15min).
Turisme Centre Cultural, C/d'Ullà (July & Aug daily 10am–2pm & 6–9pm; Sept–June Mon & Wed–Sat 10am–2pm & 5–8pm, Sun 10am–2pm; ☎972 755 180, ⓦ visitestartit.com/en).

ACCOMMODATION

Palau Lo Mirador Pg. de l'Església 1 ☎972 758 063, ⓦ palaulomirador.com. This handsome, historic hotel features a palatial interior, with spacious rooms and well-appointed bathrooms. **€120**

L'Estartit and the Illes Medes

The nearest beach to Torroella is 6km to the east at **L'ESTARTIT**, an otherwise unexceptional resort town. Call into the *turisme* for information about the nearby **Illes Medes**, Catalunya's only offshore islands – kiosks in the area sell boat trips in the summer. The tiny islands form a protected nature reserve, hosting the most important colony of herring gulls in the Mediterranean, numbering some eight thousand pairs, and offer some of the best **diving** and snorkelling on the coast.

ARRIVAL AND INFORMATION   L'ESTARTIT AND THE ILLES MEDES

By bus Hourly buses travel here from Torroella de Montgrí (15min).
Turisme At the northern end of Pg. Marítim, which runs along the seafront (summer daily 9.30am–2pm; rest of year Mon–Fri 9am–1pm & 3–6pm, Sat & Sun 10am–2pm; ☎972 751 910, ⓦ visitestartit.com).

ACCOMMODATION AND EATING

Hotel Les Illes C/Illes 55 ☎972 751 239, ⓦ hotellesilles .com. This amiable hotel, with comfortable, well-maintained rooms, organizes its own popular diving excursions and other water activities. **€110**
Restaurant Bravo Pg. Marítim 82–86 ☎972 752 116. You'll find plenty of bars and restaurants along the seafront, like this restaurant, which serves mid-priced fresh seafood, including fresh mussels and grilled fish, and aromatic rice dishes on a breezy terrace. Summer daily 1–4pm & 8–10pm; sometimes limited hours in winter.

Alt Empordà

Beyond Torroella de Montgrí, the scenery changes quite abruptly as you move into the fertile plains and wetlands of the southern part of the **Alt Empordà**, dominated by the broad swathe of the **Golf de Roses**. Coves give way to long stretches of sand as far north as **Roses**, which nestles in its own closed-in bay. The gulf is backed for the most part by flat, rural land, well watered by the Muga and Fluvià rivers. Having been left to its own quiet devices for centuries, this section of coast is distinct from the otherwise touristy Costa Brava, and has really only suffered the attentions of the developers in towns at either end of the bay, most notably in the few kilometres between Roses and the giant marina-cum-resort of Empuriabrava.

At the southern end of the gulf is the pleasant old fishing port of **L'Escala**, made more remarkable by the presence of **Empúries**, a ruined Greek and Roman settlement and one of Spain's most important archeological sites. Beyond Roses, the familiar crashing rocks and deeply indented coves return with a vengeance in the wild Cap de Creus headland. The jewel in the crown here is **Cadaqués**, eternally linked to **Salvador Dalí**, who lived for years in the neighbouring fishermen's village of **Portlligat**, now home to an absorbing museum in his bizarre former residence. For the final run to the French border, the road swoops along the coast through quieter villages such as whitewashed **El Port de la Selva**.

11

L'Escala

At the southernmost end of the sweeping billhook of the Golf de Roses, **L'ESCALA** is split between its shabby but picturesque *nucli antic*, or **old town**, favoured by local holiday-makers, and the more commercial **Riells** quarter, which has a beach and is the haunt of foreign visitors. Infinitely more appealing, the narrow pedestrianized streets of the old town huddle around the ancient port, where you'll find medieval mooring posts and a cannonball fired from a ship in May 1809, embedded in the wall of the house at C/Joan Massanet 2 (close to the seafront at the end of C/Pintor de Massanet).

A further enticement is L'Escala's proximity to the ancient site of Empúries, which lies just a couple of kilometres out of town.

ARRIVAL AND INFORMATION

L'ESCALA

By bus Buses stop on Avgda. Girona, just down the road from the *turisme*. Regular services travel to and from Barcelona (3 daily; 2hr 40min); Figueres (45 daily; 45min); Girona (2 daily; 1hr); Palafrugell (4 daily; 45min); and Pals (4 daily; 35min).

Turisme Pza. de las Escoles 1, on the edge of the old town (mid-June to mid-Sept Mon–Sat 9am–8pm, Sun 10am–1pm; mid-Sept to mid-June Mon–Fri 9am–1pm & 4–7pm, Sat 10am–1pm & 4–7pm, Sun 10am–1pm; ☎ 972 770 603, ⓦ lescala.cat).

ACCOMMODATION AND EATING

Freshly caught fish and seafood, particularly **anchovies**, are the speciality of the town's **restaurants**, with a good choice in the port and the old town. For a **drink**, head to the *nucli antic*, where you'll find a range from fishermen's taverns and bars.

THE ART OF ANCHOVIES

There are anchovies, and then there are **Catalan anchovies**. Most think of anchovies as oily, limp little items, but here on the Catalan coast, and most famously in **L'Escala**, *anchoas* (*anxoves* in Catalan) are succulent, pale in colour, and plump – almost double the size of what you may be used to. L'Escala is widely known for its canning factories where Catalunya's best anchovies are packaged.

You can sample them in most bars and restaurants – and there may be nothing better than a plate of anchovies, a hunk of bread (the better to soak up the aromatic olive-oil-laced juices) and a *cerveza* or three, enjoyed at a seaside *terraza*. And bring the taste home with you: plenty of grocery shops around town sell little jars and cans that you can pack into your bags.

Can Català Pza. de les Escoles ☎972 770 443, ⓦhotelcancatala.com. This family-run hotel has simple rooms – sturdy furnishings, basic beds, no-frills bathrooms – but each comes with a terrace and is well-maintained. Most importantly, the price is excellent for this area, and it includes a buffet breakfast in the airy dining room. **€69**

Hostal Empúries Platja de Portitxol s/n ☎972 770 207, ⓦhostalempuries.com. This lovingly run hotel places a premium on sustainability – using biodegradable products and sourcing all its electricity from renewable resources – and is the first hotel in Europe with a LEED Gold Certification. It also has an excellent location, near the beach and the main entrance to Empúries. There are two sections to the hotel: the cheaper, older, historic section and the newer, sleeker spa rooms, with terraces overlooking the sea (€191). The attached *Villa Teresita* restaurant serves tasty local organic cuisine. **€145**

Restaurant l'Avi Freu Paseo Lluis Albert 7 ☎972 771 241. This established restaurant serves a daily menu focusing on rice dishes, starting at €16, as well as fresh seafood and other regional dishes. Daily 1–4pm & 7.30–10.30pm; weekends only in winter.

Villa Teresita Hostal Empúries ☎972 770 207, ⓦhostalempuries.com. This light-filled restaurant follows *Hostal Empúries'* eco-friendly philosophy, serving what they call "eco-Mediterranean" cuisine. Feast on crayfish and prawns sourced from Palamós and Roses, grilled squid and cod with pig's ears and beans. Dishes €14–28. Daily 1–3.30pm & 8–10.30pm.

Empúries

Daily: Easter & June–Sept 10am–8pm; rest of year 10am–6pm • €3 • ☎972 770 208, ⓦwww.mac.cat/esl/Sedes/Empuries • You can enter the site via the beach in summer, but at other times the main entrance and car park lie on the road farther inland

The archeological site of **Empúries**, which lies behind a sandy bay about 2km north of L'Escala, has immense historical significance, being the first entry point of classical Mediterranean culture into Iberian Spain – its fascination derives from its distinct Greek and Roman quarters showing how one culture steadily usurped the other. You can see the ruins in a leisurely afternoon, spending the rest of your time on the pleasant duned stretch of sand nearby.

Empúries was the ancient Greek Emporion (literally "trading station"), founded in the early sixth century BC by merchants who, for three centuries, conducted a vigorous trade throughout the Mediterranean. In 218 BC, their settlement was taken by Scipio, and a Roman city – more splendid than the Greek, with an amphitheatre, fine villas and a broad marketplace – grew up above the old Greek town. The Romans were replaced in turn by the Visigoths, who built several basilicas, and Emporion disappears from the records only in the ninth century when, it is assumed, it was wrecked by either Saracen or Norman pirates.

The Greek colony

The remains of the original **Greek colony**, destroyed by a Frankish raid in the third century AD – at which stage all inhabitants moved to the Roman city – occupy the lower part of the site. Among the ruins of several **temples**, to the south on raised ground is one dedicated to Asklepios, the Greek healing god whose cult was centred on Epidauros and the island of Kos. The temple is marked by a replica of a fine third-century-BC statue of the god, the original of which (along with many finds from the site) is in the Museu Arqueològic in Barcelona. Nearby are several large water filters: Emporion had no aqueduct so water was stored here to be filtered and purified and then supplied to the town by means of long pipes, one of which has been reconstructed. Remains of the town gate, the **agora** (or central marketplace) and several streets can easily be made out, along with a mass of house foundations, some with mosaics, and the ruins of Visigoth basilicas. A small **museum** stands above, with helpful models and diagrams of the excavations, as well as a variety of archeological finds, and a digital and audiovisual display giving a brief history of the settlement.

The Roman town

Beyond the museum stretches the vast but only partially excavated **Roman town**. Here, two luxurious villas have been uncovered, and you can see their entrance halls, porticoed gardens and magnificent mosaic floors. Farther on are the remains of the **forum**, **amphitheatre** and outer walls.

Parc Natural dels Aiguamolls de l'Empordà
Daily • Free

Halfway around the Golf de Roses, in two parcels of land on either side of the resort of Empuriabrava, is one of Spain's more accessible nature reserves. The **Parc Natural dels Aiguamolls de l'Empordà** is an important wetland reserve, created by the Catalan government in 1983 to save what remained of the Empordà marshland, which once covered the entire plain here but gradually reduced over the centuries as a result of agricultural developments and cattle raising. The park attracts a wonderful selection of birds to both its coastal terrain and the paddy fields typical of the area.

The park
There are two main **paths** around the lagoons and marshes: the first takes around two hours, while a second five-hour trek crosses more open land and can be cycled. Hides have been created along the way; morning and early evening are the best times for **birdwatching** and you'll spy the largest number of species during the migration periods (March–May & Aug–Oct). You'll almost certainly see marsh harriers and various waterfowl, and might spot bee-eaters and the rare glossy ibis.

Sant Pere Pescador
The nearest village to the visitors' centre at El Cortalet is **Sant Pere Pescador**, 6km south, pleasant enough but surrounded by a glut of sprawling, extremely busy campsites. You can rent bikes here, handy given the flat countryside, but the hordes of tourists make Castelló d'Empúries, 8km farther on, a more attractive base.

ARRIVAL AND INFORMATION   PARC NATURAL DELS AIGUAMOLLS DE L'EMPORDÀ

By bus Sarfa buses travel daily to Sant Pere Pescador from Castelló d'Empúries, L'Escala and Figueres.
Visitor centre El Cortalet (daily: April–Sept 9.30am–2pm

& 4.30–7pm; Oct–March 9.30am–2pm & 3.30–6pm; ☎972 454 222, ⊛ parcsdecatalunya.net). Here you can pick up a brochure marking the recommended routes in the park.

ACCOMMODATION

Can Ceret C/Mar 1 ☎972 530 433, ⊛ canceret.com. If you decide to stay in Sant Pere Pescador, try this well-maintained eighteenth-century farmhouse, which offers comfortable rooms and good meals. **€120**
Nautic Almatà In the Parc Natural dels Aiguamolls de

l'Empordà ☎972 454 477, ⊛ almata.com. This massive campsite is one of the best for access to the park. It has well-maintained facilities, including two pools and bike rental, and can organize outdoor excursions. Closed Oct to mid-May. **€46**

Castelló d'Empúries
Formerly the capital of the counts of Empúries, the delightful small town of **CASTELLÓ D'EMPÚRIES**, halfway between the beach at Roses and Figueres, is also midway between the two halves of the Parc Natural dels Aiguamolls. A five-minute walk from where the bus halts takes you into a small medieval conglomeration that's lost little of its genteel charm. The town's narrow alleys and streets conceal some fine preserved buildings, a medieval bridge and handsome church.

Church of Santa María
Church and museum: daily 10am–2pm & 4–8pm • Museum €1.50

The towering thirteenth-century church, **Santa María**, has an ornate doorway and alabaster altarpiece which alone are reward enough for the trip. Known as the Catedral of the Empordà, the church was intended to be the centre of an episcopal city, but opposition from the bishopric of Girona meant this was never to be, thus leaving Castelló with a church out of proportion to the town.

ARRIVAL AND INFORMATION

By bus Daily Sarfa buses service Castelló d'Empúries from Figueres (15min), Cadaqués (1hr) and Barcelona (1hr 30min). It's a 10min walk from the bus stop into town.

Turisme Pza. Jaume I (summer daily 9am–9pm; rest of year Mon–Sat 9am–2pm & 4–6pm, Sun 10am–1pm; ☎ 972 156 233, ⓦ castelloempuriabrava.com).

ACCOMMODATION AND EATING

Hotel Canet Pza. Joc de la Pilota 2 ☎ 972 250 340, ⓦ hotelcanet.com. For budget beds, try this hotel with simple, economical rooms – plus a restaurant that serves Catalan cuisine, including seafood, grilled meats and local produce. Mains €15–20. Daily 1–4pm & 8–11pm. **€80**

Hotel de la Moneda Pza. de la Moneda 8–10 ☎ 972 158 602, ⓦ hoteldelamoneda.com. Elegant seventeenth-century mansion, run by the same owners as *Hotel Canet*, with cosy, brightly painted rooms. **€110**

El Molí 8km west of Castelló d'Empúries ☎ 972 525 139, ⓦ elmolidesiurana.com. Lovely *El Molí* is one of several *casas rurales* in the area. It's set among vast gardens with oaks and laurel trees, near the village of Siurana d'Empordà, between Figueres and Sant Pere Pescador. Includes breakfast. **€90**

Roses

ROSES, 9km from Castello, enjoys a lovely situation beneath medieval fortress walls at the head of the grand, sweeping bay. It's a site that's been inhabited for over three thousand years – the Greeks called the place Rhoda when they set up a trading colony around the excellent natural harbour in the ninth century BC – but apart from the ruined **Castell de la Trinitat** and the Citadel, which contains the absorbing **Museu de la Ciutadella**, there's little in present-day Roses to hint at its long history. Instead, Roses is a full-blown package resort that trades exclusively on its 4km of sandy beach, which has fostered a large and popular watersports industry. If you're staying, don't skip a day-trip to Cadaqués, which you can reach via a short bus ride over the hill.

Citadel and the Museu de la Ciutadella

April–Sept Tues–Sun 10am–9pm; Oct–March daily 10am–6pm • €4

You can walk around the **Citadel**, which contains the remains of the Greek settlement of Rhoda, an ancient Roman villa and the **Museu de la Ciutadella**, which explores the Citadel's history – and its role in the evolution of Roses – via exhibits and photographs.

ARRIVAL AND INFORMATION

By bus The bus station is on the corner of C/Gran Vía Pau Casals and Rambla Ginjolers. Sarfa buses travel regularly to and from Barcelona (2hr 15min) and Figueres (30min).

Turisme On the seafront promenade near the citadel (mid-June to mid-Sept 9am–9pm; rest of year Mon–Fri 9am–6pm, Sat 10am–2pm & 3–6pm, Sun 10am–1pm; ☎ 972 257 331, ⓦ roses.cat).

SIP YOUR WAY THROUGH EMPORDÀ

The vineyards in the **Empordà** wine region (ⓦ doemporda.cat) aren't just old. They're ancient. This lush wine region, which unfolds inland from the Costa Brava, has been producing wine since the fifth century, when the Phoenicians first settled in the area. While primarily known for its naturally sweet Garnatxa, the region is going through a renaissance, with new, progressive small-batch winemakers developing a wide variety of blends. Over fifty wineries populate the Emordà, which is flanked by the Pyrenees on one side and the Mediterranean on the other, extending from Figueres north to the French border, and south through Baix Emporda. Rich soils and a mild Mediterranean climate ensure a flourishing harvest, but there's also something else that's unique to the region: the strong Tramuntana winds, which help protect the vines from disease and frost. Turisme Costa Brava Girona has launched a **DO (Denominació d'Origen) Empordà Wine Route** (ⓦ costabrava.org/what-to-do/wine-route), which features a range of wineries, including Castell Peralada (ⓦ castilloperelada.com), Celler Martin Faixó (ⓦ cellermartinfaixo.com) and Mas Llunes (ⓦ masllunes.com), as well as participating restaurants, accommodation, wine museums and even wine-based spa treatments.

11

THE EVOLUTION OF EL BULLI

In 2011, the most famous chef in the world closed his restaurant at the height of its popularity. Why? The answer to that explains who Catalan chef Ferran Adrià is.

Adrià's legendary "molecular gastronomy" restaurant **El Bulli**, near the town of Roses, was voted best restaurant in the world numerous times by *Restaurant* magazine. At its apex, there were two million reservation requests per year – and eight thousand granted. Adrià closed *El Bulli* in July 2011, and in its place has set up a nonprofit culinary foundation and centre, in pursuit of what he calls "constant evolution" and "a permanent commitment to creativity". The new centre consists of three sections, including elBulli 1846, an overview on the history of cooking; elBulli DNA, a culinary research laboratory; and Bullipedia, a "gastronomic encyclopedia" that will hold a vast database of recipes. For up-to-date information, check the website: ⓦ elbullifoundation.org. Though *El Bulli* the restaurant has now closed its doors, you can still sample Adrià cuisine at brother Albert Adrià's cluster of restaurants in the El Paral.lel neighbourhood in Barcelona, including the lively tapas bar *Tickets* (see p.692).

Ferran Adrià is perhaps best known for his "foams" (*espumas*), scented with everything from carrot to pine nuts to smoke. One of his culinary signatures has been to re-create traditional Mediterranean flavours via very non-traditional methods, his wizardry yielding such concoctions as liquid ravioli; spherified olives; parmesan ice cream; and "caviaroli" – caviar made with *allioli*. As Adrià has said of his cuisine: "Nothing is as it seems." Adrià is also famous for his deconstruction of Spain's comfort dishes, like *tortilla de patatas*. Hot potato is transformed into foam, onion made into a thick purée and egg white becomes a whipped sabayon. It's served in a tiny sherry glass with a spoon: the flavours fill the mouth – intense, warm and startlingly familiar.

The El Bulli Foundation occupies the same space as the restaurant, which is perched over the quiet cove of **Montjoi**, at the end of a long and winding road above Roses. It's a lovely, isolated spot – a far cry from the thronged Costa Brava and its laminated, quadrilingual menus. The land on which it sits was originally purchased by a German couple, who opened a beach bar which was followed by a restaurant, which they named after their pet French bulldogs – *El Bulli*. Adrià joined the staff in 1984, and contemporary Catalan cuisine has never been quite the same since.

Adrià is sometimes compared to another famous native son of Catalunya: Salvador Dalí. One is a surrealist on canvas, the other a surrealist in the kitchen. Adrià, in eloquent fashion, summed up the relationship between art and cuisine like this:

The dialogue between art and cuisine is still young. But in the end, it's not that important if cuisine is art, but if it changes the way you look at the world.

ACCOMMODATION AND EATING

Almadraba Park Hotel Avgda. Díaz Pacheco 70, Platja de l'Almadraba ☎ 972 256 550, ⓦ almadrabapark.com. For a splurge, stay at this classy spot, which has retained its history and elegance even amid the overbuilt Costa Brava. The hotel features pretty views of the sea and stylishly comfortable rooms, while the restaurant is worth a visit in itself: It's helmed by the well-known chef Jaume Subirós of the *Hotel Empordà* in Figueres (see p.743), and serves creative Catalan cuisine; the menu is €43, and dishes start at €24. Restaurant closed mid-Oct to March. **€164**

Cadaqués

CADAQUÉS is by far the most pleasant place to stay on the northern Costa Brava, reached only by the winding road over the hills from either Roses (16km) or Port de la Selva (12km) and consequently retaining an air of isolation. With whitewashed and bougainvillea-festooned houses lining narrow, hilly streets, a tree-lined promenade and craggy headlands on either side of a working fishing port, it's genuinely picturesque. Already by the 1920s and 1930s the place had begun to attract the likes of Picasso, Man Ray, Lorca, Buñuel, Thomas Mann and Einstein, but Cadaqués really "arrived" as an **artistic-literary colony** after World War II when Surrealist painter **Salvador Dalí** and his wife Gala settled at nearby Portlligat, attracting for some years a floating bohemian community. Today, a seafront statue of Dalí provides the town's physical and spiritual focal point, haughtily gazing on the artists, well-heeled Barcelonans and art-seeking foreigners who have rolled up in his wake.

With its art galleries and studios, smart restaurants and trendy clothes shops, Cadaqués makes for an interesting stroll. At the top of the hill is the austere-looking sixteenth-century **Església de Santa María**, containing an ornate eighteenth-century altarpiece and a side chapel on the left painted by Dalí. Local **beaches** are all tiny and pebbly, but there are some enjoyable walks around the harbour and nearby coves; the helpful *turisme* has further information and maps.

Museu de Cadaqués

C/Narcis Monturiol 15 • April–June Mon–Sat 10am–1.30pm & 4–7pm; July to mid-Sept Mon, Tues & Thurs–Sun 10am–8pm, Wed 10am–1.30pm & 4–7pm; mid-Sept to Dec Mon, Tues & Thurs–Sat 10.30am–1.30pm & 3.30–6.30pm, Wed 10am–3pm; generally closed Jan–March • Entry fee varies • ☎ 972 258 877

Below the church, the **Museu de Cadaqués** features temporary exhibitions by local artists and intriguing displays relating to aspects of Dalí's work. They also occasionally showcase exhibits on other artists connected to Cadaqués, including Picasso.

11

ARRIVAL AND INFORMATION   CADAQUÉS

By bus Sarfa buses arrive at the little bus office on C/Sant Vicenç, on the edge of town, next to a large pay car park. From here, you can walk along C/Unió and C/Vigilant to the seafront or climb up through the old streets to reach it. Buses run to Barcelona (2 daily; 2hr 20min); Castelló d'Empúries (4 daily; 1hr); Figueres (3 daily; 1hr 5min); and

Roses (4 daily; 30min).
Turisme C/des Cotxe 2, just back from Pza. Frederic Rahola on the promenade (late June to mid-Sept Mon–Sat 9am–9pm, Sun 10am–1pm & 5–8pm; mid-Sept to late June Mon–Sat 9am–1pm & 3–7pm; ☎ 972 258 315, Ⓦ visitcadaques.org).

ACCOMMODATION

Cadaqués can get very busy in the peak season, and it's a good idea to book in advance. Note that many hotels close in low season, from November to February, so call ahead if you're visiting in winter.

Hostal La Residència C/Caritat Serinyana 1 ☎ 972 258 312, Ⓦ laresidencia.net. Handsome building, built in 1904 (the year that Dalí was born) and loaded with character, though the rooms are relatively ordinary – the suites are elaborately decorated with Dalí in mind, however, and the balconies have stunning views. **€95**

L'Hostalet de Cadaqués C/Miquel Rosset 13 ☎ 972 258 206, Ⓦ hostaletcadaques.com. Pleasant, small hotel with a stone-and-iron facade that gives way to stylish rooms, each named after a different *cala*, or cove; a glossy, commissioned photo of each cove hangs over the bed. **€65**

★**Hostal Vehí** C/Església 6 ☎ 972 258 470, Ⓦ hostalvehi.com. Friendly and family-owned, this excellent-value *pensió* has a lovely central location near the church and well-tended rooms, and is consequently very popular. Closed Nov–Feb. **€70**

Hotel Blaumar C/Massa d'Or 21 ☎ 972 159 020, Ⓦ hotelblaumar.com. If you've come to Cadaqués for some quiet afternoons of sprawling poolside, *Blaumar* delivers. It's about a 10min walk from the centre of town, but that gives it an intimate, tucked-away feel. Rooms are simple but well kept, most with terraces, and the staff are helpful and accommodating. Closed Nov to mid-March. **€119**

Hotel Calina On Portlligat, Avgda. Salvador Dalí 33 ☎ 972 258 851, Ⓦ hotelcalina.com. Near Portlligat Beach, about a 20min walk from town, this well-maintained hotel offers tidy rooms with terraces as well as self-catering apartments, with full kitchens, that are ideal for families. Plus, you can splash in two swimming pools that are surrounded by gardens. Doubles **€105**, apartments **€175**

Hotel Horta d'en Rahola C/Sant Vicenç ☎ 972 251 049, Ⓦ hortacadaques.com. This eighteenth-century family home has been charmingly transformed into a boutique hotel, with a lovely garden, and seven breezy rooms with local art on the walls and views over the Cadaques old town. **€130**

Llané Petit C/Dr Bartomeus 37 ☎ 972 251 020, Ⓦ llanepetit.com. Friendly, relaxing hotel at the southern end of the town. Most rooms have terraces with sea views, and there is a well-maintained pool. Closed Jan–Feb. **€124**

Playa Sol Platja Pianc 3 ☎ 972 258 100, Ⓦ playasol .com. Set in a curve of the seafront, this quiet, charming hotel offers simply furnished but comfortable rooms affording superb views of the town or over tranquil gardens. Closed Dec. **€157**

EATING AND DRINKING

Moderately priced seafood **restaurants**, any of which are worth trying, are strung along the seafront, while dotted about the old town and along C/Miquel Rosset are places to suit a wide range of tastes and budgets. **Nightlife** is a pleasurable blend of laidback idling at the beachside terraces and stylish hobnobbing around the bars and restaurants on C/Miguel Rosset.

Es Baluard Riba Nemesi Llorens ☎ 972 258 183, ⓦ esbaluard-cadaques.net. This friendly spot has the hallmarks of traditional Cadaqués: it's family-run, seafood reigns supreme and it's built into the old sea wall (*baluard* means bastion). Mid-range prices. Mid-Feb to Oct daily 2–4pm & 8–11pm.

El Barroco C/Nou 10 ☎ 972 258 632, ⓦ elbarroco.net. This long-running restaurant represents all that's unique about Cadaqués: Surrealist-tinged artwork lines the walls, while the sunny courtyard spills over with flowers and crawling vines. The menu is equally creative, with a focus on Lebanese cuisine, like mezze platters of hummus and grape leaves, as well as paellas. Dalí used to dine here with Gala, and the owner is happy to share anecdotes of the restaurant's formidable history. Dishes €11–25. Daily 2–4pm & 8–11pm; limited hours in winter.

Can Tito C/Vigilant ☎ 972 259 070. Managed by part of the same family that runs *Casa Anita*, *Can Tito* specializes in Catalan cuisine, with many dishes featuring seafood, including grilled anchovies and a robust shellfish paella. Menu starts at €15. April–Sept Mon 9–10pm, Tues–Sun 1.30–3pm & 9–10pm; Oct weekends only.

Casa Anita C/Miquel Rosset 16 ☎ 972 258 471. Cadaqués marches to the beat of its own drum, and this quirky institution is a good example. Seating is at communal tables and there are generally no menus – just the family staff rattling off the day's specials of superb Catalan cuisine. Mains €15–25. Best to reserve ahead. Tues–Sun 1.30–4pm & 8.30–10pm; closed Nov.

Casa Nun Pza. de Portitxó 6 ☎ 972 258 856. This lovely restaurant offers top-notch regional fish and meat dishes, which you can enjoy on the small, sunny terrace perched above the Pza. des Portitxó. Dishes €14–25. Easter–Oct daily 1.30–4pm & 8–11pm; Nov–Easter Fri & Sat lunch & dinner, plus Sun lunch.

★**Compartir** Riera Sant Vicenç ☎ 972 258 482, ⓦ compartircadaques.com. Founded by three former *El Bulli* chefs, this award-winning restaurant features multi-course meals that are designed for diners to share ("compartir"). Inventive dishes include everything from razor clams with apple sorbet to sardines enveloped in *horchata*. The setting matches the cuisine: the spacious restaurant is awash in the colours of Cadaqués – white and blue – as well as a sun-dappled terrace. Dishes €17–30. Tues–Sun 1–3.45pm & 8–10.45pm; closed Jan to mid-Feb.

La Sirena C/Es Call ☎ 972 258 974. Tucked away in the old town, this appropriately named restaurant – "*sirena*" means "mermaid" – serves some of the best seafood in town. Menu starts around €15. Daily 1.30–4pm & 8–11pm; limited hours in winter.

Casa-Museu Salvador Dalí

Mid-June to mid-Sept daily 9.30am–9pm; rest of year Tues–Sun 10.30am–6pm; closed Jan 7 to mid-Feb; last entry 50min before closing • Tour €11; visits must be booked in advance by phone or via the website • ☎ 972 251 015, ⓦ dali-estate.org

A well-signposted twenty-minute walk north of Cadaqués and 3km by road is the tiny harbour of **PORTLLIGAT**, former home of Salvador Dalí. The artist had spent much of his childhood and youth in Cadaqués, and later, with his wife and muse, Gala, he converted a series of waterside fishermen's cottages in Portlligat into a sumptuous home that has all the quirks you would expect of the couple, such as speckled rooftop eggs and a giant fish painted on the ground outside. The house is now open to the public as the **Casa-Museu Salvador Dalí**, and although there's not much to see in the way of art,

---

THE DALÍ TRIANGLE

There are three museums in the Costa Brava devoted to the life and work of **Salvador Dalí** and they're known locally as the Dalí Triangle. The **Teatre-Museu Dalí** in Figueres (see p.741) provides a display of the breadth of his art and his consummate creative skill, whereas the **Casa-Museu Castell Gala Dalí** (see p.740), northwest of Girona, reveals the artist's complex personal relationship with his Russian wife and muse, Gala. Famously, he was only allowed to enter her home with permission; he repaid her with mischief by painting false radiators on the covers she had insisted he install to hide the real ones. You can also gain insight into the artist at **Casa-Museu Salvador Dalí** (see above) in Portlligat, next to Cadaqués, which was his only fixed home from 1930 until 1982, when he moved into Gala's castle. The *casa* is a tortuous maze of a home made up of fishermen's huts that were successively acquired and strung together.

it's worth the visit to see first-hand how the bizarre couple lived until Gala's death in 1982, after which Dalí moved to Figueres. Visitor numbers are strictly controlled and you have to **book a visit** beforehand.

Tours take in most of the house, and include Dalí's studio, the exotically draped model's room, the couple's master bedroom and bathroom, a secondary workshop in an olive grove and, perhaps best of all, the oval-shaped sitting room that Dalí designed for Gala, which, apparently by accident, boasts stunning acoustics. You'll also see the garden and swimming pool where the couple entertained guests – they didn't like too many strangers trooping through their living quarters. The phallic-shaped pool and its various decorative features, including a giant snake and a stuffed lion, are a treat.

Cap de Creus

Museum Summer Mon–Wed, Sat & Sun 10am–7pm, Thurs & Fri 10am–2pm & 3.30–6.30pm; rest of the year Mon–Fri 9am–4.30pm, Sat & Sun 9am–5pm · Free, or small entry fee depending on the exhibit · **Creuers Cadaqués** ☎ 972 159 462, ⓦ creuerscadaques.cat

A road winds 8km from Casa-Museu Salvador Dalí past glimpses of wave-plundered coves to the wind-buffeted **Cap de Creus** headland, the easternmost tip of the Iberian Peninsula, provides breathtaking views of the coast and is topped by a lighthouse built in 1853. It's now occupied by the **Museu Espai Cap de Creus**, with a small exhibition on the surrounding *parc natural*. If you fancy viewing the Cap de Creus from the sea, you'll find a few **boats** along the seafront that do excursions, including those run by Creuers Cadaqués.

El Port de la Selva and around

Thirteen kilometres northwest of Cadaqués, **EL PORT DE LA SELVA** is centred on its fishing and pleasure **ports**, while either side is a ribbon of lovely **coves** with some of the cleanest water in the Mediterranean: those to the north are far more rugged and reached on foot or by sea, while the ones to the west are easier to get to and, therefore, more popular.

Sant Pere de Rodes

Tues–Sun: June–Sept 10am–7.30pm; Oct–May 10am–5pm; check hours with Cadaqués' turisme · €5, Tues free

It's 8km up the paved **road** from El Port de la Selva, via Selva de Mar, to the Benedictine monastery of **Sant Pere de Rodes**, just below the 670m-high summit of the Serra de Roda; approaching **by foot**, use the marked trail (1hr 30min) through the Vall de Santa Creu, which begins at Molí de la Vall.

The first written record of the monastery dates back to 879, and in 934 it became independent, answerable only to Rome: in these early years, and thanks especially to the Roman connection, the monks became tremendously rich and powerful. As the monastery was enlarged it was also fortified against attack, starting a period of splendour that lasted four hundred years before terminal decline set in. Many fine treasures were looted when it was finally abandoned in 1789, and it was also pillaged by the French during the Peninsular War; some of the rescued silver can be seen in Girona's Museu d'Art.

Once one of the most romantic ruins in all of Catalunya, its central church universally recognized to be the precursor of the Catalan Romanesque style, the monastery is being robbed of a great deal of its charm by overzealous restoration. No original columns or capitals remain in the cloister and some of the work looks too clinical. The redeeming feature, apart from the view, is the **Catedral**, which retains its original stonework from the tenth to fourteenth centuries, including eleventh-century column capitals carved with wolves' and dogs' heads. Nearby is the peaceful pre-Romanesque church of **Santa Elena**, all that remains of the small rural community that grew up around the monastery.

Castell de Sant Salvador

Above the monastery (and contemporary with it) stands the much more atmospheric, ruined **Castell de Sant Salvador**, a thirty-minute scramble up a steep, narrow path. This provided the perfect lookout site for the frequent invasions (French or

11

Moorish), which normally came from the sea; in the event of attack, fires were lit on the hill to warn the whole surrounding area.

ARRIVAL AND DEPARTURE
EL PORT DE LA SELVA AND AROUND

By bus A daily bus travels from Figueres to El Port de la Selva (30min), though there's currently no public transport to Sant Pere de Rodes.

ACCOMMODATION AND EATING

Hostal La Tina C/Mayor 15 ☎972 387 149, Ⓦ hostallatina.cat. Comfortable and central *hostal*, with a simple, brick-arched restaurant serving local cuisine, from grilled meats to seafood. The hearty menu starts at €15. Daily 2–4pm & 8–11pm. **€80**

Hotel Porto Cristo C/Major 59 ☎972 387 062, Ⓦ hotelportocristo.com. Elegant rooms, many with views of the Mediterranean, and well-outfitted bathrooms. Dine at the pleasant restaurant which features local cuisine, including fresh seafood and seasonal produce. Closed late Dec to mid-Feb. Daily 2–4pm & 8–11pm. **€160**

Port de la Vall Carretera de Llança, km 6 ☎972 387 186, Ⓦ www.campingportdelavall.com. There are a few campsites within 2km of the beach, the best being *Port de la Vall*, with well-maintained grounds. Closed Oct–Easter. **€36**

Girona and around

Medieval, beautifully preserved **Girona**, which is accessible within an hour from the sea, offers a refreshing change from the sun-and-sand hedonism of the Costa Brava. This elegant, provincial capital features a walled medieval quarter, **Barri Vell**, perched on a hill above the city – a delight to explore, with narrow cobbled alleyways, balconied houses and shady little *plaças*. Clinging to the banks of the Ríu Onyar, as it meanders through the centre of town, is a long row of picturesque pastel-hued houses, the **Cases de l'Onyar**.

Historically, Girona has seen it all – at least by Spanish standards. The Romans settled here, and called the town Gerunda. Girona then became an Islamic town after the Moors conquered Spain. A vibrant Jewish community also flourished here for more than six centuries, and Girona's **Call**, the medieval Jewish quarter, remains one of the best preserved in Spain. Elsewhere, you'll spy a fetching mix of architectural styles, from Romanesque to *modernisme*. Girona also features a range of excellent museums, a lovely Catedral and lively arts and music festivals. **Rambla de la Llibertat**, running along the river, is the city's grand promenade, where locals take their daily *paseo* past a bustling strip of shops and restaurants.

Northwest of Girona, in the town of Púbol, rises the **Casa-Museu Castell Gala Dalí**, a medieval castle-turned-museum about surreal master Salvador Dalí and his wife Gala.

Catedral

Pza. de la Catedral • Daily: April–Oct 10am–8pm; Nov–March 10am–7pm; hours may vary • €7, free Sun • ☎ 972 215 814, Ⓦ catedraldegirona.org

Looming majestically over the old quarter, Girona's **Catedral** is an elegant amalgamation of architectural styles. The Romanesque cloister and tower are the only parts remaining from the original eleventh-century building, and the Catedral was continually rebuilt and expanded up to and throughout the eighteenth century. The splendid Gothic nave, dating from the fifteenth and sixteenth centuries, is the second widest of its kind in the world (after St Peter's in Rome). Also impressive are the fourteenth-century silver altarpiece and Gothic tombs.

It's well worth visiting the twelfth-century **cloister** (same hours as Catedral), and the Tresor Capitular (Chapter Treasury), which features a wealth of religious artefacts, including medieval gold pieces, a fifteenth-century bible and the ornate sixteenth-century *retablo* of Santa Elena. The main attraction is a splendid Italian tapestry, which dates back to the twelfth century and depicts the Creation.

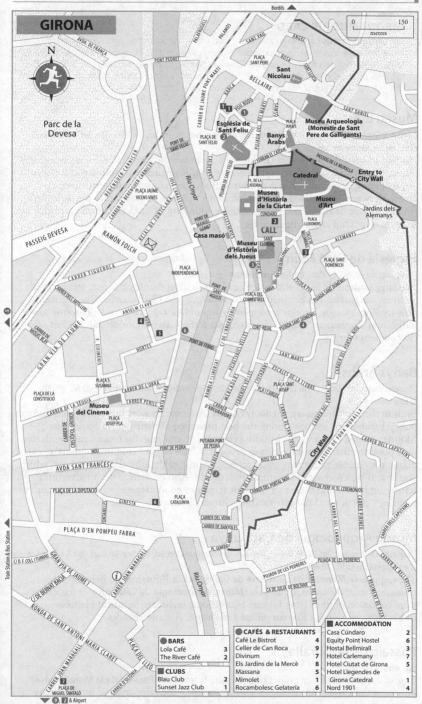

GIRONA

Parc de la Devesa

0   150
metres

N

AVDA. DE FRANÇA

Bordils

PONT PEDRET

PALAFRUGELL

PALAMÓS

SANT PAU

ANGEL

CARRER DE JAUME PONS MARTÍ

PLAÇA SANT PERE

ROSA

SANTILLECA

BELLAIRE

BARCA

POU RODÓ

Sant Nicolau

SANT DANIEL

Església de Sant Feliu

PLAÇA DE SANT FELIU

PUJADA DEL REI MARTÍ

PLAÇA JURATS

PUJADA DE SANT FELIU

Banys Àrabs

CARRER DE FERRAN EL CATÒLIC

Museu Arqueologia (Monestir de Sant Pere de Galligants)

PASSEIG DE LA MURALLA

Catedral

Entry to City Wall

PONT DE SANT FELIU

Riu Onyar

PL. DE LA CATEDRAL

Museu d'Història de la Ciutat

Museu d'Art

Jardins dels Alemanys

BERENGUER CARNISSER

CARRER DE BERENGUER CARNISSER

PLAÇA JAUME VICENS VIVES

JOSEP CANALETAS

REIAL DE FONTCLARA

PONT DE MANUEL SAUAÓ

BALLESTERIES

CÚNDARO

CALL

PLAÇA LLEDONERS

CARRER NOLMIALL

ALEMANYS

11

PASSEIG DEVESA

RAMÓN FOLCH

Casa masó

SANT LLORENÇ

Museu d'Història dels Jueus

FORÇA

CARRER DE CIUTADANS LLIBRES

PLAÇA SANT DOMÈNECH

CARRER FIGUEROLA

PLAÇA INDEPENDÈNCIA

PONT DE SANT AGUSTÍ

PLAÇA DEL CORREU VELL

ESCOLA PIA

PUJADA SANT DOMÈNECH

CARRER DELS ARTILLERS

ANSELM CLAVÉ

NORD

CORT-REIAL

PUJADA SANT DOMÈNEC

CARRER DE MIQUEL BLAI

GRAN VIA DE JAUME I

F. EIXIMENIS

HORTES

PONT DE FERRO

CARRER DE L'ARGENTERIA

BALLESTERIES VELLES

MERCADERS

SANT MARTÍ

CARRER DEL PORTAL NOU

CARRER DELS CAPUTXINS

PLAÇA S. SUSANNA

CARRER DE L'OBRA

SANTA CLARA

RAMBLA LLIBERTAT

CUIRADORS

ESCALES DE LA LLEBRE

PLAÇA DE LA CONSTITUCIÓ

CARRER PERILL

CARRER D'ABEURADORS

MERCADERS VELLES

PLAÇA SANT JOSEP

PLAT CARGOL

CARRER DE SANT JOSEP

City Wall

PASSEIG DE FORA MURALLA

CARRER DE CRISTÒFOL GROBER

Museu del Cinema

PLAÇA JOSEP PLA

PONT DE PEDRA

PUTJADA PONT DE PEDRA

NOU DEL TEATRE

CARRER DEL PORTAL NOU

CARRER DE PERE III 'EL CEREMONIÓS'

CARRER DEL CAMÍGÓ

CARRER PIRINEU

CARRER DELS CAPUTXINS

NOU

AVDA SANT FRANCESC

CARRER DE CALDERERS

PUJADA DEL PORTAL NOU

PLAÇA DE LA DIPUTACIÓ

GINESTA

PLAÇA CATALUNYA

CARRER DEL VERN

CARRER DE BANYOLES

PL. GENÈS

PUJADA DE LES PEDRERES

PUJADA DE LES PEDRERES

FONTANILLES

PLAÇA D'EN POMPEU FABRA

Riu Onyar

CREU DE JÚLIA DE BOLÍVAR

CARRER DEL SOL

REGIMENT DE BAZA

CARRER DE BELLVISTA

Train Station & Bus Station

C/ D. F. COLL ITURRAU

GRAN VIA DE JAUME I

C/ DE BERNAT BAÇA

RONDA DE SANT ANTONI MARIA CLARET

CARRER JOAN MARAGALL

CARRER D'UTÒNIA

PLAÇA DE MIGUEL SANTALÓ

PLAÇA DEL LLEÓ

Airport

■ BARS

Lola Café	3
The River Café	2

■ CLUBS

Blau Club	2
Sunset Jazz Club	1

● CAFÉS & RESTAURANTS

Café Le Bistrot	4
Celler de Can Roca	9
Divinum	1
Els Jardins de la Mercè	8
Massana	5
Mimolet	1
Rocambolesc Gelateria	6

■ ACCOMMODATION

Casa Cúndaro	2
Equity Point Hostel	6
Hostal Bellmirall	3
Hotel Carlemany	7
Hotel Ciutat de Girona	5
Hotel Llegendes de Girona Catedral	6
Nord 1901	4

GIRONAMUSEUS CARD

The **GironaMuseus** card (Ⓦ gironamuseus.cat) offers discounted entry to six of Girona's museums – the Museu d'Arqueologia de Catalunya, Museu d'Art, Museu d'Història de la Ciutat, Museu d'Història dels Jueus, Museu del Cinema and Casa Masó. Pay regular entry at any of the five, pick up the card and then you'll receive fifty percent discount to the other museums. You can get the card at any of the museums covered by the card, or at the *turisme* (see p.738).

Museu d'Art

Pujada de la Catedral 12 • March–Sept Tues–Sat 10am–7pm, Sun 10am–2pm; Oct–Feb Tues–Sat 10am–6pm, Sun 10am–2pm • €2 • Ⓣ 972 203 834, Ⓦ museuart.com

Housed in the Palau Episcopal (Bishop's Palace) near the Catedral, Girona's five storey **Museu d'Art** features a wide-ranging collection of Romanesque, Gothic and modern art, including beautifully preserved murals from local churches, fifteenth-century embroidery and rare stained-glass tables. Don't miss the tenth-century portable altar from Sant Pere de Rodes and the impressive collection of modern Catalan art, such as sculptures by Olot artist Miquel Blay.

Església de Sant Feliu

Pza. de Sant Feliu • Mon–Sat 9.30am–2pm & 4–7pm, Sun 10am–noon • Free

The large **Església de Sant Feliu** is one of Girona's most iconic churches, and it reveals an interesting transition between the Romanesque and Gothic styles. The thirteenth-century Romanesque interior is topped by a grand Gothic nave, and a Baroque tower looms over the western facade. The highlight is the Catalan Gothic statue, *Crist Jacent* (Recumbent Christ).

Banys Àrabs

C/Ferran el Catòlic • April–Sept Mon–Sat 10am–7pm, Sun 10am–2pm; Oct–March Mon–Sat 10am–2pm • €2 • Ⓣ 972 190 797, Ⓦ banysarabs.org

Built in the twelfth century, the **Banys Àrabs** (Arab baths) were inspired by the Romans' public bathhouses, and are among the best preserved of their type in Spain. The Moorish-tinged Romanesque building contains several graceful rooms, each with its own pool: the frigidarium (cold-water room), whose elegant columns support a central dome; the tepidarium (warm-water room); and the caldarium, the steam room, which was heated by a roaring fire burning underneath. Also on view is the apodyterium (changing room), and there's an outdoor terrace, a good vantage point to view both the building's exterior and the surrounding Girona cityscape.

Museu Arqueologia de Catalunya

C/Santa Llúcia 8 • June–Sept Tues–Sat 10.30am–1.30pm & 4–7pm, Sun 10am–2pm; Oct–May Tues–Sat 10am–2pm & 4–6pm, Sun 10am–2pm • €4.50 • Ⓣ 972 202 632, Ⓦ mac.cat

The impressive **Monestir de Sant Pere de Galligants**, a Romanesque Benedictine monastery near the baths, houses the **Museu Arqueologia de Catalunya**. It features a large collection of finds from Girona excavations, including beautiful Hebrew tombstones, sections of Roman pillars and Bronze Age metalworks.

Passeig de la Muralla

Daily 10am–8pm • Free

One of the finest vantage points over Girona is from the **Passeig de la Muralla**, also known as the Passeig Arqueològic, a walkway along the ramparts and medieval city wall. You can gain access to it from various points, including from near the Museu Arqueologia. As you trudge along the perimeter of the walls, you can enjoy lovely views of Girona – over the colourful rooftops to the river snaking through the centre – and the surrounding Ter valley. The walkway has several exits along the way, and it ends at Pza. Catalunya, where you can descend and amble back into the old town.

Carrer de la Força and the Jewish Quarter

Girona's Jewish community, known as the **Call** or the **Aljama**, existed for more than six hundred years, and the warren of narrow streets and alleyways around **Carrer de la Força** is widely regarded as one of the finest preserved Jewish neighbourhoods in Europe.

Centre Bonastruc ça Porta and Museu d'Història dels Jueus

C/la Força 8 • July & Aug Mon–Sat 10am–8pm, Sun 10am–2pm; Sept–June Mon–Sat 10am–6pm, Sun 10am–1pm • €4 • ☎ 972 216 761, ⓦ ajgirona.org/call

The well-run **Centre Bonastruc ça Porta**, housed in a former synagogue, is home to the **Museu d'Història dels Jueus**, which does an excellent job of curating archeological and ethnological finds from Girona's Jewish heritage. The exhibition covers themes such as festivals and tradition; the synagogue and cemetery; the diaspora; and the Inquisition, which features a display of original documents ordering the expulsion of all Jews from Spain. Other highlights include a gilded seal used for making Passover bread; a fourteenth-century limestone slab inscribed with Jewish law from a local synagogue; and a unique belt buckle, dating to between the thirteenth and fifteenth centuries, engraved with what is believed to be the mythical Leviathan, which features in the Hebrew Bible.

11

Museu d'Història de la Ciutat

C/la Força 27 • Tues–Sat 10am–2pm & 5–7pm, Sun 10am–2pm • €4 • ☎ 972 222 229, ⓦ girona.cat

Girona's history is formidable, and the excellent **Museu d'Història de la Ciutat** offers a well-organized overview under one roof. There's a wide range of Roman remains and modern arts and crafts on show, and the museum includes exhibits on the old fortified walls, and those who attacked them to plunder Girona; the history of the Catalan *sardana* dance and other folkloric traditions; and contemporary paintings by regional artists.

Casa Masó

Ballesteries 29 • Tues–Sat 10am–6pm; accessible via guided visits only; book online or by phone • €5 • ☎ 972 413 989, ⓦ rafaelmaso.org

Step into early twentieth-century Girona at the superbly restored home of acclaimed Girona architect Rafael Masó (1880–1935), who formed a key part of the Catalan *noucentisme* cultural movement. *Noucentisme*, which took its name from the "1900s" (in Catalan, *noucents*), was both a continuation of *modernisme* and a reaction to it, with

---

JEWISH GIRONA

A Jewish community first settled in Girona in the late ninth century; by the tenth century, the Jews had become a prosperous and influential sector of the city's society, but this all changed in the thirteenth century, when Gironan Jews became the victims of severe and unrelenting persecution. The entire Jewish quarter became a constant target of racist attacks and eventually became an isolated ghetto, in which the residents were virtually imprisoned, confined within neighbourhood limits and banned from the rest of the city. This continued until 1492, when all Jews were expelled from Spain. Life in the Call was bleak and presented an immense daily challenge: out of desperate necessity, residents created an underground community of tiny alleys and courtyards within which to survive.

a style that was characterized by elegant classicism as well as a renewed civic and Catalan pride. **Casa Masó** is the only one of the famous houses on the Ríu Onyar that is open to the public, and the beautifully designed interior features period furnishings, as well as paintings, sculpture, ceramics and drawings from the eighteenth to twentieth centuries.

ARRIVAL AND INFORMATION   GIRONA

By plane Girona-Costa Brava airport (ⓦbarcelona-girona-airport.com), 13km south of the city, handles flights by airlines from throughout Europe. Sagalés Barcelona Bus regularly does the 25min trip between the airport and the Girona bus station, and also to Barcelona's Estació del Nord (1hr 10min). A taxi from the airport to central Girona costs around €20.

By train The train station is near Pza. d'Espanya, a 15–25min walk southwest from the Barri Vell. Girona is well connected by train; it's on the train line between Barcelona (1hr 30min), Figueres (40min) and Portbou

(1hr). The Barcelona–Paris high-speed train (2–4 trains daily) stops in Girona and Figueres, as does the high-speed Madrid–Marseille.

By bus The bus station is next to the train station. Teisa buses operate regularly to regional cities, including Besalú (50min) and Olot (a little over 1hr). Sarfa runs several buses in the summer from the airport to the coast, including Roses (1hr 30min) and Tossa de Mar (1hr).

Turisme C/Joan Maragall 2 (Mon–Sat 9am–8pm, Sun 9am–2pm; ☎972 226 575, ⓦgirona.cat/turisme).

ACCOMMODATION

Girona has a wide variety of accommodation, from well-maintained hostels to historic hotels, many of which are central and within an easy stroll to the old quarter. In the surrounding countryside, you'll also find a range of comfortable **cases de pagés** (*casas rúrales*), including in the rustic hamlet of **Bordils**, which lies 10km northeast of town.

THE CITY

Casa Cúndaro Pujada de la Catedral 9 ☎972 223 583, ⓦcasacundaro.com. Top off your experience of medieval Girona by staying at this family-run hotel, which features elegantly restored rooms and apartments in a historic Jewish home a short stroll from the Catedral. It's an artful blend of old and new, from wood-beam ceilings and stone walls to leather sofas and, in the apartments, gleaming kitchens. **€85**

Equity Point Hostel Pza. Catalunya 23 ☎972 41 78 40, ⓦequity-point.com. This well-run hostel mini-chain has unisex dorms with shared bathrooms, and private rooms, plus welcoming details like free breakfast and common room with table football. Dorms **€21**, doubles **€60**

Hostal Bellmirall C/Bellmirall 3 ☎972 204 009, ⓦbellmirall.cat. Housed in a renovated fifteenth-century building, with comfortable rooms, stone walls, a communal living room and a hearty continental breakfast. It's right near the Catedral, so light sleepers may be woken up by the bell chimes. **€70**

Hotel Carlemany Pza. Miquel Santaló ☎972 211 212, ⓦthecarlemanyhotel.com. Modern hotel, geared more towards business travellers, but handily within walking distance of the train station. The *El Pati Verd* restaurant serves tasty Catalan cuisine. **€105**

Hotel Ciutat de Girona C/Nord 2 ☎972 483 038, ⓦhotel-ciutatdegirona.com. This boutique hotel in the centre of town has modern rooms in muted greys and red. The sleek *Blanc* restaurant serves creative Mediterranean dishes, including grilled tuna with sesame. **€150**

Hotel Llegendes de Girona Catedral Portal de la Barca 4 ☎972 220 905, ⓦllegendeshotel.com. Set in a magnificently restored eighteenth-century building, this handsome hotel is smack in the centre of town, near the Catedral (as the name indicates) and the Banys Àrabs. The comfortable rooms balance sleek amenities and crisp white linens with earthy touches like exposed brick walls and pine ceilings. Couples take note: the Eros Room is curated for couples, with furnishings like a tantric chair. **€137**

Nord 1901 C/Nord 7–9 ☎972 411 522, ⓦnord1901.com. This lovely boutique hotel offers the best of all worlds. It's central, in the heart of Girona. It's housed in a historic building that was fully renovated in 2009, with plenty of luxury, contemporary amenities. And it has one of the only gardens with private swimming pool in this part of town. Choose between handsome rooms or spacious apartments. Doubles **€150**, apartments **€290**

BORDILS

Can Carreras del Mas C/Creu 34, Bordils ☎972 490 276, ⓦcancarrerasdelmas.com. This welcoming, rustic *casa rural* has stone walls, brick-arched ceilings and a range of contemporary amenities, including a swimming pool. **€85**

Mas de la Roda C/Creu 31, Bordils ☎972 490 052, ⓦmasdelaroda.com. This cared-for stone house is a good place to relax, with a fireplace, four ample rooms and home-made meals made from locally sourced ingredients. **€80**

DINING WITH THE ROCA BROTHERS

Every year, restaurants around the world vie for first place in *Restaurant* magazine's annual Top 50 list. And in 2013, that honour went to **Celler de Can Roca** (see below). The Roca brothers – Joan, Josep and Jordi – had already been household names in Spain, but nabbing the top spot catapulted them onto the worldwide culinary stage. Their win was well-deserved, and each brother continues to work his specialty within the restaurant – Joan as the head chef, Jordi on desserts, and Josep on wine. If you don't get a reservation at the restaurant, you can still sample the Roca magic – at their **Rocambolesc Gelateria** in Girona (see below) The shop also functions as an introduction to the famous restaurant, with cookbooks and other information.

EATING

Girona has a diversity of **restaurants**, including a top-notch selection serving Catalan cuisine, most famously at the *Celler de San Roca* (see box above), just out of town. The area around C/la Força and C/Ballesteries is dotted with restaurants, while you'll find breezy outdoor cafés along Rambla de la Llibertat and Pza. del Vi.

Café Le Bistrot Pujada Sant Domènec 4 ☎ 972 218 803, ⊛ cafelebistrot.com. Inviting restaurant with a *belle époque* interior and tables outside, where you can fill up on Catalan cuisine at decent prices – dishes €14–24. Daily 1–4pm & 8pm–midnight, sometimes later at weekends.

★ **Celler de Can Roca** Can Sunyer 48, about 2.5km northwest of Girona, off the Taialà road ☎ 972 222 157, ⊛ cellercanroca.com. The menu showcases Ferran Adrià-style renderings of Catalan cuisine, from caramelized olives that arrive hanging from a small tree to steak tartare with mustard ice cream. For a superb sampling, try one of the tasting menus they offer, starting from around €155. Reservations are essential. Tues–Sat 1–3.30pm & 9–11pm; closed 3 weeks around Christmas, 1 week in Aug and for Easter.

★ **Divinum** C/Albereda 7 ☎ 872 080 218, ⊛ divinum.cat. Feast on creative contemporary Catalan cuisine at this sleek restaurant, from foie gras with vanilla and apple to steak tartare spiked with a gin-and-tonic citrus dressing. Don't miss the superb array of artisanal cheeses. This is a place where it's well worth going for the tasting menu (€45), which shows off the best of the kitchen. Dishes €14–26. Mon–Sat 1.30–3.45 & 8.30–11pm.

Els Jardins de la Mercè Pujada de la Mercè 10 ☎ 972 226 845, ⊛ elsjardinsdelamerce.com. Comfortable restaurant, with black-and-white tiled floors and a youthful appeal, in the centre of town. Enjoy well-priced, market-fresh Catalan cuisine and alfresco dining in the patio garden. Mains €15–20. Daily 1.30–3.30pm & 8.30–10.30pm; sometimes limited hours in winter.

Massana C/Bonastruc de Porta 10 ☎ 972 213 820, ⊛ www.restaurantmassana.com. This spacious, elegant restaurant takes locally sourced cuisine to a high art, serving such inventive dishes as wild mushrooms and marinated prawn in a pine-nut vinaigrette; sea bass with oysters in cava sauce; and Girona-raised beef with duck liver and apple frosting. Dishes €24–29; tasting menu €85. Tues 1.15–3.45pm, Wed–Sat 1.15–3.45pm & 8.30–10.45pm.

Mimolet C/Pou Rodó 12 ☎ 972 202 124, ⊛ mimolet .net. Classy, welcoming restaurant with a Catalan menu built around local produce, including monkfish with olives and foie with an sweet apple glaze. Menu starts at €18, while individual dishes range €18–24. Tues–Sat 1–3pm & 8.30–10.30pm.

Rocambolesc Gelateria C/Santa Clara 50 ☎ 972 416 667, ⊛ rocambolesc.com. A Willy Wonka-esque ice-cream and sweets shop that serves freshly churned, all-natural ice cream – try the ever-popular baked apple flavour – with toppings like cotton candy, guava jam and bacon. Sun–Thurs noon–10pm, Fri–Sat noon–midnight.

DRINKING AND NIGHTLIFE

Girona's nightlife caters to the sizeable university crowd, with rustic **bars** in Pza. de la Independencia and across the river along Rambla de la Llibertat, and splashier **clubs** (like *Blau Club*) further afield. The suburb of Pedret, about 700m north of the old town, also heats up at night with a string of clubs, while in the summer, everyone heads to the open-air bars, **Les Carpes**, which operate in the Parc de la Devesa, on the west side of the river in the modern part of town.

BARS

Lola Café C/Força 7 ☎ 972 228 824. This friendly, Latin-themed bar, in the middle of the old town, serves tasty tropical cocktails – mojitos, caipirinhas – and heats up with occasional live music, from rumba to salsa and more.

Daily 6pm–3am.

The River Café C/La Barca 2 ☎ 972 228 245, ⊛ rivercafegirona.com. This friendly bar and café, with a large, sun-dappled terrace, is at the foot of the lovely Església de Sant Feliu. Enjoy cocktails, chilled beer, local wine and other beverages, from fresh-squeezed juice to coffee. Plus, they'll often host various events, including live music, soccer matches, photography exhibitions and more. Tues 9am–1am, Wed 9am–2am, Thurs–Sat 9am–3am, Sun 10am–2pm.

CLUBS

Blau Club Camp de les Lloses 8 ⓦ blauclub.com. About 2km south of town, this is where the cool kids come to groove and flirt, with DJs spinning tracks all night long on the weekends. Fri & Sat 11pm/midnight–late.

Sunset Jazz Club C/Jaume Pons i Martí 12 ⓦ sunsetjazz-club.com. Near the old town, this lively joint hosts regular jazz concerts and jam sessions featuring musicians from around the country – and the world. You can enjoy potent cocktails poured with top-shelf alcohol, plus a good assortment of whiskys. Daily 9pm–closing (up to 2am).

Púbol

Salvador Dalí had many obsessions, but none quite like Gala, his beloved wife and lifelong muse, who he met when she was visiting Cadaqués in 1929 with her husband, French poet Paul Eluard. Dalí and Gala fell in love and married in 1934. Dalí lavished many gifts on her, including, in 1969, the medieval castle of Casa Púbol, which rises near the small village of **Púbol**, about 20km northeast from Girona. Gala lived here, and rumour has it that she entertained a string of lovers all the while, and imposed strict rules on Dalí, who supposedly had to get permission before he could visit. She stayed here until her death in 1982, when **Dalí** moved in. The artist made this his permanent base until 1984 when fire struck parts of the castle, prompting him to move to Figueres.

Casa-Museu Castell Gala Dalí

Mid-March to mid-June & mid-Sept to Oct Tues–Sun 10am–6pm; mid-June to mid-Sept daily 10am–8pm; Nov & Dec Tues–Sun 10am–5pm; closed Jan to mid-March • €8 • ☎ 972 488 655, ⓦ salvador-dali.org • Regular Sarfa-run Girona–Palafrugell buses stop in La Pera, from where it's 2km to Púbol (you'll need to walk or take a taxi); the Barcelona–Portbou train stops in Flaça, which is 4km from Púbol

The castle, which is now the **Casa-Museu Castell Gala Dalí**, is decorated in vintage Dalí style, though parts of it are considerably more understated than other Dalí sights – it is one of three in the region (see box, p.732). Stuffed animal heads protrude from walls, and dome ceilings are painted in quasi-religious motifs, but there are also quietly stark rooms with simple wood floors. Exhibits feature a supremely entertaining array of Dalí photos, particularly from his 1930s–40s heyday, while outside is an atmospheric swimming pool and garden, populated by sculptures of Richard Wagner, one of Dalí's favourite composers.

Figueres

It is a testament to **Dalí**'s enduring popularity that his eponymous museum, in the middle of **FIGUERES**, 35km northeast of Girona, is the most visited sight in Spain after Madrid's Prado and Bilbao's Guggenheim. There's more to Figueres, of course, but you wouldn't immediately know it from the crowds tripping over themselves to get to the museum. Native son Dalí returned to Figueres specifically to create this homage to Surrealism, and what an homage it is: wonderfully bizarre and cheekily interactive, the museum is all you'd expect from the world's most celebrated Surrealist.

By all means make the museum your first stop – but leave yourself some time to roam

---

DALÍ BY NIGHT

The **Dalí Museum** may be surreal by day, but is even more so at night (and especially after a glass of cava). In the summer, generally from late July to late August, the museum opens its doors at night (10pm–1am; last entry at 12.30am). For an admission price of €13, visitors are offered a glass of cava on one of the terraces, where they also show a film on Dalí. There is limited capacity, so it's worth booking ahead, which you can do on the museum website (ⓦ salvador-dali.org).

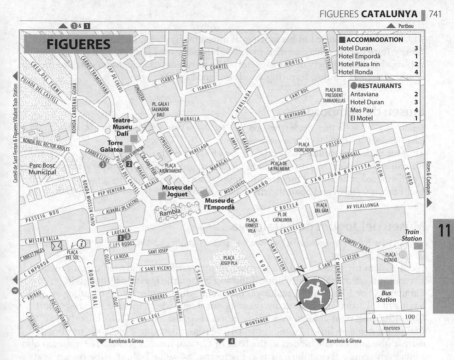

Figueres afterwards. Cutting a wide swathe through the centre of town is **La Rambla de Figueres**, a graceful, leafy pedestrian street lined with modern houses and outdoor cafés. The **Museu de l'Empordà** features local archeological finds and the nearby **Castell de Sant Ferran** is a massive fortification on sprawling grounds.

Teatre-Museu Dalí

Teatre-Museu Dalí Pza. Gala i Salvador Dalí • **Dalí Joies** Corner of C/María Àngels Vayreda and Pujada del Castell • Both: March–May Tues–Sun 9.30–6pm, June–Sept daily 9am–8pm, Oct Tues–Sun 9.30am–6pm, Nov–Feb Tues–Sun 10.30–6pm; last admission 45min before closing • €12 for Teatre includes entry to Dalí Joies • ☎ 972 677 500, ⓦ salvador-dali.org

One thing is certain: you won't have trouble spotting the **Teatre-Museu Dalí**. Just look for a roof topped with giant eggs and a red facade with protruding bread loaves. Housed in a former theatre – which is particularly apt, for this most theatrical of artists – the museum is designed around a large courtyard with white ceramic sinks and gold mannequins inspired by Oscar statues. Light streams in to the building through a transparent, geodesic dome ceiling that resembles the eye of a fly, in a nod to Dalí's fixation with insects. Incidentally, the artist had no problem with flies, but was supposedly repulsed by ants, which he depicted crawling out of eyeballs and such in his paintings.

Dalí created the museum to be an all-round sensory – and surreal – experience. Look through binoculars to see *Gala Nude Looking at the Sea Which at Twenty Metres is Transformed into a Portrait of Abraham Lincoln*, or revive a "dead" body in a coffin made of circuit boards. And check out *The Face of Mae West That Can Be Used as a Drawing Room*, in which Mae's giant nose has a fireplace (complete with logs) built into each nostril, and her fleshy red lips are a couch.

Inside the **Sala de Tresor** is housed many of Dalí's better-known works, including *The Spectre of Sex Appeal*, which explores the artist's famous sex phobia. Other emblematic works include *Soft Self-Portrait with Fried Bacon*, in which Dalí's dripping visage is held up by little sticks, and *Venus de Milo with Drawers*.

Dalí, fittingly, is buried in his fantastical museum. By 1984, he had moved to the nearby **Torre Galtea**, where he died in 1989. His body now lies behind a simple granite slab in a basement gallery of the museum. The museum ticket includes entry to the nearby **Dalí Joies** exhibit, featuring jewels designed by Dalí.

Museu de l'Empordà

Rambla 2 • May–Oct Tues–Sat 11am–8pm, Sun 11am–2pm; Nov–April Tues–Sat 11am–7pm, Sun 11am–2pm • €4, or free with Teatre-Museu Dalí ticket • ☏ 972 502 305, ⓦ museuemporda.org

The **Museu de l'Empordà** explores the region's history, with exhibits covering Greek and Roman archeological remains, frescoes, sacred art and medieval sculpture. It also features a well-curated collection of nineteenth- and twentieth-century art by an assortment of well-known Catalan and Spanish artists, from Sorolla and Miró to Tàpies to Dalí.

Museu del Joguet de Catalunya

Hotel Paris, C/Sant Pere 1 • June–Sept Mon–Sat 10am–6pm & 4–7pm, Sun 11am–7pm; Oct–May Tues–Sat 10am–6pm, Sun 11am–2pm • €6 • ☏ 972 504 508, ⓦ mjc.cat

From ancient toy wooden tops and bronze Roman rattles to candy-red cars, miniature circuses and twentieth-century optical-illusion games, the **Museu del Joguet de Catalunya** (Toy Museum of Catalunya) offers a playful glimpse into the history of having fun. Particularly curious are the religious items, which include altar boys' clothes from 1905 and mini-churches with tiny moveable priest figures. Don't miss the traditional *caganers*, little figurines of squatting peasants taking a break to "fertilize the earth", who are cheekily hidden in the back of Catalan nativity scenes. The museum also hosts lively temporary exhibits, such as the recent "Salvador Dalí: the first twenty years".

Castell de Sant Ferran

Daily: March–June & mid-Sept to Oct 10.30am–6pm; July to mid-Sept 10am–8pm; Nov–Feb 10.30am–3pm; last admission 1hr before closing • €3 • ⓦ castillosanfernando.org

The impressive eighteenth-century fortified **Castell de Sant Ferran**, one of the largest in Europe, stands 1km northwest of Figueres. Explore the sprawling castle grounds and walk its 4km perimeter and you'll get a sense of just how massive it is. It was at Sant Ferran that the last official meeting of Spain's Republican parliament took place, on February 1, 1939, before it surrendered to Franco's forces. More recently, Colonel Tejero was imprisoned here after his failed coup attempt in 1981.

ARRIVAL AND INFORMATION   FIGUERES

By train The train station is just east of the city centre. Figueres is on the train line from Barcelona, via Girona, to Portbou on the French border. Services run regularly between Figueres and Girona (up to 20 daily; 40min), and Barcelona (3–6 daily; just over 2hr). High-speed rail connects Perpignan and Figueres (2–4 daily), stopping at Figueres-Vilafant, 2km west of Figueres; the route continues on to Barcelona. Teisa buses (€2) run from the city centre, and the bus and train stations, to Figueres-Vilafant station.

By bus The bus station is east of the city centre, just south of the train station. Buses operate regularly to regional cities, including Girona (1hr) and Barcelona (2hr 30min).

Turisme Pza. del Sol (late June to mid-Sept Mon–Sat 9am–8pm, Sun 10am–3pm; mid-Sept to late June generally Mon–Sat 10am–2pm & 4–7pm, Sun 10am–2pm; ☏ 972 503 155, ⓦ figueresciutat.cat).

ACCOMMODATION

Hotel Duran C/Lausaca 5 ☏ 972 501 250, ⓦ hotelduran.com. Long-running hotel – Dalí and Gala were frequent visitors – that has been artfully updated, with inviting rooms of polished wood floors, muted colours and modern baths. Keep an eye out for original Dalí works displayed throughout. The restaurant serves tasty Catalan cuisine. €70

Hotel Empordà Avgda. Salvador Dalí i Domènech 170, 1km northwest of Figueres ☏ 972 500 562, ⓦ hotelemporda.com. While it's the restaurant that receives the accolades (see below), the hotel itself is also historical and welcoming, with comfortable rooms and a breezy terrace. It's important to book ahead. **€95**

Hotel Plaza Inn Pujada del Castell 14 ☎ 972 514 540, ⓦ plazainn.es. Bright, friendly hotel right in the centre, next to the museum, with a quirky, art-filled decor,

well-maintained rooms and a small rooftop terrace overlooking Figueres. **€65**

Hotel Ronda Avgda. Salvador Dalí 17 ☎ 972 503 911, ⓦ hotelronda.com. It looks a bit antiseptic from the outside, but this modern hotel has elegant rooms, and a friendly restaurant with terrace. **€85**

EATING AND DRINKING

Figueres, particularly in high season, can be crammed with visitors. This translates into a slew of restaurants, especially in the streets around the Museu Dalí, that cater to tourists, often with mediocre menus at inflated prices. You will find some good choices, though, slightly beyond the centre. Also, if you have your own wheels, you can opt for heading to one of the villages around Figueres, several of which have lovely, old farmhouse restaurants, such as *Mas Pau*.

Antaviana C/Llers 5–7 ☎ 972 510 377, ⓦ restaurantantaviana.cat. The airy dining room, with light woods and sleek lighting, matches the contemporary Catalan cuisine, with a focus on seafood, from fresh mussels to cod with spinach. They also serve a good selection of local Empordà wines. Dishes €11–20. Mon–Sat 1–3.30pm & 8.30–11.45pm.

Hotel Duran C/Lausaca 5 ☎ 972 501 250, ⓦ hotelduran.com. You're in good company: Dalí used to have his own dining room here, where creative regional cuisine has been prepared by the Duran family for generations. *Mar i muntanya* dishes might include cuttlefish and meatballs or prawns and sausage. Dishes €13–20. Daily 12.30–4pm & 8.30–11pm.

Mas Pau Carretera de Figueres a Besalú ☎ 972 546 154, ⓦ maspau.com. Tuck into Catalan fare in a sixteenth-century farmhouse surrounded by breezy gardens, 5km southwest of town. The restaurant, which opened in 1960, celebrates the seasons and regional produce, and might include local anchovies, suckling lamb from Ripoll and spring-onion soup with *calçotada romesco* fritters. They

also operate as a comfortable hotel. Dishes start at €26–30. The restaurant is on the road to Besalú near the turning for Avinyonet de Puigventós. Mid-March to Dec Tues 8.30–10.30pm, Wed–Sat 1.30–3.30pm & 8.30–10.30pm, Sun 1.30–3.30pm.

★**El Motel** Hotel Empordà, Avgda. Salvador Dalí i Domènech 170, 1km northwest of Figueres ☎ 972 500 562, ⓦ elmotel.cat. Before the foams of Ferran Adrià and the "emotional cuisine" of the Roca brothers, there was the *Hotel Empordà* (originally called the *Motel Ampurdan*, in part because it sits on a busy roadway), where chef Jaume Subirós is credited with elevating traditional cooking from home kitchen to restaurant quality. Considered the birthplace of modern Catalan cuisine, *El Motel* (as the restaurant is now called in homage to its roots) continues to serve some of the finest and most innovative food in the region. The chefs find inspiration in the sea, with dishes like wild sea bass from Cadaqués with lime leaves and polenta, rock lobster from Cap de Creus with fragrant rice, shrimp from Roses, and sea cucumbers. Dishes start at €24. Book ahead. Daily 1–3.30pm & 8.30–10.30pm.

La Garrotxa

The fertile landscape of **La Garrotxa**, which unfolds west of Girona and Figueres, is anchored by the historic capital of **Olot**. To the east lies lovely, quiet **Besalú**; to the north, mountain peaks march along the French border; and to the south extends the **Parc Natural de la Zona Volcànica**, a verdant, hilly terrain punctuated by volcanic cones and craters.

Besalú

Medieval **BESALÚ**, about 50km north of Girona, is a captivating sight: the impressive eleventh-century Romanesque **Pont Fortificat** spans the River Fluvià at the entrance to the town, beyond which rise church towers amid stone houses. These days, Besalú is a small, humble town, but its beautifully preserved core, with dark little streets, arcaded shops and elegant historic architecture, is testament to its formidable past. Roman, Visigothic and Muslim rulers all passed through, but Besalú's most important role came between the tenth and twelfth centuries, when it served as the capital of the region until power was transferred to Barcelona.

Església de Sant Pere and around

The thirteenth-century **Casa de la Vila**, which now houses the *ajuntament*, rises over Pza. de la Llibertat. To the west of Llibertat lies a spacious *plaça*, the Prat de Sant Pere, which is presided over by the tenth-century Benedictine monastery **Església de San Pere**. Keep an eye out for the beautiful Gothic window on the west facade. The nearby Romanesque **Església de Sant Vicenç** features impressive Gothic capitals. Both churches are usually only open for services, but guided tours are sometimes organized by the *turisme*.

Miqvé

Baixada de Mikwe • Guided tours: summer usually daily noon, 1.30pm, 4.30pm & 6pm; check with *turisme* and for times the rest of the year

Similar to Girona, Besalú had a Jewish community from the ninth century onwards, until the Jews were forced out of town in 1436 due to Christian persecution. Their **Miqvé**, said to be the only existing Jewish ritual bath in Spain, sits near the river, and features a barrel-vaulted underground stone room. The bath was also once connected to the town's **synagogue**, the remains of which were discovered nearby.

11

ARRIVAL AND INFORMATION   BESALÚ

By bus The bus stop is on the main Olot–Girona road; there are regular buses to and from Figueres (30min) and Girona (50min).
Turisme Pza. de la Llibertat (daily 10am–2pm & 4–7pm;

972 591 240, besalu.cat). In addition to guided tours of the churches and Miqvé, the *turisme* also offers tours encompassing all of Besalú's sights, usually daily at 5pm, but hours are subject to change.

ACCOMMODATION AND EATING

★ **Cúria Reial** Pza. de la Llibertat 14 972 590 263, curiareial.com. Enjoy the twin pleasures of top-notch local cuisine and the beautiful outdoors at this friendly, mid-priced restaurant, where you can dine alfresco on the terrace overlooking the historic bridge. Mains €15–20. Mon & Wed–Sun 12.30–4pm & 8.30–10.30pm; closed Mon dinner in winter.
Hotel Comte Tallaferro C/Ganganell 2 972 591 609, grupcalparent.com. This historic hotel features elegant, well-furnished rooms with wood floors, and a restaurant serving regional dishes. Daily lunch & dinner. **€125**
Els Jardins de la Martana Pont 2 972 590 009,

lamartana.com. For a feel of Besalú's history, bed down in this antique mansion, with its faded but graceful rooms and leafy gardens, that sits across from the Pont Fortificat. **€120**
Pont Vell C/Pont Vell 24 972 591 027, restaurantpontvell.com. Named after the bridge that it overlooks, this rustic restaurant with a lovely outdoor terrace offers traditional Catalan cuisine with a modern twist, including *escalivada*, a typical Catalan dish of grilled vegetables, here often picked from the restaurant's garden, and the Pont Vell speciality – sweet and sour rabbit. Mains €15–25. Wed–Mon 1.30–4pm & 8.30–10.30pm; occasionally closed Sun & Mon nights.

Beget

The tiny village of **BEGET**, about 30km northwest of Besalú, is nestled so deeply in a valley that you don't see it until you're almost upon it. And when you do, it's a handsome sight: Beget looks much as it did centuries ago, with narrow cobbled streets, little bridges and stone houses. A stillness fills the graceful twelfth-century church, **Sant Cristòfor**, which rises over the village. The church (sporadic opening times; enquire in the village) is notable for its *Majestat*, a carved-wood figure of Christ in a full-length tunic, arms outstretched.

ARRIVAL AND DEPARTURE   BEGET

By bus and taxi It's hard to reach Beget without your own transport. If you don't have your own wheels, the best

option is to take a bus to Camprodon (see p.751), and then hire a taxi.

ACCOMMODATION AND EATING

Les Barnedes Veïnat dels Grells in the village of Molló, 11km northwest of Beget 656 925 816 or 676 157 806, barnedes.com. This *casa rural* has rustic,

self-catering apartments, each equipped with a full kitchen, fireplace and a garden. In July and Aug, the apartments rent out only by the week (€1000). **€155**

Can Jeroni C/Bellaire 17–19 ☎972 741 239, Ⓦcanjeroni.net. Friendly, family-run restaurant serving seasonal Catalan cuisine (€20-plus à la carte), with seating near an old bridge and views of the church. Daily 1.30–3.30pm & 8.30–10.30pm; limited hours in winter.

Hostal El Forn C/Josep Duñach ☎972 741 230. This cosy *hostal* is one of the better budget choices in town. It's set in a rustic stone house and features brightly coloured rooms. Rate includes breakfast. **€45**

Olot

La Garrotxa's provincial capital, **OLOT**, is an amiable, mid-sized town with busy shopping streets and a breezy Pza. Mayor. Passeig d'en Blay, the central *rambla*, is flanked by lovely historic buildings and dotted with lively cafés. Olot's varied countryside, marked by sheer cliffs, verdant valleys and extinct volcanic cones and craters, inspired the highly respected nineteenth- and twentieth-century **Olot School** of landscape painters, whose works you can view in the town's Museu de la Garrotxa.

Museu de la Garrotxa

C/Hospici 8 · Summer Tues–Fri 10am–1pm & 3–6pm, Sat 11am–2pm & 4–7pm, Sun 11am–2pm; rest of year, hours may vary · €3, €4 combined ticket with Museu dels Volcans or other museum · ☎972 271 166, Ⓦolotcultura.cat

Nature was at the core of the Olot School of painters, who explored Garrotxa's unique landscape on canvas, from rolling, pastoral hills to desolate terrain punctuated by stark trees. The school, founded by Joaquim Vayreda i Vila, was also influenced by the French Impressionists. You can view many of its striking works in the well-curated **Museu de la Garrotxa**, housed in a renovated eighteenth-century hospital. The museum also features *modernista* sculptures by Miquel Blay and Josep Clarà, and exhibits on the history of Olot and Catalan arts and crafts.

Parc Nou and Museu dels Volcans

Avgda. Santa Coloma, 1km southwest of town centre · **Jardí Botànic** Daily April–Sept 9am–9pm; Oct–March 9am–7pm (sometimes 6pm) · Free · **Museu dels Volcans** Tues–Sat 10am–2pm & 3–6pm, Sun 10am–2pm; rest of year, hours may vary · €3, €4 combined ticket with Museu de la Garrotxa or other museum · ☎972 266 762, Ⓦolotcultura.cat

Parc Nou is a nine-acre municipal park that encompasses the well-tended, leafy **Jardí Botànic** and the **Casal dels Volcans**, a Palladian building that houses the helpful Centro d'Informació del Parc Natural de la Zona Volcànica, where you can pick up park maps and other information. The park also hosts a variety of open-air musical concerts and festivals, often in the summer. Also here is the **Museu dels Volcans**, which features exhibits on the volcanic history of the region, including rock samples and photos.

ARRIVAL AND INFORMATION   OLOT

By bus The bus station is at the east end of C/Bisbe Lorenzana, the main thoroughfare. Teisa runs regular buses to and from Barcelona (just under 3hr) and Girona (just over 1hr).

Turisme C/Hospici 8, inside the Museu Comarcal (summer Mon–Sat 10am–2pm & 5–7pm, Sun 10am–2pm; ☎972 260 141, Ⓦturismeolot.cat). The *turisme* has up-to-date lists of local accommodation and transport timetables, and also sells a joint ticket to the museums in the area (€3–5 depending on number of museums you visit).

CYCLING THE CARRILET

Where trains once rumbled down tracks, cyclists can now pedal amid quiet greenery. The **Ruta del Carrilet** (Ⓦviesverdes.cat) are traffic-free trails for pedestrians and cyclists that follow unused train lines, offering the chance to ride or stroll through the rolling Catalan countryside, passing small towns and villages along the way. Among the most popular is the 54km Olot-to-Girona route. In Olot, the trail starts at Fonts Sant Roc (Sant Roc Springs), just southwest of the city, near the Fluvià River; enquire at the *turisme* for further information and directions. The route is relatively flat and therefore appropriate for all levels, and is especially popular with families.

11

ACCOMMODATION AND EATING

Olot has a range of decent **hotels and hostels** in town, but some of the most appealing accommodation options are the **manors and B&Bs** in the surrounding countryside, many of which make the most of their proximity to the Parc Natural de la Zona Volcànica, with terraces, hearty breakfasts to fuel your hiking, and bikes for hire.

The volcanic Garrotxa region, famed for its fertile soil, has become known for its rich **Cuina Volcànica** (Ⓦ cuinavolcanica. cat). Traditional ingredients – all locally produced – include Santa Pau haricot beans, black radishes, mushrooms and sheep's cheese. Olot has several good *Cuina Volcànica* **restaurants**, though it's in the surrounding villages, like Besalú and Santa Pau, that you'll find the best renditions.

11

Ca l'Enric Carretera de Camprodon, Vall de Bianya, 7km northwest of Olot ☏ 972 290 015, Ⓦ restaurantcalenric .cat. Locally sourced Catalan cuisine is taken to a high art at this long-running restaurant that's set in a beautifully renovated nineteenth-century country house. Dishes range from foie gras with cacao to grilled partridge. The restaurant also hosts special dinners tied to the season, like truffles (Dec–Jan) and wild mushrooms (from April). Dishes €26–34. Tues, Wed & Sun 1.15–3.15pm, Thurs–Sat 8.45–10.30pm.

★**Les Cols** Carretera de la Canya, on the northern outskirts of Olot ☏ 973 269 209, Ⓦ lescols.com. Fresh produce reigns supreme at this elegant restaurant, where the menu might include wild asparagus in a charcoal tempura, grilled peas from the garden with bacon, the region's signature Santa Pau beans, fresh river trout, and a tangle of spaghetti in a smoked broth, that come with these instructions: "to eat whole and with fingers." It's

pricey – from €200 for two – but worth it. Reservations advised. Wed–Sat 1–3.30pm & 8.30–10.30pm, Sun 1–3.30pm; sometimes closed 2 weeks in summer.

Hotel Borrell C/Nonet Escubós, Olot ☏ 972 276 161, Ⓦ hotelborrell.com. Near the centre of town, next to Pza. Catalunya, this small, friendly hotel has simple but clean rooms with hardwood floors and decently sized bathrooms. €87

★**Mas El Guitart** Vall de Bianya, 7km northwest of Olot, just above Sant Andreu de Socarrats village ☏ 972 292 140, Ⓦ guitartrural.com. Comfortable country house, with hardwood-floor rooms and cabins, and, uniquely for these parts, a lovingly run spa, with therapies including hot-stone massages and reflexology. €70

Torre Malagrida Pg. de Barcelona 15, Olot ☏ 972 264 200, Ⓦ xanascat.cat. This central, well-kept youth hostel with simple dorms is housed in a nineteenth-century tower set amid gardens. Dorms €18

Parc Natural de la Zona Volcànica

The sprawling **Parc Natural de la Zona Volcànica** makes up much of the **Baixa Garrotxa** region. You won't see lava flows and smoke-snorting volcanoes, though – the last eruption was almost 11,000 years ago, and the park is in fact largely green and verdant, with a remarkably fertile soil. The volcanic landscape comes in the shape of the park's forty cones, which vary widely in size, the bigger ones topping 170m.

There are numerous trails through the park – if you're short on time, you can opt to take shorter trails to several of the volcanoes that start at car parks around Olot. Posted signs point out those that lead to the two easiest cones to access from town: **Volcà del Croscat**, the youngest cone in the park, and **Volcà de Santa Margarida**.

ARRIVAL AND INFORMATION

Accessing the park You'll need your own wheels to access the park; there is a regular Teisa bus service between Girona and Olot.

Centro d'Informació del Parc Natural de la Zona Volcànica Casal del Volcans, Olot (Mon–Sat 10am–2pm &

PARC NATURAL DE LA ZONA VOLCÀNICA

4–6pm, Sun 10am–2pm; ☏ 972 268 112, Ⓦ gencat.cat /parcs/garrotxa). The main park information office is in Parc Nou in Olot, where you can pick up helpful hiking maps.

Turisme Pza. Mayor, Santa Pau (Mon & Wed–Sat noon–6pm, Sun 11am–3pm; ☏ 972 680 349, Ⓦ santapau.com).

ACCOMMODATION AND EATING

Cal Sastre C/Cases Noves, near Plaçeta dels Balls, Santa Pau ☏ 972 680 049, Ⓦ calsastre.com. For a taste of the famous Santa Pau *fesols*, dine at this established Catalan restaurant, which also doubles as a handsome hotel (price includes breakfast). Tues–Sat 1–3.30pm & 9–10.30pm, Sun 1–3.30pm; closed Feb. €90

Can Blanc Passatges de la Deu, around 1.5km north of town ☏ 972 276 020, Ⓦ canblanc.es. The location here is the big draw: it's in the Parque Natural, and surrounded by greenery, yet still within easy reach of town (around 30min on foot, should you want to walk). Rooms are comfortable, and nearby is the historic *La Deu Restaurant*. €50

Can Menció Pza. Major 17, Santa Pau ☎ 972 680 014, ⓦ canmencio.com. This inviting hotel is one of the better picks in town, with alpine-style rooms and an inviting, breezy café-bar (open daily) right on the *plaça*. **€50**

La Deu Restaurant Carretera de la Deu s/n, near Can Blanc, about 1.5km south of Olot ☎ 972 261 004, ⓦ ladeu.es. This established restaurant, which sits in the Parque Natural and dates back to 1885, is helmed by the fourth and fifth generations of the Reixac family. The menu is rooted in *Cuina Volcànica*, and includes their signature La Deu potatoes; *escalivada*, a typical Catalan dish of grilled vegetables; and pig's trotters. The menu is €12. Mon–Sat 1.30–3.30pm & 8–10.30pm, Sun 1.30–3.30pm.

Santa Pau

Medieval **Santa Pau**, 9km southwest of Olot, sits right in the middle of the volcanic region, and is a great jumping-off point for exploration. The beautifully preserved village features stone houses, narrow lanes, ancient archways and the thirteenth-century **Pza. Mayor**, once the Firal dels Bous (Cattle Market). Santa Pau is also known for its *fesols* (haricot beans), which figure prominently in the local cuisine. The village celebrates its beloved bean in the Fira de Sant Antonic, also known as the **Fira de Fesol** (Fesol Festival) in mid- or late January.

11

Vic

The Serra del Montseny, a towering granite mountain range with lushly forested slopes, looms southwest of Girona. On the west of the range, 34km southwest of Olot and easily accessible as a day-trip from Barcelona, is the amiable, well-preserved town of **Vic**. Vic is considered one of the more quintessential Catalan centres, both because the locals have especially strong Catalan pride, and also because it's near the Ripoll area, cradle of Catalan history. Vic was once the capital of an Iberian tribe, and in the second century became a Roman settlement – you'll spy various Roman remains, including parts of a temple, scattered around town.

Vic also hosted a prosperous medieval market, and the town has a yearly **Mercat Medieval de Vic** (ⓦ firesifestes.com) in its old quarter in early December, celebrating its medieval past. Vic is defined by its elegant, enormous **Pza. Mayor**, ringed by historic, porticoed buildings, which features a colourful **food market** twice a week (Tues & Sat) – and if there's one thing to buy, it's Vic's famous sausages (*llonganissa* or *fuet*), which are heralded throughout Catalunya and perfect for tossing into the suitcase to bring home.

Catedral and Museu Episcopal

Catedral Pza. de la Catedral · Daily 10am–1pm & 4–7pm · €2 for cloister and crypt · **Museu Episcopal** Pza. Bisbe Oliba 3 · April–Sept Tues–Sat 10am–7pm, Sun 10am–2pm; Oct–March Tues–Fri 10am–1pm & 3–6pm, Sat 10am–7pm, Sun 10am–2pm · €7 · ☎ 938 869 360, ⓦ museuepiscopalvic.com

Vic's Neoclassical **Catedral** looms over the centre of town; inside, striking murals depict scenes from the Bible by Catalan artist Josep Maria Sert. The nearby **Museu Episcopal** features a superb collection of sacred art from the eleventh to thirteenth centuries, including an alabaster altarpiece depicting the Passion, Resurrection and Ascension of Christ. The museum also showcases an array of art and religious artefacts culled from Pyrenean churches, making it one of the most important collections of Catalan Romanesque art outside of the Museu d'Art de Catalunya in Barcelona.

ARRIVAL AND INFORMATION   VIC

By train and bus Trains and Sagalés buses run regularly to and from Barcelona (1hr 20min). It's a short walk east from the (adjacent) train and bus stations to the centre of town.

Turisme Just off Pza. Mayor (Mon–Sat 10am–2pm & 4–7pm, Sun 10.30am–1.30pm; ☎ 938 862 091, ⓦ victurisme.cat).

ACCOMMODATION AND EATING

Arròs i Peix C/la Riera 30 ☎ 938 832 564, ⓦ arrosipeix .cat. As the name suggests, this stylish restaurant excels at rice and fish, including robust paellas, ruby-red tuna tartare and ink-black *arròs negre* (rice with squid ink). Pair the meal with a local wine – they have an excellent array, including from Priorat and Empordà. Tapas and dishes €9–€15. Tues–Sat 1–3pm & 8–11pm; Sun 1–3pm.

D.O. Vic C/Sant Miquel dels Sants 16 ☎ 938 832 396, ⓦ restaurante-do-vic.com. This creative, *Cuina Catalana* restaurant lives up to its name of "Denominació d'Origen", focusing on locally sourced ingredients. Dishes might include artichoke hearts with cod and tuna tartare with golden apples. Tasting menu starts at €30. Wed–Sun 1.30–3.30pm & 8.30–10.30pm.

Estació del Nord Pza. de l'Estació 4 ☎ 935 166 292, ⓦ estaciodelnord.com. It's hard to get any more convenient than the sleek little boutique hotel on the upper level of Vic's train station. The fully refurbished hotel has well-maintained rooms, with lots of white and pale, earthy colours. **€75**

El Jardinet C/Corretgers 8 ☎ 938 862 877, ⓦ eljardinetdevic.com. Dine on seasonal Mediterranean cuisine at this welcoming restaurant which has a well-priced weekday lunchtime *menú del día* for €14, and €19 for dinner. They also offer a more gourmet menu for €26, which might include foie gras and fresh tuna. Tues–Sat 1–3.30pm & 8.30–11pm, Sun 1–3.30pm.

Seminar Allotjaments Ronda Camprodon 2 ☎ 938 861 555, ⓦ seminarivic.cat. This converted seminary, which lies a 5min stroll north of the old town, offers basic but comfortable rooms with private baths, as well as a cafeteria that serves Catalan cuisine and breakfasts (€83 half board; €97 full board).The grounds also feature a chapel and breezy garden. **€71**

The Catalan Pyrenees

Looming gracefully over northern Catalunya, the snow-tipped Pyrenees form a mighty barrier between the Iberian Peninsula and the rest of Europe. You can ski and hike throughout these mountains, making use of a range of ski centres and vast stretches of natural parkland. Imposing peaks reach more than 3400m, while fierce rivers cleave the green valleys; tucked away in the valleys and clinging to the mountains are centuries-old alpine villages, each with its own Romanesque church, collectively forming an open-air rural museum of early medieval architecture, particularly in the beautiful **Vall de Boí**.

The Pyrenees are easy to reach from Barcelona – **Ripoll**, a gateway town to the mountains, is accessible in less than three hours. The ski scene dominates the mountains northwest of Ripoll, while summer draws hikers and trekkers. North of Ripoll is the village of **Ribes de Freser**, where you can board the famous **cremallera** railway which snakes its way up to the small ski town and pilgrimage site of **Núria** – one of the most magnificent journeys in the Pyrenees.

West of here unfolds the formidable **Serra del Cadí**, which offer superb hiking and trekking around one of Catalunya's most recognizable peaks, the **Pedraforca**. To the

THE GR11 AND THE HRP

Running roughly parallel to the GR10, which runs on the French side, the **GR11** is a network of long-distance hiking trails which traverses the Spanish Pyrenees from one end to the other. Estimated to be about 850–900km in length, it runs from the Golfo de Vizcaya (Bay of Biscay) in the Basque region to the west to Cap de Creus, near Cadaqués in the east. For seasoned trekkers, there is also the **HRP** (Haute Randonnée Pyrénéenne), which follows a higher and wilder course in the Pyrenees, criss-crossing the Spanish–French border along the way. It runs largely through the Parc National des Pyrénées in France but also takes in parts of the Parc Nacional d'Aigüestortes i Estany de Sant Maurici. In Spain, you can get more general information about the GR routes from the Federación Española de Deportes de Montaña y Escalada (FEDME; Spanish Mountain Sports Federation; ⓦ fedme.es), though the website is mostly in Spanish only. Tourist offices, refuges, and many hotels in the Pyrenees can also supply maps, information on accommodation along the route, and more.

> **THE LEGEND OF THE BLOODY FLAG**
>
> Many legends swirl around the colourful **Guifré el Pélos** (Wilfred the Hairy), who established himself as the first count of Barcelona in the ninth century. One such story is the bloody creation of the **Catalan flag**. As the legend goes, Guifré el Pélos was mortally wounded in a battle against the Normans (some say the battle was against the Moors). The Frankish king Charles the Bald wanted to pay tribute to the dying Guifré's bravery by awarding him a coat of arms on the battlefield. The king is said to have dipped Guifré's hands in his own freshly drawn blood, and then ran his fingers across the golden shield; hence the four bands of red on a yellow background.

north, along the French boder, is **La Cerdanya**, a lush, sunny Pyrenean valley that's especially popular in the summer with outdoor enthusiasts. Cerdanya's capital is the lively town of **Puigcerdà**, while just across the border sits the geographical oddity of **Llívia**, a Spanish town fully enclosed by France. In winter, skiers flock to **La Molina** and **Masella**, the two big ski resorts in the area.

The mountainous terrain around **La Seu d'Urgell**, still further west, offers some of the best trekking in the Pyrenees. Whitewater aficionados get their adrenalin rush in the **Noguera Pallaresa** valley, where churning rivers offer the best rafting in the region. Finally, in the far northwest unfolds the rugged **Parc Nacional d'Aigüestortes i Estany de Sant Maurici**, and lush **Val d'Aran**, one of Spain's most chic and finest ski resorts.

11

Ripoll

The quiet mountain town of **RIPOLL**, which serves as a good starting point for exploring the Pyrenees, is known as the cradle of Catalunya, as it was here that founding father Guifré el Pélos (Wilfred the Hairy) staked his claim to what became the Autonomous Community of Catalunya. The chief reason to visit is to view the impressive Benedictine Monestir de Santa Maria, founded in 888 by Guifré el Pélos – and where he is buried. Ripoll holds an international **music festival** in July and August in the fourteenth-century church of Sant Pere, which rises over the Pza. Abat Oliba. Ripoll is also the starting point for a beautiful Via Verde (Wviesverdes.cat) – trek or cycle the 15km La Ruta del Ferro i del Carbó (Iron and Coal), which starts near the train station in the centre of town, to San Joan de les Abadesses (see p.750).

Monestir de Santa Maria

Monastery Pza. Abat Oliba • Daily: April–Sept 10am–1pm & 3–7pm; Oct–March 10am–1pm & 3–6pm • €3 • W ripoll.cat

One of the few parts to survive a tragic fire, the splendid twelfth-century facade of the west portal of the **Monestir de Santa Maria**, which was founded some four hundred years earlier, is considered one of Spain's great works of Romanesque art. The portal showcases a series of sculptures depicting the Creation and other Biblical scenes in gorgeous detail – singing angels, the stories of Moses and Solomon and mythical beasts representing the Apostles, among other scenes – giving it its nickname as the "Stone Bible" or "Ripoll Bible". The cloister has also aged beautifully, while the nave is a replica of the original structure that was built over Guifré el Pélos' tomb.

Museu Etnogràfic de Ripoll

Pza. Abat Oliba • Tues–Sat 10am–1.30pm & 4–6pm, Sun 10am–2pm • €4 • ☎ 972 703 144, W museuderipoll.org

The **Museu Etnogràfic de Ripoll** explores the history of Ripoll and inland Catalunya through its culture, society, religion and trades, with exhibits on everything from farming methods to folklore. Ripoll had a thriving metalworking industry in the Middle Ages, and later became a production centre for weapons and firearms, and exhibits include ancient keys, forged ironwork and early rifles and other weapons.

11

DRAGONS AND DEVILS

Pleasant **Berga**, 30km west of Ripoll, has the usual historical draws – an old town, the remains of a castle – but the reason that it's on the map, so to speak, is as host of one of Catalunya's most famous festivals, the **Festa del Patum**. During Corpus Christi week, Berga's otherwise staid streets fill with parade floats of pagans and fantasy creatures – the famous *gegants*, devils, dragons spewing fireworks and dragon-slayers – while revellers dance on the sidelines and behind the floats. The festival is said to be named after the sound of the drum, and you'll hear the crowd chanting "pa-tum, pa-tum!" throughout. During Patum, you must book accommodation at least a month in advance. Good places to stay include: *Hotel Berga Park*, Carretera de Solsona 1A (☎938 216 666, ⌨www.hotelbergapark.com; €61); *Hotel HCC Ciutat de Berga*, Pg. de la Industria 11 (☎938 214 422, ⌨hcchotels.es; €60).

ARRIVAL AND INFORMATION

RIPOLL

By train and bus The train and bus stations are near each other, a 10min walk from the centre of town. Regular trains from Barcelona stop in Ripoll (2hr) en route to Puigcerdà.

Turisme Pza. Abat Oliba, near the monastery (Mon–Sat 9.30am–1.30pm & 4–7pm (sometimes 8pm in Aug), Sun 10am–2pm; ☎972 702 351, ⌨ripoll.cat).

ACCOMMODATION

Masia Jaume Coll Borredà, 20km west of Ripoll, on Carretera C26, the road to Berga ☎938 239 095 or ☎670 964 751. Inviting, stone-walled *casa de pagès* ("peasant's house") in the tiny village of Borredà. They also have a small café-restaurant for guests. Rate includes breakfast and dinner. **€73**

La Trobada Pg. Compositor Honorat Vilamanyà 4 ☎972 702 353, ⌨latrobadahotel.com. This family hotel is wonderfully central – near the monastery, the train and bus stations and the Via Verde (see p.749). Quiet and simple rooms offer a variety of views, from the Pyrenees to the towering monastery. **€65**

Sant Joan de les Abadesses

Sitting in the verdant Ríu Tur valley 1km northeast of Ripoll, the petite town of **SANT JOAN DE LES ABADESSES** was built around the monastery of the same name, which was founded by Guifré el Pélos in 887 and named after his daughter. Sant Joan is a pleasant place for a stroll, particularly through the Pza. Mayor to the Gothic bridge over the Ríu Ter.

The monastery and museum

Monastery and museum daily 10am–7pm • €3

The twelfth-century **monastery** features an elegant single-nave church, a Gothic cloister and a thirteenth-century wooden sculpture depicting Christ's descent from the cross. Also a highlight is the beautiful alabaster Gothic altarpiece of Santa María la Blanca, which dates from the fourteenth century. The **Museu de Monestir** offers a well-curated overview of the town's formidable religious history, with sacred artefacts and detailed embroidery and silverware.

ARRIVAL AND INFORMATION

SANT JOAN DE LES ABADESSES

By bus Teisa buses run regularly to Sant Joan de les Abadesses (4–6 times daily, sometimes less often on weekends) on the Girona–Olot–Ripoll route.

Turisme Palau de l'Abadia, next to the Museu del Monestir (Mon–Sat 10am–2pm & 4–7pm, Sun 10am–2pm; ☎972 720 599, ⌨santjoandelesabadesses.cat).

ACCOMMODATION

Sant Joan, while pleasant for an overnight stop, has minimal accommodation. A better bet is to venture into the countryside, where you'll find several excellent rustic houses.

Can Janpere C/Mestre Andreu 3 ☎972 720 077, ⌨elripolles.com/fondajanpere. This is one of the few budget spots in town; the rooms are simple, with somewhat dated furnishings, but they're clean and well maintained, as are the bathrooms. If you fancy dining in, try their dinner menu. **€50**

Mas Mitjavila 10km northwest of Sant Joan, in Sant Martí d'Ogassa ☎972 722 020, ⓦmasmitjavila.es. Stone farmhouse that was once, along with the adjacent tenth-century church of Sant Martí, a dependency of the Sant Joan monastery. The lovely rooms are the picture of rustic-chic, with lots of gleaming dark wood – from the furnishings to the beamed ceilings – and views of the surrounding green valley. **€76**

Camprodon

CAMPRODON, 12km east of Sant Joan de les Abadesses, is where you really start to feel like you're in the mountains: the peaks loom in the distance, the air is crisp and the streets are dotted with ski- and outdoor-gear shops. Camprodon also has an upscale, alpine-holiday air to it, particularly along the broad promenade of **Passeig Maristany**, where many well-off Catalans have mountain villas. Camprodon's handsome centrepiece is the sixteenth-century **Pont Nou**, which spans the Ríu Ter in the middle of town. From here, the main street leads to the lovely Romanesque **Sant Pere church**, open generally for services only.

Museu Isaac Albéniz

Pza. d'Espanya 1 • Mon & Wed–Sun 11am–2pm & 4–7pm • €2 • ⓦ albeniz.cat

Composer and pianist Isaac Albéniz (1860–1909) was born in Camprodon, and was known for his pieces that evoked Catalan and Spanish folk songs. The small **Museu Isaac Albéniz** showcases his life and times via photographs and documents. Camprodon also hosts a music **festival** in July that celebrates Albéniz, with a range of classical music concerts.

ARRIVAL AND INFORMATION	CAMPRODON

By bus Regular Teisa buses from Ripoll stop at a shelter at the southeast edge of town.

Turisme The *turisme* is on Pza. d'Espanya 1 (Tues–Sat 10am–2pm & 4–7pm, Sun 10am–2pm; ☎972 740 010, ⓦ valldecomprodon.org).

ACCOMMODATION AND EATING

Camprodon gets busy in the peak season, when it's advisable to make reservations. You'll also find some good accommodation out of town in the Ter valley.

Cal Marques C/Catalunya 11 ☎972 740 434. Feast on local Catalan cuisine at this spacious restaurant, which serves top-notch grilled meats and game – beef, rabbit, duck – as well as seasonal vegetables and well-crafted desserts. Dishes €13–20. Daily 1–4pm & 8–11pm; occasionally closed Sun or Mon; limited hours in winter.

Hotel de Camprodon Pza. Dr Robert 3 ☎972 740 013, ⓦhotelcamprodon.com. This handsome hotel, in a *modernista* building, has a graceful interior and clean if slightly faded rooms. **€130**

Hotel Maristany Avdga. Maristany 20 ☎972 130 078, ⓦhotelmaristany.com. Just north of town, this historic building has landscaped gardens and stylish rooms. The restaurant (reserve in advance) serves local cuisine, such as veal with cuttlefish and duck with cherries. Rates include a hearty breakfast. Closed mid-Dec to Jan. **€130**

El Pont 9 Cami Cerdanya ☎972 740 521, ⓦrestaurantelpont9.com. Worth a splurge, with lovely views of the bridge, and superb market-fresh Catalan cuisine, from pungent sheep cheeses to cod and *caragols* (snails). The daily menu starts at €17–20. Mon, Tues & Sun 12.30–4pm, Wed & Thurs 12.30–4pm & 8–10pm, Fri & Sat 12.30–4pm & 8.30–10.30pm.

Around Camprodon

Beyond Camprodon, appealing mountain villages and trekking trails dot the peaks and **Ter valley**. This is hiking territory, and many visitors come to this area for outdoor adventure, whether on the trails in summer, or on the slopes of **Vallter 2000** in winter. The best way to explore is with your own wheels, though a few buses crawl through the valley. **Villalonga de Ter**, 5km from Camprodon, makes for an amiable stopover in your

11

explorations of the valley; it has a Romanesque church, Sant Martí, on the main *plaça*. Also a pleasant stop is the hilltop **Tregurá de Dalt**, 6km beyond Villalonga, where stone houses line cobbled streets and there are lovely views of the valley and peaks. Both have good accommodation options.

Vallter 2000
Ⓦ vallter2000.com

If you're looking to ski in the area, try the well-run **Vallter 2000**, which overlooks the Ter valley and has a decent range of pistes, as well as a variety of offerings for kids, from a good ski school to a Jardí de Neu (snow garden), where the wee ones can play in the snow. Check the resort website before visiting, though, because snowfall can vary. The resort also offers plenty of summer activities, from hiking to horseriding.

ACCOMMODATION	AROUND CAMPRODON
Fonda Rigà Carretera de Tregurà, Tregurà de Dalt ☎ 972 136 000, Ⓦ fondariga.com. Family-run rustic inn with inviting rooms, some with wood-beamed ceilings. The	restaurant (call ahead to check opening times), with picture windows overlooking the sloping valley, serves hearty Catalan cuisine. Breakfast included. **€60**

Ribes de Freser, Núria and around

The Freser valley extends north of Ripoll to the mountain village of **Ribes de Freser** and Queralbs before unfolding eastward through a stunning gorge. Ribes de Freser sits at the confluence of three rivers, hemmed in by verdant valleys, and features a small old town and the **church of Santa María**, which dates back to the eleventh century but was then rebuilt in the 1900s in a modernist style. The village is best known as the starting point for the famous rack-and-pinion **cremallera** train (see box below), which snakes up the mountain to the sanctuary of **Núria** and its neighbouring ski centre, offering tantalizing views along the way. Ribes de Freser also makes for a pleasant Pyrenean base, thanks to its proximity to the mountains and decent array of accommodation.

Santuari de la Mare de Déu

The Núria valley has long been visited by pilgrims, and the **Santuari de la Mare de Déu** had its beginnings in a visit by **Sant Gil of Nîmes**, who came here on retreat in the seventh century. Gil left behind a wooden statue of the Virgin Mary, which became an object of veneration, and eventually a patron saint among local shepherds. The sanctuary consists basically of a parochial **church** (built in 1911) and a hermitage – a small, ancient-looking mountain church, built in 1615 and refurbished over the years. The overall complex itself is rather plain – it includes the sanctuary, plus several straightforward bars, restaurants and self-catering apartments. Pilgrims still come to visit, and the church holds daily Mass for locals, but the devout are usually outnumbered by skiers in winter and hikers in summer.

THE CREMALLERA

The journey of the Cremallera de Vall de Núria, most often just known as the **cremallera** railway ("zipper" in Catalan), built in 1931, is spectacular: the little train follows the rushing Ríu Freser and then, quite suddenly, begins to scale steep mountainsides along stomach-churning switchbacks, from where you're rewarded with beautiful views of the river and valley far below. Trains depart from the Ribes-Enllaç station, in the southern part of Ribes, daily year-round except November, when it runs only on the weekends. In high season (July to mid-Sept, plus winter hols), trains run 10–13 times a day; in low season, it's around 6–7 times. One-way journey time is thirty-five minutes; tickets are €22.30 round-trip in high season. For the latest information, visit Ⓦ valldenuria.cat or call ☎ 972 732 020.

ARRIVAL AND INFORMATION

By train Regular trains on the Barcelona–Puigcerdà line stop at the Ribes de Freser (2hr 30min), where you can catch the *cremallera* train (see box opposite).

ACTIVITIES

Hiking The area abounds with good hikes, including the popular trek along the river gorge from Núria to the village of Queralbs (2hr 30min). Those with more stamina can go on a full-day hike through the Gorges of Freser, trekking on the GR11.7 and then returning on another signposted trail.

RIBES DE FRESER, NÚRIA AND AROUND

Turisme Pza. de l'Ajuntament 3, Ribes de Freser (Mon–Sat 10am–2pm & 5–8pm, Sun 10am–1pm; ☎ 972 727 728, ⓦ vallderibes.cat).

You can take a break along the way at *Refugi Coma de Vaca* (see below).
Skiing The Vall de Núria ski centre (ⓦ valldenuria.cat) has plenty of activities for kids, so is popular with families.

ACCOMMODATION AND EATING

RIBES DE FRESER

Hotel Caçadors C/Balandrau 24–26 ☎ 972 727 006, ⓦ hotelsderibes.com. This hotel has good-sized rooms in an earthy colour scheme. The restaurant serves tasty, mid-priced Catalan cuisine with a creative twist – and hearty portions. Meals are best value if you opt for half-board (€77). Daily 2–4pm & 8–11pm. **€55**

Hotel Resguard dels Vents Cami de Ventaiola, 1km north of town. Stylish little hotel with airy rooms, views of the surrounding quiet mountains and a small, peaceful spa. **€84**

NÚRIA

Albergue Pic de l'Àliga ☎ 972 732 048, ⓦ xanascat .cat. Location is the big draw at this youth hostel, which sits

at the top of the cable-car line of the ski centre. Basic dorms, large communal spaces, and they can help arrange outdoor activities. They also have private rooms with bath. Dorms **€27.60**, doubles **€49**

Hotel Vall de Núria ☎ 972 732 030, ⓦ valdenuria .com. This comfortable spot, with clean rooms and self-catering apartments, includes breakfast; half-board also available. Doubles **€70**, apartments **€120**

GORGES OF FRESER

Refugi Coma de Vaca ☎ 972 198 082, ⓦ comadevaca .com. This well-maintained refuge has bunk-bed dorms, an inviting common room with wooden tables and lovely mountain views. Staffed Easter and mid-June to mid-September, but call ahead to confirm. **€15**

The Serra del Cadí

Unfolding in the eastern section of the Western Pyrenees, the verdant **Parc Natural Cadí-Moixeró** encompasses the massive **Serra del Cadí**, which has the area's best hiking and trekking around one of Catalunya's most recognizable mountains, **Pedraforca**. The village of **Bagà** houses the park's tourist office. The park has a number of staffed refuges, which you can access via treks from the surrounding mountain villages. There are also superb birding opportunities, and you may spy Tengmalm's owls and the black woodpecker, the park's symbol. It's best to have your own transport, as buses pass only intermittently through the outer villages.

Bagà makes for a good base in the area. It has a tidy little medieval quarter, centred on Pza. Porxada, and a pretty Romanesque-Gothic church. Surrounded by the leafy Gòsol valley, the village of **Gòsol**, 10km to the west of Saldes (see below), is also a good base. The remains of an eleventh-century castle loom over the village, which is dotted with a few places to stay and a good campsite nearby. Gòsol celebrates its popular annual festival on August 15, with local folk dances, music and cuisine.

Pedraforca and around

Gaze up at the mighty **Pedraforca**, which rises east of Gòsol, and it's easy to see why it has become Catalunya's most iconic peak. Its name means "stone pitchfork" because the looming mountain appears cleaved down the middle, resulting in two impressive peaks. The Pedraforca is a boon for hikers; most people access it from **Saldes**, a village at the foot of the mountain.

REFUGES AND HIKES ON PEDRAFORCA

One of the best ways to negotiate the Pedraforca is by using the refuges as your nightly base – or as refuelling pit stops. A ninety-minute trek from Saldes brings you near **Refugi Lluís Estasen** (1647m; important to reserve ahead in summer), from where you can ascend the 2491m Pedraforca (the full trek up and down takes about 5–6hr). The hike up the mountain reaches the divide between the two summits, where you'll connect with the path coming up from Gòsol. You'll find a number of refuges on the mountain; the tourist office in Bagà has up-to-date information on all of them. One popular day-hike from the *Refugi Lluís Estasen* is to the **Refugi Sant Jordi** (1570m; staffed generally only in summer) to the east, with the mountain peaks rising up all around you.

REFUGES

Refugi Lluís Estasen ☎608 315 312. Generally staffed only in summer; call ahead or enquire at park information office. Dorms €15

Refugi Sant Jordi ☎619 239 860, ⌨refugisantjordi .cat. Generally staffed only in summer; call ahead or enquire at park information office. Dorms €15

ARRIVAL AND INFORMATION　　　　　　**THE SERRA DEL CADÍ**

By bus Alsa buses travel several times daily from Barcelona via Berga to Bagà (2hr 30min); buses drop you off near the centre of Bagà.

Park information office C/la Vinya 1, Bagà (summer Mon–Fri 9am–1.30pm & 4–7pm, Sat 9am–1.30pm &

4–6.30pm, Sun 9am–1pm; winter Mon–Fri 8am–3pm, Sat 9am–1.30pm & 4–6.30pm, Sun 9am–1pm; ☎938 244 151, ⌨parcsnaturals.gencat.cat). You can pick up maps and a list of refuges here.

ACCOMMODATION AND EATING

Cadí Southwest of Gòsol, off the road to Tuixént ☎973 370 143, ⌨cadivacances.com. This well-maintained complex has both a camping area and bungalows, as well as a swimming pool, playgrounds, and restaurant with fireplace. Camping €28, bungalows €110

Cal Triuet Pza. Major 4, Gòsol ☎973 370 072. This longtime hotel has decent rooms; they can offer information on hikes into the surrounding mountains. The restaurant serves good mid-priced regional cuisine. Hotel usually closed Dec–Feb. €50

Hotel Ca L'Amagat C/Clota 4, Bagà ☎938 244 032, ⌨hotelcalamagat.com. Near the centre of town, this cosy spot has comfortable rooms and a stone-and-wood-walled restaurant with hearty Catalan cuisine. Mains €15–20. Daily 2–4pm & 8–11pm. €75

Molí del Casó 2km south of Bagà ☎938 244 076, ⌨molidelcaso.es. Welcoming, rustic *casa rural* with cosy rooms, a vegetable garden and dining room (for guests only) serving regional cuisine. €90

La Cerdanya

The verdant **Cerdanya valley**, hemmed in by looming peaks to the north and south, has long shared a geo-cultural affinity with France. The border snakes its way through the middle of the valley, but you can hardly tell where Spain ends and France begins. Catalan is spoken on both sides of the border, and in many ways, Cerdanya seems to function as an independent entity, with customs all its own. As the locals say, it's not quite Spain, and it's not quite France – it's simply La Cerdanya. The only Pyrenean valley running east–west, the Cerdanya is showered with more sunlight than any other part of the range, and is therefore a popular summer spot for hikers and mountain bikers. In winter, skiers flock to **La Molina** and **Masella**, the two big ski resorts. **Puigcerdà**, the capital of Cerdanya, is the transport hub for the area, from where you can catch a train that continues into France – the only still-running trans-Pyrenean rail route, and offering lovely views along the way.

Toses

The small village of **TOSES**, about 18km west of Ribes de Freser, is perched at 1450m. Its highlight is the church of **San Cristòfol**, dating from the tenth to twelfth century (open usually for services only). The church is modest but well restored, with a handsome nave, rectangular belfry and reproduction frescoes. You'll also find several good places to stay in town as well as restaurants serving hearty regional cuisine.

ACCOMMODATION AND EATING   TOSES

Ca la Martra C/l'Església ☎ 972 736 398 or 618 475 511, ⓦ calamartra.com. Comfortable, rustic apartments with views of the leafy hills. Usually a minimum two-night stay. Apartment **€100**

Les Forques d'en Pep Pza. Estudi 2 ☎ 972 736 125. Fill up here on mid-priced regional cuisine, from steak and lamb to root vegetables and rice dishes. Mains €15–20. Summer daily 1.30–3.30pm & 8.30–10.30pm; weekends only in winter.

La Molina and La Masella

ⓦ lamolina.com, ⓦ masella.com

The combined ski resorts of **La Molina** and **La Masella** comprise one of the larger ski areas in the Spanish Pyrenees, with pistes on **Tosa d'Alp** (2537m; 15km south of Puigcerdà) and a total of 101 runs. If you're new to skiing, try La Molina, which caters to beginners and has a good ski school. La Masella also has a ski school, and offers extensive runs that appeal to more skilled skiers.

ARRIVAL AND ACCOMMODATION   LA MOLINA AND LA MASELLA

By bus It's easiest to get around with your own transport, though in the ski season there is an intermittent bus from

Puigcerdà (generally departing once in the morning to the resort, and twice in the afternoon back to Puigcerdà).

ACCOMMODATION

You'll find a few options in the area. Many skiers, if they have their own transport, opt to stay in Puigcerdà or other villages in the region.

Hotel Adserà La Molina ☎ 972 892 001, ⓦ hoteladsera .com. This alpine hotel has simple but comfortable rooms, an on-site restaurant with regional food and views of the

Cerdanya valley. Ask about discounts and packages, which they offer for ski classes and lift passes. **€60**

Puigcerdà

Perched above the breezy union of the rivers Segre and Querol (*puig* is Catalan for "hill"; *cerdà* comes from Cerdanya), with the Pyrenees looming grandly above, hilltop **PUIGCERDÀ** is one of the prettier border towns you'll come across. With its cluster of budget lodgings and proximity to ski resorts, the town is a busy stopover for skiers, hikers and mountain bikers.

Founded in 1177, Puigcerdà has a rich history, but sadly most of its old buildings

---

SKIING THE CATALAN PYRENEES

There's a good reason the Spanish royal family and other luminaries choose to ski in the Catalan Pyrenees – it's home to some of the best resorts in Spain. As with most ski regions, often the best way to save is through the **package deals** offered by many hotels, which include discounts on lift tickets. General prices are €14–25 a day for ski gear (skis, boots, poles), and €25–48 daily for lift passes, with prices varying with the length of time you buy passes for, whether it's a weekday or the weekend, and the quality of the resort. Note, also, that it's well worth checking ahead to find out the level of snow, especially in the spring.

The Catalan Pyrenees offer a surprising variety of resorts, catering both to first-timers and advanced skiers. Intermediate skiers will find plenty of thrilling terrain at **La Masella** in La Cerdanya, which now also offers skiing at night on Fridays and Saturdays along 10km on thirteen slopes. Also popular for expert skiiers is **Boí-Taüll** on the western boundary of Aigüestortes and the premiere **Baqueira-Beret** in the Val d'Aran. The best resorts for newbies and families are **Espot Esquí** on the eastern boundary of the Parc Nacional de Aigüestortes i Estany de Sant Maurici; and **La Molina** near La Masella.

11

were destroyed in the Civil War, and its aged roots are best reflected in the layout and design of its narrow streets and *plaças*. Among the monuments that were spared is the *campanaria* (bell tower) in graceful **Pza. de Santa Maria**, while the well-preserved Pza. Cabrinetty (near Pza. de l'Ajuntament) has beautiful balconies and porticoes.

Church of Sant Domènec and around

Pg. 10 d'Abril • Generally open for services only: daily 8pm, plus Sun mornings and occasional weekday mornings; church opens 1hr before the service

The **church of Sant Domènec** was built in 1291 and restored after the Civil War. The church features an elegant portal, while inside is a series of fourteenth-century Gothic paintings. Next door sits the convent of Sant Domènec, which now houses a library, a historical archive and sacred artefacts.

ARRIVAL AND INFORMATION   PUIGCERDÀ

By train and bus The train and bus stations sit at the bottom of the hill, from which a free funicular (daily 5.30am–midnight) travels up to Pza. de l'Ajuntament in the middle of town. Several trains daily connect Puigcerdà with Barcelona (3hr), via Vic and Ripoll. *Rodalies* (local) trains also run 4–5 times daily from Puigcerdà to Latour de

Carol in France (10min), from which there are connections to Toulouse (2hr 30min–3hr).
Turisme C/Querol 1, near the Pza. de l'Ajuntament (June to mid-Sept Mon–Fri 9.30am–1pm & 4–7pm, Sat 10am–1pm & 4–7pm, Sun 10am–1pm; rest of the year closed Sun & Mon; ☎ 972 880 542).

ACCOMMODATION

Fonda Cerdanya C/Ramon Cosp 7 ☎ 972 880 010, ⓦ fondacerdanya.es. This basic *fonda* has the cheapest beds in town – rooms are simple and a bit faded, but clean, and the friendly owner can fill you in on the area. **€50**
Hospes Villa Paulita Avgda. Pons i Gasch 15 ☎ 972 884 622, ⓦ hospes.com. This boutique hotel, housed in a nineteenth-century summer villa, has cheery rooms and a good restaurant serving regional cuisine. Hearty breakfast included. **€156**
Hotel del Lago Avgda. Dr Piguillem 7 ☎ 972 881 000, ⓦ hoteldellago.com. Blessed with a breezy garden, this hotel features alpine-style rooms, and a small spa offering massages and facials. **€125**
Sant Marc In the village of Les Pereres, 1.5km south of Puigcerdà ☎ 972 880 007, ⓦ santmarc.es. If you have your

own transport, stay at one of the *casas rurales* in the area, like this well-preserved mansion, which features spacious sitting rooms, cosy fireplaces, wood-floored rooms and a stone-walled restaurant that serves filling regional fare. **€80**
Torre del Remei Camí del Remei 3, about 5km southwest of Puigcerdà ☎ 972 140 182, ⓦ torredelremei .com. For a taste of the good life in the Catalan Pyrenees, stay at this modernist palace-turned-upscale hotel, surrounded by rolling gardens presided over by sequoias. The eleven rooms and suites are the picture of elegance, including the Suite Royale, with three balconies and sweeping views of La Molina and Masella. The handsome restaurant, helmed by chef/owner Josep Maria Boix, features superb Catalan cuisine, made with vegetables and herbs pulled from the hotel's gardens. **€285**

EATING AND DRINKING

Puigcerdà has a range of restaurants, most tending towards homely regional cuisine; take a twirl around Pza. de Santa Maria, which has plenty of eating spots.

El Caliu C/Alfons Primer 1 ☎ 972 140 825, ⓦ elcaliu.com. Everything from beef tenderloin to salmon and sardines is served at this inviting spot. Dishes €11–15. Daily 1–3.30pm & 8.30–10.30pm; sometimes closed Wed.

Taberna del Call Pza. del Call ☎ 972 141 036. Fill up on tasty, mid-priced regional food, including grilled fish and meats, at this popular, welcoming *taberna*, which has a terrace overlooking the *plaça*. Daily 1–3.30pm & 8.30–10.30pm.

Llívia

In 1659, the town of **LLÍVIA** officially became a Spanish enclave within France, a geographical oddity that has garnered a mention in guidebooks ever since. Though the Spanish ceded 33 villages to France that year, tiny Llívia, deemed a town, remained Spanish. Just 6km from Puigcerdà, it's easy to reach on foot, or you can take a bus. Either way, Llívia makes for a lovely day-trip, if only to lose yourself in the town's medieval aura, which becomes increasingly more apparent the higher you climb the steep streets.

Mare de Déu dels Àngels

C/dels Forns 13 • Usually daily in summer 10am–1pm & 3–7pm; more limited hours in winter – check with *turisme* • ☎ 972 896 301, ⓦ llivia.org

This sturdy **church**, dating from the fifteenth century, features Doric columns and a Baroque *retablo*. The best time to visit is during the long-running Llívia **music festival** (since 1982), which is held in and around the church on August weekends, and features orchestras, choirs and sometimes big-name stars (Catalan opera great Montserrat Caballé once performed here).

Museu Municipal

C/dels Forns 12 • Mid-June to mid-Sept Tues–Sat 10am–8pm, Sun 10am–2pm; mid-Sept to mid-June Tues–Sat 10am–6pm, Sun 10am–2pm • €3 • ☎ 972 896 011, ⓦ llivia.org

The **Museu Municipal**, which reopened after renovations in 2012, features sections of what is thought to be the oldest pharmacy in Europe, founded in the early fifteenth century. Look out for the ancient pharmaceutical implements, as well as an impressive collection of Renaissance coffers, with portraits of saints.

11

ARRIVAL AND INFORMATION	**LLÍVIA**

By bus Buses leave for Llívia from in front of Puigcerdà's train station at least twice daily on weekdays, and once daily on weekends.

Turisme C/dels Forns 10 (Mon–Fri 9am–1pm & 4–7pm, Sat 10am–1.30pm & 4–7pm, Sun 10am–1pm; shorter hours in winter; ☎ 972 896 313, ⓦ llivia.org).

ACCOMMODATION AND EATING

★**Can Ventura** Pza. Major 4 ☎ 972 896 178, ⓦ canventura.com. Helmed by father and son Josep and Jordi Pous, *Can Ventura* excels at seasonal Catalan fare that is rooted in local produce. The rustic restaurant, set in a beautifully renovated seventeenth-century townhouse, serves tender duck with Prats de Lluçanès oranges and gingerbread; thick slices of aubergine with cheese from the Pyrenees; and grilled pigs' feet with apple sauce. Top it off with a dessert of *crema catalana* along with a brisk Cerdanya white wine. Dishes €8–19. Wed–Sun 1.30–3.30pm & 8.30–10.30pm.

Fonda Mercè C/Estavar 29 ☎ 972 897 001, ⓦ fondamerce.com. On the east side of old town, this simple *fonda* has clean rooms with hardwood floors, as well as a Catalan-cuisine restaurant that serves tapas and hearty grilled meats. €85

La Formatgeria de Llívia Pla Ro, Gorguja ☎ 972 146 279, ⓦ laformatgeria.com. This inviting restaurant on the town's eastern edge is housed in a former cheese factory, and accordingly serves gooey fondues and raclettes, as well as seasonal Catalan cuisine. Mon & Thurs–Sun lunch & dinner; may close in Aug.

Hotel Bernat de So Cereja 5 ☎ 972 146 206, ⓦ hotelbernatdeso.com. Just north of town, this handsome hotel is a lovely blend of rustic and elegant, with a breezy outdoor garden, a pool and a comfortable living room with a fireplace. €126

Bellver de Cerdanya

The Pyrenean atmosphere is very evident in the historic village of **BELLVER DE CERDANYA**, where rustic, slate-roofed chalets line the cobbled streets. About 25km west of Puigcerdà, Bellver overlooks the rushing Ríu Segre – and trout fishing was once a major local industry. The elegant **Pza. Major** is graced with impressive porticoes, while nearby rises the Gothic church of **Sant Jaume**. South of town is the twelfth-century Romanesque church of **Santa Maria de Talió**, presided over by a wooden Virgin.

ARRIVAL AND INFORMATION	**BELLVER DE CERDANYA**

By bus Bellver is one of the first stops on the bus route between Puigcerdà (25min) and La Seu d'Urgell (35min).

Turisme Pza. de Sant Roc 9 (mid-June to mid-Sept Mon–Sat 11am–1pm & 6–8pm, Sun 11am–1pm; ☎ 973 510 229).

La Seu d'Urgell

Known to locals simply as Seu, the pleasant town of **LA SEU D'URGELL**, capital of the *comarca* of Alt Urgell, sits amid looming peaks, with Andorra just 10km to the north and the valleys of the rocky Serra del Cadí nearby. As the seat (*seu*) of the regional archbishopric since the sixth century and home to an outdoor market held continuously since 1029 (on Tues and Sat), Seu has a formidable history, which is revealed in its well-preserved medieval quarter, twisting alleys and imposing Catedral.

The pleasantly mysterious medieval quarter is a small warren of narrow, arcaded streets. **Carrer dels Canonges**, the oldest street, cuts through its heart, and is lined with centuries-old buildings like **Cal Roger**, believed to have been a pilgrim's hostel, and which reveals wooden ceiling beams and some fourteenth-century Gothic carvings (enquire at the *turisme* about visiting).

Catedral de Santa Maria

Pza. dels Oms • July–Aug Mon–Sat 10am–1pm & 4–7pm, Sun 10am–1.30pm; Sept–June Mon–Sat 10am–1.30pm & 4–6pm, Sun 10am–1.30pm • €3, includes cloister and Museu Diocesà

Seu's twelfth-century **Catedral de Santa Maria**, just off Pza. dels Oms, is a wonderfully preserved example of Romanesque architecture, with a thirteenth-century cloister which has columns topped with sculpted figures from medieval mythology, and the adjoining eleventh-century chapel of San Miquel. The **Museu Diocesà** features superbly preserved reliquaries and fragments of the sarcophagus of Bishop Abril Pérez.

Espai Ermengol–Museu de la Ciutat

C/Major 8 • Mon–Sat 10am–2pm & 4–7pm, Sat 10am–2pm, Sun 10am–2pm • Free • ☎ 973 353 057, ⓦ espaiermengol.cat

Next to the Catedral, the small **city museum** features four floors of exhibits on La Seu's history. Exhibits include archeological remains, videos and interactive maps and an in-depth look at local products such as the region's well-known Cadí cheese. On the top floor, you can enjoy lovely views over the rooftops of town.

ARRIVAL AND INFORMATION

LA SEU D'URGELL

By bus The bus station is on C/Joan Garriga Massó, just north of the old town. Alsina Graells runs buses to Barcelona (3–5 daily; 3hr 30min), Puigcerdà (3 daily; 1hr) and Lleida (1 daily, 2hr 30min).

Turisme Helpful, well-stocked *turisme* on C/Major 8 (summer Mon–Fri 9am–7pm, Sat 10am–2pm & 4–7pm, Sun 10am–2pm; rest of year Mon–Sat 10am–2pm & 4–6pm, Sun 10am–2pm; ☎ 973 351 511, ⓦ turismeseu.com).

ACCOMMODATION AND EATING

Seu has a number of decent hotels scattered about town. If you have your own wheels, try one of the many *casas rurales* in the area, as most are reasonably priced and have an inviting homespun ambience. The *turisme* also has a list of recommended country hotels in the area.

Arbeletxe C/Sant Ermengol 22 ☎ 610 079 782, ⓦ arbeletxe.com. The Basque Country meets Catalunya at this stylish restaurant that serves a classic menu with contemporary touches, like a fresh salad of black tomatoes with mozzarella and pesto; squid squirted with lemon vinaigrette; succulent duck; and a dessert of tart with apples from the agricultural town of Arfa. Dishes €8–18. Mon & Thurs–Sun noon–2pm & 9–11pm, Sun 9–11pm.

Casa Rural Vall del Cadí Camí del Salit, about 2km south of town ☎ 973 350 390, ⓦ valldelcadi.com. Friendly *casa rural* with wood-beamed ceilings, wrought-iron bed frames and bucolic countryside views. To reach it cross the Ríu Segre, then head east toward Ortedò/Tuixent. **€70**

El Castell de Ciutat 1.5km west of La Seu, at the foot of the Castellciutat citadel ☎ 973 350 000,

ⓦ hotel-castell-ciutat.com. This luxurious Relais & Châteaux hotel and spa is set in an ancient castle, and features elegant rooms, sumptuous spa treatments and excellent Mediterranean cuisine, which you can enjoy on the breezy terrace overlooking the Urgellet valley. **€225**

El Menjador C/Major 4 ☎ 606 922 133, ⓦ elmenjador .com. This inviting, quirky restaurant, set in a former inn and decorated with flowers and colourful local art, features market-fresh cuisine, including trout from the Ríu Segre, chicken from local farms and cheeses from Cadí's cooperative. Menu €19. Mon–Sat 1.30–3.30pm & dinner (starts at 9pm; reserve ahead); call ahead to check times.

Parador Seu d'Urgell C/Sant Domènec 6 ☎ 973 352 000, ⓦ www.parador.es. This welcoming parador has a blend of old and new – the spacious ground floor

incorporates a Romanesque cloister strewn with sofas, while rooms are modern with pale woods. €138
Les Tres Portes Avgda. Joan Garriga i Massó 7 ☎973

355 658. Mid-priced grilled meats, such as pork tenderloin with mushrooms, and well-prepared seafood served in a breezy garden. Daily 1–4pm & 8–11pm.

The Noguera Pallaresa valley

Catalunya's most famous whitewater-rafting river, the **Noguera Pallaresa**, churns through the lush valley of the same name. The river has long been an important source of hydroelectric power, and large power plants sit at various points along its banks. The *raiers* (logger-raftsmen) of **La Pobla de Segur** used to ride rafts of logs from the Pallars Forest all the way south to the lowlands.

The town of **Sort**, north of La Pobla de Segur, has become the region's whitewater-rafting hub, with a host of aquatic-adventure shops. If you're using public transport, you'll likely arrive or depart from La Pobla de Segur, which has most of the valley's connections to and from Barcelona and Lleida.

11

La Pobla de Segur

The amiable town of **LA POBLA DE SEGUR** is one of the largest in the Vall de la Noguera, and a good base for river rafting or relaxing amid valley scenery for a few days. You'll find a decent selection of simple accommodation, plus regular train and bus services.

ARRIVAL AND INFORMATION   LA POBLA DE SEGUR

By train Regular trains connect La Pobla de Segur with Lleida (1hr 50min) and Barcelona (4hr; via Lleida).
By bus Regular buses run between La Pobla de Segur and Lleida and Barcelona. Buses also head west to El Pont de Suert, Boí and Capdella, where you can access the Parc Nacional d'Aigüestortes i Estany de Sant Maurici; as well as

north to Sort and Llavorsí, from where you can also access the park.
Turisme Avgda. Verdaguer 35, at the north end of town, by the *ajuntament* (Mon–Sat 9am–2pm; ☎973 680 257, ⓦ pobladesegur.cat).

WHITEWATER ADRENALINE RUSH

The **Noguera Pallaresa**'s mighty flow is legendary, and draws thrill-seekers from around Spain and further afield. The original rafts were primitive – logs lashed together – but could withstand the frothy waters, and were ridden by *raiers* (rafters) to the sawmills of La Pobla de Segur. These days, the rafts are of the inflatable variety, and exciting whitewater trips are offered by operators throughout the region.

The most popular section of the river is between **Llavorsí** and **Rialp**, but tour companies offer a range of trips, each more rugged and scenic than the last. The rafting **season** is from April to early September; some outfitters also offer rafting programmes in March and October. In season, trips are run daily, usually in the late morning and lasting 1–2 hours on the water. Two-hour trips start at €35, and go up to €70–90 for longer rides, including lunch. The tourist office has a list of recommended **rafting operators**, including those listed below. Most offer other activities as well:

ACTIVITIES OPERATORS
Rafting Llavorsí Camí de Riberies, Llavorsí ☎973 622 158, ⓦ raftingllavorsi.com. This established operator offers rafting, kayaking (€80 for 2 days of instruction; 2hr/day) and multiple other aquatic adventures as well as canyoning (starting at €41 for a beginner course); in the winter, they can arrange snowshoe treks. Daily 9am–8pm.
Roc Roi Pza. Nostra Senyora de Biuse, Llavorsí ☎973 622 035, ⓦ rocroi.com. This friendly operator

runs a multitude of river sports, including kayak beginning classes (starting at €25) plus trekking and horseriding. Mid-Oct to Easter daily 9am–9pm.
Rubber River Diputación 14, Sort ☎973 620 220, ⓦ rubber-river.com. Sort is filled with rafting and adventure shops, including this reputable outfitter, which offers everything from rafting and canoeing (starting at €50 for a beginner class) to bungee-jumping (€30/jump) and horseriding. Offices open daily 9am–1pm & 5–9pm; closed mid-Oct to April.

TREN DELS LLACS

Never underestimate the allure of nostalgia. This historic **Tren dels Llacs** (Lake Train) is comprised of refurbished old-fashioned steam and diesel locomotives. On its 90km journey between Lleida and La Pobla de Segur, the quaint train chugs over 31 bridges and through 41 tunnels, along cliffs, mountain passes and, of course, lakes. The Tren de Llacs (1hr 50min one way, €28 round trip) operates from April to October, generally only on the weekends or on holidays. You can buy tickets only at the tourist offices in Lleida or La Pobla de Segur, or La Tienda de FGC in Barcelona on Carrer Pelai. For details, check the website: ⓦ trendelsllacs.cat.

ACCOMMODATION AND EATING

Fonda Can Fraseria C/Major 4 ☎ 973 680 245, ⓦ canfasersia.com. This former boarding house in the middle of the old town is one of several simple *fondas*, and has a range of economical rooming options, including single rooms with shared bathroom (€15) and double rooms with shared bathroom (€28) as well as double rooms with private bath. Breakfast included. There's also a restaurant that serves hearty Catalan meals. Mains €10–20. Daily 1–4pm & 8–11pm. **€48**

Gerri de la Sal

Thirteen kilometres north from La Pobla de Segur toward Sort, you'll come to the petite village of **GERRI DE LA SAL**, named after the nearby salt mines. Next to the village, an old stone bridge leads to the beautiful twelfth-century **Monasterio de Sant Maria**. Though it's closed to the public, the area around it is lovely for a wander. Just beyond Gerri de la Sal is a tunnel, alongside which the old road hugs the rocky side of the mountain and is open to hikers and bikers.

Museum de Gerri de la Sal

Pza. Àngel Esteve • Summer Tues–Sun 11am–2pm & 5.30–7.30pm; rest of year, open by reservation • Free • ☎ 973 662 040, ⓦ mnactec.cat

This small but growing **museum** explores the history of salt mining in Gerri de la Sal, an industry that dates back to the nineth century. The museum, which forms part of the European Route of Industrial Heritage, features photos, tools and implements and a video that traces the evolution of salt in Gerri de la Sal, from the salt springs to the advent of salt mines to transport – salt was carried by mules to be grinded and packed into sacks.

Sort

The capital of the *comarca* of Upper Pallars, **SORT** is a pleasant mix of old and new, with an ancient core and modern facilities catering to the outdoor adventurers (see box, p.759) who descend in the spring and summer. Every year in early July, the town hosts the **Raiers (Rafters) Festival**, celebrating the log-rafters of the past.

ARRIVAL AND INFORMATION   SORT

By bus One Alsina Graells bus departs Barcelona daily for Sort, Rialp, Llavorsí and Esterri d'Àneu. Buses stop at a shelter north of town.
Turisme Camí de la Cabanera (July & Aug Mon–Fri 9am–8pm, Sat 10am–2pm & 3–8pm, Sun 10am–1pm; Sept–June Mon–Thurs 9am–3pm, Fri 9am–3pm & 4–6.30pm, Sat 10am–2.30pm; ☎ 973 621 002, ⓦ pallarssobira.cat).

ACCOMMODATION AND EATING

El Fogony Avgda. Generalitat 45 ☎ 973 621 225, ⓦ fogony.com. This is a wonderful surprise in Sort: a handsome restaurant, run by a husband-and-wife team, that serves superlative Catalan cuisine that's locally sourced, including duck foie gras with Armagnac, roast pig with oranges and cod with spinach and onion ravioli. Dishes €20–30; menu starts at €35. Generally Wed–Sat 1–4pm & 8–10pm, Sun 1–4pm.
Hotel Florido Pza. Joan Carles Dolcet ☎ 973 620 727, ⓦ raftingsort.com. Run by the friendly and knowledgeable folks at the adventure operator Rubber River (see box, p.759), this spacious hotel is geared

towards outdoor enthusiasts, with a pool, volleyball courts, equipment rental and basic but well-maintained rooms. Closed mid-Oct to April. **€90**

Rialp and Port-Ainé

Tiny **RIALP**, which lies just 3km north of Sort, is an atmospheric jumble of old houses and new chalets. **Port-Ainé** (⟨w⟩granpallars.com), 15km northeast of Rialp, features good beginner and intermediate skiing on its thirty-plus runs, and also has a dedicated children's slope. Snow conditions are generally top-notch, even in the spring.

Hotel Condes del Pallars Avgda. Flora Cadena 2, Rialp ☎ 973 620 626, ⟨w⟩hotelcondesdelpallars.com. This long-running resort-style hotel is a favourite with families. It may be in need of a refurbishment, but it serves its purpose as a place to base yourself for winter sports, with plenty of amenities, including a restaurant (guests only), a small gym and a kids' activity centre. Rate includes breakfast. **€99**

Hotel Port Ainé 2000 Port-Ainé ☎ 973 627 627. At 2000m, this is one of the higher hotels in the Pyrenees, and, though fairly basic and a bit faded, offers awesome views of the surrounding peaks and countryside. It's also at the bottom of the ski lifts. **€95**

Llavorsí

A rugged mountain landscape surrounds the riverside **LLAVORSÍ**, 10km north of Rialp. With an attractive mix of stone houses, modern accommodation and established outdoor operators, the town makes for a good base. Sports operators offer a wide range of activities, including rafting, mountain biking, canyoning and rock climbing. Regular buses run from Barcelona to Llavorsí (5hr 30min) via Sort and Rialp.

Aigües Braves 1km north of Llavorsí ☎ 973 622 153, ⟨w⟩campingaiguesbraves.com. This campsite has a variety of facilities, including pool, bar and arranged activities. They also offer weekend deals in wooden bungalows (€70), which includes breakast and an outdoor activity. Closed Oct–April. **€20**
Hotel del Rei Avgda. Pallaresa 10 ☎ 973 622 011, ⟨w⟩hotelderei.com. This well-run hotel has an array of comfortable rooms, from doubles to triples to sizeable family rooms, many of which have views of the mountains. The restaurant serves up good breakfasts and Catalan dinners. **€66**
Hotel Riberies ☎ 973 622 051, ⟨w⟩riberies.com. This hotel features elegant rooms, a small spa with Jacuzzi and a good restaurant serving regional cuisine, from river trout to duck with pears. Breakfast included. Mains €15–20. **€75**

Vall d'Àneu and Esterri d'Àneu

The **Vall d'Àneu** stretches north of Llavorsí, sitting at the head of the Noguera Pallaresa river. The rugged valley is well placed for access to the region's great outdoors, from hiking in the Parc Nacional d'Aigüestortes i Estany de Sant Maurici to skiing at the Espot resort to the west and Baqueira-Beret to the north. The Vall d'Àneu is made up of a smattering of villages and towns, most comprising a mix of modern chalets catering to the ski crowd and traditional homes and restaurants.

Esterri d'Àneu

Once a rustic mountain community, **Esterri d'Àneu** is now angled as an alpine resort, with both contemporary apartment buildings and hotels. It has a well-restored **old town**, over which rises the elegant **Sant Vicenç** church. A lovely Romanesque bridge, dating to the early thirteenth century, arches over the river, along whose banks you can walk and take in the surrounding mountain scenery.

By bus Regular buses travel between Esterri d'Àneu and Barcelona (5hr 30min) and Lleida (3hr).
Turisme C/Major 62 (summer Mon 10am–1.45pm, Tues–Sun 10am–1.45pm & 4–8.20pm; rest of year usually Sat & Sun only; ☎ 973 626 345, ⟨w⟩vallsdaneu.org). Has information on the valley and outdoor activities.

ACCOMMODATION AND EATING

Hostal Vall d'Àneu C/Major 46 ☎973 626 097, ⓦhostalvalldaneu.com. This central refurbished inn has simple, well-tended rooms and a restaurant serving regional fare. €45

Hotel-Restaurant Els Puis Avgda. Morelló 13 ☎973 626 160. This long-running spot has six comfortable rooms, but the real draw is the inviting restaurant, where you can fill up on robust, mid-priced Catalan cuisine, from steak and lamb to rice dishes. Daily 1.30–3.30pm & 9–10.30pm; closed Mon in winter. €50

Parc Nacional d'Aigüestortes i Estany de Sant Maurici

ⓦgencat.cat/parcs/aiguestortes

One of nine in Spain, Catalunya's largest national park, the **Parc Nacional d'Aigüestortes i Estany de Sant Maurici**, encompasses soaring peaks topping 3000m and lush meadows irrigated by more than four hundred lakes, streams, waterfalls and impressive glacial valleys. Established in 1955, the park is comprised of valleys blanketed in pine and fir forests, while wild animals like the isard, a small antelope also known as the chamois, roam the terrain. You might even spot a golden eagle or black woodpecker, both common here.

Hiking and trekking opportunities abound, from easy walks around sparkling lakes to serious treks up the mountain. The **Sant Nicolas valley** in the west features numerous glacial lakes, as well as the meanders of **Aigüestortes** (Twisted Waters). In the east lies the massive **Estany de Sant Maurici** (Sant Maurici Lake), at the head of the Escrita valley. In the winter, you can also **cross-country ski** through the park, though there are no marked trails.

The park's western sector is best reached from the **Vall de Boí** – to explore Aigüestortes, the approach is generally from Boí via **El Pont de Suert**; the eastern portion, including Lake Sant Maurici, is accessed via **Espot**, which lies just beyond the eastern border of the park. The easiest starting point for the higher mountains is **Capdella**, south of the park. If you'll be hiking for several days at a time between June and September, you can stay at any of the **refuges** throughout the park (see below). Either visitor centre can give you a list.

ARRIVAL AND INFORMATION — PARC NACIONAL D'AIGÜESTORTES I ESTANY DE SANT MAURICI

By car and taxi Private cars are not allowed in the park, but 4WD taxis travel from the main square in Boí to the information booth at the entrance; taxis operate July to Sept 15 (8 or 9am–7pm) and rest of the year (9am–6pm) from €6 one-way. The closest you can get to the park in your car is La Molina car park, near the boundary. When this fills up, try the La Farga car park, about 1.5km east. You can arrange for a 4WD taxi to take you from either car park further uphill. When you arrive at the park entrance from Boí (3.5km) it's then about another 3.5km to the crashing waterfalls of Aigüestortes. It's important to keep track of the weather, as it can greatly affect accessibility. In the cold season, it can be difficult to access certain roads.

Visitor centres There are park information booths at the entrance and also above the waterfalls (both generally open July–Sept daily 9.30am–2pm & 4–7pm). You can also pick up trail guides and park maps at the visitor centres in Boí (see p.765) and Espot (see opposite).

Maps Editorial Alpina (ⓦeditorialalpina.com) has excellent, detailed topographical maps of the park.

Entrance Entry to the park is free.

Safety It's always a good idea to alert the refuge staff before you set out on treks, any time of year.

ACCOMMODATION

Refuges Accommodation in and around the park encompasses around twenty refuges, both in the park and in the park's peripheral zone. The refuges usually open in the summer (when most are staffed), Easter and sometimes Christmas, as well as on selected weekends and school holidays during the rest of the year. Refuges are usually equipped with bunk beds and have a basic meal service. Prices generally range between €17 and €40/person. Most refuges are fully booked during July and August, so you'll need to reserve ahead, which you can do via ⓦlacentralderefugis.com or by calling ☎973 641 681.

Camping Camping in the park is officially forbidden, though you can camp in the peripheral zone.

HIKES AND RIDES FROM CAPDELLA

There are a number of popular **treks** from Capdella, including the half-day hike to the inviting *Refugi Colomina,* set amid mountain lakes (see box, p.764). You'll find various treks around the *Refugi Colomina,* including to Estany Llong, by way of Estany Tort. You can also access the park on the **teleférico** (cable car; July–Sept; around 9 departures daily, 8am–6pm; €18 round trip). The cable car travels from the Saliente reservoir (about 7km north of Capdella) to the Estany Gento, which is near an entrance of the park – on its fifteen-minute trip, the cable car climbs 450m. It was originally constructed in 1981 to transport materials and workers while the Saliente power station was being built, and it's said to be one of the cable cars with the greatest transport capacities in Europe; it was opened to the public in 1991.

Vall de Fosca

The verdant **Vall de Fosca,** which extends just south of the park, received its name Fosca ("dark") because it's surrounded by steep slopes that obscure the sun. Tiny **Capdella** is perched at its northernmost point and, at 1420m, is the highest of the fifteen or so tiny villages and settlements that are sprinkled south through the valley, including **Espui** and **La Torre de Capdella.** Capdella makes for a good jumping-off point into the park, and is the village closest to the **teleférico** (see box above).

ARRIVAL AND INFORMATION   VALL DE FOSCA

By bus Buses travel from La Pobla de Segur to Capdella (30min).

Turisme The Vall de Fosca *turisme* is in the *ajuntament* of Torre de Capdella on the Pza. Major (daily Mon–Fri 9am–3pm, Mon & Thurs also 4.30–8.30pm; ☎973 663 001, ⓦvallfosca.net), 4km south of Espui.

ACCOMMODATION AND EATING

Hotel Montseny Near the village of Espui, about 4km south of Capdella; signposted from road ☎973 663 060, ⓦmontseny.com. This amiable, alpine-style hotel has cosy rooms, a swimming pool, and a bar/restaurant with filling Catalan fare, including grilled meats; mains €15–20. Breakfast included. Hotel and restaurant closed from late Dec to Easter. Daily lunch & dinner for guests; lunch only for nonguests. **€90**

Espot, Espot Esquí and around

ESPOT is a cosy mountain town hemmed in by a lovely green valley, which has increasingly been built up as a tourist centre. In the winter, skiers pass through on their way to **Espot Esquí** (ⓦgranpallars.com), just south of town, which has nearly thirty alpine trails.

You can access the park from Espot, which lies about 7km from the **Estany de Sant Maurici.** Upon arrival at the *estany* (lake), you'll want to get your camera out: it's a beautiful scene, the lake fringed by wilderness and dominated by the spires of **Els Encants** ("The Enchanted Ones"; 2700m).

ARRIVAL AND INFORMATION   ESPOT, ESPOT ESQUÍ AND AROUND

By bus and taxi The daily buses from Barcelona, Lleida and La Pobla de Segur to Esterri d'Àneu stop at the Espot turn-off. From there, it's a steep 8km uphill walk to Espot, and then another similar distance to get to the park.

By taxi The quickest and easiest way to the park is by taxi, which travel from Espot to Estany de Sant Maurici. Taxis generally depart from the park information offices.

(July–Sept 8am–6pm or 7pm, rest of year 9am–6pm; from around €7 one-way).

Casa del Parc information office C/Sant Maurici 5, at the edge of Espot (June–Sept daily 9am–1pm & 3.30–6.45pm; Oct–May Mon–Sat 9am–2pm & 3.30–5.45pm, Sun 9am–2pm; ☎973 624 036). Has maps of the park and up-to-date weather reports.

ACCOMMODATION AND EATING

Camping La Mola Carretera Estany de Sant Maurici, 3km east of Espot ☎973 624 024, ⓦcampinglamola .com. Located outside of Espot, this quality campsite features an excellent range of amenities, including a pool, tennis court, games room, bar and a small supermarket. They also have apartments with kitchens. Open Easter & July–Sept. **€20**, apartments (for four people) **€100**

Casa Felip C/Felip ☎973 624 093, ⓦcasafelip.com.

11

11

POPULAR HIKES AND REFUGES

One of the most popular (though challenging in parts) hikes is to traverse the park from east to west, starting at the **Estany de Sant Maurici**. The full trek, all the way to **Boí**, takes about 9–10 hours, but you can shorten the trek by hopping in a taxi for the last part from the park entrance to Boí. Roughly halfway along this trek sits the **Refugi de Estany Llong**.

The northern section of the park offers a wealth of treks for the adventurous and well-equipped – the Espot park information office has detailed maps of trails – as well as refuges, including the top-notch **Refugi de Colomèrs**, the **Refugi de Restanca** and the **Ventosa i Calvell**, near Estany Negre.

Another good hike from the east is to **Refugi Josep Maria Blanc**, which lies southwest of Espot and is surrounded by lush valleys. The hike from Espot to the refuge takes 3–4 hours. From here, the hike continues to the **Colomina** refuge, which you can reach in another 3–4 hours.

REFUGES

The refuges are all very similar – usually sturdy, stone houses with simple rooms and basic beds.

Refugi de Colomèrs ☎ 973 253 008, ⊛ refugi colomers.com. Daily Easter & mid-June to late Sept, weekends Feb & March. €17

Refugi Colomina ☎ 973 252 000, ⊛ lacentralderefugis.com. Early Feb, mid-March to mid-April & mid-June to mid-Sept; call ahead to confirm. €15

Refugi de Estany Llong ☎ 973 299 545, ⊛ lacentralderefugis.com. Late Feb, Easter & June to mid-Oct. From €10

Refugi Josep Maria Blanc ☎ 973 250 108, ⊛ jmblanc.com. Late May to mid-Oct. €17

Refugi de Restanca ☎ 608 035 559, ⊛ restanca .com. Weekends most of the year, plus daily Easter week & mid-June to late Sept. €17

Refugi Ventosa i Calvell ☎ 873 297 090, ⊛ refugiventosa.com. Mid-June to late Sept & some winter weekends. €17

Located in the middle of Espot, this long-running spot has comfortable rooms, a small front garden, a storage area for skis and bikes. They can also help arrange outdoor activites, in summer and winter. €55

Juquim Pza. Sant Martí 1 ☎ 973 624 009. In the centre of Espot, try this popular restaurant which serves filling mountain fare, including grilled meats, from lamb and wild boar to juicy sausages (€9–14). The menu starts at €18. Generally daily 1.30–3.30pm & 8.30–10.30pm; sometimes closes for part of winter.

Vall de Boí

Extending just west of the national park is the lush **Vall de Boí**, anchored by the mountain village of **Boí**. The highlights of the valley are its lovely **Romanesque churches**, the most remarkable of their kind in Catalunya. In 2000, the churches were designated a World Heritage Site by UNESCO, who described them as "an especially pure and consistent example of Romanesque art in a virtually untouched rural setting". And it is this setting that leaves the lasting impression – the beautiful simplicity of the early Romanesque architecture is magnified by the utter alpine stillness surrounding them. The churches, all built between the eleventh and fourteenth centuries, were constructed of local materials, like stone, slate and wood – and their most striking features are their elegant belfries which, in the case of **Taüll**, rises an impressive six storeys. Note that many of the church frescoes are reproductions – though excellent ones, to be sure – because the originals have been moved to MNAC in Barcelona. In addition to the valley's two finest churches in Taüll, other Romanesque beauties worth a visit are Sant Feliu in **Barruera**, Nativitat in **Durro** and Santa Eulàlia in **Erill la Vall**.

Boí

The pleasant town of **BOÍ** serves as a good starting point for exploring the surrounding region, both for the Romanesque churches – you can walk a variety of signposted trails from Boí to neighbouring churches – and also the national park, an entrance to which lies 3.5km from town. Boí also has a helpful park information office, and its own Romanesque church, the twelfth-century **Sant Joan**: parts of the original belfry are still intact, and the church has three naves. As with other churches in the area, the frescoes are reproductions but nonetheless eye-catching, and include images of mythical animals.

Estany de Cavallers

Five kilometres north of Boí is the **Estany de Cavallers** (Cavallers Lake), where you can pick up trails towards the lake-filled landscape in the northwest section of the park, which are presided over by the Besiberri and Montrarto peaks. A good refuge in the northwest of the park is *Ventosa i Calvell* (see box opposite).

Taüll

TAÜLL, 3km east of Boí is home to two of the valley's best-known Romanesque churches. **Sant Climent**, consecrated in 1123, features an exquisite six-storey square belfry that rises gracefully above the town. The church's emblematic Romanesque murals were created by the so-called Master of Taüll, and transferred to Barcelona in 1922. Particularly striking is the image of Pantocrator (Christ in Majesty) in the apse. Taüll's second Romanesque icon is the church of **Santa Maria**, with its four-storey belfry.

Boí-Taüll

☎ 902 406 640, ⓦ boitaullresort.es

The valley is also home to a ski centre, **Boí-Taüll**, which lies 11km southeast of Taüll. The resort has nearly fifty pistes, lifts that reach up to 2750m, and covers an area of about 45km. They offer an array of classes for beginners, and a good family ski programme. Call ahead, as the resort may be undergoing some changes and may therefore have limited hours.

ARRIVAL AND INFORMATION   VALL DE BOÍ

By bus Buses from Barcelona to La Pobla de Segur run up to three times daily throughout the year. From July to mid-September, a connecting bus travels from La Pobla de Segur to El Pont de Suert and from there to Barruera and the Boí turn-off, about 1km before Boí.
Park information office C/les Graieres 2, Boí (July &

Aug daily 9am–2pm & 3.30–6pm; rest of year closed Sun afternoon; ☎ 973 696 189, ⓦ oapn.es). Has route information, maps and a list of the refuges in the park. There are also information booths both at the park entrance and above the Aigüestortes waterfalls (see box, p.762).

ACCOMMODATION AND EATING

BOÍ

Hotel Pey Pza. Treio 3 ☎ 973 696 036, ⓦ hotelpey.com. This welcoming, family-run hotel has a range of accommodation, including alpine, wood-panelled rooms and fully equipped apartments (for two to three people). They also have a friendly restaurant, where you can refuel over thick stews and grilled meats, from rabbit to beef. Mains €15–20. Daily 2–4pm & 8–11pm. Doubles **€76**, apartments **€80**

CALDES DE BOÍ

Caldes de Boí 5km north of Boí ☎ 973 696 201, ⓦ caldesdeboi.com. If you'd like some pampering, head to this lovely spot, considered one of the best spas in the Spanish Pyrenees, with a wide range of treatments, from natural springs to massages, and two accompanying hotels, the *Manantiel* and the *Caldes*, both comfortable and well maintained. Both are usually closed Jan–March. *Manantiel* **€109**, *Caldes* **€80**

ROMANESQUE CHURCHES IN THE VALL DE BOÍ

Pick up information on all the Romanesque churches at the **Centre d'Interpretació del Romànic**, on C/Batalló in **Erill la Vall** (Daily 9am–2pm & 5–7pm; ☎ 973 696 715, ⓦ centreromanic.com), in the centre of the valley. All churches have the same general hours: July to early Sept daily 10am–2pm & 4–8pm; rest of the year daily 10am–2pm & 4–7pm. Individual churches are €2 (Sant Climent de Taüll is €5), or €7 for a combined ticket to three churches, €8 for three churches and access to the centre, €10 for five churches and the centre and €15 for three churches and access to MNAC (see p.666) in Barcelona; Santa Maria de Taüll is free.

TAÜLL

Hotel el Rantiner C/Trestaüll 5 ☎ 973 696 184, ⓦ hotelelrantiner.com. This cosy mountain hotel features simple rooms rustically done up with wood floors and sturdy furniture. **€115**

Hostal Rural Santa Maria Cap del Riu 3 ☎ 973 696 170, ⓦ taull.com. This beautifully renovated house features cosy, wood-beamed rooms, a dining room with a fireplace, and a breezy garden. **€110**

El Xalet de Taüll C/El Como 5 ☎ 973 696 095, ⓦ elxaletdetaull.com. This inviting chalet has wood-panelled rooms, mountain views and a summer garden. May be closed for part of winter so call ahead. **€115**

Val d'Aran

Nudging the French border in the far northwest of the Catalan Pyrenees, the lush **Val d'Aran** has long been geographically and culturally distinct from the rest of the Pyrenees. You can see the disparity of its architecture – French-style chalets dot the mountains – and you can hear it on the streets: the language here is Aranés, a mix of Gascon French and Catalan. The valley drains towards the Atlantic and splits into the Garonne River, whose waters eventually feed the vineyards of Bordeaux.

The Val d'Aran joined Catalunya-Aragón in the twelfth century and was fully given over to Catalunya in 1389. Completely ringed by high peaks, however – some reaching over 3000m – it has always been difficult to access. For most of the valley's history, the only routes in from the Spanish side crossed the tricky **Bonaigua** or **Bossòst** passes, both accessible only in summer. This changed only in 1948, when the first Vielha Tunnel opened on the N230 highway.

The valley's capital and commercial centre is **Vielha**, a beautiful alpine town with one foot in the past and the other in the very contemporary present, as a luxury resort. In winter, the Val d'Aran becomes upscale **skiing** country, drawing folks from all over Spain and France. While the area still reveals pockets of traditional life, it has undergone a massive shift in the last several decades, with upmarket apartments replacing family dwellings, and much of the retail catering to slick skiers. The Spanish royal family, along with the fit and fabulous, frequent **Baqueira-Beret**, one of Spain's premier ski resorts.

The Val d'Aran is divided into three sectors: **Vielha e Mijaran** (Middle Aran), **Baish Aran** (Lower Aran; northwest of Vielha near the French border) and **Nau Aran** (Upper Aran; east of Vielha). Both Upper and Lower Aran are ripe for exploration, each of their mountain villages more lovely than the last. You'll find plenty of hiking and trekking opportunities – trails meander all over the valley. You could easily spend a day or two hiking from one tiny village to the next, enjoying a country meal at one, and bedding down in a rustic farmhouse in the next. **Salardú** and **Arties** make for pleasant stopovers in Nau Aran.

Vielha

The valley centres on the bustling town of **VIELHA**, which goes through a metamorphosis in winter: when the snow descends, so too do the slickly outfitted

---

GO WILD

The Val d'Aran has long drawn the crowds for its alpine activities. And now, it's drawing crowds for its alpine animals. Wildlife-watching has been growing in popularity in the Val d'Aran, with the tourist office (see p.768) expanding its wildlife coverage and tour companies, including **WildWatching Spain** (ⓦ wildwatchingspain.com) and **Aran Experience** (ⓦ aranexperience .com) offering a variety of wildlife treks, including springtime photo treks and summer birding. Among the animals you might spot are, in spring and summer, the Pyrenean capercaillie, black woodpecker, brown bear, bearded vulture and marmot; and in winter, the spotted woodpecker, mountain passerines and golden eagle. Also, in 2013, the wildlife park **Aran Park** in Bossòst (€2; April–June & Sept–Oct daily 9.30am–6pm, July–Aug daily 9.30am–7pm; €2) opened, featuring a wide range of animals in a natural setting, including arctic wolves, deer and bears.

OPPOSITE HUMAN CASTLES AT THE SANTA TECLA FESTIVAL, TARRAGONA (P.778) >

skiers, who crowd the slopes, gear shops and restaurants. After the snow melts, Vielha reverts to its small-town self, when the hilly streets get quiet, and the bars are again the domain of the locals. The tiny old quarter features the parish church of **Sant Miquèu**, with a twelfth-century wooden *Crist de Mijaran,* a superb example of Romanesque art.

Museu dera Val d'Aran

C/Major 26 • Tues–Sat 10am–1pm & 5–8pm, Sun 11am–2pm • €2

The small **Museu dera Val d'Aran**, housed in a seventeenth-century building in the old town, features an overview of Aranese history, folklore and ethnology, from prehistoric times to today, including exhibits of old photographs, period furnishings and more.

ARRIVAL AND INFORMATION   VIELHA

By bus A couple of Alsina Graells buses travel daily between Barcelona and Vielha (5hr 30min), via Lleida and El Pont de Suert. From June to September, one daily service also runs from Barcelona to Vielha via La Pobla de Segur, Llavorsí and Salardú.

Turisme C/Sarriulera 6 (daily 9am–9pm; ☎ 973 640 110, ⓦ visitvaldaran.com). This office has up-to-date lists of accommodation in the valley.

ACCOMMODATION

Hotel El Ciervo Pza. de San Orenç 3 ☎ 973 640 165, ⓦ hotelelciervo.net. This cheerful, family-run hotel has well-maintained rooms, each individually decorated, and an excellent breakfast buffet with local specialities and fresh-brewed coffee. Closed June & Nov. €80

Parador de Vielha Carretera del Túnel ☎ 973 640 100, ⓦ www.parador.es. The draw at this modern parador is the lovely view of the mountain peaks. The granite building is very contemporary-looking – no historic charm here

– but the rooms are warmly done up in the trademark parador style, with wooden furniture. €168

Sol Vielha Aneto de Vielha ☎ 973 638 000, ⓦ melia .com. Wake up to sweeping views of the Pyrenees from this warmly run hotel, with spacious rooms and a well-equipped Wellness Center, with a gym, heated pool, saunas and a variety of services, from herbal massages to facials. The restaurant offers buffet breakfasts and dinners, or enjoy a cocktail on the bar's outdoor terrace. €80

EATING AND DRINKING

Casa Turnay 2km east, in the village of Escunhau ☎ 973 640 292. Rustic, stone-walled Aranese restaurant with hearty local food, from grilled rabbit to trout fished from local rivers to *butifarra negra* (Catalan sausage). Dishes €10–15. Mon–Sat 1.30–3.30pm & 8–11pm.

★**Era Coquela** Avgda. Garona 29 ☎ 973 642 915, ⓦ eracoquela.com. This deservedly popular restaurant serves hearty, lovingly prepared local cuisine in a cosy dining room, from suckling pig and grilled fish with romesco sauce to duck with cassis sauce and pear tart with ice cream. The menu, starting at €14, is an excellent deal, and sometimes includes a bottle of wine for two. Dishes €8–18. Mon–Sat 1.30–3.30pm & 8–11pm.

Era Mòla – Gustavo y María José C/Marrec 14 ☎ 973 642 419. This perennially popular restaurant serves rich, French-influenced Catalan cuisine, including a superb duck breast with wild mushrooms. Dishes start at €24. Mon, Tues, Thurs & Fri 8–11pm, Sat & Sun 1.30–3.30pm & 8–11pm.

Petit Basteret C/Major 6 ☎ 973 640 714. Central and casual, with simple local food, including river trout and tasty tapas. Dishes €10–20. Daily 1.30–3.30pm & 8.30–10.30pm.

Saxo Blu C/Marrec 6 ⓦ saxoblu.com. For cocktails and occasional live music, try this lively bar which has decently priced drinks and draws a mix of locals and visitors. Daily 7pm–2.30am.

Baqueira-Beret

☎ 973 639 010, ⓦ baqueira.es

The massive **Baqueira-Beret** ski resort has more development than any other in the area and imbues the valley with a stylish sheen. It's one of Spain's choicest resorts, and has the crowd to match. Discerning skiers, most famously Spain's king himself, flock to its 72 pistes, which cover up to 105km – making it one of Spain's largest resorts. The resort amenities – groomed pistes, numerous chairlifts, a top-notch ski staff – rival the Pyrenean scenery of frosted peaks piercing the bright blue sky. If you don't want to go for the pricey resort accommodation, do what many do: stay for considerably less at a nearby village, such as Salardú or Vielha.

Salardú

The Val d'Aran contains over thirty hillside villages, most with their own Romanesque church. **SALARDÚ**, which lies just west of Baqueira-Beret, is one of the largest of the valley's settlements, with the thirteenth-century **church of Sant Andreu** (open for services; enquire at *turisme* about other times) standing tall in its centre. Take a look at the detailed portal and, inside, the carefully restored frescoes.

Salardú makes for a good overnight spot. It has a decent tourist infrastructure – several options for lodging and food – but also a rugged alpine personality. Call ahead to your hotel in the non-snow season, as they sometimes close.

PyrenMuseu

Pza. Major • Mon–Sat 10.30am–1.30pm & 4.30–7.30pm; hours can be extended on request • €5 • ☎ 973 645 814, ⓦ pyrenmuseu.com

One of the oldest places to stay in town, **Refugi Rosta** (see below) also doubles as a charming small **museum** – and has therefore created the slogan, "Ahora puedes alojarte en un museo" ("Now you can sleep in a museum"). The museum, which is spread out among the *refugi's* well-preserved rooms, hallways, bar and other spaces, explores the unique history of tourism in the Val d'Aran, with exhibits featuring period furnishings and art, old photographs and maps, a timeline of the development of the famous ski resort Baqueira-Beret, and more. Entry to the museum includes a glass of wine in the atmospheric bar.

ARRIVAL AND INFORMATION

SALARDÚ

By bus From June to Sept, one daily service runs from Barcelona to Vielha via La Pobla de Segur, Llavorsí and Salardú (about 5hr 30min).

Turisme C/des Estudis (daily 9am–1pm & 4–7pm, off-season hours may be limited; ☎ 973 645 197, ⓦ visitvaldaran.com).

ACCOMMODATION AND EATING

Alberg Era Garona Carretera de Vielha ☎ 973 645 271, ⓦ tojuaran.com. Basic but fairly spacious youth hostel in a stone-and-slate building. Rooms, which have up to four beds, each have their own bathroom. **€26**

Hotel Deth Pais Pza. Dera Pica ☎ 973 645 836, ⓦ hoteldethpais.com. This comfortable, slate-roofed hotel in the village centre has clean rooms with balconies. **€70**

Prat Aloy Dera Mola ☎ 973 644 179. This place serves meaty dishes, like grilled steak, lamb and sausages. Main dishes €17–25. Daily 1–4pm & 9–11pm; usually closed March, Oct & Nov.

Refugi Rosta Pza. Major 1 ☎ 973 645 308. Comfortable refuge in a three-hundred-year-old building on the main *plaça*, catering to trekkers and skiers on a budget. It also doubles as a lovely museum (see above). Breakfast included. Sometimes closed March, Oct and Nov. The on-site restaurant serves mid-priced Pyrenean cuisine in a lovely, traditional dining room, and is also home to the bar *Delicatesen*. Restaurant open daily for dinner 8–10pm; bar daily late morning to 11pm or later; closed March, Oct & Nov. **€26**

Arties

ARTIES, 3km west of Salardú, offers a charming mix of Pyrenean history and the chance to join the locals in dining (and drinking) out. Its old town is pleasant for a stroll, featuring the signature slate-roof houses of the valley, and you can take in the Romanesque-Gothic **Santa Maria** (open for services), which has a barrel-vaulted nave and a five-storey belfry.

ACCOMMODATION AND EATING

ARTIES

Casa Irene C/Major 3 ☎ 973 644 364, ⓦ hotelcasairene. com. This well-regarded restaurant serves mountain cuisine, from grilled rabbit to thick Aranese stews; prices range from €17 to €27 for mains. They also have an adjoining hotel, with elegant, individually decorated wood-floored rooms, and a small but well-run spa. Restaurant generally open daily 2–4pm & 8–11pm; closed in winter. **€105**

Tauèrnes Urtau Pza. Urtau 12 ☎ 972 640 926, ⓦ urtau.com. There's good reason that this local tapas chain pulls in the crowds. The diverse menu is flavourful, filling and fun, including a huge array of tapas and *pintxos*, from croquettes and grilled shrimp to foie gras with caramelized apple and ham and cheese with fried artichokes. Tapas €7–15. Other locations are in Vielha and Bossòst. Daily 8am–midnight.

11

Southern Catalunya

The great triangle of land south of Barcelona may be one of the lesser-visited wedges of Catalunya – but it shouldn't be. This wonderfully varied area encompasses a sun-speckled coast, a trinity of medieval monasteries and the historically rich provincial capitals of Tarragona and Lleida.

West of Barcelona lies **cava country**, where you can tour Catalunya's best-known cava producers, especially around **Sant Sadurní d'Anoia**. On the coast, just south of Barcelona, sits vibrant **Sitges**, a major gay summer destination that's also home to some fine *modernista* architecture. Beyond this is the **Costa Daurada** – the coastline that stretches from just north of Tarragona to the Delta de l'Ebre – which suffered less exploitation than the Costa Brava. It's easy enough to see why it was so neglected – the shoreline can be drab, with beaches that are narrow and characterless, backed by sparse villages – but there are exceptions, and if all you want to do is relax by a beach for a while, there are several down-to-earth and perfectly functional possibilities.

The Costa Daurada really begins to pay dividends, however, if you can forget about the beaches temporarily and spend a couple of days in **Tarragona**. It's a city with a solid Roman past – reflected in an array of impressive ruins and monuments – and makes a handy springboard for trips inland into Lleida province. South of Tarragona, Catalunya peters out in the lagoons and marshes of the **Delta de l'Ebre**, a riverine wetland rich in birdlife – perfect for slow boat trips, fishing and sampling the local seafood.

Inland attractions are fewer, and many travelling this way are inclined to head on out of Catalunya altogether, not stopping until they reach Zaragoza. It's true that much of the region is flat, rural and dull, but nonetheless it would be a mistake to miss the outstanding monastery at **Poblet**, only an hour or so inland from Tarragona. A couple of other nearby towns and monasteries – notably medieval **Montblanc** and **Santes Creus** – add a bit more interest to the region, while by the time you've rattled across the huge plain that encircles the provincial capital of **Lleida** you'll have earned a night's rest. Pretty much off the tourist trail, Lleida is the start of the dramatic road and train routes into the western foothills of the Catalan Pyrenees, and is only two and a half hours from Zaragoza.

Vilafranca del Penedès

Pleasant **VILAFRANCA DEL PENEDÈS**, capital of the *comarca* of Alt Penedès, lies about 45km southwest of Barcelona, and offers the twin pleasures of history and wine. It was founded in the eleventh century in an attempt to attract settlers to land retaken from the expelled Moors and in time became a prosperous market centre. This character is still in evidence today, with a compact old town with narrow streets and arcaded squares adorned with restored medieval mansions. In the centre, around Pza. de Sant Joan, a Saturday market sells everything from farm-fresh produce to clothes, household goods and handicrafts. The **vineyards** of Vilafranca are all scattered in the countryside out of town – one of the closest (and most famous) is Torres (see box opposite).

The **Festa Major** (Ⓦfestamajor.info), at the end of August and the first couple of days in September, brings the place to a standstill. Dances and parades clog the streets, while the festival is most widely known for its display of *castellers* – teams of people competing to build human towers (see box, p.778).

Vinseum

Pza. Jaume I • June–Aug Tues–Sat 10am–7pm, Sun 10am–2pm; rest of year Tues–Sat 10am–2pm & 4–7pm, Sun 10am–2pm • €7 • ☎ 938 900 582, Ⓦ museosdelvino.es

Opposite the much-restored Gothic church of Santa Maria, the **Vinseum** features an impressive collection, including antique casks, wine-themed art through the ages and historic *porrons*, a traditional Catalan wine pitcher with a thin spout, designed to pour *vino* in a stream directly into your mouth, so that it can be shared around a table. (In

CAVA COUNTRY

Cava – Spain's answer to champagne – is grown largely in the Penedès region, which also produces quality white wines and robust reds. "Cava" simply means cellar, and was the word chosen when the French objected to the word champagne. The eminently drinkable, and very affordable, sparkling wine is usually defined by its sugar content: *seco* (literally "dry") has around half the sugar of a *semi-seco* ("semi-dry"). In addition to selling bottles of bubbly, the region's famous *bodegas* often offer informative tours and tastings, and are located in stunning properties, attractions in themselves. Most can be found in the Penedès region near the town of **Sant Sadurní d'Anoia**, about 30km west of Barcelona, and in the countryside around **Vilafranca de Penedès**, 15km southwest of Sant Sadurní. And, while the Penedès continues to be dominated by the big names – Condorniu, Freixenet and Torres – a wave of small-batch wineries are beginning to present strong competition, many of them offering organic bubbly, like Parés Baltà. There are regular trains from Estació-Sants Barcelona to Sant Sadurní (40min) and Vilafranca de Penedès (50min). Also, Codorniu offers bus service to and from Barcelona; see their website for details.

THE WINERIES AROUND PENEDÈS

Bodegas Torres Finca el Maset, Pacs del Penedès, 3km northwest of Vilafranca de Penedès ☏ 938 177 487, ⓦ torres.es. Torres, one of Spain's leading wine producers, leads well-organized tours, which include trundling through the fragrant vineyards in a small tourist train, slick audiovisual presentations and a tasting at the end. Oenophiles can opt for a more in-depth experience with wine-tasting classes on Saturdays (4–6.30pm; €22). Tours €6.70. Mon–Sat 9.15am–4.45pm, Sun 9.15am–1pm.

Codorniu Avgda. Jaume Codorníu, just outside Sant Sadurní d'Anoia ☏ 938 913 342, ⓦ codorniu.com. Codorníu, one of Spain's best-known cava brands, is credited with bringing sparkling wine production to Spain in 1872. On a tour, you'll explore the cellars, view the beautiful *modernista* premises designed by Josep Maria Puig i Cadafalch and enjoy a tasting at the end. Reservations are essential – you can call or book online. The winery is about 2km from the highway and well signposted. Tours €9. The winery also offers a range of culinary and cava experiences, including a full Mediterranean lunch paired with cavas (€50). Mon–Fri 9am–4pm, Sat & Sun 9am–noon.

Freixenet C/Joan Sala 2, visible from the highway ☏ 938 917 096, ⓦ freixenet.com. This celebrated producer offers interesting tours which include a visit to their oldest cellars, originally excavated in 1922, a ride on a tourist train around the winery and samples of bubbly. There's also a well-stocked shop. Tours must be booked in advance, either by phone or the website. Tours €7. Consult the website for hours.

Parés Baltà C/Masia Can Baltà, Pacs del Penedès, just west of Vilafranca ☏ 938 901 399, ⓦ paresbalta .com. Sample organic cava at the family-owned Parés Baltà, which is helmed by two women winemakers. Bump along on a 4WD guided tour across the winery's five estates, and see first hand the organic methods, like the flocks of grazing sheep that help fertilize the vineyards. In some parts, the vineyards grow amid wild parkland – Parés Baltà is one of the few producers in Spain with vineyards in a natural park, the Parc del Foix. Pick up a bottle of the award-winning rosé Parés Baltà Ros de Pacs. Book in advance, via phone or web. Tours start at €10. Generally Mon–Fri 9am–5pm, Sat & Sun 9am–1pm.

George Orwell's *Homage to Catalonia*, he humorous recounts his experience in drinking from one.) Rivalling the museum's exhibits is the building itself, a thirteenth-century royal palace that was once the seat of the Catalan-Aragon crown. After your visit, sample local wines at the *Vinmuseum Tavern*.

ARRIVAL AND INFORMATION   VILAFRANCA DEL PENEDÈS

By train Regular trains travel from Barcelona to Vilafranca (50min).
Turisme C/Cort 14 (Mon 4–7pm, Tues–Fri 9am–1pm & 4–7pm, Sat 9.30am–1.30pm & 4–7pm, Sun 10am–1pm; ☏ 938 181 254, ⓦ turismevilafranca.com).

ACCOMMODATION, EATING AND DRINKING

Casa Torner i Güell Rambla de Sant Francesc 26 ☏ 938 174 755, ⓦ casatorneriguell.com. For the full Penedès experience, bed down in this graceful *modernista* boutique hotel in the heart of the charming old town. The elegant, light-filled rooms feature gleaming woods and sleek furnishings. Take in breezes in the leafy garden and sip local wines in the handsome cocktail lounge. **€140**

Inzolia C/la Palma 21, just off C/Sant Joan ☎938 181 938, ⓦinzolia.com. An agreeable place in town to wine-taste: a range of cavas and wines are sold by the glass, and there's a good wine shop attached. Tues–Sat 10am–2pm & 5–10pm, Sun 5–10pm.

El Racó de la Calma C/Casal 1 ☎938 199 299, ⓦelracodelacalma.com. Slice into rabbit cannelloni draped in a truffle béchamel or squid stuffed with Tou dels Tillers, a lightly salted local creamy cow's cheese, at this restaurant. Don't miss the *crema Catalana* ($6), Catalonia's version of crème brûlée, but here served as an ethereal foam. Tues 1.15–3.45pm, Wed–Fri 1.15–3.45pm & 8.30–11pm, Sat 1.30–3.45pm & 8.30–11pm, Sun 1.30–3.45pm.

Sitges

SITGES, 40km from Barcelona, is definitely the highlight of this stretch of coast. Established in the 1960s as a holiday town, whose liberal attitudes openly challenged the rigidity of Franco's Spain, it has now become the great weekend escape for young Barcelonans, who have created a resort very much in their own image. It's also a noted gay holiday destination, with the nightlife to match. Indeed, if you don't like vigorous action of all kinds, you'd be wise to avoid Sitges in the summer – staid it isn't. Finding a place to stay in peak season can be a challenge, unless you arrive early in the day or book well in advance. None of this deters the varied and generally well-heeled visitors, however – nor should it, since Sitges as a sort of Barcelona-on-Sea is definitely worth experiencing for at least one night.

The town itself is appealing and attractive: a former fishing village whose well-maintained houses and narrow streets have attracted artists and opted-out intellectuals for a century or so. But, it's the **beach** that brings most people to Sitges, and it's not hard to find, with two strands right in town, to the west of the church. From here, a succession of *platjas* of varying quality and crowdedness stretches west for a couple of kilometres down the coast. A long seafront promenade flanks the beach, and all along there are beach bars, restaurants, showers and watersports facilities. Towards the end of the western stretch of beach, you'll reach nudist beaches, a couple of which are exclusively gay.

Museu Cau Ferrat

C/Fonollar • ☎938 930 464

In town, climb up the knoll overlooking the beaches, which is topped by the Baroque parish church – known as La Punta – and a street of old whitewashed mansions, locally called the Corner of Calm. One contains the **Museu Cau Ferrat**, home and workshop to the artist and writer Santiago Rusiñol (1861–1931). Its two floors contain a massive jumble of his own paintings, as well as sculpture, painted tiles, ceramic, glasswork, drawings and various collected odds and ends, such as the decorative ironwork (over eight hundred pieces) Rusiñol brought back in bulk from throughout Catalunya. Two of his better buys were the minor El Grecos at the top of the stairs on either side of a crucifix.

CARNAVAL AND FANTASY IN SITGES

Carnaval in Sitges (Feb/March) is outrageous, thanks largely to the gay populace. The official programme of parades and masked balls is complemented by an unwritten but widely recognized schedule of events. The climax is the Tuesday late-night parade, in which exquisitely dressed drag queens swan about the streets in high heels, twirling lacy parasols and coyly fanning themselves. Bar doors stand wide open, bands play, and processions and celebrations go on until four in the morning.

If you're a fan of fantasy, don't miss the annual **Sitges Film Festival** (ⓦcinemasitges.com), one of the world's premiere fantasy and horror film festivals. The festival has also expanded to embrace other genres and attracts some big-name actors and directors. It takes place over ten days in late October at venues around the town (information and venues from the *turisme*). In the summer, the city government usually hosts **outdoor concerts** at the various museums and gardens, including opera, jazz and classical guitar. Enquire at the tourist office.

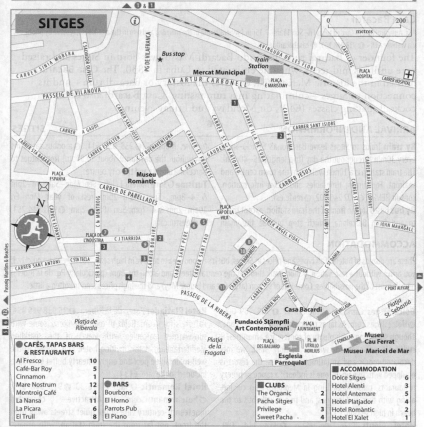

SITGES

0 ————— 200
metres

Bus stop
Train Station

PG DE VILAFRANCA
AVINGUDA DE LES FLORS
CAPELLANS

CARRER SINIA MORERA
C SALVADOR OLIVELLA

PLAÇA HOSPITAL
CARRER HOSPITAL

Mercat Municipal
AV ARTUR CARBONELL
PLAÇA E MARISTANY

PASSEIG DE VILANOVA

CARRER A GAUDI
CARRER SANT JOSEP
CARRER ST BARTOMEU
CARRER ST GAUDENC
CARRER ILLA DE CUBA
CARRER SANT ISIDRE
F GUMA

CARRER STA BARBARA
CARRER ESPALTER
C ST BUENAVENTURA

CARRER SANT FRANCESC

CARRER JESUS
CARRER RAFAEL LLOPART

PLAÇA ESPANYA
Museu Romàntic
CARRER DE PARELLADES

C SANTIAGO RUSSINOL
CARRER ST SEBASTIA
C JOAN MARAGALL

N
CARRER ESPANYA
C N MONTROIG
PLAÇA DE L'INDUSTRIA
C J TIARRIDA
CARRER BONAIRE
CARRER SANT PERE
CARRER SANT PAU
PLAÇA CAP DE LA VILA
PLAÇA AJUNTAMENT
CARRER ANGEL VIDAL
ST DAMIA

Platja Marítim & Beaches
CARRER SANT ANTONI
C STA TECLA
C 1ER DE MAIG
C ISLA LLAGARDÉ
CARRER CARRETA
C AIGUA

PASSEIG DE LA RIBERA
CARRER TACÓ
CARRER NOU
CARRER MAJOR

Platja de Riberala
Platja de la Fragata

Casa Bacardi
Fundació Stämpfli Art Contemporani
PLAÇA AJUNTAMENT
CORVALLADA
Platja St. Sebastià

PLAÇA DES BALUARD
PL. M URTILLO MORLIUS
C FONOLLAR
Museu Cau Ferrat
Museu Maricel de Mar

Esglesia Parroquial
C PORT ALEGRE

● CAFÉS, TAPAS BARS & RESTAURANTS	
Al Fresco	10
Café-Bar Roy	5
Cinnamon	1
Mare Nostrum	12
Montroig Café	4
La Nansa	11
La Picara	6
El Trull	8

● BARS	
Bourbons	2
El Horno	9
Parrots Pub	7
El Piano	3

● CLUBS	
The Organic	2
Pacha Sitges	1
Privilege	3
Sweet Pacha	4

■ ACCOMMODATION	
Dolce Sitges	6
Hotel Alenti	3
Hotel Antemare	5
Hotel Platjador	4
Hotel Romàntic	2
Hotel El Xalet	1

The museum also contains works by the artist's friends (including Picasso) who used to meet in the *Els Quatre Gats* bar in Barcelona. The museum has been going through major renovations, to be reopened at the end of 2015, so call ahead or check at the *turisme*.

Museu Maricel de Mar

C/de Fonollar • ☎ 938 940 364

The **Museu Maricel de Mar** has some minor artworks, medieval to modern, and maintains an impressive collection of Catalan ceramics and sculpture. The museum has been going through major renovations, at the time of writing it was due to reopen soon; call ahead or check at the *turisme*.

Fundació Stämpfli Art Contemporani

Pza. Ajuntament • July–Sept Fri & Sat 9.30am–2pm & 4–7pm, Sun 10am–3pm; Oct–June Fri & Sat 3.30–6.30pm, Sun 10am–3pm • €3.50 or €6.50 discount ticket for three of Sitges museums • ⓦ fundacio-stampfli.org

Fundació Stämpfli Art Contemporani, an impressive addition to the Sitges museum scene, opened in late 2010, founded by the acclaimed art foundation **La Fundació Stämpfli**, helmed by Swiss artist Peter Stämpfli, who has worked in the Catalan art world for decades. The museum, which occupies two adjoining historic buildings, one of which was the old fish market, features artwork from around the globe, from bold, colourful paintings to wooden assemblage sculptures.

Casa Bacardi

Pza. Ajuntament 11 • Guided tours Fri–Sun 11am–7.15pm (generally one in the morning and two in the afternoon); reserve by phone or via website • €8 • ☏ 938 948 151, ⓦ casabacardi.es

The founder of Bacardi rum, Facundo Bacardí Massó, was born in Sitges and raised here until his mid-teens, when he emigrated to Cuba in 1830. The **Casa Bacardi**, housed in the historic Mercat Vell, explores the history of Bacardi rum – and its connection to Sitges – culminating in a rum tasting. Casa Bacardi also offers cocktail-making classes (€40), on Mondays and Friday evenings.

ARRIVAL AND INFORMATION

By train Trains to Sitges leave Barcelona's Estació-Sants every 30min throughout the day (trip length 25–40min). The train station is a 10min walk from the town centre and seafront. For current timetables and ticket information, consult RENFE (☏ 902 240 202, ⓦ renfe.es).

By bus Buses stop in front of the train station, except those to and from Barcelona, which stop outside the main

SITGES

turisme. MonBus (☏ 938 937 511, ⓦ monbus.cat) runs throughout the day (until about 10.30pm) from Sitges to Barcelona airport and the city centre.

Turisme C/Sínia Morera 1 (July–Sept Mon–Sat 9am–2pm & 4–8pm, Sun 10am–2pm; rest of year Mon–Fri 10am–2pm & 4–7pm, Sun 10am–2pm; ☏ 938 944 251, ⓦ sitgestur.cat).

ACCOMMODATION

There are dozens of hotels of all types and prices in Sitges, but it's a good idea to reserve in high season as they fill up quickly. If you arrive without a reservation, a short walk through the central streets and along the front (particularly Pg. de la Ribera) reveals most of the possibilities. Come out of season (after Oct and before May) and the high prices tend to soften a little.

Dolce Sitges Cami del Miralpeix 12 ☏ 938 109 000, ⓦ dolcesitges.com. As far as resorts go, this is a good one. Though sprawling, with plenty of conference amenities, it still feels personalized, with a friendly staff, warmly decorated rooms and an intimate spa. Plus, the resort is equipped with five pools (one is indoor); a range of breezy restaurants, most specializing in Mediterranean cuisine, along with bars and lounges; and free shuttle bus to the beach in high season. **€174**

Hotel Alenti C/1er de Maig ☏ 938 114 790, ⓦ hotelalenti.com. Sleek boutique hotel, in an all-white, cube-shaped building, with plenty of pale wood and picture windows that let in the Sitges sunshine. Restaurant with a terrace directly onto the "Street of Sin". **€180**

Hotel Antemare C/Mare de Déu del Montserrat 50 ☏ 938 947 000, ⓦ antemare.com. One street back from the sea, about 1.5km from the centre, this classy hotel has stylish rooms at reasonable rates. Also has a thalassotherapy (sea-water) spa, with massages and body wraps. **€115**

Hotel Platjador Paseo de la Ribera, ☏ 35 938 945 054, ⓦ hotelsitges.com. Relax in colourful rooms, some with sun-warmed balconies with views of the sparkling Mediterranean, at this inviting hotel. Plus, splash in the well-maintained pool and enjoy a hearty buffet breakfast, included in the rate. **€134**

Hotel Romàntic C/Sant Isidre 33 ☏ 938 948 375, ⓦ hotelromantic.com. Attractive converted nineteenth-century villa in the quiet streets away from the front, not far from the train station, with ornate, modernista touches and rooms with plenty of character; some have a terrace overlooking the palm-shaded gardens. It's a favourite with gay visitors. Breakfast included. Closed Nov–March. **€130**

Hotel El Xalet C/Illa de Cuba 35 ☏ 938 110 070, ⓦ elxalet.com. This longtime hotel has a pretty modernista design, though it is a bit faded. Rooms are decent, there's a charming little interior courtyard and it's near the train station. **€100**

EATING AND DRINKING

Most of the **restaurants** along the promenade feature sea-view terraces and serve paella and seafood, while the side streets are dotted with inviting spots. You can get picnic supplies at the town's **market**, the Mercat Municipal, near the train station, on Avgda. Artur Carbonell.

Al Fresco C/Pau Barrabeitg 4 ☏ 938 940 600, ⓦ alfrescorestaurante.es. This welcoming restaurant serves Mediterranean cuisine with a twist, from fresh fish ceviche with toasted almonds to chicken curry with green mango. Mains €15–22. Summer daily 8.30–11.30pm; closed Mon in winter.

Café-Bar Roy C/les Parellades 9 ☏ 938 110 269. An old-fashioned café with dressed-up waiters and marble tables. Watch the world go by from its prime streetside perch, over a glass of cava or a fancy snack. Daily noon–late.

Cinnamon Pg. de Pujades 2 ☏ 938 947 166, ⓦ cinnamonsitges.com. The lovely outdoor garden terrace matches the fresh, creative Asian fusion cuisine, including their signature dish Thai Lap salad, made with minced pork with cucumber, onion and red pepper. Also tasty is the chicken curry and creamy hummus. Dishes €15–25. Wed–Sun 1.30–4pm & 8.30–11pm.

Mare Nostrum Pg. de la Ribera 60 ☎938 943 393, ⓦrestaurantmarenostrum.com. Long-established fish restaurant on the seafront, with a menu that changes according to the catch and season. Around €40 a head. March–late Dec Mon, Tues & Thurs–Sun 1–4pm & 8–11pm; closed late Dec–Feb.

Montroig Café C/Marqués de Montroig 11 ☎938 948 439, ⓦmontroigcafe.com. Large, two-level, buzzy café with a shady courtyard out back, where you can sip *cerveza* or *café con leche* while soaking up the sun and the social scene. Daily 9am–2am; closed mid-Dec to mid-Jan.

★La Nansa C/Carreta 24 ☎938 941 927, ⓦrestaurantlanansa.com. A *nansa* (fishing net) hangs in

this amiable, family-run restaurant, which has wood-panelled walls, brass lanterns and maritime paintings. The top-notch seafood- and fish-focused menu (mains €16–26) includes the regional favourite, *arroz a la Sitgetana* (rice with meat, prawns, clams, and a generous splash of Sitges Malvasia wine). Mon & Thurs–Sun 1.30–4pm & 8.30–11pm, Wed 8.30–11pm; closed Jan.

La Picara C/San Pere 3 ☎93 811 0285, ⓦlapicarasitges. com. Graze on top-notch tapas at this cheerful restaurant, from calamari to juicy shrimp to *albondigas* (meatballs) to croquettes. The wine list is also strong, featuring a superb selection of Catalan vintages. Tapas €8–18. Daily 11am–midnight.

El Trull Ptge. Mossèn Félix Clarà 3, off C/Major ☎938 944 705. Elegant French-style restaurant in the old town, with exceptional foie gras and sumptuous fish casserole. Weekly menu €22. Mon, Tues, Thurs & Fri 7.30–11pm, Sat & Sun 1.30–4.30pm & 7.30–11pm; closed Jan.

DRINKING AND NIGHTLIFE

Late-opening **bars** centre on pedestrianized Carrer 1er (Primer) de Maig (popularly known as *Calle del Pecado*, or "Street of Sin" and its continuation, C/Marqués de Montroig, while Carrer de les Parellades and Carrer Bonaire complete the block. In summer, this is basically one long run of **disco-bars**, pumping music out into the late evening, interspersed with the odd restaurant or fancier cocktail bar, all with outdoor tables vying for your euros.

Pacha Sitges C/San Dídac, Urb Valpineda, 1.5km north of town ☎938 943 812, ⓦpachasitges.com. Mother of all *Pachas*, opened in 1967 and spawning a global dynasty of mega-clubs; fans won't be disappointed – there are

two massive dancefloors, a huge sound system and big-name resident and visiting DJs. Summer generally Fri, Sat & sometimes Sun till late; winter hours depend on events.

SITGES' GAY SCENE

The frenetic and ever-changing **gay scene** in Sitges is chronicled on a gay map and guide available from *Parrots Pub*, as well as from several other bars and clubs. Most of the bars and clubs are centred around Pza. Indústria and in the triangle made up by Carrer Espalter, Carrer Sant Francesc and Carrer Parellades. Sitges' clubs are liveliest in the summer, when they're open Friday and Saturday nights and sometimes during the week; in winter, hours vary and may be limited. Most clubs open no earlier than midnight and stay hopping until the wee hours.

For more information, check out ⓦgaysitgesguide.com and ⓦgogayguide.com.

GAY BARS AND CLUBS

Bourbons C/Sant Buenaventura 13 ☎600 378 120, ⓦbourbonsbar.com. Sip cocktails, from potent mojitos to caipirinhas, at this hopping bar, with live music and electro music dance sessions. Summer daily 9pm–1am; winter hours vary.

El Horno C/Joan Tarrida 4 ☎938 940 909, ⓦsitges4men.com. This long-running bar draws crowds during happy hour and has live music. Summer daily 6pm–early morning; winter hours vary.

The Organic C/Bonaire 15 ⓦtheorganicdanceclub. com. Groove the night away at this jam-packed gay club, which has themed dance nights, including 80s music night. Daily from 2.30am; winter hours vary.

Parrots Pub Pza. de la Indústria ☎938 111 219, ⓦparrotspub.com. One of the town's best-known gay bars, at the top of C/1er de Maig, and a required stop for practically everyone at some point in the day or night; it's just one place you can pick up the free gay map of Sitges. Front bar: summer daily 10am–late; the rest of the pub 5pm–late.

El Piano C/Sant Bonaventura 37 ☎938 146 245. Join the crowd in singing show tunes at this friendly gay bar. Open daily 7pm–late; winter hours vary.

Privilege C/Bonaire 24 ⓦprivilegesitges.com. This happening club has theme nights every weekend, including 70s and 90s disco. Daily from 2am; winter hours vary.

11

Sweet Pacha Port Esportiu d´Aiguadolç ☎938 943 812, ⓦsweetpacha.com. *Sweet Pacha* offers a more chic-lounge experience than *Pacha Sitges*, with plenty of white leather, a back-lit bar, DJ tunes and a dancefloor, a seafood restaurant (*Sweet Mar*) and sea views. Summer daily 8.30pm–1am; winter hours vary.

Tarragona

Sited on a rocky hill, sheer above the sea, **TARRAGONA** has a formidable ancient past. Settled originally by Iberians and then Carthaginians, it was later used as the base for the Roman conquest of the peninsula, which began in 218 BC with Scipio's march south against Hannibal. The fortified city became an imperial resort and, under Augustus, **Tarraco** was named capital of Rome's eastern Iberian province – the most elegant and cultured city of Roman Spain, boasting at its peak a quarter of a million inhabitants. Temples and monuments were built in and around the city and, despite a history of seemingly constant sacking and looting since Roman times, it's this distinguished past which still asserts itself throughout modern Tarragona.

Time spent in the handsome upper town quickly shows what attracted the emperors to the city: strategically – and beautifully – placed, it's a fine setting for some splendid Roman remains and a few excellent museums. There's an attractive medieval section, too, while the rocky coastline below conceals a couple of reasonable beaches. If there's a downside, it's that Tarragona is today the second-largest port in Catalunya, so the views aren't always unencumbered – though the fish in the Serrallo fishing quarter is consistently good and fresh. Furthermore, the city's ugly outskirts to the south have been steadily degraded by new industries – chemical and oil refineries and a nuclear power station – which do little for Tarragona's character as a resort.

Orientation

The city divides clearly into two parts: a predominantly medieval, walled upper town (where you'll spend most of your time) known as **La Part Alta**, and the prosperous modern centre below, referred to as **Eixample**, or the Centre Urbà. Between the two cuts is the **Rambla Nova**, a sturdy provincial rival to Barcelona's, lined with fashionable cafés and restaurants, culminating at its southern end with the lovely **Balcó del Mediterràni**, overlooking the sea. Parallel, and to the east, lies the **Rambla Vella**, marking – as its name suggests – the start of the old town. To either side of the *rambles* are scattered a profusion of relics from Tarragona's Roman past, including various temples and parts of the forum, theatre and amphitheatre. Note that some of the most impressive monuments are a fair way out, but there's enough within walking distance to occupy a good day's sightseeing and to provide a vivid impression of life in Tarragona in imperial Roman times.

Museu Nacional Arqueològic

Pza. del Rei • June–Sept Tues–Sat 9.30am–8.30pm, Sun 10am–2pm; Oct–May Tues–Sat 9.30am–6pm & 4–7pm, Sun 10am–2pm • €4.50 (includes the Museu i Necròpolis Paleocristians) • ☎977 236 209, ⓦmnat.cat

The most stimulating exhibition in town is housed in adjacent buildings off Pza. del Rei. The splendid **Museu Nacional Arqueològic** is a marvellous reflection of the richness of imperial Tarraco. Its huge collection is well laid out, starting in the basement with a section of the old Roman wall preserved *in situ*. On other floors are thematic displays on the various remains and buildings around the city, accompanied by pictures, text and relics, as well as whole rooms devoted to inscriptions, sculpture, ceramics, jewellery – even a series of anchors retrieved from the sea. More importantly, there's an unusually complete collection of mosaics, exemplifying the stages of development from the plain black-and-white patterns of the first century AD to the elaborate polychrome pictures of the second and third centuries.

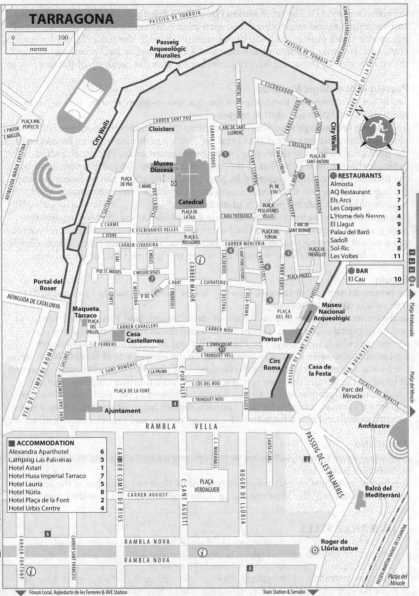

TARRAGONA

Museu i Necròpolis Paleocristians

Museum Avgda. Ramón i Cajal 78 • March–May & Oct Tues–Sat 9.30am–1.30pm & 3–6pm, Sun 10am–2pm; June–Sept Tues–Sat 10am–1.30pm & 4–8pm, Sun 10am–2pm; Nov–Feb Tues–Sat 9.30am–1.30pm & 3–5.30pm, Sun 10am–2pm • €4.50 (includes the Museu Nacional Arqueològic) • ⓦ mnat.cat • Walk 20min out of the centre down Avgda. Ramón i Cajal, which runs west off Rambla Nova

The most interesting remains in town are those of the ancient **Necropolis**. Here, both pagan and Christian tombs have been uncovered, spanning a period from the third to the sixth century AD. The small **Museu i Necropolis Paleocristians** features sarcophagi and some of the most fascinating finds, such as an ivory doll with moveable arms and legs, and you can peek at the main burial grounds through the fence. Most of the relics attest to Tarragona's importance as a centre of Christianity: St Paul preached here, and the city became an important Visigothic bishopric after the break-up of Roman power.

Passeig Arqueològic Muralles

Portal del Roser, Avgda. Catalunya • Mid-May to Sept Tues–Sat 10am–9pm, Sun 10am–3pm; rest of year Tues–Sat 10am–7pm, Sun 10am–3pm • €3.30 or €11.05 joint ticket • ☎ 977 245 796, ⓦ taragona.cat

The **Passeig Arqueològic Muralles** is a promenade that encircles the northern half of the old town. From the entrance at the Portal del Roser, a path runs between **Roman walls** of the third century BC and the sloping, **outer fortifications** erected by the British in 1709 to secure the city during the War of the Spanish Succession. Megalithic walls built by the Iberians are excellently preserved in places, too, particularly two awesome gateways; the huge blocks used in their construction are quite distinct from the more refined Roman additions. Vantage points (and occasional telescopes) give views across the plain behind the city and around to the sea, while various objects are displayed within the *passeig*: several Roman columns, a fine bronze statue of Augustus and eighteenth-century cannons still defending the city's heights. Just beyond the entrance on the right, a small doorway leads up to the battlements from where you get fine views of the old city.

Forum

Pza. del Forum • Mid-May to Sept Tues–Sat 10am–9pm, Sun 10am–3pm; rest of year Tues–Sat 10am–7pm, Sun 10am–3pm • €3.30 or €11.05 joint ticket • ☎ 977 242 501, ⓦ tarragona.cat

In the centre of town, the Roman forum, or rather forums, have also survived, since – as provincial capital – Tarragona sustained both a ceremonial **Forum Provincial** (the scant remnants of which are displayed on Plaça del Forum) and a **Forum de la Colonia** on C/-Lleida, whose more substantial remains are on the western side of Rambla Nova, near the Mercat Central. Located on the flat land near the port, this was the commercial centre of imperial Tarraco and the main meeting place for locals for three centuries. The site, which contained temples and small shops arranged around a porticoed square, has been split by a main road: a footbridge now connects the two halves where you can see a water cistern, house foundations, fragments of stone inscriptions and four elegant columns.

Amfiteatre

Parc del Miracle • Mid-May to Sept Tues–Sat 10am–9pm, Sun 10am–3pm; rest of year Tues–Sat 10am–7pm, Sun 10am–3pm • €3.30 or €11.05 joint ticket • ⓦ tarragona.cat

A group of Tarragona's tangible Roman remains lie close to each other at the seaward end of the Rambla Vella. Most rewarding is the **Amfiteatre**, built into the green slopes

---

HUMAN CASTLES

It's not often that you'll come across a group of grown men and women who willingly climb onto each other's back to form a tall, if a bit wobbly, human tower. But when you do, it's a sight to behold. Catalunya's famous *castellers* – teams of people competing to build human towers – originated in **Valls**, near Tarragona, at the end of the eighteenth century. Over time, the rest of Catalunya embraced the tradition, and *castells* now form a part of festivals throughout the region. The impressive *castells* can loom up to ten human storeys tall, and are completed by a small child scrambling to the very top.

Castells are a feature of Tarragona's annual **Festival of Santa Tecla** in mid-September. To learn more about the history, pay a visit to Tarragona's **Casa de la Festa**, Via Augusta 4 (end June to end Sept Tues–Sat 11am–2pm & 5–9pm, Sun 11am–2pm; rest of year Tues & Wed 9am–1pm, Thurs & Fri 9am–1pm & 5–7pm, Sat 10am–2pm & 5–7pm, Sun 11am–2pm; free; ☎ 977 220 086). The Festa Major of Vilafranca del Penedès in late August (see p.770) also showcases *castells*.

of Parc del Miracle. The tiered seats backing onto the sea are original, and from the top you can look north, up the coast, to the headland; the rest of the seating was reconstructed in 1969–70, along with the surviving tunnels and structural buildings.

Circ Roma and Pretori

Rambla Vella, Pza. del Rei • Mid-May to Sept Tues–Sat 10am–9pm, Sun 10am–3pm; rest of year Tues–Sat 10am–7pm, Sun 10am–3pm • €3.30 or €11.05 joint ticket • ⓦ tarragona.cat

The **Circ Roma**, or Roman Circus, was the site of chariot races. The visible sections encompass vaults that are set back from the street under the gloom of the surrounding buildings. You can exit through the Roman **Pretori** tower on Pza. del Rei.

Casa Castellarnau

C/Cavallers 14 • Mid-May to Sept Tues–Sat 10am–9pm, Sun 10am–3pm; rest of year Tues–Sat 10am–7pm, Sun 10am–3pm • €3.30 or €11.05 joint ticket • ☎ 977 242 220, ⓦ tarragona.cat

Strolling the old town's streets will also enable you to track down one of Tarragona's finest medieval mansions and lesser-known museums, the **Casa Castellarnau**. The interior courtyard alone rewards a visit, with its arches and stone coats of arms built over Roman vaults. Otherwise, the small-scale collections are largely archeological and historical (Roman jars and the like), rescued from banality by some rich eighteenth-century Catalan furniture and furnishings on the upper floor.

Catedral

Pza. de Palau 2 • Mid-March to Oct Mon 3–6pm, Tues–Sat 10am–7pm; Nov to mid-March Mon–Sat 10am–5pm • €5; guided visit €15, call ahead to book • ☎ 977 226 935, ⓦ catedraltarragona.com

The central C/Major climbs to the quarter's focal point, the **Catedral**, which sits at the top of a broad flight of steps. This, quite apart from its own grand beauty, is a perfect example of the transition from Romanesque to Gothic forms. You'll see the change highlighted in the main facade, where a soaring Gothic portal is framed by Romanesque doors, surmounted by a cross and an elaborate rose window. Except for services, entrance to the Catedral is through the **cloisters** (*claustre*; signposted up a street to the left of the facade), themselves superbly executed with pointed Gothic arches softened by smaller round divisions. The cloister also has several oddly sculpted capitals, one of which represents a cat's funeral being directed by rats. Note that the Catedral has been undergoing renovations, so parts of it may be closed to the public, and the entry fee may therefore be reduced. The ticket also gives access to the **Museu Diocesà**, which is piled high with ecclesiastical treasures.

Serrallo

A fifteen-minute walk west along the industrial harbourfront from the train station (or the same distance south from the Necropolis) takes you to the working port of **Serrallo**, Tarragona's so-called "fishermen's quarter". Built a century ago, the harbour here isn't particularly attractive, though it's authentic enough – fishing smacks tied up, nets laid out on the ground for mending. The real interest for visitors is the line of **seafood restaurants** which fronts the main Moll dels Pescadors. The warehouses nearby, back towards town, have been given a face-lift, as has the Estació Marítima (cruise-ship terminal).

11

ARRIVAL AND DEPARTURE

TARRAGONA

By train The train station is on Pg. de Espanya (☎ 902 432 343), from which it's an easy walk into town. In addition to the regular trains, there are high-speed AVE trains from Barcelona, Madrid and other main cities which arrive at the Camp de Tarragona AVE station, a 10min taxi ride from the centre.
Destinations Barcelona (every 30min; 1hr); Cambrils (12 daily; 20min); Lleida (12 daily; 2hr, *talgo* 1hr, AVE 30min); Sitges (direct every 30min; 1hr); Tortosa (13 daily; 1hr); Valencia (16 daily; 4hr, *talgo* 2hr 15min); Zaragoza (12 daily; 3hr 30min).

By bus The bus terminal is at the end of Rambla Nova, at Pza. Imperial Tarraco.
Destinations Barcelona (18 daily; 1hr 30min); Berga (July & Aug 1 daily, rest of year Sat & Sun only; 3hr 10min); La Seu d'Urgell (daily at 8am; 3hr 45min); Lleida (6 daily; 1hr 45min); Montblanc (3 daily; 50min); Poblet (Mon–Sat 3 daily; 1hr 5min); Tortosa (Mon–Fri 1 daily; 1hr 30min); Valencia (7 daily; 3hr 30min); Zaragoza (4 daily; 4hr).

INFORMATION

Turisme C/Major 39 (July–Sept Mon–Sat 9am–9pm, Sun 10am–2pm; Oct–June Mon–Sat 10am–2pm & 4–7pm, Sun 10am–2pm; ☎ 977 250 795, ⊛ tarragonaturisme.cat). There are a few other information booths/offices, including on Rambla Nova (summer daily 10am–8pm; winter Mon–

Sat 10am–2pm & 4–7pm, Sun 10am–2pm).
Regional tourist office C/Fortuny 4, just south of Rambla Nova (Mon–Fri 9am–2pm & 4–6.30pm, Sat 9am–2pm; ☎ 977 233 415, ⊛ tarragonaturisme.cat). Especially good if you're travelling farther afield.

ACCOMMODATION

Alexandra Aparthotel Rambla Nova 71 ☎ 977 248 701, ⊛ ah-alexandra.com. Outside the hotel, you're in the thick of things, right on busy Rambla Nova. Inside, the airy *Alexandra* offers a quiet retreat, with generously sized rooms and studios, many with fully equipped kitchens and dining rooms, making this an ideal spot for families and groups of friends. Doubles €80, studios €100
Camping Las Palmers ☎ 977 208 081, ⊛ laspalmeras .com. There are a number of campsites east of town including this well-maintained site at Platja Llarga, 3km northeast along the coast. €30
Hotel Astari Vía Augusta 95–97 ☎ 977 236 900, ⊛ hotelastari.com. Friendly hotel with modern rooms, a marble-floor lobby, a decent swimming pool and pleasant garden. It's a 15min walk from the old town, and less than a 10min stroll from the nearest beach. €90
Hotel Husa Imperial Tarraco Pg. de les Palmeres ☎ 977 233 040, ⊛ hotelhusaimperialtarraco.com. One of the city's finer hotels, modern but beautifully positioned, sitting on top of the cliff and facing out to sea. Relax in the breezy garden or lounge by the pool. Good online rates. €110

Hotel Lauria Rambla Nova 20 ☎ 977 236 712, ⊛ hotel-lauria.com. Well-located three-star just off the main *rambla* with modern if functional rooms, some smartly refurbished, and a small outdoor pool. Good online rates. €84
Hotel Núria Vía Augusta 145 ☎ 977 235 011, ⊛ hotelnuria.com. Amiable hotel near Arrabassada beach, 1km northeast of Tarragona – the *playa* stretches right nearby, and town is about a 25min walk away (or you can opt for one of the regular buses). The decor tends towards minimalist, and there's a restaurant-café, with a weekday lunchtime menu. €95
Hotel Plaça de la Font Pza. de la Font 26 ☎ 977 246 134, ⊛ hotelpdelafont.com. Central, cosy hotel with simple, well-scrubbed rooms, and a small restaurant with a cheery terrace on the *plaça*. €70
Hotel Urbis Centre Pza. Corsini 10 ☎ 977 240 116, ⊛ hotelurbiscentre.com. This central hotel has a contemporary style, with white marble floors in the lobby. The simple rooms are well maintained, and the regional-cuisine restaurant (closed Sun) serves a good selection of local wines. €90

EATING AND DRINKING

There are plenty of good **restaurants** in the centre of Tarragona; many – particularly in and around Pza. de la Font – have outdoor seating in the summer. Alternatively, you could try the fish and seafood places down in Serrallo – not cheap, but the food is fresh and you can find some menus for around €15–20 in the narrow street behind the main Moll dels Pescadors. Tarragona's marina (Port Esportiu) features several **clubs and bars**, which generally heat up in the summer – though note that they come and go with great regularity. It's in town – around the old quarter and the Catedral and in the streets between the train station and Rambla Nova – that you'll find spots with more historical, local appeal.

Almosta C/Ventallols ☎ 977 222 742. Organic is the name of the game at this small innovative rustic restaurant. The seasonal menu celebrates fresh produce, from rabbit

confit squirted with citrus and served with yucca flower to a cherry tartar with mascarpone ice cream. Dishes €13–25. Thurs–Mon 1–4 & 8.30–11pm.

★**AQ Restaurant** C/Les Coques 7 ☎977 215 954, ⓦaq-restaurant.com. Glossy restaurant – the sky-lit dining room sports honey-hued walls and sleek furnishings – with impressive cuisine to match (main dishes €18–25). Husband-and-wife team Quintín and Ana (after whom the restaurant is named) serve up seasonal food with flair including superb fresh fish and shellfish. Tues–Sat 1.30–3.30pm & 9–11pm; usually closed second 2 weeks of Dec.

Els Arcs Misser Sitges 13 ☎977 218 040, ⓦrestaurantarcs.com. Ancient, graceful stone arches – hence the name – preside over a cosy dining room. Fresh Mediterranean dishes include cod with a Cabrales cheese sauce and duck with sweet-and-sour cherry preserves. Expect to pay around €40/person, without drinks. Tues–Sat 1.30–3.30pm & 8.30–10.30pm.

El Cau C/Trinquet Vell 2 ☎977 239 812, ⓦelcau.net. Situated in an underground Roman vault in the old town, this dimly lit venue has strong cocktails and live indie-pop or rock on the weekends. Daily 10pm–4am.

Les Coques C/Sant Llorenç 15 ☎977 228 300, ⓦles-coques.com. Top-notch Catalan fare in a comfortable restaurant near the Catedral, with a weekday lunch menu for €25. Mon–Sat 1.30–4pm & 9–10.30pm.

L'Home dels Nassos C/Merceria 13, ⓦhdnrestaurant.wordpress.com. A creative couple run this tiny restaurant that has landed on the foodie trail, thanks to its experimental Catalan menu rooted in local produce. Enjoy everything from grilled fish with wild-flower garnishes to foie mousse on a carpaccio of strawberries. Dishes €15–25. Generally Wed–Sat 9–11.30pm.

El Llagut C/Natzaret 10 ☎977 228 938. Rice and seafood are the stars of the menu at this handsome tavern. Try *arròs negre* (rice with squid ink) and a huge array of fresh seafood, from monkfish to mussels to cuttlefish. The well-curated wine list showcases superb vintages from around Catalunya. Dishes €16–30. Tues–Sat 1–4pm & 8.30–11pm & Sun 1–4.

Palau del Baró C/Santa Anna 3 ☎977 241 464, ⓦpalaudelbaro.com. Dining rooms set in an eighteenth-century mansion with a lovely courtyard area. Well-prepared regional food includes shellfish in *romesco* sauce and *fideuà* (Catalan noodles) with clams and monkfish. Dishes €15–25. Tues–Sat 1–4pm & 8–11pm, Sun 1–4pm.

Sadoll C/Mare de Déu de la Mercè 1 ☎ 977 244 404, ⓦsadollrestaurant.com. Inviting restaurant tucked away in a quiet corner near the Catedral, and featuring fresh, creative dishes in an elegant Art Nouveau dining room. Dishes €15–20. Mon–Sat 1.30–3.30pm & 8.30–10.30pm.

Sol-Ric Vía Augusta 227, about 1km east of the city ☎977 232 032, ⓦrestaurantesolric.es. Feast on mid-priced seafood and grilled meats at this amiable restaurant that's set in an old house with antique furniture and wooden beams. Tues–Sat 1–4pm & 8.30–11pm, Sun 1–4pm.

Les Voltes C/Trinquet Vell 12 ☎977 230 651, ⓦrestaurantlesvoltes.cat. Atmospheric restaurant, with a fabulous location within Roman vaults, and recommended for its hearty seafood and meats, ranging in price from €15 to €20. Tues–Sat 1–3.30pm & 8–10.30pm, Sun 1–3.30pm.

11

Around Tarragona

The coast between Tarragona and the historic town of **Altafulla**, 11km east, is littered with Roman remains, well worth checking out, though for all but the Roman **aqueduct** you'll need your own transport. West of Tarragona, the pleasant town of **Reus** features an entertaining museum on master Catalan architect Antoni Gaudí.

Aqüeducte de les Ferreres

Open during daylight hours • Free • ☎977 242 220, ⓦtarragona.cat • Parking on-site; check with *turisme* about bus transport to the site

Perhaps the most remarkable (and least visited) of Tarragona's monuments stands 4km outside the original city walls, reached via a small, signposted road off the main Lleida highway. This is the Roman **Aqüeducte de les Ferreres**, which brought water from the Ríu Gayo, some 32km away. The most impressive extant section, nearly 220m long and 27m high, lies in an overgrown valley in the middle of nowhere: the utilitarian beauty of the aqueduct is surpassed only by the one at Segovia and the Pont du Gard, in the south of France. Popularly, it is known as El Pont del Diable (Devil's Bridge) because, remarked Richard Ford, of the Spanish habit of "giving all praise to 'the Devil', as Pontifex Maximus".

Reus

Gaudí aficionados might want to take a spin through the small, handsome city of **Reus**, 14km west of Tarragona, where the *modernisme* master, Gaudí, was born in 1852.

While Reus has no Gaudí buildings – he left at the age of 16 – it does feature a smattering of other *modernista* buildings, all of which form part of the town's **Ruta del Modernisme**. Besides Gaudí, Reus is popular for its good shopping, especially clothing, thanks in part to the town's once-thriving textile industry.

Gaudí Centre

Pza. del Mercadal • Mid-June to mid-Sept Mon–Sat 10am–8pm, Sun 11am–2pm; mid-Sept to mid-June Mon–Sat 10am–2pm & 4–7pm, Sun 11am–2pm • €7 • ⓣ 977 010 670, ⓦ gaudicentre.com

The sleek **Gaudí Centre** offers an engaging overview of the great artist via three floors of tactile and sensory exhibits. The first floor focuses on young Gaudí and his connection with Reus; look for what is believed to be the only hand-written notebook by Gaudí still in existence. The second floor, called "Gaudí the Innovator", focuses on his progressive designs. The top floor shows a film on Gaudí and covers his influence on architecture around the globe.

ARRIVAL AND INFORMATION — REUS

By bus Regular trains and buses connect Reus with Tarragona (15min) and Barcelona (1hr 40min). Buses also travel regularly between the Barcelona airport and Reus airport, which lies about 6km east of Reus and handles various budget European airlines.

Turisme Inside the Gaudí Centre (mid-June to mid-Sept Mon–Sat 9.30am–8pm, Sun 11am–2pm; mid-Sept to mid-June Mon–Sat 9.30am–2pm & 4–7pm, Sun 10am–2pm; ⓣ 977 010 670, ⓦ reus.cat/turisme). You can pick up a map at the helpful *turisme*, and they also offer a variety of good guided tours of the city, which sometimes include access to *modernista* buildings otherwise closed to the public.

ACCOMMODATION

Hotel Gaudí Raval de Robuster 49 ⓣ 977 345 545, ⓦ hotelgaudireus.com. This comfortable, mid-range hotel, one of several decent options in the city, has modern rooms in muted colours, a casual cafeteria and a lobby with a Gaudí-style decor. **€65**

Mas Passamaner Camí de la Serra 52, La Selva del Camp, 5km northwest of Reus ⓣ 977 766 333, ⓦ maspassamaner.com. For a further taste of *modernisme*, consider staying at this hotel designed by the master architect Lluis Domènech i Montaner in 1922, and converted into a five-star hotel, with elegant rooms, a pool and a spa. **€222**

Altafulla

ALTAFULLA makes a reasonable stop, for a wander about the old town, with its 400-year-old castle (privately owned), the Baroque **Església Parroquial de Sant Martí** (open for services only), which was completed in 1705 and has a distinctive octagonal dome, and a pair of gateways left standing from the original medieval walls.

Villa Romana dels Munts

C/Villa Romana • June–Sept Tues–Sat 10am–1.30pm & 4–8pm, Sun 10am–2pm; March–May & Oct Tues–Sat 10am–1.30pm & 3–6pm, Sun 10am–2pm; Jan–Feb & Nov–Dec Tues–Sat 10am–1.30 & 3–5.30pm, Sun 10am–2pm • €2.50 • ⓣ 977 652 806, ⓦ mnat.cat

Surrounded by a sleepy estate of holiday homes, the **Villa Romana dels Munts** is one of the more important finds in the region, primarily because of the exceptional mosaics and paintings that decorated its rooms and thermal baths – indicating an owner of high standing. The mosaics are preserved in the Museu Nacional Arqueològic in Tarragona and today the villa is worth a look chiefly for the ruins of its thermal baths, which include a remarkably well-preserved arch and water tank.

ARRIVAL AND INFORMATION — ALTAFULLA

By bus and train Regular buses and trains connect Altafulla with Tarragona (10min).

Turisme C/Marqués de Tamarit 16 ⓦ altafulla.cat (Jan–March Mon–Fri 9am–3pm; May, June & Sept–Dec Mon–Thurs 9am–3pm, Fri & Sat 4–7pm; July & Aug daily 10am–2pm & 4–8pm; ⓣ 977 651 426); Pza. dels Vents (summer only; ⓣ 977 650 752). Note that hours change depending on city budget.

Tortosa

The only town of any size in Catalunya's deep south is **TORTOSA**, slightly inland astride the Ríu Ebre. In the Civil War the front was outside Tortosa for several months until the Nationalists eventually took the town in April 1938. The battle cost 35,000 lives, and is commemorated by a gaunt metal monument on a huge stone plinth in the middle of the river in town. The fighting took its toll in other ways, too: there's little left of the medieval quarter, the *barri antic*, which lies on the east bank of the Ebro, north of the modern commercial district. Nonetheless, Tortosa still throws a boisterous and popular Festa del Renaixement (Renaissance Festival; ⊛festadelrenaixement.org) in late July, which celebrates the city's history, with thousands turning out in period costumes, along with theatre, street entertainment, live music, free-flowing wine and more.

Catedral de Santa Maria

C/Portal del Palau • Tues–Sat 10am–1pm & 4.30–7pm, Sun usually 12.30–2pm

The **Catedral de Santa Maria** is worth a look. Founded originally in the twelfth century on the site of an earlier mosque, it was rebuilt in the fourteenth century, and its Gothic interior and quiet cloister – although much worn – are both lovely.

11

La Suda and the Jardins del Príncep

Jardins del Príncep • May to mid-Sept Tues–Sat 10am–1.30pm & 4.30–7.30pm, Sun 11am–1.30pm; mid-Sept to April 10am–1.30pm & 3.30–6.30pm, Sun 11–1.30pm • €3 • ⊛tortosaturisme.cat

Tortosa's brightest point is also its highest. **La Suda**, the old castle, sits perched above the Catedral, glowering from behind its battlements at the Ebre valley below and the mountains beyond. Like so many in Spain, the castle has been converted into a luxury parador, but there's nothing to stop you climbing up for a magnificent view from the walls, or from going into the plush bar and having a drink.

The **Jardins del Príncep**, which sit at the base of the castle, feature an impressive collection of sculptures of the human figure by Santiago de Santiago.

ARRIVAL AND INFORMATION   TORTOSA

By train Tortosa is connected by regular trains to Barcelona (2hr) and Tarragona (1hr).

By bus Buses run from Tortosa to Vinaròs (in Castellón province to the south), from where you can reach the wonderful inland mountain town of Morella; and to Tarragona and the Delta de l'Ebre area.

Turisme Jardins del Príncep (May to mid-Sept Tues–Sat 10am–1.30pm & 4.30–7.30pm, Sun 11am–1.30pm; mid-Sept to April 10am–1.30pm & 3.30–6.30pm, Sun 11am–1.30pm; ☏977 442 005, ⊛tortosaturisme.cat).

WINE TOURING IN THE PRIORAT

Around 35km west of Tarragona lies one of Spain's emerging wine regions, the **Priorat**, which was awarded its DOC in 2001. The red wine produced here, and in the adjacent Montsany DOC, is highly sought after, and the *cellers* have started to follow their more established competitors in La Rioja by cashing in with wine tours and tastings. The *turisme* in Tarragona has up-to-date information, or you can try the local office in Falset (Mon–Fri 9am–3pm & 4–7pm, Sat 10am–2pm, Sun 11am–2pm; ☏977 831 023, ⊛turismepriorat.org). Most tours cost €5–7, and many have English-speaking guides – reservations are essential.

La Conreria de Scala Dei C/Mitja Galta 32, Scala Dei, just south of La Morera de Montsant ☏977 827 027, ⊛vinslaconreria.com. This established winery, named after the Carthusian monks of Scala Dei, offers tours through its cellars and vineyards followed by tastings. Book tours in advance. Tours €10. Mon–Fri 11am–5pm, Sat & Sun 11am–2pm.

Costers del Siurana Camí Manyetes, Gratallops ☏977 839 276, ⊛costersdelsiurana.com. This highly regarded winery offers tours through the cellars, and also runs the charming, small *Cellers de Gratallops* restaurant nearby, which serves regional cuisine – and Priorat wine, of course. Call or email ahead to enquire about tour hours and prices.

11

THE WINE CATHEDRAL

The name says it all: The Bodega Pagos de Híbera **Catedral del Vi** (Wine Cathedral; C/Pilonet, ☎977 426 234, ⊛catedraldelvi.com; €4.80; Mon–Sat 10am–6pm, Sun 10am–8pm) rises over Pinell de Brai, roughly 30km north of Tortosa, in the Terra Alta region, which is Catalunya's southernmost wine region. Designed by Gaudí disciple Cèsar Martinell, the winery is a magnificent tribute to *modernisme*, revealing its architectural hallmarks, from soaring stone arches to colourful tiling. The winery offers self-guided audio tours and wine and olive-oil tastings, as well as free guided visits at noon and 5pm on the weekends. Make a day of it, and sample local cuisine – and Pagos de Híbera wine – at the stately restaurant (open Sat–Sun for lunch only), which serves an excellent menu (€25). Dishes include grilled octopus and traditional Catalan sausage, followed by choice desserts – try the luscious *crema Catalana*. Northwest of Pinell de Brai lies the town of Gandesa, the capital of the Terra Alta wine region, and home to the **Celler Cooperatiu de Gandesa** (Avgda. Catalunya 28, ☎977 420 017, ⊛coopgandesa.com; Mon–Sat 9am–1pm & 3–7pm, Sun 9am–2pm), another magnificent building also designed by Martinell.

ACCOMMODATION AND EATING

Hotel Rural Panxampla Carretera d'Alfara, 7km west of Tortosa in the hamlet of Els Reguers ☎977 474 135, ⊛hotelruralpanxampla.com. For a taste of the Tortosa countryside, try this comfortable *hotel rural* with elegant rooms with stone walls and wood-beam ceilings. The rustic restaurant serves Catalan cuisine. Breakfast included. **€100**

Parador Nacional Castell de la Suda ☎977 444 450, ⊛www.parador.es. For a splurge, it's well worth opting for this splendid parador, where you'll feel like you've stepped into the medieval era. It also has one of the better restaurants in town, open to nonguests and specializing in fish from the Ebro delta. **€110**

La Torreta de Remolins C/David Ferrando 4, ☎977 441 893, ⊛latorretaremolins.com. Dine on traditional Catalan cuisine, from grilled meats and fish to rice dishes and salads. The wine list is culled from the Terra Alta region, including superb reds. Dishes €10–20. Mon–Thurs 1–4pm, Fri–Sat 1–4pm & 8.30–10pm.

The Delta de l'Ebre

In the bottom corner of Catalunya is the **Delta de l'Ebre** (Ebro Delta), 320 square kilometres of sandy delta constituting the biggest wetland in Catalunya and one of the most important aquatic habitats in the western Mediterranean. Designated a natural park, its brackish lagoons, marshes, dunes and reed beds are home to thousands of wintering birds and provide excellent fishing; around fifteen percent of the total Catalan catch comes from this area. The scenery is unique in Catalunya, with low roads running through field after field of rice paddies, punctuated by solitary houses and small villages, before emerging onto dune-lined beaches. Since much of the area of the **Parc Natural de Delta de l'Ebre** is a protected zone, access is limited, and it's best to visit with your own transport. Check in with the well-stocked tourist office about birdwatching opportunities and other nature tours and treks.

Deltebre

The best place to start to get a good sense of Delta de l'Ebre is the town of **DELTEBRE**, at the centre of the delta, 30km from Tortosa. There's also an interesting **Ecomuseum**, in the park information centre (Mon–Sat 10am–2pm & 3–7pm, Sun 10am–2pm, until 6pm in winter, Sun 10am–2pm; €1.20), which has an aquarium displaying species found in the delta.

Riumar

The town of **RIUMAR**, 10km east of Deltebre, also makes for a good base to explore the area. It has a couple of restaurants and good, if windy, bathing on a sandy beach, connected to the road by duckboards winding through the dunes, and more remote beaches accessible to the north.

INFORMATION AND TOURS

Park information centre Martí Buera 22, on the main highway, on the edge of Deltebre (Mon–Sat 10am–2pm & 3–7pm, Sun 10am–2pm, until 6pm in winter; ☎977 489 679, ⊚deltebre.net). The well-signposted information centre can provide you with a map of the delta and has information about tours and local walks.

River cruises A river cruise is a good way to experience

DELTA DE L'EBRE

the delta. Several boat companies, including Creuers Delta de l'Ebre (☎977 480 128, creuersdeltaebre.com), the Santa Sussanna (☎629 204 117) and Olmos (☎977 48 05 48) operate trips of an hour or so on the river. Enquire at the tourist office or call ahead, because the boats sometimes only operate for groups; prices start at around €9/trip.

ACCOMMODATION AND EATING

Casa Núri Final Goles de Ebre, Riumar ☎977 480 128, ⊚restaurantnuri.com. Dine on a wide range of seafood, from shrimp to mussels, as well as the local speciality, *arròs a banda* – similar to paella except that the rice is brought before the seafood. Dishes €13–25. Daily 10am–10.30pm; lunch only in winter.

Delta Hotel Avgda. del Canal, on the outskirts of Deltebre towards Riumar ☎977 480 046, ⊚deltahotel. net. This comfortable hotel has well-cared-for, rustic

rooms, some with wood-beam ceilings, as well as a breezy garden. **€90**

Mediterrani Blau C/l'Eucaliptus, 11km south of Deltebre towards the sea ☎977 479 079, ⊚mediterraniblau.com. This blocky, white hotel is filled with modern if rather impersonal rooms, and a restaurant serving local seafood, duck and rice dishes. Hotel & restaurant usually closed Nov–Feb. **€95**

11

Montblanc

The walled medieval town of **MONTBLANC**, 8km before the turning to the monastery at Poblet, is a surprisingly beautiful place to discover in the middle of nowhere. The Pza. Major is picturesque, and livens up for the evening *passeig*, while there are many fine little Romanesque and Gothic monuments contained within the town's tight circle of old streets; all are marked on the map in front of the town's medieval gateway, the **Torre-portal de Bové**, which is just 100m or so up from the train station. On the southern side of the walls, the **Torre-portal de Sant Jordi** marks the spot where San Jordi, or St George (patron saint of Catalunya as well as England), slew the dragon, an event commemorated with a fiesta on April 23.

Santa Maria la Major

Pza. Major • Mon–Sat 11am–1pm & 4–6pm, Sun 11am–2pm • Free • ☎977 860 110

Just above the central Pza. Major, stands the grand Gothic parish church of **Santa Maria la Major**; its elaborate facade has lions' faces on either side of the main doorway and cherubs swarming up the pillars. There's a fine view from the once fortified mound that rises behind the church (known as the Pla de Santa Bàrbara) over the rooftops, defensive towers and walls, and away across the plain.

Sant Miquel

Pza. St Miquel • Open only as part of a guided tour • Free

East from Santa Maria along C/Major, the church of **Sant Miquel** dates from the fourteenth century, and has Romanesque and Gothic elements, an impressive coffered ceiling and lovely Gothic lateral chapels. The church was the seat of the Catalan courts from 1307 to 1370.

Museu Comarcal de la Conca de Barberà

Just off Pza. Major • Tues–Sat 10am–2pm & 4–7pm, Sun 10am–2pm • Free or nominal fee (varies) • ☎977 860 349, ⊚concadebarbera.info

This fine local **history museum**, set in a medieval home dating from the thirteenth century, has well-curated exhibits on the history and culture of the region, including on the art of glassmaking, and features a reproduction of an old chemist's shop.

11

ARRIVAL AND INFORMATION

By bus Regular trains and buses connect Montblanc to Tarragona (50min) and Lleida (50min).

Turisme At the eastern end of C/Major (Mon–Sat 10am–1.30pm & 3–6.30pm, Sun 10am–2pm; ☎977 861

733, ⊛montblancmedieval.cat). Helpful *turisme* in the old church of Sant Francesc, just outside the walls. They offer guided tours of medieval Montblanc (€5, including a glass of cava).

ACCCOMMODATION

Fonda Cal Blasi C/Alenyà 11–13 ☎977 861 336, ⊛fondacalblasi.com. This warm and friendly *fonda* is in a restored nineteenth-century stone townhouse, just a short

walk from Pza. Major. They also serve home-cooked meals rooted in seasonal produce, along with local wines from Conca de Barberà. **€75**

The Monestir de Poblet

Mid-March to mid-Oct Mon–Sat 10am–12.30pm & 3–5.55pm, Sun 10.30am–12.25pm & 3–5.25pm; mid-Oct to mid-March Mon–Sat 10am–12.30pm & 3–5.25pm, Sun 10.30am–12.25pm & 3–5.25pm • €7.50; €10 with guided tour • ☎977 870 254, ⊛poblet.cat

There are few ruins more stirring than the **Monestir de Poblet**, lying in glorious open country, vast and sprawling within massive battlemented walls and towered gateways. Once *the* great monastery of Catalunya, it was in effect a complete manorial village and enjoyed scarcely credible rights, powers and wealth. Founded in 1151 by Ramón Berenguer IV, who united the kingdoms of Catalunya and Aragón, it was planned from the beginning on an immensely grand scale. The kings of Aragón-Catalunya chose to be buried in its chapel and for three centuries diverted huge sums for its endowment, a munificence that was inevitably corrupting. By the late Middle Ages Poblet had become a byword for decadence – there are lewder stories about this than any other Cistercian monastery – and so it continued, hated by the local peasantry, until the Carlist revolution of 1835 when a mob burned and tore it apart. The monastery was repopulated by Italian Cistercians in 1940 and over the decades since then it's been subject to continual – and superb – maintenance and restoration.

The cloisters

As so often, the **cloisters**, focus of monastic life, are the most evocative and beautiful part. Late Romanesque, and sporting a pavilion and fountain, they open onto a series of rooms: a splendid Gothic **chapterhouse** (with the former abbots' tombs set in the floor), wine cellars, a parlour, a **kitchen** equipped with ranges and copper pots, and a sombre, wood-panelled **refectory**.

The chapel

Beyond, you enter the **chapel** in which the twelfth- and thirteenth-century tombs of the kings of Aragón have been meticulously restored by Frederico Marès, the manic collector of Barcelona. They lie in marble sarcophagi on either side of the nave, focusing attention on the central sixteenth-century altarpiece.

The dormitory

You'll also be shown the vast old **dormitory**, to which there's direct access from the chapel choir, a poignant reminder of Cistercian discipline. From the dormitory (half of which is sealed off since it's still in use), a door leads out onto the cloister roof for views down into the cloister itself and up the chapel towers.

ARRIVAL AND INFORMATION

By bus Two to three buses a day (Mon–Sat) run to Poblet from Tarragona or Lleida, passing right by the monastery. It's an easy day-trip from either city.

By train By train, you get off at the ruined station of

L'Espluga de Francolí, from where it's a beautiful 3km walk to the monastery, much of it along a signposted country track. Since it lies on the same line, it's easy enough to combine a trip to Poblet with a stop-off at Montblanc.

Turisme Pg. Abat Conill 9, Poblet (summer Tues–Sat 10am–1.30pm & 3–6pm, Sun 10am–2pm; winter Tues–Fri 10am–2pm & 2.30–5pm, Sat 10am–1.30pm & 3–6.30pm, Sun 10am–2pm; ☎ 977 871 247).

ACCOMMODATION AND EATING

Staying overnight at **Poblet** is an attractive proposition if you have your own transport, since it makes a good base for excursion into the surrounding countryside. A kilometre up the road from Poblet, around the walls, the hamlet of **Les Masies** has a couple of hotels and restaurants, while **L'Espluga**, 2km northwest, also has a few places to stay.

★ **Hospedería del Monasterio de Poblet** Poblet ☎ 977 871 201, ⊛ www.poblet.cat. For the full monastic experience, stay at the lovely *hospedería*, opened in 2010, which rises up alongside the monastery. Designed by Spanish architect Mariano Bayón, the building blends harmoniously with its surroundings, featuring honey-hued stone, a cloister and a courtyard planted with olive trees. The monastic philosophy extends to all parts of the *hospedería*, which is quiet and soothing, with no TVs in the simply furnished rooms. Guests are invited to participate in the monastery's liturgy and services, and the restaurant even serves dishes inspired by historical monastic menus,

like cod with *allioli de membrillo* (quince). Mains €15–25. Breakfast included. Daily 1–4pm & 8–11pm. **€90**

Hostal del Senglar Pza. Montserrat Canals, L'Espluga de Francolí ☎ 977 870 121, ⊛ hostaldelsenglar.com. This welcoming *hostal* has cosy, comfortable rooms and a charming garden which features tiled benches and towering trees. **€79**

Villa Engràcia Carretera de les Masies, Les Masies ☎ 977 870 308, ⊛ villaengracia.com. This attractive former spa built in 1888, set in pleasant, leafy grounds, has elegant, well-outfitted rooms, an outdoor pool and tennis courts. **€155**

Prades

If you have time and transport, a couple of excursions into the countryside surrounding Poblet are well worth making. The red-stone walled village of **PRADES**, in the Serra de Prades, 20km from the monastery, is a beautifully sited and tranquil place that needs no other excuse for a visit. It's also the place to be during the second weekend of July, when they replace the water in the fountain with cava, and you can join in and help yourself – or order a bottle of bubbly at a terrace bar in the porticoed *plaça* and enjoy the scene. The area around Poblet is also home to two more twelfth-century Cistercian monasteries.

Reial Monestir de Santes Creus

Daily 10am–5pm, June–Sept till 6.30pm • €4.50 • ⊛ larutadelcister.info

The **Reial Monestir de Santes Creus** lies 7km north of the Barcelona–Lleida highway, and is clearly signposted. It's built in Transitional style, with a grand Gothic cloister and some Romanesque traces, and you can explore the dormitory, chapterhouse and main church.

Monestir de Vallbona de les Monges

Sat 10.30am–1.30pm & 4.30–6.30pm, Sun noon–1.30pm & 4.30–6.30pm; Nov–Feb closes 5.30pm • €4 • ⊛ larutadelcister.info

The **Monestir de Vallbona de les Monges** is about 16km north of Poblet, and reached via Montblanc. This monastery of *monges* (nuns) has been occupied continuously for over 800 years. The church, built over the twelfth to fourteenth centuries, is a particularly noteworthy example of the transition between Romanesque and Gothic, and has a rectangular nave and elegant cloisters.

Lleida

LLEIDA (Lérida), at the heart of a fertile plain in inland Catalunya, has a rich history. First a *municipium* under the Roman Empire and later the centre of a small Arab kingdom, it was reconquered by the Catalans and became the seat of a bishopric in 1149. Little of those periods survives in today's city but there is one building of

11

outstanding interest, the old Catedral, which is sufficient justification in itself to visit. Several interesting museums and a steep set of old-town streets will easily occupy any remaining time. Rooms are easy to come by, and the students at the local university fill the streets and bars on weekend evenings, including at the breezy Pza. de Sant Joan, in good-natured throngs.

Seu Vella and Castillo del Rey

Catedral Summer Tues–Sat 10am–7.30pm, Sun 10am–3pm; winter Tues–Fri 10am–1.30 & 3–5.30pm, Sat 10am–5.30pm, Sun 10am–3pm; last entry 30min before closing • ⓦ turoseuvella.cat • **Castillo del Rey** Summer Tues–Sat 10.30am–2pm & 4–7.30pm, Sun 10am–3pm; winter Tues–Sat 10am–1.30pm & 3–5.30pm, Sun 10am–3pm; last entry 30min before closing • €7 for Catedral and castle

The **Seu Vella**, or old Catedral, is enclosed within the walls of the ruined Castillo del Rey (also called La Suda), high above the Ríu Segre, a twenty-minute climb from the centre of town. It's a peculiar fortified building, which in 1707 was deconsecrated and taken over by the military, remaining in their hands until 1940. Enormous damage was inflicted over the years but the church remains a notable example of the Transitional style, similar in many respects to the Catedral of Tarragona. The Gothic cloisters are masterly, each walk comprising arches different in size and shape but sharing delicate stone tracery. They served the military as a canteen and kitchen. You can also visit parts of the reconstructed **castle**, such as the fortified walls – the views from the walls over the plain are stupendous.

Seu Nova

Mon–Fri 9.30am–1pm & 5.30–7.30pm, Sat & Sun 9.30am–1pm & 5.30–8.30pm • Free

You can climb back down from the old Catedral towards the river by way of the new Catedral, **La Seu Nova**. It's an austere eighteenth-century building with Neoclassical doorways, a main facade topped by a large crest of the Casa de Borbón and a series of minuscule, high stained-glass windows.

Museu de Lleida

C/Sant Crist 1 • June–Sept Tues–Thurs & Sat 10am–2pm & 4–7pm, Fri & Sun 10am–2pm; Oct–May Tues–Thurs & Sat 10am–2pm & 4–6pm, Fri & Sun 10am–2pm • €4 • ☎ 973 28 30 75, ⓦ museudelleida.cat

The spacious **Museu de Lleida** is the city's flagship museum. Two floors show off ancient finds from throughout Lleida and Catalunya, including Romanesque altarpieces, a Visigoth baptismal font and stone sculptures from the Seu Vella.

Centre d'Art La Panera

Pza. de la Panera 2 • Aug–June Tues–Fri 10am–2pm & 4–7pm, Sat 11am–2pm & 5–8pm, Sun 11am–2pm; July Tues–Fri 10am–2pm & 5–8pm, Sat 11am–2pm & 5–8pm, Sun 11am–2pm • Free • ☎ 973 262 185, ⓦ lapanera.cat

For top-notch exhibits of contemporary art, check out the creative **Centre d'Art La Panera**. The building's history is as interesting as the art inside: it dates back to the twelfth century, when it was Lleida's trading exchange and market, and you can still see evidence of its medieval roots in the original colonnade, made up of a line of 21 stone columns. In the early 1600s, the building was acquired by the canonry of the Catedral, who used it to store and sell food products – hence its official name, La Panera dels Canonges, or The Canons' Pantry.

ARRIVAL AND INFORMATION   LLEIDA

By train Trains regularly connect Lleida to Barcelona via Valls or Reus/Tarragona (17 daily; 2hr–4hr 15min, AVE 1hr). There are also services to: La Pobla de Segur (3 daily; 2hr 10min); Tarragona (8 daily; 1hr 30min–2hr); and Zaragoza (20 daily; 1hr 50min). For current timetables and ticket information, consult RENFE (☎ 902 240 202, ⓦ renfe.es). It's a 15–20min walk east of the train station to Pza. de Sant Joan.

By bus Lleida has regular buses to Barcelona (Mon–Sat 10 daily, Sun 4 daily; 2hr 15min); Huesca (5 daily; 2hr 30min); La Seu d'Urgell (2 daily; 3hr); Montblanc (6 daily; 1hr 30min); La Pobla de Segur (daily; 2hr); Poblet (Mon–Sat 3 daily; 1hr 15min); Tarragona (3 daily; 2hr); Vielha, via Túnel de Vielha (2 daily; 3hr); and Zaragoza (Mon–Sat 6 daily, Sun 2; 2hr 30min). It's a 15–20min walk west of the bus station, down Avgda. de Blondel, to Pza. de Sant Joan.

By plane The Lleida-Alguaire airport (☎973 032 700, ⓦaeroportlleida.cat) 15km northwest of Lleida, is a regional hub. UK charter flights also occasionally fly here, ferrying skiers to the Pyrenees.

Turisme C/Mayor 31 (Mon–Sat 10am–2pm & 4–7pm, Sun 10am–2pm; ☎973 700 402, ⓦturismedelleida.cat).

ACCOMMODATION AND EATING

There are a couple of **places to stay** right outside the train station, and more along Rambla Ferran, which leads into the centre. Otherwise, there are several options around central Pza. Sant Joan.

Lleida is famous for its **snails**, roasted over a wood fire with peppers and garlic (*caragols a la llauna*). The streets north of the church of Sant Martí hold a range of restaurants; this is where the students come to eat and hang out at the loud **music-bars** along the block formed by C/Sant Martí, C/Camp de Mart, C/Balmes and Avgda. Prat de la Riba.

El Celler del Roser C/Cavallers 24 ☎973 239 070. One of the better spots to sample the celebrated snails is at this amiable, mid-priced restaurant, with wood tables and exposed brick. There's a strong local wine list. Mon–Sat 1–4pm & 8.30–11pm.

Ferreruela C/Bobalà 8 ☎973 221 159, ⓦferreruela .com. Showcasing *cocina de la terra* (local cuisine), this jovial restaurant serves an excellent range, including Lleida's signature snails with *alioli*, grilled cod with *samfaina* (ratatouille) and juicy lamb. Plus, as part of the dessert menu, they offer an excellent assortment of local cheeses. Dishes €15–25. Wed–Sat 1–4pm & 8–11pm, Sun 1–4pm.

Hotel Real Avgda. Blondel 22 ☎973 239 405, ⓦhotelreallleida.com. One of the more comfortable hotels in the old town, in a great location facing the river. Rooms have a simple, modern design and come with tiled bathrooms. €75

Hotel Sansi Lleida C/Alcade Porqueras 4–6 ☎973 244 000, ⓦsansihotels.com. Handsome hotel on the north side of the old town with hassle-free parking and plenty of bars nearby. €65

11

Valencia
and Murcia

PEÑÍSCOLA

Valencia and Murcia

Named "El Levante" after the rising sun, this lush region is the part of Spain that wakes up first. Valencia has the Mediterranean Sea as its front yard, while the inland *huerta* is one of the most fertile in Europe, crowded with orange and lemon groves, date-palm plantations and rice fields still irrigated by systems devised by the Moors. Paella originated in these parts, and a juicy orange is named after Valencia. Evidence of the lengthy Moorish occupation can be seen throughout, in the castles, crops and place names – Benidorm, Alicante and Alcoy are all derived from Arabic. The region also encompasses the historical Murcia, which offers a fascinating contrast to the sun-and-sand debauchery on the water. Explored from one end to the other, this is a land of ancient and modern, of beauty and beastliness.

The growing self-assurance of the region is evident in the increasing presence of Valenciano – a dialect of Catalan – which challenges Castilian as the main language of education and broadcasting in the area. There are even a few extreme trains of thought that challenge the dialect's Catalan origins, but those beliefs have remained largely on the margins.

Murcia's province is quite distinct, a *comunidad autónoma* in its own right, and there could hardly be a more severe contrast with the richness of the Valencian *huerta*. This southeastern corner of Spain is virtually a desert and is some of the driest territory in Europe. It was fought over for centuries by Phoenicians, Greeks, Carthaginians and Romans, but there survives almost no physical evidence of their presence – or of five hundred years of Moorish rule, beyond an Arabic feel to some of the small towns and the odd date palm here and there. The province's capital city of **Murcia**, with its lovely Catedral and terrace tapas bars, makes for a comfortable base for exploring the region.

Much of the **coast** is marred by heavy overdevelopment, with concrete apartment blocks and sprawling holiday complexes looming over many of the best beaches. However, away from the big resorts, particularly around **Denia** and **Xàbia** (Jávea) in Valencia, there are some attractive isolated coves, while the historic hilltop settlements of **Altea** and **Peñíscola** are undeniably picturesque, if touristy. In Murcia, the resorts of the **Mar Menor** are reasonably attractive and very popular with Spanish families in high season; the best beaches are in the extreme south, around **Águilas**, where you'll find some dazzling unspoilt coves. The increasingly vibrant cities of **Valencia** and **Alicante** are the major urban centres, and there are several delightful historic small towns and villages a short way inland, such as **Morella**, **Xàtiva** and **Lorca**.

The Valencia area has a powerful tradition of **fiestas**, and there are a couple of

MORELLA

Highlights

❶ La Ciudad de las Artes y Ciencias Europe's largest cultural centre and the architectural definition of Valencia: progressive, playful, breathtaking. **See p.797**

❷ Las Fallas Witness giant effigies going up in an explosion of flames – this is one of Spain's most famous festivals. **See p.802**

❸ Horchata Cool your throat with a chilled glass of Valencia's own tiger-nut shake. **See p.809**

❹ Paella Feast on Spain's most iconic dish in its birthplace. **See p.812**

❺ Festival Benicàssim Huge annual music festival featuring the biggest names in alternative pop. **See p.817**

❻ Morella Step into medieval Spain in this fortified town crowned by a fairy-tale castle. **See p.819**

❼ Alicante A city that seems to capture the Mediterranean: elegant esplanades, *sangría* at terrace cafés, and silky-sand beaches. **See p.827**

❽ Cuatro calas Águilas' gorgeous cove beaches offer an inviting blend of sun, sea and, on some stretches in low season, solitude. **See p.843**

HIGHLIGHTS ARE MARKED ON THE MAP ON P.794

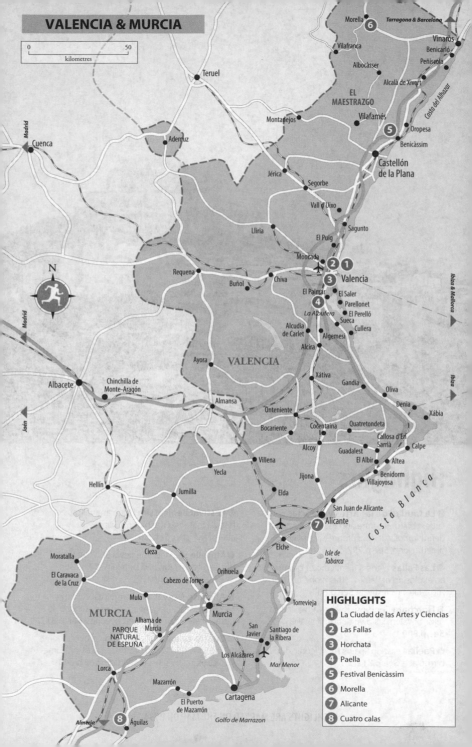

VALENCIA & MURCIA

0 ——— 50
kilometres

Tarragona & Barcelona

Morella **6**

Vilafranca

Vinaròs

Benicarló

Albocàsser

Peñíscola

Alcalà de Xivert

EL MAESTRAZGO

Vilafamés

Montanejos

Costa de Alhazor

5 Oropesa

Benicàssim

Teruel

Castellón de la Plana

Ademuz

Jérica

Segorbe

Vall d'Uixó

Cuenca

Sagunto

Lliria

El Puig

Moncada

Madrid

Requena

Chiva

2 **1**

Buñol

3 Valencia

El Palmar

El Saler

Parellonet

4

El Perelló

La Albufera

Sueca

Alcudia de Carlet

Algemesí

Cullera

Alcira

Ayora

VALENCIA

Xàtiva

Albacete

Chinchilla de Monte-Aragón

Gandía

Oliva

Almansa

Onteniente

Denia

Ibiza & Mallorca

Ibiza

Xàbia

Jaén

Bocariente

Cocentaina

Quatretondeta

Callosa d'En Sarrià

Alcoy

Guadalest

Calpe

Villena

El Albir

Altea

Jijona

Benidorm

Yecla

Villajoyosa

Hellín

Jumilla

Elda

San Juan de Alicante

7 Alicante

Costa Blanca

Moratalla

Cieza

Elche

Isle de Tabarca

Caravaca de la Cruz

El

Cabezo de Torres

Orihuela

Mula

Murcia

Torrevieja

MURCIA

Alhama de Murcia

San Javier

Santiago de la Ribera

PARQUE NATURAL DE ESPUÑA

Los Alcázares

Mar Menor

Lorca

Mazarrón

Almería

8 Águilas

El Puerto de Mazarrón

Cartagena

Golfo de Marrazon

HIGHLIGHTS

1 La Ciudad de las Artes y Ciencias

2 Las Fallas

3 Horchata

4 Paella

5 Festival Benicàssim

6 Morella

7 Alicante

8 Cuatro calas

VALENCIAN CUISINE

Gastronomy is of great cultural importance to the Valencians. Rice is the dominant ingredient in dishes of the region, grown locally in paddy fields still irrigated by the Moorish canal system (*acequias*). Gourmets tend to agree that the best **paellas** are to be found around (but not *in*) Valencia, the city where the dish originated. The genuine version doesn't mix fish and meat – it typically contains chicken, rabbit, green beans, *garrofón* (large butter beans), snails, artichokes and saffron – and should be prepared fresh and cooked over wood (*leña*), not scooped from some vast, sticky vat; most places will make it for a minimum of two people, with advance notice.

Other **rice-based dishes** vary around the region: *arroz negro* is rice cooked with squid complete with ink, which gives the dish its colour, and served with *aioli*, a strong garlic mayonnaise. *Arroz al horno* is drier, baked with chickpeas. *Fideuà* is seafood and noodles cooked paella-style. The most famous, *arroz a banda*, is found on the south coast around Denia – it's rice cooked with seafood, served as two separate dishes: soup, then rice. Around Alicante, you can try *arroz con costra*, which is a meat-based paella topped with a baked egg crust. Apart from rice, **vegetables** (best *a la plancha*, brushed with olive oil and garlic) are always fresh and plentiful.

The sweet-toothed should try **turrón** (see box, p.832), a nuts-and-honey nougat, which you could follow with a **horchata**, or *orxata*, (see box, p.809), a rich drink made from tiger nuts (*chufas*) or almonds (*almendras*).

elements unique to this part of the country. Above all, throughout the year and more or less wherever you go, there are mock battles between Muslims and Christians (*Moros y Cristianos*). Recalling the Christian Reconquest of the country – whether through symbolic processions or re-creations of specific battles – they are some of the most elaborate and colourful festivities to be seen anywhere, especially in Alcoy (see box, p.826). The other recurring feature is the *fallas* (bonfires) in which giant carnival floats and figures are paraded through the streets before being ceremoniously burned.

Getting around by public transport is relatively straightforward as there are frequent train and bus services, though you'll need your own transport to really explore the area. The motorway network is excellent, but tolls are quite pricey.

Valencia

For many, **VALENCIA**'s enviable perch on the Mediterranean would be enough of a draw. Not so for the city itself: Valencia has been reinventing itself at a heady pace, and shows no signs of slowing down. Well on the way to equalling – indeed, eclipsing in some instances – the cosmopolitan vitality of Barcelona and the cultural variety of Madrid, Spain's third-largest city has finally shaken off its slightly provincial former reputation. The vast, iconic **La Ciudad de las Artes y Ciencias** cultural complex was completed in 2005, the state-of-the-art metro is still expanding and dozens of hip new bars, restaurants and boutiques have injected new life into the historic centre. Valencia has also fully redeveloped its beach and port area, in part sparked by its hosting of prestigious yachting jamboree, the America's Cup. Nevertheless, despite its size and *stylista* cachet, Valencia retains an unpretentious if tangibly charged air.

Always an important city, Valencia was fought over for the agricultural wealth of its surrounding *huerta*. After Romans and Visigoths, it was occupied by the Moors for over four centuries with only a brief interruption (1094–1101) when **El Cid** recaptured it. He died here in 1099, but his body, propped on a horse and led out through the gates, was still enough to cause the Moorish armies – previously encouraged by news of his death – to flee in terror. It wasn't until 1238 that Jaime I of Aragón permanently wrested Valencia back. It has remained one of Spain's largest and richest cities ever since.

Valencia has long boasted some of the best **nightlife** in mainland Spain. *Vivir Sin Dormir* (Live Without Sleep) is the name of one of its bars, and it could be taken as a Valencian mantra. The city is alive with noise and colour throughout the year, with

12

FIESTAS

FEBRUARY

Week before Lent: Carnaval Águilas' *Carnaval* is one of the wildest in the country. Vinaròs also has good *Carnaval* celebrations.

MARCH/APRIL

March 12–19: Las Fallas de San José Valencia's Las Fallas (see box, p.802) is by far the biggest of the bonfire festivals, and indeed one of the most important fiestas in all Spain. The whole thing costs over €1 million, most of which goes up in smoke (literally) on the final *Nit de Foc* when the grotesque papier-mâché caricatures are burned.

March 19: Día de San José Smaller *fallas* festivals in Xàtiva, Benidorm and Denia.

Third Sunday of Lent: Fiesta de la Magdalena Castellón de la Plana celebrates the end of Moorish rule with pilgrimages and processions of huge floats.

Semana Santa (Holy Week) In Elche, there are, naturally, big Palm Sunday celebrations making use of the local palms, while throughout the week there are also religious processions in Cartagena, Lorca, Orihuela and Valencia. The **Easter processions** in Murcia are particularly famous, and they continue into the following week with, on the Tuesday, the Bando de la Huerta, a huge parade of floats celebrating local agriculture, and, on the Saturday evening, the riotous "Burial of the Sardine" which marks the end of these spring festivals.

April 22–24: Moros y Cristianos After a colourful procession in Alcoy, a huge battle commences between the two sides in the main square.

MAY

1–5: Fiestas de los Mayos *Fiesta* in Alhama de Murcia, and Moros y Cristianos in Caravaca de la Cruz.

Second Sunday: La Virgen de los Desamparados The climax of this celebration in Valencia is when the statue of the Virgin is transferred from her basilica to the Catedral.

Third Sunday: Moros y Cristianos In Altea.

JUNE

23–24: Hogueras de San Juan Magnificent festival in Alicante with processions and fireworks, culminating as huge effigies and bonfires are burnt in the streets at midnight. It's

explosions of gunpowder, fireworks and festivities punctuating the calendar. Valencia's **fiestas** are some of the most riotous in Spain and the best is Las Fallas (see box, p.802).

The most atmospheric area of the city is undoubtedly the maze-like **Barrio del Carmen** (in Valenciano "de Carmé"), roughly north of the Mercado Central to the Río Turia, extending up to the Torres de Serranos and west to the Torres de Quart. This once-neglected quarter continues to undergo regeneration, as buildings are renovated and stylish cafés open up next to crumbling townhouses, all of which makes for an incredibly vibrant, alternative neighbourhood. The **city walls**, which, judging from the two surviving gates, must have been magnificent, were pulled down in 1871 to make way for a ring road, and the beautiful church of **Santo Domingo**, in Pza. de Tetuan, has been converted into a barracks – it was from here that General Milans del Bosch ordered his tanks onto the streets during the abortive coup of 1981. This incident, however, isn't representative of the city's political inclination, which has traditionally been to the left – Valencia was the seat of the Republican government during the Civil War after it fled Madrid, and was the last city to fall to Franco.

The oldest part of Valencia is almost entirely encircled by a great loop of the **Río Turia**, which is now a landscaped **riverbed park**. In 1956, after serious flooding damaged much of the old town, the river was diverted. The ancient stone bridges remain, but the riverbed now houses cycle ways, footpaths and football pitches, as well as the astonishing Ciudad de las Artes y Ciencias, Europe's largest cultural complex. As further proof that Valencia is ever reinventing itself, the city's Central Park, a 57-acre

celebrated on a smaller scale on the beaches of Valencia (Malvarossa, Cabanyal and Aloboraya) with bonfire-jumping. Altea also celebrates with a popular tree-bearing procession and a bonfire in the old town.

JULY

Early July: Fiestas de la Santísima Sangre Dancing in the streets of Denia, plus music and mock battles.
15–20: Moros y Cristianos In Orihuela.
Second week: Feria de Julio Valencia hosts music, bullfights and above all fireworks, ending with the Battle of the Flowers in the Alameda.
Penultimate weekend: FIB Benicàssim's international music festival, a massive party bringing together the major names in alternative and electronic music.
25–31: Moros y Cristianos Villajoyosa sees battles by both land and sea.

AUGUST

4: Festa del Cristo de la Salut Festival in El Palmar with processions by boat into the lake.
Mid-August: Misteri d'Eix Elche presents a mystery play, based on a drama dating back to medieval times.
14–20: Feria de Agosto Xàtiva's fair has a very extensive cultural dimension including concerts, plays and exhibitions, plus bullfights and barrages of fireworks.
15: Local festivities in Denia.
Last week: La Tomatina (see box, p.813) A riotous free-for-all of tomato-throwing takes place in Buñol on the last Wednesday of the month. There's also a music festival in Morella.
Last Wednesday: Local fiesta in Sagunto, and at the same time the great Moros y Cristianos festival and a mystery play in Elche.

SEPTEMBER

4–9: Moros y Cristianos In Villena.
Second week: Bull-running through Segorbe's streets.
8–9: Les Danses Celebrations in Peñíscola's old quarter include a human tower construction.
22: Fiesta de Santo Tomás In Benicàssim with bands and a "blazing bull".

OCTOBER

Second Sunday: La Virgen de Suffrage Benidorm celebrates its patron saint's day.

space for promenades, gardens and an art centre, is one of Valenica's – if not Spain's – largest redevelopment projects to date.

Valencia's main beach is the **Playa de la Malvarrosa** to the east of the city centre, which becomes **Playa de las Arenas** at its southern end.

La Ciudad de las Artes y las Ciencias

Avda. Autopista del Saler • ☎ 902 100 031, ⓦ cac.es • Ⓜ Alameda (15min walk); buses #13, #14 and #35 from Carrer Roger de Lloria, just south of the Pza. del Ayuntamiento, or bus #95 at the Torres de Serrano; if you drive, you can park at the Umbracle car park (€2.30/hr, €24/day)

More than any other project, the breathtaking **Ciudad de las Artes y las Ciencias** (City of Arts and Sciences, or CAC), rising from the riverbed, symbolizes the autonomous government's vision for Valencia and its quest to establish the city as a prime tourist destination. The giant complex consists of a series of futuristic edifices designed mainly by Valencian architect Santiago Calatrava.

The architecture itself is simply stunning. Even if you only have a day or two in the city, it's well worth the effort getting here to take in the eye-catching buildings surrounded by huge, shallow pools. Calatrava's designs adopt an organic form, his technical and engineering brilliance providing the basis for his pioneering concrete, steel and glass creations. However, despite near-universal acclaim for its architecture, the complex has not completely escaped criticism. Some feel that the vast cost of constructing it should have been used to tackle the city's pressing social issues, while

VALENCIA

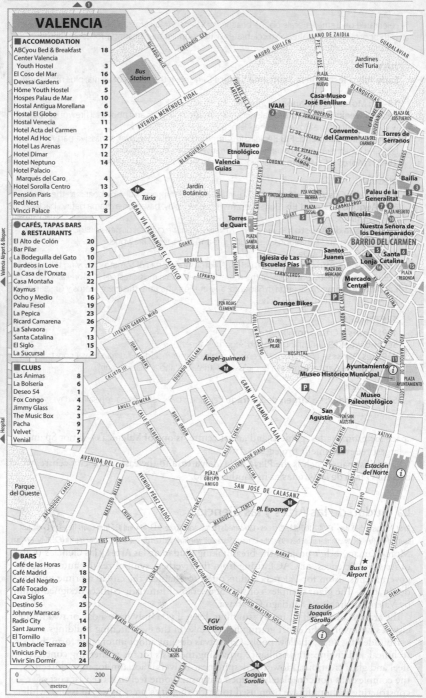

ACCOMMODATION

ABCyou Bed & Breakfast	18
Center Valencia Youth Hostel	3
El Coso del Mar	16
Devesa Gardens	19
Hôme Youth Hostel	5
Hospes Palau de Mar	10
Hostal Antigua Morellana	6
Hostal El Globo	15
Hostal Venecia	11
Hotel Acta del Carmen	1
Hotel Ad Hoc	2
Hotel Las Arenas	17
Hotel Dimar	12
Hotel Neptuno	14
Hotel Palacio Marqués del Caro	4
Hotel Sorolla Centro	13
Pensión Paris	9
Red Nest	7
Vincci Palace	8

CAFÉS, TAPAS BARS & RESTAURANTS

El Alto de Colón	20
Bar Pilar	9
La Bodeguilla del Gato	10
Burdeos in Love	17
La Casa de l'Orxata	21
Casa Montaña	22
Kaymus	1
Ocho y Medio	16
Palau Fesol	19
La Pepica	23
Ricard Camarena	26
La Salvaora	7
Santa Catalina	13
El Siglo	15
La Sucursal	2

CLUBS

Las Ánimas	8
La Bolsería	6
Deseo 54	1
Fox Congo	4
Jimmy Glass	2
The Music Box	3
Pacha	9
Velvet	7
Venial	5

BARS

Café de las Horas	3
Café Madrid	18
Café del Negrito	8
Café Tocado	27
Cava Siglos	4
Destino 56	25
Johnny Marracas	5
Radio City	14
Sant Jaume	6
El Tornillo	11
L'Umbracle Terraza	28
Vinicius Pub	12
Vivir Sin Dormir	24

12

Valencia Airport & Biopark

Hospital

0   200
metres

9 , Alicante & Albacete

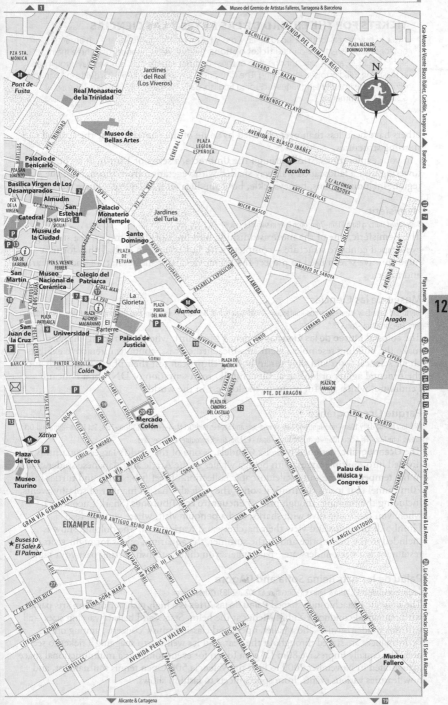

12

PZA STA. MÓNICA
Pont de Fusta
ALBORAYA
Jardines del Real (Los Viveros)
Real Monasterio de la Trinidad
Museo de Bellas Artes
BOTÁNICO
BACHILLER
AVENIDA DEL PRIMADO REIG
PLAZA ALCALDE DOMINGO TORRES
ALVARO DE BAZÁN
MENENDEZ PELAYO
N
AVENIDA DE BLASCO IBÁÑEZ
Palacio de Benicarló
PZA SAN LORENZO
Basílica Virgen de Los Desamparados
PZA DE LA VIRGEN
Almudín
Catedral
San Esteban
Museu de la Ciudad
PLAZA LEGIÓN ESPAÑOLA
Facultats
C/ ALFONSO DE CÓRDOBA
ARTES GRÁFICAS
DOCTOR MOLINER
PINTOR LÓPEZ
PTE. DEL REAL
GENERAL ELIO
Palacio Monaterio del Temple
Santo Domingo
Jardines del Turia
MICER MASCÓ
AVENIDA SUECIA
AVENIDA DE ARAGÓN
PZA DE LA REINA
San Martín
Museo Nacional de Cerámica
Colegio del Patriarca
PLAZA S. VICENTE FERRER
PLAZA DE TETUÁN
PASEO DE LA CIUDADELA
PASARELA EXPOSICIÓN
AMADEO DE SABOYA
San Juan de la Cruz
Universidad
El Parterre
La Glorieta
PLAZA PORTA DEL MAR
Alameda
NAVARRO REVERTER
SERRANO FLORES
Aragón
Palacio de Justicia
BARCAS
PINTOR SOROLLA
Colón
SORNI
GRABADOR ESTEVE
EL PONTÓ
R. CEPEDA
PLAZA DE AMÉRICA
Xàtiva
ISABEL LA CATÓLICA
JORGE JUAN
M. CORTES
C/ FÉLIX PIZCUETA
Mercado Colón
C/ SERRANO MORALES
PLAZA DE CÁNOVAS DEL CASTILLO
PTE. DE ARAGÓN
PLAZA DE ARAGÓN
A. VDA. DEL PUERTO
Plaza de Toros
Museo Taurino
COLÓN
CIRILO AMORÓS
GRAN VÍA MARQUÉS DEL TURIA
M. GODOY
CONDE DE ALTEA
SALAMANCA
ALMIRANTE CADARSO
BURRIANA
CISCAR
AVENIDA JACINTO BENAVENTE
REINA DOÑA GERMANA
Palau de la Música y Congresos
A. VDA. EDUARDO BOSCÁ
GRAN VÍA GERMANÍAS
CÁDIZ
EIXAMPLE
AVENIDA ANTIGUO REINO DE VALENCIA
PINTOR SALVADOR ABRIL
PEDRO III EL GRANDE
DOCTOR SUMSI
CENTELLES
Buses to El Saler & El Palmar
CUBA
LITERATO AZORÍN
SUECA
C/ DE PUERTO RICO
REINA DOÑA MARÍA
ZAPADORES
AVENIDA PERIS Y VALERO
LUIS OLIAG
OBISPO JAIME PÉREZ
GENERAL URRUTIA
ESCULTOR JOSÉ CAPUZ
MATÍAS PERELLÓ
PTE. ÁNGEL CUSTODIO
ALCALDE REIG
Museu Fallero

Alicante & Cartagena

TICKETS FOR THE CIUDAD DE LAS ARTES Y LAS CIENCIAS

You can buy tickets for the Ciudad de las Artes y las Ciencias individually at each attraction, or opt for one of several discounted **ticket options**. A combined entrance to all three main sights is €36.25, and is valid for one, two or three (not necessarily consecutive) days; you'll need at least one full day to see everything. The CAC offers a walking tour (€75.05/guide in Spanish, €86.25/guide in other languages including English; daily 10.30am, 12.30pm & 4.30pm, plus 6.30pm in summer).

others have been less than overwhelmed by some of the content inside the Ciudad's startling structures.

In your explorations, stroll through the **Umbracle**, a series of 18m-high arches towering over a landscaped walkway shaded with vegetation from throughout the region, including palms, honeysuckle, bougainvillea and, of course, orange trees.

Hemisfèric

Daily shows starting from 11am–7pm, open later in summer • €8.80

The **Hemisfèric**, one of the more astonishing buildings of the complex, is a striking eye-shaped concrete structure – complete with lashes, and an eyeball that forms a huge concave screen used to project IMAX movies, laser shows, nature documentaries and more.

Museo de las Ciencias

July to mid-Sept daily 10am–9pm; mid-April to June & mid-Sept to mid-Oct daily 10am–7pm; mid-Oct to mid-April Mon–Thurs 10am–6pm, Fri–Sun 10am–7pm • €8

The colossal **Museo de las Ciencias** (Science Museum), whose protruding supports make the building resemble a giant sun-bleached carcass, contains interactive exhibits about science, sport and the human body. Visitors can test their physical strength and their mental agility or look at a colourful 3D representation of DNA or a Foucault Pendulum, which at 34m is one of the longest in the world.

Parque Oceanográfico

Mid-July to Aug daily 10am–midnight; end June to mid-July and Sept to mid-Oct Mon–Fri & Sun 10am–7pm, Sat 10am–8pm; mid-Oct to end June Mon–Fri & Sun 10am–6pm, Sat 10am–8pm • €27.90, shark encounter €290 per dive

The **Oceanogràfic**, designed by Félix Candela, is one of the world's largest aquariums. It's divided into multiple zones, with beluga whales in the Arctic area, Japanese spider crabs in the temperate zone and a kaleidoscopic collection of reef fish, sharks and turtles in the 70m tunnel that forms the tropical zone. The park also has all manner of splashy events, including the thrilling (though pricey) **Encuentro con Tiburones** (Shark Encounter), where you can scuba dive with sharks; and a **penguin visit**, where you can feed Humboldt penguins and view their hatchery and rearing area. The dolphin show is included in the ticket price and in the summer, the aquarium opens for night visits. The restaurant is a sleek underwater space where you dine with fish darting past your table.

Palau de les Arts Reina Sofía and L'Àgora

Guided tours daily at 11.30am & 1pm • €8 • Box office ☎ 902 202 383, ⊛ lesarts.com

The majestic pistachio-nut-shaped **Palau de las Artes** is a high-tech performing arts palace with renowned conductor Zubin Mehta at the helm. Stages and halls of varying sizes – all with splendid acoustics – host ballet, opera and classical music concerts, among others. Performances are staged throughout the year, and it's well worth snagging a ticket to see one. The equally impressive 80m L'Àgora (open for events only), is a multifunctional space inaugurated in November 2009 to host the Valencia 500 Open tennis tournament, and now features various events, from sports meets to fashion shows.

12

Plaza del Ayuntamiento

In the heart of Valencia, just north of the train station, is the **Plaza del Ayuntamiento**, a handsome central square lined with flower stalls, an impressive floodlit fountain and the surprisingly attractive post office headquarters. The *ayuntamiento* itself houses the **Museo Histórico Municipal** (Mon–Fri 9am–2pm; €2; ☎963 525 478), whose library has an impressive eighteenth-century map of Valencia showing the city walls intact.

Estación del Norte

Built in 1917, the **Estación del Norte**, just south of the Pza. del Ayuntamiento on C/Xàtiva, is another of the city's lovely, and surprisingly well preserved, *modernista* buildings. Peer around at the detailed ceramic mosaics, tiled ceilings and carved wooden doorways, both in the main foyer and in a few side rooms.

Museo Nacional de Cerámica

Poeta Querol 2 • Tues–Sat 10am–2pm & 4–8pm, Sun 10am–2pm • €3, free Sat afternoon & Sun • ☎ 963 516 392, ✆ mnceramica.mcu.es

The distinctive feature of Valencian architecture is its elaborate Baroque facades, the most extraordinary being the entrance to the **Palacio del Marqués de Dos Aguas**. Hipólito Rovira, who helped to design its amazing alabaster doorway complete with revolving statue of the Virgin del Rosario, died insane in 1740, which should come as no surprise to anyone who sees it. Inside the *palacio* is the **Museo Nacional de Cerámica**, with a vast collection of ceramics from all over Spain, and particularly Valencia, itself a major ceramics centre, largely owing to the size of its Morisco population. Apart from an impressive display of ceramic tile works (*azulejos*), the collection contains some stunning plates with gold and copper varnishes (*reflejos*) and a trio of evocatively ornate eighteenth-century carriages.

12

Plaza Patriarca

Rising over the **Plaza Patriarca** is the Neoclassical former **Universidad**, with lovely cloisters where free classical concerts are sometimes held in the summer, and the beautiful Renaissance **Colegio del Patriarca** (daily 11am–1.30pm; €1.20; ☎963 514 176), with a small **art museum** that includes works by El Greco, Morales and Ribalta. The university **library** contains the first book printed in Spain, *Les Trobes*, in 1474.

Catedral and around

Pza. de la Reina • **Catedral** Daily 8am–8.30pm • Free • **Museum** Mon–Sat 10am–5.30pm, Sun 2–5.30pm • €4 • **Miguelete tower** Mon–Sat 10am–7.30pm, Sun 10am–1.30pm & 5.30pm–7.30pm • €2 • ☎ 963 918 127, ✆ catedraldevalencia.es

The café-rich **Pza. de la Reina** is overlooked by the florid spire of the church of Santa Catalina and octagonal tower of Valencia's **Catedral**. Founded in the thirteenth century, the Catedral embraces an eclectic combination of architectural styles (apparently including, interestingly, Jewish iconography), with the lavishly ornate Baroque main entrance leading to a largely Gothic-built interior. It's an exhausting climb up the tower, known as the **Miguelete**, but the spectacular views of the city and its many blue-domed churches more than compensate. The **museum** contains more paintings

---

THE VALENCIA CARD

If you plan on exploring the city extensively, consider buying a **Valencia Card** (€15/20/25 for one, two or three days; ☎ 900 701 818, ✆ valenciatouristcard.com), which gives you unlimited access to the entire transport system and discounted entry to many museums, and for bike rental and guided tours, as well as money off your bill at bars and restaurants – you can buy one at most *turismo* offices, at major hotels and newspaper kiosks.

FALLAS: VALENCIA ON FIRE

Valencia erupts in a blaze of colour and noise for the Fiesta de las Fallas, March 12 to 19. During the year, each *barrio* or neighbourhood builds satirical caricatures or *fallas*, some as tall as buildings. These begin to appear in the plazas at the beginning of March and are judged and awarded prizes before being set alight at midnight on March 19, the **Nit de Foc** – traditionally, carpenters celebrated the beginning of spring by decorating the torches (*foc* in Valenciano) they used over winter and adding them to a ritual bonfire. The *fallas* are ignited in succession – and the last to go up are the prizewinners. Each *falla* has a small model, or *ninot*, beside it, usually created by the children of the *barrio*. These are exhibited in La Lonja before the fiesta begins, and the best displayed in the Museu Fallero (see p.805); the rest are burned with the *fallas*.

During the fiesta, **processions** of *falleros*, dressed in traditional costume and accompanied by bands, carry flowers to the Pza. de la Virgen, where they are massed to create the skirt of a huge statue of La Virgen. The daily Las Mascaletas **firecracker display** (2pm in the Pza. del Ayuntamiento) sees the whole city racing to this central square for a ten-minute series of body-shuddering explosions. There are also nightly fireworks, bullfights, paella contests in the streets and *chocolate y buñuelos* stalls. Finally, around 1am on March 19, the *falla* of the Pza. del Ayuntamiento goes up in flames, followed by the last thunderous firework display of the Nit de Foc.

and also a 2300-kilo tabernacle made from gold, silver and jewels donated by the Valencian people. Above the structure's crossing, the Catedral's fourteenth-century lantern is another fine feature, as are its soaring windows that are glazed with thin sheets of alabaster to let in the Valencian light.

Many visitors, however, come just for the Catedral's most celebrated religious icon: a gold-and-agate chalice (the Santo Cáliz), said to be the one used by Christ at the Last Supper – the **Holy Grail** itself, and no mean asset in a post-*Da Vinci Code* era. It's certainly old and, hidden away throughout the Dark Ages in a monastery in northern Aragón, it really did inspire many of the legends associated with the Grail. Other treasures include the two Goya paintings of the San Francisco chapel, one of which depicts an exorcism (the corpse was originally naked, but after Goya's death a sheet was painted over it).

Plaza de la Virgen

The famous meeting point of the Tribunal de las Aguas is in the **Plaza de la Virgen**, just behind the Catedral. Here, the black-clad regulatory body of Valencia's water users meets at noon every Thursday to judge grievances about the irrigation system of the *huertas*. The practice dates back to Moorish times, and Blasco Ibáñez (1867–1928) describes their workings in detail in his novel *La Barraca*, which is about peasant life in the Valencian *huerta* and remains the best guide to the life of the region at that time.

Nuestra Señora de los Desamparados

Pza. de la Virgen • Mon–Fri 6.45am–1.45pm & 4.30–8.45pm, Sat & Sun 7.30–1.45pm–4.30–8.45pm • Free • ☎ 963 918 611

Two footbridges allow the clergy (only) to go straight from Valencia's Catedral into the archbishop's palace and on to the domed basilica of **Nuestra Señora de los Desamparados**, also on the Pza. de la Virgen, where thousands of candles constantly burn in front of the image of the Virgin, patron of Valencia.

Palau de la Generalitat

Pza. des Manises • Only open via reservation; enquire at the *turismo* • Free

The **Palau de la Generalitat** dates from the fifteenth century and today is the seat of the Valencian autonomous government. Inside, you can see beautifully painted ceilings and frescoes depicting a meeting of the assembly (1592) in the Salón Dorado, as well as the tiled Salón de Cortés.

La Lonja

Pza. del Mercado • Mon 10am–2pm, Tues–Sat 10am–2pm & 4.30–7pm, Sun 10am–3pm • €2 • ☎ 962 084 153

If you tire of Baroque excesses, you could head for the wonderfully sombre interior of the Gothic **La Lonja** (also known as La Lonja de la Seda, or the Silk Exchange). The main focus of this UNESCO-listed building is its superb main hall, with an elegant rib-vaulted ceiling supported by slender, spiralling columns; the orange trees in the central courtyard pay testament to Valencia's diverse heritage.

Mercado Central

Pza. del Mercado • Mon–Sat 8am–2.30pm • ☎ 963 829 101, ⓦ www.mercadocentralvalencia.es

The enormous **Mercado Central**, a *modernista* iron, girder and glass structure built in 1928, is embellished with a collage of tiles and mosaics, and crowned with swordfish and parrot weather vanes. It's one of the biggest markets in Europe – fitting for *huerta* country – with almost a thousand stalls selling fruit and vegetables, meat and seafood.

Mercado Colón

C/Jorge Juan • Daily 7.30am–1pm • ☎ 963 371 101, ⓦ mercadocolon.es

About 1km southeast of the Mercado Central, Valencia's other market, the renovated **Mercado Colón**, is an even more impressive *modernista* building. Its open-sided rectangular design loosely resembles a church, with slim wrought-iron columns supporting a steep pitched roof, and monumental arched facades at either end. However, it's the building's detail that's really outstanding, combining two-tone brickwork with broken-tile mosaic chimneys, features that reveal the influence of *modernista* architect Antoni Gaudí – indeed, the market's architect, Francisco Mora, was a close friend of the Catalan genius. The Mercado Colón also houses colourful flower stalls, a bookstore, upmarket cafés, music concerts and the lovely restaurant *El Alto de Colón* (see p.809), which has a vaulted ceiling of a Valencian mosaic, and large windows that offer glimpses of the market's eye-catching *modernista* ironwork.

Museu de Bellas Artes and the Jardines del Real

C/San Pío V 9 • **Museu de Belles Artes** Mon 11am–5pm, Tues–Sun 10am–7pm • Free • ☎ 963 870 300, ⓦ museobellasartesvalencia.gva.es • **Jardines del Real** Daily 8am–sunset • Free

The **Museu de Belles Artes**, on the far side of the river, has one of the best general collections in Spain, with works by Bosch, El Greco, Goya, Velázquez, Ribera and Ribalta, as well as large quantities of modern Valencian art. The museum takes up the southwest corner of the **Jardines del Real** (also called Los Viveros). The lovely gardens – the largest of Valencia's parks – are well worth a stroll, and host various outdoor concerts in the summer.

Torres Serranos

Pza. de los Fueros • Mon–Sat 9.30am–7pm, Sun 9.30am–3pm • €2, free Sun • ☎ 963 919 070

The fourteenth-century **Torres Serranos**, once part of Valencia's fortified walls, is an impressive gateway defending the entrance to town across the Río Turia. Climb up to the top for panoramic views over the old city; to the west, you can pick out another gateway, the Torres de Quart, which dates from the fifteenth century.

Instituto Valenciano de Arte Moderno

C/Guillém de Castro 118 • Tues–Sun 10am–7pm • €2, free Sun • ⓦ ivam.es

The **Instituto Valenciano de Arte Moderno (IVAM)** features a permanent display of works

THE PORT AND THE PLAYAS

Barcelona famously transformed its waterfront from drab to dazzling, and Valencia has done something similar to its city coastline, having significantly spruced up its beaches and boardwalk over the last decade. In 2007, Valencia became the first European port since 1851 to host the America's Cup (which was staged here again in 2010), and to celebrate the event, parts of the forgotten waterfront were redeveloped, with a gleaming new **marina** and the eye-catching **Veles e Vents** ("Sails and Winds") structure designed by British architect David Chipperfield helping to transform the area. The Valencia Street Circuit was also constructed in the port area as the site of the 2008 **Formula One European Grand Prix**, which was raced here until 2012.

As for **beaches**, you can catch some rays on the soft sand of the broad and breezy *playas* Malvarrosa and Las Arenas, which are backed by the Paseo Marítimo and extend along the waterfront. The outdoor cafés, bars and clubs here are particularly popular in the summer months. There are a number of ways to get to Malvarrosa and Las Arenas, but one easy route is to take the #5 metro from the central Colón station to Neptú (the train service becomes a tram at Marítim Serrería), from where you can walk north along the boardwalk to the sands. You can also catch buses from Pza. del Ayuntamiento, often supplemented during the summer by buses from various points in the centre; ask at the *turismo*.

El Salér, 10km south of the city, is also a pleasant beach: a long, wide stretch of sand with pine trees behind. Autocares Herca buses (T 963 491 250, W autocaresherca) leave from various points around town, including the corner of Gran Vía Germanías and C/Sueca, and C/Alcalde Reig (hourly; 30min).

by sculptor Julio González and painter Ignacio Pinazo, as well as many excellent temporary exhibitions by mainly Spanish contemporary artists. In keeping with other well-known modern-art museums, IVAM also has an excellent restaurant, *La Sucursal* (see p.810).

12

Casa-Museo José Benlliure

C/Blanquerias 23 • Tues–Sat 9.30am–2pm & 3–7pm, Sun 9.30am–3pm • €2 • T 963 919 103

Set in the beautifully renovated home of Valencian painter and sculptor José Benlliure, the **Casa-Museo José Benlliure** displays historical and religious works, from paintings and drawings to sculptures and ceramics. Pieces by his son, Pepino, are also on show, as are works by his brother, established sculptor Mariano Benlliure, and there's a lovely garden with flowers and palms.

Museu Fallero

Pza. Monteolivete 4 • Tues–Sat 10am–7pm, Sun 10am–3pm • €2 • T 963 525 478

The **Museu Fallero** offers a fascinating insight into Valencia's Fiesta de las Fallas. On display is a wacky array of *ninots* that have been voted the best of their year, and consequently saved from the flames.

Bioparc

Avda. Pío Baroja • Daily: summer 10am–9pm; rest of year until 6/7/8pm • €23.30, under-12s €18 • T 902 250 340, W bioparcvalencia.es • Metro lines #3 and #5 to Nou d'Octubre (10min walk); or buses #3, #29, #61, #67, #81 and #95 from various different points

If you're travelling with kids, the city's expansive **Bioparc**, an open-air zoo west of the city centre, might entice. As far as zoos go, this well-maintained specimen tries to be a different sort of place. The creators have made serious attempts to be as eco-aware and animal-friendly as possible, with re-created African savanna and Malagasy landscapes that are home to roaming rhinos, giraffes, antelopes, gorillas, leopards, elephants and lions.

Casa-Museo de Vicente Blasco Ibáñez

C/Isabel de Villena • Mid-March to mid-Oct Tues–Sat 10am–2pm & 3–7pm; mid-Oct to mid-March Tues–Sat 10am–2pm & 3–6pm • €2, free on Sun • ☎ 962 082 586, ⓦ casamuseoblascoibanez.com

The **Casa-Museo de Vicente Blasco Ibáñez** explores the life of the celebrated Valencian author, journalist and political activist Vicente Blasco Ibáñez (1867–1928). An outspoken antimonarchist, he was best known in the English-speaking world for his World War I novel *Los Cuatro Jinetes del Apocalipsis* (The Four Horsemen of the Apocalypse), which was later made into a film. His renovated home, just off Malvarrosa beach, has been turned into an in-depth museum featuring personal mementoes, photographs, documents and more, all of which offer insight both into Blasco Ibáñez himself and the political history of Valencia and Spain during his time.

ARRIVAL AND DEPARTURE VALENCIA

BY PLANE
Valencia airport The airport (☎ 961 598 500, ⓦ aena.es) is 8km west of town, and served by metro lines #3 & #5; the most convenient stop for the centre is Colón. Alternatively, a taxi will set you back around €16.

BY TRAIN
Estación del Norte Situated close to the town centre; walk north along Avda. Marqués de Sotelo to the Pza. del Ayuntamiento, the central square.
Destinations Alicante (11 daily; 1hr 30min–2hr 15min); Barcelona (19 daily; 2hr 50min–4hr 45min); Benicàssim (11 daily; 1hr 10min); Castellón de la Plana (18 daily; 45min–1hr); El Puig (every 20min; 20min); Gandía (every 30min; 50min); Madrid (23 daily; 2hr–4hr 30min); Málaga (6 daily; 9hr); Murcia (5 daily; 3hr 20min); Orihuela (12 daily; 3hr); Peñíscola (9 daily; 1hr 30min); Sagunto (every 30min; 30min); Segorbe (3 daily; 1hr); Teruel (3 daily; 2hr 25min); Xàtiva (every 30min; 1hr); and Zaragoza (2 daily; 5hr–6hr 45min).

Estación Joaquín Sorolla Just south of Estación del Norte, this is the station (☎ 902 432 343, ⓦ adif.es) for the Madrid–Levante high-speed AVE line. There are free shuttles from Estación del Norte to Sorolla for AVE ticket holders. There's also a metro stop, Joaquín Sorolla Station, nearby, and a taxi rank just outside.
Destinations Madrid (around 15 daily; 1hr 40min), Murcia (around 20 daily; 1hr).

BY BUS
Valencia's bus station The station is some way out on the north side of the river; take local bus #8 or #79 or the metro to Turia, or allow 30min to walk.
Destinations Alicante (20–25 daily; 2hr 30min–4hr 30min); Barcelona (13–16 daily; 4hr–5hr); Benidorm (18–23 daily; 2hr 30min–3h 45min); Cuenca (3 daily; 4hr); Denia (10–11 daily; 1hr 45min); Gandía (11–14 daily; 1hr); Madrid (16–20 daily; 4hr); Murcia (11–14 daily; 3hr 15min); and Sagunto (25 daily; 45min).

BY FERRY
Puerto de Valencia The Balearic ferry terminal connects with Pza. del Ayuntamiento via bus #4 and with Estación del Norte train station via bus #2. Ferries are operated by Acciona Trasmediterránea (☎ 902 454 645, ⓦ trasmediterranea.es), Iscomar (☎ 902 119 128, ⓦ iscomar.com) and Baleària (☎ 902 160 180, ⓦ balearia.com).
Destinations Acciona Trasmediterránea: Palma de Mallorca (June–Sept 2 daily; 5hr 45min & 7hr 15min; Oct–May weekly; 9hr); Ibiza (June–Sept daily; 2hr 45min; Oct–May weekly; 4hr 45min); Maó, Menorca (1 weekly; 14hr).
Iscomar: Palma (5 weekly; 9hr 30min); Baleària: Ibiza (daily; 3hr 45min); Palma (daily; 6hr 45min).

VALENCIA BY BIKE

With its famously balmy weather, relatively flat terrain and network of well-maintained bike lanes (including in the Río Turia riverbed park and near the beaches), Valencia is a great place to explore by bike. The city's new **public bike scheme**, ValenBiSi (☎ 902 006 598, ⓦ valenbisi.es), features 2750 bikes distributed across 275 stations throughout the city, including the centre and Barrio del Carmen. There are several options if you want to hop on one of the bikes – the shortest is the seven-day subscription (€13.04). Once you have a subscription, the first thirty minutes is free, and then it's €1.04 for the next thirty. After that, it's €3.12/hr. Credit cards are accepted.

Another option is to rent a bike from the well-run Orange Bikes on C/Guillem Sorolla, 1 (☎ 963 917 551, ⓦ orangebikes.net), with bicycles for €9–15 per day; they also do repairs.

GETTING AROUND

By metro, bus and on foot Most of Valencia's sights are centrally located and can be reached on foot, but the city also has an efficient, well-maintained public transport system – metro, trams and buses – which are helpful for reaching outlying neighbourhoods and sights (including the Ciudad de las Artes y Ciencias) and the beaches. Metro stations in the city centre include Xàtiva and Colón, where you can connect with several metro lines. Local EMT buses (ⓦemtvalencia.es) cost €1.50/journey, and they also sell various discount multi-use tickets; trams and metro are €1.50 (€2.90 return) for inner zone A, which covers central Valencia (more info on the metro system at ⓦmetrovalencia .com). If you plan on using public transport regularly, a

Valencia Card (see p.801) is a good way to save.

By tourist bus The hop-on, hop-off Valencia Bus Turístic (ⓣ963 414 400, ⓦvalenciabusturistic .com; €17/24hr, €19/48hr) offers various routes around the city, including Historic or Maritime Valencia, as well as to Albufera (see p.812).

By car Rental companies in Valencia include Avis (airport & Gran Vía de Ramón y Cajal 2, among other locations; ⓣ963 510 734, ⓦavis.com); Hertz (airport & C/Segorbe 7 ⓣ963 415 036, ⓦhertz.com); and Atesa (airport & Estación del Norte ⓣ963 517 145, ⓦatesa.es).

By taxi Radio Taxi ⓣ963 703 333; Tele Taxi ⓣ963 571 313; Cooperativa Valenciana de Taxis ⓣ963 740 202.

INFORMATION AND TOURS

Turismo The main *turismo* is at Pza. de la Reina 19 (Mon Sat 9am–7pm, Sun 10am–2pm; ⓣ963 153 931, ⓦturisvalencia.es). There are also branches in Pza. del Ayuntamiento (same hours; ⓣ963 524 908, ⓦturisvalencia.es), at the airport and at the Joaquín Sorolla train station. Valencia has helpful regional offices

including at C/Paz 48 (Mon Fri 9am 7pm, Sat 10am 2pm & Sun 11am–2pm; ⓣ963 986 422, ⓦcomunitatvalenciana .com).

Tours Valencia Guías on C/Turia 67 (ⓣ963 851 740, ⓦvalenciaguias.com) offers a range of excellent tours, including by bike, in many languages.

ACCOMMODATION

Valencia boasts a huge range of **accommodation**, from historical hotels to hip hostels and sunny beachfront properties. The city centre, between the train station and the Río Turia, is sprinkled with budget hotels and hostels.

THE CITY CENTRE AND AROUND

★**ABCyou Bed & Breakfast** C/Taquígrafo Martí 10 ⓣ963 815 560, ⓦabcyou.es. With modern white decor contrasting with old Spanish tiled floors, this cool Dutch-owned B&B has individually decorated rooms and a small garden haven. Don't miss out on the home-baked goodies and freshly squeezed juice for breakfast (€6.50). €55

Center Valencia Youth Hostel C/Samaniego 18 ⓣ963 914 915, ⓦcenter-valencia.com. Just about as central as you can get, this amiable hostel sits in Barrio del Carmen, just a stumble away from a slew of bars and cafés. €20

Hôme Youth Hostel C/La Lonja 4 ⓣ963 916 229 & Pza. Vicente Iborra ⓣ963 913 797, ⓦlikeathome.net. This lively hostel is in the historic quarter and features retro-chic furnishings and clean dorms, plus double rooms. Dorms €17, doubles €46

Hospes Palau de Mar Navarro Reverter 14 ⓣ963 162 884, ⓦhospes.com. Set in a nineteenth-century baronial mansion, this handsome hotel exudes a lovely blend of old and new, from the renovated historic facade to the sleek, white interior that borders on minimalist. Get pampered at the Bodyna Spa, and then dine on Mediterranean dishes at the restaurant. €115

Hostal Antigua Morellana C/En Bou 2 ⓣ963 915 773, ⓦhostalam.com. The quiet rooms at this cheerful, well-maintained hotel close to the Barrio del Carmen are excellent value. Book ahead. €65

Hostal Venecia C/En Llop 5 ⓣ963 524 267, ⓦhotelvenecia.com. Don't be fooled by the *hostal* tag: this is a stylish, well-managed, central hotel. Some rooms come with views over the Pza. del Ayuntamiento, and all are clean and comfy. Special parking discounts available. €73

Hotel Acta del Carmen Blanquerías 11 ⓣ962 057 700, ⓦhotel-carmenvalencia.com. This colourful, boutique-style hotel – quirky art, walls painted in red and blue – sits in the middle of the Barrio del Carmen's bustle. €57

Hotel Ad Hoc C/Boix 4 ⓣ963 919 140, ⓦadhochoteles. com. One of Valencia's first boutique hotels, this is suitably comfortable and elegant, with exposed brick walls and textile wall-hangings, in a building with plenty of period character. €96

Hotel Dimar Gran Vía del Marqués del Turia 80 ⓣ963 951 030, ⓦhotel-dimar.com. Comfy, stylish rooms in a building renovated in 2009, on the edge of the old town. €85

Hotel Palacio Marqués de Caro Almirall 14 ⓣ963 059 000, ⓦcarohotel.com. This luxury boutique hotel, in a thirteenth-century palace, reveals a gorgeous blend of history and *haute* style. The owners (one of whom is a descendant of the last Moorish King of Valencia) discovered a large section of Moorish wall when renovating the building, and incorporated it into the design of the hotel; the result is a bewitching glimpse into the Valencia of the past, with upscale amenities that are very much from the present. €156

12

FASHION FORWARD

Move over Madrid and Barcelona, and make room for style diva Valencia. The city has a rich and vibrant **fashion culture**, and twice a year, in spring and autumn, the glossy Valencia Fashion Week (Ⓦvalenciafashionweek.com) sees catwalk shows from all the latest and greatest local and national designers. Valencia's home-grown designers have made a splash in the international scene: look out for the flamboyant, gypsy-inspired pieces of Francis Montesinos; the sexy styles of Alex Vida; the urban look of Alejandro Sáez de la Torre; bold, geometric swimwear from Dolores Cortés; Higinio Mateu's frisky dresses; and the avant-garde, flouncy threads of Tonuca. Shoes and accessories rival the clothes, with such renowned designers as jeweller Vicente Gracia, whose reinvented antique brooches have been worn by the Queen of Spain herself.

Where to shop? You can find both local and international designs throughout Valencia, from small boutiques to big department stores, particularly around the old town and city centre, including the Eixample (Ensanche) district, between Calle Colón and Gran Vía del Marqués del Turia; and Calle Jorge Juan by Mercado Colón.

Hotel Sorolla Centro Convento Santa Clara 5 ☎963 523 392, Ⓦhotelsorolla.com. Comfortable, slightly Asian-influenced rooms – and well-placed for the new Joaquín Sorolla high-speed train station, which is 600m away. **€77**

Pensión Paris C/Salvá 12 ☎963 526 766, Ⓦpensionparis.com. Inviting, family-owned *pensión*. Clean, comfy rooms – some with en-suite bathrooms (€36), others with shower and shared bathroom – are simply furnished but well-tended, and have views of the old university. **€28**

Red Nest C/de la Paz 36 ☎963 427 168 & Pza. Tetuan 5 ☎963 532 561, Ⓦnesthostelsvalencia.com. Cheery, bright backpacker hostel with dorms and doubles and a bar. The busy social calendar, run alongside its sister hostel on Pza. Tetuán, features walking tours and pub crawls. Dorms **€13.50**, doubles **€30**

★Vincci Palace La Paz 42 ☎962 062 377, Ⓦvinccihoteles.com. Well-heeled hotel with the history to match, housed in a former *palacete* that offered safe lodging to intellectuals during the Civil War, with a lovely facade fronted by wrought-iron balconies. Comfortable rooms, soft beds, spic-and-span bathrooms and all the amenities. **€100**

THE PORT AND THE BEACHES

El Coso del Mar Paseo Neptuno 12 ☎963 728 213, Ⓦelcosodelmar.com. If you're in Valencia for the *playa*, then you'll like the location of this beachside hotel, with easy access to Playa Malvarrosa. Rooms are decent; ask for one with a beachside view when booking. It's about 30min into town, walking to and hopping on the tram. **€109**

Devesa Gardens Near El Saler beach and La Albufera ☎961 611 136, Ⓦdevesagardens.com. Some 15km southeast of Valencia, with spacious grounds surrounded by pine forest, and great amenities including a swimming pool, tennis courts and also simple wooden bungalows. Camping **€17.10**, bungalows **€79.50**

Hostal El Globo Paseo de Neptuno 42–44 ☎963 727 777, Ⓦhostalelglobo.com. Friendly place with simple, funky furnished rooms – some with great views – near the beach. They also run the long-established bar *Vivir Sin Dormir* (see p.811). **€75**

Hotel Las Arenas Eugenia Viñes 22–24 ☎963 120 600, Ⓦhotel-lasarenas.com. Valencia's only five-star beachside hotel maximizes its proximity to the sea: the morning light fills the cream and dark-wood rooms, sun-speckled terraces face the sea, and it's a short stroll to the beach. **€201**

Hotel Neptuno Paseo de Neptuno 2 ☎963 567 777, Ⓦhotelneptunovalencia.com. Light-flooded hotel with a minimalist, modern look: white furnishings, a glass lift, hardwood floors and a beach-facing terrace, strewn with low sofas and plump red pillows. The top-notch *Tridente* restaurant serves up creative Valencian cuisine. Rates include breakfast. **€125**

EATING

As befits Spain's third-largest city, Valencia's cuisine scene is wonderfully varied and suits all budgets. For **tapas** and cheap eats, head to the area around the Mercado Central, where there are plenty of places offering set menus for under €15; Barrio del Carmen is also sprinkled with lively tapas bars. The once-gritty, now-hip Russafa, just south of the centre, has continued to evolve into one of Valencia's liveliest multiethnic neighbourhoods, where you can find everything from Arabic tearooms to Halal butchers.

Valencia has also marched into the gourmet culinary echelons with style and swagger: witness such standouts as *Ricard Camarena*. And while the city is the home of **paella**, the finest places to eat it are, in fact, out of town, in Perellonet or El Palmar (see p.812), or along the city beach – Paseo Neptuno is lined with small paella and *marisco* restaurants.

RESTAURANTS

El Alto de Colón Mercado Colón ☎ 963 530 900, ⓦ grupoelalto.com. Elegant, vaulted restaurant with a high-end Mediterranean menu (at high-end prices) that features lots of innovative flourishes, such as fresh shellfish heaped on sticky rice. Mains from €35. Mon–Fri 2–4pm & 9–11pm, Sat & Sun 9–11pm; closed Aug.

★**Ricard Camarena** C/Sumsi 4 ☎ 963 355 418, ⓦ ricardcamarena.com. Valencian cuisine is taken to a high art at this restaurant, the latest project by chef Ricard Camarena after the Michelin-starred *Arrop* restaurant (now closed). The superb dishes include hake cheeks, Valencian oysters and chicken dumplings, all exquisitely presented. The "short menu" (€75) contains six such dishes; and the tasting menu has nine (€90) or, if you're feeling really fancy go for the menu named after the man himself with eleven plated masterpieces for €105. Tues–Sat 1.30pm–midnight.

Burdeos in Love C/Mar 4 ☎ 963 914 350, ⓦ burdeosinlove.com. Giant forks speared with wine corks flank the doorway of this stylish restaurant, where rich, creative dishes like cod with a parmesan mousse, and a mini veal burger topped with a quail egg, pair beautifully with robust Spanish reds. €30 menu. Mon–Sat 1.30–4pm & 8.30–11.30pm.

Kaymus Avda. del Mestre Rodrigo 44 ☎ 963 486 666, ⓦ kaymus.es. This classy restaurant just north of the city centre fuses modern and traditional – try the superb *arroces* (rice dishes), like cod and cauliflower. The crisp dining room, with paintings in modern stripes and swirls that play against the white walls, caters to the growing business district near the gleaming Palacio de Congresos (conference centre). Tasting menu €45; lunch and dinner menu €28/€32. Mon 2–4pm, Tues–Sun 2–4pm & 9–11pm.

Ocho y Medio Pza. Lope de Vega 5 ☎ 963 922 022, ⓦ elochoymedio.com. Named after the Fellini film, this bi-level restaurant with dusky peach walls, blonde-wood floors and views of the Santa Catalina church, excels at innovative French-tinged Mediterranean fare, from their speciality of rich foie gras to aromatic paellas or grilled squid with black risotto. Mains €17–25. Daily noon–midnight; hours can vary in winter.

★**Palau Fesol** Hernán Cortés 7 ☎ 963 529 323, ⓦ www. palacefesol.com. Feast on plump sardines, fragrant *arroces* and superb wines (at mid-range to expensive prices) at this graceful restaurant which is over a century old – proof that things do get better with age. The rustic dining room boasts a colourful mosaic, beamed ceiling and stone walls, while the gracious owner is the consummate host. Mains from €30. Daily 1–6pm, dinner generally group reservations only; closed second half of Aug.

La Pepica Paseo Neptuno 6 ☎ 963 710 366, ⓦ lapepica .com. Founded in 1898, this inviting, spacious paella restaurant has undeniable staying power: over the decades, it has hosted plenty of the rich and famous, from Hemingway and Orson Welles to swaggering bullfighters and the Spanish royal family. Settle in on the sun-speckled

12

HORCHATA

Valencia is known for its **horchata** – a drink made from *chufas* (tiger nuts) served either liquid or *granizada* (slightly frozen), and accompanied by long, thin cakes called *fartons*. Legend has it that the name *horchata* was coined by Jaime I, shortly after he conquered Valencia. He was admiring the *huerta* one hot afternoon, and an Arab girl offered him a drink so refreshing that he exclaimed, "*Aixó es or, xata*" (this is gold, girl).

HORCHATERÍAS

There are **horchaterías** all over Valencia city; traditionally, however, the best *horchata* comes from **Alboraya**, formerly a village in the Valencian suburbs, now absorbed into the city – to get there take metro line #3.

La Casa de l'Orxata Mercado de Colón ☎ 963 527 307, ⓦ casadelaorxata.com. In the historic Mercado de Colón, try the excellent *La Casa de l'Orxata*, who make their smooth *horchata* with traditional methods and organic ingredients, and sell it from street carts around town. Mon–Fri 7.30am–10.30pm, Sat & Sun 7.30am–2am.

Daniel Avda. de la Horchata 41 ☎ 961 858 866, ⓦ horchateria-daniel.es; Ⓜ Palmaret. One of the better-known spots to cool your throat, despite being slightly out of the centre of town – but the breezy terrace makes up for the journey. Daily 10am–1am; closed mid-Dec to Feb.

Santa Catalina Pza. Santa Catalina ☎ 963 912 379, ⓦ horchateriasantacatalina.com. Minutes from the Catedral, this iconic *horchateria* and *chocolatería* has over 100 years of history. Daily 8am–9pm.

El Siglo Pza. Santa Catalina ☎ 963 918 466. On Pza. Santa Cantalina is a historic *horchateria* which serves *fartons* (long cylinder doughnuts) to dip into your tiger-nut drink. Daily 8am–9pm.

Subies Carretera de Barcelona, Alboraya ☎ 961 854 673, ⓦ horchatasubies.es. One old-time spot in the Almássera neighbourhood of Alboraya where three generations have been honing their craft. Daily 8.30am–11pm.

terrace and tuck into fresh fish and seafood or aromatic paellas. Tasting menu €27.50. Daily 1–4pm & 8.30–11pm; closed second half of Nov.

La Salvaora C/Calatrava 19 ☎963 921 484, ⓦlasalvaora.com. This slender Andalucian restaurant, with high, dark-wood tables and white marble floors, pays homage to flamenco singers and stars via black-and-white photos on the walls. The creative fare includes tripe tossed with red peppers and steak with a port reduction. Their weekday lunch menu is excellent value at €11. Mon 8.30–11.30pm, Tues–Sun 1.30–3.30pm & 8.30–11.30pm.

La Sucursal C/Guillém de Castro 118 ☎963 746 665. Valencia's IVAM gallery features a superb restaurant that matches (if not sometimes trumps) the art within. The elegant, sparse *La Sucursal* serves artisanal cuisine with a twist, from saffron-scented rice studded with lobster to a cauliflower mousse. Mains are €21–35. Mon–Fri 2–3.30pm & 9–11pm, Sat 9–11pm; closed second half of Aug.

TAPAS BARS

★**Bar Pilar** Cnr C/Moro Zeit 13 ☎963 910 497. This boisterous joint, which has been around since 1917, gets packed most nights, with the beer-happy crowd spilling out onto the pavement. The speciality is *clochinas* (mussels), which you can slurp at the bar, tossing the shells into buckets on the floor. Daily noon–midnight.

La Bodeguilla del Gato C/Catalans 10 ☎963 918 235. Yes, it can sometimes seem like there are more tourists than locals, but this is an authentically lively tapas bar nonetheless, with exposed brick-and-mustard walls hung with bullfighting posters. Munch on *pulpo a la Gallega*, octopus dusted with paprika, and crisp *flamenquines*, croquettes of pork, ham and cheese. Daily 8.30pm–midnight.

Casa Montaña C/José Benlliure 69 ☎963 672 314, ⓦemilianobodega.com. This vintage, cheery tapas bar in the Cabañal fishermen's quarter is one of the oldest (and best) in the city, with one of Valencia's most impressive wine cellars to boot. Graze on a wonderful array of tapas from anchovies and *michirones* (fava beans) to cod croquettes, which get a pine nut kick. €27 menu. Mon–Sat 1–3.30pm & 8–11.30pm, Sun 1–3.30pm; closed second half of Aug.

DRINKING AND NIGHTLIFE

12

The heady days of *La Ruta del Bacalao* (when people drove hundreds of kilometres to party in Valencia's out-of-town warehouses) may be long gone, but the city still takes its **nightlife** seriously. The **Barrio del Carmen** is one of the liveliest areas at night, especially around C/Caballeros, with scores of small cafés, bars and restaurants. The whole area between Pza. de la Reina, Pza. Santa Ursula and Pza. Portal Nueva is heaving at the weekend. Calle Juan Llorenç, west of the city centre, is another popular area to bar- and club-hop, with lively Latin and salsa-style clubs. Russafa, southeast of the city centre, has evolved into one of the funkier, still relatively untouristed neighbourhoods, and bustles with cafés and bars. Across the Río Turia, near the **university**, particularly on and around C/Blasco Ibáñez, and just north, around Pza. Benicamlet, you'll find a more studenty, alternative-music-style nightlife, especially during the school year.

In **summer**, the bars lining the **Malvarrosa beach** are the places to be. Many Valencian bars serve *Agua de Valencia*, the classic Valencian cocktail, made with orange juice, cava and vodka, and served by the jug.

To get a grip on **what's going on**, you can check out local English-language websites like ⓦthisisvalencia.com and ⓦvalenciavalencia.com, which both offer updated overviews of nightlife and restaurants. For a Spanish-language lowdown on the club scene, check out *A Little Beat* magazine (ⓦalittlebeat.com). Note that the big nightclubs are generally open Thursday to Saturday, and usually get going after midnight.

BARS

Café de las Horas Conde de Almodóvar 1 ☎963 917 336. Baroque-tinged, gay-friendly bar with a gurgling fountain, tiled floors and a marble bar. Drop in early evening for a romantic glass of wine, or later in the night join the crowds getting tipsy on chilled jugs of *Agua de Valencia*. Mon–Thurs 4pm–1.30am, Fri–Sun 4pm–3am.

★**Café Madrid** C/de la Abadía de San Martín 10. This two-storey haunt is considered the birthplace of *Agua de Valencia* – and, as you might expect, the bartenders are true connoisseurs at making this fruity cocktail. The welcoming bar has managed to maintain a wonderfully old-fashioned air – dark wood, burgundy walls, antique mirrors – while still drawing a buzzy, stylish set until the small hours. Mon–Thurs 7pm–2am, Fri & Sat 7pm–3.30am.

Café del Negrito Pza. del Negrito 1 & C/Calatrava 15 ☎963 914 233. This sociable spot, in one of Valencia's loveliest plazas, is perfect for an outdoor cocktail. Come evening, a bohemian crowd gathers for conversation and *cervezas al aire libre*. Mon–Thurs & Sun 5pm–3am, Fri & Sat 5pm–3.30am.

Café Tocado C/Cádiz 44 ☎650 390 232. Enjoy cocktails and conversation at this fun, long-standing Russafa café, with a decor inspired by Paris cabarets. Daily 7pm–midnight.

Cava Siglos C/Caballeros 12 ☎963 916 271, ⓦcavasiglos.com. Stylish, minimalist wine bar, with a "look *neoyorquino*" ("New York look"), serving a creative selection of wine and cava, plus *bocadillos*. Mon noon–5pm, Tues–Sun noon–1.30am.

Destino 56 Avda. Neptuno ☎689 979 416,

GAY AND LESBIAN VALENCIA

The city has a robust **gay scene**, with plenty of bars clustered in the Barrio del Carmen, and especially along C/Quart. In general, though, much of Carmen's nightlife is gay-friendly, including amiable café-bars such as *Café de las Horas*. A general gay and lesbian resource is **Col-lectiu Lambda de lesbianes**, **gais**, **transsexuals i bisexuals** (C/Sant Dionís 8; ☎963 342 191, ⓦ lambdavalencia.org), whose focus is on Pride events, outreach and local news. The tourist office also has listings of gay-friendly nightlife.

Deseo 54 C/Pepita ⓦ deseo54.com. North of the centre, this lively club sees plenty of revellers decked out in wild outfits (or lack thereof) – think sequins on some nights, shirtless on others. Usually Thurs–Sat midnight–late.

Venial C/Quart 26 ⓦ venialvalencia.com. *Venial*, with its apt moniker "The Queen of the Night", has disco balls, laser shows and pounding music. Summer daily midnight–late; winter Fri & Sat midnight–late.

ⓦ destino56.com. Ease into the Valencia night over cocktails with views of Playa de las Arenas, followed by grooving on the dancefloor. Summer Thurs–Fri 10pm–midnight; check website for updates.

Johnny Marracas C/Caballeros 39 ☎963 915 266. Stylish locals flirt over strong cocktails at this smooth lounge. Mon–Thurs 7pm–3am, Fri–Sun 7pm–4am.

Radio City C/Santa Teresa 19 ☎963 914 15. This veteran drinking den hosts poetry, films and live music, with full-on flamenco on Tues. Daily 10.30pm–3.30am.

★ **Sant Jaume** C/Caballeros 51 ☎963 912 401. Of the many bars on this main drag, the characterful *Sant Jaume*, set in a small converted pharmacy with aged mirrors and tiles, is one of the most popular, with a great terrace that packs in the crowds nightly. Daily noon–1.30am.

El Tornillo Campoamor 42 ☎639 403 148, ⓦ eltornillo. com. Bohemian student hangout spinning indie, alternative and left-field electronica. Look for the *tornillo* (screw) that marks the spot outside. Tues & Wed 0.30pm 2.30am, Thurs Sat 8.30pm–3.30am.

L'Umbracle Terraza L'Umbracle, La Ciudad de las Artes y las Ciencias ☎671 668 000, ⓦ umbracleterraza.com. Sexy lounge where you can sip tasty cocktails under palm trees and the twinkling stars, and then head to the downstairs dance club *Mya* to finish off the night. Summer Thurs–Sat 10/11pm–late.

Vinicius Pub C/Bolsería 11 ☎607 723 219, ⓦ viniciuspub.com. Sip potent cocktails, from *Agua de Valencia* to *caipirinhas*, to a playlist of international and Spanish pop, funk and house. Wed–Sat 10pm–3.30am.

Vivir Sin Dormir Paseo Neptuno 42 ☎963 727 777, ⓦ vivirsindormir. Once a legend, and now a lively

pub-club with a long bar and an outdoor terrace, particularly popular with travellers. Daily 9pm–3am.

CLUBS

Las Ánimas Paseo Neptuno ☎902 108 527, ⓦ grupolasanimas.com. The hopping *Las Ánimas*, in the port area, is one of the places to be for late nights and early mornings. Check the website for details of DJs and events. Usually Thurs–Sat midnight–late.

La Bolsería Bolsería 41 ☎963 918 903. Sleek nightspot that can sometimes take itself too seriously. That said, it's a comfortably swish place to enjoy Valencia's nightlife, with excellent cocktails, a cool house and pop soundtrack, and a mature crowd. Daily 8pm–4am.

Fox Congo C/Caballeros 35 ☎963 925 527. On the *barrio*'s main strip, this dimly lit, funky club reveals a sexy interior of copper pillars, black banquettes and glowing onyx bar. Dance tunes and good cocktails, too. Daily 11pm–late.

Jimmy Glass C/Baja 28 ⓦ jimmyglassjazz.net. Authentically smoky, shoebox-shaped jazz club putting on quality live acts for a studenty audience. Daily 8pm–3am.

The Music Box Pinto Zariñena 16 ☎963 914 151. The cool crowd heats up the dancefloor at this busy club that pumps out soul and swing, indie and electro. Daily 1am–7am.

Pacha C/San Vicente 305 ⓦ pachavalencia.com. South of the city centre, the Valencian branch of the Spanish superclub features booming house tunes and two floors of writhing dancers in party gear. Check the website for up-to-date information. Thurs–Sat 11pm–late.

Velvet Campoamor 58. Lively student-jammed club, with tunes ranging from indie rock to Spanish pop or electronica. Tues–Sat 9pm–late.

DIRECTORY

Consulates UK C/Colón 22, 5-H ☎963 520 710; USA C/Dr Romagosa 1, 2-J ☎963 516 973.

Hospital Hospital General, Avda. del Cid, at the Tres Cruces junction (☎961 972 00; ⓜ Avenida del Cid).

Police C/Los Mestres 2 ☎963 920 607.

Post office Pza. del Ayuntamiento 24 (Mon–Fri 8.30am–8.30pm, Sat 9.30am–2pm).

12

Around Valencia

There are a number of good **day-trips** to be made from Valencia, including a visit to the monastery at **El Puig** or a meal at some of the region's very best **paella** restaurants at El Palmar, El Perelló or El Perellonet.

Real Monasterio del Puig de Santa María

Guided visits Tues–Sat 10am, 11am, noon, 4pm & 5pm • €4 • ☎ 961 470 200, ⓦ monasteriodelpuig.es.tl • Trains (every 30min; 20min) and buses (hourly; 30min) from Valencia

Eighteen kilometres north of Valencia on the road to Sagunto is the small town of **El Puig** (pronounced "pooch"), where it's well worth spending a couple of hours visiting the impressive **Real Monasterio del Puig de Santa María**, a huge fort-like structure flanked by four towers that dominates the town and surrounding countryside. The Orden de la Merced – the order that acts as guardians of the sanctuary – was founded by Pedro Nalaso in 1237 after he'd seen a vision of the Virgin Mary on the nearby hill. It is a favourite pilgrimage destination for Valencians and royalty alike, from Jaime I to the present monarchs Juan Carlos I and Doña Sofía, although in Franco's time it was put to a rather different use – as a prison.

Museum of Print and Graphics

Tues–Sat 10am–2pm & 4–6pm, Sun 10am–2pm

In the lower cloister, the **Museum of Print and Graphics** (one of the most important in Europe) contains a wealth of artefacts, including the former smallest book in the world – the size of a thumbnail. Looking at it through a magnifying glass reveals the Padre Nuestro (Lord's Prayer) in half a dozen languages. Other star exhibits include a copy of the Gutenberg Bible and a wonderful pictorial atlas of natural history, both from the sixteenth century. In the upper cloister, the **ceramics room** houses various Roman pieces, but its real treasures are the fourteenth-century plates, bowls and jars recovered from the seabed close to El Puig. Keep an eye out, too, for the neck manacles that the monks use as candle holders throughout the monastery.

La Albufera and the paella villages

La Albufera, just 12km south of Valencia, is a vast lagoon separated from the sea by a sandbank and surrounded by rice fields. Being one of the largest bodies of fresh water in Spain, it constitutes an important wetland, and attracts tens of thousands of migratory birds – a throng composed of 250 species, of which ninety breed here regularly. In the Middle Ages, it was ten times its present size but the surrounding paddies have gradually reduced it. After growing contamination by industrial waste, domestic sewage and insecticide, the area was turned into a natural park. Whether you're into birdwatching or not, the lagoon area makes a relaxing change from the city.

It's possible to "hop on, hop off" the Valencia Bus Turístic and tuck into a lunch of **paella**, or eels with *all i pebre* (piquant sauce), in the lakeside village of **El Palmar**, which is packed with restaurants. In July and August, El Palmar celebrates its **fiesta**; on the middle Sunday the image of Christ on the Cross is taken out onto the lake in a procession of boats and hymns are sung. Another 2km farther along the road to El Perelló is the village of **El Perellonet**, where you can also sample some of the best paella in Spain.

ARRIVAL AND DEPARTURE	LA ALBUFERA AND THE PAELLA VILLAGES

By bus One of the easiest ways to do La Albufera is to jump aboard the Valencia Bus Turístic, which leaves from various points in the city (11 daily in winter, 21 daily in summer; €17; ☎ 963 414 400, ⓦ valenciabusturistic.com); the trip includes a short boat ride on the lake. Additionally, regular Autocares Herca buses travel to El Saler and on to the lagoon, El Palmar and El Perelló.

ALL PULPED OUT: LA TOMATINA

La Tomatina – the tomato-throwing festival of Buñol – is about as wild and excessive as Spanish fiestas get. Picture this: 30,000 people descend on a small provincial town at the same time as a fleet of municipal trucks, carrying 120,000 tonnes of tomatoes. Tension builds. "To-ma-te, to-ma-te" yell the crowds. And then the truckers let them have it, hurling the ripe, pulpy fruit at everyone present. And everyone goes crazy, hurling the pulp back at the trucks, at each other, in the air … for an hour. It's a fantasy battle made flesh: exhausting, not pretty and not to everyone's taste. But it is Buñol's contribution to fiesta culture, and most participants will tell you that it is just about as much fun as it is possible to have with your clothes on. Not that you should wear a great deal.

La Tomatina has been going since 1944 but has got a lot bigger in recent years, following a string of articles in the press in Spain and abroad. The novelist Louis de Bernières was one of the first foreign writers to cover the event: he wrote a superb account that is reprinted in *Spain: Travelers' Tales*, and concluded that, if he planned his life well and kept his health, he could attend another nineteen Tomatinas, before he would be too enfeebled for the occasion.

If the idea appeals, then you'll need to visit Buñol on the **last Wednesday of August** (but call the Valencia tourist office just to check, as some years it takes place a week early). You can get there from the city by train or bus in around an hour, but try to arrive early, with a spare set of clothing that you should leave at a bar. The tomato trucks appear on the central Pza. del Ayuntamiento at around noon, and then the battle commences: this is no spectator sport – everyone is considered fair game. At 1pm, an explosion signals the end of the battle and nobody hurls another speck of tomato for the next twelve months. Instead, the local fire brigade arrives to hose down the combatants, buildings and streets, and a lull comes over the town. And then, miraculously, within the hour, everyone arrives back on the street, perfectly turned out, to enjoy the rest of the fiesta, which, oddly enough, includes such refined pursuits as orchestral concerts in the town's open-air auditorium. For more information, check out the festival website Ⓦlatomatina.info, or try the town's own website Ⓦbunyol.es.

As Buñol's **accommodation** options are limited, most people take in the fiesta as a day-trip from Valencia; but if you want to stay, try *Hotel Condes de Buñol*, Avda. Blasco Ibañez 13 (Ⓣ962 504 852, Ⓦhotelcondesdebunol.com; €44, or €90 during Tomatina, when it's a three-night minimum).

12

EATING AND DRINKING

Blayet Avda. Gaviotas 17, El Perellonet Ⓣ961 777 184, Ⓦblayet.com. This inviting spot, including a hotel with sea views, has been ladling out fragrant paellas and fresh seafood since 1935. Book ahead on weekends. Tues–Sun: Jan–July & Sept–Dec 1–4pm; Aug 1–4pm & 9–11pm.

Nou Raco Del Palmar 21, El Palmar Ⓣ961 620 172, Ⓦnouraco.com. Traditional cuisine meets modern sensibility (and decor) at this welcoming restaurant where seafood is the speciality, along with paella, of course. Tues–Sun 1–3pm, plus July–Aug Fri & Sat 8pm–midnight.

North of Valencia and the Costa del Alzahar

Within an hour's drive from Valencia are the fine Roman ruins at **Sagunto** as well as sweeping mountain scenery and good hiking around **Segorbe** and **Montanejos**. All three are perfect destinations for day-trips from the city. Towards the sea, the coast north of Valencia, which runs up to the pleasant port town of **Vinaròs** on the regional border, is known as the Costa del Alzahar. It is dotted with **beach resorts**; sun-seekers should head to **Benicàssim** and provincial capital **Castellón de la Plana** for the best sandy spots. Culture-lovers will appreciate the historic walled city of **Peñíscola** and its spectacular clifftop location, plus the fortified town of **Morella** which features castle and Gothic architecture and is about an hour's drive west of Vinaròs.

Sagunto

Twenty-four kilometres north of Valencia are the fine Roman remains of **SAGUNTO** (Sagunt). This town passed into Spanish legend when, in 219 BC, it was attacked by

Hannibal in one of the first acts of the war waged by Carthage on the Roman Empire. Its citizens withstood a nine-month siege before burning the city and themselves rather than surrendering. When belated help from Rome arrived, the city was recaptured and rebuilding eventually got under way. Today, Sagunto has several restored buildings to explore, especially in the well-preserved Jewish quarter, where you'll find medieval houses lining the cobbled alleyways.

Teatro Romano

C/Castillo • May–Sept Tues–Sat 10am–8pm, Sun 10am–2pm; Oct–April Tues–Sat 10am–6pm, Sun 10am–2pm • Free

Chief among Sagunto's ruins is the second-century Roman amphitheatre, the **Teatro Romano**, the basic shape of which survives intact. After years of (occasionally controversial) renovation, it's now functional and is recognized as a *Bien de Interés Cultural* national monument. In the summer (usually Aug) you can take in plays and concerts and the views from its seats are wonderful, encompassing a vast span of history – Roman stones all around, a ramshackle Moorish castle on the hill behind, medieval churches in the town below and, across the plain towards the sea, the black smoke of modern industry.

Museu Històrico de Sagunto

C/Castillo • Tues–Sat 11am–8pm, Sun 11am–3pm • Free • ☎ 962 665 581, ⓦ www.sagunt.es

The **Museu Històric de Sagunto**, which occupies two storeys of a fourteenth-century medieval house, features archeological finds from Sagunto and around, including Latin and Hebrew inscriptions and sculptures, detailed mosaics, vases and ceramics.

ARRIVAL AND INFORMATION   SAGUNTO

By train and bus There are trains every 30min and frequent buses between Sagunto and Valencia; the town centre is a 25min walk from the train station.

Turismo The main office is at Pza. Cronista Chabret (summer Mon 10am–2.30pm & 4.30–7.30pm, Tues–Fri 9am–2.30pm & 4.30–7.30pm, Sat 10.30am–2pm & 4–6.30pm, Sun 10am–2pm; winter Mon–Fri 9am–2pm &

4–6.30pm, Sat & Sun 9am–2pm; ☎ 962 655 859, ⓦ www. sagunt.es). There's another office at the Puerto de Sagunto, Avda. Mediterráneo 67 (summer Mon–Fri 9.30am–2pm & 5.30–8.30pm, Sat 10.30–2pm & 4–6.30pm, Sun 10am–2pm; winter 9.30am–2pm & 4–6.30pm, Sat 9am–2pm; ☎ 962 690 402, ⓦ sagunt.es).

ACCOMMODATION

Sweet Hotel Els Arenals C/ Felisa Longás 1 ☎ 962 608 067, ⓦ sweethotelelsarenals.com. This spacious beachfront hotel has modern rooms, a pool with sun terrace, restaurants and a gym. **€49**

Vall d'Uixo

Daily: Jan–May & Oct–Dec 11am–1.15pm & 3.30–5.45pm; June, July & Sept 11am–1.15pm & 3.30–6.30pm; Aug 11am–1.15pm & 3.30–7.15pm • €10 • ⓦ riosubterraneo.com • Frequent buses from Sagunto pass through Vall d'Uixo

Twenty-eight kilometres north of Sagunto, at **Vall d'Uixo**, is the underground river of San José, featuring caves with astonishing stalactites. Along with boat trips through the caves, the attendant tourist complex also has a swimming pool, restaurant and an auditorium which holds summer concerts.

Segorbe

About 30km inland from Sagunto is **SEGORBE**, which is worth a visit for its tranquil surrounds and ruins. It lies in the valley of the Río Palancia, among medlar and lemon orchards. Segorbe has its **fiesta** in September, including the Entrada de Toros y Caballos where bulls are run through the town by horses. One kilometre outside town on the road to Jérica, the so-called **fountain of the provinces** has fifty spouts, one for each province of Spain, each labelled with the coat of arms.

Catedral and museum

C/Santa Maria • Tues–Sun 11am–1.30pm • €3, but this may vary • ☎ 964 711 014

Segorbe's **Catedral** was begun in the thirteenth century, but suffered in the Neoclassical reforms, and only the cloister is original. Its **museum** contains a few pieces of Gothic Valencian art, with *retablos* by Vicente Maçip and his son; Flemish artwork; and a Madonna with Child in marble by the Italian master Donatello.

ARRIVAL AND INFORMATION   SEGORBE

By train and bus There are daily trains and buses between Valencia and Segorbe.
Turismo The tourist office is in Pza. Alto Palancia (Mon–Fri

9am–2pm & 4–6pm, Sat 10am–2pm & 4–6pm, Sun 10am–2pm; ☎ 964 713 254, ✆ turismo.segorbe.es).

ACCOMMODATION

Hospedería el Palen C/Franco Ricart 9 ☎ 964 710 740, ✆ elpalen.com. This renovated *hospedería*, set in a

historic building in the centre of town, has comfortable rooms. **€49**

Montanejos

Thirty-eight kilometres from Segorbe, tiny **MONTANEJOS** (not to be mistaken for Montan, the village just before) is popular with visitors for its hot springs, **Fuente de Baños**, where the water emerges at 25°C and has medicinal properties. **Walks** around the village join up with the nationwide GR (Gran Recorrido) network of trails.

ARRIVAL AND INFORMATION   MONTANEJOS   **12**

By bus Regular buses travel from Segorbe.

Information Visit ✆ montanejos.com for information.

ACCOMMODATION

Hotel Gil Avda. Fuente de Baños 28 ☎ 964 131 380, ✆ hotelgil.com. Comfortable rooms with views of the river and mountains, and a variety of spa treatments such as facial peels and massages on offer. **€28**

Hotel Rosaleda del Mijares Carretera de Tales 28 ☎ 964 131 079. Well-appointed hotel with a gym and a spa that provides a range of therapies. Closed Jan. **€67**

Castellón de la Plana

CASTELLÓN DE LA PLANA is a provincial capital and one of the main cities in the Costa del Azahar area. Important sights are mostly around Pza. Mayor, which contains a fine seventeenth-century **ayuntamiento**, the sixteenth-century **El Fadrí** bell tower and the neo-Gothic **Concatedral de Santa María** – the original eleventh-century building was destroyed in the Civil War.

The **Parque Ribalta**, dedicated to local Baroque painter Francisco Ribalta, is well worth a stroll but perhaps the main reason to visit are the nearby **beaches**, including at Castellón's *grau* (port), 5km east of the centre – and along the coastal road north to Benicàssim.

Museo de Bellas Artes

Avda. Hermanos Bou 28 • Tues–Sat 10am–8pm, Sun 10am–2pm • Free • ☎ 964 727 500, ✆ culturalcas.com

The impressive contemporary premises of the **Museo de Bellas Artes** features some valuable works by Francisco Zurbarán, José Benlliure and Vicente Salvador Gómez, such as ceramics and sculptures, and other paintings and works by a variety of regional and Spanish artists.

ARRIVAL AND INFORMATION   CASTELLÓN DE LA PLANA

By train and bus Buses and trains arrive at the combined station on Avda. Pintor Oliet. Buses for the

port and the beaches leave regularly from Pza. Borrull, and from nearby Pza. Farrell to Benicàssim.

Turismo The *turismo* on Pza. María Agustina (summer Mon–Fri 9am–7pm, Sat 10am–2pm; winter Mon–Fri 9am–2pm & 4–7pm, Sat 10am–2pm; ☎ 964 358 688, ⓦ castellonturismo.com), has a wealth of information about the city and district.

ACCOMMODATION

H2Castellón Carcagente ☎ 964 723 825, ⓦ hoteles2.com. Large, sleek hotel with gym in the city centre. Rooms are on the small side, but outfitted with all the amenities. **€40**

Hotel Herreros Avda. del Puerto 28 ☎ 964 284 264, ⓦ hotelherreros.com. This well-run hotel, about 2km from the beach, has simple, comfy rooms. **€41**

Vilafamés

VILAFAMÉS, 24km inland from Castellón, is an attractive hill town that successfully mixes the medieval, Renaissance and modern. In the highest part of town, there's an ancient ruined castle, conquered by Jaime I in 1233.

Museo de Arte Contemporáneo

Diputación Provincial 20 • Mon–Fri 10am–1.30pm & 4–7pm, Sat & Sun 10.30am–2pm & 4–7pm• €2 • ☎ 964 329 152, ⓦ turismodecastellon.com

The fifteenth-century Palau del Batlle houses the **Museo de Arte Contemporáneo**, a collection of over five hundred sculptures and paintings, from the late 1920s onwards, including works by Miró, Lozano, Chillida and Barjola.

ACCOMMODATION AND EATING	VILAFAMÉS

El Jardin Vertical C/Nou 15 ☎ 964 329 938, ⓦ eljardinvertical.com. This welcoming *casa rural*, in a five-storey seventeenth-century stone-walled house, has lovely, rustic rooms and views of the rolling countryside. The restaurant serves up a tasting dinner menu for €35; nonguests should book ahead. Restaurant generally daily 1.30–3.30pm & 8.30–10.30pm; closed Mon–Fri in winter. **€115**

El Rullo C/la Fuente 2 ☎ 964 329 384, ⓦ elrullo.es. Clean, colourful, wood-beamed rooms and a restaurant that does a daily lunch and dinner, right in the heart of the old town. **€60**

Benicàssim and around

It's music that draws the masses to **BENICÀSSIM**, a few kilometres north of Castellón, which hosts the annual, highly acclaimed alt-music **Festival Internacional de Benicàssim (FIB)**. Beyond the festival, Benicàssim is also a popular summer resort for Spaniards, with sun-kissed beaches, and a well-oiled tourist infrastructure.

Bodegas Carmelitano

C/Bodolz 12, off Avda. Castellón • Summer 9am–1.30pm & 3.30–7pm • Tours €2.50 (book in advance) • ☎ 964 300 849, ⓦ carmelitano.com

The Benicàssim area was well known as a centre for the production of Moscatel wine; very few vineyards remain today, but you can take a wine-tasting tour at **Bodegas Carmelitano**, named after the local Carmelite monks who produced an acclaimed aromatic herb liqueur here in the late seventeenth century. The *bodegas* continue to make the liqueur, using the same process and recipes as the monks, as well as Moscatel and other wines. Tours include the history of the *bodega*, a visit to the cellar and wine and liqueur tasting.

Aquarama

Mid-June to early Sept daily 11am–7pm • Full day €23.50, €17 for children under 1.4m (€20 and €13 online); half-day €15/€11 (€13/€9 online) • ☎ 964 303 321, ⓦ aquarama.net

As befits a vacation spot, Benicàssim boasts the massive **Aquarama** water park just south of town, with all the usual pools, water slides, overpriced snacks and screaming (but happy) kids.

FESTIVAL INTERNACIONAL DE BENICÀSSIM (FIB)

The annual **Festival Internacional de Benicàssim** (ⓦ fiberfib.com) in late July draws tens of thousands to hear the world's biggest names in alternative pop and rock. Over the years, it has pulled in everyone from Depeche Mode to Oasis and, more recently, The Killers and Arctic Monkeys. The dance tents are as buzzing as the live music stages, with DJs playing all night long. A four-day festival ticket is €159, including camping at the massive campsite.

Desierto de las Palmas

Six kilometres inland from Benicàssim, the **Desierto de las Palmas** is a nature reserve with a scattering of ruins (including the atmospheric *monasterio antiguo*, abandoned in the late eighteenth century) and walking circuits. The name was coined by Carmelite monks whose presence in the area dates back to 1697.

ARRIVAL AND INFORMATION   BENICÀSSIM

By train Trains for both Vinaròs and Castellón leave fairly regularly from the small station, 10min walk north of the *turismo*.

By bus There's a regular bus service between Castellón and Benicàssim: buses leave from the bus stop on Avda. Pintor Oliet roughly every 15min in summer, every 30min in winter. There are also five daily buses to and from Vinaròs, two of which stop at Peñíscola en route.

Turismo C/Santo Tomás 74–76 (summer Mon–Fri 9am–2pm & 5–8pm, Sat & Sun 10.30am–1.30pm & 5–8pm; winter Mon–Sat 9am–2pm & 4–7pm, Sun 9am–2pm; ☎ 964 300 102, ⓦ turismo.benicassim.es).

ACCOMMODATION

Although Benicàssim is heavily developed for package tourism, budget accommodation is fairly easy to come by in the streets around the *turismo*.

Camping Florida Sigalero 34 ☎ 964 392 385, ⓦ campingflorida.net. Well-run campsite close to the beach, with a pool and tennis courts. **€25.50**

Hotel Montreal C/Les Barraques 5 ☎ 964 300 681, ⓦ hotelmontreal.es. Comfy, polished-floor rooms near Terrers beach, plus a swimming pool, sun-dappled garden terrace and a buffet-style restaurant. Closed Oct–Semana Santa. **€111**

Hotel Residencia Canada C/La Pau 1 ☎ 964 304 611, ⓦ hotelcanadabenicassim.com. Sunny, well-kept rooms in the city centre, about a 20min stroll to the beach. **€45**

Hotel Termas Marinas Palasiet C/Pontazgo 11 ☎ 964 300 250, ⓦ palasiet.com. For the utmost in pampering (and prices) try this spa-hotel overlooking Playa Voramar, 3km from town. In addition to elegant, pale-toned rooms, there's a thermal centre with thalassotherapy treatments – think whirlpools with algae – along with sweet-chocolate facial peels and onyx-stone massages. **€190**

Hotel Voramar Paseo Pilar Coloma 1 ☎ 964 300 150, ⓦ voramar.net. This friendly, family-run hotel is a refreshing departure from the typical tourist trap, and also has an enviable perch right on the beach. The restaurant serves local dishes and seafood, and looks out at the sea. Minimum stays (three nights) likely. **€80**

EATING AND DRINKING

There are plenty of restaurants in the town centre, particularly on and around C/Tomás. As for nightlife, Benicàssim has its fair share of party spots: C/los Dolores is dotted with pubs, and for *discotecas* head to Avda. Gimeno Tomás.

Casa Teresa C/Estatut 23 ☎ 964 301 327. Dine on mid-priced paella, seafood, grilled meats and other regional cuisine at this family-run restaurant. Daily 1–3.30pm, Fri & Sat 8.30–11pm.

Peñíscola

Apart from the gorgeous town of **Alcalà de Xivert**, which has a Baroque church and an Arab-Christian hilltop castle, there's not too much north of Benicàssim until you reach **PEÑÍSCOLA**, 60km away. The setting is one of Spain's most stunning: a fortified promontory jutting out into the Mediterranean, zealously shielding its warren of alleys and lanes with perfectly preserved medieval walls. From here, it's easy to see why

12

Peñíscola is called the "The City in the Sea" - the spur is surrounded by water everywhere except its northeast corner.

The breezy Paseo Marítimo is a pleasant place from which to take in views of the sea, and the resort's slender **beach** is well kept, if busy. The farther north you get from the castle, the quieter it becomes. There's also a smaller cove beach, Playa Sur, 200m west of the old town.

The castle

Daily: summer 9.30am–9.30pm; winter 10.30am–5.30pm • €3.50

Peñíscola's **castle**, where part of *El Cid* was filmed, is well worth a visit to admire the colossal vaulted guards' quarters, basilica and the views from its roof. There was once a Phoenician settlement here, and later it was occupied by Greek, Carthaginian, Roman and Moorish rulers, but the present castle was built by the Knights Templar, with alterations by Pedro de la Luna. Pope Benedict XIII (Papa Luna) lived here for six years after he had been deposed from the papacy during the fifteenth-century church schisms.

Museo del Mar

C/Principe • April–June daily 10am–2pm & 4–8pm; July–Sept daily 10am–2pm & 5–9pm; Oct–March Tues–Sun 10am–2pm & 4–6pm • Free • ☎ 964 481 603

Peñíscola's **Museo de Mar** explores the town's rich maritime history in three sections: ancient seafaring and archeological finds, including anchors, old bronze diving helmets and pottery; the fishing industry and its evolution; and the area's underwater flora and fauna, comprising aquariums filled with local fish species and more.

ARRIVAL AND INFORMATION | PEÑÍSCOLA

By bus Buses shuttle between Peñíscola and Vinaròs every 30min between 7.30am and 11pm, stopping at various points along Avda. Papa Luna. For points south, you'll have to change bus at Benicarló (C/San Francisco).
Turismo Paseo Marítimo (summer Mon–Fri 9.30am–8pm,

Sat 10am–1pm & 5–8pm, Sun 10am–1pm; winter Mon–Fri 10am–1pm & 4–7pm, Sat 10am–1pm & 4–7pm, Sun 10am–1pm; ☎ 964 480 208, ⓦ peniscola.es). Both provide a good map and accommodation information.

ACCOMMODATION

Dios Esta Bien C/San Roque 22 y 24 ☎ 964 482 253, ⓦ diosestabien.com. One of the better choices in town: inviting and rustic, with comfortable rooms and a terrace; they also have an apartment with a private kitchen that's good for small groups, and a café that roasts its own coffee on-site. Doubles €70, apartments €90

Hostal Aranda C/General Aranda 3 ☎ 964 480 816, ⓦ hostalaranda.com. This comfortable spot has clean rooms with pastel walls and tiled floors. €53
Pension Casa Juanita C/Escuela 4 ⓦ pensioncasa juanita.com. Cheap-as-chips rooms with en suites and balconies, right in the middle of the old town – it's in the same block as the *ayuntamiento* building. €20

EATING AND DRINKING

The area just below the old town is thick with **restaurants**, many serving local dishes such as *suquet de peix* (fish stew).

Mandarina Avda. Papa Luna 1 ☎ 964 467 650, ⓦ mandarinaclub.net. This restaurant-lounge gets crowded in summer, but if you can nab a seat on the breezy terrace, you enjoy everything from salads and sushi to seafood and pasta – and then ease into the warm evening over cocktails. Mains €13–22, sushi tasting menu €25.

Daily noon–late; generally closed Nov–April.
El Peñón C/Santos Mártires 22 ☎ 964 480 716, ⓦ elpenyon.es. This rustic hotel and restaurant has been serving quality seafood and local specialities since 1982. Mains from €18. Daily 1–3.30pm & 8–11pm; closed late Dec–March.

Vinaròs

The **beaches** of the scruffy port-cum-resort **VINARÒS**, next along the coast, are small but rarely packed, and in town there's an elaborate Baroque church, with an excellent local produce market nearby. In the early evening, it's worth going down to the dockside **market** to watch the day's catch being auctioned and packed off to restaurants all over the region. Locally caught fish is excellent, with the *langostinos* reputedly the best in Spain. In mid-August, Vinaròs celebrates the **Fiestas del Langostino**, with plenty of outdoor seafood feasts.

ARRIVAL AND INFORMATION   VINARÒS

By train The train station, 2km west of the centre, has twelve daily services to and from Valencia via Castellón and eleven connecting to Barcelona via Tarragona.

By bus There are two buses to Morella (Mon–Fri 8am & 4pm), leaving from Pza. de Sant Esteve. Both the half-hourly service to Peñíscola, and the six daily buses to Castellón (three of which stop at Benicàssim) leave from the corner of Avda. de Leopold Querol and Pg. del 29 de Setembre.

Turismo Near the seafront, the *turismo* (Pg. de Colom; summer daily 10am–2pm & 5–8pm; winter Mon–Fri 10am–2pm & 5–7pm, Sat 10am–2pm, Sun 11am–2pm; ☎ 964 453 334, ⓦ turisme.vinaros.es) has decent maps and will help to locate accommodation.

ACCOMMODATION AND EATING

Bar Folet C/Costa y Borràs 58 ☎ 964 451 597. Almost overlooking the portside action, this is a wonderfully friendly spot for local seafood dishes and a glass of wine. Mains from €18. Daily 10.30am–4pm & 7.30–midnight; closed Tues lunch; closes around 10.30pm in winter.

El Faro Zona Portuaria ☎ 964 456 362. This converted lighthouse serves fresh seafood, and a creative array of tapas; it can be quite pricey (mains from €24), but the seafood is top-notch. Daily 1.30–3.30pm & 8.30–10.30pm; limited hours in winter.

Hotel Nou Casablanca C/Santa Ana 30 ☎ 964 450 425, ⓔ noucasablanca@gmail.com. Central, family-run hotel with comfortable rooms. **€45**

12

Morella

MORELLA, 62km inland on the road from the coast to Zaragoza, is one of the most attractive – and possibly most friendly – towns in the Castellón province. A medieval fortress town, it rises from the plain around a small hill crowned by a tall, rocky spur and a virtually impregnable **castle** that dominates the surrounding countryside. A perfectly preserved ring of ancient walls defends its lower reaches. The city was recovered from the Moors in the thirteenth century by the steward of Jaime I. He was reluctant to hand it over to the Crown, and it's said that the king came to blows with him over possession of the town. Today, Morella hosts an annual **festival of classical music** in the first two weeks of August.

Basílica de Santa María la Mayor

Pza. de la Iglesia • Tues–Sun: summer 11am–2pm & 4–7pm; winter 11am–2pm & 4–6pm • Free

Chief among the town's monuments is this beautiful **basílica**, a fourteenth-century Gothic construction with carved doorways and an unusual raised *coro* reached by a marble spiral stairway, with detailed reliefs that depict the different stages in the life of Christ.

The castle

Daily: mid-June to mid-Sept 11am–7pm; mid-Sept to mid-June 11am–5pm • €3.50

Morella **castle** itself is now in ruins, but the view up to its imposing walls from the town below is still impressive, as is the view down from the crumbling courtyard at the top – down over the monastery, bullring and town walls to the plains. In the distance are the remains of the peculiar Gothic **aqueduct** that once supplied the town's water. The splendid restored Palacio del Gobernador features an exhibit on the history of the castle and of Morella.

Museo Tiempo de los Dinosaurios

Pza. de San Miguel • Tues–Sun: May–Sept 11am–2pm & 4–7pm, Oct–April 11am–2pm & 4–6pm • €2

The curious **Museo Tiempo de los Dinosaurios** features a wide array of dinosaur fossils, from carnivores to herbivores, discovered in the area, along with audiovisual displays (mainly in Spanish) and exhibits on geological finds. Look out especially for the full-scale replica of an Iguanodon.

ARRIVAL AND INFORMATION

By bus Buses run between Morella and Vinaròs (Mon–Fri 2 daily) and Castellón (Mon–Fri 2 daily, Sat daily). Morella is one possible approach to the Maestrazgo region of southern Aragón – buses leave for Alcañiz (Mon & Fri 10am) and Cantavieja/Villafranca del Cid (Mon–Fri daily,

early evening departure).
Turismo Pza. de San Miguel (summer daily 10am–2pm & 4–7pm; winter Tues–Sat 10am–2pm & 4–6pm, Sun 10am–2pm; ☎ 964 173 032, ✆ morellaturistica.com).

ACCOMMODATION

La Fonda Moreno C/Sant Nicolau 12 ☎ 964 160 105, ✆ lafondamoreno.com. Pleasant, colourful rooms, along with an inviting restaurant serving regional cuisine. **€60**
Hostal La Muralla C/Muralla 12 ☎ 964 160 243. Relax in clean, well-kept rooms with views of the hills. Rates include breakfast. **€60**
Hotel El Cid Puerta San Mateo 3 ☎ 964 160 125,

✆ hotelelcidmorella.com. Modern, comfortable rooms with balconies. They also have a restaurant with nicely priced menus. **€54**
Hotel del Pastor San Julián 12 ☎ 964 161 016, ✆ hoteldelpastor.com. Welcoming hotel with wood-beam ceilings and cosy rooms; they also run the excellent restaurant *Mesón del Pastor*. Rates include breakfast. **€59**

EATING AND DRINKING

Calle San Julián, between the church and *ayuntamiento*, and its neighbouring streets are Morella's main destination for **food**, with bars, bakeries and cafés. Ask for *flaons*, a local pastry made from cinnamon, cheese and almonds. Morella is prime **truffle** country – the best time to try them is between February and early March, when many of the restaurants serve truffles, and the town hosts a gastronomic festival celebrating this aromatic delicacy.

Casa Roque Cuesta San Juan 1 ☎ 964 160 336, ✆ casaroque.com. For local *trufa negra* and other gourmet-rustic delicacies, head to this inviting restaurant. Tues–Sat 1.30–3.30pm & 8.30–10.30pm, Sun 1.30–3.30pm.

Mesón del Pastor Cuesta Jovani 5 & 7 ☎ 964 160 249, ✆ mesondelpastor.com. Fill up on robust dishes of grilled meats, wild mushrooms and the region's famous truffles, when in season. Mon–Fri & Sun 1–4pm & 9–11pm; Sat & 9–11pm; dinner-only in Aug.

The Costa Blanca

Stretching south of Valencia, the **Costa Blanca** (White Coast) boasts some of the **best beaches** in the region, especially between Gandía and Benidorm. Much of it, though, suffers from the worst excesses of **package tourism**, with concrete building projects looming over the sand. It pays to book ahead in summer, particularly in August. Campers have it somewhat easier – there are hundreds of campsites – but driving can be a nightmare unless you stick to the toll roads (which are nearly always deserted). If you're taking the inland route as far as **Gandía**, you'll get the opportunity to see the historic town of **Xátiva**.

Xàtiva

The ancient town of **XÀTIVA** (Játiva), 50km south of Valencia, was probably founded by the Phoenicians and certainly inhabited by the Romans. Today, it's a scenic, tranquil place and makes a great day-trip. Medieval Xàtiva was the birthplace of Alfonso de Borja, who became Pope Calixtus III, and his nephew Rodrigo, father of the infamous Lucrezia and Cesare Borgia. When Rodrigo became Pope Alexander VI, the family moved to Italy.

Xàtiva has a fine collection of mansions scattered around town, but most are private and cannot be entered. Many of the churches, though, have been renovated, and the **old town** is a pleasant place to wander. **Fiestas** are held during Semana Santa and in the second half of August, when the Feria de Agosto is celebrated with bullfights and livestock fairs.

Museo del Almudín

Corretgeria 46 • Mid-June to mid-Sept Tues–Fri 10am–2pm, Sat & Sun 10am–2pm; mid-Sept to mid-June Tues–Fri 9.30am–2.30pm & 4–6pm, Sat & Sun 10am–2.30pm • €2.40, €3.10 with the castle • ☎ 962 276 597

In the centre of town, the **Museo del Almudín** features both an archeological collection and an art museum. The latter includes several pictures by José Ribera (who was born here in 1591) and engravings by Goya – *Caprichos* and *Los Proverbios*. A portrait of Felipe V is hung upside down in retribution for his having set fire to the town in the War of the Spanish Succession and for changing its name (temporarily) to San Felipe.

The castle

Tues–Sun: March–Oct 10am–7pm; Nov–Feb 10am–6pm • €2.40, €3.10 for a joint ticket with the Museo del Almudín

From town, it's a steep uphill walk (there's the option of a tourist train for €4.20) to Xàtiva's tenth-century **castle** – follow signposts from the main square, Pza. del Españoleto, or take a taxi from outside the *turismo* (€11 one-way). It's worth the ascent, though; the castle has been renovated with exhibition rooms and leafy gardens, and there are stunning lookout points over the surrounding town and vast countryside, plus a chapel that houses the tomb of the Count of Urgell.

Església de Sant Feliu

April–Oct Tues–Sat 10am–1pm & 4–7pm, Sun 10am–1pm; Nov–March Tues–Sat 10am–1pm & 3–6pm • Free

On the hill leading to the castle is the thirteenth-century **Església de Sant Feliu**, a hermitage built in transitional Romanesque-Gothic style, and the oldest church in Xàtiva. The interior boasts ancient pillars, fine capitals and a magnificent Gothic *retablo*.

12

ARRIVAL AND INFORMATION XÀTIVA

By bus and train Xàtiva is served by buses and trains to and from Valencia; the train (1hr) is cheaper, and leaves every 30min. There are also connections with Gandía (by bus) and Alicante (by train).

Turismo C/Alameda Jaume I (summer Tues–Fri 10am–2pm & 5–7.30pm, Sat & Sun 10am–2pm; winter Tues–Fri 10am–1.30pm & 4–6pm, Sat & Sun 10am–2pm; ☎ 962 273 346, ⓦ comunitatvalenciana.com). There's also a seasonal office in front of the *ayuntamiento* (summer daily 10am–2pm; same phone).

ACCOMMODATION AND EATING

Keep an eye open for **arnadí** in the bakeries – a local speciality of Moorish origin, it's a rich (and expensive) sweet made with pumpkin, cinnamon, almonds, eggs and pine nuts.

Hostería de Mont Sant ☎ 962 275 081, ⓦ mont-sant.com. If you'd like to go the deluxe route, opt for this ancient country house on the way up to the castle, which has gorgeous jasmine gardens and a pool. €104

Hotel Murta C/Ángel Lacalle ☎ 962 276 611, ⓦ hotelmurta.com. If you're enjoying Xàtiva's peace and quiet and are looking for a decently priced spot, try this modern and comfortable hotel. They also have a restaurant specializing in local cuisine such as baked rice dishes (à la carte and set menus at lunch and dinner). €43

Gandía and around

GANDÍA, 65km south of Valencia, is a historical town and lively resort area. The town centre features the impressive Borja palace, a quiet old quarter including the attractive Colegiata de Santa María church, and plenty of shops and restaurants. The long, sun-splashed **Gandía Playa** sprawls along the coast 4km away, and draws crowds of vacationing Spaniards in the summer.

Palacio Ducal de los Borja

End March–Oct Mon–Sat 10am–1.30pm & 4–7.30pm, Sun 10am–1.30pm; Nov end to March Mon–Sat 10am–2pm & 3–6.30pm • All visits are by guided tour, €7 • ☎ 962 871 4 65, ⓦ palauducal.com

The main testimony to Gandía's heyday is the **Palacio Ducal de los Borja**, built in the fourteenth century, with Renaissance and Baroque additions and modifications later.

Duke Francisco de Borja was largely responsible for the golden age of the town (late fifteenth to early sixteenth century) in terms of urban and cultural development. Learned and pious, the duke opened colleges all over Spain and Europe, and was eventually canonized. The palace contains his paintings, tapestries and books, but parts of the building itself are of equal interest, such as the *artesonado* ceilings and the pine window shutters, so perfectly preserved by prolonged burial in soil and manure that resin still oozes from them when the hot sun beats down. There are also several beautiful sets of *azulejos*, but these are outshone by the fourteenth-century Arabesque wall tiles, whose brilliant lustre is irreparable as it was derived from pigments of plants that became extinct soon after the Muslims left. The palace also occasionally hosts excellent contemporary and international arts and theatre programmes.

ARRIVAL AND INFORMATION

By train and bus The joint bus and train station is on Avda. Marqués de Campo. Trains and buses run regularly to and from Valencia. The AVE train now connects Gandía with Madrid (via Valencia) in just over 3hr; trains run a couple of times a day in each direction; schedules may be limited in winter; contact RENFE (w renfe.com) for current updates.
Turismo The main *turismo* is opposite the station (summer

GANDÍA

Mon–Fri 9.30am–1.30pm & 4–8pm, Sat 9.30am–2.30pm; winter Mon–Fri 9.30am–1.30pm & 3.30–7.30pm, Sat 9.30am–1.30pm; ☎ 962 877 788, w visitgandia.com). There's a second office at Paseo Marítimo Nefruno, Gandía Playa (summer Mon–Sat 9.30am–8.30pm, Sun 9.30am–1.30pm; winter Tues & Thurs 9.30am–2.30pm, Fri 9.30am–2.30pm & 3.30–6.30pm, Sun 9.30am–1.30pm; ☎ 962 842 407).

GETTING AROUND

By bus Buses run every 15–20min (6am–11.30pm) from the tourist office in town to Gandía Playa.

ACCOMMODATION

Albergue Mar i Vent C/ Dr. Fleming, 10km south of Gandía town ☎ 962 831 748. This exceptionally pleasant hostel is on the beachfront at Playa de Piles. In summer, about six daily buses run there from the train station; in winter, there are fewer buses, and they drop you off about 1km from the hostel. **€18**
Hotel Bayren Paseo de Neptuno 62 ☎ 962 840 300, w hotelesrh.com. Big, glossy four-star beach hotel – if

you're in Gandía for the sun and sand, then this place delivers. Most of the rooms have balconies, plus there's a pool, restaurant/terrace and plenty of activities for kids. **€109**
Hotel Los Naranjos C/Avda. del Grau 67 ☎ 962 873 143, w losnaranjoshotel.com. In the middle of town, this decent hotel has clean, if rather faded, rooms. **€50**

EATING AND DRINKING

Gandía town has a range of restaurants, from traditional spots with a *menú del día* to tapas, while the beach zone is a good place for **seafood** and paellas; don't miss *fideuà*, a seafood paella cooked with vermicelli instead of rice.

La Gamba Carretera Nazaret-Oliva ☎ 962 841 310. A few blocks back from Gandía Playa, with a breezy terrace in the summer. Fill up on fresh seafood, from *cigalas* (crayfish) and lobster to, yes, *gambas* (shrimp). The daily menu is €30, and mains are €15–20. Tues–Sun 1.30–3.30pm, plus 8.30–10.30pm in summer.

L'Ullal C/Benicanena 12 ☎ 962 877 382. The chefs here use local ingredients to creative use, with a tasty range of seafood, grilled meats and the regional speciality of *fideuà*. Tasting menus €28–35. Mon–Sat 1.30–3.30pm & 8.30–10.30pm; closed dinner Mon & Tues.

NIGHTLIFE

For **nightlife**, head just slightly inland to Pza. del Castell for cocktails at one of the busy bars, then make for the beach area clubs, most of which are liveliest on summer weekends; some open in the low season for events and parties.

CocoLoco Paseo de Neptuno 53 ☎ 962 867 261, w cocoloco.es. The crowds here get hot and sweaty, dancing to everything from Latin beats to techno. The owners also run several other nightspots, including poolside beach club *Agua de Coco* and the sleek *Luna*, both on Paseo

Neptuno. Generally Thurs–Sat midnight until late.
Discoteca Bacarra C/Legazpi 7 ☎ 659 597 776 w bacarragandia.com. Groove to DJ-spun tunes surrounded by fresh-off-the beach locals. Thurs–Sat midnight–late.

Around the cape: Gandía to Altea

A string of attractive little towns and beaches stretches from **Gandía** to **Altea**, before you reach the developments of Benidorm and Alicante, but your own transport is essential to enjoy the best of them, and accommodation can be pricey. The least expensive option along this coast is to camp – there are scores of decent **campsites**, and a useful booklet listing them is available from local *turismos*.

Denia

DENIA, at the foot of Parque Natural Montgó, is a sizeable, sprawling town even without its summer visitors. Beneath the wooded capes beyond, bypassed by the main road, stretch probably the most beautiful **beaches** on this coastline – it's easier if you have a car to get to most of them, though there are a couple of buses that make the trip from the port.

ARRIVAL AND DEPARTURE   DENIA

By train and bus Trains depart regularly for Benidorm, where you can then connect to a tram to Alicante. Buses also run hourly to and from Alicante, departing from Pza. Archiduque Carlos, among other spots.
By ferry Daily ferries service Mallorca and Ibiza: for

information, contact Baleària (☎ 902 160 180, ⓦ balearia .com), or Iscomar (☎ 902 119 128, ⓦ iscomar.com). Departures Sant Antoni, Ibiza (2 daily; 2hr 15min); Ibiza Town (3 daily; 2hr); Palma (4 daily; 5hr); Formentera (daily; 3hr 45min).

ACCOMMODATION

Hostal Residencia Loreto C/Loreto 12 ☎ 966 435 419, ⓦ hostalloreto.com. Simple and slightly dated place, though the rooms have a certain rustic style. **€84**
La Posada del Amar Pza. Drassanes ☎ 966 432 966,

ⓦ laposadadelmar.com. Set in a nicely renovated thirteenth-century building that was a former customs house at the port, this hotel blends old and new with elegant aplomb. Price includes breakfast. **€163**

Xàbia

At the heart of this area, very near the easternmost Cabo de la Nao, is **XÀBIA** (Jávea), an attractive, prosperous town surrounded by hillside villas, with a fine beach and a very pleasant old town. In summer, both Denia and Xàbia are lively in the evenings, especially at weekends, as they're popular with *valencianos*. There are plenty of idyllic cove beaches close to Xàbia; one of the best is **Cala Portitxol** (also known as Playa la Barraca), a wonderful sand-and-pebble bay backed by high cliffs.

ACCOMMODATION   XÀBIA

Hotel Xàbia Pío X 5 ☎ 965 795 461, ⓦ hotel-javea.com. This place by the port has rooms with modern bathrooms with a touch of a maritime theme and balmy sea views. **€72**
Parador de Jávea Avda. del Mediterráneo ☎ 965 790

200, ⓦ parador.es. With an enviable perch overlooking the sea and great views, this sizeable place has all the parador hallmarks, including a restaurant serving local cuisine. Breakfast included. **€185**

EATING AND DRINKING

Nightlife is centred on the beach bars. Later in the evening, the crowds move to the out-of-town clubs on the road to Cabo de San Antonio.

La Bohême Playa Arenal ☎ 965 791 600, ⓦ bohemejavea.com. Restaurants come and go with great frequency in Xàbia, but *La Bohême* has stayed around. The Mediterranean dishes have international touches – a seafood casserole with basmati rice, or fresh tuna drizzled in teriyaki sauce. The lunch menu is a good deal at just

under €15. Daily 1–4pm and 6pm–midnight.
La Bomboneria Lepanto 20 ☎ 965 791 647. Enjoy uniquely prepared Mediterranean cuisine and fresh seafood at this friendly port restaurant. The daily menu is around €18, and there's a gourmet version for €29. Daily 1–3.30pm & 8–11pm.

Altea

Heading southeast from Xàbia, you pass the dramatic rocky outcrop known as the **Peñón de Ifach**, its natural beauty offering a stark contrast to the concrete towers of the neighbouring package resort of **Calpe** (Calp). If you'd like to enjoy the coast for a night or two, **ALTEA**, just 11km to the south, is a more attractive proposition: a small resort set below a historic hilltop village, with views overlooking the whole stretch of coastline. Tourist development is centred on the seafront, where there's a pebble beach and attractive promenade of low-rise apartment buildings interspersed with tottering old fishermen's houses.

The old village, or *poble antic*, up the hill, is even more picturesque, with its steep lanes, white houses, blue-domed church and profuse blossoms. In summer, the entire quarter is packed with pavement diners and boutique browsers.

If you need a sandy shore, head just south again to El Albir, which also has great hikes up to a lighthouse on a craggy outcrop.

INFORMATION ALTEA

Turismo C/San Pedro 9 (summer usually Mon–Fri 9.30am–2pm & 5–7.30pm, Sat 10am–1pm & 5–8pm; rest of the year reduced hours; ☎965 844 114, ⓦaltea.es).

ACCOMMODATION

It's a good idea to book ahead in the summer. Beyond staying in town, the verdant environs reveals a number of comfortable and unique *casas rurales*.

Hotel Altaya C/San Pedro 28 ☎965 840 800, ⓦhotelaltaya.com. This swanky place on the seafront has prime sea views from balustraded balconies. **€68**

El Naranjal Cami dels Morers 15 ☎965 792 989, ⓦcampingelnaranjal.com. Well-run campsite 1.5km south of Xàbia with facilities including a pool and bar and, in the summer, live music and other events. **€27**

★ **Refugio Marnes** Sierra de Bernia, Benissa ☎637 063 003, ⓦrefugiomarnes.com. Some 15km northwest of Calp, this rural *finca* (country estate), covering 50 acres, has three types of accommodation: a restored farmhouse B&B, a private cottage and a luxurious Bedouin tent (both available for weekly rentals only). Farmhouse rooms **€83**, tent (weekly) **€663**, cottage (weekly) **€765**

EATING AND DRINKING

It's a treat **to eat** in the old town, with most of the alfresco dining centred on Pza. de la Iglesia; there are also plenty of cafés and restaurants along the seafront. The best places to **drink** are to be found around the main square of the old village.

Oustau C/Mayor 5 ☎965 842 078, ⓦoustau.com. If you're feeling flush, try the French-influenced cuisine at this quality restaurant – it's one of the better-known old-town options. Tues–Sun 7pm–midnight.

Restaurante La Capella C/San Pablo 1 ☎966 880 484, ⓦlacapella-altea.com. Lovely restaurant in a historic building with stone walls and a breezy terrace with views of the surrounding countryside. Traditional mid-priced cuisine, from *arroz a la banda* to salads bursting with local produce. Mon, Tues, Thurs–Sun noon–4pm & 8pm–midnight, Wed noon–4pm; closed last 2 weeks in Sept, Nov & Feb.

Sant Pere 24 C/Sant Pere 24 ☎965 965 845 154. By the seafront, this comfortable spot serves up delicious seafood and rice combinations, including fresh shrimp, lobster and the catch of the day. Mains €11–15. Daily 1–11.30pm.

Benidorm

Hugely high-rise, vaguely Vegas and definitely dodgy, **BENIDORM** is the beach resort that everyone loves to hate. Nonetheless, the crowds keep coming, and if you're looking for package tourism, Benidorm is king. Fortunately, the reason it was so popular during the boom of the 1970s and 1980s is still present: sun-drenched sandy beaches and crystal-clear sea. This is why the British, German and Scandinavian holiday-makers who are lobster-red from the sun (and, often, the drink) still arrive in their hordes.

Decades ago, British writer Rose Macaulay described Benidorm as a small village "crowded very beautifully round its domed and tiled church on a rocky peninsula". The old part's still here, serving up fresh mojitos, delicious tapas and Mediterranean leisure, but you may need to walk past the "English" pubs screening football and rugby and the pulsating discos and bar-clubs to find it. If you want to order food from laminated,

BENIDORM'S WATER PARKS

If you're travelling with kids (or just want to get in touch with your inner child), you're spoilt for choice in Benidorm, where each amusement park seems to eclipse the next: there's the "mythical" theme park **Terra Mítica** (Mythic Land) (W terramiticapark.com); the wildlife theme park **Terra Natura** (W terranatura.com); the **Aqualandia** water park (W aqualandia.net); and, well, you get the idea.

quadrilingual menus, or if you want to meander along a cosy, covered "tapas route", Benidorm has all of it.

The connection to Benidorm from Alicante via tram is quick and easy so it's possible to do a day-trip if you want to just enjoy the beach, the bars, and then avoid the boisterous atmosphere in Avenida de Mallorca – but, when in Rome…

ARRIVAL AND INFORMATION
BENIDORM

By train, bus and tram Trains arrive at the top of town, off Avda. de Beniarda, while the main bus stop is at the junction of Avda. de Europa and C/Gerona. Moving on to Alicante, you can either take the FGV tram or a bus, but the tram is quicker and more convenient. There's also a night-train service that runs along the coast to Alicante in July and August. Regular buses travel to and from Valencia.

Turismo Pza. del Torrejó, in the old town (Mon–Fri 9am–9pm, Sat 10am–5pm, Sun 10am–2pm; ☎ 965 851 311, W visitbenidorm.es).

ACCOMMODATION

With tens of thousands of hotel beds and hundreds of apartments, finding a **place to stay** isn't a problem (except perhaps in July and Aug – when you may need to commit to a minimum of three nights or more). Budget places are clustered around the old town, and out of season many of the giant hotels slash their prices drastically, making Benidorm a cheap base from which to explore the surrounding area.

12

Barceló Asia Gardens Glorieta del Fuego, Mítica ☎ 966 818 400, W barceloasiagardens.com. If you're looking to splurge in Benidorm, this elegant, five-star hotel is the place to do it. Set back from the sea (2km from the beach) in massive grounds on the slopes of the Sierra Cortina, it boasts Balinese-style furnishings, a spa and two good Asian-themed restaurants. **€295**

Camping Raco Avda. Doctor Ochoa 19 ☎ 965 868 552, W campingraco.com. One of the best – and greenest – of Benidorm's myriad campsites. **€26.40**.

Gran Hotel Bali C/Luís Prendes ☎ 966 815 200, W granhotelbali.com. It's hard to miss this towering deluxe landmark, one of Europe's highest hotels – and the preferred choice of visiting rock royalty. Prices can plummet by half in the low season. **€190**

Hotel Iris C/Palma 47 ☎ 965 865 251, W iris-hotel.net. Comfortable, simple budget hotel. It's a nice price regardless, but especially reasonable if you consider its central location in the middle of the old town. **€38**

Hotel Rocamar C/Cuatro Esquinas 18 ☎ 965 850 552, W hotelrocamarbenidorm.es. Smack in the heart of the old town, with simple rooms boasting touches of boutique style. **€90**

Hotel Santa Faz C/Santa Faç 18 ☎ 965 854 063, W santafazhotel.com. Basic but well kept, and one of the better budget options in town. **€80**

Villa Venecia Pza. San Jaume 1 ☎ 965 855 466, W hotelvillavenecia.com. Fully updated and renovated, this welcoming beachfront property is a five-star boutique hotel, with a breezy, light-filled interior, a sunny terrace overlooking the sea, and a restaurant serving innovative local dishes. **€225**

Villa del Mar Av Armada Española 1 ☎ 965 85 45 50, W hotelvilladelmar.com.es. This beachfront hotel has a spa, restaurant and a brilliant rooftop bar where you can snuggle up on a huge sunbed and watch the world of Poniente beach go by. Modern, airy rooms with sea views and rain showers – if you're feeling flush, note that some rooms have a Jacuzzi. Spa and restaurant do breakfast, lunch and dinner daily. Price includes breakfast. **€94**

Sol Costablanca Av Alcoy ☎ 902 14 44 40, W es.melia .com. With a funky bar area and a pool 10m from the beach, this hotel has stylish summery rooms with balconies and a restaurant serving, among other things, an indulgent breakfast spread (price includes breakfast). **€112**

EATING AND DRINKING

Fish and chips and fried breakfasts can dominate in Benidorm, but local cuisine is available and surprisingly authentic if you eat in the old town around C/Santo Domingo.

Club Náutico Benidorm Paseo Colón ☎ 965 853 067, ⓦ cnbenidorm.com. For a departure from the Benidorm crowds and cacophony, amble down to this quiet waterfront restaurant south of the centre, where you can sample fresh seafood on a breezy terrace to the sounds of water slapping against the sides of boats in the dock. Daily menu €24. Daily 1–4pm & 8–11pm.

La Picaeta de Matias C/L'Alt 3 ☎ 687 239 466. Basic and friendly spot, if a bit touristy, with tasty tapas and fish. Mains €8.50–12. Mon–Sat 8pm–midnight.

Posada del Mar Paseo Colón ☎ 965 851 373. Usually crammed to the gills, this is a lively spot where you can tuck into freshly caught fish and seafood. Weekly menu €17, tasting menu €24. Daily 1–4pm & 8pm–midnight; may have limited hours in winter.

Inland from Benidorm

In total contrast to the coastal strip, the remote mountainous terrain **inland from Benidorm** harbours some of the most traditional and isolated villages in the Valencia region. Better roads and local government grants (which encourage the conversion of rural properties into guesthouses) are slowly opening up this area to tourism, but for now the austere *pueblos* retain a fairly untouched character, Castilian is very much a second language and the main visitors are hikers. The area is rich in **birdlife**, with golden eagles, and, in autumn, griffon vultures, often spotted soaring over the limestone ridges. There's no bus or train service, other than links to Alcoy and **Guadalest** (generally only once daily to and from Benidorm), so you'll need your own wheels to get around – and a leisurely drive to take it all in is well worth it. Head to the **Amadorio Reservoir**, a staggering aquamarine expanse, for a swimming experience that is nothing like that on the beach.

Continue west along the well-maintained highway to Sant Vicent del Raspeig **then travel north to Alcoy**, for a memorable contrast between hedonistic sun-and-sand coast and quiet, rural inland.

Guadalest

Twenty-one kilometres west of Benidorm, **GUADALEST** is one of the more popular tourist attractions in the area. The sixteenth-century Moorish castle town is built into the surrounding rock, and you enter through a gateway tunnelled into the mountain. If you can put up with the slew of tourists and gift shops, it's worth

---

FIESTAS DE MOROS Y CRISTIANOS

Fiestas de Moros y Cristianos are some of the most important fiestas in the region, and the three-day Fiesta de Moros y Cristianos in **Alcoy**, about 60km from Alicante, is perhaps the biggest of the lot. It's held for three days around St George's Day (Día de San Jordi); usually April 23 but this can vary slightly according to when Easter falls. Magnificent processions and mock battles for the castle culminate in the decisive intervention of St George himself – a legend that originated in the Battle of Alcoy (1276), when the town was attacked by a Muslim army. New costumes are made each year and prizes are awarded for the best, which then go into the local museum, the **Museo Alcoyano de la Fiesta**, at C/ San Miguel 60–62 (Tues–Sat 10am–2pm & 4–7pm, Sun 11am–2pm; €3; ☎ 965 540 580, ⓦ museualcoiadelafesta.com).

On the first day, the Christians make their entrance in the morning before the Moors in the afternoon; day two is dedicated to St George, with several religious processions; day three sees a gunpowder battle, leading to the saint's appearance on the battlements. Access from Alicante is easy, with five buses a day. If you decide to stay in town, you can try *Hostal Savoy*, C/Casablanca 9 (☎ 965 547 272, ⓦ hostalsavoy.com; €45), or the *Hotel Reconquista*, Puente San Jorge 1 (☎ 965 330 900, ⓦ hotelreconquista.es; €61, during fiestas €150). The *turismo*, C/Sant Llorenç 2, next to the *ayuntamiento* (Mon–Fri 10am–2pm & 4–6pm, Sat & Sun 11am–2pm; ☎ 965 537 155, ⓦ alcoy.org), can also offer suggestions for accommodation. After Alcoy's fiesta, the Moros y Cristianos fiestas in **Villena** (beginning of Sept) and **Elche** (Aug) are two of the best.

12

visiting for the view down to the reservoir (accessible via the village of Beniarda just to the west) and across the valley.

Museo Ethnològico

C/Iglesia 1 • Mon–Fri & Sun: summer 10am–8pm; winter 10am–6pm • Free • ☎ 661 152 774, ⓦ guadalest.es

Set in an eighteenth-century house on the main street, **Museo Ethnològico** explores local history via exhibits of antique tools and agricultural methods, plus audiovisual accompaniments and displays that explain the production process of local foods, "from olives to olive oil".

INFORMATION AND TOURS   GUADALEST

Turismo The office on Avda. de Alicante (Mon–Fri & Sun 10am–2pm & 3–5pm; Sat 11.30am–1.30pm & 3–5pm; ☎ 965 885 298, ⓦ guadalest.es) has maps of the town and can arrange trips on a solar-powered tourist boat which centre on the local flora and fauna.

Alicante

In the minds of many, **ALICANTE** (**Alacant**) is often lumped together with the other brash Costa Blanca resorts. It shouldn't be. Valencia's second-largest city, the thoroughly Spanish Alicante has a decidedly elegant Mediterranean air. Seafront *paseos* and wide, breezy esplanades, such as the Rambla Méndez Núñez, are peppered with cosy bars and terrace cafés; a series of well-curated museums feature everything from ancient archeology to contemporary art; the city's culinary scene is making a name for itself, just as its healthy nightlife did long ago; and its long, sandy beaches are sun-kissed for much of the year. The city's well-maintained sandy beach – **Playa del Postiguet** – has some nice *chiringuitos* but gets very crowded in summer. The beaches at **San Juan de Alicante**, about 6km out (take bus #23 from the Pza. del Mar or the FGV tram to the Costa Blanca stop), are also quite built up, while **Playa Arenales**, backed by sand dunes, is more pleasant; it's 12km south of the city and reachable by an hourly bus from the main bus station.

Founded by the Romans, who named it Lucentum (City of Light), and dominated by the Arabs in the second half of the eighth century, Alicante was finally reconquered by Alfonso X in 1246 for the Castilian Crown. In 1308, Jaime III incorporated Alicante into the kingdom of Valencia.

Today, the main fiesta, Las Hogueras de San Juan, is at the end of June, and ignites a series of cracking celebrations, second only to Las Fallas in Valencia, including over fifty individual bonfire spots around the city.

Castillo de Santa Bárbara

Castle Daily: April–Sept 10am–10pm; Oct–March 10am–8pm • Free • **Museum** Daily 10am–2.30pm & 4–8pm • **Lift** Daily: April–Sept 10am–7.30pm; Oct–March 10am–7.30pm • €2.40 • ☎ 965 927 715, ⓦ castillodesantabarbara.com

The rambling **Castillo de Santa Bárbara**, an imposing yet grand medieval fortress located on the bare rocky hill above the town beach, is Alicante's main historical sight. It's best approached from the seaward side where a 205m shaft has been cut straight up through the hill to get you to the top; the **lift** entrance is on Avda. de Jovellanos. Almost opposite are the Iberian and Roman remains that have been found on the site, but most of the present layout dates from the sixteenth century. The castle itself is home to the **Museo de la Ciudad de Alicante (MUSA)** which explores the history of Alicante and the surrounding region via a variety of exhibits. The grounds, or **Parque de la Ereta**, are attractively landscaped, with olive groves, recently renovated pathways, a café and tremendous views of the city. There's also a viaduct-style path which passes Ermita de Santa Cruz, a cute traditional whitewashed chapel.

12

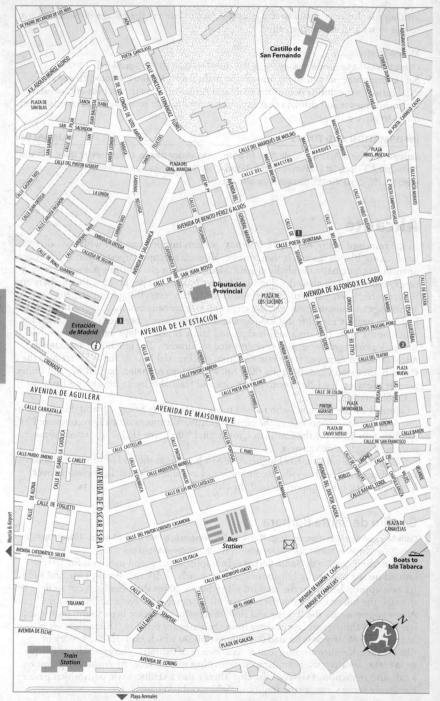

Castillo de
San Fernando

C DE PADRE RECAREDO DE LOS RÍOS

JAÉN

POETA GARCILASO

PLAZA DE
SAN BLAS

AV. ADOLFO MUÑOZ ALONSO

CALLE WENCESLAO FERNÁNDEZ FLÓREZ

AV. DE LOS CONDES DE SOTO AMENO

SANTA ISABEL
SAN JUAN BOTA

SANTA LEONOR

RABASA

SANTA FELICITAS

POETA GARCILASO

SAN GABRIEL

SAN EL PILAR

SALVADOR

AVENIDA

PLAZA DEL
GRAL MANCHA

JOSÉ Mª PÍ

CALLE DEL PINTOR GISBERT

CALLE GASPAR TATO

CALLE JUAN ORTEGA

CALLE CARLOTA FIGARÓN

LA UNIÓN

CARDENAL BELLUGA

CARDENAL TATO

CALLE CARDENAL

CALLE DE

TUCUMÁN

CALLE DEL MARQUÉS DE MOLINS

MAESTRO GAZTAMBIDE

MAESTRO BARBIERI

MAESTRO MARQUÉS

MAESTRO BRETÓN

MAESTRO

CALLE DEL

AVENIDA PBL.

PLAZA
HNOS. PASCUAL

AV. POETA CARMELO CALVO

C. POETA CAMPOS HÁSALDO

CALLE GARCÍA MORATO

SARGENTO HALLO

TENIENTE DURÁN

T. AGÜERGANO MARTÍ

ENRIQUETA ORTEGA

PINTE

CALLE DE BONO GUARNER

CALLOSA DE SEGURA

CALLE DE

NÚÑEZ DE SALAMANCA

CATEDRÁTICO FERRÉ VIDIELLA

CALLE DE SAN JUAN BOSCO

CALLE

AVENIDA DE BENITO PÉREZ GALDÓS

GENERAL MARVÁ

CALLE DE

SEGURA

CALLE POETA QUINTANA

CALLE DE BILBAO

CALLE DE PABLO IGLESIAS

CALLE DE

CALLE DE

[1]

Estación
de Madrid

[3]

Diputación
Provincial

PLAZA DE
LOS LUCEROS

AVENIDA DE ALFONSO X EL SABIO

CALLE DE ÁLVAREZ SEREIX

CALLE ÁNGEL LOZANO

LAS NAVAS

CALLE CÉSAR ELGUEZÁBAL

CALLE DE BAZÁN

AVENIDA DE LA ESTACIÓN

CALLE DE SERRANO

CREMADES

CALLE PINTOR CABRERA

GENERAL LACY

CALLE GENERAL

AVENIDA DE FEDERICO SOTO

CALLE DE

CALLE MÉDICO PASCUAL PÉREZ

CALLE DEL TEATRO

[2]

PLAZA
NUEVA

LAS NAVAS

JERUSALÉN

AVENIDA DE AGUILERA

CALLE CARRATALÁ

CALLE DE ISABEL LA CATÓLICA

C. CARLET

AVENIDA DE MAISONNAVE

CALLE POETA VILA Y BLANCO

O'DONNELL

CALLE DE COLÓN

PINTOR
AGRASOT

PLAZA
MONTAÑETA

CALLE DE GERONA

CALLE BARÓN

CALLE DE SAN FRANCISCO

CALLE CID

VELARDE

PLAZA DE
CALVO SOTELO

CALLE PARDO JIMENO

CALLE DE ALONA

CALLE DE FOGLIETTI

CALLE CASTELLAR

CALLE DE CHURRUCA

CALLE PINTOR APARICIO

C. PARÍS

CALLE PORTUGAL

CALLE ARQUITECTO MORELL

CALLE DE LOS REYES CATÓLICOS

CALLE DEL PINTOR LORENZO CASANOVA

CALLE DE ITALIA

Bus
Station

CALLE DE ALEMANIA

AVENIDA DEL DOCTOR GADEA

CALLE DE CANALEJAS

ROBLES

LIMONES

CALLE RAFAEL TEROL

C. JC. CHAPULI LAMEZA

C. VALDÉS

PLAZA DE
CANALEJAS

AVENIDA DE ÓSCAR ESPLÁ

Murcia & Airport

AVENIDA CATEDRÁTICO SOLER

TRAJANO

CALLE EUSEBIO SALA

CALLE MANUEL SEMPERE

CALLE DEL ARZOBISPO LOACES

CALLE ORENSE

AB-EL-HAMET

AVENIDA DE RAMÓN Y CAJAL

PARQUE DE CANALEJAS

Boats to
Isla Tabarca

AVENIDA DE ELCHE

PLAZA DE GALICIA

Train
Station

AVENIDA DE LORING

N

Playa Arenales

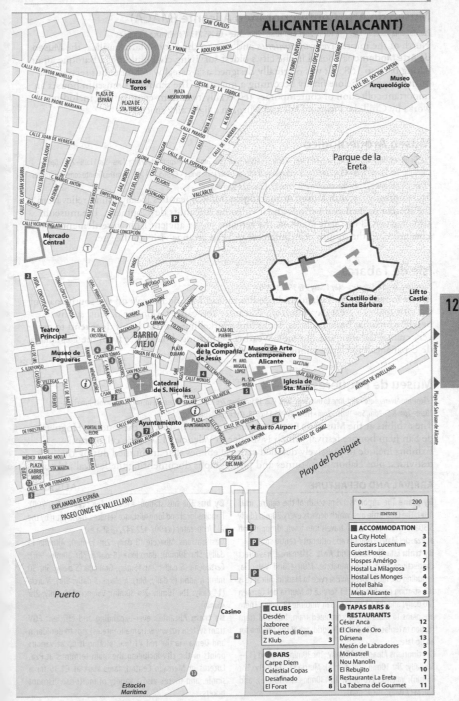

ALICANTE (ALACANT)

12

Valencia

Playa de San Juan de Alicante

Plaza de Toros

Parque de la Ereta

Museo Arqueológico

Castillo de Santa Bárbara

Lift to Castle

Mercado Central

Teatro Principal

Museo de Fogueres

BARRIO VIEJO

Real Colegio de la Compañía de Jesús

Museo de Arte Contemporáneo Alicante

Catedral de S. Nicolás

Iglesia de Sta. María

Ayuntamiento

★ Bus to Airport

Puerto

Casino

Playa del Postiguet

Estación Marítima

0	200
metres	

■ ACCOMMODATION

La City Hotel	3
Eurostars Lucentum	2
Guest House	1
Hospes Amérigo	7
Hostal La Milagrosa	5
Hostal Les Monges	4
Hotel Bahía	6
Melia Alicante	8

● CLUBS

Desdén	1
Jazboree	2
El Puerto di Roma	4
Z Klub	3

● BARS

Carpe Diem	4
Celestial Copas	6
Desafinado	5
El Forat	8

● TAPAS BARS & RESTAURANTS

César Anca	12
El Cisne de Oro	2
Dársena	13
Mesón de Labradores	3
Monastrell	9
Nou Manolín	7
El Rebujito	10
Restaurante La Ereta	1
La Taberna del Gourmet	11

Museo de Arte Contemporáneo Alicante (MACA)

Pza. de Santa María 3 • Tues–Sat 10am–8pm, Sun 10am–2pm • Free • ☎ 965 213 156, ⓦ maca-alicante.es

North of the impressive *ayuntamiento* and next to the Santa María basilica, the **Museo de Arte Moderno** is housed in the city's oldest surviving civil building, a Baroque affair dating back to 1685. It was originally designed as a cereal warehouse, but served as a business school before finally becoming a museum. The renovated museum houses an important collection of contemporary (especially twentieth-century) art, including works by Chillida, Picasso, Dalí and Miró, in a light airy space.

Museo Arqueológico

Pza. Dr Gómez Ulla • Sept–June: Tues–Fri 10am–7pm, Sat 10am–8.30pm, Sun 10am–2pm; July & Aug: Tues–Sat 11am–2pm, 6pm–midnight, Sun 11am–2pm • €3, €2 to El Tossa archeological site, or €4 for joint ticket • ☎ 965 149 000, ⓦ marqalicante.com • Bus routes #2, #6, #9, #20 and #23 pass the museum and trams L1, L3 and L4 stop nearby

The impressive, stylish **Museo Arqueológico (MARQ)** features locally found relics from the Iberian to medieval periods and a video on Alicante's development. The museum also manages **El Tossal de Manises**, the remains of the ancient Roman settlement of Lucentum, in the suburb of Albufereta, and can arrange visits to the site.

Isle de Tabarca

Boats June–Sept 6 daily; Oct–May 1 daily • ☎ 965 216 396

Isle de Tabarca, a small island and Mediterranean Marine Reserve off the south coast of the city, makes a great day-trip from Alicante. You can relax on the decent, sunny beach, which has basic facilities, including snorkelling centres, but it does tend to get very cramped during the summer. Weather permitting, boats leave from the Explanada de España; call to clarify sailing times and fares.

Museu de Fogueres

C/Teniente Álvarez Soto • Mid-June to mid-Sept: Tues–Sat 10am–2pm & 6–9pm, Sun 10am–2pm; mid-Sept to mid-June Tues–Sat 10am–2pm & 5–8pm, Sun 10am–2pm • Free • ☎ 965 146 828, ⓦ hogueras.org

The exhibits at the **Museu de Fogueres** delve into the history of the raucous Hogueras de San Juan bonfire festival, which is similar to Valencia's Las Fallas celebration. Exhibits include impressively detailed satirical effigies that are burned during the festivities, plus elaborate costumes and photographs documenting the festival's history.

ARRIVAL AND DEPARTURE

ALICANTE

By plane The airport is 12km south of the centre, in El Altet. The C6 shuttle bus, which departs every 20min (daily 5.30am–midnight; €2.70) travels into town, dropping off at Pza. del Mar, La Rambla and other city-centre spots.

By train Estación de Madrid, Avda. Salamanca, has direct connections to Madrid, Albacete, Murcia and Valencia, including the high-speed AVE service to Madrid. Alicante is the starting point for the C1 service to Murcia del Carmen (20 daily) and the C3 route to San Vincente (8 daily). There are plans to build a new combined train, bus and tram station to replace Estación de Madrid; ask at the *turismo* for an update.

Destinations Albacete (10 daily; 1hr 30min); Madrid (12–14 daily; 2hr 10min–2hr 45min); Murcia (8–14 daily; 1hr 15min); Valencia (10 daily; 1hr 30min–2hr 15min); and Xàtiva (7 daily; 1hr 15min).

By bus The bus station, Avda. Loring (☎ 965 130 700), handles local and long-distance services, mostly run by the ALSA operator (☎ 902 422 242, ⓦ alsa.es).

Destinations Albacete (8 daily; 2hr 15min); Almería (5 daily; 5hr 30min); Barcelona (8 daily; 7hr 30min–9hr); Cartagena (6 daily; 2hr 45min); Granada (5 daily; 5hr 30 min); Madrid (9 daily; 6hr); Málaga (5 daily; 8hr); Murcia (14 daily; 1hr 10min–2hr 30min); Valencia (20 daily; 2hr 45min).

By tram Alicante's ever-expanding and efficient FGV tram system (ⓦ www.tramalicante.es) zips to Benidorm and Denia via the red #1 line, picking it up at various points in the city including the main terminus at Pza. Luceros or Mercado Central; fares start at €1.35 for a single, and there's also a variety of multi-use discount tickets.

12

INFORMATION

Turismo Avda. Rambla Méndez Núñez 41 (Mon–Fri 10am–6pm, Sat–Sun 10am–2pm; ☎965 200 000, ⊛alicanteturismo.com). There are also branches at Estación de Madrid (Mon–Fri 9.30am–2pm & 4.15–7pm, Sat–Sun 10am–2pm), in Pza. del Ayuntamiento (Mon–Fri 9.30am–2pm & 4.15–7pm, Sat–Sun 10am–2pm) and at Playa de San Juan in the summer months.

ACCOMMODATION

Alicante has a wide range of **accommodation**, with plenty of hotels concentrated at the lower end of town, above the attractively tiled seafront walk, Explanada de España.

Camping El Jardín El Campello ☎965 657 580, ⊛campingeljardin.com. One of many campsites along the coast here, this inviting site is near a quiet beach, is accessible by tram and also has fetching little bungalows (sleep six people). Camping **€30.50**, bungalows **€106**

La City Hotel Avda. de Salamanca 16 ☎965 131 973, ⊛lacityhotel.com. Bright, modern, good-value hotel near the train station, with a cool-toned lobby that gives way to comfortable rooms with crisp bedspreads and blonde-wood furnishings. **€66**

Eurostars Lucentum Avda. Alfonso X El Sabio 11 ☎902 932 424, ⊛eurostarslucentum.com. Sleek and central addition to the Eurostars chain, with plenty of blonde wood, gleaming marble lobby floors, recessed lights and business-friendly amenities. **€69**

Guest House C/Segura 20 ☎650 718 353, ⊛guesthousealicante.com. A perennial budget favourite among travellers – and with good reason – this inviting, cheery guesthouse is lovingly cared for by the amiable owner. Individually decorated, spic-and-span rooms and apartments reveal personal touches, such as complimentary coffee and tea. **€50**

★**Hospes Amérigo** Rafael Altamira 7 ☎965 146 570, ⊛hospes.es. This upmarket hotel is housed in a magnificently restored seventeenth-century Dominican convent. The rooms reveal gleaming hardwood floors and delicate white curtains, while the breezy rooftop deck has a pool, sauna and spa, and a chill-out zone where you can relax under the night sky and look out to the castle and sea. One of the city's best restaurants, *Monastrell* (see p.832), is on-site. **€110**

Hostal La Milagrosa C/Villavieja 8 ☎965 216 918, ⊛lamilagrosa.eu. Efficiently run, often busy *pensión* with great-value rooms that are simple, spotless and inviting. A well-kept roof terrace, seemingly nestled just under the imposing castle silhouette, seals the deal. **€40**

★**Hostal Les Monges** C/San Agustín 4 ☎965 215 046, ⊛lesmonges.es. Named after the convent of cloistered nuns (*monges*) that sits across the street, this is one of the better – and more original – deals in Alicante, with lovely, strikingly styled rooms. Some are antique-chic, while others are Japanese influenced, and are accessed from corridors lined with vibrant *azulejos*, oddball curios and unlikely paintings – and there's a chill-out area and a roof terrace. Ask for an upstairs room if you're a light sleeper. Breakfast available for €6. **€50**

Hotel Bahia C/Juan Bautista Lafora 8 ☎965 206 522, ⊛hotelbahia.es. This friendly, unpretentious hotel on the seafront has a bright reception and unassuming, coolly comfortable rooms, some with sea views. **€50**

Internacional La Marina 33km out on the road to Torrevieja ☎965 419 200, ⊛campinglamarina.com. A pleasant location in the woods, close to a good beach, and with excellent facilities: everything from a gym and spa to fantastic lake-themed pool area, to games room, bike rental and live music. **€60**

Melia Alicante Pza del Puerto 3 ☎965 205 000, ⊛melia.com. Smack-bang in between the port and Postiguet beach, this hotel has spacious sea-view rooms with red or black hardwood decor, and a pool area with bar for seaside snacks. The charming restaurant serves modernized local food and the lounge bar has some of the best maritime panoramas in the city. **€82**

EATING

Alicante boasts a rich variety of restaurants, and is now as much a culinary destination as a seaside town: uniquely, a good number of the city's well-known chefs are women, such as María José San Román of *Monastrell* (see p.832), who is nicknamed the "Saffron Queen" for her prowess with rice dishes. Restaurants are concentrated in and around the old town, with **tapas** places on C/San Francisco. If you want to fashion your own meals, there's no better place than the enormous **Mercado Central**, housed in a wonderful old *modernista* building on Avda. Alfonso X El Sabio. The *mercado* is so well-known that it's the standard meeting point for all social activity. Another market (a major outdoor event) is held by the Pza. de Toros (Thurs & Sat 9am–2pm).

César Anca C/Ojeda 1, Pza. Gabriel Miró ☎965 201 580, ⊛cesarancahosteleria.com. Elegant restaurant where the innovative César Anca reinvents Mediterranean cuisine, with mains at €15–25. Wines from the on-site *bodega*, including an excellent selection of Valencia and Alicante *vinos*, are matched to the superb food. Mon–Thurs & Sun noon–4.30pm & 8.30–11.30pm, Fri & Sat noon–4.30pm & 8.30pm–midnight.

12

TURRÓN

Spaniards have a sweet spot for **turrón** (torró in Catalan/Valenciano), a nougat candy with almonds and honey that's perhaps most popular in the Alicante region. Turrón is believed to have originated as a Moorish delicacy in the town of **Jijona** (Xixona). You can sink your teeth into two varieties: crunchy (often called Alicante) and soft (Jijona), which has a smooth consistency almost like peanut butter. The two leading brands are Lobo and 1880, though you'll find many others throughout Spain, including small-batch boutique producers; and you'll see turrón for sale in sweet shops throughout the region, including along C/Mayor in Alicante. The **Museo del Turrón** in Jijona (Jan–June Mon–Fri 10am–1.30pm & 4–7.30pm, Sat 10am–1pm & 4–7pm, Sun 10am–1pm & 5–7pm; July–Dec Mon–Fri 10am–7.30pm, Sat 10am–1pm & 4–7pm, Sun 10am–1pm & 5–7pm; €3; ☎ 965 610 712, ⓦ museodelturron.com), traces turrón's impressive timeline – it can be traced back to the Middle Ages – and includes a view of the modern production plant on site.

El Cisne de Oro C/Teatro 5 ☎ 965 141 427. Locals crowd around the curved bar at this lively tapas place to munch on the justifiably popular signature grilled pork loin, with mushrooms, pepper and mayonnaise. Also available is the regional speciality mojama (salted tuna). Close to San Nicolas Catedral. Tues–Sun noon–late.

Dársena Muelle de Levante 6 ☎ 965 207 589, ⓦ darsena.com. This handsome nautical themed restaurant on the waterfront, complete with porthole windows, serves aromatic paellas and top-notch seafood in a genteel setting. It's pricey – but the paella is the real deal. Mains from €16, tasting menu €60. Tues–Sat 1–4pm & 8–11pm, Sun 1–4pm; open until 11.30pm July–Aug.

Mesón de Labradores C/Labradores 19 ☎ 965 204 846. Buzzing bar where you can graze on tasty tapas, including fresh seafood bites and wafer-thin ham, and wash it down with jugs of sangría. Tues–Sun 7.30pm–1am.

★ **Monastrell** Amérigo Hotel, C/Rafael Altamira 7 ☎ 965 200 363, ⓦ monastrell.com. Michelin-starred chef María José San Román creates delicious Spanish cuisine with a twist, from monkfish with rye-bread crumbs and saffron-scented tomato sauce to a superb variety of rice dishes, including one topped with red Denia prawns and white truffles. Tasting menu €79. Tues–Sat 1.30–4pm & 8pm–midnight.

Nou Manolín C/Villegas 3 ☎ 965 200 368, ⓦ noumanolin.com. Feast on market-fresh regional fare, including superb shellfish and paella in the curved terracotta restaurant space. Mains are €18–27. Daily 1–4pm & 8pm–midnight.

El Rebujito C/San Francisco ☎ 966 105 719, ⓦ gruporebujito.com. Lively little Andalucian bar-restaurant, where in the true tapas tradition, dining out is as much a social occasion as a gastronomic one. Seating is at the bar or at big barrels-turned-tables, and the menu is scrawled on a chalkboard. Try a plate of shrimp with a bottle of wine for €15, or opt for a small beer (a "caña") or a glass of sangría for the nice price of €1.50–2. Tues–Sat noon–late; may close for part of summer.

Restaurante La Ereta Parque de la Ereta ☎ 965 143 250, ⓦ laereta.es. The memorable city views are matched by the locally sourced cuisine with a designer touch, from razor clams and ruby-red hunks of tuna to cubes of watermelon sangría. Halfway up to the castle and surrounded by the greenery of Parque de la Ereta, the attractive wood-and-glass restaurant offers a refreshing change from the bustle of the city. Tasting menus €39 and €59. Summer: Mon–Wed dinner only, Thurs–Sat lunch and dinner; winter: Tues–Wed dinner only, Thurs–Sat lunch and dinner.

La Taberna del Gourmet C/San Fernando 10 ☎ 965 204 233, ⓦ latabernadelgourmet.com. Stylish modern haunt with an eye-catching rocky facade, which serves some of the more creative tapas and organic wines in Alicante, including lamb sweetbreads, chorizo croquettes and scrambled eggs with cod. Tapas and montaditos €4–5, mains €17–25. Tapas menu is €27.50; tasting menu €55. Daily 11am–late.

DRINKING AND NIGHTLIFE

For hitting the bars and **drinking** with locals, the old town – or El Barrio, as it's called – still rules, with everything from dark, cosy bars to jazz joints. Alicante also has a decent number of **gay clubs and bars**, both in the old town and just south of it, around C/ San Fernando. For a slightly more Ibiza-style night, with large bars and clubs in a small vicinity, head to the port area past the casino. This designated party village never fails to be lively even for midweek, out of season, drinking and dancing – often until sunrise.

BARS

Carpe Diem C/Santo Tomás. Busy yet welcoming bar serving beers and a dangerously tempting selection of chupitos (shots). Very popular with students including foreigners on exchange from American universities – Wednesdays are international party night. Tues–Sat 8pm–1am.

12

Celestial Copas C/San Pascual. Knock back a few cocktails in this deliciously strange and arty bar. Summer daily 10pm–3am; winter Thurs 10pm–3am, Fri & Sat 10pm–4am.

Desafinado C/San Andrés 6 ☎ 965 142 671. This lively pub heats up with live music and friendly banter. Tues–Sun 8.30pm–4.30am.

El Forat Pza. Santa Faz. Wildly popular gay (but very straight-friendly) bar with an over-the-top decor of twinkling lights, huge bunches of fake flowers and caricatures of divas and record covers on the walls. Fri & Sat 11pm–late.

CLUBS

Desdén C/Labradores 22 ☎ 965 143 323. Groove to a range of music, from jazz and house to dance and funk. Thurs–Sat 11pm–late.

Jazboree C/San José 10 ☎ 616 971 325. Music club with all sorts of live acts: jazz, ska, roots and sometimes even flamenco. Wed–Sat 11pm–late.

El Puerto di Roma Muelle de Levante ☎ 965 201 448. One of the biggest bars in the area, this venue plays contemporary pop music including Latino hits until the small hours and beyond. Tues–Sat 11pm–late.

Z Klub C/San Fernando ☎ 965 210 646. This stylish club spins laidback dance sounds, and draws a lively, youngish crowd. Thurs–Sat 11pm–late.

DIRECTORY

Consulates UK, Rbla Méndez Núñez 28–32 ☎ 902 10 93 56.   **Police** C/Médico Pascual Pérez 27 ☎ 965 20 15 26.

Around Alicante

For a distinct change from Alicante's sun and sand, head inland to the lush palm forest at the lovely town of **Elche**. Further south, explore the region's formidable history in elegant **Orihuela**, which features three medieval churches and a well-preserved old quarter.

12

Elche

ELCHE (ELX), 20km inland and south from Alicante, is famed for its exotic **palm forest**, El Palmeral, and for the ancient **stone bust** known as *La Dama de Elche*, discovered here in 1897 (and now in the Museo Arqueológico in Madrid). These two assets, plus the School Museum of Pusol, a centre for traditional culture and education, made Elche the first town in Spain to have three cultural properties registered in the different categories of the UNESCO World Heritage List.

The palm trees, originally planted by the Moors, are still the town's chief industry, and not only for tourism: the female trees produce dates, and the fronds from the males are in demand for use in Palm Sunday processions and as charms against lightning.

The **parque municipal** of Elche town is one of the most charming in the region, with palm-shaded gravel paths, a bandstand, water fountains and a huge Spanish flag, as well as sports grounds and a municipal pool, plus the amiable restaurant *Dátil de Oro* (see p.834).

Elche is also the home of a remarkable summer **fiesta**, which culminates in a centuries-old mystery play – *Misteri*, held in the eighteenth-century **Basílica Menor de Santa María** over August 14–15. Additional celebrations include one of the best examples of the *Moros y Cristianos* mock battles (see box, p.826).

Huerto del Cura

Porta de la Morera 49 • Daily: Jan–Feb & Nov–Dec Mon–Sat 10am–5pm, Sun 10am–3pm; May–Aug 10am–8.30pm; March, April, Sept & Oct Mon–Sat 10am–7.30pm, Sun 10am–6pm • €5 • ☎ 965 451 936, ⓦ visitelche.com

Elche's palm forests, unique in Europe, are all around the outskirts of the city; the finest trees are those in the **Huerto del Cura**, a beautifully landscaped private garden, where you can stroll among the sun-warmed groves.

Museu del Palmeral

Porta de la Morera 12 • Tues–Sat 10am–1.30pm & 4.30–8pm, Sun 10.30am–1.30pm • €3 • ☎ 965 422 240, ⓦ visitelche.com

Set in a traditional farmhouse near the Huerto del Cura, the **Museu del Palmeral** explores the origins, history and evolution of the beautiful palm groves via exhibits, videos and touch screens. A visit also includes a walk through the lush, adjacent palm grove and orchard.

Rio Safari Park

Daily: June, July & Sept 10.30am–7pm; Aug 10.30am–8pm; Oct–May 10.30am–6pm • Adults €22.50, children (3–12 years) €17 • ☏ 966 638 288, ⓦ riosafari.com

Ten kilometres out of town, on the way to Santa Pola, lies the **Rio Safari wildlife park**, a home to tigers, monkeys, antelopes, camels and giraffes, as well as the venue for a number of animal shows, including sea lions and parrots. There's also an extensive selection of non-creature-related activities, such as trampolines, go karts and a pool with water slide – all surrounded by the ever-present palm trees.

ARRIVAL AND INFORMATION   ELCHE

By train and bus Trains and buses run more or less hourly between Alicante and Elche.
Turismo Pza. Parque 1 (April–Oct: Mon–Fri 9am–7pm,

Sat 10am–7pm, Sun 10am–2pm; Nov–March: Mon–Fri 9am–6pm, Sat 10am–6pm, Sun 10am–2pm; ☏ 966 658 196, ⓦ visitelche.com).

ACCOMMODATION

Jardín Milenio Prolongacion de los Curtidores ☏ 966 612 033, ⓦ hotelmilenio.com. Located within the UNESCO Heritage Site of the Palmeral, this well-appointed hotel is based around an attractive courtyard with a mosaic water feature. Big beds and terracotta colour rooms, plus a restaurant, sauna and pool on-site. **€30**

Hotel Huerto del Cura Porta de la Morera 14 ☏ 966 610 011, ⓦ hotelhuertodelcura.com. One of Elche's most elegant hotels, just south of the Huerto del Cura, with wood-beamed rooms leading onto stunning gardens, and a graceful ambiance throughout. A gourmet restaurant, wine bar terrace and spa break options add to the "oasis" feeling. **€90**

EATING AND DRINKING

Keep an eye out for *arroz con costra*, a local speciality (literally "rice and crust"), made with rice, eggs, *embutidos* (cured sausage), chicken and rabbit.

El Granaino C/José María Buch 40 ☏ 966 664 080, ⓦ mesongranaino.com. For Levantine and Andalucian delicacies, head to this acclaimed restaurant, where the chefs incorporate seasonal produce in the well-crafted dishes. Pricey (mains from €24) but worth it. Daily 9.30am–4pm & 8pm–midnight, closed Sun.

Dátil de Oro Parque Municipal ☏ 965 453 415, ⓦ datildeoro.com. This massive restaurant, set amid the leafy town park, serves tasty traditional cuisine, from rice dishes to quality seafood and meats. Mains €14–20. Daily 9.30am 1–4pm & 8.30–11pm.

Orihuela

Just over 50km southwest of Alicante lies **ORIHUELA**, capital of the Vega Baja district, where Los Reyes Católicos held court in 1488. The town's aristocratic past is reflected in the restored old quarter; despite its proximity to the coast, Orihuela retains its provincial charm and embraces its Muslim and Baroque origins. One of Orihuela's hidden treasures, the Baroque **Monasterio de la Visitación Salesas** on C/Salesas Marqués Arneva, has several paintings by the nineteenth-century artist Vincente López displayed in its cloisters and a gorgeous gold altar. The building is usually open only to churchgoers during hours of worship and only very occasionally to the public; enquire at the *turismo*.

Catedral de Orihuela

C/Doctor Sarget • Tues–Fri 10am–2pm & 4–7pm, Sat & Sun 10am–2pm; winter hours may vary • €2

Right in the centre of the old town is the Catalan-Gothic medieval **Catedral**, no bigger than the average parish church, with spiralling, twisted pillars and vaulting. A painting by Velázquez, *The Temptation of St Thomas*, hangs in a museum in the nave. Don't overlook the Mudéjar (Iberian Muslim)-influenced, fourteenth-century *Puerta de las Cadenas*.

Museo Diocesano de Arte Sacro

C/Ramón y Cajal • Tues–Sat 10am–2pm & 4–7pm, Sun 10am–2pm • €4 • ☎ 966 743 627, ⊛ museodeartesacro.es

The **Palacio Episcopal**, with its impressive Baroque exterior, is home to the **Museo Diocesano de Arte Sacro**, which explores the city's formidable religious past via an unexpectedly rich collection of art and sacred treasures from throughout the town and the region, including works by the early Renaissance painter Pablo de San Leocadio.

Iglesia de Santiago

Pza. de Santiago • Tues–Fri 10am–1.30pm & 4–7pm, Sat & Sun 10am–2pm • Free

The **Iglesia de Santiago** is another of Orihuela's Catalan-Gothic churches, a style you won't find any farther south. The oldest part of the church is the front portal, the Puerta de Santiago, a spectacular example of late fifteenth-century Gothic-Hispano-Flemish architecture. Inside, the furniture is Baroque, and there's a *retablo* by Francisco Salzillo.

Iglesia de Santas Justa y Rufina

Pza. Salesas • Generally Tues–Fri 10am–1.30pm & 4–7pm, Sat & Sun 10am–2pm • Free • ☎ 965 300 622

In the town centre, just past the *ayuntamiento*, rises another of Orihuela's medieval churches, the **Iglesia de Santas Justa y Rufina** – its tower is the oldest construction in the parish and has excellent gargoyle sculptures.

Museo de Semana Santa

Pza. de la Merced 1 • Tues–Sat 10am–2pm & 4–7pm, Sun 10am–2pm • €2 • ☎ 966 744 089, ⊛ semanasantaorihuela.com

Housed in the Iglesia de Nuestra Señora de la Merced, the **Museo de Semana Santa** explores the history of the Semana Santa celebrations, with exhibits on the elaborate costumes and rituals, plus audiovisual presentations and photographs that trace the long timeline of Semana Santa.

Museo de la Muralla

C/Río • Tues–Sat 10am–2pm & 4–5pm, Sun 10am–2pm • Free • ☎ 965 304 698

Within the grounds of the Universidad Miguel Hernández, the **Museo de la Muralla** is centred on the extensive underground remains of Orihuela's impressive city walls, plus a well-preserved *baños Árabes* (Arab baths), which includes a room where the water was heated. There's also a Gothic palace and a Baroque building dating from the eighteenth century, plus displays of ancient ceramics.

Museo Fundación Pedrera

C/Doctor Sarget • Tues–Sat 10am–2pm & 4–7pm, Sun 10am–2pm • ☎ 966 736 106

The impressive **Museo Fundación Pedrera** is set in the eighteenth-century Palacio de Sorzano de Tejada. It contains a rich permanent collection that includes works by many of the Spanish greats, including Sorolla, Picasso, Murillo, Zurbarán, Goya and Dalí.

Colegio de Santo Domingo

C/Adolfo Claravana • Summer: Tues–Sat 10am–1.30pm & 5–8pm, Sun 10am–2pm; winter: Tues–Sat 10am–1.30pm & 4–7pm, Sun 10am–2pm • Free • ⊛ cdsantodomingo.com

The Baroque **Colegio de Santo Domingo**, at the entrance to town near the palm forest, was originally a Dominican monastery. It was converted into a university in 1569 by Pope Pius V, then closed down by Fernando VII in 1824. The two cloisters are well worth seeing, along with the fine eighteenth-century Valencian tiles in the refectory. For a view of the town and surrounding plains, walk up to the seminary on top of the hill – from Pza. Caturla in the centre of town, take the road leading up on the right; not far from the top, there are a couple of steeper shortcuts to the right.

12

By train and bus Orihuela is connected by regular trains and buses to Alicante, Murcia and Torrevieja, which arrive and depart from the combined station at the south end of Avda. de Teodomiro.

Turismo Pza. de la Soledad, near the Catedral (summer

Mon 8am–3pm, Tues–Fri 8am–3pm & 4–8pm, Sat & Sun 10am–2pm & 5–8pm; winter Mon 8am–4pm, Tues–Fri 8am–3pm & 4–7pm Sat & Sun 10am–2pm & 4–7pm; ☎ 965 304 645, ⊚ orihuelaturistica.es).

ACCOMMODATION AND EATING

Hostal Rey Teodomiro Avda. Teodomiro 10 ☎ 965 300 349, ⊚ hostalreyteodomiro.eu. Convenient for the bus station, and just five blocks from the train station, this decent *hostal* has clean, bright, unpretentious rooms. **€40**

Hotel Melia Palacio de Tudemir C/Alfonso XIII 1 ☎ 966 738 010, ⊚ melia.com. This handsome hotel is suitably palatial, with wall-mounted excavations inscribed in ancient Arabic, and calming rooms and corridors; the restaurants serve à la carte Mediterranean dishes as well as

bar snacks and tapas. Restaurant daily 1.30–4pm & 8.30–11pm. **€64**

Restaurante Casa Corro Avda. Doctor Garcia Rogel 23 ☎ 965 302 963 ⊚ restaurantecasacorro.es. Tuck into traditional cuisine such as the local speciality of *arroz con costra*, at this restaurant with 100 years of history, 1km out of town. The lunchtime *menú del día* is €10.10. They also operate a basic hotel, with simple, well-kept rooms. Restaurant Tues–Sun 1.30–4pm & 9–11pm. **€40**

Murcia

12

MURCIA, according to the nineteenth-century writer Augustus Hare, would "from the stagnation of its long existence, be the only place Adam would recognize if he returned to Earth". Things have certainly changed – today, Murcia is the commercial hub of the region and boasts a lively cultural scene. Founded by the Moors in the ninth century on the banks of the Río Segura (no more than a trickle now), the city soon became an important trading centre and, four centuries later, the regional capital. It was extensively rebuilt in the eighteenth century, and the buildings in the old quarter are still mostly of this era. Today, a substantial student population ensures that there's a thriving bar and club scene, plus plenty of tapas bars and restaurants to suit all budgets.

The Catedral

Pza. Cardenal Belluga • **Catedral** July & Aug: Mon–Fri 7am–1pm & 6–8pm, Sat–Sun 7am–1pm & 6–9pm; Sept–June: daily 7am–1pm & 5–8pm • Free • **Museum** July to mid-Sept: Tues–Sat 9am–3pm, Sun 10am–1pm; mid-Sept to June: Tues–Sat 10am–1pm & 4–7pm, Sun 10am–1pm • €3 • ☎ 968 219 713

The **Catedral** towers over the mansions and plazas of the centre. Begun in the fourteenth century and finally completed in the eighteenth, it's a strange mix of styles, dubbed "Mediterranean Gothic". The outside is more interesting architecturally, particularly the west side with its Baroque facade. The bell tower, the tallest campanile in Spain, features some Renaissance architecture and visitors can climb it for great views of the city. Inside, the most remarkable aspect is the florid Plateresque decoration of the chapels – particularly the **Capilla de los Vélez** (1491–1505). Originally designed as a funeral area, but never completed, it's one of the finest examples of medieval art in Murcia and one of the most interesting pieces of Hispanic Gothic; an urn in the niche of the main altar contains the heart of Alfonso the Wise. The **museum** has some fine sculptures and, above all, a giant processional monstrance – 600kg of gold and silver twirling like a musical box on its revolving stand.

The ayuntamiento

Pza. Cardenal Belluga • Generally closed to the public – enquire at the *turismo*

Looming across the Pza. Cardenal Belluga is the newest addition to Murcia's architectural heritage. Architect Rafael Moneo's extension to the **ayuntamiento** closes

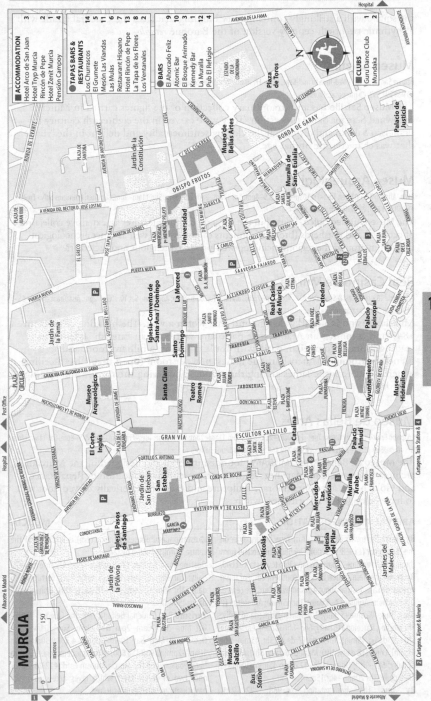

MURCIA

Hospital ▲

■ ACCOMMODATION
Hotel Arco de San Juan	3
Hotel Tryp Murcia	2
Rincón de Pepe	1
Hotel Zenit Murcia	4
Pensión Campoy	

● TAPAS BARS & RESTAURANTS
Los Churrascos	14
El Grumete	5
Mesón Las Viandas	11
Las Mulas	6
Restaurant Hispano	7
Hotel Rincón de Pepe	13
La Tapa de los Flores	8
Los Ventanales	2

■ BARS
El Ahorcado Feliz	9
Atomic Bar	10
El Bosque Animado	3
Kennedy Bar	1
La Muralla	12
Pub El Refugio	4

■ CLUBS
Guru Dance Club	1
Mundaka	2

12

the square with a strikingly contemporary building that faces the Catedral facade with a rhythmic twentieth-century version of the Baroque *retablo*.

Museo Salzillo

Pza. de San Agustín 3 • Mid-June to mid-Sept: Mon–Fri 10am–2pm; mid-Sept to mid-June: Mon–Sat 10am–5pm, Sun 11am–2pm • €5 • ☎ 968 291 893, Ⓦ museosalzillo.es

The **Museo Salzillo** has an extraordinary collection of the figures carried in Murcia's renowned Semana Santa procession. They were carved in the eighteenth century by Francisco Salzillo and display all the cloying sentimentality and delight in the "rustic" that was characteristic of that age.

Museo Arqueológico

Avda. Alfonso X 7 • Winter: Tues–Fri 10am–2pm & 5–8pm, Sat 11am–2pm & 5–8pm, Sun 11am–2pm; summer: mornings only • Free • ☎ 968 234 602, Ⓦ museosdemurcia.com

The **Museo Arqueológico**, housed in the Casa de Cultura, features an extensive collection of ceramics and potsherds (broken fragments of pottery), as well as other archeological finds from around the region, including well-preserved religious and sacred art.

Real Casino de Murcia

C/Trapería 18 • Jan–June & Sept–Dec daily 10.30am–7pm; July daily 10.30am–9pm; Aug Mon–Sat 10.30am–2pm, restaurant closed • €5 • ☎ 968 215 399, Ⓦ casinomurcia.com

Murcia's **casino** is a quirky delight and well worth a visit. The building dates from 1847 and combines an Arabic-style patio and vestibule, an English-style library reading room, a Pompeiian patio with Ionic columns, a billiard room and a French ballroom. The neo-Baroque ladies' powder room (open to all) has a ceiling which depicts angelic ladies among the clouds, powdering their noses and tidying their hair.

Museo de Bellas Artes

C/Obispo Frutos 12 • July & Aug: Tues–Fri 10am–2pm, Sat & Sun 11am–2pm; Sept–June: Tues–Fri 10am–2pm & 5–8pm, Sat 11am–2pm & 5–8pm, Sun 11am–2pm • Free • ☎ 968 239 346, Ⓦ museosdemurcia.com

The **Museo de Bellas Artes (MUBAM)**, founded in 1910 and designed by the Murcian architect Pedro Cerdán Martínez, features a representative collection of Renaissance and Golden Age art, contemporary sculpture and even an esoterically carved door said to have belonged to a Portuguese witch.

ARRIVAL AND INFORMATION   MURCIA

By plane The town's airport is 50km away in San Javier on the Mar Menor (☎ 968 172 000). City buses run to and from the airport three times a day; taxi fares into town start at €40.

By train The train station is at the southern edge of town on Pza. de La Industria, about a 20min walk into the centre. Destinations Águilas (3–5 daily; 1hr 45min); Albacete (10 daily; 2hr); Alicante (5 daily; 1hr 30min); Almería (6 daily; 3hr 30min); Barcelona (6 daily; 6hr–8hr 30min); Cartagena (20–26 daily; 45min); Granada (7 daily; 3hr 45min–5hr 30min); Lorca (18 daily; 1hr); Madrid (6 daily; 5hr); Málaga (5 daily; 6hr–9hr); Orihuela (8–12 daily; 45min); Valencia (3–5 daily; 3hr 20min–4hr 15min).

By bus The bus station (☎ 968 292 211, Ⓦ estaciondeautobusesdemurcia.com) is just west of the centre, within walking distance.

Destinations Águilas (3–5 daily; 4hr); Alicante (16–22 daily; 2hr 30min); Barcelona (5 daily; 7hr); Cartagena (5 daily; 1hr 45min); Lorca (12–18 daily; 1hr); Orihuela (14 daily; 45min).

Turismo Pza. Cardenal Belluga, near the Catedral (April–Oct Mon–Sat 10am–2pm & 5–9pm, Sun 10am–2pm; Oct–March Mon–Sat 10am–2pm & 4.30–8.30pm, Sun 10am–2pm; ☎ 968 358 600, Ⓦ turismodemurcia.es). From here, you can buy the Murcia Tourism Card (€12/18/21 for one, two or three days) which gives access to many participating tourist sights for free.

ACCOMMODATION

Hotel Arco de San Juan Pza. de Ceballos 10 ☎ 968 210 455, ⓦ arcosanjuan.com. A Neoclassical palace turned hotel, the handsome facade may be worth the price alone, and the acclaimed restaurant *Los Churrascos* is on-site. **€50**

Hotel Tryp Murcia Rincón de Pepe C/Apósteles 34 ☎ 968 212 239, ⓦ tryphotels.com. One of the finer hotels in Murcia, paved with pink Portuguese marble and featuring suitably plush rooms plus a well-regarded restaurant and atmospheric bar *La Muralla*. Discounted weekend rates. **€60**

Hotel Zenit Murcia Pza. San Pedro 5–6 ☎ 968 214 742, ⓦ zenithoteles.com. Comfortable, business-friendly three-star hotel that sits in the thick of things, a few paces from lively Pza. de las Flores. A cool-toned lobby, tidy rooms and all the amenities. **€50**

Pensión Campoy C/Diego Hernández 32 ☎ 968 254 591, ⓦ pensioncampoy.com. This basic *pensión* has clean, if somewhat spartan rooms, some with en suite. Twee lobby area and perfectly situated for the train station. **€32**

EATING

Murcia is known as *la huerta de Europa* (the orchard of Europe), and although this might be a slight exaggeration, you'll find local produce on most restaurant menus: vegetable soups, grills and paellas are the main specialities. It's also an important rice-growing region, and the local variety, Calasparra, which ripens very slowly, is used to make paella. When talk turns to **tapas**, Murcia doesn't often come up; it should. Come evening, do as the locals and *ir de tapeo* in and around Pza. de las Flores, Pza. Santa Catalina and along Gran Vía Alfonso X. For well-priced traditional Spanish food, it's also worth checking out the *mesones* in the Pza. de Julián Romea (beside the theatre) and on and around Pza. San Juan.

Los Churrascos Hotel Arco de San Juan, Pza. San Juan ☎ 968 221 200, ⓦ loschurrascos.com. Regional cuisine with a modern twist, from succulent duck with a mandarin liqueur to artisanal desserts. Various menus up to €25. Mon & Tues 7.30am–4pm, Wed–Sat 7.30am–4pm & 8.30–11.30pm.

El Grumete C/Vara de Rey 6 ☎ 968 220 080 If you're in the mood for seafood, this is the spot for tasty, fresh *mariscos*, served by weight. Mains around €26. Tues–Sun 1.30–3.30pm & 8.30–10.30pm, closed part of summer.

★ **Hotel Rincón de Pepe** C/Apósteles 34 ☎ 968 212 239, ⓦ tryphotels.com. This elegant restaurant is *the* place for a Murcian gastronomic experience. Expect to pay around €55 a head for a meal, which will invariably include some inspired combinations of local produce – be sure to leave room for dessert. Tues–Sat noon–4pm & 8–midnight, Sun noon–4pm; closed Fri & Sat in July & Aug.

Mesón Las Viandas C/Pascual ☎ 968 221 188, ⓦ mesonlasviandas.com. Friendly local restaurant with authentic, hearty food. *Menú del día* from €15. Daily 7pm–midnight; closed Sun in Aug.

Las Mulas C/Ruiperez 5 ☎ 968 220 561. An earthy tapas experience, with a delicious *patatas Real Murcia*, a scrambled egg and potato concoction named after the local football team. Daily 8am–midnight.

Restaurante Hispano C/Radio Murcia 3 ☎ 968 216 152, ⓦ restaurantehispano.es. Super-modern venue with sweeping, shining decor, serving Spanish cuisine and local tuna in sashimi style. Daily 1.30–4.30pm & 8–11.30pm.

La Tapa de los Flores Pza. de las Flores 13 ☎ 968 211 317, ⓦ latapadelasflores.com. For outdoor tapas, settle in at one of the tables scattered near the plaza fountain, and graze on tasty bites including young eel tossed with potatoes. Mains around €18. Daily noon–5pm & 8pm–midnight.

Los Ventanales C/ Jaime 7 ☎ 968 931 240, ⓦ losventanales.com. The most central of several citywide branches of this popular tapas place, cooking up five different varieties of *patatas a lo pobre*. Mon–Fri 8am–4.30pm & 7pm–midnight, Sat 10am–4.30pm & 7.30–1am, Sun 10am–4.30pm & 7–11.30pm.

DRINKING AND NIGHTLIFE

As a university town, Murcia has a disarmingly vibrant and diverse **nightlife** during termtime, and a scene that hasn't yet succumbed to across-town uniformity. To get a grip on what's hot, pick up a copy of the free listings magazine *Guía de Ocio* (ⓦ guiadelocio.com). One of the liveliest areas for **bars** is around the university, near the Museo de Bellas Artes, in particular C/Dr Fleming, C/ Saavedra Fajardo and the side streets off them.

BARS

El Ahorcado Feliz C/Cánovas del Castillo ☎ 968 934 986. This hopping bar and "gin club" pulls in an friendly local crowd and has decently priced beer and cocktails. Mon–Thurs 5.30pm–2am, Fri & Sat 5.30pm–3am.

Atomic Bar C/Simón García ☎ 968 957 767. Happening bar with live music, from blues to rock, amid low leather chairs and velvet drapes. Mon–Sat 6pm–late.

El Bosque Animado Pza. Cristo del Rescate ☎ 968 901 342, ⓦ elbosqueanimado.es. This central, aptly named "Animated Forest" has outdoor tables for evening cocktails (try the great *mojitos*) on the breezy plaza and, inside, artificial trees twinkling with lights. Mon–Sat 6pm–late.

Kennedy Bar Callejón Burruezo ☎ 968 291 680. Irish-style pubs may be ubiquitous in Spain, but this amiable spot near Jardín San Esteban is worth seeking out – not only because it

12

also does afternoon coffee. Original stone arches grace the spacious interior and an elevated church pulpit, brought over from England, makes for a romantic drinking nook. The bar also hosts comedy shows – ask at the bar for dates – which sometimes feature well-known names. Mon–Thurs 3pm–2am, Fri & Sat 3pm–3am, Sun 4pm–midnight.

★ **La Muralla** Hotel Rincón de Pepe C/Apóstoles 34 ☎ 968 212 239, ⓦ lamurallarincondepepe.com. This underground, low-lit bar below the hotel is one of Murcia's more memorable places to drink – sip cocktails while surrounded by the original Moorish city walls. They also host regular jazz sessions. Mon, Tues & Wed 3.30pm–1am, Thurs–Sat 3pm–4am.

Pub El Refugio Pza. de las Balsas. The terrace of this bar is more or less at the centre of the action for cocktails and conversation, and makes an excellent place to start off the evening. Mon–Sat 6pm–late.

CLUBS

Guru Dance Club Avda. Ciclista Mariano Rojas ⓦ gurudanceclub.com. Sprawling modern venue, fitting of its industrial park location, devoted to electronic dance music, with guest DJs and cocktails served in fruits. Thurs–Sat midnight–late.

Mundaka Carretera Santa Catalina 26 ☎ 968 34 76 99. This premier club boasts three scenes: house and techno, disco funk and a chill-out garden. Resident, national and international DJs spin tunes until sunrise. Thurs–Sat midnight–late; closed July & Aug.

DIRECTORY

Car rental Europcar, Avda. Miguel de Cervantes 7 (closed Sun; ☎ 968 283 086, ⓦ europcar.es); Atesa, C/Azarbe del Papel 16 (closed Sun; ☎ 968 200 337, ⓦ atesa.es).

Hospital Hospital General Universitario "Reina Sofía", Avda. Intendente Jorge Palacios 1 (☎ 968 359 000).

Market Mercado Las Verónicas, C/Verónicas (Mon–Sat 8am–2pm, ⓦ mercadodeveronicas.es), has stacks of wonderful local produce.

Police Policía Municipal de Murcia, Avda. San Juan de la Cruz (☎ 968 358 750).

12

Torrevieja and around

The stretch of coast around the south of **Torrevieja** has been developed at a rapid rate, and is now home to a wide mix of Europeans alongside the locals. The town itself has a nice marina with an active boating and sports scene, as well as some pleasant town squares and seaside restaurants, but beachgoers will find a more sunbathe-able setting at **Las Playas de Orihuela** (as they come within Orihuela's provincial boundary). Both Playa La Zenía and Playa Cabo Roig are good, clean options with car parks and cafés; the restaurant at Cabo Roig is also exceptionally good and enjoys wide views over the harbour.

Santiago de la Ribera

The Murcian Costa Cálida starts at **Mar Menor** (Lesser Sea), a broad lagoon whose shallow waters (ideal for kids) warm up early in the year, making this a good out-of-season destination. With its high-rise hotels, the "sleeve" (*La Manga*) looks like a diminutive Benidorm; the resort of **SANTIAGO DE LA RIBERA** on the land side of the lagoon is a more appealing place to spend a day or two by the coast, and is popular with *murcianos*. There's a good sandy beach, an attractive promenade, lookout spots to the atmospheric *Isla Mayor O del Barón* and an important sailing club – the calm sea is perfect for novices.

ARRIVAL AND INFORMATION
SANTIAGO DE LA RIBERA

By train The nearest train station is Balsicas (connected with Murcia, San Pedro and Santiago by hourly buses). Trains run direct between Barcelona, Valencia and Madrid.

By bus Buses run regularly to and from Cartagena.

Turismo C/Padre Juan, 300m back from the seafront (July to mid-Sept: Mon–Fri 10am–2pm & 5.30–8.30pm, Sat & Sun 10.30am–1.30pm; mid-Sept to Oct and Easter–July: Mon–Fri 9.30am–2.30pm & 5–7pm, Sat & Sun 10am–1.30pm; Nov–Easter: Mon–Fri 9.30am–2pm & 4–6.30pm; ☎ 968 571 704).

ACCOMMODATION AND EATING

Hotel El Marino Explanada Barnuevo 13 ☎ 968 572 121, ⓦ elmarino.es. This family-owned, nautical-themed hotel has homely, summery rooms with good sea views. Breakfast €3.50. **€65**

Lonja Mar Menor Paseo Colón ☎ 968 573 657. This lively restaurant near the beach is the perfect spot for a seafood feast. Follow the locals' example and order *fritura*, small fried fish, or go all out with a generous – and pricey – *mariscada*, with shrimp, clams and prawns. Mains €24–29. Daily 1–5pm & 8pm–midnight.

Cartagena

Whether you're approaching **CARTAGENA** from one of the numerous resorts along Mar Menor, inland from Murcia, or from Almería to the south, it's not a traditionally pretty sight, even if the rusting mineworks that scar the landscape have their own austere appeal. It's only when you reach the old part of town by the port, with its narrow medieval streets packed with bars and restaurants, that the city's real character emerges.

Cartagena was Hannibal's capital city on the Iberian peninsula, named after his Carthage in North Africa, and a strategic port and administrative centre for the Romans. Many of the old city's sights have recently been restored and made into visitor attractions, including the theatre and the wonderful **Parque Archeológico del Cerro del Molinete.**

International Nautical Week is celebrated here in June; in July, the Mar de Músicas festival showcases some of the best in world music; and in November the city hosts both a nationally famous jazz festival and an International Festival of Nautical Cinema. The **fiestas** of Semana Santa are some of the most elaborate in Spain, with processions leaving from the church of Santa María de Gracia in the early hours of Good Friday morning.

The best way to get a feel of the city's rich past is to stroll the streets: you'll see a large number of *modernista* buildings. Most of these are the work of former Cartagenian and disciple of Gaudí, Victor Beltri (1865–1935). In particular, have a look at **Casa Maestre** in Pza. San Francisco; **Casa Cervantes**, C/Mayor 15; and the old **Hotel Zapata**, Pza. de España.

12

Castillo de la Concepción

July to mid-Sept: Mon–Sun 10am–8pm; mid-Sept to Nov 4, Easter & March–June: Tues–Sun 10am–7pm; Nov 5–April Tues–Sun 10am–5.30pm • €3.75, €4.25 with lift • ☎ 968 500 093

Reached by a signposted path or a **panoramic lift**, the impressive **Castillo de la Concepción** has interesting displays exploring Cartagena's history, and you can also wander around the old walls, where lookout points afford panoramic views of the town and surrounding landscape.

Museo Naval

Paseo Alfonso XII • Tues–Sat 10am–1.30pm & 4.30–7pm, Sun 10am–2pm • Free • ☎ 968 127 138

The vast military **Arsenal** that dominates the old part of the city dates from the mid-eighteenth century. Recently moved to seafront location, the well-curated **Museo Naval** provides an in-depth look at Cartagena's naval history, from exhibits on nautical maps and navigational charts to model ships, uniforms, artillery, and a section dedicated to Cartagena-born Isaac Peral, the inventor of the submarine.

Museo del Teatro Romano de Cartagena

Pza. del Ayuntamiento 9 • May–Sept: Tues–Sat 10am–8pm, Sun 10am–2pm; Oct–April: Tues–Sat 10am–6pm, Sun 10am–2pm • €6 • ☎ 968 504 802, ⓦ teatroromanocartagena.org

The recently opened **Museo del Teatro Romano de Cartagena** features relics from Cartagena's past, starting with a tour through a "corridor of history" including the Neighbourhood of Fisherman era through the time as a Byzantine port. You move past exhibits of theatre architecture and exposed sections of the old Islamic medina before stepping out into one of the higher levels of the carefully restored 7000-capacity pink-stone theatre – a huge surprise, given the modest entrance to the museum.

Museo Archeológico Municipal

C/Ramón y Cajal 45 • Tues–Fri 10am–2pm & 5–8pm, Sat & Sun 11am–2pm • Free • ☎ 968 128 968, ⓦ museoarqueologicocartagena.es

The **Museo Archeológico Municipal** is built on a Roman burial ground and offers a good introduction to the ancient history of the city. The excellent collection of Roman artefacts includes an impressive display of glass, plus Romanesque art and sculptures.

Muralla Púnica

C/San Diego • July to mid-Sept daily 10am–8pm; mid-Sept to Nov 4, Easter & mid-March to June Tues–Sun 10am–7pm; Nov 5 to mid-March Tues–Sun 10am–5.30pm • €3.50 • ☎ 968 500 093

The **Muralla Púnica** visitor and interpretation centre, built on and around one of the city's old Punic walls, explores the city's Carthaginian and Roman history via exhibits and audiovisuals in a roughly 45-minute visit. It also provides helpful information on other sights around the city, including the **Casa de la Fortuna** and the **Military Museum**.

ARRIVAL AND INFORMATION
CARTAGENA

By train and bus The FEVE train station (with services connecting Cartagena with Los Nietos on the Mar Menor) is almost next door to the ALSA bus station, on C/Trovero Marín, and the RENFE station nearby at the end of Avda. América.

Turismo Pza. del Ayuntamiento, in the Palacio Consistorial (May–Oct: Mon–Sat 10am–2pm & 5–7pm, Sun 10.30am–1.30pm; Nov–April: Mon–Sat 10am–2pm & 4–6pm, Sun 10.30am–1.30pm ☎ 968 128 955, ⓦ cartagena.es). The Muralla Púnica also provides local information and itineraries, and offers tours and discount tickets through Cartagena Puerto de Culturas (☎ 968 500 093, ⓦ cartagenapuertodeculturas.com).

ACCOMMODATION

Hotel Los Habaneros C/San Diego 60 ☎ 968 505 250, ⓦ hotelhabaneroscartagena.com. Comfortable, well-maintained rooms, and a very central location near both the bus and train stations. **€50**

NH Cartagena Real 2 ☎ 968 120 908, ⓦ nh-hotels .com. Smart, central place with elegant rooms on Pza.

Héroes de Cavite, plus one of the chain's signature *NHube* restaurants, serving creative regional fare. **€67**

Pensión Oriente C/Jara 27 ☎ 968 502 469, ⓦ pensionoriente.es. Long-established *pensión*, with basic, clean, budget rooms in a central location. **€34**

EATING AND DRINKING

Mare Nostrum Paseo de Alfonso XII ☎ 968 522 131, ⓦ marenostrum.es. Dine on excellent seafood dishes (€14–21) by the port, including *mero marinera*, grouper with clams, and crayfish. Daily 1–4pm & 7–11pm.

El Mejillonera C/Mayor 4 ☎ 968 521 179. This lively spot near the Pza. del Ayuntamiento does tasty *mejillones* (mussels) and Gallego-style *pulpo*. Daily 1.30–3.30pm & 8.30–10.30pm.

The Golfo de Mazarrón

South of Cartagena, much of the scenic coastline down to the border with Andalucia is undeveloped, with a succession of fine coves lying beneath a backdrop of arid, serrated hills. The region's main resorts, **El Puerto de Mazarrón** and **Águilas**, are both fairly small-scale and easy-going, mainly attracting Spanish families. The better beaches are often out of town so you'll need your own vehicle; though if you don't have one, note that the south-facing Playa Poniente beach at Águilas is well-maintained and has a fantastic view up to the castle.

El Puerto de Mazarrón

There has been a large amount of development in **EL PUERTO DE MAZARRÓN** in the last few years – so much so that the port area is more of an attraction than Mazarrón town itself. The port has a sweeping, sandy beach just north of the yacht-filled marina, and there are more great **beaches** within easy reach of town. Buses head 6km southwest along the coast to Bolnuevo, where there's a superb stretch of sand. West of Bolnuevo, the route becomes a dirt track, with access to several coves popular with nudists, until you reach the headland of Punta Calnegre, 15km from El Puerto de Mazarrón, where there are more good stretches of sand. Alternatively, if you head northeast from El Puerto de Mazarrón the best beaches are around Cabo Tiñoso, 13km away. When you're tired of sunbathing, visit the nature reserve at **La Rambla de Moreras**, 2km north of Bolnuevo, which has a lagoon that attracts a variety of migratory birds.

INFORMATION — EL PUERTO DE MAZARRÓN

Turismo Pza. Toneleros 1 (Mon–Fri 9.30am–2pm & 5–8pm, Sat 10am–1pm & 5–7pm; summer also Sun 10am–1.30pm; ⓣ 968 594 426, ⓦ turismo.mazarron.es).

ACCOMMODATION AND EATING

La Barraca C/Torre 13 ⓣ 968 594 402, ⓦ restaurantelabarraca.net. Enjoy fresh seafood, from lobster and shrimp to sea bream, as well as paellas and *arroz con bogavante* at this long-established restaurant near the port. Mains €16–25. Mon, Tues & Thurs–Sun 1–3.30pm & 8.30–10.30pm, Wed 1–3.30pm; closed mid-Jan to mid-Feb.

Hotel Bahía Playa de la Reya ⓣ 968 594 000, ⓦ hotelbahia.net. It may look fairly generic and concrete from the outside, but it's near the beach, and offers colourful, comfortable rooms, a plant-filled lobby and a sun terrace. €50

Playa de Mazarrón Carretera Bolnuevo ⓣ 968 150 660, ⓦ playamazarron.com. This well-maintained, massive campsite, with good facilities, is open year-round. €28

DRINKING

Café la Sal Paseo de la Sal ⓣ 968 052 090. Situated on the pier between the beach and the marina, this trendy bar serves coffees, beers and cocktails to customers gawping at the yachts. Daily 1–11pm.

12

Águilas

ÁGUILAS, 47km from Mazarrón and almost on the border with Andalucia, is hemmed in by the parched hills of the Sierra del Contar. Along with the cultivation of tomatoes – one of the few things that can grow in this arid region – fishing is the mainstay of the economy here, and a fish auction is held at around 5pm every day in the port's large warehouse. **Carnaval** is especially wild in Águilas, and for three days and nights in February the entire population lets its hair down with processions, floats and general fancy-dress mayhem.

Águilas is also popular for its plentiful **beaches**, and the area has a superb year-round climate. The town itself has managed to escape the worst excesses of tourism, and retains much of its rural charm and port-town character. The most important tourist sights are the **Castillo de San Juan** (closed Mon) and the exquisite mosaic staircase at **Rincon Del Hornillo**; ask at the *turismo* in the port.

Cuatro calas and Águilas' beaches

You'll find sandy **beaches**, and over thirty small *calas* (coves) in the vicinity – those to the north are rockier and more often backed by low cliffs, while the best are the wonderful, fairly undeveloped **CUATRO CALAS** south of town. You'll need your own wheels to reach these beaches, which get better the farther you get away from Águilas, but all are signposted. The first two, **Calarreona** and **La Higuérica**, have fine sands and are backed by dunes and the odd villa, but 6km south of Águilas where the coast is completely wild, the ravishing back-to-back sandy coves of **Cala Carolina** and **Cala Cocedores** are simply superb.

If you don't have your own transport, you're better heading for the chain of beaches north of Águilas served by regular buses (generally July to end of Aug only). **Playa Hornillo** is a nice beach with a couple of bars (and you could actually reach it by walking from the train station), while **Playa Amarillo** is decent but in a built-up area.

The bus also passes *playas* Arroz, La Cola and finally Calabardina (7km from town). If you feel energetic, you could head across **Cabo Cope** to yet another chain of beaches beginning at Ruinas Torre Cope.

ACCOMMODATION AND EATING	**ÁGUILAS**
Hotel Restaurante El Paso C/Cartagena 13 ☎ 968 447 125, ⓦ hotelelpasoaguilas.com. This pleasant small hotel has simple but well-maintained rooms, a central interior courtyard and a bar-restaurant for guests. **€70** **Restaurante la Veleta** C/Blas Rosique Blaya 6 ☎ 968	411 798. Dine on fresh seafood, from mussels to octopus to plump shrimp, as well as grilled meats and aromatic rice dishes at this inviting restaurant with terrace bar. Daily menus from €28; tasting menu €45. Daily 1–4pm & 8pm–midnight; closed March.

Lorca and around

One of the more easily accessible historic villages of inland Murcia is **LORCA**, a former frontier town whose historic centre, on the hill between C/López Gisbert and the castle, still has a distinct aura of the past. For a time, it was part of the Córdoba caliphate, but it was retaken by the Christians in 1243, after which Muslim raids were a feature of life until the fall of Granada, the last Muslim stronghold. Most of the town's notable buildings – churches and ancestral homes – date from the sixteenth century onwards.

Today, Lorca is famed for its **Semana Santa** celebrations, which outdo those of both Murcia and Cartagena, the next best in the region. There's a distinctly operatic splendour about the dramatization of the triumph of Christianity, with characters such as Cleopatra, Julius Caesar and the royalty of Persia and Babylon attired in embroidered costumes of velvet and silk. The high point is the afternoon and evening of Good Friday.

Palacio de Guevara

C/Lope Gisbert • Tues–Sat 10.30am–2pm & 5–8.30pm, Sun 11am–2pm • Free, guided tour €3 • ☎ 968 479 003

The **Casa de los Guevara** is an excellent example of civic eighteenth-century Baroque architecture and features all the historical hallmarks of a luxurious mansion, including well-appointed rooms with paintings and period furniture, and a lovely patio and cloister – it's easy to see why the building is nicknamed the "House of Columns".

Calle Corredera

On the corner of Pza. San Vicente and **Calle Corredera**, the main shopping artery, is the **Columna Milenaria**, a Roman column dating from around 10 BC which marked the distance between Lorca and Cartagena on the *via Heraclea*, the Roman road from the Pyrenees to Cádiz. The Gothic **Porche de San Antonio**, the only gate remaining from the old city walls, lies at the far end of C/Corredera.

Plaza de España

Colegiata de San Patricio • Mon–Fri 11am–1pm & 4.30–6.30pm, Sat & Sun 11am–1pm & 4.30–8pm • Free

The **Plaza de España** is the focal point of Lorca life, and holds the imposing **Colegiata de San Patricio**, with its enormous proto-Baroque facade, built between the sixteenth and eighteenth centuries – there's a marked contrast between the outside and the sober, refined interior, which is largely Renaissance. The most important of the works inside is dedicated to the *Virgen del Alcázar*.

Nearby is the **ayuntamiento**, with its seventeenth- to eighteenth-century facade. An equally impressive front is presented by the sixteenth-century **Posito**, down a nearby side street – originally an old grain storehouse, it's now the municipal archive.

EARTHQUAKE IN LORCA

On May 11, 2011, Lorca was shaken by a 5.2-magnitude **earthquake**, said to be the most serious tremor to hit Spain in fifty years. Parts of town – particularly the old quarter – were levelled, and ten people were killed. Most parts of the town have now, fortunately, been restored, but you may still notice damage around the touristy areas.

Castillo "La Fortaleza del Sol"

Easter & mid-July to Aug: Tues–Sun 10.30am–8.30pm; April–June & Sept–Dec: Tues–Sun 10.30am–6.30pm; Jan–March Tues–Sun 10.30am–5.30pm • €5, €8 with miniature train and Centro de Visitantes • Night visits July & Aug Tues–Sat at 8.30pm, 9.30pm and 10.30pm • €8, or €20 with dinner • ☎ 968 959 646 or ☎ 902 400 047

Lorca's brooding thirteenth- to fourteenth-century **Castillo**, overlooking the town, has been turned into a medieval-themed tourist attraction, which may or may not be your cup of tea: think actors prancing around in medieval costume, and re-enacted battle scenes. There are also some well-presented exhibits about the castle's undoubtedly formidable history.

Note that although the miniature train goes up to the castle, it's perfectly possible to walk (or drive) up through the *barrio antiguo* above the Colegiata de San Patricio.

Museo de Bordados del Paso Azul

C/Nogalte • Mon–Fri 10am–1.30pm & 5–7.30pm, Sat 10am–1.30pm • €2.50 • ☎ 968 472 077

Timing your visit to coincide with Lorca's famous Semana Santa festivities makes for an unforgettable experience, but if you can't be here for the real thing, it's still worth visiting the **Museo del Paso Azul** to get some insight into the elaborate costumes, history, and the incredible devotion that the festival is known for.

Centro Regional de Artesanía

C/Lope Gisbert • Mon–Fri 9am–2pm & 5.30–7.30pm, Sat 10.30am–2pm & 5.30–8.30pm, Sun noon–2pm • Free • ☎ 968 463 912, ⓦ carm.es

If you're looking to pick up some souvenirs, it's worth popping into the spacious **Centro de Artesanía**, part of the Palacio de Guevara, which displays and sells traditional crafts, and has an area where you can watch local artists at work.

ARRIVAL AND INFORMATION   LORCA

By train and bus Hourly trains and buses connect Lorca with Murcia, although the train is cheaper and a little quicker.

Turismo Centro de Visitantes, Antiguo Convento, C/Puerta de San Ginés (summer Mon–Sat 10am–2pm & 5.30–8pm, Sun 10am–2.30pm; ☎ 902 441 914, ⓦ lorcaturismo.es).

ACCOMMODATION AND EATING

Note that hotel rates go up drastically (as much as twice) around the time of Semana Santa, and you'll have to book accommodation at least three months in advance for the festival – or stay in Murcia or Águilas.

Hotel Alameda C/Musso Valiente 8 ☎ 968 406 600, ⓦ hotel-alameda.com. A friendly hotel, which sits smack in the centre of town. The rooms are decent and have a bird's-eye view of the Semana Santa parades; rates include breakfast. **€60**

Jardines de Lorca Alameda Rafael Méndez ☎ 968 470 599, ⓦ hoteljardinesdelorca.com. This hotel sits in a restful residential zone, near the leafy park after which it's named. Prices dip to nearly half in low season. **€58**

La Parrilla de San Vicente Glorieta San Vicente ☎ 968 471 287. For hearty Lorcan cuisine, including excellent grilled meats, head to this friendly, central restaurant with terrace. Weekday *menú del día* €10. Daily 1–4pm & 8–11pm; July & Aug closed Sat.

12

The Balearic Islands

PLATJA DE SES ILLETES, FORMENTERA

The Balearic Islands

East of the Spanish mainland, the four chief Balearic Islands – Ibiza,
Formentera, Mallorca and Menorca – maintain a character distinct from the
rest of Spain and from each other. Ibiza is wholly unique: its capital Ibiza
Town is loaded with historic interest and a draw for thousands of clubbers
and gay visitors, while the north of the island has a distinctly bohemian
character. Tiny Formentera has even better beaches than its neighbour and
makes up in rustic charm what it lacks in cultural interest. Mallorca, the
largest and best-known Balearic, battles with its image as an island of little
more than sun, booze and high-rise hotels. In reality, you'll find all the
clichés, most of them crammed into the mega-resorts of the Bay of Palma
and the east coast, but there's lots more besides: mountains, lovely old
towns, some beautiful coves, and the Balearics' one real city, Palma. Mallorca
is, in fact, the one island in the group you might come to other than for
beaches and nightlife, with scope for plenty of hiking. And finally, to the east,
there's Menorca – more subdued in its clientele, and here, at least, the
modern resorts are kept at a safe distance from the two main towns, the
capital Maó, which boasts the deepest harbour in the Med, and the
charming, pocket-sized port of Ciutadella.

Access to the islands is easy from Britain and mainland Spain, with plenty of bargain-priced flights in summer, though in winter only Mallorca is really well connected. In addition, ferries and catamarans link Barcelona, Valencia and Denia with the islands, and there are plenty of inter-island ferries, too, though these can be pricey and fully booked in summer. For fuller details on **routes**, see the "Arrival and Departure" sections for individual ports and cities.

The main fly in the ointment is cost: as prime "holiday islands", the Balearics charge considerably above mainland prices for rooms and eating out can be expensive. Rental **cars** can also be hard to come by at this time. Travelling around by **bus**, **moped**, **scooter** and **bicycle** are all perfectly feasible, but note that car-rental companies do not allow their vehicles to be taken from one island to another.

Catalan is spoken throughout the Balearics, and each of the three main islands has a different dialect, though locals all speak Castilian (Spanish). For the visitor, confusion arises from the difference between the islands' road signs and street names – which are almost exclusively in Catalan – and many of the maps on sale, which are in Castilian. In particular, note that Menorca now calls its capital Maó rather than Mahón, while both the island and town of Ibiza are usually referred to as Eivissa. In this chapter we give the Catalan name for towns, beaches and streets, except for Ibiza and Ibiza Town which are not widely known by their Catalan names outside Spain.

Highlights

❶ A stroll through Dalt Vila Explore Ibiza Town's souk-like walled city, a UNESCO World Heritage Site. **See p.852**

❷ World clubbing capital Lose yourself to the music of the globe's most sought after DJs at one of Ibiza's legendary club nights. **See p.856**

❸ Explore Ibiza's hidden calas Hire a bike and spend a day cycling between exquisite cove beaches, including Benirràs and Cala Mastella. **See p.857**

❹ Formentera's beaches Sweeping white-sand beaches and pellucid waters. **See p.861**

❺ Palma's old town Charming Renaissance mansions are clustered in this delightful part of Mallorca's capital city. **See p.865**

❻ Deià, Mallorca One of Mallorca's prettiest villages, perched high above the ocean. **See p.874**

❼ Downtown Ciutadella A delightful little Menorcan town of maze-like lanes and fine old mansions. **See p.886**

HIGHLIGHTS ARE MARKED ON THE MAP ON P.850

THE BALEARIC ISLANDS

MAINLAND
SPAIN

Menorca

Fornells
Maó

Ciutadella ⑦

Mallorca

Pollença
Port d'Alcúdia
Port de Sóller
Deià ⑥
Valldemossa
PALMA ⑤

Cabrera

Ibiza

Santa Eulària
Sant Antoni ②
③
Ibiza Town ①

Formentera

La Savina
④

MEDITERRANEAN SEA

Barcelona

Barcelona

Valencia

Denia

Alicante

N

0   50
kilometres

HIGHLIGHTS

① A stroll through Dalt Vila
② World clubbing capital
③ Explore Ibiza's hidden calas
④ Formentera's beaches
⑤ Palma's old town
⑥ Deià, Mallorca
⑦ Downtown Ciutadella

13

AIRLINES AND FERRY COMPANIES

Most inter-island **flights** are operated by Iberia (☎ 902 400 500, ⓦ iberia.com).

Ferries and **catamarans** between the islands and to the Spanish mainland are operated by Trasmediterránea (☎ 902 454 645, ⓦ trasmediterranea.es), Baleària (☎ 902 160 180, ⓦ balearia .com) and Iscomar (☎ 902 119 128, ⓦ iscomar.com). Trasmapi (☎ 902 314 433, ⓦ trasmapi.com) run ferries from Ibiza Town to Formentera.

Ibiza

IBIZA, or **Eivissa** in Catalan, is an island of excess – beautiful, and blessed with scores of stunning cove beaches and dense pine forests. Nevertheless, it's the islanders (*eivissencs*) and their visitors who make it special. Ibiza has long attracted hedonistic characters and wealthy bohemians, and the locals remain determinedly blasé about the mullet-haired fashionistas and celebrities who flock to the island today.

For years, Ibiza was *the* European hippy escape, but nowadays it's the extraordinary clubbing scene that most people come here to experience. The island can lay a strong claim to being the globe's **clubbing capital**, with virtually all of the world's top house DJs and many more minor players performing here during the summer season. However, visit between October and May, and you'll find a much more peaceful island – just one club (*Pacha*) and a few funky bars remain open through the winter.

Ibiza Town, the capital, is the obvious place to base yourself: only a short bus ride from two great beaches – **Ses Salines** and **Es Cavallet** – and crammed with bars, restaurants and boutiques. The town of **Sant Antoni** is, for the most part, a sprawling concrete mass of seedy bars and unappealing restaurants, and is best avoided beyond a few choice bars and clubs. The more pleasant town of **Santa Eulària** is a good base for exploring the north of the island. Around the entire shoreline, you'll find dozens of exquisite **cove beaches** (*calas*), many all but deserted even in high season, though you'll need your own transport to reach the best spots. **Inland**, the scenery is hilly and thickly wooded, dotted with a series of tiny hamlets.

Brief history

The **Carthaginians**, who founded Ibiza Town in about 654 BC, transformed the island into a major trading port, with salt the main export. The **Romans** arrived in 123 BC and the island continued to prosper. After the fall of the Roman Empire, Ibiza was

BALEARIC CUISINE

The influx of the sea-and-sun-seeking masses has brought an **international flavour** – or lack thereof – to many Balearic cafés and restaurants. There are, perhaps, notably few dishes which are unique to the islands but that's hardly surprising given their history of foreign invasion. Typical dishes, which are often of Catalan descent, consist of hearty stews, soups and spiced meats.

Fish and shellfish are the mainstay of most menus. *Caldereta de llagosta* (a lobster stew cooked with tomatoes) is a common speciality, especially in Menorca, as is salted cod, grilled squid and prawns cooked in antisocial – but delicious – amounts of garlic.

As in mainland Spain, the most enjoyable way to experiment with local cuisine is by sampling smaller portions in the form of tapas, or *pintxos* (typical of the Basque country). *Pa amb oli* (bread rubbed with olive oil) is an obvious cheap snack and is typically eaten for lunch or breakfast. For the sweeter-toothed, another source of Balearic culinary pride is a spiral pastry dusted with icing sugar called an **ensaimada**.

Menorcans were inspired into gin-making by the British, and Xoriguer gin made in Maó has a potent kick – it's often drunk as a *pomada* (gin with lemonade). Mallorcan wine – particularly red Binissalem – is experiencing something of a resurgence and is worth seeking out.

13

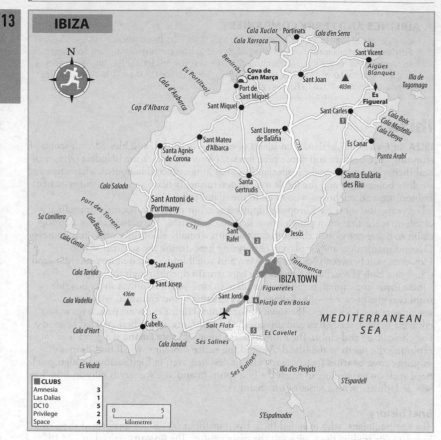

IBIZA

CLUBS
Amnesia	3
Las Dalias	1
DC10	5
Privilege	2
Space	4

conquered by the Moors in the ninth century, and their five-hundred-year reign is still evident in the island's architecture and traditional dress. But thereafter a gradual decline set in, and it wasn't until Beatniks discovered the island in the 1950s that Ibiza began to reinvent itself as one of the most chic locations in the Mediterranean.

Today more than four million tourists flock to the much-revered "white isle" every year. However, Ibiza's tourism-driven prosperity has seen more and more coastline consumed by **rampant development**. The balance between keeping the tourists coming and maintaining the island's natural allure is keenly felt by the islanders but, for now at least, it's not hard to find a pristine cove or a quiet forested trail if you make the effort.

Ibiza Town

IBIZA TOWN (Ciutat d'Eivissa) is easily the most attractive settlement on the island. Colossal medieval walls guard the maze of cobbled streets of the UNESCO-listed old town quarter of **Dalt Vila**. The walls reach a dramatic climax at the main archway entrance, the imposing **Portal de ses Taules**. Just beyond is the elegant **Pza. de Vila**, which is lined with restaurants and cafés and makes a delightful setting for some tapas or a meal. It's well worth the walk up the steep, winding streets to the Catedral, if only to enjoy the wonderful views out over the harbour.

During summer nights, the whitewashed streets of the port area are packed with people darting between chic boutiques, street market stalls and hip bars. In winter, things are much more peaceful, and the focus of activity shifts to the area around the graceful boulevard Passeig de Vara de Rey.

Catedral
Pza. de la Catedral • Daily 9.30am–1.30pm & 5–8pm; closed Mon & Sun afternoons • Free

Today's thirteenth-century **Catedral** stands at the highest point in Dalt Vila. It's pleasingly austere, with sombre, sturdy Gothic lines supported by giant buttresses, though inside, the whitewashed decor contains somewhat trite Baroque embellishments.

Museu Arqueològic d'Eivissa i Formentera
Pza. de la Seu • April–Sept Tues–Sat 10am–2pm & 6–8pm, Sun 10am–2pm; Oct–March Tues–Sat, 9am–3pm, Sun 10am–2pm • €2.40 • ☎ 971 301 231, ⓦ maef.es

Opposite the Catedral, the informative **Museu Arqueològic d'Eivissa i Formentera** has some interesting Phoenician and Carthaginian exhibits, including images of the fertility goddess Tanit. Ibiza's Moorish period is dealt with in the Centro de Interpretación Madina Yabisa (April–Sept Tues–Fri 10am–2 & 5–8pm, Sat & Sun 10am–2pm; Oct–March Tues–Fri 9am–4.30pm, Sat & Sun 10am–2pm; €2) inside La Cúria, on C/Major 2, a converted courthouse that has some flashy video displays and fine ceramics.

Outside the walls
The port areas of **Sa Penya** and **La Marina** snuggle between the harbour and the ramparts, a maze of raked passages and narrow lanes crimped by balconied, whitewashed houses. This highly atmospheric quarter is packed with boutiques, bars and restaurants. Farther to the west, the **new town** is generally of less interest, but the boulevard-like Passeig de Vara de Rey and the leafy, pedestrianized Pza. des Parc just to the south both host some fine cafés and restaurants.

Punic necropolis
Via Romana 31 • April–Sept Tues–Sat 10am–2pm & 6–8pm, Sun 10am–2pm, Oct–March Tues–Sat 9am–3pm, Sun 10am–2pm • Free • ☎ 971 301 771

Set on a rocky hillside off Vía Romana are the remains of a huge **Punic necropolis**. There's not that much to see today – though you can descend into some of the tombs – but thousands of terracotta pieces, amphorae and amulets have been uncovered here. Ibiza functioned as an A-list burial site, with wealthy Carthaginians paying by special minted currency for the shipment of their bodies to the island upon death.

ARRIVAL AND DEPARTURE   IBIZA TOWN

IBIZA AIRPORT
By plane Ibiza's international airport (☎ 913 211 000, ⓦ www.aena-aeropuertos.es) is 6km southwest of Ibiza Town.

Destinations Palma (4–5 daily; 45min).

By bus Buses leave for Ibiza Town (every 20–30min 6.30am–12.30am, every 15min July & Aug; 20min; €3.50) and also for Sant Antoni (hourly 8am–1pm, until 3pm in summer) and Santa Eulària (June–Sept only, every 2hr 8am–9pm).

By taxi A taxi to Ibiza Town will cost €15–20.

IBIZA TOWN
By bus The town's bus station – which is little more than an office next to where the buses pull up – is about 1.5km northwest of the centre, just off the inner ring road on Avgda. d'Isidor Macabich; regular buses run from here to the port area. Full timetables and ticket costs are available at ⓦ ibizabus.com. There's a good bus service between Ibiza Town, Sant Antoni, Santa Eulària, Portinatx, the airport and a few of the larger beaches. Note that services are less frequent from November to April.

Destinations Airport (every 20–30min 6.30am–12.30am, every 15min July & Aug; 20min);

IBIZA TOWN

MEDITERRANEAN SEA

Port d'Eivissa

N

Ferry terminal for Mainland, Talamanca, **1** (1.5km), Mallorca (2km), ▲ **1** & **2**   Formentera ▲   ▲ Talamanca

Bus Station (1.5km), Airport (6km) & Post Office
UK Consulate and Post Office
Internet and Hospital Can Misses
Punic Necropolis

0   100
metres

BARS
Bar Dado	4
Lo Cura	5
Rock Bar	6
Sunrise	8
Sunset	10
Teatro Pereira	9

TAPAS BARS & RESTAURANTS
Bide Bide	1
Bon Profit	12
La Brasa	11
Can Costa	2
Comidas Bar San Juan	7
El Olivo	13
Los Pasajeros	3

CLUBS
Booom!	1
Pacha	2

ACCOMMODATION
Hostal Giramundo	7
Hostal Las Nieves	2
Hostal Residencia Parque	4
Hotel La Ventana	6
Hotel Ocean Drive	1
Urban Spaces	5
Vara de Rey Guest House	3

Estació Marítim

LA MARINA

SA PENYA

Moped Rental

Teatro Pereira

Mercat

Baluard de Sant Joan

Portal de ses Taules

Museu d'Art Contemporani

Baluard de Santa Llúcia

Seminari

Sant Domingo

DALT VILA

Baluard des Portal Nou

La Cúria

Museu d'Arqueològic

Ajuntament

Catedral

Baluard de Sant Jaume

Castillo

Baluard de Santa Tecla

Baluard de Sant Jordi

Baluard de Sant Bernat

ES SOTO

7 (1.25km)

Figueretes (every 30min; 5min); Platja d'en Bossa (every 20–30min; 10min); Sant Antoni (every 15–30min; 30min); Sant Carles (3 daily; 45min); Santa Eulària (every 30–60min; 25min); Sant Joan (2–4 daily; 35min); Sant Josep (hourly; 20min); Sant Miquel (3–8 daily; 30min); Ses Salines (hourly; 20min).

By ferry There are two ferry terminals: one on Avgda. Santa Eulària (for Formentera, ⓦ trasmapi.com), and the other at Dique de Botafoc (mainland and Mallorca served

by ⓦ trasmediterranea.es, ⓦ balearia.com and ⓦ iscomar .com). All Ibiza destinations run from May–Oct only and mainland services are less frequent in winter).

Destinations Barcelona (1–2 daily; 5–10hr); Denia (daily; 3hr 30min); Es Canar (3–6 daily; 1hr 25min); Formentera (every 30min; 35min); Palma (3–4 daily; 3–5hr); Platja d'en Bossa (every 30min–1hr; 20min); Santa Eulària (3–6 daily; 1hr); Talamanca (every 25–30min; 5min); Valencia (1–2 daily; 5–6hr 30min).

INFORMATION

Turisme Pza. de la Catedral (July–Sept Mon–Sat 10am–2pm & 6–9pm, Sun 10am–2pm; April–June Mon–Sat 10am–2pm & 5–8pm, Sun 10am–2pm; Oct–March Mon–Fri 9am–3pm, Sat & Sun 10am–2pm;

☏ 971 399 232, ⓦ ibiza.travel). Helpful English-speaking staff, and good maps and leaflets. The excellent website ⓦ ibiza-spotlight.com is also highly informative.

ACCOMMODATION

Hostal Giramundo C/Ramón Muntaner 55, Figueretes ☎971 307 640, ⓦhostalgiramundoibiza.com. A brightly coloured, backpacker haven very close to Figueretes beach and a 15min walk from the centre. Bonuses include lockers, a DVD room and a popular in-house bar. Room prices drop significantly in winter months. Double **€88**, dorm **€33**

Hostal Las Nieves C/Joan d'Austria 18 ☎971 190 319, ⓦhostalibiza.com. A well-established *hostal* with clean rooms, some en suite (€15 extra) and others sleeping three, on a quiet street a 5min walk from the main drag. Closed Oct–March. **€90**

Hostal Residencia Parque Caieta Soler s/n ☎971 301 358, ⓦhostalparque.com. Stylish, smart hotel in an excellent central location, with superb views of Dalt Vila from the classy Atico penthouse suites which have their own terraces. All doubles are en suite with a/c and TVs. Also has a pleasant patio café. **€130**

Hotel Ocean Drive Port Deportivo, Playa de Talamanca-Marina Botafoch, on the north side of Ibiza's harbour ☎971 318 112, ⓦoceandrive.es. This luxury boutique hotel is one of Ibiza's most stylish. Its pristine, tasteful rooms are located across the bay from Dalt

Vila. Perks include getting your name on the guest lists at the island's most sought-after club nights. **€320**

Hotel La Ventana Sa Carrossa 13 ☎971 390 857, ⓦwww.laventanaibiza.com. Classy hotel inside Dalt Vila, with thirteen chic and beautifully furnished rooms with four-poster beds and great views, as well as an excellent restaurant (open May–Oct) and roof terrace. All rooms have satellite TV and most have private balconies. **€178**

Urban Spaces Via Punica 32 ☎871 517 174, ⓦurbanspacesibiza.com. Staying is this boutique hotel is a little like kipping down in a modern art gallery. Each room has large individual works of art from leading British and local contemporary artists including Lauren Barker. Rooms are extremely large and comfortable with great views over town, while facilities include a terrace and cocktail bar. **€220**

★**Vara de Rey Guest House** Passeig de Vara de Rey 7 ☎971 301 376, ⓦhibiza.com. Housed in an attractive former mansion, the creatively decorated rooms echo the building's grandiose charm. You'll need to climb several flights of stairs but there's a winch for your bags. Rooms all have washbasins; most bathrooms are shared. **€85**

EATING

★**Bide Bide** C/Felipe II 13 ☎971 312 680. Lively, modern bar with a superb choice of *pintxos* from about €3; sample dishes include delicious strips of pork cooked in beer and peppers stuffed with salted cod, as well as classics like *patatas bravas*. Try the excellent house red to wash them down. Open 7pm–late.

Bon Profit Pza. des Parc 5 ☎971 313 866. Bustling canteen-style place with a bargain-priced menu and really hearty, flavoursome food such as grilled lamb or squid – full meals for under €20 a head. No reservations taken and tables fill up fast but the service is extremely efficient. Mon–Sat 1–3pm and 8–10pm; closed Jan.

La Brasa C/Pere Sala 3 ☎971 301 202. Classy restaurant with a delightful garden terrace shaded by plants and palm trees. The innovative menu concentrates on Mediterranean fish and grilled meat. It's a good place to splash out, particularly on the Ibiza sea crab (around €28). Mon–Sat 1pm–late & Sun 6.30pm–late.

Can Costa Carretera Sa Creu 17. This place, in the maze of streets in the old town, serves authentic Spanish cuisine at rock-bottom prices. The daily menu at €11 is both

substantial and excellent value, or try one of the sumptuous *bocadillos*. Daily 1–3.15pm & 8–11pm.

★**Comidas Bar San Juan** C/G. de Montgri 8 ☎971 311 603. Cosy, atmospheric, bistro restaurant with dimly lit rooms and excellent-value Spanish and Ibizan cuisine (paella, calamari, gambas, etc for around €15 a head). Expect to share tables. Mon–Sat 1–3.30pm & 8.30–11pm.

El Olivo Pza. de Vila 9 ☎971 300 680, ⓦelolivoibiza. org. For a memorable meal in historic surrounds, this sophisticated Dalt Vila restaurant with a choice of Mediterranean and international cuisine (such as baked cod with chorizo) comes highly recommended. If you want to sit on the terrace, reserve in advance. Expect to pay over €40 a head. Daily noon 1pm & 7pm–1am; closed Mon Sept–June.

Los Pasajeros C/Vicent Soler s/n ☎971 3317 828. Inexpensive first-floor restaurant that's a kind of staff canteen for the hard-core club crowd. You may have to queue for a table but the atmosphere is always sociable. Cheap wine and great-value food: two courses for around €12. May–Oct only, open until 2am.

DRINKING AND NIGHTLIFE

Ibiza's **bar and club scene** is nothing short of incendiary. Drink prices at the island's clubs are astronomical but Ibiza Town offers no shortage of reasonably priced bars to get the night started. Stylish bars line the eastern end of C/Garijo, while the café/bars of Pza. des Parc are best for a quiet beer.

13

CLUBBING IN IBIZA

Some of the globe's most spectacular **clubs** are spread across the southern half of Ibiza. Clubs cost around €25–60 to get in, are open between midnight and 6am – try to blag a guest pass from one of the bars on the harbour front. The Discobus (June–Sept midnight–6.30am; €3, discobus.es) ferries partygoers from Ibiza Town to the island's major clubs, leaving from the main port.

BARS

Bar Dado C/de la Verge 40. Just along the street from the more flamboyant drinking holes of Ibiza's gay quarter, this friendly bar draws a sociable crowd. Cocktails (around €7) are cheaper than the bars closer to the port. May–Oct daily 9pm–3.30am.

Lo Cura C/Antonio Marí Ribas 4. This is a quirky local hangout with frequent DJs. Space is limited but it's fantastic for people-watching over a frozen margarita (€10). May–Oct 9pm–late.

Rock Bar C/Garijo 14 ✪therockbaribiza.com. This British-run island institution is a second home for a crowd of characterful expats and pre-clubbers. Staff are friendly and you're guaranteed to meet fellow fun-seekers. May–Oct daily 7.30pm–3.30am.

Sunrise C/de la Verge 44. Popular and stylish bar, though nothing gets going until around midnight. It's dubbed the only lesbian bar in town but actually attracts a mixed clientele. May–Oct daily 10.30pm–3.30am.

Sunset Pza. des Parc ✆971 304 448. Down-to-earth and relaxed café/bar with tables out onto the square. *Bocadillos*, pizzas and juices on offer, in addition to beers and cocktails. Often hosts visiting DJs. Daily 8am–1am.

Teatro Pereira C/Comte de Rosselló 3 ✆971 304 432, teatropereyra.com. A breath of fresh air – and alternative music – among the town's clubland-focused nightlife. A lively bar and a superb calendar of blues, reggae, rock and jazz acts. Free entry. Daily 8pm–4am.

CLUBS

Amnesia Ibiza Town–Sant Antoni road, km 5 ✆971 198 041, ✪amnesia.es; map p.852. Historically Ibiza's most innovative club, and the setting for the acid-house revolution. The atmosphere in its two giant rooms can be explosive; the best nights are Cream, Music On, and legendary gay night La Troya. Daily June–Sept.

Booom! Passeig Joan Carles I 9 ✆682 100400, ✪booom

ibiza.com; map p.854. Located in the marina, this relative newcomer to the Ibiza clubbing scene has a renowned sound system which scintillates those inside while being inaudible outside. One of the more laidback clubs with a good-sized dancefloor and appealing palm-lined outdoor terrace.

★ **Las Dalias** San Carles de Peralta, Ibiza Town–Sant Carles road, km 12 ✆971 326 825, ✪lasdalias.es; map p.852. This bar-cum-venue with a garden terrace has a legendary place in Ibiza's hippy scene past and present. There's a Saturday hippy market (10am–9pm), a summer night market (June–Aug Mon & Tues 7pm–1am), Wax da Jam club night on Tuesdays and Namaste night on Wednesdays (both June–Sept 9pm–6am).

DC10 Carretera de Las Salinas, Sant Josep de sa Talaia, ✪dc10-ibiza.ibiza-clubs.net; map p.852. Famed for its underground vibe and after-hours parties, *DC10* is out by the airport – its former open-air areas have been roofed to mask the noise of planes taking off. A long-term favourite for serious hedonists into electro music.

Pacha Avgda. 8 d'Agost, Ibiza Town ✆971 313 600, ✪pacha.com; map p.854. The *grande dame* of the scene and a world-renowned clubbing brand. Multiple rooms playing dance, funk and soul as well as a beautiful garden terrace along with visits from the world's top DJS including Pete Tong and Solomun. April–Sept daily; Oct–March weekends only.

Privilege Ibiza Town–Sant Antoni road, km 7 ✆971 198 160, ✪privilegeibiza.com; map p.852. Officially the world's largest club with a capacity for 10,000 people with a hangar-like main room, fourteen bars, a garden terrace, pool, chill-out dome and café. Not surprisingly, it usually feels less busy than most clubs. Daily June–Sept.

Space Platja d'en Bossa ✆971 396 793, ✪spaceibiza .es; map p.852. One of Ibiza's most modern clubs, with a vast main room, two huge terraces and a plethora of other chill-out zones and alternative rooms. June–Oct daily from 10pm; sometimes earlier.

DIRECTORY

Car rental Avis, Avgda. Santa Eulalia Del Rio 17 (✆971 313 163, ✪avis.com) and the airport (✆902 090 262). Hertz (✆971 809 178, ✪hertz.com at the airport). Class Rent-a-Car, Avgda. Cala Llonga 131 (✆971 196 285 ✪classrentacar. es) is also recommended and has offices around the island.

Consulates UK, Avgda. d'Isidor Macabich 45 ✆902 109 356, ✪www.gov.uk (Mon, Wed & Fri 8.30am–1.30pm).

Hospital Hospital C'an Misses, Corona 32–36, Can Misses, 2km west of the port (✆971 397 000).

Moped rental Casa Valentín, C/Bartomeu Vicent Ramón 19 (✆971 310 822, ✪casavalentin.es), from €35 a day.

Post office Avgda. d'Isidor Macabich 67 (✆971 399 769; Mon–Fri 8.30am–2pm, Sat 8.30am–1pm).

Taxi Taxi Elvissa (✆971 398 483, ✪taxi-elvissa.com).

The beaches around Ibiza Town

You'll find sea and sand close to Ibiza Town at **Figueretes**, **Platja d'en Bossa** and **Talamanca** beaches, but the first two of these are built-up continuations of the capital (Figueretes is just a 15-minute walk from Ibiza Town) and only at Talamanca is there any peace and quiet. Regular buses run to all three.

Ses Salines and Es Cavallet

To the **south of Ibiza Town**, stretching from the airport to the sea, are thousands of acres of **salt flats**. For two thousand years, Ibiza's prosperity was dependent on these salt fields (*salines*), a trade that was vital to the Carthaginians. Even today, some salt production continues. Buses from the Ibiza Town bus station leave regularly for the gorgeous beach of **SES SALINES**, whose fine white sand arcs around a bay, the crystal-clear waters fringed by pines and dunes. The beach also has a handful of superb beach bars. From Ses Salines, it's a brief walk through the dunes to **ES CAVALLET**, a popular nudist beach also favoured by gay visitors.

EATING AND DRINKING   THE BEACHES AROUND IBIZA TOWN

El Chiringuito Playa Es Cavallet ☎971 395 355, ⓦ www.elchiringuitoibiza.com. A classy beachside café-restaurant which serves everything from breakfast, coffees and cocktails to full meals. The lengthy menu features gourmet beefburgers (€20), *spaghetti frutti di mare* (€45 for two) and a sublime lobster rice (€65 for two) which you can enjoy on the terrace facing the waves. Mon–Fri 10am–9pm.

The east coast

Heading northeast from Ibiza Town, it's 15km to **SANTA EULÀRIA DES RIU**, a pleasant town with a plush marina but few obvious sights, though it does boast an attractive church – a fortified whitewashed sixteenth-century construction perched on a hilltop to the west of the town centre. **SANT CARLES**, 7km to the north, is an agreeable one-horse village.

East of Sant Carles the road passes through burnt-red fields of olive, almond and carob trees to several almost untouched beaches. **Cala Llenya**, a broad sandy cove with sparkling waters, is the nearest, and is popular with families. Tiny **Cala Mastella**, 2km farther north, is a supremely peaceful spot, with a diminutive sandy beach and crystal-clear sheltered water. Just north of Cala Mastella is **Cala Boix**, another stunning sandy cove, a little larger and more exposed.

Continuing north from Cala Boix, the coastal road follows an exhilarating, serpentine route above the shore, through thick pine forests and past the lonely nudist beach of **Aigües Blanques**.

ACCOMMODATION   THE EAST COAST

Hostal Cala Boix Cala Boix ☎971 335 224, ⓦ hostalcalaboix.com. A wonderfully tranquil setting with bright, spacious rooms just metres from a quiet beach, all rooms have a/c and private bathrooms and it has its own garden, pool and a good-value adjacent restaurant (daily 10am–midnight) where mains start from €10. Half-and-full board options available. **€95**

EATING AND DRINKING

Anita's Bar Sant Carles, on the main through road ☎971 335 090. A milestone in Ibiza's bohemian past, this vine-shaded patio remains a popular meeting point and has an inexpensive menu of burgers, pizza, tapas and a good range of drinks, including its own famous *hierbas* liqueur (full meals under €15 a head). The art on the walls allegedly dates from the times when 1960s artists donated their works in exchange for sustenance. Daily 7am–1am.

El Bigotes Cala Mastella ☎650 797 633. Perched on a rocky outcrop a short walk from the beach (follow the signs), this simple fish restaurant offers a memorable fish stew of the day (around €25) served by the chef with the eponymous *bigote* (moustache). It's a beautiful setting and quite an experience, but in high season you'll have to book a table in advance. April–Oct daily noon–2.30pm.

13

The north

Twenty kilometres from Ibiza Town, **SANT JOAN** is a pretty hilltop village home to a typically minimalist, whitewashed Ibizan church, and a sprinkling of café-bars. North of the village are some wonderful beaches, especially remote **Cala d'en Serra**, a tiny, exquisite sandy cove, with turquoise waters perfect for snorkelling. **Benirràs**, 9km northwest of Sant Joan, is another beautiful bay, backed by high, wooded cliffs. This is one of Ibiza's prime hippy-centric beaches – dozens gather here to burn herbs and pound drums to the setting sun on Sundays.

The next village to the west is **SANT MIQUEL**, where there's an imposing fortified church, and a number of simple tapas bars – try *Es Pi Ver* for an inexpensive meal. The once astonishingly beautiful inlet at **PORT DE SANT MIQUEL**, 3km north of the village, has been badly mauled by the developers, but outside high season it's not too packed here, and the sheltered bay is great for children.

ACCOMMODATION   THE NORTH

Atzaró Sant Joan, km15 ☎ 971 338 838, ⓦ atzaro.com. Serene countryside retreat dotted with orange trees, complete with a heavenly spa, various bars and a top-notch restaurant. Rooms are exquisitely decorated and the grounds breathtakingly beautiful. **€390**

Can Plannels Venda de Rubio 2, near Sant Miquel ☎ 971 334 924, ⓦ canplanells.co.uk. Away from the coast, this is a sumptuous *agroturismo*. Spacious and chic but rustic rooms nestle into this rural villa that has own extensive grounds, and a tempting pool. **€200**

EATING AND DRINKING

Restaurante Port Balansat C/Port de Sant Miquel S/N, Sant Joan de Labritja ☎ 971 334 527, restauranteportbalansat.com. Overlooking the sands of Puerto de San Miguel, this smart restaurant is famed for its superb *Bullit de Peix* fish stew, though its other dishes

– fresh fish, paella, grilled meats and the like – are equally memorable. Expect to pay €40–50 a head. May–Oct daily noon–midnight. Nov–April Tues–Fri & Sun noon–4pm, Fri and Sat noon–midnight.

The west and south coast

For years unchallenged at the top of Europe's *costa hooligania* league table, the package resort of **SANT ANTONI DE PORTMANY** on the island's west coast is trying hard to shake off its tarnished image, with a recently revamped marina. Nevertheless, the high-rise concrete skyline and gritty British pubs of the "West End" aren't at all enticing. Hordes of young British clubbers flock to San An for its plethora of bars within easy staggering distance – the Sunset Strip on the western side of town is the most appealing place for a drink.

Beaches near Sant Antoni

South of Sant Antoni, it's just a few kilometres to some exquisite coves. Sheltered **Cala Bassa** gets packed with holidaying families in high season, but it does have a campsite, while the more exposed beach of **Cala Conta** is less crowded, and is a beautiful spot to while away an afternoon. The most beguiling beach in the Balearics, **Cala d'Hort**, is in the extreme southwest of the island, with an unspoilt, quiet sand-and-pebble shoreline plus three good, moderately priced seafood restaurants. From the shore there are mesmeric vistas of **Es Vedrà**, an incisor-shaped 378-metre-high islet revered by islanders and island hippies alike, and is the subject of various myths and legends – including a claim to be Homer's island of the sirens.

Taking the scenic southern road to Ibiza Town you pass via **SANT JOSEP**, a pretty village with a selection of café-restaurants. Some 7km southwest of Sant Josep is **Cala Jondal**, a popular pebble beach.

13

INFORMATION, ARRIVAL AND DEPARTURE

Tourist office Passeig de Ses Fonts, s/n, Sant Antoni (May–Sept Mon–Fri 10am–8.30pm, Sat–Sun 10am–2pm & 5–8pm; Oct–April Mon–Fri 10am–2pm; ☎971 343 363, ⊛santantoni.net).

By bus The modern bus station at C/Paris in Sant Antoni is located just behind the main street, at the corner where the main road parallel to the beach meets the road that runs alongside the marina.

Destinations Buses leave Sant Antoni for Ibiza Town every

THE WEST AND SOUTH COAST

30–120min 7am–11.30pm, and there are frequent departures to the *calas* Vedella, Conta and Tarida (May–Oct).

By ferry Most ferry services to the island arrive and depart from Ibiza Town but there are a number of mainland services which call at Sant Antoni. The port is easily accessible at the end of the marina on the north side of the bay.

Destinations Barcelona (1–2 daily; 8hr 30min); Denia (2 daily; 2hr 30min–4hr).

ACCOMMODATION

Cala Bassa Ctra. Cala Bassa ☎931 003 167, ⊛www .campingcalabassa.com. Just 250m from the beach, this well-established campsite has mobile homes for four

people at €109/night or ready erected tents for four for €55. Closed Oct–March. €̲3̲3̲

EATING

El Destino C/Atalaya 15, Sant Josep ☎971 800 341. Tasty tapas bar with an excellent range of fresh meat, fish and vegetable dishes. Fills up fast and groups will need to book in advance. Tapas from €8. Mon–Sat 1pm–1am.

S'illa des Bosc Playa de Cala Conta ☎971 806 161, ⊛silladesbosc.com. This classy restaurant is in an idyllic location overlooking the sands of Cala Conta, and the food is equally memorable: paella is recommended from €15, and you can't fault the fresh fish of the day (from €23).

Daily 1–11pm (until sunset from Oct–April).

Sunset Ashram Cala Conta ☎661 347 222, ⊛sunsetashram.com. Looking out over the beach, this is a beautiful spot to dine at as the sun sinks into the Med. International dishes include a range of salads from €15, curries from €17, and steaks or fresh fish from €25. It also has a cocktail bar and nightly DJ sets. March–Oct daily 10am–midnight.

DRINKING AND NIGHTLIFE

Blue Marlin Playa Es Jondal ☎971 410 230, ⊛bluemarlinibiza.com. A suave beach club in an idyllic spot, attracting top DJs. A great spot for a cocktail, it also has a restaurant, though meals will set you back over €60 a head. Daily April–Oct 10am–4am.

Café Mambo C/Vara de Rey 38, Sant Antoni ☎971 346 638, ⊛cafemamboibiza.com. A classic haunt on the Sunset Strip with a deserved reputation for ambient tunes and strong cocktails (about €15). Famed for its big-name DJs, party nights and amazing sunsets. May–Oct daily 10am–4am.

Gatecrasher Avgda. C/Salvador Espriu, Sant Antoni ☎650 516 713, ⊛gatecrasher.com. After the fall of Eden – the club housed here for some fifteen years – Gatecrasher have moved into a stylish, modern club that looks like a psychedelic mosque from the outside, with regular big-name DJ nights, a mega sound-and-light system and a 3000 capacity. Open daily May–Sept 11.30pm–6am.

Ibiza Rocks Hotel C/Cervantes 27, Sant Antonio ☎971 347 774, ⊛www.ibizarocks.com. The hotel is no looker but it's the focal point of the burgeoning Ibiza Rocks brand, hosting the weekly Ibiza Rocks gigs on Wednesdays (recent acts have featured Tinie Tempah, Ed Sheeran and Lily Allen), the club night W.A.R on Fridays and a daily party in the central swimming pool area. May–Sept daily from 7pm.

Racó Verd Pza. de la Iglesia, Sant Josep ☎971 800 267, ⊛racoverdibiza.es. There is nightly live music at this great cultural centre whose outdoor terrace boasts a 1000-year-old olive tree. Music (from 10pm) varies nightly from rock to world music and flamenco. The café-bar is also recommended, serving delicious fresh juices for around €5, as well as *bocadillos*, wraps and salads. April–Sept Mon–Sat 10am–3am; Oct–March Thurs–Sat 6pm–late.

Formentera

Just eleven nautical miles south of Ibiza Town, **FORMENTERA** (population around 8000) is the smallest of the four main Balearic Islands, measuring just 20km from east to west. Formentera's history more or less parallels that of Ibiza, though between 1348 and 1697 it was left uninhabited for fear of pirate raids. Like Ibiza, it was a key part of the 1960s hippy trail (Pink Floyd made an album here), and the island retains a bohemian character.

Formentera is very arid, and mainly covered in rosemary, which grows wild everywhere; it also crawls with thousands of brilliant-green **Ibiza wall lizards** (*Podarcis pityusensis*), which flourish in parched scrubland. The economy is tourism-based, taking advantage of some of Spain's longest, whitest and least-crowded beaches. Development has been limited, and visitors come here seeking escape rather than sophistication. Nude sunbathing is the norm just about everywhere, except in Es Pujols.

La Savina

There's nothing much to keep visitors in **LA SAVINA**, Formentera's only port. Along from the ferry port, there's a smart marina which fills with a fleet of gleaming yachts in the summer. Beyond that, though, it's a rather functional place with little more than car rental kiosks and unappealing wholesale stores.

Platja de Illetes and Espalmador

Northwest of La Savina are the absolutely spectacular sands of **Platja de Illetes**, whose clear waters are ideal for watersports and diving. Across a narrow channel lies the uninhabited island of **Espalmador**, where there's another great beach, and water turquoise enough to trump any Caribbean brochure. You can get to Espalmador on one of the regular boats from La Savina (May–Oct only; €15 return) – don't be tempted to wade across, as currents are deceptive and dangerous.

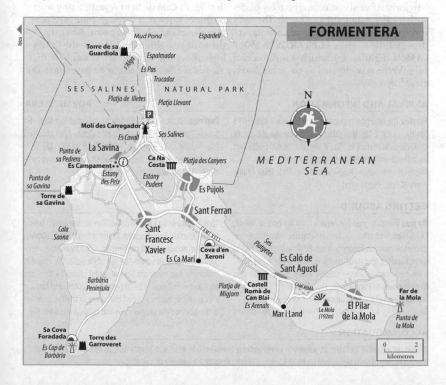

13

Sant Francesc Xavier

The island capital, **SANT FRANCESC XAVIER**, is 4km inland from La Savina and serves as Formentera's commercial and shopping centre with a handful of restaurants, cafés, street stalls and a supermarket, plus the island's main post office, at Pza. de sa Constitució 1. The only real sight here is the mighty fortified **church**, now stripped of its defensive cannon, that sits in the large central square.

Sant Ferran and Platja de Migjorn

There is little to see in the sleepy village of **SANT FERRAN** except a small nineteenth-century church. From here it is a short journey south to one of Formentera's best beaches. Taking up most of Formentera's southern coastline, **Platja de Migjorn** is a sweeping bay with 5km of pale sands and crystalline waters.

Es Pujols

From Sant Ferran, a side road leads to **ES PUJOLS**, Formentera's main resort development – though it's tiny, and tame by mainland standards. Here you'll find two fine sandy beaches and clear, shallow waters, plenty of good seafood restaurants and some late-night bars.

The east

As you head eastwards from Sant Ferran, dusty pathways and tracks – well worth exploration – dart off from the main island road to quieter spots along Platja de Migjorn. After about 6km, the road passes through **Es Caló de Sant Agustí**, a tiny inlet with a café, restaurant and hotel. The road continues eastwards through pine forests as it skirts the northern flanks of **La Mola**, at 192m the island's highest point. After the drowsy little town of **EL PILAR DE LA MOLA**, the road straightens for 2km to the **Far de La Mola** (lighthouse), which stands on cliffs high above the blue ocean. It was here that Jules Verne was inspired to write his *Journey Round the Solar System* as he gazed into the clear night sky.

ARRIVAL AND INFORMATION   FORMENTERA

Ferries The return ferry crossing from Elvissia in Ibiza to La Savina costs €40; timetable on ⓦtransmapi.com or ⓦtransmediterranea.es. There are also summer sailings from Denia with Baleária (ⓦbalearia.com).
Destinations Denia (June–Sept daily; 3hr); Ibiza (daily; every 30min; 35min–1hr).

Turisme C/Calpe s/n, La Savina (May to mid-Oct Mon–Fri 10am–7pm & Sat 10am–4pm; mid-Oct to April Mon–Fri 10am–2pm & 5–7pm, Sat 10am–3pm; ⓣ971 322 057, ⓦformentera.es), can help with accommodation and cycle routes, and provide maps.

GETTING AROUND

By bus There's a good bus service from the port of arrival, La Savina, to the main settlements; timetable on ⓦconsellinsulardeformentera.cat. Of various round island tourist routes, the most useful is Ruta Verde which runs from La Savina to Illetes roughly every 30min, with less frequent runs to Playa Pujols, Faro de La Mola and back to Savina; timetable on ⓦautocarespaya.com.
Destinations La Savina to: Es Pujols (every 20–30min;

10min); Faro de La Mola (6 daily; 50min); San Ferran (every 45min;15min); Sant Francesc Xavier (every 45min; 10min).
By bike, scooter and car Getting about by bicycle is very popular, since apart from the hill of La Mola, the island is extremely flat; there are several rental places by the ferry dock and in Es Pujols (€5–10 per day). Scooters and cars are also available but be warned that some of the tracks down to the beaches are very uneven and sand-covered terrain.

ACCOMMODATION

It's almost essential to make an **advance reservation** between late June and September, as the bulk of the island's limited supply of beds is snapped up early. Camping is not permitted anywhere on the island.

Gecko Beach Club Platja de Migjorn, Ca Mari ☎971 328 024, ⓦgeckobeachclub.com. If you want to enjoy Formentera's simple charms from a sophisticated base, this stylish hotel is one of the island's best. A picture-postcard location on the beach with gleaming floors, a garden-like pool area, an excellent restaurant, yoga classes and massage sessions. **€375**

Hostal Illes Pitiüses Juan Castelo Guasch, Sant Ferran ☎971 328 189, ⓦillespitiuses.com. A long-established family-run hotel on the main cross-island road. Rooms are comfortable and pleasantly old-fashioned; all have satellite TV, private bathrooms and a/c. **€140**

Hostal Mayans C/Punta Prima 37, Es Pujols ☎971 328 724, ⓦhostalmayans.es. Good-value, modern hotel with a large pool and shaded patio café/bar area. The best rooms have balconies overlooking the pool area. Closed Nov–March. **€140**

Hostal Rafalet Caló de Sant Agustí 1, Es Caló ☎971 327 016, ⓦhostal-rafalet.com. Overlooking a tiny fishing harbour, this hotel's spacious rooms afford magnificent sea views. With welcoming staff and a good bar and restaurant (open to the public), it's the perfect place to unwind. Closed Nov–March. **€100**

Hostal La Savina Avdga. Mediterranea 20–40, La Savina ☎971 322 279, ⓦhostal-lasavina.com. This hip *hostal* is right on the beach – rooms, with their own fridges, are bright and fresh, some (€15 extra) with balconies facing the sea, and there's a good café-bar downstairs plus live music on Saturdays. **€160**

Es Pas Venda de Ses Clotades, Es Calo ☎971 328 033. A short walk from the beach at Es Calo, this 200-year-old former *finca* is now a stylish hotel with its own substantial grounds. It has just six rooms (so it gets booked up quickly) which are large and well-equipped and there's a good outdoor pool. **€250**

EATING AND DRINKING

Blue Bar C/San Ferran-La Mola, Platja de Migjorn ☎666 758 190, ⓦbluebarformentera.com. Chilled-out beachside bar-restaurant with ambient tunes and a perfect place to enjoy a cocktail under the stars. Live music on Saturday evenings and children's entertainment on Sundays. Easter to mid-Oct Sun–Thurs noon–1am; Fri–Sat noon–4am.

Cafetería Espardell Avdga. Miramar 6, Es Pujols ☎971 328 357, ⓦespardell.com. Popular café/bar tourist haunt on the seafront with quality, international fare and a good selection of cakes and pastries. Mains from €12. April–Oct daily 8.30am–2am.

Fonda Platé C/Sant Jaume 1, San Francesc Xavier ☎971 322 313. A welcoming, traditional café next to the church with a vine-shaded patio, serving up snacks,

sandwiches and light meals, with occasional live music at night. Daily 8am–1am.

Macondo C/Major 1, Sant Ferran. At the end of the main street, this highly recommended pizzeria has modern decor, an outside terrace and a smart-looking bar area. Gets lively in the evenings; get there early to bag a table. Giant pizzas from around €10. Daily 1–3pm & 7.30–midnight; closed Nov–March.

El Mirador Pza. Del Pilar, La Mola ☎971 327 037. It is the exceptional views rather than the food that brings people here in droves. The specialities are paella and fish (around €15) – get a table on the terrace and the average quality won't matter. Daily 1–4pm & 7–11pm.

DIRECTORY

Car rental Autos Ca Marí ☎971 328 855, ⓦautoscamariformentera.com. Offices in La Savina, Ca Marí and Es Caló.

Emergencies For the police and fire brigade, call

☎092 and for general emergencies dial ☎112.

Hospital L'Hospital de Formentera, Vénda des Brolls s/n, Sant Francesc ☎971 321 212.

Taxi Radio-Taxis ☎971 322 342.

Mallorca

Few Mediterranean holiday spots are as often and as unfairly maligned as **MALLORCA**. The island is commonly perceived as little more than sun, sex, booze and high-rise. It's an image spawned by the helter-skelter development of the 1960s, yet it takes no account of Mallorca's beguiling diversity. In fact, the spread of development, even after fifty years, is essentially confined to the **Badia de Palma** (Bay of Palma), a thirty-kilometre strip flanking the island capital, and a handful of mega-resorts notching the east coast.

Elsewhere, things are very different. **Palma** itself, the Balearics' one real city, is a bustling, historic place whose grand mansions and magnificent Gothic Catedral defy

13

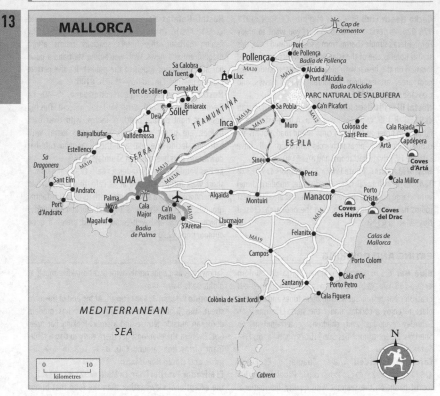

the expectations of many visitors. And so does the northwest coast, where visitors delight in the rearing peaks of the rugged **Serra de Tramuntana**, beautiful cove beaches, monasteries at Valldemossa and Lluc, and a string of delightful old towns and villages – such as Deià, Sóller and Pollença. There's a startling variety and physical beauty to the land, which has drawn tourists to visit and well-heeled expatriates to settle here since the nineteenth century, including artists and writers of many descriptions, from Robert Graves to Roger McGough.

GETTING AROUND
MALLORCA

Public transport Palma lies at the hub of an extensive public transport system – the latest timetables are on ⓦ tib.org. Bus services link the capital to all Mallorca's principal settlements and there are even a couple of train lines – one, a beautiful ride up through the mountains to Sóller (see p.872), is an attraction in itself. And with your own transport, Palma is within two hours' drive of anywhere on the island. Hiring a bike is also a popular way to seek out the island's quieter spots.

Taxis can work out a reasonable deal, too, if you're travelling in a group – the fare across the island to Port de Pollença from Palma is about €70, for instance.

ACCOMMODATION

The main constraint for travellers is **accommodation**, or lack of it. In high season (May–Oct) rooms are far less booked out in inland towns and villages. Everything is quieter in the winter months but many hotels in the main resorts close. Bear in mind also that several of Mallorca's former **monasteries** rent out renovated cells at exceptionally inexpensive rates – reckon on €40–50 per double room per night. The Monastir de Nostra Senyora at Lluc (see p.876) is reachable by public transport.

Palma

13

In 1983, **PALMA** became the capital of the newly established Balearic Islands autonomous region, since when it has developed into a go-ahead and cosmopolitan commercial hub of almost 400,000 people. The new self-confidence is plain to see in the city centre, which is a vibrant place and a world away from the heaving tourist enclaves of the surrounding bay.

Finding your way around Palma is fairly straightforward once you're in the city centre. The obvious landmark is the **Catedral**, which dominates the waterfront and backs onto the oldest part of the city, a cluster of alleys and narrow lanes whose northern and eastern limits are marked by the zigzag of avenues built beside – or in place of – the city walls. On the west side of the Catedral, Avgda. d'Antoni Maura/Passeig d'es Born cuts up from the seafront to intersect with Avgda. Jaume III/Unio at Pza. Rei Joan Carles I. These busy thoroughfares form the core of the modern town.

The Catedral

Pza. de la Almoina • April–May Mon–Fri 10am–5.15pm, Sat 10am–2.15pm; June–Sept Mon–Fri 10am–6.15pm, Sat 10am–2.15pm; Nov–March Mon–Fri 10am–3.15pm, Sat 10am–2.15pm • €6 including the Museu de la Catedral • ☎ 902 022 445, Ⓦ catedraldemallorca.info

Five hundred years in the making, Palma's **Catedral** is a magnificent building – the equal of almost any on the mainland – and a surprising one too, with its interior featuring *modernista* touches designed by Antoni Gaudí. The original church was built following the Christian Reconquest of the city, and the site taken, in fulfilment of a vow by Jaume I, was that of the Moorish Great Mosque. Essentially Gothic, with massive exterior buttresses to take the weight off the pillars within, the church derives its effect through its sheer height, impressive from any angle but startling when glimpsed from the waterside esplanade.

The nave

In the central nave, fourteen beautifully aligned, pencil-thin pillars rise to 21m before their ribs branch out – like fronded palm trees – to support the single-span, vaulted roof. The **nave**, at 44m high, is one of the tallest Gothic structures in Europe, and its length – 121m – is of matching grandeur. This open, hangar-like construction, typical of Catalan Gothic architecture, was designed to make the high altar visible to the entire congregation, and to express the mystery of the Christian faith, with kaleidoscopic floods of light filtering in through the **stained-glass windows**. For once, the light isn't trapped by the central *coro* (choir) that normally blocks the centre of Spanish cathedrals. The innovative though controversial sidelining of the *coro*, and the fantastic forms of the lighting system above the altar, were Gaudí's work, undertaken between 1904 and 1914.

Museu de la Catedral

On the way into the church, you pass through three rooms of assorted ecclesiastical bric-a-brac, which comprise the **Museu de la Catedral**. The first room's most valuable exhibit, in the glass case in the middle, is a gilded silver monstrance of extraordinary delicacy, its fairy-tale decoration dating from the late sixteenth century. The second room is mainly devoted to the Gothic works of the **Mallorcan Primitives**, a school of painters who flourished on the island in the fourteenth and fifteenth centuries, producing strikingly naive works of bold colours and cartoon-like detail.

Palau de l'Almudaina

Pza. de la Almoina • April–Sept Mon–Fri 10am–8pm, Sat 10am–1pm; Oct–March Mon–Fri 10am–8pm, Sat 10am–1pm • €9, plus €4 for audio-guide; free entry to EU citizens showing their passport on Wed and Thurs April–Sept from 3–8pm, Oct–March from 5–8pm • ☎ 971 214 134, Ⓦ patrimonionacional.es

Opposite the cathedral entrance stands the **Palau de l'Almudaina**, originally the palace of the Moorish *walis* (governors) and later of the Mallorcan kings. The interior has

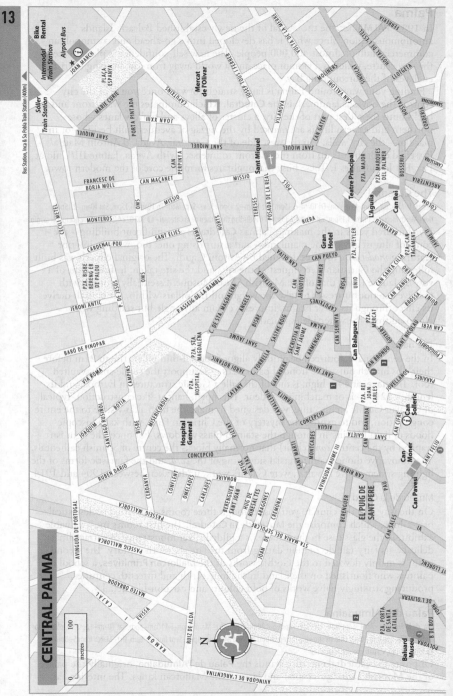

CENTRAL PALMA

metres
0   100

N

Bus Station, Inca & Sa Pobla Train Station (400m)

Sóller Train Station

Intermodal Train Station

Bike Rental

Airport Bus

JOAN MARCH

PLAÇA ESPANYA

MARIE CURIE

PORTA PINTADA

JOAN XXIII

SANT MIQUEL

Mercat de l'Olivar

CAPUTXINS

JOSEP LLUÍS FERRER

VOLTA DE LA MERÈ

MOLINERS

SINDICAT

HOSTAL DEL ESTEL

FERRERIA

LLOTGETA

CAN VALLORI

VILANOVA

HOSTALS

CORDERIA

SAMARITANA

CANÒSSIGA

FRANCESC DE BORJA MOLL

CAN MAÇANET

CAN PERPINYÀ

MISSIÓ

SANT MIQUEL

CAN GATER

PZA. MAJOR

Teatre Principal

Sant Miquel

ARGENTERIA

BOSSERIA

PZA. MARQUES DEL PALMER

L'Àguila

Can Rei

COLOM

CECILI METEL

OMS

MISSIÓ

MONTEROS

SANT ELIES

CARDENAL POU

CARME

HORTS

TERESES

POSADA DE LA REAL

POLS

RIERA

Gran Hotel

CAN PUEYO

PZA. WEYLER

PZA. SANTA CILIA

BARTOMEU

SANT

JAUME II

PZA. BISBE BERENGER DE PALOU

P. DE JESUS

OMS

PASSEIG DE LA RAMBLA

VALTIO CAN

C CAMPANER

UNIÓ

ROSA

CAN DANUS

CAN TÀGAMENT

QUINT

JERONI ANTIC

CAN JAQUOTOT

CAPUTXINES

ANGELS

BISBE

SASTRE ROIG

PALMA

CAN SERINYA

CAN BALAGUER

PZA. MERCAT

GOIXERE

CAN BRONDO

CAN VERI

BROSSA

SANT NICOLAU

PUIGDORFILA

BARÓ DE PINOPAR

VIA ROMA

CAMPINS

C DE STA. MAGDALENA

PZA. STA. MAGDALENA

C TORRELLA

SANT JAUME

SACRISTIA DE SANT JAUME

C CARMENGOL

JARDÍ BOTÀNIC

SANT JAUME

PZA. REI JOAN CARLES I

JOVELLANOS

PARAÍRES

BOTIA

JOAQUIM

SANTIAGO RUSIÑOL

BISBE

MISERICORDIA

CATANY

C CAVALLERIA

C GILABERA

GAVARRERA

ERMITA

CONCEPCIÓ

AIGUA

SANT FELIU

GRANADA

CAN GIFRE

Can Solleric

Hospital General

PZA. HOSPITAL

PIETAT

MEMÈ

METAS

SANT MARTÍ

MONTCADES

GAIETA

Can Moner

SANT FELIU

RUBEN DARIO

CONCEPCIÓ

CONFLENT

OMELADES

CARLADES

BONAIRE

BERENGUER SANT JOAN

HUG DE RIBESALTES

ARAGONÈS

CREMONA

AVINGUDA JAUME III

CAN RIBERA

BERENGUER

PAU

EL PUIG DE SANT PERE

Can Pavesi

AVINGUDA DE PORTUGAL

PASSEIG MALLORCA

PASSEIG MALLORCA

STA. MARIA DEL SEPULCRE

JOAN DE

CAN SALES

VI

ST LLORENÇ

RUIZ DE ALDA

MATEU OBRADOR

EVISSA

CABAL

RAMON

AVINGUDA DE L'ARGENTINA

POLVORA

PZA. PORTA DE SANTA CATALINA

Baluard Museu

B DE BOU

FORN DE L'OLIVERA

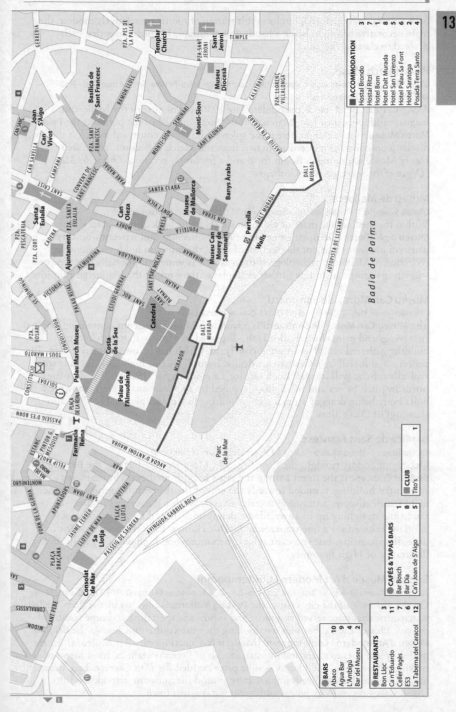

ACCOMMODATION

Hostal Brondo	3
Hostal Ritzi	7
Hotel Born	1
Hotel Dalt Murada	8
Hotel San Lorenzo	5
Hotel Palau Sa Font	6
Hotel Saratoga	2
Posada Terra Santo	4

BARS

Abaco	10
Agua Bar	9
L'Ambigú	4
Bar del Museu	2

RESTAURANTS

Bon Lloc	3
Ca n'Eduardo	11
Celler Pagès	7
ES3	6
La Taberna del Caracol	12

CAFÉS & TAPAS BARS

Bar Bosch	1
Bar Dia	8
Ca'n Joan de S'Aigo	5

CLUB

Tito's	1

Badia de Palma

13

been painstakingly restored, but its rabbit warren of rooms are relatively modest, the main decorative highlight being a handful of admirable Flemish tapestries, each devoted to classical themes.

Palau March Museu
C/Palau Reial • April–Oct Mon–Fri 10am–6.30pm, Sat 10am–2pm; Nov–March Mon–Fri 10am–5pm, Sat 10am–2pm • €4.50 • ☎ 971 711 122, ⓦ fundacionbmarch.es

Along C/Palau Reial stands the opulent late 1930s townhouse of the Mallorcan magnate and speculator Joan March (1880–1962), opened to the public as the **Palau March Museu**. The highlight here is the splendid Italianate courtyard, which is used to display a potpourri of modern art drawn from the March collection. There are two Henry Moore sculptures, a Rodin torso and a fetchingly eccentric *Orgue del Mar* (*Organ of the Sea*) by Xavier Corbero.

Museu de Mallorca
C/Portella 5 • Tues–Sat 11am–6pm, Sun 11am–2pm • Free • ☎ 971 177 838, ⓦ museudemallorca.caib.es

Within the medina-like maze of **old town** streets at the back of the Catedral is the **Museu de Mallorca**. Occupying one of the many fifteenth- and sixteenth-century patrician mansions that dot this section of town, the museum holds an extensive collection of Mallorcan archeological finds as well as some exceptionally fine medieval religious paintings, including further examples of the work of the Mallorcan Primitives.

Museu Can Morey de Santmarti
C/Portella 9 • Daily 9.30am–8.30pm • €9 • ☎ 971 724 741, ⓦ museo-santmarti.es

The **Museu Can Morey de Santmarti** is a wonderful house museum containing original engravings and prints by Salvador Dalí, displayed in a lovely sixteenth-century building gathered round an internal courtyard, which has its own attractive café. The collection, donated by a German art dealer, is not huge but highlights include some typically off-the-wall images. Look out for *La girafe en feu* (1966–67) and various prints inspired by sex and bullfights – typified by *Le piano sous la neige*, showing a bull's body being dragged from a snowy bullring in a grand piano. There are also showings of Dalí's films.

Basílica de Sant Francesc
Pza. Sant Francesc 7 • Mon–Sat 9.30am–12.30pm & 3.30–6pm, Sun 9.30am–12.30pm • €1.50

Occupying, oddly enough, the site of the old Moorish soap factory, the **Basílica de Sant Francesc** is the finest among the city's bevy of medieval churches. It's a substantial building, founded towards the end of the thirteenth century, and the main facade displays a stunning severity of style, with a great sheet of dressed sandstone stretching up to an arcaded balcony and pierced by a gigantic rose window. Entered via a fine trapezoidal Gothic cloister, the cavernous interior is a little disappointing, but you can't miss the monumental **high altar**, a gaudy affair illustrative of High Baroque.

Baluard Museu d'Art Modern i Contemporani
Pza. Porta de S.Catarina 10 • Tues–Sat 10am–8pm, Sun 10am–3pm • €6, temp exhibitions €4 extra • ☎ 971 908 200, ⓦ esbaluard.org

On the west side of the city centre, the **Passeig Mallorca** is bisected by the deep, walled watercourse that once served as a moat and is now an especially handsome feature of the city. One of the old bastions overlooking the watercourse now houses the **Baluard Museu d'Art Modern i Contemporani** (Modern & Contemporary Art Museum), where pride of place goes to a rare and unusual sample of Picasso ceramics, most memorably a striking, white, ochre and black vase-like piece entitled *Big Bird Corrida*. Take time, too, to explore the town walls immediately around the museum, remodelled into stylish walkways and viewpoints with great vistas across town.

ARRIVAL AND DEPARTURE

PALMA

BY PLANE

By plane Mallorca's whopping international airport is 11km east of Palma. It has car rental outlets, 24hr ATMs and currency exchange facilities among the package tour operator helpdesks. The airport is linked to the city and the Bay of Palma resorts by the busy MA19 highway. Bus #1 leaves for Palma every 15min from the main entrance of the terminal building, just behind the taxi rank (5.30am–2.20am; €3), and goes to Pza. Espanya, on the north side of the city centre. A taxi from the airport to the city centre will set you back around €20.

Destinations Ibiza (8–10 daily; 45min) and Maó (6–12 daily; 40min).

By bus Buses from outside Palma arrive and depart from the city's transport Intermodal hub at Pza. Espanya. Go down the escalators and follow the signs.

Destinations Alcudia (Mon–Sat 18 daily, Sun 5 daily; 1hr); Andratx (hourly; 1hr); Deià (Mon–Fri 7 daily, Sat & Sun 4–6 daily; 45min); Lluc (2 daily; 1hr 15min); Pollença (Mon–Fri 14 daily, Sat & Sun 9 daily; 1hr); Port d'Alcúdia (Mon–Sat 18 daily, Sun 5 daily; 1hr 15min); Port de Pollença (Mon–Fri 14 daily, Sat & Sun 9 daily; 1hr 15min); Port de Sóller (via the tunnel: Mon–Fri approx hourly, Sat & Sun every 2hr, 35min; via Valldemossa: 4–7 daily, 1hr 30min); Sóller (via the tunnel: Mon–Fri 14 daily, Sat & Sun 6–8 daily, 35min; via Valldemossa: 4–6 daily, 1hr 25min); Valldemossa (Mon–Fri 12 daily, Sat & Sun 6–7 daily; 30min).

By car Parking is problematic especially in the old town, though there are usually places around the seafront Parc de la Mar.

By ferry The Palma ferry terminal is about 4km west of the city centre. Bus #1 leaves every 15min from outside ferry Terminal 2 (6am–1.45am; €3) bound for the Pza. Espanya and on to the airport. The taxi fare for the same journey is about €12.

Destinations Barcelona (2–3 daily; 7–9hr); Denia (1–2 daily; 6hr) Ibiza (3–4 daily; 2–4hr) Maó (1 weekly; 6hr); Valencia (2 daily; 7–8hr). Full timetables on ⓦ transmediterranea.es, ⓜ balearia.com or ⓦ www.iscomar.com.

By train Palma has two train lines. The scenic trip on the Tren de Sóller is the most popular (see p.872) but a more functional line serves several inland towns from the modern Palma Intermodal train station (ⓣ 971 177 777, ⓦ tib.caib.es), off Pza. Espanya.

Destinations Inca (every 30min; 30min), Manacor (hourly; 1hr 15min), Sa Pobla (hourly; 1hr)

INFORMATION

Turisme In the city centre, the *turisme* nearest the old town is just off the Passeig d'es Born at Pza. de la Reina 2 (Mon–Fri 8.30am–8pm, Sat 8.30am–3pm; ⓣ 971 173 990, ⓦ infomallorca.net).

Municipal office The main office on the north edge of Pza. Espanya not far from the main bus/train station (daily 9am–8pm; ⓣ 902 102 365). Both provide island-wide information.

ACCOMMODATION

Hostal Brondo C/Ca'n Brondo 1 ⓣ 971 720 507, ⓦ hostalbrondo.com. A stylish little place in a central but quiet location, with Mallorcan antiques and neatly done-up rooms. It's probably the best bang for your buck in town. Both en-suite and shared-facility doubles, breakfast €10 extra. **€75**

★**Hostal Ritzi** C/Apuntadors 6 ⓣ 971 714 610, ⓦ hostalritzi.com. Superbly located in a fantastic five-storey former mansion off the Passeig d'es Born, the *Ritzi* is an excellent meeting point for other travellers. Ask for a room which doesn't back onto the main street as it can get noisy at night. Dorm **€25**, double **€60**, en suite **€75**

★**Hotel Born** C/Sant Jaume 3 ⓣ 971 712 942, ⓦ hotelborn.com. Comfortable and justifiably popular hotel in an excellent downtown location. It's a sixteenth-century refurbished mansion and has marvellous high-ceiling rooms and grand communal areas as well as a courtyard café. **€115**

★**Hotel Dalt Murada** C/Almudaina 6 ⓣ 971 425 300, ⓦ daltmurada.com. Set inside a former manor house with period architecture and artwork, and all modern comforts and conveniences. Great central location, too – just behind the town hall. **€150**

Hotel Palau Sa Font C/Apuntadors 38 ⓣ 971 712 277, ⓦ palausafont.com. This smooth and polished four-star hotel, decorated in earthy Italian colours and graced by sculptures and other modern works of art, manages to be both stylish and welcoming. Its roof terrace gives inspiring views of the Catedral. **€165**

★**Hotel San Lorenzo** C/San Lorenzo 14 ⓣ 971 728 200, ⓦ hotelsanlorenzo.com. The rooms in this place, in a narrow old town street, are dotted about a rambling building of various terraces on different levels. The best rooms have balconies or terraces facing a gorgeous secluded pool surrounded by bougainvillea, while a generous breakfast is served in a cool downstairs bar area. **€175**

Hotel Saratoga Pg. Mallorca 6 ⓣ 971 727 240, ⓦ hotelsaratoga.es. An excellent modern hotel with swimming pool. Most rooms have balconies overlooking either the boulevard (a bit noisy) or the interior courtyard and pool (quieter). Pluses include an in-house spa and jazz bar. **€140**

Posada Terra Santa Posada Terra Santa 5 ⓣ 971 21 47 42, ⓦ palausafont.com. This boutique hotel combines modern flare with the old-world charm of a

13

sixteenth-century manor house on a narrow side street. Rooms come with large flat-screen TVs and beds have Egyptian cotton sheets, while the bar-restaurant is adjacent to an internal courtyard. **€200**

EATING

CAFÉS AND TAPAS BARS

Bar Bosch Pza. Rei Joan Carles I ☎ 971 712 228. One of the most popular and inexpensive cafés in town (good sandwiches from €4 to €6), the traditional haunt of intellectuals, and usually humming with conversation. At peak times, you'll need to be assertive to get served. Daily 7am–12.30am.

★ **Bar Dia** C/Apuntadores 18 ☎ 971 716 264. Bustling tapas bar with delicious Spanish cuisine at reasonable prices, with a small restaurant area or stools at the bar. Tapas from €3 to €7, or larger *raciones* such as scallops from €7 to €8. Tues–Sun noon–1am.

★ **Ca'n Joan de S'Aigo** C/Can Sanç 10 ☎ 971 710 759. In a tiny alley near Pza. Santa Eulàlia, this long-established coffee house has wonderful, freshly baked *ensaimadas* (sweet spiral pastry buns). Charmingly formal, period-piece decor. Mon–Fri 8am–9pm, Sat 8am–9.15pm.

RESTAURANTS

Bon Lloc C/Sant Feliu 7 ☎ 971 718 617, ⓦ bonllocrestaurant.com. One of the few vegetarian restaurants on the island, centrally situated off the Passeig d'es Born, with an informal atmosphere and satisfying food at low prices. Good-value set menus from €18.50. Mon–Wed 1–4pm, Thurs–Sat 1–4pm & 7.30–10.30pm.

Ca n'Eduardo C/Contramoll Mollet 4 ☎ 971 721 182, ⓦ caneduardo.com. Spic-and-span restaurant located upstairs in one of the plain modern buildings looking out above the fish dock. There's an enjoyable view of the harbour, but the real treat is the fresh fish (from €21) – a wonderful range, all simply prepared; the monkfish bouillabaisse (€29) is superb. The restaurant is just across from – and east of – the foot of Avgda. Argentina. Daily 1–3.30pm & 8–11pm; closes Sun from Nov–Feb.

Celler Pagès Off C/Apuntadors at C/Felip Bauza 2 ☎ 971 726 036. Small, inexpensive restaurant with an easy-going family atmosphere serving traditional Mallorcan food – try the stuffed marrows with home-made mayonnaise. Good-value lunch menu at €13. Reserve at weekends. Tues–Sat 1–3.30pm & 8–11pm, Sun 1–3.30pm.

ES3 Pza.Drassana 12 ☎ 659 173 354. This café-restaurant serves very good value three-course meals from €10, though better are the paellas from €13. Tables spill out onto one of Palma's liveliest squares, and service is swift and friendly. Daily 10am–midnight.

La Taberna del Caracol C/Sant Alonso 2 ☎ 971 714 908. Deep in the depths of the old town, this smashing *taberna* occupies charming old premises – all wooden beams and ancient arches. Main courses are good, but recommended is the first-rate range of tapas from €5.50 to €8 – the prawns in garlic are superb. Reservations advised at peak times. Mon 7.30–11.30pm, Tues–Sat 12.15pm–3.15pm & 7.30–11.30pm.

DRINKING AND NIGHTLIFE

There's a cluster of lively **late-night bars** – mostly with music as the backdrop rather than the main event – among the narrow side streets backing onto Pza. Llotja. The **club scene** in Palma is small but worth investigating after around midnight; entry charges are between €6 and €25, depending on the night and what's happening.

BARS

Abaco C/Sant Joan 1 ☎ 971 714 939, ⓦ bar-abaco.es. Easily Palma's most unusual bar, with fruits cascading down its stairway, caged birds hidden amid patio foliage and a daily flower bill you could live on for a month. Cocktails start at €20. Everyone is often so mesmerized by the bizarre surroundings that the atmosphere is rather sedate. Mon–Thurs 8pm–midnight, Fri–Sat 8pm–3am.

Agua Bar Jaume Ferrer 6 ⓦ aguabar.com. Friendly New Yorker-run bar with a good range of beer, an impressive collection of rock 'n' roll and a relaxed vibe. Various theme nights, including an open-mic night on Sundays, attracts a crowd. Mon–Thurs 7pm–1am, Fri–Sat 7pm–3am.

L'Ambigú C/Carnissería 1 ☎ 971 572 151. Just behind Santa Eulàlia, this modern bar with wall-to-wall contemporary artwork attracts a young professional crowd. It's hidden just away from the tourist droves so is, generally speaking, a peaceful place for a relaxed drink. Flavourful tapas too. Mon–Sat 7pm–midnight.

Bar del Museu Es Baluard Museu, Pza. Porta de S. Catarina 10 ☎ 971 908 200. For a classy drink spot, head to the terrace bar of the museum restaurant. Set within the town walls, surrounded by contemporary works of art, the views towards the port over palm trees is a delight. Cocktails start at €7. Daily 8am–midnight.

CLUBS

Tito's Paseo Maritimo s/n ☎ 971 730 017, ⓦ titosmallorca.com. With its stainless steel, neon lighting and glass exterior, this long-established nightspot looks a bit like something from a sci-fi film. Outdoor lifts carry you up from Avgda. Gabriel Roca (the back entrance) to the dancefloor, which plays anything from hardcore dance to mainstream pop. Entry €20, which includes a free drink. July and Aug daily 11pm–6am; June & Sept Fri–Sun 11pm–6am; May Fri–Sat 11pm–6am.

DIRECTORY

Bike rental Palma has an excellent network of cycle lanes and is ideal for cycling round. Lock & Co, at the main Intermodal station, Pza. España ☎ 971 716 417, ⓦ palmalockandgo.com, rents bikes from €6 a day (daily: April–Oct 9am–8pm, Nov–March 9.30am–7.30pm).
Car rental Avis (☎ 971 730 720) has offices in the city and at Palma airport.

Hospital Son Dureta Hospital, Andrea Doria 55 ☎ 971 175 000.
Pharmacy Farmacia Reina, Pza. Reina I ☎ 971 715 371, Mon–Fri 9am–10pm, Sat–Sun 10am–10pm.
Post office C/Constitució 6 ☎ 971 721 867, Mon–Fri 8.30am–8.30pm, Sat 9.30am–1pm.

Around Palma

Anywhere in the west or centre of the island is readily accessible as a **day-trip** from Palma. If you're after a quick **swim** the most convenient option is to stick to the resorts strung along the neighbouring **Badia de Palma** (Bay of Palma). Locals tend to go east on the #15 bus (every 10min; 30min) from Pza. Espanya to **S'Arenal**, where there's an enormously long, albeit often very crowded, sandy beach.

Castell de Bellver

C. de Camilo José Cela, Palma • April–Sept Mon 8.30am–1pm, Tues–Sat 8.30am–8pm, Sun & hols 10am–8pm; Oct–March Mon 8.30am–1pm, Tues–Sat 8.30am–6pm, Sun & hols • 10am–6pm • €4, free on Sun • ☎ 971 735 065, ⓦ cultura.palma.es

An appealing option, though there are no buses to it, is the **Castell de Bellver**, a strikingly well-preserved fortress of canny circular design built for Jaume II at the beginning of the fourteenth century. The castle perches on a wooded hilltop some 3km west of the city centre and offers superb views of Palma and its harbour.

Andratx, Sant Elm and Sa Dragonera

Inland from the Bay of Palma, you could spend an hour or two exploring **ANDRATX**, a small, undeveloped town huddled among the hills to the west of the city – there are buses roughly every hour from Palma. From here, it's another forty minutes through a pretty, orchard-covered landscape to low-key **SANT ELM**, with its small beach.

There is not much to the place, but you can take the 15-minute ferry crossing (every 30min; April–Sept daily 9.45am–3.45pm, Oct 10.15am–3.45pm, Feb–March Mon–Sat 10.15am–1.15pm; €12; ⓦ crucerosmargarita.com) across from Sant Elm's minuscule harbour to the austere offshore islet of **Sa Dragonera**, an uninhabited chunk of rock some 4km long and 700m wide, with an imposing ridge of sea cliffs dominating its northwestern shore; the main pull here – apart from hiking on this traffic-free islet – is the birdlife.

ACCOMMODATION AND EATING   SANT ELM

Hostal Dragonera Rei Jaume I, 15 ☎ 971 239 086, ⓦ hostaldragonera.es. This very reasonably priced *hostal* is highly recommended. It's situated right on the seafront and has simple but comfortable rooms, most of which offer sea views. Closed Dec–Feb. **€60**

Vista Mar C/Jaime I 46 ☎ 971 237 547. Harbourside restaurant with a beautiful terrace and delicious paella and fish dishes. Reckon on at least €40 for a complete meal, including house wine. Wed–Mon 1–4pm & 7–11pm.

Northern Mallorca

Mallorca is at its scenic best in the gnarled ridge of the **Serra de Tramuntana**, the imposing mountain range that stretches the length of the island's western shore, its soaring peaks and plunging sea cliffs intermittently intercepted by valleys of olive and citrus groves and dotted with some of the island's most attractive towns and villages. An enjoyable way to admire this spectacular scenery at a leisurely pace is to drive or cycle along the coastal road MA10, which runs from Andratx to Pollença – though be

13

HIKING IN NORTHERN MALLORCA

The **Serra de Tramuntana** provides the best walking on Mallorca, with scores of hiking trails latticing the mountains, the most famous being the GR221 Dry Stone Route (☻ gr221.info), which runs for 135km from Port d'Andratx to Pollença. Generally speaking, paths are well marked, though apt to be clogged with thorn bushes. There are trails to suit all levels of fitness, from the easiest of strolls to the most gruelling of long-distance treks, but in all cases you should come properly equipped – certainly with an appropriate hiking **map** (available in Palma and at the Sóller *turisme*), and, for the more difficult routes, a **compass**. Spring and autumn are the best times to embark on the longer trails; in midsummer, the heat can be enervating and water is scarce. Bear in mind also that the mountains are prone to mists, though they usually lift at some point in the day.

aware that some of the twists and turns are quite precarious. If you're reliant on public transport, the easiest way to explore the north is to travel up from Palma to Sóller and use this town as a base, making selected forays along the coastal road. Sóller is within easy striking distance of the mountain village of **Deià** and the monastery of **Valldemossa** to the southwest, or it's a short haul northeast to the monastery of **Lluc**, the quaint town of **Pollença** and the resort of **Port de Pollença**.

As far as **beaches** are concerned, most of the region's coastal villages have a tiny, shingly strip, and only around the bays of Pollença and Alcúdia are there more substantial offerings. The resorts edging these bays have the greatest number of hotel and *hostal* rooms, but elsewhere **accommodation** requires some forethought.

Sóller

If you're arriving by train at **SÓLLER**, the obvious option is to take the **tram** straight through to the port. If you don't stop, however, you'll miss one of the most laidback and enjoyable towns on Mallorca, though it's the general flavour of the place that appeals rather than any specific sight: the town's narrow, sloping lanes are cramped by eighteenth- and nineteenth-century stone houses, whose fancy grilles and big wooden doors once housed the region's well-heeled fruit merchants.

Plaça Constitució

All streets lead to the main square, **Plaça Constitució**, an informal, pint-sized affair of crowded cafés just down the hill from the train station. The square is dominated by the hulking mass of the church of **Sant Bartomeu**, a crude but still somehow rather engaging neo-Gothic remodelling of the medieval original, its main saving grace being the enormous rose window cut high in the main facade.

ARRIVAL AND DEPARTURE   SÓLLER

By bus Buses to and from Port de Sóller to Palma, Deià, Valldemossa and north Mallorca call en route at the Sóller bus station at C/Cetre – about a 5min walk west of the centre. Destinations Alcúdia (2 daily; 2hr 10min); Deià (4–7 daily; 25min); Lluc (May–Oct Mon–Sat 2 daily; 1hr 5min); Palma (via Valldemossa: 4–6 daily, 1hr 25min; via the tunnel: Mon–Fri 14 daily, Sat & Sun 6–8 daily, 35min); Pollença (May–Oct Mon–Sat 2 daily; 1hr 35min); Port d'Alcúdia (2 daily; 1hr 20min); Port de Pollença (May–Oct Mon–Sat 2 daily; 2hr); Port de Sóller (4–7 daily; 5min); Valldemossa (4–6 daily; 55min).

By train Easily the best way to cross the Serra de Tramuntana is to take the train (☎ 971 630 130,

☻ trendesoller.com,) from Palma to Sóller, a 28km journey that takes about an hour on antique rolling stock that seems to have come straight out of an Agatha Christie novel. The rail line, constructed on the profits of the nineteenth-century orange and lemon trade, dips and twists through the mountains and across fertile valleys, offering magnificent views.

Destinations Palma (4–5 daily; 1hr; €19.50 return, combined with tram ticket to Port de Sóller €28).

By tram Trams leave (7am–8.20pm, 1–2 hourly; 15min; €5 each way, or €28 combined with return train fare to Palma) from outside the station down to the seashore at Port de Sóller, just 5km away.

INFORMATION

Turisme Located inside an old tram carriage on Pza de Espanya; it has a good supply of leaflets as well as a list of accommodation (Mon–Fri 9.30am–2pm & 3–5pm; Sat & Sun 10am–1pm; ☎971 638 008). The website ⓦsollernet .com is also an excellent source of information.

ACCOMMODATION

Hotel Ca'l Bisbe C/Bisbe Nadal 10 ☎971 631 228, ⓦhotelcalbisbe.com. Upmarket hotel in an immaculately restored old mansion with spacious rooms, all with a/c and cable TV, set around an attractive pool area. Check their website for discounts. Closed mid-Nov to March. **€137**
Hotel El Guía C/Castanyer 2 ☎971 630 227, ⓦsollernet.com/elguia. First opened in 1880, this smart-looking hotel just metres from the train station is a family-run Sóller institution, with an excellent and reasonably priced restaurant serving typically Mallorcan fare. Expect – and revel in – plenty of old-world charm but few mod cons. Closed Dec–Feb. **€90**

EATING AND DRINKING

Petit Celler Cas Carreter C/Cetre 4 ☎971 63 51 33, ⓦcascarreter.net. Founded in 1914, and once a carriage maker's workshop, this is now a spacious restaurant dotted with huge barrels and wooden wheels. A long list of tasty dishes on the menu includes paella (€16), fresh fish such as sea bass (€16) and rabbit with prawns and onions (€17). April–Oct daily noon–4pm & 7.30pm–11pm; Nov–March Mon–Sat noon–4pm & 7.30pm–11pm, Sun noon–4pm.
Sá Fàbrica de Gelats C/Romaguera 12 ☎971 631 708, ⓦgelatsoller.com. Heavenly ice-cream parlour with a choice of forty flavours. It's famed for its hugely refreshing orange ice-cream. Take away or enjoy in the garden terrace. Daily 10am–8pm; closed Dec–Jan.

Port de Sóller

PORT DE SÓLLER is one of the most popular and family-orientated resorts on the west coast, and its horseshoe-shaped bay must be the most photographed spot on the island after the package resorts around Palma. The best **swimming** is along the pedestrianized area of **Platja d'en Repic**, where the water is clear and the beach clean and well maintained. Also good fun is the fifty-minute walk up to the **lighthouse**, which guards the cliffs above the entrance to Port de Sóller's harbour. It's a steep climb but the views out over the wild and rocky coast are spectacular, especially at sunset, and there's even a restaurant at the cape. Directions couldn't be easier: from the centre of the resort, walk round the southern side of the bay past the Platja d'en Repic beach and keep going. At the opposite end of the bay, fifty-minute boat trips run out to Cala Calobra (2–3 daily in season, €25).

ARRIVAL AND INFORMATION   PORT DE SÓLLER

By tram Trams from Sóller clank to a halt beside the waterfront, bang in the centre of town and a couple of minutes' walk from the *turisme*.
By bus Buses arrive and depart just off C/Sa Figuera, the second roundabout out of town on the Sóller road, a 5min walk from the *turisme*.
Destinations Deià (4–7 daily; 30min); Palma (via Valldemossa: 4–7 daily, 1hr 30min; via the tunnel: Mon–Fri approx hourly, Sat & Sun every 2hr, 35min); Pollença (May–Oct Mon–Sat 2 daily; 1hr 45min); Port de Pollença (April–Oct Mon–Sat 2 daily; 2hr); Sóller (Mon–Fri approx hourly, Sat & Sun every 1–2hr; 5min); Valldemossa (4–7 daily; 55min).
Turisme Located beside the church on C/Canonge Oliver (March–Sept Mon–Fri 9.30am–3pm; ☎971 633 042). It can provide a full list of local hotels and *hostales*.

ACCOMMODATION

Hotel Marina & Wellness Spa Paseo La Playa s/n ☎971 631 461, ⓦhotelmarinasoller.com. The best of a string of modern waterfront hotels, and just a stone's throw from the crowded, but pleasant enough, beach. There are clean, functional rooms, an outdoor pool and a spa. **€140**
★**Hotel Es Port** C/Antonio Montis s/n ☎971 631 650, ⓦhotelesport.com. Outside peak season, there's a good chance of a reasonably priced room at the attractive *Hotel Es Port*, which occupies a huge old mansion with lovely gardens set back from the main part of the port. There are both indoor and outdoor pools, plus a spa. **€160**

13

EATING AND DRINKING

Las Palmeras C/Es Través ☎ 971 631 306. In an attractive old building with a vine-shaded terrace, this pleasantly traditional restaurant has a range of inexpensive dishes such as pizza, paella, chicken and grilled sardines from €7.50 to €14. There are also tables out on the promenade. Daily noon–midnight.

So Caprichos Sant Ramon de Penyafort 15 ☎ 971 630 095. A gem among the rather overpriced harbourside options. Large slabs of hot-stone-cooked steaks (€25) are the speciality among a good choice of Mallorcan and international cuisine, served up on a shaded terrace by attentive staff. Three courses will set you back around €40. May–Oct daily 11am–4pm & 6.30–11pm; Nov–April Wed–Mon noon–4pm.

Deià

It's a dramatic, ten-kilometre journey southwest from Sóller along the MA10 to the beautiful village of **DEIÀ**, where the mighty Puig des Teix mountain ramps down to the coast. At times, this thoroughfare is too congested to be much fun, but the tiny heart of the village, tumbling over a high and narrow ridge on the seaward side of the road, still preserves a surprising tranquillity. Here, labyrinthine alleys of old peasant houses curl up to a pretty country church, in the precincts of which stands the grave of **Robert Graves** (1895–1985), the village's most famous resident and author of works including *I, Claudius* and *Goodbye To All That*. The grave is marked simply "Robert Graves: Poeta, E.P.D." (*En Paz Descanse*: "Rest In Peace"), and the views from the graveyard out over the coast are truly memorable.

Ca N'Alluny

Carretera Deià a Sóller • April–Oct Mon–Fri 10am–5pm & Sat 10am–3pm; Nov Mon–Fri 9am–4pm & Sat 9am–2pm; Dec–March Mon–Fri 10.30am–1.30pm • €7 • ☎ 971 636 185, ⓦ lacasaderobertgraves.com • Bus #210 from Soller and Palma

Robert Graves put Deià on the international map, and his old home, **Ca N'Alluny**, a substantial stone building beside the main road about 500m east of the village, was opened to the public in 2006. Graves first lived here in the 1930s and returned after World War II to remain in the village until his death. For the most part, the house has been returned to its 1940s appearance, and its rooms are decorated with Graves' own furnishings and fittings. You can see the study where Graves produced much of his finest work, as well as an exhibition of manuscripts and photos of Graves posing with a few of his well-known visitors.

Cala de Deià

Cala de Deià, the nearest thing the village has to a beach, comprises some 200m of shingle at the back of a handsome rocky cove of jagged cliffs, boulders and white-crested surf. It's a great place for a swim, the water clean, deep and cool, and there's a ramshackle beach bar. It takes about thirty minutes to walk from the village to the *cala*, a delightful stroll down a wooded ravine – or a five-minute drive.

ARRIVAL AND INFORMATION   DEIÀ

By bus Buses loop through Deià, dropping passengers on the main street.
Destinations Palma (Mon–Fri 7 daily, Sat & Sun 4–6 daily; 45min); Port de Sóller (4–7 daily; 30min); Sóller

(4–7 daily; 25min); Valldemossa (4–7 daily; 15min).
Information There's no *turisme* but a useful website with information about the village is ⓦ deia.info.

ACCOMMODATION

★ **Es Molí** Carretera Valldemossa–Deià ☎ 971 639 000, ⓦ esmoli.com. One of the most agreeable hotels on Mallorca, *Es Molí* is a supremely comfortable establishment in an immaculately maintained building with superb gardens overlooking the main road at the west end of the village. It even has its own private cove, served by a free minibus shuttle. Closed Nov to mid-April. **€240**

★ **Pensión Miramar** C/de Can Oliver ☎ 971 639 084, ⓦ pensionmiramar.com. A slightly run-down-looking *pensión* in lush surroundings, reached by a short, steep walk up above the main road. Rooms are unimaginative but perfectly adequate, and there are smashing views over the village from the terrace. Closed Dec–Feb. **€98**

13

EATING AND DRINKING

Trattoria Italiana, Viña Vieja 1 ☎ 971 636 450. This sophisticated Italian restaurant has a superb terrace with mountain views. It's a good spot for a drink or the likes of steaks, salmon with dill, and various pasta dishes. Mains from €17. Mon–Sat noon–4pm & 7–10.30pm.

The Village Café C/Felip Bauça 1 ☎ 971 63 91 99. This diminutive café-restaurant is on a narrow side street off the main through road, with an attractive shaded terrace. The menu caters for the eclectic clientele of Deià, with everything from gazpacho and bruschetta (€5) to smoked salmon salads, gourmet burgers and pizzas (€12–13). Wed–Sun noon–5pm & 7–10pm.

Valldemossa

Some 10km **southwest of Deià** along the MA10 lies the ancient and intriguing hill town of **VALLDEMOSSA**, a sloping jumble of rusticated houses and monastic buildings set in a lovely valley and with a mountain backdrop. The origins of Valldemossa date to the early fourteenth century, when the asthmatic King Sancho built a royal palace here in the hills, where the air was easier to breathe. Later, in 1399, the palace was given to Carthusian monks from Tarragona, who converted and extended the original buildings into a **monastery**, now the island's most visited building after Palma Catedral.

Real Cartuja de Jesús de Nazaret

Jan & Dec Mon–Sat 9.30am–3pm, Sun 10am–1pm; Feb & Nov Mon–Sat 9.30am–5pm, Sun 10am–1pm; March & Oct Mon–Sat 9.30am–5.30pm, Sun 10am–1pm; April–Sept Mon–Sat 9.30am–6.30pm, Sun 10am–1pm • €8.50, an extra €3.50 to visit cell 4 • ☎ 971 612 986, ⓦ cartujadevalldemossa.com

Remodelled on several occasions, most of the present complex, the **Real Cartuja de Jesús de Nazaret**, as it's formally named, is of seventeenth- and eighteenth-century construction, its square and heavy church leading to the shadowy corridors of the cloisters beyond. The monastery owes its present fame almost entirely to the novelist and republican polemicist **George Sand**, who, with her companion, the composer **Frédéric Chopin**, lived here for four months during 1838–39 in a commodious set of vacant cells – their stay is commemorated in Sand's self-important work, *A Winter in Majorca*.

A visit begins in the gloomy, aisleless **church**, which is distinguished by its fanciful bishop's throne, and then continues in the adjoining cloisters, where the **prior's cell** is, despite its name, a comfortable suite of bright, sizeable rooms with splendid views down the valley. Farther along the corridor, **cell no. 2** exhibits miscellaneous curios relating to Chopin and Sand, from portraits and a lock of hair to musical scores and letters. Neighbouring **cell no. 4**, which also has its own separate entrance from the main square, includes Chopin's piano, which you have to pay an extra €3.50 to view. Upstairs, there's a small but outstanding collection of **modern art**, including work by Miró, Picasso, Francis Bacon and Henry Moore. And be sure also to take the doorway beside the prior's cell that leads outside the cloisters to the enjoyable **Palace of King Sancho**. It's not the original palace at all – that disappeared long ago – but it is the oldest part of the complex, and its fortified walls, mostly dating from the sixteenth century, accommodate a string of handsome period rooms.

ARRIVAL AND DEPARTURE   VALLDEMOSSA

By bus Valldemossa is easily reached by bus from Deià, Sóller and Palma. Buses stop beside the bypass at the west end of town; from here, it's just a couple of minutes' walk to the monastery.
Destinations Deià (4–7 daily; 15min); Palma (Mon–Fri 12 daily, Sat & Sun 6–7 daily; 30min); Port de Sóller (4–7 daily; 55min).

Turisme On the main MA1110, next to the central car park (Mon 9am–1.30pm & 3–5pm, Tues–Fri 9am–6.30pm, Sat 10am–1pm & 4.30–6.30pm, Sun 10am–2pm; ☎ 971 612 106, ⓦ valldemossa.com).

ACCOMMODATION AND EATING

C'an Molinas Via Blanquerna 15 ☎ 971 612 247. Long-established café with a pleasant garden and a display counter bursting with delicious pastries and sandwiches, all available to take away. Serves good, strong coffee and *ensaimadas* (sugar-dusted pastries) for around €2. Daily 7am–8.30pm.

13

★**Es Petit Hotel** C/Uetam 1 ☎971 612 479, ⓦespetithotel-valldemossa.com. Spacious and taste-fully decorated rooms in an attractive refurbished old house. All the rooms have a/c and satellite TV, and some have great views over the valley. The price includes an excellent buffet breakfast. **€130**

Lluc

Without doubt, the most interesting approach to the northernmost tip of the island is the 35km stretch of the MA10 northeast from Sóller to **LLUC**. The road slips through the highest and harshest section of the **Serra de Tramuntana**. Tucked away in a remote mountain valley, Lluc was Mallorca's most important place of pilgrimage from the middle of the thirteenth century, supposedly after a shepherd boy named Lluc (Luke) stumbled across a tiny, brightly painted statue of the Madonna here in the wood.

Monestir de Nostra Senyora

Daily 9am–8pm • Free • Car park €6, refunded with entry to museum

Lluc is dominated by the austere, high-sided dormitories of the **Monestir de Nostra Senyora**. At the centre of the monastery is the main shrine and architectural highlight, the **Basílica de la Mare de Déu de Lluc**, a dark and gaudily decorated church, whose heaviness is partly relieved by a dome over the central crossing. On either side of the nave, stone steps extend the aisles round the back of the Baroque high altar to a little chapel. This is the holy of holies, built to display the much-venerated statue of the Virgin, commonly known as **La Moreneta** ("The Little Dark-Skinned One") ever since the original paintwork peeled off in the fifteenth century to reveal brown stone underneath. You can also stroll along the **Camí dels Misteris del Rosari** (Way of the Mysteries of the Rosary), a pilgrims' footpath that winds its way up the rocky hillside behind the monastery. Don't miss the attractive botanical gardens (to the left of the monastery as you face it), where you can also find an extremely alluring open-air pool.

Museu de Lluc

Daily 10am–6pm • €3 • ☎971 871 525

Allow time for a visit to the monastery museum, the **Museu de Lluc**, which includes a fascinating display of archeological finds and gifts offered to the Virgin. The entry fee also allows you to see a small and underwhelming sound and light display about the monastery, adjacent to the ticket office.

ARRIVAL AND DEPARTURE   LLUC

By bus Buses stop at a large car park just a minute's walk from the monastery's main entrance.
Destinations Alcúdia (2 daily; 1hr); Palma (2 daily; 1hr 15min); Pollença (May–Oct Mon–Sat 2 daily; 30min); Port de Alcúdia (May–Oct Mon–Sat 2 daily; 1hr 10min); Port de Sóller (May–Oct Mon–Sat 2 daily; 1hr 15min); Sóller (May–Oct Mon–Sat 2 daily; 1hr 5min).

ACCOMMODATION

Santuari de Lluc Lluc ☎971 871 525, ⓦlluc.net. Spending the night at the monastery provides the perfect opportunity to experience the peace and quiet that has been sought here for centuries. Rooms are basic but comfortable, and there are also apartments available for two to six people; breakfast costs €6 extra. Note that the kitchens are not equipped with utensils. Gates shut at midnight. Two-bedroomed apartment available for €68. **€41**

EATING AND DRINKING

Sa Fonda Santuari de Lluc, Lluc ☎971 871 525. Inside the monastery, on the left as you enter, this is grander than you might expect from a former monks' refectory and the pick of Lluc's dining experiences. Lamb is the speciality, with mains for about €15. Wed–Sun 8.30am–10.30am, 1–3pm & 7.30–9.15pm.

Pollença

Heading northeast from Lluc, the MA10 twists through the mountains to travel the 20km on to **POLLENÇA**, a pretty and ancient little town that nestles among a trio of hillocks where the Serra de Tramuntana fades into the coastal flatlands. Following standard Mallorcan practice, the town was established a few kilometres from the seashore to protect it against sudden pirate attack, with its harbour, Port de Pollença (see p.878), left as an unprotected outpost. For once, the stratagem worked. Unlike most of Mallorca's old towns, Pollença avoided destruction, and the austere stone houses that cramp the twisting lanes of the centre mostly date from the eighteenth century. In the middle, **Pza. Major**, the main square, accommodates a cluster of laidback cafés and the dour facade of the church of **Nostra Senyora dels Àngels**, a sheer cliff face of sun-bleached stone pierced by a rose window.

Via Crucis

Pollença's pride and joy is its **Via Crucis** (Way of the Cross), a long, steep and beautiful stone stairway, graced by ancient cypress trees, which ascends **El Calvari** (Calvary Hill) directly north of the principal square. At the top, a much-revered statue of the **Mare de Déu del Peu de la Creu** (Mother of God at the Foot of the Cross) is lodged in a courtyard of the simple **Oratori** (Chapel), whose whitewashed walls sport some of the worst religious paintings imaginable. On Good Friday, a figure of Jesus is slowly carried by torchlight down from the Oratori to the church of Nostra Senyora dels Àngels, in the **Davallament** (Lowering), one of the most moving religious celebrations on the island.

Ermita de Nostra Senyora del Puig

There are magnificent views from the **Ermita de Nostra Senyora del Puig**, a rambling, mostly eighteenth-century monastery that occupies a serene and beautiful spot on top of the Puig de María, a 320-metre-high hump facing the south end of town. The Benedictines now own the place, but the monks are gone and today a custodian supplements the order's income by renting out cells to tourists – the views are spectacular, but the conditions pretty spartan. To get to the monastery, take the signposted turning left off the main Pollença–Inca road just south of town, then head up this steep, 1.5-kilometre lane until it fizzles out, to be replaced by a cobbled footpath that winds up to the monastery entrance. It's possible to drive to the top of the lane, but unless you've got nerves of steel, you're better off leaving your vehicle by the turning near the foot of the hill. Allow just over an hour each way if you're walking from the centre of town.

ARRIVAL AND INFORMATION   POLLENÇA

By bus Buses to Pollença from Palma and Port de Pollença halt immediately to the south of Pza. Major, just along the road from the *turisme*. But, inconveniently, buses from Lluc and Sóller drop off passengers about 1km north of the centre on the main MA10 road.
Destinations Alcúdia (Mon–Sat 2 daily; 30min); Palma (Mon–Fri 14 daily, Sat & Sun 9 daily; 1hr); Sóller (May–Oct

Mon–Sat 2 daily; 1hr 35min); Lluc (Mon–Sat 2 daily; 30min); Port de Pollença (every 20min; 15min).
Turisme C/Guillem Cifre de Colonya s/n, a block south of the main plaza (May–Oct Mon–Fri 8.30am–1.30pm & 2–6pm, Sun 10am–1pm; Nov–April Mon–Fri 8am–10.30am & 11–3pm; ☎971 535 077, ⍟pollensa .com/info).

ACCOMMODATION

L'Hostal C/Mercat 18 ☎971 535 281, ⍟pollensahotels .com. This modern hotel just off the main square has individually styled rooms with chic touches – bare stone walls, sloping ceilings etc. There's a pleasant patio and an airy lounge where breakfast is taken in winter; at other times, it is served at the sister *Hotel Juma*. €100
Hotel Juma Pza. Major 9 ☎971 535 002, ⍟hoteljuma .com. The most central place to stay is the *Hotel Juma*, with comfortable, a/c modern bedrooms, some of which

overlook the main square. Popular with cyclists, this medium-sized hotel is above a café, and has helpful staff. Closed Nov–Feb. €125
La Posada de Lluc C/Roser Vell 11 ☎971 535 220, ⍟posadalluc.com. A welcoming hotel occupying an intelligently revamped old mansion where the Lluc monks once used to stay when they were in town. The eight rooms are bright and homely, with some overlooking the pretty pool. €177

13

EATING AND DRINKING

Ca'n Moixet Pza. Major 2. ☎ 971 534 214. Partly dating back to the twelfth century when it was part of a house for the Knights Templars, this place retains a traditional ambience and is one of the less tourist-centred cafés around the main square, offering snacks, simple meals and strong coffee. It has a good choice of tapas from €3.50. Daily 8am–late.

★ **Manzanas y Peras** C/Martell 6 ☎ 971 532 292, ⓦ manzanasyperas.eu. An arty café/restaurant with tables outside on Pza. Seglars. The menu features baguettes, superb sharing platters (€20 but enough for three) and dishes such as pork, apple and sage burger (€9.50), plus a very tasty home-made chocolate brownie. Sun–Fri 11am–4pm. Sun–Fri 10am–4pm & 7–10pm.

Port de Pollença

Over at **PORT DE POLLENÇA** things are a little more touristy than at Pollença, though still pleasantly low-key. With the mountains as a backdrop, the resort arches through the flatlands behind the Badia de Pollença, a deeply indented bay whose sheltered waters are ideal for swimming. The **beach** is the focus of attention, a narrow, elongated sliver of sand that's easily long enough to accommodate the crowds. There's also a delightful three-kilometre (each way) **hike** across the neck of the Península de Formentor to the remote shingle beach of **Cala Boquer**.

ARRIVAL AND INFORMATION
PORT DE POLLENÇA

By bus Buses to Port de Pollença stop by the marina right in the centre of town – and metres from the seafront *turisme*. Destinations Palma (Mon–Fri 14 daily, Sat & Sun 9 daily; 1hr 15min); Pollença (every 15min to 1hr; 15min); Port de Sóller (April–Oct Mon–Sat 2 daily; 2hr); Sóller (May–Oct

Mon–Sat 2 daily; 2hr).
Turisme Located on the seafront by the bus stops at Passeig Saralegui s/n (May–Sept Mon–Fri 8am–8pm, Sat 9am–4pm; Oct–April Mon–Fri 8am–3pm, Sat 9am–1pm; ☎ 971 865 467).

TOURS AND ACTIVITIES

Boat trips Lanchas la Gaviota (ⓦ lanchaslagaviota.com) runs passenger ferries between the marina and the Platja de Formentor (April–Oct 4 daily; 30min; €12), one of Mallorca's most attractive beaches, as well as boat trips around the bay and over to Cap de Formentor; check

website for schedules.
Bike rental The flatlands edging the Badia de Pollença make for easy, scenic cycling, and mountain bikes can be rented from around €25 a day from March at C/Joan XXIII 89 (☎ 971 864 784, ⓦ rentmarch.com).

ACCOMMODATION

Hotel Bahía Pg. Voramar 29 ☎ 971 866 562, ⓦ hoposa. es. A few minutes' walk north of the marina, this peaceful hotel has a great location right on the seashore. It's a good choice, with small but pleasant rooms that have been recently renovated, and an excellent restaurant. Expect to pay extra for a sea view. Closed Nov–March. €124
Hotel Can Llenaire Carretera Llenaire ☎ 971 535 251, ⓦ hotelllenaire.com. The *Can Llenaire* occupies an imposing Mallorcan manor house on the brow of a hill with wide views over the Badia de Pollença. There are just eleven rooms, each decked out in period style, pretty

gardens and a lovely pool. The hotel is signposted down a country lane from the main coastal road just east of the centre of the resort. €275
Pension Bellavista C/Monges 14 ☎ 699 549 376, ⓦ pensionbellavista.es. This simple *pensión* is metres from the seafront. Rooms are small and some face a noisy side street, others open onto an attractive communal terrace at the back. Communal areas are attractively decorated with works by local artists, but the best feature is the patio garden where various vegetarian breakfasts are served under the trees from €4.50. €65

EATING AND DRINKING

Bella Verde C/Monge 14 ☎ 675 602 528. You don't have to be a vegetarian to appreciate the food at this leafy hideaway. With tables set up under shady trees in a patio garden, you can enjoy vegetarian curries, pumpkin lasagne or tomato tart with asparagus and rosemary potatoes (mains from €9.50). Lovely cakes and fresh juices, too. Tues–Sun 8am–11pm; closed during Jan or Feb.

★ **Celler la Parra** C/Juan XXIII 84 ☎ 971 685 043, ⓦ cellerlaparra.com. On the main road into town, this quirky and highly appealing space is filled with rustic knick-knacks and giant wine barrels. Once a wine cellar, it now serves good-value Mallorcan dishes. Tasty hake fillets and pork steaks from around €10–14. Daily 1.30–3.30pm & 6.30–11.30pm.

Península de Formentor

Travelling northeast out of Port de Pollença, the road soon weaves up into the craggy hills of the twenty-kilometre-long **Península de Formentor**, the final spur of the Serra de Tramuntana. At first, the road (which suffers a surfeit of tourists from mid-morning to mid-afternoon) travels inland, out of sight of the true grandeur of the scenery, but after about 4km the **Mirador de Mal Pas** rectifies matters with a string of lookout points perched on the edge of plunging, north-facing sea cliffs. From here, it's another couple of kilometres to the woods backing onto the **Platja de Formentor**, a pine-clad beach of golden sand in a pretty cove.

Alcúdia

It's just 10km round the bay from Port de Pollença to the pint-sized town of **ALCÚDIA**, whose main claim to fame is its impeccably restored medieval walls and incredibly popular open-air market (Tues & Sun), that has everything from souvenir trinkets to fruit and veg. Situated on a neck of land separating two large, sheltered bays, the site's strategic value was first recognized by the Phoenicians, and later by the Romans, who built their island capital, Pollentia, here in the first century AD.

Pollentia

Tues–Fri 10am–3.30pm, Sat 10am–1.30pm • €3 • ⓦ alcudia.net

It only takes an hour or so to walk around the antique lanes of Alcúdia's compact centre, and to explore the town walls and their fortified gates. This pleasant stroll can be extended by a visit to the meagre remains of Roman **Pollentia**, whose broken pillars and mashed foundations lie just outside the town walls. The entrance ticket includes admission to the small but excellent **Museu Monogràfic** nearby – just inside the walls.

ARRIVAL AND DEPARTURE ALCÚDIA

By bus Buses to Alcúdia stop beside – and immediately to the south of – the town walls on Avgda. dels Princeps d'Espanya. Destinations Lluc (2 daily; 1hr); Palma (Mon–Sat 18 daily, Sun 5 daily; 1hr); Pollença (Mon–Sat 2 daily; 30min); Port de Pollença (every 15min; 20 mins); Sóller (2 daily; 2hr 10min).

EATING AND DRINKING

Restaurant S'Arc C/Serra 22 ☎ 971 548 718. S'Arc, in the heart of Alcúdia, is a bright, fashionable space inside an old building, with an alluring courtyard. The menu features good tapas (from €8) and mains such as *salmon a la planca* (€14.50) or Iberian pork (€15). Daily 12.30–3pm & 6.30–11pm.

Port d'Alcúdia

PORT D'ALCÚDIA, 3km south of Alcúdia, is easily the biggest and busiest of the resorts on the Badia d'Alcúdia, its raft of restaurants and café-bars attracting crowds from a seemingly interminable string of high-rise hotels and apartment buildings. The tower blocks are, however, relatively well distributed and the streets neat and tidy. Predictably, the daytime focus is the **beach**, a superb arc of pine-studded golden sand, which stretches south for 10km from the combined marina and fishing harbour.

ARRIVAL AND DEPARTURE PORT DE ALCÚDIA

By bus Port d'Alcúdia acts as northern Mallorca's summertime transport hub, with frequent bus services to and from all the neighbouring towns and resorts, plus Palma. Destinations Alcúdia (every 15min; 10min); Lluc (May–Oct Mon–Sat 2 daily; 1hr 10min); Palma (Mon–Sat 18 daily, Sun 5 daily; 1hr 15min); Port de Pollença (every 15–30min; 30min); Sóller (2 daily; 1hr 20min).

By ferry Ferries depart from the modern ferry building on the eastern side of the bay to make the crossing to Ciutadella in Menorca (March–Sept 4–5 daily; Oct–Feb 1 daily; 2–2hr 30min). Details on ⓦ www.iscomar.com and ⓦ baleria.com.

Turisme On the seafront on Passeig Marítim (Mon–Sat 9.30am–8.30pm; ☎ 971 547 257). It can supply all sorts of information, most usefully free maps marked with all the resort's hotels and apartments.

13

Parc Natural de S'Albufera

Daily: April–Sept 9am–7pm; Oct–March 9am–5pm • Free • ☎ 971 892 250, ⓦ mallorcaweb.net/salbufera • Buses from Port d'Alcúdia to Ca'n Picafort (Mon–Sat 2–3 daily; 30min) stop beside the entrance

Heading south around the bay from Port d'Alcúdia, it's about 6km to the **Parc Natural de S'Albufera**, a slice of protected wetland, which is all that remains of the marshes that once extended round most of the bay. The signposted entrance to the park is on the MA12, but access is only on foot or cycle – so if you're driving, you'll need to use the small car park near the entrance. About 1km from the entrance, you come to the park's **reception centre**, from where footpaths radiate out into the reedy, watery tract beyond. It's a superb habitat, with ten well-appointed hides allowing excellent **birdwatching**. Over two hundred species have been spotted: resident wetland-loving birds, autumn and/or springtime migrants, and wintering species and birds of prey in their scores.

Menorca

The second largest of the Balearic Islands, boomerang-shaped **MENORCA** is the least plagued by unsavoury development. An essentially rural island, it features rolling fields, wooded ravines and humpy hills filling out the interior in between its two main – but still notably small – towns of **Maó** and **Ciutadella**. Much of this landscape looks pretty much as it did at the turn of the twentieth century, and only around the edges of the island, and then only in parts, have its rocky coves been colonized by sprawling villa complexes. Neither is the development likely to spread: determined to protect their island from the worst excesses of the tourist industry, the Menorcans have clearly demarcated development areas and are also pushing ahead with a variety of environmental schemes – the island was declared a UNESCO Biosphere Reserve in 1993, and over forty percent of it now enjoys official protection.

GETTING AROUND   MENORCA

By bus Bus routes are distinctly limited, adhering mostly to the main central road between Maó and Ciutadella, occasionally branching off to the larger coastal resorts.

By car You'll need your own vehicle to reach any of the emptier beaches, which are sometimes down a track fit only for 4WD.

ACCOMMODATION

Accommodation is at a premium, with limited options outside Maó and Ciutadella – and you can count on all the beds in all the resorts being block-booked by the tour operators from the beginning to the end of the season (May–Oct).

MENORCA'S PREHISTORY

Menorca is dotted with **prehistoric monuments**, weatherworn stone remains that are evidence of a sophisticated culture. Little is known of the island's prehistory, but the monuments are thought to be linked to those of Sardinia and are classified as examples of the **Talayotic culture**, which is usually considered to have ended with arrival of the Romans in 123 BC. **Talayots** are the rock mounds found all over the island – popular belief has it that they functioned as watchtowers, but it's a theory few experts accept. The megalithic **taulas** – huge stones topped with another to form a T, around 4m high and unique to Menorca – are even more puzzling. They have no obvious function, and they are almost always found alongside a *talayot*. Some of the best-preserved *talayot* and *taula* remains are on the edge of Maó at the **Talatí de Dalt** site. The third prehistoric structure of note is the **naveta** (dating from 1400 to 800 BC), stone-slab constructions shaped like an inverted bread tin.

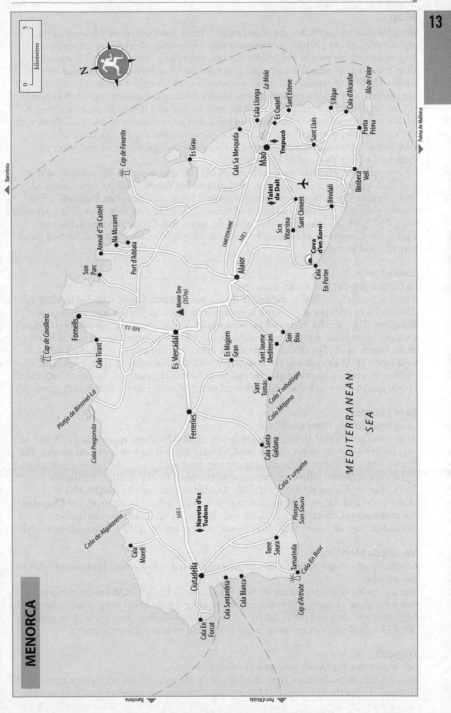

MENORCA

13 Maó

MAÓ (Mahón in Castilian), the island capital, has a place in culinary history as the eighteenth-century birthplace of **mayonnaise** (*mahonesa*). Perched high above the largest natural harbour in the Mediterranean, the town's compact centre is no more than ten minutes' walk from one end to the other. Its architecture consists of an unusual hybrid of classical Georgian townhouses, which reflect a strong British connection, and tall Spanish apartment blocks shading the narrow streets. Port it may be, but there's no real gritty side to Maó, and the harbour is now home to a string of slick – if rather sedate – restaurants and cafés that attract droves of tourists. Wandering the maze of alleyways and peering into the gateways of the city's collection of handsome old mansions are its charm, rather than any specific sight, and you can explore the place thoroughly in a day.

From near the ferry terminal, set beneath the cliff that supports the remains of the city wall, a generous stone stairway, the **Costa de Ses Voltes**, leads up to the series of small squares that comprise the heart of the old town. The first, **Pza. Espanya**, offers views right across the port and bay, and houses Maó's bustling fish market, in operation since 1927, while to the left at the top of the steps, **Pza. Carme** is home to the vast Eglésia del Carme whose cloisters house a bustling market – a good place to buy picnic supplies and souvenirs.

Santa María

Pza. Constitució • Mon–Sat 7.30am–noon & 6–8.30pm • Free

The Pza. Constitució boasts the town's main church, **Santa María**, founded in 1287 by Alfonso III to celebrate the island's Reconquest and remodelled on several subsequent occasions. The church's pride and joy is its **organ**, a monumental piece of woodwork, all trumpeting angels and pipes, built in Austria in 1810 and lugged across half of Europe at the height of the Napoleonic Wars under the concerned charge of Britain's Admiral Collingwood. Daily concerts are held here Monday to Saturday at 1pm. Next door, the eighteenth-century **ajuntament** benefited from British largesse, too, its attractive arcaded facade graced by a clock that was presented to the islanders by the first British governor.

Sant Francesc

C/Isabel II • Mon–Sat 10am–12.30pm & 5–7pm • Free

At the end of C/Isabel II, the Baroque facade of **Sant Francesc** appears as a cliff face of pale golden stone set above the rounded, Romanesque-style arches of its doorway. The church was a long time in the making, its construction spread over the seventeenth and eighteenth centuries following the razing of the town by the piratical Barbarossa in 1535. The nave is poorly lit, but it's still possible to pick out the pinkish tint in much of the stone and the unusual spiral decoration of the pillars. In contrast, the **Chapel of the Immaculate Conception** is flooded with light – an octagonal wonderland of garlanded vines and roses that offers an exquisite example of the Churrigueresque style.

Museu de Menorca

Avdga. Doctor Guàrdia s/n • April–Oct Tues–Sat 10am–2pm & 6–8.30pm, Sun 10am–2pm • €2.40, free Sat pm & Sun • ☎ 971 350 955, 🖳 dgcultur.caib.es

The monastic buildings adjacent to Sant Francesc now house the **Museu de Menorca**, easily the island's biggest and best museum, holding a wide sample of prehistoric artefacts, beginning with bits and pieces left by the Neolithic pastoralists who settled here around 4000 BC; there's also an extensive range of material from the Talayotic period.

Trepucó

Tues–Fri 9am–2.30pm, Sat & Sun 9am–3pm • €1.80; free access outside these times

It's a 35-minute walk south from the Museu de Menorca to the prehistoric remains of **Trepucó**. To get there, follow C/Moreres from the eastern corner of Pza. S'Esplanada,

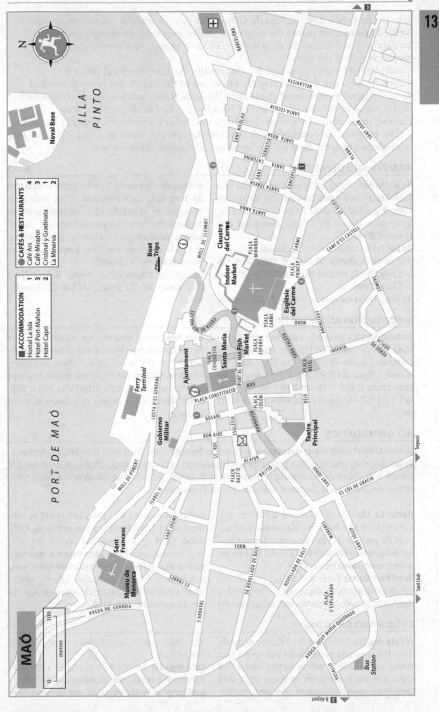

MAÓ

ILLA PINTO

Naval Base

PORT DE MAÓ

Ferry Terminal

Boat Trips

Gobierno Militar

Ajuntament

Santa Maria

Fish Market

Indoor Market

Claustre del Carme

Església del Carme

Teatre Principal

Sant Francesc

Museu de Menorca

Bus Station

PLAÇA CONSTITUCIÓ
PLAÇA CONQUESTA
PLAÇA ESPANYA
PLAÇA REIAL
PLAÇA COLÓN
PLAÇA MIRANDA
PLAÇA PRÍNCEP
PLAÇA CARME
PLAÇA BASTIÓ
PLAÇA S'ESPLANADA

■ ACCOMMODATION	
Hostal La Isla	1
Hotel Port-Mahón	3
Hotel Capri	2

● CAFÉS & RESTAURANTS	
Café Ars	4
Café Mirador	3
Cristinal y Gredinata	1
La Minerva	2

MAÓ

metres
0   100

▼ ❷ & Airport

▼ Sant Lluís

▼ Trepucó

▲ ❸

13

take the first right down C/Cós de Gràcia and then go straight on, streaming onto C/ Verge de Gràcia just before the ring road. At the ring road, go straight over the roundabout and follow the twisting lane in front of you, past the cemetery, and thereafter follow the signs.

Surrounded by olive trees and dry-stone walls, the tiny site's focal point is a 4.2-metre-high and 2.75-metre-wide **taula**, one of the largest and best preserved of these T-shaped monoliths on the island. The *taula* stands inside a circular compound that is edged by the remains of several broadly circular buildings. These were thoroughly excavated by a team of archeologists from Cambridge University in the late 1920s, but even they couldn't work out how the complex was structured. There are two cone-shaped **talayots** close by, the larger one accessible, the other not.

ARRIVAL AND DEPARTURE   MAÓ

By air Menorca's airport, just 5km southwest of Maó, has a handful of car-rental outlets. There are buses (€2.60) every 30min or so to Maó bus station; the taxi fare is about €10.
Destinations Mallorca (6–10 daily; 25min) and Ibiza (4 weekly; 50min).
By bus The bus station is on Pza. S'Esplanada.
Destinations Ciutadella (Mon–Fri 20 daily, Sat & Sun 6–8 daily; 1hr); Es Mercadal (Mon–Fri 20 daily, Sat & Sun 6–8 daily; 25min).
By ferry Ferries sail right up the inlet to Maó harbour,

mooring directly beneath the town centre. From behind the ferry dock, it's a 5min walk up the wide stone stairway to the old part of town. Ferries from Maó are run by Trasmediterranea (🖥 trasmediterranea.es), though Balearia (🖥 balearia.com) and Iscomar (🖥 www.iscomar. com) also sometimes run some winter services (see individual websites for details).
Destinations Barcelona (3–7 weekly; 8–9hr); Palma (1–2 weekly; 5hr–5hr 30min); and Valencia (1 weekly; 15hr).

INFORMATION AND BOAT TRIPS

Turisme There is a tourist information desk at the airport (daily 9am–2pm; ☎ 971 157 115), plus one office at Pza. Constitució 22 (Mon–Fri 9.30am–1pm & 5–7.30pm; Sat 9.30am–1.30pm; ☎ 971 363 790) and one down on the harbourfront, at Moll de Llevant 2 (Mon–Fri 9am–1pm; ☎ 971 355 952). The island's official website is 🖥 menorca .es.

Boat trips Several companies run boat trips along the Port de Maó that leave from the Moll de Llevant near the bottom of the main steps. Yellow Catamarans (🖥 yellowcatamarans.com; €12) run regular hour-long trips out past Es Castell to the fortress of La Mola in glass-bottom boats, with a running commentary in several languages.

ACCOMMODATION

Maó has a limited supply of **accommodation**, and excessive demand tends to inflate prices at the height of the season. Despite this, along with Ciutadella it remains the best Menorcan bet for bargain lodgings, with a small concentration of *hostales*. None of these places is inspiring, but they're reasonable enough, and convenient, though you may prefer to stay outside town in a *finca* or on the coast in nearby Cala d'Alcaufar (see opposite).

Hostal La Isla C/Santa Caterina 4 ☎ 971 366 492, 🖥 hostal-laisla.com. Rooms at this amenable *hostal* may be on the small side, but they are clean and comfortable, and all have private bathroom and TV. There's a popular bar and restaurant downstairs, too. **€56**
Hotel Port-Mahón Avgda. Port de Maó 13 ☎ 971 362 600, 🖥 sethotels.com. An elegant colonial-style hotel in a superb location overlooking the Maó inlet, with a swimming

pool and all mod cons. It's a 20min walk east of the town centre along C/Carme. Room prices vary enormously. **€200**
Hotel Capri C/San Esteban 8 ☎ 971 361 400, 🖥 artiemhotels.com. This modern three-star hotel has a good location and decent-sized comfortable rooms, many with balconies. But its crowning glory is the rooftop pool (under a glass roof in winter) and spa, with great views out over the town and harbour. **€110**

EATING AND DRINKING

★ **Café Ars** Pza. Príncipe ☎ 971 351 879, 🖥 arscafe .info. This café/music bar/restaurant puts on live jazz, theatre and comedy as well as hosting regular club nights with DJs. It also serves up decent tapas, with some good vegetarian options, and great mojitos.

Mon–Thurs noon–4.30pm Fri & Sat noon–4.30pm & 8pm–4/5am.
Café Mirador Pza. Espanya 2. Located a few steps from the fish market, this appealing café-bar offers a good range of snacks and tapas, and has great views

over the harbour from its terrace. Jazz is the favoured background music. Mon–Thurs noon–12.30am, Fri & Sat noon–1.30am.

Cristinal y Gradinata C/Isabel II 124 ☎ 971 363 316, ⓦ gradinata.es. A collection of old radios, hats and beer bottles adorn the shelves of this delightful bistro bar. The house speciality is its delicious mini-sandwiches which are among the tastiest on the island and come with a fine variety of fillings; a good selection of wines

and beer too. Mon 8.30am–3pm, Tues–Fri 8.30am–3pm & 7–11.30pm, Sat noon–3pm & 7.30–11.30pm.

La Minerva Moll de Llevant 87 ☎ 971 351 995. Decent restaurant in a great location down on the harbourfront with tables out on the water on a floating pontoon terrace. The food is mostly fish and seafood – the lobster with rice is good – and reasonable value, though service can be slow and rather indifferent. Daily 12.30–3.30pm & 7–11.30pm.

DIRECTORY

Hospital Hospital Mateu Orfila, Ronda de Malburguer 1 ☎ 971 487 000, ⓦ ibsalut.es.

Post office C/Bonaire 15, ⓦ correos.es.

Around Maó

The southeast corner of the island is pretty flat and rural, which makes it a good place for cyclists, especially as the main roads are shadowed by separate dedicated bike lanes. There's not much to detain you in this region save the odd low-key resort and what must be one of the world's most spectacularly sited nightspots.

Cala d'Alcaufar

Some 10km south of Maó, **CALA D'ALCAUFAR** is a pretty little former fishing village set beside a narrow inlet of flat-topped cliffs and backed by a small sandy beach. Impossibly picturesque, it's a low-key place consisting of little more than a few subdued holiday homes, and some whitewashed old fishermen's cottages built into the rock that tumble down to the sea. Facilities are limited to one simple hotel, a lovely *finca*, a seasonal shop and one restaurant, so don't expect lively nightlife.

ARRIVAL AND DEPARTURE   CALA D'ALCAUFAR

By bus Buses from Maó arrive in the centre of Cala d'Alcaufar, about 200m from the Hostal Xuroy (summer only; 6 daily; 25min).

ACCOMMODATION

★**Alcaufar Vell** Carretera Alcalfar, Sant Lluís ☎ 971 151 874, ⓦ alcaufarvell.com. This delightful rustic former farmhouse, 1.5km inland from Cala d'Alcaufar, is now a smart boutique-style hotel, with 21 comfortable rooms, some in the main farmhouse and some in outbuildings around the grounds with private terraces. The buffet breakfast is good, staff are friendly and

efficient and there's a lovely pool. **€282**

Hostal Xuroy ☎ 971 151 820, ⓦ xuroymenorca.com. It's the location that really sells this simple, family-run hotel – it's right on the beach, with a fine pool and restaurant on a terrace that is practically lapped by the waves. The rooms are basic, but adequate and some have balconies looking over the sea. Closed Nov–April. **€65**

Cova d'en Xoroi

Carrer de Sa Cova 2, Cala en Porter • Cave daily May 3–5.30pm; first 2 weeks of June 11.30am–5.30pm; mid-June to Sept 11.30am–4.30pm; €8, including one soft drink • Evening chill-out sessions daily May to mid-June 6–9.30pm; mid-June to Sept 5–10pm Oct Fri–Sun from 11pm; €10, including one soft drink • Check website for details of discos and club nights • ☎ 971 377 236, ⓦ covadenxoroi.com • A taxi from Maó costs around €25

The **Cova d'en Xoroi** caves are built into a high cliff face, with terraces and large open windows hewn out of the rock giving spectacular views over the Med. A winding staircase leads down from the entrance at the top, punctuated by terraces and seating areas as it links various colourfully lit caves that tunnel back into the rocks. During the day, you can wander round the caves and sit on the terraces to marvel at the view, but at night it really comes into its own as a **nightclub** showcasing some big-name DJs and club nights.

13

Across the island

The road from Maó to Ciutadella, the **Me-1**, forms the backbone of Menorca, and what little industry the island enjoys – a few shoe factories and cheese plants – is strung along it. Here also is the island's highest peak, **Monte Toro**, from the top of which there are wondrous views.

Talatí de Dalt

4km out of Maó on the Me-1 • May–Sept daily 10am–sunset • €4; Oct–April open access; free

Down a country lane, clearly signposted off the Me-1, **Talatí de Dalt** is another illuminating Talayotic remnant. Much larger than Trepucó, the site is enclosed by a Cyclopean wall and features an imposing *taula*, which is adjacent to the heaped stones of the main *talayot*. All around are the scant remains of prehistoric dwellings. The rustic setting is charming – olive and carob trees abound and a tribe of semi-wild boar root around the undergrowth.

Es Mercadal and Monte Toro

The old market town of **ES MERCADAL** squats among the hills at the very centre of the island about 20km west of Maó. It's an amiable little place of whitewashed houses and trim allotments, whose antique centre straddles a quaint watercourse.

Monte Toro

From Es Mercadal, you can set off on the ascent of **Monte Toro**, a steep 3.2-kilometre climb along a serpentine road. At 357m, the summit is the island's highest point and offers wonderful vistas. It has been a place of pilgrimage since medieval times, and the Augustinians plonked a monastery on the summit in the seventeenth century. Bits of this original construction survive in the convent there today, though much of the convent area is closed to visitors.

From this lofty vantage point, Menorca's geological division becomes apparent: to the north, Devonian rock (mostly reddish sandstone) supports a rolling, sparsely populated landscape edged by a ragged coastline; to the south, limestone predominates in a rippling plain that boasts both the island's best farmland and, as it approaches the south coast, its deepest valleys.

Naveta d'es Tudons

Just off Me-1, 6km from Ciutadella • May–Sept Mon & Tues 9am–2pm, Wed–Sun 9am–8.30pm • €2 • Oct–April open access; free

Heading on from Es Mercadal, the Me-1 swings past the village of **FERRERIES** before sliding across the agricultural flatlands of the western part of the island. There are prehistoric remains to either side of the road, but easily the most interesting is the **Naveta d'es Tudons**, Menorca's best example of a *naveta*. Seven metres high and fourteen long, the structure is made of massive stone blocks slotted together in a sophisticated dry-stone technique. The narrow entrance leads into a small antechamber, which was once sealed off by a stone slab; beyond lies the main chamber where the bones of the dead were stashed away after the flesh had been removed.

Ciutadella

Like Maó, **CIUTADELLA** sits high above its harbour, though navigation is far more difficult here, up a narrow channel too slender for anything but the smallest of cargo ships. Despite this nautical inconvenience, Ciutadella has been the island's capital for most of its history; the narrow, cobbled streets of its compact, fortified centre brim with fine old palaces, hidden away behind high walls, and a set of Baroque and Gothic churches very much in the Spanish tradition.

The main plazas, accommodation and points of interest are all within a few strides of each other, on and around the main square, **Pza. d'es Born**, in the middle

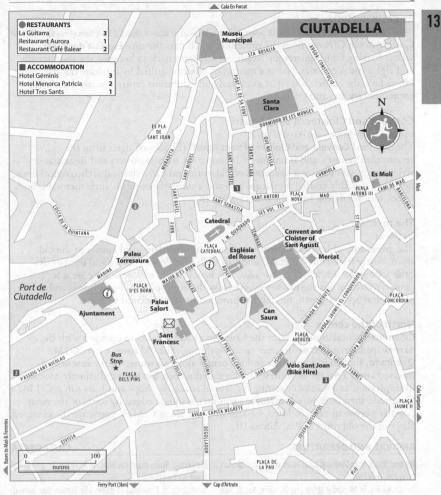

CIUTADELLA

RESTAURANTS
La Guitarra	3
Restaurant Aurora	1
Restaurant Café Balear	2

ACCOMMODATION
Hotel Géminis	3
Hotel Menorca Patricia	2
Hotel Tres Sants	1

of which a soaring obelisk commemorates the town's futile defence against the marauding Turks in 1558. To the northwest, the square is bordered by the steep harbour walls, and in the northeast lies the vast nineteenth-century Palau Torresaura. Like many of the city's grand aristocratic mansions, it is still privately owned and off limits to visitors.

Allow at least a couple of days, more if you seek out one of the charming cove beaches within easy striking distance of town – **Cala Turqueta** is the pick of the bunch.

Catedral

C/Cal Bispe 8 • May–Oct Mon–Sat 10am–4pm; Nov–April 8am–1pm & 5–9pm • €3, or €5 including entry to the Convent and Cloister of Sant Agustí • ☎ 971 380 343

From beside Palau Torresaura, C/Major d'es Born leads through to the **Catedral**, built by Alfonso III at the end of the thirteenth century on the site of the town's chief mosque. Built so soon after the Reconquest, its construction is fortress-like, with windows set high above the ground – though the effect is somewhat disturbed by the flashy columns of the Neoclassical west doorway, the principal entrance.

13

Església del Roser

C/Roser • July & Aug Mon–Sat 10.30am–1.30pm & 6–9pm; Sept–June Mon–Sat 10.30am–1.30pm & 5.30–8.30pm • Free • ☎ 971 383 563

Cutting down C/Roser from the cathedral, you'll pass the tiny **Església del Roser**, whose striking Churrigueresque facade, which dates back to between the seventeenth and eighteenth centuries, boasts a quartet of pillars engulfed by intricate tracery. Nowadays, the church is used as a cultural and exhibition centre, mostly displaying contemporary arts and crafts.

Convent and Cloister of Sant Agustí

C/Seminari 7 • Mon–Sat 10am–4pm • €3 • ☎ 971 481 297

The dignified **Convent and Cloister of Sant Agustí** (El Socors) dates from the seventeenth century, and is unique in Menorca for its twin towers and Renaissance style. Inside, you can see a collection of Talayotic and early classical archeological finds, notably a superbly crafted miniature bull and a similarly exquisite little mermaid, both Greek bronzes dating from the fifth century BC.

The mercat

Pza. Llibertat

The green-and-white-tiled **mercat** (market) is another delightful corner of the old town, where fresh fruit, vegetable and fish stalls mingle with lively and inexpensive cafés selling the freshest of *ensaimadas*. The benches and café patios are great for people-watching but the market square lacks the atmospheric chaos, bustle and colour of a typical Spanish town, though the produce on sale is second to none.

North of the centre

C/Seminari proceeds north from the Convent of Sant Agustí to intersect with the narrow, pedestrianized main street running through the old town – here **C/J.M. Quadrado**, though it goes under various names along its route. To the east of this intersection is a parade of whitewashed, vaulted arches, **Ses Voltes**, distinctly Moorish in inspiration and a suitable setting for several attractive shops and busy cafés. C/J.M. Quadrado then leads into **Pza. Nova**, a minuscule square edged by some of the most popular pavement cafés in town. Continuing east along C/Maó, you leave the cramped alleys of the old town at Pza. Alfons III.

ARRIVAL AND DEPARTURE   CIUTADELLA

By bus Buses from Maó and local buses pull in and depart from Pza. dels Pins.
Destinations Es Mercadal (Mon–Fri 20 daily, Sat & Sun 6–8 daily; 25min); Maó (Mon–Fri 20 daily, Sat & Sun 6–8 daily; 1hr).
By ferry Car ferries dock at the port about 4km south of the centre. Buses meet the boats to ferry passengers to the town centre (10min).
Destinations Barcelona (1 daily; 5 hr 30min–9hr 30min); Port de Alcúdia (March–Sept 4–5 daily; Oct–Feb 1 daily; 2–2hr 30min).

INFORMATION

Turisme The tourist office in the Ajuntament on Pza. d'es Born (Mon 9.30am–2pm, Tues–Sun 9am–8pm; ☎ 971 484 155), has buckets of information on Menorca as a whole and Ciutadella in particular. Bike hire is available at Velos Joan, C/Sant Isidre 32–34 (☎ 971 381 576, ⊛ velosjoan .com).

ACCOMMODATION

Hotel Géminis C/Josepa Rossinyol 4 ☎ 971 384 644, ⊛ hotelgeminismenorca.com. This well-tended, peaceful two-star hotel on a quiet residential street has thirty simple but comfortable rooms, and a small outdoor pool. Closed mid-Oct to March. **€120**
★ **Hotel Menorca Patricia** Pg. Sant Nicolau 90 ☎ 971 385 511, ⊛ hotelmenorcapatricia.com. Smart, family-run hotel, popular with business folk and handy for the centre. The comfortable, modern rooms are very clean and there's a great buffet breakfast and a saltwater pool outside. **€183**
Hotel Tres Sants C/Sant Cristòfol 2 ☎ 626 05 35 36, ⊛ grupelcarme.com. A boutique-style hotel sensitively

converted from an old manor house in the heart of the old town. The roof terrace has great views over the town and harbour, and there's a small pool and Turkish bath in the basement. **€210**

EATING AND DRINKING

For an early **breakfast**, make your way to the **market** on Pza. Llibertat, where a couple of simple cafés serve coffee and fresh pastries. Later in the day, around **lunchtime**, aim for C/J.M. Quadrado, Pza. Nova or Pza. Alfons III, which together hold a good selection of inexpensive café-bars, offering tapas and light meals. In the summer evenings, head to the bars around the harbour for a taste of Ciutadella nightlife.

★**La Guitarra** C/Nostra Senyora dels Dolors 1 ☎971 381 355. Located a short walk from the Catedral, and housed in an old cellar, this family-run affair features the very best of Menorcan cuisine, with main courses – anything from seafood to rabbit stew to snails – averaging a very reasonable €15–20. Daily noon–3.30pm & 7.30–11pm.

Restaurant Aurora Pza. Ses Palmeres 3 ☎971 481 994. In one of the quieter squares, opposite the windmill, this popular restaurant serves up a variety of dishes including tapas, steaks and fish – the *menu del dia* is good

value at €13 for three courses, and the staff are friendly. Daily noon–4pm & 7–11pm.

★**Restaurant Café Balear** Es Pla de Sant Joan 15 ☎971 380 005, ⓦcafe-balear.com. In a great location right on the waterfront, this justifiably popular restaurant specializes in fish and seafood which they catch daily from their own boat – expect such locally sourced treats as *calderata de langosta* (lobster stew), monkfish, prawns and John Dory. The terrace is the best place to eat, but there are tables inside, too. Around €40 a head. Daily 10am–midnight; more limited hours in winter.

Southeast of Ciutadella: Cala Turqueta

Beginning at the traffic island on C/Alfons V, the cross-country **Camí de Sant Joan de Missa** runs southeast from Ciutadella to the remote coves of the south coast. The one to head for is **Cala Turqueta**, an idyllic cove flanked by wooded limestone cliffs. About 3km from town, you reach the clearly marked farmhouse of **Son Vivó**, where the road branches into two with the more easterly (signposted) road leading to the **Ermita de Sant Joan de Missa**, a brightly whitewashed church with a dinky little bell tower. There's a fork here, too, but the signs are easy to follow, and you keep straight with the road slicing across the countryside before swerving round the **Marjal Vella** farmhouse. Shortly afterwards, about 4.3km from the church, you turn at the sign, going through the gateway to reach the car park for Cala Turqueta. The beach, a sheltered horseshoe of white sand, slopes gently into the sea and is ideal for swimming.

CHRISTOPHER COLUMBUS RECEIVED BY THE CATHOLIC MONARCHS

Contexts

History

The first Europeans of whom we have knowledge lived in southern Spain. A recent series of spectacular discoveries at Orce, 115km northeast of Granada, rocked the archeological world, as the date for the arrival of early humans in Europe was pushed back from around 700,000 years ago to perhaps a million years before this, making Orce – the findings were scientifically confirmed in 2013 – the earliest known site of human occupation in Europe by a long way. Other finds of early human remains around 800,000 years old in the Sierra de Atapuerca are further confirmation of early activity on the peninsula. Evidence of occupation by Stone Age societies stretching back some 400,000 years was already known about from discoveries at Venta Micena, close to Orce, where early inhabitants hunted elephant and rhino and left behind tools and camp fires. Some of the earliest human fossils found on the Iberian Peninsula were unearthed inside the Gibraltar caves, with evidence of Neanderthals dating from around 100,000 BC.

In the Paleolithic period, the first **homo sapiens** arrived on the Iberian Peninsula from southern France, settling around the Bay of Biscay as well as in the south. They were cave dwellers and hunter-gatherers, and, at **Altamira** in the Cordillera Cantábrica near Santander, and the Pileta and Nerja caves near Málaga, left behind remarkable **cave paintings** and deftly stylized cave murals depicting the animals they hunted. The finest examples (created about 12,000 BC) are at Altamira – now closed for general visits, though you can see similar paintings at Puente Viesgo nearby. During the later Neolithic phase, a sophisticated material culture developed in southern Spain, attested to by the finds of *esparto* sandals and baskets as well as jewellery in the **Cueva de los Murciélagos** in Granada. This period also saw the construction of **megalithic tombs** (dolmens) along the perimeter of the Iberian Peninsula, including the superbly preserved examples at Romanya de la Selva, in Catalunya, and **Antequera**, near Málaga.

Subsequent prehistory is more complex and confused, and the focus shifts from the cave cultures of the north, south to Almería, which was settled around 5000–4000 BC by the "Iberians", **Neolithic** colonists from North Africa. They had already assimilated into their culture many of the developments in Egypt and the Near East. Settling in villages, they introduced pastoral and agricultural ways of life and exploited the plentiful supply of copper. Around 1500 BC, with the onset of the **Bronze Age**, they began to spread outwards into fortified villages on the central *meseta*, the high plateau of modern Castile. At the turn of the millennium, they were joined by numerous waves of **Celtic** and **Germanic** peoples. Here, Spain's divisive physical make-up – with its network of mountain ranges – determined its social nature. The incoming tribes formed distinct and isolated groups, conquering and sometimes absorbing each other

1.5 million years ago	25,000 BC	12,000 BC
Early humans active at Orce in the province of Granada after arriving from Africa.	Cave dwellers occupy caves in Málaga province.	Cave paintings made at Altamira in Cantabria and dolmens constructed in Catalunya and Málaga.

but only on a very limited and local scale. Hence the Celtic "urnfield people" established themselves in Catalunya, the **Vascones** in the Basque Country and, near them along the Atlantic coast, the **Astures**. Pockets of earlier cultures survived, too, particularly in Galicia with its *citanias* of beehive huts.

First colonies

The Spanish coast, meanwhile, attracted colonists from different regions of the Mediterranean. The **Phoenicians** founded the port of Gadir (Cádiz) around 1100 BC and traded intensively in the metals of the Guadalquivir valley. Their wealth and success gave rise to a Spanish "Atlantis" myth, based on the lost kingdom of Tartessus, mentioned in the Bible and probably sited near Huelva. Market rivalry later brought the **Greeks**, who established their trading colonies along the eastern coast – the modern Costa Brava. There's a fine surviving site at Empúries, near Barcelona.

More significant, however, was the arrival of the **Carthaginians** in the third century BC. Expelled from Sicily by the Romans, they saw in Spain a new base for their empire, from which to regain strength and strike back at their rivals. Although making little impact inland, they occupied most of Andalucía and expanded along the Mediterranean seaboard to establish a new capital at Cartagena ("New Carthage"). Under Hannibal they prepared to invade Italy, and in 219 BC attacked Saguntum, a strategic outpost of the Roman world. It was a disastrous move, precipitating the **Second Punic War**; by 210 BC, only Cádiz remained in their control and they were forced to accept terms. A new and very different age had begun.

Romans and Visigoths

The **Roman colonization** of the peninsula was far more intense than anything previously experienced and met with great resistance from the Celtiberian tribes of the north and centre. The conquest took two centuries to complete, and indeed the Basques, although defeated, were never fully Romanized. Nonetheless, Spain became the most important centre of the Roman Empire after Italy itself, producing no fewer than three emperors, along with the writers Seneca, Lucan, Martial and Quintilian. Again, geography dictated an uneven spread of influence, at its strongest in Andalucía, southern Portugal and on the Catalan coast around Tarragona. In the first two centuries AD, the Spanish mines and the granaries of Andalucía brought unprecedented wealth and Roman Spain enjoyed a brief **"Golden Age"**. The finest monuments were built in the great provincial capitals – Córdoba, Mérida (with impressive remains) and Tarragona – but across the country more practical construction was undertaken: roads, bridges and aqueducts. Many of the latter were used into recent centuries – the most remarkable being those of Segovia and Tarragona – and many bridges, such as that crossing the Guadalquivir in Córdoba, remain in use even today.

Towards the third century, however, the Roman political framework began to show signs of decadence and corruption. Although it didn't totally collapse until the Muslim invasions of the early eighth century, it became increasingly vulnerable to **barbarian incursions** from northern Europe. The Franks and the Suevi (Swabians) swept across the Pyrenees between 264 and 276, leaving devastation in their wake. They were

2500 BC	**c.1100 BC**	**c.1000 BC**
Chalcolithic (Copper Age) sites flourish in Almería.	Phoenicians found Cádiz.	Semi-mythical kingdom of Tartessus flourishes in the southwest of the peninsula.

followed two centuries later by further waves of Suevi, Alans and Vandals. Internal strife was heightened by the arrival of the **Visigoths** from Gaul, allies of Rome and already Romanized to a large degree. The triumph of Visigothic strength in the fifth century resulted in a period of spurious unity, based upon an exclusive military rule from their capital at Toledo. But order was often fragmentary and nominal, with the bulk of the subject people kept in a state of disconsolate servility and the military elite divided by constant plots and factions – exacerbated by the Visigothic system of elected monarchy and adherence to the heretical Arian doctrine. In 589, **King Recared** converted to Catholicism but religious strife was only multiplied: forced conversions, especially within the Jewish enclaves, maintained a constant simmering of discontent.

Moorish Spain

In contrast to the drawn-out Roman campaigns, **Moorish conquest** of the peninsula was effected with extraordinary speed. This was a characteristic phenomenon of the spread of Islam – Muhammad left Mecca in 622 and by 705 his followers had established control over all of North Africa. Spain, with its political instability, wealth and fertile climate, was an inevitable extension of their aims. In 711, Tariq, governor of Tangier, led a force of seven thousand Berbers across the straits and routed the Visigothic army of King Roderic; two years later, the Visigoths made a last desperate stand at Mérida, and within a decade the Moors had conquered all but the wild mountains of Asturias. The land under their authority was dubbed "**al-Andalus**", a fluid term that expanded and shrank with the intermittent gains and losses of the Reconquest. According to region, the Moors were to remain in control for the next three to eight centuries.

It was not simply a military conquest. The Moors (a collective term for numerous waves of North African Arabs and Berbers) were often content to grant a limited autonomy in exchange for payment of tribute; their administrative system was tolerant and absorbed both Jews and Christians, who became known as "Mozarabs". And al-Andalus was a distinctly Spanish state of Islam. Though at first politically subject to the Eastern Caliphate (or empire) of Baghdad, it was soon virtually independent. In the tenth century, at the peak of its power and expansion, Abd-ar-Rahman III asserted total independence, proclaiming himself caliph of a new **Western Islamic empire**. Its capital was Córdoba – the largest, most prosperous and most civilized city in Europe. This was the great age of Muslim Spain: its scholarship, philosophy, architecture and craftsmanship were without rival and there was an unparalleled growth in urban life, in trade and agriculture, aided by magnificent irrigation projects. These and other engineering feats were not, on the whole, instigated by the Moors, who instead took Roman models and adapted and improved them. In **architecture** and the **decorative arts**, however, their contribution was original and unique – as may be seen in the fabulous monuments of Seville, Córdoba and Granada.

The Córdoban Caliphate for a while created a remarkable degree of unity. But its rulers were to become decadent and out of touch, prompting the brilliant but dictatorial **al-Mansur** to usurp control. Under this extraordinary ruler, Moorish power actually reached new heights, pushing the Christian kingdom of Asturias-León back into the Cordillera Cantábrica and sacking its most holy shrine, Santiago de Compostela. However,

c.9th–4th century BC	600–300 BC	c.5th century BC
Celts settle in the north and west of the peninsula. Greeks establish trading posts along east coast.	Greeks establish trading colonies along the Mediterranean coast.	Carthage colonizes southern Spain. Celtiberian culture develops, with Greek influence.

ALMOHAD ARCHITECTURE

In the eleventh century, Andalucía fragmented into rival kingdoms or *taifas*, allowing successive waves of Moorish invaders to move into the power vacuum. One of these, the ultra-fundamentalist **Almohads**, left behind a number of remarkable buildings of which the foremost is the magnificent **Giralda** tower in Seville, the surviving minaret of the Friday mosque demolished to construct the Gothic Catedral. At 100m high with elaborate *sebka* brickwork panels adorning its exterior walls, it was started in 1184 under architect Ahmed ibn Baso and completed twelve years later.

after his death the caliphate quickly lost its authority, and in 1031 it disintegrated into a series of small independent kingdoms, or *taifas*, the strongest of which was Seville.

Internal divisions among the *taifas* weakened their resistance to the Christian kingdoms that were rallying in the north, and twice North Africa had to be turned to for reinforcement. This resulted in two distinct new waves of Moorish invasion – first by the fanatically Islamic **Almoravids** (1086) and later by the **Almohads** (1147), who restored effective Muslim authority until their defeat at the battle of Las Navas de Tolosa in 1212.

The Christian Reconquest

The **Reconquest** of land and influence from the Moors was a slow and intermittent process. It began with a symbolic victory by a small force of Christians at Covadonga in Asturias (722) and was not completed until 1492 with the conquest of Granada by Fernando and Isabel.

The victory at Covadonga resulted in the formation of the tiny Christian kingdom of **Asturias**. Initially just 50 by 65km in area, it had by 914 reclaimed León and most of Galicia and northern Portugal. At this point, progress was temporarily halted by the devastating campaigns of al-Mansur. However, with the fall of the Córdoban Caliphate and the divine aid of Spain's Moor-slaying patron, St James the Apostle, or Santiago (see p.552), the Reconquest moved into a new and powerful phase.

The frontier castles built against Arab attack gave their name to Castile, founded in the tenth century as a county of León-Asturias. Under **Ferdinand I** (1037–65), it achieved the status of a kingdom and became the main thrust of the Reconquest. Other kingdoms were being defined in the north at the same time: the Basques founded **Navarra** (Navarre), while dynastic marriage merged **Catalunya** with **Aragón**. In 1085, this period of confident Christian expansion reached its zenith with the capture of the great Moorish city of Toledo. The following year, however, the Almoravids arrived on invitation from Seville, and military activity was effectively frozen – except, that is, for the exploits of the legendary El Cid (see p.421), a Castilian nobleman who won considerable lands around Valencia in 1095.

The next concerted phase of the Reconquest began as a response to the threat imposed by the Almohads. The kings of León, Castile, Aragón and Navarra united in a general crusade that resulted in the great victory at Las Navas de Tolosa (1212). Thereafter, Muslim power was effectively paralysed, and the Christian armies moved on to take most of al-Andalus. Ferdinand III ("El Santo", The Saint) led Castilian soldiers

c.214 BC	210 BC	27 BC	c.409–415
Second Punic War with Rome.	Roman colonization begins.	Octavian-Augustus becomes the first Roman emperor.	Vandals invade Spain.

into Córdoba in 1236 and Seville in 1248. Meanwhile, the kingdom of Portugal had expanded to near its present size, while Jaime I of Aragón was to conquer Valencia, Alicante, Murcia and the Balearic Islands. By the end of the thirteenth century, only the kingdom of Granada remained under Muslim authority, and for the following two centuries was forced to pay tribute to Castile.

Two factors should be stressed regarding the Reconquest. First, its **unifying religious nature** – the spirit of crusade, intensified by the religious zeal of the Almoravids and Almohads, and by the wider European climate (which in 1095 gave rise to the First Crusade). This powerful religious motivation is well illustrated by the subsequent canonization of Ferdinand III, and found solid expression in the part played by the military orders of Christian knights, the most important of which were the Knights Templar and the Order of Santiago. At the same time, the Reconquest was a movement of **recolonization**. The fact that the country had been in arms for so long meant that the nobility had a major social role, a trend perpetuated by the redistribution of captured land in huge packages, or *latifundia*. Heirs to this tradition still remain as landlords of the great estates, conspicuously in Andalucía. Men from the ranks were also awarded land, forming a lower stratum of nobility, the *hidalgos*. It was their particular social code that provided the material for Cervantes in *Don Quixote*.

Any spirit of mutual cooperation that had temporarily united the Christian kingdoms disintegrated during the fourteenth century, and independent lines of development were once again pursued. Attempts to merge Portugal with Castile foundered at the battle of Aljubarrota (1385), and Portuguese attention turned away from Spain towards the Atlantic. Aragón experienced a similar pull towards the markets of the Mediterranean, although pre-eminence in this area was soon passed to the Genoese. It was Castile that emerged the strongest over this period: self-sufficiency in agriculture and a flourishing wool trade with the Netherlands enabled the state to build upon the prominent military role it played under Fernando III. Politically, Castilian history was a tale of dynastic conflict until the accession of the Catholic Monarchs.

Los Reyes Católicos

Los Reyes Católicos – the **Catholic Monarchs** – was the joint title given to **Fernando of Aragón and Isabel of Castile**, whose marriage in 1469 united the two largest kingdoms in Spain. Unity was in practice more symbolic than real: Castile had underlined its rights in the marriage vows and Aragón retained its old administrative structure. So, in the beginning at least, the growth of any national unity or Spanish – as opposed to local – sentiment was very much dependent on the head of state. Nevertheless, from now on it becomes realistic to consider Spain as a single political entity.

At the heart of Fernando and Isabel's popular appeal lay a **religious bigotry** that they shared with most of their Christian subjects. The **Inquisition** was instituted in Castile in 1480 and in Aragón seven years later. Aiming to establish the purity of the Catholic faith by rooting out heresy, it was directed mainly at Jews – resented for their enterprise in commerce and influence in high places, as well as for their faith. Expression had already been given to these feelings in a pogrom in 1391, reinforced by an edict issued in 1492 that forced up to 400,000 Jews to flee the country. A similar spirit was embodied in the Reconquest of the **Kingdom of Granada**, also in 1492. As the last

c.5th–7th century	711	722
Visigoths arrive and take control of most of Spain.	Moors under Tariq invade and defeat Visigothic King Roderic near Jerez. Peninsula conquered in seven years.	Pelayo defeats Moors at Covadonga in Asturias in northern Spain marking the start of the Reconquest.

COLUMBUS AND THE CATHOLIC MONARCHS

After many frustrating years trying to find backers for his plan **to reach the Indies by sailing west**, Columbus' luck turned in 1491 when he spent a period at the Franciscan monastery of La Rabida in the province of Huelva. The abbot of La Rabida, Juan Pérez, a former confessor to Queen Isabel, was moved to write to her on Columbus' behalf. It was a timely moment as Granada had just fallen, the treasury was empty, and the promise of gold and glory for a resurgent Spain now attracted Isabel and her husband King Fernando. On August 3, 1492, Columbus set out from Palos, a port in Huelva, with three small vessels and 120 men. On October 12, he made landfall on Watling Island (aka San Salvador) in the Bahamas. After leaving a colony of men on Hispaniola (modern Haiti) he returned to Palos on March 15, 1493, to enormous acclaim. The Spanish conquest of the Americas had begun.

stronghold of Muslim authority, the religious rights of its citizens were guaranteed under the treaty of surrender. Within a decade, though, those Muslims under Christian rule had been given the choice between conversion or expulsion.

The year 1492 was symbolic in another way: it was the year that Columbus (Cristóbal Colón) discovered America, and of the papal bull entrusting Spain with the conversion of the American Indians, entrenching its sense of a mission to bring the world to the "True Faith". The next decade saw the systematic conquest, colonization and exploitation of the **New World** stretching from Labrador to Brazil, and new-found wealth pouring into the royal coffers. Important as this was for Fernando and Isabel, and their prestige, their priorities remained in Europe, and strategic marriage alliances were made with Portugal, England and the Holy Roman Empire. It was not until the accession of the Habsburg dynasty that Spain could look to the activities of Cortés, Magellan and Pizarro and claim to be the world's leading power.

Habsburg Spain

Carlos I, a **Habsburg**, came to the throne in 1516 as a beneficiary of the marriage alliances of the Catholic Monarchs. Five years later, he was elected emperor of the Holy Roman Empire as Carlos V (**Charles V**), inheriting not only Castile and Aragón, but Flanders, the Netherlands, Artois, the Franche-Comté and all the American colonies to boot. With such responsibilities it was inevitable that attention would be diverted from Spain, whose chief function became to sustain the Holy Roman Empire with gold and silver from the Americas. It was only with the accession of **Felipe II** in 1556 that Spanish politics became more centralized. Felipe lived in the centre of Castile, near Madrid, creating a monument to the values of medieval Spain in his palace, El Escorial.

Two main themes run through his reign: the preservation of his own inheritance, and the revival of the crusade in the name of the Catholic Church. In pursuit of the former, Felipe successfully claimed the Portuguese throne (through the marriage of his mother), gaining access to the additional wealth of its empire. Plots were also woven in support of Mary Queen of Scots' claim to the English throne, launching the ill-fated **Armada** in 1588, its sinking a triumph for English naval strength and Protestantism.

This was a period of unusual religious intensity: the **Inquisition** was enforced with renewed vigour, and a rising of Moriscos (subject Moors) in the Alpujarras was fiercely

756	c.9th century	967	1031
Abd-ar-Rahman I proclaims Emirate of Córdoba. Great mosque of Córdoba (Mezquita) begun.	Kingdoms of Catalunya and Navarra founded.	Al-Mansur usurps Caliphal powers of Córdoba Caliphate and forces Christians back into Asturias.	Caliphate disintegrates into *taifas* (petty kingdoms).

suppressed. Felipe III later ordered the expulsion of half the total number of Moriscos in Spain – allowing only two families to remain in each village in order to maintain irrigation techniques. The **exodus** of both Muslims and Jews created a large gulf in the labour force and in the higher echelons of commercial life – and in trying to uphold the Catholic cause, an enormous strain was put upon resources without any clear-cut victory.

By the middle of the seventeenth century, Spain was losing international credibility. Domestically, the disparity between the wealth surrounding Crown and court and the impoverishment of the masses was a source of perpetual tension. Discontent fuelled regional revolts in Catalunya and Portugal in 1640, and the latter had finally to be re-acknowledged as an independent state in 1668.

Bourbons and the Peninsular War

The **Bourbon dynasty** succeeded to the Spanish throne in the person of **Felipe V** (1700); with him began the **War of the Spanish Succession** against the rival claim of Archduke Charles of Austria, assisted by British forces. In the Treaty of Utrecht, which ended the war (1713), Spain was stripped of all territory in Belgium, Luxembourg, Italy and Sardinia, but Felipe V was recognized as king. Gibraltar was seized by the British in the course of the war. For the rest of the century, Spain fell under the French sphere of influence, which was politically defined by an alliance with the French Bourbons in 1762.

Contact with France made involvement in the **Napoleonic Wars** inevitable and led eventually to the defeat of the Spanish fleet at Trafalgar in 1805. Popular outrage was such that the powerful prime minister, Godoy, was overthrown and King Carlos IV forced to abdicate (1808). Napoleon seized the opportunity to install his brother, Joseph, on the throne.

Fierce local resistance was eventually backed by the muscle of the British army commanded by Sir John Moore, then the Duke of Wellington, and the **Peninsular War** resulted in the French being driven out. Meanwhile, however, the **American colonies** had been successfully asserting their independence from a preoccupied centre and with them went Spain's last real claim of significance on the world stage. The entire nineteenth century was dominated by the struggle between an often reactionary monarchy and the aspirations of liberal constitutional reformers.

Seeds of civil war

Between 1810 and 1813 an ad hoc Cortes (parliament) had set up a **liberal constitution** with ministers responsible to a democratically elected chamber. The first act of Ferdinand VII on being returned to the throne was to abolish this, and until his death in 1833 he continued to stamp out the least hint of liberalism. On his death, the right of succession was contested between his brother, Don Carlos, backed by the Church, conservatives and Basques, and his infant daughter, Isabel, who had the support of the liberals and the army. So began the **First Carlist War**, a civil war that lasted six years. Isabel II was eventually declared of age in 1843, her reign a long record of scandal, political crisis and constitutional compromise. Liberal army generals under the leadership of General Prim effected a coup in 1868 and the queen was forced to abdicate, but attempts to maintain a republican government foundered. The Cortes

1037	1085	1086	1147
Fernando I unites kingdoms of Castile and León-Asturias.	Christians capture Toledo.	Almoravids invade Spain from North Africa.	Invasion by Almohads from Morocco; Seville becomes new Moorish capital in Spain.

was again dissolved and the throne returned to Isabel's son, Alfonso XII. A new constitution was declared in 1876, limiting the power of the Crown through the institution of bicameral government, but again progress was halted by the lack of any tradition on which to base the constitutional theory.

The years preceding World War I merely heightened the discontent, finding expression in the growing **political movements** of the working class. The Socialist Workers' Party was founded in Madrid after the restoration of Alfonso XII, and spawned its own trade union, the UGT (1888), successful in areas of high industrial concentration such as the Basque Country and Asturias. Its anarchist counterpart, the CNT, was founded in 1911, gaining substantial support among the peasantry of Andalucía.

The loss of **Cuba** in 1898 emphasized the growing isolation of Spain in international affairs and added to economic problems with the return of soldiers seeking employment where there was none. A call-up for army reserves to fight in **Morocco** in 1909 provoked a general strike and the "Tragic Week" of rioting in Barcelona. Between 1914 and 1918, Spain was outwardly neutral but inwardly turbulent; inflated prices made the postwar recession harder to bear.

The general disillusionment with parliamentary government, together with the fears of employers and businessmen for their own security, gave **General Primo de Rivera** sufficient support for a military coup in 1923 in which the king, Alfonso XIII, was pushed into the background. Dictatorship did result in an increase in material prosperity, but the death of the dictator in 1930 revealed the apparent stability as a facade. New political factions were taking shape: the Liberal Republican Right was founded by Alcalá Zamora, while the Socialist Party was given definition under the leadership of Largo Caballero. The victory of antimonarchist parties in the 1931 municipal elections forced the abdication of the king, who went into exile, and the **Second Republic** was declared.

The Second Republic

Catalunya declared itself a republic independent of the central government and was ceded control of internal affairs by a statute in 1932. **Separatist movements** were powerful, too, in the Basque provinces and Galicia, each with their own demands for autonomy. Meanwhile, the government, set up on a tidal wave of hope, was utterly divided internally and too scared of right-wing reaction to carry out the massive tax and agrarian reforms that the left demanded, and that might have provided the resources for thoroughgoing regeneration of the economy.

The result was the increasing polarization of Spanish politics. **Anarchism**, in particular, was gaining strength among the frustrated middle classes as well as among the workers and peasantry. The **Communist Party** and left-wing **Socialists**, driven into alliance by their mutual distrust of the "moderate" socialists in government, were also forming a growing bloc. On the right, the **Falangists**, basically a youth party founded in 1923 by **José Antonio Primo de Rivera** (son of the dictator), made uneasy bedfellows with conservative traditionalists and dissident elements in the army upset by modernizing reforms.

In an atmosphere of growing confusion, the left-wing Popular Front alliance narrowly won the general election of **February 1936**. Normal life, though, became

1162	1212	1213
Alfonso II unites kingdoms of Aragón and Catalunya.	Almohad advance halted at Las Navas de Tolosa in Andalucía.	Jaime I "El Conquistador" becomes king of Aragón and leads Christian Reconquest of Balearics (1229), Valencia (1238) and Alicante (1266).

increasingly impossible: the economy was crippled by strikes, peasants took agrarian reform into their own hands, and the government failed to exert its authority over anyone. Finally, on July 17, 1936, the military garrison in Morocco rebelled under the leadership of **General Francisco Franco**, to be followed by risings at military garrisons throughout the country. It was the culmination of years of scheming but in the army, but in the event was far from the overnight success its leaders expected. The south quickly fell into Nationalist hands, but Madrid and the industrialized north and east remained loyal to the Republican government.

Civil War

The ensuing **Civil War** was undoubtedly one of the most bitter and bloody the world has seen. Violent reprisals were taken on their enemies by both sides – the Republicans shooting priests and local landowners wholesale, the Nationalists carrying out mass slaughter of the population of almost every town they took. Contradictions were legion in the way the Spanish populations found themselves divided from each other. Perhaps the greatest irony was that Franco's troops, on their "holy" mission to ensure a Catholic Spain, comprised a core of Moroccan troops from Spain's North African colony.

It was, too, the first modern war – Franco's German allies demonstrated their ability to wipe out entire civilian populations with their bombing raids on Gernika and Durango, and radio proved an important weapon, as Nationalist propagandists offered the starving Republicans "the white bread of Franco".

Despite sporadic help from Russia and thousands of volunteers in the **International Brigade**, the Republic could never compete with the professional armies and massive assistance from Fascist Italy and Nazi Germany enjoyed by the Nationalists. In addition, the left was torn by internal divisions that at times led almost to civil war within its own ranks. Nevertheless, the Republicans held out in slowly dwindling territories for nearly three years, with **Catalunya** falling in January 1939 and armed resistance in **Madrid** – which never formally surrendered – petering out over the following months. As hundreds of thousands of refugees flooded into France, General Franco, who had long before proclaimed himself head of state, took up the reins of power.

Franco's Spain

The early reprisals taken by the victors were on a massive and terrifying scale. Executions were commonplace, and upwards of two million people were put in concentration camps until "order" had been established by authoritarian means. Only one party, the **Falange**, was permitted, and censorship was rigidly enforced. By the end of World War II, during which Spain was too weak to be anything but neutral, **Franco** was Europe's only fascist head of state, one responsible for sanctioning more deaths than any other in Spanish history. Spain was economically and politically isolated and, bereft of markets, suffered – almost half the population were still tilling the soil for little or no return. When President Eisenhower visited Madrid in 1953 with the offer of huge loans, it came as water to the desert, and the price, the establishment of American nuclear bases, was one Franco was more than willing to pay. However belated, economic development was incredibly rapid, with Spain enjoying a growth

1217   **1469**

Fernando III "El Santo" crowned king of Castile, and retakes Córdoba (1236), Murcia (1241) and Seville (1248).

Castile and Aragón united by the marriage of Isabel and Fernando, Los Reyes Católicos (the Catholic Monarchs).

rate second only to that of Japan for much of the 1960s, a boom fuelled by the tourist industry and the remittances of Spanish workers abroad.

Increased **prosperity**, however, only underlined the political bankruptcy of Franco's regime and its inability to cope with popular demands. Higher incomes, the need for better education, and a creeping invasion of Western culture made the anachronism of Franco ever clearer. His only reaction was to attempt to withdraw what few signs of increased liberalism had crept through, and his last years mirrored the repression of the postwar period. Trade unions remained outlawed, and the rampant inflation of the early 1970s saw striking workers across Spain hauled out of occupied mines and factories and imprisoned, or even shot in the streets. Attempts to report these events by the liberal press resulted in suspensions, fines and censorship. **Basque nationalists**, whose assassination of Admiral Carrero Blanco in 1973 had effectively destroyed Franco's last hope of a like-minded successor, were singled out for particularly harsh treatment. Hundreds of so-called terrorists were tortured, and the Burgos trials of 1970, together with the executions of August 1975, provoked worldwide protest.

Franco finally died in November 1975, nominating **King Juan Carlos** as his successor. Groomed for the job and very much "in" with the army – of which he remained official commander-in-chief – the king's initial moves were cautious in the extreme, appointing a government dominated by loyal Francoists who had little sympathy for the growing opposition demands for "democracy without adjectives". In the summer of 1976, demonstrations in Madrid ended in violence, with the police upholding the old authoritarian ways.

The return of democracy

The violent events leading up to and following his mentor's death persuaded Juan Carlos that some real break with the past and a move towards **democratization** was now urgent and inevitable. Using the almost dictatorial powers he had inherited, he ousted Franco's reactionary prime minister, Carlos Arias Navarro, and replaced him with **Adolfo Suárez**, an ambitious lawyer and former apparatchik in Franco's ruling Movimiento party. Taking his cue from the king, in 1976 Suárez pushed a **Law of Political Reform** through the Cortes, reforming the legislature into two chambers elected by universal suffrage – a move massively endorsed by the Spanish people in a referendum. Suárez also passed legislation allowing the setting up of free trade unions, as well as legitimizing the Socialist Party (PSOE) and, controversially, the Communists. Several cabinet ministers resigned in protest, and an outraged military began planning their coup d'état.

When elections were held in June 1977, Suárez's own hastily formed centre-right party, the **Unión del Centro Democrático** (**UCD**), was rewarded with a 34 percent share of the vote, the Socialists coming in second with 28 percent, and the Communists and Francoist **Alianza Popular** marginalized at 9 percent and 8 percent respectively. Despite the overwhelming victories in Catalunya and the Basque Country of parties appealing to regional sentiment, this was a vote for democratic stability rather than for ideology, something reflected in the course of the parliament, with Suárez governing through "consensus politics", negotiating settlements on all important issues with the major parties.

1492	1516	1519	1532
Fall of Granada, the last Moorish kingdom. Discovery of America by Cristóbal Colón (Columbus).	Carlos V succeeds to the throne and becomes the Holy Roman Emperor (1520), inaugurating the Golden Age.	Cortés lands in Mexico.	Pizarro "discovers" Peru.

THE LAW OF HISTORICAL MEMORY

In Spain as well as abroad the **legacy of Franco** remains controversial. In the years following the restoration of democracy there was no national debate about the dictator's thirty-five-year rule and unlike other countries, such as Germany and Argentina, Spain has never fully come to terms with its former dictatorship. Instead, politicians on both sides of the divide tacitly agreed not to mention the legacy of the Franco regime and no war crimes trials were held. But many others were angry at a pact which meant that crimes committed in the Franco years not only went unpunished, but were not even recognized as having taken place. In 2007 the Spanish PSOE government – led by José Luís Rodrigo Zapatero, whose own grandfather was executed by Franco's forces – decided to address this issue and passed into law **La Ley de Memoria Histórica** (The Law of Historical Memory). This rules that sentences handed down by kangaroo courts during the regime – that led to the imprisonment or execution of thousands of Franco's opponents – were "illegitimate". It also decrees that local governments must locate, exhume from mass graves and identify the victims of the Franco regime. Historians claim that the remains of tens of thousands of Franco's opponents are buried in unmarked graves throughout the country.

The law also stipulates that all statues, plaques and symbols relating to the regime must be removed from public buildings (however, church property was excluded). It deals, too, with the dictatorship's monumental legacy – the vast basilica of the **Valle de los Caídos** near Madrid where the remains of Franco and the founder of the fascist Falange party, José Antonio Prima de Rivera, are interred. The law prohibits all political events at the site, thus preventing the traditional "Mass for the Caudillo" formerly celebrated each 20 November (the anniversary of Franco's death), and its celebration of the fascist cause.

The first parliament of the "New Spain" now embarked on the formidable task of drawing up a **constitution**, while the Suárez government applied for membership of the then EEC. One of the fundamental components of the new constitution was the concept of **autonomy** – the granting of substantial self-rule to the seventeen *autonomías* (autonomous regions) into which Spain was to be divided. In Franco's time, even speaking regional languages such as Catalan or Basque was banned, and the backlash against this policy ensured that nothing less than some form of independence would be acceptable for regions such as the Basque Country and Catalunya. On December 6, 1978, the new constitution was overwhelmingly endorsed in a national referendum and, remarkably, only three years after the death of Franco, Spain had become a full democracy.

Elections in March 1979 virtually duplicated the 1977 result, but when the UCD, a fractious coalition of moderates and extremists, started to crack, **Suárez resigned** in January 1981. This provided the trigger for a **military coup**, launched by a contingent of Guardia Civil loyal to Franco's memory and commanded by the tragi-comic Colonel Antonio Tejero. They stormed into the Cortes with Tejero brandishing a revolver, and submachine-gunned the ceiling as *diputados* (MPs) dived for cover. The crisis was real: tanks were brought out onto the streets of Valencia, and only three of the army's ten regional commanders remained unreservedly loyal to the government. But as it became clear that the king would not support the plotters, most of the rest then affirmed their support. Juan Carlos had taken the decision of his life and emerged with immensely enhanced prestige in the eyes of most Spaniards.

1556	1588	1605	1609
Accession of Felipe II (d.1598).	British forces defeat the Spanish Armada. Marks Spain's demise as a sea power.	Miguel de Cervantes writes *Don Quijote* (*Quixote*), considered the first modern novel.	Expulsion of Moriscos, last remaining Spanish Muslims.

The González era

On October 28, 1982, the Socialist PSOE, led by charismatic **Felipe González**, was elected with the biggest landslide victory in Spanish electoral history to rule a country that had been firmly in the hands of the right for 43 years. The Socialists captured the imagination and the votes of nearly ten million Spaniards with the simplest of appeals: "for change".

Once in power, however, the Socialist Party chose the path of pragmatism, and a relentless drift to the right followed. Four successive election victories kept the party in power for fourteen years, and by the mid-1990s the PSOE government's policies had become indistinguishable from the conservative administrations of Britain or Germany.

González himself, meanwhile, had also undergone transformation – from a radical young labour lawyer into a careworn elder statesman. Control of inflation had become a more urgent target than reducing unemployment, while loss-making heavy industries were ruthlessly overhauled and others privatized. Like most of Spain's left, González had vehemently objected to Spain's membership of NATO but when a referendum was held on the issue in 1986 – which turned out marginally in favour of staying in – his was one of the main voices in favour of continued membership. **European Union** membership came in the same year, and the pride that most Spanish people felt at this tangible proof of their acceptance by the rest of Europe bought the Socialists more valuable time.

After long years of being hopelessly divided, in the late 1980s the **Spanish right** realigned itself when former prime minister Adolfo Suárez's UCD Christian Democrats merged with the Alianza Popular to form the new right-of-centre **Partido Popular** (PP), which came a respectable runner-up in the 1989 elections; a new far-left coalition, **Izquierda Unida** (United Left), composed of the Communists and smaller leftist parties, came third, albeit with the same number of seats (18) in the Congress of Deputies as the Catalan Nationalists, barely a tenth of the PSOE's representation.

The nation's progressive disillusionment with Felipe González's government in the early 1990s saw the rise to prominence of **José María Aznar** as leader of the PP. A former tax inspector, Aznar was dogged in his criticism of government incompetence in dealing with its own sleaze and the growing economic crisis. This debilitated the PSOE's position still further in the build-up to the **1993 elections**. However, the PSOE confounded the opinion polls to hang on to power by the skin of its teeth, albeit as a minority government.

But González's victory was a poisoned chalice, for his past now began to catch up with him. Illegal financing of the PSOE and corruption and commission-taking on government projects by party officials and ministers were only some of numerous scandals now exposed. By far the most serious was the **GAL affair** (Grupo Antiterrorista de Liberación), when it was discovered that a semi-autonomous anti-terrorist unit had been carrying out a dirty war against the ETA terrorists in the 1980s, which included kidnapping and wholesale assassinations of suspected ETA members. The press – and a later judicial investigation – exposed police participation in these crimes and a clear chain of command reaching up to the highest echelons of the PSOE government. Some Guardia Civil police officers were sent to prison for offences connected with the GAL affair, as were (briefly) two ministers for covering up the plot, before being released on appeal. But despite the efforts of prosecutors, González managed to avoid being hauled before the courts.

1700	1808	1812
War of Spanish Succession brings Felipe V (1683–46), a Bourbon, to the throne. British seize Gibraltar.	French occupy Spain. Venezuela declares independence, others follow.	Liberal constitution declared in Cádiz.

The swing to the right

The ailing PSOE administration, immersed in endless scandals, limped on towards what looked likely to be a crushing defeat in the **1996 elections**. The surprise result, however, was another **hung parliament**, making everyone a loser. Aznar, the narrow victor, was denied the "absolute majority" he had believed to be his throughout the campaign, and was forced into a deal with the nationalist parties in order to secure a workable parliamentary majority. Meanwhile, the PSOE's avoidance of the expected overwhelming defeat was proclaimed as a vindication by González, who hastily dismissed ideas of retirement. However, unable to make any significant impact on changing public opinion, and with the PSOE still in turmoil, early in 1998 **González resigned** the leadership of the party he had dominated for 23 years.

Elected on a centre-right platform, during his first term in office following his narrow 1996 victory, Aznar progressively moved his party to the centre, shifting aside remaining hardliners in the hope of gaining the electorate's confidence and a working majority not dependent on alliances with the northern nationalists.

Following the resignation of Felipe González in 1998, a desperate PSOE formed an alliance with the ex-communist Izquierda Unida, but this failed to convince voters and the outcome of the March 2000 **general election** was a stunning **triumph for Aznar** and the PP, and for the first time since the death of Franco the right was in power with an overall majority.

The result was disaster for the left, and the PSOE then elected **José Luis Rodríguez Zapatero**, a relatively unknown young politician, as leader. A moderate, Zapatero admitted the PSOE's past mistakes, stating emphatically that any government led by him would be radically different. This seemed to go down well with the electorate, and the opinion polls started to move in the PSOE's favour.

The return of the PSOE

In 2001, José María Aznar announced that he would lead the PP up to the next general election but would then resign, and that it must seek a new leader. As leader designate (to take over following the election), the party chose Aznar's nominee, the less prickly, cigar-puffing **Mariano Rajoy**, minister for the interior and deputy prime minister. Early in 2004 all the indicators suggested that the following March general election would deliver a comfortable victory for the ruling PP and its new leader, Rajoy. Then, on March 11, and three days before polling day, a series of **bombs** exploded on rush-hour commuter trains travelling into Madrid, killing 191 people and injuring almost two thousand others. The nation was thrown into shock at the most savage attack seen in Spain since the Civil War. Despite the discovery by police within hours of a van linked to the bombings containing detonators and a Koranic audiotape, the PP leadership decided that the Basque terrorist group ETA had to be the culprits. This was a high-risk tactic for the government, but it seemed convinced that by pinning the responsibility on ETA it would deflect attention away from its support for the Iraq war (ninety percent of Spaniards had been against it) just long enough for the votes to be counted. No mention was to be made of any possible link with Islamic militant groups, and at the same time the blaming of ETA would conveniently vindicate Aznar's hardline stance against Basque terrorism and separatism.

1833–1839	1898	1923	1931
First Carlist War. Dissolution of the monasteries.	Loss of Cuba, Spain's last American colony.	Primo de Rivera dictatorship. Resigns (1930) due to ill health and popular agitation urges a republic.	King Alfonso XIII is forced out and Second Republic is declared.

For the three days prior to the election, the heavily state-influenced media and Spanish diplomats around the world peddled the "ETA is responsible" line. But soon doubts began to surface, and in the hours before the polls opened the electorate seems to have become highly suspicious of the government's tactic of using ETA as a scapegoat to save its skin, believing that the attack – as was subsequently proved – was the work of **Islamic terrorists** and a retaliation for Spain's participation in the unpopular Iraq war.

The nation turned out in force to give its verdict – and Zapatero and the PSOE **an unexpected victory**. Two million new young voters already angered by Aznar's unwavering support for the Iraq war appear to have been pivotal to the final result. The accusations of lies and distortion hurled at the PP intensified when it was revealed that the outgoing government, before leaving office, had hired a specialist company to destroy all computer records dealing with the bombings.

The first act by Zapatero as government leader was to announce the **immediate withdrawal of Spanish troops from Iraq**, an election promise. This aligned him firmly with the German and French governments in Europe to whom Aznar had been hostile, but incurred the displeasure of US president George W. Bush, who shunned Zapatero for the rest of his presidency. In his first four years of office leading up to elections in 2008, Zapatero's record was competent if unspectacular. He enjoyed the benefit of a favourable economic climate with consistently high growth figures and an economy producing more jobs than any other euro-zone member. But in the latter part of 2007, the impact of the world **economic downturn** was desperately felt in Spain, as one of the major drivers of the Spanish economy, the huge construction industry, went into meltdown. The **general election of March 2008** took place against a backdrop of economic uncertainty, and although the result was another **PSOE victory** the reality was that they had scraped home seven seats short of an overall parliamentary majority.

Contemporary politics

The PSOE government's second term was dominated by the world financial and economic crisis that started to unravel in 2007–2008. The recession caused unemployment to rise to alarming levels while an austerity programme aimed at dealing with the government's massive debt lost it much support as civil service and teachers' salaries were cut, benefits and pensions frozen and welfare programmes cancelled.

Despite government efforts to stem the tide of unpopularity threatening to engulf it, little changed throughout the winter of 2010 as the economy foundered and the unemployment figure passed twenty percent. The local and regional elections held in May 2011 produced a resounding victory for the opposition Partido Popular causing alarm in PSOE ranks.

Appearing weary and indecisive, Zapatero announced that he would not lead the party into the general election of 2012 and that it must seek a new leader. While he had been a capable, if undistinguished, prime minister in times of plenty, it seemed that he had little stomach for the long haul ahead to bring the Spanish economy out of deep recession. The party chose veteran Alfredo Pérez Rubalcaba – a minister in all the PSOE administrations since the 1990s – to succeed Zapatero and he assumed the

1936	1937	1939	1953
Spanish Civil War begins.	Basque town of Gernmika is destroyed by German bombers. Over 1500 civilians are killed.	Civil War ends and Franco dictatorship begins.	US makes economic deal with Franco in return for military bases.

title of leader designate. The party hoped that Rubalcaba's "safe pair of hands" might be able to thwart a massacre, if not the seemingly inevitable defeat, at the approaching general election.

At the end of July 2011 Zapatero announced that he would call an early general election for the following November. The election delivered the predicted **landslide victory** for the PP and the PSOE suffered its most crushing defeat since the return of democracy. In his victory speech the PP leader, and now prime minister, **Mariano Rajoy**, gravely announced that "Difficult times are coming" as the financial crisis continued to wreak havoc across world markets.

Difficult times

On taking power the Rajoy government first blamed the socialists for the economic mess in which they had left the country, and then set about imposing even harsher **austerity measures** than the outgoing administration, dictated by the EU in Brussels and the German government in Berlin. Promising that cutting government debt would eventually lead to prosperity, the reality for vast numbers of Spaniards has been unemployment, which soared to 27 percent in 2014, the EU's highest. The major victims of this tragedy have been the under-thirty age group, close to fifty percent of whom are out of work.

Other headaches for Rajoy's ministers included a **banking crisis** and **endemic corruption** which has left the country with unfinished airports, tramways and metro systems – all constructed during the boom years at eye-watering cost – that are unlikely ever to see a plane, tram or train. Embarrassingly for Rajoy, one of the biggest corruption scandals involved the PP's party treasurer who not only stashed away tens of millions of party funds in Swiss bank accounts, but claimed that the party's senior politicians (including Rajoy) had all received regular and illegal cash payments in brown envelopes (that is, tax free).

The perennial stone in the shoe of Madrid administrations, the autonomous region of **Catalunya**, also caused unwelcome waves by announcing its intention to hold a **referendum on independence** in November 2014. In response, Madrid flatly stated that this would be unconstitutional and therefore illegal "and will not take place". At the time of writing the Catalan autonomous government has announced that it intends to go ahead, while Madrid has stated that it will "take measures provided for in the constitution to ensure that the law is adhered to". The question now is how far the Spanish government is prepared to go to stop the vote taking place.

The monarchy, in the person of **King Juan Carlos**, posed another unwelcome distraction during Rajoy's first term. Although placed on the throne by General Franco, the king played a pivotal role during the *Transición* (the period following the dictator's death) and significantly influenced Spain's transformation into a democracy. In recent years, however, his judgement has been error-prone, typified by his unawareness – until it was too late – that his own daughter had become involved in a financial scandal involving fraud and tax evasion which came before the courts. While this scandal was making headlines, in 2012 the king flitted off to Botswana for a free elephant-hunting trip that only became news when he fell down steps at a hunting lodge, badly injuring his hip. Flown home by special aircraft, it emerged that his companion on the trip was

1975	1981	1986	2002
Death of Franco. Spain becomes a constitutional monarchy with Juan Carlos I as king.	Attempted military coup fails; members of parliament are held hostage in the Cortes (Spanish Parliament).	Spain joins the European Union.	Spain swaps peseta for euro.

not Queen Sofía but a German socialite, and that it was not their first such tryst. When a rather tasteless photo of the king standing proudly beside an elephant he had shot then hit the media, the World Wide Fund for Nature (Juan Carlos was its honorary president) promptly fired him. In June 2014 the king, hardly able to walk following numerous operations, announced that he intended to **abdicate in favour of his son** who acceded to the throne as **Felipe VI** with his spouse, Letizia, as queen.

In the spring of 2014 convulsions were also taking place in the PSOE opposition party, after a series of opinion polls ranked the party in second place to the highly unpopular PP government. Blame for their poor showing fell on leader Alfredo Pérez Rubalcaba and, following a disastrous performance by the party in the European Elections, he offered his resignation. At a special congress the party chose **Pedro Sánchez**, a telegenic university economics lecturer, as its new leader. His task will be to overhaul a party that has haemorrhaged votes in recent years and has lost the support of much of its working-class base.

Disillusion with the established political parties – particularly on the part of the young – led to a new left-wing party, **Podemos** (We Can) gaining 1.2 million votes and five seats in the European Parliament in the June 2014 elections. To the consternation of Spain's political establishment, busy preparing for a general election in 2015, Podemos's 35-year-old leader, the bearded and pony-tailed **Pablo Iglesias**, declared that he was intent on undermining the corrupt regime – including all the major political parties – that has governed Spain since the death of Franco. In a country where one in four is unemployed, where more than 150,000 families have been evicted from their homes in the last five years and where soup kitchens and food banks are features of most major towns and cities, many desperate voters seem more than willing to give the radicals a chance.

2004	2010	2014
Madrid train bombings kill 191 and injure more than 1800, influencing the outcome of the general election held three days later.	Spain wins the FIFA World Cup in South Africa for first time.	Following royal scandals, King Juan Carlos I abdicates; his son is crowned Felipe VI with consort Queen Letizia.

Wildlife

Despite its reputation as the land of the package holiday, you can't beat Spain for sheer diversity of landscape and wildlife. When the Pyrenees were squeezed from the earth's crust they created an almost impenetrable barrier stretching from the Bay of Biscay to the Mediterranean Sea. Those animals and plants already present in Spain were cut off from the rest of Europe, and have been evolving independently ever since. In the same way, the breach of the land bridge at what is now the Strait of Gibraltar, and the subsequent reflooding of the Mediterranean basin, stranded typical African species on the peninsula. The outcome was an assortment of wildlife originating from two continents, resulting in modern-day Iberia's unique flora and fauna.

Spain is the second most **mountainous** country in Europe after Switzerland. The central plateau – the *meseta* – averages 600–700m in elevation, slopes gently westwards and is surrounded and traversed by imposing sierras and cordilleras. To the north, the plateau is divided from the coast by the extensive ranges of the Cordillera Cantábrica, and in the south the towering Sierra Nevada and several lesser ranges run along the Mediterranean shore. Where these southern sierras continue across the Mediterranean basin, the unsubmerged peaks today form the Balearic Islands. The Pyrenean chain marks the border with France, and even along Spain's eastern shores the narrow coastal plain soon rises into the foothills of the sierras of Montseny, Espuña and Los Filabres, among others. The ancient sierras de Guadarrama and Gredos cross the *meseta* just north of Madrid, and the Sierra Morena and the Montes de Toledo rise out of the dusty southern plains. With such an uneven topography, it is not surprising to find an alpine element in the flora and fauna, with the most strictly montane species showing adaptations to high levels of ultraviolet light and prolonged winter snow cover.

Climatic variations have produced a corresponding diversity in Spanish wildlife. The wet, humid north is populated by species typical of northern Europe, while the southern foothills of the Sierra Nevada have more in common vegetation-wise with the Atlas Mountains of Morocco. The continental weather pattern of much of the **interior** has given rise to a community of drought-resistant shrubs, together with annual herbs that flower and set seed in the brief spring and autumn rains, or more long-lived plants that possess underground bulbs or tubers to withstand the prolonged summer drought and winter cold.

Habitat

Like most of Europe, the Iberian Peninsula was once heavily forested. Today, though, following centuries of deforestation, only about ten percent of the original **woodland** remains, mostly in the north. Historically, much of the *meseta* was covered with evergreen oaks and associated shrubs such as laurustinus and strawberry tree (*madroño* – the tree is the symbol of Madrid), but the clearance of land for arable and pastoral purposes has taken its toll, as have the ravages of war. Today, tracts of Mediterranean woodland persist only in the sierras and some parts of Extremadura. When it was realized that much of the plateau was unsuitable for permanent agricultural use, the land was abandoned, and it is now covered with low-growing, aromatic scrub vegetation, known as *matorral* (maquis). An endangered habitat, the maquis is a haven for many rare and distinctive plant and animal species, some found nowhere else in

Europe. The southeastern corner of the *meseta* is the only part of Spain that probably never supported woodland; here the arid steppe **grasslands** (*calvero*) remain basically untouched by man. In northern Spain, where vast areas are still forested, the typical tree species are more familiar: oak, beech, ash and lime on the lower slopes, grading into pine and fir at higher levels – and the appearance is distinctly northern European.

Much of the *meseta* is predominantly flat, arid and brown. Indeed, in Almería, Europe's only true **desert** is to be found, such is the lack of rainfall. But the presence of subterranean water supplies gives rise to occasional **oases** teeming with wildlife. The numerous tree-lined **watercourses** of the peninsula also attract birds and animals from the surrounding dusty plains. The great Ebro and Duero rivers of the north, and the Tajo and Guadiana in the south, have been dammed at intervals, creating **reservoirs** that attract wildfowl in winter.

The Spanish **coastline** has a little of everything: dune systems, shingle banks, rocky cliffs, salt marshes and sweeping sandy beaches. In Galicia, submerged river valleys, or *rías*, are reminiscent of the Norwegian fjords, and the offshore islands are home to noisy sea-bird colonies; the north Atlantic coast is characterized by limestone promontories and tiny, sandy coves; the Mediterranean coast, despite its reputation for wall-to-wall hotels, still boasts many undeveloped lagoons and marshes; and southwest of Seville lies perhaps the greatest of all Spain's coastal wetlands: the Coto Doñana.

While the rest of Europe strives for agricultural supremacy, in Spain much of the land is still **farmed** by traditional methods, and the **landscape** has changed little since the initial disappearance of the forests. The olive groves of the south, the extensive livestock-rearing lands of the north and even the cereal-growing and wine-producing regions of the plains, exist in relative harmony with the indigenous wildlife of the country. It is only since Spain joined the European Union that artificial pesticides and fertilizers and huge machines have made much impact. Even so, compared to its neighbours, Spain is still essentially a wild country. Apart from a few industrial areas in the northeast and around Madrid and large-scale urbanization along parts of the coast, the landscape reflects the absence of modern technology, and the low population density means that less demand is made on the wilderness areas that remain.

Flora

With such a broad range of habitats, Spain's **flora** is nothing less than superb. Excluding the Canary Islands, about eight thousand species occur on Spanish soil, approximately ten percent of which are found nowhere else in the world. The plethora of high **mountains** allows an alpine flora to persist in Spain well beyond its normal north European distribution, and because of the relative geographical isolation of the mountain ranges, plants have evolved which are specific to each. In fact, there are about 180 plants that occur only in the Pyrenees, and over forty species endemic to the Sierra Nevada.

This effect is clearly illustrated by the **buttercup** family. In the Pyrenees, endemic species include the pheasant's-eye *Adonis pyrenaica* and the meadow rue *Thalictrum macrocarpum*; the Sierra Nevada has *Delphinium nevadense* and the monkshood *Aconitum nevadense*, and of the columbines *Aquilegia nevadensis* occurs here alone. *A. discolor* is endemic to the Picos de Europa, *A. cazorlensis* is found only in the Sierra de Cazorla, and *A. pyrenaica* is unique to the Pyrenees. Other handsome montane members of this family include alpine pasqueflowers, hepatica, hellebores, clematis and a host of more obvious buttercups.

The dry Mediterranean grasslands of Spain are excellent hunting grounds for **orchids**. In spring, in the meadows of the Cordillera Cantábrica, early purple, elder-flowered, woodcock, pink butterfly, green-winged, lizard and tongue orchids are ten a penny, and a little searching will turn up sombre bee, sawfly and Provence orchids. Farther into the Mediterranean zone, exotic species to look for include Bertoloni's bee, bumblebee and mirror orchids. Lax-flowered orchids are common on the Costa Brava and high limestone areas will reveal black vanilla orchids, frog orchids and summer lady's tresses a bit later in the year.

The Mediterranean **maquis** is a delight to the eye and nose in early summer, as the cistus bushes and heaths come into flower, with wild rosemary, thyme, clary and French lavender adding to the profusion of colour. The *dehesa* grasslands of southwest Spain are carpeted with the flowers of *Dipcadi serotinum* (resembling brown bluebells), pink gladioli and twenty or so different trefoils in May. In the shade of the ancient evergreen oaks grow birthworts, with their pitcher-shaped flowers, bladder senna and a species of lupin known locally as "devil's chickpea".

Even a trip across the **northern meseta**, although reputedly through endless cereal fields, is by no means a dull experience. Arable weeds such as cornflowers, poppies, corncockle, chicory and shrubby pimpernel add a touch of colour and are sometimes more abundant than the crops themselves. Where the coastal **sand dunes** have escaped the ravages of the tourist industry you can find sea daffodils, sea holly, sea bindweed, sea squill and the large violet flowers of *Romulea clusiana*.

Mammals

The great mammalian fauna that roamed Europe in the Middle Ages today survives only as a relict population in the wildest areas of Spain. Forced to seek refuge from hunters and encroaching civilization, it is perhaps surprising that the only species to have succumbed to extinction is the little-known European beaver. Unfortunately, with elusiveness the key to their survival, the mammal species that remain can be almost impossible to see. Endangered, but common in the mountains of the north, the **wolf** (*lobo*) avoids contact with humans as much as possible. Persecuted for centuries in response to the exaggerated menace portrayed in folk tales, they are still today regarded as a major threat to livestock in some quarters, despite their dwindling numbers. Although afforded official protection, many farmers would not think twice about shooting on sight. Similarly, the omnivorous **brown bear** (*oso pardo*) shows none of the inquisitive boldness exhibited by its American cousins, and with numbers as low as a hundred in Spain, anybody catching a glimpse of one should consider themselves exceptionally fortunate.

In the **northern mountains** – the Pyrenees and the Cordillera Cantábrica – you should get at least a glimpse of chamois, roe and red deer, and possibly **wild boar** (*jabalí*), which can be seen at dusk during the winter conducting nightly raids on village potato patches. The **Spanish ibex** (*cabra montés*), the scimitar-horned wild goat, had represented the main quarry of locals since prehistoric times. However, while it was able to sustain low levels of predation, its agility was no match for modern hunters and it almost disappeared in the early years of the twentieth century. Thanks to effective conservation measures, its numbers are slowly beginning to recover and it is becoming an increasingly common sight in the sierras de Cazorla, Grazalema (both Andalucía) and Gredos (Castilla y León). Europe's answer to prairie dogs, **marmots** (*marmotas*) can occasionally be seen in the Pyrenees, where they graze in alpine meadows, while the surrounding pine forests support large numbers of their arboreal relatives – the **red squirrel**. Less well known, and considerably more difficult to see, is the bizarre **Pyrenean desman**, a large, shrew-like creature closely related to the mole, which inhabits mountain streams.

The typical mammals of **southern Spain** have more in common with Africa than Europe, the separation of the two continents leaving several species stranded to evolve in isolation. Specialities of African origin include the sleek, cat-like **spotted genet** and the adaptable, intelligent **Egyptian mongoose**, both of which are active mainly at night but can be glimpsed during the day. The undoubted jewel of the south, though, is the **Iberian lynx** (*lince ibérico*), paler, more heavily spotted and less heavily built than the northern-European species, in adaptation to the subtropical climate. Highly endangered, and now almost completely confined to parts of the Sierra Morena near Andújar and Parque Nacional Coto Doñana (although a small and previously unknown population has recently been discovered in Castilla-La Mancha), its haunting cries on spring nights are sadly becoming more and more infrequent. An emergency breeding programme set up in 2005 in Coto Doñana increased the population there to fifty or so individuals, which has remained roughly the same in the years reported since then. A similar programme in the Parque Natural Sierra de Andujár has had greater success and has more than doubled the 2002 population of 60 to over 150 individuals reported in 2009. In April 2013 it was reported that an Andalucía-wide census had found a total wild population of 310 individuals. It is hoped that both programmes – in addition to new captive breeding programmes in Portugal and Spain – will eventually aid the lynx's regeneration and remove it from the critically endangered species list.

In the air, no fewer than 27 species of **bat** occupy caves and woodlands throughout Spain. Highly visible and often attracted to artificial light sources by clouds of insects, they are among the easiest of wild mammals to see, although identification to species level is best left to experts. Most interesting are the four types of horseshoe bat and Europe's largest bat, the rare **greater noctule**, which, with a wingspan of 45cm, even feeds on small birds.

The most spectacular **aquatic mammals** are the twenty or so species of whale and dolphin, whose presence has encouraged the appearance of numerous boating companies to run trips out to see them. **Pilot whales** and **sperm whales** are common in the Straits of Gibraltar, and **dolphins** will often choose to accompany boat trips in all areas. Isolated and protected coves on the Mediterranean shores shelter some of the last breeding colonies of the **Mediterranean monk seal**, a severely threatened species perhaps doomed to extinction. **Fresh water** also supports a number of mammal species, perhaps the best known being the playful **European otter**, which is still fairly numerous in the north.

Birds

If any country in Europe qualifies as a paradise for **birdwatching**, then it must surely be Spain. Most twitchers head straight for the world-famous Parque Nacional Coto Doñana, where over half of all European bird species have been recorded, but other parts of the country are just as rewarding, even if you have to work a little harder to get a matching list.

Birds of prey are particularly visible, and as many as 25 species of raptor breed here, but it is during the spring and autumn migrations that you will see the most dramatic numbers. Clouds of honey buzzards, black kites and Egyptian vultures funnel across the Straits of Gibraltar, aided by warm currents, followed by less numerous but equally dramatic-looking species such as short-toed and booted eagles. Resident species include the widespread griffon vulture, the surprisingly common red kite and the Bonelli's eagle. Twitchers, though, are likely to have their sights set on four attention-grabbing species: the Eurasian black vulture, fighting against extinction in Extremadura; the bone-breaking bearded vulture of the Pyrenees; the diminutive but distinctive black-winged kite of the southern plains; and the endangered, endemic Spanish imperial eagle. The latter is most easily seen in Coto Doñana, where guides take great delight in pointing out this emblematic hunter.

There is no less variety in other types of bird. Woodpeckers are most abundant in the extensive forests of the **northern mountain ranges**. While white-backed woodpeckers are confined to the Pyrenees, other such rarities as black and middle-spotted woodpeckers may also be seen in the Cordillera Cantábrica, and the well-camouflaged wryneck breeds in the north and winters in the south of the country. Other typical breeding birds of these northern mountains are the turkey-like capercaillie, pied flycatcher, blue rock thrush, alpine accentor, citril and snow finches, and that most sought-after of all montane birds, the unique, butterfly-like wallcreeper.

In the open **grasslands** and cereal fields of the *meseta*, larks are particularly common. Look out for the calandra lark, easily identified by its chunky bill and the trailing white edge to the wing. More rewarding are great and little bustards – majestic at any time of year, but especially when the males fan out their plumage during the springtime courtship display. In a tiny area of the Mediterranean coast, strange nocturnal mooing calls from low-growing scrub betray the presence of the secretive **Andalucian buttonquail**, a tiny, quail-like bird, more closely related to the bustards than the quails. Look out also for the exotically patterned pin-tailed sandgrouse, one of only two European members of a family of **desert-dwelling birds**, as well as stone curlews and red-necked nightjars, the latter seen (and heard) mainly at dusk.

Olive groves are an ornithological treasure-trove playing host to a colourful assemblage of birds – hoopoes, azure-winged magpies, golden orioles, southern grey and woodchat shrikes, bee-eaters, rollers, great spotted cuckoos and black-eared wheatears. On a sunny summer's day, these birds are active and often easy to spot if you are patient.

Fluctuating water levels, particularly in the south, mean that there is no shortage of seasonally flooding **fresh-water** habitats positively teeming with birdlife. In reed beds, you may come across the vividly coloured purple gallinule, the high-stepping Bailon's crake, the thrush-sized great reed warbler or localized colonies of sociable bearded reedlings. In winter, large flocks of migrant waterfowl may gather, but it is the resident species that bring more reward: the exotic red-crested pochard, the rare ferruginous duck, the delicate marbled teal and the threatened white-headed duck among the highlights.

Coastal wetlands and **river deltas** are a must for any serious birdwatcher, with common summer occupants including black-winged stilts, avocets, greater flamingos and all but one of the European representatives of the heron family: cattle and little egrets, purple, grey, squacco and night herons, bitterns and little bitterns. In the right conditions and at the right time of year, almost all the species can be seen breeding together in vast and noisy heronries – an unforgettable sight. Wintering waders are not outstandingly distinctive, though wherever you go, even on the Atlantic coast, you should look for spoonbills. Grey phalaropes visit the northwest corner, as do whimbrels, godwits, skuas and ruffs, taking a break from their northern breeding grounds. For **sea birds**, the Illas Cíes, off the Galician coast, are unbeatable, providing breeding grounds for shags, the rare Iberian race of guillemot and the world's southernmost colony of lesser black-backed gulls.

Even **towns** have their fair share of notable species. The **white stork** (*cigüeña blanca*) is a summer visitor that has endeared itself to Andalucía and south central Spain, and few conurbations are without the unkempt nest atop a bell tower, electricity pylon or war monument. Finches such as serin and goldfinch are numerous, and the airspace above any town is usually occupied by hundreds of swifts, martins and swallows; you may be able to pick out alpine, pallid and white-rumped swifts and red-rumped swallows if you're in the southern half of the country, as well as crag martins in the north.

The **Balearic Islands** can provide you with a few more unusual cliff-nesting species, such as Eleanora's falcon, while deserted islets are ideal for hole-nesting sea birds, including Cory's shearwaters and storm petrels.

Reptiles and amphibians

Around sixty species of reptiles and amphibians occur in Spain, including some of Europe's largest and most impressive. Four species of salamander inhabit the peninsula. The brightly coloured **fire salamander**, an attractive patchwork of black and yellow, is perhaps the best known. Named for its habit of seeking solace in woodpiles and later emerging when the fire was lit, the salamander spawned the legend that it was somehow born out of the flames. The 30cm-long **sharp-ribbed salamander** of the southwest is Europe's largest, and bizarrely pierces its own skin with its ribs when attacked. The two remaining species, the drab, misnamed **golden-striped salamander** and the **Pyrenean brook salamander**, are confined to the cool, wet, mountainous north.

Closely related to the salamanders are the **newts**, of which there are only four species in Spain. If you take a trip into the high mountain pastures of the Cordillera Cantábrica, where water is present in small, peaty ponds all year round, you should see the brightly coloured **alpine newt**, while the aptly named **marbled newt** can be seen round the edges of many of Spain's inland lakes and reservoirs. Searches through tall waterside vegetation frequently turn up the tiny, lurid-green **tree frog**, striped in the north and west, but stripeless along the Mediterranean coast.

Two species of **tortoise** occur in Spain: **spur-thighed tortoises** can still be found along the southern coast and on the Balearic Islands, the latter the only Spanish locality for the other species – **Hermann's tortoise**. European **pond terrapins** and **stripe-necked terrapins** are more widely distributed, but only in fresh-water habitats. Beware of confusion between these native species and the introduced North American **red-eared terrapin**, the result of the release of unwanted pets following the decline of the Teenage Mutant Ninja Turtle craze. **Marine turtles** are uncommon visitors to the Mediterranean and Atlantic coasts – perhaps the most frequently encountered is the protected **green turtle**, especially in the waters around Gibraltar, but **loggerhead** and **leathery turtles** are very occasionally reported.

The most exotic reptilian species to occur in Spain is the **chameleon**, although again this swivel-eyed creature is confined to the extreme southern shores where its camouflage skills render it difficult to find. **Lizards** are numerous, with the most handsome species being the large **ocellated lizard** – green with blue spots along the flank. Some species are very restricted in their range, such as Ibizan and Lilford's wall lizards, which live only in the Balearic Islands. In the south, the most noticeable species are **Moorish geckos**, large-eyed nocturnal creatures usually seen on the walls of buildings both inside and out. Adhesive pads on their feet enable them to cling perilously to vertical surfaces as they search for their insect prey.

Similarly, **snakes** are common, although few are venomous and even fewer are ever likely to bite. When faced with humans, evasive action is the snake's preferred option, and in most cases a snake will be long gone before the intruder even knew it was there. The **grass snake** will even play dead rather than bite, if cornered. **Asps** and **western whip snakes** occur in the Pyrenees, while the most common species in the south is the harmless **horseshoe whip snake**, named for the distinctive horseshoe mark on the back of its head.

The most unusual Spanish reptile is undoubtedly the **amphisbaenian**, sometimes misleadingly called the blind snake. Adapted to a subterranean existence, this rarely encountered and harmless creature can sometimes be found by searching through rotten leaves and mulch in forested environments and gardens of the south.

Teresa Farino

Flamenco

Flamenco – one of the most emblematic musics of Spain and its richest musical heritage – has recently enjoyed huge exposure and today is more popular than ever before. Twenty-five years or so ago it looked like a music on the decline, preserved only in the clubs or *peñas* of its aficionados, or in travestied castanet-clicking form for tourists. However, prejudice vanished as flamenco went through a tremendous period of innovation in the 1980s and 1990s, incorporating elements of pop, rock, jazz and Latin, and today there's a new respect for the old "pure flamenco" artists and a huge joy in the new. Fittingly, in 2010 UNESCO added flamenco to its intangible cultural heritage list, as a world-class art form to be encouraged, protected and supported.

The initial impetus for flamenco's new-found energy came at the end of the 1960s, with the innovations of guitarist **Paco de Lucía** (who died in 2014) and, especially, the late, great singer **Camarón de la Isla**. These were musicians who had grown up learning flamenco but whose own musical tastes embraced international rock, jazz and blues.

They have been followed by groups such as **Ketama**, **Raimundo Amador** (ex Pata Negra), **La Barbería del Sur**, **Navajita Plateá** and **Niña Pastori**, who have all reached massive audiences that neither de Lucía nor de la Isla could have dreamt of decades before. At the end of the 1990s, there were successful comebacks from such established artists as the late **Enrique Morente** and **José Mercé**. Morente – the king of flamenco – experimentally revisited old styles and combined them with new moves, releasing a spectacular new album, *Omega*, in 1996, with **Lagarjita Nick**, one of the most emblematic bands of the Spanish indie rock scene. José Mercé collaborated with **Vicente Amigo** – recognized as the most gifted player of the moment – on *Del Amanecer*. Paco de Lucía acknowledges Amigo as his successor in the innovation of flamenco guitar.

Among others regarded as the best **contemporary singers** are the male singers El Cabrero, Juan Peña "El Lebrijano", the Sorderos, El Fosforito, José Menese, Duquende and El Potito. The most revered women include Fernanda and Bernarda de Utrera, Carmen Linares, Remedios Amaya, Estrella Morente (daughter of Enrique Morente, and the new "star" of Spanish flamenco), Montse Cortés, La Macanita and Carmen Amaya. Until his death, **Camarón** – or more fully **Camarón de la Isla** – was by far the most popular and commercially successful singer of modern flamenco. Collaborating with the guitarists and brothers Paco de Lucía and Ramón de Algeciras, and latterly, Tomatito, Camarón raised *cante jondo* to a new art. A legend in his own lifetime, he died of cancer in 1992 at the age of just 42, having almost single-handedly revitalized flamenco song, inspiring and opening the way for the current generation of flamenco artists.

Origins

Flamenco evolved in southern Spain from many sources: Morocco, Egypt, India, Pakistan, Greece and other parts of the Near and Far East. Most authorities believe the roots of the music were brought to Spain by gypsies arriving in the fifteenth century. In the following century, it was fused with elements of Arab and Jewish music in the Andalucian mountains, where Jews, Muslims and "pagan" gypsies had taken refuge from the forced conversions and clearances effected by the Catholic kings and the church. Important flamenco centres and families are still found today in quarters and towns of *gitano* and refugee origin, such as Alcalá, Jerez, Cádiz, Utrera and the Triana *barrio* of Seville.

Although flamenco is linked fundamentally to **Andalucía**, emigration from that province has long meant that flamenco thrives not only there but also in Madrid, Extremadura, the Levante and even Barcelona – wherever Andalucian migrants have settled.

Flamenco aficionados enjoy heated debate about the purity of their art and whether it is more validly performed by a *gitano* (gypsy) or a *payo* (non-gypsy). Certainly during dark times, flamenco was preserved by the oral tradition of the closed *gitano* clans. Its power and the despair that it overcomes, seem to have emerged from the lives of a people surviving for centuries at society's margins. These days, though, there are as many acclaimed *payo* as *gitano* flamenco artists, and the arrival on the scene of musicians from Barcelona such as Vicente Amigo – who has no Andalucian blood but grew up in a neighbourhood full of flamenco music – has de-centred the debate.

The concept of dynasty, however, remains fundamental for many. The veteran singer **Fernanda de Utrera**, one of the great voices of "pure flamenco", was born in 1923 into a *gitano* family in Utrera, one of the *cantaora* (flamenco singer) centres. The granddaughter of the legendary singer "Pinini", she and her younger sister Bernarda, also a notable singer, both inherited their flamenco with their genes. This concept of an active inheritance is crucial and has not been lost in contemporary developments: the members of Ketama, for example, the Madrid-based flamenco-rock group, come from two *gitano* clans.

While flamenco's exact origins are debated, it is generally agreed that its "laws" were established in the nineteenth century. Indeed, from the mid-nineteenth into the early twentieth century it enjoyed a Golden Age, the tail end of which is preserved on some of the earliest 1930s recordings. The musicians found a first home in the **café cantantes**, traditional bars that had their own groups of performers (*cuadros*). One of the most famous was the *Café de Chinitas* in Málaga, immortalized by the poet Federico García Lorca in *A las cinco de la tarde* ("At five in the afternoon"), in which he intimates the relationship between flamenco and bullfighting, both sharing root emotions and flashes of erratic genius, and both being a way to break out of social and economic marginality.

The art of flamenco

Flamenco is played at *tablaos* and fiestas, in bars and at *juergas* (informal, more or less private parties). Because the Andalucian public are so knowledgeable about flamenco, even musicians, singers and dancers found at a local club or village festival are usually very good.

Flamenco songs often express pain. Generally, the voice closely interacts with improvising guitar, which keeps the *compás* (rhythm), the two inspiring each other, aided by the **jaleo** – the hand-clapping *palmas*, finger-snapping *palillos* and shouts from participants at certain points in the song. Aficionados will shout encouragement, most commonly ¡olé! when an artist is getting deep into a song, but also a variety of other less obvious phrases. A stunning piece of dancing may, for example, be greeted with ¡Viva la maquina escribir! (Long live the typewriter!), as the heels of the dancer move so fast they sound like a clicking machine; or the cry may be ¡agua! (water!), for the scarcity of water in Andalucía has given the word a kind of glory.

The encouragement of the audience is essential for the artists, as it lets them know they are reaching deep into the emotional psyche of their listeners. They may achieve the rare quality of **duende** – total communication with their audience, and the mark of great flamenco of any style or generation. Latterly, the word *duende* has been used to describe "innovation", which, while it is significant, does not always capture its real depth.

Flamenco songs

There is a classical repertoire of more than sixty flamenco **songs** (*cantes*) and dances (*danzas*) – some solos, some group numbers, some with instrumental accompaniment, others a cappella. These different styles (or *palos*) of flamenco singing are grouped in families according to more or less common melodic themes, establishing three basic types of *cante flamenco*: **cante grande** (comprising songs of the *jondo* type), **cante chico**, and **cante intermedio** between the two. Roughly speaking, the *jondo* and *chico* represent the most and the least difficult *cantes* respectively in terms of their technical and emotional interpretation, although any form, however simple, can be sung with the maximum of complexity and depth. **Cante jondo** (deep song) comprises the oldest and "purest" songs of the flamenco tradition, and is the profound flamenco of the great artists, whose *cantes* are outpourings of the soul, delivered with an intense passion, expressed through elaborate vocal ornamentation. To a large extent, however, such categories are largely arbitrary, and few flamenco musicians talk about flamenco in this way; what matters to them is whether the flamenco is good or bad.

The basic *palos* include **soleares**, **siguiriyas**, **tangos** and **fandangos**, but the variations are endless and often referred to by their place of origin: *malagueñas* (from Málaga), for example, *granaínos* (from Granada), or *fandangos de Huelva*. *Siguiriyas*, which date from the Golden Age, and whose theme is usually death, have been described as cries of despair in the form of a funeral psalm. In contrast, there are many songs and dances such as *tangos*, *Sevillanas*, *fandangos* and *alegrías* (literally "happinesses"), which capture great joy for fiestas. The **Sevillana** originated in medieval Seville as a spring country dance, with verses improvised and sung to the accompaniment of guitar and castanets (rarely used in other forms of flamenco). In the last few years, dancing *Sevillanas* has become popular in bars and clubs throughout Spain, but their great natural habitats are Seville's Feria de Abril and the annual *romería*, or pilgrimage, to El Rocío. Each year wonderful new *Sevillanas* come onto the market in time for the fiestas.

Another powerful and more seasonal form is the **saeta**, songs in honour of the Virgins that are carried on great floats in the processions of Semana Santa (Holy Week). Traditionally, they are quite spontaneous – as the float is passing, a singer will launch into a *saeta*, a sung prayer for which silence is necessary and for which the procession will therefore come to a halt while it is sung.

Flamenco guitar

The guitar used to be simply an accompanying instrument – originally, the singers themselves played – but in the early decades of last century it developed as a solo instrument, influenced by classical and Latin American traditions. The greatest of these early guitarists was **Ramón Montoya**, who revolutionized flamenco guitar with his harmonizations and introduced a variety of *arpeggios* – techniques of right-hand playing adapted from classical guitar playing. Along with Niño Ricardo and Sabicas, he established flamenco guitar as a solo medium, an art extended from the 1960s onwards by **Manolo Sanlúcar**, whom most aficionados reckon the most technically accomplished player of his generation. Sanlúcar has kept within a "pure flamenco" orbit, and not strayed into jazz or rock, experimenting instead with orchestral backing and composing for ballet.

The best known of all contemporary flamenco guitarists, however, is undoubtedly the late **Paco de Lucía**, who made the first moves towards "new" or "fusion" flamenco. A *payo*, he won his first flamenco prize at the age of 14, and went on to accompany many of the great singers, including a long partnership with Camarón de la Isla. He started forging new rhythms for flamenco following a trip to Brazil, where he was influenced by *bossa nova*, and in the 1970s established a sextet with electric bass, Latin percussion, flute and saxophone. Over the past twenty years, he has worked with jazz-rock guitarists such as John McLaughlin and pianist Chick Corea, while his own regular band, the Paco de Lucía Sextet featuring his brother, the singer Pepe de Lucía, remains one of the most original and distinctive sounds on the flamenco scene.

Other modern-day guitarists have equally identifiable sounds and rhythms, and fall broadly into two camps, being known either as accompanists or soloists. The former include **Tomatito** (Camarón's last accompanist), Manolo Franco and Paco Cortés, while among the leading soloists are the brothers Pepe and Juan Habichuela; Rafael Riqueni, who is breaking new ground with classical influences; Enrique de Melchor; Gerardo Núñez; and Vicente Amigo. Jerónimo Maya was acclaimed by the Spanish press as the "Mozart of Flamenco" when he gave his first solo performance, aged 7, in 1984.

Nuevo flamenco

The **reinvention of flamenco** in the 1980s was initially disliked by purists, but soon gained a completely new young public. Paco de Lucía set the new parameters of innovation and commercial success, and following in his footsteps came **Lolé y Manuel** and others, updating the flamenco sound with original songs and huge success. **Jorge Pardo**, Paco de Lucía's sax and flute player, originally a jazz musician, has continued to work at the cutting edge. **Enrique Morente** and **Juan Peña "El Lebrijano"** were two of the first to work with Andalucian orchestras from Morocco, and the Mediterranean sound remains important today, together with influences from southern India.

Paco Peña's 1991 *Missa Flamenca* recording, a setting of the Catholic Mass to flamenco, with the participation of established singers including Rafael Montilla "El Chaparro" from Peña's native Córdoba and a classical academy chorus from London, has stayed a bestseller since its first appearance, remaining a benchmark for such compositions.

The encounter with rock and blues was pioneered at the end of the 1980s by Ketama and Pata Negra. **Ketama** were hailed by the Spanish press as creators of the music of the "New Spain" after their first album, which fused flamenco with rock and salsa, adding a kind of rock-jazz sensibility, a "flamenco cool" as they put it. They then pushed the frontiers of flamenco still farther by recording the two *Songhai* albums in collaboration with Malian kora player Toumani Diabate and British bassist Danny Thompson. The group **Pata Negra**, a band led by two brothers, Raimundo and Rafael Amador, introduced a more direct rock sound with a bluesy electric guitar lead, giving a radical edge to traditional styles like *bulerías*. Their *Blues de la Frontera* album caused an equal sensation. After splitting, Raimundo Amador has continued as a solo artist.

Collectively, these young and iconoclastic musicians became known, in the 1990s, as **nuevo flamenco** – a movement associated in particular with the Madrid label Nuevos Medios. They form a challenging, versatile and at times musically incestuous scene in Madrid and Andalucía, with musicians guesting at each other's gigs and on each other's records. Ketama have had massive hits nationally, bringing flamenco into the mainstream.

In the 1980s and 1990s, the music became the regular sound of **nightclubs**, through the appeal of young singers such as **Aurora** – whose salsa-rumba song *Besos de Caramelo*, written by Antonio Carmona of Ketama, was the first 1980s number to crack the pop charts. Pop singer **Martirio** (Isabel Quiñones Gutierrez) is one of the most flamboyant personalities on the scene, appearing dressed in lace mantilla and shades like a cameo from a Pedro Almodóvar film, recording songs with ironic, contemporary lyrics, full of local slang, about life in the cities. Martirio's producer, **Kiko Veneno**, who wrote Camarón's most popular song, *Volando Voy*, has been key to opening up the scene. A rock musician originally, he has a strongly defined sense of flamenco. **Rosario**, one of Spain's top female singers, has also brought a flamenco sensibility to Spanish rock music. In the mid-1990s **Radio Tarifa** emerged, leading the exploration of a flamenco-Mediterranean sound with a mix of Arabic and medieval influences. They later expanded to include African musicians.

More recently, the Barcelona-based collective, **Ojos de Brujo**, have given new flamenco fusions hip credibility and a contemporary ethos, making flamenco much more integral to Spanish musical life. Their genius has been their reworking of flamenco styles to incorporate modern musical tendencies, while expressing passionate politics embedded in issues of everyday life, championing anti-corporate concerns and challenging the negative effects of global capitalism on the small community. Other more identifiably *nuevo flamenco* bands and singers to look out for include La Barbería del Sur (who add a dash of salsa), Wili Gimenez and José el Francés.

Jan Fairly, David Loscos and Manuel Domínguez

Books

Listings below represent a highly selective reading list on Spain and Spanish matters. Most titles are in print, although we've included a few older classics, no longer in print (indicated by o/p); most of them are easy to find, in secondhand bookshops or on websites such as ⱳabebooks.co.uk. An excellent specialist source for books about Spain – new, used and out of print – is Paul Orssich, 2 St Stephens Terrace, London SW8 1DH (☏020 7787 0030, ⱳwww.orssich.com). Books marked ★ are particularly recommended.

TRAVEL AND GENERAL ACCOUNTS

THE BEST INTRODUCTIONS

★**John Hooper** *The New Spaniards*. This authoritative portrait of post-Franco Spain was originally written by *The Guardian*'s former Spanish correspondent in the 1980s. A revised second edition published in 2006 is already dated, but is still one of the best introductions to contemporary Spain.

Adam Hopkins *Spanish Journeys: A Portrait of Spain*. Published in the mid-1990s, this is an enjoyable and highly stimulating exploration of Spanish history and culture, weaving its considerable scholarship in an accessible and unforced travelogue form, and full of illuminating anecdotes.

★**Michael Jacobs** *Andalusia*. A well-crafted, opinionated and wide-ranging introduction to Andalucía, covering everything from prehistory to the Civil War with perceptive pieces on flamenco, gypsies and food and drink. A gazetteer at the back details major sights. Recently updated, this remains one of the best introductions to the region.

★**Mark Kurlansky** *The Basque History of the World*. An entertaining take on this much-maligned, misunderstood and misrepresented people. Kurlansky uses history, stories, anecdotes and recipes to concoct this heady brew.

Lucy McCauley (ed) *Spain: Travelers' Tales*. Probably the best anthology of writing on Spain, which gathers its stories and journalism mostly from the last fifteen years. Featured authors include Gabriel García Márquez, Colm Tóibín and Louis de Bernières, whose "Seeing Red", on Buñol's La Tomatina festival, is worth the purchase price alone.

★**Giles Tremlett** *Ghosts of Spain*. Tremlett (*The Guardian*'s Madrid correspondent) digs into the untold story of Spain's Civil War dead and the collective conspiracy of silence surrounding the war's terrors, and goes on to peel away the layers of the post-Franco era to present an enthralling and often disturbing study of contemporary Spain. An updated edition (2014) has a new chapter, "The Fiesta is Over".

RECENT TRAVELS AND ACCOUNTS

Christopher Howse *The Train in Spain*. A chronicle of ten railway journeys in various parts of Spain by *Daily Telegraph* columnist and hispanophile Howse. The journeys are used

as a prop for a series of witty and perceptive observations on modern Spain. His earlier *Pilgrim in Spain* records observations on the route to Santiago as well as other religious monuments in northern Spain.

★**Chris Stewart** *Driving Over Lemons – An Optimist in Andalucía*. A funny, insightful and charming account of life on a remote peasant farm, El Valero, in the Alpujarras where Stewart set up home. The sequel, *A Parrot in the Pepper Tree*, has more stories from the farm interspersed with accounts of the author's earlier adventures as a sheep shearer in Sweden, drummer with rock band Genesis and flamenco guitarist in Seville. The saga's next episode, *The Almond Blossom Appreciation Society*, delivered another cocktail of hilarious, improbable and poignant tales. The "fourth book in the trilogy" *The Last Days of the Bus Club*, was published in 2014 and ladles out another enjoyable helping of El Valero bonhomie.

TWENTIETH-CENTURY WRITERS

★**Gerald Brenan** *South from Granada*. An enduring classic. Brenan lived in a village in the Alpujarras in the 1920s, and records this period and the visits of Virginia Woolf, Lytton Strachey and Bertrand Russell.

★**Laurie Lee** *As I Walked Out One Midsummer Morning, A Rose for Winter* and *A Moment of War*. *One Midsummer Morning* is the irresistibly romantic account of Lee's walk through Spain – from Vigo to Málaga – and his gradual awareness of the forces moving the country towards civil war. As an autobiographical novel, it's a delight; as a piece of social observation, painfully sharp. In *A Rose for Winter* he describes his return, twenty years later, to Andalucía, while in *A Moment of War* he describes a winter fighting with the International Brigade in the Civil War – by turns moving, comic and tragic.

★**George Orwell** *Homage to Catalonia*. Stirring account of Orwell's participation in the early exhilaration of revolution in Barcelona, and his growing disillusionment with the factional fighting among the Republican forces during the Civil War.

OLDER CLASSICS

George Borrow *The Bible in Spain* and *The Zincali* (both o/p). On first publication in 1842, Borrow subtitled *The Bible in Spain* "Journeys, Adventures and Imprisonments of an English-man"; it is one of the most famous books on Spain – slow in places but with some very amusing stories. *The Zincali* is an account of the Spanish *gitanos* (gypsies), whom Borrow got to know pretty well.

★ **Richard Ford** *A Handbook for Travellers in Spain and Readers at Home* and *Gatherings from Spain*. This must be the best guide ever written to any country. Massively opinionated, it is extremely witty in its British, nineteenth-century manner, and worth reading for the proverbs alone. *The Gatherings* is a timid, yet entertaining, abridgement of the general pieces, intended for a female audience who wouldn't have the taste for the more cerebral stuff. A biography, *Richard Ford, Hispanophile, Connoisseur and Critic* by Ian Robertson, places the great man in context.

Washington Irving *Tales of the Alhambra* (published 1832; abridged editions are on sale in Granada). Half of Irving's book consists of oriental stories, set in the Alhambra; the rest are accounts of his own residence there.

George Sand *A Winter in Majorca*. Sand and Chopin spent their winter at the monastery of Valldemossa. They weren't entirely welcomed in which lies much of the book's appeal. Local editions, including a translation by late Mallorcan resident Robert Graves, are on sale around the island.

ANTHOLOGIES

David Mitchell *Travellers in Spain: An Illustrated Anthology* (also published under the title *Here in Spain*). A well-told story of how four centuries of travellers – and most often travel writers – saw Spain. It's interesting to see Ford, Irving, Brenan, Laurie Lee and the rest set in context.

HISTORY

PREHISTORIC AND ROMAN SPAIN

James M. Anderson *Spain: 1001 Sights, An Archeological and Historical Guide*. A good guide and gazetteer to 95 percent of Spain's archeological sites.

María Cruz Fernandez Castro *Iberia in Prehistory*. A major study of the Iberian Peninsula prior to the arrival of the Romans, which surveys recent archeological evidence relating to the remarkable technical, economic and artistic progress of the early Iberians.

John S. Richardson *The Romans in Spain*. A recent look at how Spain became part of the Roman world. It also examines the influences exchanged between Spain and Rome.

EARLY, MEDIEVAL AND BEYOND

J.M. Cohen *The Four Voyages of Christopher Columbus*. Columbus' astonishing voyages as described by Columbus himself in his log are interwoven with opinions of contemporaries on the great explorer, including his biographer son Hernando. A fascinating collection, superbly translated.

Roger Collins *The Arab Conquest of Spain 710–97*. Controversial study documenting the Moorish invasion and the significant influence that the conquered Visigoths had on early Muslim rule. Collins' earlier *Early Medieval Spain 400–1000* takes a broader overview of the same subject.

★ **J.H. Elliott** *Imperial Spain 1469–1716*. The best introduction to the "Golden Age" – academically respected, and a gripping tale.

★ **Richard Fletcher** *The Quest for El Cid* and *Moorish Spain*. Two of the best studies of their kind – fascinating and highly readable narratives. The latter is a masterly introduction to the story of the Moors in Spain.

L.P. Harvey *Islamic Spain 1250–1500*. Comprehensive account of its period – both the Islamic kingdoms and the Muslims living beyond their protection.

David Howarth *The Voyage of the Armada*. An account from the Spanish perspective of the personalities, from king to sailors, involved in the Armada.

★ **Henry Kamen** *The Spanish Inquisition*. A highly respected examination of the Inquisition and the long shadow it cast across Spanish history. *The Spanish Inquisition: An Historical Revision* returns to the subject in the light of more recent evidence, while Kamen's *Philip of Spain* is the first full biography of Felipe II, the ruler most closely associated with the Inquisition. In *Spain's Road to Empire*, Kamen skilfully dissects the conquest of the Americas and the Philippines.

Elie Kedourie *Spain and the Jews: the Sephardi Experience, 1492 and After*. A collection of essays on the three million Spanish Jews of the Middle Ages and their expulsion by Los Reyes Católicos.

John Lynch *Spain 1598–1700* and *Bourbon Spain: 1700–1808*. Two further volumes in the Blackwells project covering Spain from prehistory to modern times, written by the series' general editor and dealing with Spain's rise to empire and the critical Bourbon period.

Hugh Thomas *Rivers of Gold: The Rise of the Spanish Empire*. Thomas' scholarly but accessible history provides a snapshot of Spain's most glorious period – its meteoric rise in the late fifteenth and early sixteenth centuries, when characters such as Fernando and Isabel, Columbus and Magellan shaped the country's outlook for the next three hundred years. This is part one in the trilogy on the Spanish Empire; the second volume, *The Golden Age*, and the third, *World Without End* are equally compelling.

THE TWENTIETH CENTURY

Phil Ball *Morbo – The Story of Spanish Football* (When Saturday Comes Books, UK). Excellent account of the history of Spanish football from its nineteenth-century beginnings with British workers at the mines of Río Tinto in Huelva to the golden years of Real Madrid and the dark days of Franco.

Ever-present as a backdrop is the ferocious rivalry, or *morbo* – political, historical, regional and linguistic – that has driven the Spanish game since its birth.

★ **Gerald Brenan** *The Spanish Labyrinth*. First published in 1943, Brenan's account of the background to the Civil War is tinged by personal experience, yet still makes for an impressively rounded read.

★ **Raymond Carr** *Modern Spain 1875–1980* and *The Spanish Tragedy: the Civil War in Perspective*. Two of the best books on modern Spanish history – concise and well told.

Ronald Fraser *Blood of Spain*. Subtitled *An Oral History of the Spanish Civil War*, this is an equally impressive – and brilliantly unorthodox – piece of research allowing Spaniards to recount their experiences in their own words.

★ **Ian Gibson** *Federico García Lorca, The Assassination of Federico García Lorca* and *Lorca's Granada*. The biography is a compelling book and *The Assassination* a brilliant reconstruction of the events at the end of the writer's life, with an examination of Fascist corruption and the shaping influences on Lorca, twentieth-century Spain and the Civil War. *Granada* contains a series of walking tours around parts of the town familiar to the poet.

Sid Lowe *Fear and Loathing in La Liga: Barcelona and Real Madrid*. Proving that FC Barcelona and Real Madrid are more than mere football clubs, this book examines the explosive rivalry between the two – the wounds left by the Civil War, the games between them which encapsulate the plucky Catalan nation against the overweening Spanish state, the attempts by both clubs to achieve global domination – by means of interviews with ex-players and coaches.

★ **Paul Preston** *Franco* and *Concise History of the Spanish Civil War*. A penetrating – and monumental – biography of Franco and his regime, which provides a clear picture of how he won the Civil War and survived in power so long. *Civil War* is more accessible than Thomas' work (see below). Preston's recently published and acclaimed *The Spanish Holocaust* documents the brutal and murderous persecution of Spaniards between 1936 and 1945 when some 200,000 were murdered, mostly by Franco's new regime.

★ **Hugh Thomas** *The Spanish Civil War*. This exhaustive thousand-page study is regarded (both in Spain and abroad) as the definitive history of the Civil War.

Gamel Woolsey *Málaga Burning* (Pythia Press, US) and under its original title *Death's Other Kingdom* (Eland, UK). A long-ignored minor classic written in the late 1930s and recently reprinted (and retitled) by a US publisher, in which the American poet and wife of Gerald Brenan vividly describes the horrors of the descent of their part of Andalucía into civil war. The Eland edition includes an interesting biographical afterword by Michael Jacobs.

ART, ARCHITECTURE, PHOTOGRAPHY, FILM AND DESIGN

Marianne Barrucand and Achim Bednoz *Moorish Architecture*. A beautifully illustrated guide to the major Moorish monuments.

Bernard Bevan *History of Spanish Architecture* (o/p). Classic study of Iberian and Ibero-American architecture, including extensive coverage of the Mudéjar, Plateresque and Baroque periods.

Robert Goff *The Essential Salvador Dalí*. An enjoyable and accessible introduction to Dalí and Surrealism, which examines the artist's bizarre life and obsessions (particularly his intense attachment to Gala, his wife), as well as his most enigmatic paintings.

Godfrey Goodwin *Islamic Spain*. Portable architectural guide with descriptions of virtually every significant Islamic building in Spain, and a fair amount of background.

Gijs van Hensbergen *Gaudí: the Biography*. At last, a worthy biography of one of the world's most distinctive architects. Van Hensbergen puts substantial flesh on the man while also placing his work firmly in context.

Robert Hughes *Goya*. The celebrated author of *The Shock of the New* and *Barcelona* turns his attention to one of Spain's greatest painters in this fabulous biography, a gripping account of Goya's life and work, placed within the context of turbulent eighteenth- and early nineteenth-century Spain.

★ **Michael Jacobs** *Alhambra*. Sumptuous volume with outstanding photographs and expert commentary. Authoritatively guides you through the Alhambra's history and architecture, and concludes with a fascinating essay on the hold the palace has had on later artists, travellers and writers, from Irving and Ford to de Falla and Lorca.

John Richardson *A Life of Picasso*. The definitive biography of one of the twentieth century's major artistic driving forces, currently in three volumes with the final volume due for publication in 2015.

Gabriel Ruiz Cabrero *The Modern in Spain*. This readable book is a clear, comprehensive study of postwar Spanish architecture. The author is an architect and professor in the renowned Faculty of Architecture at Madrid's Politécnica.

Meyer Schapiro *Romanesque Art*. An excellent illustrated survey of Spanish Romanesque art and architecture – and its Visigothic and Mozarabic predecessors.

FICTION AND POETRY

SPANISH CLASSICS

Pedro de Alarcón *The Three-Cornered Hat*. Ironic nineteenth-century tales of the previous century's corruption, bureaucracy and absolutism.

Leopoldo Alas *La Regenta*. Alas' nineteenth-century novel, with its sweeping vision of the disintegrating social fabric of the period, is a kind of Spanish *Madame Bovary* (a book that it was in fact accused of plagiarizing at time of publication).

Ramón Pérez de Ayala *Belarmino and Apolonio* and *Honeymoon, Bittermoon*. A pair of tragicomic picaresque novels written around the turn of the twentieth century.

Emilia Pardo Bazán *The House of Ulloa*. Bazán was an early feminist intellectual and in this, her best-known book, she charts the decline of the old aristocracy in the time of the Glorious Revolution of 1868.

★ **Miguel de Cervantes** *Don Quixote* and *Exemplary Stories*. In 2005 Spain and the Hispanic world celebrated the four-hundredth anniversary of the publication of Cervantes' work. *Quixote* is the classic of Spanish literature and still an excellent and witty read, with much to inform about Spanish character and psychology. J.M. Cohen's fine Penguin translation or the 2005 translation by Edith Grossman, published by HarperCollins, are worth looking out for. To try Cervantes in a more modest dose, the *Stories* are a good place to start.

Benito Pérez Galdós *Fortunata and Jacinta*. Galdós wrote in the last decades of the nineteenth century, and his novels of life in Madrid combine comic scenes and social realism; he is often characterized as a "Spanish Balzac". Other Galdós novels available in translation include *Misericordia*, *Nazarín* and the epic "*I*".

★ **St Teresa of Ávila** *The Life of Saint Teresa of Ávila*. St Teresa's autobiography is said to be the most widely read Spanish classic after *Don Quixote*. It takes some wading through, but it's fascinating in parts.

MODERN FICTION

★ **Bernardo Atxaga** *Obabakoak*. This challenging novel by a Basque writer won major prizes on its Spanish publication. It is a sequence of tales of life in a Basque village and the narrator's search to give them meaning.

★ **Arturo Barea** *The Forging of a Rebel* (o/p). Superb autobiographical trilogy, taking in the Spanish war in Morocco in the 1920s, and Barea's own part in the Civil War. The books have been published in UK paperback editions under the titles *The Forge*, *The Track* and *The Clash*.

Camilo José Cela *The Family of Pascual Duarte* and *The Beehive*. Nobel Prize-winner Cela was considered integral to the revival of Spanish literature after the Civil War, though his reputation is tainted by his role as a censor in Franco's government. *Pascual Duarte*, his first novel, portrays the brutal story of a peasant murderer from Extremadura, set against the backdrop of the Civil War, while *The Beehive*, his best-known work, set in Madrid at the end of the same war depicts the poverty and misery of this period through the lives of the characters.

Ildefonso Falcones *Cathedral of the Sea*. Historical romp tracing the life of the son of a fugitive serf who makes a new life for himself in the thriving medieval port of Barcelona. The title refers to the Gothic church of Santa María del Mar, which provides the backdrop to much of the action.

★ **Juan Goytisolo** *Marks of Identity*, *Count Julian*, *Juan the Landless*, *Landscapes after the Battle* and *Quarantine*. Born in Barcelona in 1931, Goytisolo became a bitter enemy of the Franco regime, and has spent most of his life in self-exile. He is perhaps the most important modern Spanish novelist, confronting, above all in his great trilogy (comprising the first three titles listed above), the whole ambivalent idea of Spain and Spanishness, as well as being one of the first Spanish writers to deal openly with homosexuality. The more recent *Quarantine* is a journey into a Dante-esque netherworld in which the torments of hell are set against reportage of the first Gulf War.

Carmen Laforet *Nada*. Written in 1944 but only recently translated, this is a haunting tale of a Barcelona family locked in the violence and despair of post-Civil War Spain. For all the horror, there is beauty also in the portrayal of a teenage girl's longing for consolation.

★ **Javier Marías** *Tomorrow in the Battle Think on Me*. There are many who rate Marías as Spain's finest contemporary novelist – and the evidence is here in this searching, psychological thriller, with its study of the human capacity for concealment and confession. Two other Marías novels, *A Heart So White* and *All Souls*, are also available in English translation.

Ana María Matute *School of the Sun*. The loss of childhood innocence on a Balearic island, where old enmities are redefined during the Civil War.

★ **Eduardo Mendoza** *City of Marvels* and *The Truth about the Savolta Case*. Mendoza's first and best novel, *City of Marvels*, is set in the expanding Barcelona of 1880–1920, full of underworld characters and comic turns. It's a milieu repeated in *The Truth about the Savolta Case*.

★ **Manuel Vázquez Montalbán** *Murder in the Central Committee*, *Southern Seas*, *An Olympic Death*, *The Angst-Ridden Executive*, *Off Side* and *The Man of My Life*. Montalban was, until his death in 2003, one of Spain's most influential writers. A long-time member of the Communist Party, he lived in Barcelona, like his great creation, the gourmand private detective Pepe Carvalho, who stars in all of his wry and racy crime thrillers. The one to begin with – a classic – is *Murder in the Central Committee*.

Julián Ríos *Larva*. Subtitled *Midsummer Night's Babel*, *Larva* is a large, complex, postmodern novel by a leading Spanish literary figure, published to huge acclaim in Spain.

Carlos Ruiz Zafón *The Shadow of the Wind*. A wonderfully atmospheric and gripping novel in which a young boy tries to unravel the truth behind the life and death of a forgotten writer. Set in post-Civil War Barcelona. Its follow-up, *The Angel's Game*, has recently been translated.

PLAYS AND POETRY

Pedro Calderón de la Barca *Life is a Dream and other Spanish Classics* and *The Mayor of Zalamea*. Some of the best works of the great dramatist of Spain's "Golden Age".

J.M. Cohen (ed) *The Penguin Book of Spanish Verse*.

Spanish poetry from the twelfth century to the modern age, with (parallel text) translations from all the major names.

Lope de Vega Spain's first important playwright (b.1562) wrote hundreds of plays, many of which, including *Lo Cierto por lo Dudoso* and *Fuenteobvejuna*, remain standards of classic Spanish theatre.

★**Federico García Lorca** *Five Plays: Comedies and Tragicomedies*. Andalucía's great pre-Civil War playwright and poet.

SPAIN IN FOREIGN FICTION

★**Ernest Hemingway** *The Sun Also Rises* and *For Whom the Bell Tolls*. Hemingway remains a big part of the American myth of Spain and *The Sun Also Rises* – played out against the background of Pamplona's San Fermín *feria* – contains some lyrically beautiful writing, while the latter is a good deal more laboured.

★**Norman Lewis** *Voices of the Old Sea*. Lewis lived in Catalunya from 1948 to 1952, just as tourism was starting to arrive. This book is an ingenious blend of novel and social record, charting the breakdown of the old ways in the face of the "new revolution".

★**Amin Malouf** *Leo the African*. A wonderful historical novel, re-creating the life of Leo Africanus, the fifteenth-century Moorish geographer, in the last years of the kingdom of Granada and his subsequent exile in Morocco and world travels.

SPECIALIST GUIDEBOOKS

THE PILGRIM ROUTE TO SANTIAGO

Millán Bravo Lozano *A Practical Guide for Pilgrims: The Road to Santiago* (Everest). Colourful, informative guide. Includes separate map pages so you can leave the heavy guide at home.

John Higginson *Le Puy to Santiago – A Cyclist's Guide*. A cyclist's guide to the pilgrim route, which follows as closely as possible (on tarmac) the walkers' path, visiting all the major sites en route.

Edwin Mullins *The Pilgrimage to Santiago* (o/p). This is a travelogue rather than a guide, but is by far the best book on the Santiago legend and its fascinating medieval pilgrimage industry.

Alison Raju *The Way of St James: Le Puy to the Pyrenees* (vol. I) and *Pyrenees-Santiago-Finisterre* (vol. II); *Vía de la Plata – The Way of St James* (all Cicerone, UK). Walking guide to the pilgrim route divided between the French and Spanish sections and written by an experienced Iberian hiker. Both books include detailed maps, background on sights en route as well as practical information such as where to stay. In *Vía de la Plata* Raju covers the lesser-known pilgrim route to Santiago, starting out from Seville.

David Wesson *The Camino Francés* (Confraternity of St James). Annually updated basic guide to the *camino*, with directions and accommodation. The Confraternity (ⓦ csj.org.uk) publishes the most accurate guides to the route, and there's also an online bookshop.

TREKKING AND CYCLING

Tony Bishop and Eva Monika Bratek *Walking in the Ronda Mountains*. Describing thirty half-day walks in the Serranía de Ronda and the Sierra de Grazalema in Andalucía, this hiking guide contains clear maps and plenty of detail (with photos) about the flora and fauna to be seen.

David and Ros Brawn *Sierra de Aracena*. A guide covering this magnificent Andalucian sierra in 27 walks, with an accompanying map (sold separately), and all routes GPS waypointed.

Charles Davis *Costa del Sol Walks*, *Costa Blanca Walks* (both Santana, Málaga; ⓦ santanabooks.com). Well-written guides to two excellent walking zones describing 31 (32 in *Costa Blanca*) walks of between 3km and 18km; each walk has its own map. The same author's *Walk! the Axarquía* (Discovery, UK; ⓦ www.walking.demon.co.uk) is a reliable guide to the Andalucía region describing 30 walks between 5km and 22km, all GPS waypointed. *34 Alpujarras Walks*, details GPS waypointed treks and Mallorca's Drystone Way (Discovery, UK) is a guide to the Balearic island's long-distance walking route. In the latter books, each walk has its own map; also there are waterproof 1:40,000 *Axarquía/Alpujarras Tour and Trail* maps (sold separately) with all walks (and GPS points) marked.

Harry Dowdell *Cycle Touring in Spain*. Well-researched cycle-touring guide, which describes eight touring routes of varying difficulty in the north and south of Spain. Plenty of practical information on preparing your bike for the trip, transporting it, plus what to take.

★**Teresa Farino** *Picos de Europa*. An excellent walking and touring guide in the *Landscapes* series detailing a variety of hikes in this spectacular national park, with special emphasis given to flora and fauna.

★**Guy Hunter-Watts** *Walking in Andalucía*. First-rate walking guide to the natural parks of Grazalema, Cazorla, Los Alcornocales, Aracena and La Axarquía, as well as the Alpujarras and the Sierra Nevada, with 36 walks each with a colour map, and free internet updates. Regularly updated.

Jacqueline Oglesby *The Mountains of Central Spain*. Walking and scrambling guide to the magnificent sierras de Gredos and Guadarrama by resident author.

June Parker *Walking in Mallorca*. This popular and reliable guide is now in its fourth edition.

Gisela Randant Wood *Walking in Extremadura*. New hiking guide (with clear maps) to one of Spain's less-travelled regions. The guide covers 27 routes of varying length and includes three city tours – Merida, Caceres and Trujillo.

Kev Reynolds *Walks and Climbs in the Pyrenees*. User-friendly guide for trekkers and walkers, though half devoted to the French side of the frontier.

Bob Stansfield *Costa Blanca Mountain Walks*.

Two-volume set (sold separately) of walks in this little-known but spectacular area near Alicante. Vol. 1 covers the western Costa Blanca, Vol. 2 the eastern sector.

Douglas Streetfield-James et al *Trekking in the Pyrenees*. The best – and always the most current – English-language west-to-east guide to most of the GR11 and choice bits of the Camino de Santiago, though the GR10 and its variants is half the book. Easy-to-use sketch maps with (brisk) time courses and practical details for overnighting in villages.

Robin Walker *Walks and Climbs in the Picos de Europa* and *Walking in the Cordillera Cantábrica*. The first is a guide to

walks and rock climbs in the Picos by an experienced resident mountaineer, the second expands beyond this zone to detail treks in the Cordillera mountain range.

Andy Walmsley *Walking in the Sierra Nevada*. Forty-five walks of varying distance and difficulty, from three-hour strolls in the Alpujarras to the arduous Tres Mils peaks. The latest edition also caters for mountain bikers.

Editorial Alpina The Barcelona-based map publisher Editorial Alpina (ⓦ editorialalpina.com) has a reliable range of 1:25,000 to 1:40,000 walking maps and guides covering Andalucía, Catalunya, the Pyrenees, the Picos de Europa, the Costa Blanca, the Balearics and other parts of Spain.

WILDLIFE

Teresa Farino and Mike Lockwood *Travellers' Nature Guides: Spain*. Excellent illustrated wildlife guide by two Spanish-based experts (one of whom contributed this guide's wildlife section); divided into regional groupings with detailed maps, it covers all the peninsula's major habitats.

Clive Finlayson *Al-Andalus: how nature has shaped history*. Biologist and anthropologist Finlayson has produced a history of one region with its theme of interaction between man and the environment. Lavishly illustrated with excellent photos of flora and fauna.

FOOD AND WINE

Coleman Andrews *Catalan Cuisine*. The best available English-language book dealing with Spain's most adventurous regional cuisine.

Nicholas Butcher *The Spanish Kitchen*. A practical and knowledgeable guide to creating Spanish dishes, with informative detail on tapas, olive oil, *jamón serrano* and herbs.

Penelope Casas *The Foods and Wines of Spain*. Superb and now classic Spanish cookbook, covering traditional and regional dishes with equal, authoritative aplomb. By the same author is the useful *Tapas: the little dishes of Spain*.

Alan Davidson *The Tio Pepe Guide to the Seafood of Spain and Portugal*. An indispensable (and pocketable) book that details and illustrates every fish and crustacean found in restaurants and bars along the Spanish *costas*.

★**Julian Jeffs** *Sherry*. The story of sherry – history, production, blending and brands. Rightly a classic, and the best introduction to Andalucía's great wine. The same

author's *Wines of Spain* is an erudite guide to traditional and up-and-coming wine regions, with details of vineyards, grape varieties and vintages.

Jean Claude Juston *The New Spain – Vegan and Vegetarian Restaurants* (available from ⓦ vegetarianguides .co.uk). Very useful guide to vegetarian restaurants throughout Spain by the owner/chef of a vegetarian restaurant in the Alpujarras.

Jan Read *Guide to the Wines of Spain*. Encyclopedic (yet pocketable) guide to the classic and emerging wines of Spain by a leading authority. Includes maps, vintages and vineyards.

★**Paul Richardson** *Late Dinner*. A joyous dissection of the food of Spain, region by region and season by season. He even squeezes in a meal with top chef Ferran Adrià at the (now closed) culinary shrine *El Bulli*. A celebration of culture and cuisine, this is the best general introduction to what Spanish food (and life) is really all about.

LEARNING SPANISH

Breakthrough Spanish Now ageing slightly, this is still one of the best of the CD- and book-linked home-study courses, which aims to give you reasonable fluency within three months. The same series has advanced and business courses which are also good. Packages (comprising book and CDs) are cheaper and available online.

★**Collins Spanish Dictionary** Recognized as the best single-volume bookshelf dictionary. Regularly revised and updated, so make sure you get the latest edition.

Elisabeth Smith *Teach Yourself Instant Spanish*. Good book-based (CD is available) course that gets you from zero to streetwise Spanish in six weeks in thirty minutes per day.

★*Get By in Spanish* (BBC Publications, UK; ⓦ bbcactive .com/languages; book and CD). One of the BBC's excellent

crash-course introductions (at a bargain price), which gets you to survival-level Spanish in a couple of weeks. The CD content can be downloaded to an MP3 player to take on the trip.

Michel Thomas Method *Foundation Course* and *Advanced Spanish*. The revolutionary "100 percent audio" CD-based learning system devised by the late polyglot Thomas has been praised by many learners who have struggled with traditional "grammar grind" methods.

Rough Guide Spanish Dictionary Good pocket-size dictionary that should help with most travel situations.

Untza Otaola Alday *Colloquial Spanish*. Excellent book-based beginner's course (supporting CDs are sold separately) with well-structured lessons and exercises. *Colloquial Spanish 2* takes you to the next level.

Language

Once you give it a try, Spanish (Castellano or Castilian) is among the easier languages to get a grip on. English is spoken, but wherever you are you'll get a far better reception if you at least try communicating with Spaniards in their own tongue. Being understood, of course, is only half the problem – getting the gist of the reply, often rattled out at a furious pace, may prove far more difficult.

Castilian

The rules of **pronunciation** are straightforward and, once you get to know them, strictly observed. Unless there's an accent, words ending in d, l, r and z are **stressed** on the last syllable, all others on the second last. All **vowels** are pure and short; combinations have predictable results.

A somewhere between the A sound of "back" and that of "father".

E as in "get".

I as in "police".

O as in "hot".

U as in "rule".

C is lisped before E and I; otherwise, hard: *cerca* is pronounced "thairka" (though in Andalucía many natives pronounce the soft "c" as an "s").

G works the same way, a guttural "H" sound (like the ch in "loch") before E or I, a hard G elsewhere – *gigante* becomes "higante".

H is always silent.

J the same sound as a guttural G: *jamón* is pronounced "hamon".

LL sounds like an English Y or LY: *tortilla* is pronounced "torteeya/torteelya".

N is as in English unless it has a tilde (accent) over it, when it becomes NY: *mañana* sounds like "manyana".

QU is pronounced like an English K.

R is rolled, RR doubly so.

V sounds more like B, *vino* becoming "beano".

X has an S sound before consonants, normal X before vowels. More common in Catalan, Basque or Gallego words, where it's sh or zh.

Z is the same as a soft C, so *cerveza* becomes "thairvaitha" (but again much of the south prefers the "s" sound).

The list of a few essential words and phrases here should be enough to get you started, though if you're travelling for any length of time a dictionary or phrasebook is obviously a worthwhile investment. If you're using a **dictionary**, bear in mind that in Spanish CH, LL and Ñ count as separate letters and are listed after the Cs, Ls and Ns respectively.

In addition to Castilian, many Spaniards speak a second, **regional language** – we've given brief pronunciation rules and condensed glossaries for the three most widely spoken: **Catalan** (*Català*), **Basque** (*Euskara*) and **Galician** (*Galego*).

CASTILIAN WORDS AND PHRASES

BASICS

Yes, No, OK	Sí, No, Vale
Please, Thank you	Por favor, Gracias
Where, When	Dónde, Cuando
What, How much	Qué, Cuánto
Here, There	Aquí, Allí
This, That	Esto, Eso
Now, Later	Ahora, Más tarde
Open, Closed	Abierto/a, Cerrado/a
With, Without	Con, Sin
Good, Bad	Buen(o)/a, Mal(o)/a
Big, Small	Gran(de), Pequeño/a
Cheap, Expensive	Barato, Caro

Hot, Cold	Caliente, Frío
More, Less	Más, Menos
Today, Tomorrow	Hoy, Mañana
Yesterday	Ayer

GREETINGS AND RESPONSES

Hello, Goodbye	Hola, Adiós
Good morning	Buenos días
Good afternoon/ night	Buenas tardes/noches
See you later	Hasta luego
Sorry	Lo siento/disculpéme
Excuse me	perdón/Con permiso
How are you?	¿Como está (usted)?

I (don't) understand	(No) Entiendo	(arrive in …)?	(llega a…)?
Not at all/ You're welcome	De nada	What is there to eat?	¿Qué hay para comer?
Do you speak English?	¿Habla (usted) inglés?	What's that?	¿Qué es eso?
I (don't) speak Spanish	(No) Hablo español	What's this called	¿Como se llama este en
My name is …	Me llamo …	in Spanish?	español?
What's your name?	¿Como se llama usted?		
I am English/	Soy inglés(a)/	**NUMBERS AND DAYS**	
Australian/Canadian/	australiano(a)/	one	un/uno/una
American/Irish	canadiense(a)/	two	dos
	americano(a)/irlandés(a)	three	tres
		four	cuatro

HOTELS AND TRANSPORT

		five	cinco
I want	Quiero	six	seis
I'd like	Quisiera	seven	siete
Do you know …?	¿Sabe …?	eight	ocho
I don't know	No sé	nine	nueve
There is (is there)?	(¿)Hay(?)	ten	diez
Give me … (one like that)	Deme …(uno así)	eleven	once
Do you have …?	¿Tiene …?	twelve	doce
the time	la hora	thirteen	trece
a room	una habitación	fourteen	catorce
… with two beds/	… con dos camas/	fifteen	quince
double bed	cama matrimonial	sixteen	diez y seis
… with shower/bath	… con ducha/baño	twenty	veinte
It's for one person	Es para una persona	twenty-one	veintiuno
(two people)	(dos personas)	thirty	treinta
for one night	para una noche	forty	cuarenta
(one week)	(una semana)	fifty	cincuenta
It's fine, how much is it?	¿Está bien, cuánto es?	sixty	sesenta
It's too expensive	Es demasiado caro	seventy	setenta
Don't you have anything	No tiene algo más barato?	eighty	ochenta
cheaper?		ninety	noventa
Can one …? camp (near)	¿Se puede ….?	one hundred	cien(to)
here?	… acampar aquí (cerca)?	one hundred and one	ciento uno
Is there a hostel nearby?	¿Hay un hostal aquí cerca?	two hundred	doscientos
How do I get to …?	¿Por donde se va a …?	two hundred and one	doscientos uno
Left, right	Izquierda, derecha,	five hundred	quinientos
straight on	todo recto	one thousand	mil
Where is …?	¿Dónde está …?	two thousand	dos mil
… the bus station	… la estación de	two thousand and one	dos mil uno
	autobuses	two thousand and two	dos mil dos
… the train station	… la estación de station	two thousand and three	dos mil tres
	ferro-carril	first	primero/a
… the nearest bank	… el banco mas cercano	second	segundo/a
… the post office	… el correos/la oficina de	third	tercero/a
	correos	fifth	quinto/a
the toilet	el baño/aseo/servicio	tenth	décimo/a
Where does the bus to	¿De dónde sale el autobús	Monday	lunes
… leave from?	para …?	Tuesday	martes
Is this the train for	¿Es este el tren para	Wednesday	miércoles
Mérida?	Mérida?	Thursday	jueves
I'd like a (return)	Quisiera un billete (de ida	Friday	viernes
ticket to …	y vuelta) para …	Saturday	sábado
What time does it leave	¿A qué hora sale	Sunday	domingo

MENU READER

BASICS

Aceite	Oil
Ajo	Garlic
Arroz	Rice
Azúcar	Sugar
Huevos	Eggs
Mantequilla	Butter
Miel	Honey
Pan	Bread
Pimienta	Pepper
Sal	Salt
Vinagre	Vinegar

MEALS

Almuerzo/Comida	Lunch
Botella	Bottle
Carta	Menu
Cena	Dinner
Comedor	Dining room
Cuchara	Spoon
Cuchillo	Knife
La cuenta	The bill
Desayuno	Breakfast
Menú del día	Fixed-price set meal
Mesa	Table
Platos combinados	Mixed plate
Tenedor	Fork
Vaso	Glass

SOUPS (SOPAS) AND STARTERS

Ajo blanco	Chilled almond and garlic soup
Caldillo	Clear fish soup
Caldo	Broth
Caldo verde gallego	Thick cabbage-based broth
Ensalada (mixta/verde)	(Mixed/green) salad
Gazpacho	Chilled tomato, peppers and garlic soup
Pimientos rellenos	Stuffed peppers
Sopa de ajo	Garlic soup
Sopa de cocido	Meat soup
Sopa de gallina	Chicken soup
Sopa de mariscos	Seafood soup
Sopa de pescado	Fish soup
Sopa de pasta (fideos)	Noodle soup
Verduras con patatas	Boiled potatoes with greens

FISH (PESCADOS)

Anchoas	Anchovies (canned)
Anguila/Angulas	Eel/Elvers
Atún	Tuna
Bacalao	Cod (often salt)
Bonito	Tuna
Boquerones	Fresh anchovies
Chanquetes	Whitebait
Dorada	Bream
Lenguado	Sole
Lubina	Sea bass
Merluza	Hake
Mero	Grouper
Pez espada	Swordfish
Rape	Monkfish
Raya	Ray, skate
Rodaballo	Turbot
Rosada	Rockfish
Salmonete	Mullet
Sardinas	Sardines
Trucha	Trout
Urta	Bream family

SEAFOOD (MARISCOS)

Almejas	Clams
Arroz con mariscos	Rice with seafood
Calamares (en su tinta)	Squid (in ink)
Centollo	Spider crab
Cigalas	King prawns
Conchas finas	Large scallops
Gambas	Prawns/shrimps
Langosta	Lobster
Langostinos	Crayfish
Mejillones	Mussels
Nécora	Sea crab
Ostras	Oysters
Paella	Classic Valencian dish with saffron rice, chicken, seafood, etc
Percebes	Goose barnacles
Pulpo	Octopus
Sepia	Cuttlefish
Vieiras	Scallops
Zarzuela de mariscos	Seafood casserole

COMMON TERMS

al ajillo	in garlic
a la brasa	grilled over embers
a la Navarra	stuffed with ham
a la parrilla/plancha	grilled
a la Romana	fried in batter
al horno	baked
alioli	with garlic mayonnaise
asado	roasted
cazuela, cocido	stew
en salsa	in (usually tomato) sauce
frito	fried

guisado	casserole	Nabos/Grelos	Turnips
rehogado	sautéed	Patatas	Potatoes
		Patatas fritas	French fries (chips)

MEAT (CARNE) AND POULTRY (AVES)

		Pepino	Cucumber
Callos	Tripe	Pimientos	Peppers/capsicums
Carne de buey	Beef	Pisto manchego	Ratatouille
Cerdo	Pork	Puerros	Leeks
Cerdo Ibérico	Black-pig pork	Puré	Mashed potato
Choto	Baby kid	Repollo	Cabbage
Chuletas	Chops	Tomate	Tomato
Cochinillo	Suckling pig	Zanahoria	Carrot
Codorniz	Quail		
Conejo	Rabbit	**FRUITS (FRUTAS)**	
Cordero	Lamb	Albaricoques	Apricots
Escalopa	Escalope	Cerezas	Cherries
Fabada asturiana/	Hotpot with butter beans,	Chirimoyas	Custard apples
Fabes a la catalana	black pudding, etc	Ciruelas	Plums, prunes
Hamburguesa	Hamburger	Dátiles	Dates
Hígado	Liver	Fresas	Strawberries
Jabalí	Wild boar	Granada	Pomegranate
Lacón con grelos	Gammon with turnips	Higos	Figs
Lengua	Tongue	Limón	Lemon
Lomo	Loin (of pork)	Manzanas	Apples
Pato	Duck	Melocotones	Peaches
Pavo	Turkey	Melón	Melon
Perdiz	Partridge	Naranjas	Oranges
Pollo	Chicken	Nectarinas	Nectarines
Rabo de toro	Oxtail	Peras	Pears
Riñones	Kidneys	Piña	Pineapple
Solomillo	Sirloin steak	Plátanos	Bananas
Solomillo de cerdo (Ibérico)	Pork tenderloin	Sandía	Watermelon
Ternera	Beef/Veal	Toronja/Pomelo	Grapefruit
Venado	Venison	Uvas	Grapes

VEGETABLES (LEGUMBRES)

		DESSERTS (POSTRES)	
Acelga	Chard	Arroz con leche	Rice pudding
Alcachofas	Artichokes	Crema Catalana	Catalan crème
Arroz a la cubana	Rice with fried egg and		brûlée
	tomato sauce	Cuajada	Cream-based dessert
Berenjenas	Aubergine		served with honey
Cebollas	Onions	Flan	Crème caramel
Champiñones/Setas	Mushrooms	Helado	Ice cream
Coliflor	Cauliflower	Melocotón en almíbar	Peaches in syrup
Espárragos	Asparagus	Membrillo	Quince paste
Espinacas	Spinach	Nata	Whipped cream
Garbanzos	Chickpeas	Natillas	Custard
Habas	Broad/fava beans	Pan de Calatrava	Bread pudding
Judías blancas	Haricot beans	Peras al vino	Pears cooked in wine
Judías verdes,	Green, red, black beans	Pudín	Sweet pudding (varies
rojas, negras			nationwide)
Lechuga	Lettuce	Tarta de almendras	Almond tart
Lentejas	Lentils	Tarta de manzana	Apple tart
Menestra/Panache de	Mixed vegetables	Tarta de Santiago	Classic Galician almond
verduras			tart

Tocino de cielo	Syrup and egg flan (Andalucía)
Yogur	Yoghurt

CHEESE

Cheeses (*quesos*) are on the whole local, though you'll get the hard, salty *queso manchego* everywhere. Mild sheep's or goats' cheese (*queso de oveja/cabra*) from León province or the Sierra de Grazalema (Cádiz) is widely distributed and worth asking for.

STANDARD TAPAS AND RACIONES

Aceitunas	Olives
Albóndigas	Meatballs
Anchoas	Anchovies
Berberechos	Cockles
Berenjenas fritas	Fried aubergine
Bígaros	Periwinkles
Boquerones	Anchovies
Cabrillas	Large snails with tomato
Calamares	Squid
Callos	Tripe
Caracolas	Whelks
Caracoles	Snails
Carne mechada	Larded meat
Champiñones	Mushrooms, usually fried in garlic
Chocos	Deep-fried cuttlefish
Chorizo	Spicy sausage
Cocido	Stew
Costillas	pork ribs
Croquetas	Fish or meat croquettes
Empanada	Fish/meat pasty
Ensaladilla rusa	Russian salad (diced vegetables in mayonnaise)

Escalibada	Aubergine and pepper salad
Espinacas con garbanzos	Spinach with chickpeas
Garbanzos	Chickpeas
Gambas (al ajillo)	Prawns (cooked in garlic)
Habas	Broad beans
Habas con jamón	Broad beans with ham
Hígado (de pollo)	Liver (chicken liver)
Jamón Serrano	Cured ham (like Parma ham)
Jamón Ibérico	Cured black-pig ham (the best)
Langostinos	Big, deep-water prawns
Mejillones	Mussels
Morcilla	Blood sausage (black pudding)
Navajas	Razor clams
Papas arrugadas	Boiled then baked new potatoes served with spicy sauce (Canary Is.)
Patatas alioli	Potatoes in garlic mayonnaise
Patatas bravas	Spicy fried potatoes
Pimientos	Peppers
Pincho moruno	Kebab
Pintxo	Basque *tapa* (on stick)
Pulpo	Octopus
Puntillitas	Deep-fried baby squid
Riñones al Jerez	Kidneys in sherry
Salchicha	Sausage
Salchichón	Cured, peppery salami
Sepia	Cuttlefish
Tabla	*Tapa* served on a wooden board
Tortilla de camarones	Prawn fritters
Tortilla española	Potato omelette
Tortilla francesa	Plain omelette

Catalan

Catalan (Català) is spoken in Catalunya, part of Aragón, much of Valencia, the Balearic Islands and the Principality of Andorra. On paper, it looks like a cross between French and Spanish, and is generally easy to understand if you know those two, but, spoken, it has a distinct, rounded sound and is far harder to come to grips with – the language has eight vowel sounds (including three diphthongs).

The main differences from Castilian in **pronunciation** are:

A as in "hat" when stressed, as in "alone" when unstressed.

C sounds like an English S: *plaça* is pronounced "plassa".

G before E and I is like the "zh" in "Zhivago"; otherwise, hard.

J as in the French "Jean".

N is as in English, though before F or V it sometimes sounds like an M.

NY replaces the Castilian Ñ.

QU before E or I sounds like K; before A or O as in "quit".

R is rolled at the start of the word; at the end, it's often silent.

TX is like the English CH.

V sounds more like B at the start of a word; otherwise, a soft F sound.
W sounds like a B/V.

X like SH in most words, though in some it sounds like an X.
Z like the English Z.

CATALAN GLOSSARY

one	un(a)	thank you	gràcies
two	dos (dues)	today	avui
three	tres	yesterday	ahir
four	quatre	tomorrow	demà
five	cinc	day before yesterday	abans d'ahir
six	sis	day after tomorrow	demà passat
seven	set		
eight	vuit	more	més
nine	nou	a lot, very	força
ten	deu	a little	una mica
Monday	Dilluns	left	esquerre(a)
Tuesday	Dimarts	right	dret(a)
Wednesday	Dimecres	near	(a) prop
Thursday	Dijous	far	lluny
Friday	Divendres	open	obert(a)
Saturday	Dissabte	closed	tancat
Sunday	Diumenge	town square	plaça
good morning/hello	bon dia	beach	praia
good evening	bona nit	where?	¿on?
goodbye	adéu	when?	¿quan?
please	per favor	how much?	¿quant?

Basque

Basque (Euskara) is spoken in the Basque Country and Navarra. According to the official estimates in 2011 around thirty percent of the population of the Basque Country and eleven percent of Navarra are "actively bilingual", speaking Euskara as their first language but understanding Castilian.

It's worth noting a couple of **key letter changes**: notably, the Castilian CH becomes TX (*txipirones* as opposed to *chipirones*), V becomes B and Y becomes I (Bizkaia as opposed to Vizcaya). Above all, Euskara features a proliferation of Ks: this letter replaces the Castilian C (Gipuzkoa instead of Guipúzcoa) and QU (Lekeitio instead of Lequeitio) and is also used to form the plural and the possessive (eg Bilboko means "of Bilbao").

BASQUE GLOSSARY

one	bat	Friday	ostiral
two	bi	Saturday	larunbat
three	hiru	Sunday	igande
four	lau	yes, no	bai, ez
five	bost	hello	kaixo
six	sei	good morning	egun on
seven	zazpi	good night	gabon
eight	zortzi	please	mesedez
nine	bederatzi	thank you	eskerrik asko
ten	hamar	today	gaur
Monday	astelehen	yesterday	bihar
Tuesday	astearte	tomorrow	atzo
Wednesday	asteazken	more	gehiago
Thursday	ostegun	a lot	asko

a little	gutxi	town square	enpastantza
left	ezker	beach	hondartza
right	eskuin	shop	denda
near	hurbil	where?	¿daude?
far	urruti	when?	¿noiz?
open	ireki	how much?	¿zenbat?
closed	hertsi		

Galician

While superficially similar to Castilian, **Galician** (Galego) is closer to Portuguese – in fact, both Galician and Portuguese evolved from a single ancestral tongue – and the main or only language of seventy percent of the population of Galicia.

The most obvious **characteristic** of Galician is the large number of Xs, which in Castilian might be Gs, Js or Ss; these are pronounced as a soft "sh" – thus *jamón* in Castilian becomes *xamón*, pronounced "shamon", in Galician. Similarly, LL in Castilian often becomes CH in Galician. You'll also find that the Castilian "la" becomes "a" (as in A Coruña), "el" is "o" (as in O Grove), "en la" is "na", "en el" is "no", "de la" is "da" and "del" is "do".

GALICIAN GLOSSARY

one	un	thank you	grazas
two	dous	today	hoxe
three	tres	yesterday	onte
four	catro	tomorrow	mañá
five	cinco	more	mais
six	seis	a lot	moito
seven	sete	a little	pouco
eight	oito	left	esquerda
nine	nove	right	dereita
ten	dez	near	preto
Monday	Luns	far	lonxe
Tuesday	Martes	open	aberto
Wednesday	Mécores	closed	pechado
Thursday	Xoves	town square	praza
Friday	Venres	beach	praia
Saturday	Sábado	shop	tenda
Sunday	Domingo	where?	¿onde?
good morning	bos días	when?	¿cándo?
good afternoon	boas tardes	how much?	¿cánto?
good night	boas noites		

Glossary of Spanish and architectural terms

Alameda Park or grassy promenade.

Alcazaba Moorish castle.

Alcázar Moorish fortified palace.

Apse Semicircular recess at the altar (usually eastern) end of a church.

Ayuntamiento/ajuntament Town hall.

Azulejo Glazed ceramic tile work.

Barrio Suburb or quarter.

Bodega Cellar, wine bar or warehouse.

Calle Street.

Capilla mayor Chapel containing the high altar.

Capilla real Royal chapel.

Cartuja Carthusian monastery.

Castillo Castle.

Chiringuito Beach restaurant serving fish, seafood and paella.

Churrigueresque Extreme form of Baroque art named after José Churriguera (1650–1723) and his extended family, its main exponents.

Colegiata Collegiate (large parish) church.

Convento Monastery or convent.

Coro Central part of church built for the choir.

Coro alto Raised choir, often above west door of a church.

Correos Post office.

Corrida de toros Bullfight.

Cortes Spanish parliament in Madrid.

Cuadrilla A bullfighter's team of assistants.

Custodia Large receptacle for Eucharist wafers.

Dueño/a Proprietor, landlord/lady.

Ermita Hermitage.

Gitano Gypsy or Romany.

Hórreo Granary.

Iglesia Church.

Isabelline (Gothic Hispano-Flemish) Ornamental form of late Gothic developed during the reign of Isabel and Fernando.

Lonja Stock exchange building.

Mercado Market.

Mihrab Prayer niche of Moorish mosque.

Mirador Viewing point.

Modernisme (Modernista) Catalan/Spanish form of Art Nouveau, whose most famous exponent was Antoni Gaudí.

Monasterio Monastery or convent.

Morisco Muslim Spaniard subject to medieval Christian rule – and nominally baptized.

Mozarabe Christian subject to medieval Moorish rule; normally allowed freedom of worship, they built churches in an Arab-influenced manner (Mozarabic).

Mudéjar Muslim Spaniard subject to medieval Christian rule, but retaining Islamic worship; most commonly a term applied to architecture which includes buildings built by Moorish craftsmen for the Christian rulers and later designs influenced by the Moors. The 1890s to 1930s saw a Mudéjar revival, blended with Art Nouveau and Art Deco forms.

Palacio Aristocratic mansion.

Parador State-owned luxury hotel, often (but not always) converted from a minor monument.

Paseo Promenade; also the evening stroll thereon.

Patio Inner courtyard.

Plateresque Elaborate Renaissance style, the sixteenth-century successor of Isabelline forms. Named for its resemblance to silversmiths' work (*platería*).

Plaza Square.

Plaza de toros Bullring.

Posada Old name for an inn.

Puerta Gateway; also mountain pass.

Puerto Port.

Raciones Large plate of tapas, often shared.

Reja Iron screen or grille, often fronting an altar or a window.

Reliquary Receptacle for a saint's relics, usually bones; often highly decorated.

Reredos Wall or screen behind an altar.

Retablo Altarpiece.

Ría River estuary in Galicia.

Río River.

Romería Religious procession to a rural shrine.

Sacristía, sagrario Sacristy of church – room for sacred vessels and vestments.

Sardana Catalan folk dance.

Seo, Seu, Se Ancient/regional names for cathedrals.

Sidrería Bar specializing in cider.

Sierra Mountain range.

Sillería Choir stall.

Solar Aristocratic town mansion.

Taifa Small Moorish kingdom, many of which emerged after the disintegration of the Córdoba caliphate.

Transepts The wings of a cruciform church, placed at right angles to the nave and chancel.

Tympanum Area between lintel of a doorway and the arch above it.

Turismo Tourist office.

POLITICAL PARTIES AND ACRONYMS

CNT Anarchist trade union.

Convergencia I Unio Conservative party in power (with ERC) in Catalunya.

ERC (Esquerra Republicana de Catalunya) Catalan nationalist party currently sharing power in Catalunya.

ETA Basque terrorist organization.

Falange Franco's old Fascist party; now officially defunct although a number of minor political groupings still use the name for their internet ravings.

Fuerza Nueva Descendants of the above, also on the way out but also have a presence on the internet.

IU Izquierda Unida, broad-left alliance of communists and others.

MC Movimiento Comunista (Communist Movement),

small radical offshoot of the PCE.

OTAN NATO.

PCE Partido Comunista de España (Spanish Communist Party). Now defunct.

PNV Basque Nationalist Party – in control of every post-Franco right-wing autonomous government until it lost the election in 2009. Regained power in 2012.

PP Partido Popular, Centre-right party led by Mariano Rajoy. Currently the government party in the Cortes.

PSOE Partido Socialista Obrero Español, the Spanish Socialist Workers' Party. Led by Pedro Sánchez and currently the main opposition party in the Cortes.

UGT Unión General de Trabajadores, Spain's major union and the equivalent of Britain's Transport and General Workers' Union.

Small print and index

A ROUGH GUIDE TO ROUGH GUIDES

Published in 1982, the first Rough Guide – to Greece – was a student scheme that became a publishing phenomenon. Mark Ellingham, a recent graduate in English from Bristol University, had been travelling in Greece the previous summer and couldn't find the right guidebook. With a small group of friends he wrote his own guide, combining a highly contemporary, journalistic style with a thoroughly practical approach to travellers' needs.

The immediate success of the book spawned a series that rapidly covered dozens of destinations. And, in addition to impecunious backpackers, Rough Guides soon acquired a much broader readership that relished the guides' wit and inquisitiveness as much as their enthusiastic, critical approach and value-for-money ethos.

These days, Rough Guides include recommendations from budget to luxury and cover more than 120 destinations around the globe, as well as producing an ever-growing range of ebooks.

Visit **roughguides.com** to find all our latest books, read articles, get inspired and share travel tips with the Rough Guides community.

Rough Guide credits

Editors: Olivia Rawes, Tim Locke
Layout: Pradeep Thapliyal
Cartography: Rajesh Chhibber
Picture editor: Yoshimi Kanazawa
Proofreader: Susanne Hillen
Managing editors: Natasha Foges, Alice Park
Assistant editor: Sharon Sonam
Production: Janis Griffith

Cover design: Nicole Newman, Emily Taylor, Pradeep Thapliyal
Editorial assistant: Rebecca Hallett
Senior pre-press designer: Dan May
Programme manager: Gareth Lowe
Publisher: Joanna Kirby
Publishing director: Georgina Dee

Publishing information

This fifteenth edition published March 2015 by
Rough Guides Ltd,
80 Strand, London WC2R 0RL
11, Community Centre, Panchsheel Park,
New Delhi 110017, India
Distributed by Penguin Random House
Penguin Books Ltd,
80 Strand, London WC2R 0RL
Penguin Group (USA)
345 Hudson Street, NY 10014, USA
Penguin Group (Australia)
250 Camberwell Road, Camberwell,
Victoria 3124, Australia
Penguin Group (NZ)
67 Apollo Drive, Mairangi Bay, Auckland 1310,
New Zealand
Penguin Group (South Africa)
Block D, Rosebank Office Park, 181 Jan Smuts Avenue,
Parktown North, Gauteng, South Africa 2193
Rough Guides is represented in Canada by Tourmaline
Editions Inc. 662 King Street West, Suite 304, Toronto,
Ontario M5V 1M7
Printed in Singapore

Help us update

We've gone to a lot of effort to ensure that the fifteenth edition of **The Rough Guide to Spain** is accurate and up-to-date. However, things change – places get "discovered", opening hours are notoriously fickle, restaurants and rooms raise prices or lower standards. If you feel we've got it wrong or left something out, we'd like to know, and if you can remember the address, the price, the hours, the phone number, so much the better.

Please send your comments with the subject line "**Rough Guide Spain Update**" to ✉ mail@uk.roughguides .com. We'll credit all contributions and send a copy of the next edition (or any other Rough Guide if you prefer) for the very best emails.

Find more travel information, connect with fellow travellers and plan your trip on ⓦ roughguides.com.

Acknowledgements

Simon Baskett Simon Baskett would like to thank Antonio and Javier of the Hostal Gonzalo, Itziar HerrÁjn and Trini, Patrick and Laura. Thanks too to Tim Locke and Andy Turner for all their hard work and patience on the editing front.

Matthew Hancock A special thanks for the invaluable help from David Currie, David Hall and Alex Hancock-Tomlin. Thanks also to Natalia Loeffler and Coloma Jaume Campomar; Valentina Beteta and Marina del Carmen Sanchez del Campo Sanfeliciano at the Spanish Tourist Office; Olivia and Mandy for at home support; and Andy Turner and Olivia Rawes at Rough Guides.

Laurie Isola Laurie would like to thank Montse Planas of Turisme de Barcelona, Mia Palau for her invaluable insight

on all things Barcelona, and Jules Brown for all his hard work on previous editions of the guide.

Helen Ochyra Many thanks to everyone who helped put my trip together and made it such a pleasure to travel in Spain, and to the team at Rough Guides, especially Olivia Rawes for her thorough editing. Special thanks to Anna Springbett for travelling with me and acting as my unofficial driver and – as ever – to my very patient husband Douglas Whelpdale.

AnneLise Sorensen Thanks to all who invited me in, wined and dined me, and shared information, travel tips and lively evenings, including: Maite, as always, for her splendid hospitality and knowledge of Spain; my entire – and ever-entertaining – Catalan family, including

ABOUT THE AUTHORS

Simon Baskett is a writer and journalist and author of the *Pocket Rough Guide to Madrid*. He lives and works in Madrid with his wife, Trini, and two children, Patrick and Laura.

Geoff Garvey caught the Iberian bug when (hitch) hiking around Spain as a student. Quite a few years on, he now lives in the mountains of Cádiz province and co-authors the *Rough Guide to Andalucía*.

Matthew Hancock is a freelance writer and editor. He is author of the *Rough Guide to Dorset, Hampshire and the Isle of Wight*, the *Pocket Rough Guide to Lisbon* and co-author of the *Rough Guide to Portugal*. He also contributes to the Rough Guides to Britain and England.

Laurie Isola is a California-based writer and researcher whose work has appeared in various magazines and newspapers, as well as online. During the nearly three years she lived in Barcelona, she could be found treasure hunting at Els Encants Vells or sipping a *tallat* on a sunny *terrassa*.

Helen Ochyra is a freelance travel writer whose first trip abroad was to Spain. Since then she has written about the country for newspapers and magazines, as well as contributing to numerous other Rough Guides. She is based in London but is more often found on the road.

AnneLise Sorensen (ⓦannelisesorensen.com), who has Catalan-Danish roots, has penned (and wine-tasted) her way across Spain, reporting for guidebooks, magazines, and radio/TV. AnneLise grew up spending summers with her Catalan family, lived in Barcelona, and divides her time between NYC and Europe, sustained by late-night tapas and sangria on both sides of the Atlantic. AnneLise also covers Scandinavia, Central America, New York and San Francisco.

Joanna Styles is a freelance writer and author based in Marbella, which she sees as just about the perfect place to live. Since she first spotted orange trees in the sunshine and the snow on Sierra Nevada as a university student, she's been passionate about Andalucia, its people, places and culture. Twenty-five years later she's still discovering hidden corners.

Ros Walford is a custom publishing editor at Rough Guides and occasional freelance travel writer who has a healthy obsession with all things Spanish.

Greg Ward (ⓦgregward.info) has been writing about Spain since the 1980s. As well as writing sixteen travel, history and music books for Rough Guides, he has also written for a number of leading travel publications.

Simon Willmore realised that he wanted to be a travel writer when he was living in Grenoble, France – while trying desperately to complete his Masters in Engineering. Immediately after completing his thesis, he retrained in Journalism and has been working as a journalist, editor and travel writer ever since. You can follow him on Twitter @SiWillmore.

Anna and Miquel and all my wonderful *Tiets* and *Tietas*; Claire (and family) for being such a special best friend; the magnificent paradores, as well as the top-notch turismos, across Catalunya. Thanks to guapo and all the wonderful friends in New York for their support and cheery emails. A resounding thanks to my co-authors, editors Andy Turner and Olivia Rawes, and the London and Delhi Rough Guides offices. Finally, a big *gracias, mange tak* and thank you to the best companion a travel-writer could ask for, Papa Kurt; and to Mama, who welcomed us back, with truita, cava and open arms, to the home base.

Ros Walford Ros Walford would like to give special thanks to José Ignacio, the conservator at the Museo Nacional de Escultura in Valladolid for his patience and fascinating explanations; Amador, my unique guide in Astorga, who loves to show pilgrims his town and to Jesús who opened up a little church – just for me – that was stuffed full of several-hundred-year-old *pasos* (the religious figures used during Semana Santa); all the super-helpful tourist information staff, in particular Mercedes in Zamora, Alicia in Léon, Ana in Salamanca, Mari in La Alberca, Ana in Palencia, Roberto in Astorga and Loreto in Valladolid; Feliciano at Hotel Don Rodrigo in Zamora for being such a lovely host; and not least, thanks to Olivia at Rough Guides for being a brilliant editor and to Jo and Keith for giving me the opportunity to get out from behind my desk.

Greg Ward Thank you to Sam Cook, Alison Cowan and Cefn Ridout for sharing the joys, and the cheeses, of Spain; Olivia Rawes and Tim Locke at Rough Guides, for all their hard work; and Oihana Lazpita and Itziar Herrán, for invaluable help in the Basque Country.

Simon Willmore Thank you to Carola and Cathryn for their unfaltering hospitality, Rocio and Siten for being friendly faces in a new city, Irene (Nana) for providing accommodation at a moment's notice, all of my amazing hosts, and my friends and family.

Readers' updates

Thanks to all the readers who have taken the time to write in with comments and suggestions (and apologies if we've inadvertently omitted or misspelt anyone's name):

Nancy Barker, Francis Beresford, Tony Bishop, Tony Boas, Tatiana Byttebier, Derek Carr, Wendy Cave, Frederick Cotterell, Andrew Darwin, Rupert Esdaile, William Eyre, Mark Ferguson, Pepa Fernandez, Alison Fisher, John Forde, Patrick Frazer, Matej Furkan, Nigel Hedges, Katharina Heyer, David Isherwood, Eric Jiménez, Maggie King, Gregory Kipling, Bob Mills, Robert J. Misulich, Jaime Moreno, Joanna Mudie, Jim O'Rourke, Barrie Painter, Lucy Palma, Gavin Parnaby, Dante Perez, Frank Pike, Andrea Pirio, Michael Pollitt, Simon Pyars, Manuel Bordello Romero, Larrans Sagberg, Frank Selkirk, Marian Smith, Ian Spencer, Elizabeth Squires, Bryan Stevens, Brian Thomas, John Thomson, Simon Trotter, Viktoria Urbanek, Amanda Willis, Tanya Zint.

Photo credits

All photos © Rough Guides except the following:
(Key: t-top; c-centre; b-bottom; l-left; r-right)

p.1 Matteo Colombo/AWL Images
p.2 Alan Copson/AWL Images
p.4 Banana Pancake/Alamy
p.5 Sebastian Wasek/4Corners
p.9 Barbara Santoro/ 4Corners (b)
p.10 Laurent Grandadam/4Corners
p.11 SoFood/Alamy (t); Hartmut Pönitz/4Corners (c); Jose Fuste Raga/Robert Harding Picture Library (b)
p.12 Massimo Ripani/4Corners
p.13 Heidi Grassley/Axiom Photographic Agency
p.14 Paul Quayle/Axiom Photographic Agency
p.15 Lisa Linder/4Corners (t); Robert Harding/Alamy (c); Hemis/Alamy (b)
p.16 Rafael Campillo/SuperStock (tl); Victor Spinelli/ Getty Images (tr); Juan Silva/Getty Images (c); Wilmar Photography/Alamy (b)
p.17 Richard Taylor/4Corners (t); Allan Baxter/ Getty Images (b)
p.18 Jon Mikel Duralde/Alamy (t); Rafael Jauregui/Robert Harding Picture Library (c); Fernando Fernandez/Robert Harding Picture Library (b)
p.19 Gavin Hellier/AWL Images (tl); mauritius images GmbH/Alamy (tr); John Cancalosi/Alamy (br)
p.20 Hemis/Alamy (t); Ian Cumming/Axiom Photographic Agency (c);Robert Harding/Alamy (b)
p.21 Oso Media/Alamy (t); Prisma Bildagentur AG/Alamy (c); jean-pierre lescourret/Getty Images (b)
p.22 Oliver Benn/Getty Images (tl); Pietro Canali/ 4Corners (b)
p.23 Andre Maslennikov/Robert Harding Picture Library (t); LOOK Die Bildagentur der Fotografen GmbH/Alamy (b)
p.24 Gabriele Croppi/4Corners
p.26 Jeronimo Alba/Alamy
p.58–59 Slow Images/Getty Images
p.87 Jorg Greuel/Getty Images (t)
p.107 Luis Asín/Ministerio de Educación, Cultura y Deporte/Museo Arqueologico Nacional (tr)
p.124–125 Jon Arnold Images Ltd/Alamy
p.127 Jo Chambers/Alamy
p.145 Alex Segre/Alamy (t); Maremagnum/ Getty Images (b)
p.173 Neil Setchfield/Alamy
p.175 Marco Cristofori/Alamy
p.215 JMN/Getty Images (t); Martin Ruegner/Getty Images (b)
p.222–223 Ken Welsh/Alamy
p.225 Gavin Hellier/AWL Images

p.267 Lucas Vallecillos/Robert Harding Picture Library (t); Maremagnum/Getty Images (b)
p.295 Bart Pro/Alamy (t); Ian Cumming/Axiom Photographic Agency (b)
p.329 Visions Of Our Land/Getty Images (t); Hiroyuki Matsumoto/Getty Images (bl); Travel Ink/Getty Images (br)
p.368–369 Danita Delimont/Alamy
p.371 Jam World Images/Alamy
p. 381 Pat Behnke/Alamy (t); Jon Bower Spain/Alamy (b)
p.433 Xavier Fores, Joana Roncero/Alamy (t); Alberto Paredes/Alamy (b)
p.444–445 Hemis/Alamy
p.447 Alex Segre/Alamy
p.473 Ian Dagnall/Alamy (t); Bob Masters/Alamy (b)
p.496–497 Prisma Bildagentur AG/Alamy
p.499 Felix Gonzalez/Robert Harding Picture Library
p.523 Stan Kujawa/Alamy; (t); Gloria Latorre, Álvar Montes/ Alamy (b)
p.542–543 Herve Hughes/Getty Images
p.545 Paul Gordon/Alamy Images
p.555 Robert Frerck/Getty Images (t); john norman/ Alamy (bl); Hemis/Alamy (br)
p.594–595 Hemis/Alamy
p.597 Andalucia Plus Image bank/Alamy
p.625 Chad Ehlers/Alamy
p.640–641 Sylvain Sonnet/Getty Images
p.675 Kevin Foy/Alamy (tl, tr); Visions Of Our Land/Getty Images (bl)
p.704–705 Wilmar Topshots/Alamy
p.707 Oso Media/Alamy
p.729 Pierre Jacques/Corbis (t); Prisma Bildagentur AG/ Alamy (b)
p.767 Riccardo Valsecchi/Corbis
p.790–791 Wilmar Photography/Alamy
p.793 isifa Image Service s.r.o./Alamy
p.803 Marco Simoni/Getty Images (t); Martin Child/Getty Images (b)
p.846–847 Guido Cozzi/4Corners
p.849 Stuart Pearce/Alamy
p.859 Dosfotos/Getty Images (tl)
p.890 The Art Archive/Alamy

Front cover and spine Sunflowers, Finca near Jerez de la Frontera © Reinhard Schmid/4Corners
Back cover Sabine Lubenow/AWL Images (t); Mlenny Photography/Getty Images (bl); Michele Falzone/AWL Images (br)

Index

Maps are marked in grey

Map symbols

The symbols below are used on maps throughout the book

International boundary	Funicular	Ruin	Mountain refuge
Province boundary	Narrow-gauge railway	Statue	Church (regional)
Chapter division boundary	Cable car	Castle	Rocks
Major road	Ferry route	Skiing	Swamp
Minor road	Path	Lighthouse	Bridge
Motorway road	Synagogue	Monastery	Building
Pedestrian road	Parking	Spring/spa	Market
Railway	Internet café/access	Swimming pool/area	Church
Ferry route	Post office	Waterfall	Stadium
River	Information office	Gardens	Park
Airport	Telephone office	Viewpoint	Beach
Bus/taxi	Museum	Cave	Saltpan
Tram stop	Hospital	Campsite/ground	Wall
Metro station	Place of interest	Mountain range	
Cercanías RENFE station	Mosque	Mountain peak	

Listings key

- ■ Accommodation
- ● Café / restaurant
- ■ Bar / club
- ● Shop